Concise Dictionary of

WOMEN
ARTISTS

Concise Dictionary of

WOMEN
ARTISTS

Editor
DELIA GAZE

FITZROY DEARBORN PUBLISHERS
LONDON • CHICAGO

**British Library and Library of Congress Cataloguing in Publication
Data are available**

ISBN 1–57958–335–0

First published in the USA and UK 2001

Typeset by Lorraine Hodghton, Radlett, Herts, UK
Printed by Edwards Brothers, Ann Arbor, Michigan, USA

Cover illustration:
Self-Portrait in Profile Facing Left, Drawing by Käthe Kollwitz,
1933; National Gallery of Art, Washington, DC, Rosenwald
Collection

CONTENTS

Editor's Note   *page*   vii
Contributors   xi
Alphabetical List of Artists   xiii
Chronological List of Artists   xvii
Preface by Mara R. Witzling   xxi

Introductory Surveys

Women as Artists in the Middle Ages   3
Academies of Art   20
Copyists   34
Printmakers   42
Amateur Artists   50
Training and Professionalism, 19th and 20th centuries
   1. Britain and Ireland   67
   2. France   77
   3. Germany, Austria and Switzerland   89
   4. Russia   99
   5. North America   106
Modernism and Women Artists   123
Feminism and Women Artists   131

Artists   141

Notes on Contributors   711
Photographic Acknowledgements   725
(illustrations appear between pages 342 and 343)

EDITOR'S NOTE

to the complete *Dictionary of Women Artists* (1997)

The *Dictionary of Women Artists* contains substantial entries on artists working in a wide variety of media from the Middle Ages to the present day, in countries throughout Europe as well as America and Australasia. To set the work and careers of the individual artists in context, introductory essays examine training opportunities and the changing conditions of work for women since the medieval period. A survey on women as artists in the Middle Ages assesses the evidence for women's participation in the arts in earlier periods.

The book is the fruit of the extensive scholarly interest in the subject of women artists that has been manifested since the 1970s, as part of a wider re-examination of women's history. While there are already very useful works of reference in the field, no previously published dictionary has covered such a wide-ranging historical and geographical span with such detailed entries. The list of artists was initially drawn up in consultation with the advisers whose names are listed below. It was expanded and refined through the suggestions of contributors. For practical reasons, certain firm parameters were established at the outset: the project would be concerned only with the Western tradition in art, and it would exclude women born after 1945; the emphasis would be historical rather than contemporary, and no attempt would be made to cover architecture, interior or garden design, or fashion.

Major themes of the book are the problems women encountered in trying to obtain adequate training, and their endeavours to gain professional recognition and status comparable to that of men; the concentration is thus on the "fine" arts of painting and sculpture. But the areas in which women have traditionally been employed are by no means neglected. Survey essays on printmakers and copyists shed light on the activities of those who operated on the margins of the official art world, and there are entries, for example, on 16th- and 17th-century printmakers, 18th-century textile designers and goldsmiths, and 19th-century ceramists. For the most part, however, the contribution of women to the applied arts was anonymous, or at least poorly documented, and therefore unsuited to the format of the entries included here. For continuity with the earlier periods, there are also entries on the most innovative 20th-century artists and designers working in the fields of ceramics, textiles and metalwork, including important women members of the Wiener Werkstätte and the Bauhaus. But these professional women were not the only ones who aspired to be artists, and although professionalism is perhaps the most dominant theme in the book, attention is also given to the many women whose artistic activity was confined to the domestic sphere: the amateur artists from the middle and upper classes, whose work was regarded as a mere "accomplishment" and a social skill.

The selection of entrants never ceased to be problematic. Only a minority would satisfy those most obvious criteria for inclusion in a reference book: contemporary reputation or posthumous fame. And of those who do qualify on these grounds – the women artists mentioned by

Lodovico Guicciardini in the 16th century, for instance – only a handful are adequately documented or have left behind a sufficient corpus of work to warrant an individual entry.

In a book dealing with such an area as this, it is perhaps inadvisable to talk of "criteria for inclusion" in any conventional sense at all; in many cases, the race was as important as the prize, and failure no ground for exclusion. A case in point is Anne Forbes: her derivative and rather mediocre work would in no way qualify her for inclusion in a dictionary of artists judged according to traditional art-historical norms, but her career, illuminated by surviving correspondence, offers a fascinating insight into the difficulties an 18th-century woman painter experienced in trying to establish herself. Thus in many ways this *Dictionary* may be regarded as an anthology, the entries demonstrating the extremely wide range of artistic activities in which women have been engaged; the roles accorded to them in a patriarchal society; and their responses to the constraints imposed upon them.

The book contains examples of artists who worked in the context of the convent, court or city; who were active as members of a family workshop or married into one; who were pupils, relatives, lovers or wives of well-known artists; who were representative practitioners within the genres traditionally associated with women: portraiture, still life, flower painting and genre; who established successful businesses, or who were amateur artists; who had exhibiting careers and gained some degree of professional recognition; who enjoyed popular success; who were educators or campaigners for women's artistic advancement; whose art and writings influenced other artists; who were associated with an avant-garde group, movement or trend; who were instrumental in the diffusion of modernism; who were themselves pioneers; whose work was or is pertinent to women's concerns; who explored issues of gender, race and identity; and artists who followed independent paths and cannot be categorised.

With only 600 entries, the *Dictionary* is inevitably selective, but the inclusion of one name at the expense of another who may have equal claims is an unavoidable consequence of the process of putting a book of this sort together and should not be taken to imply that the list of entries constitutes some kind of canon. We endeavoured to maintain an international balance, but there is an inescapable – although not intentional – Anglo-American bias, which largely stems from the abundance of literature on the subject in these areas. In the selection process, priority was weighted towards the earlier artists, to those who have attracted critical comment in at least their own language, those whose work was particularly relevant to women's issues and, for the more recent artists, those with a strong exhibiting career and public profile.

Artists are listed under their professional name – the one that they first or most frequently worked or exhibited under – in a form current in their lifetime; cross-references are provided from alternative names that the reader is likely to come across in the literature. The entries contain basic biographical information, a list of exhibitions (where appropriate), a bibliography and a signed critical essay contributed by a specialist on the artist concerned. The headnote points to the main areas of an artist's activity; she would, for example, be described as a writer only if this formed an integral part of her work as an artist. The outline biography is intended to provide a framework for the critical discussion of the artist's work in the essay. Major awards are mentioned here, unless they accompany an exhibition cited in the list below. Every effort has been made to ensure that the information provided is accurate. In many cases, the contributor's own archival research produced results that differed considerably from published sources; dates of birth proved particularly fluid.

The list of exhibitions is intended to convey the character of the artist's exhibiting career. Posthumous exhibitions are not listed, with the exception of a major retrospective held soon after an artist's death; important later exhibitions are signposted by the inclusion of the catalogue(s) in the bibliography. For most artists with post-war careers, only individual exhibitions are listed; important group shows are either mentioned in the biography or essay, or alluded to by the presence of the catalogue in the bibliography. Exhibitions are listed in chronological order; the venue is followed by the year(s) of a show's opening. For regularly occurring group exhibitions, such as the Paris Salon and the Royal Academy, the years of participation are cited; "occasionally" points to a break, but is no comment on the frequency of showing. For touring exhibitions, only the first venue is named.

The bibliography is arranged chronologically, to give the reader an indication of the historiography of the subject. Survey books and dictionaries are rarely cited, since they appear in the general bibliography. Exhibition catalogues are listed under their title, with the first venue and the year of opening; authors are given when a single entry or essay is cited in a more general work. English-language editions of books are provided wherever possible. Any writings by an artist are listed separately, under the heading "Selected Writings"; such lists include books, as well as articles that shed light on the entrant's work as an artist. Writings that appear in a broader context, such as statements in exhibition catalogues, are listed in the bibliography. Significant manuscript collections are noted at the end of the bibliography. In the essays, references to works in the bibliography are given as follows: author and date for books and articles, venue (i.e. town/city) and date for exhibition catalogues. The locations of works are provided wherever possible; otherwise, a reference is given to a published illustration (abbreviation: "repr.").

DELIA GAZE

Advisers to the complete *Dictionary of Women Artists* (1997):
Kathleen Adler, Shulamith Behr, Annemarie Weyl Carr, Nicola Coleby, Judith Collins, Estrella de Diego, Ann Eatwell, Michelle Facos, Tamar Garb, Sara F. Matthews Grieco, Janice Helland, Alison McNeil Kettering, Anne Kirker, Nancy Mowll Mathews, Jennifer Hawkins Opie, Gill Perry, Griselda Pollock, Wendy Wassyng Roworth, Mary Schoeser, Jane Sellars, Philip Ward-Jackson, Genevieve Warwick, Mara R. Witzling.

Note on the Concise Edition

This book, a concise version of the two-volume *Dictionary of Women Artists* (Fitzroy Dearborn, 1997), contains 200 full-length entries on individual artists as well as a number of introductory essays. Although the selection represents only about a third of that in the original book, the entries on individuals cover a similar historical and geographical range and still reflect the diversity of women artists' activity. The surveys focus on the mainstream areas of Europe and North America. It is hoped that readers will turn to the larger *Dictionary* if they are interested in artists or areas not treated here. For reasons of space, it was not possible to illustrate all the entries in the concise edition. Please note that references to figures are given alongside the artist's name in the entry headings.

For the selection of entries in the *Concise Dictionary*, I would particularly like to thank Mara R. Witzling and Shulamith Behr; Nicola Coleby, John House and Daniel Kirkpatrick also provided helpful advice.

DG, 2001

CONTRIBUTORS

Kathleen Adler
David Alexander
Bruce Arnold
Karen A. Bearor
Shulamith Behr
Carl Belz
Marianne Berardi
Renate Berger
Jon Bird
Marja Bloem
Kate Bomford
Patrick Bourne
Nicola Gordon Bowe
John E. Bowlt
Bettina Brandt
Patricia Brauch
Xanthe Brooke
Betty Ann Brown
Ariella Budick
Bernard Bumpus
Vivian P. Cameron
E. A. Carmean, Jr
Flavio Caroli
Annemarie Weyl Carr
Susan P. Casteras
Madeline H. Caviness
Mary Ann Caws
Mary Chan
Robin M. Chandler
Liana De Girolami Cheney
Margot Coatts
Georgiana M. M. Colvile
Emmanuel Cooper
Elizabeth Cropper
Elizabeth Cumming
Penelope Curtis
Sabine Dahmen
Carol Damian
Brenda Danilowitz
John A. Day

Katy Deepwell
Lea Rosson DeLong
Estrella de Diego
Terence Diggory
Claire Doherty
Douglas Dreishpoon
Elizabeth Eastmond
Sarah Edge
Bridget Elliott
Michael Evans
Michelle Facos
Betsy Fahlman
Constance A. Fairchild
Alicia Craig Faxon
Phylis Floyd
Jeana K. Foley
Mary F. Francey
Tamar Garb
Andrea Garrihy
Lola B. Gellman
Margherita Giacometti
Helen Goodman
Jeffrey D. Grove
Nina Guryanova
Catherine Hall-van den Elsen
Catherine Harding
Rosemary Harris
Lisa Heer
Janice Helland
Jane Hill
Patricia Hills
Alison Hilton
Julie Berger Hochstrasser
Lena Holger
Denise Hooker
Rosella M. Huber-Spanier
Kristina Huneault
Margaret Iversen
Fredrika H. Jacobs
Deborah Jean Johnson

Amelia Jones
Britta Kaiser-Schuster
Janet A. Kaplan
Alison McNeil Kettering
Catherine King
Elaine A. King
George Knox
Ute Krebs
Cecily Langdale
Mary Tompkins Lewis
Elisabeth Lidén
Marcelo Lima
Evelyn Lincoln
Stephen Lloyd
Christina Lodder
Sarah M. Lowe
Joe Lucchesi
Heidrun Ludwig
Catherine MacKenzie
Alyce Mahon
Valerie Mainz
Joan M. Marter
Nancy Mowll Mathews
Marsha Meskimmon
Barbara L. Michaels
Lillian B. Miller
Claudine Mitchell
Adelina Modesti
Laurie J. Monahan
Gerta Moray
Elizabeth Mulley
Caroline P. Murphy
Pamela Gerrish Nunn
Annika Öhrner
Anthony Parton
Martha Moffitt Peacock
Juliet Peers
Phyllis Peet
Gill Perry
Elizabeth Prelinger
Nancy Proctor

Erich Ranfft
Christopher Reeve
Roxana Robinson
Wendy Wassyng Roworth
Wendy R. Salmond
Gill Saunders
Alette Rye Scales
Edith Schoeneck
Birgit Schulte
Miriam Seidel
Jane Sellars
Harriet F. Senie
Mary D. Sheriff
Nicola J. Shilliam
Elizabeth A. T. Smith
Richard J. Smith
Domenica Spadaro
Lesley Stevenson
Katlijne Van der Stighelen
Karin Stober
Tara Leigh Tappert
Dorcas Taylor
Paula Terra Cabo
Margo Hobbs Thompson
Joanna Thornberry
Marina Vaizey
Debra Wacks
Neil Walker
Susan Waller
Esmé Ward
Nina Weibull
Sigrid Wortmann Weltge
James A. Welu
Barbro Werkmäster
Helen Weston
Colin Wiggins
Beth Elaine Wilson
Sarah Wilson
Mara R. Witzling
Jeryldene M. Wood
Alison Yarrington

ALPHABETICAL LIST
OF ARTISTS

Magdalena Abakanowicz
Berenice Abbott
Eileen Agar
Anni Albers
Tarsila do Amaral
Anna Ancher
Sofonisba Anguissola
Rita Angus
Diane Arbus
Josefa d'Ayala de Óbidos

Harriet Backer
Marie Bashkirtseff
Mary Beale
Cecilia Beaux
Vanessa Bell
Mme Benoist
Mme Léon Bertaux
Isabel Bishop
Rosa Bonheur
Lee Bontecou
Gesina ter Borch
Louise Bourgeois
Margaret Bourke-White
Marie Bracquemond
Marianne Brandt
Romaine Brooks
Lady Butler

Claude Cahun
Julia Margaret Cameron
Margaret Carpenter
Emily Carr
Rosalba Carriera
Carrington
Leonora Carrington
Mary Cassatt
Elizabeth Catlett

Constance Charpentier
Judy Chicago
Chryssa
Fanny Churberg
Lygia Clark
Camille Claudel
Marie-Anne Collot
Maria Cosway
Imogen Cunningham

Anne Seymour Damer
Dorothy Dehner
Sonia Delaunay
Evelyn De Morgan
Françoise Duparc

Susan Macdowell Eakins
Marie Ellenrieder
Alexandra Exter

Leonor Fini
Audrey Flack
Lavinia Fontana
Helen Frankenthaler
Meta Vaux Warrick Fuller

Fede Galizia
Giovanna Garzoni
Wilhelmina Geddes
Artemisia Gentileschi
Marguerite Gérard
Gluck
Anna Golubkina
Natalya Goncharova
Eva Gonzalès
Nancy Graves
Kate Greenaway

Nina Hamnett
Grace Hartigan
Clementina, Viscountess Hawarden
Jacoba van Heemskerck
Catharina van Hemessen
Barbara Hepworth
Herrad
Eva Hesse
Hildegard of Bingen
Sigrid Hjertén
Hannah Höch
Frances Hodgkins
Harriet Hosmer

Mainie Jellett
Gwen John
Frances Benjamin Johnston
Lois Mailou Jones

Frida Kahlo
Gertrude Käsebier
Angelica Kauffman
Mary Kelly
Kitty Kielland
Hilma af Klint
Laura Knight
Käthe Kollwitz
Joyce Kozloff
Lee Krasner
Barbara Kruger

Adélaïde Labille-Guiard
Giulia Lama
Dorothea Lange
Marie Laurencin
Tamara de Lempicka
Edmonia Lewis
Judith Leyster
Anna Dorothea Lisiewska-Therbusch
Barbara Longhi

Dora Maar
Margaret Macdonald
Anita Malfatti
Maruja Mallo
Diana Mantuana
Marisol
Agnes Martin
Louisa Matthiasdóttir
Constance Mayer
Maria Sibylla Merian

Annette Messager
Lee Miller
Joan Mitchell
Paula Modersohn-Becker
Louise Moillon
Berthe Morisot
Vera Mukhina
Gabriele Münter

Alice Neel
Plautilla Nelli
Louise Nevelson
Vera Nilsson
Jenny Nyström

Georgia O'Keeffe
Maria van Oosterwijck
Meret Oppenheim

Anna Claypoole and Sarah Miriam Peale
Clara Peeters
I. Rice Pereira
Lyubov Popova
Margaret Preston

Henrietta Rae
Yvonne Rainer
Katharine Read
Anne Redpath
Paula Rego
Germaine Richier
Lucie Rie
Bridget Riley
Faith Ringgold
Adelaide Alsop Robineau
Marietta Robusti
Emy Roeder
Geertruydt Roghman
Luisa Roldán
Properzia de' Rossi
Olga Rozanova
Rachel Ruysch

Betye Saar
Kay Sage
Niki de Saint Phalle
Charlotte Salomon
Augusta Savage
Miriam Schapiro
Helene Schjerfbeck
Carolee Schneemann

Anna Maria van Schurman
Zinaida Serebryakova
Elisabetta Sirani
Sylvia Sleigh
Clarissa Sligh
Jaune Quick-to-See Smith
Joan Snyder
Rebecca Solomon
Jo Spence
Lilly Martin Spencer
Nancy Spero
Milly Steger
Varvara Stepanova
Alice Barber Stephens
Florine Stettheimer
May Stevens
Gunta Stölzl

Sophie Taeuber-Arp
Dorothea Tanning
Ellen Thesleff
Mary Thornycroft

Charley Toorop
Phoebe Traquair

Nadezhda Udaltsova

Suzanne Valadon
Anne Vallayer-Coster
Remedios Varo
Maria Elena Vieira da Silva
Elisabeth Vigée-Lebrun
Caterina Vigri

Kay WalkingStick
Henrietta Ward
Caroline Watson
Marianne Werefkin
Candace Wheeler
Joyce Wieland

Marguerite Thompson Zorach
Unica Zürn

CHRONOLOGICAL LIST
OF ARTISTS

1098–1179	Hildegard of Bingen	1760–1838	Maria Cosway
active c.1178–c.1196	Herrad	1760/61–1814	Caroline Watson
c.1413–1463	Caterina Vigri	1761–1837	Marguerite Gérard
active 1514–29	Properzia de' Rossi	1767–1849	Constance Charpentier
1523–1588	Plautilla Nelli	1768–1826	Mme Benoist
1528–after 1565	Catharina van Hemessen	1775–1821	Constance Mayer
c.1532–1625	Sofonisba Anguissola	1791–1863	Marie Ellenrieder
c.1547–1612	Diana Mantuana	1791–1878	Anna Claypoole Peale
1552–1614	Lavinia Fontana	1793–1872	Margaret Carpenter
1552–1638	Barbara Longhi	1800–1885	Sarah Miriam Peale
c.1552/60–1590	Marietta Robusti	1809–1895	Mary Thornycroft
c.1578–c.1630	Fede Galizia	1815–1879	Julia Margaret Cameron
1593–1652/3	Artemisia Gentileschi	1822–1899	Rosa Bonheur
1600–1670	Giovanna Garzoni	1822–1865	Clementina, Viscountess Hawarden
1607–1678	Anna Maria van Schurman	1822–1902	Lilly Martin Spencer
1609–1660	Judith Leyster	1825–1909	Mme Léon Bertaux
1609/10–1696	Louise Moillon	1827–1923	Candace Wheeler
active 1611–21	Clara Peeters	1830–1908	Harriet Hosmer
1625–1651	Geertruydt Roghman	1832–1886	Rebecca Solomon
1630–1693	Maria van Oosterwijck	1832–1924	Henrietta Ward
c.1630–1684	Josefa d'Ayala de Óbidos	1840–1916	Marie Bracquemond
1631–1690	Gesina ter Borch	1841–1895	Berthe Morisot
1633–1699	Mary Beale	1843–1914	Kitty Kielland
1638–1665	Elisabetta Sirani	1844–1926	Mary Cassatt
1647–1717	Maria Sibylla Merian	c.1844–after 1911	Edmonia Lewis
1652–1706	Luisa Roldán	1845–1932	Harriet Backer
1664–1750	Rachel Ruysch	1845–1892	Fanny Churberg
1675–1757	Rosalba Carriera	1846–1933	Lady Butler
1681–1747	Giulia Lama	1846–1901	Kate Greenaway
1721–1782	Anna Dorothea Lisiewska-Therbusch	1849–1883	Eva Gonzalès
1723–1778	Katharine Read	1851–1938	Susan Macdowell Eakins
1726–1778	Françoise Duparc	1852–1934	Gertrude Käsebier
1741–1807	Angelica Kauffman	1852–1936	Phoebe Traquair
1744–1818	Anne Vallayer-Coster	1854–1946	Jenny Nyström
1748–1821	Marie-Anne Collot	1855–1942	Cecilia Beaux
1748–1828	Anne Seymour Damer	1855–1919	Evelyn De Morgan
1749–1803	Adélaïde Labille-Guiard	1858–1932	Alice Barber Stephens
1755–1842	Elisabeth Vigée-Lebrun	1859–1935	Anna Ancher

1859–1928	Henrietta Rae	1894–1954	Claude Cahun
1860–1884	Marie Bashkirtseff	1894–1958	Varvara Stepanova
1860–1938	Marianne Werefkin	1895–1978	Gluck
1862–1944	Hilma af Klint	1895–1965	Dorothea Lange
1862–1946	Helene Schjerfbeck	1895–1965	Anne Redpath
1864–1943	Camille Claudel	1897–1944	Mainie Jellett
1864–1927	Anna Golubkina	1897–1983	Gunta Stölzl
1864–1952	Frances Benjamin Johnston	1898–1991	Berenice Abbott
1864–1933	Margaret Macdonald	1898–1980	Tamara de Lempicka
1865–1929	Adelaide Alsop Robineau	1898–1963	Kay Sage
1865–1938	Suzanne Valadon	1899–1991	Eileen Agar
1867–1945	Käthe Kollwitz	1899–1994	Anni Albers
1869–1947	Frances Hodgkins	1900–1984	Alice Neel
1869–1954	Ellen Thesleff	1900–1988	Louise Nevelson
1871–1945	Emily Carr	1901–1994	Dorothy Dehner
1871–1944	Florine Stettheimer	1902–1988	Isabel Bishop
1874–1970	Romaine Brooks	1902–1995	Maruja Mallo
1875–1963	Margaret Preston	1902–1971	I. Rice Pereira
1876–1923	Jacoba van Heemskerck	1902–1959	Germaine Richier
1876–1939	Gwen John	1902–1995	Lucie Rie
1876–1907	Paula Modersohn-Becker	1903–1975	Barbara Hepworth
1877–1968	Meta Vaux Warrick Fuller	1904–1971	Margaret Bourke-White
1877–1970	Laura Knight	1905–1998	Lois Mailou Jones
1877–1962	Gabriele Münter	1907–1954	Frida Kahlo
1879–1961	Vanessa Bell	1907–1997	Dora Maar
1881–1962	Natalya Goncharova	1907–1977	Lee Miller
1881–1948	Milly Steger	1908–1970	Rita Angus
1882–1949	Alexandra Exter	1908–1996	Leonor Fini
1883–1976	Imogen Cunningham	1908–1984	Lee Krasner
1883–1956	Marie Laurencin	1908–1963	Remedios Varo
1884–1967	Zinaida Serebryakova	1908–1992	Maria Elena Vieira da Silva
1885–1979	Sonia Delaunay	1910–	Dorothea Tanning
1885–1948	Sigrid Hjertén	1911–	Louise Bourgeois
1886–1973	Tarsila do Amaral	1912–	Agnes Martin
1886–1918	Olga Rozanova	1913–1985	Meret Oppenheim
1886–1961	Nadezhda Udaltsova	1915–	Elizabeth Catlett
1887–1955	Wilhelmina Geddes	1916–	Sylvia Sleigh
1887–1986	Georgia O'Keeffe	1916–1970	Unica Zürn
1887–1968	Marguerite Thompson Zorach	1917–	Leonora Carrington
1888–1979	Vera Nilsson	1917–2000	Louisa Matthíasdóttir
1889–1978	Hannah Höch	1917–1943	Charlotte Salomon
1889–1964	Anita Malfatti	1920–1988	Lygia Clark
1889–1953	Vera Mukhina	1922–	Grace Hartigan
1889–1924	Lyubov Popova	1923–1971	Diane Arbus
1889–1943	Sophie Taeuber-Arp	1923–	Miriam Schapiro
1890–1956	Nina Hamnett	1924–	May Stevens
1890–1971	Emy Roeder	1926–1992	Joan Mitchell
1891–1955	Charley Toorop	1926–	Betye Saar
1892–1962	Augusta Savage	1926–	Nancy Spero
1893–1983	Marianne Brandt	1928–	Helen Frankenthaler
1893–1932	Carrington	1930–	Magdalena Abakanowicz

1930–	Marisol	1936–1970	Eva Hesse
1930–	Faith Ringgold	1939–	Judy Chicago
1930–	Niki de Saint Phalle	1939–	Carolee Schneemann
1931–	Lee Bontecou	1939–	Clarissa Sligh
1931–	Audrey Flack	1940–1995	Nancy Graves
1931–	Bridget Riley	1940–	Jaune Quick-to-See Smith
1931–1998	Joyce Wieland	1940–	Joan Snyder
1933–	Chryssa	1941–	Mary Kelly
1934–	Yvonne Rainer	1942–	Joyce Kozloff
1934–1992	Jo Spence	1943–	Annette Messager
1935–	Paula Rego	1945–	Barbara Kruger
1935–	Kay WalkingStick		

PREFACE

Why a dictionary of women artists at this time?

This dictionary embodies the vast shift that has occurred over the past 25 years concerning our knowledge and interpretation of women as artistic producers. By its size, scope, depth and breadth it obviates the question asked by Linda Nochlin in 1971: "Why have there been no great women artists?"[1] Even a cursory glance through its pages reveals that since the Middle Ages women have, indeed, been active makers of art in diverse media and geographical locales. Our purpose here is to consolidate and make available to both researchers and students the wealth of information that has been uncovered and recovered, as scholars have attempted to write women artists back into art history.

The scope of this work is limited to the Western tradition, from the medieval to the modern periods, including persons born before 1945; those born later have been omitted for practical reasons. Several hundred artists are presented in individual entries of varying lengths, incorporating details of their biographies and assessment of their art, as well as basic bibliographical information and exhibition chronology. The *Dictionary* also contains some 20 introductory surveys in order to contextualise these individual entries. These surveys differ somewhat in purpose and scope, depending on their subject. While the dictionary includes entries on women photographers and those who worked in the so-called applied arts, its emphasis is most definitely on painters and sculptors. Architects and interior designers, for example, have been omitted, not because of some judgement about the worthiness of their contribution, but rather to keep the scope of the project manageable. Likewise, the inclusion of only a few women who have worked in the more traditionally "female" areas such as needlework should be interpreted as the result of logistical constraints.

Our primary aim in this volume is historical, not theoretical. Nevertheless, it would be useful to present, at the outset, a brief overview of the process by which women artists and their artistic productions have been made visible over the past 25 years. In her discussion of the multifaceted impact of writing women into history, Joan Wallach Scott said that "the effort goes far beyond the naive search for the heroic ancestors of the contemporary women's movement to a re-evaluation of established standards of historical significance".[2] While the first investigations by art historians mostly consisted of the search for "lost" women artists, as in analogous research by historians and literary critics, subsequent analyses have questioned or revised the basic paradigms of art history. Their primary purpose was the collection of information that established women as producers of art, and these early endeavours accepted as given a fixed "canon" of artists, a traditional subdivision of art-historical "periods" and conventional categories of appropriate artistic practice. Such an approach illustrates the limitations of the process of recovery, according to Scott, which fails to bring about any real change in the conventional historical (or in this case art-historical) narrative.[3] As Peggy McIntosh has asserted, this historical method is problematic because it "assumes that the discipline is perfect as constructed" and that "women don't count" except for those few who have achieved within it.[4]

Subsequent analyses looked to social factors that might have accounted for women's exclusion from the art-historical canon. One critical stance emphasised women's hardships and exclusions – their "struggles" as they pursued the "obstacle race".[5] In the introduction to her book of this title, Germaine Greer says that her intention is to show how women artists as a "group" were "tormented by the same conflicts of motivation and the same practical difficulties, the obstacles both external and surmountable, internal and insurmountable of the race for achievement".[6] At this stage, women artists were perceived as a universal cohort whose difference from the "norm" was constructed as a liability. Their differing position was problematic: the disadvantages of women artists were stressed and women artists were perceived as "victims" of a misogynistic system. One drawback of this stage of historical analysis is that it leads to anger and resentment,[7] and while observation of the cultural barriers to women's achievement encourages us to question the construction of the canon, it does not necessarily revise it. Instead, it tends to ghetto-ise women's accomplishments, still considering them as exceptions, as outside the norm.

Like their counterparts in historical and literary analysis, more recent art-historical reassessments have focused on the social construction of gender, the "comparative location and activities of men and women ... [and] what representations of sexual difference suggest about the structure of social, economic and political authority".[8] Critics and historians have emphasised the actual achievements of women artists, understanding that "since there have always been women artists, the issue is ... how they worked despite these restraints".[9] Taking into account that women's cultural positions differed from those of their male counterparts, researchers have identified how artists adopted "enabling strategies" that allowed them to work when they found their gender in conflict with accepted conventions about the nature of art and its culturally sanctioned producers.[10] Furthermore, when viewed from this perspective, the production of women artists, which often differed from that of canonical male artists, forces contemporary scholars to reassess that canon and its assumptions. Scott's discussion regarding the "usefulness" of gender as a historical category is absolutely to the point here. As she says:

> feminist desires to make woman a historical subject cannot be realized simply by making her the agent or principal character of a historical narrative. To discover where women have been throughout history it is necessary to examine what gender and sexual difference have had to do with the workings of power.

She continues:

> the realization of the radical potential of women's history comes in the writing of narratives that focus on women's experience and analyze the ways in which politics construct gender and gender constructs politics. Female agency then becomes not the recounting of great deeds performed by women, but the exposure of the often silent and hidden operations of gender which are nonetheless present and defining forces of politics and political life.[11]

While this volume, with its chronological orientation, its periodic surveys and its biographical organisation might seem to be a product of the older approach in which women are made "historical subjects" and their "great deeds" are emphasised, in actuality it exemplifies the more sophisticated methodology in which discrete events are carefully examined through the lens of gender. No attempt has been made to "fit" the artists discussed herein into a pre-packaged canon of artistic "greats". No attempt is made to create an alternative canon of "great" women artists. While the canon itself is not questioned from a polemical stance, the essays in this volume look at the specifics of the circumstances under which women engaged in art. In that way the presence of women practitioners is written back into the history of art. And at the same time a more accurate sense of such questions as how the art market functioned, or what standards were prevalent at different times, is communicated.

Thus, one could say that simply by its weight the information herein challenges conventional readings of art history. First, the *Dictionary* makes very clear that women always were involved in the production of art in some way. It is also clear that there were a good number of women artists and patrons who achieved a certain amount of repute during their lifetimes. Furthermore, the analyses are specific and take their subjects on their own terms, without trying to fit the artists into a pre-existing paradigm. By considering, instead, the specific circumstances under which women made art they conclude, along with Annemarie Weyl Carr regarding women as artists during the Middle Ages, that the "dark is light enough". The forceful, but previously unacknowledged presence of women during that allegedly unenlightened period provides a good illustration of how the work encompassed in this volume expands our understanding of the role of women in the production of art. Contrary to popular misconception, during the medieval period many women were prominent cultural patrons. Furthermore, although a signature need not imply authorship in the way we would conceive it, at that time patrons played a more active role in the conception of works of art. As Carr and her associates also point out, the materials of high art differed during that period, so that two sisters noted for their work in gold and gems were not "minor" artists, as a contemporary bias would seem to indicate; rather they were working with the most valued media of their time. Additionally, women's names appear in guild lists consistently, particularly those associated with the production of textiles, also not merely a "decorative" art. By looking beyond the established art-historical preconceptions of what constituted art and art-making, the actual contributions of numerous women artists can now be chronicled.

But if women artists were there all along, how could it be that their accomplishments are only now being recovered? This volume also helps to answer and explain this predicament. Although women did play a more active role in the production of art than they have been traditionally granted – and many achieved high status within their lifetimes – this volume documents the very real cultural and institutional impediments that have prevented women as a group from being on "equal" terms with their male counterparts. Women could not study from live models until the end of the 19th century, so they were precluded from practising history painting, then viewed as the ultimate in the hierarchy of artistic worthiness.[12] The woman who was able to have access to the necessary education to compete in that arena was the exception. This explains why, as Nochlin observed at the outset, so many early women artists were the daughters of artists who were able to learn their crafts through their fathers. In all centuries from the 15th through the 18th there are instances of women who gained access to artistic education through the position and influence of their fathers (or other family members), which opened a route that would not have been otherwise available to them. The necessity for male protection or patronage continued, actually, into the 20th century, when women artists gained access to public forums through the influence of a spouse or a lover whose high status in the art world helped her career to progress.

Although, in actuality, women produced art during all post-medieval periods, their presence as creators with authority equivalent to that of their male counterparts was only grudgingly acknowledged in the public discourse. Women artists were constructed as "different" from their male colleagues, who constituted the norm while the woman of achievement was considered exceptional. The complicated and persistent attempts to exclude women from the academies or to limit their membership, as discussed in the survey on Academies of Art, provide an excellent case in point. The academies were agencies of both education and legitimisation, whose "over-riding concern was to raise the dignity of the profession". Women were excluded from full participation in most major European academies from the Renaissance through the 19th century via several different strategies. When women were allowed membership in an academy at all their fellow academicians took steps to ensure that they would comprise only a small fraction of the membership, as in the Académie Royale de Peinture et de Sculpture in France, which agreed in 1770 to receive no more than four women at one time (and hastened to point out that they were in no way obliged to fulfil that entire number). Furthermore, women were often accorded different status that prohibited them from being perceived as "true" members that held the same standards as their male counterparts. In the French Academy, for example, female academicians were not allowed to take the same public oaths as men, and were thus perceived as "foreign in some fashion to its constitution".

The gendered nature of artistic practice has also hindered the ability of women to produce art with significant impact in the public sphere. The post-Renaissance construction of the concept of "artist" has been gendered as male, whether conceived in Renaissance terms as the genius reflecting God's genius or in the 19th-century context of the bohemian who expresses his scorn for the bourgeoisie by having numerous sexual exploits.[13] According to the 18th-century system of aesthetics, the work of women was delicate – the pleasing – whereas that of men was powerful – the sublime. The nature of high art has also been gendered, as has the classification of the relative worthiness of various genres of painting. From the 16th to the 19th centuries paintings whose subjects were drawn from history and mythology were deemed to be more "important" art productions than landscapes, portraiture or still lifes, lesser subjects because they focused on the specific, the individual or the domestic. When this model changed during the latter part of the 19th century, and artists were exhorted to find their subject matter in "modern life", for the most part that implied the modern city to which women did not have the same access as men. During the 20th century abstraction, "pure art", was given a higher worth than art with residual narrative content; this way of seeing was also gendered. Finally, as time progressed from the Middle Ages to the present day, the rift between high art and the so-called crafts has widened. Those areas in which women had long excelled – such as needlework – were devalued accordingly. The Arts and Crafts movements of the later part of the 19th century were a solid attempt to return to a more medieval convention, not only in stylistic motifs, but in terms of recognising the "artfulness" that could characterise various objects of use.

These very real impediments explain how a conventional history of art that excluded the presence of women could have been written. Because the contributors to this *Dictionary* have taken a nuanced regard of history, a picture of women's place within it is allowed to emerge: "the rich world that is revealed when you look at women's lives starting from women's own ground, rather than assuming that we are victims or deprived".[14] The space in which women were active as creators, patrons and entrepreneurs in a variety of traditional and non-traditional media is opened up and made visible. In so doing, a different response to Nochlin's question is provided, one that makes clear that perhaps the long-accepted parameters for assessing "great" art and artists are not strictly or unilaterally valid, nor do they give the most full and subtle interpretation of the historical data.

MARA R. WITZLING

Notes

1   Linda Nochlin, "Why have there been no great women artists?", *Woman in Sexist Society: Studies in Power and Powerlessness,* ed. Vivian Gornick and Barbara K. Moran, New York: Basic Books, 1971; reprinted in *Women, Art and Power and Other Essays*, New York: Harper, and London: Thames and Hudson, 1988, pp.145–78. Nochlin's essay and the question it asks has stood as a benchmark for the feminist reassessment of art history. Numerous subsequent writers have used this question as the starting point of their investigations, which over the years have pushed its boundaries, showing why other questions need to be asked. Nochlin herself has pointed out that other questions are more relevant and productive. None the less, if one could cite a starting point for the project on which all others are based – this is it.

2   Joan Wallach Scott, "Women in history: The modern period", *Past and Present*, no.101, November 1983, p.145.

3   *ibid.*, p.147.

4   Peggy McIntosh, "Interactive phases of curricular re-vision: A feminist perspective", *Traditions and Translations: Women's Studies and a Balanced Curriculum*, conference held at Claremont College, CA, February 1983, p.26.

5   Germaine Greer, *The Obstacle Race: The Fortunes of Women Painters and Their Work*, London: Secker and Warburg, and New York: Farrar Straus, 1979. Greer mentions Nochlin's essay specifically, and says that it asks a "false question". According to Greer, the real questions are "What is the contribution of women to the visual arts?" "If there were any women artists, why were there not more?" "If we can find one good painting by a woman, where is the rest of her work?" "How good were the women who earned a living by painting?"

6   *ibid.*, p.6.

7   McIntosh op. cit., p.27.

8   Scott op. cit., p.153.

9   Rozsika Parker and Griselda Pollock, *Old Mistresses: Women, Art and Ideology,* London and New York: Routledge, 1981. Parker and Pollock make this statement in response to Nochlin's assertion, as they characterise it, that "institutional restraints were responsible for women's 'problems' in art practice".

10 Griselda Pollock's essay "Modernity and the spaces of femininity" in *Vision and Difference: Femininity, Feminism and the Histories of Art* (London and New York: Routledge, 1988) is an early example of a study of women artists' positional negotiations. The term "enabling strategies" is used by Bridget Elliot and Jo-Ann Wallace in *Women Artists and Writers: Modern (Im)Positionings* (London and New York: Routledge, 1994) with reference to the "diverse strategies" developed by women artists "for negotiating what were unequal, and thus frequently uneasy, relationships with their male modernist counterparts" (p.17).

11 Scott op. cit., p.156.

12 Nochlin calls attention to this institutional barrier in her germinal article cited above: "By examining in detail a single deprivation or disadvantage, the unavailability of the nude model, I have suggested that it was indeed made institutionally impossible for women to achieve artistic excellence or success on the same footing as men" (p.176).

13 For a history of the conflation of genius and masculinity that extends back to the Roman empire, see Christina Battersby, *Gender and Genius: Towards a Feminist Aesthetic*, Bloomington: Indiana University Press, 1989.

14 McIntosh op. cit., p.32.

INTRODUCTORY
SURVEYS

Women as Artists in the Middle Ages
"The Dark Is Light Enough"

This essay surveys the evidence of women as artists in the Western Middle Ages in the centuries between about 600 and 1400 (for Byzantium, see the complete *Dictionary of Women Artists*). Dorothy Miner's *Anastaise and Her Sisters* (1974) laid the foundation for current inquiry into medieval women's art.[1] Much of the data that she – and indeed that we today – rely upon was noted already in 19th- and early 20th-century sources.[2] Our task has been its assembly and, more importantly, its interpretation. Composing a fabric within which to understand the widely scattered women whom we discover challenges many of our preconceptions about the production, the consumption and indeed the very definition of art in the Middle Ages. The job of interpreting women as artists has been enriched by recent insights into women's prominent role as cultural patrons in the Middle Ages.[3] The work of women as creators of rich and significant artefacts takes its place within this broader rediscovery of women as arbiters of medieval culture.

Inevitably the search for medieval women artists depends to a fair extent upon the search for signed works. But signatures are notoriously slippery in medieval art. Although medieval works are more often signed than we generally imagine (see Bergmann 1985 and Legner 1985, both with bibliographies), names do not necessarily appear in the same contexts or carry the same messages as they do in more modern arts, and they lead less often to the agonistic heroes of self-expression whom groups in search of a history hunger to own. Signatures are problematic not only because of the longstanding reluctance of modern scholars to credit women with the production of the works on which their names actually appear, but because of a genuine ambiguity in medieval attributions of authorship. Craftsperson, designer, entrepreneur and patron may all be identified as the one who "made" a work, and the presence of a name is no guarantee that it singles out the person closest to the modern conception of that work's "creator". Questions of gender more often complicate than clarify this situation. Thus the embroidery of the superb 13th-century Göss vestments in the Museum für Kunst und Industrie, Vienna, is traditionally attributed to the Kunigunde whose name is inscribed in purple silk on the pluvial: "Heavenly Mother receive the gift of Kunigunde, may the pluvial with an alb be pleasing to you, heavenly patron" (*celi matrona Chunegundis suscipe dona, casula cum cappa placeat tibi celica [patrona]*; Bock 1856–71, ii, pp.47 and 296). Had the inscription named a man, he would have been read at once as the vestment's donor; Kunigunde was imagined as an artist because more women than men are known by name as embroiderers. Today scholars regard Kunigunde, too, as the donor. But should this attribution imply the same relationship to the work that we would assume for a man? Might women, whose names appear with such notable frequency as donors of fine textiles, have been more closely involved and so have assumed more authority than men in the design of such works? Can we assume that they had equal access to the cultural resources that are deployed in the often intricate iconographic programmes of these works? Might they, indeed, have had even greater access to images than men, as Hamburger (1989 and 1991) suggests?

Such issues of interpretation lead us to search beyond the testimony of signatures to the contexts of medieval luxury production. Legal texts – guild and tax lists, cases at law, deeds of contract, inheritance and sale – have proved to be especially informative about the ways in which work was distributed and valued, but texts that lurk on the edge of legend can offer insights into mentality, as well. Thus, the 9th-century *Vita* of the sainted 7th-century Mosan sisters Harlinde and Renilde is well known for its claim that the sisters wrote and copied so much that it would be laborious for robust men (Eckenstein 1896, p.231). It is less often cited for the way in which it describes their surviving works: a book sparkling with new gold and shining gems, and an embroidery ornate with gold and jewels. The sisters were embroiderers in precious materials, then, as well as scribes; moreover, their work in both media is described with nearly the same words: both are luminous with gold and precious stones. That the "new gold and shining gems" seem in the case of the book to refer to a new, 9th-century cover and not to the sisters' pages is unimportant; what matters in the *Vita* is that golden splendour characterises all their work. It is an aesthetic attribute, a way of conferring greatness. Luminous materials assumed great power in the medieval eye, and metalwork and embroidery were the media that deployed such materials in their purest and most compelling form. Even monumental media such as architecture and sculpture were affected by this. From the silver- and gem-clad chapels of the Merovingians to the glazed and mosaiced churches of the later medieval West, buildings were assimilated to the quality of fine metalwork and its dazzling, mobile manifestation in the pliant coats of embroidered gold that vested clergy, rulers and ritual spaces. As Dodwell (1982) has shown so vividly, works in gold and gems were the high arts of the Middle Ages. This is precisely what their *Vita* attributes to the sisters Harlinde and Renilde. Their scribal labour was virtuous; their work in gold was great.

These examples illustrate some of the challenges of interpretation that confront one in the quest for women artists in the Middle Ages. There is the question of the extent to which women and women's work were distinct from men and their work; there is the question of women's access to cultural resources; there is the question of what – in the medieval scheme of value – most nearly corresponds to a conception of art and of the artist that we can accept; and there is the question of modes of production and their relation to the names that do appear in inscriptions, documents and narrative sources.

The most explicit documentation on the distribution of labour within the trades comes from the guild lists that survive from Paris, Cologne and London (Uitz 1990; Baron 1968; Michaëlsson 1951), although they appear only towards the end of the period treated here, from the 1290s onwards. Relating their testimony to the patterns of production that preceded them has not been done on a systematic basis for women's work. The implica-

tions for women of the mature guild system, in turn, extend well beyond the period covered here. Two things are striking in the evidence offered by the guild lists. One is the pervasiveness of women's presence: women figure in 108 of the 321 professions found in Paris in the years around 1300 (Uitz 1990, p.52). In addition to the guilds engaged in the production of silk and linen cloth that were limited in law or in practice to women alone, we find women in many other trades, including those of painter, glazier, sculptor and metalworker, where they may comprise as many as 12 per cent of the names (Lillich 1985, pp.80–82). Many of the women who appear are widows who inherited their husbands' shops. But others were masters in their own right, and Edith Ennen (1989, p.186) has suggested that the incomes of employed wives helped to finance their husbands' engagement in the otherwise unpaid offices of civic government. If women appear pervasively in the lists, however, the guild lists are equally notable for the numerical dominance they give to men, especially as masters. Both phenomena must to some extent reflect the patterns of work that preceded the guilds during the centuries that dominate this chapter, but it is far from clear just how.

The guilds bring out a fact of medieval evidence: where names appear, women's names appear among them. Book art and textile arts are the skills in which one can most consistently find women named, and so it is in these that one can best ponder the issues of women's artistic productivity. This essay will focus heavily upon these media. This said, it remains to be ascertained to what extent women in fact gravitated to the skills in which their names appear, or whether their names appear in these skills simply because more names of all types are associated with them.

Textile arts

The association of women with textiles and especially needlework is found too persistently throughout the Middle Ages to have escaped commentary, though this commentary, as Rozsika Parker has shown (Parker 1984, pp.13–59), has varied widely, from the Victorian adulation of the myth of cloistered womanhood through the affirmative interest of Parker herself to the opprobrium of Germaine Greer (1979, pp.151–68), who saw in it a confinement of women's ingenuity to a minor and repressive craft. Textiles that bear attributions are characteristically the great ones – large and intricate floor or wall coverings or opulent embroideries in gold and precious gems. Works such as these were exceptional in their own time for their high cost in both materials and labour, and the people associated with them are often of correspondingly elite social status, making it difficult to distinguish patronage from active participation in the design and production of the works: one wonders how many of the 20 crowned women cited in Franz Bock's index (Bock 1856–71, ii, pp.363–77) actually themselves made the gold-gorgeous textiles assigned by legend or inscription to their hands (though see Dodwell 1982, p.70, on Edith, queen of Edward the Confessor of England). None the less, there is enough evidence to make it clear that the association of women and fine textiles was neither a figment of Victorian imagination nor a matter simply of women's exile from the major arts into the realm of craft. This association was as characteristic of Byzantium as it was of the West.

Already in the 5th century, the *Notitia dignitatum*, a Roman inventory of the empire's cities, referred to cloth-manufactories as "gynaecea"; the term continues in the early medieval centuries, and it is as gynaecea that Paul Grimm identifies two rooms at the Ottonian palace at Tilleda in which loom weights and foundations for upright looms were found (Grimm 1963). Their name implies that these were staffed by women, and indeed one hears in 9th-century Augsburg of an estate that employed 24 women in a cloth workshop and at Reichenau of taxes paid in kind with *textura feminae* – women's textile work (Uitz 1990, pp.18–19). There is no evidence that the gynaecea produced fine textiles, but the production of fine textiles, too, is associated with women from the very beginning of the Middle Ages. Caesarius of Arles in 6th-century France and the Council of Clovesho of 747 in England both objected to the amount of time spent by nuns in the production of fine embroidery (such complaints are so frequent that they must be a topos: see Dodwell 1982, p.57, and Eckenstein 1896, p.226), and references to gifts of fine textiles by women are frequent in the early Church.

This is especially true in England, where women figure recurrently in early saints' lives as the source of fine textiles. Thus, the silken shroud of St Wilfrid (d. 709 or 710) and the fine shroud of St Guthlac (d. 715) were both provided by abbesses, and St Cuthbert (d. 687) is said by the *Liber Eliensis* to

have received silks magnificently embroidered with gold and precious gems by St Etheldreda of Ely (Dodwell 1982, p.49, though he doubts the report on Etheldreda since it is not recorded by Bede; Eckenstein 1896, p.225). Etheldreda belonged to the royal elite of the realm, and it is around such noble figures that reports of wondrous works of textile art cluster most richly. We see this at Etheldreda's Ely itself. We hear not only of Etheldreda's skill in the 7th century, but later of Aelfflaed, widow of Byrhtnoth, earldorman of Ely (d. 991 at the Battle of Maldon), who gave the abbey church of Ely a woven or embroidered hanging that was figured with her dead husband's deeds (Budny 1991; Dodwell 1982, p.135). A generation later Aethelswitha, daughter of King Canute, refused marriage and retired to a dwelling near Ely, where, *cum puellulis* – with a group of young girls – she devoted herself to the production of gold embroidery for the abbey; a headband made with her own hands still survived in the late 12th century (Bock 1856–71, i, p.153; Dodwell 1982, p.70). These accounts from Ely embrace lay and cloistered women, large works and small, and sacred and secular subject matter. All, however, are recorded because of their splendour. How impressive such pieces could be is indicated by the account of an altar frontal embroidered in 1016 by Aethelswitha's mother, Queen Aelgiva, which was so richly studded with gold, pearls and gems that it was said to resemble the monumental medium of gold mosaic (Thieme and Becker 1907–50, i, p.96). The surviving stole of St Cuthbert (Durham Cathedral Treasury; repr. Dodwell 1982, pl.F; Staniland 1991, fig.5), produced between 909 and 916 at the instigation of Queen Aethelfleda, can still give an impression of this work. Who actually made the Cuthbert stole is unknown, but we know of queens commissioning such work from other women. Thus, in 1083 Matilda, queen of William the Conqueror, gave to her foundation of La Trinité at Caen a chasuble embroidered at Winchester by Alderet's wife (Staniland 1991, p.8). A married woman and therefore clearly a lay person, Alderet's wife must have been a professional embroiderer like two women cited in the great inventory of 1086–7 recording property in England known as Domesday Book: Leofgyd, who held an estate in Wiltshire "because she used to make, and still makes, the embroidery of the King and Queen", and Aelfgyd, given land by the sheriff of Buckinghamshire "on condition of her teaching his daughter embroidery work" (*idem*).

The examples cited are assembled from different kinds of evidence, but they are striking in the fact that – as Budny notes – the surviving evidence for the Anglo-Saxon period names women – not men – in conjunction with the production of fine textiles (1991, p.272); women of various social levels practised this work. Their skill is clear; their authority is more complicated. Many of these people probably worked to designs developed by men; we hear, for instance, of the artistically gifted St Dunstan in the 10th century providing a design for a noble lady named Aethelwynn, who embroidered it in gold and jewels (Dodwell 1982, p.70). But in other instances women must have worked to their own designs. The case of Aelfflaed is especially tantalising, for her hanging for Ely anticipates that other great textile war-narrative, the Bayeux Tapestry. A 70-metre-long embroidered narrative of the Norman Conquest of England of 1066 (Wilson 1985; Bernstein 1986), the Bayeux Tapestry is often claimed for women. It can illuminate the question of authorship. Bernstein has traced many of its motifs persuasively to manuscript sources at Canterbury, and so to male designers. Like Queen Matilda, they very probably relied on professional embroiderers – including women – associated with Canterbury to execute their designs (Parker 1984, p.27). A large number of the motifs, however, derive ultimately from the early 9th-century Utrecht Psalter (Bibliotheek der Rijksuniversiteit te Utrecht, MS 32), which in 1066 was in the great (male) monastic library at Christ Church, Canterbury. But it is important to remember that its exceptionally rich visual imagery has suggested to modern scholars that it was initially made for a woman, the Carolingian queen Judith (McKitterick 1990, p.311). If such books were indeed made for them, early medieval women would scarcely have lacked the iconographic repertoire to design elaborately figured textiles such as Aelfflaed's.

It seems clear that early medieval women participated extensively in the production of fine textiles, and that aristocratic women must have commanded both the craft and the iconographic resources required for the creation of remarkable designs. Evidence from the early medieval Continent only corroborates the role of women as producers of fine textile art. The so-called battle flag of Gerberga of *c.*962 survives as concrete testimony (Backes and Dölling 1971, pp.198–9). A square of silk (33 × 33 cm.) preserved in the treasury of Cologne Cathedral, it is embroidered in gold with figures of Christ, the Archangels and saints, to whom a prostrate Count Ragenardus is shown praying. Beneath him in large letters are the words GERBERGA ME FECIT (Gerberga made me). The name – clearly that of a woman – lies close to his form, suggesting that Gerberga was his wife; if so, she was assuredly a noblewoman.

Women's names continue to appear in conjunction with fine textiles as one moves into the 12th and 13th centuries. At this point, however, the more complex and costly types of production were increasingly dominated by professional ateliers. This is certainly the case with the technique of the knotted carpet, seen in a sequence of 12th-century survivals in Germany culminating in the famous carpet at St Servatius, Quedlinburg, which bears in a metric inscription the name of Agnes of Meissen (d. 1203), noble abbess of the Ottonian imperial convent of Quedlinburg (Wilckens 1992; Stuttgart 1977, i, pp.641–4, ii, figs 597–8). It is unlikely that her nuns themselves practised the new and specialised craft of the pile carpet. But Agnes probably was responsible for the carpet's learned theme, which repeats the subject of Martianus Capellus's *Marriage of Mercury to Philology* already used earlier in a carpet of 995 given by the nun Hedwig to the monastery of St Gall (Eckenstein 1896, p.233).

Mounting professionalism affected both lay and monastic production. In the urban world of lay craftspeople it generated ever-greater specialisation. This is demonstrated in the realm of gold embroidery. Associated particularly with England, as the generic term *opus anglicanum* indicates, gold embroidery was practised in a number of urban centres by the end of the 13th century (see London 1963; Brel-Bordaz 1982; Cologne 1985, ii, pp.140–45). Earlier, as our examples from Ely have shown, costly production had gathered into monastic centres: it may well have been among such groups as the *puellulae* of Ely that the lay embroiderers mentioned in the Domesday Book were trained. In the first half of the 12th century we hear of the pope acquiring embroidery from the mystic and nun Christina of Markyate (Eckenstein 1896, p.227). The signed embroideries by Abbess Iohanna of Beverly in England (an altar frontal of *c.*1290–1340, signed on the back DOMNA IOHANNA

BEVERLAI MONACA ME FECIT; Victoria and Albert Museum, London; London 1963), and those from 13th-century Cologne by the Abbess Iulia (a horizontal border embroidered DOMINA IVLIA ABBATISA; Kunstgewerbemuseum, Berlin; Cologne 1985, ii, pp.441, 443, no.F82) and by Odelia (a border of *c.*1290–1340 signed ODILIA ME FECIT; Victoria and Albert Museum; *ibid.*, p.441), who was probably also a nun, although she does not give a title, show that convents continued to produce fine work. Monasteries did, too, as demonstrated by the embroiderers John of Thanet (active 1300–20; Staniland 1991, p.58; London 1963) and Thomas of Selmiston (d. 1419; Parker 1984, p.44).

In 1246, on the other hand, when the pope was impressed by the splendid vestments of the English clergy and sent to England to acquire comparable ones, his request was turned over to the merchants of London (Staniland 1991, pp.10–12). It is to them, also, that the extraordinarily prodigal patronage of the court was committed in the 13th and 14th centuries. Among the embroiderers were many women; their names – most notably that of Mabel of Bury St Edmunds, embroiderer for King Henry III – appear in contracts (*ibid.*, p.10; Lancaster 1972, pp.83–5). But alongside the women were many men: men and women belonged together to long-lived family dynasties of needleworkers, such as the Settere family, and one cannot in any sense designate embroidery as a gender-specific task of women; it was a professional speciality. Thus, Mabel's work was judged by "discreet men and women with knowledge of embroidery"; 112 people – 70 men and 42 women – were engaged in 1330 to embroider counterpanes for Queen Philippa of England (Staniland 1991, pp.13–14, 23); and more men than women are named in the London court records known as the Hustings Rolls from the years around 1300 (Fitch 1976, pp.288–96; Brel-Bordaz 1982, p.21).

One by one, women of real authority who worked as master embroiderers and weavers emerge from these documents: we find women taking on apprentices (Parker 1984, p.47) and occasionally being sued (for a suit against one Katherine Duchewoman who was accused of weaving a tapestry deceptively in 1374, see Amt 1993, p.205). Some tasks seem to have been dominated by women: in Paris the ribbon-makers and braid-makers were all women (Uitz 1990, p.51). But specialisation was not wholly conducive to the woman artist. One notes in the contract for Queen Philippa's counterpanes that the women were paid two-thirds what the men were; moreover, men and women alike worked not to their own designs but to those of professional artists who were hired at twice the needleworkers' wages. Major works were contracted not with the embroiderers themselves but with entrepreneurs who assembled the requisite teams of artists and craftspeople; their exploitative and often biased behaviour is illustrated vividly in the case brought in 1286 against the Douai wool merchant Jehan Boinebroke by 40 employees including the dyer, Agnes li Patiniere, for defrauding her and a number of other women (Gies and Gies 1978, pp.165–74), and only rarely do women seem to have assumed the status of merchant entrepreneur: just one woman – Rose of Burford, wool merchant and wife of a London wool merchant – is known among those who managed the lucrative embroidery trade in London (Parker 1984, pp.47–8). The statutes of Parisian embroiderers of 1316 – in which nearly half of the 200 names are women's – and the guild lists of Cologne both corroborate the English evidence that women were prominent in the craft of fine textiles; at the same time they confirm the close interaction of men and women, and the very high degree of specialisation that tended to make needlework a craft pursued in hired groups, anonymously, under the hegemony of named artists and commercial entrepreneurs.

Urbanisation and the attendant professional specialisation of trades had an effect upon monastic production as well, and especially upon the urban convents founded with increasing bourgeois support under the aegis of the mendicant and reformed orders. Here, the effect was less specialisation as such than self-sufficiency. One can study this especially in Germany, where Catholic convents were often passed on to Protestant sodalities and so escaped destruction. Recent catalogues on the urban development of Osnabrück, Freiburg, Cologne and Nuremberg all give remarkable vistas into the richness and intensity of the visual culture in the local convents (Braunschweig 1985, Freiburg im Breisgau 1970, Cologne 1985 and Schraut 1987, respectively). Textiles – though unsigned – are prominent. Both the *Ancren riwle*, a devotional text composed around 1200 in England for women anchorites, and the great secular writer Christine de Pisan (or Pizan) around 1400 spoke of nuns producing woven or embroidered objects for sale to help support their houses (Parker 1984, p.43). In the same period we find nuns producing within their own communities the beautiful textiles that outfitted their churches: wall hangings, huge curtains to veil the sanctuary during Lent (*Fastentücher*), garments for their devotional figures of Christ, the Virgin and the saints, and covers for the choir benches. Varied techniques were used – a 14th-century border for an altar that survives at, and was probably produced in, the convent of Isenhagen is entirely embroidered in beads of coral, pearls and other semi-precious stones, recalling Queen Aelgiva's altar frontal in its mosaic-like opulence (Braunschweig 1985, i, pp.472–3, no.389). But the most characteristic technique is the brightly coloured wool embroidery known significantly as *Klosterstich* – that is, convent stitch.[4] A late but fully documented picture of this work is offered by the Saxon convent of Lüne, where some 85 square metres of colourful woollen embroidery were produced by the sisters of the community in the 16 years between 1492 and 1508. Seventeen sisters took part in shifting groups of six to nine at once, signing their work with initials that can – in the one case of Margarete Rosenhagen – be matched with a name in the task-book (Appuhn 1983, p.12). There were celebrations when a piece was finished, but the work was undertaken as a form of devotion and reflects the devotional themes of the sisters' spiritual life. The surviving records at Lüne post-date our period, but big, beautifully embroidered *Fastentücher* survive at Lüne from as early as the beginning of the 14th century, and it seems likely that they, too, were produced internally by members of the convent (*ibid.*, p.21). (The 13th-century *Fastentuch* of Richmod von Adocht, formerly in the church of the Holy Apostles, Cologne, and recorded in the sketchbook of Matthias Joseph de Noël, had the prominent praying figure of a nun in the lower border; repr. Cologne 1985, ii, pp.196–7, no.E15.) How pervasive this model of self-sufficient convent production actually was is debated, as illustrated especially clearly by Moessner's considered treatment of the rich legacy of embroideries – including the famous late 14th-century Tristan tapestry – preserved at the Cistercian convent of Wienhausen (Moessner 1987). In the mid-15th century, however, it is clear that a number of houses – including Wienhausen itself, St Katherine's and the Clarissan convent in Nuremberg, and Heilig Grab in Bamberg – had become significant purveyors of fine textiles, not only adorning their own buildings but filling commissions for secular institutions in their cities.[5] The nine-part tapestry of 1508 (Diözesanmuseum, Bamberg) with its tiny marginal image of nuns at their great upright loom offers a pictorial signature of this kind of convent-industrial women's art (Baumgärtel-Fleischmann 1983, pp.54–5).

The evidence of fine textiles is both rich and elusive. It confirms the fact that, as noted, where names appear, women's names appear among them. Neither types of work nor roles within them – patron, entrepreneur, master, labourer – are gender-segregated. Creative authority, on the other hand, remains harder to assign.

Book arts

Book art is another area in which names – and with them women's names – appear in fair number. It can cast further light on questions posed by the evidence of textiles: of the degree of authority assumed by women in works associated with them, of the relation of women and women's work to men and their work, of the role of monastic as opposed to secular life in women's expression, and of the relative importance of different media.

Testimony to the role of women in the production of books, like that in the production of fine textiles, runs back in hagiographic sources to the very beginning of our period, when the 6th-century Caesaria of Arles is reported both to have copied books and to have trained her nuns to do so, especially the works of her brother Caesarius (Heinrich 1924, p.149; Casa 1993). Already more than a century earlier St Melania had made fair copies of the biblical commentaries and translations of her mentor St Jerome; again later, in the 8th century, we hear of St Boniface giving Eadburg, Abbess of Thanet, a silver stylus so that she could produce books for him, including a copy of the Epistle of Peter in gold (Heinrich 1924, p.150; for Eadburg's embroidery for Boniface, see Dodwell 1982, p.57). Writing in gold was an activity requiring highly developed skill and judgement. At the same time, however, these accounts indicate that women's scribal work, like that with textiles, was dominated from the beginning by utility.

The earliest surviving group of books that can be assigned to women is the cluster of 13 codices attributed to the convent of Charlemagne's sister, Gisela, at Chelles (Bischoff 1957). Among the 13 is a three-volume copy of Augustine's commentary on the Psalms (Cologne, Dombibliothek, MSS 63, 65 and 67) that preserves the signatures of nine of its ten scribes; all are women. Like the career of Gisela herself, a correspondent and confidante of the scholar Alcuin, the books reflect a learned community. There are no painted ornaments in these volumes, but Bernhard Bischoff (*ibid.*, p.401) would like to attribute to Chelles, as well, the superbly illuminated Gelassy Sacramentary (Biblioteca Apostolica Vaticana, MS Reg.lat. 316). This would not automatically assure its illumination by a woman, for Chelles was a double monastery, twinned with a male institution. We know, however, that women did paint such books. This is indicated by the Gelassy Sacramentary's famous contemporary, the Gellone Sacramentary (Paris, Bibliothèque Nationale, MS lat.12048), produced around 800 at Meaux. The Gellone Sacramentary itself is signed in one of its initials by a man, David. However, its sister manuscript (Cambrai, Bibliothèque Municipale, MS 300), a codex of 198 folios incorporating St Augustine's *De trinitate*, contains in an initial on folio 155r the similar signature of one Madalberta, clearly a woman (*ibid.*, p.410; Lowe 1934–72, v, p.12, no.739). Women no less than men moved from calligraphy to design in their manual meditations on sacred Scripture (on the manual meditations of great scribes, see Lewis 1980).

The manuscripts from Chelles confirm the high calligraphic accomplishment at least of a very elite community of early medieval women; they also alert us to key themes of our quest. One is its scribes' role as nuns; Harlinde and Renilde, too, were nuns, and the books of nuns figure throughout the history of medieval women's art. No less significant, however, is its nuns' contact with male religious. Chelles was a double monastery, and Gisela received spiritual advice from Alcuin. Recurrently, we find male spiritual writers turning to women to replicate their works (and so to assure their fame): like Melania and Caesaria, so in the 12th century we find Irmgard and Regelinde of Admont copying the Admont scholar Irembert's commentary on Joshua, Judges and Ruth, a work of more than 1000 pages, and a certain Brother Idung sent his work to be "clearly copied and diligently edited" by the nuns of Niedermünster in Regensburg (Heinrich 1924, p.151). Conversely, the women who were educated in these circumstances became educators of women, and the double monastery plays repeatedly through the history of the medieval bookwoman.

The earliest surviving cycle of figural paintings securely associated with a woman is the rich illumination of the Spanish Beatus of Girona (Girona Cathedral, MS 7), signed in 975 by the scribe Señor and the painters Emeterius and Ende. Ende was most probably a nun. Efforts to isolate Ende's contribution to this magnificent book have been fraught on the one hand by efforts to distinguish some inherently "female" quality in her art, and on the other by a deep reluctance to credit the colophon's clear statement that a woman was a painter. This reluctance runs recurrently – though not always so ill-advisedly – through the scholarship of the middle third of the 20th century in particular.

The Girona Apocalypse was produced in the double monastery of Tábara in León, and it may well be that Ende lived there. We do, however, know of nuns who worked for houses other than their own. This is the case with the Spanish Benedictine, Londegonda, nun of Bobadilla, who in 912 produced a compilation of monastic rules for the monastery of Samos (cited in Marques Casanovas, Dubler and Neuss 1962, p.71, note 1, quoting Francisco de Asis de Bofarull y Sans, *Conferencias publicas relativas a la Exposición Universal de Barcelona*, Barcelona, 1889). This surely also applies to the elusive German nun, Diemud of Wessobrunn, who produced some 45 manuscripts in the years between 1075 and her death around 1130. Cited as a contemporary of Pope Gregory VII (1073–85) in a manuscript account of the Abbots of Wessobrunn, Diemud is described more fully in the text of an anonymous 16th-century monk of Wessobrunn, who writes of her:

> Diemudis was formerly a most devout nun of this our monastery of Wessobrunn. For our monastery was formerly double, or divided into two parts – that is to say, of monks and nuns ... This virgin was most skilful in the art of writing. For though she is not known to have composed any work, yet she wrote with her own hand many volumes in a most beautiful and legible character, both for divine service and for the public library of the monastery, which are enumerated in a list written by herself in a certain plenarius. For in that list the following books pertaining to divine service are enumerated ... [translated in Maitland 1844, pp.419–20].

There follows a list of five missals, some with

Epistles, Gospels, a gradual and sequences for the entire year, two books of offices, two Gospel books and a book of Epistles. One of the missals is listed as having been given to the Bishop of Trier, and the large number of missals suggests that Diemud took orders for them. After the service books, the account goes on to list a further 35 volumes of biblical and patristic texts by Diemud, of which one, a bible in two volumes, was given in exchange for an estate of land in Pisinberch. The Anonymous concludes:

> These are the volumes written with her own hand by the aforesaid handmaid of God, Diemudis ... But at what period she lived I could never discover, since, in all the books (we charitably hope from humility), she omitted to mention her name and the time when she finished.

The account of the Wessobrunn monk is as interesting for its evaluation as for its enumeration of Diemud's books: while admiring her labour as a copyist he notes that she did not compose texts. As with Harlinde and Renilde, her scribal work was more virtuous than great. None the less, his account has captivated historians, who have hoped to find surviving evidence of Diemud's work. Volumes signed by "Diemud" have, indeed, emerged – volumes not only written but painted in a beautiful and legible character. One of them (Munich, Bayerische Staatsbibliothek, clm.23056) has a picture of a nun named Diemud (repr. Greer 1979, p.157), but belongs to the 13th century; a second, a handsomely illuminated missal of the 12th century (Bayerische Staatsbibliothek, clm.11004), bears an enigmatic colophon usually believed to identify Diemud as the scribe but in fact stating that "pious Diemud made the material of the book" (Swarzenski 1908–13, p.62, gives the colophon as: *Materiam libri fecit Diemuod pia scribi / Seo Rudberto celi pro munere certo / Celestis vite scribuntur in ordine scribe*). This book has been the subject of extensive debate; rather late in character for our Diemud, it contains a text arranged for Salzburg use, and the nun of its colophon – whatever her role – may have been Diemud, Abbess of Nonnberg in Salzburg (d. 1136; *idem*). Yet a third Diemud appears in a 12th-century manuscript (Bayerische Staatsbibliothek, clm.23044) that came to Munich from Wessobrunn (*ibid.*, p.63).

Diemud (Demut) – that is, Humility – is in fact a frequent monastic name. Also at Admont, noted for its learned women, we find among the necrologies one "Diemud, member of our congregation and scribe" (*Diemudis conversa nostrae congregationis et scriptrix*; Heinrich 1924, p.151). Whether or not the Diemud described by the Anonymous of Wessobrunn will ever be identified, her name has proved to be a mine of generosity. In the first place, her name has yielded not just one but in fact four or even five bookwomen: the scribe of Admont, the illuminator of clm.23056, the nun in the colophon of clm.11004, the scribe of clm. 23044 and the scribe of the Wessobrunn Anonymous. The copyist-nun thus emerges in striking numbers. In the second place, Diemud illuminates a modern preoccupation. The Anonymous described Diemud as a scribe. All the books that have jockeyed for her name, however, have been illuminated. Like the Anonymous, who had hesitated to lend the aura of fame to a "mere" copyist, we, too, demand more than "mere" calligraphy of an artist.

The colophon page of a manuscript in Strasbourg (Bibliothèque du Grand Séminaire, MS 78; repr. Alexander 1992, pl.28; Cologne 1985, iii, p.245, no.B44) may be a medieval dialogue on this very issue. A voluminous martyrology, it was copied in 1154 by an excellent calligrapher, the nun Guta of Schwarzenthann. She has given her name – prominently written and highlighted with colours – in an elaborate, full-page colophon. She does not include the name of the book's more modestly skilled illuminator, Sintram, a monk at Marbach, Schwarzenthann's brother monastery. Sintram, however, had his own way of claiming pre-eminence. In the miniature that accompanies the colophon it is he, and not the scribe Guta of the proud text, who stands at the right hand of the Virgin.

The pride of achievement that radiates from both Guta's colophon and Sintram's miniature finds a compelling expression in the well-known self-portrait of the nun Guda, who stands, her artist's right hand large before her breast, in an initial on folio 110v of a 12th-century homiliary (Frankfurt am Main, Stadt-und Universitätsbibliothek, MS Barth. 42; Cologne 1985, iii, p.244, no.43; Legner 1985, p.213). Her banderole tells us that she both copied the volume and illuminated it with initials. Only two of the initials contain figures, but they show vividly how the skilled bookwoman could assume expressive and even self-expressive control of her craft, turning her products into statements of her own creative power. Diemud of Wessobrunn had not signed her books, as was usual for monastic labour; Guda's eloquent initial forces one to stop and ask how many other unsigned medieval initials are the work of women, since women obviously were scribes, and some like Ende and Guta had the opportunity to develop very high levels of skill and self-awareness.

Guda makes visible a kind of creative engagement that unquestionably existed also in textile work but has been harder to demonstrate there. A second major conceptual model that emerges with particular clarity in book art is offered by the works of the famous 12th-century abbesses, Hildegard of Bingen (q.v.) and Herrad (q.v.). Both were women of encyclopaedic learning; both owed their education to their monastic upbringing; and both composed books unique in their own time in which images played a central role. Neither book has survived in the original: Hildegard's *Scivias* described, interpreted and illustrated 35 of her complex, powerful visions; Herrad's *Hortus deliciarum* was a pictorial encyclopaedia for her nuns at Hohenbourg that traced the history of salvation through 636 elaborately glossed images. Neither author illuminated the finished book with her own hand, and several quite different hands appear in the *Hortus deliciarum*. None the less, it must have been the authors themselves who conceived the exceptional interdependence of image and text in their books and directed its realisation. As such, they emerge as towering visual innovators. Madeline Caviness's vigorous claim for Hildegard's status as a great artist is one of the most significant contributions to this *Dictionary*.

The image of the artist that these two great figures present is a distinctively medieval one, given its clearest definition, perhaps, by Sandra Hindman in her book on that great secular woman intellectual and author, Christine de Pisan (1364–1431):

Christine seems to have been involved to a considerable degree in the make-up of the pictorial cycle. The degree of her involvement fully justifies claims that the illuminators worked under Christine's direction, following her verbal instructions. It is clear, moreover, that she gave explicit instructions in the form of the purple rubrics to the illuminators. She certainly supervised the illustration.

Evidence concerning manuscript production in Paris suggests that this sort of involvement on the part of the author may have been common. Christine's own writings on art show her to have been more outspoken in the role of the artist than her contemporaries and, further, to have perceived the artist as an imitator of reality, not an inventor of pictures. A study of the various pictorial sources for the Epistre reveals that probably the author, not the miniaturists, studied related illuminated manuscripts and selectively adapted their models to the Epistre. In some cases, such as the Ovide, these models were close to Christine's ends and therefore were retained unchanged. In many other cases modifications were introduced so as to express the themes emphasized in the text ...

We can now turn to these manuscripts, confident that the overall characteristics and the individual details of their particular programs were worked out by Christine, not by her illuminators [Hindman 1986, pp.98–9].

It must be in much the same way that the *Scivias* and the *Hortus deliciarum* were produced. The acknowledgement of the formative role of their authors in the conception and design of their novel, imaginative illumination and the recognition of them as artists open valuable vistas on to artistic invention in the domain of textiles, too: how many major patrons – such as Kunigunde or Agnes of Meissen – directed their craftspeople in this formative way? It also opens up new realms of historical inquiry into the way the intellectual imagination of the great medieval woman of learning was furnished. Several scholars have concluded that richly imaged books were associated especially closely with the education of women and with women's devotional practices in the Middle Ages, as has been intimated already in the reference to the Utrecht Psalter (McKitterick 1990, p.311; Hamburger 1991; Camille 1985, pp.41–2). A vast pictorial encyclopaedia such as Herrad's would thus assume a logical place in a convent noted for its learned women, as was Hohenbourg. Herrad's mentor and predecessor as abbess, Reglindis, is variously associated with the convents of Bergen and Admont, famous for their learned communities and bound by close mutual ties (Cames 1971, p.138; Radspieler 1962). Hohenbourg's intellectual roots thus run back to the great double monastery of Admont; it is perhaps time to study the genealogy of its visual culture, as well.

This image of the artist as instigator unites three of the most brilliant names among medieval women. More than 200 years stretch between them, Hildegard and Herrad in the 12th century and Christine in the late 14th. It has been a source of consternation, even anger, that these centuries have not yielded more visible women of their stature. Major developments in the patterns of production occurred in these centuries and each has been blamed for this dearth. On the one hand, during these centuries production was urbanised, as attested by the guilds. The guild lists of painters and illuminators, like those of embroiderers, show a steady if less numerous flow of women's names. In Italy before the 15th century professional women almost always figure as scribes (Frugoni 1992, p.400, cites Montanaria, a scribe, wife of Onesto, who received a contract from a Florentine named Bencivenne in 1271–2; Antonia, a scribe, daughter of Rodolfo del fu Gandolfo, 1275; Allegra, a scribe, wife of Ivano, 1279; Flandina di Tebaldino, scribe, active 1268; Uliana di Beneventu da Faenza, scribe, 1289; and Branca, scribe, 1329, wife of the scribe Anastasio). But the guild list of 1339 for the Florentine painters' guild, the Compagnia di San Luca, does imply the membership of women, though they paid only two-thirds the dues of the male members (Los Angeles 1976, p.15), and a few women emerge in other documents to assert their presence: Donatella miniatrix, wife of a miniaturist, is cited in a document in Bologna in 1271 (*ibid.*, p.14; Miner 1974, p.11); a Florentine woman identified as "the woman [or, Domina] the wife of Acco the painter" is documented in 1295 when she took a (male) apprentice for four years (the Latin is *domina uxore Acci pictoris.* "Domina" may be a proper name, or simply "the woman"; London 1989, p.9), and a portrait of *St Francis* in San Francesco a Ripa, Rome, was attributed in the 17th century to a Lady Jacoba (Cook 1994, pp.23–4).

In Paris, on the other hand, ten of the 229 painters and sculptors in the guild lists from the decades around 1300 were women (Baron 1968, nos 1, 2, 19, 29, 74, 79, 146, 160bis, 215 and 219); in the lists of painters in Bruges Farquhuar found that 12 per cent in 1454 and by 1480 nearer to 25 per cent of those named were women (cited in Miner 1974, p.24). Five of the women in the Paris lists are associated with deceased husbands of the same trade and so may have been heirs rather than practitioners of the husband's business: one notes in the self-portrait (1512) of the illuminator Nicholaus Bertschi with his wife, Margaret (Stuttgart, Württembergische Landesbibliothek, MS mus.1, fol.65 [fol.236v], repr. Alexander 1992, pl.50), that he alone paints, while she serves him. Others, however, were unquestionably professionals, either living by themselves or married to men with different trades. (See in Baron 1968: no.2, Aalis *l'ymagiere* [=sculptor?, see pp.40–41], married to Thybaut the carpenter; no.74, Eremboure, *enlumineresse*; no.215, Thiephaine, *peintresse*, and Thomasse, *enluminerresse* and *taverniere*, all cited without spouses; for a review of the evidence for women as master illuminators in Paris, see Farber 1993, p.37, note 2.) Even within marriage, as the textile trades have shown, crafts were family specialities and not the personal career of the male alone. So, for instance, we saw the Florentine *domina* taking on a (male) apprentice quite independently of her painter husband. More famous, if not as yet traced to identifiable work, was Bourgot, daughter of the painter Jehan de Noir. Cited as an *enlumineresse* in a contract of her father's in 1353, she went on to share his commissions for the courts of France and Berry (Meiss 1969, p.168; Miner 1974, pp.18–19). In Bourgot we encounter the pattern so familiar from the post-medieval world, of the painter who is the daughter of a painter.

These data leave no doubt that women practised as professional painters in the late medieval cities of Europe. Among them was the title figure of Dorothy Miner's essay, the painter Anastaise, of whom Christine de Pisan wrote: "she is so skillful and experienced in painting borders and miniatures of manuscripts that no one can cite an artist in the city of Paris ... who in these endeavors surpasses her" (quoted in Miner 1974, p.8). What Christine praised Anastaise for were her borders and backgrounds, though, and not her creative initiative. As Hindman's reconstruction of Christine's own methods of book design show, it is as trained producers rather than as inventors of illuminations that guild members of either sex generally worked. Here as in the realm of fine textiles it is certain that a portion of the artfulness of late medieval art – its consummate skill and sophisticated beauty – was due to the highly professional women who made it. Women who took projects in hand as conceptual overseers, as Christine herself did, remained rare.

The women who do emerge as candidates for this role in the later medieval centuries are monastic.

They can be found particularly in Germany and the Low Countries. Cistercian, Clarissan and especially Dominican houses in the wake of the wide-ranging Dominican reform movement of the late 14th and 15th centuries produced many books, culminating in the great 15th-century library of 500 volumes at the Dominican convent of St Katherine, Nuremberg: repeated Dominican proscriptions of women's copying must reflect its vitality rather than its absence.[6] Christian von Heusinger (1959) has identified almost a dozen Dominican convents in south Germany with active scriptoria, and Elisabeth Schraut (1988) has identified a range of volumes produced in Cistercian houses. Women illuminators are fewer than scribes – among its many scribes, St Katherine's produced only one illuminator who is known by name and oeuvre. This is Barbara Gwichtmacherin (d. 1491), known to have illuminated a gradual of 1459 (Nuremberg, Stadtbibliothek, MS Cent.V, App.34q) not because of her own signature but from the records of the book's binder (Fischer 1928, pp.69–70; Schraut 1991, pp.100–01; Schraut also attributes Stadtbibliothek, MS Cent.V 10a to Gwichtmacherin). Women illuminators do appear throughout the later Middle Ages, though, both in decorated documents like the indulgence of 1363 at Herkenrode (Oliver 1995) and a charter of 1362 at St Katherine's itself (now Nuremberg, Stadtarchiv, Alte Urkunden, no.234; repr. Schraut 1987, no.52, pl.5), and in illuminated books. Especially impressive is Gisle von Kerzenbroeck, named in an inscription at the beginning of a magnificently written and illuminated gradual (Osnabrück, Gymnasium Carolinum and Bischöfliches Generalvikariat MS) from the Cistercian convent of Rulle near Osnabrück: "The venerable and devout virgin Gisle of Kerzenbroeck wrote, illuminated, notated, paginated and decorated with pictures and golden initials this excellent book in her own memory. In the year of Our Lord 1300 her soul rested in holy peace. Amen."[7] Gisle herself appears in two of the volume's sonorous initials, confirming its close connection with her. Despite the carefully inventoried inscription, however, her authorship has been challenged, for both script and painting display the work not of one but of several hands. Oliver has argued in response that these may belong to Gisle's monastic sisters under her direction. The convent did engage in book work – four scribe-nuns are known there, including the prolific Cristina von Haltern, who signed the two-volume Rulle Bible (Osnabrück, Gymnasium Carolinum MS 90) in 1278 (Oliver 1997, notes 20 and 22) – and it is possible that one or more sisters in such a community also practised illumination at a professional level of skill.

This possibility is demonstrated by the convent of the Poor Clares in Cologne. Members of the convent produced a number of musical manuscripts in the 13th and early 14th centuries, among them several with very beautiful illuminations (Galley 1961). Of these, a gradual (Cologne, Wallraf-Richartz Museum, Graphische Sammlung Inv. Nrs 67–71) of the 1330s copied by Sister Gertrude van dem Uorst may have been illuminated in the scriptorium of the Franciscan friary of Cologne, where in 1299 a Brother Johannes von Valkenburg "scripsi et notavi et illu[m]i[n]avi" two handsome graduals (Cologne, Diözesanbibliothek, MS 1B; Bonn, Universitätsbibliothek, MS 384; Oliver 1997, note 13). A cluster of comparably fine musical manuscripts from the 1350s, on the other hand, are signed by the Clarissan sister Loppa de Speculo. Among them an antiphonary (Stockholm, Kungl. Bibliothek, MS 172A), contains, on folio 106, the explicit inscription: "Sister Jutta Alfter paid for this book with her money and alms; pray for her and for those she remembers. Sister Loppa de Speculo completed it, writing, ruling, notating, illuminating it so that she would not be excluded from your hearts …".[8] Like her Franciscan counterpart, Johannes, Loppa lists her responsibilities in the book. That she herself provided the illuminations as well as the filigree initials has been challenged: not only are they of professional calibre, but the missals attributed to Loppa (Cologne, Domarchiv, MS 149; Brussels, Bibliothèque Royale, MSS 209, 212) were made for use not in her own convent, but elsewhere (Beer 1965, p.150). Nuns' production for other monastic houses is long-attested, however: in 1366, at much the time that Loppa was working, we find the Cistercian monk Jacob of Lindau ordering an antiphonary (Heidelberg, MS Sale IX 66) from Sister Catherine de Brugg of Rothenmünster near Lake Konstanz, who is portrayed in a large initial at the beginning of the book in what may be a self-portrait (Wattenbach 1875, p.376). Moreover, as Galley (1961, pp.16 and 18) has shown, among Loppa's sisters was one with the same family name as the Franciscan painter Johannes von Valkenburg, and it seems entirely plausible that the children of highly skilled professional clans would have brought their family skills with them into their monastic houses. Italy, too, yields painter-nuns in the 14th century, such as Sister Giovanna Petroni of the Sienese convent of Santa Maria (Bradley 1887–9, iii, p.61). Gisle, Loppa and Giovanna suggest that, if women are to be identified as initiators of major painting projects, they should be sought in the religious life.

During the 13th century there was an escalation in the number and intensity of women seeking a spiritual life, either in cloistered monasticism or in a form such as that of the beguine movement, which was more integrated into secular life (Oliver 1988, pp.130–32; Oliver 1997, p.106). Beguines were lay women who gathered in devotional associations only loosely recognised by the established Church. The religious community thus acquired a vitality that made it a major focus of women's artistic production. Here as in textile work the convent responded to the shifting conditions of late medieval production, developing a self-sufficient answer to its distinctive needs. Convents carried on – as male monasteries rarely did – the earlier medieval model of the self-contained, in-house scriptorium (Oliver 1997, p.116). That convents produced illuminated books in the Gothic centuries has been widely recognised, as the currency of the term *Nonnenbücher* proves. Like the word *Klosterstich*, encountered in embroidery, it is a German term, identifying the area most richly informative about these works. And like the term *Klosterstich* it is dismissive in tone, indicating a technical and often an iconographic simplicity that looks painfully naive next to the sophisticated productions of urban professionals. Yet it is precisely in this area of convent production that the most vividly interesting scholarship on medieval women artists is being done.

Indicative of the interest of this material is the seemingly exiguous fact that the later medieval manuscripts discussed so far have been almost entirely musical manuscripts; so, too, is the exuberantly decorated manuscript (Bornem, Abdij Sint Bernardus, MS 1) produced in 1244 at the convent of Nazareth in Lier, Belgium, and notated by a nun named Christina, perhaps the sister of the great Nazareth mystic, Beatrice (Oliver 1997, p.106). Already Wilhelm Wattenbach in 1875 had noted the association of women and musical manuscripts (p.376), observing that musical manuscripts need to be made by the musicians who know and use their music. The musical manuscripts are, in short, a sign

that these books by nuns were intimately woven into their lives and worship. This is even truer of the psalter, the great devotional book of the Middle Ages. In the 12th century the devotional psalter had emerged as one of the major recipients of illumination. Already at this time the owners of these luxurious books were predominantly women,[9] and women continue in the ensuing centuries to appear repeatedly as the owners of devotional psalters (Oliver 1992). Psalters, in turn, as Oliver has shown, appear with striking frequency among books made by women's religious groups (Oliver 1997, p.106). She notes the 13th-century psalters produced at the Cistercian convent of Engelsberg in Switzerland (Beer 1959, pp.25–6), the group of psalters from mid-13th-century Liège in Belgium that she attributes to beguines of that city, and the bequest left in 1266 by a Liège beguine to fund the production of psalters. Liturgical books, in turn, dominate the later Cistercian book production that Schraut examines (1988, p.49), and here again it is a musical book – an antiphonary (Stuttgart, Württembergischer Landesbibliothek, HB XVII 17), copied and illuminated in 1344 with numerous signatures by Alheid Quidenbeumen at Billigheim – that bears the fullest illumination (*ibid.*, pl.I).

The books produced by women's communities prove to be not only closely bound to their religious life, but illuminated in ways that cast a unique light upon that life. Oliver (1997, pp.111–16) has shown this particularly finely in her analysis of a type of ornament that recurs in books associated with women's communities. In books as widely varied as Gisle von Kerzenbroeck's gradual discussed above, and a modest little homiliary (Baltimore, Walters MS W148; repr. Miner 1974, figs 4–5) redecorated in the early 14th century, she finds rich adornment, often recalling gold and coloured embroidery, applied to particular words that play a strategic role in the performance of the liturgy. This sort of liturgically based embellishment is not usual in manuscripts made in male communities, but it does reflect the practice of pious reading, *lectio divina*, that characterised monastic life. It permeates especially the writings of Mechtild of Hackeborn (d. 1298), whose *Book of Special Grace* dwells with delectation upon individual words and their many resonances of meaning and instruction. As Oliver notes:

> Words were thus laden individually with great spiritual merit and Mechtild visualized them as jewels. On the feast of Saint Agnes, Christ

and the saint appeared to Mechtild in red robes. All the saint's words (that is, the text of her office) were embroidered in golden letters on Christ's robe and gave off light which entered the hearts of the choir singing the psalms ... At the memorial service for Abbess Gertrude, Mechtild saw the apostles bearing large, richly ornamented books, acknowledging the abbess' apostolic calling as spiritual teacher of her nuns. Abbess Gertrude herself appeared adorned in a vestment of green embellished with innumerable golden stars, its seams studded with white pearls and small rubies. Such splendor immediately recalls embroidery, the art form in which German nuns excelled in the Gothic period ... [1997, p.115].

The white pearls and little rubies recall the pearl- and coral-studded embroidery from Isenhagen. In the rich pages of the nuns' manuscripts, *lectio divina*, illumination and embroidery come together in a luminous visual feast, a spiritual delectation that was distinctive to women's expression. It was a women's art.

Hamburger (1990), in turn, has begun to explore the figural images in such books. Often decried – by Greer (1979), for example – because they remained inbred and out of fashion, copied and recopied over many decades without stylistic or qualitative modification (e.g. the pages discussed in Oliver 1997, p.107, fig.54), the miniatures in nuns' books none the less bear a particular weight of significance in Hamburger's view (1989 and 1991), for in the later medieval centuries especially, images were regarded as peculiarly appropriate to women and their ways of thinking. Thus, images assumed an expressive licence that they rarely had in men's institutions. Formulated by women to speak to women of the powerful affections of their own hearts in devotion, the images in women's devotional books often carry an intensity of content that is unique and uniquely tailored to them. While certainly not claiming all women's devotional imagery for women artists, Hamburger has nevertheless found many miniatures that were painted by women, opening up a whole class of devotional book that has been neglected by historians seeking art as traditionally defined. The devotional intensity of Hamburger's images will lend a new interest to the distinctive themes of women's textile art, as well, leading historians to look beyond the cheerful simplicity of their *Klosterstich* to the devotional impetus behind it.

Monumental arts

In the figures of Guda with her vigorous, self-expressive craft, of Hildegard, Herrad and Christine with their creative authority, and of the anonymous artists of the *Nonnenbücher* with their intense expressive imagery, the art of the book has given clear formulation to types of women artists known also, if less clearly, from textiles. Only in tapestry, however, have these media yielded evidence of women as creators of art on a monumental scale. Where names appear in the Middle Ages, women's names appear among them, but names are extremely rare in the monumental arts of the Middle Ages, and women are correspondingly elusive. The only reasonably securely identified woman monumental artist is Teresa Díaz, named in the inscription in the choir frescoes of *c.*1316 at Santa Clara in Toro (Zamora) in Spain and presented for the first time by Pamela Patton in the complete edition of the *Dictionary of Women Artists*. The inscription, TERESA DIEÇ ME FECIT, repeats exactly that of Gislebertus on the tympanum at Autun; to query it would require considering the possibility – as only few have done – that Gislebertus, too, was a patron, not a sculptor. Díaz's signature may have bearing on fresco cycles like those from the 14th century in the convent church at Wienhausen in Germany that have traditionally been attributed to nuns. It also reinforces insights offered by other media: Lillich's evidence from the guild lists of Paris glaziers, where 12 per cent of those named are women (1985, pp.80–82); the women, Aalis and Perronelle, listed between 1292 and 1316 as *imagiere* – sculptor – in Paris (Baron 1968, nos 2 and 19); and Alexander Neckham's report from his own late 12th-century London of women goldsmiths (Amt 1993, p.198). In addition, there is a tantalising inscription on a reliquary cross (*c.*1150–70; Metropolitan Museum of Art, New York; [IN HO]NORE: S[AN]C[T]I; SALVATORIS: SANCCIA: GUIDISALVI: ME; FECIT; New York 1993) from the church of San Salvador de Fuentes (Asturias) in Spain, which may point to a woman goldsmith, although its similarity to donors' inscriptions is problematic. These scanty data imply that here as elsewhere, women joined in their families' craft. The greatest woman sculptor of the Middle Ages, however – Sabine, daughter of Erwin von Steinbach, the late 13th-century master builder of

Strasbourg Cathedral – has been shown in a remarkable deconstruction by Geyer (1989) to be a component of her father's florid, high Romantic myth.

Conclusions

The evidence assembled here has treated women as artists in the medieval West. More extensive than evidence from Byzantium, where names are rarely given, it offers certain rules of thumb to use in assessing the place of women in medieval art. At no time in the Middle Ages were women excluded from the media in which their society forged its visual imagery of faith and prestige. Fine textiles were the most consistent and costly medium in which their work is found: kings and priests were vested in these fabrics; saints were propitiated; spaces were made numinous; and the stories of husbands and heroes were consecrated to history. But women are attested, too, as scribes and illuminators, goldsmiths and glaziers, sculptors and mural painters. Media as such offer few barriers to women.

Corollary to this is the rarity of gender-specific tasks. While textile work seems in the early Middle Ages to have been associated especially with women, the medieval guilds show both men and women engaged in most aspects of cloth-making and working; women, in turn, practised even heavy tasks like glass-making and stone-carving alongside their husbands and brothers in family businesses. Even monastic production is most visible in the double monasteries – Chelles, San Salvatore, Marbach/Schwarzenthann, Wessobrunn, Admont – where male and female religious often worked together on major projects. The tendency to look for women's enclaves, whether in segregated secular tasks or cloistered retreats, is rewarded only rarely and then at the chronological extremes of the Middle Ages, at the beginning or the end.

Authority itself is hard to divide on gendered lines. The medieval divisions of responsibility in creative tasks do not coincide with our own, and this makes it difficult for us to assign artistic authority. At all points in the Middle Ages, however, it is clear that women functioned in a vast range of different capacities, and no one definition of "artist" will embrace a critical cross-section of them.

If media and métier in themselves offered few barriers to women, however, it is also true that patterns of greater and lesser visibility play across the data that are offered here. The convent recurs in every period discussed and obviously offered contexts conducive to women's art. At the same time, it is notable how heavily weighted the evidence is towards Germany and the Low Countries. Spain, Italy and even France make far more reticent appearances.[10] While survival of documentation may condition this distribution, especially in the later Middle Ages when the passage of German convents to Protestant sodalities protected their contents and continuity, it very probably reflects genuine conditions of medieval existence, as well. Both the canonical houses with their double monasteries and the reformed mendicant houses in the later Middle Ages were stronger in Germany than elsewhere; the canonical double houses had been discouraged in the Carolingian territories already under Louis the Pious in the early 9th century. It is the double monasteries in particular that come to the forefront of the evidence about women as artists. This suggests the rule that it is not monasticism itself but the *type* of monasticism available to women that affected their opportunities for artistic expression.[11]

After the monasteries, the lists of the medieval urban guilds are the most valuable resource we have for tracing women's roles in the production of fine things, and they expand the monastic evidence especially in the range of media represented. There are many media, including glazing and sculpture, in which women are known only from the guild lists, and it is Alexander Neckham's observations of his own urban surroundings that yield our most concrete testimony to women as metalworkers. The testimony of the cities makes it clear that women worked in most media that we embrace in the broad category of art. None the less, the distribution of evidence across media remains uneven. Conspicuously slim throughout most of the Middle Ages is evidence of women's participation in the seasonal arts of masonry, mural painting and monumental sculpture; rare, too, are the extremely expensive arts such as work in precious metals, for which – until cities created an ongoing demand – the need in any one place was limited and artists were engaged only sporadically over the span of centuries. If gender as such offered little impediment to women's participation, it may be that itinerancy did: that except where flourishing monastic houses or urban development offered steady employment that removed the need for itinerancy, the seasonal and sporadic arts were not practised widely by women.

The urbanisation of production reflected by the guilds, on the other hand, shows an extensive engagement of women in the professions: as indicated, few tasks were closed to them. The growth of the towns thus can certainly be seen as offering opportunities to women, engaging them in the sophisticated and excellently regulated skilled labour that distinguishes so much of later medieval art. At the same time, it is true that the entrepreneurial patterns of urban production favoured male control of both families and businesses. It can be no accident that the types of women's artistic expression most defined by gender – the late medieval cloister arts – occurred as a counterpoint to the late medieval city, for all its large numbers of working women.

ANNEMARIE WEYL CARR
with the help of ANNE DERBES (Hood College, Frederick, MD), PAULA GERSON (International Center of Medieval Art, New York), JUDITH H. OLIVER (Colgate University, Hamilton, NY) and PAMELA A. PATTON (Southern Methodist University, Dallas)

Notes

1 See since then Carr 1976 and 1985; Ludwigshaven 1983; Parker 1984; Schraut 1987; Chadwick 1990; Yawn-Bonghi 1992; Oliver 1997; Hamburger (in preparation). I owe my thanks to Professor Eleanor Tufts, who first engaged me in the issue of women as artists, and to Maria Hopewell, who introduced me to the literature on Sabine von Steinbach.

2 See especially Maitland 1844; Bock 1856–71; Wattenbach 1875; Bradley 1887–9; Eckenstein 1896; Thieme and Becker 1907–50; Heinrich 1924.

3 As an *entré* into this by now very richly documented material, see Bell 1982; Berman 1985; Sekules 1987; Caviness 1993; Jeffreys 1980; Laiou 1981.

4 See Kroos 1970; Freiburg im Breisgau 1970; Braunschweig 1985; Cologne 1985; Schraut 1987; and, with colour plates, Appuhn 1963.

5 For Wienhausen, see Appuhn 1983, p.13, and Moessner 1987; for Nuremberg, see Schraut 1991, pp.94, 106–10; for Heilig Grab, see Baumgärtel-Fleischmann 1983, p.54.

6 The literature on these houses is by now quite extensive. For the beguines, see Oliver 1988; for the Cistercians, see Schraut 1988; for the Clarissans, see Galley 1961, Schraut 1991 and Steingräber 1952; for the Dominicans, see Fischer 1928; Raspe 1905, pp.10–31; Schraut 1987 and Heusinger 1959; for the oeuvre of a group of Brigittine or Cistercian nuns in Westphalia, see Oliver 1997. For the Dominican

proscriptions against women's production of books, in 1249, 1254 and again in 1263, see Oliver 1997.

7 *Istu[m] egregiu[m] libru[m] scripsit, ill[um]inavit, notavit, i[m]paginavit, aureis litteris et imaginibus pulchris decoravit venerabilis ac devota virgo Gysela de Kerzenbroeck i[n] sui memoria[m]. Anno d[omi]ni MCCC cui[us] a[n]i[m]a req[ui]escat i[n] s[an]c[t]a pace*; on the Gisle Codex, see Kroos 1973; and Oliver 1997, where she translates the inscription, p.109, and reproduces it, fig.56.

8 *Soror Jutta de Alft[er] p[er]solvit ist[um] lib[rum] cu[m] suis expe[n]sis et el[eemosyn]is orate p[ro] ea et p[ro] q[ui]b[u]s devote i[n]te[n]di[t] et Soror Loppa de Spec[u]lo p[er]fecit scr[i]bendo, liniando, nota[n]do, illu[m]i[n]ando q[ui]a n[on] excludatis ex cordib[us] v[est]ris ...*; Galley 1961; among the other manuscripts attributed to Loppa, in addition to the Stockholm antiphonary and the missals cited below, is a fragmentary antiphonary, Cologne, Wallraf-Richartz Museum, inv. nos 56 and 66.

9 Thus the earliest of the devotional psalters with their distinctive full-page multiple frontispieces and calendars were made for women, identified currently as Christina of Markyate and Queen Melisende of Jerusalem, and women continue to be prominent among their owners. For the kind of text included in these books, see the woman's psalter and commentary published in Gregory 1990.

10 Thus see Bomford in London 1989, who comments, p.9: "As far as is known, the painters in medieval Italy were nearly all men ... Unlike Northern painting, there are no illustrations from Italy of women at the easel". Of Spain, Patton wrote in notes for this project: "I found no literature treating the topic of women artists in Spain ... One area which I had hoped might yield evidence of artistic activity by women was that of textile arts ... I found no indication that the possibility of female artists had even been considered". Even in England the number of women known in the book arts is scant in the later centuries; hence the interest with which Mary C. Erler (book review in *Scriptorium*, xlviii, 1994, p.350) noted Christopher de Hamel's attribution of one of the early 15th-century prayer books from Syon Abbey to its owner, Anna Kaarlsdottir, in *Syon Abbey ... 1991*.

11 For the impact of varied types of monasticism, see Wemple 1990.

Bibliography

Christine de Pisan (1364–1431), *The Book of the City of Ladies*, New York: Persea, 1982

S[amuel] R[offey] Maitland, *The Dark Ages: Essays Illustrating the State of Religion and Literature in the Ninth, Tenth, Eleventh and Twelfth Centuries*, London: Rivington, 1844; reprint, with introduction by Frederick Stokes, Port Washington, NY: Kennikat Press, 1969

Franz Bock, *Geschichte der liturgischen Gewänder des Mittelalters*, 3 vols, Bonn: Henry & Cohen, 1856–71;

reprinted Graz: Akademische Druck- und
Verlagsanstalt, 1970

Wilhelm Wattenbach, *Das Schriftwesen im Mittelalter*,
Leipzig: Hirzel, 1875

John W. Bradley, *A Dictionary of Miniaturists,
Illuminators, Calligraphers and Copyists*, 3 vols,
London: Quaritch, 1887–9

Lina Eckenstein, *Woman under Monasticism: Chapters
on Saint-Lore and Convent Life Between* AD 500 *and*
AD 1500, Cambridge: Cambridge University Press,
1896; reprinted New York: Russell and Russell, 1963

Theodor Raspe, *Studien zur deutschen Kunstgeschichte:
Die Nürnberger Miniaturmalerei bis 1515*, Studien zur
deutschen Kunstgeschichte, 60, Strasbourg: Heitz,
1905

Ulrich Thieme and Felix Becker, *Allgemeines Lexikon der
bildenden Künstler von der Antike bis zur Gegenwart*,
37 vols, Leipzig: Seeman, 1907–50

Georg Swarzenski, *Die Salzburger Malerei*, 2 vols,
Leipzig: Hiersemann, 1908–13

Maria Pia Heinrich, *The Canonesses and Education in
the Early Middle Ages*, PhD dissertation, Catholic
University of America, Washington, DC, 1924

Karl Fischer, *Die Buchmalerei in den beiden
Dominikanerklöstern Nürnbergs*, Nuremberg, 1928

E. A. Lowe, ed., *Codices latini antiquiores:
A Palaeographical Guide to the Ninth Century*, 2nd
edition, 11 vols, Oxford: Clarendon Press, 1934–72

Karl Michaëlsson, "Le livre de la taille de Paris, l'an de
grace 1313", *Göteborgs Högskolas Årsskrift*, lvii/3,
1951, pp.1–349

Erich Steingräber, "Neun Miniaturen einer Franziskus-
Vita", *Zeitschrift für schweizerischen Architektur und
Kunstgeschichte*, xiii, 1952, pp.237–45

Bernhard Bischoff, "Die Kölner Nonnenhandschriften
und das Skriptorium von Chelles", *Karolingische und
Ottonische Kunst: Werden, Wesen, Wirkung*,
Forschungen zur Kunstgeschichte und christlichen
Archäologie, 3, Wiesbaden: Steiner, 1957, pp.395–411

Ellen Beer, *Beiträge zur oberrheinischen Buchmalerei in
der erste Hälfte des 14. Jahrhunderts, unter besonderer
Berücksichtigung der Initialornamentik*, Basel:
Birkhauser, 1959

Christian von Heusinger, "Spätmittelalterliche
Buchmalerei im oberrheinischen Frauenklostern",
Zeitschrift für die Geschichte des Oberrheins, new
series, lxviii (=cvii), 1959, pp.136–60

Eberhard Galley, "Miniaturen aus dem Kölner
Klarissenkloster: Ein Kapitel rheinischen Buchmalerei
des 14. Jahrhunderts", *Aus der Welt des Bibliothekars
(Festschrift für Rudolf Juchhoff)*, ed. Kurt Ohly,
Cologne: Greven, 1961, pp.15–28

Jaime Marques Casanovas, César E. Dubler and Wilhelm
Neuss, *Sancti Beati a Liebana in Apocalypsin: Codex
Gerundensis*, 2 vols, Oltun: Graf, 1962

H. Radspieler, "Reglind aus Admont, Abtissin von Bergen
und Hohenburg", *Neuburger Kollektaneenblatt*, cxv,
1962, pp.33–48

Horst Appuhn, *Meisterwerke der niedersächsischen Kunst
des Mittelalters*, Bad Honnef Rhein: Peters, 1963

Paul Grimm, "Zwei bemerkenswerte Gebäude in der
Pfalz Tilleda: Eine zweite Tuchmacherei",
Prähistorische Zeitschrift, xli, 1963, pp.62–82

Opus anglicanum: English Medieval Embroidery, exh.
cat., Arts Council at the Victoria and Albert Museum,
London, 1963

Ellen Beer, "Literaturbericht: Gotische Buchmalerei.
Literatur von 1945 bis 1961", *Zeitschrift für
Kunstgeschichte*, xxviii, 1965

Françoise Baron, "Enlumineurs, peintres et sculpteurs
parisiens des XIIIe et XIVe siècle d'après les rôles de la
taille", *Bulletin Archéologique du Comité des Travaux
Historiques et Scientifiques*, iv, 1968, pp.37–121

Millard Meiss, *French Painting in the Time of Jean de
Berry*, 2 vols, 2nd edition, London: Phaidon, 1969

Renate Kroos, *Niedersächsische Bildstickereien des
Mittelalters*, Berlin: Deutscher Verlag für
Kunstwissenschaft, 1970

*Kunstepochen der Stadt Freiburg: Ausstellung zur 850-
Jahrfeier*, exh. cat., Städtliche Museen, Freiburg im
Breisgau, 1970

Magnus Backes and Regine Dölling, *Art of the Dark
Ages*, New York: Abrams, 1971

Gérard Cames, *Allégories et symboles dans l'Hortus deliciarum*, Leiden: Brill, 1971

R. Kent Lancaster, "Artists, suppliers, clerks: The human
factors in the art patronage of King Henry III",
Journal of the Warburg and Courtauld Institutes,
xxxv, 1972, pp.81–107

Renate Kroos, "Der Codex Gisle I: Forschungsbericht
und Datierung", *Niederdeutsche Beiträge zur
Kunstgeschichte*, xii, 1973, pp.117–34

Dorothy Miner, *Anastaise and Her Sisters: Women Artists
of the Middle Ages*, Baltimore: Walters Art Gallery,
1974

Annemarie Weyl Carr, "Women as artists in the Middle
Ages", *Feminist Art Journal*, v, 1976, pp.5–9, 26

Marc Fitch, "The London makers of *opus anglicanum*",
*Transactions of the London and Middlesex
Archaeological Society*, xxvii, 1976, pp.228–96

Women Artists, 1550–1950, exh. cat., Los Angeles
County Museum of Art, and elsewhere, 1976

Die Zeit der Staufer: Geschichte, Kunst, Kultur, 5 vols,
exh. cat., Württembergisches Landesmuseum,
Stuttgart, 1977

Frances Gies and Joseph Gies, *Women in the Middle
Ages*, New York: Crowell, 1978

Germaine Greer, *The Obstacle Race: The Fortunes of
Women Painters and Their Work*, London: Secker and
Warburg, and New York: Farrar Straus, 1979

Suzanne Lewis, "Sacred calligraphy: The chi rho page in
the Book of Kells", *Traditio*, xxxvi, 1980, pp.139–59

S. G. Bell, "Medieval women book owners: Arbiters of
lay piety and ambassadors of culture", *Signs*, vii,
1982, pp.742–68

Odile Brel-Bordaz, *Broderies d'ornements liturgiques*

XIIIe–XIVe siècles, Paris: Nouvelles Editions Latines, 1982

C.R. Dodwell, *Anglo-Saxon Art: A New Perspective*, Ithaca, NY: Cornell University Press, and Manchester: Manchester University Press, 1982

Horst Appuhn, *Bildstickereien des Mittelalters in Kloster Lüne*, Dortmund: Harenberg, 1983

Renate Baumgärtel-Fleischmann, *Ausgewählte Kunstwerke aus dem Diözesanmuseum Bamberg*, Bamberg: Bayerische Verlagsanstalt, 1983

Frauen und Kunst im Mittelalter, exh. cat., Wilhelm-Hack-Museum, Ludwigshaven, 1983

Rozsika Parker, *The Subversive Stitch: Embroidery and the Making of the Feminine*, London: Women's Press, 1984; New York: Routledge, 1989

Ulrike Bergmann, "PRIOR OMNIBUS AUCTOR – an höchster Stelle aber steht der Stifter", *Ornamenta ecclesiae: Kunst und Künstler der Romanik*, 3 vols, exh. cat., Schnütgen-Museum, Cologne, 1985, i, pp.117–48

Constance H. Berman, "Women as donors and patrons to southern French monasteries in the twelfth and thirteenth centuries", *The Worlds of Medieval Women: Creativity, Influence, Imagination*, ed. Constance H. Berman and others, Morgantown: West Virginia University Press, 1985, pp.53–68

Michael Camille, "Seeing and reading: Some visual implications of medieval literacy and illiteracy", *Art History*, viii, 1985, pp.26–49

Anton Legner, "Illustres Manus", *Ornamenta ecclesiae: Kunst und Künstler der Romanik*, 3 vols, exh. cat., Schnütgen-Museum, Cologne, 1985, i, pp.187–230

Meredith Parsons Lillich, "Gothic glaziers: Monks, Jews, taxpayers, Bretons, women", *Journal of Glass Studies*, xxvii, 1985, pp.72–92

Ornamenta ecclesiae: Kunst und Künstler der Romanik, 3 vols., exh. cat., Schnütgen-Museum, Cologne, 1985

Stadt im Wandel: Kunst und Kultur des Bürgertums in Norddeutschland, 1150–1650, 4 vols, exh. cat., Herzog Anton Ulrich-Museum, Braunschweig, 1985

David M. Wilson, *The Bayeux Tapestry: The Complete Tapestry in Colour*, London: Thames and Hudson, and New York: Knopf, 1985

David J. Bernstein, *The Mystery of the Bayeux Tapestry*, London: Weidenfeld and Nicolson, 1986; Chicago: University of Chicago Press, 1987

Sandra L. Hindman, *Christine de Pizan's "Epistre d'Othéa": Painting and Politics at the Court of Charles VI*, Toronto: Pontifical Institute of Mediaeval Studies, 1986

V. Moessner, "The medieval embroideries of Convent Wienhausen", *Studies in Cistercian Art and Architecture*, iii, 1987, pp.161–77

Elisabeth Schraut, ed., *Stifterinnen und Künstlerinnen im mittelalterlichen Nürnberg*, Nuremberg: Selbstverlag der Stadt Nürnberg, 1987

Veronica Sekules, "Women and art in England in the thirteenth and fourteenth centuries", *Age of Chivalry*, exh. cat., Royal Academy, London, 1987, pp.41–8

Judith H. Oliver, *Gothic Manuscript Illumination in the Diocese of Liège, c.1250–1330*, 2 vols, Leuven: Peeters, 1988

Elisabeth Schraut, "Zum Bildungszustand fränkischer Zisterzienserinnenkonvente", *Württembergische Franken*, lxxii, 1988, pp.42–67

Art in the Making: Italian Painting Before 1400, exh. cat., National Gallery, London, 1989

Edith Ennen, *The Medieval Woman*, Oxford: Blackwell, 1989

Marie-Jeanne Geyer, "Le mythe d'Erwin de Steinbach", *Exposition de bâtisseurs de cathédrals gothiques*, exh. cat., Strasbourg, 1989, pp.322–9, 477–9

Jeffrey Hamburger, "The visual and the visionary: The image in late medieval monastic devotions", *Viator*, xx, 1989, pp.161–82

Whitney Chadwick, *Women, Art and Society*, New York and London: Thames and Hudson, 1990

Stewart Gregory, ed., *The Twelfth-Century Psalter Commentary in French for Laurette d'Alsace (An Edition of Psalms, I–L)*, 2 vols, London: Modern Humanities Research Association, 1990

Jeffrey F. Hamburger, *The Rothschild Canticles: Art and Mysticism in Flanders and the Rhineland circa 1300*, New Haven and London: Yale University Press, 1990

Rosamond McKitterick, ed., *The Uses of Literacy in Early Mediaeval Europe*, Cambridge and New York: Cambridge University Press, 1990

Erika Uitz, *The Legend of Good Women: Medieval Women in Towns and Cities*, Mt Kisco, NY: Moyer Bell, 1990; as *Women in the Medieval Town*, London: Barrie and Jenkins, 1990 (German original, 1988)

Suzanne Fonay Wemple, "Female monasticism in Italy and its comparison with France and Germany from the ninth through the eleventh eenturies", *Frauen in Spätantike und Frühmittelalter*, ed. Werner Affeldt, Sigmaringen: Thorbecke, 1990, pp.291–310

Mildred Budny, "The Byrhtnoth tapestry or embroidery", *The Battle of Maldon, AD 991*, ed. Donald Scragg, Oxford: Blackwell, 1991, pp.263–78

Jeffrey Hamburger, "A *Liber Precum* in Silestat and the development of the illustrated prayer book in Germany", *Art Bulletin*, lxxiii, 1991, pp.209–36

Elisabeth Schraut, "Überlegungen zu den Möglichkeiten der Frauen im mittelalterlichen Kunstbetrieb am Beispiel Nürnberg", *Auf der Suche nach der Frau im Mittelalter: Fragen, Quellen, Antworten*, ed. Bea Lundt, Munich: Fink, 1991, pp.81–114

Kay Staniland, *Embroiderers*, London: British Museum Press, and Toronto: University of Toronto Press, 1991

Syon Abbey: The Library of the Brigettine Nuns and Their Peregrinations after the Reformation: An Essay by Christopher de Hamel, with the Manuscript at Arundel Castle, Otley: Roxburghe Club, 1991

Jonathan J.G. Alexander, *Medieval Illuminators and Their Methods of Work*, New Haven and London: Yale University Press, 1992

C. Frugoni, "The imagined woman", *A History of Women in the West, II: Silences of the Middle Ages*, ed. Christiane Klapisch-Zuber, Cambridge, MA: Harvard University Press, 1992

Jeffrey F. Hamburger, "Art, enclosure and the 'Cura Monialium': Prolegomena in the guise of a post-script", *Gesta*, xxxi, 1992, pp.108–34

Judith Oliver, "Devotional psalters and the study of beguine spirituality", *Vox Benedictina*, ix, 1992, pp.198–225

Leonie von Wilckens, "The Quedlinburg carpet", *Hali*, xiv/5, 1992, pp.97–128

Lila Yawn-Bonghi, "Medieval women artists and modern historians", *Medieval Feminist Newsletter*, xii, 1992, pp.10–19

Emilie Amt, ed., *Women's Lives in Medieval Europe: A Sourcebook*, New York and London: Routledge, 1993

The Art of Medieval Spain, AD 500–1200, exh. cat., Metropolitan Museum of Art, New York, 1993

Lorena Casa, *Religious Women as Scribes and Artists in Early Anglo-Saxon England*, MA thesis, University of London, 1993

Madeline H. Caviness, "Patron or matron: A Capetian bride and a *vade mecum* for her marriage", *Speculum*, lxviii, 1993, pp.333–63

Allen S. Farber, "Considering a marginal master: The work of an early fifteenth-century Parisian manuscript decorator", *Gesta*, xxxii, 1993, pp.21–39

William Cook, "Early images of St Francis of Assisi in Rome", *Exegisti monumentum aere perennius: Essays in Honor of John Frederick Charles*, ed. Bruce R. Baker and John E. Fischer, Indianapolis: Guild Press of Indiana, 1994

Judith Oliver, "The Herkenrode indulgence, Avignon and pre-Eyckian painting of the mid-fourteenth-century Low Countries", *Flanders in a European Perspective: Manuscript Illumination around 1400 in Flanders and Abroad: Proceedings of the International Colloquium, Leuven, 7–10 September 1993*, ed. M. Smeyers and B. Cardon, Leuven: Peeters, 1995, pp.187–206

——, "The Walters homiliary and Westphalian manuscripts", *Journal of the Walters Art Gallery*, liv, 1996, pp.69–85

——, "Worship of the word: Some Gothic Nonnenbücher in their devotional context", *Women and the Book: Assessing the Visual Evidence*, ed. Jane Taylor and Lesley Smith, London: British Library, and Toronto: University of Toronto, 1997

Jeffrey Hamburger, *Nuns as Artists: The Visual Culture of a German Convent at the End of the Middle Ages* (in preparation)

Academies of Art

Italy

The first academies of painting and sculpture were founded in Italy during the second half of the 16th century. Formed under the protection of a prince or state, art academies were intended as instruments of artistic reform, and their members included scholars, art lovers and art patrons as well as painters, sculptors and architects. They were modelled on literary and scientific academies, societies of humanist scholars and gentlemen who shared an interest in ancient culture. Part of the purpose of art academies was to free artists from the exclusive control of the guilds to which they had traditionally belonged (painters to the Arte de' Medici e Speziali, sculptors and architects to the Università dei Fabbricanti). Nevertheless, they continued to share many of the same functions and aims, and the first art academies co-existed with the system of guilds and artists' confraternities (Compagnia di San Luca). There were also private academies that were less formal associations of artists who trained and worked together, such as the Accademia degli Incamminati founded by the Carracci in Bologna (1584). But both public and private academies differed from guilds and medieval workshops in their focus on art theory and classical ideals in addition to studio practice.

As practical institutions, academies set standards, laid down rules and regulations for the business of art production and provided instruction; however, their overriding concern was to raise the dignity of the profession. This emphasis on the intellectual foundations of the visual arts, the application of the mind as well as the hand in the perfect union of theory and practice, was the fundamental principle underlying the academic programme. According to academic theory, the artist's idea or concept was developed and perfected through *disegno*, a term that meant both drawing and design.

By the middle of the 17th century a hierarchy of the arts became institutionalised in academies. The fine arts of painting, sculpture and architecture with their intellectual basis in *disegno* were considered superior to the manually produced mechanical arts and crafts. The art of painting was itself subdivided into higher and lesser categories, with history painting considered the highest because its purpose was to provide instruction and delight to the mind through the representation of morally uplifting themes. Based on Leon Battista Alberti's concept of *historia* (*De pictura*, 1435), history paintings portrayed significant human actions in narratives taken from biblical and classical literature and history. Its didactic purpose distinguished it from less lofty subjects that simply imitated nature in order to please the eye and lacked moral values: portraiture, themes from everyday life (genre), landscape and still-life painting. This division of the arts into higher and lower categories, with their attendant qualities of social and intellectual status, had consequences for the position of women within the profession.

Both the theoretical and practical programmes of art academies made life drawing from nude models one of their primary activities; in fact, the term "academy" still signifies life drawing. Proficiency in drawing the human figure in action and knowledge of anatomy were essential for training as a history painter. Young artists began to develop these skills by copying old master paintings and engravings. Parts of bodies, limbs and faces were practised first, followed by whole figures, and eventually the student moved on to three-dimensional objects in the form of sculptures or casts of antique statuary. Only after these were fully mastered could an artist advance to life studies from the draped and nude model. Women artists could follow the early stages of study by copying paintings, prints, statuary or plaster casts, which might include nude or nearly nude figures, but at this level of training, when male artists advanced to life classes, women were left behind. Drawing directly from the nude, especially the male nude, was thought to be unsuitable for them. The very idea of a woman artist taking the male prerogative to study living nude figures, male or female, and to create them herself, her pencil or brush stroking the portrayed flesh, could be construed as both titillating and distracting to the male students. Thus, the academic emphasis on the male nude made it difficult for women to pursue history painting and restricted most of them to the lesser genres of portraiture and still life.

The first formal art academy, the Accademia del Disegno, was created in Florence in 1563 under the inspiration of the artist-writer Giorgio Vasari and with the support of Cosimo I de' Medici, Grand Duke of Tuscany. Its members were selected from among the best painters, sculptors and architects in Florence, and its statutes were drawn up by a group of artists and humanist scholars. The curriculum they developed aimed to provide a broad liberal education for artists, and included mathematics, perspective, anatomy, life drawing and natural philosophy.

During its first 50 years the Accademia del Disegno had no women members. In 1616 Artemisia Gentileschi (q.v.) was accepted as the first female academician, although she and her husband had been permitted to use the facilities for the previous two years. Gentileschi's acceptance was undoubtedly tied to the patronage and support she received from the Medici family. Later in the 17th century the names of three more women appear in academy records: Rosa Maria Setterni (1662), Caterina Angiola Corsi Pierozzi (1691) and Colomba Agrani (1691).

In Rome the Accademia di San Luca, dedicated to St Luke, the patron saint of artists, was founded in 1593 by the painter and theorist Federigo Zuccari with the support of Cardinal Federigo Borromeo. As in the Florentine academy, Zuccari's principal aim was to promote the intellectual basis of art, *disegno*, and also to enhance the status and respectability of artists in society. The Academy set standards for admission, collected dues from members, held exhibitions and competitions (*concorsi*), and awarded prizes, which were a mark of official approval for young artists. The basic activity of the academy was the training of artists, so facilities for copying paintings, a study collection of plaster casts of antique sculpture and models for life drawing were provided. There was to be an ambitious programme of lectures and theoretical debates on various subjects such as the meaning of *disegno*, decorum in composition, the rendering of human movements in painting and the qualities of architecture.

Although membership of the Academy was not at first a prerequisite for a successful artistic career, if artists joined they had to abide by its regulations. These included restrictions on selling work below a fixed price, painting licentious subjects, attracting other artists' pupils and keeping a model. Members were required to present the Academy with one of their works, a reception piece. It is not entirely clear, however, whether such rules, which were rewritten several times during the course of the 17th century, were ever fully operational.

According to the rules of the Accademia di San Luca of 1607, women could be elected to membership but were prohibited from attending meetings.

Caterina Ginnasi, one of the few female members, is recorded in 1638 as having paid dues for the annual banquet held by the academicians in honour of St Luke. The name of the still-life painter Giovanna Garzoni (q.v.) appears on a list of academicians created in April 1633. Although this list is not considered reliable, she may have been admitted under the informal procedures of the 1620s and 1630s. After 1654 Garzoni is also noted on six occasions as a contributor to the annual celebration feast for the patron saint. In 1656, and later in 1669–70, she was treated to the special cakes that were customarily given to members who were ill. At her death she bequeathed her belongings to the Academy (Harris in Los Angeles 1976, p.15). After 1617 members of the nobility, scholars and distinguished foreign artists, including women, could be nominated for honorary membership as "accademici d'onore e di grazia" or "accademico di merito", to distinguish them from the local professional members.

In the 18th century more women were elected to membership in academies, but they were primarily foreigners who had established themselves as accomplished artists before coming to Italy. On 10 October 1762, just a few months after her arrival in Florence, the Swiss-born Angelica Kauffman (q.v.), already a celebrated artist at the age of 21, was elected to the Accademia del Disegno. Payment of her entrance fee was recorded several days later; however, her membership was more of an honour than an expectation of full participation in academy business. The Italian-born British painter Maria Cosway (q.v.) was similarly elected to membership in the Florentine Accademia del Disegno before the age of 20 on 27 September 1778. Kauffman was also honoured in 1762 with membership in the Accademia Clementina in Bologna (founded in 1709), and almost 20 years later, on her return to Italy from England in 1781, she was made an honorary member of the Accademia delle Belle Arti in Venice, which had been founded in 1750 as the first public art school in that city.

The Venetian Rosalba Carriera (q.v.) was elected Accademica di Merito in the Roman Accademia di San Luca on 27 September 1705. As a reception piece for their collection, she presented the institution with a small painting on ivory representing *Innocence*. When Kauffman became a member on 17 November 1765, she donated an allegorical painting of *Hope*. Other women artists listed as

members in the 18th century, most of whom were either foreigners or related to important male artists by birth or marriage, include Luisa Roldán (q.v., 1706), Maria Tibaldi Subleray (1742), Veronika Stern (1742), Maria Maini, daughter of the painter Giovanni Battista Maini (no date), Maria Vien, wife of the Director of the French Academy in Rome (1757), Caterina Preziado, "daughter of a prince" (1760), Theresa Concordia Maron-Mengs (1766) and Elisabeth Vigée-Lebrun (q.v., 1790). Despite their increasing numbers, women were still not allowed to vote or to draw from nude models.

Women artists and academies of art in Rome

The exclusion of women from full participation in the Roman Academy was due primarily to its continuing emphasis on life drawing, although the academy's stress on the theoretical basis of art and the supremacy of history painting also played a part. In reality, during much of the 17th and the 18th centuries in Rome, drawing from models took place in private studios rather than in the Accademia di San Luca, which did not consistently provide classes. One place at which artists could draw from nude models was the Académie de France, the French Academy in Rome, which had been founded in 1666 as a branch of the Parisian Academy and where life drawing classes were held every day. In any case, models were generally male, for although female models were occasionally used in Italian academies, this did not become standard practice until the 19th century (see Bignamini in Boschloo 1989). In 1754 Pope Benedict XIV established the Accademia del Nudo in Rome as a place for art students to draw from nude and draped models on a regular basis without paying a fee. Members of the Accademia di San Luca, to which the school was affiliated, took turns supervising classes, posing models and correcting students' work. Competitions (*concorsi*) were held at the end of each year for the best drawing and sculpted figure, and medals were awarded. Women, who were excluded from these classes, were at a distinct disadvantage in the advancement of their careers, especially those who aspired to pursue history painting. In 1752 the British painter Katharine Read (q.v.) was in Italy to further her artistic training. Her situation was described in a letter from one of her patrons (Abbé Grant): "... was it not for the restrictions her sex obliges her to be under, ... she would shine wonderfully in history painting, too, but it is impossible for her to attend public academies or even design or draw from nature ...".

Among Kauffman's early sketches made in Rome in the early 1760s are a few nude or nearly nude male figures. One drawing (Kupferstichkabinett, Berlin, repr. Baumgärtel 1990, p.81), proudly and perhaps defiantly signed "Designée par moi Marianne Angélique Kauffman l'an 1763", represents a nude man tied to a tree trunk with a sweep of drapery behind him. The figure's pose, as if viewed from slightly below, his left side towards the picture plane, resembles a standard life-class attitude with one arm behind his back and the other outstretched. While it is conceivable that Kauffman drew from a live model, perhaps in the privacy of her own studio, it is much more likely that this was copied from a drawing by another artist. She did in fact copy at least one nude study from an engraving after a drawing by the French artist Fragonard (c.1760; Städelsches Kunstinstitut und Städtische Galerie, Frankfurt am Main, repr. Baumgärtel 1990, p.85). She knew many artists in Rome, including Nathaniel Dance and Gavin Hamilton, who may well have allowed her to copy their studies.

Academies of art outside Florence and Rome

With the support of Church and State, the Accademia del Disegno in Florence and the Accademia di San Luca in Rome remained the most important and influential art academies in Italy. During the 17th and 18th centuries dozens of new public and private academies modelled on those of Florence and Rome were founded in other Italian cities such as Bologna, Milan, Lucca, Parma and Venice. The intellectual ideals and emphasis on life drawing and the study of antiquities also inspired the formation of academies in other European cities, including Haarlem, Utrecht, Amsterdam, Paris, Nuremberg, Berlin, Dresden, Munich, Vienna, Copenhagen, Edinburgh, Dublin, Lisbon, Madrid and St Petersburg, although most remained provincial (see Pevsner 1940).

Artists from all over Europe, including such women as Anne Forbes, whose trip abroad between c.1768 and 1771 was financed by subscription among friends and relations in Edinburgh, continued to travel to the artistic centres of Italy, especially Florence and Rome, to learn from the art of the "old masters" and classical antiquity. Some women artists were able to participate in exhibitions and competitions in the newer academies, and a few

even became members. Nevertheless, the only academy that could rival the Florentine Accademia del Disegno and the Roman Accademia di San Luca in influence and prestige was the French Académie Royale de Peinture et de Sculpture, and it was in the Academy in Paris that the role of women as artists was seriously challenged.

WENDY WASSYNG ROWORTH

France

The Académie Royale de Peinture et de Sculpture was founded in France in 1648 during the reign of Louis XIV. In contrast to the artists' guild or Maîtrise, the Academy stressed its honorific, rather than commercial function. Academicians could not keep a shop or display works for sale in their studios, and their regulations stressed decorum and learning. The Crown, moreover, gave the newly formed Academy the privilege of posing the nude (male) model for public instruction and provided a system of government patronage that would make the Académie Royale into a powerful arts institution. The finance minister Colbert was the first official protector of the Academy, and he used this position not only to ensure the flow of government patronage, but also to control art production in the interests of the state.

In 1737 the Academy solidified its control over the visual arts by holding official art exhibitions, known as Salons, in the Salon carrée of the Louvre in the autumn, in alternate years. Although the Academy had earlier sponsored sporadic exhibitions, in 1737 the Salon was regularised as a biennial event. Only academicians could show their works at the Salon, which was one of the very few public exhibition spaces in 18th-century Paris. The Salon grew increasingly important as the exhibitions encouraged a flowering of art criticism, which increased as the century progressed.

Acceptance procedures and the admission of women

It was during Colbert's tenure of office, on 14 April 1663, that the Academy accepted its first woman member: Cathérine Duchemin, wife of the sculptor François Girardon. The painter Charles Le Brun presented to the academicians a flower painting by Duchemin, and "the Company, affected by their esteem for this work and recognising the merit of this young woman, resolved to give her the position of Académicienne" (*Procès-verbaux*, i, pp.222–3). The institution's official rationale for accepting Duchemin rested on interpreting the king's intention in founding the Academy. In assessing her case for admission, the academicians deemed it their duty to abide by the king's wish to honour "all those who excel in the arts of painting and sculpture and those judged worthy, regardless of their sex" (*idem*). But women were not honoured in the same way as their male contemporaries. For example, at the same meeting in which Duchemin was accepted, the company also received 14 male artists. Whereas she was sent letters of appointment, they were ordered to take the oath in which they swore to uphold "religiously" the rules and statutes of the Academy. Oath-taking in France during the Ancien Régime formalised and added force to commitments, but women were banned from swearing them, except-ing, of course, the vow of marriage. Beyond requir-ing oath-taking, in the 17th century admission procedures were not regularised nor were admis-sions systematically recorded. Later, however, the differences between the admissions of men and women became more evident.

Male painters usually went through the Academy's training programme, which they concluded by presenting for evaluation a work of their choice. If the work was accepted, they entered the Academy as a provisional member or *agréé*, with the evaluated work designated as their *morceau d'agrément*. To obtain final acceptance, the aspiring academician completed a second "masterpiece" called the *morceau de réception*. The subject of this work was usually assigned by the Academy, which gave the artist a specific period of time, normally a year, to complete it. These procedures governed the admission of nearly all male artists, although a few were excepted from them in one way or another. The *morceau de réception* was especially important since its subject determined the category in which a painter was received. Once received as a painter of a particular genre, the artist could never change his or her designated place. At the top of the academic hierarchy was history painting (subjects drawn from history, myth, religion as well as allegory) and below that portraiture, genre painting, landscape and still life. Although the system of apprenticeship and admission was regularised by the 18th century, women were never received in the "normal" way.

The Academy usually made them *agréée* and *académicienne* on the same day. Most, although not all, brought to the session several paintings from which the academicians could "find" appropriate reception pieces.

Women and the status of the Academy

The acceptance of women moved the Académie Royale de Peinture et de Sculpture closer to the Maîtrise than to the other honorific institutions, such as the Académie des Sciences and the Académie Française, which did not admit women. This partly explains why women were kept in an equivocal position within the arts institution. The presence of women in the corporation bespoke a lowered status and evoked the mixed body of the guild, which admitted not only women but also art dealers and artisans. The Academy was also anxious to stress its difference from the Maîtrise since on several other counts the two functioned in a similar way. For example, both encouraged a long apprenticeship for students in the atelier of an established master and both asked for a masterpiece (which the Academy called a *morceau de réception*). Most significantly, both institutions (like all other guilds) gave prefer-ence to the sons of its members, and some consider-ation to their daughters and widows. For the history of women in the Academy this last point is signifi-cant, especially since family connections seem to have played a role in opening the Academy to women. Indeed, the first three women received into the Academy were the daughters or wives of acade-micians. After Cathérine Duchemin, Geneviève and Madeleine Boulogne, daughters of Louis Boulogne, were accepted in 1669. In total, one-third of all women admitted were relatives of academic artists. Marie-Thérèse Reboul, wife of Joseph Vien, was accepted in 1754, and Marie-Suzanne Giroust, wife of Alexandre Roslin, in 1770.

Although the Academy could not exclude women entirely, it could maintain them in an equivocal posi-tion – as foreign elements – since they were not allowed to swear allegiance to the institution and its rules. The Academy records suggest that it was never eager to admit women and always did so as "exceptions". This was the case even though women were admitted infrequently and comprised a very small proportion of the membership. Indeed, between 1648 and 1792, when the Academy was disbanded and reorganised, the royal institution admitted more than 450 artists. Of that number, 15

(3 per cent) were women. The collective anxiety about these women is encoded in certain phrases that appear repeatedly in the *Procès-verbaux*; specifically, those indicating that the acceptance of a particular woman was not meant to set a precedent. For example, in 1680 Dorothée Massée was accepted "in the position of academician, without allowing her to be a precedent for the future" (*Procès-verbaux*, ii, pp.175–6). In 1682 the admission of Cathérine Pérot was qualified with the phrase: "ce sans tirer consequence" (*ibid.*, ii, p.215), which appeared again in recording the election of Rosalba Carriera in 1720 (*ibid.*, iv, p.303). In 1722 the same phrase marks the record of admitting a second foreign woman, Margareta Haverman (*ibid.*, iv, p.328). Although it was another 32 years before the next woman was admitted, the Academy still felt compelled to point out that the admission of Madame Vien, on 30 July 1754, was not to set a precedent (*ibid.*, vii, p.41).

These standards of recording the admission of women are punctuated in the Academy's history by the record of official efforts to restrict the number of women who could enter the academic body. On 25 September 1706 the *Procès-verbaux* recorded only one item of business at the regular meeting: "Règlement général que l'on ne recevra aucune Damoiselle en qualité d'Académicienne". The rule was allegedly prompted by the fact that the Academy had learned that "several ladies who have applied themselves to painting have planned to present themselves to be received as académiciennes". After "une sérieuse réflexion" the company decided to forestall the presentations of these women by resolving that henceforth they would receive no woman as academician and that this resolution would serve as the "règlement général" (*ibid.*, iii, p.34). This rule may also have been promoted because in 1706 six women – the largest group at any one time – were current members of the Academy. Besides the sisters Boulogne, in 1672 the Academy had received Elisabeth-Sophie Chéron, the first woman admitted who was not the wife or daughter of an academician. Chéron, not incidentally, was the most distinguished and learned woman artist of 17th-century France, one whose works the academicians distinguished as "very exceptional and surpassing the ordinary power (force) of her sex" (*ibid.*, i, p.388). Three other women had also been admitted: Anne Strésor in 1677, Dorothée Massée in 1680 and Cathérine

Pérot in 1682. The rule of 1706 that closed the Academy to women, however, was not long-lasting; it was enacted without the king's order and did not have the force of law. Fourteen years later the resolution was broken and two foreign women were received: the Italian Carriera (1720) and the Dutchwoman Haverman (1722). Foreign women might have been doubly alien to the French Academy, but they were much less threatening than local ones. The foreigner was usually passing through; she did not disrupt the established circuits of patronage, or challenge male monopolies over academic enterprise.

Between 1706, when the first rule for prohibiting the admission of women was enacted, and 1770, when a second one was suggested, the Academy admitted women sporadically. With one notable exception, all the women admitted during this period were either foreigners, such as Carriera, Haverman and the Prussian Terbouche (1767), or artists' wives, such as Madame Vien (1757) and Madame Roslin (1770). The exception was Mlle Vallayer (q.v.), also admitted in 1770, whose father was goldsmith to the king. Two months after her admission on 28 September 1770, Pierre, the first painter, proposed another *Règlement pour l'admission des femmes l'Académie*:

> Although [the Academy] is pleased to encourage talent in women by admitting some into our body, nevertheless, these admissions, foreign in some fashion to its constitution must not be repeated too often. [The Academy] has agreed that it will receive no more than four women. It will, however, receive women only in cases in which their extraordinarily distinguished talents lead the Academy to wish, with a unanimous voice, to crown them with particular distinction. The Academy does not pretend to oblige itself always to fill the number of four, reserving for itself the right to choose only those whose talents are truly distinguished [*Procès-verbaux*, vii, p.53].

Like the resolution of 1706, however, Pierre's regulation lacked the official sanction of the Crown, and it was not until 13 years later that the Academy obtained officially the longed-for limitation on the number of women. This came in conjunction with the acceptance, in 1783, of two women, the last who would ever be members of that royal institution: Elisabeth Vigée-Lebrun (q.v.) and Adélaïde Labille-Guiard (q.v.). The decree limiting the number of women is inseparable from the controversy that surrounded the admission of one of those women, Vigée-Lebrun. Because she was married to an art dealer, the Academy, represented by its director d'Angiviller, held her in violation of the statute forbidding artists from engaging in commerce, and refused to admit her. At the request of the queen, Marie-Antoinette, the king ordered an exception to the rule, which opened the way for the artist to be accepted as *académicienne*. In contrast to this example, on the same day the academicians conducted and recorded the acceptance of Labille-Guiard according to the practices established for accepting women. But the double admission did more than stress the differences in how the two candidates were admitted. Receiving Labille-Guiard brought the number of women in the Academy to four (the other two were Mme Vien and Mme Vallayer-Coster). Moreover, four was precisely the number that Pierre had selected as the appropriate limit for women more than a decade before. In addition to the order admitting Vigée-Lebrun, d'Angiviller persuaded the king to give a second order, "limiting to four the number of women who can, in the future, be admitted into the Academy". The academicians responded by sending "a letter of thanks to M. d'Angiviller for having preserved the rights of the Academy and the force of its statutes, and for having fixed the number of women academicians at four" (*Procès-verbaux*, ix, p.153). The director's justification for limiting the number of women to four was as follows: "this number is sufficient to honour their talent; women can not be useful to the progress of the arts because the modesty of their sex forbids them from being able to study after nature and in the public school established and founded by your Majesty" (*ibid.*, ix, p.157). What d'Angiviller meant by the progress of the arts was, of course, the progress of history painting.

Women and academic training in France

It has been more than two decades since Linda Nochlin (1971) argued in her ground-breaking work that women were excluded from the highest achievements in painting because they could not receive the necessary academic training. Women were excluded from two learning situations – drawing after nature and attending the Academy

school. Modesty dictated that women should not look at the nude male body, which is what study after nature meant in this context. Posing the male model was the only life drawing sanctioned in the Academy, and it was this privilege that distinguished the Academy from the Maîtrise. Modesty kept women from other aspects of artistic education, as well. They could not attend schools such as the Ecole Royale des Elèves Protégés, where aspiring artists not only learned the finer points of practice, but also acquired intellectual knowledge in subjects thought essential to history painting: geography, history, literature, anatomy and perspective. This exclusion exemplifies the general situation in France where young men and women were educated separately and learned different kinds of subjects and skills thought *convenable* to their sex.

In comparison to the noble genre of history painting, the lesser genres were theoretically feminised since their only function was to please. History paintings, on the other hand, were made to instruct, to edify, to instil virtue and to capture *gloire*. A fear of the emasculating effect of women was one factor in the prevention of women – always foreign to the academic body – from entering the Académie Royale in too great a number. Too many women would dilute the proportion of history painters, which was one measure of the Academy's manliness. It was not, d'Angiviller argued, in society's interests to promote women as members of such institutions as the Académie Royale. Women, he implies, would impede the progress of art by taking academic positions that might otherwise be filled by (male) history painters. But this is a specious argument – there was no limit on the number of academicians, and so an alteration in the ratio of male to female artists entering the Academy could not affect the "progress of the arts".

At the same time that d'Angiviller was working to close admission to the Academy to women, other avenues for women's advancement in the arts were also being closed. For example, women had formerly been allowed to train in the studios of academic painters who had their lodgings and ateliers in the Louvre (an atelier in the Louvre was one of the rewards available to academicians). Only one woman artist, Vallayer-Coster, had lodgings there and the pains taken over them show that she, like Vigée-Lebrun, had a powerful protector in Marie-Antoinette. D'Angiviller, moreover, had no reason to fear that Vallayer-Coster (then Mlle

Vallayer) might pose a threat to the "decency" of the Louvre. He wrote to her that, as director of the Academy, he wanted her to have an apartment where she could "cultivate in peace" her distinguished talents (Michel 1970). When a second woman, Labille-Guiard, asked for lodgings in the Louvre, however, d'Angiviller was not so accommodating. She was not asking for solitude, but for a place to hold her art school for young women. In a letter of November 1785 to the king concerning Labille-Guiard's request for lodgings in the Louvre, d'Angiviller points out that because the artist "has a school for young students of her sex", allowing her to bring her studio and students to the Louvre would present great dangers. He reminds the king that "all the artists have their lodging in the Louvre and as one only gets to all these lodgings through vast corridors that are often dark, this mixing of young artists of different sexes would be very inconvenient for morals and for the decency of your majesty's palace" (Passez 1973, p.301). The point, of course, ignores the fact that the Louvre already housed a mixed-sex community, because artists had wives and daughters and other women relatives living there. But perhaps d'Angiviller could accept this mixing because the women residing there were located firmly under the roof of male authority (of a father or husband).

Even more pernicious than denying Labille-Guiard's request for lodgings was d'Angiviller's order prohibiting artists from teaching women students in the Louvre. He was so adamant about the issue that in 1785 he went so far as to get an official order from the king forbidding these classes (Guiffrey 1874). It is important to bear in mind that it was through such private lessons that many young women artists, Vigée-Lebrun for example, received their early education. Thus d'Angiviller closed an important avenue for the training of women artists who were not the wives or daughters of academicians. The director's zeal in enforcing the ban is evident in the letters exchanged in 1787 between d'Angiviller and the artists Jacques-Louis David and Joseph-Benoît Suvée who had taken on women students in their ateliers. D'Angiviller reminded both artists that the Louvre was a "place where it is particularly necessary that decency should reign, so we cannot allow ourselves to close our eyes to this abuse" (19 July 1787; Silvestre de Sacy 1953, p.176). Even when one of the girls' guardians wrote to d'Angiviller, he received a curt and officious reply.

D'Angiviller told him in no uncertain terms that his daughter's exclusion was not motivated by a mistaken impression of her conduct, but by a general consideration of the trouble that could follow from holding a school for girls. He said quite bluntly that even if all precautions possible were taken to ensure decency, this would not justify a departure from the rule (*ibid.*, p.177). One suspects that the rule was meant to ensure something other than decency.

Women, Academy, Revolution

Labille-Guiard's attempts to gain for women students an official training-ground at the Louvre were thwarted by d'Angiviller. During the Revolutionary period her attempts to gain other privileges for women also failed, this time thwarted by the leader of the so-called "progressive" painters, Joseph Vien. In 1790 the Academy would use the same strategies to keep women in an equivocal position that they had used a century earlier. The oath again became a point that separated the women from the men.

In 1790 the officers banned women from discussions about re-organising the Academy because they had not taken the oath. That this ban followed Labille-Guiard's attempts to gain for women an unlimited number of seats in the Academy is significant. It demonstrates again that when under threat from women – as it had been already in 1706 and 1783 – the Academy would act to limit their role, even though the records and reports suggest that the academicians were by no means unanimous in their resolve to keep women out. Moreover, the timing of this ban also supports the historian Geneviève Fraisse's argument that the ideology of liberty and equality fostered by the Revolution raised in a glaring way the problem of women's rights (*La Raison des femmes*, Paris: Plon, 1992, pp.49–62). Indeed, an appeal to the new principles fuelled Labille-Guiard's attempts to gain equality for women.

Little about these attempts is recorded in the Academy's *Procès-verbaux*, but more is suggested in the memoirs of the engraver Wille. His entry for 23 September 1790 begins: "Madame Guiard, seated next to me, made a very well justified speech on the admission of women artists to the Academy and proved that accepting an unlimited number must be the only admissible rule" (Duplessis 1857, ii, p.268). Wille also described a second motion made by Labille-Guiard and supported by the painter Vincent that would allow some women to be distinguished with particular honours. Labille-Guiard justified the request by arguing that because women could neither participate in the governance of the Academy nor be professors in its schools, there was no way in which they could elevate themselves within the existing hierarchy. Commenting on the fate of the proposal, Wille wrote: "This article, despite the opposition of M. LeBarbier, was approved and passed the vote, as did the first" (*idem*). Again we see that the members of the Academy were by no means united in their opposition to women, and it was left to the officers to stop their efforts to gain more equal power. And it shows that the admission of artists' wives and daughters was by no means a cue that those academicians supported women's rights. For the artist who seems to have led the move to suppress Labille-Guiard's efforts was none other than Vien, whose wife had been admitted to the Academy in 1757.

Although the minutes in the *Procès-verbaux* do not record the meeting cited by Wille, the record does include a letter dated 23 September 1790 from the officers to the academicians that refers to the meeting. The officers – and chief among them Vien – seem to have separated themselves from the academicians for the purpose of enacting new statutes. To justify the move they argued that it was impossible to continue work with the entire Assembly because, among other things, several members supported their opinions with a "chaleur immodéré" and because:

> ... we do not find it appropriate that women mix themselves in a work that is foreign to them, it being only a question of redrafting the Statutes, which do not concern them at all since they have not submitted to them, never having taken the oath to obey them [*Procès-verbaux*, x, p.81].

How convenient that women are foreign to the Academy because they have not taken the oath! Oath-taking, it seems, both in the Ancien Régime and during the Revolution, was a male prerogative. After all the revolutionary dust had settled and the Academy was reorganised, there were no more exceptional women in that corporate body, for the Academy had closed its doors to them.

MARY D. SHERIFF

Britain

A state-sponsored academy of art was not established in Britain until 1768. The history of the formation of the Royal Academy of Arts and its forerunners, which included private academies run by artists themselves and societies of artists who banded together to produce public art exhibitions, must be seen as part of a search for a national identity in the arts that was closely tied to the commercial concerns of British artists who decried the lack of a native school of art and the importation of continental art and artists (see Bignamini 1989).

In the latter years of the 17th century a few private art academies set up for both professional and amateur artists provided training through the study of antique statuary and live models. Although traditional studios and workshops continued to provide training on an individual basis, by the middle of the 18th century a few academies were established to foster common artistic goals and standards under the guidance of a single instructor. A number of British artists, many of whom had travelled on the Continent and observed artistic training there, felt the need to organise life drawing classes along the lines of Italian and French theory and practice. The most important academic predecessor of the Royal Academy in London was the Academy in St Martin's Lane (1735–68), in which William Hogarth played a major role. Outside London, academies developed in Edinburgh (1729 and 1760), Dublin (1742), Birmingham (1754) and Glasgow (1754), providing instruction through the copying of paintings, prints and casts.

A unique feature of British academies was the regular employment of both female and male nude models in the life class. Since the Renaissance, European artists had studied from female models in the privacy of their studios, and they were occasionally used in some of the early Italian and German academies, but they did not become part of regular academic practice in Europe and America until the 19th century. In fact, throughout the 17th and 18th centuries the Académie Royale in Paris and the Académie Française in Rome forbade the use of naked female models at the same time that study of the nude male was the essential foundation of artistic theory and practice. For artists who could not afford to hire a woman to model in private, female anatomy was studied from antique sculpture and old master paintings, engravings or drawing books. Ironically, the British, who were so late in the development of an official academy, led the way in the systematic study of female anatomy through living models (see Nottingham and London 1991).

Societies for the promotion of the arts

The Society for the Encouragement of Arts, Manufactures and Commerce (Society of Arts), founded in London in 1754 to encourage inventions and improvements in the "Arts and Sciences", awarded premiums (prizes) for the best paintings in different categories, such as history or landscape, and to boys and girls under the age of 16 who produced the best drawings. In 1759 they also offered premiums for drawings from "Living Models at the Academy of Artists in St Martin's Lane ... by young men under 24 years". The practice of drawing from the live human figure, which was becoming standard practice for young male artists, was not considered appropriate for young women.

In the years just preceding the creation of the Royal Academy of Arts several groups of artists came together for the purposes of promoting contemporary British art through public exhibitions and raising money through admissions and the sale of catalogues. In 1760 the Society for the Encouragement of Arts, Manufactures and Commerce provided a room in London for an exhibition by one such group; however, the independent-minded artists wanted more autonomy than the Society was willing to allow in the charging of admission fees and the selection and hanging of their pictures, so in 1762 they broke away to form the Free Society of Artists and held their own exhibitions until 1783. Several women, such as Angelica Kauffman (1765, 1766 and 1783), were among the exhibitors. This group also formed a charitable fund to help artists and their families in times of need. Another breakaway rival group, the Society of Artists of Great Britain (1761), which became the Incorporated Society of Artists in 1765, held their own exhibitions until 1791, and these also included works by women artists such as Mary Moser and Katharine Read (q.v.).

Foundation of the Royal Academy of Arts

After this long and sometimes bitter campaign by different factions of British artists, on 10 December 1768 the Royal Academy of Arts was founded under the protection of George III (see Bignamini and Hutchison in Boschloo 1989). The *Instrument of Foundation* laid down regulations for membership of the Academy and its governance under a Council and an elected President, a position first filled by Joshua Reynolds. During his presidency (1768–92) Reynolds delivered a series of lectures, later published as *Discourses on Art*, in which he laid out his ideas for the theory and practice of academic art. The *Instrument of Foundation* also specified how business should be conducted, the establishment of an annual public exhibition of paintings, sculptures and designs, and a programme of instruction patterned on the Italian and French academies that stressed mathematics and perspective, as well as anatomy studied from the antique and from living models. Instruction in the Academy schools was supervised by artists called Visitors who were elected from the membership, in addition to professors of anatomy, perspective and geometry, painting and architecture. A Keeper of the Royal Academy fulfilled the responsibility of providing life models, books, casts and other items essential for artistic education. Admission to the school was restricted to students who could demonstrate their abilities to the Visitors, the Keeper and the Council.

Membership in the Royal Academy consisted of 40 painters, sculptors and architects. After the initial appointment of the founding members, all future vacancies were to be filled by election from among the participants in the annual exhibitions, which were open to "all Artists of distinguished merit", as judged by a committee of academicians. After 1770 a separate category called Associates of the Royal Academy was established. This was limited to 20 in number and was originally intended as a way to add more engravers to the membership, albeit with lesser status. Another adjunct group were honorary members, which included antiquaries and professors of ancient literature and history.

Women in the Royal Academy

Among the 40 founding members were two highly accomplished women artists, Kauffman and Moser, the latter the daughter of the first Keeper of the Royal Academy, George Moser. The Swiss-born and Italian-trained Kauffman had arrived in London just two years earlier, but had already made a major impression on a number of influential artists and patrons. Although a foreigner, Kauffman's background and skills as a history painter, the highest category of painting, which Reynolds and others hoped to promote, made her a valuable asset in the struggle to cultivate patrons and to gain recognition for art produced in Britain. The fact that she was a woman and a foreigner seemed less important than her status as a history painter who could serve as role model for the type of artist Britain needed. Among the founding members, Moser was one of only two flower painters, a much lower rank in the hierarchy of painting; however, the combination of her father's influence and her precocious talent gained her a place within this elite group. She had been awarded a silver prize by the Society of Arts in 1759, at the age of 15.

While Kauffman and Moser were not expected to attend meetings, they did take part in the judging for gold medals and travelling scholarships by sending in marked lists. They also voted in elections. Kauffman mailed her votes in the form of letters to the President, but between 1779 and 1810 Moser often attended general assemblies and participated in Academy proceedings. No doubt inspired by the two female academicians, the Incorporated Society of Artists, which continued to exist as a separate body, elected several women to honorary memberships in 1769. These were the painters Read, Mary Grace, Mary Benwell, Eliza Gardiner and Mary Black, the last a skilful copyist of old master paintings.

Before the mid-19th century there seems to have been an unofficial limit on the admission of women to the Academy schools. There was, in fact, by that time a separate government Female School of Art and Design (1843) to which the Academy contributed money, a factor that discouraged women applicants to the Royal Academy Schools. Nevertheless, in 1860 a female artist, Laura Anne Herford, was admitted to the Antique School by judges who did not suspect she was a woman because her drawings had been identified only by her initials. Soon after, a few more women students were accepted, including Louisa Starr, who won medals in 1865 and 1867. With the admission of even a limited number of women students, the Council acted to ensure observation of the strictest propriety.

Women artists and the life class

The best-known early representation of the Royal Academy is Johann Zoffany's informal group portrait of 1771–2 (Royal Collection) in which the members are portrayed in Old Somerset House, London, the first home of the Academy. Casts of antique statues are arranged along the wall behind the artists, but the primary function of this room was life drawing, an activity central to the Academy's programme. All the artists can be identified, and include the painter Zoffany at the far left and the first President, Sir Joshua Reynolds, who stands near the centre of the picture with his characteristic ear trumpet. He is one of the few figures who does not direct his attention towards the two male models at the far right of the picture, one disrobing in the foreground and the other posing under the direction of the Keeper, George Moser. The two female founding members of the Royal Academy are physically absent from this scene and are represented only by their portraits hanging on the wall above the male models. Despite Kauffman's and Moser's participation in just about every function of the Academy, as Linda Nochlin observed in her essay "Why have there been no great women artists?" (1971), Zoffany's decision to set the scene in the life class made their marginalisation very apparent.

The Royal Academy held winter and summer terms for the "Academy of Living Models, men and women of different characters" provided by the Keeper. Four male models were employed daily to sit for two hours, the established practice in European academies, holding the same pose aided by a rope or staff, as seen in Zoffany's picture. A female model sat three nights a week, every other week. They were better paid than the men but were regarded with curiosity and suspicion, considered no better than prostitutes, which many of them may have been. To ensure proper decorum no unmarried men under the age of 20 were permitted to draw from the female nude, and no others except members of the royal family were admitted during the time the model was sitting. Women artists were not allowed to draw from the nude model in the Royal Academy until 1893, when the partially draped figure was introduced into the female life class.

Under these circumstances Moser and Kauffman did not attend life class; nevertheless, an unusual drawing by Moser of a full-length standing female nude (Fitzwilliam Museum, Cambridge, repr. Nottingham 1982, p.45) suggests that she may have had the opportunity to study from a female model, perhaps at the St Martin's Lane Academy, where her father had provided models as he did in his later role as Keeper of the Royal Academy. However, this drawing may simply have been copied from the work of a male colleague. Similarly, Kauffman managed to overcome the obstacle of exclusion from the life class – a serious drawback for a history painter – by copying academy drawings by other artists, casts of Classical sculpture, and the heads and limbs of clothed living models.

In later years malicious rumours suggested that Kauffman had disguised herself as a man so that she could slip into the Academy to attend the life class, or that she hired male models to pose in the privacy of her studio. J.T. Smith wrote in *Nollekens and His Times* (London, 1824) that he asked the model Charles Cranmer, the same man who sat for Reynolds, if this were true. Cranmer assured him that although he had modelled for Kauffman many years earlier, her father was always present, and he had only bared his arms, shoulders and legs for her to draw. Kauffman's biographer had decried a similar method and insisted that she always adhered to the strictest propriety in her work. Women artists were forced to tread a fine line between mastering necessary academic skills and maintaining their reputations.

Frances Reynolds, the sister of Sir Joshua Reynolds and a painter herself, was said to have expressed the opinion that it was a great pity drawing from nude models should be a necessary part of the education of a painter. Her view was noted by James Northcote, Joshua Reynolds's pupil and assistant, in a letter dated 21 December 1771, in which he added: "Miss Reynolds drew all her figures clothed except infants". In Northcote's own opinion, it was "impossible to make a good history painter and not know the human figure well, for many great painters drew the outlines of the body always before they did the drapery on them" (Whitley 1928, ii, p.287).

Women in the Royal Academy exhibitions in the 18th century

The Academy annual exhibitions continued to grow so that by 1779 more than 400 works were shown. The hanging committee was quite strict in their control over the appropriateness of submissions. The "high" arts of painting and sculpture were favoured over the "low" arts and crafts, and while any professional or amateur was allowed to submit work, the standard was biased in favour of academically trained artists. Needlework, artificial flowers and models in coloured wax were displayed in other contemporary exhibitions, but after 1771 they were specifically excluded from the Royal Academy. In 1791 a Miss Lane tried to submit a picture made of hair but was rejected. Other types of art excluded from consideration were drawings copied after paintings, and in some cases engravings after works of art were not allowed. This emphasis on originality and academic training made it almost impossible for most women artists to gain acceptance even though they were not officially excluded by the rules.

Despite these rigid restrictions some women artists apart from the academicians Kauffman and Moser were able to show their work at the annual exhibitions. One of them was the prodigy Helen Beatson, who in 1779 exhibited a picture at the tender age of eleven years. Read was also a frequent exhibitor, and Maria Cosway (q.v.) showed 42 portraits and subject paintings from mythology and literature between 1781 and 1801.

Frances Reynolds exhibited two pictures at the Royal Academy in 1774, *Children Going to Bed* (no.354) and *The Garland, from Prior* (no.355). They are officially identified as by "A Lady" with no indication of her name, but we know that they were hers because a reviewer commented on no.354:

> We do not remember ever to have seen a prettier subject for the exercise of a lady's pencil …, nor could it perhaps be better made use of in the hands of a more experienced artist … The public are indebted for this picture to Miss Reynolds, sister to the President of the Royal Academy.

The following year she exhibited *Lace Makers* (no.382), a miniature, described by a critic as "a pretty, elegant, feeling picture". Unfortunately, her brother's view was that her pictures made him cry and others laugh (Whitley 1928, i, pp.297–8). Unlike Kauffman, Moser and Cosway, who pursued painting as a profession and were taken more or less seriously, Frances Reynolds felt herself relegated to amateur status by her brother's attitude and social aspirations, which restricted her to the role of a proper gentlewoman and frustrated her artistic ambitions. She confessed in a letter to a friend that she "envyd the female competitors in the exhibition" and pointed out that there were "other female competitors besides those who made it a profession" (Wendorf 1996, pp.80–81).

Kauffman exhibited numerous portraits and history paintings during her years in London and even after her return to Italy in 1781, often sending in as many as five or six a year. In 1771 the artist Mrs Delany wrote: "This morning we have been to see Mr [Benjamin] West's and Mrs Angelica's paintings ... My partiality leans to my sister painter. She certainly has a great deal of merit, but I like her history still better than her portraits" (*The Autobiography and Correspondence of Mary Granville, Mrs Delany*, ed. Lady Llanover, 6 vols, London: Bentley, 1861–2; reprinted New York: AMS Press, 1974). Kauffman generally received very favourable notices for her works, especially history paintings. The reviewers' high regard may be interpreted as expressions in support of that genre's importance as much as praise for Kauffman herself. In addition, even positive reviews were sometimes moderated by criticism of certain weaknesses, especially the "effeminacy" of the male characters. With their smooth contours and covered limbs, her painted men may have reflected her lack of study of male anatomy, or they could have been deliberately modelled to resemble the Roman relief sculptures of beautiful young men so admired by antiquarians.

In 1775 a notorious incident involving Kauffman caused a stir in the Academy. Another artist, Nathaniel Hone, sent a painting to the annual exhibition called *The Conjuror* (National Gallery of Ireland, Dublin). This picture showed an old bearded magician waving his wand over a group of engravings of famous old master paintings, while a little girl leaned coyly on his knee looking at a large open book. Viewers recognised it immediately as a satiric attack on Reynolds's method of borrowing motifs from well-known works of art to incorporate into his compositions, and the little girl may have been understood to represent his friend and inspiration, Kauffman. However, the reason it was finally removed from public view in the Royal Academy was Kauffman's written objection to what she believed was a small nude female figure intended to represent her. The figure in question was in the background among a group of artists waving paintbrushes towards St Paul's Cathedral, an allusion to a decorative project in which Kauffman was to take part. After a group from the Royal Academy tried to persuade her to allow Hone's picture, she wrote

indignantly with threats to remove her own paintings if *The Conjuror* remained. In the end Kauffman won, the painting was removed and the offending figure painted out.

Kauffman's decorative paintings for the Royal Academy

In 1780 the Academy moved to new quarters in Somerset House in the Strand, and plans were developed for a series of allegorical ceiling paintings to represent the theoretical basis of academic art. Kauffman, who was included in this important scheme, was assigned four oval paintings of allegorical images to represent the four parts of painting: *Invention*, *Composition*, *Design* and *Colour*. They were set into the ceiling of the Council Chamber around a central painting by Benjamin West that represented *Nature*, the *Three Graces* and the *Four Elements*. Kauffman's complex and subtle female personifications characterise the theory of art as expressed in Reynolds's lectures, which were originally delivered in this room. In 1837 the paintings were moved to the library of the Academy's new premises in Trafalgar Square. Since 1899 these paintings and the ones by West have been on the ceiling of the entrance hall of the Royal Academy's current home in Burlington House.

Women academicians after Kauffman and Moser

The status and respect granted to Kauffman and Moser as female academicians were never real issues within the Royal Academy, but it was a very long time before another woman was elected to their ranks. In 1879 the admission of women to membership of the Royal Academy was seriously considered when Lady Butler (q.v.) missed election by a narrow margin. The Council decided that since the *Instrument of Foundation* (1768) had specified that members must be "men of fair moral character" as well as artists of "high reputation in their profession" – the historical status of Kauffman and Moser notwithstanding – women were ineligible. Nevertheless, at the request of the General Assembly a resolution was put forward to allow for the election of women but with limited "privileges". In fact no female members were elected until Annie Swynnerton and Laura Knight (q.v.) became Associates, in 1922 and 1927 respectively. Knight achieved full status as Royal Academician in 1936, more than 150 years after the two women founding members.

WENDY WASSYNG ROWORTH

Bibliography

General

Nikolaus Pevsner, *Academies of Art Past and Present*, Cambridge: Cambridge University Press, and New York: Macon, 1940; reprinted New York: Da Capo, 1973 (important study of the history of academies of art with extensive bibliography)

Linda Nochlin, "Why have there been no great women artists?", *Woman in Sexist Society: Studies in Power and Powerlessness*, ed. Vivian Gornick and Barbara K. Moran, New York: Basic Books, 1971; reprinted New American Library, 1972, pp.480–510

Ann Sutherland Harris, "Introduction", *Women Artists, 1550–1950*, exh. cat., Los Angeles County Museum of Art, and elsewhere, 1976, pp.15–44

Jennifer M. Fletcher, "The glory of the female sex: Women artists, *c.*1500–1800", *The Women's Art Show, 1550–1970*, exh. cat., Nottingham Castle Museum, 1982, pp.8–10

Cynthia E. Roman, "Academic ideals of art education", *Children of Mercury: The Education of Artists in the Sixteenth and Seventeenth Centuries*, exh. cat., Brown University, Providence, RI, 1984, pp.81–95

Laura Olmstead Tonelli, "Academic practice in the sixteenth and seventeenth centuries", *ibid.*, pp.95–107

Anton W.A. Boschloo and others, eds, *Academies of Art Between Renaissance and Romanticism*, The Hague: SDU, 1989 (an important source, with extensive bibliographies on academies in Europe, although there is no specific discussion of women)

Bettina Baumgärtel, *Angelika Kauffmann (1741–1807): Bedingungen weiblicher Kreativität in der Malerei des 18. Jahrhunderts*, Weinheim and Basel, 1990 (Kauffman and other women artists in academies)

Italy

Melchior Missirini, *Memorie per servire alla storia della Romana Accademia di San Luca fino alla morte di Antonio Canova*, Rome, 1823

Jean Arnaud, *L'Académie de Saint-Luc à Rome (Considerations historiques depuis son origine jusqu'à nos jours)*, Rome: Loescher, 1886

Vincenzo Golzio, *La galleria e le collezioni dell'Accademia di San Luca in Rome*, Rome: La Libreria dello Stato, 1966

Italo Faldi, "Dipinti di figura dal rinascimento al neoclassicism", *L'Accademia Nazionale di San Luca*, ed. C. Petrangeli and others, Rome: De Luca, 1974, pp.158–70 (paintings by Rosalba Carriera and Angelica Kauffman in the Accademia di San Luca, Rome)

Stefano Susinno, "I ritratti degli academici", *ibid.*, pp.201–70 (portraits and self-portraits of various women artists in the Accademia di San Luca, Rome)

A. Cipriani, "L'Accademia di San Luca dai Concorsi dei Giovani ai Concorsi Clementini" in Boschloo 1989, pp.61–76

France

Georges Duplessis, ed., *Mémoires et journal de J. G. Wille*, 2 vols, Paris: Renouard, 1857

J.J. Guiffrey, "Ecoles de demoiselles dans les ateliers de David et de Suvée au Louvre", *Nouvelles Archives de l'Art Français*, 1874–5, pp.396–7

Procès-verbaux de l'Académie Royale de Peinture et de Sculpture, ed. Anatole de Montaiglon, 11 vols, Paris: J. Baur and Charavay Frères, 1875–92; reprinted Paris: Nobele, 1972 (minutes of meetings of the French Academy; invaluable source for information on women in the Academy)

Octave Fidière, *Les Femmes artistes à l'Académie Royale de Peinture et de Sculpture*, Paris: Charavay Frères, 1885 (factual overview of women in the French Academy based on primary sources)

Etienne Charavay, "Réception de Mmes Vigée-Lebrun et Guiard à l'Académie de peinture", *Nouvelles Archives de l'Art Français*, vi, 1890, Paris: Dumolin, pp. 181–2

J.J. Guiffrey, *Histoire de l'Académie de Saint-Luc*, published as vol.ix of *Archives de l'Art Français*, Paris: Champion, 1915 (history of the painters' guild, the Académie de Saint-Luc, which included many women artists)

Jacques Silvestre de Sacy, *Le Comte d'Angiviller, dernier Directeur Général des Bâtiments du Roi*, Paris: Plon, 1953

Marianne Roland Michel, *Anne Vallayer-Coster, 1744–1818*, Paris: CIL, 1970 (contains extensive discussion of Vallayer-Coster's association with the Academy)

Anne-Marie Passez, *Adélaïde Labille-Guiard (1749–1803): Biographie et catalogue raisonné de son oeuvre*, Paris: Arts et Métiers Graphiques, 1973 (includes substantial discussion of Labille-Guiard and Vigée-Lebrun in relation to the Academy)

Elisabeth Vigée-Lebrun, *Souvenirs*, ed. Claudine Herrmann, 2 vols, Paris: Des Femmes, 1984

Thomas E. Crow, *Painters and Public Life in Eighteenth-Century Paris*, New Haven: Yale University Press, 1985 (no specific discussion of women, but considers many other aspects of academic practice from the founding of the Academy to the French Revolution; particularly strong on relation between Academy and political events)

Albert Boime, *The Academy and French Painting in the Nineteenth Century*, revised edition, New Haven, Yale University Press, 1986 (although there is no specific analysis of women in the Academy, this book provides a full discussion of academic practices in the 19th century)

Candace Clements, "The Academy and the other: Les graces and le genre galant", *Eighteenth-Century Studies*, xxv, 1992, pp.469–94 (discusses practices of life drawing in the Academy)

Reed Benhamou, *Public and Private Art Education in*

France, published as volume of *Studies on Voltaire and the Eighteenth Century*, Oxford: Siden Press, 1993 (discusses all aspects of artistic education throughout France, including both the Académie Royale and provincial academies; extensive bibliography)

Mary D. Sheriff, *The Exceptional Woman: Elisabeth Vigée-Lebrun and the Cultural Politics of Art*, Chicago: University of Chicago Press, 1996 (includes analysis of the Academy's attitudes towards women artists and a short history of women in the Academy; extensive bibliography)

Britain

G. Baretti, *A Guide Through the Royal Academy*, London, 1781 (includes description of ceiling paintings by Angelica Kauffman)

Algernon Graves, *The Royal Academy of Arts: A Complete Dictionary of Contributors and Their Work from Its Foundation in 1769 to 1904*, 8 vols, London: Graves, 1905–6; reprinted New York: Franklin, 1972

William T. Whitley, *Artists and Their Friends in England, 1700–1799*, 2 vols, London, 1928; reprinted New York: Blom, 1968

M. Butlin, "An eighteenth-century art scandal: Nathaniel Hone's 'The Conjuror'", *Connoisseur*, clxxiv, 1970, pp.1–9 (includes Kauffman's correspondence with the Royal Academy with her objections to this satirical painting)

Sidney C. Hutchison, *The History of the Royal Academy, 1768–1986*, 2nd edition, London: Royce, 1986

John Newman, "Reynolds and Hone: 'The Conjuror'", *Reynolds*, exh. cat., Royal Academy, London, 1986, pp.344–54 (discussion of satirical painting attacking Reynolds and Kauffman)

Ilaria Bignamini, "The 'Academy of Art' in Britain before the foundation of the Royal Academy" in Boschloo 1989, pp.434–50

Sidney C. Hutchison, "The Royal Academy of Arts in London: Its history and activities" in Boschloo 1989, pp.451–63

The Artist's Model: Its Role in British Art from Lely to Etty, exh. cat., University Art Gallery, Nottingham, and Iveagh Bequest, Kenwood, London, 1991 (examines British artists' use of life models and antique statuary in academies and private studios)

Richard Wendorf, *Sir Joshua Reynolds: The Painter in Society*, Cambridge, MA: Harvard University Press, 1996 (on Frances Reynolds; also Reynolds's friendship with Kauffman)

Copyists

Copies and the reproductive arts

Throughout the early modern period, copies played an important reproductive role in the visual culture of Western Europe. Although prints could and did duplicate the subject matter and format of an image, the colour, style and particular qualities of the original medium were absent. Before the 19th-century development of planographic and photo-mechanical techniques of reproduction, copying a painting in the same medium as the original was one of the few viable means to achieve a close replication of all its qualities. The copy and copying were thus important both to the practices of the consumers who commissioned or purchased such images and to those of the artists who made them.

During the Renaissance, as paintings became greatly esteemed for their aesthetic qualities, political or ideological significance, and as costly, class-marking commodities, the demand for copies of acclaimed works of art grew quickly. Copies enabled the development of a unique identity for each individual painting and also allowed the dissemination of the image to a wider audience. Regardless of the particular organising principle motivating the patron or collector – indexical, historical, monographic, geographic or purely decorative – copies served to fill important lacunae in the collections of many important connoisseurs. As northern Europeans from France, Britain and the German and Nordic countries sought to emulate the opulent habits of the picture-collecting Italian nobility, copies enabled an exact appropriation of many of the visual components of this culture. Indeed, copies were in many ways preferable to original paintings in that they had the added value of illustrating the published histories and theoretical texts that formed the basis of a pan-European polite discourse on art. Moreover, they maintained reference to the contextual significance of the original as well as to those of the entire network of other similar copies. Well into the 19th and 20th centuries, this pattern of cultural arrogation continued to be an important model for the *nouveau riche* of the Americas and other European colonies who sought acceptance from the cultural mainstream of Europe. Once installed within these new colonial contexts, copies, particularly those of important religious paintings, royal or official portraits, or ideologically-charged history paintings, contributed greatly to the processes of acculturation and control imposed upon subservient nations.

For the artist, copying was a primary step in his or her training. Academic theory dictated that the student first learn to draw by copying prints and drawings before taking models from life. When facility in drawing had been attained, students then learned an understanding of colour and the application of paint by copying the work of their teachers as well as that of famous masters. Students were frequently restricted to copying until they had attained the necessary skill and command of their master's technique and style. They were then judged able and ready to challenge or surpass the accomplishments of their predecessors with their own unique vision. Many artists continued to copy throughout their lifetimes in order to practise, to learn from or to pay homage to other masters' work. Even though modernist ideologies of artistic production privileged original work above all else, copying and the graphic reproductive arts continued to be important (although often concealed) elements of the workshop practices of many prominent artists until well into the 19th century. Consumer demand for versions or replications of the master's more popular works was the economic foundation of most workshops, especially those of portrait painters. Many artists followed the examples set by Raphael, Titian and Rubens, who had all recognised the importance of artistic reproduction for the augmentation and propagation of their reputations. The work and reputation of women artists in particular have been intimately tied to both the production and the concept of the copy from the Renaissance until the recent past.

Copying and the education of the artist

Traditional academic practice advocated that both male and female students should learn drawing by first copying, from other drawings or prints, the simplest outlines of bodily components such as heads, eyes, hands, limbs, etc. Once these were mastered and synthesised into entire bodies, the student advanced to the copying of finished drawings, prints and plaster casts, while at the same time developing expertise in the techniques of shading, working in ink, chalk or pastel, and painting in washes. Only then did the student draw from life or raw nature. Female art students often completed these early stages of artistic training only to be

discouraged from continuing their studies at the next level – that of figure drawing. Women were prevented on the grounds of morality from participating in these drawing classes, which, in general, focused on the study of the nude male body, and were deemed the basis for the expressive portrayal of human thought and action in that highest genre of subject matter, history painting. Such classes were sponsored and regulated by the many academies of art established throughout Europe during the 17th, 18th and 19th centuries, and which were generally structured to favour male over female students (see Academies of Art survey). Female participation was not only prohibited in the life-drawing class, but was also increasingly discouraged or rigidly controlled in many of the other aspects of the curriculum, prize-givings or exhibitions institutionalised by most academies of art. Ambitious women attempted to circumvent this restriction by copying other students' figure studies, by moving on to the next stage of training (which consisted of learning the theory and application of paint and colour by copying from pre-existing paintings), or by surreptitiously hiring their own models. However, as authentic knowledge of the human body was considered essential for the skilled artist, critics held this lack of training against women artists, regardless of their real ability or accomplishment. Consequently, many women were prevented from taking the educational steps that would enable them to rise from the immature status of the journeyman or amateur to the level of the professional artist fully legitimised with academic credentials.

Workshop practices

Copying was an important component of the work performed in the collaborative system of the studio, *bottega* or workshop, the most prevalent structure for the production of paintings in Europe before the 20th century. Headed by a prominent master who was personally unable to supply the demand for his pictures, these workshops served both to educate and employ other artists who were collectively responsible for its production of images. Such studios not only provided for the reproduction of the master's original work but also the continued care and conservation of images that had already left the workshop. Women artists often participated in these collaborations, either as students or as assistants. The actual division of labour within such organisations varied; masters either assigned work as it was needed or contracted skilled individuals to specialise in particular tasks. Such responsibilities included the preparation of pigments and canvases, the blocking-in and under-painting of the figures, the painting of costumes, landscape elements, draperies and backgrounds, the cleaning and conservation of older works, and the production of studio copies. Portrait studios in particular were responsible for a tremendous number of copies and versions of a master's work (or those of other artists). Studio work would then be finished (perhaps) and signed by the master whose signature attested to a certain standard of style or execution.

An easily exploitable workforce – both inexpensive and available – for the studio of a painter was that of his female relatives. Several women artists of the early modern period received their training in the arts as a result of being related to male artists. Some managed to become independent and professional artists in their own right, but many remained as assistants in the studios of their fathers, brothers or husbands. Marriages between the daughters or sisters of artists and other artists served not only to form familial as well as professional bonds between various workshops, but also to transfer skills and labour from one studio to another. Many of these daughters, sisters and wives specialised in the reproductive aspects of the workshop's practice, freeing their male relations for more creative work. These women not only painted, but also often drew, etched and engraved, in full-scale or miniature, their copies of the more popular images of the master. While an artist's male offspring were also frequently trained to follow in their father's footsteps, they would eventually be expected to challenge, surpass and leave behind their parent/teachers; daughters by training and social convention were not expected to advance to this stage of creative autonomy. The best that many could expect to accomplish was to imitate their fathers' style and technique so expertly and closely as to be indistinguishable from them. The work of these women was thus marked with the identity of their male relatives and not their own. Marietta Robusti (q.v.), the daughter of Tintoretto, worked in a style so closely modelled on her father's that only one picture is today attributed to her. The "faithful" and exact copyist whose work could not be distinguished from that of her father became a *topos* for the praise of daughter-artists such as Anne Louise de Deyster (1690–1747) who further merged her identity with that of her father by becoming his

biographer as well as his copyist. Indeed, it was by no means unusual for male artists to appropriate the works of their talented female relatives; both Orazio Gentileschi and Johann Joseph Kauffman claimed to have done paintings actually produced by their daughters, Artemisia Gentileschi and Angelica Kauffman (both q.v.).

The inclusion of wives, daughters and sisters in the family business (albeit in the more mechanical aspects of it) was typical throughout Europe during the 16th, 17th and even 18th centuries. As most middle-class businesses were conducted on the same premises as domestic life, women of the early modern period often contributed to a broader range of the family's business activities than mere care of the family. Preparation of canvases, the laying-in of backgrounds, the painting of drapery or landscape elements, as well as responsibility for the reproduction of the studio's more popular or important works, were frequently the province of female family members. In Italy, Agnese Dolci (d. 1689) was trained by her father Carlo to be a successful copyist in his style; other less-known daughter-artists include Vittoria Farinato and Rosalia Novelli who both copied for their fathers. In Spain, Dorotea Joanes (d. 1609) and Margarita Joanes (d. 1613) collaborated with their father Vicente Juan Macip, as did Isabel Sanchez Coello (1564–1612), who produced the tremendous number of copies of the royal portraits painted by her father, Claudio Coello, for the Spanish court. In England, Susanna Penelope Rosse, the daughter of the court dwarf/painter Richard Gibson, was instructed by her father in watercolour and oil painting and her copies in miniature of many of the paintings in the royal collection were highly praised by contemporary critics. In the later 18th century, Maria Cosway (q.v.) reproduced much of her husband's work for him in soft-ground etching. In France, Madelaine Hérault (1635–82), daughter of the landscape painter, Antoine Hérault, was trained by her father and served as a copyist first for his studio and then, after her marriage to Noël Coypel, for her husband's studio. Her sister Antoinette was a successful copyist in miniature of old master paintings whose marriage to Guillaume Chastel provided an important connection for her family with the prestigious engraving family. Their niece Marie Cathérine, daughter of their painter-brother Charles Antoine, also married a painter, Silvestre le Jeune, who was called to Dresden to serve as court painter to

Augustus II. There, Marie Cathérine, like many of the other women of her family, helped her husband with the preliminary tasks of the workshop as well as with the numerous copies required of the official court portraits. Their daughter Marie Maximilienne Silvestre (1708–97) continued the family tradition by copying in the workshops of her male relatives as had her female forebears. In Florence, Anna Bacherini Piattoli (1720–88), wife and mother to two other painters, Gaetano and Giuseppe Piattoli, served as a court painter specialising in pastel and miniature portraits and religious scenes, many of which seem to have been copies of other masters' works. Her work is known today only through three self-portraits, one of which was completed in 1776 for the famous Medici collection of self-portraits. Here she modestly portrays herself at her work table, copying Andrea del Sarto's *Madonna del Sacco* in miniature. A most extreme example of family collaboration was that of the Edinburgh Nasmyth family, in the early 19th century. Alexander Nasmyth trained and employed all of his four sons and his daughters Anne, Barbara, Charlotte, Elizabeth, Jane and Margaret in his combined drawing school/picture manufactory. While the sons were trained as professional painters within the academic system, each of the daughters was put to work teaching drawing to ladies or in the mass production of the generic "Claudian" Scottish landscape paintings associated with the family. This familial organisation of studio labour continued well into the 19th century: Lucy Madox Brown and her sister Catherine (later Mrs Hueffer), daughters of the painter Ford Madox Brown, did preparatory work and produced copies for their father.

For many artists, skill in the arts was the only training they could give their daughters to ensure their future living. Teaching art also became a professional option as watercolour painting and drawing developed during the 18th century into important drawing-room accomplishments for young women of the upper classes. Mary Black, the daughter of Thomas Black, served as an assistant to the portrait painter Allan Ramsay and supported herself as a portrait painter, as a copyist of contemporary portraits and old master paintings, and as a teacher of painting for fashionable young women. Another of Ramsay's studio assistants, Philip Reinagle, trained his two daughters Fanny and Charlotte in miniature copying and both displayed their work at the Royal Academy and British Institution exhibitions. The sister of the painter Hugh Douglas Hamilton, Maria Bell (later Lady Bell), as well as his daughter Harriott Hamilton (later Mrs John Way), were both successful copyists of old master paintings and contemporary portraits. Anne Forbes, the granddaughter of William Aikman, was trained as a portrait painter and copyist and served as the copyist of old master paintings in the Roman studio of the Neo-classical painter Gavin Hamilton between c.1768 and 1771.

Not all women copyists served as useful and convenient appendages to the practices of their families. Mary Beale (q.v.) was the daughter of John Cradock, a Suffolk parson and enthusiastic amateur painter from whom she may have received some early training. She married Charles Beale, a Deputy Clerk in the Patents Office, in 1652 and the young couple settled in Covent Garden, the centre for London's artistic community from which they made several friends. Mary took a more serious interest in painting at this point, studying with Walker, and possibly Lely, two of the most prominent portrait painters of the day. By 1670 Charles's career in the Patents Office had faltered and Mary began painting professionally in order to support her young family. Her social connections among the clergy formed the basis for a clientele and her artist-friends obliged her by throwing other commissions and much copying work in her way. She soon became the centre of a busy studio modelled closely upon those of her male associates. Her husband, Charles, stretched canvases, ground colours and served as her business manager by keeping records of her work and acting as her public intermediary. Her two sons, Charles and Bartholomew, both trained by their mother, assisted her by painting backgrounds and draperies. She also took students, including two young women, Keaty Tioche and Sarah Curtis. Curtis, who married the Revd Benjamin Hoadley in 1701, modelled her own professional practice (focused for the most part on portraiture and copying) after that of her teacher and soon became a rival. Both women attracted attention through their unusual career choices. Mary Beale's work was studied with great interest and curiosity by the art chroniclers George Vertue and Horace Walpole, who wrote favourably concerning her style and production during the mid-18th century. Beale's success was due not only to her talent, but also because she never challenged or stepped over contemporary boundaries constraining male and female social spheres. Her genteel social class provided her with a clientele, the scale of her work was small and not very costly, she frequently took as sitters children, women and servants (subjects not threatening to her male rivals), and was not overly fastidious about accepting excess work from other artists' studios. Moreover, she modestly allowed her husband to represent her in the more public aspects of the business. Throughout the 18th and 19th centuries, women such as Mary Beale with artistic talent turned to copying as a marginal, but viable profession.

Within the studios of those women artists who achieved a modicum of fame, such as the Swiss painter Angelica Kauffman, copying still played an important role. Kauffman, like most of her male contemporaries, spent a considerable period of training in Italy, copying in the leading collections there. Even after establishing herself as one of the leading history painters in London, she was frequently requested by her clientele to copy not only her own work but that of other masters as well. Several decorative programmes undertaken by Kauffman included copies after artists such as Titian, Guercino, Domenichino and Guido Reni as well as her own work. Kauffman's decorative work in particular found favour with her fashionable clientele; in order to take advantage of the popularity of her work, Kauffman worked closely with printmakers and publishers of reproductive prints. Several of her designs were reproduced in Matthew Boulton's and Francis Eginton's "Mechanical Paintings" project (1770s–80s), and used as decorative panels on furniture or in architecture.

Amateur painting

During the 18th and 19th centuries, the growing perception of painting as a drawing-room accomplishment for young ladies encouraged many women of the upper and middle classes to participate in the arts (see Amateur Artists survey). Such activities filled leisure hours, served as an entertainment, provided a means of documenting personal experience, and allowed young women to participate knowledgeably in the fashionable discourses of art. As in the training of the professional artist, the young lady learned much of her skill by copying the works of others. The models for such endeavours could range from prints and drawings to the paintings from the family collection. Amateur artists noted for their copying included Mrs Anne Carlisle,

a protégée of King Charles I; Mrs Rhoda Astley (1725–57), whose copies were hung at Seaton Delavel, Northumberland; Mrs Eglinton Margaret Pearson (d. 1823), who made two sets of copies after the Raphael Cartoons; Lady Helena Percival, daughter of the 1st Earl of Egremont; and Lady Caroline Stanhope, a relative of the Earl of Harrington whose copy of the portrait of *Mary, Queen of Scots* hung in the family seat in Derbyshire.

For many amateurs, copying the works of the old masters or other artists was the height of their ambition, and their work would be displayed in family rooms to demonstrate their "accomplishment". For others, the copies they made themselves, acquired from friends or purchased from professional artists often allowed them to form small art collections or to decorate their personal apartments. George Vertue reports that Lady Burlington made copies of her husband's collection for her boudoir, and that Miss Da Costa copied paintings by Rubens, van Dyck and others for her "ladys Cabinet". The Boudoir at Wardour Castle, Wiltshire, the seat of Lord Arundell was richly decorated with a collection of drawings and miniatures, many of them copies after Guido Reni, Raphael and Pannini. A Mrs Corbet decorated the ante-drawing-room of Sundorne Castle in Shropshire with her own copies after Cuyp, Vandevelde, Barroccio and Raphael.

One of the best-known amateur painters of the 18th century, Mary Delany (1700–88), was an avid copier of paintings. Sophie von la Roche described her as a "remarkable lady close to 90 years" seated in a room decorated with pictures from galleries in Italy, the Netherlands and France, "abundant evidence of her noble industry and intellect". She also records Mrs Delany as stating: "There are no masterpieces you see there, merely copies I made while on my travels." Mrs Delany's high birth and court connections gave her access to many important collections from which she borrowed and copied extensively, including paintings by Veronese, Lely, Claude, Soldi, Guido Reni, Salvator Rosa, Rembrandt, Correggio and Hogarth. Copying seems to have functioned for her as an opportunity for close repeated analysis and meditation on either the subject of the representation itself or of the skill and technique of the original artists. Upon finishing a copy of a Veronese in 1744, she wrote to a friend: "I have finished it as high as possible for me to finish, because it will be a sort of study for me when I can't get better pictures to copy." Often copying served as a basis for experiencing nostalgic memories of times past; in 1745 she wrote: "I have copied in large one of the sketches of Dovedale that I took when we were there together. How many tender ideas did it raise whilst I was drawing it." Many of the copies she produced went as gifts to her women friends. She gave her copy of Hogarth's *Sigismunda* to the Duchess of Portland, a half-length of the Duchess of Mazarin to a Miss Bushe, and a copy of her mother's portrait to her close friend Mrs Dawes. Her will, dated 22 February 1788, distributed her remaining pictures, for the most part copies, among her circle of women friends

Many women lacking training or painting materials translated such paintings into other materials. Particularly popular at the end of the 18th century were needlework pictures, many of which were copies of old master and contemporary paintings. Mary Linwood, Harriet Frankland and Anne Morritt all made and exhibited pictures in needlework, that most acceptable of female leisure activities. The high critical acclaim they received was as much in response to their audacious appropriation of male masterpieces into a medium heavily associated with female domesticity as for the skill of their undertaking. Harriet Frankland's copy in needlework of Tenier's *Prodigal Son* was exhibited at the tenth Spring Gardens exhibition of the Society of Artists in 1769. Mary Linwood's copies after Morland, Reynolds, Stubbs, Gainsborough and Raphael went on display in an exhibition touring London and the surrounding counties at the end of the 18th century. Anne Eliza Morritt's tapestry copies after Zuccarelli, Poussin, Pietro da Cortona, Rubens, Annibale Carracci and Salvator Rosa were exhibited in York and highly praised by Arthur Young in his account of *A Six Month's Tour Through the North of England* (1771). This translation of creative and artistic work into an acceptable feminine medium allowed these women to participate in cultural and intellectual matters that might otherwise have rendered them unfeminine, or "unnatural" in the eyes of their contemporaries.

For many young women of the leisured classes, the drawing-room accomplishments of painting and drawing could also provide them with a marketable skill should they need it. Ellen Sharples (1769–1849) was not born into an artistic family, but instead was trained in painting and drawing as amateur activities befitting a young woman of the

gentry. However, after marrying her drawing master James Sharples around 1787, Ellen soon put her training in a "ladies accomplishment" to profitable use in her husband's practice. The couple journeyed to America with their young children between 1794 and 1801 and again between 1809 and 1811. There, they travelled through the new country as itinerant artists, offering their services as portraitists and copyists to elite patrons. Their miniature portraits of *George Washington* (of which more than 40 were produced, including at least 6 copies by Ellen) and other prominent members of American society were in great demand and proved to be extremely remunerative. Upon the family's return to England, Ellen continued to produce both original and copies of miniature portraits on ivory and even exhibited at the Royal Academy in 1807. After the death of her husband in 1811, she returned with her family to Bristol, where, with her son James, she continued to be a mainstay of the family business. Ellen was also responsible for the artistic education of her young daughter Rolinda, whose talent and training soon enabled her to study with Philip Reinagle and to become a professional artist in her own right.

The feminisation of the copy

With the growth of the middle classes and the industrialisation of Western Europe during the 19th century, European society was increasingly divided into gender-based spheres of activity. The male realm was that of public interaction, politics and manufacture, one in which male identity was defined by the individual's production, speech and action. The female domain was defined by reproduction, passivity, silence and a domestic economy in which women became the major consumers of the products of mass culture manufactured by men. Unacknowledged, but essential to such ideological constructions was the importance of woman's reproductive capacity to the filiation and kinship ties between men. Women were responsible not only for the biological continuation of their class/race/species, but also for the cultural reproduction and transmission of social ideologies through their maintenance of the family and their responsibility for the moral indoctrination and education of the young. Such larger ideological concerns shaped modern conceptions of creativity, the role of the artist, and notions of originality.

The feminisation and marginalisation of the copy played an important role in the modernist notion of the male artist as a creative genius, a conception constructed and institutionalised in the 19th-century art market and academic practice. The autonomy and reputation of the modern artist was threatened by the dominance of the classical canon and the market's reiteration of that canon through copies and prints. The most frequent mode for classifying the copy with "after" yielded identity, authority and financial gain to the name of the original master rather than that of the copyist. During the 18th century the definition of taste was transformed from the ability to recognise and discuss the subject of the representation to the recognition and discussion of the singularity of the artist. Originality and authenticity became the criteria for selection or judgement in order to protect such concepts of intellectual property. The elevation of the modern artist was enabled by the exclusion of artisans and certain practices within the institutions of museum and academy. Throughout Europe, academic regulations maintained the practice of copying, but only in a marginal capacity. Copying was increasingly discouraged except by: 1) students for whom copying was important to the process of learning through emulation; 2) the reproductive arts such as printmaking where replication was an inherent part of the processes of production; 3) artisans or failed artists who were pushed by lack of talent to the margins of the profession; and 4) women whose access to original art was increasingly limited, whose training was frequently halted at the stage of the copy, and whose basic social role was considered to be innately "reproductive". Moreover, the discourse of the copy takes on a connotation of amateurism and femininity just as the making of the copy is devalued as an occupation. The access to the copy allowed to women artists both in the making of images and habits of consuming them tends to contribute to and reinforce this depreciation.

During the 19th century, copying thus became a legitimate career for women artists once it had been discarded as an appropriate activity for the male artist. While women's access to the academic stages of training that enabled originality were limited, their access to institutions where copying was approved became fairly easy. Organisations founded to enable student study of the old masters (such as the British Institution in London) and museums such as the National Gallery in London and the Louvre in Paris were constantly filled with copyists, often with waiting lists for the more popular paintings. Women were a significant presence among these painters, both as students learning from the old masters and as professional copyists producing copies either for private collectors or public institutions. In France during the Second Empire, a special government office sponsored a large number of copies after official portraits or history paintings for display in various state institutions. It also commissioned copies of religious paintings for distribution to provincial churches, according to an agreement made between Church and State. Women artists were considered equally capable of providing such copies as male artists, and several such as Juliette de Ribeiro, Zoe Laura de Chatillon, Ernestine Froidure de Pelleport, Henriette and Clara Fournier, and Justine de Janvry received regular and well-paid commissions from the government to paint the required images.

While copying did allow women access to a realm of male activity and knowledge and did at times enable them to form their own intimate spheres of intellect and conversation, their association with a discourse of copying and reproduction prohibited or made their creativity extremely difficult on a professional level. Stopped at an adolescent stage in the training of the artist, women were discouraged from expressing their subjectivity and autonomy in their work, and their copying served most strongly to contrast with male originality and genius. Indeed, as an act of study, translation or interpretation, copying was seen as transforming the woman artist into an ideal spectator or audience for the appreciation of male genius. This conception is best illustrated in Nathaniel Hawthorne's character of Hilda in his novel *The Marble Faun* (1860). Hilda, a young virginal American artist, travels to Rome to study from the art of the past. There she is so overwhelmed by her confrontation with the old masters that she discards all ambition to conceive "great pictures" with her "feminine mind". She shuts herself away in a tower where she is untarnished by any authentic experience, her identity completely subsumed by the paintings she copies, feeling rather than intellectualising her response; through her copying she thus becomes the perfect receptor for the male artist:

> Hilda had ceased to consider herself as an original artist ... she had the gift of discerning and worshipping excellence in a most unusual measure. She saw – no, not saw, but felt – through and through a picture ... she

went straight to the central point, in which the master had conceived his work. Thus, she viewed it, as it were, with his own eyes, and hence her comprehension of any picture that interested her was perfect.

She thus becomes the "handmaid of Raphael". Her role is again that of reproduction, her copying of a great work "by patient faith and self-devotion … multiplied it for mankind".

The 20th century

By the 20th century the copy had become so completely marginal within the practices of art that it was generally equated with failure, poor judgement, unsavoury market practices, and the fraudulence and deceit of forgery. The ideologies of modernism dictated that the artist strive to be of the avant-garde and to express only those original and unique aspects of his (or her) personal vision. The reproductive functions of the copy were relegated to photography, while the previous importance placed on copying to learn was now seen as antithetical to the development of originality and personal expression in the neophyte artist. Women artists, like the male artists of the 18th century, abnegated the copy in order to avoid its contamination of their reputations and ambitions and to validate their tenuous position as professionals. The copy was allowed a partial legitimacy through Pop Art, but only as kitsch or a tongue-in-cheek reference on the part of the superiorly-placed, informed artist to his or her position relative to the traditions of representation and the art of the past. However, recent feminist critique and revision of modernism (its gendered constructions of originality and genius in particular) has challenged many women artists to address these aspects in their work. The post-modern work of artists such as Sherrie Levine, Cindy Sherman and Dottie Attie questions how patriarchal assumptions and the traditions of art structure their roles as both artists and women. Dottie Attie's small copies of sections of paintings by past masters are reassembled and re-contextualised by text panels through which the artist imposes her own personal narrative and interpretation of the Western art tradition. Sherrie Levine has re-photographed the work of Walker Evans, Edward Weston, Andreas Feininger and Eliot Porter in order to examine the importance our culture places on originality and intellectual property. Cindy Sherman's work, in which she photographs herself appropriating the forms of advertising, film images and old masters, probes Western conventions of representing women as well as her own position as an artist within a tradition that has previously privileged only men.

LISA HEER

Bibliography

Nathaniel Hawthorne, *The Marble Faun*, Boston: Ticknor and Fields, 1860

Lady Llanover, ed., *The Autobiography and Correspondence of Mary Granville, Mrs Delany*, 6 vols, London: Bentley, 1861–2; reprinted New York: AMS Press, 1974

Bea Howe, "Pioneer of the woolwork picture", *Country Life*, cxi, March 1952, pp.656-8

"The Excellent Mrs Mary Beale", exh. cat., Geffrye Museum, London, and elsewhere, 1975

Germaine Greer, *The Obstacle Race: The Fortunes of Women Painters and Their Work*, London: Secker and Warburg, and New York: Farrar Straus, 1979

Rozsika Parker and Griselda Pollock, *Old Mistresses: Women, Art and Ideology*, London and New York: Routledge, 1981

Paul Duro, *The Copy in French Nineteenth-Century Painting*, PhD dissertation, University of Essex, 1983

Rozsika Parker, *The Subversive Stitch: Embroidery and the Making of the Feminine*, London: Women's Press, 1984; New York: Routledge, 1989

Charlotte Yeldham, *Women Artists in Nineteenth-Century France and England*, 2 vols, New York: Garland, 1984

Rosalind E. Krauss, *The Originality of the Avant-Garde and Other Modernist Myths*, Cambridge: Massachusetts Institute of Technology Press, 1985

Griselda Pollock, "Art, artschool, culture: Individualism after the death of the author", *Block*, no.11, 1985–6, pp.8-18

Paul Duro, "The *Demoiselles à Copier* in the Second Empire", *Woman's Art Journal*, vii/1, Spring–Summer 1986, pp.1–7

Andreas Huyssen, *After the Great Divide: Modernism, Mass Culture, Postmodernism*, Bloomington: Indiana University Press, 1986

Leonore Davidoff and Catherine Hall, *Family Fortunes: Men and Women of the English Middle Class, 1780–1850*, London: Hutchinson, and Chicago: University of Chicago Press, 1987

Susan Lambert, *The Image Multiplied: Five Centuries of Printed Reproductions of Paintings and Drawings*, London: Trefoil, 1987

Griselda Pollock, *Vision and Difference: Femininity, Feminism and the Histories of Art*, London and New York: Routledge, 1988

Wendy Steiner, *Pictures of Romance: Form Against Context in Painting and Literature*, Chicago: University of Chicago Press, 1988

Christine Battersby, *Gender and Genius: Towards a*

Feminist Aesthetic, Bloomington: Indiana University Press, and London: Women's Press, 1989

Retaining the Original: Multiple Originals, Copies and Reproductions, Studies in the History of Art, 20, Washington, DC: National Gallery of Art, 1989

Whitney Chadwick, *Women, Art and Society*, London and New York: Thames and Hudson, 1990; revised edition, 1996

Ann Bermingham, "The origins of painting and the ends of art: Wright of Derby's *Corinthian Maid*", *Painting and the Politics of Culture: New Essays on British Art, 1700–1850*, ed. John Barrell, Oxford and New York: Oxford University Press, 1992, pp.135–65

Susan P. Casteras, "Excluding women: The cult of the male genius in Victorian painting", *Rewriting the Victorians: Theory, History and the Politics of Gender*, ed. Linda M. Shires, New York and London: Routledge, 1992

Wendy Wassyng Roworth, ed., *Angelica Kauffman: A Continental Artist in Georgian England*, London: Reaktion, 1992

Deborah Cherry, *Painting Women: Victorian Women Artists*, London and New York: Routledge, 1993

Gill Perry and Michael Rossington, eds, *Femininity and Masculinity in Eighteenth-Century Art and Culture*, Manchester: Manchester University Press, 1994

A Struggle for Fame: Victorian Women Artists and Authors, exh. cat., Yale Center for British Art, New Haven, 1994

Lisa Heer, *Problems in Copies: The Production, Consumption and Criticism of Copies after the Old Masters in Eighteenth-Century England*, PhD dissertation, Bryn Mawr College, 1995

Kathryn Metz, "Ellen and Rolinda Sharples: Mother and daughter painters", *Woman's Art Journal*, xvi/1, 1995, pp.3–11

Printmakers

From the first days of printmaking, following the development of the woodcut in the 15th century, women have been involved in the print trade as members of printmaking families. It is easily forgotten that in the past printmaking had a primary function in transmitting information, whether religious, technical, commercial, artistic or scientific, and that much printmaking was only secondarily an artistic activity in its own right. Nuns in the Low Countries who were involved in the cutting and printing of religious woodcuts in the 15th century would not have considered themselves to be artists. Women were crucial to certain aspects of the print trade; for example, the colouring of prints was often done by women and their children, and women often ran shops or stalls selling prints. Many women continued their husbands' workshops as widows, employing journeymen to carry out tasks that were beyond their abilities or strengths. There were many strenuous activities connected with printmaking, especially plate printing; thus there were physical barriers against the entry of women into printmaking in addition to the cultural obstacles that prevented them from making independent careers; these did not begin to be surmounted until the end of the 19th century.

Reproductive printmakers of the early modern period

The first identifiable women printmakers were members of families involved in engraving; their unpaid skill could be used to strengthen the family as an economic unit and reduce the need to employ strangers who might be disruptive or disloyal as well as expensive. Although on occasion a daughter might show sufficient artistic ability to repay the effort of additional training, this had to be balanced against the likelihood that when she married her skills would be lost, possibly to a rival family of engravers. Sometimes, however, a young woman would show such exceptional skill or initiative that her work had to be recognised and her name allowed to appear on the plates. The best-known woman engraver in Renaissance Italy was Diana Mantuana (q.v.), daughter of an engraver and stucco-worker in Mantua who worked for Giulio Romano and who also made engravings of Romano's works to promote his reputation. She learned from her father to do likewise and signed 46 plates; these were either engraved to promote the work of living artists or to provide plates to inform others about antique works of art; in other words they were primarily bought for their information. This is not to deny that they might have additional value because they were well engraved, but the plates made by reproductive printmakers were initially bought as images of works of art.

In northern Europe Magdalena van de Passe (Cologne, 1600–Utrecht, 1637) was trained in Utrecht by her father Crispijn van de Passe the Elder, as were her three brothers. Her name is on 25 plates, a small output even for a relatively short life, and she probably assisted family members on others. A generation later in Paris the Flemish family of van der Stella produced an able woman engraver, Claudine Bouzonnet (Lyon, 1636–Paris, 1698). With two brothers and two sisters she trained as a painter under her uncle, the painter Jacques de Stella, but she concentrated on etching and engraving. She produced 125 plates, in particular after Poussin and her uncle, whose name she later took. In Spain María Eugenia de Beer (active 1630s–1652), daughter of the Flemish engraver Cornelio de Beer, produced engravings for illustrated books.

Painter-etchers

The women discussed above worked as reproductive engravers, but there are also women who used printmaking for original work. In Amsterdam there was Geetruydt Roghman (q.v.), daughter of the engraver Hendrik Lambertz. Roghman and great-niece of the painter and etcher Roelant Saverij. She signed only 13 plates, including a few landscapes designed and initially etched by her brother Roelant, but she also designed and engraved five interesting prints of women engaged in domestic tasks. They are perhaps the first example both of a woman designing prints and also making prints of specifically female subjects. These were issued by the Amsterdam engraver and publisher Claes Jansz. Visscher, and the fact that they were engraved rather than etched would have meant that, if there was a demand for the prints, large editions could be printed.

17th-century Italy

In Italy there continued to be women printmakers drawn from artistic families. Teresia del Po, daughter of the painter Pietro del Po, learned painting from her father and became a member of the Roman Accademia di San Luca in 1678. He also taught her printmaking; her best-known print was an engraving of one of his *Nativity* pictures. She died in Rome in 1716, and was roughly contemporary with the long-lived Suor Isabella Piccini (Venice, 1644–?1735), daughter of an engraver of the second rank, Jacopo Piccini. She became a nun, using her skills, such as they were, to engrave portraits of eminent Italians for G.B. Fabri's *Conchilia celeste* (Venice, 1690), as well as a number of religious

prints; some of these are important because they were distributed by Antonio Remondini, whose inexpensive prints reached all over Europe.

Very different from Suor Isabella was Elisabetta Sirani (q.v.), daughter of Giovan Andrea Sirani, an assistant of Guido Reni and contemporary of the important painter-etcher Simone Cantarini. She trained as a painter and attracted early attention; she also, like so many painters of the time, tried her hand at etching and her 14 known prints stand comparison with the best of her contemporaries. Her best-known print, a memorable *Holy Family* after her own design, was done at the age of 19.

18th-century France

In the 18th century it was in Paris that much of the most important printmaking in Europe took place. The tradition of line engraving produced singly issued prints of portraits and history paintings of superb quality as well as elegant book illustrations; at the same time there were opportunities for painter-etchers. There were many important families of engravers and many of these had female members who showed engraving skills. Three Hortheemels sisters, whose brother was the engraver Frederic, were all printmakers: Louise Madeleine married the reproductive engraver Charles Nicolas Cochin the Elder, and did a great deal to help the career of their son, who became a celebrated designer and etcher, famous for his portrait medallions of well-known figures. She engraved several of his works as well as providing plates for J.B. Monicart's *Versailles immortalisé* (1720). Marie Anne married the engraver Nicolas Tardieu, and Marie Nicolle married the painter Alexis Simon Belle.

Among women of the next generation one can single out Renée Elisabeth Lepicie, wife of the engraver Bernard Lepicie, and Cathérine Cousinet, who studied engraving under L. Cars and Etienne Fessard before her marriage to the engraver L.S. Lempereur; like several other women she continued to sign plates with her maiden name after her marriage. As the century went on there were increasing numbers of women engaged in printmaking in Paris; admittedly most worked only on an intermittent basis and generally on plates of secondary importance, but their total output is impressive. Some women, however, did receive academic recognition, which was crucial given the very regimented and centralised organisation of engraving in Paris. Anne Philiberte Coulet, a pupil of Aliamet and

Lempereur, who became known for her landscape prints, was received at the Vienna Academy in 1770. The short-lived Cathérine Deschamps was another well-regarded figure, who engraved both before and after her marriage in 1761 to her instructor, the engraver Jacques-Firmin Beauvarlet. Among those working immediately before the Revolution were Marguerite Hemery, sister of the engraver François-Antoine Hemery; she married Nicolas Ponce – one of the leading engravers of the *estampe galante* that pictured the life of the rich – and made a name for herself with her book illustrations; her sister Thérèse Eléonore, who married the engraver C.L. Lingée, and whose artistic talents were recognised by membership of the Marseille Academy, was successful in the crayon manner, developed to produce decorative facsimiles of drawings; Marie Catherine Riollet, who was the third wife of Beauvarlet, publisher of her *Mauvaise Riche* after Teniers; and Marie Rosalie Bertaud, pupil of Augustin Saint-Aubin and Pierre Philippe Choffard, who engraved a number of landscapes after Joseph Vernet.

All these women can be classed as reproductive engravers; there was little market for etchings by unknown artists, and one of the few women of the time who showed the freedom of handling associated with the painter-etcher was Marguerite Gérard (q.v.). She studied both painting and etching under her brother-in-law Jean-Honoré Fragonard, and in 1779 etched his drawing *Au génie de Franklin*. This was perhaps the most important print by a woman made in 18th-century Paris, and admirably conveyed all the force and drama of the original, and was well received by collectors of etchings. Gérard was sufficiently talented to have a successful career as a painter and etched only six prints, all after Fragonard and all done in her early years. By their nature etchings of this kind had only a limited sale and much valuable painting time could be spent trying to sell them. The process of etching was of course easier than engraving and it is therefore no surprise that it was taken up by artistic amateurs, as well as by a few professional artists, notably Saint-Aubin and Jean Baptiste Le Prince.

French amateurs

The prints made by amateurs were generally distributed privately among friends and acquaintances, though the fame of their makers might occasionally attract a more general curiosity. The most celebrated exponent was the Marquise de Pompadour, mistress of Louis XV, who made nearly 80 prints, mostly in the 1750s, and her lead was followed by others. This was by no means the first time that leisured women had amused themselves making prints. The accomplished Anna Maria van Schurman (q.v.), savante and musician, made half a dozen prints, and her contemporary the Dutch poet Anna Maria de Koker etched some ten landscapes in the style of Jan van Goyen and others. Others who experimented included royalty, notably Queen Christina of Sweden, who abdicated on converting to Catholicism and settled in Rome. Often amateurs left the messy side of printmaking, such as biting and proving, to their professional teachers, who would often, openly or surreptitiously, improve the plates, so that it is difficult for posterity to be able to judge the artistic abilities of, say, Madame de Pompadour; at least one of her plates was retouched by Charles Nicolas Cochin. On the other hand there can be no doubting the talents of Maria Anna, Archduchess of Austria, who had a wide interest in the arts and sciences. She studied under the painter Friedrich August Brand and became a member of the Imperial Academy of copperplate-engravers in the year following its foundation in 1767. In 1772 she issued a series of landscapes and genre scenes, *Sechzehn radirte Blätter*.

Angelica Kauffman

The constraints upon women meant that very few had genuinely independent careers as artists. Most of the printmakers, it is clear, were members of families of engravers engaged in reproductive work, and did not use printmaking for their personal artistic expression. In the 18th century the most remarkable example of a woman who did make her own way was Angelica Kauffman (q.v.). Her formative years were spent in Italy, where the tradition of the painter-etcher was the most powerful in Europe. She took up etching in her early twenties and made a number of plates, some after other painters but others after her own designs. Initially these were distributed privately, but after she went to London in 1766 she took advantage of the great interest she aroused and herself published a set of prints for a guinea (£1 1s.). She continued to make etchings for sale. When she left England for Italy she sold her plates, many of which were re-issued by the important London printseller John Boydell and therefore became widely known.

British amateurs

Kauffman's example helped to encourage fashionable women, many of whom had taken drawing lessons, to take up printmaking. This had in fact already been given encouragement by the fledgling Society of Arts; its primary purpose was to encourage the arts of design for commercial reasons, and it offered "premiums" (prizes) for drawing, but it also advertised premiums for etchings made by women. The motive may have been to secure the goodwill towards the Society from the families of the nobility and gentry whose daughters were most likely to be able to compete. One keen amateur was Lady Louisa Greville, daughter of the Earl of Warwick, whose many etchings after landscapes by the Carracci, Salvator Rosa and Marco Ricci, as well as figure studies after Guercino, are mostly dated 1758–62, before her marriage to William Churchill in 1770. Public exhibitions began in 1760 and she exhibited one etching, a landscape after Salvator Rosa, at the Free Society in 1762. Unlike the Royal Academy, founded in 1768, the Society of Artists and the breakaway Free Society both allowed prints to be exhibited, though only a few women took advantage of this opportunity. As in France such prints were not usually sold but were instead given away or exchanged in aristocratic circles. Horace Walpole, who tended to exaggerate the talents of well-born artists, assembled two albums of etchings (Lewis Walpole Library, Farmington) by men and women who etched as a pastime, as did another collector, Richard Bull (two albums in the British Museum, London). Among the few amateur prints that were sold were aquatints by Catherine Maria Fanshawe, who did a number of charming studies of children around 1800, and sold some prints in aid of charitable causes. Aquatint was a form of tonal etching introduced in the 1770s for the reproduction of wash drawings; it was more difficult than traditional etching, which simply called for the design to be scratched with a needle through the hard ground coating the copper plate, and was therefore seldom used by amateurs.

Drawing masters now started to teach etching; prominent among these was William Austin, who actually advertised that he taught etching; among the women who were probably taught by him was Miss Catherine St Aubin who made several etchings and whose drawings of her family home, St Michael's Mount, Cornwall, were etched by Austin. One woman who advertised as a teacher of etching was Mary Darly, wife of the designer and etcher Matthew Darly. It is difficult to separate their work; together they etched and published the political satires of George Townshend, who pioneered the combination of personal caricature and political satire. Darly kept a shop – as did many engravers' wives – in the early 1760s and her name appears as publisher on a number of satires, mostly directed against the Scots-born minister Lord Bute. In 1762 she published a booklet: *A Book of Caricatures, on 60 Copper Plates, with the Principles of Designing … with Sundry Ancient & Modern Examples … for the Use of Young Gentlemen and Ladies*.

Professional women engravers in Britain

There were very few professional women engravers in Britain, and those there were generally did not sign many plates. Angélique Ravenet, daughter of a French-born line engraver, may have been instructed by her father; after her marriage to the engraver V.-M. Picot she exhibited a mezzotint of *Cervetti* (the cellist G. Basseri) at the Society of Artists (1771), but did not sign many other plates and, although she may have assisted her husband, she was probably engaged in the printselling side of his business. At the Society of Artists Miss Elizabeth Judkins exhibited mezzotints after Joshua Reynolds in 1772 and 1775; she was undoubtedly instructed by her uncle, the mezzotint engraver James Watson, but did not become a professional engraver. It was Watson's daughter Caroline (q.v.) who became the only British-born woman professional; she did not engrave in mezzotint but in the new technique of stipple or dotted manner, which was developed out of the French crayon manner and was initially used in Britain from the mid-1770s to reproduce drawings by Kauffman. It was very difficult, in Britain as elsewhere, for a young woman to learn printmaking as a career except within the family. The only British engraver who appears to have had female apprentices was John Raphael Smith, who took on Ann Probin and Caroline Kirkley in 1789; they were probably engaged to learn print colouring rather than engraving, though Kirkley did sign one mezzotint. A few other women signed occasional stipples, for example Mary Ann Rigg, who was probably taught by Edmund Scott, whom she married. Later on Marie Anne Bourlier engraved a considerable number of stipples between 1806, when she engraved ten of the *Portraits … of the Royal Family* (Abbey 1952, "Life" 278), published by E. Harding, and about 1815. There were also a few line engravers, notably Elisabeth Ellis and Letitia Byrne, who assisted her father, the engraver William Byrne, and became an accomplished etcher. These two women both had their names on many plates; this was not so in the case of the daughters of Isaac Taylor, the line engraver who trained his daughters alongside his apprentices. Their talents lay elsewhere as writers and they did not progress to signing plates; we only know of their training because Mary Taylor mentions it in her autobiography (*Autobiography and Other Memorials of Mrs Gilbert*, ed. Josiah Gilbert, London: King, 1874, i, p.103).

One last professional engraver in 18th-century Britain remains to be mentioned: Maria Catherine Hull, who married the engraver Theophilus Prestel in Nuremberg in 1769 and assisted him, initially on the crayon manner facsimiles he made of drawings and later with his aquatints. She left him in 1786 and went to London, which had taken over from Paris as the most important centre of printmaking. In the eight years remaining to her she engraved some very large and impressive landscape plates, which, like many London prints of the time, had a wide sale in Germany and the rest of continental Europe.

Women were becoming more important as buyers of prints by the end of the 18th century, and there was a greater market for prints with a feminine appeal. The best example of this is perhaps the edition of Mary Robinson's poem *The Winter Day* published in 1804 by Rudolph Ackermann with aquatint plates by Caroline Watson after designs by Maria Cosway (q.v.). Ackermann had in 1800 published *Imitations in Chalk* etched by Cosway, a drawing book of softground etchings by Maria of sketches by her husband Richard Cosway. Another group of etchings that she made were of eight paintings in the Louvre, sketched on a short visit to Paris following the Peace of Amiens in 1802, and originally intended to illustrate a description of the Louvre and its new treasures which had been commandeered from all the newly conquered lands.

The introduction of lithography

Until the early 19th century printmaking was, except for relief methods of woodcut and wood-engraving, done on copper, using intaglio methods whereby the image was printed from ink retained on the plate in lines or rough areas produced mechani-cally or by acid. The first planographic technique, lithography, involved drawing on limestone – which repelled ink when wet – with a wax crayon whose marks held the ink.

Ackermann was one of the first printsellers to take an interest in lithography, or "polyautography" as the process was initially called following its discovery in 1798 by a German, Aloys Senefelder. He visited London in 1800–01, and, after he obtained a patent, several lithographs drawn on the stone by various artists were published in 1803 as *Specimens of Polyautography*. The artists included one woman amateur, Lady Cawdor, née Caroline Howard, who contributed two pen lithograph landscapes. The same year Ackermann issued *Twelve Views of Scotland* by Miss F. Waring, which were chalk lithographs; their extreme rarity today suggests they did not sell very well, and the interest in lithography did not really develop in Britain until after Ackermann published an English edition of Senefelder's *Complete Course in Lithography* (1819). It was in fact in Munich and then Paris that the earliest commercial lithographs were made. When interest was revived in Britain it opened up much greater opportunities for women printmakers, as it was much easier to work on stone than with the etching needle. There are numerous examples made by women, several of whom illustrated their own travel books with lithographs.

There were few women who could be called professional lithographers. There is little doubt that the prejudice against "trade" in 19th-century Europe inhibited many women from taking up such a career. Therefore most lithographs made by women were either by amateurs, such as Princess Charlotte Bonaparte, whose work included a series of American landscapes, or by women painters, such as Elise Journet, who made lithographs of some of her paintings for publication in *L'Artiste*. One French professional was Cécile Marechal Marchand, who assisted her lithographer husband Jacques Marchand and signed at least 36 lithographs herself. The most important woman lithographer was Fanny Palmer, who turned to the process as a way of supporting her family after it ran into financial trouble. Her earliest lithographs were made in Leicester in 1842 (Abbey 1952, "Scenery" 199), but in 1844 she and her family emigrated from Britain to the USA. There she first worked as an independent lithographer, but she was before long recruited by the publisher Nathaniel Currier and became one of the mainstays of the firm of Currier & Ives; she is credited with some 200 lithographs, drawn on the stone by herself, between 1849 and 1868. Most of the purchasers of these popular prints, which give such an evocative picture of America, were quite unaware that she was a woman since she simply signed herself "F. F. Palmer".

The "etching revival"

Despite the interest in and ease of lithography, etching remained a popular pastime. In Britain the list of amateurs was headed by Queen Victoria, who had lessons from George Hayter, who became her Painter in Ordinary in 1841. A number of British women made prints in distant parts of the Empire; for example, in 1826, Countess Amherst, wife of the Governor-General of India, made an etching of Sir Charles D'Oyly's painting room in Patna (Sir Charles himself later took up lithography and involved several British women in his Bihar Lithographic Press). In Paris the painter Frédérique O'Connell began in 1853 to teach art, including etching, to ladies and produced several etchings herself.

It was in Paris that the Etching Revival began, and major artists began to take a new interest in producing prints. The most active printmaker was the American painter Mary Cassatt (q.v.), who made 220 etchings and 2 lithographs from about 1878; among these her colour etchings, many of them of women and children, attracted most notice. Her example seems to have encouraged Berthe Morisot (q.v.), but, although the latter made a few drypoints and a lithograph based on existing draw-ings, she did not maintain her interest. Another important artist who made prints was Suzanne Valadon (q.v.). She made some 30 etchings and drypoints, mostly studies of women, but they were largely unknown until her later fame as a painter aroused interest in them. In Britain the growing status of etching was reflected by the foundation in 1880 of the Society of Painter-Etchers, which was to have many women members (after the Society received a royal charter members were denoted as "RE" and associates "ARE"). Among the first full members was Mary Nimmo Moran, who, with Cassatt, was one of the main exhibitors in a display of the *Work of Women Etchers of America* at the Museum of Fine Arts, Boston, in 1887–8. One of the most influential of women etchers was Constance Pott, known for her landscape prints,

who became a full member of the Society in 1898. She was assistant to Frank Short, one of the leading printmakers of his day, at the Royal College of Art, London, where a number of women trained, such as Mary Anne Sloane. Other women, such as Margaret Kemp-Welch, ARE, were taught printmaking at the art school at Bushey run by the painter and print-maker Herbert Herkomer.

The etching boom

There could hardly be a greater contrast between the pastoral, often cosy subject matter of much British and American printmaking and the prints produced by Käthe Kollwitz (q.v.). She turned to printmaking principally to express her distress about the condition of the poor, which she saw as the wife of a Berlin doctor, but she also produced some extraordinarily powerful self-portraits. Kollwitz worked in a number of techniques and after World War I also took up woodcut, influenced by the powerful work of Ernst Barlach. However, the European public was not really interested in work of such a disturbing nature as she produced – after the horrors of the war more reassuring images were in demand.

During the immediate post-war period there was a tremendous surge of demand for etchings on both sides of the Atlantic, and many women artists were ready to respond, from painters such as Laura Knight (q.v.) with her etchings of the stage or of circus life, to Berthe Jacques, who was one of the founders of the Chicago Society of Etchers. Chicago emerged as an important centre for printmaking, and etchers from all over the world sent prints to its annual exhibitions. Among the most interesting women etchers in Britain were those influenced by Walter Sickert, such as Edna Clarke Hall; his pupils included Sylvia Gosse, RE and Wendela Boreel, ARE. In 1920 the Society of Graphic Artists was founded, with annual exhibitions held until 1940, when it had 46 women members, many of them printmakers.

Colour prints

The colour etchings produced by Mary Cassatt have already been mentioned: in the early years of the 20th century there was a great vogue for colour prints of various kinds. There was a resurgence in colour lithography in Paris in the 1890s in which women played little part, but women played a major part in the production of colour prints that had their inspiration in Japanese art, in particular in colour woodcuts. In the USA Arthur Wesley Dow, who taught in New York, was a central figure, and those who produced colour prints as a result, either directly or indirectly, of his example included Helen Hyde and Georgia O'Keeffe (q.v.).

In Britain an important influence was Mabel Royds, who was inspired by Japanese colour woodblocks and began to produce colour prints just before World War I. She taught the American printmaker Norma Bassett Hall, who was the sole woman founding member of the Prairie Print Makers, a society that distributed an annual gift print to its members between 1931 and 1965, five of them by women. Colour woodcuts were also popular in Australia, largely through the example and teaching of Thea Proctor.

The boldness inherent in woodcut had already made its impact on the Continent, most notably at the fifth exhibition of the Vienna Secession in 1899. Among those who turned to the colour woodcut as a consequence was Norbertine von Bresslern-Roth, who made an impact with her colour woodcuts of animals. One prolific exponent of the woodcut was Emma Boorman, who also trained in Vienna. After World War I she travelled extensively, not only in Europe but also in Asia, and made many powerful prints, many of which are on a large scale, and mostly of the cities she visited. She was one of the printmakers who was not deterred by the Depression of the 1930s; the collapse of the boom was most felt by traditional etchers and many of those who produced colour prints continued in work. One individual talent who emerged at the time was Elyse Ashe Lord, who made many distinctive colour prints, many with drypoint, under the influence of Chinese painting.

Another technique that attracted interest despite the Depression was the colour linocut. This was pioneered by Claude Flight, who taught at the Grosvenor School of Modern Art, London, from 1926; among his pupils, and a major exhibitor at the annual British Lino-Cut exhibitions of the Grosvenor School's students held from 1930, was Sybil Andrews, whose work, influenced by Futurism, seemed appropriately "modern". In Australia several women, notably Ethleen Palmer, used linocut very effectively.

Wood engraving

If women were in the clear minority as artists in previous centuries, there was one specialised area in which they held the lead during the 20th century: wood-engraving. The greatest of the group trained in London was Clare Leighton, who studied under Noel Rooke at the Central School and was one of the early members of the Society of Wood Engravers founded in 1920. Some of her prints, notably those in her book *Four Hedges* (1935), have an important part in the British pastoral tradition. She settled permanently in the USA in 1939. Gertrude Hermes, Agnes Miller Parker, Gwen Raverat and Joan Hassall all became well known, largely because so much of their work was reproduced by means of photolithography as book illustrations.

Printmaking and the avant-garde

Most of the British wood-engravers were traditional in their aims and subject matter, but Hermes was a more radical artist and was one of six women printmakers who were included in an exhibition at the British Museum of avant-garde printmakers, the others being Sybil Andrews, Eileen Agar (q.v.), Gillian Ayres, Prunella Clough and Lill Tschudi. Bringing such a list up to date would lead to the addition of such artists as Paula Rego (q.v.). In the 20th century printmaking has everywhere moved into a more central position in contemporary art, becoming a means of expression for many major artists. Nowhere is this seen more powerfully than in the USA, where the important artists who have been printmakers include such figures as Isabel Bishop (q.v.) and Peggy Bacon. Many artists have come to printmaking thanks to the establishment of printing workshops: Tamarind, for example, was important for Anni Albers (q.v.), Louise Nevelson (q.v.) and Miriam Schapiro (q.v.). Universal Limited Art Editions, sustained for so long by Tatyana Grosman, helped the careers of several artists, such as Mary Callery, Grace Hartigan (q.v.) and Helen Frankenthaler (q.v.).

DAVID ALEXANDER

Bibliography
(excluding references to artists with their own entries in the *Concise Dictionary*; for Magdalena van de Passe, María Eugenia de Beer, Edna Clarke Hall, Sylvia Gosse, Gertrude Hermes, Gwen Raverat, Gillian Ayres and Prunella Clough, see the complete edition of the *Dictionary of Women Artists*)

General

Adam von Bartsch, *Le Peintre-graveur*, 21 vols, Vienne, 1803–21

Charles Le Blanc, *Manuel de l'amateur d'estampes, 1550–1820*, 4 vols, Paris: Bouillon, 1854–89

Catalogue of a Collection of Engravings, Etchings and Lithographs by Women, exh. cat., The Grolier Club, New York, 1901

Malcolm C. Salaman, *The New Woodcut*, London: The Studio, and New York: Boni, 1930

Timothy A. Riggs, *The Print Council Index to Oeuvre-Catalogues of Prints by European and American Artists*, Millwood, NY: Kraus, 1983

Allgemeines Kunstler-Lexikon, Munich: Saur, 1990–

Elizabeth Harvey-Lee, *Mistresses of the Graphic Arts: Famous and Forgotten Women Printmakers, c.1550–c.1950*, dealer's cat., North Aston, Oxford, 1995

Italy

Alexandre de Vesme, *Le Peintre-graveur italien*, Milan: Hoepli, 1906

Donne artiste nelle collezioni del Museo di Bassano, exh. cat., Museo Civico di Bassano di Grappa, 1986

Italian Etchers of the Renaissance and Baroque, exh. cat., Museum of Fine Arts, Boston, 1989

The Netherlands

F.W.H. Hollstein, *Dutch and Flemish Etchings, Engravings and Woodcuts, c.1450–1700*, Amsterdam: Hertzberger, 1949–

"Dames Gaan Voor": De Vrouw in de prentkunst, 1500–1800 ["Ladies first": Women in printmaking, 1500–1800], exh. cat., Museum Boymans-van Beuningen, Rotterdam, 1975

Printmaking in the Age of Rembrandt, exh. cat., Museum of Fine Arts, Boston, 1980

Germany and Austria

Andreas Andresen, *Der Deutsche Peintre-Graveur*, 5 vols, Leipzig: Weigel, 1864–78

F.W.H. Hollstein, *German Engravings, Etchings and Woodcuts, c.1400–1700*, Amsterdam: Hertzberger, 1954–

France

Inventaire du Fonds Français: Graveurs du XVIIe siècle, 11 vols, Paris: Bibliothèque Nationale, 1939–

Inventaire du Fonds Français: Graveurs du XVIIIe siècle, 14 vols, Paris: Bibliothèque Nationale, 1939–69

Inventaire du Fonds Français: Graveurs après 1800, 14 vols, Paris: Bibliothèque Nationale, 1930–77

Britain

Harold J. Wright, "The lithographs of Ethel Gabain", *Print Collector's Quarterly*, x, 1923, pp.254–87

C.A. Nicholson, "The etchings of Orovida [Pisarro]", *Print Collector's Quarterly*, xii, 1926, pp.176–202

Clare Stuart Wortley, "Amateur etchers", *Print Collector's Quarterly*, xix, 1932, pp.189–

J.R. Abbey, *Scenery of Great Britain and Ireland in Aquatint and Lithography, 1770–1860, from the Library of J.R. Abbey*, London: Curwen Press, 1952; reprinted Folkestone: Dawsons, 1972, and San Francisco: Wofsy, 1991

George Mackley, *Monica Poole: Wood-Engraver*, Biddenden, Kent: Florin Press, 1984

Garton and Cooke, Catalogue 28, dealer's cat., London, 1984 (with a full list of the colour woodcuts of Mabel Royds)

David Chambers, *Joan Hassall: Engravings and Drawings*, Pinner: Private Libraries Association, 1985

Patricia Jaffé, *Women Engravers*, London: Virago, 1988 (wood-engravers only)

British Avante-Garde Printmaking, exh. cat., British Museum, London, 1990

James Hamilton, *Wood Engraving and the Woodcut in Britain, c.1890–1990*, London: Barrie and Jenkins, 1994

Stephen Coppel, *Linocuts of the Machine Age: Claude Flight and the Grosvenor School*, Aldershot: Scolar Press, 1995

North America

George C. Groce and David H. Wallace, *The New-York Historical Society's Dictionary of Artists in America, 1564–1860*, New Haven: Yale University Press, 1957

Mary B. Cowdrey, "Fanny Palmer, an American lithographer", *Prints: Thirteen Illustrated Essays on the Art of the Print*, ed. Carl Zigrosser, New York: Holt Rinehart, 1962, pp.218–34

Richard S. Field and Ruth E. Fine, *A Graphic Muse: Prints by Contemporary American Women*, New York: Hudson Hills Press, 1987

Esther Sparks, *Universal Limited Art Editions: A History and Catalogue, the First Twenty-Five Years*, Chicago: Art Institute, 1989

Arthur Wesley Dow and His Influence, exh. cat., Herbert F. Johnson Museum of Art, Cornell, Ithaca, 1990

Mary Evans O'Keefe Gravalos and Carol Pulin, *Bertha Lum*, Washington, DC: Smithsonian Institution Press, 1991

Tim Mason and Lynn Mason, *Helen Hyde*, Washington, DC: Smithsonian Institution Press, 1991

Martha R. Severens, *Alice Ravenel Huger Smith: An Artist, a Place and a Time*, Charleston, SC: Carolina Art Association, 1993

C.S. Rubinstein, "Fanny Palmer", *The Dictionary of Art*, ed. Jane Turner, xxiii, London and New York: Grove, 1996

Australia

Sydney by Design: Wood and Linoblock Prints by Sydney Women Artists Between the Wars, exh. cat., National Gallery of Australia, Canberra, 1995

Amateur Artists
Amateur art as a social skill and a female preserve

16th and 17th centuries

Any discussion of amateur art must begin with a definition of the term. According to the *Encyclopaedia Britannica*, the original meaning of the word "amateur" is "someone who participates in any art, craft, game, sport or other activity solely for pleasure and enjoyment". Indeed, the root of the word derives from the Latin *amare* (to love) and *amatorem*, which means essentially "one who has a taste for anything". The second meaning of the word is more judgemental: it indicates "a person of inferior or superficial skill, ability or proficiency, as compared with others who specialise in and are expert in any field". Those who practise art for pleasure are distinguished from those who practise the same art for other reasons, to which category belong the specialists or experts, who are motivated by professional ambition rather than by love of the field.

In practice, the term amateur usually has a double meaning. An art amateur is someone who practises the arts for his or her pleasure and does this without explicitly specialising. This implies that he or she does not apply him or herself professionally, and practises the arts alongside other activities. As far as we know, the term was first used at the court of Louis XIV (1642–1715) to indicate "a connoisseur of the fine arts". It was apparently initially used in the literal sense of the word: an amateur loves the arts and in this sense is a "connoisseur". The term is also encountered with the same meaning in 18th-century England. In 1784 the word "amateur" was used for "one who appreciated the polite arts of painting and music". This introduction may make it clear that the use of the term "amateur artists" for the 16th and 17th centuries is an anachronism. However, the absence of the term during this period does not imply that the phenomenon now associated with it did not exist.

"Amateur" or "Amateuse"?

Both the interpretations of "amateurs" quoted above have to do with men, and it is worthy of note that the word spread only in its masculine form. The feminine variant *amateuse* is not found in France, Britain or the Netherlands. How can one come to an understanding of the content of the term that is applicable to women as well? Were women active as amateurs in the visual arts? The following perspectives enable the profile of the amateur to be defined with greater exactitude.

1. An amateur is someone who is not professionally involved with the arts. Consequently, the amateur activity is practised alongside other activities that may or may not be professional. This expression seems to imply that amateurs could not be members of professional organisations, such as the guilds of St Luke.

2. The status of "amateur" assumes a certain socio-economic situation. Someone who practises the arts for pleasure has no intention of providing a living for himself or herself with this activity. Thus amateurs are found primarily in the upper social classes. An abundance of free time is required for it.

3. An important exception must be made for women who came from artist families. The practice of art on a non-professional basis then takes place in the context of the family. Here artistic practice is the result of having an atelier at hand and of possible "natural" aptitude. That an artist has a daughter who develops into an amateur artist is in this case the result of practical circumstances. Here we are dealing with "circumstantial" amateur artists.

4. The practice of the arts as a hobby was often the result of an educational process whereby handicraft skills were practised alongside music, dancing and horseback riding. The practice of the arts by the dilettante thus fits within a broader notion of the upbringing thought necessary for women if they were to prepare for a role in society. These one might call "intentional" amateur artists.

5. The practice of the arts as a hobby is sometimes also classified as "amateurish" on the basis of the genre employed. The more decorative genres (the minor arts, flower-pieces, still lifes, etc.) were associated with amateurism more than was history painting. Copying after the models of the "great masters" was likewise seen as a mark of dilettantism. Sometimes also copying took place

as a means of schooling when teachers were lacking.

The origins of the phenomenon

Important in this context is the question of the origin of the phenomenon. From what point was amateur artistic practice a criterion for the evaluation of a woman's upbringing?

Among the Greeks and Romans little intellectual ambition was attributed to women. The woman's education stopped in the gynaeceum, from which point she was occupied with the administration of the household. In the early Renaissance this thread was taken up once more. Leon Battista Alberti wrote in his treatise *Della famiglia*: "women are by nature timid, soft, slow, and therefore more useful when they watch over things". Alberti does not say that they should benefit from this opportunity to practise the skills of handicrafts. When Baldassare Castiglione published *Il libro del cortegiano* in 1528, he also paid a great deal of attention to the role women had to fulfil in the milieu of the court. A woman must not be intelligent so much as modest and courteous in conversation. It was also good if she could dance, play a musical instrument and have some schooling in painting. While a number of exceptionally learned women are known about in detail, information about their artistic activities is rarely found. An exception is Isabella d'Este, who spoke Latin, Greek and various "modern" languages, danced well, and played both the clavecimbel and the lute. We are told that she designed objects for embroidery work and also executed these herself.

Instruction versus the "interests of conversation"

The 16th-century French poet Louise Labé, who opened the first bourgeois salon in France, spoke several languages and learned dancing and horseback riding, music and handicrafts. Painting or drawing were apparently not among her accomplishments. Margaret, one of the daughters of Sir Thomas More, was still more versatile: she studied logic, arithmetic, physics and philosophy; she, too, played music. The most important advocate of a "total education" for women was Juan Luis Vives, who was the tutor of, among others, Mary Tudor, daughter of Catherine of Aragon, to whom he dedicated his treatise on the education of women in 1523; the English translation, *Instruction of a Christian Woman*, appeared in 1540. Certainly, some education of girls could do no harm, but what was taught had to conform to the housewifely tasks of women. Neither Erasmus nor Vives was an advocate of "the fashionable court lady of the Italian mode". In their eyes, such women, who aspired to appropriate a social role at court, had forsaken the necessary modesty. There is no mention of explicit artistic training.

The "industrial" arts such as spinning and weaving on the other hand could indeed have a certain practical utility. In Catholic lands the upbringing of girls was managed by prominent orders of nuns such as the Ursulines. In 1596 the first French convent of the order was founded in Avignon. Here girls from both the upper and lower classes went to school. Sewing was almost always on the programme. For less wealthy girls, a craft such as lace-making was sometimes also taught. The girls recruited from better social ranks also learned some Latin and Italian and were instructed in dancing and music.

The composition of the programme indicates that the upbringing of girls was still inspired by the Renaissance ideal as articulated by Castiglione. Both in England and in France the education of women was focused on the *arts d'agrément*, which were intended to turn women into socially useful partners. Inspired by the example of the early 15th-century writer Christine de Pisan in her *Livre de la Cité des Dames*, by the beginning of the 17th century a discussion had originated on the supposed inferiority of women. "Male and female are the same creature, with the same capabilities", wrote Marie Le Jars de Gournay in 1622. The Netherlandish Anna Maria van Schurman (q.v.) answered in 1641 with a treatise on the question of whether it was fitting for the Christian woman to occupy herself with the study of literature. She also held that condemning women to the needle and the scissors was the result of custom and nothing else. The English translation of van Schurman's text (1659) inspired the linguist Bathshua Makin to write the *Essay to Revive the Ancient Education of Gentlewomen in Religion, Manners, Arts and Tongues* (1673). Van Schurman also maintained contact with Madeleine de Scudéry. In one of the ten parts of *Le Grand Cyrus* (Paris, 1649–53) the latter wrote:

Is there anything more bizarre than to see how one approaches the education of women. One does not wish them to become coquettes, and yet one permits them to learn carefully all that is appropriate to coquetry without allowing them to learn anything that could occupy their mind or fortify their virtue … Up to now, with rare exceptions, the education of girls goes no further than reading, writing, dancing and singing.

Madeleine de Scudéry comes out in favour of a broader intellectual training in which the "musical" plays only a limited role. In that province, according to her, there were already plenty of opportunities. Thus de Scudéry apparently felt that artistic activities did not contribute to the upbringing of women. One encounters precisely the same point of view from Mary Astell, who in *An Essay in Defence of the Female Sex* (1696) considers painting as one of those

> mindless occupations that kept women from real learning. [Men] have endeavoured to train us up altogether to Ease and Ignorance … about the age of six or seven [the sexes] begin to be separated, and the boys are sent to the Grammar school and the girls to Boarding Schools, and other places, to learn needlework, Dancing, Singing, Music, Drawing, Painting and other Accomplishments … Reading and Writing are the main Interests of Conversation, though Music and Painting may be allow'd to contribute something toward it, as they give us an Insight into the Arts that make up a great Part of the Pleasures and Diversions of Mankind.

Astell sees artistic occupation as a social skill and not as something that can enrich women as such. According to Iain Pears (1988), the number of women active as amateur artists in 17th-century England was significantly greater than the number of men who knew how to ply the brush. Nevertheless, he assumes that the phenomenon of the woman dilettante was fully developed only during the course of the 18th century. Painting and drawing were decent pastimes for women, because they were clearly more useful to them than the other specifically feminine occupations. For men this was quite obviously not the case.

On the basis of the views of both de Scudéry and Astell one deduces that "intentional" amateur artists are to be sought in a privileged aristocratic milieu that was anything but feminist in its inspira-

tion. Women with some feminist engagement reacted against this form of "pastime" because they functioned expressly to stereotype the sexes.

Nevertheless, there were also "intentional" amateur artists who drew an emphatic distinction between the traditional feminine pastimes such as weaving and embroidery and the more explicitly artistic ones of drawing, painting and sculpture. The real discussion in which women also took part did not take place until the 17th century. Anna Maria van Schurman, for example, recommended these last media together with a whole range of minor arts as a sensible and emancipatory occupation. It cannot be determined with certainty whether the type of the "intentional" woman dilettante with great artistic versatility is found earlier than the 17th century. "Circumstantial" female artists were certainly to be found earlier, in the antique prototypes that had played their own role in the thinking about women and art from the early Renaissance. No indication of any expressly "amateur" women artists can be found in Pliny the Elder's *Historia naturalis* of AD 70. In his paragraph on *Pinxere et mulieres* he indicates five different women artists, of whom at least two belong to the category of circumstantial artists. They include Timarete, daughter of Micon the younger; Irene, daughter and pupil of the painter Cratinus; Aristarete, daughter of the painter Nearchus, as the teacher of Autubulus; and finally Iaia of Cyzicus, who was active as an unmarried woman in Rome and painted primarily portraits. Pliny further remarks that she – living at the time with Marcus Varro – asked prices for her portraits that were as high as those of such prominent painters as Sopolis and Dionysus. As far as we know, this last woman cannot in any way be described as an amateur.

Examples

In order to elucidate the complex concept of amateur artist, two case-studies are presented here. For the 16th century Catharina van Hemessen (q.v.), who came from a trade milieu and applied herself to painting, exemplifies the "circumstantial" amateur artist. Anna Maria van Schurman, who was situated in an aristocratic-humanist environment and cultivated the ambition of absolute versatility, functions as an example of the "intentional" amateur artist for the 17th century. The selection is justified by the fact that the careers of both women are relatively well documented. Both their position and their work make clear how difficult it is to articulate and apply the distinction between professional and non-professional.

Catharina van Hemessen was born in 1528 as the daughter of Jan Sanders van Hemessen and Barbe de Fevre. Four years earlier her father had become a member of the Antwerp Guild of St Luke. She herself appears not to have had relations with the painters' guild. Her known oeuvre is limited in number, and all her known works date from the years 1548–55. Among her most attractive paintings are her self-portrait at the easel of 1548 (Kunstmuseum, Basel) and the portrait of a 22-year-old woman at the clavier from the same year (Wallraf-Richartz-Museum, Cologne); the portraits were probably originally pendants. Van Hemessen married the musician Chrétien de Morien, who in 1552 had become the organist for the Onze-Lieve-Vrouwekerk in Antwerp. In 1556 the couple was invited to the court of Mary of Hungary in Spain, but it is not known how long they stayed there.

Van Hemessen was not a guild member and, as far as we know, produced very little. Her sitters seem to have been recruited from her immediate surroundings and there are several reasons to suppose that she practised the arts explicitly as an amateur. Mary of Hungary provided the couple with a pension at her death, but this does not in itself necessarily imply that van Hemessen was active as an artist at the Spanish court. On the other hand it is indeed remarkable that she is still expressly mentioned in the first edition of Lodovico Guicciardini's *Descrittione di tutti i paesi bassi, altrimenti detti Germania Inferiore* (1567) as among

> the most outstanding women in this art [of painting] that are still alive today … Catharine daughter of the most outstanding master Jan van Hemssen, housewife of Kerstiaen, the very excellent player of instruments: so that they both have practised their great virtues and arts for the Queen of Hungary in Spain and she has even provided them both with good support for the rest of their lives after her death.

As the daughter of an amateur artist, van Hemessen may be compared with Susanna, the daughter of Gerard Horenbout. Albrecht Dürer met this painter-miniaturist, among others, when he was living in Antwerp in 1521. In his daybook he noted:

"Item master Gerhart, illuminist, has a daughter 18 years old, named Susanna, who has illuminated a little plate, a Saviour, for which I have given her one guilder". His judgement at once praises and deprecates: "It is a wonder that a Woman's picture can be of such quality". Given that little more is known about the woman, one can assume that her amateurish skill left no historical trace.

Like many of her Italian contemporaries, van Hemessen was taught by her father. An analysis of women artists known by name in the period between the 15th century and the 19th shows that some three-quarters came from an artistic milieu. Their activities in surroundings where several family members were also active as artists often make it difficult to distinguish their works from those of their family. This distinction was made only exceptionally in the past, largely because it was professional production that was evaluated – and not the amateur work of daughters or spouses. On the other hand, Alison Kettering's *Drawings from the Ter Borch Studio Estate in the Rijksmuseum* (2 vols, The Hague: Staatsuitgeverij, 1988) demonstrates that through fundamental detailed study the drawings can be attributed to Gerard, Harmen, Moses, Anna and Gesina ter Borch (q.v.).

The female amateur artists examined here did not practise the arts because their fathers prized the educational value of drawing and/or painting. The training happened as it were by itself. Experience taught and stimulated. So it is no surprise that in his *Gulden Cabinet vande edel vry schilderconst* (Golden cabinet of the noble free art of painting; 1661) Cornelis de Bie refers emphatically to the daughters of great artists:

> In Brabant Fame also praises the beautiful minds
> Of the fragile women who pawn their spirits
> To the pleasant Brush, wherein they are experienced
> As shown to us by the art of the Daughter of Pepijn,
> Of d'Egmont, and Van Dijck, so elegant, clever and powerful
> Vigorous and colourful, and wondrously masterful …

Sofonisba Anguissola (q.v.) was the oldest daughter of an impoverished nobleman from Cremona. In accord with Italian custom, the daughters, of whom there were six in the family, received instruction in drawing and music. When Anna Maria van Schurman was born in Cologne in 1607 to a father who had come from Antwerp and a noble German mother, a "humanist" education for the girl was to be expected. In an autobiographical apologia entitled *Eukleria seu melioris partis electio*, published in 1673, she tells of her lessons in Latin, music and various arts to verify herself finally as a linguist, theologian, philosopher and artist. She experimented with an array of arts. She virtually invented the pastel portrait in the Netherlands and also made portraits in graphite and wash, on ivory and buckskin. There are decoratively written pages and also runners preserved from her hand, as well as exceptionally skilful cuttings, etchings and embroidery.

In her dissertation about whether or not the Christian woman should become a scholar, van Schurman recommends the arts and sciences. Yet she finds that not all women are suited to take up this invitation. Only women of at least average intelligence and with adequate free time would be considered eligible. This last implies an unmarried state or sufficient financial means to employ servants. According to van Schurman, mathematics, poetry, painting and "other fine arts" not listed further formed a suitable "feminine pastime". With this she smoothed a path that must have ensured the peace of mind of women who were both Christian and creative. She herself was the role model. Her self-portraits were unusually popular as prints. At an advanced age she joined the sect of the Genevan reformer Jean de Labadie, through which her intellectual and artistic activities received a severe blow.

The exception: Being amateur without being artist

The term amateur artist indicates practitioners at the margin of the official artistic circuit. In this same margin lay the art critics, who in the 17th century were also connoisseurs. "Intentional" dilettantes and connoisseurs of art were often in the same circle, though it must be remarked here that women were seldom to be found among the recognised connoisseurs. The humanist tradition itself invited but few 17th-century women to take part in a discourse in which art became an intellectual affair. Even Schurman in her *Dissertatio* – despite her extensive philosophical schooling – does not go so far as to discuss the theory of art.

For this reason one is surprised by the initiative of Carola Catharina Patina, who published a luxurious folio written in Latin: *Tabellae selectae ac explicatae* (1694). She was the daughter of the famous Paris-born doctor and numismatist Carolus Patin who became professor of medicine in Padua in 1676. She was at home in history, mathematics and archaeology, and spoke Latin as well as French and Italian. The book contained a selection of paintings elucidated by her, primarily by Italian masters who are all also portrayed in print. In 1684 the Rouen artist Noël III Jouvenet did a portrait of the learned family. The print after this portrait ends the *Tabellae selectae*, and the accompanying commentary is particularly detailed. Patina emphasises the simplicity of her own hairdo in contrast to the fashionable coiffures of her mother and sister, who were likewise intellectually active: *Sexum nostrum reprehendebat vetus quidam; autor, comuntur, plectuntur, annus est*. Patina found that she used her time well; she certainly did not need a "year" to do her make-up and her hair! A clearer proof of distinction can scarcely be given. This difference becomes still more evident through the celestial globe in her right hand, an attribute about which her parents had some doubt. Patina responds, however, with a quote from a letter written by Thomas More to his daughter Margaret in which he specifically advises the study of the *sphaera*. Earlier in the book Patina also discusses Holbein's portrait of More's family, in which the oldest daughter is naturally included.

So the circle is complete: one learned woman becomes the inspirational example for another. The importance of connoisseurship would become more widely recognised only in the course of the 18th century. Women connoisseurs remained rare even then. Carola Catharina Patina constitutes a rare early example of a dilettante who was indeed delighted but was herself not artistically active.

KATLIJNE VAN DER STIGHELEN

18th and 19th centuries

The classification of many women artists of the 18th and 19th centuries as "amateur" rather than "professional" is extremely problematic and generally involves the imposition of 20th-century categorisations of artistic quality on work produced by women operating within a very different cultural milieu. The categories of "amateur" and "professional" were not always clearly defined for the male artists of this period, let alone for women seeking access to or parity in a male-dominated field. Today, the term "amateur" takes much of its meaning from its opposition to "professional", and often implies a performance of marginal proficiency practised by those who lack commitment, are partially trained, or want in talent. In the past, art historians have often relegated many women artists to amateur status because the "professional" conditions of production have, since the early modern period, been defined by the artist's ability to claim a certain level of training and expertise, to receive some monetary compensation for his or her work, or, better still, to make a living or reputation because of the high level of skill and knowledge in the realm in which he or she "professed" expertise. These expectations were generally attainable for the men who specified such criteria, but often extremely difficult to realise for women whose other social roles prevented them from partaking in such activities. Equally problematic have been recent attempts to compensate for the past neglect of women artists by over-stressing the professional status or quality of work produced by women who were not necessarily as concerned with such qualifications as we are today.

During the 18th century, the term "amateur" also connoted another – perhaps more important – meaning, one that lingers in today's usage and which is important for an understanding of the situation of many "amateur" women artists of earlier periods. In the early modern period, "amateur" had come to indicate a member of the upper classes, one who loved, who had a passionate, even obsessive interest in art but primarily as a connoisseur – a collector or expert in the knowledge of art. Members of this class needed no recompense for the practice of art and, in general, preferred not to dirty or disfigure their hands with manual labour. The "professional" making of art was stigmatised as a lower- or middle-class activity, and upper-class amateurs of this sort learned the practice of art only in so far as it advanced their expertise in the understanding and knowledge of artistic matters. Since the Renaissance, many women, such as Isabella d'Este and Queen Christina of Sweden, had taken great delight in the arts and, participating as patrons, collectors and connoisseurs in the artistic cultures of their periods, had qualified as "amateurs" according to this usage of the term. During the 18th century, this royal model for the amateur was continued with Sophie Albertine, Princess of Sweden; Christiane Louise, Countess of Solms-Laubach and the wife of Prince Friedrich Carl Ludwig von Hohenlohe-Kirchberg; and Caroline Luise, Margravine of Baden. Certainly, the love of and desire for knowledge in artistic matters continued to be a major motivation for many women artists through the 19th and 20th centuries.

The term "amateur" began to take on a more marginal connotation towards the end of the 18th century. Seeking to elevate their profession and to ensure their autonomous control over the production and interpretation of art, the men regulating the professional status of male artists through institutions such as art schools and academies protected their occupation by increasingly placing limitations on various types of artists and the works they produced. As well as male amateurs and practitioners of non-academic genre and media, upper- and middle-class women (many of whom were receiving a greater education in art and art-related matters than they had previously) were restricted from partaking in the privileges of such professional organisations. For example, in 1770 the French Académie Royale decreed that no more than four women at a time could be members, and although two women artists were among the founding members of the Royal Academy in England in 1768, no others were accorded such privileges until well into the 20th century (see Academies of Art survey). Many women, whose skills and knowledge might have qualified them to work on a level consistent with their male counterparts, were thus denied the professional certification and access to the modes of training, production and marketing that would have potentially enabled them to compete as equals. Consequently, women artists, save for an exceptional few, were unable to rise above the amateur level. In addition, the association of women with this status had a reciprocal feminising and marginalising effect on social perceptions of amateur work in general.

Cultural constructions of gender and contemporary definitions of women's social and biological functions and acceptable behaviour and activities contributed greatly to perceptions of women as "professional" or "amateur" during the 18th and 19th centuries. The ideologies of gender delineated by contemporary philosophers and cultural critics such as Jean-Jacques Rousseau stressed that a woman's "natural" place, because of her child-bearing capability, was linked to the private and domestic sphere – the home – this being the site of motherhood and the care of the family. Just as a woman's place was thus restricted to the privacy of her home, the male's place was to provide for her by labouring in the public world. The industrial revolution and capitalism encouraged the growth of professionalism throughout most male occupations of the bourgeois classes. This concept of professionalism encouraged the individual (usually one of male gender) to declare an avocation for a particular activity, to seek education in the necessary "science" and skills and, finally, to have his validity endorsed and accredited by the certifying institutions of university or academy. Indeed, such systems were inherently dependent upon a division of labour in which the male professional worked for a wage in the public world while his female dependants remained at home providing for the domestic needs of the family. These divisions of public and private spheres according to differences in gender were increasingly manifested and promoted throughout Western Europe and America by changes in the urban fabric, particularly in the separation of the home from the place of work. The situation differed from that of periods before industrialisation, when work and domestic life frequently shared the same space and women might take part as vital participants in various aspects of a family business. Even in the exceptional case that a woman artist was talented and received adequate training, she was generally expected to relegate her artistic interests to a position secondary to her domestic duties, especially after marriage and the birth of children. Consequently many women artists were, by definition, not professional and therefore amateur and, despite their relative skill or knowledge, able to practise art only as an interest ancillary to their basic social function or their domestic roles as daughters, mothers and wives.

18th century

Both the making of art objects and connoisseurship became widespread and acceptable "amateur" activities for upper-class women to fill their free time during this period. The economic prosperity, diversity of consumer goods and services, and greater leisure time generated by agricultural innovation and the growing industrialism and commerce of the 18th century enabled well-born men and women to pursue and develop a variety of educated interests and skills. At this time art and connoisseurship also became important components of the cultural exchange among and throughout the greater European community. As more and more members of the upper classes took advantage of the new transportation and mobility and travelled through the major cities of Western Europe for reasons of pleasure, business or education (institutionalised as the Grand Tour), the knowledge of and the ability to discuss art, architecture and archaeology became important indications of upper-class status and heritage while abroad. Seeing the appropriate monuments and collections, learning to discuss personal experiences and responses in a seemly and knowledgeable manner, and collecting souvenirs and art objects to attest to their travels on their return home became the goal of many Grand Tourists. Although the personal pleasure and educational development of individual women were seldom the motivating factors for this type of travel as they were for young gentlemen, many women accompanied their male relatives on such journeys and were subject to and influenced by these cultural preoccupations and "amateur" activities no less than their male companions. An exceptional few, such as Elizabeth Percy, Duchess of Northumberland, who assembled a small collection of paintings for herself during her tour of the Netherlands in 1771, were able to make purchases according to their own tastes only if in possession of their own fortunes or generous allowances. In general, however, very few women had the personal economic resources that enabled them to indulge their interests to quite the same extent as men. They were able to view those important monuments that were considered appropriate for their sight. Ancient art and archaeology, linked with the male dominion of classical language and literature, were often deemed inappropriate topics for women to study. "Modern" art (art made during and after the 16th century) was considered more comprehensible for female understanding as long as the subject matter was not too violent or sexual, and women could acquire an extensive knowledge of this material in the public and private collections they saw during their travels, thus qualifying as "amateurs" in one of the contemporary usages of the term.

In the expatriate circles in which Grand Tourists found themselves during their travels abroad, class restrictions normally observed at home became more relaxed and there were greater mobility and interchange between people of different classes. Rome, with its rich treasures of art and architecture from both ancient and modern eras, was a primary goal not only for aristocratic tourists but also for artists. Many young artists of different nationalities journeyed there in order to study the art of the past, to advance their reputations and to make themselves known to potential patrons. In this foreign context, men and women of the upper classes mingled socially and shared interests with artists of their own nationalities as well as with those of their host country. The patronage and purchase of art – particularly portraits and landscapes commemorative of their experiences – were also important activities that brought these two segments of society together. Indeed, social visits to the ateliers of the leading masters became desirable tourist attractions, integral components of the spectacle of the Grand Tour, and further stimulus for developing general interest and connoisseurship in the arts. These connections and intellectual pursuits, both amateur and professional, were carefully maintained and nurtured by both artists and patrons on their return home. Once at home, women as well as male "amateurs" developed similar relationships of patronage and intellectual exchange with the artists of their localities. Viewing habits that had developed on the Grand Tour were continued on their return; the commissioning of portraits and other genres of painting, visits to artists' studios, and attendance at collections, exhibitions, museums and picture-auctions all continued to be popular entertainments. In France during the early to mid-18th century, such women amateurs played important roles as purveyors of culture through the new social convention of the salon. Within the public rooms and boudoirs of many great Parisian houses, the *salonnières* – educated upper-class hostesses, many of whom qualified as amateurs because of their strong intellectual interests in the arts – brought together artists, writers, *philosophes* and scientists with members of the upper classes for entertainment, polite conversation and intellectual exchange. The *salonnières*' pursuit and encouragement of the arts were reflected not only by the hospitality they offered to artists, architects and connoisseurs, but also in the patronage they extended in their careful and elaborate decoration of the salons and boudoirs in which such assemblies and conversations were held.

For upper-class art lovers, the motivation to understand and be knowledgeable about artistic matters led to their experimentation with the actual making of images and objects. Authority over the arts for both connoisseurs and artists was divided between those who claimed expertise in the *scientia* – the science or knowledge of art – and *arte* – the technical skill and dexterity necessary for the production of art. Artists claimed both distinctions, and consequently amateurs often extended their study to the actual production of images and objects in order both to enhance and validate their critical judgement and expertise. Many women amateurs began their practice of art for just such reasons. An excellent example of this type of female amateur was Caroline Luise, Margravine of Baden. She was born Landgravine of Hesse-Darmstadt, and in 1751 married Margrave Carl Friedrich of Baden-Durlach. Her interest in collecting art led her to study painting with Liotard and she became known as the Hessian Minerva. She was made a member of the Royal Danish Academy of Fine Arts in 1763 and of the Accademia degli Arcadi in Rome in 1776. Another amateur similarly motivated was Jeanne Poisson, Marquise de Pompadour, the mistress of Louis XV, whose interests in philosophy, music, architecture and the arts led her to the extensive study and patronage of a variety of arts and artists. Her intellectual passions also induced her to become first an accomplished draughtswoman, and later to develop proficiencies in painting and printmaking as well. Such women were true "amateurs" in every aspect of the 18th-century usage of the word; their connoisseurship and strong interests in the history and discourse of art were passionately combined and manifested in their physical and personal involvement with the actual creative feat. Indeed, Mme de Pompadour's myriad interests, personal expertise and the connections she nurtured within the cultural milieu enabled her to be a powerful mediator between the king, court and contemporary intellectuals and artists, and transformed her patronage and favour into an influential force in the Parisian art world.

The ability to manoeuvre successfully within elite circles, to have sufficient knowledge of the cultural concerns of this stratum of society in order to engage in polite conversation, led many of the upper classes to provide their daughters with at least rudimentary skills in the visual arts, music, literature and contemporary languages. Concerning amateur painting and other "harmless amusements for young people", the amateur artist Mary Delany noted in 1753: "*Painting* has *fewer objections*, and generally *leads people into much better company*." In England, several women of the upper classes were noted for their artistic work, including Lady Diana Beauclerk; Lady Anson (née Lady Elizabeth Hardwick), whose painting was praised by Mrs Delany; Mrs Rhoda Astley, whose portraits of family members were displayed at Seaton Delavel, Northumberland, and commented upon by Bishop Pococke in 1760; Lady Fitzwilliam, whose work was displayed at Wentworth House; Lady Caroline Stanhope, a relative of the Earl of Harrington, whose paintings hung at Elvaston Castle, Derbyshire; and Margaret, Countess of Lucan, whose miniature work was commented upon by both Horace Walpole and Sir Joshua Reynolds.

Artistic "accomplishments", as ladies' amateur art work came to be called, were considered desirable and encouraged for several reasons. As noted above, these activities provided women of the leisured classes with entertainment, an outlet for their creative impulses and intellectual curiosity, served as busy work or diversion to fill excess time, or escapist solace for those whose personal life was unhappy. For the widowed Mrs Delany, painting and drawing not only occupied much of her day but also complemented and augmented her intellectual interest in the art she saw (and frequently borrowed for further study) in the collections of her friends and relatives. The talented Maria Cosway (q.v.), forbidden from painting professionally by her jealous husband, the miniaturist Richard Cosway, distracted herself from her unhappy marriage in the private pursuit of painting and music. But painting was also a social activity that many women practised in the company of other women. Commenting upon a visit from a young friend, Mrs Delany wrote:

> I am happy to have her; she has spread before me some of her drawings that she has done since I saw her, and they are charming. I lent her some prints of Claude, that she has copied to great perfection; and now we shall paint and draw and chatter together as fast as our hands, eyes and tongues can go.

Women amateurs gathered not only to work together, but to discuss art and to show one another their works. Many women hung their own work in the rooms set aside for their use, and this served several functions. No formal or public venue for the display of amateur achievements existed for either men or women; many women lacked the economic resources to purchase works by professional artists and thus decorated empty domestic spaces with their own work; others were thereby enabled to inject an element of self-expression or to assert personal control over their immediate environment. In these boudoirs, drawing-rooms and informal workrooms, women visited, discussed and exchanged work with one another. Mrs Delany, whose rooms were decorated with her own work ("abundant evidence of her noble industry and intellect", as the diarist Sophie von la Roche commented), shared her artistic interests with Lady Andover, also an amateur painter; the Duchess of Leeds brought Lady Vanburgh and then later Lady Cardigan and Lady Westmorland to see her pictures. She herself became an attraction or curiosity for well-connected foreign tourists, including Sophie von la Roche, to visit when in London. At her death in 1788, most of her work was willed to various friends, many of whom were noblewomen who had shared her interests. Indeed, the amateur context of women's drawing-rooms extended beyond the discussion and making of art to the trade and exchange of pictures as well. Elizabeth Percy, Duchess of Northumberland, described her visit while touring the Netherlands to see the "fine pictures" of a Mme Boshart: "she is a woman of fashion but notwithstanding, would (which is almost the case in general here) part with them for a good price."

While the knowledge and practice of art were important mechanisms of social bonding for many women, they could also operate as exclusionary tactics as well. Ladies' "accomplishments" served to provide a basis of class differentiation from the encroachment of the increasingly wealthy middle classes who sought affiliation with the aristocracy. Knowledge of the arts, the ability to perform, to purchase and to converse appropriately, constituted a constantly changing coded system of taste controlled by the upper classes who had the time and resources to participate in such activities. To a certain degree, the free time of upper-class women, the leisure activities and hobbies with which they filled that free time, and the changing criteria for women's education during this period served as exclusionary devices to shut out those who wished to enter higher social circles. Attempts by the middle classes to cross class boundaries were thwarted by subtle strategic changes within these cultural codes, which served to exclude those who might have the wealth and leisure time, but who had not been born, raised or educated within the class that regulated cultural practices. Women, as well as men, had increasingly decisive roles in this process, and the well-born, educated lady "amateur" thus served as an important component in the maintenance of class distinctions.

Within the elite circles of the aristocracy, the development of women's interest and education in the arts served another important social function, that of making the lady amateur a more attractive commodity in the matrimonial marketplace. Not only were her accomplishments, social graces and leisure activities capable of reflecting and augmenting her husband's social status, but as romantic love and mutual attraction rather than the unification of political and landed interests became the basis of matrimonial choice during the 18th century, the lady amateur made an attractive companion for the gentleman amateur, whose interests and education her knowledge complemented. Within the ritual of courtship, the performative spectacle of the young woman dancing, drawing, singing or playing a musical instrument allowed male attention to be focused on her person, while "maidenly modesty" was maintained in a socially acceptable manner through her concentration and preoccupation with her immediate task. In her absence, the exhibition of a young lady's accomplishments – by means of musical instruments, drawings, watercolours, needlework and other "busy" work within the public rooms of her family's residence – formed an important element in the process of her debut into society and the proclamation of her marriageability. For example, the early 18th-century English art chronicler George Vertue reported that when the Princess Augusta arrived in London to marry Frederick, Prince of Wales, her paintings were prominently displayed to the court for a year after her marriage. Such exhibitions of a young lady's artistic skill and accomplishment also served as important models for imitation within the descending ranks of the aristocracy, gentry and middle classes who sought to prepare their daughters for socially advantageous marriages by having them trained in fashionable accomplishments; Vertue also noted that the paintings of Miss Da Costa (the daughter of a London merchant and businessman) decorated an entire cabinet of her family's house.

As the knowledge and practice of art became important social assets, art training became an important part of women's education. Young women were often trained in the practice of art on an individual basis at home and by private instructors. These tutors were artists who were employed by great noble families to care for their various artistic needs, including the maintenance and restoration of collections, decoration and the painting of portraits as well as the artistic education of the younger members of the family, or they were artists who were either desirous of supplementing their income (as did Bernard Lens with Mrs Delany, the Misses Da Costa and Lady Helena Percival, the daughter of the 1st Earl of Egremont) or unable to subsist from the sale of their own work and thus reduced to teaching in order to earn a living. The daughters of families less wealthy or prominent received art instruction within the confines of one of the many new boarding and finishing schools often founded towards the end of the century by impoverished gentlewomen. In this context, drawing, languages, music and dancing were supplements to the regular curriculum and required additional fees. Women with economic means, previous training and a strong commitment to the arts could also seek instruction from more prominent artists if any were willing to accept female students; thus Mary Delany studied with William Hogarth and Mme de Pompadour with Boucher.

Women's training in the arts differed greatly from that of male artists. Distinct media and techniques for women's practice were stressed: line-drawing, crayon, watercolour, pastel and occasionally miniature painting on ivory were advocated as the most seemly media for women's performance; their perceived qualities of delicacy, meticulous execution and preciosity were considered to be innately feminine. In general, women, even those of the upper classes, seldom had the privilege of a specially assigned room to serve as their studio; the spaces for both their domestic duties and their amusements had to overlap and be multi-functional. The cleanliness and daintiness of the female hands and body had to be maintained as well. Consequently, amateur women artists sought and were encouraged to pursue artistic recreations that had a certain ease of execution, were tidy, and that used easily prepared, fast-drying materials such as ready-to-use watercolours and tube paint. Besides requiring compact workspace, these artistic activities had to employ equipment that was limited in quantity, portable and easily stored away so that such personal occupations would not interfere with the other activities of the family. Work in pastel was perceived to be especially appropriate for women because it was associated with the work of the Venetian artist Rosalba Carriera (q.v.), a woman artist who had excelled in the technique. Its light palette was also reminiscent of the rococo interiors dominated by the female *salonnières*; its delicacy of touch was viewed as akin to that of lace-work (the production of which had long been the domain of women) and its chalk pigments were similar to those used in women's make-up. Miniature painting, with its costly materials and minutely detailed finish, was not only seen as jewel-like in its execution and scale, but was frequently enframed by gems and metal-work and functioned as jewellery for the adornment of the female body. It, too, became a highly popular medium for women's amateur work.

Many exceptional women did work on a grander scale in the messier, smellier and technically more complicated medium of oil-painting, such as Mrs Delany (who had a servant to grind and mix colours and to clean up after her); printmaking, as practised by Mme de Pompadour and Isabella Howard (the second wife of the 3rd Earl Howard); and even in sculpture, in which Anne Seymour Damer (q.v.) excelled. But these media were seen as requiring an education, intelligence and physical strength not believed to be present in the female body. Moreover, painting and sculpture, especially in the genres of history and figure painting, were increasingly privileged as high art and elevated above other media, techniques and subject matter by the institutions of academy and museum, both dominated by professional male artists. For women to work at this level was felt during the late 18th century to demonstrate an ambition that was both defeminising and "unnatural".

Much of the artistic training that women received was by no means intended to prepare them to work at a level commensurate with that of male professionals. Frequently, women's training followed that of their male counterparts only through the earliest stages of the usual curriculum, deliberately leaving them at an adolescent level of expertise, which, to a large degree, pre-determined their amateur status. Instruction for both men and women began with the learning of draughtsmanship. Starting with pen or pencil, novices learned first to draw by copying simple shapes and outlines, advancing from these to more complicated forms using the techniques of chiaroscuro and colouring with crayon, pastel or watercolour washes. Whereas male students then usually progressed to working in oil or stone, the training for most women stopped at this intermediary stage and most lady amateurs continued to work only in these "lesser" media. Indeed, when the French Academy limited the number of female academicians to four in 1770, it concurrently opened its enrolment of women amateurs in its drawing classes. Not only were drawing and watercolour often ranked as preliminary stages in the training of artists, they also continued to be used by professional artists for working up preparatory designs and sketches before beginning the final finished product in oil and stone. This also contributed to the perception of the media most frequently used by women as preparatory and peripheral.

Apart from the more traditional media of "high art", women artists worked in a variety of materials and methods ranging from embroidery and needlework, wax modelling, shell and beadwork, cut-paper work and collage, the painting of fans, china, small furniture and other decorative objects, to the construction of jewellery and other artistic *objets* with unusual material such as hair and feathers. Mrs Delany, who spent most of her artistic life painting, is better known today for the delicate paper mosaic flower studies she made in the latter years of her life. She also produced several shellwork pictures as well as silhouettes, embroidered pictures and featherwork. Several of these media – particularly textile work – were considered to be appropriate for female practice because of their applicability to the functioning or decoration of the domestic context. Their focus on small minute detail also called forth – and served to display – the female virtues of patience, diligence and perseverance. Indeed, many of these techniques and materials – such as pastel portraiture and watercolour washes – came to be seen as rather feminine activities because of their marked popularity with women practitioners.

For many women amateurs, however, the choice of odd materials or techniques was simply an ingenious and imaginative way to provide for creative aspirations within their limited contexts. In general, women amateurs demonstrated a remarkable ability to compensate for their lack of resources in the assembly, reshaping and personalisation of their immediate visual experience. The techniques of collage and *découpage* – the piecing together of images appropriated from other sources – particularly satisfied amateur desires for both viewing and making images and reached their most monumental manifestation in the late 18th-century decorative fad, the "print room". A selection of reproductive prints was pasted directly on to the walls of a special room or cabinet in imitation of picture galleries and then framed with engraved or cut-out paper swags, bows, medallions and borders. Lady Louisa Conolly constructed a print room (the Small Dining-Room) in the 1760s and 1770s at Castletown (Co. Kildare, Ireland); the Countess of Egremont (wife of the 3rd Earl) decorated the Great North Dressing-Room at Petworth, Sussex, in this manner around 1801; Mrs Chute and her nieces were responsible for pasting up the print room at The Vyne, Hampshire, in 1815. For amateurs such as these, the print room offered a relatively inexpensive way of practising the aesthetic judgements of connoisseurship in the collecting, indexing and arranging of important works of art; for other women, the design, assembly and decoration of the spaces around the prints provided them with a means for creative expression. Collage and the print room gave women the opportunity to appropriate and make their own the images and ideas generally controlled by men; similarly, the choice of the new and strange materials that many employed in their work allowed women artists to carve out their own sphere of artistic production. Moreover, women's artistic skills displayed in "marginal" materials (beads, shells, hair, etc.) were more acceptable in that they did not compete with the work of male artists on either a professional or an amateur level.

Subject matter as well as media took on gendered implications as certain genres were both favoured by women and advocated for their use. Women, even those who excelled in the early stages of their training, were effectively prevented from progressing to professional status by their prohibition from attending the life-drawing classes, as many scholars have noted. Up to this point in the artist's education, the student learned first by copying earlier masters' works, or from drawing subjects within the minor genres of still-life, landscape and animal painting. Life-drawing classes, in which the student learned to draw the human body from a nude live model, was conducted and regulated by the official art schools and academies that were dedicated to the production of professional artists. Female students were banned from attending these classes on moral grounds. As the understanding of and proficiency in the depiction of the workings of the human body were deemed essential to an artist's ability to manipulate the expressive potential of the figure in history painting, the highest of genres, women were effectively prevented from participating in this domain. Lack of life-class training discouraged women from figure drawing except on an amateur basis. Moreover, critics generally held women's lack of this crucial step in the training of the professional artists against them regardless of whatever their real skill or achievement might be. Instead, both professional and amateur women artists produced works in the lower genres of still-life, flower-painting, landscape, domestic topics and portraiture. This limiting range of subject matter both contributed and responded to contemporary polarisations of female and male spheres that in turn were linked to the gendered opposition of the feminine nature and emotion versus masculine culture and reason. Women's art was on a small, precious and intimate scale, portraying their personal, particular experience of botanical subjects, animals, landscape and the "natural" human topics found in the home, while men's art was more typified by the generalising, intellectualising, philosophically elevated "grand style" of history painting.

19th century

During the 19th century women of the elite classes continued to draw and paint much as they had during the 18th. Princess Eugenie of Sweden, Princess Marie Christine d'Orléans and Queen Victoria and her daughters were all committed amateur artists as were many women of the aristocracy, such as Louise de Broglie, Comtesse d'Haussonville; Catherine Maria, Countess of Charleville; and Louisa, Marchioness of Waterford. However, as men of mercantile or professional occupation attained greater wealth and independence, many from the middle classes sought to demonstrate their new social mobility through imitation of upper-class behaviour and patterns of consumption. Their wives and daughters were encouraged to partake in the leisure activities of aristocratic women (albeit on a more limited basis) and to become accomplished in the arts. Indeed, the disciplined instruction of most women of the higher classes in drawing and painting, regardless of their personal inclination or skill, resulted in much art of mediocre quality, which contributed to the deflating value of amateur work during the 19th century. Social biases against women earning their living remained and became even stronger during this period as women's roles became more entrenched within the domestic context. However, their artistic training did allow women a marginally acceptable professional option if they were orphaned, widowed or faced with destitution. In such circumstances, most women with a modicum of education and possessing some accomplishment sought employment as governesses. Book illustration, decorative painting, the hand-colouring of prints and the teaching of art also offered semi-professional options to make a living, of which many in such situations took advantage. Emily Mary Osborn's painting *Nameless and Friendless* (1857) depicts one such woman, accompanied by her young son, forced by widowhood or poverty to leave her "proper" domestic context. She has ventured into the public marketplace, in the attempt to sell the paintings or drawings previously produced solely for her own or her husband's amusement. Mary P. Harrison, an amateur painter of flower pictures, eventually supported her invalid husband and three children with botanical illustration. Clara Maria Wheatley Pope illustrated botanical texts following the death of her painter husband in 1801, and even after remarrying continued to teach painting to young women, including Princess Sophia of Gloucester and the Duchess of St Albans. For the most part, however, amateur work was the only completely legitimised artistic activity for women, and women amateur painters proliferated during the 19th century.

Middle-class women of the Victorian period were increasingly held responsible for the consumption of material goods for their family's immediate needs as well as for the decoration and maintenance – "the arranging" – of the family domicile. With the greater restrictions on the resources, leisure time and domestic environment of the middle-class woman, much of her effort was expended upon artistic activities that affected her family's lifestyle, the early training and education of her children, and the decoration of her clothing and domestic environment. Indeed, many of the earliest art schools were established to train women for employment, such as the French Ecole Gratuite de Dessin pour les Jeunes Filles (opened in 1803), which focused on

teaching the design and decoration of feminine and domestic artefacts such as textiles, painted wallpaper, lace, artificial flowers, fans, lampshades, cameos, vignettes, ceramic and enamel painting, book bindings and tapestries. The watercolours of the Irish artist Louisa Payne Gallway depicted a variety of topics and were set in a screen that was entitled *Memoirs of Old Haunts and Happy Days* (1867) and given as a present to her cousin. Idleness in women, even those of the leisured classes, was a social vice to be avoided or masked by the artistic construction or improvement of such functional objects. This linkage of female work with the design and decoration of functional household items would contribute to the marginalisation of "craft" (as opposed to "art") that underpins evaluations of much of Western visual culture. Wives and daughters were encouraged to spend a portion of their day in the parlour or the morning-room at the small worktables assigned to their personal use. Pencil or pen-and-ink sketching, watercolour and gouache remained popular media for women's work as they had in the late 18th century.

Even within the privacy of the home, a woman's work was not conducted without scrutiny or restriction. She was schooled to be sensitive and submissive to those around her. Many women served as amateur assistants to their husbands and fathers, as did the British woman Jane Webb Loudon, who illustrated her husband's *Encyclopaedia of Gardening* (1834), or as Lady Wilkinson did with her husband, Sir Gardiner Wilkinson, in his *Desert Plants of Egypt*. The time, expenditure and even the choice of subject matter of many amateur women artists were often closely supervised and regulated by their husbands or fathers. Amateur art was for the most part anonymously produced, and frequently, if exhibited or published, ascribed as "By a Lady". The American flower painter Susan Fenimore Cooper published her illustrated *Rural Hours by a Lady* in 1850 anonymously; her name is never given, but her father, James Fenimore Cooper, is frequently credited as "The Author of *The Deerslayer*". Consequently, much amateur work has been ignored because of the difficulty of attributing it to any specific artist.

Nineteenth-century attitudes concerning women held that their natural emotional and responsive sensitivities equipped them to play a central and refining role within the family and the home – and by extension society in general. Female accomplishments, even on an amateur level, served not only as entertainment for themselves, but also to provide a comfortable and elegant home for the benefit of the husband and children. As women's lives became increasingly restricted to the domestic and the interior, their role within this limited context was to respond to the emotional, physical and material needs of the members of their household. As in the 18th century, painting and sketching were social activities, undertaken in the company of other women, usually a sister, mother, daughter or close personal friend. Many women practised art only during their childhood and adolescence, abandoning these activities when they married and had children, while others kept up their interests throughout their lifetime. Even those who had received an excellent and advanced education in the arts and had briefly attempted to paint on a professional standing, such as Edma Pontillon, sister of Berthe Morisot, often practised only on an amateur level after marriage. The resulting drawings and paintings depict the specific places and activities with which women associated themselves and manifest the boundaries placed upon their social experience and domain. The watercolours of the English artist Mary Ellen Best recorded the rooms of the house she lived in, depicting the furnishings, occupants and activities of each, as did an entire album produced by Charlotte Bosanquet and the pen-and-ink washes produced by the Irish artist Caroline Hamilton. Much of women's amateur art was characterised by a more personal, intimate and particularised response to their individual situation, focusing on their emotive response to the everyday circumstances of domestic family life and to their restricted views of nature. Moreover, 19th-century ideologies of gender held that women were innately closer to nature. Local landscape, domestic animals and garden plants and flowers were easily accessible and, as in earlier centuries, popular choices as subject matter for amateur women artists. Studies of vegetable and animal matter were also easily adapted to textile design and interior decoration. Paintings of flowers, in particular, became highly popular and feminised with a poetical and sentimental language of their own. For many women, however, close study of animals and flowers led to a greater intellectual interest and knowledge of natural history, zoology, entomology and botany – topics of inquiry not usually encouraged in women. English amateurs such as Priscilla Susan Bury, Elizabeth Twining,

Lady Harriet Anne Hooker Thiselton Dyer, Beatrix Potter and Marianne North; Americans such as Susan Fenimore Cooper and Mrs E.W. Wirt; the Irish amateurs Lydia Shackleton and Lady Blake; the French amateur Natalie, Baronne Renaud; and the Australian Louisa Anne Meredith all became renowned naturalists through their amateur artistic study, and several became published authors and illustrators.

Domestic subject matter was also deemed singularly appropriate for women artists, besides being that which was most readily available for study. Genre paintings of the rituals of a woman's life – household work, courtship, motherhood, family life and children – or cautionary tales warning against the transgression of these norms, were extremely popular with both professional and amateur women artists throughout the 19th century. Such topics both reiterated the "natural" domestic sphere of femininity, and painters such as the four Hayllar sisters, Edith and Jessica in particular, produced and exhibited images depicting a serene and highly ordered domesticity in which the preferred female roles were carefully represented. Although these women could and did at times exhibit at venues such as the Royal Academy, they were considered to offer little or no challenge to the subject matter, techniques and economic success of male artists of professional status. By means of their sketched notes of family life, many women became responsible for the unofficial recording of family memory, thereby extending their genetic and reproductive functions into the artistic context. Portraits of relatives or close connections, such as those produced by Cassandra Austen of her sister Jane (c.1810), by Amelia Curran of Percy Bysshe Shelley (1819) and by Adèle Hugo in 1838 of her children, helped to document family likenesses, connections and lineage. Not only were the appearances of their family members and immediate environment preserved, but women's amateur sketching recorded the events of day-to-day home life, special occasions, or journeys both local and abroad and further served to form an archive of family memory.

Of growing popularity through the course of the 19th century was the organisation of women's drawings, designs and vignettes into sketchbooks and albums. These collections of small pictures were usually arranged according to a general organising principle: they held only a particular type of image, such as portraits of family members, or a record of botanical study, studies from other artists' work, or they served as a souvenir by recording a particular event or journey. Sometimes the work was by a single artist, while at other times such albums brought together samples of others' work as well. Either way, they served as small-scale records of taste and personal response on the part of an individual woman. Many albums were simple sketchbooks while others could be richly-bound compilations of watercolours, sketches, drawings and portraits made by their owners together with similar images exchanged with other amateur artists. They also frequently contained reproductive prints, postcards and images drawn from the popular press.

After the development of photography, such women amateurs as Julia Margaret Cameron (q.v.) and Clementina, Viscountess Hawarden (q.v.) practised the new technology as well as collecting the images that were most often housed in such albums. When Adolphe Alfonse Diseri introduced the relatively inexpensive *carte-de-visite* portrait photographs in the mid-19th century, the collection of these small, easily exchangeable images in albums became a tremendous fad, quickly replacing the collections of drawn and painted portraits, and eventually developing into the traditional photograph album. In Switzerland, the Russian Marguerite de Krüdener brought her paintings and drawings of her home, holidays and portraits of her family members in discrete albums, while her sister Marie included in hers a *mélange* of materials including pen and ink drawings, watercolours, maps, photographs, prints, pressed flowers and butterflies. Such accretions, in which female "amateur" response to the visual environment and artistic culture was collaged on to the pages of a book, bear a resemblance to the 18th-century print rooms. Both allowed women to imitate the larger collections of old masters and ancient sculpture in which their male relatives were able to indulge themselves. The difference in scale between such collections as the print room and the album reflects both the increased restriction on women's activities during the 19th century as well as the extension of such activities for women from the upper classes to the small-scale endeavours of the middle classes. In such albums female response was easily contained, privatised or stored away, to be brought out later for display and discussion in the company of other women, with male admirers, or for the amusement of visitors and relatives. Many albums were frequently exchanged or given away as gifts to female family members and close friends. Albums and the types of images they contained became a peculiarly feminine genre of art production that in turn largely shaped the art made for them. Julia Margaret Cameron, for example, produced her photographs as unique objects, but always with an eye to their inclusion in the albums she presented to her friends and family. The containment and concealment of women's artistic work within such albums point to the relative unimportance of their particular vision frozen on paper and indicates instead the greater importance placed on the spectacle or display of the lady artists as they sketched, painted or looked at these albums under the gaze of their male relations or acquaintances.

Many of the educational strategies for teaching young women proper accomplishments – private drawing masters, governesses and finishing schools – remained the same from the 18th century to the mid-19th. However, the middle classes were not always able to afford these more expensive forms of training for their daughters. In such cases, responsibility for teaching drawing and painting to the young girls of a household often fell to their mother or another female family member who had some skill in such matters. The Barker sisters, Leila, Octavia and Lucette, all amateur painters of animals, flowers and landscape topics, were taught to draw by their father, Thomas Barker, a Yorkshire vicar who objected to their working for recompense. By the end of the 18th century, a burgeoning trade in popular literature for female audiences had developed, and it continued to expand in the 19th century. Drawing manuals and "how-to" books such as *The Lady's Drawing Book and Compleat Florist* of 1755 and *The Student's Treasure, A New Drawing Book ...* of 1804, ladies' magazines and periodicals ranging from Rudolph Ackermann's *Repository of Arts* and the *Ladies Monthly Museum* to *Gazette des Femmes* and *La Mode Illustrée* provided elementary lessons in drawing and watercolour, instructions in the appropriate response to and appreciation of art, and frequently household hints, botanical information, sewing and embroidery patterns, fashion plates and social gossip. Entrepreneurs such as Ackermann, who capitalised on the popularity of his own magazine by opening a London shop of the same name, specialised in art supplies, prints, art books and other commodities to exploit the women's market for art goods. Such literature and resources not only helped to provide an inexpensive education in the arts, but also enabled women to work within the seclusion of their own homes, thereby preserving domestic sanctity.

In general, speciality or professional training for women artists went against bourgeois definitions of feminine respectability. In Britain (as was typical of most Western nations) women were not allowed into the Royal Academy schools until the late 1850s, after a long feminist campaign. Meanwhile, many women attended the informal ateliers or academies founded by artists of both sexes who wished to profit from the tremendous amateur demand for instruction. Young women from both Britain and America whose parents could support their ambitions both financially and ideologically travelled to Paris and Rome, where masters were accepting of female students and society was less concerned with the transgressions of foreigners. Others took advantage of the local and national schools of design that, starting in the 1840s, were established to train and make employable women without other means of support, in the more mundane aspects of commercial design and illustration. Women who wished to practise art on the more serious basis associated with male professionalism agitated for art schools modelled after those for men – including carefully monitored life classes – and were quick to differentiate their goals from those of their amateur sisters.

Art classes conducted for amateurs allowed women an option to leave their domestic environments in order to extend their social circle and to participate in the public sphere on a limited basis. Another opportunity to leave the safe environment of the home was membership in one of the many amateur sketching and watercolour societies that were founded during the 19th century. These clubs, whose organisation ranged from the local to the national levels, brought amateur ladies, or ladies and gentlemen, together for the "mutual improvement in painting and drawing and the cultivation of a taste for art" (as was stated by the founders of the Irish Amateur Drawing Society). Apart from offering convivial social advantages, these groups brought together people of similar interests for lectures, discussion and sketching expeditions, disseminated interest in art, dispensed instruction for their members, and also provided opportunities for exhibition.

Exhibition became increasingly difficult for both male and female amateur painters over the course of the 19th century. While women were not completely banned from showing works even in venues as prestigious as the Paris Salon or the Royal Academy's annual exhibition, amateur work in general was increasingly marginalised in order to protect the primacy of the male professionals. With the mid-19th-century foundation of academies for the serious training of professional women artists throughout Western Europe and America, women artists also attempted to control and elevate their position in the art world to match the standards of male professional artists. Like the male academicians of the previous century, they, too, sought to emphasise the legitimacy of their occupation through the certification of their members and dissociation from the mediocrity connoted by the female amateur tradition. Young women whose strongest motivation for the study of art was to become "accomplished" according to social convention, or to develop a moderate interest in a pleasurable time-filling activity, became known as "academy belles". Their tenuous commitment, undeveloped or lack of talent, and conventional taste for predictable subject matter (often of sentimental or domestic topics) led to their ostracism first by male artists, and then by their more committed sisters who sought to separate themselves from this marginalised group. Outside the venue of their own amateur associations, women amateurs were frequently either charged to exhibit with their professional colleagues or ostracised completely.

As the system of workshop and private patronage typical of early modern artistic production was replaced by galleries and the public exhibition of art as the primary conduits through which an artist's work could become known, the institutions that sponsored and regulated such displays increasingly restricted both female and male amateur painters. The economic exigencies of the life of the professional artist necessitated the ability to seek out and woo patrons, dealers and publicity, and involved aggressive qualities that contradicted the virtues of womanly modesty and were deemed socially unacceptable as well as actively discouraged. Women, even those who had overcome the difficulties of obtaining professional instruction, were pushed back into amateur status by the denial of access to the major venues of visual consumption and profitable exchange: academic exhibitions and gallery salerooms. Amateur women artists, particularly those of the upper classes, could and did exhibit or donate their work for charitable causes. Lady Waterford designed the cartoons for the stained-glass windows of the church of Clonegan and produced a series of frescoes for a Northumberland village school; the Princess Royal contributed one of her etchings to an auction benefiting the Crimean War effort; and Francesca Alexanders sold a series of her Tuscan drawings to benefit charity (New Haven 1994, pp.18–19). Such attempts generally only contributed to the association of amateur work with charitable and community volunteerism.

Towards the end of the 19th century, the domestic subject matter and focus of most amateur women's work found a legitimate place with the Arts and Crafts Movement. Sponsored by male aesthetes such as the members of the Pre-Raphaelite group and William Morris, this movement promulgated a return to a pre-industrial artisanship in which art, design and function were to be integrally united in the making of the craft object. Ornamental needlework, crewelwork, lace-making, wood-engraving, wallpaper design, ceramic tiles and pottery were revived and produced in the Morris firm, helped by the female members of his family, his wife Jane, his daughter May Morris, his sister-in-law Elizabeth and others. This workshop and the many that imitated it not only provided many women with professional work, but also helped to give a greater dignity, aesthetic and monetary value to the feminine "arranging" of household interior decoration for which amateur women had long been held responsible.

By the end of the 19th century a clear qualitative differentiation had been made between amateur and professional status for women as well as men. The term had come to connote a level of mediocrity, domesticity, lack of commitment and an association with volunteerism and the social hobbies of the leisured woman. For women engaged seriously in the production of art, "amateur" had become a label carefully to be avoided.

LISA HEER

Bibliography

Baldassare Castiglione, *Il libro del cortegiano*, 1528; as *The Book of the Courtier*, 1561

M. A. Vente, "De illustre Lieve-Vrouwe Broederschay te 's Hertogenbosch, 1541–1615" [The illustrious brotherhood of Our Lady in 's Hertogenbosch, 1541–1615],

Tidschrift van de Vereniging voor Nederlandse muziekgeschiedenis, xix, 1960–61, pp.32–43

Carola Catharina Patina, *Tabellae selectae ac explicatae*, Patavii [Padua], 1691

Christian Gottlieb Jöcher, *Allgemeines Gelehrten-Lexikon*, iii, Leipzig, 1715, columns 1300–01

Elizabeth Percy, Duchess of Northumberland, *A Short Tour Made in the Year One Thousand Seven Hundred and Seventy-One*, London, 1775

J.P. Neale, *Views of the Seats of Noblemen and Gentlemen in England, Wales, Scotland and Ireland*, London, 1818

The Autobiography and Correspondence of Mary Granville, Mrs Delany, ed. Lady Llanover, 6 vols, London: Bentley, 1861–2; reprinted New York: AMS Press, 1974

Edmond Vander Straeten, *La Musique aux Pays-Bas avant le XIXe siècle*, vii, Brussels: Van Trigt, 1885, p.426

George Vertue, "The Vertue note books" in *The Walpole Society*, xviii, xx, xxii, xxiv, xxvi and xxix, London: Oxford University Press, 1929–47

Claire Williams, ed., *Sophie in London, 1786: Being the Diary of Sophie von la Roche*, London: Cape, 1933

Ruth Kelso, *Doctrine for the Lady of the Renaissance*, Urbana: University of Illinois Press, 1956; reprinted 1978

M. A. Vente, "De illustre Lieve- Vrouwe Broederschay te 's Hertogenbosch, 1541–1615", *Tidschrift van de Vereniging voor Nederlandse muziekgeschiedenis*, xix, 1960–61, pp.32–43

Women Artists, 1550–1950, exh. cat., Los Angeles County Museum of Art, and elsewhere, 1976

Ian Maclean, *Woman Triumphant: Feminism in French Literature, 1610–1652*, Oxford: Clarendon Press, 1977

Desmond Guinness, "The revival of the print room", *Antique Collector*, vi, 1978, pp.88-91

Phyllis Stock, *Better than Rubies: A History of Women's Education*, New York: Putnam, 1978

Anthea Callen, *Angel in the Studio: Women in the Arts and Crafts Movement, 1870–1914*, London: Astragal, 1979; as *Women Artists of the Arts and Crafts Movement*, New York: Pantheon, 1979

Germaine Greer, *The Obstacle Race: The Fortunes of Women Painters and Their Work*, London: Secker and Warburg, and New York: Farrar Straus, 1979

Ruth Hayden, *Mrs Delany: Her Life and Her Flowers*, London: British Museum Publications, 1980; revised as *Mrs Delany's Flower Collages*, 1992

Rozsika Parker and Griselda Pollock, *Old Mistresses: Women, Art and Ideology*, London: Routledge, 1981

Rozsika Parker, *The Subversive Stitch: Embroidery and the Making of the Feminine*, London: Women's Press, 1984; New York: Routledge, 1989

Linda Woodbridge, *Women and the English Renaissance: Literature and the Nature of Womankind, 1540 to 1620*, Urbana: University of Illinois Press, 1984

Charlotte Yeldham, *Women Artists in Nineteenth-*

Century France and England, 2 vols, New York: Garland, 1984

R.J. Schoeck, "Margaret More", *Contemporaries of Erasmus: A Biographical Register of the Renaissance and Reformation*, 3 vols, Toronto: University of Toronto Press, 1985–7, ii, pp.455–6

Stevie Davies, *The Idea of Woman in Renaissance Literature: The Feminine Reclaimed*, Brighton: Harvester, 1986

Karel Moens, "De vrouw in de huismuziek: Een iconografische studie naar 16de- en 17de-eeuwse schilderijen en prenten uit de Nederlanden" [Women in family music-making: An iconographical study of 16th- and 17th-century paintings and prints from the Netherlands], *Jaarboek van het Vlaams Centrum voor Oude Muziek*, ii, 1986, pp.43–63

Leonore Davidoff and Catherine Hall, *Family Fortunes: Men and Women of the English Middle Class, 1780–1850*, London: Hutchinson, and Chicago: University of Chicago Press, 1987

Gilpin to Ruskin: Drawing Masters and Their Manuals, exh. cat., Fitzwilliam Museum, Cambridge, 1987

Iain Pears, *The Discovery of Painting: The Growth of Interest in the Arts in England, 1680–1768*, New Haven and London: Yale University Press, 1988

Whitney Chadwick, *Women, Art and Society*, London and New York: Thames and Hudson, 1990; revised edition, 1996

Anne Higonnet, "Secluded vision: Images of feminine experience in nineteenth-century Europe", *The Expanding Discourse: Feminism and Art History*, ed. Norma Broude and Mary D. Garrard, New York: HarperCollins, 1992, pp.170–85

Ann Pullen, "*Conversations on the Arts*: Writing a space for the female viewer in the *Repository of Arts*, 1809–15", *Oxford Art Journal*, xv/2, 1992, pp.15–26

Ann Bermingham, "The aesthetics of ignorance: The accomplished woman in the culture of connoisseurship", *Oxford Art Journal*, xvi/2, 1993, pp.3–20

Deborah Cherry, *Painting Women: Victorian Women Artists*, London and New York: Routledge, 1993

Wayne E. Franits, *Paragons of Virtue: Women and Domesticity in Seventeenth-Century Dutch Art*, Cambridge and New York: Cambridge University Press, 1993

Gerda Lerner, *The Creation of Feminist Consciousness: From the Middle Ages to Eighteen-Seventy*, New York and Oxford: Oxford University Press, 1993

Anne Crookshank and the Knight of Glin, *The Watercolours of Ireland*, London: Barrie and Jenkins, 1994

Els Kloek, Nicole Teeuwen and Marijke Huisman, *Women of the Golden Age: An International Debate on Women in Seventeenth-Century Holland, England and Italy*, Hilversum: Verloren, 1994

A Struggle for Fame: Victorian Women Artists and Authors, exh. cat., Yale Center for British Art, New Haven, 1994

Mirjam de Baar and others, eds, *Choosing the Better Part: Anna Maria van Schurman, 1607–1678*, Dordrecht and London: Kluwer Academic Publishers, 1996 (Dutch original, 1992)

Jack Kramer, *Women of Flowers: A Tribute to Victorian Women Illustrators*, New York: Stewart Tabori and Chang, 1996

Training and Professionalism

19th and 20th centuries

1. Britain and Ireland
2. France
3. Germany, Austria and Switzerland
4. Russia
5. North America

1. Britain and Ireland

19th century

The professional female artist emerged in 19th-century Britain as an apparently new feature of the domestic art scene. Seeming to be preceded only by a few individuals such as Angelica Kauffman (q.v.), she was a product of the developments that made the 19th century a different era from the 18th: that is to say, first of industrialisation and urbanisation,

and subsequently of the women's rights movement and the commodification of art. Although little remarked upon before the 1840s, she posed a challenge to the economy of art and the assumed role and character of high culture and to the sexual politics of Victorian society. The controversy about women's ability to achieve in this field and the propriety and convenience of her attempting to do so was huge, lasting beyond the end of the century, although census figures suggest the ranks of female artists to have been small and the growth in their numbers to have slowed steadily after the middle of the century (e.g. 1841: 278; 1851: 548; 1861: 853; 1871: 1069).

1800–1837

During the first decades of the 19th century, the upper- and middle-class woman was expected to treat creative work as a hobby or accomplishment, making no distinction between, say, musical performance, embroidery and painting, while the working-class woman was presumed to possess neither creativity nor cultural aspirations. All women were expected to have a capacity for needle-work and a taste for the decorative, but they were equally assumed to possess no ambition for public acknowledgement, no originality of thought and little intellectual or physical rigour. The tradition of amateurism, typified by copies and miniature portraits, obscured the fact that such activities were carried on professionally by such women artists as the Sharpe sisters. The only female artist with a national reputation was the portraitist Margaret Carpenter (q.v.), though professional families such as the landscapist Nasmyths and Rayners included women. Confounding the stereotype of the delicate watercolourist animated by personal associations, all these women produced a steady output of oil paintings on commission.

Obtaining a fine-art training was difficult. Although there was no systematic art education for women, some fine-art institutions in provincial cities had an educational arm and might admit women, though they had about them the aura of upper-class amateurism. Relatives in the profession and private drawing teachers were the readiest source of fine-art instruction for women. The establishment of provincial art exhibitions from the 1820s on allowed women to gain some local exposure, reputation and professional standing, depending on the liberalism of the civic leaders in the region: thus, for instance, Rolinda Sharples gained a great reputation in Bath and Bristol, and women were allowed to participate in the exhibitions of the Royal Hibernian Academy in Dublin from their inception in 1829. Where women were allowed to participate in these new arenas, however, their position was usually signalled as an aberration from an implied male norm: the Society of Painters in Watercolours, or Old Watercolour Society (established 1804; Royal Watercolour Society from 1881),

classed women as "lady members", which it saw as synonymous with "honorary members", a status imposed on women also by the Society of British Artists (established 1823).

1838–1869

The practice of art was one that middle-class women, socialised into a feminine amateurism in artistic activities, increasingly tried to turn to professional use. Their motivation ranged from the need of an income to the search for greater fulfilment or independence than convention allowed them. Since Victorian ideology restricted all respectable women's usefulness to the family, home and factory, and yet economic and demographic reality made such ghettoisation difficult to sustain, the issues raised by the increase in numbers and visibility of women artists were not only aesthetic but social and political. They pivoted on the division of activity and experience into private and public spheres and the alleged symbiosis between the domestic and the professional worlds. The specific questions debated from the 1850s against a background of the "woman question" were of woman's innate abilities, her proper or desired roles in society generally and culture in particular, her moral probity and her intellectual worth. Prejudices concerning woman's natural and necessary nature and function remained persuasive to a large number of Victorians, whose society exaggerated sexual difference wherever it could.

The development of Realism, with its emphasis on observation and rejection of classical learning, opened art up to female practitioners, and Pre-Raphaelitism in particular promised validation of the genres to which women commonly had greater access: still life, landscape, portraiture and scenes of mundane reality. The growth in popularity of genre – anecdotal scenes of everyday life – was significant for women, whose social immobility and poor training opportunities left them generally ill-equipped for the traditionally prestigious types of work, such as history painting. Convention allowed that the domestic world, along with still life, portraiture and landscape, was a legitimate subject for women artists.

The most prestigious sources of fine-art education – the Royal Academy of Arts in London, the Royal Scottish Academy in Edinburgh and the Royal Hibernian Academy in Dublin – either prohibited or did not welcome women students. A campaign to open the educational opportunities offered by the Royal Academy to women on an equal basis with men was launched by women artists, writers and social reformers in 1859 and was partially successful by 1861, when female students were conditionally accepted.

All other training options were second best. They included the Government Schools of Design, established from the 1840s throughout Britain and Ireland and including a Female School in London (threatened with closure in 1859), although these institutions offered an applied-art training meant to raise the aesthetic level of manufacture rather than preparation for the career of painter, sculptor or architect. It was, indeed, much easier to get a design training than a fine-art one, even when the demand among middle-class women for marketable skills was reluctantly recognised: the Queen's Institute for the Training and Employment of Educated Women was set up in Dublin in 1861 for this express purpose, but went along the road to fine art only as far as still-life and landscape painting. Some private art schools such as Cary's or Leigh's (both London) accepted women, though their aim of preparing students for application to the Royal Academy Schools limited their relevance to female students until 1861. Another possibility was the drawing teacher who was privately employed to teach in the pupil's home or his/her own rooms. Even more dependent on the availability of family finance was tuition in the schools or studios of such continental centres as Paris, Munich and Rome; academies were closed to women throughout Europe, but the atelier system functioning in other European countries, though little favoured in Britain, depended only on a woman finding a practising artist willing to teach female students, as Anna Mary Howitt and Jane Benham found when seeking an art education in Munich in 1850. Self-help was a widespread source of training for women, which could include learning from instruction manuals, copying from private or public art collections, arranging private study from the life (the Society of Female Artists attempted some collective self-help in respect of this particular problem) or sketching excursions.

In the absence of reliable accessible training provision, it was women in artistic families who could most easily become artists themselves, whether in painting, engraving or sculpture. Certainly, nearly all the women artists who became best known in this period, such as Henrietta Ward

(q.v.), Mary Thornycroft (q.v.), Rebecca Solomon (q.v.) and Joanna Boyce, were daughters, wives or sisters of male artists. Although the family gave practical assistance and access to professional networks, it could also predetermine and restrict the kind of work a woman practised and keep her in the shadow of her male relatives through their shared name. The categorisation in the census of 1861 of artists as professionals would have encouraged such female artists as these to claim their identity, though deterring others still bound by the etiquette of "fine-ladyism".

Exhibition and membership of exhibiting bodies was often categorically denied to women (e.g. the Glasgow Institute of Fine Arts, established in 1861). Exhibition opportunity depended in most cases on membership of the exhibiting body, and the establishment in London in 1857 of the Society of Female Artists was a response to the discriminatory, restrictive membership generally allowed to women. Anti-academic and anti-institutional feeling grew from the middle of the century, giving rise to the Free Exhibition (established 1848, later the National Institution), more accessible to women because less costly, the Dudley Gallery (established 1865), more congenial to women because it favoured water-colour and had no membership system, and others. Photographic societies and exhibitions were set up in the 1850s, and appear to have been generally open to women, though not necessarily welcoming. The exposure sought by women graphic artists was, of course, of a different kind, and several female illustrators such as Mary Ellen Edwards and Adelaide and Florence Claxton established themselves as regular contributors to medium-range weeklies, monthlies and annuals.

Women were active in art writing at most levels. Anna Jameson and Elizabeth (Lady) Eastlake became prominent in the 1850s for their learned books and articles, while many lesser-known women published art history for adults and for children, translations of art-historical classics, biographies, handbooks and manuals. The feminist press obviously offered express opportunities for female journalists. Art critics, however, were nearly all men until the 1880s, and tended to treat women's work with condescension or paternalism if they did not simply ignore it as unimportant, unskilled and unoriginal. Though a liberal trend of sincere encouragement was discernible on the establishment of the Society of Female Artists, this tailed off in the mid-1860s. The inferior status of women's art was generally perpetuated in all kinds of writing about art, whether by men or women, typified by the common journalistic habit of reviewing women's exhibits as a separate category even where they were not in fact hung together.

The rise of such commercial dealers as Ernest Gambart and Henry Wallis in the 1850s and 1860s brought little advantage to female artists as a group, although a few crowd-pleasing individuals whose novelty value could command high prices (the French painter Rosa Bonheur, q.v., stands out) did find success with a wide public in this way. Women who were construed as semi-amateur, such as the landscapist Barbara Bodichon and the photographer Julia Margaret Cameron (q.v.), were, perversely, as likely to be given solo shows in this milieu, no doubt because they were neither serious challengers for the patronage that men guarded jealously nor claiming more than a marginal role for women in the delineation of mainstream taste and trends. While old master (sic) collections, private and public, contained hardly any women's work, the principal collectors of contemporary art, such as Richard Vernon, also bought very little work by women, with isolated examples by the portraitist Margaret Carpenter, landscapists the Nasmyth sisters, topographer Louise Rayner and the history painter Henrietta Ward being the exceptions that proved the rule. This generalisation applies also to the avant-garde taste for Pre-Raphaelitism. Few women were in command of the wealth needed to form an art collection, and those who are documented, such as Queen Victoria, the heiress Angela Burdett-Coutts and Ruskin's friend Ellen Heaton, showed no partiality for (though no prejudice against) women's work. Royal patronage was premised on a conventional sexual division of labour that allocated to sculptor Mary Thornycroft, for example, the portrayal of the royal babies in statuette form. A more fruitful source of patronage for women artists were the Art Unions, whose prizewinners, though routinely castigated as possessing low-brow, narrow taste, looked for works at the cheaper end of the market. Public commissions such as the interior decorations of the Palace of Westminster and statues of local worthies did not go to women.

1870–1900

In her book *Modern Painters and Their Paintings* (1874) Sarah Tytler remarked:

> I may observe, in proof of the difficulty which the technicalities of art must present to women, that of all the women painters whom I have chronicled, I am not aware of one … who did not overcome the difficulty, by the advantage of an early familiarity with art, from having been the daughter of a painter, or, at least, of an engraver.

This was a situation reflected by the case studies in Ellen Clayton's *English Female Artists* (1876), but it became less so as, with improving opportunities and a greater general resignation to the fact of women artists, preparing for a career in painting (still much more feasible than sculpture) was less of a challenge to convention and propriety. The best-known women artists of this period, Lady Butler (q.v.), Henrietta Rae (q.v.), Kate Greenaway (q.v.) and Helen Allingham, had no family connection to the profession. One of the factors behind this change in climate was the opening in 1871 of the Slade School of Fine Art, London, which, in distinguishing itself from the Royal Academy Schools, promised better opportunities for women from the start.

Although Louisa Starr and Jessie McGregor appeared to have proved the case for women by winning the gold medal for history painting at the Royal Academy Schools in 1867 and 1872 respectively, the Royal Academy continued to limit women's training with special regulations until 1893, when a life class for women was introduced (and when the Royal Hibernian Academy finally admitted women students), and to deny women membership of the Academy itself until 1923. Women continued to seek art training abroad, especially if looking for modern art: an example is Sarah Purser, whose French connections became an important influence in late 19th-century Irish art. The retardataire wish to see women content with the less prestigious and arguably amateur pursuits classed as applied arts was evidenced in the reception of the Royal School of Art Needlework (established 1872) and the Ladies' Work Society (established 1875), which attempted to play the emergence of women as creative talents and the contemporary revival of the "arts and crafts" off against each other to conservative purpose. The Arts and Crafts Movements in Scotland and Ireland, by contrast, effected a broadening of the spectrum of women's creativity, bringing prominence to individual female artists and craftswomen alike.

The revival of classicism established by the late 1860s and pre-eminent by the 1880s, though unsuited to women's education and experience, attracted many ambitious women artists by its cultural cachet, especially after their access to improved fine-art training gave them greater confidence in tackling the nude. Even as the Royal Academy tried to reassert its importance through the classical revival, independent exhibition fora proliferated and the Grosvenor Gallery (established in 1877 by Sir Coutts and Lady Lindsay) was by contrast welcoming to female artists, who, like the male exhibitors, were hand-picked. But independent initiatives did not necessarily exhibit progressive sexual politics, and the same range of attitudes to women could be seen towards the end of the 19th century as at the middle: the Watercolour Society of Ireland (founded in 1870 as the Amateur Drawing Society) was dominated by women; the Old Watercolour Society elected its first woman member in 1890; but the Dublin Art Club (established 1886) categorised women still as "lady members" and the Glasgow Art Club (established 1880), the Art Workers' Guild (established 1884) and the New English Art Club (established 1886) were for men only. Thus there was still an argument for women-only organisations such as the Glasgow Society of Lady Artists (established 1882). In the commercial sector, Elizabeth Thompson, later Lady Butler, and Helen Allingham were made conspicuous by solo shows at the Fine Art Society, though the most famous female artist of the period, Kate Greenaway, found success in the less weighty field of illustration, made more feminine by her specialisation in material for children.

Female journalists became common in this period. The poet Alice Meynell and the columnist Florence Fenwick-Miller were among the women whose writings displayed a special interest in art during the last two decades of the 19th century. Reviews of the Society of Female Artists (renamed the Society of Lady Artists in 1874), the only regular exhibition where women's work was in the majority, became fewer and more cursory in this period as an anti-feminist backlash manifested itself in the 1880s, remobilising the misogynistic arguments of the mid-19th century. There was a revival of interest in Kauffman and her French contemporaries such as

Elisabeth Vigée-Lebrun (q.v.), which set them up as the exemplars of a feminine art. A similarly retrogressive use was made of Princess Louise's much-publicised example of upper-class amateurism, which extended to exhibition while eschewing professionalism.

Collectors, whether mainstream or avant-garde, such as Edmund Davies, Mr and Mrs George McCulloch and George Holt, showed greater willingness to purchase women's work though usually via one favourite individual artist. Some progress in public patronage was marked by Amelia Paton Hill's statue of *David Livingstone* in Princes Street, Edinburgh, described on its erection in 1876 as "the first public work of the kind to be executed by a woman". The first purchases of women's work for a public institution occurred in the Liverpool Corporation's acquisition in 1871 of the painting *Elaine* by Sophie Anderson, and in 1873 of Louisa Starr's *Sintram*, and for a national institution in the Chantrey Bequest's acquisition in 1890 of *Love Locked Out* by Anna Lea Merritt for the new Tate Gallery. The persistence and escalation of the women's rights movement in the 1890s, embodied for many in the "New Woman", ensured that the century ended on a note of challenge and resistance as strong as when women artists first emerged as an issue in mid-century.

Pamela Gerrish Nunn

20th century

The visibility of women artists in Britain and Ireland in the 20th century is marked by a contradiction – a seemingly steady increase in the number of women working in all areas of art and design work matched by a corresponding decrease in their appearance in art-history books until the 1970s, when feminist art historians started to look again at women's work. At the centre of this problem is the representation of women in modern art collections (e.g. Tate Gallery, London; Arts Council Collection) and standard modernist art history books (e.g. Charles Harrison's *English Art and Modernism, 1900–1939*, Denis Farr's *English Art, 1870–1940* and Frances Spalding's *British Art since 1900*) of 10–20 per cent, while their representation within contemporary art exhibitions in the course of the century has fluctuated between 25 and 50 per cent. The representation of women artists' work in art criticism and art history needs to be separated from the actual patterns of social and historical change in order to reassess women's position as artists. Two contributory factors to this picture of social and historical change in the 20th century are the expansion and development of general education (from which women benefited as both pupils and teachers) and women's changing status in the labour market (where the numbers of women, single and married, has steadily increased in the course of the century).

Since the 1890s women have formed the majority of students educated in British and Irish art schools, fluctuating between 50 and 75 per cent of all art students. This pattern varies considerably from school to school: at the Royal Academy Schools in London, for instance, women students formed less than 25 per cent of the student intake between 1901 and 1914, whereas at the Slade School of Fine Art, London (from its foundation in 1871 to 1945), the ratio was reversed, with women students forming 75 per cent of the student intake. In the same period, at the Glasgow School of Art, women students formed a fluctuating 33 to 47 per cent of the intake, rising to 50 per cent after 1920. If access to art education was no longer the major obstacle to women that it had been in the 19th century, access to institutions did not equate with equality of opportunity within the art school or in professional life.

While certain Victorian and Edwardian stereotypes about the lady amateur were abandoned in the 20th century, the suspicion persisted until well into the 1960s that the large numbers of women in art education were merely filling in time between school and marriage. The low expectations of many male lecturers in fine art (from Professor Tonks to Reg Butler) about the lack of seriousness of women students are matched by the frequency of accounts in autobiographies of women artists who had to "prove" their commitment to male tutors (e.g. Laura Knight, q.v., Nina Hamnett, q.v.). By 1910 the nude, rather than the draped model, which had been so central to any form of academic training in the 19th century, was offered to women as an object of study in life-drawing classes in most London art schools, but many provincial art schools continued the convention of the draped model in the name of "propriety" until 1945. Women were largely taught in sex-segregated classes until 1918 and this fashion continued in some art schools until 1945.

During the period 1900–18 art education became increasingly diversified as the distinctions between fine art and the applied and commercial arts became more marked. At the turn of the century, particularly in the applied arts under the impetus of the Arts and Crafts Movement, more enlightened educators such as W.R. Lethaby (Central School of Art, London) and Francis Newbery (Glasgow School of Art) encouraged women students as professional artists and designers while maintaining that certain areas of design were more suited to women; they thus perpetuated a different form of gender stereotyping of women's abilities at the same time as opening up opportunities for women. Val Williams (1986, p.90) has emphasised the role a formal training played in enabling women to pursue a career in photography, and the ways in which studio portrait photography and providing editorial coverage for "women's interests" in magazines were seen as the means to earn a living in photography. A similar argument was made by Lorna Green (1990) about the role of art schools in providing limited and specialised opportunities for women to work in certain areas of sculpture.

As education remained fee-paying, these prejudices were also reinforced by the pattern that emerged in most schools of a predominance of fee-paying "daughters of educated men" studying in day classes, when compared with the large number of men enrolled in part-time evening classes after a day's work elsewhere. Working-class women also entered the art and design fields through evening classes and so gained opportunities to develop as designers. Scholarships were highly prized, especially the Prix de Rome, which was first awarded to a woman, Winifred Knights (Monnington), in 1920, and many women benefited from the opportunities offered by county or school scholarships and medals. In 1933 the diversity of diplomas and teaching certificates offered by individual schools was replaced first by the Art Teacher's Diploma, then in 1946 by the National Diploma of Design; this was followed in 1961 by the Diploma of Art and Design, and in the 1970s by the introduction of degrees, equivalent in academic status to those of universities. The expansion of private secondary education for middle- and upper-class girls since the 1870s, followed by the expansion of state provision and the slow raising of the school-leaving age in the first half of the 20th century, also contributed to the increasing general extension of women's education into higher education, particularly into teacher training. In 1918, when women were partially enfranchised for the first time, the universities (with the exception of Cambridge) opened their doors to women. Art education, as with higher education in general, became more than a finishing school for middle-class women – it was a means to a "room of one's own", an independent income and professional status.

The high number of women students in art education was not mirrored by the number of women teachers and lecturers in higher education – and this remains one of the foremost problems of inequality in art education. No woman taught at the Royal Academy Schools before the 1960s, a reflection of the fact that only four women were elected to its ranks between 1922 and 1945. At the Slade, only one woman teacher was employed before 1945, Margaret Alexander (who taught there 1928–46). By contrast, the Glasgow School of Art, in the period 1892–1920, employed 27 women artists: 7 in painting and drawing, and 20 in the applied-arts section, among them Jessie M. King, Ann Macbeth, Frances Macdonald and Dorothy and Olive Carleton Smyth. The same pattern can be found at the Metropolitan School of Art in Dublin, where Alice Jacob headed the Design School (c.1900–21), and where women students, alongside lace and needlework, excelled in the applied arts of enamelling and stained glass. By the 1960s art schools offered diplomas in an increasingly wide and more highly specialised variety of fields from textiles to jewellery, printmaking to pottery, graphic design to fine art, film and photography. While the opportunities to teach in art schools remained highly limited until 1945, many women ran their own schools and classes, for example Mainie Jellett (q.v.), Lucy Kemp-Welch and Sylvia Gosse. Education continued to play a crucial role in the large number of independent workshops established by women in the first half of the 20th century, such as those of Evelyn Gleeson, Evie Hone and Susie Cooper. By the 1960s an increasing number of women artists could be found lecturing in art schools and participating in what has become the dominant model of the (male) fine artist, who both exhibits and teaches.

A further aspect to women's education is the frequency with which women artists trained or studied abroad. Paris remained a magnet for aspiring artists before 1945 and the main opportunity to meet and learn about modernist artists and to live *la vie bohème* (e.g. Mainie Jellett, Eileen Agar, q.v., Nina Hamnett). There have, however, been many prominent women artists both pre- and post-1945 who have not taught or held posts in art schools (e.g. Barbara Hepworth, q.v., Eileen Agar), a pattern in direct contrast to the "norm" for male artists in the 20th century, and it is within the art school system – and its particular relationship to the art market – that a "structural" discrimination against women has been both established and maintained.

While most of the well-known women artists who trained in the 1900s and 1910s were middle- or upper-class women who were able to continue their practice either because of a private income or through the support of family or husband, this pattern changed in the 1920s as a more diverse cross-section of the daughters of "professional and educated men" entered the labour market. Career books for girls and young women written between the 1900s and 1930s encouraged those interested in fine art to consider both teacher training and a specialism in an area of craft, design or applied arts as the most likely means through which a woman could find employment. This "realism" was both a reflection of knowledge about women's actual employment prospects and the generally low aspirations of women's abilities. A large number of women trained at art school went to work in the expanding primary and secondary education system as the state both raised the school-leaving age and made primary education compulsory. Equal pay was not introduced until 1945 and women were forced to leave their teaching jobs on marriage by law. The work of women artists in this sector included both major reforms and innovations in the training of children and the development of art in schools (e.g. Evelyn Gibbs, Nan Youngman) but its generally low status did not change until the Depression in the 1930s increasingly encouraged men to start seeking employment in schools.

Negative stereotyping of women artists in the press is another characteristic between 1900 and 1960, and the legacy of this continues to mar the perception of women's considerable achievements as artists today. Women were frequently told in the late 19th and early 20th centuries that they must choose between a career and marriage (with the presumption of motherhood) and that it was impossible to combine the two. While the reputations of many women artists have in the 20th century been overshadowed by that of their partners, their lives and careers show that this "choice" has been increasingly refused in so far as many women artists married and, of these, some, but by no means all, had children. Married women, in general, have entered the wage-labour market in increasing numbers throughout the 20th century but the social prejudices against women continuing to work once married continued – an ideology reinforced in the 1920s and 1930s by legal dismissal on marriage in both teaching and the civil service. This general social prejudice, which has its more positive characterisations in the 1950s as "housewife as career", has contributed to some of the most marked prejudices of the 20th century against women who were known to be partners of male artists, trivialising their labour as a "hobby" , the result of "frustrated maternity" (Brighton and Morris 1977, p.228), or by characterising women's work as simply derivative of their male partners, rather than the result of mutual exchanges.

During the course of the 20th century the "ideology" of separate and appropriate spheres of public activity for men and private/domestic activity for women has shifted from the separation of home and work into more complex patterns of horizontal and vertical segregation amongst women and men at work. These patterns of segregation, where women are either confined to particular areas of labour (horizontal) or "cluster" at the bottom of the profession with only a select minority rising to the top (vertical), are typical of women artists' careers when compared to their male peers, both in terms of their limited entry into a hierarchical and increasingly segmented and specialised fine-art market, and the clustering of women in often devalued branches of the arts, crafts and design industries. If one also bases an assessment of sex discrimination upon the marks of recognition given by the art world to its leading artists, a pattern of belated recognition is also visible in terms of the granting of awards, prizes or one-person exhibitions at prestigious galleries to men earlier and more frequently than their women colleagues. Discrimination along gender lines is also reflected in the actual market values for the works of women artists, which have generally sold for lower prices than equivalent works by their male peers.

The diversity of work undertaken by women artists through the course of the 20th century is one of the key indicators of women's ingenuity, since wherever opportunities opened up women artists have taken them. The rise in women in other professions such as architecture, law, medicine, even engineering, is used repeatedly as an indication of this general trend. Fine-art printmaking is one area where women's participation grew rapidly (Gertrude Hermes, Clare Leighton) – a pattern at odds with the almost exclusively male-dominated commercial printers. Women nevertheless continued to find opportunities to exhibit, while keeping their eye on possibilities to work as graphic artists, illustrators, craftspersons or designers. Vanessa Bell (q.v.), Nina Hamnett, Frances Hodgkins (q.v.) and Gertrude Hermes all worked as applied artists and designers alongside the exhibition of their paintings. Banners, posters, illustrations and applied art were made for the fight for the vote, for example, the work of Sylvia Pankhurst for the Women's Social and Political Union; of the Artists Suffrage League (from 1907, chaired by Mary Lowndes); and the Suffrage Atelier (from 1909).

In the 1920s and 1930s the four women artists' exhibiting groups – the Society of Women Artists, the Women's International Art Club, the Glasgow Society of Women Artists and the Scottish Society of Women Artists – all offered their members the opportunity to exhibit both paintings and sculpture alongside craft objects in recognition of this aspect of women artists' work. At a time when the fine-art market was increasingly specialised into print, painting, sculpture and drawing exhibitions, the mixing of fine art and craft brought only the rebuke that these exhibitions were not professional enough, regardless of the fact that the same women artists sent their fine-art exhibits to other major group exhibitions. The Royal Academy, which separated art forms, abolished the display of miniatures in 1940 – one area in which women artists *had* dominated.

At the turn of the 19th and 20th centuries the dominant model of the fine artist was centred on regular participation in large group exhibitions and selection to membership of prestigious artists' groups. London remained the largest community of artists and the centre of the art market in contemporary art. Flourishing art communities could also be found throughout Britain and Ireland with the combination of an art school, a local academy and competing groups of younger or more avant-garde artists, as in Glasgow, Edinburgh, Manchester and Dublin, and more rural communities, such as Newlyn and St Ives in Cornwall. The submission of works to large-scale metropolitan exhibitions attracted commissions as well as building critical reputations and would be supplemented by one-person exhibitions at individual London dealers and auction houses (even the few exhibitions of Gwen John, q.v., in London, for example, fit this pattern). Between 1900 and 1930 women artists gained considerably both in the numbers participating in these exhibition forums and the numbers elected to these large artists' groups, which averaged between 25 and 33 per cent in the inter-war years – a figure directly opposed to their majority presence as students. The election of the first four women to the Royal Academy can be seen in this light, but the minority of women selected has remained tiny as women formed only 10 per cent of all Associates (ARA) and Academicians (RA) by the 1980s and tokenistic, when compared with the London Group, where women's participation in the exhibitions reached 50 per cent by 1930 but their membership was confined to 30 per cent. The Royal Academy did host a rare prize in its open exhibition for women sculptors, the Lady Feodora Gleichen memorial prize (Gleichen had been a sculptor and bequested the money) from 1926 to the 1940s.

Women artists were given war commissions in both world wars, in the schemes initiated by the British Government, though the scale and the type of commission was never on the same terms as those of their male counterparts. Anna Airy was the only woman offered commissions of munitions factories on the same basis as men in World War I. The remaining commissions came from the Women's War Committee (1918–20), set up to document and celebrate women's contribution to the war effort, and these were displayed during the 1920s at the Imperial War Museum as a separate part of the collection, the Women's Section. Art works by women artists form 5 per cent of the First World War Collection and 10 per cent of the Second World War Collection at the Imperial War Museum, London. The Second World War collection was commissioned by Kenneth Clark under the War Artists Advisory committee. Laura Knight, Evelyn Gibbs and Evelyn Dunbar were among the women who received commissions.

By the 1930s artists no longer relied on large group exhibitions to build their critical reputation and instead concentrated on the public exhibition of their work in one-person or small peer-group exhibitions organised by dealers. Large-scale group exhibitions became increasingly criticised for the inconsistent and poorly arranged hanging of the exhibits, which drowned the few decent works considered to be on show. This criticism has to be seen in the context of the belated arrival in Britain of both the dealer-critic system from France and a growing interest in modernism, where small exhibitions of one artist or a small group demonstrating their shared and common interests were becoming a more formidable method of gaining critical attention. The establishment of the Irish Living Art exhibitions in 1943 is another extension of this "modernist" pattern. While many women artists did exhibit over a long period with one particular dealer (Ethel Walker at Redfern; Laura Knight at the Leicester Galleries; Barbara Hepworth at Gimpel Fils and Marlborough, all in London), a consistent long-term relationship with one dealer is frequently what marks out those who are considered the most prominent and successful women of the period. The development of modernist groups, such as the Seven and Five Society and the English Surrealist group, did little to promote women artists into their ranks, and the numbers of women in these groups remained very small (around 10 per cent). The emergence of modernism in the 1930s in Britain was combined with a deep recession in the art market following the slump. In this context, the exclusion of women could be seen as one means through which a newly emergent modernist and male-dominated group could assert its "professionalism", but it is also possible to recognise sexist practices within the ideology of modernism. There have, however, been many notable women dealers in this period. Peggy Guggenheim had galleries in both London and Manchester in the 1930s, and after World War II Halima Nalech and Annely Juda. In the post-1945 expansion of the art market and publicly funded gallery system, there has been a steady rise in women's participation in the art world as administrators and curators. By the early 1990s women formed 75 per cent of arts administrators, although the inequality of vertical segregation remains an issue.

Art criticism in contemporary art journals and newspapers was until the 1960s a male-dominated endeavour, although there were some notable women art critics before World War II, for example, Gwen Raverat (*Time and Tide*), Myfanwy (née Evans) Piper (*Axis*), E.H. Ramsden and Mary Chamot (also a curator at the Tate Gallery). Many women artists also participated in the production of avant-garde journals and publications (e.g. Jessica Dismorr, Eileen Agar and Barbara Hepworth).

The art infrastructure in Britain changed considerably in 1945 with the establishment of the Arts Council of Great Britain. While the dealer-critic system continued to develop, it did so in relationship to a new network of both private and publicly funded art centres and institutions that showed contemporary art independently of the city art museums and galleries established in the Victorian era. The art centre movement of the 1960s and the growth since the 1970s of sculpture parks and temporary site-specific art works are two other factors in the expansion of opportunities to show work in the regions in a context other than a large group exhibition. Increasingly exhibition internationally either under the aegis of the British Council's touring exhibitions or representation at the Venice or São Paulo Biennales or through reciprocal relationships with galleries in Paris or New York became an important feature of an artist's profile. The selection of women artists to represent Britain has been poor with some notable exceptions, for example Barbara Hepworth and Bridget Riley (q.v.); the Irish sent two women painters, Norah McGuinness and Nano Reid, to the Venice Biennale in 1950, and a woman sculptor, Hilary Heron, in 1956. Another factor in the development of post-war exhibition was the model of exhibition and catalogues set by the Museum of Modern Art in New York. Whereas before 1945 most exhibitions were accompanied by a short essay and/or a hand-list, during the 1950s and 1960s increasingly well-illustrated catalogues with extended critical essays became the norm. Few women artists have benefited from this kind of scholarly attention and the representation of women in large-scale retrospectives is both mixed and very poor. Only eight one-person shows of women artists were held at the Tate Gallery between 1910 and 1986 compared with 214 for men. Although several women have been short-listed for the Turner Prize, introduced in the 1980s by the Tate, Rachel Whiteread has been the only woman to win in a decade. Institutions of contemporary art such as the Whitechapel Art Gallery and the Institute of Contemporary Arts in London, or publicly funded galleries such as the Camden Arts Centre in London, Ikon in Birmingham, Arnolfini in Bristol, Cornerhouse in Manchester and others, have since the 1950s become increasingly important as venues for both thematic presentations of contemporary art and retrospectives of mid-career artists. It is generally in their shows that increasing numbers of contemporary women artists can be seen, and many feminist exhibitions were held at these venues in the 1970s and 1980s.

While the women's movement has brought women together for many different initiatives in the visual arts since the early 1970s, access to resources (both material and intellectual) and institutional recognition remain key problems for many women. Insights from feminist art theory and history have challenged many assumptions about values in the critical assessment of art practices and initiated new directions in art practice. But the question of who gets written into the history books remains.

KATY DEEPWELL

Bibliography

Vrynwy Biscoe, *300 Careers for Women*, London: Lovat, Fraser and Nicholson, 1932

Winifred Kirkland and Frances Kirkland, *Girls Who Became Artists*, New York and London: Harper, 1934

Mary Chamot, *Modern Painting in England*, London: Country Life, and New York: Scribner, 1937

Stuart Macdonald, *The History and Philosophy of Art Education*, London: University of London Press, 1970

Grant M. Waters, *Dictionary of British Artists Working 1900–1950*, 2 vols, Eastbourne: Eastbourne Fine Art, 1975

Jane Johnson and A. Greutzner, *The Dictionary of British Artists, 1880–1940*, Woodbridge, Suffolk: Antique Collectors' Club/Baron, 1976

Janet Minihan, *The Nationalization of Culture: The Development of State Subsidies to the Arts in Great Britain*, London: Hamish Hamilton, and New York: New York University Press, 1977

Andrew Brighton and Lynda Morris, eds, *Towards Another Picture*, Nottingham: Midland Group, 1977

Anthea Callen, *Angel in the Studio: Women in the Arts and Crafts Movement, 1870–1914*, London: Astragal, 1979; as *Women Artists of the Arts and Crafts Movement, 1870–1914*, New York: Pantheon, 1979

Germaine Greer, *The Obstacle Race: The Fortunes of Women Painters and Their Work*, London: Secker and Warburg, and New York: Farrar Straus, 1979

Carol Dyhouse, *Girls Growing Up in Late Victorian and Edwardian England*, London and Boston: Routledge 1981

Grant Longman, *The Herkomer Art School and Subsequent Developments, 1901–1918*, Bushey Reference Paper no.2, Bushey: Longman, 1981

AIA: The Story of the Artists' International Association, 1933–1953, exh. cat., Museum of Modern Art, Oxford, 1983

Jane Lewis, *Women in England, 1870–1950: Sexual*

Divisions and Social Change, Brighton: Wheatsheaf, and Bloomington: Indiana University Press, 1984

Charlotte Yeldham, *Women Artists in Nineteenth-Century France and England*, 2 vols, New York: Garland, 1984

Chris Petteys, *An International Dictionary of Women Artists Born Before 1900*, Boston: Hall, 1985

Pamela Gerrish Nunn, ed., *Canvassing Women: Recollections by Six Victorian Women Artists*, London: Camden, 1986

Val Williams, *Women Photographers: The Other Observers, 1900 to the Present*, London: Virago, 1986; as *The Other Observers: Women Photographers in Britain, 1900 to the Present*, 1991

Gail Braybon and Penny Summerfield, *Out of the Cage: Women's Experiences in Two World Wars*, London and New York: Pandora, 1987

Jane Beckett and Deborah Cherry, *The Edwardian Era*, London: Phaidon, 1987

Irish Women Artists from the Eighteenth Century to the Present Day, exh. cat., National Gallery of Ireland, Dublin, and elsewhere, 1987

Pamela Gerrish Nunn, *Victorian Women Artists*, London: Women's Press, 1987

Rozsika Parker and Griselda Pollock, *Framing Feminism: Art and the Woman's Movement, 1970–1985*, London and New York: Pandora, 1987

Robert Radford, *Art for a Purpose: The Artists' International Association, 1933–1953*, Winchester: Winchester School of Art Press, 1987

Lisa Tickner, *The Spectacle of Women: Imagery of the Suffrage Campaign, 1907–1914*, London: Chatto and Windus, 1987; Chicago: University of Chicago Press, 1988

Pauline Barrie, "The art machine", *Women Artists Slide Library Journal*, no.20, December 1988–January 1989, p.9

Deirdre Beddoe, *Back to Home and Duty: Women Between the Wars, 1918–1939*, London and Boston: Pandora, 1989

Jan Marsh and Pamela Gerrish Nunn, *Women Artists and the Pre-Raphaelite Movement*, London: Virago, 1989

Cheryl Buckley, *Potters and Paintresses: Women Designers in the Pottery Industry, 1870–1955*, London: Women's Press, 1990

Mary Ann Caws, *Women of Bloomsbury: Virginia, Vanessa and Carrington*, New York and London: Routledge, 1990

Penny Dunford, *A Biographical Dictionary of Women Artists in Europe and America since 1850*, New York and London: Wheatsheaf, 1990

Lorna Green, *The Position and Attitudes of Contemporary Women Sculptors in Britain, 1987–1989*, M.Phil. dissertation, Department of Fine Art, Leeds University, 1990

Ten Decades: Careers of Ten Women Artists Born 1897–1906, exh. cat., Norwich Gallery, Norfolk Institute of Art and Design, Norwich, 1992

Jude Burkhauser, ed., *Glasgow Girls: Women in Art and Design, 1880–1920*, 2nd edition, Edinburgh: Canongate, and Cape May, NJ: Red Ochre, 1993

Deborah Cherry, *Painting Women: Victorian Women Artists,* London and New York: Routledge, 1993

Sybil Oldfield, ed., *This Working-Day World: Women's Lives and Culture(s) in Britain, 1914–1945*, London: Taylor and Francis, 1994

A Struggle for Fame: Victorian Women Artists and Authors, exh. cat., Yale Center for British Art, New Haven, 1994

Clarissa Campbell Orr, ed., *Women in the Victorian Art World*, Manchester: Manchester University Press, 1995

2. France

19th century

During the 19th century all the world looked to France for leadership in the fine arts. For the professional artist of either sex, the opportunities for training, exhibiting and selling art in Paris were unrivalled. For women, the highly competitive atmosphere of this art capital meant that they faced extreme obstacles in training and professional activities, but at the same time it propelled such ambitious women as Elisabeth Vigée-Lebrun (q.v.), Rosa Bonheur (q.v.), Marie Bashkirtseff (q.v.), Berthe Morisot (q.v.) and Mary Cassatt (q.v.) to rare international fame.

In the century ushered in by Napoleon, there were seen the blossoming of a government-sponsored system for the production of art during the early decades and then, at the mid-point, the growth of a free art market to displace it. Both systems helped large numbers of artists to attain the status of such professionals as doctors, lawyers and professors in terms of education and income. But neither system could support all those who aspired to be artists, particularly as the high status of the arts attracted an increasing number of applicants from outside as well as inside France. Women found that they could be easily eliminated from competition for the many reasons that kept them out of professional life in general, but women's desire to participate in the arts was so great that persistence and politicking allowed many of them to force open the closed door.

The central obstacle for women artists in France was their exclusion from the Ecole des Beaux-Arts, the primary training facility for the inner circle of artists whose careers would be assured by government and private patronage. The school was run by the French government for the purpose of testing and refining the most promising students and ultimately sending the best each year to study at the French Academy in Rome. Although many men such as Gustave Courbet were rejected from this prestigious school and went on to become successful artists, not even being allowed to apply roused the ire of women artists all through the century. The admission of women to the Ecole des Beaux-Arts was finally granted in 1897 as the direct result of the efforts of the sculptor Mme Léon Bertaux (q.v.) and the Union des Femmes Peintres et Sculpteurs, which she had founded in 1881.

Until that victory was won, however, women found other avenues of artistic training. For the most part this meant private lessons, but an important state art school, the Ecole Gratuite de Dessin pour les Jeunes Filles, was opened in 1803, assuring talented women without money a basic level of artistic training. As Charlotte Yeldham (1984) points out, the schools of design for boys and girls in Paris, as well as the provincial schools that followed, were primarily established to train budding artists in the decorative and industrial arts, but they also provided courses in drawing, painting and sculpture. With fine-art training, a young woman could move on to more advanced work in a private studio or she could turn to teaching in one of the many public grammar schools. Rosa Bonheur was the most famous of the directors of the Ecole Gratuite de Dessin pour les Jeunes Filles during her tenure from 1848 to 1859.

The women who rose to prominence in the Paris art world, however, tended to have the means and the connections to study in the private studios of the greatest artists of their day. The women in the early 19th century who exhibited regularly in the Salons (opened to women in 1791) and who received the patronage of the emperors, kings and the wealthiest collectors of that era learned their craft from such masters as David (Mme Benoist, q.v.), Regnault (Pauline Auzou), Greuze (Constance Mayer, q.v.) and Fragonard (Marguerite Gérard, q.v.). Adélaïde Labille-Guiard (q.v.), one of the most successful women artists of the 18th century, was also a teacher of important artists of the early 19th century, such as Gabrielle Capet. Mme Benoist, Pauline Auzou and Lizinka de Mirbel followed in her footsteps by opening their own ateliers for women students. An example of women handing down their skills through several generations is that of Marie Godefroid, a portraitist from a prominent artistic family, who taught at an exclusive girls' school outside Paris run by Mme Jeanne Campan. An American student of Mme Campan later set up her own school in Pittsburgh and taught Mary Cassatt's mother, who was in turn instrumental in promoting her daughter's career.

By far the most dominant figure of the first decades of the 19th century was Vigée-Lebrun, whose rise to the top epitomises the unusual paths that women often followed to achieve rare international fame. She was a child prodigy. Her father provided her earliest training, and by the age of 15 she was able to support the family with her commissions for copies and portraits. She married one of the most active art dealers of the day who promoted her work. When her patron, Queen Marie-Antoinette, was beheaded in 1790, she spent the next decade painting all over Europe in exile from France. Forever identified with Mme de Staël's novel *Corinne; ou, L'Italie* (1807) because of her portrait of de Staël in the guise of her heroine (1808; Musée d'Art et d'Histoire, Geneva), Vigée-Lebrun published her memoirs of her own peripatetic life in 1835. Her example, primarily transmitted through her writings, influenced many women in the 19th century to pursue careers in the arts, including the young Rosa Bonheur.

Vigée-Lebrun thus combined all the strategies of the marginalised woman artist to circumvent the system: she used the influence of her father and husband, she found success abroad, she capitalised on the sensationalism of one of the most popular novels of her day, and she assured her legacy by publishing her own account of her life. Few women could afford to be quite so independent, but most found that success came from marketing their art outside the bureaucracy that served the interests of male artists more than their own.

By mid-century, the new emperor Napoleon III began to have a profound influence on the French art world. Napoleon's belief in the importance of visual symbols of power not only transformed the city of Paris into an impressive display of monumental buildings and sweeping boulevards, but it created an unprecedented demand for public art of all kinds. Painters, sculptors, printmakers and decorative artists found work making portraits and religious scenes to spread the glory of Napoleon's reign throughout France. The industry of making copies alone kept dozens of artists on the government payroll. While the most prestigious commissions went to male artists, there were sufficient jobs on the lower levels to bring increasing numbers of women into the fold. In addition, the government enthusiasm for art also spurred the cosmopolitan population of Paris to collect privately. By the accounting of Harrison and Cynthia White (1965), about 200,000 paintings were being produced each year. The Whites estimated that approximately one third of the artists were women.

By and large the women at mid-century trained and conducted their careers in the same manner that women had in the early 19th century. They studied in the ateliers of prominent artists, exhibited at the Salon and used their connections to attract government and private commissions. The primary difference was the spirit in which women approached art. Social movements and feminist groups such as the St Simonistes that were underway by the 1830s protested at the exclusion of women from the workplace and the resulting inability of women to improve their circumstances by honest labour. The dilemma was most keenly felt by educated middle-class women who were barred from the professional world inhabited by their brothers and husbands. For these women art became a viable alternative to the genteel servitude of being a governess. Flora Tristan, the social activist and grandmother of Paul Gauguin, was apprenticed in a lithography shop. The novelist George Sand tried her hand at painting to support herself during the 1830s.

Art continued to be thought of as a source of income for the gentlewoman in reduced circumstances in novels throughout the 19th century, such as Emile Zola's Comtesse de Beauvilliers and her daughter Alice in *L'Argent*, first published in 1891: "Behind the thin muslin curtains she could vaguely distinguish the figure of the Countess, who was mending some linen, whilst Alice was busy with some water-colour sketches, which she painted hurriedly by the dozen and secretly sold" (*Money*, 1894, p.233). This image of the woman artist working behind the scenes for much-needed money was a far cry from Mme de Staël's romantic Corinne.

Rosa Bonheur, the most famous woman artist at mid-century, was equally far from the idol of her youth, Vigée-Lebrun. Although she also trained with her father and owed much of her worldwide fame to the efforts of a dealer, the Belgian Ernest Gambart, rather than to the French academic system, Bonheur's fame rested on her down-to-earth hard work as opposed to the cosmopolitan glamour of Vigée-Lebrun. Her ten years as director of the Ecole Gratuite de Dessin pour les Jeunes Filles endorsed the prosaic side of studying and teaching art. Bonheur's speciality, monumental animal paintings, was gender-neutral, as were her studies in the stables and abattoirs of Paris. The Empress Eugénie celebrated Bonheur's neutrality by saying, as she bestowed the red ribbon of the Légion d'Honneur on her in 1865: "Genius has no sex".

In the 1860s the old system of private study in the atelier of an established artist began to give way to a new method of learning. Increasingly the young art student could enrol in a class, sometimes organised by a prominent artist, but more often at a new type of "academy". Beginning in 1862 young women could attend a school of decorative arts in Paris that had numerous branches, called Les Ecoles Professionelles d'Elisa Lemonnier. In painting, starting in 1868, both men and women could attend classes at the Académie Julian. For the next ten years, until they were separated into their own classes, there existed in Paris the unique opportunity for women to receive their training alongside men.

Rodolphe Julian, who had studied with Cabanel and Cogniet but had not been accepted at the Ecole des Beaux-Arts, accurately gauged the demand for training created by the burgeoning of the arts during the Second Empire. He was especially canny in opening the doors of his school to women since they had so few other choices. Women made up a growing percentage of his first mixed classes, but the price they paid for studying from the nude model "side by side with the Frenchmen" was high. May Alcott Nieriker (1879) described the patience that women in those classes had to have to endure the gazing of the men:

> One remembers the brave efforts made by a band of American ladies ... who supported one another with such dignity and modesty, in a steadfast purpose under this ordeal, that even Parisians, to whom such a type of womanly character was unknown and almost incomprehensible, were forced into respect and admiration of the simple earnestness and purity which proved a sufficient protection from even their evil tongues.

Julian found that although some women were steadfast enough to brave the harassment, most found it too uncomfortable – particularly the Frenchwomen who probably understood more of the insults. Once he separated the sexes the school flourished; although the peace women gained was mitigated by the fact that they paid higher fees and felt they received less rigorous instruction. In spite of these complaints, the Salon success of the women who studied at Julian's was undeniable, and the determined student received a high level of professional training.

In addition to the Académie Julian, classes for women were offered by such artists as Charles Chaplin, Carolus-Duran and William Bouguereau in Paris and Thomas Couture in his studio in suburban Villiers-le-Bel. Of the women who would be prominent in Paris in the second half of the 19th century, Eva Gonzalès (q.v.) and Mary Cassatt studied with Chaplin, Cassatt went on to study with Couture, and Marie Bashkirtseff studied at the Académie Julian. From that same generation, Berthe Morisot sought the advice of a number of teachers including Corot, and Marie Bracquemond (q.v.) was a pupil of Ingres.

Women seeking instruction in sculpture had fewer choices apart from the Ecole Gratuite de Dessin. In 1873 Mme Léon Bertaux began holding classes, and in 1879 she built her own sculpture school in the avenue de Villiers. Bertaux's influence extended far beyond her own classes, however. In 1881 she founded the first professional organisation for women artists in Paris, the Union des Femmes Peintres et Sculpteurs. Taking Rosa Bonheur as their model, just as Bonheur had taken Vigée-Lebrun, the women who flocked to the Union sought equal opportunities. To this end they began petitioning the Ecole des Beaux-Arts for women's classes, they instituted the first annual exhibitions for women and, in 1890, founded their own journal, the *Gazette des Femmes*. As Tamar Garb (1994) points out, the organisation grew to 450 members by the end of the 19th century and the exhibitions were as large as 1000 works. All the women artists in Paris benefited from the activism of this group whether they chose to participate or not. Some of the better-known members and exhibitors were Eva Gonzalès, Marie Bashkirtseff, and Virginie Demont-Breton, who became the second president of the Union.

However, the organisation's adherence to the professional structure of the French government system – training at the Ecole des Beaux-Arts and pursuit of medals in the Salon – set it at odds with the more modern system of art production and distribution that had been gaining ground since the mid-19th century. After the fall of the Second Empire in 1870, government support of the arts declined precipitously. Without this centralised patronage, the stylistic standards for government works of art as well as the monolithic Ecole des Beaux-Arts and the Salon began to succumb to the pressures of the large and unruly community of artists, patrons and dealers that had assembled in Paris. The conservative art style and professional strategy promoted by the Union des Femmes Peintres et Sculpteurs represented only one of many options available to women in the later 19th century.

The growth of private art dealers and the proliferation of exhibiting societies in Paris increased artists' exposure to the buying public. Instead of using the Salon as the annual clearing-house in which artists proved themselves to collectors, dealers and government juries, artists in the 1870s began to seek such opportunities more often and in a variety of settings. The new art-buying public was extraordinarily diverse, from the newly rich to the foreign tourist to the modest middle-class professional. Thus works of art for sale began to appear in "exhibitions" in business offices, restaurants, jewellery stores and art-supply shops in addition to art dealers and auction houses. Naturally the diversity of audience spawned a diversity of styles unheard of in the past.

The most famous outgrowth of this chaotic period in French culture was the style known as Impressionism. One of many exhibition societies that sprang up in the 1870s, the Impressionist group gained attention because of its link to contemporary naturalist literature, notably that of Zola, which brought their art an intellectual and avant-garde audience. The presence of three highly visible women in the group, Berthe Morisot, Mary Cassatt and Marie Bracquemond, accentuated the "modern" image they wanted to project. To show their total freedom from the old government art systems, they vowed not to exhibit at the Salon. Instead they trusted their fate to journalists and newspaper art critics and an interested dealer, Paul Durand-Ruel, to help get their paintings into the hands of collectors. At certain times, when he could afford it, Durand-Ruel offered his artists a regular income in exchange for a regular flow of paintings to the gallery. He handled the work of the women in the group as well as the men and for Mary Cassatt he eventually became exclusive dealer. When the old French academic system finally collapsed after the turn of the 19th and 20th centuries, the Impressionist women, unlike most of their sister artists who had tied their fate to the traditional style, became the only women from their period to achieve lasting fame.

The welter of styles, exhibiting groups and dealers continued to increase as the century drew to a close. The presence of many foreign artists and art collectors in Paris contributed to the instability of the situation. Training was less a matter of lengthy study in one atelier or *académie* and more a sampling of approaches that could be gained from private lessons, study at Julian's or at the Académie Colarossi, which had recently opened to women, or attendance at one of the small art schools set up by women for women students. Study of the nude model, both male and female, was *de rigueur*. Some women, such as Suzanne Valadon (q.v.), were able to begin as models and then take up painting. Women had the choice of exhibiting at either the government Salon or the new Salon of the Société Nationale des Beaux-Arts. Furthermore, an annual exhibition of Indépendants was hung without jury selection. As Garb (1994) points out, women could also show their work in the private exhibitions of such societies as the Société des Aquarellistes, Paris, or in one of the numerous groups just for women, such as the Société des Femmes Artistes, the Association des Femmes Artistes Américaines, the Femmes Pastellistes and Les XII.

An example of the successful woman at the end of the 19th century is Camille Claudel (q.v.), a sculptor who studied at the Académie Colarossi, in a co-operative studio with other women, and finally with Rodin. Her work was promoted by several dealers including Samuel Bing and Eugéne Blot and she had a crowning Salon success in 1893. She concentrated on small-scale sculptures that would have a wider market among collectors, and she allied herself with the Symbolist intelligentsia with her themes of love and death. By 1900 she was hailed as one of the greatest sculptors of her day. Claudel did not have the benefit of the Ecole des Beaux-Arts, nor was her income secure through large-scale public sculptures. She advanced her career instead by training in the best schools and ateliers available to her and reached the public primarily through the efforts of a dealer even though she continued to show at the Salons. As the successful women throughout the 19th century had done, she patched together both conventional and unconventional elements from the array available to her to appeal to the tastes and desires of her own time.

NANCY MOWLL MATHEWS

20th century

1900-1930

Lady art students of the present day are going to Paris in increasing numbers. That the life they lead there differs from that led by their male companions, both as regards its freedom and its strenuousness, goes without saying; but it is sufficiently Bohemian for the most enterprising feminine searcher after novelty.

Thus wrote the reviewer Clive Holland in *The Studio* of December 1903. Despite the social constraints of gender that are acknowledged here, at the beginning of the 20th century Paris offered women artists better opportunities for exhibiting and training than those available in most provincial French towns and in many other European art centres. The capital attracted many aspiring women artists from the French provinces, from Europe and America, who came to study and exhibit their work, and who subsequently settled in the city. This group, which includes French names such as Marie Laurencin (q.v.) and Jacqueline Marval, as well as Tamara de Lempicka (q.v.) and Sonia Delaunay (q.v.) from Russia and María Blanchard from Spain, forms part of a broader international artistic culture, shared by both male and female artists, for whom Paris had become an undisputed artistic centre and the cradle of so-called avant-garde developments. Many other women artists came to Paris for shorter periods to work, study, and/or exhibit. Among the better-known names are Paula Modersohn-Becker, Käthe Kollwitz, Gabriele Münter and Marianne Werefkin from Germany, and Natalya Goncharova and Lyubov Popova from Russia (all q.v.).

Although the Ecole des Beaux-Arts was fully open to women by 1900 (when they were finally allowed to enter the ateliers), its influence was already on the wane. Increasingly, public interest and critical attention seem to have shifted from the official, government-sponsored salons and art schools towards the more commercial arena of the private galleries and academies and the independent exhibiting societies. For artists of both sexes who were interested in pursuing more "progressive" forms of art that could feed the growing network of private galleries, dealers and collectors, the many private Parisian academies were a popular training ground. Between 1900 and 1914 a large number of such academies were springing up under the leadership of well-known or established artists, including the Académie Matisse (founded by Henri Matisse), the Académie de la Palette (whose teachers included Amédée Ozenfant and Dunoyer de Segonzac) and the Académie Ranson (whose teachers included Paul Sérusier and Maurice Denis). The Académie Russe, a school founded exclusively for Russian art students in Paris, attracted many women who worked alongside other emigré artists such as Soutine and Zadkine.

Most of these institutions admitted women and included large numbers of foreign students. By 1900 the Académie Colarossi was competing with the Académie Julian as one of the most popular art schools for women students, attracting a truly international clientele. Clive Holland described a morning class at Colarossi's in 1903, in which

> there were five girls and half a score of men working on sketches of a Spaniard in matador costume: except that 50 per cent of the men were Americans, there was scarcely another instance of two of the same workers being of the same nationality.

As Colarossi's became one of the most popular venues for foreign students, conditions could be crowded. The Russian artist Marevna, who moved to Paris in 1912, has provided a vivid description of a mixed life-drawing class that she joined one evening that year:

> The crowd there was thicker still; the building was filled with a whole army of young students of all nationalities, and all the rooms were packed. In the one where we were drawing from the nude the air was stifling, because of an inferno permeated by the strong smell of perspiring bodies mixed with scent, fresh paint, damp waterproofs and dirty feet; all this was intensified by the thick smoke from cigarettes and the strong tobacco of pipe smokers. The model under the electric light was perspiring heavily and looked at times like a swimmer coming up out of the sea. The

> post was altered every five minutes, and the enthusiasm and industry with which we all worked had to be seen to be believed [*Life in Two Worlds*, 1962, p.122].

Women's access to the growing number of private academies also provided a context within which they might be associated with, or become aware of, some of the early modernist groups and networks. Although the educational culture and the conditions of artistic production continued to favour a male-dominated profession, the atmosphere of the private academies – and some of the bohemian artistic circles associated with them – helped to expand the educational and artistic alternatives for women during the first decade of the century. Many of these institutions increased the possibilities for acquiring less "academic" forms of training, and allowed women to work alongside male artists who have now come to be seen as "heroes" of the Parisian avant-garde. For example, Kees van Dongen's influence on many of his female students who graduated from the Académie Vitti is now well known, encouraging a widespread pursuit of "Fauve" interests during this period. And in 1907 Georges Braque, who had been a fellow pupil with Laurencin at the Académie Humbert, first introduced her to Picasso and his circle of friends around the Bateau Lavoir.

Access to exhibiting space and the support of a dealer were, of course, crucial factors in the establishment of a career in art. For women seeking such a career during the first two decades of the 20th century, there were still professional obstacles to be overcome. However, the success of the so-called "independent" salons during this period helped to make available more exhibiting opportunities for both male and female artists. Since its foundation in 1884, the Salon des Indépendants had provided an outlet for those artists whose work did not meet the more traditional standards required in the official salons. Moreover, the Indépendants was open to anyone, and (in theory at least) did not employ a jury system. This encouraged submissions from women who might otherwise have been thwarted by professional prejudice. This society became one of the most important exhibiting spaces for women during the first two decades of the 20th century, when Jacqueline Marval, Emilie Charmy, Laurencin, Suzanne Valadon (q.v.) and others showed there regularly. Valadon was well known for her outspoken support of the "open" exhibiting policies of the society, although she deplored what she saw as its decline in the late 1910s. Most of the women associated with the Cubist movement, including Sonia Delaunay, Alice Halicka, Marevna and Blanchard, showed regularly at the Indépendants during the 1910s.

Another outlet popular with lesser known artists was the Salon d'Automne, founded in 1903. Unlike the Salon des Indépendants, admissions were controlled by an elected jury, but in its early years it encouraged submissions from "beginners" and "those modern artists who found it so difficult to gain the publicity they deserved" (Franz Jourdain, first president, 1905). Many women artists working on the fringes of the Fauve movement, including Charmy and Marval, submitted regularly to the annual Salon d'Automne show. In fact, both women had exhibits in the famous Salon d'Automne of 1905 and 1906 (seminal shows in the history of Fauve painting), although their works were hung separately from the now notorious Fauve galleries. In terms of their aesthetic interests both women were producing canvases that would now qualify as Fauve, but they did not participate directly within the Fauve circle that exhibited together. Evidence from catalogues and reviews suggests that this circle was organised into a recognisable exhibiting group largely by Matisse, and that its self-image as a group of "radical" artists involved a sense of predominantly masculine creative roles. Thus the many women painters who adopted similar styles and technical interests were rarely represented in the group hanging space or seldom participated in collective studio activity.

With the growth of the commercial market during the pre-war period, the support of a dealer became a vital source of economic and professional security for artists. Powerful dealers such as Bernheim-Jeune, Ambroise Vollard and Daniel Kahnweiler played significant roles in the sale and promotion of work by artists such as Matisse, Derain, Picasso and Braque, who are now seen as key figures in the early history of modernism. Although the work of many women artists was taken up by dealers, and some received contracts, memories and accounts by several women suggest that relationships between female artists and male dealers were often vulnerable to exploitation by the latter. In her autobiography *Life in Two Worlds* Marevna expressed her anger at the sexually exploitative relationships that were often on offer (to her) in return for a dealer's support.

By the 1920s, however, increasing numbers of women had entered the male-dominated profession of dealer. These included Berthe Weill, Jeanne Bucher, Blanche Guillot, Colette Weil and Katia Granoff. Weill, who first established her famous gallery in 1901, made her name as one of the first dealers to buy the work of Picasso and Matisse. She was continually dogged by financial problems and lacked the capital resources of major dealers such as Vollard, but her commitment to promote the work of young and little-known artists involved the patronage of several women artists who were beginning to achieve limited success in the 1900s, 1910s and 1920s, including Marval, Charmy, Laurencin, Valadon and Halicka. But in her accounts of her days as a dealer Weill continually complains about the difficulties that she experienced as a woman trying to survive in a competitive and predominantly masculine world, writing in 1917: "A woman's struggle is hard and requires an exceptionally strong will."

A more conventional way in which women could relate (as patrons) to the world of culture at the beginning of the 20th century was as hostesses of artistic "salons", a form of patronage that echoed the wealthy *salonnières* of the 18th century, and which was traditionally dominated by women from the *haute bourgeoisie* or aristocracy. During the period before World War I the influx of many wealthy American women to Paris began to swell the ranks of this group of female patrons and collectors, of whom the best known is probably Gertrude Stein. While Stein became a key figure within those bohemian avant-garde groups that flourished around the now mythical figure of Picasso, and an important collector of Cubist works, she showed little interest in the work of contemporary women artists. Although her public display of an unconventional lesbian sexuality and her committed pursuit of a career as a professional writer undermined certain masculine codes of artistic and sexual behaviour, she seems to have shown little concern to promote the roles of other women artists and writers.

Public perceptions of such roles were closely tied up with contemporary ideas (moral, social, political and aesthetic) on what constituted a desirable femininity. The increasing numbers of women entering the profession during the first decade of the 20th century helped to generate a critical discourse on the most desirable forms of art practice for *les femmes peintres* (a distinct category that clearly separated women from the largely male notion of *peintre*). The improvement in educational and exhibiting possibilities for women, and their increased visibility within professional spaces, also provoked a misogynistic fear (in some quarters) that they were somehow destabilising the profession. In his book *Parisiennes de ce temps*, published in 1910, Octave Uzanne wrote:

> Women authors, painters and musicians have multiplied during the last twenty years in bourgeois circles, and even in the demi monde. In painting especially they do not meet with the violent opposition they endured in former times. One may even say that they are too much in favour, too much encouraged by the pride and ambition of their families, for they threaten to become a veritable plague, a fearful confusion, and a terrifying stream of mediocrity. A perfect army of women painters invades the studios and the Salons, and they have even opened an exhibition of "women painters and sculptors" where their works monopolise whole galleries.

Much of the critical writing that surrounded the activities of women painters in the first three decades of the century reveals a concern to categorise some notion of "feminine" art, which is defined according to a set of assumptions about the "stronger" or more "intellectual" qualities of "masculine" art. Women's traditional association with the decorative arts, especially in areas such as fabric design, fashion design and embroidery, itself affected public perceptions of what might constitute "women's art", and encouraged notions of "feminine" art as somehow more decorative or "delicate". But such stereotypes have long and complicated histories, which can be traced back to 18th- and 19th-century characterisations of women's roles and artistic practices. Such categories were subject to constant re-negotiation and debate during the first decades of the 20th century, when increasing numbers of women were engaging with modernist concerns in painting, and competing with men for comparable professional status.

Public perceptions of the nature and status of women's art was, of course, directly affected by its visibility in the influential salons and private galleries. During World War I, when many male artists were mobilised, women's names are (not surprisingly) more visible on exhibition lists. Although larger salons such as the Indépendants and the Salon d'Automne closed for the duration of the war, many private dealers continued to buy and sell. After the initial slump of the first year of the war, business picked up, and several important exhibitions of modern art were organised. Perhaps the most publicised of these was the famous Salon d'Antin of July 1916, which was titled "L'Art moderne en France", and organised by André Salmon, an influential critic of avant-garde art. The show included Picasso's notorious *Les Demoiselles d'Avignon* of 1907 and works by Matisse, Derain, van Dongen, Max Jacob, Fernand Léger, Gino Severini and Giorgio De Chirico. Unusually for a show that claimed to represent the avant-garde, around one-fifth of the exhibits were by women artists, including Marevna, Blanchard, Marval and Marie Vassiliev.

GILL PERRY

1930–1945

There is no distinct break in the story of women artists and their training in Paris after 1930, at least before World War II. Unfortunately, much basic archival work on less prominent figures remains to be done, and this account can only begin to build up a picture through contrasting examples. Certain figures became more prominent in the mid-1930s, such as the dealer Jeanne Bucher, whose stable included the female artists of the already international movement of geometric abstract painting and sculpture called Abstraction-Création – women such as Sophie Taeuber-Arp (q.v.), wife of Jean Arp, Paule Vézelay and Marlow Moss. Abstraction-Création, taking the name Réalités Nouvelles from an exhibition at the Galerie Charpentier in 1939, transformed itself into the Salon des Réalités Nouvelles after World War II. The changes in the prestige of "modernism" as such in the 1930s of course had an impact. As life and art in the Soviet Union became more repressive, dealers such as Katia Granoff came to Paris, where she ran a very successful gallery through to the 1960s and beyond. Another ambitious young Russian woman was Nadia Khodossievitch. Having trained with Malevich and the leader of the so-called Polish Unists, Wladislaw Streminski, in Russia, Khodossievitch was horrified by the turn from

Suprematism to "productionism" and resolved to abandon an increasingly utilitarian ethos to work in Paris under Fernand Léger. Escaping via marriage to Stanislas Grabowski, she met Léger at the Académie Moderne with Ozenfant and her fellow Russian, Alexandra Exter (q.v.), in 1924. Paradoxically, as she acquired greater prestige, changing from pupil to teacher in Léger's academy, which she ran for him during his trips to America in the late 1930s, her work responded to the Communist call for realism and she exhibited realist works in the left-wing venue that opened in 1934, the Maison de la Culture.

The 1930s was a time of severe economic crisis in France, especially for artists whose market, with the exception of figures such as Picasso, collapsed. It is interesting that one of the chief organisers of the Communist-orientated Association des Ecrivains et des Artistes Révolutionnaires, Boris Taslitzky, the companion of Amrita Sher-Gil, came as she did from Lucien Simon's atelier in the Ecole des Beaux-Arts. However, under the auspices of the Maison de la Culture, which absorbed the AEAR organisation, a new strain of autodidactic painters came to a certain prominence, such as Edouard Pignon and André Fougeron; their working-class origins meant that they frequented the "Université Nouvelle" or "Université Ouvrière" for political instruction, and at the same time evening drawing classes (such as the one in the working-class *arrondissement* of Belleville) and copied in the Louvre – a practice recommended by Léger and Jacques Lipchitz, both of whom ran open studios of a kind under the auspices of the AEAR. The ethos of the "worker" and "proletarian painting" was, however, very masculine, despite the presence of women artists such as Gisèle Delsinne, Andrée Viollis and Nadia Khodossievitch, and influential younger art historians such as Agnès Humbert, whose book on *David* was one of the first to offer a "Marxist" vision of the revolutionary artist. This was the time of Popular Front reform and democratisation of art structures and institutions in general. Madeleine Rousseau was a driving force, along with Georges-Henri Rivière, of the Association Populaire des Amis des Musées. The photographer Gisèle Freund politicised her art, with photocollages such as *La Misère de Paris* shown at the third Exposition d'Habitation at the Salon des Art Menagers in 1936; while the glamorous Charlotte Perriand, who visited the Soviet Union in 1934 to supervise the construc-

tion of Le Corbusier's Centrosoya building, worked on the Popular Front-inspired Centre Rural with Léger for the Paris Exposition Internationale of 1937, and would help Le Corbusier with the design of the working-class kitchen for his Maison d'Habitation in Marseille after the war.

The anti-fascist, pro-Communist movement of the 1930s was international, Parisian organisations having their counterparts in London or Amsterdam. Thus the artists Kowalska, Yvette Guibert and the Swede Greta Knutson (wife of Tristan Tzara) were among those who sent works from Paris to the Artists' International Association anti-fascist exhibition in London in 1935, while reciprocally Nan Youngman, Misha Black, Elisabeth Watson and Betty Rea came from the London AIA to Paris to work on James Holland's statistically-orientated murals for the League of Nations room and the International Peace Campaign room in the Peace Pavilion at the Paris Exposition Internationale of 1937: here the political tensions were massively intensified in the light of the Spanish Civil War and the bombing of Guernica. Ironically, the most memorable of all sculptures at the exhibition was the gigantic industrial worker and peasant woman, brandishing hammer and sickle respectively, atop the Russian Pavilion, a sculpture by Vera Mukhina (q.v.), who had trained with Rodin's epigone, Emile Bourdelle, and at the Académie de la Grande Chaumière before 1914.

After 1945

The generation of female artists of the 1940s continued to espouse traditional techniques and the ethos of the School of Paris. Painters such as the Romanian Natalia Dumitrescu and the Portuguese Maria Elena Vieira da Silva (q.v.) continued with traditional easel paintings, conventional formats and the emphasis on *belle peinture*, the sensuality of the *tache* (dab) of paint, respecting the conventions of their pre-war training. Vieira da Silva had trained at La Grande Chaumière, the Académie Fernand Léger and Stanley William Hayter's Atelier 17 (for engraving); now a new and vertiginous sense of dissolving depths and perspectives gave her work a contemporary "existentialist" feel. The division of the Parisian scene into a series of conflicting styles with their own Salons continued: the Salon des Tuileries, the Salon des Indépendants, the Salon des Réalités Nouvelles, which started up again in 1946 for abstract geometric art and was international in scope (663 exhibits from 16 countries by 1948); the new and more eclectic Salon de Mai, founded in 1945, at first under an existentialist aegis (the writings of Camus and Sartre were exhibited), later a forum for new works by Matisse and Picasso as well as the host of epigones. The Salon des Moins de Trente Ans, founded during the German occupation, was a forum for young talent with a sense of political commitment: together with such artists as Bernard Buffet, female artists, totally forgotten today, such as Angèle Macles-Herment, exhibited there, while Mireille Miailhe came to prominence in 1948 at this salon with the vengeful widows of *Les Veuves* in 1946; her satirical painting, *La Visite de l'atelier (les amateurs)*, was again the star of the salon in 1948. A generation of painters affected by the impact of the Communist Resistance after 1941 and the electoral success of the Party in 1944 – very often either trained to paint figuratively, or autodidacts – joined the wave of realist painters with socialist-realist themes that, surprisingly enough, started to dominate the Salon d'Automne, former birthplace of Fauvism, from 1947–8. Despite accusations of an art controlled and directed by Stalin's cultural spokesman A.A. Zhdanov, many artists such as Geneviève Zondervan and Marie-Anne Lansiaux exhibited canvases with themes such as unemployment, strikes, protest marches, in good faith, until the situation changed to become one of deliberate provocation. In 1951 the French police removed seven canvases from the Salon d'Automne, including Lansiaux's *1 May 1951*, of the Communist protest marches; this gave symbolic dimensions to the Party's confrontation with the government over policy. Major exhibitions such as *Algérie 52*, sponsored by the French Communist Party, demonstrated the importance of painting as a medium in this kind of debate, a medium more effective at the time than journalism, cinema or television, still a luxury in France. Mireille Miailhe continued the tradition of orientalist painters in *Algérie 52* (which she shared with Boris Taslitzky) in the steps of her 20th-century female orientalist precursors. Before 1939 women such as Lucie Ranvier-Chartier, Elisabeth Faure, Jeanne Thil or the remarkable official sculptor Anna Quinquaud had received their training, commissions and honours from the French state. Miailhe, too, ventured into the far-flung reaches of French colonial territory, but to report on resistance, political rebellion and shocking poverty, adopting the

djellabah in order to penetrate sequestered female spaces and to sketch more inconspicuously. Special exhibitions aside, realism, to a greater or lesser extent politically engaged, continued to dominate the Salon d'Automne until 1953; the Salon des Moins de Trente Ans metamorphosed (inevitably!) into the Salon de la Jeune Peinture in 1953, which would become the hotbed of the politically engaged post-Stalinist "New Figuration" movement in the 1960s (again a "macho" movement with less scope for female painters).

The Communists and the Surrealists were long-standing ideological enemies in France; one confrontation that exemplifies attitudes towards style and technique was their differing interpretation of the poet Lautréamont's famous maxim: "Poetry should be made by all and not by one". For the Communists, this meant a democratisation of art involving easy legibility of style and a clear "message". Often, alas, a "levelling down" was involved, and paintings of great banality were produced. For the Surrealists, however, Lautréamont's dictum was translated as performative: everyone should *make* art. Though so many painters who ended up as Surrealists were professionally trained, the "Surrealist object" in combination, later, with Marcel Duchamp's "ready-made", vitiated both the purpose and the necessity for such training. While Eileen Agar (q.v.), for example, was trained as a painter at the Slade, her two versions of *Angel of Anarchy*, exhibited at the International Surrealist exhibitions in Amsterdam and London in 1938 and 1940 respectively, were examples of *bricolage*: improvisations (over a classical cast) using silk, feathers, diamanté, and in homage to Surrealism's inspirations of ethnographic origin, Oceanic art "fetishes", cowrie shells and African bark. Surrealism was marketed in many private galleries in Paris in the 1940s but, as always, had no Salon. International Surrealist exhibitions, however, were held again in 1947, 1959 and 1965. Importantly, the renewal of Surrealism in Paris coincided with the discovery of so-called psychopathological art in Paris, shown at the Sainte-Anne psychiatric hospital in 1946 and on an international scale in 1950, and, at the same time, Jean Dubuffet's promotion of Art Brut, art by "outsiders", the untrained, the mentally ill. Many Art Brut artists who now have a "classic" status were discovered for the first time in this post-war period at the Sainte-Anne hospital, at the exhibition *Art Brut préféré aux arts culturels* at the

Galerie René Drouin in 1947, and the great retrospective at the Musée des Arts Décoratifs in 1967. These shows included such women as "Aloyse", the medium Jeanne Tripier, and the British woman Madge Gill, while in the international Surrealist exhibition devoted to Eros at the Galerie Daniel Cordier in 1957 slightly "deranged" artists such as Leonora Carrington (q.v.) and Hans Bellmer's companion Unica Zürn (q.v.), who figured alongside the Art Brut artist Aloyse. Carrington had been academically trained in Italy and London, while Zürn became severely mentally disturbed, discovered the chance technique of decalcomania independently from the Surrealists, and produced automatic drawings as well as superb anagrammatic poetry. Meret Oppenheim's "cannibal feast" at the opening, a living woman bedecked with food, prone on the banquet table, epitomised the Surrealist attitude to Eros; no training was necessary here.

These important changes in sensibility, which involved a fundamental shift regarding notions of both "modernism" and "professionalism" transform one's understanding of major artists of the 1960s such as Niki de Saint Phalle (q.v.). Genuinely successful professional women artists in the postwar period were few: Vieira da Silva and Germaine Richier (q.v.) come most strongly to mind; the dealers Jeanne Bucher to 1947, Collete Allendy, Denise René – who has promoted abstract geometric art (including Aurélie Nemours) in her gallery since 1945, and in the 1960s Iris Clert, doyenne for the Nouveaux Réalistes, had extremely important roles. In a situation of such stylistic plurality, various registers of realism coexisted: Bernard Buffet, Francis Gruber, Balthus, Jean Hélion were important artists remote from the socialist realist arguments. Moreover, in a context of political attacks on abstraction (as incomprehensible and elitist), "modernism" by this time – not a term used in post-war France as it is today – was a historical concept. The "second" modernism, in the Greenbergian sense, of the New York School was yet to have its impact in France. Certainly the figurative work of Germaine Richier, in bronze, with its deliberate evocation not only of her 16th-century precursor Filigier Richier but also the great tradition exemplified and continuing with Rodin and Bourdelle, has nothing to do with "modernism" and everything to do with continuity, from her use of Rodin's model Nardone to her use of the same

skilled families, Rudier, Valsuani and Susse, to cast her pieces.

Turning to Niki de Saint Phalle, who was initially so insecure about her lack of training, it was precisely the "extra-professional" sources that gave her work its strength and uniqueness and, in turn, one could argue, reinvigorated the "canon" itself, as the work of Jean Dubuffet had done before her. Hence she joined no school or immediate artistic community, but with encouragement retained her essentially autodidact style, reinforced by the eccentricity of Gaudí's ceramics (discovered in 1955) and the Palais du Facteur Cheval – a Surrealist favourite. To what extent is the evocation of such "female" qualities as abundance, decorativeness, hysteria and "schizophrenia" in her work deliberate? Such works include: the *Joan of Arc* door (1959); the "homemade" aspect of *St Sebastian or Portrait of My Lover*, with "ready-made" shirt and dartboard; the "kitchen" element of the first meat-cleaver assemblages and the *Tirs* (shooting paintings) of spaghetti, eggs and tomatoes that spilled out of the ruptured plaster; and the fertility goddess Nanas, covered in plastic fruit and flowers as well as children's toys – out of the 16th-century painter Arcimboldo but certainly recalling Oppenheim's living "cannibal feast". As always when the ratios are so imbalanced, Niki's status within the Nouveau Réaliste group of Arman, César, Gérard Deschamps and Martial Raysse, Raymond Hains, Daniel Spoerri and the *affichistes* (torn poster artists) Raymond Hains and Jacques de la Villéglé was that of a female "supplement", a mascot. More telling of the overwhelming ideological and institutional odds facing women artists – who in ateliers and even the large Salons were quite numerous, is the proportional statistics of men to women artists in the retrospective 72 *pour 72: Douze ans d'art contémporain* held in Paris in 1972, which purported to summarise the achievements of the last 12 years – the liberated 1960s, no less. Seventy men were exhibited; there were two women artists, Niki de Saint Phalle and the Nebraska-born textile artist Sheila Hicks. Niki's great supporter Pontus Hulten continued this stance in his quasi-millennial survey *Territorium artis*, which opened at the Kunst- und Ausstellungshalle in Bonn in 1992, which showed 4 female artists and 106 men! The show was topped on the upper and roof garden with Niki's retrospective – again a demonstration of the curious "supplementary" status of the woman artist. While Niki's collaborative works with the Swiss kinetic sculptor Jean Tinguely were hugely successful, such reciprocity was extremely rare: one has only to mention the cramping effect of Picasso on the independence of the photographer Dora Maar (q.v.) or the painter Françoise Gilot; even Roland Penrose – hardly a great painter – dampened the *élan* of the American photographer Lee Miller (q.v.), who became wife, cook, hostess – and the aggression revealed in the themes of the later work of Dorothea Tanning (q.v) expresses to some extent the mixed emotions she experienced, living perpetually in the orbit of Max Ernst.

It is the lesser-known artists whose careers are sometimes the most informative of the lost stories of the institutions of artistic practice beyond the commercial gallery world. In Marie-Anne Lansiaux's archives, for example, are documents relating to official purchases by the French State: in 1947 the Ministère de l'Education Nationale, Direction Générale des Arts et des Lettres, bought *A Little Kitchen* (*c.*1942) for 4,000 francs; in 1951, at the height of her political engagement, the same education ministry acting for Arts et Lettres, Direction de l'Enseignement et de la Production Artistique, bought *The Yard*, exhibited at the Salon Populiste, for 30,000 francs, and the Communist municipality of Saint-Denis bought a political work, *Departure of a Peace Demonstration in the Suburbs*, for 60,000 francs; in 1953 a still life was bought after being exhibited at the Salon des Indépendants for the State for 20,000 francs, and *The Street* from the Salon Populiste by the Ville de Paris for 100,000 francs. Lansiaux's contemporary and friend Geneviève Zondervan served on the committee and continued to exhibit in the international Biennale des Femmes Peintres et Sculpteurs: 108 salons took place between 1882, when Mme Léon Bertaux (q.v.) launched the first, and 1992. One third of the 230 women exhibiting in that last Salon did so for the first time. The president, Janine Canault, declared: "This Salon has existed since 1882, and yet ... There are still too few women painters in the galleries, little interest in their work in the media, a hesitant attitude on the part of speculators and art amateurs as far as they are concerned."

While immense contrasts exist between countries, between the now-equalising opportunities for training at least in the affluent West, it is significant that the most "equal" of democracies, America, should have spawned the Guerrilla Girls: "a bunch of masked avengers", who "fight sexism and racism in the art world with facts, humour and fake fur". They materialised in their gorilla masks "mysteriously in the dark night of 1988" in response to "An international survey of painting and sculpture" at the Museum of Modern Art in New York, a show in which a mere 13 of the 169 artists were women. No single woman has yet come forward to betray an identity behind the mask: they call themselves Romaine Brooks, Frida Kahlo, Tina Modotti, Gertrude Stein; they campaign on political issues as well as art. Lee Krasner declared: "We secretly suspect that all women are born Guerrilla girls. It's just a question of helping them discover it ... " Guerrilla Girls have travelled to Barcelona, Basel, Berlin, Dublin, Graz, Helsinki, Oslo and Vienna in Europe: they have featured recently in the review *Blocnotes* in Paris. Will they make a difference?

SARAH WILSON

Bibliography

Madame de Staël (Anne Louise Germaine), *Corinne; ou, L'Italie*, 1807; English translation, New Brunswick, NJ: Rutgers University Press, 1987

Louise-Elisabeth Vigée-Lebrun, *Souvenirs de Mme Louise-Elisabeth Vigée Lebrun*, 3 vols, Paris: Fournier, 1835–7; as *Memoirs of Madame Vigée Lebrun*, ed. Lionel Strachey, New York: Doubleday, 1903; London: Grant Richards, 1904; abridged edition with introduction by John Russell, New York: Braziller, 1989

May Alcott Nieriker, *Studying Art Abroad and How To Do It Cheaply*, Boston: Roberts, 1879

E. Somerville, "An 'atelier des dames'", *Magazine of Art*, 1886, pp.152–7

Marie Bashkirtseff, *Le Journal de Marie Bashkirtseff*, ed. A. Theuriet, 2 vols, Paris, 1887; as *The Journal of Marie Bashkirtseff*, London: Cassell, 1890; ed. Rozsika Parker and Griselda Pollock, London: Virago, 1985

Emile Zola, *L'Argent*, 1891; as *Money*, 1894

Octave Uzanne, *Parisiennes de ce temps*, Paris: Mercure de France, 1910

Berthe Weill, *Pan! dans l'oeil! (Ou trente ans dans les coulisses de la peinture contemporaine, 1900–1930)*, Paris: Lipschutz, 1933

Ambroise Vollard, *Recollections of a Picture Dealer*, Boston: Little Brown, and London: Constable, 1936; reprinted New York: Dover, 1978

Deux peintres et un poète retour d'Algérie: Boris Taslitzky, Mireille Miailhe et Jacques Dubois, Paris: Editions Cercle d'Art, 1952

Marevna Vorobëv, *Life in Two Worlds*, London and New York: Abelard Schuman, 1962

Harrison C. White and Cynthia A. White, *Canvases and*

Careers: Institutional Change in the French Painting World, New York: Wiley, 1965

Women Artists, 1550–1950, exh. cat., Los Angeles County Museum of Art, and elsewhere, 1976

Sharon Flescher, "Women artists at the Paris Salon of 1870: An avant-garde view", *Arts Magazine*, lii/3, 1977, pp.99–101

Abstraction-Création, 1931–1936, exh. cat., Westfälisches Landesmuseum, Münster, and Musée d'Art Moderne de la Ville de Paris, 1978

Iris Clert, *Iris-Time: L'artventure*, Paris: Denoel, 1978

L'altra metà dell'avanguardia, 1910–1940: Pittrici e scultrici nei movimenti delle avanguardie storiche, exh. cat., Palazzo Reale, Milan, and elsewhere, 1980

Malcolm Gee, *Dealers, Critics and Collectors of Modern Painting: Aspects of the Parisian Art Market Between 1910 and 1930*, New York: Garland, 1981

Katia Granoff, *Ma vie et mes rencontres*, Paris: Bourgeois, 1981

Paris-Paris, 1937–1957: Créations en France, exh. cat., Centre Georges Pompidou, Paris, 1981

J. Diane Radycki, "The life of lady art students: Changing art education at the turn of the century", *Art Journal*, xlii, Spring 1982, pp.9–13

AIA: The Story of the Artists' International Association, 1933–1953, exh. cat., Museum of Modern Art, Oxford, 1983

Carte blanche à Denise Réné: Aventure géométrique et sinétique, exh. cat., Paris Art Center, 1984

Charlotte Yeldham, *Women Artists in Nineteenth-Century France and England*, 2 vols, New York: Garland, 1984

Guy Vighnot, *La Jeune Peinture, 1941–1961*, Paris: Edition Terre des Peintres, 1985

Paul Duro, "The 'Demoiselles à Copier' in the Second Empire", *Woman's Art Journal*, vii/1, 1986, pp.1–7

Shari Benstock, *Women of the Left Bank: Paris, 1900–1940*, Austin: University of Texas Press, 1986; London: Virago, 1987

Michèle Lefrançais, "Art et aventure au féminin", *Coloniales, 1920–1940*, exh. cat., Musée Municipale, Boulogne-Billancourt, 1989, pp.53–66

Marina Sauer, *L'Entrée des femmes à l'Ecole des Beaux-Arts, 1880–1923*, Paris: Ecole Nationale Supérieure des Beaux-Arts, 1990

Catherine Millet, *Conversations avec Denise René*, Paris: Biro, 1991

Biennale des femmes peintres et sculpteurs, 1882–1992: 108ème Salon, exh. cat., Grand Palais, Paris, 1992

Hommage à Nadia Léger: Retrospective, 1967–1992, exh. cat., Musée National Fernand Léger, Biot, 1992

Catherine Fehrer "Women at the Académie Julian in Paris", *Burlington Magazine*, cxxxvi, 1994, pp.752–7

Tamar Garb, *Sisters of the Brush: Women's Artistic Culture in Late Nineteenth-Century Paris*, New Haven and London: Yale University Press, 1994

Jeanne Bucher: Une galerie d'avant-garde, 1925–1946, exh. cat., Les Musées de la Ville de Strasbourg, 1994

Nancy Mowll Mathews, *Mary Cassatt: A Life*, New York: Villard, 1994

Gill Perry, *Women Artists and the Parisian Avant-Garde*, Manchester: Manchester University Press, and New York: St Martin's Press, 1995

Sarah Wilson, "Femininities/Mascarades", *Rrose is a Rrose is a Rrose: Gender Performance in Photography*, exh. cat., Solomon R. Guggenheim Museum, New York, 1997

3. Germany, Austria and Switzerland

The fact that so little is known about the history of women artists has to do with the way in which women have been perceived and evaluated. With a few exceptions, art made by women in the German-speaking countries was not purchased in any quantity, collected systematically or carefully preserved; it was not accurately labelled in collections or made the subject of scholarly research. It has thus been difficult to identify the body of art created by women, so that our knowledge of their legacy is incomplete.

The study of women artists did not form part of the usual art-historical syllabus at universities, and interest in the subject increased only with the advent of the modern women's movement. In the mid-1970s exhibitions were organised, beginning with *Künstlerinnen international, 1877–1977*, held at the Neue Gesellschaft für Bildende Kunst in Berlin (1977), and for the first time there were scholarly discussions about women artists and the way in which women were perceived and represented by (male) artists, especially at the congresses of female art historians held in Marburg (1983), Zürich (1984), Vienna (1986), Berlin (1988), Hamburg (1991) and Trier (1995). The first Frauenmuseum was founded in 1981, in Bonn, but it lacked the resources and the opportunities available to an established museum to make acquisitions. At first women artists were regarded as guarantors of female authenticity and less as parts of a context to be reconstructed, so there was concentration on biographical information. Since the political context of work by women (including artistic work) was fundamentally different from the work opportunities for men, a lengthy process of research was required for each period, each country, and each region.

The problems involved in working closely with the received biographical data, of keeping in view the basic differences in the circumstances of female and male artists, and the examination of the conventions and deficits of art history have led to the recognition that ways of seeing can be just as "constructed" as relationships. A critical reassessment of the methodology is needed if we are to grasp the underlying structures of power and patterns of argument behind the testimonies of oppression, silence, and the falsification and marginalisation of female creativity.

In the early 19th century the ideas of the Enlightenment took on a particular significance for women artists who had been born in the previous century. These were mainly the daughters of artist families, whose talents were recognised and encouraged by their fathers or by other relatives. In this way women surmounted the first hurdle in a career as a court artist or a respectable portrait painter that was often carefully planned. Women artists of the 18th century not only provided proof of their talent and their mobility, but they were also sought after, so long as they could be identified as an "exception", that is, distinct from other women, and could be controlled in their ambitions. Not infrequently, male "encouragement" concealed a substantial financial interest; the income might go to the artist's father or husband, for example, or she might have to provide for a family without male support. Even Angelica Kauffman (q.v.) ended up complaining that she was "tired of painting for sale" (quoted in Bremen 1993, p.46), an indication of artistic ambition that rebelled against the expectations of relatives and patrons.

The international status and the high esteem that women artists of previous eras had enjoyed seem to have vanished from the collective consciousness by the beginning of the 19th century. For young girls in the German-speaking world, the only role model of any significance was Angelica Kauffman (ibid., pp.41–4; Memoirs of Johanna Schopenhauer, "Jugendleben und Wanderbilder" (1848) in Berger 1987, pp.60–64). In art centres such as Weimar, Dresden, Berlin, Munich, Vienna, Paris, London and Rome the fame of admired women artists survived longer than elsewhere through commissions, contacts and works accessible to the public. But of greater importance for prospective women artists, who had the greatest difficulty in appealing to female precursors, were the conditions for training in a middle-class environment. Here girls were perceived in terms of their future usefulness as wives

or mothers, and any desire that deviated from this and reached beyond narrow utility received a reprimand. If a woman's appearance made her future role as a wife seem unlikely, then her wish to be trained as an artist might be taken seriously, and she would be encouraged, within limits (as Käthe Kollwitz, q.v., was by her father). In Goethe's circle Caroline Bardua, Louise Seidler and Julie von Egloffstein, and in Konstanz Marie Ellenrieder (q.v.), belong to this category. To be taken seriously in their desire to work as artists, especially if they did not come from artistic families, such women had to flatter and win over famous men or women patrons, and rely on aristocratic or middle-class patronage.

The art academies and their life classes were closed to women, who instead had to rely on overpriced and unsystematic private lessons, and on scholarships and patronage with conditions attached, which seldom allowed them to pursue their own interests and often kept them in the role of permanent petitioners. Women artists had to acquire skills by studying for themselves, but they found that the results of their inadequate training were used to support the thesis that they were a deficient sex unsuited for art. Those who sought to escape from these attitudes by going abroad, leaving behind the provincialism of the little courts in the hope of finding the freedom to develop, discovered, as did Anna Dorothea Lisiewska-Therbusch (q.v.) in the 18th century, that male artists at their destinations also held these double standards. As Diderot wrote with obvious sympathy for Lisiewska-Therbusch:

> She does not lack the talent to arouse interest in a country like ours, she lacks youth, beauty, modesty, coquetterie. She could have been enthusiastic about the merits of our great artists, taken lessons from them, had more bosom and a handsome posterior and have had to offer both to the artists [quoted in Bremen 1993, p.54].

How strongly envy and competitiveness determined the judgement of male colleagues is shown by a remark made by Daniel Chodowiecki in relation to Lisiewska-Therbusch's attempt to go beyond the areas traditionally allotted to women – portraiture and copies of old masters – when she turned to mythological subjects:

It was especially when she had the notion to arouse voluptuous ideas that she was insufferable, particularly when I reflected that this was an old woman who wished to arouse these ideas in order to earn money [ibid., p.51].

Both these sources show that already in the 18th century sexual attitudes were being cited to ward off female competition: members of the French Académie Royale had rejected Lisiewska-Therbusch's *Jupiter Transforms Himself into Pan to Surprise the Sleeping Antiope* on the grounds that it was "obscene". The fact that one of these academicians was Boucher, who openly and without scruple catered for the sexual proclivities of his clientele in his choice of themes, shows clearly that male and female artists were measured by two different standards (*idem*; Nobs-Greter 1984, pp.121–45). This tendency increased in the 19th century. To get training, women artists from middle-class backgrounds who did not come from artist families and who had to rely on patrons, such as Ellenrieder, Bardua and Seidler, had to submit to excessive, constantly monitored respectability. For a woman artist the loss of her reputation meant the loss of everything. Forced into the role of petitioner, she had to earn for herself every concession, every "support", however modest, however wounding to her self-respect. Flattery and a pupil's imitation of a "master" were the tributes that women had to pay in order to gain a minimum of professional attention. If a woman was without youth and beauty – or at least the signals of sexual subjugation – interest in a female artist, as Diderot correctly observed, remained cerebral and unfledged, or else turned to rejection mixed with competitive envy and resentment. The young sculptor Elisabet Ney experienced this when she fought her way from provincial Westphalia to a place as a student at the Munich Academy (1852–4); as an "exception" she was taken into the circle of Varnhagen von Ense, Rahel Varnhagen's widower, and once Christian Daniel Rauch had accepted her as a pupil, she was one of the few women sculptors of her time to obtain public commissions; she made portrait busts of such politicians as *Otto von Bismarck* and *Giuseppe Garibaldi*, of scientists, intellectuals and *Arthur Schopenhauer*, who was impressed by her appearance. Women artists such as Ney found that, as a matter of survival, they had to use their phase of youthful beauty to get themselves professionally established. Beauty, the knack of attracting people's interest, and being prepared to move around – not only on tours to France, England, Greece, Italy, Spain or Egypt, but also from town to town, court to court, pursuing commissions and keeping up contacts – were essential ingredients of success (Emily Fourmy Cutrer, *The Art of the Woman: The Life and Work of Elisabet Ney*, Lincoln: University of Nebraska Press, 1988).

Women artists of the early 19th century found some support and limited patronage in the social circles of sisters and women friends, and – like Seidler or Ellenrieder – in the strict fulfilment of duties and in religiosity. It was to sisters or female friends – such as Bettina von Arnim and Karoline von Günderode – that they felt bound spiritually, in response to their desire to experience the world directly, and to give this experience an appropriate form, one that was not imposed and censored from the outside (Bremen 1993, pp.31–41). Goethe had set an example when he fled to Italy to escape the restrictions of home. In the succeeding decades Rome became the longed-for destination. Those women artists who through grants or commissions were able to make their way there and make contact with other artists (for example, some of the Nazarenes) were mostly noblewomen. Although there is evidence of women taking lodgings together, no circle of women artists at this period made its presence felt in Rome as a corporate body.

It is apparent that in the early 19th century contemporaries and critics were incapable or unwilling to separate the gender of the artist from artistic achievement. What was reviewed was not the work but the gender of its maker. The high-minded and uninhibited treatment of such questions such as Diderot had shown (he posed in the nude for his friend Lisiewska-Therbusch) was to be the exception. Women were measured by conventions; their deficiencies, the result of their lack of education and training, were held against them as part of their "nature". The mental anguish created by these contradictory demands has left traces in the diaries, letters and memoirs of individual women artists (Berger 1987).

The "surplus of women" created by the waves of emigration after 1848 meant that there were fewer and fewer women in the educated middle classes and *petite bourgeoisie* who could be supported by their families. The existing ban on training and a career for members of the middle classes made it increasingly hard to conceal this difficulty by work at home. The Allgemeiner Deutscher Frauenverein, founded in 1865 in the consciousness that women had no political rights, thus concentrated on obtaining access to educational institutions and paid public work to enable women to support themselves.

Women artists were invariably excluded from lucrative commissions because of their poor training, and only a few fields, such as portrait painting and work as copyists, were open to them. Under the pretext of decency they were kept away from life classes, and they were also prevented from displaying their work in public. The extensive network of relationships that characterised the courtly and bourgeois salon culture did, however, enable women to obtain not only a livelihood but also a modest reputation (Susanne Jensen, "'Wo sind die weiblichen Mäzene ... ?' Private Kunstförderung im Verein der Künstlerinnen und Kunstfreundinnen zu Berlin", in Berlin 1992, pp.299–310; Petra Wilhelmy-Dollinger, 'Die Berliner Salons und der Verein der Künstlerinnen und Kunstfreundinnen zu Berlin", *ibid.*, pp.339–52). But the drive towards greater professionalism brought new problems.

If industrialisation had exposed women and girls of the lower classes to the extremes of physical hardship and marginalisation, women from the educated middle classes, *petite bourgeoisie* and the office-holding nobility had a different problem: once they were seen publicly to be contributing to the financial support of a family that could no longer support itself, they found that not only was their own respectability damaged, but also that of their relatives. Unstintingly committed to a pattern of life that only a tiny upper class could maintain, they had to preserve the appearance of leisure without being able to be leisured.

Women's handiwork, which had largely lost its practical function in the family and had degenerated to a status symbol, now took on a new value. In a society that had only recently introduced universal compulsory schooling for girls, without making provision for any further, vocational training, women's handicrafts became a means of survival: the work could be done under family control without having to leave the house, and agencies could be used in order to preserve anonymity – that is, to conceal the fact that women were relying on their earnings. The collapse of such conditions was only a question of time. Numerous women from the middle classes attempted to earn their living without loss of respectability, drawing on their meagre and unsystematic education, which gave them only a basic knowledge of music, drawing, painting and languages. Since they could not be distinguished from the more affluent female amateurs, this was a fatal kind of competition. From now on any woman artist was under suspicion of amateurism, which was the more perfidious when male artists were doing their utmost to keep female competition to a minimum by excluding women from the academies and charging huge training fees.

From 1865, the year in which the organised women's movement emerged with the Allgemeiner Deutscher Frauenverein, Berlin developed into a centre for efforts to create public and paid work for women from middle-class backgrounds. Almost all the professions that were "appropriate to their status" were developed from the range of duties of "higher daughters". The first training centres were aimed at governesses and female amateurs. Among them was the Lette-Verein, founded in 1865. Its liberal founder was a severe opponent of women's emancipation, but in order to mitigate the worst poverty the association offered unmarried women training in painting, sculpture, graphics, illustration and pattern-drawing. The orientation towards the applied arts at the Lette-Verein was also apparent at the Institut für höheren weiblichen Zeichenunterricht, which opened in 1867; in courses for women at the Berlin Gewerbemuseum; and at the Schule für Kunststickerei founded in 1879, which sought to professionalise women's handiwork.

Competition to these institutions, which reacted to the boom in the applied arts, arose with the creation in 1868 of the Zeichen- und Malschule des Vereins der Künstlerinnen und Kunstfreundinnen zu Berlin. This coming together of women artists and society ladies, influential feminists and women patrons, was to continue for many years. The encouragement of young women artists was just as important to them as the task of organising exhibitions, sales and scholarships. Although the school also opened a section for women drawing teachers and employed respected women artists such as Jeanne Bauck and Käthe Kollwitz as teachers, it could not offer the full training programme of an academy.

Meanwhile the art academies followed the common principle of reserving the admission of women not as a right but merely as a favour – if at all (a summary sketch is given in Lehman 1914); their admission was seen mainly in terms of its advantage to the men from uneducated classes who were studying there, and whose cultural level could be raised through a female presence, and not in terms of the well-being of the young women artists (Wolff-Arndt 1929, pp.8, 60–63). The undignified manoeuvring of the academicians can be explained not least as stemming from the anxiety that they might lose the sinecure of their private schools that were crowded with "ladies", women who came almost exclusively from the privileged classes, and who could provide valuable contacts and commissions. (These academicians were mostly young artists who, after finishing their academic training at low cost – set to enable men from the lower classes to study at the academies – opened "schools" in order to finance their own artistic careers.) Such schools also represented a marriage market for rising or older artists (such as Lovis Corinth and Rodolphe Julian), in which the pupils' dowries were as welcome as their social contacts or their organisation of the artist's household. Many teachers were concerned with eliminating competition or attracting female imitators without any prospects. The innumerable secondary intentions of such teachers would have made a meaningful programme of study difficult or impossible.

Marriage in general, and – perversely enough – marriage to artists in particular, endangered the artistic development of women artists more than any other way of life. Celibacy was therefore to be recommended. Yet it was not just young aspiring women artists who were thrust into a contemptuous light by their new freedom of movement in the public and bohemian worlds. The mockery of writers, critics and male artists who drew for such magazines as *Simplicissimus* and *Jugend* was directed indiscriminately against young women, whose beauty was interpreted as lack of seriousness, against "Malweiber" and "Ölschwestern" or the "third sex" (lesbians), who made no secret of their rejection of "unfair" men, but imitated them in their dress and gestures.

In works such as Otto Weininger's *Geschlecht und Character* (1903) writers, academics, philosophers and politicians reveal an ideology of contempt for or hatred of women – and artists of all movements provided a visual affirmation of this. Many caricatures were concerned with the life classes. An unspoken motive of the academicians in excluding female students from life study concerned the sexual relationships that they and their students had with female models. Life study stood at the summit of the academic hierarchy of training, and its highest level was marked by the sexual use made of the model by the teacher and advanced students. The mere presence of female students would have exposed the sexual camaraderie between professors and pupils as well as the double standards of the academicians, who were so severe in their criticism of women.

Three institutions sought to oppose these appalling conditions: the Zeichen- und Malschule der Künstlerinnen und Kunstfreundinnen in Berlin, founded in 1868; the Damenakademie des Münchner Künstlerinnenvereins, established in 1882; and the Malerinnenschule in Karlsruhe, founded in 1885. Although such institutions did not have the means to offer a fully comprehensive academic programme, they were credible and successful as far as professionalism was concerned. They offered women artists the opportunity to teach, and provided their pupils with female role models. The experience of organising such schools, of maintaining the teaching programme and putting on exhibitions and festivals also stood women artists in good stead, since it gave teachers and pupils the opportunity of breaking through the traditional connection between creativity and masculinity and of concentrating on what mattered. Since the schools had to finance themselves through members' subscriptions, school fees, exhibitions and donations, they inevitably recorded a high turnover of younger teachers, who often used them as a springboard for posts in the state-financed and opulently equipped academies or else to build up an independent livelihood. The art academies in Germany and Austria (Switzerland had no art academy) remained exclusively for men until almost the end of the 19th century, and some even into the early 20th century. Here, unlike the USA, the few academically orientated women's schools failed to provide an alternative. The same applies to the three above-mentioned art schools for women if they are compared to academies, but it is notable that some of the best-known women artists emerged from such schools, including Käthe Kollwitz and Paula Modersohn-Becker (q.v.).

The number of women from the middle classes who could no longer be supported by their families must have been considerable; this is the most likely explanation for the demand for the few existing educational opportunities on offer. If women artists were tormented by being placed on the same level as lazy or inept dilettanti, Alfred Lichtwark, the director of the Hamburger Kunsthalle, attempted to play female amateurs against women artists and use them for his own purposes. Lichtwark saw the meagre artistic training of the middle-class male as a reason for the uncompetitiveness of applied art manufactures on an international level. Like his mentors – Justus Brinckmann, director of the Museum für Kunst und Gewerbe in Hamburg, who was married to the painter Henriette Hahn, and Julius Lessing, the head of the Berlin Kunstgewerbemuseum and its school – Lichtwark was in favour of the strict limitation of artistic work for women. He was attracted by the potential of leisured, well-to-do women amateurs, who in his view constituted a high-ranking public. Lichtwark's understanding of art history was slight, and his knowledge of important women artists of earlier centuries even slighter; any serious art not controlled by male interests was regarded with suspicion not only by Lichtwark, but also by the directors of large museums and by critics such as Karl Scheffler (Berger 1982, pp.78–87, 66–72). Since Lichtwark believed that through rich female dilettanti he could gain influence over their husbands, he gave them a programme in the hope of raising the standard of German applied art.

Schools of applied art and organisations of amateurs also had their status in Austria, before the Zeichenschule of the Wiener Frauen-Erwerbs-Verein was founded in 1867 with the aim of "raising taste" and providing women with "new sources of income through drawing and painting" (Plakolm-Forsthuber 1994, pp.32, 39–44). Rudolf von Eitelberger ensured that attached to the K.K. Museum für Kunst und Industrie, established in 1864, was a Kunstgewerbeschule, founded in 1867 and also open to selected young women. He was concerned with the use of culture in the formation of a national identity. In this framework even women who would not otherwise have had the opportunity had a modest "place", though one that was always being questioned. Here parallels with German developments are clear. Craftwork and applied art had a high national status in the consciousness of the reformers. The admission of female students remained restrictive, and for important specialist subjects it was purely a matter of rhet-

oric. Eitelberger's strategy of keeping women away from the specialist classes was successful – as was the later attempt by Gropius at the Bauhaus. Like Lichtwark, Eitelberger believed that "the vocation of women to high art is very limited" (ibid., p.42).

Although here it was only a matter of commercial application and not fine art, women realised to their amazement that the same arguments that had excluded them from the art academies were being directed against them in the sphere of applied art, and they were exposed to the same irritation, scepticism and mockery that they had met from fine artists. The Viennese academy even reinforced the rejection of female pupils. As in Germany, here too there were arrangements between the heads of schools regarding relations with women artists or craftswomen. In the 1880s consideration was even given to excluding women from schools that had just started to accept female pupils.

Twenty years later the rising generation of female craftworkers in Austria profited from a development that in 1900 had led to Austrian handicrafts being presented for the first time in international competition, at the 8th Secession Exhibition in Vienna. The growing demand led in 1903 to the founding of the Wiener Werkstätte. This offered young craftswomen the opportunity of contributing designs that would then be marketed under the firm's name or issued by leading artists as their own work. The strong involvement of trainees/new recruits soon led to the accusation of "feminisation". The assumption so often formulated for art, that male artists were creative and women artists imitative, was transferred in full to applied art and aimed as a reproach against women. Yet they made no official protests against the second-class status assigned to them in the hierarchy of the sexes, and contributed considerably to the success of the Wiener Werkstätte. The poor wages there and the economic hardship that followed World War I, and which lasted until the early 1930s, led to many craftswomen becoming independent. They set up studios and workshops. Emmy Zweybrück-Prochaska established the Kunstgewerbliche Werkstätte in 1913, and in 1915 she combined it with a Kunstgewerbliche Privatlehranstalt, where she trained female pupils – as did Elfriede Berbalk in her Metallwerkstätte. To some critics, women's involvement in craftwork, with its practical use, was merely a modern version of amateurism, and this too damaged the reputation of women artists who had been forced to earn their living in the applied arts in order to survive.

Such foundations, however, marked the first commercial successes. The only parallels elsewhere were in the world of photography. Since 1890, one section of the Lette-Verein had consisted of female photographers, and in Munich the Fotoatelier Elvira (1887–1908), run by Sophia Goudstikker and Anita Augspurg, set standards for portrait, court and society photography for years and brought in its wake comparable firms also run by female photographers. In Vienna Dora Kallmus at the Atelier d'Ora (1907–27) built up a similar clientele consisting of intellectuals, artists, dancers, women writers, etc., and it was to be only a few years before the first women photo-journalists – such as Gerta Taro in the Spanish Civil War – moved beyond the framework of portrait and fashion photography to new areas of work.

Austrian women artists went abroad, to the Munich Damenakademie, for instance, to study or to teach. In 1897, the year in which the Vienna Secession was founded, the Wiener Kunstschule für Frauen und Mädchen was opened. Unlike Germany, here the initiative came not from an association of women artists, but from a painter, Olga Prager. Among the founder-members of the Damenakademie was the Austrian artist Bertha Tarnoczy; later Tina Blau and Carola von Bär-Mathes taught there. On the strength of her experience as a teacher in Munich, Blau, a landscape painter, was recruited as one of the first teachers at the new schools in Vienna. The supporting association was proud of its low student fees. Other teachers were "secessionists and artists of second quality" (ibid., pp.52–3).

Many aspiring women artists lost energy in struggles with their families, with sceptical teachers, with husbands who undermined their work (as Justus Brinckmann did when as a museum director he forbade his wife, Henriette Hahn, to paint) or who allotted them second place (as Lovis Corinth did to Charlotte Berend-Corinth), and with art dealers and critics who did not believe that works by women were worthy of any serious consideration (as Philippine Wolff-Arndt describes in her memoirs). Such prejudices encroached on their own thoughts and feelings (Wolff-Arndt 1929, pp.49, 50–52, 64–5, 96). It was hard to escape the chorus of "important" artists, dignitaries and official representatives who were constantly evoking female inca-

pacity and valued women only as their public or as paying guests, as patrons and copyists.

How were women to keep away from family life, the petty competition for the favour of self-proclaimed "masters" in private ateliers, the chaos of state-imposed restrictions, and actually achieve something? How could young women artists use their money sensibly? How could they gain space for experiments, and develop beyond the barren discussions about the "place" of women artists? How were they to evade the guidance of content, the censorship, the control and the gossip of the "masters" on whom they had to rely for basic training? These and similar questions became all the more pressing as the patronage of the aristocracy and the churches declined in importance. Dora Hitz must have discovered just how difficult it was to go back to the experiences of earlier centuries when she went to the court of Princess Elisabeth of Romania (who had published poetry under the pseudonym of Carmen Sylva and supported the training of women). Neither the court nor the church offered opportunities to gain access to the avant-garde, so Hitz gave up her life at court for the freedom of Paris, where she could study the newest artistic developments.

Before 1900 very few Austrian women made use of the advantages of Paris. Munich had remained the preferred destination for them: it provided respected private ateliers, the Damenakademie and the opportunity on summer courses at the Neu-Dachauto school to study from the nude and to concentrate on landscape painting. Rome had been the destination favoured by German women artists in the early 19th century, but from the late 1860s and early 1870s into the early 20th century German and Swiss women artists sought opportunities in the French capital.

Artists, men and women, from all over Europe and America, went to Paris for the training available there. As far as access to the institutions went, the situation for women hardly differed from that at home: the Ecole des Beaux-Arts was as closed to them as were the academies at home. Here too there was the most undignified struggle, which reached its climax in a public protest organised by students against the presence of the first female students, when in 1897 they were driven out of the school building with a howl of "Down with women!" (Garb 1994, p.103). Private ateliers such as the Académie Julian provided a separate ladies' class, but women had to pay twice as much as men. Nevertheless, Paris offered something that hardly any other city could offer: a lively art scene delighting in innovation, an international body of students, more effective private schools and, as well as exhibitions and publications, participation in the most recent developments in painting and sculpture.

In 1881 French women artists had founded the Union des Femmes Peintres et Sculpteurs, and under the direction of Mme Léon Bertaux (q.v.) and Virginie Demont-Breton had waged a relentless struggle for opportunities in training, exhibitions and commissions. In Paris the Salon des Femmes was founded, as was the *Journal des Femmes Artistes*. The alternation of *galanterie* and contempt with which female students from all over the world were treated at the Académie Julian or Académie Colarossi did not prevent women artists from spending the most productive time of their lives there.

With its descriptions of the teaching at the Académie Julian, the journal of Marie Bashkirtseff (q.v.), which circulated in various versions and translations, also made an impact in Germany. It presented problems of identity with which young women artists such as Paula Modersohn-Becker and Clara Rilke-Westhoff were already familiar from their own experience, before they set off for Paris at the turn of the 20th century. The journals also show that it was not so much the teachers who were the students' role models as their fellow pupils, such as Louise Breslau, because of their professionalism and determination to achieve something.

Ambition, the struggle for prizes and state commissions, for official recognition and support – all this could be experienced and assessed on the spot, in contact with teachers, colleagues, French feminists and fellow pupils from all over the world. Towards the end of the 19th century Paris was more than the sum of the talents assembled there. It offered few opportunities for integration, but rather a sense of alienation, of loneliness and of being unrecognised, which resulted in some of the best works by German and Austrian women artists.

The oeuvre of women artists in the 19th century was created outside the world of academies. Artists, academicians, museum directors, politicians and publicists comprised a network of contacts that women artists as a group were unable to penetrate, and only in isolated instances were they able to set up something in opposition. The women artists of the 19th century could not count on pertinent critique, one that did not lead into a review of the "feminine", on an appropriate reception or on the correct storage of their works; Ernst Guhl (1858), Karl Scheffler (1908) and Hans Hildebrandt (1928) represented the level on which the "discussion" or approach to a "historiography" of female cultural achievements was played. A feature in common among critics was the repetition of clichés, the assertion that women were in principle incapable and the stereotyped pointing to the "place" of women – unattractive, contemptible areas away from interesting developments. Women were suspect as a sex, so no trust was put in their art, and there was no issue that was not sexualised. In 1908 women had joined together in the Bund Deutscher und Österreichischer Künstlerinnenvereine; some were able to exhibit in the Hagenbund, from 1906, or, like Charlotte Berend-Corinth and Käthe Kollwitz, were appointed to the committee and jury of the Berlin Secession; and in 1913 a Frauenkunstverband was planned in order to create an equivalent to the Verein Berliner Künstler, which did not accept female members. But despite such steps forward it is obvious that the struggle of the art academies against women artists was successful. Ironically, when the historic moment for women to enter the academies as students and teachers arrived, the institutions suffered the most radical loss of importance in their history.

One exception to this was the Bauhaus, which flourished during the years of the Weimar Republic (1919–33). Its locations – Weimar, Dessau and Berlin – also marked stages in its internal development. The Bauhaus was linked to democratic hopes. According to its founding programme, it was to be a modern training centre combining the strengths of handicraft, art and industry and, in contrast to the traditional academies, it was to be innovative. The rules adopted in 1919 stipulated that the Bauhaus must accept female students. In the post-war period many young women artists took advantage of this opportunity, although female handicraft traditions were foreign to industrial production (see Anja Baumhoff, "Zwischen Berufung und Beruf: Frauen am Bauhaus" in Berlin 1992, pp.113–120).

There could be no talk of the conquest of new fields. The tolerance of women students was paid for with a strict restriction to "feminine" areas of activity: weaving. It was the architecture departments of traditional academies and technical high schools that trained the first women architects, and in the open market they were initially tied down to interior design, especially for kitchens. Later such women architects as Margarete Schütte-Lihotzky, Liane Zimbler, Friedl Dicker, Ella Briggs-Baumfeld and Lucy Hillebrand concentrated on the building of housing estates and residential projects, and set great store on answering the architectural needs of working women (Plakolm-Forsthuber 1994, pp.237–65; Berlin 1991).

Women artists appeared late as teachers at academies and art schools, occasionally in the 1920s and following World War II; in the 1940s the sculptor Renée Sintenis and the tapestry-maker Woty Werner were appointed to the Hochschule der Künste in Berlin, which succeeded the old Berlin Academy. National Socialism marked a break, with the dissolution of feminist organisations, the exiling of Jewish women artists and the exclusion of "degenerate" women artists. The proscribing of the existing associations of the women's movement, and an ideology that reduced women to motherhood, meant that everything that women artists had hitherto attained was now in doubt: the way ahead was indicated by the exclusion of such renowned figures as Käthe Kollwitz and Renée Sintenis from the Prussian Academy. Women sculptors such as Hanna Cauer profited from their accommodation to the new regime; others passed their lives as unobtrusively as possible in impoverished conditions or in opposition. The most eloquent testimony of these years was left by the Jewish woman painter Charlotte Salomon (q.v.) in a series of drawings *Leben? oder Theater? Ein autobiographisches Singspiel*. Everything that had been built up with infinite struggle was wiped out within a few years. Further damage was done by the bombs of World War II; they destroyed not only the studios of women artists and the work of lifetimes, but also such valuable material as the original diary of Paula Modersohn-Becker.

From the last years of the 19th century until the 1930s there were repeated attempts to raise public awareness of the situation of women as subjects and objects of art through exhibitions, a tradition that was taken up again by the modern women's movement. In 1977 the first survey exhibition *Künstlerinnen international, 1877–1977* was held in Berlin, in Vienna the exhibition *Kunst mit Eigensinn: Aktuelle Kunst von Frauen* (1985) and in Wiesbaden *Künstlerinnen des 20. Jahrhunderts*

(1990). Attempts were made to address the museum policies that had been so disastrous for women artists in the past, a task that the Verborgenes Museum in Berlin took up in 1987 with its *Dokumente von Frauen in Berliner öffentlichen Sammlungen*, assuming the long-overdue reappraisal of the Verein der Künstlerinnen und Kunstfreundinnen zu Berlin with the exhibition *Profession ohne Tradition*. In addition to such thematic exhibitions, there was also a desire to foster co-operation between women artists and women art historians in approaching women artists of the past, and two exhibitions in which female artists and art historians worked together were held in Berlin: *Ich bin nicht ich, wenn ich sehe* (1991) and *Muse küsst Muse* (1995). This was preceded by autobiographical declarations by Judy Chicago (q.v.) in *Through the Flower: My Struggles as an Artist* (1975) and Gisela Breitling in *Die Spuren des Schiffs in den Wellen: Eine autobiographische Suche nach den Frauen in der Kunstgeschichte* (1980), the resonance of which can be compared with the journals of Marie Bashkirtseff.

To sum up, it can be said that the continuum of the history of women artists lies in discontinuity: in ever-new attempts to overcome obstacles, to develop a world view and to give it public value. In the 19th century the function of great patrons, male and female, was gradually assumed by members of the family, friends, salon ladies and organised female connoisseurs of art. Instead of small, educated circles that knew how to assess and encourage art, there soon emerged a new public shaped by the media. The expanding press offered many new opportunities for those opposed to women artists to air their views; this was, however, linked with a rapid decline in the standard of art criticism.

Despite all this, it is all the more surprising to see what and how much was achieved. One explanation is that there was one place in which women artists could think, dream, experiment, give an account of themselves – in their writings (Berger 1987, pp.15–32). In diaries, letters, memoirs, autobiographies, poems and novels a picture emerged of what women artists hoped to become in spite of hostility and contempt, a picture of themselves and a picture of the world seen through their eyes. The written word leaves room for visual imaginings, wishes and hopes, self-doubt and certainties, room for the future. Here – sometimes more strongly than in the world of images created by women artists – what was unseen, un-experienced and new had its first anchoring in reality. For women artists writing meant survival. The writings left by women artists gain in significance in the 19th century. They not only provide clarification but also reflect the attempt to escape alien control, male directives and androcentric systems.

In the midst of the everyday challenges and demands with which women artists had to reckon as women, their publicly silenced voice finds expression in a record for posterity. Without these writings, without the hidden knowledge behind the publicly displayed consciousness, nothing of significance could be created; the diary was necessary for this to become reality. Diaries contain formulations of what threatens the creation of art: external and internal resistance, conventions, prejudices, antifeminism and – yet more dangerous – trivialisation. Diaries are at once the trace of a life and a warning: "To die, oh God, to die having left nothing behind!" wrote Marie Bashkirtseff. "To die like a dog!!! To die like hundreds of thousands of other women, whose names can barely be read on their gravestones" (*ibid.*, p.170). The autobiographical writings left by women artists of the 19th and 20th centuries delineate a topography of genesis, which the scant visual material that survives can reveal to us only occasionally.

RENATE BERGER

Bibliography

General

Ernst Guhl, *Die Frauen in der Kunstgeschichte*, Berlin: Guttentag, 1858
Georg Voss, *Die Frauen in der Kunst*, Berlin, 1895
Karl Scheffler, *Die Frau und die Kunst*, Berlin: Bard, 1908
Henni Lehmann, *Das Kunststudium der Frauen: Ein Vortrag gehalten zu Frankfurt am Main*, Darmstadt: Koch, 1914
Lu Märten, *Die Künstlerin*, Munich: Langen, 1919
Hans Hildebrandt, *Die Frau als Künstlerin*, Berlin: Mosse, 1928
Maria Weese and Doris Wild, *Die Schweizer Frau in Kunstgewerbe und bildender Kunst*, Zürich and Leipzig, 1928
Künstlerinnen international, 1877–1977, exh. cat., Neue Gesellschaft für Bildende Kunst, Berlin, 1977
Germaine Greer, *The Obstacle Race: The Fortunes of Women Painters and Their Work*, London: Secker and Warburg, and New York: Farrar Straus, 1979
Gislind Nabakowski, Helke Sander and Peter Gorsen, *Frauen in der Kunst*, 2 vols, Frankfurt am Main: Suhrkamp, 1980

Renate Berger, *Malerinnen auf dem Weg ins 20. Jahrhundert: Kunstgeschichte als Sozialgeschichte*, Cologne: DuMont, 1982
Grethe Jürgens, Gerta Overbeck: Bilder der zwanziger Jahre, exh. cat., Bonner Kunstverein, Bonn, 1982
Ulrika Evers, *Deutsche Künstlerinnen des 20. Jahrhunderts: Malerei, Bildhauerei, Tapisserie*, Hamburg: Schultheis, 1983
Cordula Bischoff and others, eds, *Frauen Kunst Geschichte: Zur Korrektur des herrschenden Blicks*, Giessen: Anabas, 1984 (transactions of a conference held in Marburg, 1983)
Ruth Nobs-Greter, *Die Künstlerin und ihr Werk in der deutschsprachigen Kunstgeschichtsschreibung*, Zürich: Juris, 1984
Silvia Eiblmayr and others, eds, *Kunst mit Eigensinn: Aktuelle Kunst von Frauen: Texte und Dokumentation*, Vienna: Löcker, 1985
Hof-Atelier Elvira, 1887–1928: Ästheten, Emanzen, Aristokraten, exh. cat., Stadtmuseum, Munich, 1985
Verena Dietrich, *Architektinnen: Ideen, Projekte, Bauten*, Stuttgart: Kohlhammer, 1986
Ilsebill Barta and others, eds, *Frauen, Bilder, Männer, Mythen: Kunsthistorische Beiträge*, Berlin: Reimer, 1987 (transactions of a conference held in Vienna, 1986)
Renate Berger, *"Und ich sehe nichts, nichts als die Malerei": Autobiographische Texte von Künstlerinnen des 18.–20. Jahrhunderts*, Frankfurt am Main: Fischer, 1987
Das Verborgene Museum I: Dokumente von Frauen in Berliner öffentlichen Sammlungen, exh. cat., Akademie der Künste, Berlin, 1987
Denise Noël, *L'Académie Julian: Les Ateliers pour dames, 1868–1907*, thesis, Sorbonne, Paris, 1988
Heidemarie Seblatnig, ed., *Einfach den Gefahren ins Auge sehen: Künstlerinnen im Gespräch*, Vienna: Böhlau, 1988
Edith Krull, *Women in Art*, London: Studio Vista, 1989 (German original)
Ines Lindner and others, eds, *Blick-Wechsel: Konstruktionen von Männlichkeit und Weiblichkeit in Kunst und Kunstgeschichte*, Berlin: Reimer, 1989 (transactions of a conference held in Berlin, 1988)
Christiane Müller, *Bildende Künstlerinnen in der DDR – Soziales Umfeld und Werk: Versuch einer Situationsanalyse zu Beginn der 80er Jahre*, dissertation, Humboldt University, Berlin, 1989
Künstlerinnen des 20. Jahrhunderts, exh. cat., Museum Wiesbaden, 1990
Theresa Georgen and others, eds, *Ich bin nicht ich, wenn ich sehe: Dialoge: Ästhetische Praxis in Kunst und Wissenschaft von Frauen*, Berlin: Reimer, 1991
Domesticity and Dissent: The Role of Women Artists in Germany, 1918–1938, exh. cat., Leicester Museum and Art Gallery, and elsewhere, 1992
Renate Herter, *Visuelle Dialoge: Zum Verhältnis von Weiblichkeit und Kunst*, Berlin: Orlanda Frauenverlag, 1992

*Medaillenkünstlerinnen in Deutschland: Kreativität in
    Geschichte und Gegenwart*, exh. cat., Staatliche
    Galerie Moritzburg, Halle, 1992
Carola Muysers and others, eds, *Käthe, Paula und der
    ganze Rest: Ein Nachschlagewerk*, Berlin: Berlinische
    Galerie, 1992
*Profession ohne Tradition: 125 Jahre Verein der Berliner
    Künstlerinnen*, exh. cat., Berlinische Galerie, Berlin,
    1992
Gunther Salje, Ulrike Schaz and Bernhard Watka,
    *Bildende Künstlerinnen heute: Lebenslage und
    Selbstverständnis*, Frankfurt am Main: Lang, 1992
*"... und hat als Weib unglaubliches Talent" (Goethe):
    Angelika Kauffmann (1741–1807), Marie Ellenrieder
    (1791–1863)*, exh. cat., Rosgartenmuseum, Konstanz,
    1992
Silvia Baumgart and others, eds, *Denkräume zwischen
    Kunst und Wissenschaft, no.5:
    Kunsthistorikerinnentagung in Hamburg*, Berlin:
    Reimer, 1993 (transactions of a conference held in
    Hamburg, 1991)
Frauen Kunst Geschichte, Forschungsgruppe Marburg,
    ed., *Feministische Bibliografie zur Frauenforschung in
    der Kunstgeschichte*, Pfaffenweiler: Centaurus, 1993
*"... ihr werten Frauenzimmer, auf!": Malerinnen der
    Aufklärung*, exh. cat., Roselius-Haus, Bremen, 1993
Rheinische Expressionistinnen, Schriftenreihe des Vereins
    August Macke-Haus, no.10, Bonn, 1993
Tamar Garb, *Sisters of the Brush: Women's Artistic
    Culture in Late Nineteenth-Century Paris*, New Haven
    and London: Yale University Press, 1994
Sabine Plakolm-Forsthuber, *Künstlerinnen in Österreich,
    1897–1938: Malerei, Plastik, Architektur*, Vienna:
    Picus, 1994
Marsha Meskimmon and Shearer West, eds, *Visions of
    the "Neue Frau": Women and the Visual Arts in
    Weimar Germany*, Aldershot: Scolar Press, 1995
*Muse küsst Muse: Eine zeitgenössische Reflexion über
    historische Künstlerinnen*, exh. cat., Lindenau-
    Museum, Altenberg, 1995

Individuals
(excluding references to artists with their own entries in
the complete edition of *Dictionary of Women Artists*)
Hermione von Preuschen, *Der Roman meines Lebens:
    Ein Frauenleben um die Jahrhundertwende*, Berlin:
    1926
Philippine Wolff-Arndt, *Wir Frauen von einst:
    Erinnerungen einer Malerin*, Munich: Reinhardt, 1929
Ida Dehmel, exh. cat., Staats- und Universitätsbibliothek,
    Hamburg, 1970 (founder of GEDOK, an association
    of women artists in Germany with local clubs)
Sabine Lepsius, *Ein Berliner Künstlerleben um die
    Jahrhundertwende*, Munich: Muller, 1972
Gisela Breitling, *Die Spuren des Schiffs in den Wellen:
    Eine autobiographische Suche nach den Frauen in der
    Kunstgeschichte*, Berlin: Oberbaum, 1980
Ulrike Rosenbach, *Videokunst-Foto-Aktion/Performance,
    Feministische Kunst*, Frankfurt am Main: Rosenbach,
    1982

*Maria Slavona, 1865–1931: Eine deutsche
    Impressionistin*, exh. cat., Sammlung Bröhan, Berlin,
    1982
Gisela Breitling, "Sprechen und Stummsein: Die künst-
    lerische Rede: Gedanken über Redekonventionen und
    weibliches Selbstverständnis", *Die Horen*, no.132,
    1983
Monika Faver, *Madame d'Ora: Wien-Paris; Portraits aus
    Kunst und Gesellschaft, 1907–1957*, Vienna and
    Munich: Brandstetter, 1983
*Johanna Ey und ihr Künstlerkreis: Zum 120. Geburtstag
    der Düsseldorfer Kunsthändlerin*, exh. cat., Galerie
    Remmert und Barth, Düsseldorf, 1984
Gisela Breitling, Stuttgart: Parkland, 1987
Margarete Geiger, *Briefe der Malerin aus Würzburg,
    Bamberg, München und Wien an ihre Familie in
    Schweinfurt, 1804–1809*, ed. Friederike Kotuc,
    Nuremberg: Spätlese, 1987
*Madame d'Ora, Vienna and Paris, 1907–1957: The
    Photography of Dora Kallmus*, exh. cat., Vassar
    College Art Gallery, Poughkeepsie, 1987
Carmen Oberst, *Kairos: Der günstige Augenblick*,
    Hamburg: Blauflug, 1987
*Helen Ernst, 1904–1948: Berlin, Amsterdam,
    Ravensbrück: Stationen einer antifaschistischen
    Künstlerin*, exh. cat., Das Verborgene Museum, Berlin,
    1988
Anita Prammer, *Valie Export: Eine multimediale
    Künstlerin*, Vienna: Wiener Frauenverlag, 1988
Johannes Grützke, *Gisela Breitling: Szenen aus dem
    Leben einer Malerin*, Berlin: Ladengalerie, 1989
Marta Astfalck-Vietz: Photographien, 1922–1935, exh.
    cat., Berlinische Galerie, 1991
Raum-Spiel: Spiel-Räume: Lucy Hillebrand, exh. cat.,
    Das Verborgene Museum, Berlin, 1991
Annegret Rittmann, ed., *Ida Gerhardi (1862–1927): Eine
    westfälische Malerin zwischen Paris und Berlin*,
    Münster: Ardey, 1993
Brigitte Doppagne, *Ottilie Reyländer: Stationen einer
    Malerin*, Worpswede: Worpsweder Verlag, 1994
Irme Schaber, *Gerta Taro, Fotoreporterin im Spanischen
    Bürgerkrieg: Eine Biografie*, Marburg: Jonas, 1994

4. Russia

Modernity and the industrial era came several decades later to Russia, which was retarded by the institution of serfdom (abolished in 1861) and a population split between a tiny educated class and a vast illiterate peasantry. In the 19th century the call for women's rights to education and equality emerged in the 1860s, when wider issues of social and political reform were being debated. It was not until the 1870s that a first generation of profes-sional women artists appeared in Russia. As their opportunities improved, women emerged as crucial participants in the art movements of the late imperial and early Soviet periods, to a degree unparalleled in other countries. The cultural and political extremes that marked Russian life in the second half of the 19th century contributed to the radicalisation of educated women, many of whom became active participants in women's education, the populist and revolutionary movements, and social reform. These earlier precedents may help to explain why a relatively large proportion of major Russian artists of the early 20th century were women, and why women were accustomed to leadership roles within the artistic community as patrons, collectors, entrepreneurs and organisers of a wide range of cultural endeavours.

Before 1842

After centuries of seclusion in the *terem* (women's chamber), bound by the feudal teachings of the *Domostroy* (a 16th-century tract on family life), and restricted in their creative outlets to the production of ecclesiastical embroideries, upper-class Russian women found their lives fundamentally changed by the reforms of Peter the Great (1689–1725). Peter's rapid westernisation of Russian society brought women into public life and offered them the rudiments of education. For most of the 18th century Russia was ruled by a succession of three powerful women – Anna (1730–40), Elizabeth (1741–62) and Catherine (1762–96) – and it was during their reigns that the major art institutions were established – the Imperial Porcelain Factory (1744) and the Academy of Fine Arts (1757) – as well as the imperial art collections that helped to form Western taste in Russia. But while it was possible by the end of the 18th century for a few women to make a mark in the world of letters and humanities, as did Princess Ekaterina Dashkova, President of the Academy of Sciences, in the more professionally oriented visual arts girls from the nobility learned just enough proficiency in drawing and watercolour as was appropriate to a finishing-school education, in institutes such as the Smolny Institute for Noble Girls in St Petersburg (established 1764). The only women artists to attain any professional acclaim in Russia during this period were both foreigners: Elisabeth Vigée-Lebrun (q.v.), who spent six years in St Petersburg portraying members of the Russian aristocracy, and Christina Robertson, a Scotswoman who was much sought after in the 1840s for her

society portraits at the court of Nicholas I. Russian women of good family were expected rather to follow the example of the Empress Marya Fyodorovna, the German-born wife of Paul I, whose skill as a medallionist and silhouettist established a tradition of respectable and proficient amateurism. At the other end of the social spectrum, some serf women could expect to be trained in a number of luxury handicrafts (lace, weaving, beading, embroidery) at their owner's behest, for his or her personal consumption and profit. (Male serfs were more likely to be sent to the Academy of Fine Arts in St Petersburg for training in architecture, painting, sculpture and the applied arts.)

1842–1861

An institutional art training first became available to Russian women in the 1840s, as a direct result of a new governmental campaign to stimulate industrial growth by improving the industrial arts through the spread of art education. The new emphasis on developing the taste of artist and consumer alike made it possible for middle-class women to consider professions in the handicrafts and as drawing teachers. The first two drawing schools to be established in Russia outside the Academy of Fine Arts both offered limited professional training to women from the working and lower-middle classes. In 1842 a women's section was added to the small drawing school that the Ministry of Finance had set up in St Petersburg three years earlier. Located in the Customs House building and known as the School at the Stock Exchange (*Shkola na Birzhe*), the Women's Drawing Classes subsequently became part of the School of the Society for the Encouragement of the Arts (established 1857), the institution at which the majority of Russian women received their art education until the end of the 19th century. In Moscow, beginning in 1843, women were admitted to the Women's Drawing Section of the Drawing School Related to the Arts and Crafts (established 1825), later renamed the Stroganov School of Technical Drawing. Here the curriculum for women was limited to drawing flowers, ornament, landscapes and in exceptional cases the human head. The student body (40 in the first year) was divided between young girls from the lower classes who were trained for professional work in handicrafts and ladies "from the upper class" who had no such practical goals in mind and were taught separately.

Of the former group a handful became certified drawing teachers and some also distinguished themselves as painters. Among noblewomen only the most energetic went beyond cultivating art as a social grace, such as Princess Marya Volkonskaya, who organised a small drawing circle where she and her friends painted saints and church ornament under the tutelage of the academician Fyodor Solntsev. On the other hand, throughout the 19th century those with administrative abilities could use them in the capacity of president or honorary patron of cultural organisations, as did Grand Duchess Marya Nikolayevna, who was president of both the Society for the Encouragement of the Arts and the Academy of Fine Arts, and Countess Praskovya Uvarova, who succeeded her husband as president of the Moscow Archaeological Society on his death in 1885.

By the mid-19th century limited access to the Academy of Fine Arts became available to women, as higher education in general came within their reach. In 1858 Alexander II approved the establishment of gymnasia for girls and the following year women were admitted as auditors to university courses. By the 1850s women could also audit drawing classes at the Academy and take part in its exhibitions in the categories open to them. The academic hierarchy of genres allowed women to work in portraiture, landscape, still-life and genre painting. In 1854 Sofya Sukhovo-Kobylina won the academy's first-class gold medal for a landscape, an event that she recorded for posterity in a painting of 1859, now in the Tretyakov Gallery, Moscow. Another Academy pupil and the daughter of an artist, the 12-year-old Vera Meyer, received a silver medal in 1859 for her self-portrait, but after her marriage to the academician Pavel Chistyakov, a popular drawing teacher for many women artists, she gave up painting altogether.

1861–1891

Opportunities for women to study, exhibit and make a living from art improved during the reigns of Alexander II (1855–81) and Alexander III (1881–94), but they did so against a background of political and social upheaval that fundamentally affected the way in which women saw their role as artists in relation to society as a whole. By the 1870s there was already a recognisable group of "lady artists" from the upper classes who operated on the periphery of the Academy, restricted in medium to watercolour, drawing and pastel, and in subject to genre, landscape, portraiture and still life. But there was also an alternative group of women who rejected the idea of art for its own sake and in its traditional forms as a selfish indulgence. For these "women of the sixties" the ideal of personal freedom and collective work, embodied in Vera Pavlovna, the heroine of Nikolai Chernyshevsky's novel *Chto delat?* (What is to be done? 1863), inspired them to place their talents at the service of the public good. In this context prejudices against the applied arts held less sway as the relevance of "high art" to the common people came into question. The artist Elena Polenova typified this spirit of self-sacrifice throughout the 1870s, serving as a nurse in the Russo-Turkish war, training as a governess, and volunteering to teach drawing and dressmaking in a St Petersburg charity school before she finally enrolled in majolica and watercolour courses at the School of the Society for the Encouragement of the Arts in 1880. Others became professional drawing teachers or opened their own schools, as did the Kharkov artist Marya Rayevskaya-Ivanova, who also published her own primer, *Azbuka risovaniya dlya semi i dlya shkoly* (A drawing ABC for family and school), in 1879. Still others, mostly the wives of landowners with estates in the provinces, laid the foundation for a nationwide revival of peasant arts and crafts when they established training workshops on their estates, in the hope of winning peasants away from the cities and factories and back to their abandoned handicrafts with the promise of a steady income. Elizaveta Mamontova, wife of the railway magnate and maecenas Savva Mamontov, guaranteed the success of her Abramtsevo workshop for peasant boys (established 1876) when Polenova became its artistic director, designing art furniture based on folk ornament, in 1885.

The most vocal supporter of women artists during these years was the critic Vladimir Stasov (brother of the feminist Nadezhda Stasova), whose protégées included Elizaveta Bem, the sculptor Marya Ditrikh, Varvara and Aleksandra Shneyder, and Tatyana Semechkina. The most professionally active of these was Elizaveta Bem, whose silhouettes and watercolours of children in national garb won her a national and international reputation in the 1870s and 1880s. Stasov hailed her as "part of an emerging generation of women artists" at a time when "there are very few women [in Russia] who contemplate getting involved in anything but family affairs and everyday trivia" (V.V. Stasov, "Novyye khudozhestvennyye izdaniya" [New art publications], *Sobraniye sochineniy* [Collected works], St Petersburg, 1894, ii, p.298). For women seeking other forms of employment in the art world he encouraged serious collecting and scholarship in areas of national art traditionally considered a woman's domain. Thus, Natalya Shabelskaya's collection of Russian textiles and women's work was unparalleled in its breadth and quality, while Sofya Davydova pioneered the study of Russian lacemaking and was responsible for the foundation of the Mariynsky Lace School in St Petersburg in 1883.

The number of women seeking a formal art training increased in the 1870s, in step with the general movement for higher education that culminated in the inauguration in 1878 of the Bestuzhev Women's Higher Courses, which provided university-level training in medicine, the natural sciences, history and mathematics. With full equality in the Academy still denied them (access to live models was off-limits as was eligibility to study abroad as an Academy pensioner), women gravitated in growing numbers to the schools of industrial art. Not only did these schools offer an increasingly rigorous art education, modelled on the best industrial arts schools of Europe, but because the emphasis on decoration rather than intellectual content coincided with existing ideas about femininity they placed fewer restrictions on women than did the more prestigious fine arts schools. In his exhibition reviews of the 1870s Stasov particularly stressed the attainments of women students, noting that they excelled in "one of the most difficult architectural projects", the design of church iconostases (icon screens), whereas before "they knew only how to draw flowers, or at best sentimental landscapes and smarmy portraits". At the same time, however, women were still taught separately from men and until the end of the 19th century their fees continued to be twice those of the male students.

A major challenge to the authority and hierarchy of the Academy was the foundation in 1870 of the Association of Travelling Exhibitions, whose members (the Wanderers or Peredvizhniki) championed the painting of contemporary Russian life and its problems. The Association members Ivan Kramskoy, Ivan Shishkin and Kirill Lemokh became influential teachers at the School of the Society for the Encouragement of the Arts and a number of their women students, such as Polenova, went on to become professional artists, as did some of their own daughters and wives, for example, Sofya Yunker (née Kramskaya), Olga Lagoda-Shishkina and Elena Makovskaya-Luksch. While the Association allowed women to take part in its annual exhibitions, however, it drew the line at granting them full membership.

The first arts association to be established by women was the First Ladies' Art Circle, founded in St Petersburg in 1882 by Pelagaya Kuriar as a charitable organisation to support needy artists, but also to "develop artistic aspirations among Russian lady amateurs, allowing them to benefit from the advice of various artists, to observe them at work and to work themselves under their supervision during the circle's Wednesday meetings". With a membership dominated by such upper-class amateurs as Baronesses Marya von der Pahlen and Elena Vrangel, the circle provided women with exhibition opportunities and its charitable goals guaranteed sales for the exhibitors, primarily among members of the imperial family and the aristocracy. But it also reinforced condescending attitudes towards the "lady artist" as a "frequently bored, relatively rich, not terribly well educated, not overly cultivated woman" flirting with art to kill time and *ennui*.

Since study in one of the great European art centres was considered essential to an artist's education and women were not eligible to be Academy pensioners in Rome or Paris, only those with some financial resources could afford to travel independently to Europe to see the museums or to study with an acknowledged master. Thus, Marya Rayevskaya-Ivanova studied in Dresden with Professor Ergardt, the sculptor Teresa Ris both studied and eventually settled in Vienna, Sofya Kramskaya spent several months in Paris where she could draw from the live model, and Marya von der Pahlen spent a year in Paris studying under Trelat, Gérôme and Léon Bonnard. It was not until 1879 that the School of the Society for the Encouragement of the Arts sent its first pensioner, Polenova, to Paris to study ceramics.

1891–1905

After three decades in which liberal ideals and reform gave way to anarchism and harsh reaction, during the 1890s many younger Russian artists turned away from social concerns and realism to the world of subjective states, intuition and emotion. These were spheres of experience universally associated with female psychology and they were considered most fully expressed in the non-narrative genres of landscape, still life, portraiture and ornament, also the acknowledged domain of women. After eight years working for the Abramtsevo workshop, for example, in 1893 Polenova abandoned her work with peasant boys and turned increasingly to symbolic paintings, the illustration of fairy tales in the style of Walter Crane, and to ornamental designs that conveyed complex "musical" emotions. Her close friend Marya Yakunchikova also experimented throughout the decade with ways to express the inexpressible, using pyrogravure, woodcut and appliqué embroidery, as well as oil painting, to convey such moods as anxiety, euphoria and nostalgic longing. The expanded opportunities for experimenting with new media typical of the Symbolist era also worked to women's advantage. Art embroidery became not only acceptable in progressive art circles like the Mir Iskusstva (World of Art) and Blue Rose groups, but as practised by Natalya Davydova, Agnessa Lindeman, Tatyana Lugovskaya-Dyagileva, Vera Wulf and others it epitomised the aesthetic ideals of Symbolism with its emphasis on flatness, stylisation and expressive line. Classes in the stylisation of flowers and plants were added to the curriculum of the leading industrial arts schools and all offered classes in porcelain painting, majolica and ceramics where many of the teachers as well as the students were women. In the commercial, guild-controlled field of gold- and silver-work a number of women owned and operated successful workshops, usually the legacy of a deceased father or husband. Among the most prominent were Marya Adler, whose Moscow firm employed 74 workers and had its own drawing school, Evdokya Sazikova, Marya Semyonova and Pavla Mishukova.

In 1891 the Academy of Arts admitted the first class of women to be eligible for the title of Artist (first class). The teachers most supportive of women were Nikolai Dubovskoy, Dmitry Kardovsky and Ilya Repin, who was a member of the Association of Travelling Exhibitions with strong sympathies for progressive trends in painting and for women – Marianne Werefkin (q.v.), Anna Ostroumova-Lebedeva and Zinaida Serebryakova (q.v.) were all his pupils. Even so, in 1896 only 34 of the Academy's 388 pupils were women, compared to 84 of the 189 at the Stieglitz (Shtiglits) school (estab-

lished 1876) in St Petersburg. The most prestigious rival fine arts school was the Moscow School of Painting, Sculpture and Architecture, whose more liberal faculty attracted students disillusioned with academicism and realism alike. Yet as the biographies in this *Dictionary* seem to suggest, the Moscow school did not admit large numbers of full-time women students, perhaps because few of them had the foundation training needed to pass the gruelling entrance exams. Instead, most women artists in this period moved frequently between private studios and public schools, from the provinces to the capitals, and from Russia to Europe and back again. Particularly popular was the Moscow studio of Konstantin Yuon and Ivan Yudin, which prepared students for the Moscow School entrance exams, but affordable alternatives were also provided by other women. In 1893 Princess Marya Tenisheva opened the Tenisheva School in St Petersburg, with Repin as its foremost teacher and Marya Chembers, Elena Makovskaya-Luksch and Serebryakova among its pupils. In 1899 Elizaveta Zvantseva, herself a former Repin pupil at the Academy, opened a school in Moscow (moved to St Petersburg in 1906) where men and women worked together from nude models and whose graduates included Sofya Dymshits-Tolstaya, Elena Guro, Olga Rozanova (q.v.) and Margarita Sabashnikova (later the wife of the poet Max Voloshin). Study abroad also became easier and more acceptable for women artists. Ostroumova-Lebedeva, Yakunchikova and Anna Golubkina (q.v.) all studied with important teachers in Paris, and Elizaveta Kruglikova and Olga Mechnikova were co-founders of the Montparnas society (1903), an organisation that informed Russian artists who had recently arrived in Paris about study and exhibition opportunities.

A handful of women attained varying degrees of success in the traditionally masculine field of sculpture, in genres other than the portrait busts for which a woman's powers of observation were thought best suited. One of the first women sculptors in Russia was the academy-trained Marya Dillon, who specialised in portraits, allegorical figures and monuments on literary themes and in whose studio Natalya Danko worked. Teresa Ris, initially an auditor at the Moscow School, won the Karl Ludwig medal in 1896 for her plaster figure *Lucifer*. And despite her peasant origins, Anna Golubkina was able to obtain an excellent training at the Moscow School and the Academy of Arts, followed by two periods of study in Paris. Her reputation was confirmed in 1901 when she was commissioned to sculpt a panel in high relief (*The Wave*) for the entrance of the new Moscow Art Theatre.

By the beginning of the 20th century only the architectural profession still remained beyond the reach of women, although courses in architectural ornament and styles had long been an important component of the curriculum in the industrial arts schools. It was not until 1904 that a Society to Investigate Avenues for the Technical Education of Women was formed in St Petersburg by Praskovya Aryan and in 1906 the Women's Polytechnical Courses were opened, with an architecture department whose faculty included the leading architects of the day. Two years later women were finally admitted to the architecture department of the Academy of Fine Arts, and the same year E. Bagayeva opened her own four-year Women's Architectural Courses (from 1913 the Women's Polytechnical Institute).

The rise of merchant-class art patronage affected women artists as well as men by the turn of the 19th and 20th centuries. Throughout the 1890s Pavel Tretyakov collected work by Polenova and Yakunchikova, as well as by such lesser-known women as Emilya Shanks, Ekaterina Yunge (daughter of the sculptor Count Fyodor Tolstoy) and Marya Fyodorova, all of whom specialised in intimate genre scenes or mood landscapes. Women also became influential collectors and patrons themselves. Marya F. Yakunchikova (Marya Yakunchikova's sister-in-law) was one of Valentin Serov's first patrons, but was best known for her Solomenko embroidery workshops in Tambov province, where peasant women produced both traditional and modernised embroideries designed by Polenova, Yakunchikova and Natalya Davydova. Princess Marya Tenisheva, initially an aspiring singer who had also studied art at the Académie Julian in Paris, utilised the resources of her wealthy industrialist husband in a number of artistic and philanthropic enterprises. She assembled a collection of watercolours; founded an excellent museum of Russian antiquities in Smolensk; co-funded the art journal *Mir iskusstva* (World of Art) with Savva Mamontov; and at Talashkino, her estate in Smolensk province, she created both a summer colony for visiting artists and a network of work-

shops where peasant crafts were revived and sold through a store in Moscow.

With the spread of literacy and the growth of a consumer economy, women who specialised in the graphic arts and illustration found employment in various branches of the publishing industry, from designing covers for such popular magazines as *Niva* (e.g. Elena Samokish-Sudkovskaya), to illustrating postcards for the series put out by the Red Cross and the Community of St Evgeny (Rimma Braylovskaya, Marya Chembers, Agnessa Lindeman, Anna Ostroumova-Lebedeva, Aleksandra Shneyder and even Grand Duchess Olga Alexandrovna, sister of Nicholas II). Thanks to the World of Art group's special affection for the art of the book, the design of graphic elements such as the *ex-libris*, vignette, silhouette and cover-page became acceptable, even innovative genres in which many women trained in the industrial arts excelled.

1905–1917

By the year of the First Russian Revolution in 1905 the old centres of artistic authority – the Academy and the Association of Travelling Exhibitions – had lost all credibility with a younger generation of Russian artists. Not until 1916 did the Academy give way to the inevitable by electing four uncontroversial women artists to the rank of academician – Serebryakova, Ostroumova-Lebedeva, Olga Della-Vos-Kardovskaya and the flower painter Aleksandra Shneyder. While many women gladly took advantage of these new privileges, others still preferred the freedom of frequent moves between art schools and private studios at home and abroad. With its well-equipped workshops and close ties to Moscow industries, the Stroganov School offered such students as Lyudmila Mayakovskaya, Rozanova and Varvara Stepanova (q.v.) the design skills and practical training that each would draw on in the Soviet period. In 1906 the School of the Society for the Encouragement of the Arts adopted many of the Stroganov's innovations, under the directorship of Nicholas Roerich and new faculty such as Agnessa Lindeman (art embroidery) and Ivan Bilibin, whose graphic arts students included two women whom he would later marry: Marya Chembers and Aleksandra Shchekatikhina-Pototskaya. The quality and number of provincial art schools also improved during this period and many women received a solid training before moving to the capitals, for example Alexandra Exter (q.v.) and Evgenya Pribylskaya at the Kiev Art Institute, Stepanova at the Kazan Art School and Danko at the Vilnius Art School.

Russian women continued to study abroad until the outbreak of World War I. While some gravitated towards Munich where a small Russian community studied at the Ažbè and Hollosy Schools (Marianne Werefkin), the studios of pre-war Paris (La Grande Chaumière, La Palette, Académie Ranson, Académie Julian) became the mecca for aspiring women painters such as Lyubov Popova (q.v.) and Nadezhda Udaltsova (q.v.). In 1908 the painter Marya Vasileva established her own art school in Paris (the Académie Russe or Académie Vassiliev), which became the centre of cultural life for Russians. Even the Academy of Fine Arts sent its first woman pensioner (Elena Kiseleva) to Paris in 1907.

Young women artists figured with unprecedented prominence in the avant-garde art circles that formed and reformed during this period. With their rejection not simply of artistic conventions but often of the entire social and philosophical structure that supported them, the close-knit groups of the pre-revolutionary decade offered women an equality and visibility rarely found in contemporary Russian society. The experiments with modern French art of Natalya Goncharova (q.v.) placed her beyond the pale of acceptable behaviour for artists and women alike, giving her an outsider status that she cultivated by her active participation in the Cubo-Futurists' face-painting, public performances and cabaret culture of the pre-war era. Women were particularly active in the Supremus group formed by Kazimir Malevich during the war years (seven of the 14 artists who took part in the *First Futurist Exhibition: 0.10* in 1915 were women). With interests ranging far beyond the pursuit of abstract painting for its own sake, Rozanova, Popova and Exter applied the principles of Malevich's Suprematism to the decoration of women's accessories, theatre design, and experimental typography and book illustration. Women also continued to play important entrepreneurial and organisational roles during the war years. For example, between 1911 and 1919 Natalya Dobychina's Bureau in Petrograd was Russia's leading private commercial gallery, hosting the *0.10* exhibition in 1915–16.

After 1917

When the Russian Empire toppled in 1917, many of the values and institutions it had maintained fell with it. The official equality of women was proclaimed and so too was the right of all citizens to an art education free of academic elitism and authoritarianism. The central organisation in charge of all art issues was Narkompros (the People's Commissariat of Enlightenment), and the women who had been so active in the avant-garde groups of the war years immediately stepped into positions of authority, reorganising the decimated industrial arts centres, restructuring the education system and teaching in the new State Free Art Studios (Svomas) and Higher State Artistic and Technical Workshops (Vkhutemas), setting up museums and organising exhibitions, public spectacles and propaganda. In Kiev Exter was an influential teacher and organiser, and in Smolensk and Vitebsk Vera Yermolayeva and Nina Kogan were active members of Unovis (Affirmers of the New in Art), teaching a new generation of artists in which women were offered the same rights and opportunities as men.

With studio art and easel painting temporarily discredited as bourgeois and elitist, it was those artists who embraced the tenets of Constructivism and production art who shaped Soviet culture during the first half of the decade. Popova and Stepanova used stage and costume design as a laboratory for their very successful work as textile and clothing designers, and joined forces with proponents of the folk art revival (Evgenya Pribylskaya, Natalya Davydova), the couturier Nadezhda Lamanova and the sculptor Vera Mukhina (q.v.) to create new clothing prototypes for the Soviet woman. The promotion of literacy and political awareness gave print media (magazines, posters, advertising, books) an unprecedented social importance that women artists accustomed to working in these formerly minor areas quickly exploited. Outside the Constructivist camp more palatable images of Soviet culture were created by women working in porcelain, a medium whose potential for disseminating powerful ideological messages that were also decorative and accessible was quickly recognised. Danko and Shchekatikhina-Pototskaya were both considered important revolutionary artists, a sign that political change had indeed brought about a re-evaluation of artistic values. The zenith of women's contributions to early Soviet art and art policy was undoubtedly the Soviet contribution to the Paris Exposition des Arts Décoratifs et Industriels Modernes of 1925. But as political control over cultural life tightened in the late 1920s and the fine arts and realism were proclaimed the principal repositories of Soviet values, women once again found themselves part of a monolithic, academy-controlled art world that perpetuated sex-role stereotypes even as they proclaimed female emancipation (e.g. Mukhina's *Industrial Worker and Collective Farm Girl* of 1939). As for all those who rejected the Revolution or could not endure its consequences. emigration was the only alternative. Some women left for Berlin or Paris immediately in 1917 (Rimma Braylovskaya, Princess Tenisheva), others participated fully in Soviet artistic life for several years before deciding to leave for uncertain futures in the West (Exter, Ksenya Boguslavskaya, Serebryakova, Shchekatikhina-Pototskaya).

WENDY R. SALMOND

Bibliography

Aleksandr Somov, "Zhenshchiny-khudozhnitsy" [Women artists], *Vestnik iziashchnikh iskusstv*, no.1, 1883, pp.517–24

Isabel F. Hapgood, "Russian women, I", *Chautauguan*, xxxii/6, March 1901, pp.589–94

Nina Moleva and E.M. Belyutin, *Russkaya khudozh-estvennaya shkola vtoroy poloviny XIX–nachala XX veka* [The Russian art school of the second half of the 19th century to the beginning of the 20th], Moscow: Iskusstvo, 1967

Richard Stites, *The Women's Liberation Movement in Russia: Feminism, Nihilism and Bolshevism, 1860–1930*, Princeton, NJ: Princeton University Press, 1978

Künstlerinnen der russischen Avantgarde/Russian Women Artists of the Avant-Garde, 1910–1930, exh. cat., Galerie Gmurzynska, Cologne, 1979

Alison Hilton, "'Bases of the new creation': Women artists and Constructivism", *Arts Magazine*, October 1980, pp.142–5

Nina Smurova, "Iz istoriy vysshego zhenskogo arkhitek-turnogo obrazovaniya v Rossiy" [From the history of women's higher architectural education in Russia], *Problemy istoriy sovetskoy arkhitektury (Sbornik nauchnykh trudov)* [Problems of the history of Soviet architecture (collection of scholarly papers)], Moscow: TsNIIT gradostroitelstva, 1980, pp.110–18

M.N. Yablonskaya, *Women Artists of Russia's New Age, 1900–1935*, New York: Rizzoli, and London: Thames and Hudson, 1990

D.Ya. Severyukhin and O.L. Leykind, *Khudozhniki russkoy emigratsiy (1917–1941): Biograficheskiy slovar* [Artists of the Russian emigration (1917–1941): Biographical dictionary], St Petersburg: Chernysheva, 1994

Alison Hilton, "Domestic crafts and creative freedom: Russian women's art", *Russia – Women – Culture*, ed. Helena Goscilo and Beth Holmgren, Bloomington: Indiana University Press, 1996

Wendy R. Salmond, *Arts and Crafts in Late Imperial Russia: Reviving the Kustar Art Industries, 1870–1917*, Cambridge and New York: Cambridge University Press, 1996

5. North America

19th century

In the 19th century women artists in the USA found themselves in a different situation from that in Europe. Unlike France, the country lacked a strong centralised government that used the arts as a prop-aganda tool. And unlike Europe in general, it lacked an upper class with a long tradition of art patron-age. Therefore, the training and professional oppor-tunities for women were stereotypically American: regional, pragmatic and entrepreneurial.

Three major art centres on the East Coast – Philadelphia, New York and Boston – vied for leadership in the American fine arts, yet many important women artists emerged from Chicago, Cincinnati, St Louis, San Francisco and many lesser art centres across the country. Not one but two academies arose to train the country's elite artists – the Pennsylvania Academy of the Fine Arts in Philadelphia (1805) and the National Academy of Design in New York (1808) – but training on an equally effective level could be gained from many other institutions and individual teachers. Clubs, exhibiting societies and galleries could be found in every reasonably-sized town. Furthermore, American artists took full advantage of European training and professional opportunities when the offerings of their own country no longer satisfied them. The multiplicity of training and professional organisations available in 19th-century America was a sign of the earnestness with which local arts communities organised themselves to bring culture to a nation of modest artistic patronage.

Unlike France, where a professional class of fine artists could be supported by a combination of government and private patrons, artists in America were forced to be entrepreneurial – offering to the general public a combination of fine, reproductive and decorative art skills, while teaching on the side. As in Europe, the few artists who attained the highest status and greatest fame in the fine arts were men, but, below that small group, both men and women had to take advantage of whatever opportunities came their way. Those American women who could truly claim to have succeeded as fine artists, such as Harriet Hosmer (q.v.), Elizabeth Gardner and Mary Cassatt (q.v.), tended to live abroad.

In spite of these difficulties, women throughout the 19th century pieced together sufficient training and financial support to be able to practise as artists on a number of levels. In some regions, such as the state of Maine, they accounted for 50 per cent of the professional artists recorded during that period. The cultural patterns and institutions changed, but the desire of American women to find employment in art was constant. In the early part of the 19th century an upper class of British descent still held power in the USA, despite the War of Independence (1776–81) from Britain. Artists who had trained in Britain, such as Gilbert Stuart, Charles Willson Peale and Thomas Sully, set the standards for portraiture, both private and official. They in turn paved the way for some of the first prominent women artists of the century, Jane Stuart (Gilbert Stuart's daughter), Sarah Miriam and Anna Claypoole Peale (q.v., daughters of the miniaturist James Peale and nieces of Charles Willson Peale) and Jane Sully (daughter of Thomas Sully). These women trained with their fathers and found many doors open to them. Jane Stuart practised mainly as a copyist filling the seemingly endless demand for her father's famous portraits of *George Washington*, but Sarah Peale shaped an impressive career for herself as a portraitist and still-life painter in Baltimore and later St Louis. Peale and her sister Anna Claypoole were the first women to be elected academicians of the Pennsylvania Academy of the Fine Arts in 1824, and their friend, Jane Sully, was elected in 1831.

Women were also instrumental in shaping a very different type of art that was prominent in the early 19th century and is very popular today: "naive" or "schoolgirl" art. These images were either painted in watercolour or worked in embroidery, but the bold patterns and exaggerations of form gave them a distinctive style. Although called "naive", the style was taught in private girls' schools through a process of copying engravings of famous paintings, many by Angelica Kauffman (q.v.), simplifying and flattening the composition, and adding dramatic colouring. That these works were highly regarded is

signalled by the care taken in framing and preserving the finest examples. Some of the best-known artists who continued to paint in this style were Eunice Pinney and Mary Ann Willson. Because biblical and other religious imagery was especially effective, related watercolours can be found in the art of religious sects such as the Shakers where it was practised primarily by women. The influence of this type of folk art may be equated with the popular "Images d'Epinal" of France.

But the more typical women artists of the early 19th century were neither daughters of famous male artists nor practitioners of a "folk" style, but women such as Sophia Peabody Hawthorne or Susannah Paine whose careers encompassed a range of art endeavours. Hawthorne studied with the best Boston painters, Chester Harding, Thomas Doughty and Washington Allston, in the 1820s. She developed a modest market for her own landscape paintings as well as copies of Doughty's. However, after her marriage to the writer Nathaniel Hawthorne, who encouraged her art, she did not hesitate to paint such mundane objects as fire screens and lampshades when necessary to help support the family. Susannah Paine became an artist when a divorce left her on her own. With only the training she acquired in a private school, she developed a career as a portraitist in Portland, Maine, and travelled around the state as an itinerant artist.

A similar pioneering spirit could be found in Lilly Martin Spencer (q.v.), one of the first women to achieve national recognition. Spencer developed her skills among local artists in the small town of Marietta, Ohio, where she held her first exhibition at the age of 19. She later studied in Cincinnati and at the National Academy of Design in New York. Her fame was spread throughout the country in the 1850s and 1860s by means of reproductive engravings that were distributed by subscription to a large middle-class audience.

The generation of American women who came of age in the late 1840s was strongly affected by the emergence of feminist activism that culminated in the Women's Rights Convention, Seneca Falls, New York, in 1848. As in Europe, a woman's right to earn a living was part of the feminist platform, and the arts were perceived as a worthy field to enter. The first training schools for women in the decorative and industrial arts were founded in this spirit, including the Philadelphia School of Design for Women (1844), the Cooper Union Free Art School,

New York (1854), and the Pratt Institute, Brooklyn (1877). Many other schools were founded for men and women, but women quickly assumed as high as 80 per cent of the student body. These included the Yale School of the Fine Arts, New Haven (1867), the College of Fine Arts, Syracuse University (1873, which became the John Crouse Memorial College for Women in 1889), and the Massachusetts Normal Art School, Boston (for the training of art teachers, 1873). In addition to the other arts that women could practise as a trade at this time – design and decoration of household objects, sewing and fashion design, reproductive printmaking (lithography and wood-engraving, illustration) – came the invention of photography in 1839. As the first commercially successful photographic processes swept the world, women set up their own businesses as practitioners and teachers.

Ambitious women were also inspired by the women's movement of the 1840s and 1850s to strive for greater success in the fine arts. The example of Rosa Bonheur (q.v.) in France fired the imagination of more than one American woman, including the most colourful and effective of this consciously feminist generation of American artists, Harriet Hosmer. After studying with the sculptor Paul Stephenson in Boston, Hosmer studied anatomy in the Missouri Medical College, St Louis, and then returned home to Massachusetts to set up her own sculpture studio in 1851. Convinced that she needed to go beyond the resources of her own country, she travelled to Rome to study with the British sculptor John Gibson. Through Gibson she developed an English clientele and had her first success in Britain. She executed monumental marble sculptures as well as small-scale garden pieces and, when she became financially pressed, she created an appealing version of *Puck* sitting on a toadstool that was so popular that she supported herself well for years with commissions for copies. She was at the centre of a group of foreign women sculptors in Rome, mostly Americans, who attracted attention in the international art community. Hosmer and another American sculptor, Louise Lander, were the models for the main characters in Nathaniel Hawthorne's *The Marble Faun* (1860), in which he eulogised the woman artist as the epitome of the independent modern woman.

The phenomenon of women sculptors in Rome acting as a group or, as Henry James referred to them, "a white marmorean flock", was repeated in other centres where American women artists congregated. In Boston, students of the painter William Morris Hunt, who held art classes for women between 1868 and 1879, formed a well-known, if informal circle of professional painters and teachers who exhibited together in 1888. In New York, the Ladies Art Association was founded in 1867 to promote women artists through exhibitions and instruction. They also established a studio building in 1881 for women to live and work and had branches in Washington, DC, and Paris. They were succeeded by the National Association of Women Artists in 1889 and by numerous similar associations across the country including the Sketch Club of San Francisco, founded in the 1880s, and the Plastic Club of Philadelphia in 1895.

The most important outcome of women organising to promote their work in the middle decades of the 19th century was the Women's Pavilion at the Centennial Exposition held in Philadelphia in 1876. Organised and funded by women across the country, this building, located on the centennial fair grounds, exhibited women's achievements in such fields as journalism, medicine, science, literature, inventions, teaching, business, social work and art. Women's art ranged from the industrial to the decorative to the fine arts. Sculptures were shown by several members of the women sculptors' group in Rome, including Harriet Hosmer, Blanche Nevins, Florence Freeman and Margaret Foley. Members of the Ladies Art Association, such as Eliza Greatorex, also sent work, as did such prominent Philadelphia artists as Emily Sartain, who became principal of the Philadelphia School of Design for Women. Since the decentralised American art world did not allow any one group to hold national, much less international exhibitions of women artists – as did the Union des Femmes Peintres et Sculpteurs in Paris – the Women's Pavilion offered a rare opportunity for women from all over the country to be united.

The Women's Pavilion also marked the end of an era. After the Civil War (1861–5) a group of women emerged who had inherited the gains made by their activist mothers; they took professionalism in the arts as their right. Instead of attempting to solve societal problems through art education or activism, these women were less willing to settle for design, decorative or industrial arts and more interested in strategies for a successful fine art career. They tended not to join associations of women artists, but concentrated on the bastions of male authority in the arts – exclusive academies and prestigious exhibitions. They also had the means and desire to spend long periods abroad and occasionally expatriated to benefit their own careers rather than work for the betterment of women artists at home. They represented only a small segment of the total number of women making a living in the arts in the late 19th century, but their influence was enormous. Of this group the best known today are Elizabeth Gardner and Mary Cassatt.

Gardner and Cassatt continued an American tradition of artist expatriation beginning with Benjamin West in the 18th century. Like their predecessors and their contemporaries, Whistler and Sargent, they found that the opportunities for recognition in the fine arts were more plentiful in a world art capital such as Paris. Although Gardner followed a Salon career path and Cassatt joined the Impressionists, they each found a niche in Paris that did not exist at home. Elizabeth Gardner was inspired to become an artist by her art teacher at boarding school, Imogene Robinson, with whom she later taught at the Worcester School of Design and Fine Arts in Massachusetts. When their school closed in 1864 because of the Civil War, they went to Paris to become professional painters. Gardner quickly gravitated to the polished academic style of William Bouguereau and studied with Jean-Baptiste-Ange Tissier and Hughes Merle as well as in a women's co-operative studio. In 1871 she moved to an artist's enclave on the rue Notre-Dame des Champs where she was the neighbour of William Bouguereau and by 1879 announced her engagement to him. She concentrated on moving up in the Salon hierarchy, exhibiting frequently after 1868, winning an honourable mention in 1879, which made her *hors concours* (able to enter pictures without submitting to the jury), and medals in the Salon of 1887 (third-class) and the Exposition Universelle of 1889 (bronze). But her success in the Salon world was not enough to promote and sustain her in the public eye. In order to support herself she also executed and sold copies of paintings in the Louvre, painted portraits and "pot boilers" (inexpensive paintings on popular themes) for American tourists, wrote articles on events in Paris for American newspapers, held a weekly "afternoon" in her studio, and facilitated the sale of French paintings, including works by Bouguereau, to American collectors. She was the entrepreneurial American woman artist transplanted to Paris.

In comparison Mary Cassatt had her earliest art training in private schools in France and Germany before the age of 11, and studied at the elite Pennsylvania Academy of the Fine Arts for four years before arriving in Paris in late 1865. In Paris she attended Charles Chaplin's well-known class for women and had lessons from Jean-Léon Gérôme. She also began exhibiting at the Salon in 1868 but, rather than relying exclusively on an official career, by 1871 she began placing works with dealers in New York (Goupil) and Philadelphia (Bailey's jewellery store and Ernst Teubner). She cultivated art critics to receive greater attention in the press and sought out mentors among European artists in France, Italy and Spain. Her interest in contemporary trends in art led her to the Impressionists, among whom she formed many lasting friendships and a mentor relationship with Degas. In 1879 she withdrew from Salon competitions and began participating in the annual Impressionist exhibitions, highly publicised forums in which she could show as many works as she wanted. The Impressionist exhibitions also introduced her to a French circle of patrons that few American artists succeeded in attracting. Her work was handled by such French dealers as Durand-Ruel and Alphonse Portier and eventually Ambroise Vollard, and by 1894 her earnings allowed her to purchase a country house. Like Elizabeth Gardner, she also painted copies, pot boilers and portraits, and advised American collectors on purchases of French art.

The many other American women who established fine art careers abroad in the late 19th century represent variations on the themes established by Gardner and Cassatt. Elizabeth Boott Duveneck, Mary MacMonnies, Elizabeth Nourse, Anna Klumpke, Lilla Cabot Perry, Sarah Dodson and Anna Lea Merritt are a few who became identified with artists and movements in Europe. The many American women who came to Paris just to study at the *académies* Julian, Colarossi and others are too numerous to count.

In the USA at this time, the traditional fine arts institutions were changing under pressure from the artists who had studied abroad. While the Pennsylvania Academy of the Fine Arts had admitted women as members as early as 1824 and the National Academy of Design in New York soon after in 1826, their classes remained the few that still restricted female attendance. In the 1860s only

20 per cent of the students were women (as opposed to 75 per cent at the Yale School of the Fine Arts) and life classes were closed to women at the Pennsylvania Academy until 1868 and at the National Academy of Design until 1871. In 1875 the Art Students League was founded in New York to oppose the conservative policies of the National Academy of Design and promote equal opportunities for men and women. In 1877 women spearheaded the founding of the Society of American Artists, which offered an alternative exhibiting opportunity for the women excluded from the National Academy.

In 1893 another truly international exhibition of women's art was held in the Woman's Building of the World's Columbian Exposition in Chicago. This was modelled on the Women's Pavilion of the Philadelphia Centennial Exposition of 1876, and its organisers displayed the talents of women artists in all media with a nod to the newly successful American women in the fine arts. The design of the building, by Sophia Hayden, provided for monumental decorations in painting and sculpture as well as exhibition halls for industrial, decorative and fine arts. Taking as its theme "women gathering fruits from the tree of knowledge", the display emphasised the role of newly improved educational opportunities in making women an effective force in modern society. When Elizabeth Gardner declined the commission to paint the key murals illustrating this theme, the two opposing subjects, *Primitive Woman* and *Modern Woman*, were given to Mary MacMonnies and Mary Cassatt. Sculptors for the architectural decorations included Alice Rideout, Enid Yandell and Anne Whitney. In addition to the Woman's Building, the work of American women artists could be seen in the Department of Fine Arts of the fair as well as throughout the pavilions erected by each state.

In 1895 Cecilia Beaux (q.v.) became the first full-time teacher at the Pennsylvania Academy of the Fine Arts. She had studied with Catherine Drinker, Adolf Van der Wielan and William Sartain in Philadelphia before entering the Académie Julian, Paris, in 1888 as an established artist. In 1890 she set up her studio in Philadelphia as a portraitist and in 1899 moved to New York where she had gained the support of New York artists around Helena de Kay Gilder, a founder of the Society of American Artists, and her husband Richard Watson Gilder, publisher of the *Century* magazine. With her contacts in the press and exhibitions she established not only a powerful private clientele but a public presence. By the turn of the 20th century she was the most famous woman in the fine arts in the USA.

When modernist art theories swept the American art world in the early 20th century, most of the women who had gained a foothold in the fine arts were unceremoniously dropped from histories of American art. The only woman positioned to keep her place in a modernist re-writing of the 19th century was the Impressionist Mary Cassatt who, unlike her contemporaries, has held public attention to this day. Apart from this accident of taste and values, Cassatt should not be isolated from the field of women artists produced by the USA in the 19th century. As a group they showed a high level of talent, dedication and common sense to make careers for themselves out of the patchwork of opportunities and avenues that were open to them.

NANCY MOWLL MATHEWS

20th century

Critics have noted the emergence of a new female type in North American literary fiction of the 1890s. Invented by such authors as Kate Chopin, this woman drank, smoked, spoke her mind and moved about freely. A result of the commingling of politics and art, she was a caricature of contemporary feminists, and she lived a life of unprecedented personal freedom. This new heroine did not in any way reflect the reality of women's lives or feminist concerns; she signals, however, that women's lives were changing. While female social and familial roles remained constant (and continue to resist change even today), women had won a new visibility in the public sphere. If she were white and wealthy, a woman could obtain a sound education. By 1890, fully 10 per cent of all American graduate students were women, and by 1910 the American Census Bureau logged more than 9000 female physicians.

As part of this general phenomenon, most major North American art academies were open to women, though instruction of men and women was rarely comparable. By the third quarter of the 19th century, even life drawing classes, previously available only to men, began to admit women. This accommodation equalised a critical aspect of academic art training, but came at a time when the importance and influence of traditional academic training had permanently waned. Moreover, there were significant exceptions. At the National Academy of Design in New York, for example, it was not until 1903 that women were allowed to compete for the prestigious Prix de Rome, and the Academy continued to bar women from anatomy classes until 1914.

The National Academy was America's answer to the official art schools and exhibition networks of Europe. During the high point of academic influence in the 19th century, entrée into the European academies could establish artistic reputation; thus, it was training abroad in either the academies or the studios of recognised masters that remained the ambition of talented American and, especially, Canadian artists throughout the 19th century. Consistently lagging behind American art schools in equal opportunity, European academies were largely closed to women. In 1896 the Union des Femmes Peintres et Sculpteurs in Paris, established for just this purpose, stormed Europe's leading art institution, the Ecole des Beaux-Arts, and won the admission of women. Even when European training was available to women, however, it, too, was typically in a more compromised form than that offered to men, or in the studios of minor artists.

In response, women set about establishing options for themselves and others. The most extraordinary and vital alternative to traditional academic art instruction was the Art Students League of New York, founded in 1875 by, among others, the painter Helena de Kay Gardner. The ASL was characterised by strong liberal leanings from its founding, including women not only as fully matriculating students, but as faculty and policy makers on its governing boards. For the first several decades of operation, women effectively dominated the Board of Control and, through such artists as Alice Beach Winter and Cornelia Barnes, associated the institution with radical women's causes from suffrage to birth control. Rather than a formal curriculum, the ASL provided studios in which students could train with established artists for as long or as little as they chose. Isabel Bishop (q.v.) remembers the ASL in the 1920s as still "exciting! The students were arguing in the lunchroom. The teachers were having feuds … And you could study whatever you wanted, pay for a month and go where you wished" (Munro 1979, p.148). Although the sculptor Marisol (q.v.) remembered the ASL as somewhat tired by the time of her matriculation in the 1950s, at least through World War II it remained

a leading centre of progressive art teaching and governance. It is in operation to this day, and counts among its alumnae almost every major American woman artist of the first half of the 20th century, from Georgia O'Keeffe (q.v.) to Lee Krasner (q.v.), and many significant women artists, American and Canadian, thereafter.

Official support networks were equally closed to women. America's National Institute of Arts and Letters, founded in 1898, did not count a woman among its 250 members until 1907, when Julia Ward Howe, author of *The Battle Hymn of the Republic*, was elected. It took 19 years for a second woman to be admitted, the writer Mary Deland in 1926. Women visual artists were not represented until 1927, and according to statistics available in 1980, there were still only 12 living female artist-members, and seven deceased. That same year (1980), the American Academy, founded in 1905 with 50 members, could count among its living female artist-members only Georgia O'Keeffe and Isabel Bishop. Similarly, though women exhibited at the Royal Academy of Arts in Canada from its inception in 1880, women were not admitted to membership until well into the 20th century, and remain sparsely represented on its governing board.

Once again, in the absence of recognition and collegiality, women established their own alternatives. Occasionally, a cohesive group of artist-friends, both men and women, could serve as the kind of community that male artists had enjoyed since the time of the medieval guilds. Such was the case with the New York "14th Street Gang" of urban realists in the 1930s, also known as the Union Square group. Students and alumni of the ASL inspired by the teacher Kenneth Hayes Miller, the group counted among its numbers Minna Citron and Isabel Bishop. In Canada, a tradition of local, gender-blind artist-societies became the basic unit of Canadian arts organisations otherwise resistant to unification on a national or regional level. These have ranged in type from artists' groups such as the Painters Eleven in Ontario in the early 1950s to the more structured Emma Lake art camp in northern Saskatchewan in the late 1950s through the 1960s.

The integration of women into these groups was atypical, none the less. A more reliable community for women artists – and one that had persisted in female-dominated form since the 18th century – was the private salon. Social gatherings of like-minded people, salons provided male and female participants, as well as women organisers, with a much-needed sense of context. Without such a structure, the isolation and reticence that women artists experienced in each other's company could be numbing, as Miriam Schapiro (q.v.) recalled in 1975: "[Women] never discussed problems of ambition and ruthlessness. The spirit of the times did not permit such frankness ... When Helen [Frankenthaler, q.v.] and I were together ... we never discussed our paintings. We were in the same gallery and didn't discuss our work" (San Diego 1975, p.11).

In contrast, Romaine Brooks (q.v.) and Natalie Barney, together in Paris from 1915, made their salon famous for its commitment to serious art debate, as well as providing a special haven for lesbian artists. The New York salon of Florine Stettheimer (q.v.) became not only a gathering place for the international avant-garde, but the only site where she would exhibit her new work. The Whitney Studio Club, conducted from 1918 to 1930 in the Greenwich Village studios of Gertrude Vanderbilt Whitney, served to gather and promote both male and female artists. Isabel Bishop remembered its impact in 1927: "I had no artist friends. No art life. Eventually, however, the Whitney Studio Club run by Gertrude Whitney was a resource ... I became a member and showed my still lifes there" (Munro 1979, p.150). Bishop also recalled the salon of the women's rights activist Katherine Dreier: "There was the Société Anonyme, where Katherine Dreier held forth ... The place was an inspiration" (ibid., p.148).

The salonnières were usually women of wealth and culture, and their contacts with artists transformed several into keen and influential patrons. In the depths of the Depression and after, these women founded the most significant museums of modern art in the world, completely transforming the North American art scene. Katherine Dreier was one of the major impresarios of the avant-garde in the 1920s, and an advanced painter in her own right. Her exhibitions of radical European art were the first of their kind, and her establishment of the Société Anonyme collection, now at the Yale University Art Gallery in New Haven, functioned as North America's first museum of modern art. Similarly, the artist and patron Gertrude Vanderbilt Whitney became the founder of the Whitney Museum of American Art, established expressly to provide a stage for neglected modern American artists. In the 1940s

Peggy Guggenheim's gallery cum salon, Art of this Century, became the birthplace of the Abstract Expressionist movement, and often provided these artists' only source of income. When Guggenheim moved to Venice in 1946, the museum she established there served as the first introduction of contemporary North American art to Europe.

Many other women contributed to this trend, thereby extending into our own time women's historical role as patrons of the arts. Most notably, Baroness Hilla Rebay became the driving force behind the creation of the Guggenheim Museum of Non-Objective Art in New York; the collection of Lillie Bliss became the core of the Museum of Modern Art, also in New York; and Etta and Dr Claribel Cone established the Cone Wing at the Baltimore Museum of Art. In this way, women who were not artists exercised a decisive impact on world art.

It is not inevitable, however, that female entrepreneurs will support female artists. None of the women cited above promoted art by women exclusively, or even aggressively. Hilla Rebay's collection was notably weak in work by women, and Peggy Guggenheim, though organising such important exhibitions as 31 Women in 1943, was recorded as being hostile to women artists. This phenomenon was not restricted in time or place. When Jackson Pollock left Betty Parsons's stable of artists in the 1940s, she summarily dropped his wife, Lee Krasner, having given her exhibitions only grudgingly in the first place. As late as 1989, at least one major New York art dealer, Mary Boone, openly refused to handle women artists, citing the absence of collectors of "women's work".

During the first half of the 20th century, the most active promoter of art by women may have been Alfred Stieglitz in his New York galleries: 291, An Intimate Gallery and An American Place. Even before his well-known association with Georgia O'Keeffe, he had exhibited the work of such avant-garde women artists as Marguerite Thompson Zorach (q.v.), and a full range of women photographers, including Annie Brigman, Gertrude Käsebier (q.v.) and Jan Reece. His policies could hardly be described as gender-blind, however. He is reported to have remarked to Anita Pollitzer, who had brought him O'Keeffe's drawings: "Finally a woman on paper!" and continued to conflate sexuality and creativity as his relationship with O'Keeffe grew. He must be held at least partially accountable for the sexualised readings of O'Keeffe's work, since he often showed them alongside his own subtly erotic photographs of her. At one point, as O'Keeffe summered without him in New Mexico, he was said to have found "another young woman artist" to be his bright new star in her absence. Finally, although he gave O'Keeffe one-person shows each year for at least 20 years, he did not sell her work eagerly. When she once remarked to him that she "would like to make a living this year", he simply refused to part with her work. Stieglitz also stood in the way of O'Keeffe's decision to paint a mural for the Radio City Music Hall, New York, during the 1930s. She seems to have accepted these impediments resignedly, explaining in a later interview: "You try arguing with him and see where it gets you" (*O'Keeffe* 1977).

By the eve of World War I, women artists had broken down most institutional barriers to equal education. The Armory Show, the controversial watershed exhibition of avant-garde European and American art held in New York in 1913, had included more than 40 women artists. Among them, Marguerite Zorach was recognised as producing the most radical paintings in America to that date; Edith Dimmock Glackens sold all eight of her exhibited paintings; and Ethel Myers and Abastenia St Leger Eberle attracted significant critical attention. That same year, these women and several others formed the artists' contingent in the suffrage parade down Fifth Avenue, led by Eberle and joined by hundreds of female (and male) workers and professionals. Like the progressive political policies of the Art Students League, the professional lives of women artists were often inseparable from – or at least circumscribed by – issues of gender in both the private and public spheres.

During this same period, O'Keeffe was living a typical female, middle-class American life, characterised by expanded educational opportunities and internalised gender limitations. She received her first art instruction as a routine part of the girls' curriculum at a convent school in Madison, Wisconsin. By 1905, with the youthful dream of "being an artist" and the encouragement of her art teacher, Elizabeth May Willis, she attended specialised classes at the Art Institute of Chicago. She described her first experience in the life drawing class there in terms that recreate the psycho-social barriers with which young women struggled: the male model was "... naked except for a small loincloth. I was surprised –

I was shocked – blushed a hot and uncomfortable blush – didn't look around in my embarrassment and don't remember anything about the anatomy lesson. It was a suffering" (Slatkin 1993, p.217).

In 1907, with uneven training, O'Keeffe moved to New York to enrol at the Art Students League. She joined the studio of William Merritt Chase, who had established an environment particularly sympathetic to women. None the less, two years later, O'Keeffe still did not regard herself as an artist. With her family in financial crisis in Virginia and disillusionment about her abilities, she left New York for a position in Chicago as a commercial artist. This episode marked a major shift in her ambitions. In 1911 she returned to the family home, eyes weakened by a recent bout of measles, and prepared to abandon her dream of "being an artist". From the start, this notion had been predicated on masculinist ideas of "genius" for which there were almost no female role models. Once in Virginia, O'Keeffe turned her attention to teaching, the single career option for educated middle-class North American women at the beginning of the 20th century. Over the next several years, she taught at institutions in Virginia, South Carolina and Texas. As a sideline, she continued to study, pressed by her sisters and inspired by the principles of Arthur Wesley Dow, whose theories of abstract design and the expression of emotion renewed her interest in art. None the less, in 1915, when Stieglitz agreed to show her work, O'Keeffe wrote to Anita Pollitzer from South Carolina that she worried "there wasn't any use ruining good paper", that she "wasn't even sure that [she] had anything worth expressing" and that she had "almost decided never to try anymore" (Witzling 1991, p.213). O'Keeffe continued to be burdened by doubt throughout her life, as when she took to her bed following every major exhibition at Stieglitz's gallery, or when she was hospitalised in the 1930s for "nervous exhaustion". On the occasion of her retrospective at the Museum of Modern Art in 1946 (the first for a woman at that institution), O'Keeffe was asked what the primary requirement for an artist was; she replied: "Nerve" (Rubinstein 1982, p.185).

The first exhibition of O'Keeffe's work at Stieglitz's gallery in 1916 – a remarkable opportunity for a 29-year-old female artist – was a personal as well as a professional turning point. In 1917 she stopped teaching; more importantly, she later recalled:

I found myself saying to myself – I can't live where I want to – I can't go where I want to – I can't do what I want to – I can't even say what I want to … I decided I was a very stupid fool not to at least paint as I wanted to … as that seemed to be the only thing … that didn't concern anybody [Witzling 1991, p.222].

While O'Keeffe was apparently wilful from a young age, she also had within her family a number of self-sufficient, independent female role models: both her grandmothers had been frontier women who had raised their families alone, and two unmarried aunts had professional careers. At crucial points in her life, it was women to whom she turned, or who provided critical support: Elizabeth May Willis, her first art teacher and mentor; her sisters, who had urged her to return to study following her depression of 1911; her friend, Anita Pollitzer, who offered help and advice over several decades; and later, Mabel Dodge Luhan, who introduced her to New Mexico and provided both comfort and stimulation. It was Luhan whom she contacted when the press response to her work began to revolve around the perception of sexuality, and asked her for a piece of written criticism: "A woman might say something that a man can't – I feel there is something unexplored about woman that only a woman can explore" (*ibid.*, p.225).

O'Keeffe's strong identity precluded the stereotype of the quiescent female. To the charge by a critic that her flowers were imitations of Stieglitz's photographs, she countered that while they occasionally worked with similar motifs, she had influenced Stieglitz at least as much as he had influenced her. At the height of the political battle for the passage of the Equal Rights Amendment in the 1940s, she wrote to Eleanor Roosevelt, who opposed the bill: "The ERA would write into the highest law of our land, legal equality for all. At present women do not have it and I believe we are considered – half the people" (*ibid.*, p.228). Perhaps one of the surest indicators of O'Keeffe's independence – and one of the few uncharacteristic aspects of her education – is her disregard of European art and training; she did not even begin to travel abroad until late in life.

Of all women artists in the 20th century, O'Keeffe has been the most readily accepted into the mainstream canon of art history. Her first major retrospective (outside Stieglitz's galleries) was held in 1943 at the Art Institute of Chicago, followed by the Museum of Modern Art in 1946, and the Whitney Museum of American Art in 1970. The Whitney retrospective propelled her to star-status, and from that point on she was both well-exhibited and well-published, regarded as the *grande dame* of American painting. Also in 1970, she was awarded the prestigious gold medal for painting by the National Institute of Arts and Letters, a thoroughly male-based institution. None the less, neither O'Keeffe nor any other woman artist was mentioned in Horst W. Jansen's standard *History of Art* textbook, which was reprinted throughout the 1970s. Jansen opined in 1979 that he had "not been able to find a woman artist who clearly belongs in a one volume history of art" (Broude and Garrard 1994, p.16).

Following World War I, mounting feminist activity culminated in the passage of women's suffrage in Canada in 1918, and in America in 1920. Perhaps as a result, the decade of the 1920s has been seen as one of extraordinary female liberation. In fact, unprecedented numbers of American women moved out of the home and into the female labour force, which grew in this decade by 26 per cent to slightly more than two million. Despite this, there is little evidence that a real revolution occurred in women's economic or social roles; the employment statistics reflected a primary increase in traditional, low-paying, clerical and domestic occupations. Women who had been employed in non-gender-based positions during the war were quickly demobilised after it, and between 1910 and 1930 the number of female physicians in America actually declined from 9015 to 6825.

One theory holds that this failure of economic and social progress was the result of the decline of feminist activism following the victory of suffrage. This may also help to explain the decreased numbers of large-scale mural commissions offered to women at the end of the 1920s in anticipation of the World's Fairs from those offered on the occasion of the Panama-Pacific Exposition in 1915: by the later date, feminist agitation was simply not in evidence. The phenomenon of the "flapper" of the 1920s, a kind of materialisation of the "liberated" fantasies of 19th-century pulp fiction writers, obscured the stagnation into which American women had slipped. Newly stringent immigration quotas, the sanctioning of racist organisations and practices, and a dead halt to legislation positively effecting the status of women were all related issues in this decade.

In both Canada and the USA, female art students turned increasingly for their training to institutions that stressed "practical" employment, such as the School of Applied Design for Women in New York. The School prepared women for commercial fields from interior design to needlework, thus supporting traditionally female domestic arts and crafts. While women attended these and other art schools in growing numbers, however, very few made the transition from amateur, or student status, to professional artist. This transition was facilitated in America in the 1930s with progressive federal legislation meant to combat the economic crisis of the Depression. The best that can be said of the status of women artists in the 1920s is that the decade produced an army of well-trained young women prepared to take on the challenges of professionalism offered during the presidency of Franklin Delano Roosevelt.

The variety of work-relief programmes developed by the Roosevelt administration during the Depression, known generally as the Works Progress Administration (WPA), was remarkable on at least two levels. To begin with, they acknowledged artists as workers, were committed to supporting them, and thereby established the first systematic episode of public patronage in North American history. Second, by all accounts, official and anecdotal, the federal programmes were gender-neutral. The first Canadian programme to present this level of national, bias-free support was established only in 1957 as the Canada Council, though it is now stronger than its contemporary American counterpart, the National Endowment for the Arts and the Humanities.

An individual qualified for the WPA art unit, the Federal Art Project, by taking a general exam or submitting proof of professional activities. Not only were large numbers of female art students automatically qualified, those women unable or unwilling to participate in higher education could still display expertise. Artists who met the additional qualification of financial need (roughly 90 per cent) submitted their work on a monthly basis to regional supervisors and were provided with regular salaries. Ten per cent were admitted on the basis of skill alone, and were almost invariably placed in the Mural Division of the programme. Major mural commissions were then awarded from anonymous competitions of unsigned sketches. Isabel Bishop, Alice Neel (q.v.), Louise Nevelson (q.v.) and Lee Krasner, among others, won their first major commissions through the mural division of the WPA. Krasner had abandoned painting in 1933 at the peak of the Depression to pursue a more practical occupation: she enrolled in a teacher-training course at the City College of New York. Like many artists, she was able to return to painting in 1935 due to FAP support.

It is probable that Eleanor Roosevelt was responsible for the non-discriminatory policies of the WPA, just as she was responsible for the influx of female government officials around the President. Women comprised 41 per cent of all artists on work-relief, not only as practitioners, but also as teachers and, importantly, administrators. The photographer Berenice Abbott (q.v.) was supervisor of the Photography Division; the African-American artists Augusta Savage (q.v.) and Gwendolyn Bennett were directors of the Harlem Art Center, New York, a pulse point for the Harlem Renaissance; Ruth Reeves was national co-ordinator of the Index of American Design, a permanent archive of American folk arts directly benefiting anonymous work by women and African-Americans; Lee Krasner, Elizabeth Olds and Helen Lundeberg were local supervisors; and Audrey McMahon was the New York regional director of the Federal Art Project. This position gave McMahon supreme authority over the biggest and most productive art-producing region in North America: almost half of all American artists lived in New York. While many women were engaged in political activity through these government positions, others worked outside official networks by returning to earlier female traditions of unionisation and group activism: Alice Neel aided in the founding of the Unemployed Artists Association, Bernarda Bryson was one of the founders of the Artists' Union, and Margaret Bourke-White (q.v.) was vice-chairman of the American Artists Congress.

Women experienced in this period an unprecedented opportunity to work at their art as professionals. Commenting on this in the context of the Art Students League, Isabel Bishop remarked: "There was absolutely no feeling in those days … about my being a girl. It just didn't come up" (Munro 1979, p.148). The assumption of professionalism and the spirit of camaraderie facilitated an explosion of work by women. These factors may also have helped to generate the phenomenon of the egalitarian art colony during and after the period of government support. In Woodstock, New York, Provincetown and Gloucester, Massachusetts, Ogunquit, Maine, Laguna Beach, California, and Taos, New Mexico, women artists played an equal role and benefited equally from the support and friendship these communities offered. Similarly, the founding of American Abstract Artists (AAA) in New York during this period, ostensibly to provide a context for artists working outside the dominant realist trend, provided an unusual number of women artists and artist couples with shared visibility and responsibility. It was at AAA, for example, that Lee Krasner secured her reputation as a major player in the American abstract art movement.

None the less, it would be naive to suggest that gender-bias and discrimination could be exorcised from the individual consciousness through legislation. In fact, there had been a dark underbelly to the support of working women in the 1930s, ironically promoted by Roosevelt's female Secretary of Labor, Frances Perkins, who called throughout her tenure for the return of married women to the home. This idea dominated the later 1940s, and remained a key obstacle to the acceptance and advancement of the working wife and mother, both socially and psychologically.

The generation of women artists to come to maturity before World War II was the first to have experienced equal access to artistic training and professional support. In 1943, when federal programmes were terminated to focus energy on the war, these women lost the firm footing of government patronage. Almost simultaneously, the dominance of the New York School of painters, later known as the Abstract Expressionists and predicated on the machismo mystique of explosive genius, served to undercut women further. The rejection of women artists by the New York School was both individual and programmatic; it was supported by reactionary social trends following World War II, and quickly snapped shut the window of opportunity for women opened by the Depression. Throughout this period, the painter Lee Krasner was in a unique position as an artist of reputation and the wife of the leading star of the New York School, Jackson Pollock.

Krasner's training was rigorous and systematic. Recognised as a prodigy, she won a scholarship to the Women's Art School of Cooper Union, an institution whose popularity grew rapidly after World War II, and later entered the traditional National Academy of Design. In 1934 she joined the Federal Art Project, studied at the Art Students League, and from 1937 to 1940 painted in the studio of Hans Hofmann. Throughout the 1930s and 1940s, Hofmann's School of Fine Arts trained several of the soon-to-be prominent painters of the New York School. He also became a popular teacher to many of the most gifted women of the period. The sculptor Louise Nevelson, fresh from the Art Students League, travelled to Munich in 1931 to study with him, and joined him again in New York after his emigration. Krasner remained a devotee, despite what she described as his straightforward male chauvinist posture. She recalled his critiques of her work as the same back-handed praise that earlier women artists had experienced: "This painting is so good you'd never know it was done by a woman!" (Chadwick 1990, p.302).

These attitudes extended beyond professional contacts into art-social networks. The 8th Street Club, with the Cedar Bar, the two major meeting places for the New York School painters, admitted women only as audience. Women were effectively silenced – excluded from active participation in the intense discussions with critics and curators that the male artists found so inspiring. Women were never allowed to attend board meetings or policy discussions, even as non-participants. At the Cedar, Krasner remembered being told by Barnett Newman: "we don't need dames", and felt that women were generally "treated like cattle" (*ibid.*, p.303). For women working in non-traditional media, the sense of threat on the part of male artists could be even greater. Nevelson was told by a colleague that she "had to have balls to be a sculptor" (Slatkin 1993, p.250). More significantly, she received press critiques such as the following: "We learned the artist was a woman in time to check our enthusiasm. Had it been otherwise, we might have hailed these sculptural expressions as by surely a great figure amongst the moderns" (Chadwick 1990, p.308).

Interestingly, two female members of the group loosely identified as the second generation of Abstract Expressionists – though they were painting alongside their male colleagues in the first generation – do not recollect any significant bias. Helen Frankenthaler wrote: "It was a relatively trusting and beautiful period ... there seemed to be little that was motivated, threatening, or contaminating ... It was lucky to be in one's early 20s with a group of painters to argue painting with" (Munro 1979, p.216). It is difficult to contextualise Frankenthaler's perceptions, but she came to the group with many of the traditional accoutrements by which females seemed benign even while trespassing in a man's world: she was both wealthy and attractive; she had not yet made a significant artistic reputation (especially relative to a figure such as Krasner); and she was introduced into these circles by her close friend, the "Kingmaker" (sic) of critics, Clement Greenberg.

Grace Hartigan (q.v.), who corroborated Frankenthaler's impressions with her own, could not be characterised as similarly non-threatening. In 1952 she became one of the first artists of this generation to earn an international reputation when her painting, *Persian Jacket,* was purchased by the Museum of Modern Art in New York. Hartigan may have compensated by presenting herself as "one of the boys", painting for a brief period under the name of George and severing ties with her husband and children. As in centuries past, the neutering of one's female identity was not an uncommon strategy: the painter Gertrude Greene also adopted a male persona, Peter G. Greene, and Elaine de Kooning and Lee Krasner (whose real name was Lenore, not the androgynous Lee) signed their paintings only with their initials. Alice Neel and Louise Nevelson, who, like Hartigan, could not juggle the pressures of their art with those of motherhood, also gave up their children. Nevelson even felt compelled to promote her machismo by responding to the remark about her lack of "balls" with the protest: "I have balls!"

Following Hartigan, Frankenthaler was the next woman artist of this period to win widespread recognition. By the early 1960s, Frankenthaler had been featured in *Life, Look* and *Time,* attaining a prominence that was climaxed in 1969 by one of the first full-scale retrospectives of a woman artist at the Whitney. In contrast, such artists as Krasner and Nevelson, who came into the New York School as artistic contenders, did not fare so well. It was only in 1978 with the Whitney Museum exhibition *Abstract Expressionism: The Formative Years* that Krasner was restored to her pivotal place as a leading abstractionist of the early 1940s. Following a flurry of rediscovery, she received a long-overdue

retrospective one year before her death, declaring it "too late". Similarly, Nevelson fell into obscurity during the Abstract Expressionist episode and worked for long periods in isolation and neglect. At one point, she had not sold a piece for more than 30 years and, for lack of space, burned much of the contents of her studio. Since the 1970s and the purposeful reclamation of women artists, Nevelson has been recognised as one of the leading sculptors of the 20th century.

As in the 1930s, the appropriateness of combining family and career became a crucial issue for many female artists of this generation. Early in the century, ambitious, educated women often made the self-conscious decision not to marry. Between 1877 and 1924, 75 per cent of all American women who earned the PhD were single; in 1920, 88 per cent of all professional women were single, and the female workforce itself was overwhelmingly dominated by unmarried women under 25 until World War II. Those career women who married usually gave up their ambitions at this time, or certainly with the arrival of a baby. Marjorie Organ Henri's transition from painter to "muse" is characteristic of the early part of the century. After marrying the prominent Ash Can School painter, Robert Henri, she spent most of her time posing for him. When asked about her own work, she said that she did not have "the extra grain of ego she needed" to persevere and that if she had, she "might have spoiled her understanding disposition" (Rubinstein 1982, p.168). She referred to her husband as "The Boss", asserted that he had enough ego for both of them, and that his art was simply more important than hers.

Forty years later, Lee Krasner was still significantly derailed as an artist by her marriage. Despite her memories of shabby treatment by the New York School coterie, Krasner insisted that her husband Jackson Pollock was neither misogynist nor chauvinist. None the less, she said of their relationship: "he was the important thing. I couldn't do enough for him" and admitted that her own work began to seem "irrelevant" (Cincinnati 1989, p.28). She found corroboration for this view all around her. In 1949 Krasner and Pollock showed their work together in an exhibition at the Sidney Janis Gallery, *Artists: Man and Wife.* Predictably, the exhibition title defined her role as dependent and subsidiary. This experience, and subsequent reviews, discouraged Krasner from exhibiting again until 1951, and she later destroyed most of her works from this period. She did not recover her pre-Pollock productivity until his death.

Even Georgia O'Keeffe, who remained consistently committed to painting throughout her life, struggled with the tension of her public and private roles. Between 1917 and 1937 she posed for more than 500 photographs by her husband, a task that drained her of time and energy. In the 1930s, as her independence grew, she met with increasing resistance from Stieglitz. She wrote in 1932: "I am divided between my man and a life with him ... I have to get along with my divided self the best way I can" (Slatkin 1993, p.227). In contrast, the African-American artist Alma Thomas described the freedoms her choice to remain childless and unmarried allowed: "I paint when I feel like it. I didn't have to come home. Or I could come home late and there was nobody to interfere with what I wanted ... It was what I wanted, and no argument. That is what allowed me to develop" (Munro 1979, pp.195–6).

Nevertheless, a woman artist's professional life could be compromised by the demands of daily life without the additional complications of family. The Canadian painter Emily Carr (q.v.) was a promising young art student and, like many Canadians, especially from the West Coast, she looked for training abroad. Between 1890 and 1911 she studied in San Francisco, London and Paris. On her return to British Columbia, she decided to run a boarding house as a means of support while devoting herself to her art. Ironically, domestic duties overwhelmed her, and she entered a long period of artistic dormancy. It was only when she was "discovered" by the director of the National Gallery in Ottawa in 1927 that she was relieved of major economic concerns and returned fully to creative life. Loosely affiliated with the Group of Seven, and encouraged by them, Carr was a prolific painter until a stroke ten years later, when she transferred her attention primarily to writing. Carr's circuitous path was characteristic of the necessarily erratic lives of many women professionals, married or single.

For many of these artists, the decision not to marry, not to have children, or to abandon either or both, was based not only in practicality but in the deeply ingrained belief that a woman was fundamentally circumscribed by her social and biological roles. This, in turn, was supported by social legislation. In 1940, for example, a married woman could not hold her own earnings in 11 US states and could

not make contracts in 16 US states. In several states, she could be divorced if she were not a virgin upon marriage, could be sued for damages in the case of adultery, could not sue for child support, did not have guardianship rights, and could not serve on juries. By the 1950s, through the new medium of television, the image of woman as solely devoted wife and mother in such programmes as *The Donna Reed Show* and *Father Knows Best* became iconic. The sculptor Louise Bourgeois (q.v.) wrote: "I have had a guilt complex about pushing my art, so much so that every time I was about to show I would have some sort of attack. So I decided it was better simply not to try ... the work was done and hidden away" (Munro 1979, p.156).

The conflict of homemaker and career woman, while still a challenge for many women, was a significant impediment well into the 1960s. The oeuvre of Eva Hesse (q.v.) was produced just before her premature death in 1970, and she is an important transitional figure on many levels. On the one hand, like so many women before her, Hesse received formative training at the Art Students League. She also studied at the Pratt Institute of New York and Yale University, two rigorously professional institutions whose popularity at this point placed them among the most competitive contemporary art schools. Hesse was an aggressive and successful student. In the matter of separate identity, however, she struggled as had older women artists:

> I think at the time I met the man I married, I shouldn't say I went backwards, but I did, because he was a more mature and developed artist. He would push me in his direction and I would be unconsciously somewhat influenced by him. Yet when I met him, I had already had a drawing show which was much more me [Cincinnati 1989, p.269].

There was increasing recognition in Hesse's self-analysis that this conflict was at least partly predetermined by socially constructed gender roles. According to Alice Neel, women artists of the 1940s and 1950s did not care "to fight the fight in the streets" (*ibid.*, p.40). With Hesse's generation, the fight for recognition, like that prior to 1920, became political.

In 1966 NOW (National Organization for Women) was founded in acknowledgement of the need for a watchdog organisation to monitor gender bias. Three years later, this awareness led to the first organised protests against racism and sexism in the American art world, initially and specifically aimed at the three leading American art museums: the Metropolitan Museum of Art, the Museum of Modern Art and the Whitney Museum of American Art in New York. Throughout the 1970s, artist/activist groups such as WAR (Women Artists in Revolution), Where We At, Black Women Artists, WSBAL (Women, Students and Artists for Black Art Liberation), the Ad Hoc Women Artists Group, Women in the Arts, the Los Angeles Council of Women Artists, Ariadne and the Women's Caucus for Art conducted political actions demanding equal representation in schools, exhibitions and legislative bodies. The most successful Canadian counterpart, CAR (Canadian Artists' Representation), founded in 1968, successfully lobbied the government to legislate protection from unfair or unremunerated exploitation of both male and female artists' names and works. By 1981 there were more than 40 artist-run co-operatives in Canada, several of which, such as the Women's Cultural Building in Toronto, Womanspirit in London, Ontario, Manitoba Women in the Arts, Powerhouse in Montreal and Vancouver Women in Focus maintain a specifically feminist orientation.

As conceded by one Whitney curator, the pressure was effective. The activists Betye Saar (q.v.) and Barbara Chase-Riboud were included in the first major exhibition of African-American women at the Whitney in 1970; the percentage of women artists shown in the Whitney Annual exhibition rose from 15 per cent in 1969 to 22 per cent in 1970; the percentage of solo exhibitions by women artists in New York galleries rose from an average of 9 per cent in 1970 to 24 per cent by 1980; and supportive services such as the international liaison network, WEB (West-East Bag), the Women's Art Registry of slides, and the Women's Caucus's Job Roster were established across the country. These developments were not restricted to the USA. The end of the 1970s represented a high point in the exhibiting, critical discussion and the recognition of North American women artists in general. It is not coincidental that renewed feminist visibility at this time, combined with institutional fiscal crises, led to the shift towards co-education on the part of many gender-segregated American and Canadian colleges and universities.

As they had in the past, women also set about establishing options to traditional educational and professional venues, especially of a feminist nature. Judy Chicago (q.v.) organised the first feminist art curriculum at the California State College at Fresno in 1970, a model programme providing context, support and training by and for women. She wrote: "I realized that if the art community as it existed could not provide me with what I needed in order to realize myself, then I would have to commit myself to developing an alternative" (Slatkin 1993, p.284). In 1971 Chicago and her colleague Miriam Schapiro expanded the programme and re-established it at the California Institute of the Arts, a cutting-edge institution on the West Coast well-known for its progressive ideas and policies. Although Chicago resigned in 1973 in protest against CalArts' failure to provide adequate financial support, and Schapiro resigned in 1975 to return to New York, the programme left an enduring educational, artistic and social legacy. In 1973 Chicago, Sheila de Bretteville and Arlene Raven founded the Woman's Building, which remained an active force in Los Angeles until 1991, housing the Feminist Studio Workshop and a women's art gallery, Womanspace. In 1975 Chicago also published her autobiography *Through the Flower*. This ground-breaking text recorded the development of Chicago's personal and artistic maturity from the point of view of feminist awareness. That same year Chicago began a work that is widely acknowledged as the first piece of feminist art, *The Dinner Party*, created as a collaborative project reclaiming the lives of forgotten women in history.

Chicago had previous experience with collaboration and workshop practice in a project that became the most significant component of the CalArts programme, Womanhouse. Here, Chicago, Schapiro and a group of female graduate students rehabilitated a dilapidated Los Angeles mansion, utilising the spaces as exhibition sites for installation and performance art. These media had begun to emerge in Los Angeles in the 1960s, ultimately derived from the 1950s concepts of the Happening and multimedia presentation. The latter had been developed, in particular, at Black Mountain College, North Carolina, a short-lived, post-World War II art school where many of the most exciting inter-disciplinary collaborations among students, teachers and professional artists first occurred.

Throughout the 1970s women not only dominated the performance and installation genres, but were its leaders. Issues specific to women's bodies and experience were explored through subjects such as the goddess, female sexuality, fertility and gender roles, and paralleled the international trend towards "écriture feminine", or "writing the female body". Similarly, many women in this period also attempted to recover women's traditional "craft" media for high art, resulting in stylistic episodes known as Pattern and Decoration, Femmage and the resurgence of collage, assemblage and photomontage.

Some of the most innovative work in this context was produced by Faith Ringgold (q.v.). As a middle-class, African-American female, Ringgold knew at a young age that she would need to work to live, but, more importantly, her mother – a fashion designer – expected her to "be somebody" (*Faith Ringgold* 1991). Ringgold was aware of her artistic ambitions in her early teens, but does not recall specific encouragement from her teachers. In fact, she was once told that she did not know how to draw; it was from that moment, she says, that she knew she was an artist, because no one had the power to delimit who she could be. Ringgold enrolled at the City College of New York, and since the liberal arts programme was closed to women, she majored in education, receiving an undergraduate degree in 1955 and a master's degree in 1959. From 1955 she taught in the New York City public schools, resigning only in 1973 to devote herself full-time to her art.

Ringgold had begun to work seriously as an independent artist in the early 1960s, turning her dining room into studio space. By the late 1960s, she was politically active in both the African-American and women's rights movements, founding a series of organisations including Where We At and WSBAL. She also produced several of the most significant, politically charged paintings of this period in the Pop mode. None the less, like the lives of so many artists, hers was a balancing act. She said of this time:

> Had it not been for Mother taking the girls [Ringgold's daughters] to Europe that summer, I would not have been able to complete those paintings ... That was why I walked out [from her marriage] ... I didn't want to spend my summer cleaning the house and cooking ... I spent my days at the gallery painting till well into the night. At the end of the summer [her husband] had left. Who

could blame him? I needed him, but I needed my freedom too ... If I called him now he would just say, "Don't let those girls go away alone. Keep them with you. Give up the art" [Slatkin 1993, p.366].

Shortly after this period, Ringgold became deeply interested in African culture, teaching courses on African art and integrating African motifs into her compositions. The difficulty of transporting her work led her to soft, cloth supports and inspired by a family – and cultural – tradition of story-telling, she began to produce story quilts in the early 1980s. The use of fabric brought personal, ethnic and political identification to her art. Her mother had worked with fabric all her life, and the quilt had been an early African-American woman's medium. Like Chicago in *The Dinner Party*, Ringgold was consciously aware that she was blurring the traditional boundaries between craft – "female art" – and fine art – "male art". When asked if people called her sewn pieces "crafts", she answered: "Claes Oldenburg's soft typewriters are sewn pieces, and I never heard anyone call them craft. It's who's doing it that makes it craft" (*ibid.*, p.322).

Throughout the 1970s, women played a catalytic role in redirecting mainstream art currents. Not only did women artists introduce new genres, techniques and subject matter, they effectively brought to a close the "pure painting" movements that had dominated modernism since about 1870. As artists working from female experience, they went far in completing the historical record, moving women out of the role of passive theme into that of active speaker. One author has written that, in the past: "it has been possible to construct a history of mainstream art without women. In the future, this will not be so, in large part because of the contributions made during this period" (Randy Rosen in Cincinnati 1989, p.22). None the less, there is significant evidence that the 1980s brought with it a reactionary trend like that documented in Susan Faludi's broad socio-cultural study, *Backlash* (1991).

The emergence of the American New Right – the Moral Majority – at the end of the 1970s renewed the conflict around the "appropriate" role of women, and was founded at least in part on a platform of anti-feminism. Although during the decade the barriers in law, and even custom, to a woman's autonomy were substantially eliminated, the female role of child-bearer and family caretaker became a prominent issue once again. Reflecting the social climate, a number of the most important New York galleries refused to carry the work of women, citing the absence of collectors, or the likelihood of an artist's distracting pregnancies. Museum statistics reflect a similar trend. Throughout the 1980s, there was a marked decline of women artists included in the Whitney Biennial, experiencing an initial rapid drop from 32 per cent in 1979 to 20 per cent in 1981. In 1984, when the Museum of Modern Art opened its new facilities with the exhibition *An International Survey of Painting and Sculpture*, only 13 of 164 artists were women. This clearly had an impact on an artist's earning capacity. During the period 1980–85, 40 per cent of those classifying themselves as professional artists in the USA were women; during the same period, a National Endowment for the Arts survey recorded the average annual income from art of men at $13,000 compared to $5700 for women.

It was in response to the Museum of Modern Art's exhibition that a group of artists and art historians came together to form an activist group known as the Guerrilla Girls. Concealing their identities in gorilla costumes, they post data throughout the art districts of Manhattan documenting, among other issues, sexism and racism in New York galleries and museums. They insist upon the profound and often damaging connection between a woman artist's professional life and gender role expectations on the part of society. They have kept "the fight in the streets" by picketing art institutions, attracting the news media with information-based performances and promoting their activities through sets of slides and videos. In the arena of mainstream art developments, the opening of the National Museum of Women in the Arts in 1987 in Washington, DC, has also served to impede the backlash. Although criticised as exclusive and exclusionary, it is the first museum in North America to be solely devoted to art by women, and founded by a private collector, Wilhelmina Cole Holliday, it has kept alive the tradition of female patronage of the arts.

Women artists have struggled inordinately with the conflicting demands of female identity and artistic identity. Throughout the 1960s, at least, art has exacted a high psychic toll on women: in the 20th century, this would include the depressions and alcoholism of Alice Trumbull Mason; Alice Neel's breakdowns and suicide attempts; Nevelson's persistent but never-acted-upon desire to kill herself; Grace Hartigan's relinquishing of her name and children; even Georgia O'Keeffe's "nervous exhaustion" following exhibitions. Perhaps the greatest shift for women in the final decade of the 20th century – despite resistance to the contrary – is the decline of institutionalised scorn towards the working wife and mother. Consequently, young women artists do not document the same intensity of conflicting social roles with which earlier artists were so heavily burdened. Even now, however, a gap separates ideals of equal opportunity from realities of economic discrimination. Along with new freedoms, the feminisation of poverty in North America has also grown. Fully 70 per cent of the adult poor are women, and women artists continue to earn less than 50 per cent of the income of male counterparts.

DEBORAH JEAN JOHNSON

Bibliography

Elizabeth Fries Ellet, *Women Artists in All Ages and Countries*, New York: Harper, 1859; London: Bentley, 1860

"Woman's position in art", *The Crayon*, viii, 1861, pp.25–8

H. W., "Lady-artists in Rome", *Art Journal*, v, 1866, pp.177–8

Harriet Ford, "The Royal Canadian Academy of Arts", *Canadian Magazine*, iii, 1894, p.48

M. E. Dignam, "Canadian women and the development of art", *Women of Canada: Their Life and Work*, Toronto: National Council of Women, 1900; reprinted 1975

Anna Lea Merritt, "A letter to artists: Especially women artists", *Lippincott's Monthly Magazine*, lxv, 1900, pp.463–9; reprinted in *Love Locked Out: The Memoirs of Anna Lea Merritt*, ed. Galina Gorokhoff, Boston: Museum of Fine Arts, 1982

31 Women, exh. cat., Art of the Century, New York, 1943

Jane C. Giffen, "Susanna Rowson and her academy", *Magazine Antiques*, xcviii, 1970, pp.436–40

Paul Duval, *Four Decades: The Canadian Group of Painters and Their Contemporaries, 1930–1970*, Toronto: Clarke Irwin, 1972

Doris Cole, *From Tipi to Skyscraper: A History of Women in Architecture*, Boston: I Press, 1973

Francis V. O'Connor, ed., *Art for the Millions: Essays from the 1930s by Artists and Administrators of the WPA Federal Art Project*, Greenwich, CT: New York Graphic Society, 1973

Judy Chicago, *Through the Flower: My Struggle as a Woman Artist*, New York: Doubleday, 1975; 2nd edition, New York: Doubleday, and London: Women's Press, 1982

From Women's Eyes: Women Painters in Canada, exh. cat., Agnes Etherington Art Centre, Kingston, 1975

Miriam Schapiro: The Shrine, the Computer and the Dollhouse, exh. cat., Mandeville Art Gallery, University of California at San Diego, 1975

Some Canadian Women Artists, exh. cat., National Gallery of Canada, Ottawa, 1975

Judith Paine, "The Women's Pavilion of 1876", *Feminist Art Journal*, iv/4, 1975–6, pp.5–12

7 American Women: The Depression Decade, exh. cat., Vassar College Art Gallery, Poughkeepsie, NY, 1976

Jane C. Nylander, "Some print sources of New England schoolgirl art", *Magazine Antiques*, cx, 1976, pp.292–301

Women Artists, 1550–1950, exh. cat., Los Angeles County Museum of Art, and elsewhere, 1976

Marie Elwood, "The state dinner service of Canada, 1898", *Material History Bulletin*, Spring 1977, p.41

O'Keeffe, video, produced and directed by Perry Miller Adato, WNET 13 Production, 1977

Guy Robert, *L'Art au Québec depuis 1940*, Montreal: La Presse, 1977

Women in American Architecture: A Historic and Contemporary Perspective, exh. cat., Whitney Library of Design, 1977

Abstract Expressionism: The Formative Years, exh. cat., Herbert F. Johnson Museum of Art, Ithaca, NY, and elsewhere, 1978

Terry Fenton and Karen Wilkin, *Modern Painting in Canada*, Edmonton: Hurtig, 1978

Great Expectations: The European Vision of Nova Scotia, 1749–1848, exh. cat., Mount Saint Vincent Art Gallery, Halifax, 1978

Anthea Callen, *Angel in the Studio: Women in the Arts and Crafts Movement, 1870–1914*, London: Astragal, 1979; as *Women Artists of the Arts and Crafts Movement, 1870–1914*, New York: Pantheon, 1979

Eleanor Munro, *Originals: American Women Artists*, New York: Simon and Schuster, 1979

Painters Eleven in Retrospect, exh. cat., Robert McLaughlin Gallery, Oshawa, Ontario, 1979

Julie Graham, "American women artists' groups: 1867–1930", *Woman's Art Journal*, i/1, 1980, pp.7–12

Martha J. Hoppin, "Women artists in Boston, 1870–1900: The pupils of William Morris Hunt", *American Art Journal*, xiii/1, 1981, pp.17–46

Evelyn de R. McMann, *Royal Canadian Academy of Arts: Exhibitions and Members, 1880–1979*, Toronto: University of Toronto Press, 1981

Charlotte Streifer Rubinstein, *American Women Artists from Early Times to the Present*, Boston: Hall, 1982

Mary Ann Stankiewicz, "The creative sister: An historical look at women, the arts, and higher education", *Studies in Art Education*, xxiv/1, 1982, pp.49–55

Kenneth W. Wheeler and Virginia Lee Lussier, eds, *Women, the Arts and the 1920s in Paris and New York*, New Brunswick, NJ: Transaction, 1982

Robert Bringhurst and others, eds, *Visions:*

Contemporary Art in Canada, Vancouver: Douglas and McIntyre, 1983

Lee Krasner: A Retrospective, exh. cat., Museum of Fine Arts, Houston, and elsewhere, 1983

Rediscovery: Canadian Women Photographers, 1841–1941, exh. cat., London Regional Art Gallery, London, Ontario, 1983

Social Concern and Urban Realism: American Painting of the 1930s, exh. cat., Boston University Art Gallery, 1983

Madeleine Fidell-Beaufort, "Elizabeth Jane Gardner Bouguereau: A Parisian artist from New Hampshire", *Archives of American Art Journal*, xxiv/2, 1984, pp.2–9

David Rubinstein, *Before the Suffragettes: Women's Emancipation in the 1890s*, Brighton: Harvester, and New York: St Martin's Press, 1986

American Women Artists, 1830–1930, exh. cat., National Museum of Women in the Arts, Washington, DC, and elsewhere, 1987

Paula Blanchard, *The Life of Emily Carr*, Vancouver: Douglas and McIntyre, and Seattle: University of Washington Press, 1987

Alicia Faxon and Sylvia Moore, eds, *Pilgrims and Pioneers: New England Women in the Arts*, New York: Midmarch Arts Press, 1987

Helen Goodman, "Emily Sartain: Her career", *Arts Magazine*, lxi, 1987, pp.61–5

—, "Women illustrators of the golden age of American illustration", *Woman's Art Journal*, viii/1, 1987, pp.13–22

American Women of the Etching Revival, exh. cat., High Museum of Art, Atlanta, 1988

Wendy Beckett, *Contemporary Women Artists*, New York: Universe, and Oxford: Phaidon, 1988

Sally L. Kitch, "'As a sign that all may understand': Shaker gift drawings and female spiritual power", *Winterthur Portfolio*, xxiv, 1989, pp.1–28

Making Their Mark: Women Artists Move into the Mainstream, 1970–85, Cincinnati Art Museum, and elsewhere, 1989

Whitney Chadwick, *Women, Art and Society*, New York and London: Thames and Hudson, 1990; revised edition, 1996

Dangerous Goods: Feminist Visual Art Practices, exh. cat., Edmonton Art Gallery and elsewhere, 1990

Frances Anne Hopkins, 1838–1919: Canadian Scenery, exh. cat., Thunder Bay National Exhibition Centre, 1990

Nancy Mowll Mathews, "American women artists at the turn of the century: Opportunities and choices", *Lilla Cabot Perry: An American Impressionist*, exh. cat., National Museum for Women in the Arts, Washington, DC, 1990, pp.105–14

Doris Shadbolt, *Emily Carr*, Vancouver: Douglas and McIntyre, and Seattle: University of Washington Press, 1990

Patricia Dunlavy Valenti, "Sophia Peabody Hawthorne: A

study of artistic influence", *Studies in the American Renaissance*, 1990, pp.1–21

William Chafe, *American Women in the 20th Century*, New York: Oxford University Press, 1991

Hélène Cixous, "The laugh of the Medusa", *Feminisms: An Anthology of Literary Theory and Criticism*, ed. Robyn R. Warhol and Diane Price Herndl, New Brunswick, NJ: Rutgers University Press, 1991

Betsy Fahlman, "Women art students at Yale, 1869–1913", *Woman's Art Journal*, xii/1, 1991, pp.15–23

Faith Ringgold: The Last Story Quilt, video, created and produced by Linda Freeman, L and S Video Enterprises, Inc., 1991

Mara R. Witzling, ed., *Voicing Our Visions: Writings by Women Artists*, New York: Universe, 1991; London: Women's Press, 1992

Maria Tippett, *By a Lady: Celebrating Three Centuries of Art by Canadian Women*, Toronto: Viking, 1992

Whitney Chadwick and Isabelle de Courtivron, eds,*SignificantOthers: Creativity and Intimate Partnership*, New York and London: Thames and Hudson, 1993

Wendy Slatkin, ed., *The Voices of Women Artists*, Englewood Cliffs, NJ: Prentice Hall, 1993Norma Broude and Mary D. Garrard, eds, *The Power of Feminist Art: The American Movement of the 1970s*, New York: Abrams, and London: Thames and Hudson, 1994

Nancy Mowll Mathews, *Mary Cassatt: A Life*, New York: Villard, 1994

Maria Tippett, *Emily Carr: A Biography*, revised edition, Toronto: Stoddard, 1994

Stephanie Walker, *This Woman in Particular: Biographical Images of Emily Carr*, Waterloo, Ontario: Wilfrid Laurier University Press, 1996

Modernism and Women Artists

Modernism remains a vexed and slippery term designating a cultural field usually defined by various combinations of the following: 1) particular notions of periodisation; 2) relationships to broader philosophical and historical conceptions of modernity; and 3) the rise of various avant-garde groups and/or innovative cultural practices that paradoxically break with and perpetuate Western traditions. This essay will outline some of the theoretical problems posed by women working in various visual fields during the years between 1890 and 1945. It will, however, also address the continued legacy of modernist paradigms during the heyday of Abstract Expressionism in the 1940s and 1950s and during the feminist movements of the 1960s and 1970s.

The period opens with the first wave of women's suffrage activity and the growing fragmentation of an increasingly competitive cultural marketplace for both sexes. It also encompasses the outbreak of World War II, during which there was not only a reorientation of the art market from Paris and London to New York, but also significant shifts in the perception of gender roles as career opportunities for women first expanded during the war, then disappeared as part of a reinscription of domestic femininity in the late 1940s and the 1950s. It should be stressed that there are wide divergences between pre- and post-war conceptions of modernism. Before the war, during the period often called "early modernism" (Butler 1994), the term was a fluid one that was widely debated by a number of writers, artists and critics, particularly those associated with the avant-garde. During and after the war, especially during the 1950s, 1960s and 1970s, the term modernism in the visual arts was used in increasingly narrow ways by critics such as Alfred Barr and Clement Greenberg who, drawing upon the earlier writings of philosophers such as Immanuel Kant and critics such as Roger Fry and Clive Bell, redefined the avant-garde project as one of formalist innovation. As numerous art historians have pointed out, their redefinition of the term was achieved by overlooking the complex socio-political agendas of earlier generations. Such an ostensibly apolitical construction of modernism appealed to champions of a newly emerging American avant-garde whose cultural "freedoms" were celebrated as democratic alternatives to Stalinist Socialist Realism during the Cold War (see, for example, the essays by Kozloff, Cockcroft, Guilbaut, and Schapiro and Schapiro, collected together in Frascina 1985). As Barr's and Greenberg's accounts of modernism achieved ascendency in the North American art world and became associated with the increasingly marketable and narrowly formalist movements of post-painterly abstraction and minimalism, a second wave of cultural critics, including many feminists, challenged its limitations as well as some of the more conservative ways it had become institutionalised. Such critiques have often been associated (more or less problematically) with the emergence of post-modern cultural forms and practices during the 1980s and 1990s.

In some senses it might be argued that feminist analyses of modernism have contributed to and built upon the growing critique of artistic autonomy mounted by literary critics, social historians of art and by post-modern, post-colonial and queer studies critics. Recent discussions of modernism by such critics as T.J. Clark (1973), Peter Bürger (1984), Matei Calinescu (1987), Raymond Williams (1989), Susan Buck-Morss (1989), Kenneth E. Silver (1989) and Jeffrey Weiss (1994) – a selective list – have attempted to restore some of modernism's lost socio-political complexities by returning to more politicised accounts of modernism by early 20th-century critics such as Bertold Brecht, Walter Benjamin and Theodor Adorno. While some individuals have been more attentive to gender issues than others, such criticism has been characterised by explorations of the social, political, racial and psychic stakes in cultural production under what David Harvey (1989), Raymond Williams (1989) and others have characterised as the conditions of modernity. Some of the widely acknowledged structural conditions that characterise the modern period are: the ambivalent relationship to Enlightenment promises of liberation through the scientific domination of nature and the rational ordering of society; tensions between national and international perspectives in an age of continuing colonial expansion; a compressed sense of time and space; rapid urbanisation; the rise of the mass media and industrial models of mass production, contributing to an extensive commodification of the cultural marketplace; the breakdown and/or rejection of traditional systems of representation and the proliferation of experimental avant-garde groups; and, last but not least, the emergence of socialist, feminist and anti- or post-colonial politics. As we shall see, feminist critics concentrating on questions related to women's artistic production have generated different (albeit sometimes interrelated) problematics and historical points of focus.

Feminist politics of one sort or another has played a central role in recent studies of women's relationship to modernism and modernity, in shaping the questions that are posed and/or fixing the historical ground to be covered. Not surprisingly, given the respective sizes of the disciplines of literary studies and art history, surveys recuperating women's participation in literary modernism have been more numerous. Although such surveys have tended to concentrate on women artists only as their work and lives relate to those of women writers, they have generated interesting insights into alternative and/or transgressive models of creativity, as well as a shared experimentation with identities, lifestyles, communities, motifs, genres, media, stylistic conventions and audiences (see, for example, Hanscombe and Smyers 1987; Benstock 1986; Gilbert and Gubar 1988–94; Kime 1990 and 1995). Of course, there have been many more focused literary studies addressing problematics that often spill over into visual forms of cultural production. Citing only a few examples, one could list: the operation of sexual difference and figures of the feminine in literary texts (Jardine 1985), the marginalisation of sentimental discourses (Clark 1991), the figures of the grotesque (Russo 1995) and the primitive (Torgovnick 1990), as well as the cultural transcription of political desires that range from progressive (DeKoven 1991) to conservative (Light 1991).

Surveys of women's visual work during this period are less numerous and have usually taken the form of exhibition catalogues (Paris 1983), documentary sources (Waller 1991; Witzling 1991), monographs on individual artists and studies focusing on women involved with particular artistic movements. Useful introductory overviews of the activities of women artists during the period 1900–40/45 are provided in a number of more general studies (see, for example, chapters in Fine 1978, Chadwick 1990 and Slatkin 1997). Useful reproductions of their work can be found in the exhibition catalogue *Women Artists, 1550–1950* (Los Angeles County Museum of Art, 1976) and biographical profiles and interviews with a number of important American women artists in Eleanor Munro's *Originals: American Women Artists* (New York: Simon and Schuster, 1979).

Although these introductory texts vary in the ways in which they organise the material, which can be grouped by nationality (e.g. European and American), artistic movement or media, the central figures are largely the same. Käthe Kollwitz (q.v.) and Paula Modersohn-Becker (q.v.) are usually discussed in relation to German Expressionism, although the politically committed "realism" of the former and the self-consciously "primitivising" maternal imagery of the latter strike out in new directions. More recent studies of women associated with German Expressionism (e.g. Behr 1988) have also explored the work of Marianne Werefkin (q.v.) and Gabriele Münter (q.v.) in more detail as well as introducing a number of less well-known artists. Women associated with movements that critically explored various notions of the decorative include Sonia Delaunay (q.v.) with her Orphist and Dada connections, and Vanessa Bell (q.v.) with her work for the Omega Workshops. Both of these artists provide fascinating examples of an integrated art practice that crosses the divisions of high/low, art/craft as well as abstract/decorative. Other examples of such border crossing can be found in the Russian Constructivist work of Lyubov Popova (q.v.) and Varvara Stepanova (q.v.) and the textile work of Gunta Stölzl (q.v.), who was part of the Bauhaus weaving workshop. While the important contribution of Hannah Höch (q.v.) to collage and photo-montage is connected with Dada, her exploration of the relation of the "new woman" to the consumerist ideology of mass culture has a slightly different focus (see Lavin 1993).

In her intriguing studies of women artists connected with the Parisian avant-garde between 1900 and the late 1920s (Maria Gutiérriez Blanchard, Alice Halicka, Marie Laurencin, q.v., Jacqueline Marval, Suzanne Valadon, q.v., and others) Gill Perry explores how gender inflected their relations with the Cubist and Fauve movements as well as their training, the marketing of their work under a "feminised" School of Paris label and their representations of other women and female nudes. Another book that usefully situates women's production both inside and outside a leading avant-garde movement is Whitney Chadwick's study (1985) of Surrealist women artists (Meret Oppenheim, Frida Kahlo, Dorothea Tanning, Leonora Carrington, Leonor Fini, Kay Sage, all q.v., and others), which considers how they ambivalently negotiated the Surrealists' fascination with Woman as a figure of repressed irrational and natural powers and their fetishistic celebration of the *femme-enfant* by turning to different sources of identification and inspiration. Other important European painters such as the British portraitist Gwen John (q.v.) cannot be so easily situated in the context of any particular movement, although her life was typical of many expatriate women artists working in Paris.

In the USA some of the most frequently discussed women artists of the early 20th century include Romaine Brooks (q.v.), Georgia O'Keeffe (q.v.) and Florine Stettheimer (q.v.). Brooks was an expatriate who produced most of her work in Paris, and is best known for her striking portraits of members of the lesbian coterie surrounding the American poet Natalie Barney. Through her marriage to Alfred Stieglitz O'Keeffe was closely associated with his 291 circle in New York, but she nevertheless established her own highly distinctive style and developed large-format flower paintings and highly abstracted cityscapes and desert landscapes. Florine Stettheimer's eccentrically decorative compositions are also hard to connect to any artistic group and belong instead to her own wealthy upper-class milieu of New York that she often parodied in her paintings.

The extensive excavation and appreciation of women's artistic activity from the early 20th century was assisted by the work of a feminist art criticism during the 1970s that discussed the limitations of those modernist paradigms that had prevailed up to that point. In particular, this feminist critique rejected the fetishisation of a limited canon of formally innovative work that had neglected or dismissed much of women's artistic production described in the last few paragraphs. Lillian Robinson and Lise Vogel (1971) noted that modernist critics tended to focus on the autonomy of the work of art, broadly detaching culture from history and ignoring the "contextual" considerations of race, sex and class. Using a similar logic, Carol Duncan (1973) stressed that the much-vaunted bohemian "freedoms" of the early 20th-century avant-garde were often based on the sexual exploitation of female models in both representational and material terms. During the same period, Linda Nochlin (1971) wondered about the criteria that excluded women artists from being considered "great", and Lucy Lippard (1976) explored the sorts of imagery and issues that she felt characterised women's art. For many writers in the 1970s, a feminist perspective offered a welcome escape from the sterility of the modernist mainstream. In Lucy Lippard's words:

> Feminism's greatest contribution to the future of art has probably been its lack of contribution to modernism. Feminist methods and theories have instead offered a socially concerned alternative to the increasingly mechanical "evolution" of art about art [Lippard 1984, p.149].

Continuing this critique of Greenbergian modernism in the early 1980s, artists such as Mary Kelly and art historians such as Rozsika Parker and Griselda Pollock drew attention to the production and valuing of gendered positions across a wide range of institutional sites. Drawing upon semiotic and psychoanalytic theories, these writers argued that meanings were produced not only by the artist in her/his studio but also by a network of other commentators, including dealers, critics, teachers and members of the general public. The fact that these writers placed a strong material emphasis on socially and psychically situating artistic statements meant that they refuted any notions of female, feminine or feminist essentialisms. As Parker and Pollock explained: "(r)ather we are concerned to discover the relationships between women artists and the institutions of art and ideology throughout historical shifts and changes" (Parker and Pollock 1981, p.136; see also Kelly 1981). In more recent work, Pollock has continued to explore the constructed nature of gender categories, asserting that the "practices which constitute the most visible feminist interventions in culture are not to be defined according to the gender of their expressive subject" (1992, pp.152–3).

The refusal of fixed, stable and biologically rooted feminine identities has characterised the work of many post-structuralist/anti-essentialist feminist critics, including Judith Butler who argues that such terms as "women" must be understood as performative constructions and permanent sites of political contest. She stresses that although it might be tactically expedient to identify oneself provisionally as a "woman" in local struggles, it is important to remain aware of the term's limitations and exclusions (Butler 1993, pp.222–3). Butler's observations can help us come to terms with some of the more acrimonious and problematic generational debates between those feminist artists, critics, theorists and historians who launched various critiques of modernism during the 1970s and 1980s. Many critics from the 1970s have subsequently defended themselves against charges of naive essentialism by accusing critics from the 1980s of taking up "male" theory and abandoning political activism. As Amelia Jones has pointed out, the overly reductive nature of this debate becomes apparent when one situates the particular struggles of the different generations historically. Such false divisions between mind and body, theory and activism, and

different generations, cannot be sustained when one realises that the theoretical arguments of the 1980s have had material consequences and that many writers and artists of the 1970s were already theoretically sophisticated, even if their terminology and paradigms were not those of the 1980s (see Jones 1995; Broude and Garrard 1994; Pollock 1993). I, too, have argued that the modernist period can be more productively reassessed by considering how women from earlier generations conceptualised their artistic and interpretive agencies and horizons in ways that acknowledge late 20th-century theoretical agendas without invoking them as judgemental criteria (Elliott 1996).

One of the most important contributions of post-structuralist feminism has been the realisation that women artists are not the only ones interested in the discursive manipulation and destabilisation of gendered identities and signifiers. Many recent studies have demonstrated that certain male artists and writers belonging to various sub-cultural groups have also disrupted the binary logic of gender construction (see, for example, Jardine 1985; Jones 1994; Reed 1991; Werth 1990; Chave 1994). While such developments have radically extended the scope of feminist inquiry, a number of critics have worried that the necessary theoretical gap between discursive and experiential femininities might once again result in the marginalisation of women artists and writers who often have fewer resources and less room to manoeuvre than many of their male counterparts (Jardine 1985, p.37; see also Huyssen 1986 and Suleiman 1990). Because social, ideological and psychic inequalities have persisted well into the late 20th century, when conservative governments in many Western countries are reversing the movement towards equality and widening the gender gap by repealing equity legislation and down-sizing social services, it is essential for those pursuing feminist political agendas to relate discursive configurations of femininity to the material possibilities that exist for women at any given historical moment. Although in this essay I am focusing on writing that deals with women artists, it is important to relate this material to other feminist interrogations of modernist gender construction. Again, it is worth stressing that I am uncomfortable with hierarchical manoeuvres that set theorising about visual and rhetorical constructions of gender above and against gathering historical information about women artists. Both activities need to be at once theoretically informed *and* historically grounded. Finally, given the enormous amount of activity in the modernist field, I am only able to introduce a few important areas of research and cite a limited number of sources.

Much interesting work has focused on the first wave of feminist activism surrounding the issues of women's suffrage and the demands of the "New Woman" that emerged in the 1890s and continued through the 1930s. Lisa Tickner's richly detailed and theoretically sophisticated study (1987) of the British suffrage movement is essential reading. Tickner addresses not only the formation and day-to-day operation of suffrage artists' ateliers, but also considers the way in which women manipulated existing representations of femininity to forge new political meanings and identities. In the USA Ellen Wiley Todd (1993) has explored representations of the "New Woman" in the work of several New York artists, including Isabel Bishop (q.v.), during the 1920s and 1930s. It should be stressed that controversies over the "New Woman" often touched upon questions of sexual orientation and the problematic figure of the mannish lesbian woman. This issue is raised in Maud Lavin's study of Hannah Höch (1993), which broadly explores the crisis of gendered identities in the context of Weimar Germany, and also by Emmanuel Cooper (1994), who provides a chapter on the "New Woman" that looks at the work of artists such as Tamara de Lempicka (q.v.; see also Diana Souhami's monograph of 1988 on the British artist Gluck, q.v.). Susan Fillin-Yeh (1995) has also recently addressed women's dandyism through case studies of Georgia O'Keeffe and Florine Stetthemer. Susan Gubar (1981) and Marjorie Garber (1992) have also theorised the complicated politics of women's cross-dressing.

Another important area of activity has been an exploration of women artists' relationships to the various avant-garde groups and theories. Addressing revisionist accounts of the politics of French Impressionist painting made by social historians of art such as T.J. Clark (1973), Griselda Pollock (1988) examined how the spaces of modernity were differently configured for women and women artists such as Berthe Morisot (q.v.) and Mary Cassatt (q.v.). Building on Janet Wolff's notion of the invisible *flâneuse*, Pollock points out that the avant-garde's fetishisation of Baudelaire's notion of the artist as *flâneur* marginalises women's experiences of modernity. Instead, Pollock conceptualises cultural mobility and agency in new ways that take questions of gender into account (see her essay "Modernity and the spaces of femininity" in Pollock 1988). Elizabeth Wilson (1995) has addressed the limitations of Wolff's notion of the invisible *flâneuse* by pointing out that women experienced increasing social mobility during the period. Recent studies that also address women's agency in relation to modernist avant-garde movements and discourses have been published by Gill Perry (1993 and 1995) and by Bridget Elliott and Jo-Ann Wallace (1994). Perry, as mentioned earlier, focuses on women artists working in Paris from c.1900 to the late 1920s, critically addressing how constructions of femininity were constantly negotiated in the professional context of the atelier, the exhibition and in various sites of critical discourse as well as in the practice of executing portraits and female nudes. Focusing on the collaboration of women artists and writers (e.g. Romaine Brooks, Vanessa Bell, Marie Laurencin, Nina Hamnett and Djuna Barnes) in the same period in France and England, Elliott and Wallace identify several key modernist discourses, including those of avant-gardism, professionalism, genius and purity. In particular, they consider how women artists were differently positioned (e.g. wealthy, poor, immigrant, lesbian, heterosexual) and how this positioning inflected their artistic practice, particularly in the areas of self-portraiture and portraits of other women. Another book that spans the literary and visual is a collection of essays edited by Gabriele Griffin (1994), which looks at Djuna Barnes, Leonora Carrington, Susan Hiller and Lee Krasner (q.v.). At the time of writing, two further edited collections of essays addressing women artists and modernism, by Katy Deepwell, and Caroline Howlett and Hugh Stevens, are in press.

Taking a different tack and criticising much recent post-structuralist feminist theorising, a study by Christine Battersby (1989) focuses more closely on the issue of genius, which she feels needs to be reappropriated in order to generate a feminist aesthetic that is based upon great, individual female artists. In a wide-ranging book that moves from Surrealism to women's writing and artistic production during the 1980s, Susan Suleiman (1990) explores the subversive figures of the female body and the laughing mother, arguing that certain postmodern women artists (e.g. Leonora Carrington, Barbara Kruger, q.v., Cindy Sherman, Jenny Holzer) and writers have continued the more radical and irreverent spirit of the historical avant-gardes. Johanna Drucker (1994) similarly explores how post-modern women artists have critically engaged with the legacy of modernist subjectivity in a discussion of the works of Sherrie Levine, Cindy Sherman and Barbara Kruger. Three other articles that offer intriguing insights into how notions of avant-gardism have been rhetorically gendered are Andreas Huyssen's study of modernism and mass culture, Anne Wagner's study (1989) of Lee Krasner's contradictory positioning in the modernist and feminist canons, and Lisa Tickner's essays (1993 and 1994) on masculinity and modernism in which she looks at the work of Gwen John, Vanessa Bell, Kate Lechmere and Helen Saunders.

All of the sources I have cited in my discussion of women and the avant-garde have relied on Western European and North American case studies. As Jo-Anna Isaak has pointed out (1989), another set of theoretical assumptions might be extrapolated from a different range of case studies, such as the work of women artists associated with various sectors of the Russian avant-garde (see Briony Fer's helpful introduction of 1993 to some of these issues) and Latin America (see Baddeley and Fraser 1989). As Isaak rightly notes, most theorising about modernism is usually based on a limited Eurocentric perspective, often privileging England and France. Certainly, given spatial constraints and my own area of research, the same limitations frame this essay.

Also of crucial importance is a growing body of research exploring the ways in which women artists secured access to training, patronage, exhibiting space, models, critical reviews and other kinds of support networks. Since I cannot do justice to the huge volume of research in this field, I will mention only a handful of recent studies that, in addition to unearthing new historical information, also offer new insights into women's agency in the modernist cultural field. In terms of the Victorian art world, one might turn to the studies of Deborah Cherry (1993), Clarissa Campbell Orr (1995) and Janice Helland (1996), who show how women's day-to-day working conditions and institutional affiliations affected their representational practices. Turning to late 19th-century France, Tamar Garb's study (1994) of the Union des Femmes Peintres et Sculpteurs provides invaluable insights into various intersecting discourses of art and femininity, as does Debora Silverman's (1989), which examines how

the rhetoric of femininity played an integral role in the decorative Art Nouveau movements of France. Pen Dalton (1995) discusses the ways in which a traditional modernist bias has shaped more recent art education. (See also the studies exploring the relationships between women artists and their models by Betterton 1987; Mathews 1991; Garb 1993; Elliott 1996; and others.)

An interest in the decorative or applied arts has traditionally been associated with women, as Rozsika Parker (1984), Anthea Callen (1979) and other feminist critics have observed. Here I will discuss only a few sources that address these areas of activity in relation to modernist artistic production. Both Nancy Troy (1991) and Christopher Reed (1991) have published studies that broadly address the function of the decorative and domestic in modernist artistic discourses. Although neither study offers a sustained analysis of the works of women artists, both explore the gendered inflections of a new, increasingly consumer-oriented aesthetic. More specifically on the subject of fashion, one should refer to Elizabeth Wilson's analysis (1985) of fashion and modernity, which not only deals with women as workers in the fashion industry but also looks at them as highly sophisticated urban consumers. Also important is Peter Wollen's analysis (1993) of the role that such concepts as fashion, orientalism and decoration played in modernist discourses. More broadly considering women's involvement in the sphere of design is Judy Attfield and Pat Kirkham's collection of essays (1989), which includes not only fashion but also furniture and interior design, architecture and town-planning. Further explorations of fashion and architecture can be found in a collection of essays compiled by Lynne Walker (1994), which are drawn from a conference organised by the Design History Society. (The extensive literature on theoretical questions related to the practices of women photographers and film-makers is too complex to raise here.)

Finally, it seems useful to conclude this brief overview of modernism and women artists by considering how questions of racial and cultural difference are reshaping the field. Certainly, there is much evidence to suggest that certain women artists adopted self-consciously "primitive" references and styles of painting, as Gill Perry analyses in the case of Paula Modersohn-Becker. Whether women artists mobilised "primitive" sources in ways that differed from their male counterparts awaits further investigation. If white women artists were usually excluded from early formulations of the modernist canon, women artists of colour were almost invisible. Much has changed over the past few years as an emerging body of criticism by writers such as Bell Hooks (1995), Maud Sulter (1990) and Rasheed Araeen (London 1989) discuss the political and cultural agendas of artists including Carrie Mae Weems, Alison Saar, Emma Amos, Mona Hatoum, Lubaina Himid and Sonia Boyce. Although this "other story" focuses on contemporary practices that are usually considered more "post-modern" than "modernist", there are important links between this work and that of earlier artists such as Meta Vaux Warrick Fuller (q.v.) who was part of the Harlem Renaissance (Driskell 1987). As increasingly sophisticated and multivalent critical paradigms are applied to investigations of modernism, many of its continuities and affinities with postmodernism will become more evident.

BRIDGET ELLIOTT

Bibliography

Alfred H. Barr, Jr, *Cubism and Abstract Art*, New York: Museum of Modern Art, 1936; reprinted Cambridge, MA: Harvard University Press, 1986

Clement Greenberg, *Art and Culture: Critical Essays*, Boston: Beacon Press, 1961

——, "Modernist painting", *Art and Literature*, iv, Spring 1965, pp.193–201

Walter Benjamin, *Illuminations*, ed. Hannah Arendt, New York: Harcourt Brace, 1968; London: Collins, 1973 (German original)

Linda Nochlin, "Why have there been no great women artists?", *Woman in Sexist Society: Studies in Power and Powerlessness*, ed. Vivian Gornick and Barbara K. Moran, New York: Basic Books, 1971; reprinted New American Library, 1972, pp.480–510

Lillian S. Robinson and Lise Vogel, "Modernism and history", *New Literary History*, iii/1, 1971–2, pp.177–99

T. J. Clark, *Image of the People: Gustave Courbet and the 1848 Revolution*, London: Thames and Hudson, 1973; Princeton: Princeton University Press, 1982

Carol Duncan, "Virility and domination in early 20th-century vanguard painting", *Artforum*, December 1973, pp.30–39

Lucy R. Lippard, *From the Center: Feminist Essays on Women's Art*, New York: Dutton, 1976

Elsa Honig Fine, *Women and Art: A History of Women Painters and Sculptors from the Renaissance to the 20th Century*, Montclair, NJ: Allanheld and Schram, and London: Prior, 1978

Anthea Callen, *Angel in the Studio: Women in the Arts and Crafts Movement, 1870–1914*, London: Astragal, 1979; as *Women Artists of the Arts and Crafts Movement, 1870–1914*, New York: Pantheon, 1979

Roger Fry, *Vision and Design*, ed. J.B. Bullen, London and New York: Oxford University Press, 1981 (first published 1920)

Susan Gubar, "Blessings in disguise: Cross-dressings as redressing for female modernists", *Massachusetts Review*, xxii, 1981, pp.477–508

Rozsika Parker and Griselda Pollock, *Old Mistresses: Women, Art and Ideology*, London: Routledge, 1981

Mary Kelly, "Re-viewing modernist criticism", *Screen*, no.22, Autumn 1981, pp.41–62

L'Avant-garde au feminin: Moscou, Saint-Petersbourg, Paris, 1907–1930, exh. cat., Centre d'art plastique contemporain, Paris, 1983

Peter Bürger, *Theory of the Avant-Garde*, Minneapolis: University of Minnesota Press, 1984 (German original, 1974)

Lucy R. Lippard, "Sweeping exchanges: The contribution of feminism to the art of the 1970s", *Get the Message? A Decade of Art for Social Change*, New York: Dutton, 1984

Rozsika Parker, *The Subversive Stitch: Embroidery and the Making of the Feminine*, London: Women's Press, 1984; New York: Routledge, 1989

Whitney Chadwick, *Women Artists and the Surrealist Movement*, Boston: Little Brown, and London: Thames and Hudson, 1985

Francis Frascina, ed., *Pollock and After: The Critical Debate*, New York: Harper, 1985

Alice Jardine, *Gynesis: Configurations of Woman and Modernity*, Ithaca, NY: Cornell University Press, 1985

Elizabeth Wilson, *Adorned in Dreams: Fashion and Modernity*, London: Virago, 1985

Shari Benstock, *Women of the Left Bank, Paris 1900–1940*, Austin: University of Texas Press, 1986

Andreas Huyssen, *After the Great Divide: Modernism, Mass Culture, Postmodernism*, Bloomington: Indiana University Press, 1986

Rosemary Betterton, "How do women look? The female nude in the work of Suzanne Valadon", *Looking On: Images of Femininity in the Visual Arts and Media*, ed. Rosemary Betterton, London and New York: Pandora, 1987, pp.217–34 (expanded version of article first published in *Feminist Review*, no.19, March 1985)

Matei Calinescu, *Five Faces of Modernity: Modernism, Avant-Garde, Decadence, Kitsch, Postmodernism*, Durham: Duke University Press, 1987 (revised edition of *Faces of Modernity*, 1977)

David Driskell, "The Flowering of the Harlem Renaissance: The art of Aaron Douglas, Meta Warrick Fuller, Palmer Hayden and William H. Johnson", *The Harlem Renaissance: Art of Black America*, exh. cat., Studio Museum in Harlem, New York, 1987, pp.105–54

Gillian Hanscombe and Virginia L. Smyers, *Writing for Their Lives: The Modernist Women, 1910–1940*, London: Women's Press, 1987

Lisa Tickner, *The Spectacle of Women: Imagery of the Suffrage Campaign, 1907–14*, London: Chatto and Windus, 1987; Chicago: University of Chicago Press, 1988

Shulamith Behr, *Women Expressionists*, Oxford: Phaidon, and New York: Rizzoli, 1988

Griselda Pollock, *Vision and Difference: Femininity, Feminism and the Histories of Art*, London: Routledge, 1988

Diana Souhami, *Gluck, 1895–1978: Her Biography*, London: Pandora, 1988

Sandra M. Gilbert and Susan Gubar, *No Man's Land: The Place of the Woman Writer in the Twentieth Century*, 3 vols, New Haven: Yale University Press, 1988–94

Judy Attfield and Pat Kirkham, eds, *A View from the Interior: Feminism, Women and Design*, London: Women's Press, 1989

Oriana Baddeley and Valerie Fraser, *Drawing the Line: Art and Cultural Identity in Contemporary Latin America*, London and New York: Verso, 1989

Christine Battersby, *Gender and Genius: Towards a Feminist Aesthetic*, Bloomington: Indiana University Press, and London: Women's Press, 1989

Susan Buck-Morss, *The Dialectics of Seeing: Walter Benjamin and the Arcades Project*, Cambridge: Massachusetts Institute of Technology Press, 1989

David Harvey, *The Condition of Postmodernity: An Enquiry into the Origins of Cultural Change*, Oxford and Cambridge, MA: Blackwell, 1989

Jo-Anna Isaak, "Representation and its (dis)contents [a review of Griselda Pollock's *Vision and Difference*]", *Art History*, xii, 1989, pp.362–6

The Other Story: Afro-Asian Artists in Post-War Britain, exh. cat., South Bank Centre, London, 1989

Kenneth E. Silver, *Esprit de Corps: The Art of the Parisian Avant-Garde and the First World War, 1914–1925*, Princeton: Princeton University Press, 1989

Debora Silverman, *Art Nouveau in Fin-de-Siècle France: Politics, Psychology and Style*, Berkeley: University of California Press, 1989

Anne Wagner, "Lee Krasner as L.K.", *Representations*, no.25, 1989, pp.42–57

Raymond Williams, *The Politics of Modernism: Against the New Conformists*, ed. Tony Pinkney, London: Verso, 1989

Whitney Chadwick, *Women, Art and Society*, London and New York: Thames and Hudson, 1990

Bonnie Scott Kime, ed., *The Gender of Modernism: A Critical Anthology*, Bloomington: Indiana University Press, 1990

Susan Rubin Suleiman, *Subversive Intent: Gender, Politics and the Avant-Garde*, Cambridge, MA: Harvard University Press, 1990

Maud Sulter, ed., *Passion: Discourses on Blackwomen's Creativity*, Hebden Bridge, Yorks: Urban Fox Press, 1990

Marianna Torgovnick, *Gone Primitive: Savage Intellects, Modern Lives*, Chicago: University of Chicago Press, 1990

Margaret Werth, "Engendering imaginary modernism: Henri Matisse's *Bonheur de vivre*", *Genders*, no.9, November 1990, pp.49–74

Suzanne Clark, *Sentimental Modernism: Women Writers and the Revolution of the Word*, Bloomington: Indiana University Press, 1991

Marianne DeKoven, *Rich and Strange: Gender, History, Modernism*, Princeton: Princeton University Press, 1991

Alison Light, *Forever England: Femininity, Literature and Conservatism Between the Wars*, London: Routledge, 1991

Patricia Mathews, "Returning the gaze: Diverse representations of the nude in the art of Suzanne Valadon", *Art Bulletin*, lxxiii, 1991, pp.415–30

Christopher Reed, "Bloomsbury bashing: Homophobia and the politics of criticism in the eighties", *Gender*, no.11, 1991, pp.58–80

Nancy J. Troy, *Modernism and the Decorative Arts in France: Art Nouveau to Le Corbusier*, New Haven: Yale University Press, 1991

Susan Waller, *Women Artists in the Modern Era: A Documentary History*, Metuchen, NJ: Scarecrow Press, 1991

Mara R. Witzling, ed., *Voicing Our Visions: Writings by Women Artists*, New York: Universe, 1991; London: Women's Press, 1992

Marjorie Garber, *Vested Interests: Cross Dressing and Cultural Anxiety*, New York: Routledge, 1992

Griselda Pollock, "Painting, feminism, history", *Destabilizing Theory: Contemporary Feminist Debates*, ed. Michèle Barrett and Anne Phillips, Stanford: Stanford University Press, 1992

Judith Butler, *Bodies that Matter: On the Discursive Limits of "Sex"*, New York: Routledge, 1993

Deborah Cherry, *Painting Women: Victorian Women Artists*, London and New York: Routledge, 1993

Briony Fer, "The language of construction", *Realism, Rationalism, Surrealism: Art Between the Wars*, New Haven and London: Yale University Press/Open University, 1993, pp.87–169

Tamar Garb, "Gender and representation", *Modernity and Modernism: French Painting in the Nineteenth Century*, New Haven and London: Yale University Press/Open University, 1993, pp.219–90

Maud Lavin, *Cut with the Kitchen Knife: The Weimar Photomontages of Hannah Höch*, New Haven and London: Yale University Press, 1993

Gill Perry, "Primitivism and the 'Modern'", *Primitivism, Cubism, Abstraction: The Early Twentieth Century*, New Haven and London: Yale University Press/Open University, 1993, pp.3–85

Lisa Tickner, "Now and then: The hieratic head of Ezra Pound", *Oxford Art Journal*, xvi/2, 1993, pp.55–61

Ellen Wiley Todd, *The "New Woman" Revised: Painting and Gender Politics on Fourteenth Street*, Berkeley: University of California Press, 1993

Peter Wollen, "Out of the past: Fashion/orientalism/the body", *Raiding the Icebox: Reflections on Twentieth-Century Culture*, Bloomington: Indiana University Press, and London: Verso, 1993, pp.1–34

Griselda Pollock, "The politics of theory: Generations and geographies", *Genders*, no.17, Fall 1993, pp.99–119

Norma Broude and Mary D. Garrard, eds, *The Power of Feminist Art: The American Movement of the 1970s*, New York: Abrams, and London: Thames and Hudson, 1994

Christopher Butler, *Early Modernism: Literature, Music and Painting in Europe, 1900–1916*, Oxford: Clarendon Press, 1994

Anna C. Chave, "New encounters with *Les Demoiselles d'Avignon*: Gender, race and the origins of Cubism", *Art Bulletin*, lxxvi, 1994, pp.597–611

Emmanuel Cooper, *The Sexual Perspective: Homosexuality and Art in the Last 100 Years in the West*, 2nd edition, London and New York: Routledge, 1994

Johanna Drucker, *Theorizing Modernism: Visual Art and the Critical Tradition*, New York: Columbia University Press, 1994

Bridget Elliott and Jo-Ann Wallace, *Women Artists and Writers: Modernist (Im)positionings*, London: Routledge, 1994

Tamar Garb, *Sisters of the Brush: Women's Artistic Culture in Late Nineteenth-Century Paris*, New Haven and London: Yale University Press, 1994

Gabriele Griffin, ed., *Difference in View: Women and Modernism*, London: Taylor and Francis, 1994

Amelia Jones, *Postmodernism and the En-gendering of Marcel Duchamp*, Cambridge and New York: Cambridge University Press, 1994

Lisa Tickner, "Men's work? Masculinity and modernism", *Visual Culture: Images and Interpretations*, ed. Norman Bryson, Michael Ann Holly and Keith Moxey, Hanover, NH: University Press of New England, 1994, pp.42–82

Lynne Walker, ed., *Cracks in the Pavements: Gender/Fashion/ Architecture*, London: Sorella Press, 1994

Jeffrey S. Weiss, *The Popular Culture of Modern Art: Picasso, Duchamp and Avant-Gardism*, New Haven: Yale University Press, 1994

Pen Dalton, "Modernism, art education and sexual difference", *New Feminist Art Criticism: Critical Strategies*, ed. Katy Deepwell, Manchester: Manchester University Press, 1995

Susan Fillin-Yeh, "Dandies, marginality and modernism: Georgia O'Keeffe, Marcel Duchamp and other cross-dressers", *Oxford Art Journal*, xviii/2, 1995, pp.33–44

Bell Hooks, *Art on My Mind: Visual Politics*, New York: New Press, 1995

Amelia Jones, "Power and feminist art (history) [a review of Norma Broude's and Mary D. Garrard's *The Power of Feminist Art: Emergence, Impact and Triumph of the American Feminist Art Movement*]", *Art History*, xvi, 1995, pp.435–43

Bonnie Scott Kime, *Refiguring Modernism*, i: *The Women of 1928*, Bloomington: Indiana University Press, 1995

Clarissa Campbell Orr, ed., *Women in the Victorian Art World*, Manchester: Manchester University Press, 1995

Gill Perry, *Women Artists and the Parisian Avant-Garde*, Manchester: Manchester University Press, and New York: St Martin's Press, 1995

Mary Russo, *The Female Grotesque: Risk, Excess and Modernity*, New York: Routledge, 1995

E. Wilson, "The invisible *flâneur*", *Postmodern Cities and Spaces*, ed. Sophie Watson and Katherine Gibson, Oxford and Cambridge, MA: Blackwell, 1995, pp.59–79

Bridget Elliott, "'The strength of the weak' as portrayed by Marie Laurencin", *On Your Left: New Historical Materialism in the 1990s*, ed. Ann Kibbey and others, New York: New York University Press, 1996, pp.69–109

Janice Helland, *The Studios of Frances and Margaret Macdonald*, Manchester: Manchester University Press, 1996

Wendy Slatkin, *Women Artists in History: From Antiquity to the Present*, 3rd edition, Upper Saddle River, NJ: Prentice Hall, 1997

Katy Deepwell, ed., *Women and Modernism* (in preparation)

Caroline Howlett and Hugh Stevens, eds, *Borderlines: Gender, Sexuality and the Margins of Modernism* (in preparation)

Feminism and Women Artists

An important difference between art produced by earlier women artists and by those who have been active since the 1970s is that, in recent years, many women artists have been engaged in a deliberate dialogue with the Western art-historical tradition. Despite their widely differing goals and means of attaining them, most of these artists have sought to redress, through their art, fissures and lacunae in the Western canon – particularly with regard to women's positioning within it. While many contemporary women artists have been influenced by the feminist movement and have identified themselves as "feminists", their work has assumed diverse forms and has encompassed a variety of different strategies to achieve so-called feminist goals. In fact, in speaking of developments from this period, it is more accurate to refer to "feminisms" in the plural, rather than to a monolithic "feminist" agenda.

This essay will present an overview of art produced in response to contemporary feminism, beginning with the so-called first generation of feminist artists in the early 1970s, continuing through their successors in the 1980s and early 1990s. Some critics have found it expedient to subdivide the major developments in the art of this period into two "waves", each proscribed by a corresponding decade, the first wave of the 1970s perceived as more "activist" and the second wave of the 1980s as more "theoretical", thus tending to polarise the aims of these "generations" (e.g. Cincinnati 1989, pp.19–20). While feminist artistic interventions of the 1970s might seem to have had more overtly political motivations than those of later years, there is no clear-cut division based on chronology. As a case in point, two of the pieces most definitively associated with each methodology – Judy Chicago's *Dinner Party* (1974–9) and Mary Kelly's *Post-Partum Document* (1973–9) – are almost exactly contemporaneous. It is more useful, instead, to define the differences in terms of contrasting, but not mutually exclusive strategies employed in order to achieve a similar end: art that "represents" the point of view of its female creators more effectively than that produced in the past.

During the late 1960s and early 1970s there was a resurgence of feminist consciousness, combined with an increase in specific political activities, the era of (so-called) Women's Liberation. Numerous women artists active during this period, including May Stevens, Mary Kelly, Judy Chicago (all q.v.), Harmony Hammond and Monica Sjöö, have acknowledged the impact of the political feminist movement on the direction of their art. These artists and others, in both Britain and the USA, participated in feminist collectives, exhibition spaces and discussion groups. The same political phenomena influenced the future development of art history, both in the birth of so-called feminist art history and in the subsequent "deconstruction" of the received art-historical canon, under the influence of post-modernist thought. Mary Kelly's group in London, for example, included such important theorists as Laura Mulvey and Griselda Pollock. Linda

Nochlin's germinal article "Why have there been no great women artists?" appeared in 1971, calling for a critique that would reformulate "the crucial questions of the discipline" (Nochlin 1971, p.146). This process has taken place ever since through the work of feminist art historians and other scholars who have attempted to restructure the field of art history, and through feminist artists themselves who have brought about changes to the canon through their art.

Judy Chicago's early work constitutes an excellent example of the strategies and concerns of some women artists who sought to fulfil an overtly polemical agenda through their art. As she has documented in her autobiography *Through the Flower*, Chicago felt herself alienated from the Western art-historical tradition by the assumption that "to be a woman and an artist was contradictory" (Chicago 1975, p.43). She came to realise that she was forced to hide "the real content" of her art, a sentiment that was shared by other artists during the early 1970s including Harmony Hammond, who described her understanding that "if [she] wanted to be taken seriously as an artist [she] had to paint what the boys painted" (quoted in Witzling 1994, p.249) and, as a result, painted herself out of her own work.

Chicago set out to find a visual structure that would allow her to express her "femininity" through her art, and ended up formulating the much touted but little understood concept of vaginal iconography. Chicago, along with Miriam Schapiro (q.v.) with whom she collaborated, asserted that in the work of diverse earlier women artists they had observed "a frequent use of the central image ... sometimes surrounded by folds or undulations, as in the structure of the vagina" (Chicago 1975, p.143). In her own work, in paintings such as *Big Ox, No.2* (1968), Schapiro had also begun to seek a centripetal structure. The art critic Lucy Lippard further defined the recurring elements of "central core" imagery as "the preponderance of circular forms, central focus, inner space" (Lippard 1976, pp.49, 143–5). Schapiro and Chicago were particularly impressed with women artists' use of the central space as "the framework for an imagery which allows for the complete reversal of the ways in which women are seen in the culture" (Chicago 1975, pp.143–4). In order to effect this perceptual reversal, Chicago worked with Schapiro, and with students in their class at the California Institute of the Arts, on the environmental *Womanhouse* whose motifs were identified during the process of "consciousness raising". Issues involved with domesticity, with women's traditional culture, with the repetitive nature of women's traditional lives were explored. Following this period, in *The Dinner Party*, her *magnum opus*, Chicago represented 39 important women in history through ceramic plates that epitomise central core imagery, and runners embellished with embroidery styles typical of the periods in which these women lived. Chicago described this work, based on both the triangle, an ancient symbol of female power, and the iconography of the Last Supper, as "a people's history – the history of women in Western civilization" (quoted in Witzling 1991, p.380).

Many other women artists who did not necessarily accept the premise that there was a particular pictorial construct based on "female" experience sought to establish a dialogue with the Western tradition by posing alternative approaches to representing the female body. Joan Semmel, for example, in her paintings and her writings explored a female erotic, consisting of undulating transparent layers, stimulated by the female body as literally seen from the point of view of its possessor. In *Hand Down*, for example, the viewer looks past folds of breasts and belly, to a female hand reaching between its owner's crotch. Semmel said that she wanted to create "an imagery that would respond to female feelings" rather than one that stemmed from male sexual fantasies. She continued: "My paintings deal with communication, how a hand touches a body … sensuality with the power factor eliminated" (quoted in Seiberling 1974, p.55). Hannah Wilke began making wall hangings of undulating layers of pink latex, and then went on to explore her "starification series": vaginal forms, made from such malleable materials as chewing gum and kneaded erasers, adhered first to the artist's body and then to photographs. She described her art as "a very female thing … about multilayered forms … organic like flowers" (*ibid.*, p.58). Hammond similarly identified "a feeling of touching oneself [that] is directly connected to women's art-making" ("A sense of touch", quoted in Witzling 1994, p.254). For her, this feeling was expressed in sculptures made by obsessively wrapping layers of fabric, a sensual experience, "pushing out from the center" ("Spiral", quoted in *ibid.*, p.256). Although these artists did not claim that they were influenced by her

writings, during the same period the film critic Laura Mulvey wrote her influential essay "Visual pleasure and narrative cinema" (1975), in which she characterised the "determining male gaze" through which women's image has "continually been stolen". The projects of the artists discussed above offered methods of redressing the situation identified by Mulvey, or of taking back what the critic Lisa Tickner slightly later referred to as "colonized territory" by reversing the usual situation in which the female body is the object of art produced by male artists for a masculine audience (Tickner 1978, p.239).

Performance and environmental art provided women artists with other strategies to wrest the female body from the controlling male gaze and to enable its inhabitant to become a speaking subject. The live performances and films of Carolee Schneemann (q.v.), the earliest of which actually predate the feminist movement, were born from a desire to "make a gift of [her] body to other women: giving our bodies back to ourselves" (*ibid.*, p.247). In *Eye Body* (1963) she placed snakes on her naked body, suggestive of Minoan rituals; in *Meat Joy* (1964) she and several other actors, both male and female, engaged in an orgy involving pieces of raw meat. *Interior Scroll* (1975), in which she appeared on stage nude and proceeded to pull a scroll from her vagina and read from it, in particular spoke to the issue of women's ownership of their own bodies as a source of sexual pleasure. After painting on her body and establishing a correlation with the idea of a painter's live model, Schneemann read from the scroll in which "a happy man/a structuralist filmmaker" says: "don't ask us/to look at your films … /there are certain films/we cannot look at/the personal clutter/the persistence of feeling …" (quoted in Broude and Garrard 1994, p.163). In this work, as in others, Schneemann asserted the right to present the female body in its own terms, unmediated by the male gaze.

Several other women performance artists used their bodies as a site of artistic activity during the 1970s. In her early work the German Rebecca Horn manipulated and extended parts of her body during such performances and installations as *Cornucopia: Seance for Two Breasts* (1970) and *Finger-Gloves: An Instrument to Extend the Manual Sensibilities* (1972). In France, Gina Pane evolved several performances that challenged the stereotypical view of the female body as a site of pleasure by their stress on pain. In *Escalade non anaesthesié* (1971) she climbed up and down a ladder decked with sharp protrusions until her bare hands and feet were bleeding; in other works she transformed herself into a slab of meat (*Sentimental Action*, 1973) or chewed raw meat until she vomited. More recently, the Prague-born artist Jana Sterbak created performances that played upon the metaphorical identification of meat and the female body. In *Vanitas: Flesh Dress for an Albino Anorectic* (1987) she clothed a female body in a "dress" composed of 60 pounds of rotting flank steak. Eleanor Antin performed *Carving* (1973) over a period of a month during which she lost ten pounds, documenting the change through daily photographs.

Change to the actual body of the artist through weight loss has also been explored by Adrian Piper and more recently by Faith Ringgold (q.v.) in her several story quilts on that subject. Earlier, Piper had participated in a series of street performances called *Catalysis* (1970), in which she altered her physical appearance to depart radically from socially acceptable norms of personal comportment as, for example, when she rode on a subway train in New York garbed in clothing saturated with stale vinegar, eggs and milk. Martha Rosler performed and videotaped numerous works that challenged the acceptance of the objectification of the female body. In *Vital Statistics of a Citizen, Simply Obtained* (1973), for example, a woman (Rosler herself) was stripped, interrogated, her body measured and then videotaped while preparing food in a kitchen. More recently, in her videos, performances and installations, the Lebanese-born Mona Hatoum has gone beyond exploration of the external bodily surface. *Corps étranger* (1994) provides the viewer with a video tour of her interior vital organs, which are viewed on a screen on the floor of a dark circular booth, thanks to the technique of endoscopy.

Another approach adopted by women performance artists during the 1970s was to use their bodies in rituals that asserted women's strength and power through identification with imagery associated with prehistoric goddess worship. Cuban-born Ana Mendieta made several series of images, which she documented photographically, in which she covered her body with mud, flowers or burned her silhouette into the earth. "My art is the way I re-establish the bonds that unite me to the universe", she wrote. "It is a return to the maternal source. Through my earth/body sculptures I become one with the earth"

(Gadon 1989, p.278). Through several performances and their photographic documentation, Mary Beth Edelson sought to establish links with traditional sites and images of the goddess. She used her own image as a "stand-in" for the goddess in private rituals at various coastal sites – Montauk, Long Island, the Outer Banks of North Carolina and the Neolithic Grapçeva cave, off the coast of the former Yugoslavia. She enhanced the photographic records of these events with drawing and collage, as the energy waves that radiate from her head in *Woman Rising* from North Carolina. Of her pilgrimage to the Yugoslavian cave where she surrounded her body, submerged to the waist, with a "fire ring" she said: "I felt like the center of the universe..." (*ibid.*, p.273).

In recent decades numerous other women artists have sought to re-establish a positive image of female power through the depiction of the goddess in her many guises. An early example of a work that illustrates such concerns was the temporary environmental sculpture *La Hon* ("She" in Swedish), built by Niki de Saint Phalle (q.v.) in collaboration with Jean Tinguely and installed at the Moderna Museet in Stockholm in 1966. Viewers were able to enter and exit this brightly painted, colossal, recumbent female figure through a vaginal portal, reiterating prehistoric reverence for the sacred feminine by recreating the primal experiences of birth and death, of moving from womb to tomb. A milk bar was housed in one breast and a cinema in her head. Like many of Saint Phalle's smaller *Venus* and *Nana* figures, the shape of this figure echoed the bulbous, fecund forms of the many prehistoric sculptures of women believed by some to be depictions of maternal deities. Soon after, Monica Sjöö painted a controversial image of *God Giving Birth* (1968), a black woman silhouetted against the sky with a baby's head emerging from her vulval area. This was the earliest of many images of the goddess made by Sjöö, a writer concerned with the lost tradition of the goddess, who has made numerous pilgrimages to various sacred sites, which she has incorporated into her paintings and drawings. Likewise Meinrad Craighead, who lived for 14 years as a cloistered nun in a Benedictine abbey, published a book, *The Mother's Songs* (1986), containing 40 of her paintings of the great Mother in which the maternal principle is associated with the continuous, generative power of the earth. In her scrolls Nancy Spero (q.v.) has used repeating images of powerful female deities such as the Celtic Shelagh-na-gig (*Chorus Line I*, 1985) and the Egyptian Nut (*To the Revolution*, 1983), images of "freedom from every kind of physical, mental and social constraint; a freedom we don't possess but need to nurture, as an idea of a feeling..." (Gadon 1989, p.338). Audrey Flack (q.v.), a leading photo-realist painter, turned to sculpting images of "contemporary goddesses for a new age" (Gouma-Peterson's phrase in Los Angeles 1992) – reinterpreting traditional figures such as Medusa and Athena and creating hybrids such as the *Egyptian Rocket Goddess* and *Islandia: Goddess of Healing Waters*, images that celebrate women's strength and power.

Other artists in the 1970s employed political strategies in their attempts to insert a female presence into the history of art. To this end, Sylvia Sleigh (q.v.) created paintings in which the traditional relationship between artist (male) and subject (female) was deliberately reversed. In such paintings as *Reclining Nude: Paul Rossano*, *Philip Golub Reclining* and most especially *Turkish Bath* (1973), a parody of Ingres's work of the same title, Sleigh placed the image of naked males in poses that were typical of those of the female nude in the post-Renaissance tradition. In a moving essay, May Stevens argued that "art should be taken to the revolution" (quoted in Witzling 1994, pp.71–3), a position that she had exercised in her own work for several decades, beginning in the 1970s with her series of "Big Daddy" images. In these works, based on a caricatured image of her father seated watching television with his pug dog on his lap, Stevens expressed her outrage at the militaristic, racist and patriarchal oppression that had become characteristic of American culture. During the 1980s she explored her matrilineage in a series of images juxtaposing the "ordinary" life of her mother with the "extraordinary" life of the radical Rosa Luxemburg, both of whom had been silenced by the patriarchy. Sleigh and Stevens both painted heroised images of their female contemporaries, and Sleigh, with four other artists, contributed paintings to the never-constructed "Sister Chapel", a recreation of the Sistine Chapel celebrating heroic women.

Some feminist artists sought to differentiate themselves and their works from the approaches chronicled above, considering them to be manifestations of "essentialism", in that, as in the past, women appeared to be designated in terms of their biological characteristics. Works that stressed a vaginal iconography were chided for once more defining women by their body parts. Likewise, performance art has been criticised as an ambiguous strategy, at risk for "the recuperation of the female body to the patriarchal spectacle" (Nead 1992, p.68). Similar accusations have been made against the movement to reclaim great goddess imagery, which critics see as based on the misguided belief that there is such a thing as a "feminine essence". Although it can be argued that looking back to cultures in which female strength was celebrated rather than denigrated hardly constitutes the acceptance of an essential femininity (as does Gloria Orenstein in *The Reflowering of the Goddess*, 1990), there has been a mounting chorus of voices that refuse to accept any universal construction of the category "woman".

Many feminist artists believe that because the female image has been over-determined in Western culture all representations of women are doomed to recreate stereotypes. This stance has been aligned with other post-modernist deconstructions of the history of art, and its practitioners have adopted strategies that subvert the common construction of the sign "woman" in the Western tradition. Mary Kelly, an American who did much of her early work in London, was an important proponent of this approach, which "uses multiple representational modes" (Owens 1983, p.491) by combining text, artefacts and natural fragments, presented as if on exhibition at an anthropological museum, to allow viewers to construct their own images. In *Post-Partum Document*, her first mature work, she examined the mother-child relationship, and particularly the construction of motherhood and loss of maternal authority, by presenting a series of "mother's artefacts" including stained nappy liners, hand prints and recordings of early speech utterances. She avoided "the literal figuration of mother and child" as a "historical strategy...to cut across the predominant representation of the look...and to picture the woman as the subject of her own desire" (Kelly 1983, pp.xxvii-xxviii). In her next major work, *Interim* (1984–9), Kelly confronted the problem of "representing" the middle-aged woman, no longer useful in the patriarchy as a sex object or child-bearer, by offering the viewer a variety of textual narratives interspersed with images of women's clothing, graphs and advertising fragments. Here, too, she avoided the literal depiction of the female figure, allowing, instead, for multiple possible readings. Similarly, the French artist Annette Messager (q.v.) mixes various media – objects such as dolls, photographs and textual fragments – to encourage the viewer to examine critically cultural definitions of gender. Working in series, in small books (as in *My Jealousies* or *My Approaches*) or mixed-media installations (*Histories of Dresses*), Messager forces the viewer to piece together "ethnological" fragments, to reconstruct bodily experience, without depending on stereotyped images of femininity. Rosemarie Trockel, in Germany, also used fetishised imagery to encourage the viewer to construct "the feminine" through mechanically embroidered objects of clothing – hats, tights and "dead-pan" drawing.

Like other post-modern authors and artists, Kelly challenges viewers to construct the meaning of her works from shifting, unstable signifiers that often subvert accepted visual expectations. In this, her endeavour is similar to that of several American photographers. Lorna Simpson, like Kelly, "refuses the literal figuration" of her subject, often a black female, by presenting her figures from the rear without allowing us to see their faces and, like Kelly, accompanies her images with destabilising textual elements, as in *Twenty Questions (A Sampler)* (1986), where the accompanying text asks: "Is she pretty as a picture/Or clear as crystal/or pure as a lily/or black as coal/or sharp as a razor"? Of course, these questions have no simple answers, if any at all. Barbara Kruger (q.v.) collects "found" commercial photographic images and pairs them with provocative phrases built of "pronomial shifters" (I, we, you, they) that disrupt the power imbalance associated with the gaze in Western culture while at the same time revealing that "masculinity and femininity are not stable identities, but subject to exchange" (*ibid.*, p.499). Kruger has stated that one major goal in her work is "to welcome a female spectator into the world of men", which she achieves by inserting a female presence as the speaking and seeing subject, in such works as an untitled photograph of a stone face, affixed with the phrase "your gaze hits the side of my face". Sherrie Levine re-photographs works by such famous photographers as Walker Evans and Edward Weston, subverting the modernist and masculinist concept of the "great author". In her early photographs Cindy Sherman used her own image as model, mimicking "stills" from movies of the 1940s and 1950s, depicting stereotyped images of women, making "self-portraits" that destabilised

the selfhood of their author, and reveal the extent to which "femininity is a masquerade" in this popular culture (*idem*). In her more recent work, Sherman has made huge coloured images of dismembered female figures, accompanied by such images of pollution as used condoms, rubbish and dildos. In these works Sherman contradicts the stereotyped image of women – glossy, contained, antiseptic.

While acknowledging how strategies such as Kelly's "explore desire and identity without colluding in the objectification of women", Lynda Nead also points out that the bodily norm Kelly assumes is one that is "both valued and exhibited within patriarchal culture". She continues:

> Denying visibility to "the female body" as a universal category perpetuates the invisibility of women whose bodies do not conform to the ideals of the dominant culture and who may be struggling for the right to physical and public visibility [Nead 1992, p.76].

Thus, some women artists have recently presented aspects of the female body that make visible what has been considered an "inappropriate" image of femininity. For example, the images of the British photographer Jo Spence (q.v.) "concern a working-class woman, aging and with a scarred body". Particularly in *Narratives of Dis-ease*, Spence explores some of her "feelings and experiences since being diagnosed and treated for breast cancer" (*ibid.*, p.80). Spence's process of making visible what has been taboo is related to the work of the young American sculptor Kiki Smith, most of whose works focus on the body in the process of breaking its boundaries of containment: bleeding, crying, lactating, defecating, birthing. Smith chose the theme of "the open, protruding, extended, secreting body" because she believes that "our bodies are basically stolen from us" and she "wanted to reclaim one's own turf" (Schliefer 1991, p.86).

One other tactic used by women artists to recast history with women's perspective included is related to the process of story-telling. This is a significant process, because so many stories in the Western tradition are deficient in female protagonists, both in sheer number and in how they are permitted to act. By telling stories in which women and other oppressed groups are given full voice as protagonists, artists "challenge the pervasive 'master narratives' of the culture that would contain them" (Lippard 1990, p.57). Artists and writers see that "speaking from the margins" can be a strategy of resistance to cultural obliteration (Hooks 1990, p.145). The African-American artist Faith Ringgold exemplifies this process in her story quilts, combining visual images and narrative text in a single frame, each spoken from the point of view of an African-American female protagonist. In *Tar Beach*, for example, Ringgold tells the story of eight-year-old Cassie Louise Lightfoot, a girl from Harlem, a segregated New York ghetto, who claims the George Washington Bridge, Union Hall and an ice-cream factory simply by flying over them, concluding that "anyone can fly". In her subsequent series *The French Collection*, Ringgold constructs a protagonist, Willia Marie Simone, a black American painter living in Paris, whose story "intersects" with many of the major monuments and practitioners of modern art history. Like the work of many earlier artists, this series of quilts by Ringgold is a deliberate attempt to insert a female – and in this case – an African-American presence into the standard historical narrative.

The de-centring, de-stabilising aim of feminist artistic practice has been compared to similar practices in post-modernism. Just as post-modern artists and writers have challenged the hegemony of Western culture and its master narratives, so too have feminist artists questioned the Western privileging of the authority of the visible and its equation with "maleness" (cf. Owens 1983). But one way in which feminist projects are distinguished from other post-modern endeavours is that, despite their "deconstruction" of entrenched ways of seeing, rather than closing off possibilities through ambiguity they seek to open them up. Barbara Kruger "welcome[s] a female spectator" into the visible by giving the previously objectified female a voice with which to "talk back", to speak. Thus, it could be argued that much of the work described above is "reconstructive" in that its goal in subverting the Western tradition is to offer more balanced, less monolithic, more inclusive means of representing the visible world.

MARA R. WITZLING

Bibliography

Linda Nochlin, "Why have there been no great women artists?", *Woman in Sexist Society: Studies in Power and Powerlessness*, ed. Vivian Gornick and Barbara K. Moran, New York: Basic Books, 1971; reprinted New American Library, 1972, pp.480–510

John Berger, *Ways of Seeing*, New York: Viking, 1973

Judy Chicago and Miriam Schapiro, "Female imagery", *Womanspace Journal*, i/1, Summer 1973, pp.11–17

Dorothy Seiberling, "The female view of Erotica", *New York*, 14 February 1974

Judy Chicago, *Through the Flower: My Struggle as a Woman Artist*, New York: Doubleday, 1975; 2nd edition, New York: Doubleday, and London: Women's Press, 1982

Laura Mulvey, "Visual pleasure and the narrative cinema", *Screen*, no.16, Autumn 1975, pp.6–18; reprinted in *Visual and Other Pleasures*, Bloomington: Indiana University Press, and London: Macmillan, 1989

Cindy Nemser, *Art Talk: Conversations with 12 Women Artists*, New York: Scribner, 1975

Lucy R. Lippard, *From the Center: Feminist Essays on Women's Art*, New York: Dutton, 1976

Sara Ruddick and Pamela Daniels, *Working It Out: Twenty-Three Women Writers, Artists, Scientists and Scholars Talk about Their Lives and Work*, New York: Pantheon, 1977

Lisa Tickner, "The body politic: Female sexuality and women artists since 1970", *Art History*, i, 1978, pp.236-49; reprinted in *Looking On: Images of Femininity in the Visual Arts and Media*, ed. Rosemary Betterton, London and New York: Pandora, 1987

Judy Chicago, *The Dinner Party: A Symbol of Our Heritage*, New York: Doubleday, 1979

Eleanor Munro, *Originals: American Women Artists*, New York: Simon and Schuster, 1979

Carolee Schneemann , *More than Meat Joy: Complete Performance Works and Selected Writings*, ed. Bruce McPherson, New Paltz, NY: Documentext, 1979

The Ancient Religion of the Great Cosmic Mother of All, edited and extended by Barbara Mor, Trondheim, Norway: Rainbow Press, 1981; revised as *The Great Cosmic Mother: Rediscovering the Religion of the Earth*, San Francisco: Harper, 1987; 2nd edition, 1991

Rozsika Parker and Griselda Pollock, *Old Mistresses: Women, Art and Ideology*, London: Routledge, 1981

Charlotte Streifer Rubinstein, *American Women Artists from Early Times to the Present*, Boston: Hall, 1982

Mary Kelly, *Post-Partum Document*, London: Routledge, 1983

Craig Owens, "The discourse of others: Feminists and postmodernists", *The Anti-Aesthetic: Essays on Postmodern Culture*, ed. Hal Foster, Port Townsend: Bay Press, 1983; reprinted in Broude and Garrard 1992

Moira Roth, *The Amazing Decade: Women and Performance Art in America, 1970–80*, Los Angeles: Astro Artz, 1983

Art after Modernism: Rethinking Representation, exh. cat., New Museum of Contemporary Art, New York, 1984

Harmony Hammond, *Wrappings: Essays on Feminism, Art and the Martial Arts*, New York: TSL Press, 1984

Meinrad Craighead, *The Mother's Songs*, Mahwah, NJ: Paulist Press, 1986

Rozsika Parker and Griselda Pollock, *Framing Feminism: Art and the Women's Movement, 1970–85*, London and New York: Pandora Press, 1987

Griselda Pollock, *Vision and Difference: Femininity, Feminism and the Histories of Art*, London: Routledge, 1988

Christine Battersby, *Gender and Genius: Towards a Feminist Aesthetic*, Bloomington: Indiana University Press, and London: Women's Press, 1989

Elinor Gadon, *The Once and Future Goddess: A Symbol for Our Time*, San Francisco: Harper, and Wellingborough: Aquarian, 1989

Making Their Mark: Women Artists Move into the Mainstream, 1970–85, exh. cat., Cincinnati Art Museum, and elsewhere, 1989

Whitney Chadwick, *Women, Art and Society*, London and New York: Thames and Hudson, 1990; revised edition, 1996

Bell Hooks, *Yearning: Race, Gender and Cultural Politics*, Boston: South End Press, 1990

Mary Kelly: Interim, exh. cat., New Museum of Contemporary Art, New York, and elsewhere, 1990

Lucy R. Lippard, *Mixed Blessings: New Art in a Multicultural America*, New York: Pantheon, 1990

Gloria Feman Orenstein, *The Reflowering of the Goddess*, Oxford: Pergamon Press, 1990

Susan Rubin Suleiman, *Subversive Intent: Gender, Politics and the Avant-Garde*, Cambridge, MA: Harvard University Press, 1990

Suzi Gablik, *The Reenchantment of Art*, New York and London: Thames and Hudson, 1991

Faith Ringgold, *Tar Beach*, New York: Crown, 1991

Kristen Brooke Schliefer, "Inside and out: An interview with Kiki Smith", *Print Collector's Newsletter*, July 1991, pp.84-7

Mara R. Witzling, ed., *Voicing Our Visions: Writings by Women Artists*, New York: Universe, 1991; London: Women's Press, 1992

Breaking the Rules: Audrey Flack: A Retrospective, 1950–1990, exh. cat., Frederick S. Wight Art Gallery, University of California, Los Angeles, and elsewhere, 1992

Norma Broude and Mary D. Garrard, eds, *The Expanding Discourse: Feminism and Art History*, New York: Icon, 1992

Lynda Nead, *The Female Nude*, London and New York: Routledge, 1992

Norma Broude and Mary D. Garrard, eds, *The Power of Feminist Art: The American Movement of the 1970s*, New York: Abrams, and London: Thames and Hudson, 1994

Joanna Frueh, Cassandra L. Langer and Arlene Raven, eds, *New Feminist Criticism: Art, Identity, Action*, New York: HarperCollins, 1994

Mara R. Witzling, ed., *Voicing Today's Visions: Writings by Contemporary Women Artists*, New York: Universe, 1994

ARTISTS

A

Abakanowicz, Magdalena
Polish sculptor and graphic artist, 1930–

Born in Falenty, 20 June 1930. Studied at School of Fine Art, Sopot, 1949–50; Academy of Fine Arts, Warsaw, 1950–54. Married Jan Kosmowski, 1956. First travelled to the West, 1958, to the USA and Mexico, 1970–71, to Australasia and the Far East, 1976. Taught at the Academy of Fine Arts, Poznań, 1965–90. Recipient of gold medal, São Paulo Bienal, 1965; Grand Prize, World Crafts Council, New York, 1974; Gottfried-von-Herder Foundation prize, Vienna, 1979; Polonia Restituta medal, 1980; Alfred Jurzykowski Foundation award, New York, 1983; Francis Greenburger Foundation award, 1990; award for Distinction in Sculpture, Sculpture Center, New York, 1993; honorary doctorates from Royal College of Art, London, 1974, and Rhode Island School of Design, Providence, 1993. Chevalier, Ordre des Arts et Lettres, France, 1985. Lives in Warsaw.

Selected Individual Exhibitions
Galerie Kordegarda, Warsaw: 1960
Galerie Dautzenberg, Paris: 1962
Galerie Alice Pauli, Lausanne: 1967, 1969, 1971, 1975, 1977, 1979 (retrospective), 1981, 1983, 1985
Kunstindustrimuseet, Oslo: 1967 (touring)
Stedelijk van Abbemuseum, Eindhoven: 1968–9 (touring)
Kunsthalle, Mannheim: 1969
Konsthall, Södertälje, Sweden: 1970
Pasadena Art Museum, CA: 1971
Kunstverein für die Rheinlande und Westfalen, Düsseldorf: 1972
Muzeum Sztuki, Łódź: 1974, 1991
Whitechapel Art Gallery, London: 1975
Art Gallery of New South Wales, Sydney: 1976 (touring, organised by Australian Council for the Arts)
Konsthall, Malmö: 1977 (*Organic Structures*, touring)
Polish Pavilion, Venice Biennale: 1980
Museum of Contemporary Art, Chicago: 1982–4 (touring retrospective)
Xavier Fourcade, New York: 1985
Palace of Exhibitions, Mücsarnok, Budapest: 1988
Städelsches Kunstinstitut und Städtische Galerie, Frankfurt am Main: 1989
Marlborough Gallery, New York: 1989, 1992, 1993, 1994
Sezon Museum of Art, Tokyo: 1991 (touring)
Institute for Contemporary Art, PS 1 Museum, Long Island City, NY: 1993

Bibliography
Judith Bumpus, "Rope environments", *Art and Artists*, ix, October 1974, pp.36–41
Magdalena Abakanowicz, exh. cat., Museum of Contemporary Art, Chicago, and elsewhere, 1982
Hunter Drohojowska, "Magical mystery tours", *Art News*, lxxxiv, September 1985, pp.108–13
Leslie Milosky, "Art essay: Magdalena Abakanowicz", *Feminist Studies*, xiii, Summer 1987, pp.363–78
Magdalena Abakanowicz: Skulpturen, 1967–90, exh. cat., Städelsches Kunstinstitut und Städtische Galerie, Frankfurt am Main, 1989
Magdalena Abakanowicz, exh. cat., Richard Gray Gallery, Chicago, 1990 (contains bibliography)
Nancy Princenthal, "Abakanowicz: Memories and monuments", *Art in America*, lxxviii, March 1990, pp.178–83
Douglas Dreishpoon, "Monumental intimacy: An interview with Magdalena Abakanowicz", *Arts Magazine*, lxv, December 1990, pp.45–9
Michael Brenson, "Survivor art", *New York Times Magazine*, 29 November 1992, pp.46–54
Magdalena Abakanowicz: Recent Sculpture, exh. cat., Museum of Art, Rhode Island School of Design, Providence, and elsewhere, 1993
Magdalena Abakanowicz: War Games, exh. cat., Institute for Contemporary Art, PS 1 Museum, Long Island City, NY, 1993
Barbara Rose, *Magdalena Abakanowicz*, New York: Abrams, 1994 (contains bibliography)
Mara R. Witzling, ed., *Voicing Today's Visions: Writings by Contemporary Women Artists*, New York: Universe, 1994
Michael Brenson, "Magdalena Abakanowicz's 'Abakans'", *Art Journal*, liv, Spring 1995, pp.56–61

Magdalena Abakanowicz entered the art world through the back door, so to speak, when she exhibited, in 1962, at the first Biennale International de la Tapisserie, in Lausanne, Switzerland. Even as a so-called weaver, she consciously defied traditional rules and techniques, eventually transforming this humble craft into some of the most memorable sculptures ever made. Defying rules has always been the artist's *modus operandi*, and the work that she has produced over the past 33 years – beginning with the *Abakans* and including her numerous rope installations, various *Heads*, *Seated Figures*, *Crowds*, *Backs*, *Embryology*, site-specific commissions and *War Games* – asks existential questions at the same time as it posits resolute truths. Her sculpture takes nothing for granted, except the human condition, with its foibles and contradictions, resilience and potential for change.

Abakanowicz described herself to the critic Michael Brenson as a "gypsie" who could "work in any place and in any part of the world" (Brenson 1992, p.50). She also told him that she wanted her work to affect everyone in some way, to "touch universal problems". However, despite her cosmopolitan intentions and the work's archetypal implications, the artist acknowledges that she and her art are by-products of a particular cultural history. As a young girl living in Poland, she survived World War II and, subsequently, a series of political upheavals that dramatically altered her world view. Her work is inextricably bound to these unsettling circumstances. And still, as an expression rich in levels of meaning, her sculpture transcends the autobiographical.

From the outset of her career, Abakanowicz stretched the limits of whatever her medium was. In the early 1960s she rebelled against the technical constraints of the loom and experimented with disparate materials, weaving together composite wall hangings whose designs recalled earlier paintings – an enchanted world she referred to as "my rain forest" – but whose surface density pushed towards the third dimension. These were trying times for the artist, who laboured long hours in the cramped quarters of Maria Laszkiewicz's Warsaw studio. It did not take long, however, to realise the sculptural potential of her circumstances. She recalled in an interview: "It was becoming clear to me that I could build a three-dimensional reality; soft, full of secrets, protecting me, being a shield to me, and at the same time being my own creation, an

integral part of myself. So the *Abakans* came into being" (Dreishpoon 1990, p.47).

The *Abakans*, begun around 1967, set the tenor for many of Abakanowicz's subsequent cycles. No one had ever used the loom to produce such monumental, free-standing entities, whose pliable constitution questioned traditional sculptural values. Massive beings with multiple personalities, these hollow personages possess a sense of mystery and association that distinguishes most of Abakanowicz's ideas regardless of medium. "Like all of Abakanowicz's cycles", wrote Michael Brenson, "the 'Abakans' lead outward, away from what they might appear to represent, into psychology and history, toward fundamental links between human beings and nature that are always waiting to be recognised and explored by the imagination" (Brenson 1995, p.58).

Whether one is confronting an installation of *Abakans*, *Standing Figures* or the more recent series of *War Games*, inside/outside is an apt metaphor for the multiple ways in which Abakanowicz's work can be perceived. Inside signifies the work's psychological centre, an allusive spirit, a place of refuge. Outside denotes its public persona, phenomenology, the way it interacts with viewers, its place in history. Whereas inside implies a personality that is shy, self-effacing and humble, outside suggests a more resilient, confident and ambitious entity. Such characterisations, however, are relative. That they coexist and are often interchangeable within any given piece reinforces its complex nature.

Early on Abakanowicz moved beyond weaving. Her rope installations at the Södertälje Konsthall in Sweden and the Nationalmuseum in Stockholm (both in 1970), as well as at the Pasadena Art Museum in California and the Malmö Konsthall in Sweden, in 1971 and 1977 respectively, were a *tour de force*. They transformed their environment, like theatre, and introduced a narrative dimension as well. Rope had a special place in the artist's material repertoire. Composed of many intertwined fibres or threads, rope could symbolise unitary strength and community. When twisted into convoluted knots, it signified chaos and disorder. Rope had multiple meanings for Abakanowicz, whose installations, when compared with contemporaneous work being done by Eva Hesse (q.v.) and Jackie Winsor in the USA, were by far the most ambitious in terms of their monumentality and scope.

By the late 1970s Abakanowicz was well known in international art circles. But it was not until 1980, when she represented Poland at the Venice Biennale, that her career accelerated. The work she exhibited there, a series of free-standing burlap figures, finally liberated her from what she called the "ghetto of weavers" (Brenson 1992, p.50), and since then her sculpture has developed in a number of directions. Never one to limit the ideological extensions of her ideas, she uses whatever materials and techniques seem appropriate for a given project. A series of *Sagacious Heads* (1989) was cast in bronze. For an installation in the Negev desert, in 1987, she carved seven huge disks out of limestone. Some of her standing figures (*Crowds*, 1986–91) were also cast in bronze, while others – a remarkable series of *Backs* begun in 1976 – were assembled with burlap and glue. The *War Games* (1989) are disregarded tree trunks stripped of their bark, whose extremities are capped with steel or bandaged with burlap. Materials are selected for their associative potential – fibre and burlap signify vulnerability and impermanence; bronze and stone strength and durability; wood and steel the collision between nature and technology – and their ability to embody grand themes (*Ancestor*, 1989). The same can be said of her subjects, which gravitate between images of dissolution, death and disfigurement, and the possibility of rebirth, growth and perseverance. Her simple, iconic forms, posed alone or in communities, traverse a vast metaphorical terrain – isolation and solitude, meditation and prayer, ritual, judgement and incarceration – and straddle the line between abstraction and representation. Ultimately, her work can be seen as part of a vitalist tradition extending back to Henry Moore, Alberto Giacometti, Constantin Brancusi and Auguste Rodin. Within this sculptural continuum, Abakanowicz creates her own analogues for an ever-changing human condition.

Abakanowicz's work is represented in numerous international collections, including the Art Institute of Chicago; Detroit Institute of the Arts; Hirshhorn Museum, Washington, DC; Metropolitan Museum of Art and Museum of Modern Art, New York; Stedelijk Museum, Amsterdam; Centre Georges Pompidou, Paris; National Museum, Warsaw; National Museum of Modern Art, Kyoto; and the National Gallery of Australia, Canberra.

DOUGLAS DREISHPOON

Abbott, Berenice
American photographer, 1898–1991

Born in Springfield, Ohio, 17 July 1898. Attended Ohio State University, Columbus, 1917–18; received some training in journalism at Columbia University, New York, 1918. Studied sculpture independently in New York, 1918–21, then in the Paris studios of Emile Bourdelle and Constantin Brancusi, 1921–3, and at the Kunstschule, Berlin, 1923. Worked as studio assistant to Surrealist photographer Man Ray in Paris, 1923–5; introduced to the work of photographer Eugène Atget, 1925; opened own studio in Paris, 1926. Purchased prints and negatives from Atget's estate after his death in 1927. Returned to USA, 1929. Worked for *Fortune* and *Life* magazines, and for the Works Progress Administration Federal Art Project (WPA/FAP), 1935–9. Instructor in photography, New School for Social Research, New York, 1935–58. Worked for Physical Science Study Committee of Educational Services Inc., New York, 1958–61. Left New York for Maine, 1968. Recipient of honorary doctorates from University of Maine, Orono, 1971; Smith College, Northampton, Massachusetts, 1973; New School for Social Research, 1981; Bates College, Lewiston, Maine, 1981; Bowdoin College, Brunswick, Maine, 1982. Died in Monson, Maine, 9 December 1991.

Selected Individual Exhibitions
Julian Levy Gallery, New York: 1932
Museum of the City of New York: 1934, 1937
Yale University, New Haven: 1934 (touring), 1937
Springfield Museum of Fine Arts, MA: 1935
Massachusetts Institute of Technology, Cambridge: 1941, 1959, 1985
Galérie l'Epoque, Paris: 1947
Art Institute of Chicago: 1951
San Francisco Museum of Modern Art: 1953
Currier Gallery of Art, Manchester, NH: 1955, 1960
Toronto Art Museum: 1956
Smithsonian Institution, Washington, DC: 1960 (*Image of Physics*, touring), 1969 (retrospective), 1982
Museum of Modern Art, New York: 1970 (retrospective)
Witkin Gallery, New York: 1973
Marlborough Gallery, New York: 1976 (touring)
Galerie Zabriskie, Paris: 1977 (with Eugène Atget)
International Center of Photography, New York: 1981–2 (*The 20's and 30's*, touring)
New York Academy of Sciences: 1987
New York Public Library: 1989–90 (touring retrospective)

Selected Writings

"Eugène Atget", *Creative Art*, v, 1929, pp.651–6; reprinted in *Photography, Essays and Images: Illustrated Readings in the History of Photography*, ed. Beaumont Newhall, New York: Museum of Modern Art, 1980

A Guide to Better Photography, New York: Crown, 1941; revised as *New Guide to Better Photography*, 1953

The View Camera Made Simple, Chicago: Ziff-Davis, 1948

"What the camera and I see", *Art News*, l, September 1951, pp.36–7, 52

"The image of science", *Art in America*, xlvii/4, 1959, pp.76–9

The World of Atget, New York: Horizon, 1964

Bibliography

Elizabeth McCausland, *Changing New York*, New York: Dutton, 1939; reissued as *New York in the Thirties*, New York: Dover, and London: Constable, 1973

—, "Berenice Abbott – realist", *Photo Arts*, ii, Spring 1948, pp.46–50

Henry W. Lanier, *Greenwich Village Today and Yesterday*, New York: Harper, 1949

E.G. Valens, *Magnet*, Cleveland: World, 1964; London: Longman, 1970

—, *Motion*, Cleveland: World, 1965; London: Longman, 1970

Nathan Lyons, ed., *Photographers on Photography*, Englewood Cliffs, NJ: Prentice Hall, 1966

Chenoweth Hall, *A Portrait of Maine*, New York: Macmillan, 1968

E.G. Valens, *The Attractive Universe*, Cleveland: World, 1969

Anne Tucker, ed., *The Woman's Eye*, New York: Knopf, 1973

Women of Photography, exh. cat., San Francisco Museum of Art and elsewhere, 1975

Berenice Abbott, exh. cat., Marlborough Gallery, New York, and elsewhere, 1976

Alice C. Steinbach, "Berenice Abbott's point of view", *Art in America*, lxiv, November–December 1976, pp.77–81

Margaretta K. Mitchell, *Recollections: Ten Women of Photography*, New York: Viking, 1979

Berenice Abbott: Documentary Photographs of the 1930s, exh. cat., New Gallery of Contemporary Art, Cleveland, 1980

Michael G. Sundell, "Berenice Abbott's work in the thirties", *Prospects: An Annual of American Cultural Studies*, v, 1980, pp.269–92

Berenice Abbott: The 20's and 30's, exh. cat., International Center of Photography, New York, and elsewhere, 1981

Avis Berman, "The unflinching eye of Berenice Abbott", *Art News*, lxxx, January 1981, pp.86–93

Hank O'Neal, *Berenice Abbott: American Photographer*, New York: McGraw-Hill, 1982; as *Berenice Abbott: Sixty Years of Photography*, London: Thames and Hudson, 1982

David M. Maxfield, "Berenice Abbott: A photographer of the twentieth century", *Arts in Virginia*, xxiv/1–2, 1983–4, pp.30–39

Julia van Haaften, ed., *Berenice Abbott*, New York: Aperture, 1988

Berenice Abbott, Photographer: A Modern Vision, exh. cat., New York Public Library and elsewhere, 1989

David Vestal and others, *Berenice Abbott: Photographer*, 2nd edition, Washington, DC: Smithsonian Institution Press, 1990 (first published as exh. cat., Museum of Modern Art, New York, 1970)

Joann Prosyniuk, ed., *Modern Arts Criticism*, ii, Detroit: Gale Research, 1992

Although Berenice Abbott made her mark as a documentary photographer, she originally trained as a sculptor with Emile Bourdelle and Constantin Brancusi in Paris and Berlin. After deciding to devote her life to photography, she became Man Ray's photographic assistant in 1923, and in 1926 she opened her own portrait studio in Paris. For three years she photographed creative celebrities including James Joyce, Neil Fujita, Jean Cocteau, André Gide, Marie Laurencin (q.v.), André Siegfried and Eugène Atget. She also photographed many of the expatriate American artists and writers who were in Paris in this period. Her first exhibition of portrait photographs was held at the Au Sacre du Printemps gallery in Paris in 1926.

Abbott had encountered Atget's documentary photographs of Paris in 1925 and was immediately captivated by his work, so different from her own. Her embracing of his aesthetic marked a watershed in her career: exposed to the authority of his visual conception and purity of form, she appeared to refute the exotic and Surrealist influence evident in her earlier portraits. After Atget's death, in 1927, she determined to save his work and to bring it to international attention. With the financial backing of the New York art dealer Julian Levy, in 1928 she purchased 5000 of Atget's photographs from his estate.

In 1929 Abbott visited New York and was so impressed by the city's complexity and vitality that she decided to close her Paris studio and return there to live. She brought with her a portion of Atget's oeuvre, and in 1930 she arranged publication of a book, *Atget Photographe de Paris*. The effect of Atget's straightforward, uninflected documentary style is evident in her photographic work after her return to the USA. By the mid-1930s Abbott, with Edward and Brett Weston, Charles Sheeler and Paul Outerbridge, spearheaded the American Realist photographic style.

Deeply affected by Atget's style and by his commitment to recording the streets of historical Paris, Abbott determined to undertake a comprehensive portrait of New York, to document its changing appearance and interpret its vital spirit through the camera. She worked alone on this project, using an 8 × 10-inch (20.3 × 25.4 cm.) camera. In contrast to her exploration of human character in the Paris portraits, in urban landscapes she eliminated the human face wherever possible, attempting to produce compositions devoid of sentimentality and psychological overtones. A selection of early images was shown at the Museum of the City of New York in 1932, and a major one-woman exhibition of her photographs was held there in 1934. As arts funding was scarce in this period – there was no official patronage – in 1935 Abbott applied to the Works Progress Administration (WPA), and obtained support through the US government's New Deal program. In her proposal to the WPA Abbott wrote:

> To photograph New York City means to seek to catch in the sensitive and delicate photographic emulsion the spirit of the metropolis, while remaining true to its essential fact, its hurrying tempo, its congested streets, the past jostling the present. The concern is not with an architectural rendering of detail, the buildings of 1935 overshadowing everything else, but with a synthesis which shows the skyscraper in relation to the less colossal edifices which preceded it …

Abbott's images from this period of Manhattan shop windows, such as *Chicken Market, 55 Hester Street* (1937), *Blossom Restaurant, 103 Bowery* (1935) and *Bread Store, 259 Bleecker Street* (1937) reveal a visual sensibility reminiscent of Atget. She always denied the influence of Atget's photographs of French culture, however, citing her inclusion of printed texts as well as her treatment of the diffused reflections of mirrored objects. In many of the New York photographs the words become part of a larger object and carry more impact than their original, literal meaning. During a period of nine years she took hundreds of photographs of New York,

recording streets, residences, commercial buildings, windows, parks, bridges, roads, cemeteries and civic monuments. Among the best known are *Newsstand, 32nd Street and 3rd Avenue, 19 November 1935* and *Father Duffy, Times Square* (1937), both of which use a wealth of detail to describe the subject as well as the moment of recording. Throughout the work the story is one of contrast and change: old is next to new; decay invades beauty.

Abbott's photographs of New York have become a valuable historical resource, because many of the landmarks she documented no longer exist. In 1939 a book of her photographs titled *Changing New York* was published under the auspices of the Federal Art Project, with captions by Elizabeth McCausland. The negatives and a set of master prints from the project are housed in the Museum of the City of New York.

Much of Abbott's work in the 1940s and 1950s was devoted to scientific experimental photography. She published an instruction manual, *A Guide to Better Photography*, in 1941, a book of photographs titled *Greenwich Village Today and Yesterday* in 1949 and *A New Guide to Better Photography* in 1953. Her studies of motion and light contributed to the understanding of physical laws and the properties of liquids and solids. A series of photographs she made between 1958 and 1961 for Educational Services Inc. was circulated as an exhibition, the *Image of Physics*, by them and the Smithsonian Institution. Other scientific books for which she provided photographs included *Magnet* (1964) and *Motion* (1965), both by E. G. Valens.

Abbott continued to promote Atget's work in this period. She produced 100 copies of the *Eugène Atget Portfolio*, a selection of prints made from his original glass negatives, in 1956, and her *World of Atget* was published in 1964. Her efforts to secure his reputation culminated in the sale to the Museum of Modern Art, New York, in 1968 of the vast collection of Atget photographs, which became known as the Abbott-Levy Collection; four exhibitions from the Collection were later held there. Two books of Abbott's own photographs were published in the late 1960s: *A Portrait of Maine* (1968) and *The Attractive Universe* (1969). A retrospective exhibition of her work was held at the Museum of Modern Art in 1970. She was also awarded several honorary doctoral degrees. Despite her long and prolific career, Berenice Abbott will be remembered mainly for her distinctive architectural record of

New York in the 1930s and her powerfully revealing portraits of American expatriates and the fashionable/intellectual world of Paris in the 1920s.

ELAINE A. KING

Agar, Eileen
British painter, 1899–1991

Born in Buenos Aires, Argentina, 1 December 1899. Moved to England, 1906. Attended weekly classes at Byam Shaw School of Art, London, 1919–20; studied at Leon Underwood School of Painting and Sculpture, London, 1920–21; Slade School of Fine Art, London, 1922–4. Father died, leaving her a private income, 1925. Eloped to France with fellow student Robin Bartlett, 1925; divorced 1929. Lived with Hungarian writer Joseph Bard from 1926; married him 1940; he died 1975. Lived in France, 1928–30; studied briefly under Cubist painter Frantisek Foltyn in Paris, returning to London in 1930. Contributed to literary magazine the *Island*, edited by Bard, 1930–31. Joined London Group, 1933. Affair with Paul Nash, 1935–40. Spent summer of 1937 in Mougins with Nash, Nusch Eluard and Picasso. Included in *International Surrealist Exhibition*, New Burlington Galleries, London, 1936; also participated in International Surrealist exhibitions in New York (1936), Tokyo (1937), Paris (1938), Amsterdam (1938) and London (1940). Ceased painting during World War II. Lived in Kensington, London, from 1957, often spending winters in Canary Islands. Associate member, Royal Academy, 1990. Died in London, 17 November 1991.

Selected Individual Exhibitions
Bloomsbury Gallery, London: 1933
Redfern Gallery, London: 1942 (with Michael Rothenstein)
Leger Gallery, London: 1947
Hanover Gallery, London: 1949, 1951
Obelisk Gallery, London: 1957
Brook Street Gallery, London: 1962, 1964 (retrospective)
Galleria Billico, Rome: 1963
Commonwealth Art Gallery, London: 1971 (retrospective)
New Art Centre, London: 1975, 1976, 1978, 1981, 1983, 1984
Birch and Conran Fine Art, London: 1987 (retrospective)

Selected Writings
"Womb magic", *Island*, December 1931
A Look at My Life, London: Methuen, 1988 (with Andrew Lambirth)

Bibliography
International Surrealist Exhibition, exh. cat., New Burlington Galleries, London, 1936
Herbert Read, ed., *Surrealism*, London: Faber, and New York: Harcourt Brace, 1936
Eileen Agar: Retrospective, exh. cat., Commonwealth Art Gallery, London, 1971
Dada and Surrealism Reviewed, exh. cat., Arts Council of Great Britain, London, 1978
Thirties: British Art and Design Before the War, exh. cat., Arts Council of Great Britain, London, 1979
Dawn Ades, "Notes on two women Surrealist painters: Eileen Agar and Ithell Colquhoun", *Oxford Art Journal*, iii/1, 1980, pp.36–42
Eileen Agar: Paintings and Drawings, exh. cat., New Art Centre, London, 1981
Whitney Chadwick, *Women Artists and the Surrealist Movement*, London: Thames and Hudson, and Boston: Little Brown, 1985
A Salute to British Surrealism, 1930–1950, exh. cat., The Minories, Colchester, and elsewhere, 1985
Angels of Anarchy and Machines for Making Clouds: Surrealism in Britain in the Thirties, exh. cat., Leeds City Art Galleries, 1986
Eileen Agar: A Retrospective, exh. cat., Birch and Conran Fine Art, London, 1987
La Femme et le surréalisme, exh. cat., Musée Cantonal des Beaux-Arts, Lausanne, 1987
Teresa Grimes, Judith Collins and Oriana Baddeley, *Five Women Painters*, London: Lennard, 1989
Andrew Wilson, "The spirit of Surrealism", *Art Line Magazine*, 1989 (special supplement, with Birch and Conran Gallery, London)
Gill Houghton and Pauline Barrie, "Eileen Agar", *Women Artists Slide Library Journal*, no.27, February–March 1989, pp.5–7; no.28, April–May 1989, pp.20–21
Judith Young Mallin, "Eileen Agar", *Surrealism and Women*, ed. Mary Ann Caws and others, Cambridge: Massachusetts Institute of Technology Press, 1991, pp.213–27
Lillian Gethic, "Blazing a trail", *Feminist Art News*, iv/4, 1992, pp.8–9
Ten Decades: Careers of Ten Women Artists Born 1897–1906, exh. cat., Norwich Gallery, Norfolk Institute of Art and Design, Norwich, 1992
Brigitte Libmann, "British women Surrealists: Deviants from deviance", *This Working Day World: Social, Political and Cultural History of Women's Lives, 1914–45*, ed. Sybil Oldfield, London: Taylor and Francis, 1994, pp.156–8

Eileen Agar has the distinction of being the only British woman painter included in the International Surrealist exhibition of 1936, which launched Surrealism in Britain. With Emmy Bridgwater and Edith Rimmington, she remained one of the few women members of the British Surrealist Group organised around E.L.T. Mesens during the late 1930s and early 1940s. She survived the notorious argument in 1940 at the Barcelona Restaurant in London, when Mesens demanded that members exhibit only in Surrealist shows, because she alone was allowed dual membership of the Surrealist Group and the London Group. Many other artists, including Ithell Colquhoun, Toni del Renzio, Grace Pailthorpe and Reuben Mednikoff left at this point. Agar's adherence to Surrealist principles has resulted in her work appearing in nearly every retrospective and overview of British Surrealism since the 1930s.

Agar's early work of the late 1920s consisted of portraits and self-portraits produced in a loosely post-Impressionist style (e.g. *Self-Portrait*, 1927; National Portrait Gallery, London). Her early training was with Leon Underwood, where her peers included Henry Moore, Gertrude Hermes and the architect Rodney Thomas. She then moved to the Slade, and in 1925 eloped with a fellow student, Robin Bartlett, escaping her family and travelling to Paris and then Spain before settling in Normandy for the brief time that the marriage lasted. In 1926 she met Joseph Bard, a Hungarian writer and poet, moving to Paris with him in 1929. Here she studied briefly with the Cubist painter Foltyn, and met many avant-garde artists and writers. In the early 1930s she began experimenting with abstraction and the representation of space, producing such works as *Movement in Space* (1930–31), and began using collage and paper cut-outs in her work (*Three Symbols*, 1930; Tate Gallery, London). In her short essay "Womb magic" (1931) Agar discussed the dominance of a feminine type of imagination:

> Apart from rampant and hysterical militarism, there is no male element left in Europe, for the rational and intellectual conception of life has given way to a more miraculous creative interpretation and artistic imaginative life is under the sway of womb magic [quoted in Wilson 1989].

Many of the themes in her article are realised in *Autobiography of an Embryo* (1933–4; Tate Gallery), which mixes imagery of womb, egg and foetus and the languages of procreation and creation yet retains an organised classical structure. *Quadriga* (1935; Collection Roland Penrose) uses the horse motif from a Greek frieze, repeating the motif in each of the four divisions of the canvas and modulating the treatment of each.

Agar was selected for the Surrealist exhibition of 1936 by Paul Nash and Herbert Read, who were both "enchanted by the rare quality of her talent, the product of a highly sensitive imagination and a feminine clairvoyance" (Ades 1980, p.37). She showed three paintings and five objects at this exhibition. *Modern Muse* (1931), for example, offers a pictographic merging of male and female active and passive elements, linking both sexual and artistic imagery. She had met Nash in Swanage in the summer of 1935, and through him she developed her long-standing interest in the study of shells, fossils, plant life and the symbolic function of the natural world. Agar's *Seashore Monster* is a found object – an encrusted anchor chain – but it becomes a metaphor for Surrealist artistic creativity, created by nature, chance and man in equal combination.

In the late 1930s Agar made other experiments with found objects. Her work, including the first version of *Angel of Anarchy* (1937; destroyed), was illustrated in the *London (Gallery) Bulletin* and shown in the International Surrealist exhibition in Amsterdam in 1938. The second version (1940; Tate Gallery) has become widely reproduced as an iconic Surrealist object. In both, a plaster cast of Bard's head is transformed, in the first case through the addition of paint, feathers and collage, while in the second version the face is entirely wrapped in silk fabric and beads with additional feathers both "luxuriant and vaguely threatening". Other Surrealist objects include *Marine Object* (1939; Tate Gallery), *Ceremonial Hat for Eating Bouillabaisse* (1936; artist's estate) and *Fishbaskets* (1965; Tate Gallery). Collage and chance effects were also increasingly incorporated into her painting, as in *Battle Cry/Bullet-Proof Painting* (1938; Collection Gordon Onslow Ford), which uses lead paint and plaster on a metal surface, and *Precious Stones* (1936; Leeds City Art Galleries).

Agar's work was interrupted by the war effort, and she had great difficulty in re-establishing herself after it ended. In 1957 she painted *Bomber* (repr. London 1981), a memory of a holiday spent in the Canary Islands in the early 1950s, the first of many painting trips there. After 1965 she began painting in acrylics rather than oils and on a larger scale (122 × 152cm. as opposed to 50 × 76cm.), as in *Creatures of the Sea*, *Room with a View of the Moon*, *War Bride* and *Sleepwalkers*, all of which were exhibited in Agar's retrospective of 1987 that revived her career in the late 1980s, although *Slow Movement* (1970; Scottish National Gallery of Modern Art, Edinburgh) is executed in oil and pencil on canvas. Agar's works are often described as depending on auto-suggestion. She also represents the abstract wing of Surrealist painting. Her affairs with Nash and Eluard and her contact with most of the Surrealist circle in Paris during the 1930s have led to her characterisation as an archetypal Surrealist muse or "free and adored" woman. Although she was an independent woman with a private income, she nevertheless retained her commitment to painting throughout her life.

KATY DEEPWELL

Albers, Anni

German designer, weaver and graphic artist, 1899–1994

Born Annelise Fleischmann in Berlin, 12 June 1899. Studied art in Berlin under Martin Brandenburg, 1916–19. Studied at Kunstgewerbeschule, Hamburg, 1919–20; Bauhaus in Weimar, 1922–5, in Dessau, 1925–9 (Bauhaus diploma 1930). Worked independently in Dessau then Berlin, 1930–33; also part-time instructor and acting director of the Bauhaus weaving workshop. Married artist Josef Albers, 1925; he died 1976. Emigrated to USA, November 1933; became US citizen, 1937. Assistant professor of art, Black Mountain College, North Carolina, 1933–49. Moved to New York, 1949; first weaver to have a solo exhibition at Museum of Modern Art. Moved to New Haven, on Josef Albers's appointment to Chair of Design at Yale University, 1950. Turned to printmaking, 1963. Recipient of medal for craftsmanship, American Institute of Architects, 1961; fellowship, Tamarind Lithography Workshop, Los Angeles, 1964; gold medal for "uncompromising excellence", American Crafts Council, 1980; honorary doctorates from Maryland Institute College of Art, Baltimore, 1972; York University, Toronto, 1973; Philadelphia

College of Art, 1976; University of Hartford, Connecticut, 1979; Rhode Island School of Design, Providence, 1990; Royal College of Art, London, 1990. Died 9 May 1994.

Selected Individual Exhibitions

Museum of Modern Art, New York: 1949, 1990
Wadsworth Atheneum, Hartford: 1953
Massachusetts Institute of Technology, Cambridge: 1959
Carnegie Institute, Pittsburgh: 1959
Yale University Art Gallery, New Haven: 1959
Colorado Springs Fine Arts Center: 1959
Contemporary Art Museum, Houston: 1960
Kunstmuseum der Stadt, Düsseldorf: 1975
Bauhaus-Archiv, Museum für Gestaltung, Berlin: 1975
Brooklyn Museum, NY: 1977
Queen's College Library, New York: 1979
Galerie Denise René, Paris: 1984
Renwick Gallery, National Museum of American Art, Smithsonian Institution, Washington, DC: 1985–6 (touring retrospective)
Mary Ryan Gallery, New York: 1989
Villa Stuck, Munich: 1989 (with Josef Albers)

Selected Writings

"Work with material", *Black Mountain College Bulletin*, v, 1938; reprinted in *College Art Journal*, iii, January 1944, pp.51–4
"Handweaving today: Textile work at Black Mountain College", *Weaver*, vi, January–February 1941, pp.3–7
"We need crafts for their contact with materials", *Design*, xlvi, December 1944, pp.21–2
"Fabrics", *Arts and Architecture*, lxv, March 1948, p.33
"Weavings", *Arts and Architecture*, lxvi, February 1949, p.24
"Ben Nicholson: Paintings, reliefs, drawings … 1948", *Magazine of Art*, xliii, January 1950, p.36 (review)
"Fabric: The pliable plane", *Craft Horizons*, xviii, July–August 1958, pp.15–17
On Designing, New Haven: Pellango Press, 1959
On Weaving, Middletown, CT: Wesleyan University Press, 1965; London: Studio Vista, 1966
Pre-Columbian Mexican Miniatures: The Josef and Anni Albers Collection, New York: Praeger, and London: Lund Humphries, 1970

Bibliography

Bauhaus, 1919–1928, exh. cat., Museum of Modern Art, New York, 1938; reprinted New York: Arno Press, and London: Secker and Warburg, 1975
Josef and Anni Albers: Paintings, Tapestries and Woven Textiles, exh. cat., Wadsworth Atheneum, Hartford, 1953
Anni Albers: Pictorial Weavings, exh. cat., Massachusetts Institute of Technology, Cambridge, 1959
Nell Welliver, "A conversation with Anni Albers", *Craft Horizons*, xxv, July–August 1965, pp.17–21, 40–45

Wall Hangings, 2 vols, exh. cat., Museum of Modern Art, New York, 1969

Louise Bourgeois, "The fabric of construction", *Craft Horizons*, xxix, March–April 1969, pp.30–31

Eckhard Neumann, *Bauhaus and Bauhaus People*, New York: Van Nostrand Reinhold, 1970

Martin Duberman, *Black Mountain: An Exploration in Community*, New York: Dutton, 1972; London: Wildwood House, 1974

Nicholas Fox Weber, "Anni Albers and the printerly image", *Art in America*, lxiii, July–August 1975, p.89

Hans M. Wingler, *The Bauhaus: Weimar, Dessau, Berlin, Chicago*, 3rd edition, Cambridge: Massachusetts Institute of Technology Press, 1976 (German original)

Anni Albers: Drawings and Prints, exh. cat., Brooklyn Museum, NY, 1977

Anni Albers: Prints and Drawings, exh. cat., University Art Gallery, University of California, Riverside, 1980

Mildred Constantine and Jack Lenor Larsen, *The Art Fabric: Mainstream*, New York: Van Nostrand Reinhold, 1980

Nicholas Fox Weber, "Weaving wonders", *House and Garden*, clvii, July 1985, pp.58–63

The Woven and Graphic Art of Anni Albers, exh. cat., Renwick Gallery, National Museum of American Art, Smithsonian Institution, Washington, DC, and elsewhere, 1985 (contains extensive bibliography)

Howard Dearstyne, *Inside the Bauhaus*, ed. David Spaeth, New York: Rizzoli, and London: Architectural Press, 1986

Bauhaus Weaving Workshop: Source and Influence for American Textiles, exh. cat., Philadelphia College of Textiles and Science, 1987

Mary Emma Harris, *The Arts at Black Mountain College*, Cambridge: Massachusetts Institute of Technology Press, 1987

Karl Taube, *The Albers Collection of Pre-Columbian Art*, New York: Hudson Hills Press, 1988

Anni und Josef Albers: Eine Retrospektive, exh. cat., Villa Stuck, Munich, 1989

Sigrid Wortmann Weltge, *Bauhaus Textiles: Women Artists and the Weaving Workshop*, London: Thames and Hudson, 1993; as *Women's Work: Textile Art from the Bauhaus*, San Francisco: Chronicle, 1993

In 1922, when the world seemed to her "a tangle of hopelessness" and "undirected energy", Anni Albers, newly arrived at the Bauhaus in Weimar, recognised that here was a place for "taking chances", for experimentation, which, though often "groping and fumbling", had purpose and direction. In the ten years that followed, Annelise Fleischmann, neophyte and student, grew to be Anni Albers, artist, designer and teacher. Her early sense of the order and clarity that art offered crystallised into a clear comprehension of the primacy and potential of materials and of the enduring aesthetic power of good design. In 1984, towards the end of a creatively rich, varied and eventful working life, she would write: "… to comprehend art is to confide in a constant" (Washington 1985, p.13). Although she did not choose it, once assigned to the Bauhaus weaving workshop, Albers quickly recognised that weaving was a medium that, far from being "sissy" and weak as she had suspected, engaged the artist in an intense struggle. Weaving started from a zero point. Its material, the thread, was a simple yet infinite line. Unlike a line drawn or painted on a surface it was tangible. Its matrix, the loom – a simple structure of lines and intervals (warp and weft) – challenged and teased the artist into "building a fabric out of thread" (*On Designing* 1959, p.14). Weaving provided "the stimulation and source for inventiveness that may come in the course of struggling with a hard-to-handle material" (*ibid.*, p.63).

Albers's weavings from the Bauhaus period, and the delicate, intricately beautiful designs in gouache on graph paper on which they were based, reveal a clear and logical development. The relative simplicity of an early piece such as *Untitled Wall Hanging* (1924; Busch-Reisinger Museum, Harvard University, Cambridge, MA) – with its flat, symmetrical, undifferentiated bands of muted beiges and greys – soon evolved into the complexity of the originally brilliantly coloured, though now faded, triple weave *Black-White-Red* (1927; private collection, Germany). A limited edition of five reproductions was made in 1964 (example in Bauhaus-Archiv, Berlin). As the eye scrutinises such works as *Black-White-Red* and *Black-White-Grey* (1927; Bauhaus-Archiv, Berlin), it searches to reconstruct the underlying patterns. The seeming clarity of composition is undercut by the tantalising and elusive configurations that defy easy assimilation. An apparently ordered, rectilinear arrangement turns out to be a challenging visual exploration. The viewer is held to attention and not let off the hook lightly. For her diploma project at the Bauhaus in 1930 Albers produced a drapery fabric of cotton chenille and cellophane to be used as a stage curtain in the Bundeschule auditorium in Bernau. This innovative material was not simply a demonstration of virtuosity but in perfect accord with the function of the drapes. The outer shiny surface reflected light into the auditorium, while the sound-absorbent underside concealed behind-the-stage noises from the audience.

In the USA, at Black Mountain College from 1933 to 1949, and then in New Haven, Albers continued to teach, to write about her work and to test the limits of her art. She revered the ancient textile artists of Peru whose work she studied, collected and treasured. It provided lessons in versatility and inventiveness that she regarded as the essence of hand-weaving. By the 1940s, however, she believed that the increasing mechanisation of industrial production was seriously diminishing the weaver's capacity for invention. Although advanced technology had produced marvellous, sparkling synthetic fibres and finishes as well as newly brilliant colours, "the spontaneous shaping of a material has been lost and the blueprint has taken over" (*ibid.*, p.13). To counteract the resulting "barrenness in today's weaving", Albers advocated a rapprochement between hand-weaving and industrial production. The revolutionary fibres would benefit from innovative methods of construction that only the hand-weaver could develop. Her own work was a practical demonstration of these beliefs. She pioneered the use of non-traditional materials. Working with textile manufacturers, she executed architectural commissions – among them the design of drapery materials of cotton chenille, copper Lurex and white plastic thread (1944) for Philip Johnson's Rockefeller Guest House in Manhattan, and draperies and bedspreads for dormitory rooms in Walter Gropius's Harvard Graduate Center (1949–50). Similar ground-breaking fabrics were shown in the exhibition of her work at the Museum of Modern Art in 1949. Convinced of the links between well-designed textiles and architecture – between the aesthetic and the practical – Albers had her materials fashioned into room-dividing screens. These, uniquely, combined complicated open-weave patterns, shimmering synthetic fibres and dust-repellent finishes. At the same time she took her more private work in a new direction and made "pictorial weavings" – small-scale pieces that asserted their own integrity as complete works of art. In *Development in Rose II* (1952; Art Institute of Chicago) a subtle and delicate range of coloured linen threads – beiges, pinks, greys, blacks and touches of green – unfolds in a virtuoso array of weaving patterns. Tightly woven borders are juxtaposed with an irregular open-weave matrix traversed by horizontal lines tied together by looping threads – all in a small

(63 × 45 cm.) format. Stacks of horizontal lines created by looped weft threads first appeared in *Ancient Writing* (1936; National Museum of American Art, Smithsonian Institution, Washington, DC) and Albers developed the calligraphic associations of the woven line further in a pair of small works, *Haiku* and *Code* (both 1961; Josef and Anni Albers Foundation, Orange), and in the large composite *Six Prayers* (1967; Jewish Museum, New York).

In 1963, at the Tamarind Lithography Workshop in California, Albers made her first prints. In 1947 she had created gouaches in which magnified, intricately looped images of threads were delineated against a painterly background. Now she translated these into a pair of lithographs, *Enmeshed I and II*, and a pair of screenprints *Untitled I and II*. These were followed in 1964 by a portfolio of seven *Line Involvements*. Freed from the constraints of warp and weft Albers could now, in Paul Klee's phrase, "take a line for a walk". As she had done in her weaving, Albers produced prints of great spatial and textural complexity from a deliberately limited vocabulary of forms. In the *Meander* prints (repr. Washington 1985, pl.40) the ancient motif is repeated and superimposed in subtly modulated tones to create an abstract surface that continually invites the eye to explore depth and surface. In the screenprints *Camino Real* (1967–9; *ibid.*, pl.35), *GRI* and other related series, she used simple repeated triangles and the intervals between them to conjure dynamic symphonies of colour, form and space in which background and foreground are linked in pulsating relationships. In *Orchestra I* (1979; *ibid.*, fig.85) and *Letter* (1980; *ibid.*, fig.86) it is the outlines of the familiar triangles that serve as musical and calligraphic metaphors. Whether weaving, drawing or making prints, Anni Albers was a fearless artist, living and working according to her own stated tenets: "We learn courage from art work ... We learn to dare to make a choice, to be independent" (*On Designing* 1959, p.31).

BRENDA DANILOWITZ

Alletit *see* Bertaux

Amaral, Tarsila do [fig. 1]
Brazilian painter, 1886–1973

Born on a farm in Capivari, in the interior of São Paulo state, 1886. Studied painting in São Paulo, 1916–17, and at the Académie Julian, Paris, 1920–21. Formed Grupo dos Cinco in São Paulo, 1922. Further studies in Paris under André Lhôte, Fernand Léger and Albert Gleizes, 1922 and 1922–3. Joined Pau-Brasil group to explore artistic heritage of Brazil, 1923. Married poet Oswald de Andrade in São Paulo, 1926; divorced 1930. Visited Soviet Union, 1931. Represented Brazil at Venice Biennale, 1960. Died in São Paulo, 1973.

Selected Individual Exhibitions
Galerie Percier, Paris: 1926, 1928
Museum of Modern Western Art, Moscow: 1931
Museu de Arte Moderna, São Paulo: 1950 (retrospective)
São Paulo Bienal: 1963
Museu de Arte Moderna, Rio de Janeiro: 1969–70
  (touring retrospective)

Bibliography

Oswald de Andrade, "Manifesto da Poesia Pau-Brasil", *Correo da Manha* (Rio de Janeiro), 18 March 1924
——, "Manifesto Antropofago", *Revista de Antropofagia* (São Paulo), no.1, 1928
Mário de Andrade and others, *Revista Academica: Homenagem a Tarsila*, Rio de Janeiro, 1940
Sérgio Milliet, *Tarsila do Amaral*, São Paulo: Artistas Brasileiros Contemporaneos, 1953
Aracy Amaral, *Desenhos de Tarsila*, São Paulo: Cultrix, 1971
——, *Tarsila: Sua obra e seu tempo*, 2 vols, São Paulo: Perspectiva, 1975
Tarsila: Obras, 1920/1930, exh. cat., IBM do Brasil, São Paulo, 1982
Nadia Batella Gotlib, *Tarsila do Amaral: A musa radiante*, São Paulo: Editora Brasiliense, 1983
Carlos Lemos and others, *The Art of Brazil*, New York: Harper, 1983
Marcos A. Marcondes, *Tarsila*, São Paulo: Art, 1986
Art of the Fantastic: Latin America, 1920–1987, exh. cat., Indianapolis Museum of Art and elsewhere, 1987
Art in Latin America: The Modern Era, 1820–1980, exh. cat., South Bank Centre, London, and elsewhere, 1989
Oriana Baddeley and Valerie Fraser, *Drawing the Line: Art and Cultural Identity in Contemporary Latin America*, London and New York: Verso, 1989
Stella de Sá Rego, "Pau-Brasil: Tarsila do Amaral", *Latin American Art*, ii, Winter 1990, pp.18–22
Latin American Artists of the Twentieth Century, exh. cat., Museum of Modern Art, New York, 1993

It was in Paris that the Brazilian artist Tarsila do Amaral awakened to the significance of exotic and primitive subject matter for the avant-garde and realised that she could look to her own country for inspiration. Tarsila do Amaral and her future husband, the poet Oswald de Andrade, went to Paris for the first of many visits in 1920, when the fascination with the exotic cultures and art forms of the New World and Africa was at its height. It was a period dominated by the masters of Cubism, Futurism and Expressionism, and Tarsila took advantage of her stays in Paris to study with Fernand Léger and Albert Gleizes. She learned the basic tenets of abstract composition and how to create flat arrangements of pictorial construction.

In 1923 Amaral and Andrade returned to São Paulo, where a young group of artists and intellectuals had already begun to question the realities of Brazil's identity and the controlling forms of European art and culture that had little to do with the country in the 20th century. Their activism and desire for renewal in Brazilian culture encouraged the first movement towards modernism in the country and the use of new forms of technique and expression outside the rules of the academic system. Inspired by their message, the two artists became active in this burgeoning avant-garde and the highly creative environment of São Paulo in the 1920s. In keeping with the group's interest in Brazil's indigenous culture, Amaral and Andrade were determined to explore their own land, its vibrant ethnic mixture, the colonial architecture, festivals and African rhythms. In 1924 they embarked on a voyage of discovery that took them from Carnival in Rio to the gold-filled colonial churches of Minas Girais to the remote interior. Filled with a new visual aesthetic, Amaral wanted to apply the lessons of European modernism to create a unique vocabulary based on Brazilian nativist themes and subjects. In 1924 Andrade wrote the "Manifesto da Poesia Pau-Brasil" presenting their avant-garde attitudes regarding the popular and nativist culture of the country. Pau-Brasil is a reference to the indigenous dye-wood (Brazilwood) that gave the country its name and was the first important resource for export in colonial trade. Amaral gave artistic form to Andrade's words by creating paintings celebrating the landscape, the impact of industrialisation and modernisation, and the traditions of the indigenous people. The first of her Pau-Brasil paintings is *EFCB (Estrada de Ferro Central do Brasil/Brazilian*

Central Railway) (1924; Museu de Arte Contemporânea da Universidade de São Paulo, Brazil). The industrialised city with its railway spans, telephone lines and traffic signals is reduced to flat patterns of bright colours and given a Brazilian flavour by the addition of palm trees and the silhouette of a colonial church on the horizon. The intense colours of the tropics, the festivals and folk arts and crafts contrast vividly with the heavy black contours symbolising industrialisation and make an obvious comment about the duality of living in a tropical/primitivist environment that is also modern. Rapidly perfecting a method of stylised representation of Brazilian subjects set within solid Cubist compositions, Amaral incorporated tropical flora and fauna, the *mestizo* and black populations of the small towns, rural villages and city boundaries in an intense palette based on the popular arts and crafts of the people. She painted a number of cityscapes and landscapes during this period, including *Hillside of Shanty Towns* (1924; private collection) and *São Paulo* (1924; private collection), that are specific to São Paulo, with its colonial city sprawling outwards to incorporate the shanty towns (*favelas*) crawling up its hillsides with their predominantly Afro and mulatto populations.

After her marriage to Andrade in 1926, Amaral began the next series of works, a tropical-surrealist approach to her nativist aesthetic described as Antropofagia. The Antropofagia movement occupied the São Paulo avant-garde in the mid-1920s and stood for artistic independence from European domination. Tarsila's first work in the series was a present to her husband entitled *Abaporú* (1928; Collection Maria Anna and Raul de Souza Dantas Forbes, São Paulo). Translated "man who eats" from the Tupi-Guarani Indian language, *Abaporú* is a huge solitary figure with enormous feet sitting on a bright green patch of land and leaning his tiny head on his hand. Behind him a blazing lemon-slice moon and simplified cactus plant dominate the landscape. Rooted to the soil with his foot, he may be an imaginary descendant of mythical creatures called *sciapods* described in classical mythology as members of monstrous races that entered into the lore of the voyages of exploration and became conflated with stories of cannibals. Amaral used the image as a symbol of the primordial people rooted in the earth and inspired Andrade to publish his "Manifesto Antropofagia" or "Cannibalist Manifesto" two months later, initiating a more

aggressive attitude towards nativist subjects for both of them. As a metaphor for Brazil's dependency on European culture, the cannibal represents the conquering, not the conquered people, and calls for Brazilians to revolt against those elements that represent European aesthetics, past and present. The sequel painting, *Antropofagia* (1929; Foundation José and Paulina Nemirovsky), celebrates the fertility of the land with the *Abaporú* entwined with a female creature whose enlarged breast hangs over his knee. Tropical plants, banana leaves and cacti frame the background and the lemon-slice sun shines benevolently above. Rendered with the utmost simplicity, devoid of all extraneous details, the canvas is painted with smooth strokes and minimal colours, placing emphasis on the iconography of the land that is inseparable from its creatures. The same attention to a fantasy landscape with surreal creatures and distortions is present in *Setting Sun* (1929; Collection Jean Boghici, Rio de Janeiro). The world of nature appears untouched by human beings and sways with rhythmic grace as the flora and fauna come to life under the watchful gaze of the setting sun. Five Amazon otters (*ariranhas*) swim placidly through the water, the only occupants of the dreamlike scene.

Amaral's surreal representations of the land pay tribute to the beauty of the Brazilian environment and make a prophetic statement about the disastrous consequences of man's careless exploitation of nature, 50 years before the destruction of Brazil's rain forests was an issue of international concern. The same message appears as a subtle undercurrent in *Forest* (1929; Museu de Arte Contemporánea da Universidade de São Paulo), in which the pristine and elemental forces of nature are reduced to four abstract elements: eggs, trees, land and dead tree trunks. Each one is symbolic in the cycle of nature, from the fertility of the land represented by the egg to its death and destruction represented by the dead tree trunks. The contrast between life and death, before and after, is a powerful statement about the value of nature. The dead trunks, standing like sentinels on the horizon, fade into the distance of the desolate landscape, marking the future of the eggs in time and space.

In 1931 Amaral visited the Soviet Union to organise an exhibition in Moscow and was deeply affected by the social conditions suffered by the Russian people. On her return to Brazil she began a series of works based on social commentary. The faces of the people change with the palette as she captures Russian poverty in *2nd Class* (1931; Collection Fanny Feffer, São Paulo). Working with the same sensitivity she applied to representations of the people of Brazil, Tarsila paints a portrait of dejection and sadness of universal significance. After her divorce from Andrade in 1930 interrupted the production of her painting, Amaral continued with themes of social realism in her paintings of the late 1930s and 1940s. The 1950s were years of widespread acceptance with successful exhibitions in Brazil, and in 1960 she represented Brazil at the Venice Biennale. She worked in the country outside São Paulo until her death.

The paintings of Tarsila do Amaral represent more than a break from rigid and conservative academic standards. As one of the most important early modernists of South America, she sought themes and subjects based on her own land and people and depicted them according to contemporary systems of abstraction and expression. She worked with a sincerity of purpose and unique vision and style to create an image of an ideal, invented world that was quintessentially Brazilian.

CAROL DAMIAN

Ancher, Anna [fig. 2]
Danish painter, 1859–1935

Born Anna Kirstine Brøndum in Skagen, 18 August 1859; father a hotelier. Studied drawing and colour theory at Vilhelm Kyhn's academy in Copenhagen, winters 1875–8. Married painter Michael Ancher, 1880; daughter Helga, also a painter, born 1883; husband died 1927. Visited Göteborg, Sweden, 1881; Germany and Vienna, 1882; Paris, Amsterdam and Belgium, 1885. Spent winter of 1888–9 in Paris; studied under Puvis de Chavannes in Léon Bonnat's studio. Trips to Berlin and the Netherlands, 1891; Italy, 1897 and 1924; Germany (Berlin, Dresden), 1900. Recipient of first-class medal, Royal Danish Academy of Fine Arts, Copenhagen, 1903; second-class Eckersberg medal, Copenhagen, 1904; Ingenio et Arti medal, Copenhagen, 1913. Member of Academy Plenum Assembly (Plenarforsamling), Copenhagen, 1904. Died in Skagen, 15 April 1935.

Principal Exhibitions

Charlottenborg, Copenhagen: 1880–1927, 1929–35 (salons), 1935 (retrospective)
Exposition Universelle, Paris: 1889 (silver medal), 1900 (medal)
Kunstforening, Copenhagen: 1890 (*En samling moderne dansk kunst* [A collection of modern Danish art])
Internationale Kunstausstellung, Berlin: 1891 (honourable mention)
World's Columbian Exposition, Chicago: 1893
Industriforeningen, Copenhagen: 1895 (*Kvindernes udstilling – fra fortid til nutid* [Women's exhibition – from the past to the present])
Guildhall, London: 1907 (*Works by Danish Painters*)
Landsudstilling (National Exhibition), Århus: 1909
Esposizione Internazionale, Rome: 1911
Public Art Galleries, Brighton, Sussex: 1912 (*Modern Danish Artists*)
Den frie udstillingsbygning, Copenhagen: 1920 (*Kvindelige kunstneres retrospektive udstilling* [Women artists' retrospective]), 1930 (*Kvindelige kunstneres Samfund* [Society of Women Artists])
Brooklyn Museum, NY: 1927 (*Danish National Exhibition of Paintings, Sculpture, Architecture and Applied Art*)
Jeu de Paume, Paris: 1928 (*L'Art danois*)

Selected Writings

Breve fra Anna Ancher [Letters from Anna Ancher], ed. Knud Voss, Copenhagen: Herluf Stokholm, 1984

Bibliography

Alba Schwartz, *Skagen: Den svundne tid i sagn og billeder* [Skagen: Legends and pictures of times gone by], 1912; revised edition, Skagen: Skagens Museum, 1992
——, *Skagen: Før og nu* [Skagen: Before and now], 1913; revised edition, Skagen: Skagens Museum, 1992
Karl Madsen, *Skagens malere* [Skagen painters], Copenhagen: Gyldendal, 1929
Walther Schwartz, "Skagens datter" [Skagen's daughter], *Politiken*, 1939; reprinted in *De glade farvers fest* [Festival of gay colours], Copenhagen: Schwartz & Fisker, 1989, pp.41–53
Ernst Mentze, *P.S. Krøyer*, Copenhagen: Det Schønbergske Forlag, 1969
Knud Voss, *Skagensmaleren Anna Ancher, 1859–1935* [The Skagen painter Anna Ancher], Tølløse: Stok-Art, 1974
Margrethe Loerges, *Et solstrejf i en stue i Skagen: Portræt af Anna Ancher* [Flickering sunlight in a room in Skagen: A portrait of Anna Ancher], Copenhagen: Hernov, 1978
Henri Usselmann, *Complexité et importance des contacts des peintres nordiques avec l'impressionisme*, PhD dissertation, University of Göteborg, 1979
Danske kvindelige kunstnere fra det 19. og 20. århundrede repræsenteret på Statens Museum for Kunst

[Danish women artists from the 19th and 20th centuries represented in the Statens Art Museum], exh. cat., Statens Museum for Kunst, Copenhagen, 1980

Knud Voss, *Mennesker og kunst på Skagen* [People and art in Skagen], Skagen: Skagens Museum, 1982

Bente Scavenius, *Fremsyn – snœversyn: Dansk Dagbladskunstkritik, 1880–1901* [Forward looking – inward looking: Danish newspaper art criticism, 1880–1901], Copenhagen: Borgen, 1983

Margrethe Loerges, *Anna Ancher*, Copenhagen: Andersen, 1984

1880-årene i nordisk maleri [The 1880s in Nordic painting], exh. cat., Nasjonalgalleriet, Oslo, and elsewhere, 1985

Dreams of a Summer Night: Scandinavian Painting at the Turn of the Century, exh. cat., Arts Council of Great Britain, London, 1986

Kvindelige kunstnere på Skagen: Anna Ancher, Oda Krohg, Marie Krøyer [Women artists in Skagen], exh. cat., Moss (Oslo), Skagens Museum, Skagen, and elsewhere, 1987

Ole Wivel, *Anna Ancher*, Tølløse: Stok-Art, 1987 (in Danish and English)

De drogo till Paris: Nordiska konstnärinnor på 1880-talet [They went to Paris: Nordic women artists in the 1880s], exh. cat., Liljevalchs Konsthall, Stockholm, 1988

Kirk Varnedoe, *Northern Light: Nordic Art at the Turn of the Century*, New Haven and London: Yale University Press, 1988

Alessandra Comini, "Nordic luminism and the Scandinavian recasting of Impressionism", *World Impressionism: The International Movement, 1860–1920*, ed. Norma Broude, New York: Abrams, 1992, pp.274–313

Elisabeth Fabritius, *Michael Anchers ungdom, 1865–1880* [Michael Ancher's youth], 2 vols, Skagen: Helga Anchers Fond, 1992– (second volume in preparation)

Hans Dam Christensen, "Anna Ancher og den kunsthistoriske litteratur" [Anna Ancher and the art historical literature], *Periskop*, i/1, June 1993, pp.9–23

Anna Ancher, 1859–1935, exh. cat., Niedersächsisches Landesmuseum, Hannover, and elsewhere, 1994

Anna Ancher occupies a special place in Danish art. She was the only accomplished woman painter and native *Skagener* in the influential colony of artists that flourished in Skagen, Denmark's northernmost peninsula, during the 1880s and early 1890s. As a summer destination, Skagen attracted artists from all over Scandinavia who came to practise the radical new French figure and plein-air painting in the brilliant northern light and to exchange ideas from their foreign travels. From the time that P.S. Krøyer – the only member of the colony with an international reputation – returned from his extensive foreign travels in 1882, the nucleus of the colony was formed by Anna, her husband Michael Ancher and Krøyer. Michael Ancher had left the Academy in Copenhagen without a diploma and gone to Skagen in search of primitivist motifs in 1874. His heroic portrayals of Skagen fishermen and Krøyer's impressionistic paintings of artists' lunch parties and evening strolls on beaches have created a mythology for the area. Ancher was at the centre of this mythology, the pivot around which the drama of the artists' lives was wound, who managed to find time to paint in between her duties as wife, hostess, mother and daughter. She observed from nature and absorbed from her male colleagues what she needed in order to find her own expressive voice. Her artistic independence was remarkable. and all the more remarkable is the modernity of her idiom, with its reduced, abstracting forms and bold expressive colours, singling her out as one of the most innovative painters of her generation, exceeding most of her male colleagues, including her husband.

Her achievements and contribution to the modern breakthrough in Danish art were recognised during her lifetime. In Paris she was awarded medals for her entries in the Expositions Universelles of 1889 and 1900, when she was one of only two Danish painters to be mentioned favourably by the French critics. She won medals at other international exhibitions and in Denmark, where she regularly entered her work for the Charlottenborg exhibitions and at the various other venues that began to appear from the early 1890s; she was generally well reviewed. She was awarded membership of the Academy Plenum Assembly and in 1913 she received the Ingenio et Arti medal from the Danish king. She won the respect and admiration of her male colleagues for the sincerity of her human portrayal as well as the simplified form and light-suffused colour that lend mood and atmosphere to her mostly small and intimate oil paintings. Her increasing interest in mood and Symbolism is reflected in a small number of interiors and landscapes that are empty of human presence, but the human figure remained central to her work. Her family and the working people of her immediate surroundings provided her with subject matter.

After Ancher's death her reputation waned. After the discovery, in the artist's family house in Skagen in 1964, of a chest full of unknown works by her – mainly studies and sketches in oil – a renewed interest manifested itself in a number of exhibitions over the next three decades, culminating in a major retrospective mounted in Germany in 1994 and touring to Copenhagen and Skagen in 1995.

There has been a consistent failure to address seriously the issues of gender and representation that affected Ancher's work, yet the issue of gender is important in a critical appraisal of it. As a woman she would never have become a painter if it were not for her exceptional circumstances. At a time when Danish women did not have the vote and were barred from entry to the Academy schools, it was unthinkable for a woman outside an inner circle to pursue art professionally. Prevailing prejudices combined with women's own internalised expectations and demands made it difficult and frightening for women to compete as equals with men. The fact that Ancher was born and brought up in Brøndum's Inn, Skagen, owned by her family and later to win fame as a home and meeting place for artists, gave her an unusual entrée to the exclusive male domain of art. In her own home she was able to learn from the visiting artists, watch them work and see their copies of the great masters brought home from foreign trips. She received drawing lessons from Karl Madsen, who was to become an influential critic and the Skagen Museum's first director, and at the age of 16 she became engaged to Michael Ancher. From then on his support and encouragement were crucial to Ancher's development, although she never allowed him or anyone else to influence her to the exclusion of her own inner vision. When she married Michael Ancher on her 21st birthday she had spent three successive winters in Copenhagen taking classes in drawing and colour theory at the school run by the academic professor and landscape painter Vilhelm Kyhn, who had little faith in her talent and advised her to give up painting and devote herself to her domestic responsibilities as a wife. Kyhn's lack of support was compensated for by her husband's encouragement. The painting *Assessing the Day's Work* (1883; Statens Museum for Kunst, Copenhagen), on which both artists worked, is an exceptional visual record of a husband-and-wife team of painters. Without Michael's support, it is doubtful that Ancher would have had the confidence and courage to exhibit her works at the Charlottenborg exhibitions in Copenhagen – the Danish equivalent of the Paris Salon. Most of the women who exhibited at the Academy were flower painters. As such, they were acknowledged as professional artists but were not valued highly by the critics.

Ancher, on the other hand, enjoyed critical and popular acclaim from an early age. Aged only 19 she had her exhibition début at the Academy (Charlottenborg) with a rather naive composition of an old couple in a landscape. It was, somewhat mercifully, ignored by the critics, but the following year she had her first excellent review for the portrait of *Lars Gaihede Whittling a Stick* (1880; Skagens Museum). Its detailed drawing and mixed browns and blues show the influence of Michael Ancher, but the psychological depth of the characterisation exceeded Michael's own portrayals of the same sitter. Ancher did not pursue the style, however, but was far more attracted to the new French ideas introduced to her by Krøyer and the Norwegian painter Christian Krohg, friend of the Impressionists in Paris and teacher and mentor of Edvard Munch. Krøyer's lighter palette and fine understanding of figure and light as well as Krohg's fuller and more vibrant use of colour and the way he cut his compositions at the edges became part of Ancher's vocabulary.

The winter she spent in Paris (1888–9) increased her confidence. She won a silver medal at the Exposition Universelle and spent much time absorbing impressions of Paris. She enjoyed watching the faces of the customers when dining in a coachmen's café and was altogether enchanted, as she wrote, with the indigenous working people who reminded her of her favourite characters in Zola's novels. Sadly, the only work that has come to light from this extended visit to Paris is a portrait of the Norwegian woman painter *Kitty Kielland* (1889; Michael og Anna Anchers Hus, Skagen), which excels in the psychological depth of its characterisation. Ancher enrolled for classes with Puvis de Chavannes at a studio run by Léon Bonnat, a favourite with the Nordic artists. Her interest in modern colour theory and Symbolism would account for this choice; Puvis's colour treatment was considered very modern by Danish critics. When painting her subsequent group compositions, the best of which is *A Funeral* (1890; Statens Museum for Kunst), composed in clear pinks and dark blues, Ancher may have been influenced by Puvis. But her contact with French Impressionism exerted an even greater influence. It has been said that she was deeply impressed with the work of Manet, Degas and the other Impressionists. *Sunshine in the Blue Room* (1891; Skagens Museum), painted not long after her return from Paris, can be seen as an important Impressionist breakthrough in Skagen. It depicts a domestic interior with a child: a rhapsody of colour and light in which the room and the little girl, sitting in a chair below the window, are subordinated to the colours of the light that falls in from the window, across the girl's blonde hair on to the wall and the carpet. The colours are applied directly on to the canvas, not mixed first. Coloured light guides our gaze from the detailed yellows, gold and blues of the window side of the composition across to the wall and down to the solitary little figure in her chair, where the pale blues of the reflected light on the wall are echoed on the back of her dress.

The sitter for the painting was Ancher and Michael's only child, Helga. When she was born in 1883 Ancher had recently started painting the *Maid in the Kitchen* (1883–6; Hirschsprung Collection, Copenhagen), but she did not finish it until three years later. Its colours are brilliant and vibrant: the kitchen interior is bathed in a warm, diffused sunlight, filtered through a yellow curtain that highlights the contrasting red and black of the clothes worn by the maid, who is shown from the back. Ancher had seen works by Vermeer and de Hooch in Vienna before starting the painting, but although the picture owes a debt to the Dutch masters, her experience of motherhood during the intervening years may have given her a heightened awareness of the isolation of the woman's sphere that may account for the quiet melancholy of the composition. The ray of light from the window creates the same sense of distinction between the exterior and the interior that is such a strong feature of the painting she had done the previous year, *Sunshine in the Blind Woman's Room* (1885; Hirschsprung Collection). The sense of remoteness and isolation created by this distinction between the public and private spheres is a recurrent feature of Ancher's paintings of women in interiors. From *Young Girl Arranging Flowers* (1885; Aarhus Kunstmuseum, Århus) and *Young Girl Before a Lamp* (1887) to *Young Girl in front of a Mirror* (1899; both Skagens Museum), Ancher depicts women who seem remote, isolated and evasive as subjects. Portrayed from the back, looking down or with their faces hidden, they are never part of the light and joy that Ancher always locates outside their sphere.

Nevertheless, there is in all these interiors also a poignant sense of intimacy, created by the way the end wall of the composition is always parallel to the picture plane, reminding us that these are flat surfaces of paint. After the turn of the century, Ancher's concern with the surface of the canvas led her to paint increasingly reduced forms and to use bolder colours. The interiors that she now painted are often empty of people and she attempted landscapes, which are rare among her oeuvre and hardly count for anything in her reputation as an artist. She seems to compose in abstract masses of colour and light. *Interior with Chair and Plant* (undated) reveals her awareness of both Fauvism and Expressionism, as do the two empty interiors *Midday Hour, Interior* (1914) and *Interior with Sunlight and Red Door* (1918; all Skagens Museum). In her late landscapes there is a strong atmospheric quality; one senses the midday heat of the burning golden-reds of the quiet street in *Daphnesvej, Motif from Skagen Østerby* (c.1915), in which the narrow shadow effect on the right confirms the time of day, while the cooler, violet tones of the long shadows cast by the houses on the left side of the composition in *Østerbyvej in Skagen-Østerby* (1915; both Skagens Museum) suggest the still mood of late afternoon.

The only known self-portrait by Anna Ancher is a tiny painting in three-quarter profile (c.1877–8; Helga Anchers Fond, Skagen). It reveals a strong face with a full, sensuous mouth, a slightly crooked nose and a pair of large, piercing dark eyes. Characteristically, her gaze does not meet ours. She is evasive as a subject – as she was in character. The colours are rich and the facial expression determined and spirited. She was a sensual, not an intellectual artist. She sought in her art to create a synthesis of Naturalism and a kind of Symbolism that was not really Symbolism, since its point of departure was always an observation of her immediate surroundings; but it suggested an atmosphere. This synthesis, combined with the simple perception and the painterly emphasis on the surface, anticipates later Danish modernist painting and singles out Anna Ancher as one of the most forward-looking painters of her generation.

ALETTE RYE SCALES

Anguissola, Sofonisba [fig.5]
Italian painter, *c.*1532–1625

Born in Cremona, *c.*1532, into a noble family; her sisters Elena (died after 1584), Anna Maria (died after 1585) and Lucia (died ?1565) were also painters. Studied in Cremona under Bernardino Campi, *c.*1546–9, and Il Sojaro, 1549–*c.*1552/3. Lady-in-waiting and portrait painter at the Spanish court in Madrid, 1559–73. Married (1) Don Fabrizio de Moncado, brother of the viceroy of Sicily, after August 1569; later resided in Palermo; (2) Orazio Lomellino, a Genoese nobleman, 1579 or 1580; living in Genoa by October 1583. Living in Palermo by 1624, when Anthony van Dyck made a sketch of her (British Museum, London), recording that her eyesight was weakened. Buried in San Giorgio dei Genovesi, Palermo, 16 November 1625; survived by Orazio, who dedicated the inscription on her tomb, 1632.

Bibliography
Giorgio Vasari, *Le vite de' più eccellenti pittori, scultori ed architettori*, Florence, 1568; ed. Gaetano Milanesi, 9 vols, Florence: Sansoni, 1878–85, v, p.81; vi, pp.498–502; vii, p.133; as *Lives of the Most Eminent Painters, Sculptors and Architects*, 10 vols, London: Macmillan-Medici Society, 1912–15; reprinted New York: AMS, 1976

Giambattista Zaist, *Notizie istoriche de' pittori, scultori ed architetti cremonesi, con un appendice d'altre notizie, il discorso di Alessandro Lamo intorno alla scoltura, e pittura ...* (1584), 2 vols, Cremona, 1774; reprinted Cremona, 1975

Antonio Campi, *Cremona fedelissima città et nobilissima colonia de Romani ...*, Cremona, 1585; reprinted Bologna: Forni, 1974

Raffaello Soprani, *Le vite de' pittori, scolturi ed architetti genovesi ...*, Genoa, 1674; 2nd edition, 2 vols, ed. Carlo Giuseppe Ratti, Genoa, 1768–9; reprinted Genoa, 1965

Filippo Baldinucci, *Notizie de' professori del disegno da Cimabue in qua*, Florence, 1681–1728; reprint, ed. F. Ranalli and Paola Barocchi, 7 vols, Florence, 1974–5

M. Fournier-Sarlovèze, "Sofonisba Anguissola et ses soeurs", *Revue de l'Art Ancien et Moderne*, v, 1899, pp.313–24, 379–92

Charles de Tolnay, "Sofonisba Anguissola and her relations with Michelangelo", *Journal of the Walters Art Gallery*, iv, 1941, pp.115–19

Women Artists, 1550–1950, exh. cat., Los Angeles County Museum of Art, and elsewhere, 1976

Flavio Caroli, *Sofonisba Anguissola e le sue sorelle*, Milan: Mondadori, 1987

Rossana Sacchi, "Documenti per Sofonisba Anguissola", *Paragone*, xxxix/457, 1988, pp.73–89

María Kusche, "Sofonisba Anguissola en España: Retrattista en la corte de Felipe II junto a Alonso Sánchez Coello y Jorge de la Rúa", *Archivo Español de Arte*, lxii/248, 1989, pp.391–420 (with English summary)

Lionello Puppi, "Un tassello archivistico (e un quesito) per la biografia di Sofonisba Anguissola", *Paragone*, xl/473, 1989, pp.105–8

Flavio Caroli, "Aggiunte a Sofonisba Anguissola e Fede Galizia", *Notizie da Palazzo Albani*, xx, 1991, pp.143–8

María Kusche, "Sofonisba Anguissola: Vuelta a Italia: Continuación de sus relaciónes con la corte Española", *Paragone*, xliii/513, 1992, pp.10–35

Ilya Sandra Perlingieri, *Sofonisba Anguissola: The First Great Woman Artist of the Renaissance*, New York: Rizzoli, 1992

Sofonisba Anguissola e le sue sorelle, exh. cat., Centro Culturale, Cremona, and elsewhere, 1994

Mary Garrard, "Here's looking at me: Sofonisba Anguissola and the problem of the woman artist", *Renaissance Quarterly*, xlvii, 1994, pp.556–622

Fredrika Jacobs, "Woman's capacity to create: The unusual case of Sofonisba Anguissola", *ibid.*, pp.74–101

Sofonisba Anguissola: A Renaissance Woman, exh. cat., National Museum of Women in the Arts, Washington, DC, 1995

Of the nearly 40 women now known to have been active in visual arts professions in Italy during the 16th century, Sofonisba Anguissola holds a singular place. Internationally renowned in her lifetime, she, in contrast to other women artists, never fell from critical grace. In the history of art, Anguissola's name has appeared with regularity since Marco Gerolamo Vida counted her among the most significant painters in his *Cremonensium Orationes III adversus Papienses in controversia Principatus* (1550) and Giorgio Vasari included her in the second edition of his *Vite* (1568). It was only in 1994, however, that the major retrospective *Sofonisba Anguissola e le sue sorelle* brought together a significant number of her works.

While critical acknowledgement has accorded this artist an unusual position in the annals of art history, there is much about her early career that strikes a familiar chord. The oldest in a family of six daughters and one son, Sofonisba Anguissola was born to parents of Cremonese nobility – Amilcare Anguissola and Bianca Ponzone. In her early teens, she and her sister Elena were sent to study painting with Bernardino Campi. If the association, which lasted from *c.*1546 to 1549, was not typically that of apprentice to master but resembled more the relationship of paying guest to instructional host, Anguissola's artistic training seems to have followed conventional lines. She was taught the fundamentals of materials and technique which she practised with copying exercises. The compositional affinity of Anguissola's early works to those of Campi indicates the orthodoxy of her training. Contemporary discussions of other women, such as Lucrezia Quistelli and Suor Plautilla Nelli (q.v.), suggest that this was the *modus operandi* for women. The recent attribution by Giulio Bora (Cremona 1994) of seven studies of figures in diverse poses (one in Kupferstichkabinett, Berlin; six in Louvre, Paris), all of which have been squared for transfer, points out that she, like her male peers, was also schooled in the essential principles of *l'arte del disegno*. These drawings also reveal her exposure to and assimilation of Leonardo da Vinci's classically idealising manner via such artists as Bernardino Luini. Campi's departure for Milan in 1549 resulted in Anguissola's approximate three-year affiliation with Bernardino Gatti, called Il Sojaro. It was through Il Sojaro, who tempered Correggio's fluid Emilian style with that of Pordenone's hardened Mannerism, that Anguissola was exposed to the Parmesan mode of imaging. Sometime around 1554 she arrived in Rome. Her exposure to Roman Mannerism reinforced what she had learned from Il Sojaro, as is evident in the attenuated figure of the languidly posed Virgin in *Holy Family* (1559; Accademia Carrara, Bergamo).

The extant correspondence between Amilcare Anguissola and an array of influential humanists and potential patrons reveals the role of promoter played by Sofonisba's father. Letters to Michelangelo also disclose Amilcare's paternal zeal in securing the best possible guidance for his artist-daughter. In a letter to Michelangelo dated 7 May 1557 Amilcare thanks the master for the "innate courtesy and goodness" that prompted him "in the past to introduce her" to art. He goes on to request Michelangelo "to guide her again" and to ask that he send to Sofonisba "one of your drawings that she may colour it in oil, with the obligation to return it to you faithfully finished by her own hand". Given Michelangelo's acknowledged assistance to other artists, it is more than reasonable to assume his willingness to grant Amilcare this favour. While no image has been identified in connection with this specific request, Anguissola's drawing of *Asdrubale Bitten by a Crayfish* (late 1550s; Museo di Capodimonte, Naples) links her name to that of Michelangelo. In a letter to Cosimo de' Medici dated 20 January 1562, Tomaso Cavalieri explained his gift of the Capodimonte drawing in the following terms: "... the divine Michelangelo having seen a drawing done by [Sofonisba's] hand of a smiling girl, said that he would have liked to see a weeping boy as a subject more difficult to draw" (Tolnay 1941, p.117). *Asdrubale Bitten by a Crayfish* not only meets the challenge, it goes one better, juxtaposing the smiling girl with the weeping boy.

Cavalieri's coupling of Anguissola's name with that of Michelangelo, a pairing that is also found in Vasari's life of Anguissola, is, perhaps, understandable. While Michelangelo was singular as *Il divino*, Anguissola was unique among 16th-century women artists in being praised as men's creative equal. Certainly, she was a much sought-after painter. Paintings by her hand were requested by and subsequently entered the collections of Pope Julius III and members of the Este, Farnese, Medici and Borghese families. By 1559 her reputation had spread beyond the Italian peninsula. In that year she entered the Spanish court as lady-in-waiting and portrait painter to the queen, Isabel of Valois. She would remain in Spain until 1573, sharing with Antonis Mor and Alonso Sanchez Coello the prestige of being a member of the triumvirate of Spanish court painters.

While Anguissola executed a few devotional panels during her tenure in Spain, most of her time was devoted to painting portraits of members of the royal court and family, including *Philip II* and *Anne of Austria* (both Prado, Madrid), *Isabel of Valois* (Kunsthistorisches Museum, Vienna) and *Infanta Isabella Clara Eugenia* (Spanish Embassy, Paris, property of the Prado). In keeping with the decorum of courtly taste and reflecting the austerity of the religious climate, these portraits are marked by an almost formulaic restraint in composition, colour and light. Because other artists at the Spanish court not only painted similarly restrained images but also reproduced some of Anguissola's portraits, questions of attribution have arisen. Comparison of problematical works with those securely attributed to Sofonisba combined with technical examination have in recent years clarified most of these questions. Despite the reserved formality, poised elegance and almost petrified stiffness of Anguissola's Spanish works, qualities found also in paintings by Mor and Sanchez Coello, the physiognomies that Sofonisba recorded reveal distinctive personalities behind the decorous mask, or what Leonardo da Vinci called "the motions of the mind". In this respect, Anguissola's roots in Lombard traditions, specifically the mimetic melding of unidealised naturalism with a calculated style so evident in the works of Moretto da Brescia and Giovanni Moroni, are clearly visible. While such critics as Baldinucci and Zaist may be guilty of hyperbole in their praise of Anguissola as the equal of Titian in the art of portraiture, there can be little doubt that she mastered the art of capturing a sitter's psyche. Nowhere is this more apparent than in her more casual portrait conversation pieces.

As Vasari observed when he visited the Anguissola home in 1566, the enlivened individuality seen in Sofonisba's portraits of Italian and Spanish nobility had been given free rein in images of family members, or so-called portrait conversation pieces. Indeed, such paintings as *Amilcare Anguissola with His Son Asdrubale and Daughter Minerva* (Nivaagaards Malierisamling, Nivaa) and *The Artist's Sisters Playing Chess* (Muzeum Narodowe, Poznań) are intimate and perceptive studies of the complexities of interpersonal relationships and arrested motion. Compositionally ambitious, these portraits are particularly notable for their inventiveness, specifically Anguissola's sympathetic unification of multiple figures through a shared feeling; familial devotion in the former, jocularity and wit in the latter. In this regard, they display the vitality and freshness of her drawings *Asdrubale Bitten by a Crayfish* and the *Old Woman and Young Girl Studying the Alphabet* (Uffizi, Florence), which was subsequently engraved by Jacob Bos. On the one hand, these images reflect Flemish precedent modulated by Leonardo's concern with the symbiotic relationship of action-to-reaction; on the other, they look forward to Caravaggio's early profane works (e.g. *Boy Bitten by a Lizard*, c.1597; Fondazione Roberto Longhi, Florence).

The more than a dozen self-portraits by Anguissola stand midway between the reserve of her formal presentations of Italian nobility and Spanish royalty and her engaging portrait conversation pieces. Most, such as *Self-Portrait Before an Easel* (Muzeum Zamek, Lancut) and *Self-Portrait Before a Spinet* (Museo di Capodimonte), are images of self-fashioning in accordance with contemporary prescriptions for the ideal lady. *Bernardino Campi*

Painting a Portrait of Sofonisba Anguissola (late 1550s; Pinacoteca Nazionale, Siena) is, by contrast, an ingenious double-portrait inversion of the usual male mentor/female protégée relationship. Standing in front of a portrait of Anguissola resting on an easel, Campi, his right hand steadied by a mahlstick, turns to gaze at the artist who, of course, is Anguissola. So positioned, Anguissola holds a double place, at once within the pictorial frame as object yet also outside the pictorial space as the objectifier. Ultimately and most importantly, she assumes all agency, an assumption made clear by the greater vivacity she has imparted to Campi's countenance in comparison to the static and stiff image he has supposedly painted of her. Given Anguissola's occupation, an occupation that one contemporary humanist described as "the profession of gentlemen", this image can only be viewed as the statement of an assured and self-possessed artist.

Following her return to Italy, Anguissola resided in Palermo and Genoa. Early sources indicate that her late oeuvre consisted primarily of devotional panels. Although many of these works have yet to be identified, those that do survive, such as the *Virgin Nursing Her Child* (1588; Museum of Fine Arts, Budapest) and *Holy Family with St Anne and the Young John the Baptist* (1592; Lowe Art Museum, Coral Gables), suggest that she responded to the impress of Counter-Reformation sobriety and the influence of Luca Cambiaso's use of chiaroscuro and nocturnal luminosity. As is the case with her early figure studies, these panels also attest to her awareness of current trends in late 16th-century art theory. As Cardinal Gabriele Paleotti advised, Anguissola rendered her subjects in a manner that delights (*dilettare*), teaches (*insegnare*) and moves (*movere*) the viewer to feelings of devotion.

Sofonisba was not the only Anguissola daughter to receive artistic training and to gain renown as a painter. Like Sofonisba, Elena studied with Campi and Gatti. The third sister, Lucia, who was probably taught by her oldest sister, had the potential, according to Filippo Baldinucci, to "become a better artist than even Sofonisba" had she not died so young. Lucia's signed portrait of *Dr Pietro Manna* (c.1560; Prado) suggests that she was at least her sister's equal in pictorial realism. Not only did Lucia capture the physician's probing mind through the rendering of his penetrating gaze, the Aesculapian snake coiled around the staff he holds in his left hand has been identified as the type (*Coluber virid-iflavus*) most commonly found in Lombardy.

FREDRIKA H. JACOBS

Angus, Rita
New Zealand painter, 1908–1970

Born Henrietta Catherine Angus in Hastings, North Island, 12 March 1908; grew up in Hawke's Bay and Manawatu district. Studied intermittently at Canterbury College School of Art, Christchurch, under Leonard Booth and Cecil Kelly, 1927–33; attended lectures at Elam School of Art, Auckland, 1930. Married commercial artist Alfred Cook, 1930; divorced 1934. Worked as an illustrator for the *Press Junior*, Christchurch, 1934–7. Joined Peace Pledge Union, 1939; avoided work connected with the war effort. Patient in psychiatric hospital, 1949–50. Worked in both North Island and South Island, settling in a cottage in Thorndon, Wellington, in 1953; spent several months each year with her parents in Napier during 1960s. Travelled to Europe on a New Zealand Art Societies fellowship, 1958–9. Suffered from ill health after a back injury in 1962. Died in Wellington, 26 January 1970.

Principal Exhibitions

Individual
Centre Gallery, Wellington: 1957, 1961, 1963, 1964, 1967 (with Jean and Tim Angus)
Victoria University Library, Wellington: 1968
National Art Gallery, Wellington: 1983–4 (touring retrospective)

Group
Canterbury Society of Arts, Christchurch: occasionally 1930–65
Auckland Society of Arts: occasionally 1932–68
The Group Show, Christchurch: occasionally 1932–69
New Zealand Academy of Fine Arts, Wellington: occasionally 1932–63 (annuals), 1969 (*Five New Zealand Painters*)
Centennial Pavilion, Wellington: 1940 (*National Centennial Exhibition of New Zealand Art*)
Auckland City Art Gallery: 1957 (*Eight New Zealand Painters*), 1958 (*Five New Zealand Watercourists*), 1960 (*New Zealand Realist Tradition*), 1960 (*Contemporary New Zealand Painting*)
Commonwealth Institute, London: 1965 (*Contemporary Painting in New Zealand*)

Smithsonian Institution, Washington, DC: 1969 (*New Zealand Modern Art*)

Writings
Text in *Year Book of the Arts*, no.3, 1947, pp.67–8

Bibliography
Gordon H. Brown, *New Zealand Painting, 1920–1940: Adaption and Nationalism*, Wellington, 1975
"Rita Angus: Impressions by some friends", *Art New Zealand*, no.3, 1976–7, pp.12–20, 43
Ronald Brownson, *Rita Angus*, MA thesis, University of Auckland, 1977
Gordon H. Brown, *New Zealand Painting, 1940–1960: Conformity and Dissension*, Wellington: Queen Elizabeth II Arts Council, 1981
Gordon H. Brown and Hamish Keith, *An Introduction to New Zealand Painting, 1839–1980*, 2nd edition, Auckland: Collins, 1982
Rita Angus, exh. cat., National Art Gallery, Wellington, and elsewhere, 1983 (contains bibliography)
Janet Paul, "What makes Rita Angus different?", *Art New Zealand*, no.26, 1983, pp.28–31
Elizabeth Eastmond and Merimeri Penfold, *Women and the Arts in New Zealand: Forty Works, 1936–86*, Auckland: Penguin, 1986
Laurence Simmons, "'Tracing the self': The self-portraits of Rita Angus", *ANTIC*, no.4, October 1988, pp.39–51
Gil Docking and Michael Dunn, *Two Hundred Years of New Zealand Painting*, 2nd edition, Auckland: Bateman, 1990
Michael Dunn, *A Concise History of New Zealand Painting*, Auckland: Bateman, 1991
Francis Pound, "Nationalism, the goddess and the landscape of maternal embrace", manuscript, 1992, Elam School of Fine Arts Library, University of Auckland
Anne Kirker, *New Zealand Women Artists: A Survey of 150 Years*, 2nd edition, Tortola, BVI: Craftsman House, 1993

Rita Angus Papers, 1399, 1937–1970, are in the Alexander Turnbull Library, Wellington.

Rita Angus's reputation as New Zealand's leading Regionalist artist is largely based on her major touring retrospective of 1983–4 and the accompanying publication *Rita Angus* (Wellington 1983). Previously, there had been little detailed critical commentary on the work of this artist, who was active from the late 1920s to the late 1960s. Her significance for New Zealand art history has now been reassessed and her influence has impacted on a number of recent and contemporary New Zealand artists. Angus's Regionalism was part of the dominant strand of New Zealand art practice, yet her contribution, while in part exemplary of the movement, also provided a unique and different voice in certain respects. Her self-portraits, for instance, where symbolism is incorporated, and especially her goddess "portraits" lie outside mainstream Regionalism's emphasis on landscape.

The social and artistic contexts in which Angus worked were neither altogether conducive to life as an artist nor, more specifically, to that of a woman artist and a "separated" woman: New Zealand's major exhibiting venues over this period were few and largely dominated by the Art Societies; the one arts magazine, *Art in New Zealand*, while including some coverage of Angus, was somewhat limited, while the rigid gender roles prescribed by society made it difficult, except for the most determined women artists, to follow a career in the arts. A clear awareness of inequalities was articulated by the artist herself in an early image, a bookplate, where she depicts herself as Cleopatra confronting a snake, with a dagger above her head and her hands bound by a heavy ball and chain (private collection, Christchurch, repr. Wellington 1983, p.17). They are also expressed in writing, on the subject of "Divorce" (she divorced after four years of marriage to the painter Alfred Cook), where she stated that as a result of "the female half of the population emotionally frustrated, religiously unsublimated, disappointed in her liberty, weaned of her employment, there is present a restlessness and a resentment (all the more massive because repressed)" (Alexander Turnbull Library, Wellington, MS Papers 1399:3/3).

Despite these difficulties, and often living frugally and in isolation, Angus produced a substantial oeuvre over four decades. She studied at the Canterbury College School of Art, held her first solo exhibition at the age of 49 and lived and worked in both the South and North Islands. She wrote of her aims in art: "… as a woman painter I work to represent love of humanity and faith in mankind, in a world, which is, to me, richly variable and infinitely beautiful …" (*Year Book of the Arts*, 1947).

Her style, variations of which she used throughout her career, depends on crisp outline, an emphasis on structure, often iconic in its arrangement, rich colour and detailed brushwork, whose seamlessness reveals little of its application. Such emigrant British painters as Christopher Perkins advocated a clarity of style in opposition to the then prevailing diluted form of Impressionism, together with a focus on "modern" subjects. And local literary figures such as A.R.D. Fairburn noted how, in New Zealand: "There is no golden mist in the air, no merlin in our woods … We must learn to draw rather than paint, even if we are using a brush, or we shall not be perfectly truthful" (*Some Aspects of New Zealand Art and Letters*, London, 1934). Other factors important for the formation of Angus's characteristically chiselled style included Chinese art, Early Renaissance Italian art and the work of such old masters as Vermeer, accessible to her through reproductions.

While she produced a substantial number of highly lyrical watercolours over her career – *Untitled (Kapiti from Waikanae)* (1951; Auckland City Art Gallery) is one, and the O'Keeffian close-focus purple flower, *Untitled (Passionflower)* (1943; Rita Angus Loan Collection, Museum of New Zealand, Wellington) is another – Angus's reputation largely rests on her larger-scale oils. Of landscape subjects, the early *Cass* (1936; Robert McDougall Art Gallery, Christchurch) has become emblematic of the notion of the "invention of New Zealand". It depicts a tiny rural railway station in central, iconic fashion within the typically isolated mountainous South Island landscape. A pile of timber suggests construction in progress, while the small size of the lone figure in relation to the landscape speaks of the dominance of the land in relation to the efforts of a descendant of the European pioneer settlers. While specific in their detail, later landscapes such as *Central Otago* (1954–6/1969; Museum of New Zealand) in fact artfully combine disparate views into one composite image. Other later landscapes, while continuing a naturalistic attention to detail, demonstrate a play on Cubist and Surrealist pictorial strategies: *Landscape with Arum Lily* (1953; private collection, Wellington, repr. Wellington 1983, p.178) and *Untitled (Two Stones in Landscape)* (1966; Rita Angus Loan Collection, Museum of New Zealand) are two such works. Both contain, like so many of Angus's landscapes, the simplified shape of a dwelling, suggesting, as with Georgia O'Keeffe's shelter/habitats, a womb-like container within a landscape arguably gendered feminine. Certainly New Zealand poets of the period saw it in such terms when they addressed "Fairest earth … let us come to you barefoot, as befits love, as the boy to the trembling girl …" (A.R.D. Fairburn, "The Dominion", 1938, quoted in an unpublished text by Francis Pound).

Painted at the same period as *Cass*, Angus's *Self-Portrait* (1936–7; Dunedin Public Art Gallery) is one of many variations on self-representation by this artist. Here she presents herself gloved, holding a cigarette and gazing out with an unsettlingly direct and acerbic look. The emphatic, contoured style has much in common with the portraiture of Wyndham Lewis, while there is an unusual connection here of "woman" with notions of culture (rather than the more usual nature) in the deployment of an urban setting, together with strong suggestions of the iconography of the "new woman" in the prominence of the motif of the cigarette and absence of signs of conventional femininity. Other portraits from this earlier stage of her career include portraits of children, for instance the double portrait *Fay and Jane Birkinshaw* (1938; Rita Angus Loan Collection, Museum of New Zealand) – *Fay* later to be the novelist Fay Weldon – and the important *Portrait (Betty Curnow)* (1942; Auckland City Art Gallery), depicting Betty Curnow, wife of the poet Allen Curnow and mother of the contemporary New Zealand critic Wystan Curnow. This work was produced soon after the Centennial Exhibition of New Zealand (1940), for which Allen Curnow had been commissioned to write "Landfall in Unknown Seas". Painted at a time when the history of New Zealand was being reassessed, this powerful portrait of a significant figure is given further resonance through the use of symbolism and telling detail and has come to be seen as a portrait of a New Zealand generation.

Most unusual iconographically in the context of New Zealand Regional realist portraiture, and within the wider context of Regional realism in other countries, are three "goddess portraits" by Rita Angus: *A Goddess of Mercy* (1946–7; Robert McDougall Art Gallery), *Sun Goddess* (1949; private collection, Christchurch, repr. Wellington 1983, p.117) and *Rutu* (1951; Rita Angus Loan Collection, Museum of New Zealand). Each sets a female figure, variously garbed and with varying attributes suggesting mysticism and peace, and whose features recall those of Angus, before a landscape setting. *Rutu* depicts a blond-haired, dark-skinned woman, a sun/halo behind her head against a tropical setting, her hands gently touching a lotus. Both a play on the Maori version of her name and recalling the biblical Ruth, this hieratic representation denotes spirituality and, in the signs of racial mix, a clearly positivist, utopian view, from the 1950s, of the melding of the two dominant races within Aotearoa/ New Zealand, the indigenous Maori with the European, or Pakeha. Within the context of contemporary New Zealand where bi-culturalism is a major political issue, it functions as a particularly bold and provocative image.

ELIZABETH EASTMOND

Arbus, Diane
American photographer, 1923–1971

Born Diane Nemerov in New York, 14 March 1923; sister of the poet Howard Nemerov. Took a short course in basic photographic techniques under Berenice Abbott (q.v.), 1943; later studied photography under Alexey Brodovitch, 1954, then under Lisette Model at the New School for Social Research, New York. Married fashion photographer Allan Arbus, 1941; two daughters; separated 1959; divorced. Initially worked as assistant to husband, then as his partner; pursued independent career from 1957. Photographer for *Harper's Bazaar*, *Show*, *Glamour*, *Vogue* and various other fashion magazines, as well as the *New York Times*. Part-time instructor at Parsons School of Design, New York, 1965–6; Cooper Union, New York, 1968–9; Rhode Island School of Design, Providence, 1970–71. Lived and taught at Westbeth, an artists' cooperative in New York, 1970–71. Recipient of Guggenheim fellowships, 1963 and 1966; Robert Leavitt award, New York, 1970. First American photographer to be given an individual exhibition at the Venice Biennale, posthumously 1972. Committed suicide in New York, 26 July 1971.

Principal Exhibitions
Museum of Modern Art, New York: 1967–75 (*New Documents*, with Garry Winogrand and Lee Friedlander, touring), 1971 (*New Photography USA*, touring), 1972–5 (touring retrospective)
Seibu Museum, Tokyo: 1973–9 (touring retrospective)

Selected Writings
"The full circle", *Harper's Bazaar*, November 1961
"Mae West: Emotion in motion", *Show*, January 1965, pp.42–5
"Tokyo Rose is home", *Esquire*, May 1969, pp.168–9

Bibliography

Diane Arbus, exh. cat., Museum of Modern Art, New York, and elsewhere, 1972

Doon Arbus and Marvin Israel, eds, *Diane Arbus*, Millerton, NY: Aperture, 1972; London: Allen Lane, 1974

Amy Goldin, "Diane Arbus: Playing with conventions", *Art in America*, lxi, March–April 1973, pp.72–5

Max Kozloff, "The uncanny portrait: Sander, Arbus, Samaras", *Artforum*, xi, June 1973, pp.58–66

Ian Jeffrey, "Diane Arbus and American freaks", *Studio International*, clxxxvii, 1974, pp.133–4

Judith Goldman, "Diane Arbus: The gap between intention and effect", *Art Journal*, xxxiv, Fall 1974, pp.30–35

Susan Sontag, *On Photography*, New York: Farrar Straus and Giroux, 1977; London: Allen Lane, 1978

Shelley Rice, "Essential differences: A comparison of the portraits of Lisette Model and Diane Arbus", *Artforum*, xviii, May 1980, pp.66–71

Diana Hulick, *The Photography of Diane Arbus*, PhD dissertation, Princeton University, 1982

Doon Arbus and Marvin Israel, eds, *Diane Arbus: Magazine Work*, Millerton, NY: Aperture, 1984; London: Bloomsbury, 1992

Patricia Bosworth, *Diane Arbus: A Biography*, New York: Knopf, 1984

Patrick Roegiers, *Diane Arbus, ou, le rêve du naufrage*, Paris: Chêne, 1985

Catherine Lord, "What becomes a legend most? The short, sad career of Diane Arbus", *The Contest of Meaning: Critical Histories of Photography*, ed. Richard Bolton, Cambridge: Massachusetts Institute of Technology Press, 1990, pp.111–23

James Guimond, *American Photography and the American Dream*, Chapel Hill: University of North Carolina Press, 1991

Diana Emery Hulick, "Diane Arbus's women and transvestites: Separate selves", *History of Photography*, xvi/1, 1992, pp.34–9

Jane Livingston, *The New York School: Photographs, 1936–1963*, New York: Stewart, Tabori and Chang, 1992

Carol Armstrong, "Biology, destiny, photography: Difference according to Diane Arbus", *October*, no.66, Fall 1993, pp.29–54

"Diane Arbus", *History of Photography*, xix/2, 1995 (special issue; contains extensive bibliography)

Doon Arbus and Yolanda Cuomo, eds, *Diane Arbus: Untitled*, New York: Aperture, 1995

In the late 1950s and early 1960s Diane Arbus used her camera as a critical tool to undermine many of America's most sacredly held values and beliefs. Critics, reading backwards from her suicide in 1971, have tended to discuss Arbus as an expressionist who voiced her own existential angst through the suffering and alienation of her subjects. But Arbus's oeuvre also offers an incisive and profound commentary on the social, cultural and political realities of America in the years around 1960.

Arbus's professional career began around 1943, when she and her husband, Allan Arbus, started a fashion photography business together. While Allan actually shot and developed the pictures, she choreographed them – set the scene, acquired the props, chose and posed the models. Their fashion work, while not artistically interesting, heightened her sensitivity to the camera's ability to falsify and invent, and it was from these years that Arbus retained the directorial conventions of carefully posing her subjects in relatively static compositions and illuminating them with a flash. Almost all her later pictures show a studied intentionality, a calculated effect of confrontational, monumental symmetry that differs radically from the spontaneity valued by such contemporary street photographers as Garry Winogrand and Lee Friedlander.

Between 1956, when her partnership with Allan was winding down, and about 1961, Arbus experimented with a 35mm. camera, favoured by Henri Cartier-Bresson, William Klein and Robert Frank. Ultimately, though, she preferred 2¼-inch cameras like the Rolleiflex and Mamiyaflex, which permitted a greater range of detail and nuance; the waist-level viewfinder enabled her to engage more intensely with her subjects, and the large, square format allowed more darkroom control (Diana Hulick, "Diane Arbus's expressive methods", *History of Photography*, 1995, p.107).

Arbus's most famous works were published in an Aperture monograph in 1972, the year after her death. The book, which includes pictures taken between 1962 and 1971, is not organised chronologically and invites a thematic analysis. In 1984 Aperture published another collection entitled *Diane Arbus: Magazine Work*, which features images (including some that also appear in the monograph) taken on assignment for such glossy magazines as *Esquire* and *Harper's Bazaar*. Arbus, whose commercial fashion photographs had appeared in *Glamour* and *Vogue*, and who continued to rely on popular magazines as both outlets and sources of income, straddled the divide between the market-place and the museum. Her work was included in the *New Documents* exhibition (1967) at the Museum of Modern Art in New York and many of her "mass-market" photographs resurfaced in the museum's retrospective of her career in 1972.

In the mid- or late 1950s Arbus studied photography with Lisette Model, known for her unsentimental images of often ungainly, disfigured men and women, of gamblers and drunks. Under Model's tutelage, she found the subjects who really interested her: outsiders, freaks, transvestites, the self-invented – "singular people", she wrote, "who appear like metaphors somewhere further out than we do" ("The full circle", 1961). She became fascinated with those at the margins of society, but also revealed the hidden eccentricities of "normal people", pinpointing what she called "the gap between intention and effect" – the difference between the way people see themselves and the way that they are perceived by others (Arbus and Israel 1972, p.2).

Arbus began photographing transvestites in 1957, suggesting – at a time when *Life* magazine was able to cite a battery of experts to the effect that sex roles were exclusively biological in origin – that one's gender is a matter of personal choice. Even in the following decade, her work continued to comment on the rigidity of gender roles and the ideology of domesticity that she herself had rejected as a career woman in the 1950s. Among many other works, *Naked Man Being a Woman* (1968; *ibid.*), a picture of a male nude wearing make-up, his penis tucked between his legs and out of sight, implies that gender can be adopted, taken on or off at the whim or will of the individual and cannot be absolutely dictated by society.

The idealised images of the nuclear family that had been so popular in the 1950s also became targets of Arbus's mordant wit, metamorphosing, in her interpretations, into pictures of estranged parents and bizarre children. Her grotesque version of a Madonna and Child, *Woman with Her Baby Monkey, NJ* (1971; *ibid.*), cuts to the quick of American culture's veneration of motherhood (Guimond 1991, p.223). The woman preens with maternal pride as she cradles the monkey in her arms. In *A Jewish Giant at Home with His Parents* (1970; *ibid.*) the father gazes straight ahead while the mother tentatively confronts her outsized progeny. Images such as these challenged the prevalent ideologies of domesticity and "togetherness" that had been promoted both in the popular press and in such exhibitions as Edward Steichen's *Family of Man* at the Museum of Modern Art (1955).

Arbus used art-historical references to examine critically aspects of American culture. In *Retired Man and His Wife at Home in a Nudist Camp One Morning, New Jersey, 1963*, one of a series of photographs of nudists, she takes aim at traditional representations of Adam and Eve, re-imagining them standing, awkward and unglamorously naked, in the thin, scraggly woods of New Jersey. Her visual allusion to the graceful figures of Dürer and Michelangelo heightens the disparity between today's and yesterday's paradise. Arbus wrote about the nudist colonies:

> There is an empty pop bottle or rusty bobby pin underfoot, the lake bottom oozes mud in a particularly nasty way ... It is as if way back in the Garden of Eden ... Adam and Eve had begged the Lord to forgive them; and God, in his boundless exasperation, had said, 'all right, then. STAY. Stay in the Garden, Get civilized. Procreate. Muck it up.' And they did ["Notes on the nudist camp" in Arbus and Israel 1984, p.69].

The nudists in this series emerge as literal embodiments of contemporary American cultural utopianism. They are, like America itself, ingenuous and open, but also bloated and corrupt, searching vainly for a lost innocence.

Towards the end of her life, between 1969 and 1971, Arbus moved outdoors, photographing at residences for the mentally retarded. In these last works, known as the *Untitled* series, she rejected the characteristic stillness of her portraiture in order to capture the expressive gestures of human bodies – albeit still strange bodies – in motion. These subjects, free of the constraints of ideology and culture, are both mysterious and pure.

ARIELLA BUDICK

Arp, Sophie *see* Taeuber-Arp

Ayala de Óbidos, Josefa d'
Portuguese painter and printmaker,
c.1630–1684

Born in the parish of San Vicente, Seville, c.1630, to Baltasar Gómes Figueira, painter, and his Spanish wife Catalina de Ayala. Moved with her family to Óbidos, central Portugal, April 1634. Educated at the Augustinian convent of Santa Ana, Coimbra, from 1644. Returned to Óbidos, 1653; lived both at the family home in Rua Nova and on a farmstead, Casal da Capeleira, just outside the town's medieval walls, until her death, 22 July 1684.

Bibliography

Manuel Barreto da Silveira, "Informaçao que tirei das egrejas de Santa M. e S. Pedro da Villa de Óbidos", 20 February 1693, Bibliothèque Nationale, Paris, MS Portuguese 32, fols 237–9

Felix Da Costa, *Antiguidade da arte da pintura*, Lisbon, 1696; as *The Antiquity of the Art of Painting*, ed. George Kubler, New Haven: Yale University Press, 1967, p.467

Damião Froes Perym, *Theatro heroino, abecedario histórico e catálogo das mulheres illustres en armas, letras accoens heróicas, e artes liberais*, i, Lisbon, 1734, pp.493–5

Luiz Xavier da Costa, *Uma águafortista do século XVII: Josefa d'Ayala*, Coimbra, 1931

Esposicão das pinturas de Josefa de Óbidos (Ayala), exh. cat., Museo Nacional de Arte Antiga, Lisbon, 1949

Luís Reis-Santos, *Josefa d'Óbidos (Ayala)*, Lisbon [1956] (first comprehensive study, with list of signed and dated works)

José Hernández Díaz, *Josefa de Ayala: Pintora ibérica del siglo XVII*, Seville, 1967

Edward J. Sullivan, "Josefa de Ayala: A woman painter of the Portuguese Baroque", *Journal of the Walters Art Gallery*, xxvii, 1978, pp.22–35

——, "Obras de Josefa de Ayala", *Archivo Español de Arte*, liv, 1981, pp.87–93

Luís de Moura Sobral, "Três *bodegones* do Museu de Evora: Algumas considerações", *Colóquio: Artes*, no.55, 1982, pp.5–13

Edward J. Sullivan, "*Herod and Salome with the Head of John the Baptist* by Josefa de Ayala", *Source*, ii/1, 1982, pp.26–9

Luís de Moura Sobral, "Un nuevo cuadro de Josefa de Ayala", *Archivo Español de Arte*, lvii, 1984, pp.386–7

Vitor Serrão, "Josefa d'Ayala e a pintura portuguesa do século XVII", *Estudos de Pintura Maneirista e Barroca*, Lisbon: Caminho, 1986, pp.181–203

Josefa de Óbidos e o Tempo Barroco, exh. cat., Galeria de Pintura do Rei D. Luis, Lisbon, 1991

Josefa d'Ayala's career coincided with Portugal's struggle to free itself from Spanish control. Even her parentage underlines the artistic and economic links of the two countries. Her father Baltasar Gómes Figueira trained as a painter in Seville before returning to his home town of Óbidos in central Portugal with his Spanish wife and Josefa, aged four. He became a noted painter of tenebrist altarpieces and still lifes. Josefa's maternal uncle was probably Bernabé Ayala, a follower of the Spaniard Francisco de Zurbarán; her godfather was Seville's leading painter of religious art, Francisco Herrera the Elder; her Sevillian grandfather had a large picture collection; and one of her sisters married a Portuguese painter.

Ayala began working in 1646 from the convent of Santa Ana in the university town of Coimbra, producing engravings of half-length saints and then painting intimate devotional scenes, on a similar small scale, on copper. For the latter she used Flemish and Dutch prints as a compositional design source. Together with a hot colouring with a distinctive use of pinks, lilacs and oranges, decorative textiles and idiosyncratic doll-like faces with arched eyebrows, they remained her trademarks. She continued to produce engravings (e.g. *Insignia of the University of Coimbra*, 1653, frontispiece to the University's *Estatutos* of 1654; repr. Sullivan 1978, fig.2) and religious paintings on copper throughout the 1650s, branching out in the 1660s into larger-scale altarpieces on canvas and the still lifes on which her reputation now rests. St Catherine, her mother's name saint, was a favourite figure of Ayala's. Her earliest etching, dated 1646 (private collection, Lisbon, *ibid.*, fig.1), was a bust-length version of the saint, and her first major commission (1661) was for five canvases for the altar of St Catherine of Alexandria in Santa Maria, Óbidos (*in situ*). The Zurbaránesque paintings set into a two-storeyed columned altarpiece around a statue of St Catherine show an unusual iconography, combining typical themes such as her *Mystic Marriage* with the less common *Coronation of St Catherine* and also half-lengths of the *Penitent Magdalene* and the *Inspiration of St Teresa of Ávila*.

Ayala's Sevillian-style naturalistic tenebrism was probably learned from her father and it has been suggested that the *Month of March* (private collection, Lisbon, *ibid.*, fig.13 as Alenquer), one of a series of large *Months* painted in 1668, was a collaborative work between them, Josefa painting the foreground still life and her father the beach landscape behind. Her father's still lifes were influenced by those he had seen by Zurbarán in Seville and possibly even by the now lost still lifes of Herrera the Elder. Although she followed her father's compositional style, Ayala employed a different technique, revealed by X-rays, preferring a spontaneous brushwork to her father's preparatory underdrawing.

The Baltimore *Paschal Lamb* (1660–70; Walters Art Gallery) has become Ayala's best-known still life, perhaps because it is her only known work outside Portugal and compositionally close to Zurbarán's treatment of the subject (1635–40; San Diego Museum of Fine Arts). The painting is untypically stark: most of her other versions (Igrega dos Congregados, Braga; private collection, Estoril; Museo Regional, Evora (two versions); Paco dos Duques de Bragança, Guimarães) of this iconic image of the sacrificial, bound Lamb of God are garlanded with flowers. Her practice of adding bouquets of flowers to religiously symbolic motifs may have been influenced by Spanish paintings, or reflected the common Iberian practice of decorating altars with bouquets on feast days.

By the 1670s, her most productive decade, Ayala's reputation had spread and she gained numerous major commissions from churches and religious houses. Large altarpieces were never her strength. Several show evidence of slack design, perhaps through pressure of work engendered by economic responsibilities for her mother and two nieces after her father's death in 1674. Her skill was better expressed in the naturalistic details of dress, jewellery, books and papers that furnish the saint's study in *St Teresa Inspired by the Holy Spirit* for the altarpiece of the *Life of St Teresa* (1672; Our Lady of the Assumption, Cascais) for the Discalced Carmelites of Cascais. Such altarpieces were public statements of Counter Reformation orthodoxy for which Ayala used conventional imagery. Appropriately she reserved more inventive iconography for single easel paintings, probably private commissions. She was always more at ease on an intimate scale, producing some of her best devotional work in small scenes, often candle-lit, worthy of Northern Caravaggesque artists, such as the *Mary Magdalene* (1653; Museu de Machado de Castro, Coimbra). In her tender candle-lit *Holy Family* (1674; Museu Regional, Évora, on deposit in Portuguese Embassy, Brazil), a small easel painting probably for a private patron, a toddler Christ Child blesses the simple peasant meal of fish and radishes in front of the praying family. Ayala minutely described the table setting with the eye of a consummate still-life artist.

Ayala's modern reputation rests on her still lifes. In contrast, the earliest description of her work, in her compatriot Felix Da Costa's *Antiguidade da arte da pintura* of 1696, makes only a brief and tangential reference to them, and they were not mentioned at all in the more fulsome biographical entry in Froes Perym's *Theatro heroino* of 1734. This probably reflects the low status of the genre among art theorists. Perym's entry accompanies those on regal, aristocratic, religious and legendary women and eulogises her art, devotion and international fame. His account suggests that her curiosity value as a woman artist attracted commissions from ladies visiting the fashionable royal spa at nearby Caldas da Rainha. Perym particularly mentioned a visit by Queen Maria Francisca for the portrait of her daughter Isabel, but the portraits of the queen and infanta, once considered Ayala's (Museu do Coches, Lisbon), are now attributed to other Portuguese artists. The one portrait firmly attributed to Ayala, of the *Beneficiado Faustino das Neves* (c.1670; Museu Municipal, Óbidos), is of a distinguished member of the Colegiada of Santa Maria in Óbidos, and shows that she was one of Portugal's leading portraitists.

Ayala's early celebrity, and her status as the only Portuguese woman artist remembered in print in the 17th and 18th centuries, followed by the decline of her fame in the early 20th century, may have both clouded and exaggerated her significance. The fact that Portuguese Baroque painting was until recently an unknown quantity has added to the confusion. Only recently have biographical details been clarified, a corpus of paintings identified and her work evaluated. Her artistic development was further confused by the assumption that Óbidos was a provincial backwater. In fact it had important contacts with the court and ecclesiastical hierarchy, as it lay on the lands of the rich and culturally powerful royal monastery of Alcobaça, which commissioned works from both father and daughter. Ayala used those links, her father's connections and her devout reputation to gain religious and court patronage. The habitual reference to Óbidos in her signature, "Josepha em Óbidos", may also have enhanced her reputation, adding a rural cachet to her still lifes. The solemn, later literary descriptions of Ayala as pious, solitary and mystic are contradicted by contemporary legal documents that show her as an active landowner who affectionately named three of her cows Elegant, Cherry and Beauty.

XANTHE BROOKE

B

Backer, Harriet
Norwegian painter, 1845–1932

Born in Holmestrand, 21 January 1845; father a wealthy ship owner. Moved with her family to Christiania (Oslo), 1857. Studied painting in Christiania under Johan Fredrik Eckersberg, 1861–5, and Christen Brun, 1867–8; in Bergen under Knud Bergslien, 1872–4. Private student of Norwegian painter Eilif Peterssen in Munich, 1874–8. Lived in Paris, 1878–88, studying briefly under Léon Bonnat, Jean-Léon Gérôme and Jules Bastien-Lepage; spent most summers in Norway; stayed in Brittany 1881 and 1882; on Fleskum in Bærum, 1886. Returned to Norway, 1888. Lived in Sandvika, 1889–93, then settled in Christiania. Ran painting school, 1889–1912. Friend of Kitty Kielland (q.v.). Recipient of National scholarship, 1886–7; King's gold medal of merit, 1908; state pension, 1921. Member, board of directors of National Gallery, Christiania, 1898–1918; honorary member, Royal Academy of Fine Arts, Stockholm, 1930. Knight of First Class, Royal Order of St Olav, 1925. Died in Oslo, 25 March 1932.

Principal Exhibitions

Individual
Kunstforeningen, Christiania: 1907, 1925
Kunstnerforbundet, Christiania: 1914, 1922
Kunstforeningen, Bergen: 1916
Konstnärshuset, Stockholm: 1925
Kunstnernes Hus, Oslo: 1933 (retrospective)

Group
Christiania Kunstforening (Art Association): 1877–8, 1887, 1891
München Kunstverein, Munich: 1877–8, 1891
Bergen Kunstforening (Art Association): 1877–8, 1886
Paris Salon: 1880–82 (honourable mention 1880)

Høstutstillingen (Autumn Salon), Christiania/Oslo: occasionally 1884–1930
Exposition Universelle, Paris: 1889 (silver medal), 1900
Munich: 1890 (*Münchener II Jahresausstellung*), 1895 (*Nordische Ausstellung*)
World's Columbian Exposition, Chicago: 1893
Internationale Kunstausstellung, Berlin: 1896
Stockholm: 1897 (*Allmänna konst- och industriutställningen* [Universal art and industry exhibition])
Internationale Ausstellung, Munich: 1901
Berlin Secession: 1904
Vienna: 1913 (*Sezession Norwegische Kunst*)

Bibliography

Erling Lone, *Harriet Backer*, Christiania: Aschehoug, 1924
K. Haug, "Norway's great woman artist", *American-Scandinavian Review*, 1925, pp.735–40
Henning Alsvik and Leif Ostby, *Norges Billedkunst* [Norwegian painting], i, Oslo, 1951
Else Christie Kielland, *Harriet Backer, 1845–1932*, Oslo: Aschehoug, 1958
Harriet Backer, exh. cat., Kunstnernes Hus, Oslo, and elsewhere, 1964
U. Hamran, "Harriet Backer og Kitty L. Kielland på Bosvik sommeren 1885" [Harriet Backer and Kitty L. Kielland in Bosvik in the summer of 1885], *Aust-Agder arv: Aust-Agder Museum Årbok*, 1977, pp.117–26
R. Bowman, "The art of Harriet Backer", *Scanorama*, October–November 1978
Anne Wichstrøm, "Blant likemenn: Søkelys på Harriet Backers og Kitty L. Kiellands karrierer" [Among equals: Spotlight on the careers of Harriet Backer and Kitty L. Kielland], *Den skjulte tradisjon* [The hidden tradition], Bergen, 1982, pp.172–91
Harriet Backer, 1845–1932, Kitty L. Kielland, 1843–1914, exh. cat., Stiftelsen Modums Blaafarvevaerk, Drammen, 1983
Anne Wichstrøm, *Kvinner ved staffeliet: Kvinnelige malere i Norge før 1900* [Women at the easel: Women painters in Norway before 1900], Oslo: Universitetsforlaget, 1983 (revised edition in preparation)

Michele Vishny, "Harriet Backer: A 'northern light'", *Arts Magazine*, lvii, May 1983, pp.78–80

1880-årene i nordisk maleri [The 1880s in Nordic painting], exh. cat., Nasjongalleriet, Oslo, and elsewhere, 1985

Marit Lange, *Harriet Backer*, Oslo: Norske Klassikere, 1985

Dreams of a Summer Night: Scandinavian Painting at the Turn of the Century, exh. cat., Arts Council of Great Britain, London, 1986

De drogo till Paris: Nordiska konstnärinnor på 1880-talet [They went to Paris: Nordic women artists in the 1880s], exh. cat., Liljevalchs Konsthall, Stockholm, 1988

Kirk Varnedoe, *Northern Light: Nordic Art at the Turn of the Century*, New Haven and London: Yale University Press, 1988

Marit Lange, "Et nyoppdaget maleri av Harriet Backer" [A recently discovered painting by Harriet Backer], *Kunst og Kultur*, lxxii, 1989, pp.244–7

Alessandra Comini, "Nordic luminism and the Scandinavian recasting of Impressionism", *World Impressionism: The International Movement, 1860–1920*, ed. Norma Broude, New York: Abrams, 1992, pp.274–313

Knut Berg, "Naturalisme og nyromanrikk" [Naturalism and Neo-romanticism], *Norges Malerkunst*, ed. Knut Berg, Oslo: Gyldendal, 1993

Anne Wichstrøm, "At century's end: Harriet Backer, Kitty Kielland, Asta Nørregaard", *At Century's End: Norwegian Artists and the Figurative Tradition, 1880/1990*, exh. cat, Henie-Onstad Art Center, Høvikodden, and National Museum of Women in the Arts, Washington, DC, 1995, pp.21–67

Marit Lange, *Harriet Backer* (in preparation)

Harriet Backer belonged to the National Romantic generation of Norwegian artists and intellectuals. In the 1880s she was a pioneer in developing a moody style of painting that corresponded to the emotional resonances sought by National Romantics. As their country had been dominated for several centuries by Denmark, and since 1814 by Sweden, 19th-century Norwegian intellectuals struggled to define a uniquely Norwegian national identity. While linguistics and literature were the primary fora for these inquiries, towards the end of the century painters, too, became active participants. Where many National Romantic painters concentrated on unique or typical aspects of the Nordic landscape, Backer focused on interiors. Her works are typically small in scale, appropriately unpretentious for the village cottages and churches she so often depicted. During her own lifetime, Backer was hailed as the greatest Norwegian woman artist, and the technical virtuosity of her substantial oeuvre supports this

estimation. Her paintings are distinguished by an interest in the effects of light, both natural and artificial. *By Lamplight* (1890; Nasjonalgalleriet, Oslo) depicts a woman seated at a sewing table and concentrating on threading a needle by candlelight. The drawn window shade is aglow with a yellow light, and details of the woman's face and clothing are illuminated. Backer sought to adapt the principles of outdoor painting to interior scenes. *By Lamplight* is executed in the sketchy brush strokes of Naturalism, with far greater attention to lighting effects than to descriptive detail.

Backer began experimenting with Naturalism during the decade she spent in Paris (1878–88), where she associated with the large colony of Nordic expatriates. Within the group were many women artists, and they formed strong bonds of friendship. In 1879 Backer, with the Norwegian painters Hildegard Thorell, Anna Norstedt and Julia Beck, rented a studio in Montparnasse where the French academicians Léon Bonnat and Jules Bastien-Lepage came to criticise their work. Although these teachers practised a traditional, hard-edged realistic style characteristic of the venerable Ecole des Beaux-Arts, Backer evidenced greater interest in the looser styles of such artists as Claude Monet, whose works she saw at the Impressionist exhibitions. In 1880 the acceptance of *Solitude* (1878; untraced) at the Paris Salon confirmed for her the critical merit of her work. Although progressive French artists eschewed this time-honoured annual exhibition of painting and sculpture, the Salon was still the place where foreign artists proved their worth. While the interior in *Solitude* was executed in 1878, the figures were not added until 1880, at the behest of Bonnat. This modification produced an emotional tenor suited to Backer's increasing desire for works expressing her subjective response to a motif.

Backer's preference for rendering Norwegian village life may have been nurtured by her attachment to her home town of Holmestrand, but it was reinforced by other factors. Since 1814, when Norway had been ceded to Sweden, a strong impetus had emerged to define a Norwegian national identity. For Norwegian intellectuals, this identity resided in traditional village life and customs, which they zealously fought to preserve. In this context, Backer's placid images of daily rituals, peasant interiors and handicraft assumed ideological significance. She recorded the kinds of places and activities that socially ambitious, modern Norwegians were anxious to leave behind. The gentle emotional tenor of her works is intended to evoke a nostalgic longing for, and appreciation of, Norwegian folk life – to revalue that which was considered old fashioned and lower class. This intra-cultural specificity is a hallmark of National Romanticism and is found in the works of other Nordic artists, including Kitty Kielland (q.v.) and Hanna Hirsch Pauli.

Peasant interiors were also popular in the circle of Munich artists around Wilhelm Leibl. It was there that Backer painted *Solitude*, and studied from 1874 to 1878, when Leibl was at the height of his career. The painstaking detail of his imagery found its way into Backer's early paintings, and the unassuming simplicity of his peasant interiors established a formula that she subsequently used in her own work.

In the 1890s Backer painted the series of "blue interiors" for which she is best known. This was the decade of mood painting (*stämningsmaleri*) in Norway, a time when artists sought to represent aspects of Scandinavian nature that were either unique or typical. They fastened on the pervasive blue tonalities of Nordic summer evenings, when a Whistlerian harmony softened the contours of objects that coalesced in a decorative unity. Another *By Lamplight* (1890; Rasmus Meyers Collection, Bergen Kommune) is perhaps the best known of these works. Here a lone woman sits reading at a kitchen table in front of a lit heating stove. Although the table is set before a large window, it is dark outside, and the only light comes from an oil lamp on the table. Her face is brightly illuminated and the single light source creates dramatic contrasts of light and shadow. While the room's furnishings are quite spartan, this is clearly a middle-class interior, as indicated by the high ceilings, large window, heating stove and Rococo-style chair. *By Lamplight* combines an atmosphere of dignity and seriousness with one of cosiness and security.

In the last 20 years of her life Backer, who never married, painted sunny landscapes and still lifes in addition to interior scenes. Most of these are in private collections. Always working in a small scale, her reserved subjects reflected the modest ambitions considered appropriate for women artists in conservative Norwegian society. Her penultimate painting, *Music* (1917; private collection), depicts a young girl deeply absorbed in her piano playing in the living room of the village parish house in Loiten, where Backer was visiting her friend, the poet Ivar Mortensson Egnund. Backer's works can be found in all major Norwegian public collections, as well as in many other public collections in Scandinavia.

MICHELLE FACOS

Barber, Alice *see* Stephens

Bashkirtseff, Marie [fig. 3]
Russian painter, 1860–1884

Born in Havrontsi, Poltava province, Ukraine, 11 November (Old Style calendar)/23 November (New Style calendar) 1860. Travelled widely with her mother and family after 1870, settling in Paris in 1877. Studied in the women's class at the Académie Julian under Tony Robert-Fleury and later Jules Bastien-Lepage. Visited Spain, 1881. Contributed articles to the feminist journal *La Citoyenne* under the pseudonym Pauline Orell. Member, Union des Femmes Peintres et Sculpteurs, Paris. Died in Paris from tuberculosis, 31 October 1884. (In 1908 Bashkirtseff's mother donated works to the Russian Museum, St Petersburg; these were exhibited in 1930.)

Principal Exhibitions
Paris Salon: 1880–81, 1883–5
Union des Femmes Peintres et Sculpteurs, Paris: 1884, 1885 (retrospective)

Selected Writings
Le Journal de Marie Bashkirtseff, ed. A. Theuriet, 2 vols, Paris, 1887; as *The Journal of Marie Bashkirtseff*, London: Cassell, 1890; ed. Rozsika Parker and Griselda Pollock, London: Virago, 1985
Les Lettres de Marie Bashkirtseff, ed. François Coppée, Paris, 1891; as *Letters*, London: Cassell, 1891
I Kiss Your Hands: The Letters of Guy de Maupassant and Marie Bashkirtseff, London: Rodale Press, 1954

Bibliography
Marie Bashkirtseff, exh. cat., Union des Femmes Peintres et Sculpteurs, Paris, 1885

Mathilde Blind, "A study of Marie Bashkirtseff", *Jules Bastien-Lepage and His Art*, ed. A. Theuriet, London: Unwin, 1892, pp.149–90 (French original, 1892)

M.L. Breakell, "Marie Bashkirtseff: The reminiscence of a fellow-student", *Nineteenth Century and After*, lxii, 1907, pp.110–25

P. Borel, "L'idyll mélancolique, histoire de Maria Bashkirtseff et de Jules Bastien-Lepage", *Annales Politiques et Littéraires*, lxxviii, 1922, pp.535–6, 563–5, 591–2, 617–18, 643–4

Albéric Cahuet, *Moussia: The Life and Death of Marie Bashkirtseff*, New York: Macaulay, 1929 (French original, 1926)

Dormer Creston [D.J. Baynes], *Fountains of Youth: The Life of Marie Bashkirtseff*, London: Butterworth, 1936; New York: Dutton, 1937; as *The Life of Marie Bashkirtseff*, London: Eyre and Spottiswoode, 1943

Doris Langley Moore, *Marie and the Duke of H.: The Daydream Love Affair of Marie Bashkirtseff*, London: Cassell, and Philadelphia: Lippincott, 1966

Women Artists, 1550–1950, exh. cat., Los Angeles County Museum of Art, and elsewhere, 1976

Charlotte Yeldham, *Women Artists in Nineteenth-Century France and England*, 2 vols, New York: Garland, 1984

Colette Cosnier, *Marie Bashkirtseff: Un Portrait sans retouches*, Paris: Horay, 1985

Tamar Garb, "'Unpicking the seams of her disguise': Self-representation in the case of Marie Bashkirtseff", *Block*, xiii, 1987–8, pp.79–86; reprinted in *The Block Reader in Visual Culture*, London and New York: Routledge, 1996

John Milner, *The Studios of Paris: The Capital of Art in the Late Nineteenth Century*, New Haven and London: Yale University Press, 1988

Mara R. Witzling, ed., *Voicing Our Visions: Writings by Women Artists*, New York: Universe, 1991; London: Women's Press, 1992

Tamar Garb, *Sisters of the Brush: Women's Artistic Culture in Late Nineteenth-Century Paris*, New Haven and London: Yale University Press, 1994

John O'Grady, *The Life and Work of Sarah Purser*, Dublin: Four Courts Press, 1996

Manuscript volumes of Bashkirtseff's journals are in the Bibliothèque Nationale, Paris.

Naturalist painter, feminist sympathiser, art critic, sculptor, amateur musician and renowned diarist, Marie Bashkirtseff was an extraordinary 19th-century woman. Born of Russian aristocratic parents who were surrounded by scandal (her mother was separated, her father mysteriously absent), she spent most of her childhood and adolescence travelling in various Italian and French cities until settling eventually in Paris. She died at an early age after having suffered from tuberculosis for some years, but her posthumously published journals were widely recognised as an extraordinary document of the life and aspirations of a 19th-century woman artist and *femme du monde*. First published in France in 1887 and in Britain in 1890, the journal was one of the first published documents to articulate the stresses under which aspirant women professionals lived as they tried to reconcile the demands of a socially constructed "femininity" with the exigencies of a life devoted to art and the pursuit of public recognition. Indeed, Bashkirtseff's serious attitude to her art permeated her diaries and was reflected in the substantial output of work that she managed to produce between 1877 (when she decided to become an artist) and 1884 (the year of her death).

In the year after her death Bashkirtseff was honoured with a posthumous retrospective at the annual exhibition of the Union des Femmes Peintres et Sculpteurs, of which she had been a member. Two rooms containing some 230 pastels, paintings and sculptures were devoted to her alone. To mark the occasion, the Union published a dossier of critical writings containing extracts from some 42 articles that had commented on Bashkirtseff's work and a number of obituaries that had appeared in the general as well as the art and feminist press. From these it is apparent that Bashkirtseff was one of the best-known women artists of her time in Paris, one who was widely regarded as a woman of precocious talent and a suitably "feminine" sensibility. Critics such as Paul de Charry, writing for *Le Pays* in 1883, urged her not to be frightened of raising herself above the standards usually reached by women. She, he believed, had the talent and intelligence to pit herself against her male contemporaries (*Le Pays*, 7 May 1883).

Committed to naturalistic pictorial principles, Bashkirtseff set out to give a "truthful" rendering of contemporary life, painting everyday scenes and people. She identified with such Salon naturalists as Jules Bastien-Lepage and those painters of contemporary life who preferred smoothly polished surfaces and a high degree of finish. She chose to show her work at the Paris Salon and at women-only exhibitions. Most famous among Bashkirtseff's works was her highly polished rendering of a life class in the women's studio at the Académie Julian, exhibited under the pseudonym Mlle Andrey at the Salon of 1881 and now in the Hermitage, St Petersburg; her rendering of a group of Paris street urchins, *The Meeting* (Musée d'Orsay, Paris), shown at the Salon of 1884 and again at the Bashkirtseff retrospective in 1885, when it was purchased by the State; and her *Self-Portrait with a Palette* (Musée Cheret, Nice).

In *The Meeting* Bashkirtseff turns her gaze on to the urban poor with all the unselfconscious detachment of a wealthy woman. Exoticised as representatives of "local colour", her youthful subjects are glamorised, even sentimentalised in the smoothly licked, highly finished surface of the oil painting. It was precisely this palatable and prettified poverty that appealed to contemporary audiences, and the painting was highly acclaimed. In the self-portrait Bashkirtseff shows herself soberly attired, palette in hand, her gaze purposefully directed at the viewer. Her professional identity is stressed here, undermined only by the insertion of a harp behind her, which threatens the seriousness of her painting by making it signify as one among a number of female accomplishments. As her journals show, Bashkirtseff was painfully aware of the difficulties a woman faced in embracing a professional identity. She knew that success was always at some cost to her femininity. Her need to retain the aura of a desirable woman, a suitably feminine woman, at the same time as realising her professional goals, remained a source of continued anxiety for her throughout her short life.

Bashkirtseff's commitment to women's advancement went far beyond the norm for fashionable society artists. Unlike the majority of women of her time, she was sympathetic to the call for female suffrage. She wrote for the important feminist journal *La Citoyenne* under the pseudonym Pauline Orell. Under this name she not only wrote art criticism, on one occasion even offering a critique of one of her own works that she had exhibited under the name of Mlle Andrey, but also important analyses of the constraints on women's art education. She was a vociferous campaigner for the opening of the Ecole des Beaux-Arts to women and a fierce defender of women's capacities and talents. It was not only for the feminist press that she wrote; she also became a regular correspondent for a St Petersburg daily, *Nouveau Temps*, with her articles on contemporary Paris painters.

Bashkirtseff's significance goes far beyond her output as a painter. Hailed as a *cause célèbre* during and just after her lifetime, she has functioned subsequently as an important model and type for succes-sive critics and chroniclers interested in the changing construction of "femininity" in modern times.

TAMAR GARB

Beale, Mary
British painter, 1633–1699

Born Mary Cradock in Barrow, near Bury St Edmunds, Suffolk, eldest child of John Cradock BD, Rector of Barrow, and Dorothy Brunton (or Brinton); baptised 26 March 1633. Married Charles Beale, 8 March 1652; three sons (the first died 1654, two others born 1656 and 1660). Moved to Covent Garden, London, by 1656. Began career as a professional portrait painter, 1670; assisted by husband and sons Charles and Bartholomew. Had two pupils in 1681; later taught Sarah Curtis (Mrs Hoadley). Died at home in Pall Mall; buried at St James's, Piccadilly, London, 8 October 1699.

Bibliography

Sir William Sanderson, *Graphice: The Use of the Pen and Pencil; or, the Most Excellent Art of Painting*, London, 1658

C.H. Collins Baker, *Lely and the Stuart Portrait Painters*, 2 vols, London: Warner, 1912

Gery Milner-Gibson-Cullum, "Mary Beale", *Suffolk Institute of Archaeology and Natural History*, xvi, 1918, pp.238–51; as *Mary Beale*, Ipswich: Harrison, 1918

George Vertue, *Note Books*, i–v; index volume, Oxford: Walpole Society, 1930–55

Elizabeth Walsh, "Mrs Mary Beale, paintress", *Connoisseur*, cxxxi, 1953, pp.3–8

——, "Charles Beale 3d Book, 1680", *Connoisseur*, cxlix, 1962, pp.248–52

Daphne Foskett, *British Portrait Miniatures*, London: Methuen, 1963

"The Excellent Mrs Mary Beale", exh. cat., Geffrye Museum, London, and elsewhere, 1975

Mary Edmond, "Bury St Edmunds: A seventeenth-century art centre", *Volume of the Walpole Society*, liii, 1987, pp.106–18

Mrs Mary Beale, Paintress, 1633–1699, exh. cat., Manor House Museum, Bury St Edmunds, 1994

Charles Beale's notebook for 1677 is in the Bodleian Library, Oxford (MS Rawl 8° 572); his notebook for 1681, Richard Jeffree's *Mary Beale* and miscellaneous documentary material are in the National Portrait Gallery Archives, London.

Mary Beale was the most prolific and successful of the small number of professional female painters working in Britain in the 17th century. She is also one of the best documented of all 17th-century artists as a result of the extant notebooks in which her husband Charles Beale recorded her portrait commissions, payments, working practice and much other incidental information. Her success was due to various factors, including the help she received from her husband and father, both of whom were amateur artists, the support of a wide circle of friends and the encouragement of the court painter Sir Peter Lely; but, more importantly, her own determination to make painting not just a hobby, as it was for many gentlewomen of the period, but a serious career.

Beale's father John Cradock, Rector of Barrow, Suffolk, must initially have instructed her in the rudiments of drawing and oil painting. He obviously did not consider that she would pursue the interest, because he bequeathed his painting materials to his nephew, the professional artist Nathaniel Thach. Beale's interest would also have been stimulated by the circle of professional artists with whom her father was acquainted, including Thach, Robert Walker and Matthew Snelling. In 1652 she married Charles Beale and it seems likely that she had already become a semi-professional painter by 1656, when the couple were living in Covent Garden, London. Her husband recorded that she was being supplied with artists' colours, and she is included among the small number of female artists in Sir William Sanderson's *The Most Excellent Art of Painting*, published in 1658. Early attributed works, *Lady Penelope Hervey* (c.1655; Manor House Museum, Bury St Edmunds) and *"Catherine Gage"* (c.1658; Christchurch Mansion, Ipswich), are in the style of Anthony van Dyck and suggest the influence of Robert Walker, thought to have been Beale's tutor, but, as they do not relate clearly to her mature style, they remain problematic. The earliest references to individual portraits are recorded in the journals of Samuel Woodforde of 1664–5, but no firmly attributed works are known before the small head-and-shoulders portrait of her husband (National Portrait Gallery, London), which can be dated c.1663. Around this time the Beales became friendly with Thomas Flatman, who probably instructed Mary in the art of miniature painting; a few examples survive, two of which are signed "MB" (private collections, repr. London 1975). The

frequently illustrated three-quarter-length *Self-Portrait* (National Portrait Gallery), in which the artist is represented holding a canvas depicting her two sons, can be dated c.1666. The likely companion portrait of her husband (Manor House Museum) is the most eloquent and ambitious of the many extant portraits of him, and conveys a sensual charm and relaxed mood that tend to set it apart from the usual formal male portraiture of the period.

In 1670, after Charles had lost his lucrative job as Deputy Clerk in the Patents Office, Beale set herself up as a professional portrait painter, living and working in Pall Mall. In a role reversal not common in the 17th century, she now became the family bread-winner, Charles acting as her assistant, dealing with clients, accounts and artists' materials. She seems rapidly to have acquired a successful practice, with clients from the aristocracy and landed middle-classes and, in particular, the Protestant clergy, many of whom were personal friends of the Beales. One of the earliest of the numerous portraits of clergymen that she painted throughout her career is *John Wilkins DD* (c.1670; Bodleian Library, Oxford). The three-quarter-length seated figure proved a popular formula and was repeated in later portraits of bishops.

It is not known how the Beales became acquainted with Sir Peter Lely, but by 1672 Charles was recording that Lely had visited Mary in her studio, and praised her work. Later he lent her paintings from his extensive collection of old masters, including a van Dyck, to copy and even allowed her to watch him at work in order to study his technique. Beale also built up a lucrative trade making copies of Lely's portraits as well as using his poses in her own compositions, for example *Jane Fox, Lady Leigh, as a Shepherdess* (c.1676; Manor House Museum). Her success is indicated by the earnings carefully recorded in her husband's notebooks, which rose from £202 5s. 0d. in 1672 to a peak of £429 for 83 commissions in 1677. Her fees, £5 for head and shoulders and £10 for three-quarter lengths, are similar to those of the lesser male artists of the period.

Although Lely's influence was financially advantageous, it tended to force Beale's talent into a mould for which it was not best suited, and the resulting figures often appear awkward and doll-like as well as being derivative. The same criticism does not apply to the head-and-shoulders portraits for which she is now best known. Painted in warm brown tones and with a characteristic feigned stone oval cartouche surround, the formula can be tediously repetitive, but the sitters are presented in a straightforward and honest manner and with considerable charm. The largest single collection of this type is in the Manor House Museum, Bury St Edmunds. Other examples are at Temple Newsam House (Leeds City Council), Felbrigg Hall, Norfolk (National Trust), and various Cambridge colleges.

In between commissions Beale experimented with portraits of family and friends "for study and improvement", using more informal poses and replacing expensive artists' canvas with sacking and bed ticking. These are among her finest works and include the elegant *Self-Portrait* (*c*.1675–80; Manor House Museum), painted in bright hues and with a decorative style influenced by William Wissing. Her sensitive and noted portrayal of children and adolescents is apparent, for example, in the fancy portrait *Child as Bacchus* (*c*.1679; Manor House Museum) and the profile study of a young girl, possibly Keaty Trioche, one of several studio assistants (*c*.1682; Tate Gallery, London). Beale's practice tended to decline after Lely's death, but she continued to produce works full of character until the end of her career, for instance, *Samuel Woodforde DD* (1692; private collection, repr. London 1975, p.40).

Although Beale was a well-patronised artist in her lifetime, and favourably compared with her male competitors by the 18th-century art historian George Vertue, her reputation subsequently declined, and she has been derided by 20th-century critics for a slavish dependence on Lely. It is apparent that the necessity of having to conform to his style in order to support her family did not allow her to develop her talents fully. The exhibition *"The Excellent Mrs Mary Beale"* held at the Geffrye Museum, London, in 1975 and the more individual and distinguished works that have subsequently come to light have served to enhance her current status.

CHRISTOPHER REEVE

See also Copyists survey

Beaux, (Eliza) Cecilia

American painter and graphic artist,
1855–1942

Born in Philadelphia, Pennsylvania, 1 May 1855. Studied under Catharine Ann Drinker, 1871–2; studied at the Van der Wielen School under Francis Adolf Van der Wielen, 1872–4; Pennsylvania Academy of the Fine Arts, 1876–8; National Art Training School under Camille Piton, 1879; under William Sartain, 1881–3, all in Philadelphia; studied at Académie Julian, Paris, under Tony Robert-Fleury, William Bouguereau and Benjamin Constant, 1888–9; under Thomas Alexander Harrison and Charles Lasar in Concarneau, summer 1888; at Académie Colarossi, Paris, under Gustave Courtois and P.A.J. Dagnan-Bouveret, 1889. Subsequently taught at the Pennsylvania Academy of the Fine Arts, 1895–1916, and in The Portrait Class, New York, managed by Elizabeth Cady (Stanton) Blake, 1918–28. Lived in Philadelphia until 1898, then divided the year between apartment in New York and summer home and studio, Green Alley, in Gloucester, Massachusetts. Member, Society of American Artists, 1893; Associate member, 1894, and Member, 1902, National Academy of Design; founder-member, Plastic Club, Philadelphia, 1897; Associée, Société Nationale des Beaux-Arts, Paris, 1900; member, National Institute of Arts and Letters, 1930; American Academy of Arts and Letters, 1933; honorary life member, Arts Club of Washington, DC, 1941. Elected one of the 12 most eminent American women, National League of Women Voters, 1922. Recipient of honorary degrees from University of Pennsylvania, Philadelphia, 1908, and Yale University, New Haven, 1912; lifetime achievement awards from American Academy of Arts and Letters, 1926; National Institute of Arts and Letters, 1941. Died in Gloucester, Massachusetts, 17 September 1942.

Principal Exhibitions

Individual
St Botolph Club, Boston: 1897, 1904
Durand-Ruel Galleries, New York: 1903
Macbeth Gallery, New York: 1910
Corcoran Gallery of Art, Washington, DC: 1912
M. Knoedler & Co., New York: 1915, 1917, 1925
Syracuse Museum of Fine Art, NY: 1931 (retrospective)
American Academy of Arts and Letters, New York: 1935
   (retrospective)

Group
Pennsylvania Academy of the Fine Arts, Philadelphia:
   occasionally 1879–1935 (Mary Smith prize 1885,
   1887, 1891 and 1892, Temple gold medal 1900)
Paris Salon: occasionally 1887–1923
Exposition Universelle, Paris: 1889, 1900 (gold medal)

Art Club of Philadelphia: 1891–4 (gold medal 1892)
National Academy of Design, New York: occasionally
    1892–1934 (Dodge prize 1893, Saltus gold medal
    1914, Proctor portrait prize 1915)
World's Columbian Exposition, Chicago: 1893
Carnegie Institute, Pittsburgh: occasionally 1896–1940
    (bronze medal 1896, gold medal 1899)
International Society of Painters, Sculptors and Gravers,
    London: 1897–1900, 1908
Art Institute of Chicago: 1899, 1921 (Logan gold medal),
    1932, 1934
Pan-American Exposition, Buffalo, NY: 1901 (gold
    medal)
Louisiana Purchase Exposition, St Louis: 1904 (gold
    medal)
Corcoran Gallery of Art, Washington, DC: occasionally
    1907–39
Panama-Pacific Exposition, San Francisco: 1915 (medal
    of honour)

Selected Writings

"Uncle John's coat", *St Nicholas: An Illustrated Magazine
    for Young Folk*, xii, 1885, p.203
"Why the girl art student fails", *Harper's Bazar*, xlvii,
    May 1913, pp.221, 249
"Professional art schools", *Art and Progress*, vii/1,
    November 1915, pp.3–8
"What should the college AB course offer to the future
    artist?", *American Magazine of Art*, vii, 1916,
    pp.479–84
"Sargent", *Boston Transcript*, 2 May 1925
Background with Figures: An Autobiography, Boston:
    Houghton Mifflin, 1930

Bibliography

"'The Century's American artist series: Cecilia Beaux",
    Century Magazine, n.s., xxvi, 1894, pp.797–8
William Walton, "Cecilia Beaux", *Scribner's Magazine*,
    xxii, 1897, pp.477–85
Mrs Arthur Bell, "The work of Cecilia Beaux",
    International Studio, viii, 1899, pp.215–22
Pauline King, "Cecilia Beaux", *Harper's Bazar*, xxxii, 11
    March 1899, pp.208–9
—, "The paintings of Cecilia Beaux", *House Beautiful*,
    xi, February 1902, pp.175–81
Homer Saint Gaudens, "Cecilia Beaux", *Critic and
    Literary World*, xlvii, July 1905, pp.38–9
Hildegarde Hawthorne, "A garden of the Heart: 'Green
    Alley', the home of Miss Cecilia Beaux", *Century
    Magazine*, n.s., lviii, 1910, pp.581–7
Leila Mechlin, "The art of Cecilia Beaux", *International
    Studio*, xli/161, July 1910, pp.iii–x
Anne O'Hagan, "Miss Cecilia Beaux", *Harper's Bazar*,
    xlv, March 1911, p.119
Gutzon Borglum, "Cecilia Beaux: Painter of heroes",
    Delineator, xcviii, June 1921, pp.16–17
Allison Gray, "The extraordinary career of Cecilia
    Beaux", *American Magazine*, xcvi, October 1923,
    pp.61–3, 195–8
Carlyle Burrows, "The portraits of Cecilia Beaux",
    International Studio, lxxxv, 1926, pp.74–80
Alice Booth, "America's twelve greatest women: Cecilia
    Beaux, who has given back to the world almost as
    much beauty as she has received from it", *Good
    Housekeeping*, xciii/6, December 1931, pp.34–5,
    165–7
Thornton Oakley, *Cecilia Beaux*, Philadelphia: Biddle,
    1943
Henry S. Drinker, *The Paintings and Drawings of Cecilia
    Beaux*, Philadelphia: Pennsylvania Academy of the
    Fine Arts, 1955
Catherine Drinker Bowen, *Family Portrait*, Boston: Little
    Brown, 1970
Elizabeth Graham Bailey, "The Cecilia Beaux Papers",
    Archives of American Art Journal, xiii/4, 1973,
    pp.4–19
Cecilia Beaux: Portrait of an Artist, exh. cat.,
    Pennsylvania Academy of the Fine Arts, Philadelphia,
    1974
Judith E. Stein, "Profile of Cecilia Beaux", *Feminist Art
    Journal*, iv/4, Winter 1975–6, pp.25–31, 33
Cecilia Beaux: Early Drawings, exh. cat., Alfred J.
    Walker Fine Art, Boston, 1985
Tara L. Tappert, "Cecilia Beaux: A career as a
    portraitist", *Women's Studies: An Interdisciplinary
    Journal*, xiv, 1988, pp.389–411
Cecilia Beaux, exh. cat., Alfred J. Walker Fine Art,
    Boston, 1990
Tara L. Tappert, *Choices: The Life and Career of Cecilia
    Beaux: A Professional Biography*, PhD dissertation,
    George Washington University, 1990
Sarah Burns, "The 'earnest, untiring worker' and the
    'magician of the brush': Gender politics in the criti-
    cism of Cecilia Beaux and John Singer Sargent",
    Oxford Art Journal, xv/1, 1992, pp.36–53
Cecilia Beaux and the Art of Portraiture, exh. cat.,
    National Portrait Gallery, Smithsonian Institution,
    Washington, DC, 1995
Tara Leigh Tappert, *Out of the Background: Cecilia
    Beaux and the Art of Portraiture* (in preparation)

Cecilia Beaux Papers are in the Archives of American Art,
Smithsonian Institution, Washington, DC, and in the
Archives, Pennsylvania Academy of the Fine Arts,
Philadelphia.

At the turn of the 19th and 20th centuries, contemporary art critics identified the international style,
grand manner portraits of American upper-class
men, women and children painted by Cecilia Beaux
as eminently effective expressions analogous to
those by John Singer Sargent and William Merritt
Chase. Beaux's position as "the one woman in a
thousand who has no man standing between her

and her productions" (Saint Gaudens 1905, p.39) was based on her recognisable impressionistic style and sympathetic approach to her sitters.

In the 1870s Beaux's initial art training had prepared her for a career in the decorative arts. Her earliest commissions included the execution of carefully drawn lithographs, *Brighton Cats* (1874; private collection, repr. Philadelphia 1974, p.43) and *Cionondon Arctatus* (1875; repr. Ferdinand V. Hayden, *Report of the United States Geological Survey of the Territories*, ii, 1875, see Tappert 1988, p.396); the portrayal of small children on china plates, *Clara Hoopes* (1882; private collection, repr. Tappert 1988, p.396) and *Margaretta Wood* (c.1887; private collection, repr. *Philadelphia: Three Centuries of American Art*, exh. cat., Philadelphia Museum of Art, 1976, pp.426–7); and the creation of copy portraits from photographs, using crayon, watercolour and charcoal, *Frances Morton McCullough* (1883; private collection, repr. Tappert 1990, p.491) and *Edmund James Drifton Coxe* (1886; Pennsylvania Academy of the Fine Arts, Philadelphia). While this work perfected Beaux's drawing skills and developed her abilities in various artistic media, her broad interest in depicting figurative images equally prepared her for a career as a high-style portraitist.

During the 1880s, following training at the Pennsylvania Academy of the Fine Arts, where she refused to study with Thomas Eakins, and after work in a private class, with instruction from William Sartain, Beaux began painting portraits from her own stylistic perspective. Her earliest award-winning portrait, *Les Derniers Jours d'enfance* (1883–4; Pennsylvania Academy of the Fine Arts), a painting of her sister and nephew, displays the cumulative influences of the Philadelphia art training and indicates an awareness of the art styles in vogue in the 1880s. Her drawing experiences with Van der Wielen and her work as a lithographer are evident in the meticulous details of the setting, while the two artfully arranged flower sprigs in the vase on the table suggest an awareness of Oriental art gained from study with Catharine Ann Drinker, Camille Piton and Sartain. Her understanding of the Aesthetic movement's abstract approach to painting, popularised by James McNeill Whistler, is evident in the portrait's formal arrangement of masses, colours and tones, while her portrayal of a heart-rending moment between mother and child acknowledges her appreciation of the psychological

realism employed by Eakins. Beaux's portraits in the 1880s exhibited either the "art for art's sake" tenets of the Aesthetic movement (*Ethel Page as Undine*, 1885; private collection, repr. Tappert 1990, p.506), the realist's documentation of everyday life (*Reverend William Henry Furness*, 1886; First Unitarian Church, Philadelphia) or the decorative artist's incorporation of various techniques – the impasto of china painting in the background of *George Burnham* (1886; Philadelphia Museum of Art) and the reliance on the accuracy of photography in *Fanny Travis Cochran* (1887; Pennsylvania Academy of the Fine Arts).

Even though Beaux was emerging as a gifted portraitist in Philadelphia in the 1880s, she decided to spend the year 1888–9 in France, enhancing her artistic credentials. She pursued formal art training in Paris at the Académie Julian and Académie Colarossi, executing life studies such as *Figure Study, Standing Male* (1888–9; private collection, repr. Tappert 1990, p.508) and rendering biblical configurations such as *Supper at Emmaus* (1888–9; Pennsylvania Academy of the Fine Arts), work that taught her anatomy and composition. She further augmented her academy studies with copy work at the Louvre, creating her own version (1888; untraced) of Velázquez's *Infanta Marguerite*. During the summer of 1888 Beaux worked in the art colony at Concarneau on the Brittany coast, painting in a plein-air style under the tutelage of Thomas Alexander Harrison and Charles Lasar. In *Twilight Confidences* (1888; private collection; studies for this painting repr. in Philadelphia 1974, p.63) and the portrait of *Thomas Alexander Harrison* (1888; private collection, repr. Carter Ratcliff, "Americans Abroad", *Art & Auction*, October 1994, p.123) her palette brightened, her brushwork became more fluid and she experimented with colour values and light. While Beaux also produced a few landscapes and figure studies that summer, her overriding interest in painting "heads" helped her to recognise that her talents were best applied to portraiture.

The first painting that she made after this decision was the idealised, Aesthetic-style and dark-toned portrait of *Louise Kinsella* (1889; untraced), which was layered with autobiographical meaning. Beaux had rejected a marriage proposal that summer and had decided to pursue an art career single-mindedly, a commitment that she examined in her portrayal of the ethereal blonde. Created for the Paris Salon of 1889, this picture is one of the few instances in Beaux's oeuvre where she clearly addressed the personal and professional issues of her own life. Before returning to Philadelphia in the summer of 1889 Beaux travelled to Cambridge, England, to fulfil portrait commissions for members of the Darwin family. While there she discovered pastel as a medium especially good for women's portraits (*Maud (Du Puy) Darwin*, 1889; private collection, repr. Tappert 1990, p.519), a medium that she continued to use for a few years after she returned to Philadelphia (*Helen Biddle Griscom*, 1893; Pennsylvania Academy of the Fine Arts).

In the 1890s the numerous portraits that Beaux painted of various members of her family solidified her style and provided her with opportunities not only to portray "likeness" but also to embed into her paintings the prevailing roles and characteristics of American upper-class men, women and children. While the serene portrayal of her sister, *Aimée Ernesta (Beaux) Drinker* (1891; private collection, repr. Philadelphia 1974, p.71), and the cocky image of her nephew, *Cecil* (1891; Philadelphia Museum of Art), recall the precise dark-toned paintings of the 1880s, the incorporation of underlying messages regarding the proper demeanour of a thriving matron and the self-confidence of a well-bred boy suggest a new thematic direction. By the time Beaux painted portraits of her niece, *Ernesta with Nurse* (1894; Metropolitan Museum of Art, New York), and a cousin, *Sita and Sarita* (1894; Musée d'Orsay, Paris), a facile impressionistic style had emerged, as had even more sophisticated thematic content. These two paintings capture the moment an innocent toddler is in the safe guidance of a protective nurse, and portray the timeless contemplation of a beguiling beauty and her enigmatic cat. The following year, in the painting *New England Woman* (1895; Pennsylvania Academy of the Fine Arts), a portrait of an older second cousin, Beaux executed a bravura display of the various hues in the colour white, and a convincing portrayal of a selflessly devoted woman dedicated to the values of a bygone era. Beaux experimented with perspective and the illustration of a dimly rendered background setting in *Ernesta and Philip* (1897; private collection, repr. Bowen 1970, p.42), a double portrait of her niece and nephew that conveys the relationship of an older sister to a younger brother. Beaux also painted *At Home* or *Man with a Cat* (1898–9; National Museum of American Art, Smithsonian Institution, Washington, DC), another brilliant white painting of her brother-in-law, Henry Sturgis Drinker, depicted as a genteel man at leisure.

The lessons that Beaux learned in painting portraits of her family were applied throughout the 1890s to the numerous images she created of Philadelphia's genteel upper class. Similar issues of beauty, intelligence and sexuality are embedded in *The Dreamer* (1894; Butler Institute of American Art, Youngstown, OH), a companion piece to *Sita and Sarita*, which displays the artist's skill in the use of the colour white and her ability to create perspective in a dimly sketched background space. *Mrs Thomas A. Scott* (1897; private collection, repr. Tappert 1990, p.575), a portrait of a wealthy Philadelphia matron surrounded by colonial furnishings, recalls the old-fashioned values associated with *New England Woman*. The double portrait of two young sisters, *Gertrude and Elizabeth Henry* (1898–9; Pennsylvania Academy of the Fine Arts), is painted from the same high-point perspective as *Ernesta and Philip*, while the bright green parrot perched on Gertrude's finger adds an Aesthetic colour note similar to the dash of red on the cane in *Cecil* and the pink hat in *Ernesta with Nurse*.

In addition to the individual sitters that Beaux portrayed in the 1890s, she also painted several double portraits that reveal some of her own attitudes and biases. *Mrs Beauveau Borie and Her Son Adolphe* (1896; Amon Carter Museum, Fort Worth) is an ambivalent rendition on the mother and child theme that displays the artist's conflicted feelings about motherhood. The regal presentation, *Mrs Clement A. Griscom and Daughter Frances Canby* (1898; Pennsylvania Academy of the Fine Arts), a portrait of an aristocratic mother and debutante daughter, focuses on the sumptuous fur cloaks worn for a social event rather than the relationship of the two women. The portrait of *Dorothea and Francesca* (1898; Art Institute of Chicago), Beaux's aesthetic interpretation of sisterhood, captures the elegant dance steps of the children of Richard Watson Gilder, editor of *Century Magazine*, and is also one of the finest examples of her ability to combine portraiture and narrative.

Around 1900 Beaux's clientele widened to include sitters in Boston, New York and Washington, DC, and when she built Green Alley in 1905 people throughout the USA began coming to her for their portraits. She preferred to paint studies of people that she knew, but as her clientele expanded beyond her own social world she began to rely on the genre's current styles and conventions. While she still incorporated the Aesthetic, Impressionist and academic styles, she also added the classical elements of 18th-century British grand manner portraiture, for which there was then a resurgent interest. Her portraits were filled with identifiable references to lineage, race, status and proper gender roles, as well as her own preoccupations with beauty, intelligence and social or professional standing. Her particular expertise was an ability to balance the sitter's characteristics – both personal and societal – with the costumes and settings to create a straightforward presentation.

In the first decade of the 20th century Beaux explored different stylistic approaches and fitting narrative messages. Her portraits in the manner of John Singer Sargent, *Harriet Sears Amory* (1903; private collection, repr. Tappert 1990, p.569) and *Henry Parsons (Jimmy) King, Jr* (1905; Cape Ann Historical Museum, Gloucester, MA), were depictions of pure and innocent children – a shy young girl in a rich kimono and a self-assured boy of seven in a lavish interior. She created canvases of young women in their roles as hostesses and debutantes – the sumptuous *Mrs Larz Anderson* (1900; The Society of the Cincinnati, Anderson House), the elegant *Bertha Vaughn* (1901; Radcliffe College) and the Reynolds-like *Dorothy Perkins* (1909; Butler Institute of American Art). She dramatised maternal affection in the Whistler-inspired rendition of the elongated *Mrs Alexander Sedgwick and Daughter Christina* (1902; private collection, repr. *Background with Figures* 1930, p.258) and in the impressionistic interpretation of *Mrs Theodore Roosevelt and Daughter Ethel* (1902; private collection, *ibid.*, p.228). Beaux portrayed older women as society matrons – the glowing *Mrs Richard Low Divine* (1907; Columbus Museum of Art), selflessly devoted maiden aunts – the nearly abstract *Aunt Eliza Leavitt* (1905; private collection, repr. Philadelphia 1974, p.103) and unmarried professional women committed to their vocations – the monochromatic study of *Nurse M. Adelaide Nutting* (1906; Alan Mason Chesney Medical Archives, Johns Hopkins Medical Institutions, repr. Tappert 1990, p.577). The men that she depicted were manly (*A. Piatt Andrew*, 1902–3; Cape Ann Historical Museum) and thoughtful (*Richard Watson Gilder*, 1902–3; private collection, repr. *Background with Figures* 1930, p.210).

During the 1910s Beaux fulfilled portrait commissions for various institutions and individuals and also executed a number of paintings for her own satisfaction. In the official commissions, which were generally formal renditions, she regularly incorporated emblematic elements. The intelligent leadership of *Honorable Sereno E. Payne* (1912; US Capitol, Office of the Architect of the Capitol, House Ways and Means Committee, US House of Representatives, Washington, DC) was indicated by the magnificent, boldly lit head, while the educational career of *Dean Andrew Fleming West* (1916; Princeton University Art Museum) was highlighted by accoutrements of his profession – an academic robe and a marble bust in the background. Her lofty ambitions in the sketches of *Henry James* (1911; National Portrait Gallery, Washington, DC) and *George Arliss* (1913; American Academy of Arts and Letters) were to capture the soulful essence of a creative thinker and the theatrical élan of a vibrant actor. In fulfilling a promise to her nephew, Henry Sandwith Drinker, to paint a portrait of him and his bride when he married, Beaux completed *Portraits in Summer* (1911; private collection, repr. Tappert 1990, p.543). This picture – styled after 18th-century British grand manner portraits – suggests the beginning of a day and a new life together. Twenty years after Beaux painted *Sita and Sarita* and *The Dreamer*, she again returned to the theme of the modern woman, painting two of her finest portraits, *After the Meeting* (1914; Toledo Museum of Art), a highly patterned picture depicting the purposeful Dorothea Gilder at the close of a suffragist meeting, and *Ernesta* (1914; Metropolitan Museum of Art), a cool image of Ernesta Drinker as an ideal of regal privilege and elegant simplicity.

In the years surrounding World War I Beaux expressed patriotic sentiment through a variety of artistic renditions. On the eve of the war she painted *The Portent* (1914; Bryn Mawr College Art Collection), a classical feminine idealisation of liberty and patriotism. In *Lieutenant Leslie Buswell* (1918; private collection, repr. *Exhibition of Paintings and Sculpture Contributed by the Founders of the Galleries*, exh. cat., Grand Central Galleries Painters and Sculptors Gallery Association, New York, 1923, no.203) she paid recognition to a neighbour in Gloucester, Massachusetts, memorialising his war service as an ambulance driver for the American Field Service, representing him in a khaki Red Cross uniform with the Croix de Guerre that he had been awarded in 1915 in full display on his jacket. At the end of the war she was one of eight American artists commissioned by the National Art Committee to paint "portraits of all the great men of this war – those who have led up to a military success and led up to peace". Beaux travelled to Europe to fulfil this assignment, painting the portraits of *Cardinal Desiré Joseph Mercier* (1919), *Admiral Sir David Beatty* (1919–20) and *Premier Georges Clemenceau* (1920; all National Museum of American Art), formal images infused with a sense of political idealism.

In the 1920s and 1930s, while the initial waves of modernism were making an impact on American art, Beaux continued to paint portraits in her established style. An accident on the streets of Paris in 1924 – Beaux broke her hip – significantly slowed her production. The following year she completed a sombre painting of herself, a *Self-Portrait No.4* (1925; Uffizi, Florence), surrounded by paint pots and palette, the accoutrements of her profession. Her last public commission was the portrait of *Dr Rufus Ivory Cole* (1933; Rockefeller Institute for Medical Research), an airy interpretation of the man in his laboratory coat.

TARA LEIGH TAPPERT

Bell, Vanessa
British painter and designer, 1879–1961

Born Vanessa Stephen in London, 30 May 1879; daughter of Leslie Stephen and sister of Virginia Woolf. Studied under Sir Arthur Cope RA at his school in Kensington, London, 1896–1900; under John Singer Sargent at Royal Academy Schools, London, 1901–4; briefly attended Slade School of Fine Art, London, 1904. First visited Italy, 1902. Moved to 46 Gordon Square, Bloomsbury, 1904. Organised Friday Club, 1905 (resigned 1914). Married writer Clive Bell, 1907; sons Julian born 1908 (killed in Spain, 1937), Quentin born 1910; separated from husband. Moved to Charleston, Firle, Sussex, with Duncan Grant, 1916; daughter Angelica born 1918. Contributed to Roger Fry's Omega Workshops, London, 1913–19. Member of London Group, 1919. Taught at Euston Road School, London, from 1938. Visited Paris

frequently from *c*.1920. Rented La Bergère, near Cassis, southern France, 1927–39. Lived at Charleston, 1939–45; in Islington, London, 1949–55; also travelled widely. Member, Society of Mural Painters, 1950. Died at Charleston, 7 April 1961.

Principal Exhibitions

Individual
Independent Gallery, London: 1920 (with Duncan Grant and Robert Lotiron), 1922
Cooling Galleries, London: 1930
Thomas Agnew and Sons, London: 1932 (with Duncan Grant and Keith Baynes)
Lefevre Galleries, London: 1934, 1937
Leicester Galleries, London: 1941 (with Frank Dobson and Algernon Newton)
Adams Gallery, London: 1956, 1961 (retrospective)
Arts Council Gallery, London: 1964 (retrospective)

Group
London Salon of the Allied Artists Association: 1908, 1912
New English Art Club, London: from 1909
Alpine Club Gallery, London: 1910–12 (with Friday Club), 1913–14 (with Grafton Group)
Grafton Galleries, London: 1912 (*Second Post-Impressionist Exhibition*)
Galerie Barbazanges, Paris: 1912 (*Quelques indépendants anglais*)
Whitechapel Art Gallery, London: 1914 (*Twentieth-Century Art*)
Mansard Gallery, Heal & Sons, London: 1917 (*New Movement in Art*)
Kunsthaus, Zürich: 1918 (*Englische Moderne Malerei*)
London Group: from 1919
London Artists Association: 1926
Marie Sterner Galleries, New York: 1928 (*Modern English Pictures*)

Selected Writings
Notes on Virginia's Childhood: A Memoir, ed. Richard F. Schaubeck, Jr, New York: Hallman, 1974
Vanessa Bell's Family Album, ed. Quentin Bell and Angelica Garnett, London: Norman and Hobhouse, 1991
The Selected Letters of Vanessa Bell, ed. Regina Marler, London: Bloomsbury, and New York: Pantheon, 1993

Bibliography
Recent Paintings by Vanessa Bell, exh. cat., London Artists Association, 1930 (foreword by Virginia Woolf)
Catalogue of Recent Paintings by Vanessa Bell, exh. cat., Lefevre Galleries, London, 1934
Quentin Bell and Stephen Chaplin, "The ideal home rumpus", *Apollo*, lxxx, 1964, pp.284–91

Vanessa Bell: A Memorial Exhibition of Paintings, exh. cat., Arts Council of Great Britain, London, 1964

Quentin Bell, *Virginia Woolf: A Biography*, 2 vols, London: Hogarth Press, and New York: Harcourt Brace Jovanovich, 1972

Vanessa Bell: Paintings and Drawings, exh. cat., Anthony d'Offay Gallery, London, 1973

Richard Cork, *Vorticism and Abstract Art in the First Machine Age, 1: Origins and Development*, London: Gordon Fraser Gallery, and Berkeley: University of California Press, 1976

Vanessa Bell, 1879–1961: An Exhibition to Mark the Centenary of Her Birth, exh. cat., Mappin Art Gallery, Sheffield, 1979

Diane Filby Gillespie, "Vanessa Bell, Virginia Woolf and Duncan Grant: Conversation with Angelica Garnett", *Modernist Studies: Literature and Culture*, iii, 1979, pp.151–8

Vanessa Bell, 1879–1961: A Retrospective Exhibition, exh. cat., Davis and Long, New York, 1980

Simon Watney, *English Post-Impressionism*, London: Studio Vista, 1980

Colin Franck Ball, *Vanessa Bell: A Bibliography*, Canterbury: Canterbury College of Art, 1983

Frances Spalding, *Vanessa Bell*, London: Weidenfeld and Nicolson, and New Haven, CT: Ticknor and Fields, 1983

Vanessa Bell, 1879–1961, exh. cat., Vassar College Art Gallery, Poughkeepsie, NY, and elsewhere, 1984

Gillian Elinor, "Vanessa Bell and Dora Carrington: Bloomsbury painters", *Woman's Art Journal*, v/1, 1984, pp.28–34

The Omega Workshops: Alliance and Enmity in English Art, 1911–1920, exh. cat., Anthony d'Offay Gallery, London, 1984

Diane Filby Gillespie, *The Sisters' Arts: The Writings and Paintings of Virginia Woolf and Vanessa Bell*, Syracuse, NY: Syracuse University Press, 1988

Mary Ann Caws, *Women of Bloomsbury: Virginia, Vanessa and Carrington*, New York and London: Routledge, 1990

Jane Dunn: *A Very Close Conspiracy: Vanessa Bell and Virginia Woolf*, London: Cape, and Boston: Little Brown, 1990

Gillian Naylor, ed., *Bloomsbury: Its Artists, Authors and Designers by Themselves*, London: Pyramid, and Boston: Little Brown, 1990

Richard Shone, *Bloomsbury Portraits: Vanessa Bell, Duncan Grant and Their Circle*, 2nd edition, London: Phaidon, 1993

Lisa Tickner, "The 'left-handed marriage': Vanessa Bell and Duncan Grant", *Significant Others: Creativity and Intimate Partnership*, ed. Whitney Chadwick and Isabelle de Courtivron, New York and London: Thames and Hudson, 1993, pp.65–81

Jan Marsh, *Bloomsbury Women: Distinct Figures in Life and Art*, London: Pavilion, 1995

Hermione Lee, *Virginia Woolf*, London: Chatto and Windus, 1996

Vanessa Bell e Virginia Woolf: Disegnare la vita, exh. cat., Civiche Gallerie d'Arte Moderna e Contemporanea, Ferrara, 1996

See also numerous articles in *Charleston Newsletter*, 1982–9; *Charleston Magazine*, 1990–; and catalogues produced by Bloomsbury Workshop, London, 1988–. The Charleston Papers are in the Tate Gallery Archives, London.

Vanessa Bell is thought of mainly as a "Bloomsbury" artist, from that intellectual and witty group gathered around Virginia and Leonard Woolf, Vanessa and Clive Bell in London, and Duncan Grant in Sussex, in the early and middle years of the 20th century, with Roger Fry as the mediator between things and arts French and English. Her work seemed sometimes overshadowed, for others and for herself, by her lifelong association with the prolific painter Duncan Grant, and sometimes by the extraordinary fame of her sister Virginia Woolf. Bell was an artist with a very remarkable family, life and talent: that the last has waited until the late 20th century to be recognised is due, to a large extent, to the vivid and celebrated details of the collective biography of Bloomsbury, as well as to the widespread passion for Virginia Woolf's writing and being.

Desperately and lengthily loved by the critic and painter Roger Fry, whose acknowledged praise of her work contrasts with his lukewarm support of Carrington (q.v.), the other woman painter in the Bloomsbury group, Bell herself had an abiding and frequently selfabasing love for the homosexual Duncan Grant, which is thought of as a major consideration in her own attitude to her work. She did much of her painting at Charleston, a home that she shared with her husband Clive Bell and Grant and, at times, his various lovers; her particular torment over her necessarily unequal love affected her work. It meant that she took ultimate refuge in that work, which, like her life, was rich in aesthetic relations of all sorts, whether at Charleston or in the south of France, where she painted at Cassis alongside Duncan (whose family had a home there), overcome by the light and colours in contrast to the dark of England. About her long love of and problematic relationship with Duncan Grant, she was endlessly courageous and self-denying ("It seems better not to feel more than one can help", she said to him on 5 February 1930), determining to go on with her work as the only solution to living "without getting upset". As she wrote in a letter to Roger Fry: "It will be an odd life ... but it seems to me it ought to be a good one for painting." There is a sense of melancholy hanging over the finest of her pictures, a sense of loneliness, frequently even a sense of exile, of not being at one with her surroundings.

As for the public reaction to her work, it was certainly at a high point in the 1930s, when she had several solo exhibitions, accepted a commission to paint panels for the liner *Queen Mary* and did the sets for ballets by Frederick Ashton and Ethel Smyth. Bell was no longer experimenting with pure abstraction, as she had earlier, nor was she associated with the avant-garde movements of her time, such as Surrealism; she was and remained something of a quiet classic. She is perhaps best known, however, for her very simple designs for the jacket covers of many of Virginia Woolf's books for the Hogarth Press, such as *Jacob's Room* (1922), *To the Lighthouse* (1927), *Three Guineas* (1938), *Granite and Rainbow* (1938) and *Between the Acts* (1941). These designs show not only a profound understanding of the works, but a sense of colour and design all her own. She was also gifted at collaborative work: with Roger Fry's Omega Group she decorated tables and other furniture; with Duncan Grant she decorated houses and the little church at Berwick.

Her own work has many parts to it. Her whole life long, she did portraits, among which her faceless portrait of her sister in an armchair at Asheham (*Virginia Woolf*, 1912) stands out as singularly close to the spirit of Virginia Woolf. After a first period of figurative painting, Bell experimented with a non-representational series of decorations and paintings that may seem, to some, the highlight of her career of portraitist, mural painter, set designer and still-life painter. Her still lifes are among her most successful works, in large part because of her extreme sensitivity to colours and forms. That sensitivity is visible in such paintings as *46 Gordon Square* (1911; Charleston, East Sussex), with the three greenishyellow apples arranged in a long octagonal Chinese platter, the space around them emphasising the sparseness and a kind of discretion. This still life is set diagonally in the lower left-hand corner of the painting, on a ledge bordered by an iron-work railing between whose upright poles a fence outside can be glimpsed, with some thin brownish branches of the tree behind it just visible above – this opening of the inside on to the world beyond being central to the picture. The strange and plunging perspective remains somehow as quiet as the colours, subtle as the play of inside and out. It is often true that Bell experiments more with the oddness of perspective in her earlier works than in her later ones, which are altogether less abstract. On many occasions she painted further pictures of windows, revealing her fascination with the interplay between inner and outer scenes (e.g. *Garden Window, Roquebrune*, 1960; Royal West of England Academy, Bristol).

The British critic Simon Watney, regretting the return of Bell and Grant from their abstract experimental paintings of, say, 1911–14, to a more classical tradition, blames this to some extent on their great interest in France and in such French painters as Cézanne and Matisse. They could have remained at home in their influences, he said, and not treated Britain and British art as a lesser thing than France and French art.

Bell's immense and permanent attraction to France includes the light of the south, of Provence, as well as French art. Writing to Roger Fry on 24 March 1920, she explains what he knows already, that "one is always convinced one must live in France when one gets there. So many things that have to be repressed in one seem to expand and develop" there. The connections with France and French art cannot be overstated. Bell's attachment to Cézanne in particular ("the holy man of Aix") was notable – she would rush over to Paris to see an exhibition, she said to Duncan, because "before long you will have to go to Finland and Germany to see him". Although in her eyes Matisse, Segonzac and Picasso were all wonderful, Cézanne represented for her, as for all the Bloomsbury group, the pinnacle of art: his apples, his mountains, his eye – he is "so extraordinarily solid and alive" (letter to Roger Fry, 3 April 1918).

That, of course, is the way enthusiasts may well feel about Vanessa Bell the person and the painter. The preservation of solidity, interestingly enough, may be one of the most crucial things about her art, for, as she wrote to Roger Fry on 19 September 1923, when there had been the most intense excitement about colour a few years previously, so that many artists were tempted to change everything into colour: "It certainly made me inclined also to destroy the solidity of objects, but I wonder whether now one couldn't get more of that sort of intensity of colours without losing solidity of objects and space."

In any case, Bell was always addicted to the colourful, in her art and her life, setting off her own beauty with an Italian blue hat that would have been out of place in London, say, or enjoying a pair of red espadrilles in Provence precisely for their hue. When Duncan sent her a basket of oranges and lemons, for instance, she immediately reacted as a painter, defying contemporary custom:

> They were so lovely that against all modern theories I suppose I stuck some into my yellow Italian pot and at once began to paint them. I mean one isn't supposed nowadays to paint what one thinks beautiful. But the colour was so exciting that I couldn't resist it [25 March 1914].

Her feeling for colour was intense; but her feeling for feeling is what sets her apart from other equally talented colourists. Writing to Leonard Woolf on 22 January 1913, she entered the argument about significant form (a term used by Roger Fry, and Clive Bell after him) with her own point of view clearly stated: "it can't be the object of a great artist to tell you facts at the cost of telling you what he feels about them". And indeed the greatest of her paintings are perhaps those slightly mysterious scenes with female figures, lending themselves to multiple readings, for example *Studland Beach* (1912; Tate Gallery, London), with the hieratic tall figure standing against the sea, observed by figures faceless and crouching; *The Conversation* (1913–15; Courtauld Institute Galleries, London), with its three women conversing in the frame of a window; and *The Tub* (1917; Tate Gallery), Bell's response to the long pictorial tradition of women bathers, especially the tub paintings of Edgar Degas and, nearer home, Duncan Grant's several paintings of women standing or crouching in their tubs. In Bell's painting the naked woman stands meditatively, with the three flowers in the background against the windowsill, analysed by some commentators as representing Vanessa's difficult position with Duncan and his lover then at Charleston. The almost circular tub stands upended in the empty interior, its top circular line echoing the arch of the window opening, against which stands the vase. It is oddly reminiscent of the series of Carpaccio's *St Ursula* paintings in Venice, of which John Ruskin was so enamoured: the lily on the window ledge a sort of symbol of the Annunciation here, as there; a sense of a self-involvement mysterious in its import;

and the Oriental quality of the woman's face, as she plaits her blond hair. Although the naked woman is modelled on Mary Hutchinson, Clive Bell's mistress, and originally wore a shirt, the present statement comes over as a mixture of solitude and the kind of brave stance that requires a self-aware meditation. The strength of feeling comes through inescapably in the figure of the woman alone, standing, with a clarity of profile stark against the background.

Fry, who never stopped loving or admiring Bell, found her art far more valid and lively than his own, praised her sense of colour, calling her a realist by contrast with Grant, whose vision, he said, came from within. In fact, her vision appears to come as much from within as from without, but this is not immediately apparent. There seems visible in her work a certain kind of compassion, as well as strength. These qualities were also present in her dealings with others, as demonstrated in her letter to Carrington the painter, who was very much in Bell's situation, loving and living with the homosexual Lytton Strachey. After his death Bell wrote, in a letter of 25 January 1932, that Carrington should come and "talk to us, for we loved him very much, enough to understand … But I know it is useless. I know that the many people who loved him cannot help you, who loved him more, and perhaps it is selfish to write, but I think you will forgive me and understand." Although Carrington was to kill herself six weeks later, the sincerity of Bell's feelings and, indeed, her ability to understand, are visible.

It has often been said that Bell's tormented relationship with Grant provoked her self-denigration and excessive humility towards her own work, which Grant seems often to have valued more than she herself did. Already in 1911, Vanessa Bell wrote to Roger Fry: "But all my pictures are failures now I'm very much depressed about them". Yet her self-doubt gives depth to her self-portraits without detracting from the strength and shine of her best work.

MARY ANN CAWS

Benoist, Mme   [fig. 4]
French painter, 1768–1826

Born Marie Guillemine Leroulx-Delaville in Paris, 18 December 1768; father a government official.

Studied first with Elisabeth Vigée-Lebrun, from 1781 or 1782, then trained under Jacques-Louis David, from 1786. Married royalist lawyer Pierre Vincent Benoist, 1793; two sons, born 1794 and 1796, one daughter, born 1801. Honorary member, Société des Arts de Gand (Ghent), 1809. Died in Paris, 8 October 1826.

Principal Exhibitions

Exposition de la Jeunesse, Paris: 1784–8, 1791
Paris Salon: 1791, 1795–6, 1800, 1802, 1804 (gold medal), 1806, 1810, 1812

Bibliography

Marie-Juliette Ballot, *Une élève de David: La Comtesse Benoist, L'Emilie de Demoustier, 1768–1826*, Paris: Plon, 1914

Women Artists, 1550–1950, exh. cat., Los Angeles County Museum of Art, and elsewhere, 1976

Elsa Honig Fine, *Women and Art: A History of Women Painters and Sculptors from the Renaissance to the 20th Century*, Montclair, NJ: Allanheld and Schram, and London: Prior, 1978

Germaine Greer, *The Obstacle Race: The Fortunes of Women Painters and Their Work*, London: Secker and Warburg, and New York: Farrar Straus, 1979

La Femme artiste d'Elisabeth Vigée-Lebrun à Rosa Bonheur, exh. cat., Musée Despiau-Wlerick, Donjon Lacataye, Mont-de-Marsan, 1981

Vivian Cameron, *Woman as Image and Image-Maker in Paris During the French Revolution*, PhD dissertation, Yale University, 1983

Susan Waller, *Women Artists in the Modern Era: A Documentary History*, Metuchen, NJ: Scarecrow Press, 1991

Claire Constans, *Musée National du Château de Versailles: Les Peintures*, 2 vols, Paris: Réunion des Musées Nationaux, 1995

Madame Benoist, best known for her *Portrait of a Negress* (Musée d'Orsay, Paris), dared to produce and exhibit history painting of a high quality at a time when women were not deemed capable of executing such work. Daughter of a Parisian administrative official, Marie Guillemine Leroulx-Delaville began her career as a painter at a young age, becoming a pupil of Elisabeth Vigée-Lebrun (q.v.), who was accepted into the Academy in 1783. In 1784 Leroulx-Delaville exhibited her first works, a portrait of her father and two pastel studies of heads, at the Exposition de la Jeunesse. In 1786 she, her sister and another female student were transferred to Jacques-Louis David's studio while Vigée-Lebrun had a new studio constructed for herself. Under David, Leroulx-Delaville's style changed. The softer modelling and paler colours favoured by Vigée-Lebrun were replaced by a more rigorous linear style combined with more intense colouring. An early *Self-Portrait* (private collection, France, repr. Ballot 1914, pp.34–6 and ill. opposite p.32), exhibited in 1786, is an intermediary work, showing the influence of both. The ambitious artist joined history painting with portraiture as she depicted herself in classical garb, her right shoulder bare, her hair loosely bound with a ribbon. As she paints a copy of Belisarius and his youthful attendant on the canvas to her left, she looks at the viewer, who occupies the space of David's study for his *Belisarius Begging for Alms* (for a reproduction of the study, presumably by David, see Antoine Schnapper and others, *Jacques-Louis David, 1748–1825*, Paris: Réunion des Musées Nationaux, 1989, fig.48). With that Classical costume, the artist represented not only herself but also La Pittura. In this self-image, she combined the influence of Vigée-Lebrun – in the soft lighting and shading, pale colours and sweeping strokes of paint – with that of David, visible in the weighty drapery folds, which accentuate certain anatomical parts, such as the belly and thigh. Although this portrait has been compared to that of *Vigée-Lebrun with Her Daughter* (1789), a closer comparison can be made with Andromache in David's *Andromache Mourning Hector* (both Louvre), although Leroulx-Delaville's figure is not as robust. Both share, however, the same drapery, a tan material with a quite similar border, also to be found on Sabina in David's *Oath of the Horatii* (Louvre). The frankness and intensity of this ambitious self-portrait earned her much critical acclaim from the *Journal de Paris* as well as the *Mercure de France*, which praised its "grace" as well as its "nobility" (Ballot 1914, p.38).

At the Exposition de la Jeunesse of 1787, Leroulx-Delaville exhibited an even more ambitious work, a genre scene taken from Samuel Richardson's *Clarissa*, which had been the favourite novel of Vigée-Lebrun. In *Clarissa Harlowe at Archer's* (untraced) the heroine, on her knees before a table loaded with letters, expresses both sorrow and courage, a complexity of emotions highly lauded by the reviewer of the *Mercure de France* (23 June 1787, p.189). Like the novel, and like history painting, the work offered several moral messages: warnings against the male sex who made specious offers; against women preferring men of pleasure to men of probity; against "mésalliances"; against the excessive authority of parents. The pendant to this work, entitled the *Visit that Captain Morden, Presented by Belfort, Makes to Clarissa the Eve Before Her Death* (untraced), exhibited in 1788, won further attention by its complexity. Morden, with his expression of indignant sorrow, was much appreciated, but the reviewer, wanting Clarissa awake and frightened, failed to understand that sleep expressed her withdrawal from life, her only possible escape from her dreadful situation (*Mercure de France*, 7 June 1788, pp.44–5).

Like Vigée-Lebrun, who had executed history paintings, Leroulx-Delaville was ambitious, and took the next step forward into history painting. The topics of her subsequent works dealt with the liminal state of a young woman either passing from her family into a sexual or marital relationship, or choosing between that relationship and a career. For one painting, she drew on Apuleius' *Golden Ass*. The *Farewell of Psyche to Her Family* (untraced) was first exhibited in July 1791 at the gallery of Monsieur Lebrun (the husband of Vigée-Lebrun, who had emigrated), and then in September 1791 at the Salon, thrown open for the first time to all artists. A drawing in a private collection represents Psyche weeping in the arms of her mother while her father folds his arms in resignation; behind this group Psyche's sisters sob with grief next to the chariot that will transport her to her bridegroom. Although metaphorically the work was about the approaching union of the soul with love, more literally it represented the departure of a daughter/sister, with all of that scene's attendant emotions. One critic was rapturous about the painting: "I thought that women were hardly capable of composing history painting and especially with this degree of perfection. How everything talks in your painting! how interesting your beautiful and unhappy Psyche is!" (*La Béquille de Voltaire au Salon*, Paris [1791], Deloynes Collection, xvii, no.438, pp.292–3). But, for another (*Lettres analytiques, critiques et philosophiques*, Paris, 1791, Deloynes Collection, xvii, no.441, pp.422–3), the exhibition of this painting offered an occasion to condemn works by female artists. For this critic, the quality of the painting meant that others had had to retouch it; that is, it was, according to him, painted by "thirty-six hands". Furthermore, in this arch-conservative critic's opinion, to achieve this level of expertise the artist had had to be in compromising situations, studying with boys and from male models, all of

which made her morally unacceptable, even to the worst libertine.

Such vituperative criticism may well have been caused by the fact that Leroulx-Delaville exhibited *two* history paintings at the Salon of 1791. Her other subject was a feminist reworking of the theme of *Hercules at the Crossroads* (or *Hercules Between Virtue and Vice*), a theme popularised in the 18th century through the publication of the Earl of Shaftesbury's commentary in *Characteristiks*. In *Innocence Between Virtue and Vice* (repr. Ballot 1914, ill. opposite p.64; detail in Los Angeles 1976, ill.7) a young blonde woman, classically garbed, resists the advances of the virile and handsome man who represents Vice (the perennial attribute of a snake representing evil is at his feet, as are roses, the flowers of love) and flees to the protecting arms of the rather stern female figure of Virtue, who points the difficult way to a temple of glory or immortality. In its conception, in the expert handling of both male and female figures, which are decidedly Davidian in appearance, in the rich and varied colouring, as well as in the complicated landscape, Leroulx-Delaville demonstrated a remarkable expertise for an artist only 21 years old. Nevertheless, the unsold work remained within the family.

Two years later, married to Pierre Vincent Benoist, a royalist lawyer from Angers, Leroulx-Delaville missed the Salon of 1793, spending that year and the following one escaping Terrorist authorities. In 1795 she obtained a studio at the Louvre and exhibited at the Salon of that year a portrait of a man, as well as another *Self-Portrait* (private collection, France, repr. Ballot 1914, frontispiece) and two paintings representing *Sappho*, the last history works that she exhibited. Although these remain untraced, sketches in an unpublished album (private collection, Paris) indicate that in one work the poetess, holding a lyre, was seated under a tree; in the other, her dead body, lying on the ground, was surrounded by mourners. Other sketches of 1804–6 of such subjects as *Regulus Returning from Carthage* indicate that Benoist was still interested in history painting.

In late 1797–8, relatively poor, Benoist was reduced to illustrating books translated by her husband, which included *Marie or the Unhappiness of Being a Woman* (ibid., p.145) and *Memoirs of Miss Bellamy*. She missed exhibiting at the Salon of 1798, but returned in 1799 with further portraits.

Her renowned *Portrait of a Negress*, exhibited at the Salon of 1800, was possibly inspired by Girodet's portrait of *Jean-Baptiste Belley* (Château, Versailles), exhibited at the Salon of 1798. Benoist's painting represents a woman probably encountered at the home of her brother-in-law Benoist-Cavy, a naval officer who had married in Guadeloupe and travelled to Guyana. Its formal counterpart in David's work is his portrait of *Anne-Marie Thelusson* (Alte Pinakothek, Munich). Benoist's picture is a study of dark and light, a picture of contrasts with the black woman dressed in a white costume, turbaned in white, with one breast exposed, while gazing serenely at the viewer. Although one critic applauded the gracious attitude, the correct drawing and pose – particularly the beautifully drawn right arm – as well as the gracefully arranged drapery, he was far less sanguine about the choice of sitter, since he felt that African faces were ugly ([Baron Jean-Baptiste Boutard], "Salon de l'an VIII", *Journal des Débats*, Collection Deloynes, xxii, no.632, pp.684–5). Unfortunately he was not alone in his prejudice (see, for example, *La Vérité au Museum* …, Paris, 1800, Deloynes Collection, xxii, no.623, p.309). He further complained that "the air could not circulate around her", that is, the effect of painting this woman was to flatten the picture, make it more abstract, an attitude shared by Benoist's biographer, Marie Ballot (1914, pp.149–50).

During Napoleon's reign in the 1800s, Benoist not only exhibited portraits and genre paintings at the Salons, but also executed a number of official portraits. In 1803 she received her first commission to paint a portrait of *Napoleon* (Palais de Justice, Ghent) as first Consul for the city of Ghent, a work apparently quite similar to Ingres's *Portrait of Bonaparte as the First Consul* (Musée des Beaux-Arts, Liège). In the following years she did other portraits of Napoleon for the cities of Brest, Le Mans and Angers. For the Minister of the Interior in 1804 she executed a portrait of his mother. Other commissions followed, including portraits of *Maréchal Brune* (destroyed) for the Tuileries, *Princess Borghese* (Versailles, repr. Constans 1995, i, p.81) and the phrenologist *Dr Gall* (private collection, France, *ibid.*, ill. opposite p.192).

Benoist's genre subjects included sentimental themes dealing with children, such as *Two Young Children with a Bird's Nest* (exh. Salon 1806; private collection, France), executed in a hard, linear style. This represents a seated young boy looking at the viewer, while a young girl, seen in profile, kneels and reaches towards a nest in his lap. In the opinion of one critic, the painting was full of "spirit and grace" (*Journal des Débats*, 7 November 1806, p.1). At the Salon of 1810, she offered a more moral, Greuzian theme, the *Reading of the Bible* (Musée Municipal, Louviers, repr. Ballot 1914, ill. opposite p.224), showing an old Swiss soldier with his granddaughter on his lap while his daughter reads the Bible. The work was proclaimed to be "painted with truth" (*Le Moniteur Universel*, 6 February 1811, p.143), and a scene in which the costumes, figures and scenes were all "in harmony" ([Pierre Gueffier], *Entretien sur les Ouvrages de Peinture, Sculpture et Gravure*, Paris, 1811, p.62). For the Salon of 1812, the last at which she exhibited, Benoist included with two portraits a work entitled *Fortune Teller* (Musée des Beaux-Arts, Saintes, repr. Mont-de-Marsan 1981, pl.12). In this moderately sized canvas (1.95 × 1.14 m.), in front of a fountain and rural landscape (painted by M. Mongin), an old woman, looking attentively at a young shepherdess, tells her fortune while the recipient casts her eyes down, reflecting on her words. By the side of the fountain a young man listens attentively to her prognostications. In this theme, undertaken earlier by a Madame d'Anne for the Salon of 1806 (untraced) and later by David, Benoist returned to the sub-themes of her earlier paintings of *Psyche* and *Innocence Between Virtue and Vice*, focusing on a pivotal moment in a young woman's life when her future remains in the balance and her life will be changed. On the succession of Louis XVIII to the throne and her husband's promotion to Conseiller d'Etat, Benoist was prohibited from exhibiting at the Salons.

VIVIAN P. CAMERON

Bertaux, Mme Léon

French sculptor, 1825–1909

Born Hélène Pilate in Paris, 4 July 1825. Studied under her stepfather, the sculptor Pierre Hébert, and Augustin Dumont. Married (1) Alletit, *c.*1847; one son; separated from husband before his death; (2) Léon Bertaux. Founder, 1881, and first president, 1881–94, Union des Femmes Peintres et

Sculpteurs (UFPS), Paris. Officier de l'Académie, 1881; officier de l'Instruction Publique, 1888. Died at Château de Lassay, Saint-Michel-de-Chavaignes, Sarthe, 20 April 1909.

Principal Exhibitions

Paris Salon: 1849 (under the name Alletit), occasionally 1857–1909 (honourable mention 1863, medals 1864, 1867 and 1873, exemption from jury 1873)
Royal Academy, London: 1874 (bronze medal)
Exposition des Arts Décoratifs, Paris: 1877 (first-class medal)
Union des Femmes Peintres et Sculpteurs, Paris: from 1882
Exposition Universelle, Paris: 1889 (gold medal), 1900
Woman's Building, World's Columbian Exposition, Chicago: 1893

Bibliography

Maria Lamer de Vits, *Les Femmes sculpteurs, graveurs et leurs oeuvres*, 1905
A. D[alligny], obituary, *Journal des Arts*, 24 April 1909, p.3
Edouard Lepage, *Une conquête féministe: Mme Léon Bertaux*, Paris: Dangon, 1911
Tamar Garb, "*L'art féminin*: The formation of a critical category in late nineteenth-century France", *Art History*, xii, 1989, pp.39–65
Susan Waller, *Women Artists in the Modern Era: A Documentary History*, Metuchen, NJ: Scarecrow Press, 1991
Tamar Garb, *Sisters of the Brush: Women's Artistic Culture in Late Nineteenth-Century Paris*, New Haven and London: Yale University Press, 1994

In an article published in the literary and cultural journal *Le Papillon* in March 1883, Mme Léon Bertaux was heralded as "the best and most brilliant living proof that genius has no sex". Such a position could be occupied, claimed this writer, as much by a woman as by a man. Claims such as this surrounded Mme Bertaux's life and career. Famous during her lifetime as a sculptor, educator and indefatigable campaigner for women's artistic advancement, her name was regularly invoked at discussions on public acknowledgement for women's achievements. And yet Mme Bertaux occupies a strange position in relation to the question of "art" and "sex". Committed, as were many ambitious women artists, to traditional skills and values in art, she defended these in the name of her "feminine mission", convinced that she, as a woman, had a particular role to play in the preserving of time-honoured skills and techniques, now more than ever threatened by the onslaught of modernity. She became therefore a spokesperson for the institutional advancement of her sex while invoking women's natural conservatism as their strength. Nothing was beyond a woman's capacities, claimed Mme Bertaux, but it was *as a woman* that she should make her contribution, neither reneging on her "nature" nor selling short her female destiny. It was women's duty to harness their natural womanly skills – their tenderness, sensitivity, caution and respect for tradition – to the elevated task of Art. Art needed their protection and they needed Art's transcendent mission to elevate and give meaning to their lives.

As a sculptor, Mme Bertaux had a considerable career. She first exhibited at the Salon in 1849 under the name of Alletit but from 1857 signed her work Bertaux. (She, like a number of artists, had married her student, but, in a telling inversion of convention, in this case it was the "master" who took on the name of the student not the reverse, as like all 19th-century French women she accepted her husband's name as her own.) She was a regular exhibitor at public exhibitions and a number of her works were acquired by the State relatively early on in her career. Important examples include the *Assumption of the Virgin*, shown in the Salon of 1861 and bought in 1868, and *Young Gallic Prisoner*, bought in 1867. She received a number of State commissions, notably for *Young Girl Bathing*, shown in the Salon of 1876 and at the Exposition Universelle of 1878, and executed prestigious works for the city of Paris and numerous churches. Her works are to be seen on the exteriors of the churches of Saint-Laurent and Saint François-Xavier, on the façade of the Hôtel de Ville (for which she executed a bust of the painter *Chardin*), at the "palais du Sénat", the Opéra, the Musée du Luxembourg and the Petit Palais. She received numerous awards in her long career including the prestigious Médaille d'Or at the Exposition Universelle of 1889. In 1892 she put her name forward as a candidate for the recently vacated seat in the all-male Académie des Beaux-Arts, fourth class of the Institut de France; she was not elected, although her candidature provoked heated debate. Many critics were convinced that had she been a man, she would have had no difficulty in being elected.

Three works, all in public collections, serve to illustrate the ambition and achievement of Mme Bertaux's work as a sculptor. Her *Young Gallic Prisoner* (1867; Musée des Beaux-Arts, Nantes) shows a rare instance of a woman artist broaching the subject of the male nude, a theme that was, for the most part, forbidden to female artists, who found it extremely difficult to find opportunity to work from the naked figure, particularly the male model. Propriety, decorum and the preservation of both female modesty and male dignity were thought to be at stake in these debates. Most importantly, the entry of women into the life class threatened to expose the repressed sexuality of the life room, which was hailed as a space in which the spiritual and transcendent values of art overshadowed the earthly and base desires of the flesh. Mme Bertaux was not the type to be deterred by such considerations. Rather than seeing herself as a threat to the potential spiritual nature of Art, she felt especially well equipped as a woman to safeguard it, and her highly skilled traditional rendering in marble of a naked young man was, appropriately, purchased by the State for the respectable sum of 5000 francs. The idealised rendering of the body, its non-specificity and illegibility as a specific person (it reads as the generic body of "Art", not a living contemporary man) clothe it in a protective sheath that diffuses its power as a sexualised body. It stands for Youth, France, Innocence, Purity and the Ideal, qualities that, according to Mme Bertaux, were intuitively understood by women. Mme Bertaux's *Young Girl Bathing* of nearly ten years later is a more sensual and titillating exercise in the nude. The model in plaster of this work was shown at the Salon of 1873 and was acquired by the State for 3500 francs in that year. The marble version was installed in the "palais du Sénat" and the sculpture later appeared in bronze at the Salon of 1882 and at the Exposition Universelle of 1889. The sculpture is of a pubescent woman, a typical nymph or bather, with elongated back, graceful gestures, nubile body and self-conscious demeanour, sitting on a grassy bank with a small snail crawling slowly up her back. The slimy trail of the insect is suggested if not depicted and serves to draw attention to the surface of the body, invoking its tactility. But the invitation to touch here borders on an invitation to caress, the body of the woman and the surface of the sculpture becoming one in this moment. The work cannot help but be a sexualised object, notwithstanding the critics' determined claims for its spirituality and pure transcendent value. It was in these terms that the critics greeted Mme Bertaux's most famous work, her *Psyché sous l'empire du mystère*, first exhibited at

the Salon of 1889, shown in the same year at the Exposition Universelle and repeatedly shown and reproduced thereafter. Once again, Mme Bertaux turns her hand to the pubescent female nude, here producing the standing figure of a young woman, idealised, remote and abstracted. Highly skilled as an academic sculptor, Mme Bertaux found in the traditional language of sculpture a means of demonstrating her talent while remaining, she contended, true to her mission as a woman. The fact that there were some critics who thought that the aspirations of Mme Bertaux and other women artists to "Grand Art" was unbecoming for French women, who should content themselves with humbler aspirations and traditional women's genres and media, served only to fuel her ambitions and strengthen her resolve to combine a life that was at one time devoted to the elevation of Art and the amelioration of women's lot.

In this context, Mme Bertaux could not confine herself to the life of a practising artist alone. Her activities as a teacher and campaigner were crucial to the project that she had set herself. In 1873 she had opened the "ateliers d'études", courses in sculpture for young girls and women, having become aware of the paltry training facilities available to aspirant women sculptors in Paris. The success of these led her, in 1879, to build a sculpture school for women. She later became an indefatigable campaigner for the entry of women into the Ecole des Beaux-Arts, seeing this as the only acceptable channel for becoming a respectable artist in France. It was through her involvement with her students and her awareness of the difficulties that aspiring women artists faced that she conceived of the idea of an organisation that could represent the interests of all serious women artists and facilitate the exhibition of their work, irrespective of the level of competence they had reached. To this end she founded the first all-women's exhibition society in France, the Union des Femmes Peintres et Sculpteurs, in 1881, and remained president of this organisation from its inception until 1894, when she was succeeded by the younger naturalist painter Virginie Demont-Breton. The Union was a unique organisation devoted to the display and sale of its members' works at its annual exhibitions, but it also set up a support network for women. It published a fortnightly journal, provided a meeting place for women artists, which was located at Mme Bertaux's home, and was at the forefront of campaigns for professional representation of women, women's educational campaigns and the advancement of women's reputation throughout the 1880s and 1890s. Mme Bertaux envisaged the Union as a non-competitive exhibiting forum for women. She remained resolutely opposed to jury selection, hierarchical hanging of shows and elitism of any kind, and envisaged an inclusive, eclectic and catholic organisation that would help women to counter some of the disadvantages that they faced in a generally hostile art world. As such she was unique, and although her strong personality and personal conviction formed the basis of Union policy in the early years, the pervasive ethos of individualism and competition gradually inserted itself into the Union's policy-making. By the time Mme Bertaux resigned as president of the Union, it was a well-established and prestigious exhibition forum with nearly 1000 works on show at its sumptuous annual exhibitions. Openings were glittering affairs attended by well-known artists, politicians and members of the press. Mme Bertaux had been a tireless promoter of women's art, ensuring extensive critical coverage of the exhibitions. She had even managed to persuade the State to include the Salons des Femmes as one of the annual exhibition forums from which they chose State purchases.

Mme Bertaux was devoted to women's professional advancement but in many ways remained a political and ideological conservative. She never embraced the more far-reaching feminist campaigns, such as the agitation for political rights currently on the agenda in French political circles, nor could she stomach the changes in artistic style and technique that modernism had heralded. She set her sights on traditional institutions and markers of excellence, making the Ecole des Beaux-Arts, the Salon jury, the French Academy and the French School in Rome the focus of her institutional campaigns.

In retrospect it would be easy to construct her as a strangely misguided figure, one who backed the wrong causes and has therefore been relegated, legitimately, to the margins of history. Such a reading does not do justice to the complex situation in which Mme Bertaux and women artists of her time functioned. Excluded for so long from traditional positions of power and privilege, they had learned to believe that it was via such channels that their redemption lay. That these routes have been historically discredited and shown to be marginal to the central project of a society relentlessly bent on modernisation makes them no less worthy of our scholarly attention.

TAMAR GARB

Bingen, Hildegard of *see* Hildegard of Bingen

Bishop, Isabel
American painter, 1902–1988

Born in Cincinnati, Ohio, 3 March 1902. Studied illustration at the New York School of Applied Design for Women, 1918–20; painting at the Art Students League, New York, under Kenneth Hayes Miller, 1920–24. Travelled to Europe with Miller, Reginald Marsh and Edward Laning, 1931. Established studio in Union Square, New York, 1934. Married neurologist Harold G. Wolff, 1934; son born 1940; husband died 1962. Lived in Riverdale, New York, after marriage, but continued to work at Union Square studio until 1984. Taught at Art Students League, New York, 1936–7 (the only full-time woman member of staff); Skowhegan School of Painting and Sculpture, Maine, 1956–8 and 1963; Yale University School of Fine Arts, New Haven, 1963. Recipient of numerous awards and prizes, including American Academy of Arts and Letters award, 1943; National Arts Club gold medal, 1968 and 1970; Purchase prize, Mount Holyoke College Art Museum, South Hadley, Massachusetts, 1974; Creative Arts award medal, Brandeis University, Waltham, Massachusetts, 1975; Outstanding Achievement in the Arts award, presented by President Jimmy Carter, 1979; gold medal for painting, American Academy and Institute of Arts and Letters, 1987; honorary doctorates from Moore College of Art, Philadelphia, 1954; Bates College, Lewiston, Maine, 1979; Syracuse University, New York, 1982; Mount Holyoke College, 1983. Associate Member, 1940, and Member, 1941, National Academy of Design; member, 1944, and vice-president, 1946, National Institute of Arts and Letters (first woman officer since 1898); Benjamin Franklin fellow, Royal

Society of Arts, London, 1964; member, American Academy of Arts and Letters, New York, 1971. Died in the Bronx, New York, 19 February 1988.

Selected Individual Exhibitions

Midtown Galleries, New York: 1933, 1935, 1936, 1939, 1942, 1949, 1955, 1960, 1967, 1974, 1984, 1986
Herbert Institute, Atlanta: 1939
Smithsonian Institution, Washington, DC: 1945
Berkshire Museum, Pittsfield, MA: 1957
Virginia Museum of Fine Arts, Richmond: 1960
Wood Art Gallery, Montpelier, VT: 1972
University of Arizona Museum of Art, Tucson: 1974–5 (touring retrospective)
Associated American Artists Gallery, New York: 1981 (retrospective)
St Gaudens Museum, St Gaudens, NH: 1983
Laband Art Gallery, Loyola Marymount University, Los Angeles: 1985

Selected Writings

"Concerning edges", *Magazine of Art*, xxxviii, May 1945, pp.168–73
"Kenneth Hayes Miller", *Magazine of Art*, April 1952, pp.162–9

Bibliography

Patricia Paull Newsom, "Isabel Bishop", *American Artist*, xlix, September 1925, pp.42–5, 90
Dorothy Seckler, "Bishop paints a picture", *Art News*, l, November 1951, pp.38–41, 63–4
Fairfield Porter in *The Nation*, 21 May 1960
Ernest Harms, "Light is the beginning: The art of Isabel Bishop", *American Artist*, xxv, February 1961, pp.28–33, 60–62
Isabel Bishop: Prints and Drawings, 1925–1964, exh. cat., Brooklyn Museum, NY, 1964
Isabel Bishop, exh. cat., University of Arizona Museum of Art, Tucson, and elsewhere, 1974
Lawrence Alloway, "Isabel Bishop: The grand manner and the working girl", *Art in America*, lxiii, September–October 1975, pp.61–5
Karl Lunde, *Isabel Bishop*, New York: Abrams, 1975
Sheldon Reich, "Isabel Bishop: The 'ballet' of everyday life", *Art News*, lxxiv, September 1975, pp.92–3
Cindy Nemser, "Conversation with Isabel Bishop", *Feminist Art Journal*, no.5, Spring 1976, pp.14–20
Eleanor Munro, *Originals: American Women Artists*, New York: Simon and Schuster, 1979
Mahonri Sharp Young, "The Fourteenth Street School", *Apollo*, cxiii, 1981, pp.164–71
Isabel Bishop: The Affectionate Eye, exh. cat., Laband Art Gallery, Loyola Marymount University, Los Angeles, 1985
Susan Pirpiris Teller, ed., *Isabel Bishop: Etchings and Aquatints: A Catalogue Raisonné*, 2nd edition, New York: Associated American Artists, 1985
Helen Yglesias, *Isabel Bishop*, New York: Rizzoli, 1989 (contains bibliography)
Ellen Wiley Todd, "Isabel Bishop: The question of difference", *Smithsonian Studies in American Art*, iii/4, 1989, pp.24–41
—, *The "New Woman" Revised: Painting and Gender Politics on Fourteenth Street*, Berkeley: University of California Press, 1993

Had Stephen Sondheim never heard of Georges Seurat, he might very well have been attracted to the idea of writing a Broadway musical about the work of Isabel Bishop, frequently referred to as America's best woman painter. He would have had to shift the focus somewhat, since for this artist "color was not the original motif for me. My fundamentals are form, space and light", but emphases on the painstakingly slow crafting of an image and the structural importance of the human figure, moving or resting in New York's Union Square or subways rather than on La Grande Jatte, could have remained the same. Guided by the artist's recorded thoughts, the revised version of *Sunday in the Park with George* could have maintained its relative lack of interest in situating art within a specific social context. Appealing as this idea might be, however, much of what can be said about Bishop, the first woman to have held an executive position in the National Institute of Arts and Letters, would be lost, just as it was with Seurat.

Bishop, educated at the Art Students League under the tutelage of Kenneth Hayes Miller, clearly came to see herself as a "painter's painter". Her now highly prized drawings and etchings were created only to serve the handful of small gessoed panels produced each year. She resisted any pressure she might have felt from her contemporaries to turn her figurative art towards direct social criticism and, as a woman, felt no compunction whatsoever in affiliating herself with the European tradition of the female nude. Whatever may now be said about issues of representation, she is responsible for an impressive oeuvre, many formal qualities of which were brilliantly summarised by Fairfield Porter in a passage on her *Subway Scene* (1957–8; Whitney Museum of American Art, New York):

> The materiality of the box that frames the mirror is bright, strong, ugly, the girl herself is passing, but her image, her sublimation, of the thinnest substance of all, holds you by its subtlety … Her paradox consists in saying that the part of art which represents the outer

world, and which criticism associates with reality, is a sublimation; and that the abstract part that represents nothing, and that criticism associates with non-objectivity, is the part that stands for reality, for the object, for being awake [*The Nation*, 21 May 1960].

These words, which resist the many "realist" analyses offered by critics, apply equally well to any of her paintings from the 1940s on, as can be seen in such works as *Preparation* (1944; Marjorie and Charles Benton Collection, repr. Yglesias 1989, p.61), depicting a massive yet opalescent female nude cutting her toenails, and *Self-Portrait* (1986; Collection Mr and Mrs McCauley Conner; *ibid.*, p.41), in which the somewhat ghost-like, aged artist brings to mind Titian's fragile *Pope Julius III* (Capodimonte, Naples).

Attempts to describe Bishop's panels almost invariably include references to European painting of the 16th to 18th centuries, and this is as she would have wanted. Her nudes often evoke the work of Rubens or Rembrandt, the artist she appreciated above all, and the carefully constructed unfinished/worn appearance of her surfaces are suggestive of many pasts. Yet the word "timeless" sometimes used in conjunction with her work is only part of the story. Just as important are the changes in her picturing of the resolutely white America she observed for decades.

After leaving Miller's classroom in 1923, Bishop struggled alone for a number of years in a rented studio to find her own voice which, by the early 1930s, led her to abandon the crowded, often frieze-like urban scenes that were among Miller's specialities. Unable to persuade those she called the "bums" of Union Square to serve as her models, she settled on the working-class women of the area for her principal subjects – in some respects literally, as she spoke of having "corralled them" into her studio. They were monumentalised, singly or in pairs, in even their most mundane moments and were set within milky-grey spaces bearing few specific indicators of location. As has been convincingly argued by Ellen Wiley Todd (1993), Bishop's young women fulfilled the expectations of the office worker defined in the 1920s and 1930s; they were fashionably attired, modest in their aspirations and showed little of the exhaustion one might have anticipated in a period during which working hours increased and wages declined. *At the Noon Hour* (1939; tempera and pencil on composition board; Museum

of Fine Arts, Springfield, MA) offered an appealing image of two healthy, if slightly rumpled female office workers leaning against a wall, alert and engaged in an intimate and obviously pleasurable conversation. Some of the paintings from the early 1940s seem to anticipate the verbal intervention of a viewer: the woman wiping lipstick from her teeth in *Tidying Up* (1941; Indianapolis Museum of Art) is like a friend who, when finished, will turn and ask "did I get it all?", while the open-mouthed *Girl with Frankfurter* (1945; Collection Harold William Brown, repr. Yglesias 1989, p.104) depends on someone to warn her of any impending ketchup spills.

Bishop's women remained in fashion as they moved through the 1950s and 1960s, but were even less tied to the immediate environs of the workplace. Generally in profile, they travelled through the subways or streets, eventually losing not only their recognisable identities as a class of employees, but also the intimacy of contact with one another. *Five Women Walking, No.2* (1967; Edwin A. Ulrich Museum of Art, Wichita State University, KS) contains a grouping of three at its centre, but one that is formed by the exigencies of motion rather than any desire for companionship. By 1970 her women had once again become classifiable "workers". They had metamorphosed into miniskirted and be-jeaned students who, with their male peers, walked or sat reading in apparent isolation, knit together only by their placement in a variegated web of horizontal striations that sometimes resulted in surfaces reminiscent of crazy-quilts (*High School Students, No.3*, 1974; *ibid.*, p.138).

If Bishop's female figures had been separated from one another by the mid-1960s, shortly to become equal participants in a Seurat-like world of the non-verbal, another associated change can also be observed. Withdrawn from the female viewer was what Todd has characterised as a privileged invitation to enter the spaces of friendship forged by the young office workers of the 1930s and 1940s. The implied, though class-blind, camaraderie of female artist, subject and viewer had dissipated. Bishop lived long enough to witness the collective spirit of second-wave feminism, cautiously inserting herself into some of its activities, but chose to ignore it in her production. Possible explanations for the disappearance of a special place for women in and before her art are numerous, ranging from the personal – an artist no longer requiring from her subjects evidence of the intimacy she believed herself to have been deprived of by a father whose fortunes had fallen and by a distant, suffragist mother – to the aesthetic – the by-then unquenchable nature of her search for a way of articulating the actuality of movement, of physical and social becoming, in all human beings. The unique blend of tradition and modernism that constituted the formal character of Bishop's work erased neither the human figure nor its participation in some form of everyday drama, and her paintings still elicit more questions than answers about what those changing images of the social signified for and about her.

CATHERINE MACKENZIE

Bologna, Catherine of *see* Vigri

Bonheur, Rosa   [fig. 6]
French painter and sculptor, 1822–1899

Born in Bordeaux, 16 March 1822, to Raymond Bonheur, drawing instructor and landscape painter, and his wife Sophie. Moved to Paris with her family, 1829. Trained by her father, copying from casts at the Louvre. Met Natalie Micas, who became close friend and companion, 1836. Made sketching trips to the Auvergne, 1846 and 1847, to the Pyrenees, 1850; visited London, Birmingham and Scotland and met Edwin Landseer, 1856. Directed the state-sponsored Ecole Gratuite de Dessin pour les Jeunes Filles, assisted by her sister Juliette (later Juliette Peyrol), 1848–59. Retired with Micas to the Château de By, near Fontaine-bleau, 1860; spent summers in the south of France, 1875–89. Micas died, 1889. Met Anna Klumpke, 1889; Klumpke became her companion at By, 1898. Cross of Légion d'Honneur conferred by the Empress Eugénie, 1865; member, Order of San Carlos of Mexico, 1865; member, Institut d'Anvers (Antwerp), 1868; Commander's cross, Royal Order of Isabella the Catholic, Spain, 1880; Order of Merit for Fine Arts, Saxe-Coburg-Gotha, 1885; Order of Saint-Jacques of Portugal, 1890 (nominated officer 1894); Officier, Légion d'Honneur, 1894; honorary president, Union des Femmes Peintres et Sculpteurs, Paris. Died at Château de By, Seine-et-Marne, 25 May 1899.

Principal Exhibitions
Paris Salon: 1841–50, 1853, 1867, 1899 (third-class medal 1845, gold medal 1848, exemption from jury 1853)
Rouen Salon: 1843 (bronze medal), 1845 (silver medal), 1847 (silver medal)
Brussels Salon: 1851, 1858, 1881
Exposition Universelle, Paris: 1855 (gold medal), 1867 (second-class medal), 1889
German Gallery, London: 1860 (individual)
Society of Female Artists, London: 1861–2, 1865, 1867, 1870, 1873
New Society of Painters in Watercolours, London: 1867–8, 1875
Royal Academy, London: 1869
Lefevre Gallery, London: 1881, 1882, 1896 (all individual)
Woman's Building, World's Columbian Exposition, Chicago: 1893
Galerie Georges Petit, Paris: 1897 (individual), 1900 (retrospective)

Selected Writings
"Fragments of my autobiography", *Magazine of Art*, xxvi, 1902, pp.531–6

Bibliography
John Forbes-Robertson, "Rosa Bonheur", *Magazine of Art*, v, 1882, pp.45–50

Henry Bacon, "Rosa Bonheur", *Century Magazine*, xxviii (new series vi), 1884, pp.833–40

L. Roger-Miles, *Rosa Bonheur: Sa vie, son oeuvre*, Paris: Société d'Edition Artistique, 1900

Anna Klumpke, *Rosa Bonheur: Sa vie, son oeuvre*, Paris: Flammarion, 1908

Theodore Stanton, ed., *Reminiscences of Rosa Bonheur*, London: Melrose, and New York: Appleton, 1910; reprinted New York: Hacker, 1976

Anna Klumpke, *Memoirs of an Artist*, ed. Lilian Whiting, Boston: Wright and Potter, 1940

Women Artists, 1550–1950, exh. cat., Los Angeles County Museum of Art, and elsewhere, 1976

Danielle Digne, *Rosa Bonheur ou l'insolence: L'Histoire d'une vie, 1822–1899*, Paris: Denoël/Gonthier, 1980

Dore Ashton, *Rosa Bonheur: A Life and Legend*, New York: Viking, and London: Secker and Warburg, 1981

Albert Boime, "The case of Rosa Bonheur: Why should a woman want to be more like a man?", *Art History*, iv, 1981, pp.384–409

La Femme artiste d'Elisabeth Vigée-Lebrun à Rosa Bonheur, exh. cat., Musée Despiau-Wlerick, Donjon Lacataye, Mont-de-Marsan, 1981

Rosalia Shriver, *Rosa Bonheur, with a Checklist of Works in American Collections*, Philadelphia: Art Alliance Press, 1982

Charlotte Yeldham, *Women Artists in Nineteenth-Century France and England*, 2 vols, New York: Garland, 1984

Rosa Bonheur: Selected Works from American Collections, exh. cat., Meadows Museum, Southern Methodist University, Dallas, and elsewhere, 1989

Susan Waller, *Women Artists in the Modern Era: A Documentary History*, Metuchen, NJ: Scarecrow Press, 1991

Mara R. Witzling, ed., *Voicing Our Visions: Writings by Women Artists*, New York: Universe, 1991; London: Women's Press, 1992

Tamar Garb, "*L'art féminin*: The formation of a critical category in late nineteenth-century France", *The Expanding Discourse: Feminism and Art History*, ed. Norma Broude and Mary D. Garrard, New York: HarperCollins, 1992, pp.207–30

James M. Saslow, "Disagreeably hidden: Construction and constriction of the lesbian body in Rosa Bonheur's *Horse Fair*", *ibid.*, pp.187–206

Whitney Chadwick, "The fine art of gentling: Horses and women and Rosa Bonheur in Victorian England", *The Body Imaged: The Human Form and Visual Culture since the Renaissance*, ed. Kathleen Adler and Marcia Pointon, Cambridge and New York: Cambridge University Press, 1993, pp.89–107

Wendy Slatkin, *The Voices of Women Artists*, Englewood Cliffs, NJ: Prentice Hall, 1993

Rosa Bonheur correspondence is in the Jake and Nancy Hamon Arts Library, Southern Methodist University, Dallas.

Rosa Bonheur was not only the first woman artist to be awarded the Légion d'Honneur, which was established by Napoleon I to honour the most accomplished French citizens, but also the most prominent woman artist in Europe and America of her time, an example for women artists of a younger generation.

Bonheur was the oldest child of Raymond Bonheur, an artist, drawing instructor and follower of Saint-Simon, whose utopian theories questioned traditional social structures, including gender norms, and his wife Sophie, the child of a middle-class Bordeaux family and a former student of her husband. After Sophie Bonheur's untimely death in 1833, Rosa Bonheur found solace and affection in the Micas family; Natalie Micas would become her lifelong friend and companion. Bonheur's father initially sent her to the school at which he taught and later attempted to apprentice her to a seamstress; she, however, wanted to become a painter, and eventually her father relented, at first teaching

her himself and later sending her to the Louvre to copy. He held up Elisabeth Vigée-Lebrun (q.v.) as the model of a successful woman artist and allowed his daughter to bring animals into the family studio so that she could study them. When Bonheur determined to become an *animalier,* she went to the slaughter-house at Roule to study animal anatomy.

Bonheur made her debut at the Salon in 1841 with two paintings, including *Rabbits Nibbling Carrots* (Musée des Beaux-Arts, Bordeaux). In 1845 she was awarded a third-class medal and three years later received a first-class medal. In 1849 she exhibited *Ploughing at Nivernais* (Musée Nationale du Château de Fontainebleau), which had been commissioned by the government of the Second Republic. This monumental work was said to be inspired by the opening chapter of George Sand's novel, *La Mare au diable*. Two teams of oxen strain forward as they draw ploughs through the rich red soil, their scale and power overshadowing their four handlers. As an evocation of rural productivity, the painting was welcomed by government officials and critics. In 1851 Bonheur began preparations for another ambitious work with twice-weekly visits to the Paris horse market. *The Horse Fair* (1853; Metropolitan Museum of Art, New York) depicts a line of percherons at the market at the Boulevard de l'Hôpital near Salpêtrière. Under a blue sky, a great wheel of rearing and lunging horses surges past as grooms struggle to control them. In the centre of the canvas a rider in blue cap astride one of the horses looks out at the viewer: it has been suggested that this androgynous figure is a self-portrait that Bonheur inserted into the composition as a way of publicly questioning and resisting conventional feminine gender roles.

When it was exhibited at the Salon of 1853 *The Horse Fair* was widely admired. It recalled the work of Théodore Géricault and the frieze of the Parthenon, and Bonheur's precise naturalism and painstaking technique set her apart from other artists who painted the French countryside – particularly the group that included Millet, Théodore Rousseau and Constant Troyon and which came to be known as the Barbizon School. The painting found favour with such conservative critics as Etienne Delécluze, but others argued that her transcription of nature was too literal, that in contrast to Troyon, she merely copied nature. At the close of the exhibition, Bonheur and another woman artist were awarded *hors concours* status and granted the privilege of exhibiting whatever they wished in future Salons, a privilege that after 1852 had been reserved for members of the Légion d'Honneur and the Académie des Beaux-Arts. Although the percheron horses, native to Normandy, were particularly favoured by Louis Napoléon, who used them in his imperial coaches, the large work was not purchased by the government. It was exhibited in Bordeaux and Ghent and purchased by Ernest Gambart, a dealer of prints and paintings who had established a gallery in London to exhibit works by French artists. Gambart arranged for Bonheur to visit Britain while the painting was on view and introduced her to Charles Eastlake, the President of the Royal Academy; Elizabeth Rigby, the discerning art critic married to Eastlake; John Ruskin; and Edwin Landseer, Britain's foremost *animalier*, whom Bonheur greatly respected.

Bonheur's visit to Britain, which also introduced her to new breeds of animals and new subjects, led to such works as *Gathering for the Hunt* (1856; Haggin Museum, Stockton, CA), which represents a group of horses, dogs and riders in the early morning countryside. Ruskin complained that Bonheur's animals lacked the "gleam of humanity, a flash of light through which their life looks out and up to our great mystery of command over them" (quoted in Ashton 1981, p.112). For British audiences especially, representations of animals served as a symbolic zone of mediation between the natural and the human. Horses in particular were often endowed with qualities similar to those considered characteristic of women – docility, patience, courage, perseverance, strength – and representations of horse training thus evoked complex meanings about unruly nature subjected to man's will.

Bonheur's popularity in Britain and the USA enabled her dealers – Gambart and the Tedesco brothers – to place most of her works with collectors, and she had little need to participate in exhibitions in France. She sent *Haymaking at Auvergne* (Musée National du Château de Fontainebleau) to the Exposition Universelle in Paris in 1855, where it was hung as a pendant to *Ploughing at Nivernais* and received a gold medal. This, however, was the last Salon she participated in until the Exposition Universelle of 1867. In 1865 she was visited by the Empress Eugénie – the empress was temporarily acting as regent in Louis Napoléon's absence and

she took advantage of the powers conferred on her to award Bonheur the red ribbon of the Légion d'Honneur with the feminist slogan: "Genius has no sex".

Bonheur did not sentimentalise or anthropomorphise her subjects but portrayed them in their natural habitat. *Stag Listening to the Wind* (1867; Vassar College Art Gallery, Poughkeepsie, NY) represents a deer standing on the slope of a hillside where open fields give way to heavy woods: the beast is poised looking towards the field as though ready at the first suspicious noise to dash for cover in the woods. It contrasts markedly with Landseer's popular and much reproduced *Monarch of the Glen* (1851; John Dewar and Sons Ltd), in which a stag turns to confront the viewer, his antlers silhouetted against the distant mountain horizon. In many of Bonheur's works, as in *Returning from the Fields* (1851; Columbus Museum of Art, OH), which shows two ox-drawn carts, and *Pastoral Landscape with Cattle* (Philadelphia Museum of Art), animals are represented standing or travelling down a road, isolated against a flat, open landscape that allows a clear view of Bonheur's careful study of their physiognomy. Bonheur's letters suggest her strong identification with animals: she frequently refers to herself or her correspondents as "my poor little wren" or "your old animal of a sister".

In order to study the animals at the Paris markets and slaughter-houses Bonheur routinely entered highly masculine environments: perhaps as early as the 1840s, and certainly by the early 1850s, when she was preparing *The Horse Fair*, she adopted a form of masculinised dress – trousers and a loose smock (*blouse*). Her preferred costume may have owed something to Saint-Simonian utopian dress experiments, but it was most similar to the dress of male peasants and the studio dress worn by many male artists. By the 1850s this had become her habitual costume in the studio and at home, and she obtained necessary police permission to wear masculine clothing in public. Although she wore *blouse* and trousers in informal photographs, she avoided having formal photographs or portraits made of her in this dress, which she maintained she wore largely for convenience. For more public occasions she developed a style of provincial dress that she wore when necessary, and continually complained that it was uncomfortable. Edouard Dubufe's portrait of *Rosa Bonheur at 34* (1857;

repr. Ashton 1981, p.75) showed her with her arm resting on the shoulders of a bull, dressed in a full skirt and velvet jacket with lace collar.

A public precedent had been established for cross-dressing in the 1830s by George Sand, who had adopted upper-class male dress – a dark suit – when she wanted to attend the theatre. Sand had been satirised in the press for her costume; Bonheur, although she admired Sand, shunned such notoriety. In the 1860s, when her transvestism became a matter of public knowledge, critics treated Bonheur's *blouse* and trousers with amusement as the dress of an absent-minded but well-meaning eccentric whose studio-stable with its stalls for horses and sheep was known from a lithographic view (*ibid.*, p.72). By the end of the century, however, her costume came to be viewed with hostility and she was called a "masculinised" woman. As increasing numbers of young women entered studios where they could work from the nude model, exhibited at the Salon and embarked on careers that called into question traditional feminine roles, attitudes towards Bonheur's resistance to conventional constraints on feminine behaviour became more complex and conflicted. At the Salon of 1893, Mme Achille Fould represented Bonheur in her studio in male dress, surrounded by well-known works and other signs of her professional status and accomplishment (see Garb 1992, p.219), but in such magazines as *Le Monde Illustré* she was satirised and her dress ridiculed (see Saslow 1992, p.194). Bonheur was greatly admired by such younger artists as Virginie Demont-Breton, who in her memoirs recalled the day in her childhood when she learned that the famous artist Rosa Bonheur was a woman, and by the American Anna Klumpke, who had been given a Rosa Bonheur doll as a child. An account of Bonheur's visit to Britain was included in the *English Woman's Journal*, one of the earliest feminist journals, in 1858; in the 1890s she participated occasionally in the exhibitions of the Union des Femmes Peintres et Sculpteurs and was honoured by the organisation by being named honorary life president.

In 1860, as Bonheur's markets in Britain and the USA became well established, she bought an estate with a château at By, near the forest of Fontainebleau. There she established a household with Natalie and Mme Micas that she called a "domain of perfect friendship". This woman-centred household provided the three women with emotional and practical support and was in keeping with Bonheur's resistance to the traditional constraining roles assigned to women by French law and convention. Although in the later 19th century sexologists would formulate theories of homosexuality and gender variance to explain long-term, highly romanticised relationships between women, earlier in the century such commitments were frequently idealised as a form of elevated and passionate friendship. Bonheur was deeply saddened at the death of Natalie Micas in 1889, but in her later years was consoled by a close association with Anna Klumpke, a young painter who eventually shared her home and studio and who edited and published her memoirs.

Bonheur's estate also provided a home for her collection of animals. In the 1860s most of her paintings represented the deer, horses and dogs from the preserve at By; in the 1870s she turned her attention to lions – some of which she raised on her estate and others that she studied in zoological gardens. These became the subjects of oil paintings and watercolours, such as *Royalty at Home* (1885; Minneapolis Institute of Arts). In her notebooks Bonheur recorded multiple views of animals; as she explained: "I would study an animal and draw it in the position it took, and when it changed to another position I would draw that" (quoted in Ashton 1981, p.98). In her later years she turned to subjects from the American West. When Buffalo Bill Cody brought his Wild West show to Paris for the Exposition Universelle of 1889, she visited the encampment, making sketches of Native Americans and buffalo that would become the basis for such paintings as *Buffalo Hunt* (1889; *ibid.*, pl.155). Her friendship with Cody was commemorated in a portrait of him on horseback, *"Buffalo Bill" Cody* (1889; Whitney Gallery of Western Art, Cody, WY). In Bonheur's final years Anna Klumpke helped her to take up *Wheat Threshing at the Camargue* (Musée National de Château du Fontainbleau), a monumental canvas of a group of fiery horses that she wanted to represent "an infernal waltz". She had begun the painting in 1864 as a companion to the *Horse Fair*, but later set it aside. It remained unfinished at her death.

SUSAN WALLER

Bontecou, Lee
American sculptor and graphic artist, 1931–

Born in Providence, Rhode Island, 15 January
1931. Studied at the Art Students League, New
York, under William Zorach and John Hovannes,
1952–5; Skowhegan School of Art, Maine, 1954;
studied in Rome on Fulbright fellowships, 1955–9.
Taught in art department, Brooklyn College, New
York. Recipient of Louis Comfort Tiffany award,
1959; Competition award, Corcoran Gallery of Art
Biennial, Washington, DC, 1963; first prize,
National Institute of Arts and Letters, 1966. Has
one daughter. Lives in western Pennsylvania.

Selected Individual Exhibitions
G Gallery, New York: 1959
Leo Castelli Gallery, New York: 1960, 1962, 1966, 1971
Galerie Ileana Sonnabend, Paris: 1965
Museum Boymans-van Beuningen, Rotterdam: 1968
Städtisches Museum Schloss Morsbroich, Leverkusen:
    1968 (touring)
Kunstverein, Berlin: 1968
Museum of Contemporary Art, Chicago: 1972 (retro-
    spective)
Davison Art Center, Wesleyan University, Middletown,
    CT: 1975
Hawthorne Gallery, Skidmore College, Saratoga Springs,
    NY: 1977 (retrospective)
Museum of Contemporary Art, Los Angeles: 1993–4
    (touring)

Bibliography
Americans 1963, exh. cat., Museum of Modern Art, New
    York, 1963
Dore Ashton, "Illusion and fantasy: Lee [Magica fantasia
    di Lee]", Metro, no.8, April 1963, pp.28–33
New American Sculpture, exh. cat., Pasedena Art
    Museum, CA, 1964
Recent American Sculpture, exh. cat., Jewish Museum,
    New York, 1964
John Coplans, "Higgins, Price, Chamberlain, Bontecou,
    Westermann", Artforum, ii, April 1964, pp.38–40
Lee Bontecou, exh. cat., Galerie Ileana Sonnabend, Paris,
    1965
Donald Judd, "Lee Bontecou", Arts Magazine, xxxix,
    April 1965, pp.17–21
Lee Bontecou, exh. cat., Städtisches Museum Schloss
    Morsbroich, Leverkusen, and elsewhere, 1968
Lee Bontecou: Sculpturen, tekeningen, litho's, exh. cat.,
    Museum Boymans-van Beuningen, Rotterdam, 1968
"Lee Bontecou, untitled", Bulletin of the Cleveland
    Museum of Art, lvi, February 1969, pp.78–80
Tony Towle, "Two conversations with Lee Bontecou",
    Print Collector's Newsletter, ii, 1971, pp.25–8
James R. Mellow, "Bontecou's well-fed fish and malevo-
    lent flowers", New York Times, 6 June 1971, D19
Lee Bontecou, exh. cat., Museum of Contemporary Art,
    Chicago, 1972
Lincoln F. Johnson, "A diversity of approaches in
    contemporary art: Rauschenberg, Bontecou and
    Noland", Honolulu Academy of Arts Journal, i, 1974,
    pp.51–67
Prints and Drawings by Lee Bontecou, exh. cat., Davison
    Art Center, Wesleyan University, Middleton, CT, 1975
Eleanor Munro, Originals: American Women Artists,
    New York: Simon and Schuster, 1979
The Sculptural Membrane, exh. cat., Sculpture Center,
    New York, 1986
Charlotte Streifer Rubinstein, American Women
    Sculptors, Boston: Hall, 1990
Terry R. Myers, "From the junk aesthetic to the junk
    mentality", Arts Magazine, lxiv, February 1990,
    pp.60–64
Mona Hadler, "Lee Bontecou: Heart of a conquering
    darkness", Source: Notes in the History of Art, xii,
    Fall 1992, pp.38–44
Elizabeth A.T. Smith, "Abstract sinister", Art in America,
    lxxxi, September 1993, pp.82–7
Mona Hadler, "Lee Bontecou's 'Warnings'", Art Journal,
    liii, Winter 1994, pp.56–61

The work of the American artist Lee Bontecou was
widely acclaimed, collected and exhibited in the
USA and Europe during the 1960s and early 1970s.
Hailed as one of the most promising young sculptors of her generation, Bontecou created a startlingly original body of work that has stood apart
from the art historical mainstream and remains little
known from a contemporary perspective.

One of the few women artists to achieve broad
recognition in the 1960s, Bontecou first distinguished herself in 1959 with a body of small to mid-
sized abstract constructions of salvaged canvas and
burlap stretched over welded steel frames, held in
place by pieces of twisted wire (Untitled, 1959;
Moderna Museet, Stockholm). In 1960, the year
that her work was first shown at Leo Castelli
Gallery, Bontecou markedly increased the size and
three-dimensionality of many of these predominantly wall-mounted works. She also began to
incorporate into her sculpture an array of materials
such as rope, denim, leather and black velvet – the
last used to create the backdrops for deep voids
constructed within many of the works. In untitled
pieces of 1961 and 1962, found metal parts and
objects ranging from fan blades and industrial saw-
tooth components to war-surplus materials such as
gas masks and helmets came to be positioned within

and across the surfaces of the increasingly eccentrically configured canvas and steel armatures.

While remaining emphatically non-specific, the objects embedded within Bontecou's sculpture endow it with overtones of figurative and mechanistic imagery. In many of these resolutely abstract and persistently disquieting sculptures, a strongly implied human presence – heads, gaping mouths, eye sockets and teeth evoked by deep openings often containing jagged saw-toothed blades and metal grilles – is consistently countered by a seemingly random dispersal of visual detail and an almost cubistic fragmentation of form. The intense three-dimensionality of the works imparts a map-like quality; their relatively vast expanses and deep voids seem also to indicate environmental scale and significance.

Co-existent with the dominant tendencies of the late 1950s to early 1970s – Abstract Expressionism, assemblage, Minimalism, Pop Art and eccentric abstraction – Bontecou's sculpture resists categorisation. Furthermore, the often heroic scale, commanding physicality and brutal quality of her work attracted particular attention because these characteristics seemed at odds with the conventionally defined products of a "feminine" sensibility. Yet discussion of her sculpture often revolved around its perceived sensuality and pointedly female sexuality; critics frequently interpreted the persistent circular openings within the work as body cavities and even as symbolic "vagina dentata" due to their threatening containment of objects. Such allusions rarely acknowledged either the presence or implications of the more substantially representational aspects of Bontecou's sculpture, nor the heterogeneous, multivalent quality of its imagery and overall sculptural character.

To a contemporary viewer, the presence in many of the works of small machines, guns, zippers, rivets, metal grates, gas masks and helmets clearly refers to the materials and activities of war, and more broadly to destruction, brutality and annihilation. Although Bontecou consistently declined to explain the sources of her imagery, she alluded early on to a "concern to build things that express our relation to this country – to other countries – to this world – to other worlds – in terms of myself" (New York 1963, p.12). Not until much later in her career did she expressly reveal that a need to respond to the menacing spectres of war and global destruction had, in part, given shape to much of her early work.

The visual and visceral power of Bontecou's sculpture of the 1960s extends to a body of work on paper produced in tandem with it. Often rendered in almost hyper-realistic detail and configured in dense, all-over compositions, the drawings give evidence of a fascination with relationships between forms and images, particularly in terms of mutation or transformation between the natural and the man-made. Here, the military imagery that found its way obliquely into certain sculptures can be more easily discerned; for example, a highly detailed drawing of 1961 (D26; pencil on paper, Menil Collection, Houston) shows eerily anthropomorphic gas masks dispersed across the emptiness of a white background.

Bontecou's sculpture of the mid-1960s departs from the brutal character of much of her earlier work. Formally more complex in terms of three-dimensionality and texture, this body of work incorporates a wide range of tonalities from black to red to gold to ivory. Using epoxy to build up certain key parts of the works, Bontecou further developed her tendency towards painterly effects that she had previously achieved by shading and modelling form with soot. Invoking a palpable sensation of dynamism and organic profusion, these sculptures (e.g. *Untitled*, 1966; mixed media; 81 × 81 × 45.7 cm.; private collection) present a florid preponderance of faceted, overlapping parts; references to flora and fauna and to such images as billowing sails are apparent in both sculptures and drawings (*Untitled*, 1967; pencil and pen and ink on flocked paper; Hirshhorn Museum and Sculpture Garden, Washington, DC) executed between 1965 and 1967. Exuberant and disarmingly lyrical, these works posed an even greater challenge to critics than Bontecou's earlier works in their lack of both an identifiable content and an affinity to recognisable styles and movements.

In the late 1960s and early 1970s Bontecou's work took a frankly figurative turn. Strongly evoking but without directly representing actual species, she sculpted in vacuum-formed plastic and drew startling images of fish and flowering plants, such as *Three Fish* (1970; chalk on black paper; Museum of Modern Art, New York). Combining elements of crystalline physical perfection with qualities of sinister decrepitude, these figurative pieces share other essential characteristics with Bontecou's earlier work, such as a fascination with processes of transformation and with personification of phantasmagoria – whether observed, remembered or felt. The implicit savagery of these works also functioned as a kind of social and political statement about Bontecou's environmental concerns.

Commingling the organic and inorganic in form, imagery and technique, Bontecou's sculpture and drawings address mutation and transformation within and outside the domain of the human body. The conceptual and visual relationships between a medieval helmet and a flower, the mechanistic teeth of an industrial saw blade and those of a fish, the wretched twist of a piece of wire precariously joining a corner of canvas to a bent steel frame and the sleek, metallic mechanical parts of a found automobile engine, the stencilled name of an identifiable army private on a piece of canvas duffel bag and the abstract, even cosmic implications of blackness at the bottom of a crater-like void function as resonant elements of Bontecou's highly personal artistic vocabulary. One writer noted of Bontecou's compelling, disturbing and profoundly authentic body of work: "The best thing about her work when it hits is that it has nothing to do with anything. It is suffocating, which is the best praise I can give" (John Perreault, "Art", *Village Voice*, 10 June 1971, p.28).

Since the 1970s Bontecou has continued to work two-dimensionally while teaching in the art department of Brooklyn College. Since her recent retirement, she has once again begun to make sculpture but has exhibited very little, living and working quietly in western Pennsylvania. Her work is represented in numerous museum collections, including the Museum of Modern Art, Whitney Museum of American Art and Solomon R. Guggenheim Museum, New York; Art Institute of Chicago; Walker Art Center, Minneapolis; Museum of Fine Arts, Houston; Hirshhorn Museum and Sculpture Garden, Washington, DC; Moderna Museet, Stockholm; and the Stedelijk Museum, Amsterdam.

ELIZABETH A.T. SMITH

Borch, Gesina ter
Dutch amateur painter, 1631–1690

Born in Deventer, 15 November 1631, the daughter of Gerard ter Borch the Elder, and half-sister of Gerard ter Borch the Younger. Resided all her life in Zwolle, except for visits to Gerard the Younger in Deventer and several stays with her sister Jenneken Schellinger in Amsterdam. After Jenneken's death in 1675, the three children of the Schellinger family came to live with her in Zwolle. Died 16(?) April 1690.

Bibliography
M.E. Houck, "Mededelingen betreffende Ter Borch en anderen, benevens aantekeningen omtrent hunne familieleden" [Information concerning Ter Borch and others, with notes on members of his family], *Verslagen en Mededelingen van de Vereeniging tot Beoefening van Overijsselsch Regt en Geschiedenis*, xx, 1899, pp.1–172

S.J. Gudlaugsson, *Katalog der Gemälde Gerard ter Borchs, sowie biographisches Material*, 2 vols, The Hague: Nijhoff, 1959–60

Alison M. Kettering, *Drawings from the Ter Borch Studio Estate in the Rijksmuseum*, 2 vols, The Hague: Staatsuitgeverij, 1988

G. Luijten, "De *Triomf van de Schilderkunst*: Een titeltekening van Gesina ter Borch en een toneelstuk" [The *Triumph of Painting*: A frontispiece by Gesina ter Borch and a stage play], *Bulletin van het Rijksmuseum*, xxxvi, 1988, pp.283–314 (English summary, pp.354–6)

H. Luijten, "Swiren vol van leer, amblemsche wijs geduijt: Een opmerkelijk zeventiende-eeuws poëzie-album van Gesina ter Borch" [Elegancies replete with lessons, shown emblematically: A remarkable 17th-century poetry album by Gesina ter Borch], *ibid.*, pp.315–42 (English summary, pp.356–7, 360)

Alison M. Kettering, "Ter Borch's ladies in satin", *Art History*, xvi, 1993, pp.95–124

Gesina ter Borch was an illustrator and painter of scenes of everyday life, who enjoyed some local recognition. Her less-professional orientation to painting in watercolour led her to explore a variety of subjects and approaches largely unhindered by the conventions of contemporary fine art. Her responsiveness to the more popular artistic currents of her day meant the survival of a considerable body of material reflecting Dutch domestic taste, both visual and literary. Not least among her contributions was the preservation of many drawings by family members, among them drawings by her well-known half-brother, Gerard the Younger.

Like so many girls from artistic families during the early modern period, Gesina ter Borch took advantage both of the intellectual stimulation and the materials available in the parental home. Her father, Gerard the Elder, who had given up an artistic career to become Licence Master of Zwolle (receiver of import and export duties), encouraged the artistic education of his three sons far more vigorously than that of his daughters. Instead, Gesina developed her skills at handwriting (*schoonschrijfkunst*), probably under the supervision of the Zwolle schoolmaster. She preserved her earliest exercises – beautifully penned poems and aphorisms copied from various sources – in a *Materi-Boeck* (Theme book; begun 1646; Rijksmuseum, Amsterdam). Nevertheless, the booklet quickly turned into an album for watercolour drawings and poem illustrations, anticipating Gesina's focus on pictorial art rather than calligraphy in the years ahead. One of these sheets bears the sign of her father's approval, his annotation of the date of execution. (By contrast, Gerard the Elder annotated hundreds of juvenile drawings by his sons.)

Despite the restrictions imposed on young women at the time, Gesina proved to be strongly motivated to develop her artistic talents. She essentially learned to draw by the side of her younger brothers Harmen and Moses. In 1652, shortly after her 21st birthday, she began work on an ambitious album (Rijksmuseum) for her favourite poems, which she illustrated with delicate watercolours, heightened with gold and silver, a medium considered at the time more suitable for women than oil painting. Many of these were fully worked miniatures, loosely based on the illustrations in such contemporary songbooks and emblem collections as J.H. Krul's *Eerlyke Tytkorting* (Honourable pastime; 1634) and Jacob Cats's *Spiegel vanden ouden ende nieuwen tijdt* (Mirror of old and new times; 1632). Such books were the sources, as well, for the poems she copied into her album. Her selection from this literary material was quite diverse, although Petrarchan love themes predominated: songs featuring lovelorn suitors of hard-hearted beauties. In addition, laudatory poems written in Gesina's honour were entered into the poetry album, most significantly, those by Henrik Jordis, her possible suitor.

Jordis added the dedicatory verses to the poetry album just as Gesina was completing it in 1660. His contribution to Gesina's largest endeavour, the "Art Book" (begun 1660; Rijksmuseum), as he named it, is even more significant. An experienced writer of occasional verse, Jordis was an Amsterdam merchant with connections to literary circles. To this Art Book he contributed an original allegorical play, the *Triomphe der Schilderconst over de Doodt* (Triumph of painting over death), as well as the iconographical programme for Gesina's large title drawing directly based on the play. By 1662 no trace of Gesina's friendship with Jordis remained and she never did marry.

Gesina's major work in the Art Book dates from the 1660s. In a bold style she chronicled the manners, customs and costumes of small-town life in full-size watercolours that provide a wealth of detail about contemporary society and its attitudes. After about 20 pages she transformed the album into a scrapbook. Here can be found many drawings by her brothers and family memorabilia.

The artistic relationship between Gerard the Younger and Gesina was especially close between c.1648 and the mid-1660s. These were the years during which she frequently modelled for his paintings, and they also corresponded to the most intense period of her own artistic activity. Just as Gerard the Younger appears to have encouraged her art, Gesina's very choice of love poetry may have provided inspiration in turn for his genre paintings. During the mid-1660s Gesina also tried oil painting. The most conspicuous example of her efforts can be seen in the posthumous portrait of *Moses ter Borch* (c.1668; Rijksmuseum), on which she collaborated with Gerard.

The local acclaim that Gesina ter Borch enjoyed for her artistic accomplishments is conveyed through the many laudatory poems written in the albums by her admirers. Here the vividness of her personality and character emerge, her cleverness, quickness of mind and devotion to the pursuit of art and knowledge. She can also be credited with preserving the Ter Borch family's work on paper. She stipulated in her will that none of these drawings would leave the family. When the last of the descendants died in 1886, the Rijksmuseum in Amsterdam was able to buy nearly the entire estate intact. This also allowed the rediscovery of an amateur's works, a rare occurrence among 17th-century women amateurs.

ALISON MCNEIL KETTERING

Bourgeois, Louise [fig. 7]
American sculptor, 1911–

Born in Paris, France, 25 December 1911; natura-lised US citizen 1951. Studied in Paris at Sorbonne University, 1932–5 (baccalaureate); Ecole du Louvre, 1936–7; Ecole des Beaux-Arts, 1936–8; Atelier Bissière, 1936–7; Académie de la Grande Chaumière, 1937–8; Atelier Fernand Léger, 1938. Married American art historian Robert Goldwater, 1938; three sons; husband died 1973. Moved to New York, 1938; studied at Art Students League under Vaclav Vytlacil, 1939–40. Taught at Great Neck public schools, New York, 1960; Brooklyn College, New York, 1963 and 1968; Pratt Institute, Brooklyn, 1965–7; Maryland Art Institute, Baltimore, 1984; New School for Social Research, New York, 1987. Recipient of National Endowment for the Arts (NEA) grant, 1973; Outstanding Achievement award, Women's Caucus for Art, 1980; Skowhegan medal for sculpture, 1985; Distinguished Artist award, 1987, and Lifetime Achievement award, 1989, College Art Association; gold medal of honor, National Arts Club, 1987; Creative Arts medal award, Brandeis University, Waltham, 1989; Award for Distinction in Sculpture, Sculpture Center, New York, 1990; Lifetime Achievement award, International Sculpture Center, Washington, DC, 1991; Grand Prix National de Sculpture, French Ministry of Culture, 1991; honorary doctorates from Yale University, New Haven, 1977; Bard College, Annandale-on-Hudson, 1981; Massachusetts College of Art, Boston, 1983; Maryland Art Institute, Baltimore, 1984; New School, New York, 1987; Pratt Institute, Brooklyn, 1993; Art Institute of Chicago, 1995. Officier de l'Ordre des Arts et Lettres, French Ministry of Culture, 1984. Fellow for Life, Metropolitan Museum of Art, New York, 1987. Fellow, American Academy of Arts and Sciences, 1981. Member, American Academy and Institute of Arts and Letters, 1983; Sculptors Guild; American Abstract Artists; College Art Association. Lives in New York.

Selected Individual Exhibitions
Bertha Schaefer Gallery, New York: 1945
Norlyst Gallery, New York: 1947
Peridot Gallery, New York: 1949, 1950, 1953
Rose Fried Gallery, New York: 1963
Stable Gallery, New York: 1964
112 Greene Street, New York: 1974
Xavier Fourcade Gallery, New York: 1978, 1979, 1980
Max Hutchinson Gallery, New York: 1980
Robert Miller Gallery, New York: 1982, 1984, 1986, 1987, 1988, 1989, 1991
Museum of Modern Art, New York: 1982–3 (touring retrospective), 1994–5 (touring)
Daniel Weinberg Gallery, Los Angeles: 1984
Serpentine Gallery, London: 1985
Maeght-Lelong, Paris and Zürich: 1985 (retrospective)
Taft Museum, Cincinnati: 1987–9 (touring)
Museum Overholland, Amsterdam: 1988
Henry Art Gallery, University of Washington, Seattle: 1988
Sperone-Westwater Gallery, New York: 1989
Frankfurter Kunstverein, Frankfurt am Main: 1989–91 (touring retrospective)
Galerie Karsten Greve, Paris: 1992
American Pavilion, Venice Biennale: 1993
Brooklyn Museum, NY: 1993–6 (touring retrospective)
Musée d'Art Moderne de la Ville de Paris: 1995 (retro-spective)
Museum of Modern Art, Oxford: 1995–6 (touring)

Selected Writings
"Freud's toys", *Artforum*, January 1990, pp.111–13
"Louise Bourgeois", *Balcon* (Madrid), no.8–9, 1992, pp.44–50

Bibliography
Lucy R. Lippard, "Louise Bourgeois: From the inside out", *Artforum*, xiii, March 1975, pp.26–33; reprinted in Lucy R. Lippard, *From the Center: Feminist Essays on Women's Art*, New York: Dutton, 1976
Louise Bourgeois, exh. cat., Museum of Modern Art, New York, and elsewhere, 1982
Robert Storr, "Louise Bourgeois: Gender and posses-sion", *Art in America*, lxxi, April 1983, pp.128–37
Donald Kuspit, "Louise Bourgeois: Where angels fear to tread", *Artforum*, xxv, March 1987, pp.115–20
Bourgeois, New York: Avendon/Vintage Contemporary Artists, 1988 (interview with Donald Kuspit)
Louise Bourgeois Drawings, exh. cat., Robert Miller Gallery, New York, and Galerie Lelong, Paris, 1988
Stuart Morgan, "Taking cover: Louise Bourgeois inter-viewed", *Artscribe International*, no.67, January–February 1988, pp.30–34
Louise Bourgeois, exh. cat., Frankfurter Kunstverein, Frankfurt am Main, and elsewhere, 1989
Robert C. Morgan, "Eccentric abstraction and Postminimalism", *Flash Art*, no.144, January–February 1989, pp.73–81
Alain Kirili, "The passion for sculpture: A conversation with Louise Bourgeois", *Arts Magazine*, lxiii, March 1989, pp.68–75
Parkett, no.27, March 1991 (special issue)

Christiane Meyer-Thoss, *Louise Bourgeois: Konstruktionen für den freien Fall (Designing for Free Fall)*, Zürich: Ammann, 1992

Holland Cotter, "Dislocating the modern", *Art in America*, lxxx, January 1992, pp.100–06

David Deitcher, "Art of the installation plan", *Artforum*, xxx, January 1992, pp.78–84

Lisa Liebmann, "Mr Hoet's holiday", *Artforum*, xxxi, September 1992, pp.87–9

Paul Gardner, *Louise Bourgeois*, New York: Universe, 1993

Louise Bourgeois: The Locus of Memory, Works, 1982–1993, exh. cat., Brooklyn Museum, NY, and elsewhere, 1993

Andrew Graham-Dixon, "Totem and taboo", *Vogue* (UK), June 1993, pp.132–7

Connie Butler, "Terrible beauty and the enormity of space", *Art & Text*, no.46, September 1993, pp.60–65

Deborah Wye and Carol Smith, *The Prints of Louise Bourgeois*, New York: Museum of Modern Art, and London: Thames and Hudson, 1994

Francesco Bonami, "Louise Bourgeois: In a strange way, things are getting better and better", *Flash Art*, no.174, January–February 1994, pp.36–9

Ann Gibson, "Louise Bourgeois's retroactive politics of gender", *Art Journal*, liii, Winter 1994, pp.44–7

Louise Bourgeois, exh. cat., Musée National d'Art Moderne Centre Georges Pompidou, and Musée d'Art Moderne de la Ville de Paris, 1995

Marie-Laure Bernadac, *Louise Bourgeois*, Paris: Flammarion, 1996

Louise Bourgeois was born in Paris in 1911. The following year the family moved their tapestry gallery to Choisy-le-Roi and then later settled in the Parisian suburb of Antony on the River Bièvres, where her father established a workshop for restoring old tapestries. Bourgeois's childhood was, in her own account, dominated by her father's ten-year relationship with the children's English nurse, Sadie, and her own feelings of anger and rejection. Initially, she studied mathematics at the Sorbonne (1932) and then enrolled at the Ecole des Beaux-Arts, but she found the academic structure too conservative for her developing artistic interests and took to frequenting the numerous private studios and drawing academies, being taught by, among others, Paul Colin, André Lhôte, Yves Brayer and Fernand Léger. Bourgeois also studied art history at the Ecole du Louvre and lectured in the museum. In 1938 she married the art historian Robert Goldwater and together they joined the flow of refugee artists fleeing Europe for America who were to exert such a profound influence upon American modernism.

Such are the basic historical facts of Bourgeois's early biography. However, as Roland Barthes has observed, history tends to be naturalised by the processes of myth. Artists' lives have always provided a mythic structure for the idealisation of the individual, the cult of the genius describing a range of subject positions from a privileged marginality, through bohemian counter-cultures, to the possession of visionary "truths". Mostly these narratives have inscribed a specific, gendered identity, and have focused upon moments of biography as the keys with which to decipher the hermeneutic code of artistic production: "lives of the artist" that read the passage of experience off and into the works of art. The repetitive tropes of artistic biography partly define the humanistic impulse in Western culture. Bourgeois, as much as any other living artist, has been the subject of such mythic constructions; indeed, she appears to be a willing participant in the narrativisation of experience as mythic moments that symbolically invest the forms and relationships of her art.

The contradictions of childhood, of imaginary completeness and terrible loss, the domestic space as both secure and threatening and the vividness of the Oedipal drama explicitly and recurrently figured in works of catharsis and disavowal, describe an artistic identity constructed at the margins of the avant-garde and across geographical and linguistic boundaries, until the recognition and acclaim for her work that has grown since the beginning of the 1980s. (For example, childhood memory figures prominently in such works as *Cell (Choisy)*, 1990–93; Collection Ydessa Hendeles Foundation, Tokyo, repr. Paris 1995, p.184, where a guillotine presides ominously over the paternal mansion, while the explicit expression of murderous rage occurs in the installation *Destruction of the Father*, 1974; artist's collection, *ibid.*, p.130.) However, her antagonism towards paternal figures and the repressive metaphors of feminine sexuality that characterised Surrealist representations provided the context for a powerful expression of sublimated sexuality in her own work. These themes are worked out in the drawings, paintings and prints she made in the period between her arrival in New York until she began experimenting with sculptural materials a decade later. Their immediacy, graphic range and narrative qualities – a working out and a working through of memory and desire – have been a corollary to her sculptural practice and her increasingly large-scale installations for almost half a century.

The repetitive motif of this period is the combination of a female lower body grafted on to the childlike image of a building that forms the torso and head of the figure: the *Femme Maison* series. The most familiar of the series is the drawing of 1947 (Solomon R. Guggenheim Museum, New York), the image used for the cover illustration of the critic Lucy Lippard's collection of essays *From the Center* (1976). A schematically rendered nude figure faces the viewer, the hips surmounted by a multi-storeyed house with arms attached, the right hand upraised, perhaps in greeting. The ambivalence of this hybrid form, of femininity constrained by the cage of domesticity or, alternatively, emerging from the home into a wider and more public arena, combines themes that repeat throughout Bourgeois's subsequent oeuvre. Perhaps the most characteristic element in her drawings is the repeated patterning of parallel and cross-hatched strokes – of a line that has the quality of the trace of hair or cotton, saturated in ink and drawn or flicked across the surface of the paper. A diary entry records: "Hair in water, hair in flames, hair that dries before the fire ...", and an early memory she recounts is of repairing the frayed edges of the Gobelin tapestries in her father's workshop, replacing the excised genitals of cupids (removed by her mother in recognition of the preferences of collectors) with flowers.

As Bourgeois's life spans most of the 20th century, her meetings, associations and friendships map the major artistic currents of Western modernism. She recalls conversations with Brancusi and Giacometti, collaborations with Duchamp and arguments with André Breton. She was one of the few women artists to attend meetings held by the Abstract Expressionists and was a member of their group, the "Irascibles". She participated in the anti-war activities of the 1960s, had discussions with Minimalist artists, was associated with Arte Povera, and her work has consistently, though problematically, occupied a pivotal position in feminist art history and theory. (In Robert Mapplethorpe's 1982 photograph of her, dressed in furs and clutching an oversized phallus – her sculpture *Fillette* (1968; Museum of Modern Art, New York) – and laughing at the viewer, Bourgeois adopts the very image of a "bad mother", mocking patriarchal authority.) Myths and fables have a long tradition of connection to the feminine. The curiosity attributed to women that, in the narratives of Eve or Pandora carry a negative connotation, frequently revolves around the forbidden or the secretive. Bourgeois has always been drawn to the socially repressed and the taboo, looking in those secret places and recesses where the knowledge of the self is intimately related to sexuality and the body.

During the 1950s and early 1960s her predominant sculptural form was the vertical – structures that revolve around a central axis or spine to produce totems or pillars that refer to the figure in isolation or in groupings that suggest familial or communal relations (e.g. *Femme Volage*, 1951; Solomon R. Guggenheim Museum; *Quarantania*, 1947–53; Museum of Modern Art, New York). Wood, patinated bronze or plaster are the working materials, the clustering forms, often the subject of compositional readjustment, figure masculinity across a range from aggressive virility to the threat of castration. As she experimented with other materials – plaster, latex and the recurrent use of marble – the sexual body flows between the poles of gender in a palpable materialisation of flesh and skin, interiority and exteriority, attesting to the mutability of sexual identity. Frequently figured as nests, layers and orifices, the constant play of binary terms: masculine/ feminine, interior/exterior, penis/breast, hard/soft, open/closed, rough/smooth, etc., create formal and symbolic relationships and oppositions suggesting both the possibilities of antithesis and the longing for merger. Phallic forms soften into breasts, implode into sexually charged recesses and inner volumes, inscribe the body as the metaphor for plural genders and identities, charting the difficult play between sameness and difference (*Le Regard*, 1966; artist's collection, repr. Paris 1995, p.103; *Janus Fleuri*, 1968; bronze; artist's collection, *ibid.*, p.47; *Cumul*, 1969; marble; Musée National d'Art Moderne, Centre Georges Pompidou, Paris). Bourgeois's female imagery describes the boundaries of the feminine-masculine and masculine-feminine, hybrid spaces and surfaces that symbolise the attraction and repulsion between the sexes, and the loss that prefigures desire. For example, in *Nature Study* (1984; versions exist in red wax, plaster and bronze, the last in Whitney Museum of American Art, New York) sexual difference collapses in the figure of a crouching animal, possibly a griffin, which displays both male and female attributes. A fetishistic expression of polymorphous sexuality, the animal's truncated neck suggests a dismembered phallus, cut-off at the tip. For Bourgeois, fantasy is just another way of connecting reality and history.

In the 1980s Bourgeois started to produce the series of installations called *Cells*, works that combine found objects with carved or cast forms and which create spaces for the enactment of the dramas of family life. Again the influence of her association with the Surrealist movement comes through in the unlikely juxtaposition of objects, combinations that create new and deeper meanings, that tap the source of fantasy and desire. These works are the artist's attempt to manage the emotional traumas that underlie her most profound physical and psychological experiences – obsession, love, hate, tenderness, cruelty; the expression of identity in the recognition of the other: "I love you, do you love me?" Messages of love and pain are inscribed across the surfaces of these assemblages: "Love makes the world go round", "Fear makes the world go round" on the shutters of *Bullet Hole* (1992; repr. Paris 1995, pp.202–3); "Je t'aime" sewn into the cover of the bed supporting the arched body in *Cell (Arch of Hysteria)* (1992–3; artist's collection, *ibid.*, p.206) and embroidered across the pillow in the child's bedroom in *Red Rooms* (1994); "Do you love me?" carved into the marble base of *Untitled (With Foot, "Do You Love Me?")* (1989). A cell is an enclosed space with either religious or penal connotations, a micro-organism or the component of a battery. Cells are building blocks, transmitters of energy, or places of containment. Condensed, emotionally charged, populated with part-objects (eyes, hands, ears, breasts, in marble, glass, wood and bronze), in these domestic spaces history clings to the architectural remnants that enclose and support the objects that embody memory as a material reality.

Bourgeois's application of technique to material emphasises the craft of making, of hand-skills and co-ordination at the service of the imagination, but with her an imagination that consistently challenges the viewer to reflect upon vision as both an aesthetic and an ethical experience. If this is "woman's work", then it is a conjoining of the pleasure and the pain that accompany gender roles and divisions in order to undo our cultural stereotypes. The giant needles that pierce space (*Needle (Fuseau)*, 1992; *ibid.*, p.201), the repetitive piercing of latex or wooden forms (*Articulated Lair*, 1986; Museum of Modern Art), are constant reminders of the social violence that threatens the feminine in the fantasy of

castration. These elements are combined in *Cell (Arch of Hysteria)*. Old and weathered shuttering encloses a claustrophobic space in which two objects are juxtaposed – a disused industrial bandsaw that menaces the bronze cast of a headless, arched male body upon a bed covered with a cloth bearing, in red, the repeated phrase "Je t'aime". This extraordinary image of anger and desire, of castration and unbearable longing, expresses the violence of representation in the wish to incorporate and destroy the other. Bourgeois's consummate technical ability, her control over materials most evident in carved stone, suggests a kind of deception – that the stone has abandoned its intransigent materiality to become viscous, flowing into the shapes and volumes that define the final form. This fluidity might be taken as a metaphor for the rhythms and pulsions of the sexual body, the dissolution of boundaries that has been particularly associated with the maternal body. Bourgeois has herself spoken of the fluids of the body as metaphors of the unconscious – sweat, tears, saliva, urine, milk – and of the corporeal rites of passage that mark the stages of womanhood. The huge installation *Precious Liquids*, first shown at Documenta IX in Kassel (1992), and acquired by the Centre Georges Pompidou, Paris, is a complex arrangement of glass containers attached to stands suggesting something between an alchemical experiment and a surgical operation: of the processes of transformation and renewal.

Glass has become, since the early 1980s, a crucial material for Bourgeois, possessing as it does the qualities of resistance, fragility and strength in its solid state, and of extreme flexibility when molten. Glass can be densely opaque, translucent to the point of invisibility, or reflective when silvered. The mirrors, glass balls, containers – or the rich scarlet blown and cast forms in the *Red Rooms* (the colours of the body's interior spaces and the connotation of passion or danger) – are, for Bourgeois, the material expression of the self's complex identities. In *Cell (Glass Spheres and Hands)* (1990–93; National Gallery of Victoria, Melbourne) the compartment houses five large, clear glass spheres placed on chairs and stools surrounding a table that provides the surface for two hands, carved in white marble. Again the dialectic of pleasure and pain shifts the meanings between the tenderness expressed in the gesture of the touching hands and an allegory of the isolated and alienated self – the emptiness of the spheres. In many of the other installations, the presence of mirrors signifies, for Bourgeois, the acceptance of the real. But mirrors also mark the imaginary, the narcissistic identification with an image that conceals absence, or loss. The viewer is invited into spaces suffused with melancholy and the objects of desire. These spaces recode the domestic setting as both secure and dangerous, as refuge and incarceration, spaces for the giving and the withholding of love. A caress is shadowed by the objects that affirm the pressure of the past upon the present: the prison-house of memory.

The work of Louise Bourgeois, spanning the century as it does, has become increasingly and profoundly emblematic of the emotional and social landscapes that define the formation of our identities in the passage from childhood into a tenuous and fragile adulthood. History, as both personal experience and public memory, determines who we are and, in what Julia Kristeva describes as a deeply psychotic culture, Bourgeois's recognition that "self-knowledge is the only reward" constantly returns her and the viewer to the fundamental need for acceptance, and the acceptance of what is.

JON BIRD

Bourke-White, Margaret   [fig.8]
American photographer, 1904–1971

Born Margaret White in New York, 14 June 1904; appended mother's maiden name Bourke, 1927. Attended Columbia University, New York, for one semester, studying photography under Clarence H. White, 1921–2 (left after father's death). Studied at University of Michigan, Ann Arbor, 1922–3; Purdue University, Lafayette, Indiana, 1924; Case Western Reserve University, Cleveland, 1925; Cornell University, Ithaca, New York, 1926–7 (BA). Married (1) Everett Chapman, 1924, divorced 1926; (2) writer Erskine Caldwell, 1939, divorced 1942. Freelance photographer with studio in Cleveland, 1927; in Chrysler Building, New York, 1930; decided to abandon advertising photography, 1936. Associate editor and staff photographer, *Fortune* magazine, New York, 1929–35. Staff photographer for *Life* magazine, New York, 1936–40, 1941–2 and 1945–69 (semi-retired 1957). Chief photographer for Ralph

Ingersoll's magazine *PM*, New York, 1940. Travelled to Germany and Soviet Union, 1930 (first foreign photographer permitted to take pictures of Soviet industry); Soviet Union again, 1931 and 1932; Czechoslovakia and Hungary, 1938; London, Romania, Turkey, Syria and Egypt, 1939–40; China and Soviet Union, 1941. First woman war correspondent, US Air Force, 1942; assignments in Britain, North Africa, Italy and Germany, 1942–5. Trips to India, 1946 and 1947; South Africa, 1949–50; Japan and Korea, 1952–3. Recipient of honorary doctorates from Rutgers University, New Brunswick, New Jersey, 1948; University of Michigan, Ann Arbor, 1951; Achievement award, *US Camera*, 1963; Honor Roll award, American Society of Magazine Photographers, 1964. First symptoms of Parkinson's disease, 1953; operations 1959 and 1961. Died in Darien, Connecticut, 27 August 1971.

Principal Exhibitions

Individual
John Becker Gallery, New York: 1931 (*Photographs by Three Americans*, with Ralph Steiner and Walker Evans)
Annual Exhibition of Advertising Art, New York: 1931 (with Anton Bruehl; art works by others)
Little Carnegie Playhouse, New York: 1932
Rockefeller Center, New York: 1934
Art Institute of Chicago: 1956
Syracuse University, NY: 1966
Carl Siembab Gallery, Boston: 1971
Witkin Gallery, New York: 1971
Andrew Dickson White Museum of Art, Cornell University, Ithaca: 1972 (retrospective)

Group
Museum of Modern Art, New York: 1949 (*Six Women Photographers*), 1951 (*Memorable Life Photographs*)

Selected Writings
Eyes on Russia, New York: Simon and Schuster, 1931
Photographs of the USSR with an Introduction by the Artist, Albany, NY: Argus Press, 1934
"Dust changes America", *Nation*, cxl, 22 May 1935, pp.597–8
"Photographing this world", *Nation*, cxlii/3685, 1936, pp.217–18
You Have Seen Their Faces, New York: Viking, 1937 (with Erskine Caldwell); reprinted Athens: University of Georgia Press, 1995
North of the Danube, New York: Viking, 1939 (with Erskine Caldwell)

"How the pictures were made", *Popular Photography*, ii, March 1939, pp.15–16, 94–5

Say, Is This the USA? New York: Duell Sloan and Pearce, 1941 (with Erskine Caldwell)

Shooting the Russian War, New York: Simon and Schuster, 1942; reprinted as *The Taste of War*, ed. Jonathan Silverman, London: Century, 1985

"Photographer in Moscow", *Harper's Bazaar*, clxxxiv, March 1942, pp.414–20

They Called It "Purple Heart Valley": A Combat Chronicle of the War in Italy, New York: Simon and Schuster, 1944

"Dear Fatherland, Rest Quietly": A Report on the Collapse of Hitler's "Thousand Years", New York: Simon and Schuster, 1946

Halfway to Freedom: A Report on the New India in the Words and Photographs of Margaret Bourke-White, New York: Simon and Schuster, 1949; as *Interview with India in Words and Pictures*, London: Phoenix House, 1950

A Report on the American Jesuits, New York: Farrar Straus and Cudahy, 1956 (with John La Farge)

"Assignments for publication", *Encyclopedia of Photography*, ii, New York, 1963, pp.274–80

Portrait of Myself, New York: Simon and Schuster, 1963 (autobiography)

Bibliography

Winifred and Frances Kirkland, *Girls Who Became Artists*, New York: Harper, 1934

T. Otto Nall, "The camera is a candid machine: An interview with Margaret Bourke-White", *Scholastic*, 15 May 1937

Rosa Reilly, "Why Margaret Bourke-White is at the top", *Popular Photography*, July 1937

"American aces: Margaret Bourke-White", *US Camera*, May 1940

Lesley Blanch, "At the other end of the lens", *Vogue* (UK), January 1943

Etna M. Kelley, "Margaret Bourke-White", *Photography*, xxxi, August 1952, pp.34–43, 85

"Bourke-White's twenty-five years", *Life*, xxxviii, 16 May 1955, pp.16–18

Robert E. Hood, *Twelve at War: Great Photographers under Fire*, New York: Putnam, 1967

Margaret Bourke-White: Photojournalist, exh. cat., Andrew Dickson White Museum of Art, Cornell University, Ithaca, NY, 1972

Sean Callahan, ed., *The Photographs of Margaret Bourke-White*, Greenwich, CT: New York Graphic Society, 1972 (contains extensive bibliography)

Margaret Bourke-White: The Cleveland Years, 1928–1930, exh. cat., New Gallery of Contemporary Art, Cleveland, 1976

Margaret Bourke-White: The Deco Lens, exh. cat., Joe and Emily Lowe Art Gallery, Syracuse University, NY, 1978

Margaret Bourke-White: The Humanitarian Vision, exh. cat., Joe and Emily Lowe Art Gallery, Syracuse University, NY, 1983

Jonathan Silverman, *For the World to See: The Life of Margaret Bourke-White*, New York: Viking, and London: Secker and Warburg, 1983

Vicki Goldberg, *Margaret Bourke-White: A Biography*, New York: Harper, 1986; London: Heinemann, 1987

David E. James, "Estheticizing the Machine Age", *Artweek*, xviii, 3 October 1987

Margaret Bourke-White, exh. cat., Jane Corkin Gallery, Toronto, 1988

Bourke-White: A Retrospective, exh. cat., International Center of Photography, New York, and elsewhere, 1988

Double Exposure: The Story of Margaret Bourke-White, 94-minute video, Turner Home Entertainment, 1989

Jozef Gross, "Changing the world", *British Journal of Photography*, cxxxvi, 6 April 1989, pp.16–19

Jeanette Ross, "Transcending personality", *Artweek*, xxi, 11 January 1990

Val Williams, *Warworks: Women, Photography and the Iconography of War*, London: Virago, 1994

Manuscripts and correspondence are in the George Arents Research Library for Special Collections, Syracuse University, NY.

Margaret Bourke-White's work presents a definitive vision of mid-20th-century American photographic practice, bringing together the two primary directions of the medium from the 1920s through the 1940s – the overtly modernist conception that emphasises abstract design with the creation of an elegant and luscious formal visual surface, and the development of socially conscious documentary intended to provoke sympathy for (and ultimately action on behalf of) its disadvantaged subjects. The fusion of these two very different approaches to photography creates an almost intractable tension that is very nearly resolved in some of her finest work.

Her first major contribution to visual culture was her invention of the genre of industrial photography. After graduating from Cornell University in 1927, she settled in Cleveland, the home of steel mills and other heavy industry that captivated her imagination. Working primarily as an architectural photographer, she developed her contacts with the business community to gain entry to the Otis Steel Mill, where she learned through much trial and error how to negotiate the technical difficulties of photographing the pouring of red hot molten metal in a nearly pitch-black interior. Bourke-White brought to this undertaking some early training with the photographer Clarence H. White, who emphasised abstract design and composition. With this approach and the new technical advances of faster film speed, higher contrast paper and magnesium flare lighting, she was able to create beautiful, abstract images of the plant in all its dramatic, fiery glory. Her success at the Otis Mill drew an avalanche of clients seeking her unexpectedly glamorous photographs of industry for use in their advertisements and annual reports. Her work for the Republic Steel Corporation in 1929 quickly caught the eye of Henry Luce, publisher of *Time* magazine, who was just launching *Fortune*, a new magazine aimed at the business world. Bourke-White's photographs of everything from bank vaults to hog slaughtering, reproduced in fine detail, were to become the visual signature of the magazine, and launched her career as a photo-journalist as well.

Moving to New York in 1930, Bourke-White divided her time between *Fortune* and private advertising clients. She leased space for her studio in the Chrysler Building, which she had documented as it was under construction. She was particularly taken with the aluminium gargoyles (translated from Chrysler car ornaments) placed at the four corners of the building on the 61st floor, and made certain that her studio overlooked two of them. Her photograph of one of these gargoyles rings with her belief in the power and beauty of modern industry as she saw it transforming the world. This vision made her extremely popular with corporate clients, who clamoured for her time and talents to provide convincing, formally elegant pictures to elevate their images.

The development of sympathetic human interest in her work grew out of her dissatisfaction with the increasingly ludicrous demands of advertising work, and a growing sense that she wanted to be in touch with "real life". In 1936 she grasped the opportunity to collaborate with Erskine Caldwell (author of *Tobacco Road*) on a book documenting the destitute conditions of share-croppers in the South. *You Have Seen Their Faces*, published in 1937, was widely hailed as a social document of the time. Although she was never employed by the Farm Security Administration (FSA), Bourke-White's work with Caldwell accommodates the themes and general approach found in the contemporary social documentary work of such photographers as Dorothea Lange (q.v.), Walker Evans and Marion Post Wolcott. She shared with them the belief that if only

the ills of the world could be made known through the camera, society would necessarily act to correct them.

Bourke-White carried her new-found human interest into her assignments for *Life* magazine, which Henry Luce founded in 1936. Her photograph of the Fort Peck dam, a WPA project in Montana, with its monumental, repeated concrete towers, graced the cover of the first issue. Inside, her story on the raucous night life of the local boomtown workers caught even the magazine's editors by surprise. With the wealth of material she had sent back to New York, they organised what was probably the first true photo-essay ever published.

With the outbreak of World War II, Bourke-White was inexorably drawn to cover the conflict, beginning in Russia just before and during the German invasion of June 1940. She recounted her experiences, illustrated with her photographs, in her book *Shooting the Russian War* (1942). Continuing as a *Life* correspondent in Europe for the duration of the war, she captured one of her best-known images in 1945 at Buchenwald concentration camp. A line of emaciated, grimy camp survivors in what remains of their tattered, striped uniforms stare with vacant expressions towards the viewer, as they press up feebly against the grid of a welded-wire fence. The photograph is cropped off at either side, so it seems as though these few individuals represent just a small piece of an interminable line of survivors, multiplying the horror indefinitely. The tension arising from the contrast of the deep pathos of the men's faces and the starkly abstract design created by the fence makes this one of Bourke-White's most unforgettable photographs.

The objectification of her subjects through her intensely aesthetic gaze provides one of the greatest points of criticism for her documentary work. On assignment in apartheid South Africa in 1950, Bourke-White accompanied gold miners into the sweltering heat over a mile beneath the surface of the earth, where she reported feeling as though she were operating "in slow motion", rendered unable to speak by the oppressive conditions. There she photographed two miners, sweat glinting beautifully off their black skin as they fill the frame, their safety helmets and bodies carefully forming a repetitive, undulating abstract pattern across the image. The sheer aesthetic beauty of this photograph threatens to overwhelm the fundamental humanity of the bold, forthright gazes that they turn towards the camera, and, as a result, the grotesque working conditions and social inequities forced upon these men become almost detached from history. Grappling with the contradictions inherent in both the medium and her own artistic vision, Margaret Bourke-White's work thus provides a quintessential summary of American photography on the cusp of its shift during the 1950s into the subjective, candid snapshot-mode of such artists as Helen Leavitt and Robert Frank.

As virtually all of her photographs were made for publication, the number of vintage and/or "artistic" prints of Bourke-White's work is rather small. Most of the negatives and prints for *Life* magazine are held in the Time-Warner archives, New York. Other collections of note include the George Arents Research Library for Special Collections, Syracuse University, New York, and the private collection of her brother, Roger White.

BETH ELAINE WILSON

Bracquemond, Marie
French painter, 1840–1916

Born Marie Quiveron at Argenton near Quimper, Brittany, 1 December 1840; her father, a sea captain, died soon after her birth, and her mother remarried. Spent youth in the Jura, in Switzerland and the Auvergne before settling with her family in Etampes, south of Paris. Studied under a local restorer, M. Wassor; later in Ingres's studio in Paris. Married Félix Bracquemond, 1869; son Pierre, also an artist, born 1870; husband died 1914. Moved to Sèvres after Félix appointed artistic director of the Haviland porcelain works, Auteuil, 1871. Abandoned professional career, 1890. Died in Sèvres, 1916.

Principal Exhibitions
Paris Salon: 1857, 1874–5
Exposition Universelle, Paris: 1878 (faience tile panels)
Impressionist group, Paris: 1879, 1880, 1886
Dudley Gallery, London: 1881
Exposition des Peintre-Graveurs, Paris: 1890
Galerie Bernheim-Jeune, Paris: 1919 (retrospective, organised by Pierre Bracquemond)

Bibliography
Pierre Bracquemond, "La vie de Félix et Marie Bracquemond", undated manuscript, private collection, Paris
Gustave Geffroy, *La Vie artistique*, Paris: Floury, 1894, pp.268–74
Clara Erskine Clement, *Women in the Fine Arts*, Boston: Houghton Mifflin, 1904; reprinted New York, Hacker, 1974
Oeuvres de Marie Bracquemond (1841–1916), exh. cat., Galerie Bernheim-Jeune, Paris, 1919
Félix Bracquemond: Gravures, dessins, céramiques; Marie Bracquemond: Tableaux, exh. cat., Mortagne, 1972
The Crisis of Impressionism, 1878–1882, exh. cat., University of Michigan Museum of Art, Ann Arbor, 1979
Elizabeth Kane, "Marie Bracquemond: The artist time forgot", *Apollo*, cxvii, 1983, pp.118–21
Jean-Paul Bouillon and Elizabeth Kane, "Marie Bracquemond", *Woman's Art Journal*, v/2, 1984–5, pp.21–7
Tamar Garb, *Women Impressionists*, Oxford: Phaidon, and New York: Rizzoli, 1986

Marie Bracquemond was one of the four women artists associated with the Impressionists. With Berthe Morisot (q.v.) and Mary Cassatt (q.v.) she exhibited in the Impressionist exhibitions, showing altogether three times, in 1879, 1880 and 1886. (Eva Gonzalès, q.v., like her mentor Manet, preferred not to use this forum of display.) Unlike the other three "women Impressionists", however, she did not come from a prosperous, cultured milieu. As a young woman she was admitted to Ingres's studio where she gained the reputation of being one of his most intelligent pupils. In 1869 Marie married the successful engraver Félix Bracquemond, who introduced her to his own circle of friends comprising important contemporary artists and critics. This enabled the young artist to make important contacts. Ironically, the marriage seems also to have inhibited her development as an artist and she has come to be seen as the archetypal female casualty of an oppressive husband.

Bracquemond's own interests led her away from the stylistic conservatism of her husband towards the plein-air painting that was becoming popular among younger artists. Influenced by Monet and Renoir, she became increasingly committed to the Impressionist aesthetic of rendering contemporary life in unmodulated colour and painterly brush marks. Light became her obsession, and she experimented with different light effects, moving from pictures that explore natural daylight, such as *Tea*

Time (1880; Musée du Petit Palais, Geneva), to essays in artificial light, as in *Under the Lamp* (1887; private collection). To her husband's disapproval, Marie Bracquemond was a fervent defender of Impressionism to the end of her life. "Impressionism has produced ... not only a new, but a very useful way of looking at things. It is as though all at once a window opens and the sun and air enter your house in torrents", she declared when Félix attacked what he termed the "folly" of painting out of doors.

Tea Time is a typical Impressionist portrait. The sitter is a young woman placed in a garden setting. The quiet domestic scene, so typical of bourgeois suburban life as portrayed by the artists of the Third Republic, was the perfect subject for a woman artist seeking plein-air subjects. It provided a fitting context for the exploration of natural light effects but provided none of the threats to safety or propriety of more ambitious landscape painting. Here the artist and her model can proceed unchaperoned in the context of the home and still produce interesting and technically adventurous work.

Bracquemond's sitters were usually her family members or friends. Her son, sister and close friends are her most common models. The intimate relationship between artist and sitter presented particular problems for women artists, especially with male sitters. For a woman artist to scrutinise the face and body of a man she needed to overcome the cultural prohibitions against women looking intently and to cast aside the demure and modest glancing that was deemed appropriate for bourgeois women. This was more easily done with a family member or friend than with a stranger. *Under the Lamp* depicts Alfred Sisley and his wife who were regular guests at the Bracquemond home and formed part of the intimate circle of family and friends that surrounded them in the 1880s.

Despite the "Impressionist" appearance of works executed between 1880 and 1890, Bracquemond prepared her paintings in the traditional way, producing many preparatory drawings and sketches before starting on the canvas. A finished painting such as the ambitious, sun-filled *On the Terrace at Sèvres with Fantin-Latour* (1880; Musée du Petit Palais) is no spontaneous sketch. Like many of her Impressionist colleagues, the effect of spontaneity and immediacy that Bracquemond strove to achieve was hard won. It was the product of slow and deliberate work.

In 1890 the domestic conflict that her painting provoked resulted in Marie Bracquemond's giving up painting almost completely (except for a few watercolours and drawings). Throughout her married life, she had been a committed mother and home-maker and was constantly aware of the conflicts between these roles and her wish to be an artist. Eventually these were too much to bear and she relinquished her role as an artist to devote herself to being the wife that her husband wanted. It was her son Pierre who documented his mother's life in an unpublished manuscript, "La vie de Félix et Marie Bracquemond". In it he records the pain and difficulties that his mother suffered because of the conflicting demands of her responsibilities as a wife and her needs as an artist. He records, too, his father's jealousy of his mother's talent and his inability to accept her criticism. Bracquemond, the artist, became a casualty of her marriage, spending the last two decades of her life as a virtual recluse in the family home at Sèvres, rarely visiting Paris and never exhibiting her work in public again.

TAMAR GARB

Brandt, Marianne   [fig. 9]
German designer and photographer, 1893–1983

Born Marianne Liebe in Chemnitz, 6 October 1893. Studied painting and sculpture at Grossherzogliche Sächsische Hochschule für Bildende Kunst, Weimar, under Fritz Mackensen and Richard Engelmann, 1911–17. Independent artist in Weimar, 1917–23. Spent time in Norway and France after her marriage to Norwegian painter Erik Brandt in 1919; separated 1926; divorced 1935. Studied at the Bauhaus, Weimar, then Dessau, from 1924; deputy head of metal workshop, 1928; Bauhaus diploma, 1929. Subsequently worked with architect Walter Gropius in Berlin. Head of design department, Ruppelwerk hardware factory, Gotha, 1929–33. Member, Deutscher Werkbund. Independent artist in Chemnitz, 1933–49. Teacher for Industrial Design, Staatliche Hochschule für Werkkunst (State High School for Industrial Art), Dresden, under Mart Stam, 1949–51. Collaborated with Stam at the Institut für Industrielle Gestaltung (Institute for

Industrial Design), Hochschule für Angewandte Kunst, Berlin-Weissensee, 1951–4. Organised *Deutsche Angewandte Kunst* (German applied art) exhibition in Peking and Shanghai, China, 1953–4. Independent artist in Chemnitz (Karl-Marx-Stadt) from 1954; in Kirchberg, Saxony, from 1976. Died in Kirchberg, 16 June 1983.

Principal Exhibitions
Galerie Gerstenberger, Chemnitz: 1918 (individual)
Deutscher Werkbund, Stuttgart: 1929 (*Film und Foto*, touring)
Bauhaus-Archiv, Berlin: 1993 (retrospective)

Selected Writings
"Bauhausstil", *Bauhaus*, iii/1, 1929, p.21
"Modelle für die Serie", *Form & Zweck*, xi/3, 1979, pp.68–70
"Brief an die junge Generation", *Bauhaus und Bauhäusler*, ed. Eckhard Neumann, Cologne: DuMont, 1985, pp.156–61

Bibliography
Gisela Schulz and Hans-Peter Schulz, "Marianne Brandt", *Bauhaus 2*, 6, exh. cat., Galerie am Sachsenplatz, Leipzig, 1977, pp.8–9
Drei Künstler aus dem Bauhaus, exh. cat., Kupferstichkabinett der Staatlichen Kunstsammlungen, Dresden, 1978
L'altra metà dell'avanguardia, 1910–1940: Pittrici e scultrici nei movimenti delle avanguardie storiche, exh. cat., Palazzo Reale, Milan, and elsewhere, 1980
Karsten Kruppa, "Gestalten – ohne an Kunst zu denken", *Bildende Kunst*, xxxi, 1983, pp.373–5
——, "Marianne Brandt: Annäherung an ein Leben", *Die Metallwerkstatt am Bauhaus*, exh. cat., Bauhaus-Archiv, Berlin, 1992, pp.48–55
Anne-Kathrin Weise, *Leben und Werk von Marianne Brandt*, PhD dissertation, Humboldt-Universität, Berlin, 1995

In the 1920s, while she was working at the Bauhaus metal workshop, Marianne Brandt created her famous constructive designs for everyday items: ashtrays, tea and coffee sets, and tea-extract pots. She developed types of lamps that were put into production and thus realised Gropius's programme for the development of standard types in collaboration with industry. At the Bauhaus Brandt also occupied herself with a thorough study of the photographic medium. Like most of the Bauhaus photographers, she was self-taught – there were no regular classes in photography at the Bauhaus before 1929. It was above all her self-portraits, in which she

reflected her identity as a woman at the Bauhaus, and her still-life compositions, which are closely connected to the Neues Sehen (New Vision), that became famous. Reflection, distortion, close-up views and cut-outs are typical of these photographs, in which Brandt experimented with the effects of alienation. In her numerous collages and photomontages, which in their representation of simultaneity are comparable with the work of the Berlin Dadaists, she made a critical statement not so much about purely political matters as about the situation of women in modern society and in the context of current issues.

In 1911 Brandt began her painting studies at the Grossherzogliche Sächsische Hochschule für Bildende Kunst in Weimar under Fritz Mackensen. In 1917 she obtained a studio of her own for the first time. Her early pictures bore an Expressionist stamp and were mainly female and mother-and-child portraits. They shared a general basic mood of suppression and melancholy as, for example, in her picture *Pietà* and the early *Self-Portrait* (1917–19; photograph in Bauhaus-Archiv, Berlin). In 1918 Brandt displayed her work for the first time at the Galerie Gerstenberger in Chemnitz. After her marriage to the Norwegian painter Erik Brandt, who had also studied in Weimar, the couple lived in Norway and France, returning to Weimar in 1921.

Brandt entered the Bauhaus on 1 January 1924, when she was 31 years old; she left her academic work behind her – in fact, she burned most of it. On her preliminary course she learned about works and materials from Josef Albers and László Moholy-Nagy. She studied artistic creation under Wassily Kandinsky and Paul Klee. Her study on the subject of *Relationships Between the Primary Colours and the Basic Shapes – Circle, Triangle, Square* (1924; Musée Nationale d'Art Moderne, Paris) survives from her classes with Kandinsky on "elementary instruction in form".

In 1924, following Moholy-Nagy's advice, Brandt was accepted as an apprentice in the silversmiths' and metal workshop – the work in the carpenters' shop was too heavy for her and she was not interested in weaving, which was the proper "women's department" at the Bauhaus. At first she had to carry out subordinate tasks; she was the only woman in the workshop and the men did not like her being there. She nevertheless produced her first prototypes and models for metal objects to be manufactured by machine. Her first executed design was a simple, small hand-chased ashtray (1924; Bauhaus-Archiv). For herself, she made an inkstand with pen-rest out of sheet copper plated with argentine (1924; Bauhaus-Archiv), which showed strong modernist influence, reflecting her studies under Moholy-Nagy. In 1924 alone Brandt produced an amazing quantity of lamps, pots and small pieces of equipment from different materials. Teapots, for example, appeared in a wide variety of different styles (such as her tea-extract pot, *MT49*). She made spherical models with lids set in at an angle and then, in the same year, she made the style that became famous – hemispherical in shape, with a smooth, sharp-edged top and a similarly round off-centre lid with a wooden knob. The handle was a semicircular slice of wood; the body of the pot rested on cross-pieces rather than on the usual circular stand. This model, in its consistent limitation to almost exclusively geometric shapes, was made in many versions and in a wide range of different materials; it became a veritable incunabulum of modernist Bauhaus work (in silver; 1924; British Museum, London). The silver tea and coffee service (*MT50–55a*; 1924; Bauhaus-Archiv), probably the most expensive item that Brandt produced in the metal shop, and requiring the most work, was made for her friend Marli Ehrmann, a weaver at the Bauhaus. The individual vessels were based on geometric shapes: the cylinder, sphere, circle and cross.

Brandt's designs for ashtrays also explore these basic ideas; the ashtray with triangular lid-opening (*MT36*; 1924; Bauhaus-Archiv) is a variant on the shape of the teapot. The categorisation with model number indicates that the objects were sold as products from the metal workshop of the Bauhaus company. Between 1924 and 1929 Brandt developed 31 practical metal utensils for industrial manufacture, 28 lamps, as well as stools and cupboards. The objects she made from 1926 onwards were of course noticeably more conventional; the avant-garde shape was given up in favour of an extremely simple and functional one (e.g. milk jug, *ME11*; 1926; Bauhaus-Archiv).

After an intervening six-month stay in Paris (1926–7), where she made numerous photo-collages, such as *Paris Impressions* (1926; repr. Leipzig 1977), Brandt joined the metal workshop as a full member of staff. She led technical trials for lamp production and made contacts in the lighting industry, particularly with the firms of Körting &

Mathiesen (Kandem) in Leipzig and Schwintzer & Gräff in Berlin for the purpose of adapting and developing functional lighting for industrial production. In 1928, with Hin Bredendieck, she designed the mass-produced Kandem bedside lights and writing-desk lamps (Bauhaus-Archiv).

In 1925 the programmatic Bauhaus book *Malerei, Photographie, Film* by Moholy-Nagy appeared. This stimulated Brandt's photographic activity, which resulted especially in self-portraits and still-life pictures. She repeatedly depicted reflections in glass and metal, and also included her self-portrait, as in the self-portrait with camera, *Reflections Between the Doors of the Bauhaus in Dessau* (c.1926; Bauhaus-Archiv). Her profile *Self-Portrait with Jewellery in the Hair and Around the Neck at the Metallic Festival* (1929; Bauhaus-Archiv) also plays with reflected light. Another strikingly frequent motif is that of reflections in a glass ball. Georg Muche introduced this idea to Weimar in 1921 and Brandt used it in numerous pictures, such as *Self-Portrait in Studio* (1928–9; Bauhaus-Archiv). The factor common to all of these photographs is a serious expression of self-questioning, but this is an honest documentation of Brandt's own position in life.

In the international exhibition of the Deutscher Werkbund, *Film und Foto*, or *FiFo* (1929), Brandt, among others, represented the Neues Sehen at the Bauhaus with five photographs. These included the still-life *Clock with Ball* and *Street in the Thaw* (1928–9; Bauhaus-Archiv). Her photomontages were not exhibited. After she left the Bauhaus, Brandt took *Self-Portrait in Double Exposure* (1930–31; Bauhaus-Archiv) while she was working as a designer at the metal factory in Gotha. It shows her in her office, wearing her work clothes, with an expression of extreme self-doubt.

Under the influence of Moholy-Nagy, Brandt was also confronted with the Dadaist principle of collage, which offered her a counterbalance to the strictness of her design activities. In her collages, which she started to create from 1923 onwards, she devoted herself to themes that concerned her as a woman, and worked out her role as the only woman in the Bauhaus metal workshop: the photo-montage *Me* (c.1927–8; Bauhaus-Archiv) shows the artist on the periphery of her metal lampshade under the eye of her teacher Moholy-Nagy. The title defines the identification of object and person. The montage *Help Me!* (1926; Staatliche Kunstsammlungen,

Dresden) is dominated by the portrait of a modern woman who seems to be casting a critical gaze on the dubious achievements of progress and technology. In the collage *Our Irritating City* (1926; Galerie Berinson, Berlin) Brandt presents a completely different type of city woman – one represented by a 1920s beauty who stares wide-eyed and annoyed at the viewer. After she left the Bauhaus, during her undoubtedly unsatisfying spell in Gotha, Brandt still continued to express her feelings and wishes on the theme of the male/female relationship through the medium of collage. *Captive Balloon* (1931; Staatliche Kunstsammlungen, Dresden) contains in the form of facets a picture of a couple kissing. The man smiles tenderly and the young woman presses a bunch of roses dreamily to her bosom. After 1933 Brandt stopped using the photo-collage technique; in the 1930s the themes of the 1920s – progress, speed, the city, and technology in connection with the new role of women – ceased to stir her.

In 1928–9, after Moholy-Nagy's departure, Brandt had become deputy head of the Bauhaus metal workshop. She resigned in July 1929 because Hannes Meyer had merged the carpentry, wall-painting and metalwork departments into a new consolidated workshop. On 10 September 1929 she left the Bauhaus, receiving a Bauhaus diploma issued by Meyer and Albers as evidence of her completed studies in the metal workshop. The diploma testified to her great creative gifts, her thoroughness and energy, as well as to her feel for organic relationships, linked to a healthy sense of the practical. Brandt subsequently worked in Gropius's architect's practice, where she designed furniture and interior fittings, particularly for housing estates. Gropius, too, acknowledged her inventive gifts, first-rate technical knowledge and outstanding personal qualities.

At the end of 1929 Brandt became head of the design department in the Ruppelwerk hardware factory in Gotha, where she took on and improved the quality of design and colour of mass-produced utensils to such an extent that she was able to exhibit the products at the Grassi-Messe trade fair in Leipzig. During this period she created designs for gift and everyday items that were necessarily unspectacular and constrained to follow the style of the firm. Of these, the writing set with a spherical inkpot and the functional tea-warmer in red-lacquered sheet steel (both 1930–33; Bauhaus-

Archiv) are worthy of special notice; these are in the same mould as Brandt's Bauhaus designs.

Because of the world slump, Brandt had to give up this post in 1933 and was forced for financial reasons to return to her parents' house in Chemnitz. As a Norwegian citizen and a former member of the Bauhaus she had very little chance of finding another job. She divorced Erik Brandt at his request in 1935 (they had been separated since 1926). Moholy-Nagy tried to stand up for her in the mid-1930s, and encouraged her to take up designing again, but no lasting link with industry developed, although through Moholy-Nagy she did obtain, in 1932, a design contract with the firm Schweizerische Wohnbedarf AG, who took a design of hers of 1928 for a shallow bowl (Bauhaus-Archiv).

In the 1930s and 1940s Brandt lived with her family; after her parents' death she lived with her sister. During this period she was isolated from her fellow artists and spent her time painting, drawing and weaving. After World War II she tried to get a foothold in the newly founded art schools of East Germany as a designer, first in Dresden and later in Berlin-Weissensee. Her endeavours were unsuccessful, however, because her conception of products, which was based on functionalist principles, was regarded as formalism and therefore undesirable.

In 1947 Moholy-Nagy recommended Brandt as head for the metal workshop in the Staatliche Hochschule für Werkkunst, and in April 1949 she took up this post under Mart Stam. She was responsible for creating industrial designs for the metal, ceramic and wooden-toy workshops, and Stam got her to work on light-fittings as well. Some examples of her work from around 1950 survive: simple jewellery made out of bent wire and perforated sheet brass (1950; Sammlungen Bauhaus Dessau) and some earthenware pottery (1950; Sammlung Industrielle Gestaltung, Berlin, and Sammlungen Bauhaus Dessau).

In 1951 Brandt followed Stam to the Hochschule für Angewandte Kunst in Berlin-Weissensee with its associated Institut für Industrielle Gestaltung (Institute for Industrial Design), where simple but beautiful everyday items were to be designed. Brandt's sketches for shoes, buckles, bags and wall-paper – and for the gavel of the president of the Volkskammer – survive, but the items were never made. The "discussion of formalism" soon put an end to design that owed anything to functionalism, and Stam was sacked in 1952. Marianne Brandt went to China for a year as curator of the exhibition *Deutsche Angewandte Kunst*. She then returned to Chemnitz (Karl-Marx-Stadt), where she lived in complete isolation, able only to work as a painter, sculptor and weaver.

BRITTA KAISER-SCHUSTER

Brooks, Romaine [fig. 11]
American painter, 1874–1970

Born Beatrice Romaine Goddard in Rome, Italy, 1874, to Ella Waterman and Major Harry Goddard of Philadelphia. Joined mother and brother St Mar in London, 1886; subsequently educated in north Italy and Switzerland. Studied voice in Neuilly, 1895–6, and Paris, 1896–8; painting at La Scuola Nazionale and Circolo Artistico, Rome, 1898–9, and Académie Colarossi, Paris, 1899–1900. Rented studio on island of Capri, c.1900–02; also lived in Nice and Villa Grimaldi, Menton. Inherited a fortune after deaths of mother and brother, 1902. Brief marriage of convenience to pianist and homosexual dilettante John Ellingham Brooks, 1902. Lived in London, 1902–4, spending time in St Ives, Cornwall. Returned to Paris and studied briefly in studio of Gustave Courtois, 1905. Met Gabriele D'Annunzio, 1910, Natalie Clifford Barney, 1915. Set up studio in Venice, 1916. Exhibited at Salon des Indépendants, Paris, 1923. Visited New York briefly in 1925; rented studio in Carnegie Hall, New York, 1935–6. Living on French Riviera with Barney at outbreak of World War II. Purchased Villa Sant'Agnese, Florence, 1940; lived there until mid-1950s, when she bought Villa Gaia, Fiesole. Moved to studio apartment in Nice, 1967. Croix, Légion d'Honneur, France, 1920. Died in Nice, 7 December 1970.

Selected Individual Exhibitions
Galeries Durand-Ruel, Paris: 1910
Goupil Gallery, London: 1911
Galerie Jean Charpentier, Paris: 1925
Alpine Club Gallery, London: 1925
Wildenstein Galleries, New York: 1925
Galerie Th. Briant, Paris: 1931
Arts Club of Chicago: 1935

National Museum of American Art, Washington, DC: 1971 (retrospective)

Selected Writings
"No pleasant memories" and "A war interlude", undated manuscripts, National Archives of American Art, Smithsonian Institution, Washington, DC
"No pleasant memories", *Life and Letters Today*, xviii/12, Summer 1938, pp.38–44
"The convent", *Life and Letters Today*, xix/18, 1938, pp.14–30

Bibliography
Romaine Brooks, exh. cat., Galeries Durand-Ruel, Paris, 1910
Robert de Montesquiou, "Cambrioleur d'âmes", *Le Figaro*, May 1910
Gustave Kahn, "Romaine Brooks", *L'Art et les Artistes*, xxxvii, May 1923, pp.3, 7 and 14
John Usher, "True painter of personality", *International Studio*, lxxxiii, 1926, pp.46–50
Romaine Brooks, exh. cat., Arts Club of Chicago, 1935
Elisabeth de Gramont, *Romaine Brooks: Portraits, Tableaux, Dessins*, Paris: Braun, 1952; reprinted New York: Arno Press, 1975
Michel Desbruères, "Commentaires", *Bizarre*, xliv, March 1968, pp.13–48
Romaine Brooks: "Thief of Souls", exh. cat., National Museum of American Art, Washington, DC, 1971; reissued with revised essay by Adelyn D. Breeskin, 1986
Meryle Secrest, *Between Me and Life: A Biography of Romaine Brooks*, New York: Doubleday, 1974; London: Macdonald and Jane's, 1976
Pierre de Montera, "Gabriele D'Annunzio, Romaine Brooks et Natalie Barney", *D'Annunzio e il simbolismo europeo*, Milan: Il Saggiatore, 1976
Women Artists, 1550–1950, exh. cat., Los Angeles County Museum of Art, and elsewhere, 1976
Susan Gubar, "Blessings in disguise: Cross-dressing as re-dressing for female modernists", *Massachusetts Review*, xxii/3–4, Autumn 1981, pp.477–508
Giuditta Villa, *Romaine Brooks, (1874–1970)*, PhD dissertation, Università degli Studi, Rome, 1983
Shari Benstock, *Women of the Left Bank: Paris, 1900–1940*, Austin: University of Texas Press, 1986; London: Virago, 1987
Romaine Brooks, 1874–1970, exh. cat., Musée Sainte-Croix, Poitiers, 1987
Catherine Texier, *Analyse et recherche iconographique de l'oeuvre de Romaine Brooks*, PhD dissertation, Université de Paris VIII – Vincennes à Saint-Denis, 1987
Karla Jay, *The Amazon and the Page: Natalie Clifford Barney and Renée Vivien*, Bloomington: Indiana University Press, 1988
Françoise Werner, *Romaine Brooks*, Paris: Plon, 1990

Natalie Barney, *Adventures of the Mind*, New York: New York University Press, 1992 (French original, 1929)

Bridget Elliott and Jo-Ann Wallace, *Women Artists and Writers: Modernist (im)positionings*, London and New York: Routledge, 1994

Catherine McNickle Chastain, "Romaine Brooks: A new look at her drawings", *Woman's Art Journal*, xvii/2, 1996–7, pp.9–14

Joe Lucchesi, *Romaine Brooks' Self-Portraits and the Performance of Lesbian Identity*, PhD dissertation, University of North Carolina (in preparation)

Romaine Brooks was a wealthy American expatriate who specialised in portraiture. After training briefly at the Scuola Nazionale in Rome and the Académie Colarossi in Paris, she began an artistic career that took her through some of the most privileged cultural circles of early 20th-century Europe: the Anglo-American artistic and intellectual colony on Capri; the Parisian society of Comte Robert de Montesquiou, so-called Prince of Aesthetes; the literary Left Bank community of American writer Natalie Barney. Despite her continuous participation in a variety of cultural realms, Brooks cultivated the image of the *lapidé*, the outcast, and this image added rhetorical force to the psychologically penetrating, slightly mocking and judgmental character that critics discovered in her portraits.

The large fortune that Brooks inherited after the death of her mother and brother in 1902 allowed her to begin her continually shifting movements through these rarefied European social realms. A series of self-portraits spanning her career charts both her development as a portraitist and her changing social, intellectual and artistic concerns. These images explore a theme that becomes a leitmotif in Brooks's work: an interior sense of self-identity that also continually references the role external appearances, and particularly clothing, play in constructing a "coherent" and legible internal self. In her first *Self-Portrait* (c.1905; private collection, repr. Poitiers 1987, p.103) she presents herself in an elaborately layered black costume and enormous veiled hat typical of the refined circles of Parisian *mondaines*. By contrast, in *Artist on the Seashore* (1912) Brooks appears in a turbulent and windswept seaside landscape. The painting is imbued with a romantic symbolism that coincides with her close association with the Italian aesthetic poet Gabriele D'Annunzio, whom Brooks portrayed in an identical format as the *Poet in Exile* (both Musée National d'Art Moderne, Paris). By 1923 she had replaced this airy romanticism with a psycho-logically acute and powerfully androgynous self-presentation (National Museum of American Art, Washington, DC). Here Brooks wears an oversized riding hat whose brim partially shadows her challenging and unflinching gaze, and her masculinely tailored outfit reflects that of her contemporary lesbian associates.

Brooks also produced a series of photographic self-portraits, visually sophisticated and compositionally complex images in which she specifically addresses the self-conscious construction of identities through clothing and external signifiers (1910–20; private collection, *ibid.*, pp.65–73). Brooks models in various poses and elegant costumes. Some photographs resemble the contemporary fashionable portraits of her friend the British pictorialist photographer Baron de Meyer, while in others she photographs herself reflected and refracted in an array of mirrors, always including the camera apparatus in the picture and often her own paintings reflected in the background.

Around 1900 Brooks settled on Capri and became part of the expatriate community that formed around the British male homosexuals, such as her friend Somerset Maugham, who had fled the backlash against homosexuality after Oscar Wilde's sodomy trial (1895). Soon after meeting there James McNeill Whistler's patron, the American industrialist Charles Lang Freer, Brooks moved to London, took a Tite Street studio near Whistler's and developed her extremely nuanced colour sense, eventually settling on modulations of black, white and greys that reviewers often called "Whistlerian". Her painting of a young girl absorbed by music, *The Piano* (1910; National Museum of American Art), employs this trademark palette and also resonates with Whistler's aestheticised symbolism. Similarly, her early portraits of such *mondaines* as the Chilean hostess *Mme Errazuris* (c.1908; National Museum of American Art) and *Princess Lucien Murat* (c.1910; private collection, *ibid.*, p.114) follow closely Whistler's tradition of elegant society portraiture.

When she moved to France in 1905, Brooks entered the aristocratic, intellectual salons of Paris through her brief lesbian relationship with the art patron Winnaretta Singer, Princesse de Polignac. De Montesquiou soon became an ardent supporter of her painting. He was the undisputed leader of this cultural milieu, and his poetry and essays typify the refined, esoteric and literary symbolism associated with "the Aesthetes". Brooks's contemporary work shows the influence of this symbolist sensibility. Her first one-woman exhibition at the prestigious Galeries Durand-Ruel consisted entirely of female genre figures – charwomen, a young consumptive, girls in fashionable dresses – executed in refined colour harmonies and delicate handling that matched contemporary "Aesthetic" tastes. An underlying sobriety and a lack of idealisation, however, suggested unseen layers of meaning behind the anonymous faces of the models, prompting de Montesquiou, in his published review of the exhibition, to give Brooks the nickname *cambrioleur d'âmes* ("thief of souls") for her ability to capture "inner truths" behind outward appearances.

Distinctly Symbolist underpinnings and a pervasive psychological exposure also inform her contemporary portraits. Her subjects appear in dark, atmospheric settings, and Brooks often included small objects existing in ambiguous relation to the sitter. In *The Debutante* (1910–11; National Museum of American Art) a turkey statuette stands near an awkward, oddly dressed girl whom Brooks herself described as "ugly". In the portrait of the decorator *Elsie de Wolfe* (*c*.1914; Musée National d'Art Moderne, Paris) the sitter shares space with a small, delicate porcelain goat that bears a slight resemblance to her. Similarly, Brooks painted the young Jean Cocteau on her studio balcony with the Eiffel Tower looming behind him. In these portraits a connection between object and sitter is suggested but never explained, adding a mysterious and slightly surreal note to otherwise faithful representations.

Apart from several male portraits, Brooks's paintings focus exclusively on women. With the haunting and enigmatic figure of Ida Rubinstein as her model, around 1910 Brooks began to infuse the female body with a dense symbolic iconography and to explore both the erotic possibilities of the female nude and the performative nature of continually shifting identities. Through de Montesquiou, Brooks met Rubinstein, a Russian dancer who had appeared in several Parisian Ballets Russes productions as exotic, tragic – and always erotic – characters, including Salome, Cleopatra and Zobéïde in *Schéhérazade*. Her expressive, attenuated limbs and ghostly pale skin furnished Brooks with a visual icon of female sexuality that continued the tradition of late 19th-century Symbolists. Brooks's themes range from the association of feminine sexuality

with death in *The Journey* (1912; National Museum of American Art), where Rubinstein's extremely emaciated and cadaverous figure floats in an inky void; to the *femme fatale* of *White Azaleas* (1910; National Museum of American Art), in which she reclines seductively on a couch, her gaze shrouded by murky shadows. Brooks continues her reading of the female body in explicitly sexual terms in her portrait of the eccentric *Marchesa Luisa Casati* (1920; private collection, repr. Desbruères 1968, pp.46–7), the only major nude not inspired by Rubinstein. In contrast to Rubinstein, the Marchesa Casati is presented as the Symbolist feminine virago, a Medusa figure whose huge eyes stare balefully from beneath her writhing, flame-like corona of auburn hair and whose thin body emerges from a loosely flung purplish cloak.

Rubinstein also appeared in more elaborately allegorical paintings permeated with themes of female sexuality and erotic desire. In a collaborative project with Barney, Brooks painted Rubinstein as the *Weeping Venus* (1916–17; Musée Sainte-Croix, Poitiers), and Barney's accompanying poem makes explicit the interconnection between female eroticism and death that appeared regularly in Symbolist literature and painting. The more enigmatic *Masked Archer* (1910–11; destroyed, repr. Poitiers 1987, p.121) presents Rubinstein's nude form bound to a post, the target of an arrow already released by a male figure. Brooks intended the archer to represent D'Annunzio, and the painting is her response to his drama *The Martyrdom of St Sebastian*, written for Rubinstein and performed in Paris in 1911. The play is an arcane mixture of androgynous sensuality and symbolic Christian melodrama whose underlying gender ambiguity infuriated the Catholic Church and intrigued Parisian audiences. Brooks's painting reworks the gendered themes of ambiguity and power embedded in *St Sebastian*. Rubinstein's exposed, listless and effete Sebastian awaits the arrow shot by the masked, active, yet dwarfish D'Annunzio. In contrast to these images, Brooks also painted Rubinstein as a personification of French war-time courage and duty in *La France croisée* (1915; Museum of American Art), wearing the uniform of a Red Cross nurse and standing defiantly in a decimated landscape before a burning city. D'Annunzio wrote four accompanying poems of explicitly Symbolist allegory, and both were exhibited as part of a fund-raising effort that earned

Brooks a medal from the Légion d'Honneur after World War I.

Brooks continued to explore these issues of feminine identity in a portrait series that she produced during the early 1920s. The overt eroticism and sensuality of her earlier nudes, however, is replaced by an iconoclastic androgyny. During World War I Brooks met and began a 50-year personal and professional collaboration with Natalie Barney, who had long been a leader of the Parisian lesbian community, maintaining an openly lesbian lifestyle in the face of public disapproval and censure. Brooks's subsequent sitters reflect not only her closer involvement in a "lesbian *haute monde*", as the British painter Gluck (q.v.) called them, but also a heightened self-consciousness about the public aesthetics of an ambiguously gendered identity.

Apart from her own self-portrait, Brooks's subjects included *Una, Lady Troubridge, Gluck*, the Italian pianist *Renata Borgatti* and the French writer *Elisabeth de Gramont, duchesse de Clermont-Tonnerre* (all 1920–25; National Museum of American Art). Although the mood of the portraits varied – from the austere gravity of Gluck's portrayal to the satiric overtones of Una Troubridge – each woman appears against minimal and spatially compressed backgrounds, and each is dressed in similar, masculinely tailored costumes. Brooks exhibited Gluck's portrait under the name *Peter, a Young English Girl*, a title that suggests the contradictory and oscillating terms under which the portrait constructs an identity for the sitter. Peter's androgynous figure slips across the codes and boundaries of gendered representation, referencing both masculinity and femininity but settling on neither. Brooks installs this same sense of powerful ambiguity in *Una Troubridge*. A play with appearances is everywhere evident, from the rigidity of her exaggeratedly arch collar, binding cravat and oversized monocle, to the stereotypical feminine accents of her large pin curls, delicate pearl earrings and pink lipstick. Brooks often referred to the humour she found in Troubridge's outfits, suggesting both an underlying irony and a self-consciousness about this rhetoric of androgynous self-presentation.

With these portraits Brooks records a sartorial strategy that many lesbians used in order to gain increased cultural visibility in early 20th-century Europe, a visual interpretation and recoding of the so-called "mannish woman" that the pseudo-scientific discourse of sexologists attempted to diagnose

and cure. As exhibition reviews suggest, however, these paintings were not necessarily self-evident lesbian representations, and in fact a more complex network of cultural discourses intersected them. On the one hand, the wearing of masculinely tailored jackets, pants and tuxedos enjoyed considerable vogue associated with the fashionable and problematic "modern woman", largely a heterosexual, bourgeois phenomenon that upset traditionally assigned gender roles. On the other hand, both this clothing style and the portraits themselves echo the traditional iconography of the aristocratic dandy. Gluck's incisive comment indicates the crucial vector of class that inflected Brooks's cultural associations, patrons, subjects and self-image. The elevated class status of these women afforded them more social freedoms than their bourgeois counterparts but, paradoxically, subjected them to more intricate and firmly established rituals of public performance and propriety. Much of the visual tension of Brooks's portraits derives from the dilemma of women caught within this social and sexual rubric.

During the late 1920s Brooks's primary artistic interest shifted from painting to drawing, and after producing only two portraits in the 1930s (during a trip to New York) she stopped painting altogether. The drawings are constructed from a continuous line that wanders across the page and is then reformed into various objects and figures. The elegant, fluid arabesques and complex patterns of Brooks's drawings often weave together multiple figures in tortuous and inextricable masses, like the snout-nosed, vaporous creatures and the female figure they menace in *Caught* (1930; National Museum of American Art). Although these works have a broad thematic range, subject matter usually revolves around familial images (*Sorrow of Rebirth, or Les Parents entraînent leurs enfants*), death (*Dead Too Long*) and conflicts between terrestrial and spiritual forces (*Mother Nature*; all before 1935; National Museum of American Art). Her drawings share stylistic and conceptual ground with contemporary Surrealist automatic writing, and Brooks underlined the connection to an unconscious process of production when, in the preface to the catalogue of her exhibition in Chicago (1935), she described these drawings as "inevitable", and consistently characterised them as attempts to exorcise the nightmares of a difficult early life.

The autobiographical impulse that motivated Brooks's drawings became explicit when she produced 13 works that illustrate her unpublished manuscript "No pleasant memories" (extracts in Secrest 1974 and Werner 1990), a text that she wrote and revised for over 20 years. In this text Brooks re-presents her life as primarily a struggle against her domineering and nearly demonic mother. As this extraordinary document recounts in excruciating detail the continuous conflicts and oppression of the young artist in trying to sever her family ties, the tone and imagery that Brooks employs wavers between objective, autobiographical description and the fantastic and surreal evocations of a fairy tale. In later chapters she summarily treats her artistic career and personal life; a second volume, "A war interlude", recounts her life in Florence with Natalie Barney during World War II. This volume mixes lengthy accounts of the women's daily activities with affirmations of the Fascist ideology that Brooks fostered through her relationship with D'Annunzio, who in later years became an Italian nationalist hero.

Throughout her career and through the changes in style, themes and personal and professional allegiances, Romaine Brooks's primary artistic interest remained the exploration of identities. Her portraits and drawings are visual resolutions of the socio-psychological and sexual factors that constitute identities and often focus on the performative artifice of visible identities. Her work is a provocative exploration of the links between portraiture, visual imagery, the creation of gendered identities and the problem of the "homosexual subject" in early 20th-century Europe.

JOE LUCCHESI

Butler, Lady   [fig. 10]
British painter, 1846–1933

Born Elizabeth Southerden Thompson in Lausanne, Switzerland, 3 November 1846. Brought up with her sister Alice (the poet Alice Meynell) in England and various other European countries. Studied privately under William Standish in London, then attended the Female School of Art, South Kensington, 1861–3 and 1866–70; independent study in Italy, 1869–70. Exhibited widely from

1867. Became nationally famous after *Calling the Roll after an Engagement, Crimea* was bought by Queen Victoria, 1874. Converted to Catholicism with her mother and sister, 1873. Married Irish Catholic Major William Butler (later General Sir William Butler GCB, KCB), 1877; three sons, three daughters; first surviving child born 1879; became Lady Butler when husband knighted, 1886; he died 1910. Travelled in Europe, 1878; subsequently resided where her husband's regiment was stationed: Devonport, 1881–4; Egypt, 1885, 1890–91 and 1892; Brittany, 1886–8; Aldershot, 1893–5; South Africa, 1899, and elsewhere; acquired home at Delgany, Co. Wicklow, Ireland, 1888; returned to Britain, 1901; moved to Bansha Castle, Co. Tipperary, on Butler's retirement in 1905; to Gormanston Castle, Co. Meath, 1922. Proposed for election to the Royal Academy, 1879; narrowly defeated. Painted for war charities during World War I. Died at Gormanston Castle, 2 October 1933.

Principal Exhibitions

Dudley Gallery, London: 1867, 1871–4 (watercolour); 1868, 1872–3 (oil); 1872, 1874 (black and white)
Society of Female (later Lady) Artists, London: 1867–9, 1871–5, 1877
Royal Academy, London: occasionally 1873–1905
New Society of Painters in Watercolours, London: 1874–7
Fine Art Society, London: 1877 (individual)
Exposition Universelle, Paris: 1878
Egyptian Hall, Piccadilly, London: 1881 (individual)
Royal Hibernian Academy, Dublin: 1892, 1899, 1929–30
Paris Salon: 1894
New Gallery, London: 1896
Leicester Galleries, London: 1912, 1915, 1917, 1919 (all individual)

Selected Writings

Letters from the Holy Land, London: A. & C. Black, 1903
From Sketch-Book and Diary, London: A. & C. Black, 1909
An Autobiography, London: Constable, 1922; Boston: Houghton Mifflin, 1923

Bibliography

John Oldcastle, "Our living artists: Elizabeth Butler (née Thompson)", *Magazine of Art*, ii, 1879, pp.257–62
Wilfrid Meynell, "The life and work of Lady Butler", *Art Annual*, xviii, 1898, pp.1–31
Chronique des Arts, no.39, 10 December 1898, pp.355–6
The Times, 4 October 1933 (obituary)

Great Victorian Pictures: Their Paths to Fame, exh. cat., Arts Council of Great Britain, London, 1978

Mathew Paul Lalumia, "Lady Elizabeth Thompson Butler in the 1870s", *Woman's Art Journal*, iv/1, 1983, pp.9–14

Charlotte Yeldham, *Women Artists in Nineteenth-Century France and England*, 2 vols, New York: Garland, 1984

Joan Hichberger, *Military Themes in British Painting, 1815–1914*, PhD dissertation, University of London, 1985

Pamela Gerrish Nunn, *Canvassing: Recollections by Six Victorian Women Artists*, London: Camden Press, 1986

Lady Butler, Battle Artist, 1846–1933, exh. cat., National Army Museum, London, 1987

Paul Usherwood, "Elizabeth Thompson Butler: The consequences of marriage", *Woman's Art Journal*, ix/1, 1988, pp.30–34

——, "Elizabeth Thompson Butler: A case of tokenism", *Woman's Art Journal*, xi/2, 1990–91, pp.14–18

Wendy Slatkin, *The Voices of Women Artists*, Englewood Cliffs, NJ: Prentice Hall, 1993

Elizabeth Thompson, later Lady Butler, was by the end of the 19th century the most famous woman artist in Britain. She achieved such visibility because she was the first known woman battle painter. Previously, women artists had tended to work in genres considered feminine and/or in which the female figure and experience provided the main theme. In addition, Butler worked on a large scale, which was still not usual for women painters. In a period in which nationalism became imperialism, she drew patriotic support although she claimed to be critical of some aspects of the military establishment and army life.

From her first exhibition appearances, Elizabeth Thompson showed a preference for military subject matter and, though she vowed in 1876 to abjure such themes in favour of religious topics, this was a specialism to which she adhered throughout her career. Her first commission, *Calling the Roll after an Engagement, Crimea*, familiarly known as *The Roll Call* (1874; Royal Collection), was an overnight success and one of the most popular paintings in the history of the Royal Academy exhibitions. It set the tone for all her major works: a medium-large canvas showing numerous less-than-life-size figures of rank-and-file soldiers in an exterior setting on or near the battlefield. Her emphasis on the soldier rather than the officer was not only new in the genre, but coincided with the Cardwell Reforms of the British Army, begun in 1870. The

artist's command of her subject was marvelled at, the sentiment of her scene approved and her technical excellence admired. While Queen Victoria was an immediate admirer, feminists could also hold up Thompson as an example of what women could achieve in fine art. Her gallery-going public was augmented by the engraving of her annual exhibits, which brought the artist considerable copyright fees, greater than any woman artist before her had been able to command.

Though a keen observer from her student days, Butler had leaned considerably on the example of 19th-century French battle painting for her early work. Marrying a military man in 1877, she was able to deepen her observation of army psychology, battle locations and historical details. Her realism was tempered with an eye for the dramatic and the sentimental that gave her best works, such as *Balaclava* (1876; Manchester City Art Galleries) and *Scotland for Ever!* (1880–81; Leeds City Art Gallery), formal impact and emotional conviction. These works were complimented simultaneously for being equal to those of a man and for displaying a womanly sensibility. This perceived combination of masculine excellences and feminine virtues assured her sales and success with a wide range of viewers until the early 1880s. For nearly a decade she produced annual military dramas for the Academy or for solo exhibition with the Fine Art Society: *Quatre Bras* (1875; National Gallery of Victoria, Melbourne), *Balaclava* (1876), *Return from Inkerman* (1877; Ferens Art Gallery, Hull), *Remnants of an Army* (1879; Tate Gallery, London), *Scotland for Ever!* (1880–81), *Defence of Rorke's Drift* (1880–81; Royal Collection), *Floreat Etona!* (1882; private collection, Britain, repr. London 1987, pl.9). The impression she made with her set-piece celebrations of British soldiery was such that her admirers within the Academy put her up for election to membership of that body in 1879, even though women were not officially eligible.

By the 1880s Butler was working in conscious opposition to the aesthetic, anti-academic art that had grown up at the Grosvenor Gallery, representing what she believed were the virtues of realism and moral purpose in art. *Scotland for Ever!* was meant as a deliberate counter to a trend that she despised, but in which she perhaps foresaw the displacement of her own aesthetic. Although in 1883 the writer John Ruskin declared Butler to have converted him, with *The Roll Call* and *Quatre Bras*, to the belief that women could paint, her following waned in this decade, as French battle painters such as Alphonse de Neuville were taken up by her erstwhile audience and her own work declined technically, becoming predictable and florid. The demands of Butler's married life undermined her earlier absorption in the London art world, removing her to the provinces and various foreign outposts and diffusing her concentration, energy and application. It can be supposed that her husband's idiosyncratically liberal views on military matters, which brought him into conflict with the authorities, also confused her interpretation of her subject matter. Her rare attempts to broaden her base, such as *To the Front: French Cavalry Leaving a Breton City on the Declaration of War* (1889; private collection, *ibid.*, pl.11) and *Evicted* (1890; University College Dublin), the only major works in which she included female characters, were not well received.

Through the 1890s Butler concentrated on producing paintings and watercolours of the Napoleonic Wars. The political climate brought her renewed commercial success with these works, though critics attended less and less to her exhibits. Several British male artists had by this time established themselves in battle painting, and were seen to perform better in this genre, which men would always claim as essentially theirs. This became emphatically the case during World War I, which Butler commemorated in watercolours, mostly exhibited in solo shows at the Leicester Galleries, such as her *Waterloo Centenary* exhibition in 1915 and *Some Records of the World War* in 1919. Butler lived in Ireland after the war's end, and by her death in 1933 she had become a figure of the past.

PAMELA GERRISH NUNN

C

Cahun, Claude [fig. 12]
French photographer, mixed-media artist and writer, 1894–1954

Born Lucy Schwob in Nantes, 25 October 1894, into a Jewish intellectual family; daughter of Maurice Schwob, publisher of the newspaper *Le Phare de la Loire*, and niece of Symbolist writer Marcel Schwob. Distanced herself from her famous family by adopting the sexually ambiguous name Claude Cahun, 1918; published under this name in *Mercure de France*, reporting on the trial of Oscar Wilde. Moved from Nantes to Paris with stepsister and lifelong lover Suzanne Malherbe, also an artist. Befriended writer-publishers Adrienne Monnier and Sylvia Beach, and poet-artists Robert Desnos, Henri Michaux and Pierre Morhange; wrote for a variety of journals, including *Philosophies*, *Disque Vert* and the avant-garde homosexual review, *L'Amitié*. Joined Association des Ecrivains et Artistes Révolutionnaires (AEAR), 1932; left the following year, disenchanted with its close affiliation to the French Communist Party (PCF) and hostility to any aesthetic other than social realism. Joined anti-fascist Contre-Attaque group founded by Georges Bataille and André Breton, 1934. Left Paris permanently by 1938, moving to the Schwob family summer retreat on Jersey, Channel Islands. Active in the Resistance during the Nazi occupation; arrested and condemned to death, 1944; spared with the island's liberation, 1945; never recovered from incarceration. Continued to live in Jersey with Malherbe. Visited Paris, 1953. Died in Jersey, 8 December 1954.

Principal Exhibitions
Galerie Charles Ratton, Paris: 1936 (*Exposition surréaliste d'objets*)

Selected Writings
"La Salomé d'Oscar Wilde: Le procès Billing et les 47.000 pervertis du Livre noir", *Mercure de France*, no.481, 1 July 1918
"Heroïnes", *Mercure de France*, no.639, February 1925
Aveux non avenus, Paris: Carrefour, 1930
"Réponse à l'enquête: 'Pour qui écrivez-vous?'", *Commune*, no 4, December 1933
Les Paris sont ouverts, 1934 (tract)
"Prenez garde aux objets domestiques", *Cahiers d'Art*, i, ii, 1936

Bibliography
Edouard Jaguer, *Les Mystères de la chambre noire: Le Surréalisme et la photographie*, Paris: Flammarion, 1982
L'Amour Fou: Photography and Surrealism, exh. cat., Corcoran Gallery of Art, Washington, DC, and elsewhere, 1985
Nanda van den Berg, *Claude Cahun*, doctoral dissertation, Moderne Kunst, Utrecht, 1987
Sidra Stich, ed., *Anxious Visions*, New York: Abbeville, 1990
Paris des années 30: Le Surréalisme et le livre, exh. cat., Galerie Zabriskie, Paris, and elsewhere, 1991
François Leperlier, "Dossier Claude Cahun", *Pleine Marge*, no.14, December 1991
—, *Claude Cahun: L'Ecart et la métamorphose*, Paris: Michel Place, 1992
Honor Lasalle and Abigail Solomon-Godeau, "Surrealist confession: Claude Cahun's photomontages", *Afterimage*, xix, March 1992
Therese Lichtenstein, "A mutable mirror: Claude Cahun", *Artforum*, xxx, April 1992, pp.64–7
Mise en scène, exh. cat., Institute of Contemporary Arts, London, 1994
Le Rêve d'une ville: Nantes et le surréalisme, exh. cat., Musée des Beaux-Arts and Bibliothéque Municipale, Nantes, 1994
Claude Cahun photographe, exh. cat., Musée d'Art Moderne de la Ville de Paris, 1995 (includes extensive bibliography and catalogue raisonné)
François Leperlier, *Claude Cahun, 1894–1954*, Paris: Michel Place, 1995

Issues of gender and identity troubles may be taken to frame the work of the writer/artist/photographer Claude Cahun. Active in the prominent literary and artistic circles in Paris between the two world wars, Cahun produced a wide range of Surrealist-inspired objects, collages, photographs and writings that explored gender and identity by focusing on her own image and autobiography. Ironically, at the onset of World War II, Cahun fell into complete obscurity. Indeed, her identity became so uncertain that for a time it was unclear whether she was male or female; her works were attributed to an anonymous artist; and the circumstances of her life were essentially unknown. It is, then, a further irony that the first extensive scholarly work on Cahun should be a biography (Leperlier 1992), for if Cahun's entire oeuvre was devoted to investigating the very notion of a stable subject position through her own autobiographical inquiry, Leperlier – drawing on an interesting array of unpublished letters, manuscripts and documents – sought to fix the identity of Claude Cahun by explaining her through those very ambiguities she took up as her own critical project.

As early as 1919 Cahun consciously spurned conventions of femininity by shaving her head, and then took to dyeing in pink or green the crewcut that was sometimes allowed to sprout; she stained her skin and wore outlandish batiked, vaguely orientalised clothing. The Surrealist Marcel Jean noted in his memoirs that Cahun's appearance – "her face like that of a small bird of prey" – with her companion Malherbe at her side at the Café Cyrano was enough to drive André Breton into temporary exile, forcing him to give up his favourite café and regular meeting place.

The uneasy tension that Cahun inspired was as much cultural as it was personal, and linked to a more general anxiety around identity itself. In this respect, Cahun's work engages current feminist concerns as well as providing an opportunity to examine the ways in which her own avant-garde aspirations converge and intersect with contemporary debates around sexuality and identity.

The strength and difficulty of Cahun's work are still sensed in her self-portraits from this period. For example, in a photograph appearing in an issue of Ribemont-Dessaigne's *Bifur* in 1930, Cahun depicts herself in stark profile, her expression cold, almost menacing; harsh lighting underscores her severe, unadorned appearance, stripped of any mediating "props" – including hair – that might soften her

image. This portrait aggressively militates against the "normative ideals" of femininity and, more broadly, exposes the viewer's expectations of intelligible identity as they are grounded, specifically, in gender. Cahun made it her business to keep the question "So who is this, anyway?" constantly in play by exposing her "self" as nothing but a series of constructions.

Cahun takes her own subjectivity as the means of revealing the very impossibility of fixing the self: her texts and images speak to its dissolution, fragmentation and transformations, and biography itself becomes suspect, one more mask among many. Cahun's writings suggest that without a mask there can be no identity – not even human form. Or, alternatively, the self is nothing but masks, a point reiterated in a photo-montage in *Aveux non avenus* where we see a series of faces – all Cahun's – in various guises, springing from a single neck and framed by the handwritten words: "Under this mask, another mask. I will never finish removing all these faces". The succession of painted eyes and lips underscores the artifice and versatility of a single face, becoming a series of masks that in and of themselves obscure their own "identities": male here, female there, and elsewhere impossible to determine. In any case, revealing is never to be confused with knowing: Cahun insisted that the mystery of the masks remain intact.

Cahun's constantly shifting and transforming self sought to make gender itself ambiguous. Her work revels in the uncertainties afforded by the fluidity of "womanliness"; it was precisely through this indistinct subject-position that the coherence of the "self" was most vulnerable, and therein lay the revolutionary potential of subjectivity itself. Cahun's constructed, shifting identities were but a prelude to the radical dissolution of the individual subjectivity itself – a desire to dissolve the body, to become nothing but a heartbeat. To reach Cahun's imaginary centre, recognisable features are transformed, effaced, producing a subjectivity that turns on its own ambiguities and then, through these, attempts to transcend its own limits. The viewer, too, is asked to engage in this process: a striking self-portrait from the late 1920s underscores Cahun's sexual ambiguity, forcing the viewer to consider the elements comprising gender and identity through an ostensibly transparent and revealing means – the photographed self-portrait. Cahun's expression conveys a certainty of purpose, as determined as her commitment to obscure her own identity. She appears androgynous, her features made artificial with the black liner outlining an invented hairline, a single eyebrow or the tinted flesh of her arms. And beyond the confusion provoked in the viewer in her attempts to "place" Cahun, the image suggests that the viewer herself is implicated in the uncertainties of identity, something that is reinforced by the reflective orb she holds. Appearing as a convex mirror, the sphere reveals obscure light and shadows, rather than a clear reflection, which furthers the sense of disorientation. And even where Cahun depicts herself in particularly gendered roles (e.g. the dandy, the sailor, the debutante), the certainties on which we claim knowledge of gender and sexuality are destabilised. Thus, when she appears in feminine guise – as, for example, in a self-portrait from the early 1930s, where her bared shoulders evoke vulnerability, her expression is tentative and her eyes averted – she counters these elements with the jarring effect of her distorted and shaved head. The conventional feminine pose is transformed by her alien appearance, as though this figure could not be of this world.

In what might seem paradoxical, the individual became the site on which a kind of "collectivity" was to be founded – but only through a radical reconceptualisation, a being deconstructed through its own self-scrutiny. Not alone in this desire to "dematerialise" the limits of the self, Cahun joined other contemporary leftist intellectuals who sought alternatives to the straightforward political agitation advocated by the Communist Party. For them, a potential space of disruption was the subjective transcending its own bounds; in a society where the coherent subject was central to social stability – its structure, moral codes, rules – a radical re-conceptualisation of the self promised fundamental and profound change. To this end, Cahun began exploring the radical possibilities inherent in material objects and the viewer's relationship to them, an interest she shared with the Surrealists. Exhibiting with them in 1936, Cahun included two objects that sought to create disjunctures through juxtapositions of "found objects" and, on occasion, the addition of texts. Her *Un air de famille* – known only through photographs – consisted of a doll's bed filled with a variety of miniature toys and what appear to be matchbooks, enclosed within a veil. A cryptic message appears on a small sign tacked on to a mock bedpost, reading "dANGEr – *manger* – m

Ange z – menge – je mens – mange – gé manje". The words, taken in their entirety, make no sense, although the fragments are suggestive: danger, angel, to eat, my angel, I am lying, etc. The impulse is to make sense of these words through associations with the objects, thereby creating narrative links that make the objects more comprehensible. And yet this is precisely what Cahun's objects refuse. The space of safety and comfort is transformed into a potentially menacing and dangerous one, but the dangers and lies that the text indicates are elusive and unknown. Here the process of viewing parallels that of observing Cahun's self-portraits: one is forced to examine one's own conceptions against the image presented, a comparison that is inevitably disrupted. Cut loose from the literary, narrative elements that struggle to make sense of the world, Cahun's objects emphasise the disparate and disjunctive. Reinforcing this sense of disorder is Cahun's *Qui ne craint pas le grand méchant loup remet la barque sur sa quille et vogue à la dérive*, a variation on her lost *Souris valseuses* from the exhibition of 1936. Nestled in the jaws of an unidentified animal, small unrelated toys are crammed into the skeletal "boat": a tiny doll, a small model church, a light bulb, a pacifier and a menacing humming bird comprise a modern variant of the nonsensical ship of fools. At the base of the bones a caterpillar emerges from its cocoon, perhaps reappearing as the butterfly at the bow of the "ship", about to fly away. Although this aspect of escape and rebirth verges on sentimental cliché, it is offset by the sinister effect produced through the chaotic jumble of toys, many perched precariously on the skeletal jaws. The boat appears ominous rather than whimsical, and the seemingly childlike world is transformed into a space of potential nightmare. The mirror on which the object is placed, encircled with peacock feathers suggestive of non-seeing eyes, reinforces the impression that the sense of the object eludes the viewer, revealing nothing but the surface of appearance.

The ways in which Cahun's contemporary "external" world impinged on her personal experience were no doubt most sizeable: as a woman, as a lesbian, as a Jew, her own identity was particularly circumscribed by existing social labels and stereotypes. Yet while these categories imposed constraints, the fact that they were themselves somewhat unstable and ambiguous allowed Cahun to imagine a radically re-configured identity, grounded not only in her experience as a woman but as a lesbian as well: if the "experts" were baffled in their attempts to define "woman", then the gay woman was an even more vexing issue. Being a lesbian – separate from the "norms" of heterosexuality – enabled Cahun to produce work that so insistently turned on gender ambiguities. In this sense, although Cahun never directly addressed her personal sexuality, her own experience in this ambiguous space as a lesbian was very much an impetus for her artistic production. Furthermore, the fact that lesbian women were a prominent presence in Paris (some of the most fashionable literary circles of the inter-war period were made up of "notorious" lesbians) provided both a community and an avenue for public expression. Yet, at the same time, this heightened visibility invited what Michel Foucault termed "the policing of sex". If lesbians were able finally to come out of the closet, this also occasioned an opportunity to categorise, study and then control them further. The seemingly permissive culture was quick to reassert control with rising unemployment, declining birth rate and war on the horizon. By the early 1930s the period of cultural flexibility seemed to be coming to a close, and Cahun herself produced far fewer of her enigmatic self-portraits, turning instead to the production of objects.

To shift from the confines of the individual into a space that may be described only through negation – a world without barriers, where identity itself becomes impossible to distinguish – could this exist in any space other than the imaginary? For Cahun, the point was not to imagine what this might "look like" as a reality, but simply to indicate its possibilities, as she clarified in her texts on writing as revolutionary practice. Her access to this revolutionary space was made through the instabilities embodied in her own identity configured around gender and sexuality; she believed that these might lead to a radical re-thinking of the subject, beyond regulatory constraints of gender.

In an age in which identification with a particular group or cause too often replaces revolutionary political and radical thought, Cahun's example is still instructive, encouraging us to imagine a different kind of world in which identity does not fix and freeze the individual, but rather radically transforms the culture that would define her or him.

LAURIE J. MONAHAN

Cameron, Julia Margaret [fig. 13]
British photographer, 1815–1879

Born Julia Margaret Pattle in Calcutta, India, 11 June 1815, to James Pattle, an East India Company official, and Adeline de l'Etang. Educated in Europe, living with her maternal grandmother in Versailles; returned to Calcutta, 1834. Married Charles Hay Cameron, jurist and member of the Supreme Council of India, 1838; several children. Returned to England on husband's retirement in 1848, settling in Tunbridge Wells, Kent, before moving to Surrey, 1850; spent time on the Isle of Wight from 1860. Given first camera by her daughter, 1863. Elected member of the Photographic Societies of London and Scotland, 1864. Moved with husband to family plantation in Ceylon, 1875; visited England briefly, 1878. Died in Ceylon, 26 January 1879.

Principal Exhibitions

Individual
French Gallery, Pall Mall, London: 1865
Colnaghi's Gallery, London: 1865
German Gallery, London: 1868
9 Conduit Street, London: 1873

Group
Photographic Society of London: from 1864
Berlin International Photographic Exhibition: 1865 (bronze medal), 1866 (gold medal)
International Exhibition, Dublin: 1865 (honourable mention)
Exposition Universelle, Paris: 1867 (honourable mention)
Photography Exhibition, Groningen, Netherlands: 1869 (bronze medal)
International Exhibition, London: 1871, 1872, 1873
Weltausstellung, Vienna: 1873 (medal)
Centennial Exposition, Philadelphia: 1876 (medal)

Bibliography
Coventry Patmore, "Mrs Cameron's photographs", *Macmillan's Magazine*, xiii, January 1866, pp.230–31
Peter Henry Emerson, "Mrs Cameron", *Sun Artists*, no.5, 1890, pp.33–43
Frederick H. Evans, "Exhibition of photographs of Julia Margaret Cameron", *Amateur Photographer*, xl, 21 July 1904, pp.43–4
Alvin Langdon Coburn, "The old masters of photography", *The Century*, xc, 1915, pp.909–20
Una Taylor, *Guests and Memories: Annals of a Seaside Villa*, London: Oxford University Press, 1924
Victorian Photographs of Famous Men and Fair Women, London: Leonard and Virginia Woolf, and New York:

Harcourt Brace, 1926; revised editon, ed. Tristram Powell, London: Hogarth Press, 1973

Brian Hill, *Julia Margaret Cameron: A Victorian Family Portrait*, London: Owen, and New York: St Martin's Press, 1973

Charles W. Millard, "Julia Margaret Cameron and Tennyson's *Idylls of the King*", *Harvard Library Bulletin*, xxi, 1973, pp.187–201

Mrs Cameron's Photographs from the Life, exh. cat., Stanford University Museum of Art, CA, 1974

Colin Ford, *The Cameron Collection: An Album of Photographs Presented to Sir John Herschel*, Wokingham and New York: Van Nostrand Reinhold, 1975

Helmut Gernsheim, *Julia Margaret Cameron: Her Life and Photographic Work*, 2nd edition, London: Gordon Fraser, and Millerton, NY: Aperture, 1975

Graham Ovenden, ed., *A Victorian Album: Julia Margaret Cameron and Her Circle*, London: Secker and Warburg, and New York: Da Capo Press, 1975

Margaret Harker, *Julia Margaret Cameron*, London: Collins, 1983

Golden Age of British Photography, exh. cat., Victoria and Albert Museum, London, and elsewhere, 1984

Mike Weaver, *Julia Margaret Cameron, 1815–1879*, Boston: Little Brown, and London: Herbert Press, 1984 (expanded Italian edition, Rome, 1985)

Cameron: Her Work and Career, exh. cat., International Museum of Photography at George Eastman House, Rochester, NY, and elsewhere, 1986

Amanda Hopkinson, *Julia Margaret Cameron*, London: Virago, 1986

Whisper of the Muse: The Overstone Album and Other Photographs, exh. cat., J. Paul Getty Museum, Malibu, CA, 1986

Jan Marsh and Pamela Gerrish Nunn, *Women Artists and the Pre-Raphaelite Movement*, London: Virago, 1989

A.N. Wilson, *Eminent Victorians*, London: BBC Books, 1989; New York: Norton, 1990

Whisper of the Muse: The World of Julia Margaret Cameron, exh. cat., Royal Photographic Society, London, 1990

Pam Roberts, "Julia Margaret Cameron: A triumph over criticism", *The Portrait in Photography*, ed. Graham Clarke, London: Reaktion, and Seattle: University of Washington Press, 1992, pp.47–70

For My Best Beloved Sister, Mia: An Album of Photographs, exh. cat., University of New Mexico Art Museum, Albuquerque, 1994

Carol Armstrong, "Cupid's pencil of light: Julia Margaret Cameron and the maternalization of photography", *October*, no.76, Spring 1996, pp.115–41

In Focus: Julia Margaret Cameron: Photographs from the J. Paul Getty Museum, Getty Trust Publications, 1996

Julia Margaret Cameron's life, and what we would now call her career, was set firmly in the tradition of High Victorian amateurism that in her period trans-formed the practices of both the sciences and the arts. She was an amateur in two senses: first, she had no professional training, was an auto-didact, and did not support herself or others in her family by her "professional" activity as a photographer; second, in the love, perhaps even obsession, she had for the practice of photography. She has left behind a legacy of influential portraits of her peers – the mandarins of Empire and of government, writers, scholars, politicians, historians and poets. To a very real extent, her work has defined for us what we take to be the appearance of the grandees of Victorian Britain, while other Victorian attitudes are presented with careful artifice in what are now her period pieces of exquisitely contrived set tableaux – "art" photographs in which both servants and the eminent were pressed into hard-held poses by the force of her formidable will.

Cameron was born in Calcutta, her father, James Pattle, a member of the Bengal civil service, the family an integral and integrated part of the imperial ruling classes of the British Empire; her six sisters also married well, and of their seven husbands, a jurist, a general, an aristocrat, a landowner among them, the majority have been commemorated in the *Dictionary of National Biography*, as has Mrs Cameron herself. Julia was said not to be as beautiful as her half-dozen sisters; at 22 she married the very rich and distinguished 45-year-old Charles Hay Cameron who owned vast plantations in Ceylon, was a member of the Council of India, and an eminent jurist who codified the Indian legal system. Plain, plump, overwhelmingly charming and determined, Julia was for a while the leading British hostess in India, by virtue of her husband's position and her own social energy.

Ten years after the marriage the Camerons came to live in England, finally settling at Freshwater on the Isle of Wight. Her family connections provided a strikingly artistic and intellectual milieu; her sister was married to Thoby Prinsep and the Prinseps' salon at Little Holland House in London in the 1840s included the Pre-Raphaelites, while the artist in residence was G.F. Watts, husband of the actress Ellen Terry. Watts painted Julia Margaret Cameron, as well as Terry (*Choosing*), while Mrs Cameron photographed Terry (*Alithea*). The interchanges could be complex: Cameron translated Burger's romantic poem *Leonore*, which was published with illustrations by Daniel Maclise; Maclise also illustrated Tennyson, and his illustration for the dying

King Arthur influenced Cameron's photograph the *Passing of Arthur*; in 1874 Cameron made a set of photographs as illustrations for Tennyson's *Idylls of the King* and other poems, at the poet's request. Cameron was generally acknowledged as benevolent, even overwhelmingly so; with unusual energy, enthusiasm and high spirits that were apparently unquenchable, she could also be almost impossibly high-handed. Her very excesses became virtues when faced with the technical complexities of the mechanics of early portrait photography.

Cameron began serious photography in her fiftieth year, her eventful life three-quarters over – her memorable achievement must give hope to all late starters. It was the present of a big camera from her daughter that spurred her interest and energy in this new direction. She transformed an old glazed hen-house on the Cameron property into her studio – the coalhouse was the darkroom – and learned by hard hours of trial and error; she coerced and bullied her sitters. Servants, locals and relatives posed for illustrative tableaux, related to the subject pictures so beloved of the Victorians, and celebrity friends and acquaintances were not only integrated into these set pieces but were persuaded to sit for their individual portraits. She was successful, professionally, in her own life; she had a solo exhibition of her photographs at the art dealer, Colnaghi's, in London in 1865, and the gallery suggests that it was Colnaghi's publications of prints after the old masters that influenced Mrs Cameron's art photography.

A great deal of her work has survived. Of about 3000 images, the photographic historian Helmut Gernsheim estimated that some 60 are outstanding, milestones in Victorian portraiture. There are various significant accounts of her character, personality and working methods – for this we must thank her huge acquaintanceship and network of friends and relations, although surprisingly there is no substantial late 20th-century biography of her. A vivid, even picturesque if somewhat inaccurate account of Cameron was published in 1926 with a selection of her photographs (*Victorian Photographs of Famous Men and Fair Women*) by Virginia Woolf, Cameron's great-niece, accompanied by a fine appreciation of her photography by the Bloomsbury critic, curator and painter Roger Fry. From Woolf we learn of Cameron's indefatigable letter writing (to one friend, Sir Henry Taylor, she wrote every day), her half-realised ambitions to

write fiction – she certainly specialised in her "art" photography in the portrayal of visual fiction – and her immense generosity. Taylor observed that Cameron had a great genius, and that "she lives upon superlatives as upon her daily bread".

Perhaps her enthusiasm and energy were excessive, but she could and did exercise extraordinary patience; the elaborate chemical processes of the wet collodion process, which required not only lengthy sittings but the immediate development of the image on a wet glass plate – probably a large surface, 12×15 inches (30×38 cm.) – were handled by Cameron with uncustomary grace. She worked "fruitlessly but not hopelessly", as she said herself of her early experiments.

Her portraits were among the first photographs to challenge the painted image. According to Tennyson, her photographs of him destroyed his anonymity. Tennyson brought the American poet Longfellow to sit for Cameron, telling him that he would have to obey the imperious artist. Thomas Carlyle, who thought his photographic image "terrifically ugly and woebegone", Charles Darwin, the classical scholar Benjamin Jowett, Robert Browning, the painters Holman Hunt and G.F. Watts, and the actress Ellen Terry were among her sitters. The portraits of men are usually comparatively straightforward. The bulk of her work was not composed of portraiture, however, but of illustrations, to Tennyson's poetry, to Shakespeare and to allegorical scenes of her own devising, with women and girls posing as characters and heroines. Her heroes were usually middle-aged even elderly great men, typically posed so that their hair acted as a kind of aureole. Her compositions were heavily influenced by the biblical and historical scenes of the Pre-Raphaelite artists, and other relatively contemporary painters, as well as the old masters. For example, Sir Joshua Reynolds's portrait of *Mrs Siddons as the Tragic Muse* was a direct precursor of Cameron's *Hark, Hark*. But there was also a Zeitgeist at work: Cameron's own *Call, I Follow, I Follow, Let Me Die* pre-dates Dante Gabriel Rossetti's *Beata Beatrix*.

Cameron's generosity, combined with the decline in revenue from Charles Cameron's estates in Ceylon, added to her husband's intense desire to revisit the East. In 1875, accompanied by their two coffins, in case Ceylon did not provide such necessities, they set sail; Cameron revisited England in the spring of 1878; seven months later, she was to die in the East, back in Ceylon. She had continued her photography in the East, photographing for instance *Marianne Thornton*, the indefatigable traveller (and E.M. Forster's aunt), whose paintings on glass of horticultural subjects are housed in a special museum at Kew. But her work in Ceylon did not match the quality of her work executed in England.

Julia Margaret Cameron's portraits of "Famous Men and Fair Women" demonstrated the powerful personalities of her selected subjects, and her own personality. Creatively turning disadvantage to advantage, the awkwardness, difficulty and long time-span of early photographic techniques, Cameron deployed technical imperfections into interesting evidence of character. She liked imperfection; she deliberately refused to refine her focus. It is this bravura, dramatic element in her portraiture that has lifted that aspect of her work beyond reportage.

MARINA VAIZEY

Carpenter, Margaret (Sarah)
British painter, 1793–1872

Born Margaret Sarah Geddes in Salisbury, Wiltshire, 1 February 1793, to Alexander Geddes, a retired army officer, and Harriet Easton. Moved with her family to a farm at nearby Alderbury, 1798. Taught to paint in oils by Thomas Guest in Salisbury, c.1805, then copied old masters in the Earl of Radnor's collection at Longford Castle near her family home. Visited London, 1810–12; received financial help from Lord Radnor to move there permanently, 1813. Awarded silver medal, 1812, lesser gold medal, 1813, and principal gold medal, 1814, Society of Arts. Married William Hookham Carpenter, son of Bond Street bookseller and art dealer James Carpenter, 1817; eight children, only five surviving infancy, of whom three, William, Percy and Henrietta, also became artists. Husband appointed Keeper of Prints and Drawings, British Museum, 1845; lived in museum residence, 1852–66; received pension after his death in 1866. Died in London, 13 November 1872.

Principal Exhibitions
Royal Academy, London: 1814–25, 1828–63, 1865–6

British Institution, London: 1814–17, 1819–24, 1826–33, 1835, 1837–40, 1842–53
Royal Institution, Edinburgh: 1822–9
Paris Salon: 1827
Society of British Artists, London: 1831–6
Exposition Universelle, Paris: 1855
Art Treasures Exhibition, Manchester: 1857
Society of Female Artists, London: 1858, 1863
National Portrait Exhibition, London: 1868

Bibliography
Ellen C. Clayton, *English Female Artists*, 2 vols, London: Tinsley, 1876

Walter Shaw Sparrow, ed., *Women Painters of the World*, London: Hodder and Stoughton, and New York: Stokes, 1905; reprinted New York: Hacker, 1976

Donald C. Whitton, *The Grays of Salisbury*, San Francisco: Whitton, 1976

Charlotte Yeldham, *Women Artists in Nineteenth-Century France and England*, 2 vols, New York: Garland, 1984

Catherine Peters, *The King of Inventors: A Life of Wilkie Collins*, London: Secker and Warburg, 1991; Princeton: Princeton University Press, 1993

Margaret Carpenter Bicentenary Exhibition, exh. cat., Salisbury Museum, 1993

Richard J. Smith, *Margaret Sarah Carpenter (1793–1872): A Brief Biography*, Salisbury: Salisbury Museum, 1993

——, "Margaret Carpenter (1793–1872): A Salisbury artist restored", *Hatcher Review*, iv/36, 1993, pp.2–32

Margaret Carpenter's career bridges what some historians call the "vacuum" in British art between the Georgian school of portrait painters, culminating in Thomas Lawrence, and the later Victorian schools, from the Pre-Raphaelites onwards. She was at her peak during the 1830s and 1840s, when she was seen by many as the natural successor to Lawrence. This timing, as well as the fact that she was a somewhat lone figure and a woman, helps to account for her quite unjustified neglect ever since her death.

Even as a child, Margaret showed a prodigious talent for drawing portraits, and was in demand from families in the surrounding area. Her parents were not especially artistic, and apart from some limited instruction from Thomas Guest in Salisbury she was largely self-taught. The Earl of Radnor recognised her talent and allowed her to copy the old masters in his collection at Longford Castle. In her early days in London, she was part of a circle of young artists that included William Collins (her future brother-in-law and father of novelist Wilkie), the Scottish painter Andrew Geddes (no relation), David Wilkie and James Stark. Her oil portrait of *James Stark* (c.1814–19; Castle Museum, Norwich) shows a confidence and quality also seen in the smaller oil portrait of her future husband *William Carpenter* (1816; National Portrait Gallery, Bodelwyddan) and the watercolours of herself and William (1817; British Museum, London). The claim that Thomas Lawrence was her teacher has not been fully substantiated. She was, however, influenced by his work and that of Reynolds, although she spoke with an individual voice and was never accused of imitating either.

Lord Radnor's early patronage was important, but Carpenter's determination and ambition, combined with her talent, ensured that she continued to build on it all through her life. Her Account Book (copy in National Portrait Gallery, London) lists almost 600 clients from all walks of life – and even that is not exhaustive: in all she produced more than 1100 pictures, mostly portraits in oils, but many in chalks, and some watercolour landscapes. There were also subject pictures, many of which she exhibited at the British Institution. Two good examples are *A Gleaner* (1820; South London Gallery, Camberwell) and *The Young Artist* (1829; private collection), showing a young girl drawing her dog.

In her day Carpenter was one of the few women painting full-scale canvases, as opposed to miniatures, and it is remarkable how she managed to obtain her commissions. As a woman she could not call upon the nobility and gentry, as her brother-in-law used to do, although occasionally Collins recommended her. Yet in spite of marriage and several children, her professional output rarely flagged. With an unbusiness-like husband, and the need to help support her poverty-stricken parents, money was a crucial factor; but Carpenter's work was also driven by a streak of compulsiveness, resulting in conflict with her family responsibilities, which attracted critical comment. In 1825 John Constable noted that her painting was clearly giving her physical problems, and he suspected that her children were neglected for it (John Constable, *Correspondence*, ed. Ronald Brymer Beckett, iv, London: HMSO, 1966, p.137). Not only that, for most of her career she earned more than her husband.

Eton College was a fruitful source of work, through the influence of the Revd Edward Coleridge, for many years an assistant master. Carpenter painted up to 26 "leaving portraits" of boys, which are now in the official College collection, besides some 60 small oil panels for Coleridge himself. After his death, these were dispersed to the families of the sitters; a good example is *The 6th Duke of Roxburghe* (1831; Floors Castle, Kelso).

Carpenter's subjects all have a straightforward reality and energy. She concentrates on bringing the face, and especially the eyes, to the fore. She lights the forehead and hair, and softens the mouth and chin to give the whole face a warmth of personality. It is almost as if she and the sitter were having an animated conversation while she worked. She was also a superb draughtswoman; her small paintings often have the qualities of a miniature, while she could capture equally the swagger of a full-length portrait. From a small panel such as *John Tregonwell* (1833; 25.5 × 20.3 cm.; Russell-Cotes Gallery, Bournemouth) to the magnificent portrait of *Ada, Countess of Lovelace* (1836; 213 × 122 cm.; Government Art Collection, London), she is in total command of her medium. Her qualities were neatly summed up by Walter Shaw Sparrow: "[she is] among those quiet unpretentious portrait-painters whose thoughts are so wrapped up in their determination to be true that they never think of striving after exhibition-room effects." We see "the character of her sitters, and not technical displays of her own cleverness" (Sparrow 1905, p.60).

After Lawrence's death in 1830, Carpenter's career reached new heights. Her work was constantly praised in the art press as being "unaffectedly natural", "gracefully managed", "of classic simplicity". Her pictures of women and children, for example, *The Sisters*, a portrait of her two daughters Henrietta and Jane (1839; Victoria and Albert Museum, London), and *Spring Nosegay* (1831; Castle Museum, Nottingham), found especial favour. Her children are always natural and engaged in their own activities – a spontaneity born of the artist's years of observation of her five siblings and of her own children, unstifled by academic schooling. Over and over again, reviewers asked why she was not a member of the Royal Academy (she exhibited 156 pictures there, more than almost any other woman artist in the 19th century). Eventually in 1844 she was nominated, but as the only woman among some 60 candidates for two vacancies, she never really stood a chance.

Of the tiny fraction of Carpenter's work hanging in public galleries today, most are portraits of men. Of these, the portrait of the sculptor *John Gibson* (1857; National Portrait Gallery, Bodelwyddan) is very fine, but the posthumous portrait of the painter *Richard Bonington* (c.1833; National Portrait Gallery, London) is disappointing and untypical. Most of Carpenter's portraits of women and children are still with the families who commissioned them, but among those in collections open to the public are the beautiful *Lady Musgrave* (1825; Dalemain, Cumbria), the striking *Lady Eastnor* (1828; Eastnor Castle, Herefordshire), the softly delicate *Lady Mary Vyner* (1836; Newby Hall, Yorkshire), *Mrs John Marshall and Her Son* (1838; Leeds City Art Gallery), *Anna Maria Theobald* (1840) and her sister *Georgiana Thellusson* (1850; both Brodsworth Hall, Yorkshire), *Henrietta Baillie* (1845; Royal College of Physicians, London), two lovely portraits of members of the Frewen family (1846 and 1853; Brickwall House, Northiam, Sussex) and *Mrs Collins*, the mother of William Collins, RA (1826; National Gallery of New Zealand, Wellington). No pupils or "followers" of Carpenter have been identified, apart from her daughter Henrietta, although she probably influenced a number of her contemporaries. Often misattributed, Carpenter's work is gradually coming to light, to show her true stature and importance.

RICHARD J. SMITH

Carr, Emily   [fig. 14]
Canadian painter, 1871–1945

Born in Victoria, British Columbia, 13 December 1871. Attended California School of Design, San Francisco, 1890–93. Taught art to children in Victoria, 1893–5. First visited Northwest Coast Indian villages, 1899. Studied at Westminster School of Art, London, 1900–03, leaving to paint in St Ives, Cornwall, and in Hertfordshire. Spent 15 months in a sanatorium in England, 1903–4. Returned to Victoria, 1904. Lived in Vancouver, c.1906–10. Attended Académie Colarossi, Paris, 1910. Recuperated from illness in Sweden and painted in Brittany and Concarneau, 1911. Returned to Vancouver and opened studio at 1465 West Broadway, 1912. Built a studio and apartment house, "The House of All Sorts", in Victoria,

1913; later ran it as a boarding house (sold 1936). Visited New York, 1930. Lived with sister Alice after second heart attack, 1940. Died at St Mary's Priory, Victoria, 2 March 1945. Recipient of posthumous honorary doctorate, University of British Columbia, 1945.

Principal Exhibitions

Individual
1465 West Broadway, Vancouver: 1912
Drummond Hall, Vancouver: 1913
Women's Canadian Club, Crystal Gardens Gallery, Victoria: 1930
Seattle Art Museum: 1930, 1943
Lyceum Club and Women's Art Association, Toronto: 1936, 1941
Art Gallery of Toronto: 1937, 1940, 1943
Vancouver Art Gallery: 1938, 1939, 1940, 1941, 1943
University of British Columbia, Vancouver: 1938, 1939, 1940
National Gallery of Canada, Ottawa: 1945 (touring retrospective)

Group
Studio Club, Vancouver: 1907–9, 1912
British Columbia Society of Fine Arts: 1909–10, 1929, 1936–43
Salon d'Automne, Paris: 1911
Island Arts and Crafts Club, Victoria: occasionally 1911–37
National Gallery of Canada, Ottawa: 1927 (*Canadian West Coast Art: Native and Modern*, touring), 1928, 1930–33 (annuals), 1933 (*Contemporary Canadian Painting*, touring)
Group of Seven, Toronto: 1930, 1931
Ontario Society of Artists, Toronto: 1930, 1931
Baltimore Museum of Art: 1931 (*Baltimore Pan-American Exhibition*, touring)
Canadian Group of Painters, Toronto (touring): 1933, 1936–9, 1942
Stedelijk Museum, Amsterdam: 1933 (*Works by Women Artists*)

Selected Writings
"Modern and Indian art of the West Coast", *McGill News* (supplement), June 1929, pp.18–22
Klee Wyck, Toronto: Oxford University Press, 1941
The Book of Small, Toronto: Oxford University Press, 1942; London: Oxford University Press, 1943
The House of All Sorts, Toronto: Oxford University Press, 1944
Growing Pains: The Autobiography of Emily Carr, Toronto: Oxford University Press, 1946
The Heart of a Peacock, ed. Ira Dilworth, Toronto: Oxford University Press, 1953
Pause: A Sketch Book, Toronto: Clarke Irwin, 1953

Hundreds and Thousands: The Journals of Emily Carr,
Toronto: Clarke Irwin, 1966
Fresh Seeing: Two Addresses by Emily Carr, Toronto:
Clarke Irwin, 1972
*Dear Nan: Letters of Emily Carr, Nan Cheney and
Humphrey Toms*, ed. Doreen Walker, Vancouver:
University of British Columbia Press, 1990

Bibliography

Lawren Harris, "Emily Carr and her work", *Canadian
Forum*, no.21, December 1941, pp.277–8
Emily Carr: Her Paintings and Sketches, exh. cat.,
National Gallery of Canada, Ottawa, and elsewhere,
1945
Carol Pearson, *Emily Carr as I Knew Her*, Toronto:
Clarke Irwin, 1954
Edythe Hembroff-Schleicher, *M.E.: A Portrayal of Emily
Carr*, Toronto: Clarke Irwin, 1969
William Wylie Thom, *The Fine Arts in Vancouver,
1886–1930: An Historical Study*, MA thesis,
Department of Fine Arts, University of British
Columbia, 1969
Emily Carr: A Centennial Exhibition, exh. cat.,
Vancouver Art Gallery and elsewhere, 1971; 2nd
edition, 1975
Northrop Frye, *The Bush Garden: Essays on the
Canadian Imagination*, Toronto: Anansi, 1971
Maria Tippett and Douglas Cole, *From Desolation to
Splendour: Changing Perceptions of the British
Columbia Landscape*, Toronto: Clarke Irwin, 1977
Edythe Hembroff-Schleicher, *Emily Carr: The Untold
Story*, Saanichton, BC: Hancock House, 1978
Doris Shadbolt, *The Art of Emily Carr*, Vancouver:
Douglas and McIntyre, and Seattle: University of
Washington Press, 1979
Russell Keziere, "Emily Carr: Kultur der Neuen Welt und
Widersprüche der Alten Welt", *OKanada*, exh. cat.,
Akademie der Künste, Berlin, 1982, pp.80–87
Paula Blanchard, *The Life of Emily Carr*, Vancouver:
Douglas and McIntyre, and Seattle, University of
Washington Press, 1987
*The Expressionist Landscape: North American Modernist
Painting, 1920–1947*, exh. cat., Birmingham Museum
of Art, AL, 1988
Ruth Ann Stevens Appelhof, *Emily Carr: Canadian
Modernist*, PhD dissertation, Syracuse University, NY,
1988
Terry Goldie, *Fear and Temptation: The Image of the
Indigene in Canadian, Australian and New Zealand
Literatures*, Kingston: McGill-Queen's University
Press, 1989
Doris Shadbolt, *Emily Carr*, Vancouver: Douglas and
McIntyre, and Seattle: University of Washington Press,
1990
Emily Carr in France/Emily Carr en France, exh. cat.,
Vancouver Art Gallery, 1991
Marcia Crosby, "Construction of the imaginary Indian",
*Vancouver Anthology: The Institutional Politics of
Art*, ed. Stan Douglas, Vancouver: Talonbooks, 1991,
pp.272–6
*The True North: Canadian Landscape Painting,
1896–1939*, exh. cat., Barbican Art Gallery, London,
1991
Scott Watson, "Disfigured nature: The origins of the
modern Canadian landscape", *Eye of Nature*, exh.
cat., Walter Phillips Gallery, Banff, 1991, pp.103–12
Mara R. Witzling, ed., *Voicing Our Visions: Writings by
Women Artists*, New York: Universe, 1991; London:
Women's Press, 1992
Gerta Moray, *Northwest Coast Native Culture and the
Early Indian Paintings of Emily Carr, 1899–1913*,
PhD dissertation, University of Toronto, 1993
Maria Tippett, *Emily Carr: A Biography*, revised edition,
Toronto: Stoddard, 1994
Robert Linsley, "Landscapes in motion: Lawren Harris,
Emily Carr and the heterogeneous modern nation",
Oxford Art Journal, xix/1, 1996, pp.80–95
Stephanie Walker, *This Woman in Particular: Contexts
for the Biographical Image of Emily Carr*, Waterloo,
Ont.: Wilfrid Laurier University Press, 1996

Emily Carr is one of the most celebrated figures in
Canadian culture, a position due equally to her
outstanding modernist landscape paintings and to
her writings. Daughter of a successful English
importer-wholesaler who brought his family to
British Columbia in 1858, Carr was orphaned in her
mid-teens. With the decline of the family's
fortunes, she saved her earnings as an art teacher to
pursue further art training in Britain and France.
She travelled boldly into frontier areas of the
province to record the villages and totem poles of
the Northwest Coast native peoples. From 1928 on
she forged a distinctive modern idiom in paintings
of the landscape of British Columbia, which
have ever since defined its image in Canadian
consciousness.

Carr has attained almost legendary status, as a
"little old woman on the edge of nowhere" who
transcended local rejection of her modern paintings
to achieve national fame, as an eccentric spinster
landlady who kept a household of animals (a
monkey, parrots, dogs, a pet rat and various wild
creatures she tamed), and as a mystic who
communed with nature and "lived among the
Indians". She contributed substantially to her own
legend with seven volumes of autobiographical tales
and with her journals and letters (most published
posthumously). This has tended to occlude the fact
that she was a highly professional and dedicated
artist who maintained contact with avant-garde

developments after her training in France through available books and magazines and through correspondence with fellow artists.

Carr's landscape paintings eventually won her a place alongside the Group of Seven, the eastern Canadian painters who from 1911 developed images of wilderness landscape that were seen as the expression of a modern Canadian national identity. In oil paintings such as *Indian War Canoe, Alert Bay* (1912; Museum of Fine Arts, Montreal) Carr had independently applied the Post-Impressionist colouring and Fauve linear arabesques she learned in France to the landscape of British Columbia and to the villages and totem poles of the Northwest Coast native peoples. By the time of her death in 1945, Carr was acclaimed as a Canadian van Gogh, and the memorial exhibition mounted of her work became the largest exhibition ever held for a Canadian artist.

Carr has since also been recognised as a significant contributor to the first generation of modernism in North America (see Appelhof in Birmingham 1988). From a feminist art-historical perspective, she emerges as a figure comparable to Georgia O'Keeffe (q.v.), whom she met briefly on her only visit to New York in 1930. As with O'Keeffe, Carr's critical reception has recurrently emphasised her affinity as a woman artist with nature, the expression in her work of a personal and sexual symbology, and her search for spiritual meaning through art. She has been claimed as a precursor of feminist spirituality and ecological consciousness (Walker 1996).

Early in her career, Carr's interests diverged from the types of painting expected from women artists at the time. Like Rosa Bonheur (q.v.) and Lady Butler (q.v.), she is a woman artist whose ambition caused her to be characterised as "painting like a man". She focused her attention on two main concerns, to render the specific qualities of the Northwest Coast landscape and to record the visible legacy of aboriginal culture there. Carr's periods of study abroad kindled her interest first of all in the French-derived naturalism of the St Ives and Newlyn artists during her stay in England, and then in the Post-Impressionist and Fauve techniques she learned from English-speaking teachers in France (the Scot J.D. Fergusson, the English Henry Phelan Gibb and the Australian Frances Hodgkins, q.v., all followers of Gauguin and Matisse). Her resulting interest in strong colour and rhythmic brushwork can be seen in *Autumn in France* (1911; oil on cardboard; National Gallery of Canada, Ottawa), which was exhibited at the Paris Salon d'Automne. Her experience in Europe, however, strongly confirmed Carr's Canadian loyalties and her ambition to make a significant artistic contribution to her home province of British Columbia.

Critics and art historians have seen in Carr an artist whose vision was rooted in a formal language and a spiritual wisdom she learned through "deep understanding" of a "vanishing" Indian culture (Shadbolt 1979). As the Canadian painter Lawren Harris exclaimed: "Her art in subject matter has no contact with white peoples. It is an art whose full sustenance is drawn from the soil and the sea ... [I]t embodies an almost primitive oneness with nature, identical one feels with the Indian sympathy with nature" (Harris 1941). This image of the artist as "gone Indian" and inheriting the aborigine's bond to the land is now seen as an example of a recurrent myth in colonial literatures (Goldie 1989, p.16). Carr's representation of Northwest Coast native culture has come under critical scrutiny with the recent awareness that images of aboriginal peoples have reflected Eurocentric, imperialist and often racist attitudes (Crosby 1991, Moray 1993). It is significant that Carr's work gained its first wide recognition in 1927, when it was co-opted for the Canadian National Gallery's exhibition, *Canadian West Coast Art: Native and Modern*. The curators' agenda was to show off Northwest Coast native artefacts as a Canadian national treasure and as a resource for Canadian artists and designers. Their discovery of the aesthetic properties of these artefacts came at an historical moment when decades of aggressively assimilationist Canadian state policy had rendered illegal native social institutions such as the potlatch, had enforced residential schooling for native children, and in 1927 had declared null and void the land claims that British Columbia's aboriginal tribes had been pursuing since the province's entry into Confederation. In this context, the validation of native artefacts as aesthetic objects and their preservation for the white community were further acts of colonial appropriation.

Carr's own earlier paintings and her involvement with Indian subjects were, however, more complex and ambiguous. Their full implications at a time when the "Indian problem" was a heated local social and political issue, as Carr was well aware, have only recently been realised (Moray 1993). Carr had first decided to specialise in documenting aboriginal culture when she was establishing her career in the competitive climate of the new art community of Vancouver. Between 1907 and 1913 she undertook an extensive project to make water-colours and oils of "totem poles in their own village settings, as complete a collection of them as I could" (*Growing Pains* 1946, p.211). Through her contact with modernist primitivism in Paris, Carr became convinced that native carvings had high artistic merit, and she studied their forms carefully in her documentary sketches and paintings, most of which are now in the Vancouver Art Gallery and the British Columbia Archives and Records Service. She made sketching trips during summer breaks from teaching, including a long journey in 1912 among the Kwakiutl islands at the northern end of Vancouver Island, to Gitksan villages on the Skeena River, and to Haida settlements in the Queen Charlotte Islands. By 1913 she was able to mount a huge exhibition with over 200 documentary paintings in a large assembly hall in Vancouver that she hired at her own expense.

An unpublished "Lecture on totems", which Carr delivered at this exhibition to explain aspects of native culture to her white Vancouver audience, shows that during the course of her project she developed great sympathy and respect for the native people, and formed a picture of their culture as a system in which villages, way of life and landscape were interconnected, and many links with the past still maintained. Though not always free herself from the patronising language of her own times, Carr's writings and paintings assert a critical view of the contempt shown by many missionaries and administrators towards native traditional culture, which they represented as a dark and superstitious past. Carr deliberately contested this picture, usually showing the villages as living entities, peopled with figures in contemporary dress, with washing lines between the houses (e.g. *Totem Poles, Kitseukla*, 1912; oil on canvas; Vancouver Art Gallery) or, in the case of the Haida villages that had been abandoned because of smallpox epidemics, as tragic and defiant ruins (e.g. *Tanoo, Queen Charlotte Islands*, 1913; oil on canvas; British Columbia Archives and Records Service). She stated that she intended her documentary record as much for the natives' future as for the settler community. She did her work, she said, "for the honor of the Indian". She usually exhibited the sketches she had made in the native villages before leaving, and made copies for people there who wanted them. In 1912 she approached the Government of British Columbia to support and acquire her record for the provincial museum and art gallery that was being developed in Victoria. Nothing came of this, partly because an economic depression hit the province in 1913, and partly because Carr's testimonies to the value, the past achievements and the presence of the province's native population were not welcome at a moment when increasingly active presentation of native land claims and grievances was causing anxiety to the settler community.

Unlike her American contemporaries – William S. Taylor, who made sketches and photographs for the murals at the American Museum of Natural History, and Edward S. Curtis of Seattle, who made his Northwest Coast photographs for volume 10 of *The North American Indian* in Kwakiutl territory in the same years as Carr did her paintings there – Carr did not seek to recreate the image of an apparently authentic native life unaffected by contact with Europeans. In her paintings, and even more in her later stories, Carr always acknowledged the tensions between tradition and change. The fact that Carr's documentary project gained no effective support either from the provincial government or from private patrons in British Columbia at this time was due to her refusal to conform to popular museological and artistic conventions, as well as to her modernist style, which was ahead of the local climate of taste. This led to a period of acute discouragement and financial difficulty for Carr, and she virtually ceased painting between the years 1913 and 1926. When her professional career resumed in 1927, she turned away from documentation to convey what she saw as the underlying spirit of native culture. Potlatch figures and totem poles were now rendered in close-up with dramatic scale and three-dimensional volume, to make "strong talk" of their owners' pride in lineage. Carr's choice of motifs fitted her own subjective concerns, such as her admiration for native women as mothers, seen in *Totem Mother, Kitwancool* (1928; oil on canvas; Vancouver Art Gallery). She was fascinated by the Kwakiutl mythical figure Dsonokwa, a wild woman of the woods, both frightening and benefic-ent, whom she celebrated in several paintings such as *Gwayasdoms d'Sonoqua* (1928–30; Art Gallery of Ontario, Toronto) and adopted as a guardian spirit (see Carr's story "Dsonoqua" in *Klee Wyck* 1941).

After 1930 Carr concentrated primarily on landscape painting. Entering a new phase of formal experiment, she drew on elements from a variety of available sources, including books by Ralph Pearson, Jay Hambidge and Katherine Dreier. The overlapping planes and rhythmic repetitions that she found in reproductions of Cubism and the multiplication of stylised elements used in native design are found in a series of oil paintings that use dark colours and heavy, sculpted forms, such as *Indian Church* (1929; Art Gallery of Ontario). Carr often projected anthropomorphic and emotional associations on to natural forms, as in *Grey* (1930; private collection, repr. Shadbolt 1979), where a young tree is shown enfolded in a sombre, womb-like forest interior. Because of the darkness, density and power she gave to these images of the forest, they were seen as expressing the "malignant and somber nature" that Northrop Frye (1971) has argued characterises Canadian experience.

By the mid-1930s Carr had developed a special sketching technique in oil on paper that enabled her to paint more freely and spontaneously. She worked on large sheets of inexpensive manila paper, in oil paints thinned with white house paint and gasoline. *Tree (Spiralling Upward)* (1932–3; Vancouver Art Gallery) shows how, in this quick drying medium, she developed a calligraphic brush stroke that could indicate a variety of local forms and textures, unified by a dominant rhythmic flow. As an avid reader of Walt Whitman and follower of syncretic religious currents, Carr now thought of her paintings as the expression of the omnipresence of God, and of the forces of growth and life in nature. She extended her subjects from trees and forest interiors to the movement of the sky, then to the open spaces of the seashore and of tree-clothed hillsides, and occasionally to the massive forms of the coastal mountains. An extraordinary variety of expressive effects are generated by the flow of calligraphic marks that structure the entire surface plane of her late paintings, such as *Stumps and Sky* (1934–5; Art Gallery of Ontario).

GERTA MORAY

Carriera, Rosalba [fig. 15]
Italian painter, 1675–1757

Born in the parish of San Basilio, Venice, 7 October 1675, to Andrea Carriera, clerk, and his wife Alba Foresti, a lacemaker. Admitted to the Accademia di San Luca, Rome, 1705. Stayed in Paris, 1720–21; elected member of the Académie Royale, 1720. Stayed in Modena, 1723. Visited Vienna to work for Emperor Charles VI, 1730. Assisted by her younger sister Giovanna (d.1737). Elected member of the Bologna Academy, 1720. Went blind during the last decade of her life. Died in the parish of SS Vito e Modesto, Venice, 15 April 1757.

Selected Writings

Journal de Rosalba Carriera: Pendant son séjour à Paris en 1720 et 1721, ed. Albert Sensier, Paris: Techeur, 1865
Rosalba's Journal and Other Papers, ed. Austin Dobson, London: Chatto and Windus, 1915; reprinted Freeport, NY: Books for Libraries Press, 1970
Lettere, diari, frammenti, ed. Bernardina Sani, 2 vols, Florence: Olschki, 1985

Bibliography

Antonio Maria Zanetti, *Della pittura veneziana e delle opere pubbliche de' veneziani maestri*, 5 vols, Venice, 1771; reprinted Venice: Filippi, 1972
P.J. Mariette, *Abecedario*, i, 1851, pp.329–32
Vittorio Malamani, "Rosalba Carriera", *Le gallerie nazionali italiani*, iv, 1899, pp.27–149
Emilie von Hoerschelmann, *Rosalba Carriera: Die Meisterin der Pastellmalerei, und Bilder aus der Kunst- und Kulturgeschichte des 18. Jahrhunderts*, Leipzig, 1908
Rosalba Carriera, exh. cat., Istituto Italiano d'Arti Grafiche, Bergamo, 1910 (contains abridged version of Malamani 1899)
Carlo Jeannerat, "Le origini del ritratto a miniatura in avorio", *Dedalo*, year 11, ii, 1931, pp.767–81
Torben Holck Colding, *Aspects of Miniature Painting: Its Origins and Development*, Copenhagen: Munksgaard, 1953
Francesco Cessi, *Rosalba Carriera*, Milan: Fabbri, 1965
Gabriella Gatto, "Per la cronologia di Rosalba Carriera", *Arte Veneta*, xxv, 1971, pp.182–93
Eleanor Tufts, *Our Hidden Heritage: Five Centuries of Women Artists*, New York and London: Paddington Press, 1974
Women Artists, 1550–1950, exh. cat., Los Angeles County Museum of Art, and elsewhere, 1976
Angelo Walther, "Zu den Werken der Rosalba Carriera in der Dresdener Gemäldegalerie", *Beiträge und Berichte der Staatlichen Kunstsammlungen Dresden,*

1972–1975, Dresden: Staatliche Kunstsammlungen Dresden, 1978, pp.65–90

Franca Zava Boccazzi, "Un disegno inedito di Rosalba Carriera", *Arte Veneta*, xxxiii, 1979, pp.146–8

Bernard Aikema, "The 1733 art exhibition at San Rocco in Venice", *Mededelingen van het Nederlands Instituut te Rome*, xliii, 1981, pp.143–8

Franca Zava Boccazzi, "Per Rosalba Carriera e famiglia: Nuovi documenti veneziani", *Arte Veneta*, xxxv, 1981, pp.217–26

Bernardina Sani, "Pastelli e miniature di Rosalba Carriera nella collezione di Giovanni Guglielmo Pfalz", *Itinerari contributi alla storia dell'arte in memoria di Maria Luisa Ferrari*, ed. Antonio Boschetto, ii, Florence: SPES, 1981, pp.133–43

Franco Moro, "Un ritratto di Rosalba Carriera nella pinacoteca di Cremona e un problema inerente la grafica", *Arte Veneta*, xli, 1987, pp.155–8

J. de Bruijn Kops, "Een portretminiatuur door Rosalba Carriera (1675–1757) en de oorsprong van haar schilderkunst op ivoor" [A portrait miniature by Rosalba Carriera and the origin of her painting on ivory], *Bulletin van het Rijksmuseum*, xxxvi, 1988, pp.181–210, 268–71 (with English summary)

Bernardina Sani, *Rosalba Carriera*, Turin: Allemandi, 1988

Wendy Slatkin, *The Voices of Women Artists*, Englewood Cliffs, NJ: Prentice Hall, 1993

The Glory of Venice: Art in the Eighteenth Century, exh. cat., Royal Academy, London, and National Gallery of Art, Washington, DC, 1994

Michael Levey, *Painting in Eighteenth-Century Venice*, 3rd edition, New Haven and London: Yale University Press, 1994

Rosalba Carriera, one of the most successful of all women artists, holds an important position in the history of 18th-century portraiture. She introduced a new intimate elegance in her work, which gave a significant stimulus to that genre of painting, particularly in France, where she was greatly admired. With her original and innovative exploration of the pastel medium, applied with new freedom and delicacy of touch, she was able to catch the flavour and character of the age. Her portraits and allegories were collected all over Europe by enthusiastic patrons and connoisseurs.

Carriera's artistic formation is poorly documented and still quite uncertain. With her two sisters Giovanna and Angela she received a humanist education at home by studying French, history, literature and music. According to Mariette (1851), she started painting snuff boxes and miniatures on ivory. Her correspondence, dating from 1700 onwards, reveals that she was personally acquainted with the painters Antonio Balestra and Federico Bencovich, whose work definitely had some influence on her early production. She also knew the late 17thcentury Italian tradition of pastel drawing, represented by such artists as Baldassare Franceschini called il Volterrano and the Florentines Benedetto Luti and Domenico Tempesti, the latter a pupil of Robert Nanteuil. This is clearly shown by her first documented pastel, the portrait of *Anton Maria Zanetti the Younger* (c.1700; Nationalmuseum, Stockholm). This work reveals a light and soft touch, but still a precise and firm under-drawing that makes it quite similar to an oil painting. In the following years Carriera's technique gradually attained a supreme delicacy and finesse for which her style was unique among her contemporaries. She was also inspired by the Rococo artists who were active in Venice in the first decade of the 18th century, in particular Sebastiano Ricci and her brother-in-law Giovanni Antonio Pellegrini. Their lighter palette and new technical freedom determined the development of her style.

Alongside her pastels, the Venetian artist produced an extensive range of miniatures that, from the beginning of her career, made her name famous in Italy and abroad. Even in this genre she was able to render the lightness and softness of the Rococo with an accomplished technique that was her own personal invention. It was with a miniature as a reception piece that Carriera was accepted as a member of the Accademia di San Luca, Rome, in 1705. This work, depicting a *Girl Holding a Dove* (Accademia di San Luca), a white figure on a blue background, is painted in tempera on ivory, with minute, loose brush strokes and subtle light effects that aroused great admiration among the Academicians. This miniature was followed by many others, the intimate or allegorical subjects of which reveal the artist's acute perception of the life and culture of her century. In fresh and delicate sketches reflecting Rococo sensibility and frivolity, she portrayed a *Lady at Her Dressing Table* (Cleveland Museum of Art), *Flute Player* (Hermitage, St Petersburg) and *The Gardener* (Bayerisches Nationalmuseum, Munich).

Carriera's work was appreciated and collected all over Europe. At first her major commissions came from the German princes. Maximilian of Bavaria, during his stay in Venice in 1704, had his portrait made and commissioned those of the most beautiful women in Venice. Duke Christian Ludwig of Mecklenburgh commissioned several miniatures in 1706 and Frederick IV of Denmark, in Venice in the winter of 1708–9, sat for his portrait and commissioned pastels and miniatures. Another very important patron was the Elector Palatine Johann Wilhem von der Platz, a great admirer and collector of Italian Rococo painting, who in 1706 invited Carriera to his court in Düsseldorf. She did not accept, but between 1706 and 1713 produced for him a series of miniatures of arcadian subjects (Bayerisches Nationalmuseum) that reflect contemporary taste; among them is *The Gardener* mentioned above. Carriera's activity for the Elector Palatine is recorded in detail by her regular correspondence with his secretary, Giorgio Maria Rapparini. Her greatest admirer, however, was the Prince Elector of Saxony, later Augustus III of Poland, who first sat for his portrait in 1713, and then acquired Carriera's work throughout his reign. By the end of his life he owned over 150 pastels by her, all displayed in a gallery dedicated to the Venetian artist at his court in Dresden. They then became an important nucleus of the Dresden Gemäldegalerie.

In 1707, in Venice, Carriera met the French artist Nicolas Vleughels, whose pastel drawings, heads in particular, executed with a high degree of finish, had some influence on her. Her contact with Vleughels helped to keep her in touch with contemporary French portraiture and might have drawn her attention to the work of Watteau, who was to have a significant impact on her style, especially after her visits to his studio during her stay in Paris. Carriera's interest in French painting was also encouraged by her friendship with the connoisseurs and collectors Pierre Crozat, who visited Venice in 1715, and Pierre-Jean Mariette, who arrived in 1718.

Another significant contribution to Carriera's artistic development in these years was made by the work of the 16th-century artist Federico Barocci, whose luminous and graceful pastel drawings were much admired in the 18th century and were certainly present in contemporary Venetian collections. The influence of French portraiture, and of Nicolas de Largillière in particular, combined with Barocci's luministic approach, is shown for example in the portrait of a *Venetian Procurator* (Gemäldegalerie, Dresden). Carriera depicts the sitter in a formal pose appropriate to his social position, but at the same time she reveals his inner personality. The pastels are used with extreme subtlety, using broader and looser strokes for the procurator's sumptuous robe and minute and delicate ones for the face, whose character is rendered by an effective play of light and shadow. The realistic depiction of the face contrasts with the powdery white whig, which enhances the official presentation of the sitter.

A crucial experience for the further development of Carriera's style was her trip to Paris, where she stayed as the guest of the banker Pierre Crozat, from April 1720 to March 1721. There she visited all the major collections and met several leading painters, including Jean François de Troy, Joseph Vivien, Hyacinthe Rigaud, Nicolas de Largillière, Antoine and Charles Coypel, and Watteau. At the same time, the delicate and subtle flattery of her informal portraits and miniatures was greatly appreciated by Parisian society, then reacting strongly against the stiff formality promoted by Louis XIV and his court. Carriera dutifully recorded in her diary the important commissions that she received from the French court and aristocracy, almost competing for their portraits or little mythological pictures. She portrayed the Prince Regent, Philippe d'Orléans, and the young king himself several times, in pastel and miniature. The portrait of *Louis XV* (Gemäldegalerie) is painted with great spontaneity, aiming at rendering the youth and lively personality of the boy much more than his royal state. His formal attire is given a fresh and vivacious note by the sparkling contrast between the bright red of the embroidered jacket and the luminous transparent white of the lace jabot.

In the portrait of *Mademoiselle de Clermont* (Musée Condé, Chantilly) Carriera catches in a rapid impression the refined, mundane and frivolous culture of 18th-century Parisian high society. The attention is focused on the lovely young face, which looks straight at us with confidence and grace, while the girl's fresh beauty is given a sensuous note by the transparent veil just covering her bosom and a frivolous one by the delicate little flowers embellishing her curly hair. Rosalba's Parisian success was officially confirmed by her admission to the Académie Royale in October 1720, only four months after her arrival. When, after leaving Paris in March 1721, she sent a *Nymph* to the Academy as her reception piece, the *Mercure Galant* of February 1722 published an "Eloge de Rosalba Carriera", praising her work for the "gracefulness" of the image, the "lightness" of touch and the gemlike quality of the colour. Never before had the technical possibilities of pastel been exploited with such original invention and finesse. In France Carriera established a fashion for pastel portraits that not only characterised French Rococo painting but also persisted in the 19th century. Her technical innovations were taken up and perfected by several French artists, such as Maurice Quentin de la Tour, Charles Natoire, Jean-Baptiste Perroneau, the German Anton Raphael Mengs and the Swiss Jean Etienne Liotard.

After her return to Venice, Carriera seems to have reflected on and assimilated the French experience, achieving a further evolution and maturity in her art. The portraits painted in the 1730s reveal a deeper psychological insight and judgement of character, while still flattering the sitters. These aspects of her style are largely due to a renewed study of Watteau, most probably also encouraged by the publication of the *Figures de différents caractères, de paysage et d'études dessinées d'après nature par Antoine Watteau*, which Jean de Julienne sent to Carriera in 1728. Superb examples of these "psychological" portraits are the works painted during Rosalba's stay in Vienna in 1730, such as the portrait of *Amalia of Austria*, the little portrait of *Metastasio* (both Gemäldegalerie, Dresden) and the portrait of *Count Daniele Antonio Bertoli* (Badoglio Rota collection, Flambruzzo, Udine). In these works Carriera depicts her subjects with acute and sober realism, rendering their physiognomy with crystalline purity, yet preserving a few subtle details that suggest their distinguished social or intellectual standing. The unattractiveness of the Empress Amalia is tempered by her soft and intelligent gaze and the superb jewels decorating her dress; the poet Metastasio, who was then enjoying great success in Vienna, looks confidently out of the picture, expressing his lively creative genius; the Italian count, Superintendent of the Galleries of Emperor Charles VI in Vienna, appears in all his distinguished and sober elegance. In the last portrait in particular Carriera's technique achieves a spectacular effect by contrasting the luminous head and upper bust of the sitter with a dark background and a dark supporting drapery. The count's face is modelled with a subtle play of chiaroscuro, his powdered hair seems to float softly around his face and the fine texture of his lace jabot is suggested by dragging the flat edge of white chalk lightly over a finished under-drawing of darker tones.

Another significant series of portraits painted in the 1730s and 1740s was commissioned by the numerous British tourists who visited Venice during their Italian grand tour. Carriera's informal representations appealed in particular to the intellectual English aristocrats who were seeking a new, truthful, yet seducing image of themselves. Among them, *Charles Sackville, 2nd Duke of Dorset* (Lord Sackville's Collection, Sevenoaks, Kent), who participated in the intense Venetian social scene in 1730, is impressively portrayed in all his charming youth, wearing a preciously patterned brocade silk jacket and the typical Venetian hat called "tricorno".

In the 1740s two female figures reflect poignantly Carriera's extraordinary power of observation and understanding of the human character. Her moving *Self-Portrait as an Old Woman* (Royal Collection), painted for another great friend and patron, Joseph Smith, from 1744 British Consul in Venice, a few years before she went blind, shows the artist gazing beyond the observer, withdrawn into a world of her own, her lips firmly set. The prevailing sombre mood of the picture, conveyed by the dark fur robes that the artist is wearing, is just broken by her sparkling earrings and the fine lace that softens her décolleté. An entirely different character dominates the portrait of *Caterina Sagredo Barbarigo* (Gemäldegalerie Alte Meister, Dresden), an eccentric, widely travelled noblewoman and a skilled horsewoman, well known in Venice for her beauty. She looks directly out of the picture, in a lively and flirtatious way, her little hat worn daringly askew over her right ear. Her beautiful face is given shape by a subtle chiaroscuro, while fashionable pearls adorn her ears and neck. In this extraordinary portrait Carriera conveys the whole wordly and refined mood of the Settecento. In 1746 Carriera lost her sight, and this sad condition afflicted her for the last ten years of her life, putting a premature end to her long artistic career.

MARGHERITA GIACOMETTI

Carrington
British painter and designer, 1893–1932

Born Dora de Houghton Carrington in Hereford, 29 March 1893. Studied at the Slade School of Fine Art, London, under Henry Tonks and Fred

Brown, 1910–14 (Slade scholarship 1912). Worked for Roger Fry's Omega Workshops, c.1914–17, and Hogarth Press, 1917 and 1921. Sold work regularly through Birrell and Garnett bookshop, Bloomsbury, London, c.1923–32. Met Lytton Strachey, writer and member of Bloomsbury Group, 1915; lived with him at Tidmarsh Mill, near Pangbourne, Berkshire, 1917–24, then at Ham Spray House, Wiltshire. Married Ralph Partridge, 1921. Shot herself at Ham Spray, 11 March 1932, soon after Strachey's death.

Principal Exhibitions
New English Art Club, London: 1913, 1916
London Group: 1920
Grosvenor Galleries, London: 1921 (*Nameless Exhibition of Modern British Painting*)

Selected Writings
Carrington: Letters and Extracts from Her Diaries, ed. David Garnett, London: Cape, 1970; New York: Holt Rinehart, 1971

Bibliography
Noel Carrington, *Carrington: Paintings, Drawings and Decorations*, 2nd edition, London and New York: Thames and Hudson, 1980
Frances Partridge, *Memories*, London: Gollancz, 1981; as *Love in Bloomsbury: Memories*, Boston: Little Brown, 1981
Gillian Elinor, "Vanessa Bell and Dora Carrington: Bloomsbury painters", *Woman's Art Journal*, v/1, 1984, pp.28–34
Gretchen Gerzina, *Carrington: A Life of Dora Carrington*, London: Murray, and New York: Norton, 1989
Teresa Grimes, Judith Collins and Oriana Baddeley, *Five Women Painters*, London: Lennard, 1989
Mary Ann Caws, *Women of Bloomsbury: Virginia, Vanessa and Carrington*, New York and London: Routledge, 1990
Jane Hill, *The Art of Dora Carrington*, London: Herbert Press, and New York: Thames and Hudson, 1994
Michael Holroyd, *Lytton Strachey: A Critical Biography*, revised edition, London: Chatto and Windus, 1994; New York: Farrar Straus, 1995
Jan Marsh, *Bloomsbury Women: Distinct Figures in Life and Art*, London: Pavilion, 1995

Dora Carrington's decision to be known always by her surname; the notorious arrangement of her "Triangular trinity of happiness" with Lytton Strachey and her husband Ralph Partridge; her changeling appearance in the mythology of her generation; and her suicide before she was 40 have helped to obscure the contribution of a dedicated artist with a streak of creative genius.

Carrington was a conspicuous, prize-winning student at the Slade School of Fine Art (*Standing Nude*, 1913; oil on canvas; University College London, repr. Hill 1994, p.22) and a dramatic character, repeatedly portrayed in fiction of the day. Although the spirit of the age dictated that artists find their role models in continental Europe, Carrington remained remote from these impulses. Her work was informed by Cézanne but inspired by the English pastoral tradition. She believed that William Blake had made all the advances credited to Matisse (*The Feetbathers*, 1919; watercolour on paper; private collection, *ibid.*, p.116). She was a poetic realist and a quintessentially English artist. She painted several inn signs and wrote that painting signboards for Pangbourne shopkeepers was "a greater honour than becoming a member of the London Group" (*The Greyhound*, 1921; *ibid.*, p.66). She rarely signed, dated or exhibited her work and became an isolated worker.

At the Slade Carrington headed a revival in fresco painting. Her first commission was to provide a larger-than-life-size mural in true fresco for the library of Lord Brownlow's 19th-century gothic palace, Ashridge House, Berkhamsted, Hertfordshire. Local bucolic scenes were chosen and rendered in Pre-Raphaelite detail (*Hoeing*, 1912; *ibid.*, p.49).

Her work was inherently autobiographical; she painted the places, people and possessions she loved. Drawing and watercolour were considered preparations for painting on canvas (an explanation for the ubiquitous folds found in Carrington's works on paper) and have a very different sensibility to finished oils. Her fascination with the abstract forms of landscape created intimate place portraits. Her fish-eye image of the *Hill in Snow at Hurstbourne Tarrant* (1916; watercolour on paper; private collection, *ibid.*, p.27), "like the bony ridge of the backbone of a whale", is an accurate rendition as well as a lyrical study, whereas her depiction of what Gerald Brenan called his "yellow oxhide land" in *Yegen "Landscape"* (1924; oil on canvas; private collection, *ibid.*, p.78), of which she wrote: "I am trying a new plan, an entire underpainting in brilliant colours", is a visionary improvisation on a store of remembered images from Spain. *Farm at Watendlath* (1921; oil on canvas; Tate Gallery, London, *ibid.*, p.77) has a similar psychological power and ingeniously employs Lilliputian figures as a foil to balance the picture. *Fishing Boat in the Mediterranean* (*c*.1929; oil on canvas; private collection, *ibid*., p.114) has different concerns. Carrington jettisoned line in favour of an exquisite procession of colours that define form and suggest the depths of the sea.

Carrington wrote: "the discovery of a person, of an affection, of a new emotion is to me next to my painting, the greatest thing I care about". She had a watchful temperament and she painted people perceptively, treating subjects according to the role they played in her life. She painted *Lytton Strachey* (1916; oil on canvas; private collection, *ibid*., p.56) in loving detail with warm squirrel reds, echoed in the roof tiles of *Tidmarsh Mill* (*c*.1918; private collection, *ibid*.). She drew her own image in a *Self-Portrait* (*c*.1910; pencil on paper; private collection, *ibid*., p.18) that was utterly without vanity and unusually revealing. With the exception of Strachey, Carrington's finest portraits are of women of character and she painted a Cornish farmer, *Mrs Box* (1919; oil on canvas; private collection, *ibid*., p.73), as if she were a Gypsy queen from the New Forest. She also made a frankly erotic drawing of *Julia Strachey* (*c*.1925; pencil on paper; private collection, *ibid*., p.103), which hinted at her sexual duality. Julia was one of Paul Poiret's famously slender models. Carrington, however, pictured her as she fantasised: "very fat, and like a Veronese beauty".

Carrington's introduction to the decorative arts began around 1914 when she worked for Roger Fry's Omega Workshops, decorating objects in the "new" style, providing everything needed for the home but unlike anything ever seen there before. This ephemeral legacy of her taste was established when she decorated her Wiltshire home, Ham Spray, like a bower-bird, with the accumulated souvenirs of her life. Her eclectic collection of "treasures" furnished her with objects for paintings in the vanitas tradition (*Tulips in a Staffordshire Jug*, *c*.1921; oil on canvas; private collection, *ibid*., p. 55). Her quest for variety was tireless. She painted tiles and tea sets, made patchwork quilts, each one a calendar of her life; marbled papers for bookbinding; discovered a new technique for patterning on leather; printed book-plates from woodblocks and provided illustrations for five books, establishing a distinguishing feature for the Hogarth Press with her woodcuts for its first publication (*The Servant Girl*, 1917; *ibid*., p.45). Her skills extended to film-making, and in all these media she explored the themes that preoccupied her contemporaries.

Carrington's decorations of furniture often involved complete transformations. An *HMV Gramophone Cabinet* (1927; Portsmouth City Museum and Art Gallery, *ibid*., p.115) was painted with an odalisque, a serpent and a cornet; sportive youths, pages and greyhounds cavorted on a tin trunk and the base of a sewing machine formed the mount for a Rococo fantasy of shells. Working from squared-up drawings and templates she made a full-scale classical decoration (1928; *ibid*., p.126) for George Rylands, brightening his bleak north-facing rooms at King's College, Cambridge, with colours that complemented his collection of Crown Derby china. Her scheme for Faith Henderson's Wiltshire cottage (since painted out) was bold and fanciful with tumbling cornucopias, entwining vines and orange peacocks on mauve door panels edged with jambs in green. Oddities such as cut oranges were used to apply paint, on top of which she scratched and marked patterns.

Julia Strachey described Carrington as being "by nature a lover of marvels" and her love of theatricality can be seen in the false bookcase that she devised for Strachey's library with titles such as *False Appearances by Dora Wood*. Carrington painted a *trompe-l'oeil* picture of a ghostly *Cook and the Cat* (1931; *ibid*., p.128) in a blind window of Biddesden, a Vanbrugh-Hawksmoor-style house. The tableau curtains were a recurrent theme in Carrington's seemingly alchemical paintings on glass, backed with silver sweet papers, like moons. Carrington listed some of her subjects: "Flowerpieces, boxers, balloons, volcanoes, tightrope dancers, Victorian beauties, soldiers, tropical botanical flowers, birds and fruits", which she sold, in the 1920s, at the Birrell and Garnett bookshop in Bloomsbury.

Carrington's tinselled pictures (*"Rouen Ware"*, *c*.1923; oil, ink and silver foil on glass; private collection, *ibid*., p.54) were in the same tradition of popular art as the ornamental opulence of the saloon bar and the costume of the Pearly Kings and Queens. They were inspired by the "demountable baroque" of the fairground, the scrim-shandy work of mariners and the rose and castle of canal boats (fireplace tiles painted for the marriage of Alec and Frances Penrose, 1930; private collection, *ibid*., p.72). Carrington's appreciation of local peculiarities was before her time. They all gave form to her love of things made for country needs and tastes.

Carrington was a poet-painter. Her vivid, painterly, illuminated letters became a vehicle for focusing her mind for painting (*Gamekeeper's Sons*, 1919; Harry Ransom Humanities Research Center, University of Texas at Austin, *ibid.*, p.99). They have a quirkiness and wit that became the signature of her work and life. In the 1920s, as the bias of her friendships was with writers, Carrington lost the stimulation and encouragement of painters. Incapable of self-praise she became diffident about her work, writing: "It's rather maddening to have the ambition of Tintoretto and to paint like a diseased dormouse". Her artist's discipline was eroded as it became hopelessly undermined by her devotion to Strachey's talent above her own. Concern for his welfare, combined with running their home, left increasingly scant reserves for her work. Despite the fact that Carrington knew that the "vexations of life" disappeared when she was in her studio, conflicting emotions destroyed her purpose. She felt she was "not strong enough to live in this world of people and paint", and lost the facility to work out the harmony that can exist in living, loving and creating. Carrington was constantly conceiving ideas for paintings, walking on the Hampshire downs, plucking visions from the air, but they were not always realised. She rejected many paintings and invariably took completed canvases off the stretchers, ostensibly to use them again (she painted thinly, using a dry mixture without much oil; consequently paintings on rolled canvases are friable). Her identity had become so fragile that it depended upon Lytton's knowledge of her existence. When Lytton died, her own lights went out. Yet when Iris Tree said of Carrington: "you are like a tin of mixed biscuits, your parents were Huntley and Palmers", it was a tribute to her industriousness and the diversity of her work and vision.

JANE HILL

Carrington, Leonora   [fig. 16]
British painter and writer, 1917–

Born in Clayton Green, Lancashire, 6 April 1917. Educated in England, Florence and France; debutante at court of George V, 1935. Studied drawing and painting at Amedée Ozenfant Academy, London, 1936–7. Met Max Ernst, followed him to Paris and joined André Breton's Surrealist group, 1937; exhibited with the Surrealists in Paris (1938), Amsterdam (1938), New York (1942) and Paris (1947). Settled in Saint-Martin d'Ardèche with Ernst, 1938. Fled to Spain after his second internment as an enemy alien, and admitted to a mental asylum in Santander after a nervous breakdown, 1940. Escaped to New York after marrying Mexican diplomat Renato Leduc in Lisbon, 1941; renewed association with Surrealists in New York and contributed to *View* and *VVV* magazines. Settled in Mexico City in 1942, divorced Leduc and joined group of European Surrealists. Met her first collector, Edward James, in 1944. Married Hungarian newspaper photographer Emerico (Chiki) Weisz in Mexico, 1946; two sons, born 1946 and 1947. Joined a Gurdjieff group, and with Remedios Varo (q.v.) experimented with alchemy, witchcraft and dream interpretation, 1950s. Left Mexico for a year in protest against government repression of student unrest, 1968. Studied under exiled Tibetan lama in Canada and Scotland, 1971. After 1985, divided her time between Mexico City and USA (New York, Chicago and Richmond, Virginia).

Selected Individual Exhibitions
Pierre Matisse Gallery, New York: 1948
Galería Clardecor, Mexico City: 1950
Galería de Arte Mexicano, Mexico City: 1952
Galería Antonio Souza, Mexico City: 1957
Instituto Nacional de Bellas Artes, Sala Nacional, Mexico City: 1960 (retrospective)
Galería de Arte Mexicano and Instituto Cultural Anglo-Mexican, Mexico City: 1965
Galería de Arte Mexicano/Florencia, Mexico City: 1969
Alexander Iolas Gallery, New York: 1975
Center for Inter-American Relations, New York: 1976 (touring retrospective)
Brewster Gallery, New York: 1978, 1988, 1995
Space Mirage, Tokyo: 1988
Museo Nacional de la Estampa INBA, Mexico City: 1989
Serpentine Gallery, London: 1991–2 (touring retrospective)
Mexican Museum, San Francisco: 1991
Museo de Arte Contemporáneo de Monterrey, Mexico: 1994 (retrospective)

Selected Writings
La Maison de la peur, Paris: Parisot, 1938 (booklet, illustrated by Max Ernst; first written in English, 1937)

La Dame ovale, Paris: GLM, 1939 (illustrated by Max Ernst; first written in English, 1938)

"Down Below", *VVV*, no.4, 1944; as *En Bas*, Paris: Fontaine, 1945; 2nd edition, Paris: Eric Losfeld, 1973; English version, Chicago: Black Swan Press, 1983

"Pénélope", *Les Quatre vents*, vi, Paris, 1946 (play)

Une chemise de nuit de flanelle, Paris: Librairie Les Pas Perdus, 1951 (play)

El mundo mágico de los Mayas, Mexico City: Instituto Nacional de Antropologia y Historia, 1964 (with Andrés Medina and Laurette Séjourné)

Le Cornet acoustique, Paris: Flammarion, 1974; as *The Hearing Trumpet*, New York: St Martin's Press, 1976; London: Routledge, 1977; reprinted London: Virago, 1991

The Oval Lady and Other Stories: Six Surreal Stories, Santa Barbara: Capra, 1975

La Porte de pierre, Paris: Flammarion, 1976; as *The Stone Door*, New York: St Martin's Press, 1977; London: Routledge, 1978

Le Septième Cheval, Montpellier: Coprah, 1977 (first written in English, 1941)

Pigeon vole/contes retrouvés, ed. Jacqueline Chénieux-Gendron, Paris: Le Temps Qu'Il Fait, 1986 (short stories)

The House of Fear: Notes from Down Below, New York: Dutton, 1988; London: Virago, 1989

The Seventh Horse and Other Stories, New York: Dutton, 1988; London: Virago, 1989

Bibliography

André Breton, *Le Surréalisme et la peinture, 1928–1965*, Paris: Gallimard, 1965

——, *Anthologie de l'humour noir, 1896–1966*, Paris: Pauvert, 1966

Gloria Feman Orenstein, "Leonora Carrington: Another reality", *MS*, iii, August 1974, pp.27–31

Leonora Carrington: A Retrospective Exhibition, exh. cat., Center for Inter-American Relations, New York, and elsewhere, 1976

Bettina Knapp, "Leonora Carrington's whimsical dream-world: Animals talk, children are gods, a black swan lays an Orphic egg", *World Literature Today*, li, 1977, pp.525–30

Obliques, no.14–15, 1977 (special issue: *La Femme surréaliste*)

Gloria Feman Orenstein, "Leonora Carrington's visionary art for the New Age", *Chrysalis*, no.3, 1977, pp.66–77

Jacqueline Chénieux-Gendron, "Les contes de Leonora Carrington: Le tissage d'une intersubjectivité", *Le Surréalisme et le roman, 1922–1950*, Lausanne: L'Age d'Homme, 1983, pp.254–63

Whitney Chadwick, *Women Artists and the Surrealist Movement*, Boston: Little Brown, and London: Thames and Hudson, 1985

La Femme et le surréalisme, exh. cat., Musée Cantonal des Beaux-Arts, Lausanne, 1987

Janice Helland, "Surrealism and esoteric feminism in the paintings of Leonora Carrington", *Canadian Art Review*, xvi, 1989, pp.53–61

Susan Rubin Suleiman, *Subversive Intent: Gender, Politics and the Avant-Garde*, Cambridge, MA: Harvard University Press, 1990

Sonia Assa, "Gardens of earthly delight or, what's cookin? Leonora Carrington in the kitchen", *Studies in Twentieth-Century Literature*, xv, 1991, pp.213–27

Leonora Carrington, exh. cat., Serpentine Gallery, London, and elsewhere, 1991

Leonora Carrington: The Mexican Years, 1943–1985, exh. cat., Mexican Museum, San Francisco, 1991

Mary Ann Caws and others, eds, *Surrealism and Women*, Cambridge: Massachusetts Institute of Technology Press, 1991 (essays on Carrington by Peter Christensen, Georgiana M.M. Colvile and Madeleine Cottenet-Hage)

Mara R. Witzling, ed., *Voicing Our Visions: Writings by Women Artists*, New York: Universe, 1991; London: Women's Press, 1992

Leonora Carrington: Uno retrospectiva, exh. cat., Museo de Arte Contemporáneo de Monterrey, Mexico, 1994

Whitney Chadwick, *Leonora Carrington*, Mexico City: Consejo Nacional de la Cultura y los Artes, Ediciones ERA, 1994

Renée Riese Hubert, *Magnifying Mirrors: Women, Surrealism and Partnership*, Lincoln: University of Nebraska Press, 1994

Leonora Carrington, exh. cat., Brewster Gallery, New York, 1995

Leonora Carrington was barely 20 when she encountered Surrealism in the person of Max Ernst. Her youth, eccentricity and wild imagination prompted André Breton and his cohorts to consider her as a perfect example of the "femme-enfant" or child-woman, the Alice-in-Wonderland figure that they were forever looking for. Unlike Alice Rahon, however, Carrington soon transgressed that role. Her rebellion against her English upper-class upbringing was the first sign of her need to establish her individual freedom, so that she could develop her talents as a painter and writer. As a child, her love of painting animals and such eccentric practices as mirror-writing were already manifest, and during her finishing school years in Florence and Paris she discovered not only the Italian masters but also Hieronymus Bosch, whose influence is most clearly expressed in her remarkable *Temptation of St Antony* (1947; oil on canvas; private collection, repr. Monterrey 1994). There, as in so many of her pictures, Carrington achieves a surreal, uncanny effect by juxtaposing the fantastic proportions of the content (St Anthony's face and beard are tripled like Russian dolls within the gigantic, umbrella-shaped folds of his cloak; tiny delicately painted figures surround him; and the water that one of them pours from an amphora becomes a huge river beneath the holy man's feet) with a classical, well-mastered drawing technique and a subtle sense of colour. The strange blending of the protagonist's clothing with the raw material constituting the background landscape of the world around him and the figure of St Anthony himself evoke the affinity between Carrington and Remedios Varo (q.v.) in Mexico, leading to certain similarities in their styles of painting from the mid-1940s until Varo's death in 1963.

In the early, pre-Mexican years Carrington experimented with portraits and self-portraits (the latter genre being especially characteristic of the Surrealist women artists), in which she metamorphosed and occulted the figures represented, usually giving them a semi-animal form. In childhood, Carrington and her brothers were generally confined to the nursery and entrusted to the care of servants they disliked, which led them to seek out the company of animals. The young Leonora's totem creature was undoubtedly the horse. Her two early self-portraits, *Inn of the Dawn Horse (Self-Portrait)* (1936–7; oil on canvas; 65 × 81.2 cm.; Collection Pierre Matisse, repr. New York 1976) and *Woman and Bird* (1937; oil on canvas; 38 × 31 cm.; private collection, repr. London 1991), both represent Carrington in equine form. The first accentuates her mane-like hair and riding breeches and provides her with a triple animal *alter ego*: a face-on female hyena (this beast reappears in the story "The debutante" of 1939 as the autobiographical girl protagonist's unpresentable smelly animal "id", which ruins a debutante ball), a rocking-horse reminiscent of the nursery and a live horse seen through the window in the background, galloping away to freedom. In the second self-portrait Carrington's head and neck are those of a horse, with her human features and expression. Not only did the young Carrington love to ride horses, but her imagination also fed on the folk tales told by her Irish nanny, including several about the Celtic goddess who could take on any animal shape and about the mare-goddess Epona. In the colours of alchemy, like the other two, the portrait of *Max Ernst* (1939; Young-Mallin Archive Collection, New York) depicts the latter, with his normal human head, hands and feet, as a kind of seahorse

shaman in an arctic landscape, clad in a strange merman-shaped fur coat of purplish red, holding a green lantern containing a miniature prancing horse, a representation of Carrington perhaps, with a large white iceberg horse behind him. Several of Carrington's early stories, such as "The House of Fear" (1937), "The Oval Lady" (1938) and "The Seventh Horse" (1941) include horse-people and other hybrid creatures.

Surrealism provided a context for Carrington's fantasy world. At Saint-Martin d'Ardèche, she and Ernst produced plastic and literary works abundantly, in a mutually inspirational close collaboration, including a jointly painted oil *Meeting* (1940; Collection François Petit, Paris), portraits of each other and fantastic tales by Carrington, illustrated by Ernst. After her traumatising experience of mental illness (1940), described in her novella *Down Below* (1944), Carrington's visionary perception of both her inner and outer worlds was sharpened and intensified. Mexico, which Breton called "The Surrealist country par excellence", added new landscapes, faces and folk tales to those of her Irish heritage, although those early influences continued to dominate Carrington's art, reinforced by a careful study of Robert Graves's book *The White Goddess* (1948). When Carrington was commissioned to paint a large mural, the *Magical World of the Maya* (1963; casein on panel; 2.1 × 4.6 m.; Museo Regional, Tuxtla Gutiérrez, Mexico), celebrating the beliefs of the Chiapas Indians, whose culture and mores she studied closely during several stays in southern Mexico, she nevertheless produced a work that appears far more influenced by Celtic myths of rainbows, unicorns, dragons, animal-drawn chariots etc. than by those of Mexico. As Whitney Chadwick put it: "she herself has characterized her sensibility as caught between Catholic and Celtic" (Chadwick 1985, p.75).

While Frida Kahlo (q.v.) revived and secularised the old Mexican religious tradition of the *retablo*, Carrington discovered and adopted a medieval technique, consisting of using egg tempera on gessoed wooden panels (Chadwick 1994), thus highlighting the delicacy of her miniature forms in numerous Bosch-influenced compositions, such as *Tuesday* (1946; Collection Isaac Lif), *Palatine Predella* (1946; George Nader Gallery) and *Dog Child of Monkton Priori* (1950; private collection, repr. San Francisco 1991). In later years Carrington continued to use both oil painting and egg tempera, occasionally watercolour, as well as acrylic. She has made lithographs from some of her best paintings, for example *Tuesday* (1987; Collection Georgiana Colvile) and *Crookhey Hall* (oil painting, 1947; private collection, repr. Monterrey 1994; lithograph, 1987; Collection Whitney Chadwick).

Carrington alludes to her friendship and creative collaboration with Remedios Varo in her novel *Le Cornet acoustique* (1974). The two women shared the Parisian and then the Mexican Surrealist experience, a strong interest in magic, alchemy, dreams and culinary experiments. As Sonia Assa has shown (1991), cooking plays an important part and acquires a magic aura in Carrington's work. In some of her stories, such as "White Rabbits" and "The Sisters", eating tends to be a carnivorous and even cannibalistic practice, whereas the feasting creatures in her paintings more often than not seem to be peaceful vegetarians, as in the oils *Edwardian Hunt Breakfast* (1956; private collection, repr. New York 1976) and *Lepidoptera* (1969; private collection, Mexico, *ibid.*).

During the 1970s Carrington became interested in Tibetan culture, thus adding a new mystical facet to her art, and she also expressed a strong solidarity with the various women's movements. *The Godmother* (1970; oil on canvas; Collection Mr and Mrs Nesuhi Ertegun, *ibid.*) portrays a rotund goddess figure in the colours of alchemy, with a dark owl-like head and shoulders, birds perching on her branch-like arms, a globe in her middle, her body made up of the heads of golden-haired women. The culinary motif recurs in a tribute to her mother, *Grandmother Moorhead's Aromatic Kitchen* (1975; oil on canvas; Charles B. Goddard Center for Visual and Performing Arts, Ardmore, Oklahoma). Most of the figures in her later paintings are female, and her later work deals increasingly with the theme of women's old age, as in *The Magdalenes* (1986; egg tempera on panel; private collection). Carrington's later work includes drawings, statuettes (e.g. *Old Magdalena*, 1988; bronze; Brewster Gallery, New York) and tapestries, all alive with magic, exotic colours, dreamlike situations, mythical personae and an indomitable sense of humour. She no longer considers herself to be a Surrealist, although she has expressed and continues to express an alternative fantasy world, which goes further afield even than the work of Ernst or Breton. The exhibition at the Serpentine Gallery, London, in 1991 was her first long-overdue European retrospective and at last revealed her highly original work to her fellow countrymen and women, but she remains to date far better known in Mexico and the USA than in Britain or even France.

GEORGIANA M.M. COLVILE

Cassatt, Mary   [fig. 17]
American painter and printmaker, 1844–1926

Born in Allegheny City (now part of Pittsburgh), Pennsylvania, 22 May 1844; father a banker; eldest brother Alexander Johnston became president of Pennsylvania Railroad (1899). Travelled in Europe with her family, attending schools in Paris, Heidelberg and Darmstadt, 1851–5. Studied at the Pennsylvania Academy of the Fine Arts, Philadelphia, 1860–64. Went to Europe for further art training, 1865; remained there for the rest of her life, with return trips to USA in 1870–71, 1875, 1898 and 1908. Studied under Charles Chaplin and Jean-Léon Gérôme in Paris, 1866; Edouard Frère, Paul Soyer and other masters in art colonies at Courances and Ecouen, 1867–8; Thomas Couture at Villiers-le-Bel near Ecouen, 1868 and 1874; Charles Bellay in Rome, 1870; friend of Degas. Also made sketching trip to Piedmont, 1869; worked in Parma, Madrid and Seville, 1872–3; visited the Netherlands and Belgium, 1873; Rome again, 1874. Settled in Paris, 1874; joined there by her parents and sister Lydia, 1877. Purchased château at Mesnil-Beaufresne, north of Paris, 1894. Travelled to Italy, 1893; to Italy and Spain on collecting trip with friends Henry O. and Louisine Elder Havemeyer, 1901. Lived in Grasse, near Nice, during the winters of 1912–24 and during World War I. Chevalier, Légion d'Honneur, France, 1904. Died at Mesnil-Beaufresne, 14 June 1926.

Principal Exhibitions

Individual
Galeries Durand-Ruel, Paris: 1891, 1893 (retrospective), 1908, 1914
F. Keppel and Co., New York: 1891
Durand-Ruel Gallery, New York: 1895, 1898, 1903, 1907, 1927
Philadelphia: 1927 (memorial)
Chicago: 1927 (memorial)
New York: 1927 (memorial)

Galerie A.-M. Reitlinger, Paris: 1927, 1931 (retrospective)

Group
Paris Salon: 1868, 1870, 1872–6
National Academy of Design, New York: 1874, 1878 (annuals), 1886 (Impressionist group, special exhibition)
Pennsylvania Academy of the Fine Arts, Philadelphia: 1876–9, 1885, 1898–1907, 1910–12, 1915–17, 1920
Society of American Artists, New York: from 1879
Impressionist group, Paris: 1879, 1880, 1881, 1886
Dowdeswell Galleries, London: 1883 (*Impressionist Art*)
Exposition des Peintre-Graveurs, Paris: 1889, 1890
Woman's Building, World's Columbian Exposition, Chicago: 1893
M. Knoedler, New York: 1915 (*Suffrage Loan Exhibition*)

Selected Writings
Cassatt and Her Circle: Selected Letters, ed. Nancy Mowll Mathews, New York: Abbeville, 1984

Bibliography
Joris-Karl Huysmans, *L'Art moderne*, Paris: Charpentier, 1883
Rambaud Yveling, "Miss Cassatt", *L'Art dans les deux mondes*, no.1, 22 November 1890, p.7
Félix Fénéon, "Cassatt, Pissarro", *Le Chat Noir*, 11 April 1891; reprinted in *Félix Fénéon: Oeuvres plus que complètes*, ed. Joan Halperin, Geneva: Droz, 1970
Exposition Mary Cassatt, exh. cat., Galeries Durand-Ruel, Paris, 1893
Achille Ségard, *Mary Cassatt: Un peintre des enfants et des mères*, Paris: Ollendorff, 1913
George Biddle, "Some memories of Mary Cassatt", *The Arts*, August 1926, pp.107–11
Adelyn Dohme Breeskin, *The Graphic Work of Mary Cassatt: A Catalogue Raisonné*, New York: Bittner, 1948; reissued as *A Catalogue Raisonné of the Graphic Work*, Washington, DC: Smithsonian Institution Press, 1979
Anna Thorne, "My afternoon with Mary Cassatt", *School Arts*, May 1960, pp.10–12
Frederick A. Sweet, *Miss Mary Cassatt, Impressionist from Pennsylvania*, Norman: University of Oklahoma Press, 1966
Adelyn Dohme Breeskin, *Mary Cassatt: A Catalogue Raisonné of the Oils, Pastels, Watercolors and Drawings*, Washington, DC: Smithsonian Institution Press, 1970
Patricia T. Davis, *End of the Line: Alexander J. Cassatt and the Pennsylvania Railroad*, New York: Neale Watson, 1978
Nancy Mowll Mathews, *Mary Cassatt and the "Modern Madonna" of the Nineteenth Century*, PhD dissertation, New York University, 1980
Griselda Pollock, *Mary Cassatt*, New York: Harper, and London: Jupiter, 1980
Mary Cassatt and Philadelphia, exh. cat., Philadelphia Museum of Art, 1985
The New Painting: Impressionism, 1874–1886, exh. cat., Fine Arts Museums of San Francisco, 1986
Frances Weitzenhoffer, *The Havemeyers: Impressionism Comes to America*, New York: Abrams, 1986
Nancy Mowll Mathews, *Mary Cassatt*, New York: Abrams, 1987
Mary Cassatt: The Color Prints, exh. cat., National Gallery of Art, Washington, DC, and elsewhere, 1989
Louisine Havemeyer, *Sixteen to Sixty: Memoirs of a Collector*, ed. Susan Alyson Stein, revised edition, New York: Ursus, 1993
Nancy Mowll Mathews, *Mary Cassatt: A Life*, New York: Villard, 1994 (contains bibliography)
—, *Cassatt: A Retrospective*, New York: Levin, 1996

Best known for her participation in the French Impressionist group and for her paintings of mothers and children, Mary Cassatt is one of the few women artists to have gained an international reputation during her lifetime and to have kept it to the present day. Since it is hard for women to rise to the top of this field and harder still for them to be remembered by posterity, her success offers an object lesson to all. The ingredients contributing to her success were these: a family that was financially and emotionally supportive; a deep reserve of intelligence, energy and talent; an instinct for styles and subjects that was both fresh and lasting; and strong friendships with artists and writers who could both enrich her art and promote it to the outside world. Cassatt marshalled these resources to navigate an entrenched art establishment and to create an art that would inspire artists and amateurs the world over.

Cassatt practised as an artist for more than 50 years, beginning her formal art studies at the Pennsylvania Academy of the Fine Arts in 1860. Romanticism was still the dominant style in the USA during her student days and in some ways can be seen in her approach to subject matter throughout her career. Her earliest endeavours culminated in such paintings as the *Mandolin Player* (private collection, on loan to Philadelphia Museum of Art), which was exhibited at the Paris Salon of 1868. This painting shows the theme of love as expressed by a single monumental figure of a contemplative woman – an interest that would be eventually translated into the mother and child subject and continue into Cassatt's later years.

Women of Cassatt's generation were extremely fortunate in that the wave of feminism that had swept Europe and the USA in the 1840s opened many professional doors for them. Cassatt took advantage of the new educational opportunities, particularly in art academies that from the mid-19th century accepted increasing numbers of women. The availability of high-level training in the fine arts corresponded to the newly co-educational colleges and public universities such as Oberlin and the University of Michigan as well as the founding of women's colleges such as Vassar (1865), Smith (1871) and Wellesley (1875). Cassatt and her friends were outspoken advocates of equal rights all their lives. They campaigned for equal travel scholarships in their student days in the 1860s and campaigned for the vote in their old age in the 1910s. While it is hard to see such clear political statements of women's rights in Cassatt's art, there is no question that she painted women with dignity and the suggestion of a rich inner life.

In addition to confronting the feminist issues of her day, Cassatt also thought deeply about issues of modern art and came to her own conclusions about the reforms that were needed. From the unfair exclusion of women from the official Ecole des Beaux-Arts to the failings of the Salon jury system, Cassatt addressed in impassioned diatribes the wrongs of the French art establishment that set international standards in the 1860s and 1870s. As for the current trends in painting, she felt that acknowledged masters such as Bonnat and Cabanel misinterpreted the old masters and produced work that was "washy, unfleshlike, and grey", as she wrote to her friend Emily Sartain. During the first ten years that she painted in Europe (1866–76) she tried to adapt what teachers called her natural "talent of the brush" to current styles of costume genre painting and fashionable portraiture. She became, however, increasingly interested in the new techniques developed by the Impressionists and found that her own experiments with a lightened palette and a more spontaneous, sketch-like approach were quickly rejected by the Salon juries she was still trying to please in 1875, 1876 and 1877.

Cassatt's reputation as an outspoken critic of the establishment brought her to the attention of the Impressionists and, in 1877, Edgar Degas invited her to exhibit with the group. Her debut among these radical artists took place two years later in the fourth Impressionist exhibition held in a temporary gallery on the avenue de l'Opéra. Cassatt had studied the work of her new colleagues, particularly Degas, Berthe Morisot (q.v.) and Auguste Renoir, and developed a new style that translated her contemplative women from costumed "folk" into modern Parisians enacting the rituals of 19th-century society. Now, instead of showing veiled Spanish women on a balcony during Carnival, she captured well-dressed young Parisians on a balcony at the Théâtre Français. Ritual flirtation was still her theme, but she adjusted her style to show the ephemeral world of contemporary romance and popular entertainment.

From 1879 to 1886 Cassatt was an active member of the Impressionist group both professionally and socially. Her friendships with Degas and Morisot as well as the Impressionist dealer Paul Durand-Ruel and such patrons and supporters as M. and Mme Paul Bérard and Stéphane Mallarmé attest to her integration into rarefied Parisian intellectual and cultural circles – an unusual feat for an American. She was also friendly with both Whistler and Sargent as well as the many other American painters who visited Paris regularly, even though she made it a habit to avoid the American "colony". Thus her art references both French and American values in a mix that defies neat national categorisation. A painting such as The Loge (National Gallery of Art, Washington, DC), for example, mixes the French tradition of the cocotte with a stolid American innocence.

During the years that Cassatt exhibited with the Impressionists, she also turned her eye to her own family for scenes of contemporary Parisian life. Using a sketchbook approach, she captured her parents and older sister Lydia (who had left Philadelphia in 1877 to live with her in Paris) in their quiet domestic pursuits in their elegant fifth-floor apartment on the avenue Trudaine near the Place Clichy. These good-natured, privileged Americans often found themselves "exposed" on the walls of exhibitions or studied by collectors coming to Cassatt's studio to make a purchase. Cassatt used her family extensively in a series of etchings and drypoints she produced in 1879–80, such as Lydia and Her Mother at Tea (1880; National Gallery of Art, Washington, DC). This sudden foray into printmaking was inspired by Degas and the prospect of a new art journal, to be called Le Jour et la nuit, which would include original prints by the Impressionists. Although the journal was never published, Cassatt nevertheless came out of the experience with a significant body of new work and polished skills in a new medium.

Cassatt's experiments with printmaking gave her a new respect for the craft of drawing, which, given her natural facility with a brush, had never interested her enough to become an accomplished draughtswoman. Even as she continued to work within the Impressionist context, however, she began to emphasise the linear structure of her painting and, towards the mid-1880s, a new, more tightly composed style took the place of her earlier, freer Impressionist works. The spare depiction of her mother's cousin, Mary Dickinson Riddle, in a work called *Lady at the Tea Table* (1883; Metropolitan Museum of Art, New York) marks Cassatt's growing fascination with the power of line. The delicate web Cassatt spins to portray the elderly woman's hand curved lightly but masterfully around the handle of a teapot conveys Mrs Riddle's age, social status and personality in a single gesture. It was at this time that Cassatt also developed her own technique in pastel, which she would alternate with painting from that point on.

With Cassatt's search for a stable, linear structure to her compositions came a similar desire to simplify her subject matter. In the late 1880s she confined herself either to portraits or the mother and child theme. Symbolist trends in art and literature brought back into modern painting many subjects drawn from religious art, such as the Virgin and Child, the Temptation of Eve and the Crucifixion. For the most part, these images were derived from peasant life studied by artists of all nationalities in the villages throughout Europe, from Pont-Aven to Murnau. But although Cassatt often painted in the country during the summer months, she found her own idiom for her "modern Madonna" that combined the Impressionist insistence on modern life with a simplified, monumental composition. She adapted her highly developed devices for depicting the contemplative woman (shadowed face, eyes turned away, calm pose) to the intertwined relationship of woman and child. *Hélène de Septeuil* (William Benton Museum of Art, University of Connecticut) is a pastel based on studies made of a child model from Septeuil where Cassatt spent the summer of 1889. The simple costume of the "mother" (in reality, Cassatt's maid Mathilde Valet) and the golden brim of the child's hat encircling her head suggest the images of peasant "Madonnas" painted by such contemporaries as the Frenchman Charles Filiger and the American Gari Melchers. But Cassatt's references are seldom so obvious. Many others suggest old master sources from Botticelli to Rubens or are so openly portrait-like that it seems futile to search for sources at all. Regardless of art-historical references, Cassatt's calm, thoughtful treatment of the subject – so different from the melodrama of her main Parisian rival, Eugène Carrière – made a woman's relationship with a child one of the most compelling images to come out of this period.

From the first, these mother and child compositions were enthusiastically received by critics and collectors alike, affirming Cassatt's direction and setting her on a lifelong path that she was not always sure she wanted to follow. At this time Cassatt's business relationship with the dealer Paul Durand-Ruel was regularised, giving him exclusive rights to her annual output. This meant that he made her work readily available to the public in Paris, both in group and one-person shows as well as through his frequent publications. In 1886 Durand-Ruel began to have an annual presence in New York through large exhibitions and, by 1890, he had opened a branch of his Paris gallery on Fifth Avenue. Durand-Ruel benefited from Cassatt's connections to the art-buying public in the USA and, in turn, he promoted Cassatt on both sides of the Atlantic. The relationship had its occasional rough spots as with any artist and dealer, but, for the most part, each was crucial to the long-term success of the other. While it is probably true that Durand-Ruel encouraged Cassatt to continue painting the mother and child subject long after she had exhausted its possibilities, nevertheless it was he who gave her the professional and financial support to bring the theme to its first full flowering and opened the door for her lasting fame.

Not long after Cassatt had begun to explore the mother and child theme, she embarked on a series of large-scale colour prints modelled after the immensely popular portfolios of Japanese *ukiyo-e* woodblocks. The series included ten images (four were mother and child subjects) that followed Parisian women through a typical day of bathing and dressing, performing errands around town via the omnibus, visiting the dressmaker and entertaining at home. There are two major models depicted, and the viewer becomes acquainted with each as she appears in changing settings.

Cassatt was in the forefront of artists who were just turning to colour prints as a new means of expression. They were partly inspired by Japanese prints and partly by such popular graphic images as posters and other advertising. The small black-and-white images so popular during the "Etching Revival" of the 1860s and 1870s were associated with the print connoisseur, whereas in the more democratic 1890s artists, including Cassatt, wanted to reach a larger audience. With the work of Toulouse-Lautrec, Henri Rivière and others, colour prints in a variety of graphic media began to appear. Although inspired by woodblock prints, Cassatt chose to draw her composition in a clear drypoint line and then apply areas of colour by using aquatint tones from a second and third plate. The delicacy of the colours she achieved, along with the decorative patterning and the sinuous lines, heighten the senses of touch in such tender scenes as *Maternal Caress* and even of taste as the woman licks the envelope in *The Letter* (1890–91).

The ten colour prints were presented in 1891 in what constituted Cassatt's first solo exhibition at Durand-Ruel's gallery in Paris. Although Pissarro complained that her prints were not fully appreciated, they were well reviewed and were quickly in demand among collectors in France and the USA. A review by Félix Fénéon in *Le Chat Noir* was highly complimentary, noting that the large, masculine hands that Cassatt loves to give her women help to make the composition flow in long, linear arabesques.

The following year Cassatt went from this print project to a painting project that was just as demanding of her creative and physical energies as the prints had been. Now considered one of the most important American women painters, she was asked to paint one of two central murals for the Woman's Building of the World's Columbian Exposition of 1893. These two murals defined the overarching theme of the pavilion: women's rise from slavery and ignorance in primitive times to her current state of education and accomplishment in the modern day. The mural *Primitive Woman* was commissioned from Mary Fairchild MacMonnies, a younger American who had recently taken up residence in Paris with her husband, the sculptor Frederick MacMonnies. The mural *Modern Woman* was commissioned from the 48-year-old Cassatt. Both murals are now known only from photographs (repr. Maud Howe Elliott, *Art and Handicraft in the*

Woman's Building of the World's Columbian Exposition, Chicago, 1893, Chicago and New York: Rand McNally, 1894, p.35), since the original canvases dropped out of sight in the early 20th century. Nevertheless, the scope of the undertaking and the originality of the designs make them a constant object of study. MacMonnies's *Primitive Woman* was the more successful of the two at the time since she strove for and achieved the effect of, as she called it, "glorified wallpaper". Cassatt's mural, on the other hand, used jarring colours and small isolated figures engaged in activities that were somewhat hard to understand. She had chosen to portray "women picking fruit from the Tree of Knowledge", as she wrote to the organiser Berthe Palmer. On the sides were scenes showing young girls pursuing fame and women and the arts. Both the daring colours and symbolist subject matter were out of context in Chicago, but were well appreciated by those who saw the mural or photographs of it in Paris. Cassatt's reference to women's pursuit of knowledge and fame was both timely in light of the advances in women's education and personal, considering her own open desire for public recognition.

As the century drew to a close, Cassatt found herself increasingly drawn back into the art world of her own country. After giving her a major retrospective in Paris in 1893, Durand-Ruel held a similar exhibition of her work in New York in 1895. Three years later he held another exhibition in New York, tempting her at long last to voyage back home. In the more than 20 years since she had been to the USA much had changed, but she was particularly gratified to learn that her art was firmly rooted there among artists, collectors and critics. She had even begun to have a popular presence in such magazines as *Frank Leslie's Popular Monthly* – a fate that she would never have foreseen given her radical beginnings.

Outside the families of her two brothers in Philadelphia, Cassatt was closest to Louisine and Harry Havemeyer, wealthy New York collectors whom she had known since the 1870s. In the late 1880s the Havemeyers began coming regularly to Paris to study and purchase art of all kinds, old master to modern, Asian and Western. Cassatt was happy to share her knowledge of modern French painting and led them to some extraordinary purchases of Impressionist and realist paintings over the next 30 years. After Harry Havemeyer's death in

1907, the two best friends continued to shape the collection together, combining the best of the old and the new into one of the most significant early 20th-century American collections, most of which was bequeathed to the Metropolitan Museum of Art. Because of Cassatt's work with the Havemeyers and a few other American collectors such as the Alfred Popes, the John Whittemores and her own brother, Alexander, she has been given credit for much of the Impressionist art now found in the USA. It may be more correct to say that her role as an adviser, as well as her own presence as an Impressionist artist, made an important contribution to the development of American taste at a time when major public and private collections were being formed.

Cassatt practised as an artist until 1914 when cataracts and a series of unsuccessful operations drastically impaired her vision. But in the last ten years before she put away her brushes she created a large body of work that included monumental mothers and children based on her new interest in old master painting, portraits of friends and family, and a series of studies of children, which set a new standard for popular child portraiture that continues to the present. She vehemently rejected modernist reforms of painting as developed by Matisse and the Cubists, even though her own colours became more brilliant and she used bold decorative patterning in her later work such as *Sleepy Baby* (*c*.1910; Dallas Museum of Fine Arts). Encouraged by her dealers, the stalwart Paul Durand-Ruel and the newcomer Ambroise Vollard, Cassatt painted subjects that appealed to the more conservative taste of the emerging new American art public. She loved her chosen subjects but even she could see that she was pushed to do work that was no longer fresh; she later said to an American visitor: "I sold my soul to the dealers".

Nevertheless, her reputation grew to international proportions during these years and she was lauded by both French and American critics. Her financial success was such that it enabled her to maintain three residences – an apartment in Paris, a château at Mesnil-Beaufresne and a villa in Grasse. Even after she stopped painting she was a well-known figure at exhibitions and the object of many an art student's pilgrimage. During her lifetime her works entered such major museum collections as the Musée du Luxembourg (now the Louvre) and the Petit Palais in Paris, the Metropolitan Museum of Art, New York, the Philadelphia Museum of Art and many more in the USA. Today these four museums are the primary repositories of her work, with the National Gallery of Art, Washington, DC, the Art Institute of Chicago and the Museum of Fine Arts, Boston. Cassatt died in 1926, but her art has never fallen from public estimation, nor has the number of exhibitions or publications diminished in the intervening years. Contemporary judgements range from suspicion towards her stereotypical female subject matter to respect for her heroic struggle for recognition and belief in the radical art of the Impressionists. But at either end of the scale, Cassatt is accorded a place of prominence shared by very few.

NANCY MOWLL MATHEWS

See also Training and Professionalism survey 5

Catherine of Bologna *see* Vigri

Catlett, Elizabeth   [fig. 18]
American sculptor and printmaker, 1915–

Born in Washington, DC, 15 April 1915; naturalised Mexican citizen, early 1960s. Married (1) printmaker Charles White, 1941; divorced; (2) painter and printmaker Francisco Mora, 1947; three sons. Studied at Howard University School of Art, Washington, DC (BS cum laude 1937); University of Iowa, Iowa City, under Grant Wood (MFA 1940). Subsequently studied ceramics at Art Institute of Chicago, 1941; lithography at Art Students League, New York, 1942–3; woodcarving under José L. Ruiz and ceramic sculpture under Francisco Zuniga at Escuela de Pintura y Escultura, Esmeralda, Mexico, 1947–8; also studied privately with Ossip Zadkine in New York, 1943. Head of art department, Dillard University, New Orleans, 1940–42; instructor, Hampton Institute, Virginia, 1943; George Washington Carver School, New York, 1944–5; professor of sculpture, 1958–76, and head of sculpture department, 1959–76, Escuela Nacional de Bellas Artes, Universidad Nacional Autonoma de Mexico, Mexico City; artist-in-residence, University of

Michigan, Ann Arbor, 1990. Recipient of first prize, American Negro Exposition, Chicago, 1941; Tlatilco prize, 1962, and Xipe Totec prize, 1964, Sculpture Biennial, Mexico; first prize in sculpture, Atlanta University annual, 1965; first purchase prize, National Print Salon, Mexico, 1969; Alumni award, Howard University, Washington, DC, 1979; outstanding achievement award, National Women's Caucus for Art, San Francisco, 1981; James Van der Zee award, Philadelphia Museum of Art, 1983; honoree, National Sculpture Conference: Works by Women, Cincinnati, 1987; Amistad Research Center award, New Orleans, 1990; Candace award for art, National Coalition of 100 Black Women, New York, 1991; honorary doctorate, Morgan State University, Baltimore, 1993. Lives in Cuernavaca, Mexico, and New York.

Selected Individual Exhibitions
Barnett-Aden Gallery, Washington, DC: 1947
National School of Fine Arts (San Carlos), Mexico City: 1962
Museo de Arte Moderno, Mexico City: 1970
Brockman Gallery, Los Angeles: 1971
Studio Museum in Harlem, NY: 1971
National Center of Afro-American Artists, Dorchester, MA: 1972
Howard University Galleries, Washington, DC: 1972, 1984
Fisk University, Nashville: 1973
Scripps College, Claremont: 1975
Tobey Moss Gallery, Los Angeles: 1981 (with Lynd Ward)
Gallery Tanner, Los Angeles: 1982
New Orleans Museum of Art: 1983
Spelman College, Atlanta: 1985
Mississippi Museum of Art, Jackson: 1986, 1990–92 (A Courtyard Apart, with Francisco Mora, touring)
Montgomery Museum of Art, AL: 1991
Hampton University Museum, VA: 1993 (touring retrospective)
June Kelly Gallery, New York: 1993
Isobel Neal Gallery, Chicago: 1994 (In the Hemisphere of Love, with Francisco Mora)

Selected Writings
(as Elizabeth Catlett Mora) "The Negro people and American art", Freedomways, no.1, Spring 1961, pp.74–80
"The role of the black artist", Black Scholar, vi, June 1975, pp.10–14

Bibliography
Elton C. Fax, Seventeen Black Artists, New York: Dodd Mead, 1971
Samella Lewis and Ruth Waddy, Black Artists on Art, ii, Los Angeles: Contemporary Crafts, 1971
Charlotte Streifer Rubinstein, American Women Artists from Early Times to the Present, Boston: Hall, 1982
Shifra Goldman, "Six women artists of Mexico", Woman's Art Journal, iii/2, 1982–3, pp.1–9
Thalia Gouma-Peterson, "Elizabeth Catlett: The power of human feeling and of art", Woman's Art Journal, iv/1, 1983, pp.48–56
Samella Lewis, The Art of Elizabeth Catlett, Claremont, CA: Hancraft Studios, 1984
Freida High Tesfagiorgis, "Afrofemcentrism and its fruition in the art of Elizabeth Catlett and Faith Ringgold", SAGE, iv, Spring 1987, pp.25–32
A Courtyard Apart: The Art of Elizabeth Catlett and Francisco Mora, exh. cat., Mississippi Museum of Art, Jackson, and elsewhere, 1990
Samella Lewis, Art: African American, revised edition, Los Angeles: Hancraft Studios, 1990
"Elizabeth Catlett: Sculptor, printmaker", Artist and Influence, x, 1991, pp.1–27 (interviews by Glory Van Scott, Cuernava, Mexico, 8 December 1981, and Camille Billops, 1 October 1989, New York)
Mara R. Witzling, ed., Voicing Our Visions: Writings by Women Artists, New York: Universe, 1991; London: Women's Press, 1992
Romare Bearden and Harry Henderson, A History of African-American Artists from 1792 to the Present, New York: Pantheon, 1993
Elizabeth Catlett: Works on Paper, 1944–92, exh. cat., Hampton University Museum, VA, and elsewhere, 1993
Freida High Tesfagiorgis, "Elizabeth Catlett", Black Women in America: An Historical Encyclopedia, i, ed. Darlene Clark Hine, Elsa Barklay Brown and Rosalyn Terborg-Penn, New York: Carlson, 1993
Patricia Hills, "Interview with Elizabeth Catlett", unpublished audiotape, 3 June 1995

To African Americans and to Mexicans, although not necessarily to the New York art world, Elizabeth Catlett for many decades has had a secure place in the history of American art – as a teacher, a progressive thinker, a sculptor and a printmaker. That she is not better known to patrons of the commercial art world is hardly surprising, given her independent thinking and her desire to reach the masses of everyday people with her public sculpture and her prints.

Brought up in a poor, but middle-class home in Washington, DC, Catlett distinguished herself at high school as a talented artist. Her ambitions to pursue her art training at the Carnegie Institute of

Technology in Pittsburgh were dashed when her scholarship was revoked because of her race (Bearden and Henderson 1993, p.419). She then enrolled at Howard University, the black college in her home town, which provided her with a supportive environment in which to develop her skills. She studied design for two years under Lois Mailou Jones (q.v.) and then switched to painting with James Porter. Her art history professor, James V. Herring, introduced her to African sculpture. Inspired by Diego Rivera, she attempted to paint a mural for a restaurant near the campus (Hills 1995), and she was briefly on the Federal Art Project of the Works Progress Administration (FAP/WPA).

Like many educated African-American women, Catlett went into teaching after graduation, spending two years in the segregated school system in Durham, North Carolina, where she became controversial by raising such issues as the inequities of educational facilities for African-American children and pay differentials between the black and the white teachers (Fax 1971, pp.18–19). The next year she enrolled in the graduate programme at the University of Iowa, and studied with the regionalist painter Grant Wood. Wood encouraged her to achieve competence in all artistic media, and she began making sculpture. He also urged her to express in her art her own personal experiences, including her racial identification with issues of the black community.

Her career took off in 1941 when the judges of the American Negro Exposition awarded her first prize in sculpture for her Iowa Master's thesis sculpture, *Mother and Child* (1939; repr. Bearden and Henderson 1993, p.420). After teaching briefly at a black college, Prairie View College in Texas, Catlett was called to Dillard University, a black college in New Orleans, to direct their art department (*ibid.*, p.421). When she returned to Chicago in the summer of 1941 to take a course in ceramics at the Art Institute, she met Charles White, whom she later married. After two years at Dillard, Catlett and White moved to New York where Catlett began taking private lessons with the modernist, figurative French sculptor Ossip Zadkine, then in exile there. Zadkine had great vitality, and the older sculptor encouraged her to approach art from a "humanistic international viewpoint". She recalled to Bearden: "I felt the contrary – that it should begin as a nationalistic experience and be projected towards international understanding, as our blues and spiri-

tuals do. They are our experience, but they are understood and felt everywhere" (*ibid.*, p.420).

In 1943 Catlett joined the teaching staff of the Hampton Institute, Virginia, when White received a commission to paint a mural. Returning to New York the following year, she began working for the George Washington Carver School, a progressive community art centre, run on a shoestring, that emerged to fill the vacuum when the art centres of the government's WPA had folded. She taught sculpture and dressmaking, and that experience of working with the poor, proud and struggling people of Harlem made a lasting impression on her. During the second year of her employment at the Carver School she supported herself with a Julius Rosenwald Fund fellowship, a fellowship renewed in 1946 only on the condition that she devote herself full time to her art.

In 1946 she and White moved to Mexico, where she embarked on her Rosenwald project, *Negro Woman*, a series of 15 linocuts (Tesfagiorgis 1993, p.230). She took up printmaking with the Taller de Gráfica Popular, a collective of artists, and studied the work of the great Mexican muralists, Diego Rivera, David Siqueiros and José Clemente Orozco. Having divorced Charles White, Catlett married the painter and printmaker Francisco Mora and settled into life in Mexico. She brought up her three sons and enjoyed working collectively with other artists. As she recalled to Bearden: "I learned that art is not something that people learn to do individually, that who does it is not important, but its use and its effects on people are what is most important" (quoted in Bearden and Henderson 1993, p.423). In 1956 she began to study with the sculptors Francisco Zuniga, José Elarese and José L. Ruiz, and in 1958 was employed as a professor of sculpture at the Escuela Nacional de Bellas Artes, Universidad Nacional Autonoma de Mexico. Promoted to head of the sculpture department, she remained at the Escuela Nacional until her retirement in 1976.

Always sympathetic to the travails of poor people and the injuries of class, she and her husband moved within radical, artistic and literary circles in Mexico. During the mid-1950s she found herself harassed by government officials hunting "subversives" and was even jailed for two nights (Hills 1995). When she eventually became a Mexican citizen, the United States government would not issue her with a visa to enter the country, a ban not lifted until her exhibition at the Studio Museum in

Harlem in 1971. Always outspoken in her views, Catlett delivered a speech, "The Negro people and American art", to a conference of the National Congress of Negro Artists held in Washington, DC, in 1961. She felt that black artists could contribute to the struggles against discrimination through their subject matter, and exhorted her fellow black artists to shun segregated exhibitions and to make art that would reach a large audience: "If we are to reach the mass of Negro people with our art, we must learn from them; then let us seek inspiration in the Negro people – a principal and never-ending source" (p.80).

Catlett's sculptures are sometimes carved from wood and sometimes cast in bronze. When she chooses single women or mother and child pairings, she uses a modernist, reductive vocabulary of simplified planes and curves that imparts to the pieces a serenity, quiet sensuality and grace: smoothly carved body types of broad hips, rounded bellies, tapering legs, prominent foreheads, generalised hair and symmetrical faces. Yet she has also done moving political works, such as *Homage to My Young Black Sisters* (1968; private collection, repr. Bearden and Henderson 1993, p.420), wherein a female figure lifts up her head and raises her fist in the gesture of solidarity. *Target* (1970; Amistad Research Center, Tulane University, *ibid.*, p.425), inspired by the civil rights struggles, consists of a realistic head of a black man facing an enlarged circular metal band intersected by a metal cross-bar – the enlarged sight from a gun barrel – as if he were the target. *Political Prisoner* (1971; Schomburg Center for Research in Black Culture, New York) is an over-life-size standing female figure, dressed in a stylised shift, who looks upwards with her arms manacled behind her. Her mid-section is gently folded open to reveal equal bands of black, red and green – the flag used to designate Black Power in the 1960s and 1970s – now unfurled to declare her identity.

Some of Catlett's large sculpture pieces are in public spaces: *Olmec Bather* (1966) is placed at the National Polytechnical Institute in Mexico; *Phillis Wheatley* (1973) is at Jackson State College in Mississippi; *Louis Armstrong* (1975–6) is in New Orleans; *People of Atlanta* (1989–91) in City Hall, Atlanta.

In almost all of her linocut prints and lithographs Catlett has been concerned with representing powerful images of black people, the workers of Mexico or political figures. *Sharecropper* (1970; colour linocut; repr. Hampton 1993, cover) depicts a white-haired African-American woman with strongly chiselled features and wearing a straw hat, looking up and over her shoulder. The large safety-pin that holds her coat together hints at the poverty concealed by her proud visage. *Malcolm X Speaks for Us* (1969; colour linocut; *ibid.*, p.20) uses the repeating heads of three images, which surround the face of Malcolm. *Negro Es Bello II* (1969; lithograph; *ibid.*, p.21) represents two mask-like faces of Africans facing rows of Black Panther buttons inscribed "Black is Beautiful", a slogan of the Black Power movement of the 1960s. More recent prints have been less political and explore themes of African-American music and dance.

In the mid-1990s both Catlett and her husband continue to work in Mexico. A tall, handsome woman with a commanding presence and a deep, sonorous voice, Catlett has never flagged in her passion to present the truth of the many facets of the black experience. Her integrity and professionalism have inspired younger artists through both her art and her example.

PATRICIA HILLS

Charpentier, Constance
French painter, 1767–1849

Born Constance Marie Blondelu in Paris, 1767. According to 19th-century dictionaries, studied under Wilk (?Wille), David, Lafitte, Gérard and Bouillon. Recipient of prix d'encouragement, 1788; gold medal, Musée Royal, 1819. Died in Paris, 3 August 1849

Principal Exhibitions
Paris Salon: 1795, 1798, 1800–01, 1804, 1806, 1808, 1810, 1812, 1814, 1819

Bibliography
Clara Erskine Clement, *Women in the Fine Arts*, Boston: Houghton Mifflin, 1904; reprinted New York: Hacker, 1974
Charles Sterling, "A fine 'David' reattributed", *Metropolitan Museum of Art Bulletin*, ix, 1951, pp.121–32
French Painting, 1774–1830: The Age of Revolution, exh. cat., Grand Palais, Paris, and elsewhere, 1974

Women Artists, 1550–1950, exh. cat., Los Angeles County Museum of Art, and elsewhere, 1976

Viktoria Schmidt-Linsenhoff, "Gleichheit für Künstlerinnen?", *Sklavin oder Bürgerin? Französische Revolution und Neue Weiblichkeit, 1760–1830*, exh. cat., Historisches Museum, Frankfurt am Main, 1989, pp.114–32

Although Constance Charpentier exhibited about 30 works at the Paris Salons in the period 1795 to 1819, only one painting, *Melancholy* (1801; Musée de Picardie, Amiens), can be firmly attributed to her today. This painting shows the obvious influence of the artists Jacques-Louis David and François Gérard with whom Charpentier had studied. The profile pose of the figure of Melancholy is that of David's Camilla in his famously successful history painting the *Oath of the Horatii* (1784; Louvre, Paris). The landscape setting of Charpentier's dejected female figure, resting by a pool of water in front of a weeping willow is, however, very different to that of the history painting.

Melancholy, first exhibited at the Paris Salon of 1801, has no obvious narrative cause and is of a more generalised abstract and emblematic nature than that of the history painting. It does not incorporate a specific action, gesture or passion, but explores and communicates mood and mystery. The passive, limp pose of the woman can be associated with 18th-century tomb sculpture, but it can also be linked forward to Romanticism and the pleasures of sensibility that might be induced from an observation of the outward expression of inner pain and emotion. Another, now lost, painting on the same subject by François Vincent was also exhibited at the Salon of 1801 and contemporary critics made associations between these visual images and the lyrical poetry of the Abbé Delille.

On the basis of this work, an engraving by Monsaldy and Devisme of the Salon of 1801 and the register of deliveries to the jury of that Salon, Charles Sterling (1951) proposed that a portrait of *Mademoiselle Charlotte du Val d'Ognes* (1801; Metropolitan Museum of Art, New York) should also be attributed to Charpentier. This portrait, though, is much more contrived; there is a challenging mystery about it and its luminosity is more transparent and complex. The fluent, abstract contours of the sitter, her attenuated anatomy, smoothly chiselled flesh and illuminated silhouette are all features of the mannered and discordant trend associated with the Primitifs, a group of students who had emerged, as rebels, from David's studio.

Mlle du Val d'Ognes is shown in the bare room of an artist's studio, looking up at the spectator as if she is using him or her as a model for the drawing she is in the process of producing. Behind her, a broken window pane is a *tour de force* of the painter's art distinguishing, in its *trompe-l'oeil* effect, the view of the scene outside as to be seen as only partly through glass. The unglazed area encompasses the two small figures of a seemingly compliant woman and her seemingly masterful male companion on the terrace of an austere building. The figure of Val d'Ognes is lit from behind with much of her body in shadow, but she has a transparency, grace and fragility that give an unsettling, almost surreal quality to the work as a whole. Sterling noted that the anatomy and certain anecdotal details of the contemporary setting and draperies can be compared to that of the figure of *Melancholy*. The handling of the anatomy is mannered – the legs and thighs are too long, the shoulder and wrist joints are weak and unconvincing, and both women have similarly curved backs and fingertips bent back. White draperies trail on the ground, while the tassels of Melancholy's shawl and the tapes of the drawing portfolio of Mlle du Val d'Ognes are specifically similar, as is the violet colour used for shoes and sash.

Although no further paintings have been attributed to Charpentier, we can still situate her as a woman artist who benefited from the greater exposure that the open Salon exhibitions of the Revolution offered to women, and from the greater public recognition that could be gained thereby. In his review of the Salon of 1801, the critic Ducray-Duminil commended the works of this pleasing painter for their firm and decisive execution, the arrangement of the poses and the choice of mass formations (*Les Petites Affiches de Paris*, September 1801). *Melancholy* was purchased by the State after the Salon of 1801.

Charpentier apparently received three times a week young artists who wished to hear her advice on painting and drawing, and in 1819, the year of her last Salon, she was awarded the gold medal by the Musée Royal. Salon catalogue entries reveal that she specialised in portraits, particularly of women and children, and in sentimental genre scenes. An entry to the Salon of 1806, *A Blindman, Surrounded by His Children, Is Consoled by the Four Other*

Senses, and one to the Salon of 1808, the *First Cure of a Young Doctor*, indicate that she was concerned to invent her own iconography and does not necessarily conform to Sterling's damningly faint appraisal and highly gendered conclusion:

> Meanwhile the notion that our portrait of Mlle Charlotte may have been painted by a woman is, let us confess, an attractive idea. Its poetry, literary rather than plastic, its very evident charms, and its cleverly concealed weaknesses, its ensemble made up from a thousand subtle artifices, all seem to reveal the feminine spirit [Sterling 1951].

VALERIE MAINZ

Chicago, Judy [fig. 19]

American multi-media artist, 1939–

Born Judy Cohen in Chicago, Illinois, 20 July 1939. Studied at University of California, Los Angeles, 1960–64 (BA 1962, MFA 1964). Married (1) writer Jerry Gerowitz, 1961; killed in a road accident, 1962; (2) sculptor Lloyd Hamrol, 1969; (3) photographer Donald Woodman. Adopted name Chicago, 1970. Taught at University of California Extension, Los Angeles, 1963–9; University of California Institute Extension, Irvine, 1966–9; California State University, Fresno, 1969–71 (founded first Feminist Art Program); California Institute of the Arts, Valencia, 1971–3 (moved Feminist Art Program here and co-directed it with Miriam Schapiro, and with students produced *Womanhouse*, exhibited in Los Angeles in 1972). Co-founder, Feminist Studio Workshop and Woman's Building, Los Angeles, 1973. Recipient of Woman of the Year award, *Mademoiselle* magazine, 1973; National Endowment for the Arts (NEA) grants, 1976 and 1977; honorary doctorate, Russell Sage College, Troy, New York, 1992. Lives in New Mexico.

Selected Individual Exhibitions

Pasadena Art Museum, CA: 1969 (as Judy Gerowitz)
Faculty Club, California State College, Fullerton, CA: 1970
Jack Glenn Gallery, Corona del Mar, CA: 1972
Artemisia Gallery, Chicago: 1974
JPL Fine Arts, London: 1975

San Francisco Museum of Modern Art: 1979– (*Dinner Party*, touring)
Parco Gallery, Japan: 1980
Fine Arts Gallery, Irvine, CA: 1981
Musée d'Art Contemporain, Montreal: 1982
ACA Galleries, New York: 1984, 1985, 1986
Schirn Kunsthalle, Frankfurt am Main: 1987
Spertus Museum, Chicago: 1993– (*Holocaust Project*, touring)

Selected Writings

"Female imagery", *Womanspace Journal*, i/1, Summer 1973, pp.11–17 (with Miriam Schapiro)
Through the Flower: My Struggle as a Woman Artist, New York: Doubleday, 1975; 2nd edition, New York: Doubleday, and London: Women's Press, 1982
The Dinner Party: A Symbol of Our Heritage, New York: Doubleday, 1979
Embroidering Our Heritage: The Dinner Party Needlework, New York: Doubleday, 1980 (with Susan Hill)
The Birth Project, New York: Doubleday, 1985
The Dinner Party, New York: Atheneum, 1987
Holocaust Project: From Darkness into Light, New York and London: Viking Penguin, 1993
Beyond the Flower: The Autobiography of a Feminist Artist (in preparation)

Bibliography

Lucy R. Lippard, "Judy Chicago talking to Lucy R. Lippard", *Artforum*, xiii, September 1974, pp.60–65; reprinted in Lucy R. Lippard, *From the Center: Feminist Essays on Women's Art*, New York: Dutton, 1976
Arlene Raven and Susan Rennie, "Interview with Judy Chicago", *Chrysalis*, no.4, 1978, pp.89–101
Lucy R. Lippard, "Judy Chicago's 'Dinner Party'", *Art in America*, lxviii, April 1980, pp.114–26
Judy Chicago: The Second Decade, 1973–1983, exh. cat., ACA Galleries, New York, 1984
Judy Chicago: Powerplay, exh. cat., ACA Galleries, New York, 1986
Hilary Robinson, ed., *Visibly Female: Feminism and Art: An Anthology*, London: Camden, 1987; New York: Universe, 1988
Moira Roth, ed., *Connecting Conversations: Interviews with 28 Bay Area Women Artists*, Oakland, CA: Eucalyptus Press, 1988
Mara R. Witzling, ed., *Voicing Our Visions: Writings by Women Artists*, New York: Universe, 1991; London: Women's Press, 1992
Norma Broude and Mary D. Garrard, eds, *The Expanding Discourse: Feminism and Art History*, New York: Icon, 1992
Judy Chicago: Holocaust Project: From Darkness into Light, exh. cat., Spertus Museum, Chicago, and elsewhere, 1993

Norma Broude and Mary D. Garrard, eds, *The Power of Feminist Art: The American Movement of the 1970s*, New York: Abrams, and London: Thames and Hudson, 1994

Amelia Jones, ed., *Sexual Politics: Judy Chicago's Dinner Party in Feminist Art History*, Berkeley: University of California Press, 1996

Since its first installation at the San Francisco Museum of Modern Art in 1979, Judy Chicago's monumental *Dinner Party* has come to be one of the most controversial works in the history of Western art. Supporters and critics of the piece alike, however, have tended to neglect the rich diversity of Chicago's oeuvre.

In the late 1950s the artist moved to Los Angeles from Chicago, where she had taken art classes from the age of five. By the mid-1960s her nascent feminism began to simmer in the context of her exploration of "finish fetish", the particular fusion by Los Angeles artists of Minimalist and Pop forms and techniques, involving the use of plastics, bright local colour, vacuum technologies and abstract forms. Chicago's spray-painted *Car Hood* (1964; Collection Mr and Mrs Radoslar L. Sutnar, Los Angeles) showed her mastery of such technical skills as auto-body painting. Signalling her conviction that women artists must demonstrate their competence in the crafts of art-making, this mastery gave Chicago the authority to compete with her male colleagues.

In connection with an exhibition of her work at California State College, Fullerton, in 1970, Chicago publicly proclaimed her intention of challenging discrimination in the art world. Overtly parodying the machismo of "The Studs", the name half-seriously adopted by her male finish-fetish colleagues, Chicago posed in short hair and boxer shorts, standing aggressively in the corner of a boxing ring, for a full-page advertisement for the show in *Artforum* (December 1970). The entrance wall of the exhibition itself was inscribed: "*Judy Gerowitz* [the surname of her first husband] hereby divests herself of all names imposed upon her through male social dominance and freely chooses her own name *Judy Chicago*".

Motivated by her rage at the discrimination she experienced in the art world and driven by a new conviction that her experience as a woman and her sexuality were central to her art, Chicago began openly to express her goal of forging a feminist art practice. The next decade of her career would be shaped by her attempt to define the particularity of this experience through abstract and then increasingly recognisable representational forms. This turn towards "content" was an explicit attempt to expose the biases behind the formalist privileging of the transcendent "universality" of male abstraction.

Chicago's pictures of the late 1960s, abstract and highly polished in appearance, were nascent formulations of the hotly debated theory of "central core" that she would develop with Miriam Schapiro (q.v.) in the early 1970s. The abstracted, centralised forms of *Pasadena Lifesavers*, *Star Cunts* and *Donut* series (all 1968–70) were theorised as expressive symbols of the central "cavity" that defines women's experience of sexuality. The 15 *Lifesaver* paintings, informed by Chicago's interest in using colour to evoke particular emotional states, are particularly subversive in that they feminise the slick, high-tech hipness of finish-fetish works: each consists of an enormous slab of acrylic on which hover four throbbing, radiating wheels of colour.

During this transitional period Chicago also experimented with pyrotechnics, another process that conventionally excludes women practitioners. After studying with a fireworks company, Chicago produced a series of *Atmospheres* (repr. Lippard 1976, p.225), performances documented through photographs that involved the firing of colour flares in strategic patterns in natural or cultural public sites (see *Pasadena Museum Atmosphere*, 1970). Chicago saw these dramatic plumes of coloured smoke as feminising the landscape, an effect she exaggerated with pieces that included naked women performing goddess-rituals (*Goddess*, 1970; all documentation in artist's collection).

In the early 1970s Chicago also created several photographically-based lithographs exploring explicitly feminist subject matter. *Red Flag* (1971) depicts a woman pulling a bloody tampon (tinted a vibrant red) from her vaginal canal; *Love Story* (1970; both artist's collection) presents a sadomasochistic text from *The Story of O* underneath the unsettling image – in deep blue – of a man's hand holding a gun up to a woman's naked rear end. *Love Story* complicates the view of Chicago's work developed later by some anti-essentialist feminists who criticised her for producing only positive images of women without critiquing patriarchy.

One of Chicago's important contributions to the feminist art movement has been her conviction that women must develop strategies of making, exhibiting, teaching and writing about art in order to transform mainstream art institutions. Offered a teaching job at California State University, Fresno, in 1970, Chicago established a "Feminist Art Program" there, moving her students (all women) off campus in the hopes of establishing an environment in which they could express themselves more freely. Merging principles of cooperative education, involving aggressive interpersonal exploration through consciousness-raising techniques, with confidence-building strategies and technical training, Chicago developed a ground-breaking, multifaceted approach to art pedagogy. During the Fresno period she produced two series of paintings that expanded on the techniques and abstract symbology of her earlier work: the *Fresno Fan* and *Flesh Garden* paintings were large-scale sprayed acrylic bands of modulated colour on acrylic (e.g. *Desert Fan*, 1970–71; Collection Mary Ross Taylor, Houston). With the other members of the Feminist Art Program, Chicago also developed a number of performances, including her slapstick send-up of patriarchal sex-roles, *Cock and Cunt Play* (1970; script in *Through the Flower*).

In 1971 Chicago, at the invitation and with the support of her collaborator Miriam Schapiro, moved the Feminist Art Program with the Fresno students to the California Institute of the Arts in Valencia, where they were joined by art historian Paula Harper, designer Sheila de Bretteville, and aided by student assistants Faith Wilding, Suzanne Lacy and Sherry Brody. After the Program's climactic staging of *Womanhouse*, a derelict house in Los Angeles that they transformed into a feminist environment in 1972, Chicago became increasingly convinced that such an alternative program could not develop fruitfully within the confines of such an institution. In 1973 she withdrew from the Cal Arts faculty, moving on to co-found the Feminist Studio Workshop (with Arlene Raven and de Bretteville), an independent studio program in Los Angeles.

Chicago's works of the mid-1970s, which show a gradual development of the iconography that would come to be so controversial in the *Dinner Party* plates, are visually compelling attempts to arrive at a positive and explicit "female imagery". In her central core *Through the Flower* series and four *Great Ladies* paintings of 1973, she explored both the symbolic effects of abstracted, centralised forms (as expressive of women's sexual experience) and, with *Great Ladies*, the idea of using works of art to

reinstall important women in history. In the "great lady" *Marie Antoinette* (whereabouts unknown; related piece from *Great Ladies* series repr. Lippard 1976 and *Through the Flower*), in which intense, pulsating orange rays radiate from a soft open core, Chicago uses the title to give the abstracted form a specific historical content. She has been criticised for this attempt to construct a "universal" sign for femininity, particularly in that it might be seen to imply that women's experiences can be summed up through the morphology of their sexual anatomy.

This contentious issue of central core, as well as the question of attempting to legitimate women through masculinist notions of "greatness", came to the fore with the *Dinner Party*. Aided by hundreds of assistants, Chicago laboured for five years on the project, which quickly expanded to a grand-scale installation modelled loosely after the exclusively male Last Supper. Introduced by large woven banners calling for a utopian merging of differences, the three-sided equilateral table is a large centralised form that symbolises the egalitarianism that Chicago saw as one of the goals of feminism (the 13 settings on each side also refer to the number of men at the Last Supper and the number of members of a witches' coven). A porcelain floor with an additional 999 women's names broadens Chicago's revised history of the Western world.

As the general concept of the piece grew, so did Chicago's ambitions for the plates and for the needlework runners surrounding them and her need for assistance (though she never claimed the project to be collaborative as far as its authorship was concerned, she has been criticised for her hypocrisy in depending on the help of volunteers). Ultimately, each place setting was completed to include an elaborately modelled and painted porcelain plate, 35.5 centimetres in diameter (designed by Chicago and executed by Leonard Skuro and a team of ceramists), placed on an exquisite needlework runner representing Chicago's vision of each woman's special contribution to history (these were completed by teams headed by Susan Hill in stitches common to the period of the woman commemorated). Running from the "Primordial Goddess" through Greek culture (Sappho) up to the Enlightenment (Mary Wollstonecraft) and the 19th century (Sojourner Truth – one of the few women of colour at the table – Susan B. Anthony and others), the final "guest" is Georgia O'Keeffe (q.v.) – served by a floral plate with flesh-coloured, labial folds lunging off the surface – an artist whose flower paintings Chicago found particularly inspirational.

The *Dinner Party* has been shown in venues across Europe, North America and Australia (a 15th public exhibition of the piece took place in 1996 at the UCLA/Hammer Museum). By and large rejected by the art world for its unabashed populism, many of these venues have been non-museum sites; the exhibitions were organised by international networks of supporters (initially spearheaded by Diane Gelon, who lectured and raised money for the piece). In this sense, the piece is a successful realisation of Chicago's attempt to expand the reception of art beyond an art-world elite.

As the *Dinner Party* made its rounds, Chicago began to organise another cooperative, alternative art work: the *Birth Project* (1980–85). Growing out of her new-found interest in designing patterns for needlework and her desire to counter the iconographic void surrounding the birth process, the *Birth Project* drew on the extensive network of supporters that had arisen in response to the *Dinner Party*. Chicago designed more than 150 needlework patterns, sent these out to women to stitch in their homes and worked closely with them in the completion of each piece. The most monumental of these, a tapestry entitled *Creation of the Universe* (1984; 107 × 427 cm.; Collection Judy Chicago and Audrey Cowan), was designed by Chicago and executed by Cowan, who had assisted her on the *Dinner Party*. This is a dramatic, decorative scene of an abstracted female body, legs spread, absorbing the vitality of the sun and earth around her to nurture a foetus.

While completing the *Birth Project*, Chicago began another series of works: *Powerplay*, which shifts the focus of her feminism to an interrogation of masculinity. Produced this time primarily in her own studio, *Powerplay* includes prismacolour drawings, tapestries (woven by Cowan), sprayed acrylic paintings and cast paper and bronze reliefs. Here, anguished male bodies and faces are depicted in various violent acts, as in *Trying to Kill the Woman Inside Him* (1983; whereabouts unknown, repr. New York 1986) and *Crippled by the Need to Control* (1983; artist's collection). The iconographically direct *Three Faces of Man* (1985; artist's collection) is composed of three images of male heads grimacing in violent rage, malevolent glee and painful anguish. "Man" is shown here not as singular abuser of power but as himself riven from within, subject to the violence of patriarchy.

Extending her exploration of masculinity and the abuse of power in *Powerplay*, Chicago's most recent project explores the patriarchal ideology underlying the Holocaust. Produced in collaboration with her husband, the photographer Donald Woodman, the *Holocaust Project: From Darkness into Light* consists of a number of painting/photo combines on photo-linen, a tapestry (woven by Cowan) and a stained-glass piece (executed by several artisans). Merging painting with Woodman's manipulated pictures of Holocaust sites and other historical imagery, Chicago highlights particular intersections among various modes of oppression – misogyny, homophobia, white racism, anti-semitism, class warfare – in order to expose the larger systems of injustice out of which she believes the Holocaust emerged.

In this traumatic but ultimately hopeful project, Chicago complicates her feminist identity by exploring her relationship to the Jewish tradition, relating her desire to "teach through art" to the Jewish concept of *tikkun*, the "process of healing and repairing the world". Depicting struggling Jews, women and homosexuals, piles of bones and bodies, and Nazis committing atrocities, the piece as a whole is a dark rumination on the human potential for evil, but also – especially with the utopian image of inter-ethnic harmony in the final stained-glass panel of the piece, *Rainbow Shabbat* – proposes, optimistically, that the feminine can be "an essential step toward the humanization of our world" (*Holocaust Project* 1993, pp.3 and 11).

Chicago's ambitious project intervenes in the history of the Holocaust in a controversial way. Using her signature crude representational style, developed as a counter to what she perceives to be the elitist, coded language of modernist practice, Chicago deliberately simplifies a complex history to present a bold – some would say reductive – message about the ideology of fascism. Her linking of Nazism to sexism or even more broadly defined modes of oppression (the imagery includes pictures from the Vietnam War, the US slave trade and animal testing) raises the important question of whether such connections defuse and dehistoricise the specificity of the Holocaust.

As a contemporary version of historical allegory, such a project clearly fulfils Chicago's career-long goal of reaching a broad audience with work that is both accessible and polemical. At the same time, the very directness with which she approaches complex and highly charged issues (the utopianism of her desire to speak transparently through visual symbols in order to change consciousness) just as clearly creates discomfort within an art audience now critical of such transformative ideals. It is not surprising, then, that Chicago's *Holocaust Project*, like her *Dinner Party*, has not been fully appreciated by the art world. But it may well become a major monument in the popular imagination.

AMELIA JONES

See also Training and Professionalism survey 5

Chryssa
American sculptor, 1933–

Born in Athens, Greece, 31 December 1933; later naturalised US citizen. Took a bachelor's degree in sociology in Athens, then studied under Greek painter Anghelos Prokopion. Studied at Académie de la Grande Chaumière, Paris, 1953–4; California School of Fine Arts, San Francisco, 1954–5. Settled in New York, 1955. Exhibited at Documenta, Kassel, Germany, 1968 and 1977. Recipient of Guggenheim fellowship, 1973. Lives in New York.

Selected Individual Exhibitions
Solomon R. Guggenheim Museum, New York: 1961
Museum of Modern Art, New York: 1963
Institute of Contemporary Art, University of
    Pennsylvania, Philadelphia: 1965
Pace Gallery, New York: 1966, 1968
Department of Fine Arts, Harvard University, Cambridge,
    MA: 1968
Walker Art Center, Minneapolis: 1968
Galerie Rive Droite, Paris: 1968
Galerie Der Spiegel, Cologne: 1969
Graphic Arts Gallery, San Francisco: 1970
Galleria d'Arte Contemporanea, Turin: 1970
Whitney Museum of American Art, New York: 1972
Musée d'Art Contemporain, Montreal: 1974
Galerie Denise René, Paris: 1974
André Emmerich Gallery, Zürich: 1974, 1975
Musée d'Art Moderne de la Ville de Paris: 1979
Pinacothèque Nacional Museum Alexandre Soutzos,
    Athens: 1980
Albright-Knox Art Gallery, Buffalo: 1982
Leo Castelli Gallery, New York: 1988, 1991

Bibliography
10 American Sculptors, exh. cat., Walker Art Center,
    Minneapolis, 1964
Chryssa, exh. cat., Galerie Denise René, New York, 1973
Sam Hunter, *Chryssa*, New York: Abrams, and London:
    Thames and Hudson, 1974
Pierre Restany, *Chryssa*, New York: Abrams, 1977
    (contains bibliography)
Chryssa: Oeuvres récents, exh. cat., Musée d'Art
    Moderne de la Ville de Paris, 1979
Chryssa: Urban Icons, exh. cat., Albright-Knox Art
    Gallery, Buffalo, NY, 1982
*The Tremaine Collection: 20th-Century Masters: The
    Spirit of Modernism*, exh. cat., Wadsworth Atheneum,
    Hartford, CT, 1984
Miranda McClintic, "Chryssa: Cityscapes and icons",
    Arts Magazine, lxii, Summer 1988, pp.74–5
Donald Kuspit, "Chryssa", *Art in America*, lxxvi,
    September 1988, p.189
Chryssa: Cityscapes, New York: Thames and Hudson,
    1990
Charlotte Streifer Rubinstein, *American Women
    Sculptors*, Boston: Hall, 1990
Amei Wallach, "Chryssa retraces her steps", *Newsday*, 3
    February 1991, part ii, p.17

By 1955, as America enjoyed post-war prosperity, Chryssa had left her homeland, Greece, for Paris and had settled in New York. The effects of this move immediately manifested themselves in the artist's work. The influence of American commercial culture became apparent in *Cycladic Books* (1955; several casts made; private collections, repr. Restany 1977, figs 3, 55 and 56), where Chryssa poured plaster into a packaging box. The subsequent cast is barely three-dimensional (foreshadowing Minimalism) except for the presence of a T-shaped ridge. This ridge reminded Chryssa of the forms found on ancient Cycladic figures, allowing the work to illustrate the confluence of contemporary American and ancient Greek cultures.

The bright lights and visual language of Manhattan became a dominant source of inspiration for Chryssa's art. In *Arrow: Homage to Times Square* (1958; Empire State Collection, Albany, NY) Chryssa used small bars of aluminium to form an arrow shape. Each bar casts a shadow, which allowed her to experiment with the "static light" of the piece. In *Study of Light* (1958; painted aluminium; private collection, *ibid.*, fig.65) she cast a relief that looks like alphabet soup. When the light hitting the work changes, different forms are produced by the letters. Chryssa continued to study the structural potential of lettering in her oil painting *Newspaper No.3* (1961; Solomon R. Guggenheim Museum, New York), which is part of a series exploring patterns in newspapers. By working with such banal subject-matter, she echoed Pop Art's irreverence towards the separation of "popular" culture from "fine" art. She anticipated Warhol's multiple images with *Car Tires* (1958–62; Harry N. Abrams Family Collection, New York), in which she employed a stamp to repeat the image of a tyre within a grid.

On deciding to work with signboards in the early 1960s, Chryssa apprenticed herself to a sign maker. In *Times Square Sky* (1962; Walker Art Center, Minneapolis) she created an unintelligible message by layering decontextualised metal letters on to the wall. To balance the mélange, she used blue neon to write the word *air* above the work. Not only does this mark the first occurrence of neon in a sculpture (Hunter 1974, p.11), but it also points to Chryssa's strategic use of language. Henceforth, she experimented with the many artistic possibilities of neon. Symbols and letters were analysed via multicoloured neon, as in *Five Variations on the Ampersand* (1966; Museum of Modern Art, New York). Each ampersand stands over 60 centimetres high and is encased in grey Plexiglas, which creates a night-time effect. Emphasising the processes of the work, and her ability to control them, Chryssa exposed the mechanisms required to operate the neon. This manoeuvre complemented her claim that her sculptures are not dependent on technology, because they remain complete even after the transformers break down (*ibid.*, p.12).

In preparation for her *Gates to Times Square*, Chryssa produced a series of neon studies, most of which became individual works of art. Although *Clytemnestra II* (moulded plastic tubes with inserted neon and timer; Nationalgalerie, Berlin) began as study No.14, this neon *S*, 4.57 metres high, caused a sensation when it was exhibited at Documenta IV in 1968. Unusually expressive, the work was inspired by Irene Papas's portrayal of Clytemnestra in Euripides' tragedy *Iphigenia in Aulis*. As Chryssa relates, when the protagonist learned of her daughter's sacrifice, the curves of her body convoluted as she screamed in horror (Restany 1977, p.69). The escalating sound of anguish is visually echoed by the sculpture, which requires several timed sequences before the boldly coloured neon is completely perceivable.

Combining the knowledge gained through her studies with her interest in the city, Chryssa started to build the *Gates to Times Square* (1964–6; Albright-Knox Art Gallery, Buffalo). As she has

stated: "America is very stimulating, intoxicating for me … The vulgarity of America as seen in the lights of Times Square is poetic" (Hunter 1974, p.10). For two years of intense activity, she worked to integrate metal, signs, neon and plastic into a three-metre cube that pays homage to communication, advertising and hence to the visual mechanics of capitalism. Art and technology unite in order to produce a light that is now dynamic. At both the entrance and the exit stands a giant letter *A*, which provides structural and symbolic support to the jumble of unreadable signs. Thus, what might be understood as chaotic, becomes logical (poetic) in form.

Works of the early 1970s are dominated by a triptych that furthers the analysis of linguistic codes. In one segment entitled *That's All* (1970–73; Plexiglas, neon, electrodes, asbestos, paper; Metropolitan Museum of Art, New York) Chryssa employed coloured neon to draw fragmented letters. The result, suggests Restany, is purely gestural, for the meaning of the fractured letters is suppressed by the visuality of the irregular lines. Although the triptych contains neon tubing and cut-aluminium shapes, the two-dimensionality of the work is emphasised through fields of colour. This graphic aesthetic reappears in a commission Chryssa received to transform the interior of a castle, known as the *Metternich Project* (1973–89; Schloss Adelsleben, Germany). After eliminating all natural light from the space, she recreated the exterior landscape by fabricating the passage of time. Cool blue and white neon is superimposed over warm yellows and foggy, grey-coloured paint to evoke the sensation of evening and daylight. The synthetic environment is then brought to life by a timer that moves the neon to a slow rhythm.

Chryssa continued to explore the use of language and light in New York. In addition to Times Square, she was newly inspired by Chinatown. Throughout the 1980s she produced paintings and large wall reliefs based on Chinese calligraphy and Roman script, as in *Mott Street No.2* (1985; sheet metal, mixed media, metallic paint; artist's collection, repr. *Chryssa: Cityscapes* 1990, fig.14). Instead of neon, she relied on aluminium to convey the structural qualities of the Chinese characters, while the highly polished surfaces reflect the surrounding light independently. By the 1990s Chryssa had returned to the topic of time with *Summer* (1988–90; honeycomb aluminium, paint, neon; artist's collection, repr. Wallach 1991). This complex sculpture, however, does not refer to the "natural" season, but rather, Vivaldi's musical construction.

Light, form, language and culture remain the constant themes in Chryssa's diverse work. Yet her concerns extend beyond that of the formal. By exploring language, she repossesses a domain once considered "masculine". Moreover, when she connotes the artificiality of "nature", she is actually questioning the presumption of an inherent "female" nature. Indeed, Chryssa may be seen as an overt feminist in the scream of *Clytemnestra* but, more subtly, she repeatedly contradicts theories of essentialism with her gender-neutral art. Quite often, the only way one could ascertain that Chryssa is a *woman* artist is by her unjust lack of art-historical recognition.

DEBRA WACKS

Churberg, Fanny (Maria)
Finnish painter, 1845–1892

Born in Vaasa, Österbotten, 12 December 1845. Educated at Emma Peranders's boarding school for girls, Porvoo, 1857–9, and in Viborg, 1860–61. Studied art privately in Helsinki under Finnish painters Alexandra Frosterus, Emma Gyldén and Berndt Lindholm, 1865–6; in Düsseldorf under landscape painter Carl Ludwig, 1867–8 and 1871–4; in Paris under Swedish landscape painter Wilhelm von Gegerfelt, 1876. Painted in Finland, 1877–80. Visited the Paris Exposition Universelle, 1878. Stopped painting, 1880; devoted herself to the Finska Handarbetets Vänner (Friends of Finnish Handicraft) and campaigned for an improvement in taste; wrote reviews and art criticism for Finnish newspapers and magazines, 1886–92. Lived, unmarried, partly with her brother's family in Sweden and partly in Finland. Died in Helsinki, 5 May 1892.

Principal Exhibitions
Finnish Art Society, Helsinki: 1869, 1879–80 (first prize 1879)
Art Exhibition, Kuopio: 1891
Stenman Gallery, Helsinki: 1919 (retrospective)

Selected Writings
"Konstföreningens exposition hösten, 1887" [The Art Association's autumn exhibition], *Finland*, 30 October 1887
"Konstföreningens årsexposition, 1888" [The Art Association's annual exhibition], *Finland*, 25 November 1888
"Atelier-besök" [Studio visit], *Finland*, 6 February 1889
"Konstexpositionen i Ateneum, 1889" [The art exhibition in the Ateneum], *Finland*, 23 and 26 October 1889

Bibliography
Carl Gustaf Estlander, "Konstföreningens exposition" [The Art Association's exhibition], *Finsk Tidskrift*, 1877, pp.383–5
——, "Finska Konstföreningens exposition" [The Finnish Art Association's exhibition], *Finsk Tidskrift*, 1878, p.460
J. Ahrenberg, "Ofversigt: Bildande konst" [A survey: Didactic art], *Finsk Tidskrift*, 1879
J.J. Tikkanen, "Finska konstföreningens exposition" [The Finnish Art Association's exhibition], *Finsk Tidskrift*, 1880
Fredrik Ahlstedt, "Fanny Maria Churberg", *Finska Qvinnor på olika arbetsområden* [Finnish women in different spheres], Helsinki: Finnish Women's Association, 1892
Signe Tandefelt, "Fanny Churberg", *Arena* (Helsinki), no.1, 1920
Sigrid Schauman, "Fanny Churbergs teckningar" [Fanny Churberg's drawings], *Svenska Pressen* (Helsinki), 11 February 1922
Helena Westermarck, "Fanny Churberg: Anteckningar om hennes insats i vår målarkonst" [Fanny Churberg: Notes on her contribution to our painting], *Finsk Tidskrift*, 1935, p.315
——, *Tre konstnärinnor: Fanny Churberg, Maria Wiik och Sigrid af Forselles* [Three women artists: Fanny Churberg, Maria Wiik and Sigrid af Forselles], Helsinki: Söderström, Förlagsaktiebolag, 1937
Aune Lindstrom, *Fanny Churberg: Elämö ja teokset*, Porvoo, 1938
Målarinnor från Finland: Seitsemän Suomalaista Taiteilijaa [Women painters from Finland], exh. cat., Nationalmuseum, Stockholm, and elsewhere, 1981
Leena Ahtola-Moorhouse, *Fanny Churberg: Myttin ainekset*, Helsinki, 1988

The last decades of the 19th century were a turbulent time for art in the Nordic countries. Artists rebelled against ingrown traditions in cultural life. Fanny Churberg belonged to the generation that started this process, but she ended her painting career when she was 35 years old. She had been chastised by critics for her almost brutal paintings and dramatic visions. Although she did enjoy some measure of success, her self-confidence was shattered and in 1880 she put away her brushes for good. She continued with art by writing articles and she was the organiser and one of the founders in 1881 of the Friends of Finnish Handicraft, an organisation that helped women in particular to get an economic basis of their own. She also worked for the "Fennomanien", encouraging the Finnish people to accept their culture, language and country. She never married.

In the late 1870s Churberg tried to live as a free artist. She was strong-willed, had considerable creative powers and took great pleasure in her work. Her high moral standards did not allow her to compromise and accept half-hearted work, but neither Finnish society nor that of Germany or France could accept a woman of such strong character. Churberg accepted the consequences and stopped painting, turning her creative talents to social ends. Her breakthrough as a painter did not come until 1919, when a retrospective exhibition was held in Helsinki by the eccentric art dealer Gösta Stenman. By that time Churberg had been dead for almost 30 years. At her death her brother took care of what he thought was a bunch of worthless paintings. He kept them, but had almost forgotten their existence when Stenman happened to ask him if he knew of the whereabouts of any of Churberg's paintings. Today her works have a firm place in Finnish art history.

Churberg was able to study painting because her family had sufficient money: her father was the town doctor in Vaasa. Both her parents died before she was 20 years old, but they left their children financially secure. After some years of private art training in Helsinki, in 1867 she headed for Düsseldorf in Germany, where the landscape painter Carl Ludwig became her private teacher. She remained his pupil until 1874, spending the summers in Finland. Churberg was a romantic soul with a passionate temperament and a great love for the Finnish landscape, particularly in late autumn and winter. She had a predilection for the dramatic in nature and loved the wild forests with rocks and broken trees and water.

In 1875–6 Churberg studied in France. It was not the work of the Impressionists as such that turned her mind to Paris, but the opportunity to paint her beloved nature in plein air. She chose the Swedish landscape painter Wilhelm von Gegerfelt as her teacher. In Paris she discovered the combination of light and colour values and the intensity of the still-life motifs in the work of the 18th-century painter Chardin. In 1876 she painted *Still Life with Vegetables and Fish* (Ateneum, Helsinki) and the following year *Still Life with Mushrooms* (Österbottens Museum of Vaasa), both technically extremely well painted and with that extra light in the colours that gives even a dead fish or a freshly-picked mushroom a soul.

Churberg's career as a painter was short. She painted for only ten years, yet almost 300 paintings by her are known. In a way she was a rebel. She was energetic, passionate and expressionistic. Her touch was free and uncurbed and far from the academic style she must have learned in Düsseldorf. The fact that she was a non-conformist may have given her the opportunity to go her own way. In the end it was too much of a burden for her to continue alone.

Although she never knew the work of Vincent van Gogh, who started his ten-year career at the time she ended hers, in their feelings and wild expression they are close to each other, although different in the landscapes they chose to paint. Churberg saw the unique and barren beauty of Finnish nature, and painted the heavy grey climate of the north (e.g. *Moonlight, Study*, 1878; *Winter*, 1880; both Ateneum). No one expected anything of her, which gave her a certain freedom to do what she most wanted. She felt strongly about her work and overstepped the bounds of convention. She never completed her paintings in a realistic or naturalistic way, but left them with stormy skylines, captured the open air and powerful emotions. She was romantic in one way, but never sentimental. Churberg inspired artists for generations after her; Helene Schjerfbeck (q.v.) saw her paintings in the exhibitions of 1879–80 in Helsinki and never forgot them.

LENA HOLGER

Clark, Lygia
Brazilian artist, 1920–1988

Born Lygia Pimentel Lins in Belo Horizonte, Minas Gerais, Brazil, 23 October 1920. Married Aloizio Clark c.1938; one daughter, two sons; divorced. Studied under landscape architect Robert Burle Marx in Rio de Janeiro, 1947, and under Fernand

Léger, Dobrinsky and Arpad Szénes in Paris,
1950–52. Member of the Brazilian Concrete Art
group, Grupo Frente, Rio de Janeiro, 1954–6.
Founder-member, Neo-Concrete group, Rio de
Janeiro, 1959–61. Lived in Rio de Janeiro for most
of the 1960s. Taught courses on "gestural communication" at St Charles I, Sorbonne, Paris,
1970–75. Returned to Rio, 1976; began referring
to herself as a therapist. Recipient of artist of the
year award, Rio de Janeiro, 1952; Augusto
Frederico Schmidt prize, Rio de Janeiro, 1953; first
prize, Primeira Exposição Nacional de Arte
Abstrata, Petrópolis, Rio de Janeiro, 1953; acquisition prize, São Paulo Bienal, 1957; Guggenheim
fellowships, 1958 and 1960; best national sculpture, São Paulo Bienal, 1961; first prize, Bahia
Bienal, Salvador, 1966; honorary doctorate and
gold medal, Parma, Italy, 1980. Died in Rio de
Janeiro, 1988.

Selected Individual Exhibitions

Galerie de l'Institut Endoplastique, Paris: 1952 (retro-
spective)
Ministério da Educação e Cultura, Rio de Janeiro: 1952
Galeria Bonino, Rio de Janeiro: 1960
Museu de Arte Moderna, Rio de Janeiro: 1963, 1968
Technische Hochschule, Stuttgart: 1964
Signals Gallery, London: 1965
Venice Biennale: 1968 (retrospective)
Galeria Ralph Camargo, São Paulo: 1971
Galeria Funarte, Rio de Janeiro: 1980
Gabinete de Arte Raquel Arnaud, São Paulo: 1982
Galeria Paulo Klabin, Rio de Janeiro: 1984
Salão Nacional de Artes Plásticas da Funarte, Paço
Imperial, Rio de Janeiro: 1986 (touring retrospective,
with Hélio Oiticica)
São Paulo Bienal: 1994 (retrospective)

Selected Writings

Book-Oeuvre, limited edition A–Z, 1964–83, private
collections (Portuguese original)
"Un mythe moderne: La mise en évidence de l'instant
comme nostalgie du cosmos", Robho, no.4, 1965,
p.18
"L'homme, structure vivant d'une architecture biologique
et céllulaire", Robho, no.5–6, 1969, p.12
"Le corps est la maison-sexualité: Envahissement du
'territoire' individuel", Robho, no.8, 1971, pp.12–13
"L'art, c'est le corps", Preuves, 1975, p.138
"De la suppression de l'objet", Mácula, 1976
"The relational object in a therapeutic context", Flue,
ii/3, Spring 1983, pp.26–7

Bibliography

29 Esculturas de Lygia Clark, exh. cat., Galeria Bonino,
Rio de Janeiro, 1960
Lygia Clark: Abstract Reliefs and Articulated Sculpture,
exh. cat., Signals Gallery, London, 1965
Guy Brett, Kinetic Art: The Language of Movement,
London: Studio Vista, and New York: Rienhold Book
Company, 1968
Gaelle Basser, La Quête de la mère dans l'oeuvre de
Lygia Clark, MA thesis, Ecole de St Charles, Paris,
1978
Suely Rolnyk, La Mémoire du corps, MA thesis, VER de
Sciences Humaines Cliniques, Sorbonne, Université de
Paris VII 1978
Lygia Clark, exh. cat., Galeria Funarte, Rio de Janeiro,
1980
Daisy Ribeiro de Resende, Dedans et dehors: Evolution
de l'oeuvre de Lygia Clark, MA thesis, VER d'Arts
Plastiques, Université de Paris, VII, 1984
Lygia Clark e Hélio Oiticica, Salão Nacional de Artes
Plásticas da Funarte, Paço Imperial, Rio de Janeiro,
and elsewhere, 1986
Guy Brett, "Lygia Clark: The borderline between art and
life", Third Text, no.1, Autumn 1987, pp.65–94
Art in Latin America: The Modern Era, 1820–1980, exh.
cat., South Bank Centre, London, and elsewhere,
1989, pp.264–6
Maria Alice Milliet, Lygia Clark: Obra-Trajeto, São
Paulo: Editora da Universidade de São Paulo, 1992
Brasil: Segni d'Arte: Libri e video, 1950–1993, exh. cat.,
Fondazione Scientifica Querini-Stampalia, Venice, and
elsewhere, 1993
Latin American Artists of the Twentieth Century, exh.
cat., Museum of Modern Art, New York, 1993
Ultramodern: The Art of Contemporary Brazil, exh. cat.,
National Museum of Women in the Arts, Washington,
DC, 1993
Guy Brett, "Lygia Clark: In search of the body", Art in
America, lxxxii, July 1994, pp.56–63, 108
Yves Alain Bois, "Lygia Clark: Nostalgia of the body",
October, no.69, Summer 1994, pp.85–109 (includes
extracts from Clark's writings)
Paula Terra Cabo, Resignifying Modernity: Clark,
Oiticica and Categories of the Modern in Brazil, PhD
dissertation, University of Essex, 1996

Lygia Clark's unorthodox attitude towards art
combined analytical rigour and philosophical questioning with a transgressive practice based on existential, sensorial, ludic and psychological experiences. Her work, which is unclassifiable, has
touched upon all the pressing questions of recent
art: of movement, the body, the environment, the
relation of the visual to other senses, space-time,
authorship, the status of the object and, above all,
art's relationship with the viewer (see Brett 1987,
p.65). In her trajectory each future work can be seen

as the next step of a self-contained process and each rupture as an analytical development of the preceding stage.

In the 1950s she produced a series of constructive paintings: *Compositions* (1954–5), *Modulated Surfaces* (1956–7), *Constellations* and *Unities* (1958; all private collections). In *Compositions* she broke away from the conventional schemes of perception and representation by incorporating the frame into the work. In *Modulated Surfaces* (repr. Washington 1993, p.9; New York 1993, p.209) there is no longer any distinction between painting and frame or figure and background. She abolished the use of colour and texture and changed medium and technique – from oil on canvas to nitro-cellulose paint air-brushed on to veneer.

Clark's experimentation with the dynamics of the surface soon led her to reduce surfaces to black and white; she achieved complete emptiness of surface in *Constellations* and *Unities* (1958). The last of these, called *Egg* (private collection, repr. London 1989, p.264), represents a conceptual development of her experiences of visual perception in relation to other senses. In *Egg*, a circular black surface incompletely enclosed by a white border, she explored the idea that if an almost complete circle is presented on a surface our visual perception will tend to close the circle, according to gestalt laws, but the "outline of a light line in actual space" prevents us from doing so. Expressing her concerns with the way the object occupies space and the traditional notions of the object-subject relationship, she said: "what I wanted was for the spectator to take an active part in this created space: to have the sensation of being himself within it, experiencing it as an organism" (*Book-Oeuvre*, 1964–83, see Venice 1993, p.35).

In the early 1960s Clark's work extended beyond painting. In the earliest wall-reliefs planes were juxtaposed, overlapped and unfolded to surge forth over space, as in *Cocoon* (iron; 30.4 × 30.4 cm.; private collection, repr. Washington 1993, pp.44–5). In the manifesto of the Neo-Concrete movement the art critic Ferreira Gullar, inspired by Clark's work, defined the concept of non-object as a "quasi corpus". As examples of the quasi-corpus, Clark's *Beasts* (1959–64; private collections, repr. London 1989, p.265; New York 1993, p. 210) – hinged manipulable planar structures, interweaving clusters of

aluminium sheets – are designed to be unfolded, brought to life, by the spectator.

Her production in the 1960s marked a point in her trajectory when the values of intuition, of active perception, of the re-introduction of expressive forces into art assumed a crucial role, reflecting a change of perception about the role played by Subject and Object. Painting was then replaced by wall-sculptures (*Cocoon*, 1958; *Rubber Grubs*, 1964), objects (*Beasts*, 1959–64; *Air and Stone*, 1966; *Sensorial Masks*, 1967–9), vestiary sculptures (*Ceasarean*, 1967; *I and You*, 1967), environments (*The House is the Body*, 1968; whereabouts unknown) and propositions/dematerialised art (*Going*, 1964; *Dialogue of Hands*, 1966; *Breathe with Me*, 1966; *Mandala*, 1969; repr. Brett 1987, Brett 1994 and Bois 1994).

In the trajectory of her work from abstract-geometric painting in the 1950s through participative art from the mid-1960s to the end of the 1970s – when her work developed into a form of psychotherapy – the issue of the "status of the object" was always addressed. The object itself assumed an increasingly secondary and incomplete role. Working in close collaboration with other Neo-Concrete artists such as Hélio Oiticica, Clark reinvested what can be called "conceptual" art with existential, psychological and ethical meanings. In *Going* (1964) the object's material existence was only an excuse for spectator action. This ephemeral work is made of a white strip of paper about 40 cm. wide, to be twisted and its ends joined to form a Moebius strip, and to be continually cut with scissors from the centre of the strip along its length. In Clark's words: "the *Going* left me in a kind of void: the immanence of the act, the abandonment of any transference to the object, the dissolution even of the concept of 'the artist's work' produced in me a very deep crisis" ("About the act" in *Book-Oeuvre*).

The "crisis" to which she refers is not only "hers" but a broader crisis of modern art, of the "object itself" and even the crisis of a traditional model of opposition between signifier and signified, and the Moebius strip is the subversive model of these paradoxes. After the disintegration of the object the next step was to question the subject's relationship to the world, the continuity between the Ego and the Other. Clark proposed that "the artist loses his or her uniqueness and expressive power. He or she is content to propose to others that they be themselves, that they achieve the singular condition of art without art" (quoted in Bois 1994, p.102).

In the *I and You/Clothing-Body-Clothing* (1967) vestiary sculptures, Clark uses clothing to denude the body. The work consists of two plastic suits, which are put on by a blindfolded couple, who, by opening the zippers, make all sorts of sensorial discoveries, including that of their gender. From that stage onwards the body incorporates the object and the body's expression assumes the essential role. As Clark wrote:

in the sensorial phase of my work ... the object was still an indispensable medium ... Then, I incorporated the object by making it disappear ... and what remains of the object (some elastic bands, sheet of plastic, jute bags, string) is quite empty of meaning and can only be brought to life with human support [quoted in Brett 1987, p.85].

From the early 1970s until 1984 Clark worked with "group-propositions" and developed a kind of psychotherapy that involved the senses and the body. Although she developed the major part of her work called *Body Phantasmatic* in Paris (1968–75), and particularly the group experiences during the time she taught at the Sorbonne (*Biological Architecture*, 1972; *Cannibalism*, 1973; *Anthropophagic Dribble*, 1973; *Tunnel*, 1973; artist's estate, on loan to Museu de Arte Moderna, Rio de Janeiro; *Net of Elastic Bands*, 1974; repr. Brett 1994, pp.61–3), her position differed substantially from other forms of "participation art" or "body art". She discussed how both tendencies failed to address fully the crucial question of the prevailing notion of the artist in "De la suppression de l'objet" (1976, p.118). At this stage notions of object-subject, the art object and authorship were meaningless to her. She started referring to herself as a therapist and producing what she afterwards called "relational objects". According to the theories of Donald Winnicott and Melanie Klein, the relational object only exists within the relationship with the subject, becoming a depository of the subject's affections, fears, emotions and phantasies.

Clark's works from 1976 to 1984 were explorations of human subject issues, such as the precarious limits of personal memory and collective experiences. The relational objects – stones of a great variety of textures and heaviness, mattresses, shells, air bags, elastic strips, mirrors, cotton sacks – were

a way of facilitating the reparative impulses of the participants by re-awakening their senses, the "memories" of the body, the pre-verbal experiences. Although she was not a qualified psychotherapist, Clark's therapeutic method of establishing the phenomenological contact between the participant and the relational-object, the subject and the other, rescued many "borderliners", as she called her patients, from their psychological disturbances. Affirming the subjective character of human lived-through experience as a non-codifiable one and the impossibility of translating primal experiences into verbal signs, Clark, with the relational objects, re-affirms the possibility of dissolving the boundaries between art and life.

The development of the artist, who led a provincial life as a socialite, daughter of a distinguished judge, wife of a successful engineer and mother-of-three, changed radically after she left her home town of Belo Horizonte in the late 1940s. She spent several years in psychoanalysis. Each rupture in her search to define art-without-art was lived through as an existential-psychological crisis, and this quality was intrinsic to her development. Certainly the work she produced over almost four decades has a broader significance for the changing condition of art even if it does not fit easily into galleries (see New York 1993, Brett 1994 and Bois 1994, p.85).

PAULA TERRA CABO

Claudel, Camille   [fig. 21]
French sculptor, 1864–1943

Born in Fère-en-Tardenois, Aisne, 8 December 1864; father a government official, brother the writer Paul Claudel. Moved to Paris with her family, *c*.1881. Studied sculpture at the Académie Colarossi and in an independent studio shared with Jessie Lipscomb and other sculptors, where Alfred Boucher and Rodin came to give tuition. Later became assistant in Rodin's studio; relationship with him broke up by 1893. Took first independent Paris studio, 1888, moving to Quai Bourbon, 1899. Sociétaire, Société Nationale des Beaux-Arts, Paris, 1895. State of health declining by 1907. Confined to a mental asylum at Ville-Evrard, 10 March 1913, eight days after her father's death; remained in mental institutions for the rest of her life. Died in the Montdevergues asylum, near Avignon, 19 October 1943.

Principal Exhibitions

Paris Salon: 1882–3, 1885–9, 1903, 1905 (honourable mention 1888)

Société Nationale des Beaux-Arts, Paris: 1892–9, 1902

Exposition de la Libre Esthétique, Brussels: 1894

Salon de l'Art Nouveau, Paris: 1896

Exposition Universelle, Paris: 1900 (bronze medal)

Salon de la Plume, Paris: 1900

Salon d'Automne, Paris: 1904–5

Galerie Eugène Blot, Paris: 1905 (with Bernard Hoetger), 1907, 1908 (both individual)

Salon des Femmes Artistes Modernes, Paris: 1934

Musée Rodin, Paris: 1951 (retrospective)

Bibliography

Gustave Geffroy, *La Vie artistique*, 8 vols, Paris: Floury, 1892–1903

Roger Marx, "Les salons", *Le Voltaire*, 10 May 1893

Mathias Morhardt, "Mademoiselle Camille Claudel", *Mercure de France*, March 1898, pp.709–55

Roger Marx in *Revue Encyclopédique*, 15 July 1899, p.560

Exposition d'oeuvres de Camille Claudel et de Bernard Hoetger, exh. cat., Galerie Eugène Blot, Paris, 1905

Paul Claudel, "Camille Claudel, statuaire", *Occident*, August 1905

Camille Claudel, exh. cat., Musée Rodin, Paris, 1951 (with introduction by Paul Claudel)

Paul Claudel, *Mémoires improvisés*, Paris: Gallimard, 1969

Anne Delbée, *Une Femme*, Paris, 1982 (novel and play)

Anne Pingeot, "Le chef-d'oeuvre de Camille Claudel: *L'Age mûr*", *Revue du Louvre et des Musées de France*, xxxi (i.e. xxxii), 1982, pp.287–95

Anne Rivière, *L'Interdite: Camille Claudel, 1864–1943*, Paris: Tierce, 1983

Camille Claudel (1864–1943), exh. cat., Musée Rodin, Paris, and Musée Sainte-Croix, Poitiers, 1984

Louise R. Witherell, "Camille Claudel rediscovered", *Woman's Art Journal*, vi/1, 1985, pp.1–7

Camille Claudel, exh. cat., National Museum of Women in the Arts, Washington, DC, and elsewhere, 1987

Jacques Cassar, *Dossier Camille Claudel*, Paris: Séguier, 1987

Renate Flagmeier, "Camille Claudel: Bildhauerin", *Kritische Berichte*, xvi/1, 1988, pp.36–45

Bruno Nuttyen, *Camille Claudel*, film, 1988

Reine-Marie Paris, *Camille: The Life of Camille Claudel, Rodin's Muse and Mistress*, London: Aurum, and New York: Seaver, 1988 (contains extensive bibliography; French original, 1984)

"'*L'Age mûr*' de Camille Claudel", exh. cat., Musée d'Orsay, Paris, and Musée des Beaux-Arts, Lyon, 1989

Claudine Mitchell, "Intellectuality/sexuality: Camille Claudel, the *fin de siècle* sculptress", *Art History*, xii, 1989, pp.419–47

C. Claudel, exh. cat., Fondation Pierre Gianadda, Martigny, 1990

Reine-Marie Paris and Arnaud de la Chapelle, *L'Oeuvre de Camille Claudel: Catalogue raisonné*, 2nd edition, Paris: Biro, 1991

Anne Higonnet, "Myths of creation: Camille Claudel and Auguste Rodin", *Significant Others: Creativity and Intimate Partnership*, ed. Whitney Chadwick and Isabelle de Courtivron, New York and London: Thames and Hudson, 1993, pp.14–29

Octave Mirbeau, *Combats ésthetiques*, Paris: Séguier, 1993

Gail McIntyre and Mike Kenny, *The Waltz*, Leeds, 1994 (play)

J.A. Schmoll, *Auguste Rodin and Camille Claudel*, Munich: Prestel, 1994 (German original)

In the Paris of the mid-1890s Camille Claudel was hailed as one of the five outstanding sculptors in the age of Rodin. Those who promoted her works believed that she had brought to sculpture a dimension of intellectuality and pathos usually found only in poetry. Her reputation rested on her imaginative compositions and the expressive and narrative technique that she developed to convey emotions and concepts.

Claudel's career – the period in which she exhibited regularly, sold her sculptures and was written about – spans a period of 25 years, from the mid-1880s, when she began to exhibit regularly at the annual Paris Salons, until 1910. Her first works, as was customary with young sculptors, included modelling sections of the human body, *Torso* (1884–8; private collection, repr. Paris and de la Chapelle 1991, no.5), and a series of portrait busts for which she enlisted the collaboration of relatives and anonymous models. She immediately attracted the attention of a private collector, Baron de Rothschild, who bought *My Brother* (1884; bronze; Musée d'Art, Toulon) and continued to purchase her works, donating them to public collections. By 1888 she was capable of contrasting the male and female nudes in one composition entitled *Sakountala* (plaster; Musée de Châteauroux). Drawn from the epic poem of the Hindu writer K ālidāsa, it represents the reunion of the heroine with her husband who rescues her from a spell. In choosing an unfamiliar mythological subject Claudel made claim to originality and intellectual sophistication.

The rendering of a famous artist signalled a sculptor's status; in 1892 Claudel exhibited the portrait of a sculptor few of her colleagues had tackled, so eminent had he become: Rodin. Her effigy of *Rodin* (1892, plaster; 1895, bronze; Musée Rodin, Paris), transposed in lithograph and published many times, attested to the esteem in which she was held in professional circles. She had studied under him in the 1880s and subsequently joined his workshop as an assistant. This was a period of intense passionate relationship for both of them. In 1892 Claudel had determined to set up an independent practice. Rodin honoured her in prefacing the first monograph on Claudel with the words: "I showed her where to find gold, but the gold she finds is her own" (Morhardt 1898, p.709).

In the 1890s Claudel contributed sculptures on the themes of fate, love and destiny, death's omnipresence and the importance of mental and private experience, for which she was ranked as an outstanding contributor to Symbolist art. Fate was represented by her in a sculpture named *Clotho* (1893; plaster; Musée Rodin) after Greek mythology, as a woman rendered skeletal with age. In 1893 *Clotho* (plaster) was coupled with *The Waltz* (plaster), and in 1899 *Clotho* (marble) with *Maturity* (plaster; both untraced). *The Waltz* represented the human couple embracing face to face in a sculpture where equilibrium is attained at the limits of balance, while *Maturity* symbolised destiny. As she explained to her brother: "I am still working hard at my group of three ... to represent destiny."

In all these sculptures the human body is envisaged as a signifying process. In *The Waltz* (1895; bronze; Musée Rodin) the illusion of movement freed from gravity relates thematically to the portrayal of a relationship signified in the sculpture by facial expressions, physical contact and yet restraint. The fact that the man's lips no more touch the woman's flesh than his hands are shown pressing into it and the elegant gesture of their hands displaying self-control contribute to an expression of love as a spiritual as much as a physical union. The narrative techniques that Claudel elaborated give much scope for interpretation. Contemporary art critics who valued her work responded accordingly by publishing narrative descriptions showing that, like poetry, her sculptures were open to interpretation in a chain of associated ideas. The writer Octave Mirbeau interpreted *The Waltz* as narrating an escape from the material world: "Voluptuous

and chaste they fly away, lost in the exaltation of their soul and flesh, closely united towards love or towards death" (*Journal*, 9 May 1893). The writer Léon Daudet considered *Clotho* a potent symbol for *fin-de-siècle* culture, calling to mind Baudelairian imagery of mental suffering and decay.

The figure of *Clotho* placed to the left of *Maturity* (1903; bronze; Musée d'Orsay, Paris; another cast after 1913; Musée Rodin) is shown leading forward an ageing man; in the male nude the ageing process is registered by rendering flabby tissues and stiff articulations. To the right of the composition the figure of a young woman is shown kneeling, a version of which was first completed as the *Lost God* (private collection, repr. Paris and de la Chapelle 1991, no.44), a title referring to the myth of Psyche. When the Inspector of Fine Art, Silvestre, discovered the composition in the artist's studio in 1895, he strongly recommended its purchase by the State as a good example of Symbolist art that "represents maturity as a man drawn forward by Old Age while Youth sends a last farewell." *Maturity* interweaves connoted meanings and narrative to the allegory of life decoded by Silvestre. The base, an integral part of the sculpture, depicts patterns of waves rising or breaking on the seashore. The sea imagery combines with the floating drapery to evoke the image of a ghost ship, recurrent symbol of fate in Western art. The compositional structure itself has a symbolic meaning with the movement from left to right underlying the passage of time, while the oblique line described in space by the gaze of the young woman towards the departing group signifies the cycle of life. To spell out that her sculpture did not represent a scene in its moment of occurrence but a "vision", a figment of the artist's mind, Claudel subtitled *Maturity* "un groupe fantastique". These three sculptures fulfilled the demand that art, across disciplines, should give form to an anxious questioning of the individual's relation to existence, the characteristic mode of consciousness in *fin-de-siècle* culture.

Claudel elaborated a series of unprecedented scenic compositions, in which small-scale figures were placed within a sculptural environment that promised new departures. In the first of these, *The Gossip* (1897; onyx; Musée Rodin), two slabs positioned at right angles define an intimate corner where four naked women sit on opposite benches. One of them signals that she is about to speak by raising her hands to her mouth, and the way in which her companions stretch to gaze at her lips explains that her speech will remain a whisper. Narrative combines with the indeterminate nature of the environment to convey an overall climate of secrecy, mystery and potential threat. When exhibiting the plaster version in 1895, Claudel called it *Sketch from Nature* and confirmed in an interview (Morhardt 1898) that this work was based on a scene she observed while travelling by train. The creative process for Claudel did not, however, consist in recording such visual data as the naturalist ethos would require, but in transforming concrete material into conceptual rather than visual reality. Thus from her repertory of female figures she created two very different works *The Gossip* and *The Wave* (1900; onyx and bronze; Musée Rodin). The latter integrates three of the figures of the former, with a few modifications, in a construction suggestive of a huge wave rising nearly vertically and about to fall. The facial anatomy of these figures as well as their more compact sculptural volumes reveal Claudel's interest in Eastern art studied at the Musée Guimet, as does the image of the wave, inspired by Hokusai's famous print. It is this capacity for transforming figurative art into an imaginative experience that won her the admiration of eminent critics of the Symbolist era, such as Roger Marx who celebrated in 1899 the "tragic and fantastic imagination that enthrals us", as well as some emerging advocates of formalism such as Louis Vauxcelles, who praised "the tragic power that emanates from her art" (*Gil Blas*, 10 July 1913).

Claudel specialised in small-scale works that would find a suitable environment in the homes of private collectors. In Rodin's studio she learned of sculpture practised in the tradition of the workshop system, whereby the process of making the definitive plaster model on the basis of the clay designed by the sculptor, as well as the work of transferring the plaster model into durable material, were subcontracted to specialised technicians. The quality of the sculpture might depend on how well she or he supervised the work but the "sculptor" was not expected to carry out the carving. Claudel pioneered a new definition of sculpture in carrying out a greater part of the technical processes herself and demanding that her "originality" be evaluated on the carving technique she deployed. Through her exhibition policies she forced attention on this issue, for instance when coupling a version of *The Gossip*

in onyx, a brittle material reputedly difficult to carve, with a portrait of *Mme D* (marble; untraced), publicised as "carved by herself in front of the model" (Geffroy 1897). Involving a time-consuming method, the viability of her practice depended on her ability to enrol a network of clients to finance the transfer of her designs into durable material. Most of her famous sculptures were indebted to private sponsorship, for instance the onyx version of *The Gossip*, commissioned by the banker Peytell, *Maturity*, commissioned in bronze by Capitaine Tissier, and the marble of *Sakountala* and *Perseus and the Gorgon*, both by Comtesse Maigret. The editor Mathias Morhardt organised several sponsorships on her behalf, the marble of *Clotho* and the edition of her bust of *Rodin*. Financial viability in the practice of sculpture came from the sale of bronze multiple editions. The art dealer Eugène Blot, whom she met in 1900, undertook the edition of 12 of her designs from the 1890s. Besides permanent display of some of her works in his Paris gallery, Blot organised much publicity for Claudel with private shows held in 1905, 1907 and 1908. According to Blot, Claudel did not prove a financial success, in spite of the low prices he conceded. In 1907 some critics and administrators felt it proper to call attention to the precarious situation in which she found herself.

As Claudel understood her career, her major difficulty was to establish the originality of her practice in relation to Rodin. In 1893 she decided to isolate herself, and so that no-one could say he helped produce her work, let it be known that he never visited her studio. Her other strategy was to claim authorship for the entire production of a sculpture, carving included. Rodin caused problems to many young practitioners because of his very stature, his work and persona, seemingly a constant subject of preoccupation in French culture. As "Rodin's student" her position was particularly insecure, and an easy target for his opponents anxious to detect his pernicious influence. Hostility to Claudel, directed both towards her expressionist technique and her themes, noticeably increased at the time when the French cultural establishment violently split over Rodin's *Balzac* (1898–9).

A major area of difficulty for Claudel was the sexual dimension of her work in a period when women's claims of access to the public debate on sexuality were a source of conflict and institutionalised oppression. The proposal to exhibit

Sakountala in Châteauroux Museum in 1895 caused a public uproar echoed in the Parisian press. *The Waltz* fell under censorship from the State art establishment as Inspector Dayot advised that the sculpture should not be exhibited in a public gallery without added draperies because of "the violent accent of reality which comes from it ... the proximity of the sexes being conveyed with a surprising sensuality of expression" (Archives Nationales, F21 4299). A clear sign of Claudel's insecure position in culture was the contrast between the high esteem in which she was held in professional circles and the recurrently oppressive attitude of the State establishment towards her. Her request for the purchase of *Sakountala* (1888) and *Petite Châteleine* (1894) was rejected; the contracts for commissioning the bronze of *The Waltz* and *Maturity* drawn in March 1893 and June 1899 were never signed; *Clotho* offered on Rodin's behalf to the Musée du Luxembourg in 1905 somehow got lost. More damaging to her career, *Maturity* and a bust she considered particularly important works were refused at the art section of the Exposition Universelle of 1900, thus depriving her of a unique opportunity to receive the international recognition she deserved. The set of problems that Claudel encountered at the turn of the century while she was trying to secure her career was brutal enough to provoke a state of mental depression. Her illness, signs of which were evident in her correspondence of 1907, was never treated as such. On 10 March 1913 she was confined to a mental asylum, and remained in the custody of such institutions for the rest of her life.

In 1951 her brother, the famous poet Paul Claudel, in the introduction to the catalogue of her retrospective at the Musée Rodin, offered a biographical interpretation of her work that contradicted his Symbolist interpretation of 1905. This text has inspired many imaginative interpretations of Claudel's work and life in the 1980s. In 1914 Rodin agreed to Morhardt's idea that a room of the projected Musée Rodin should be dedicated to Claudel to exhibit the work left in her studio. This became a reality long after her death, thanks to donations of the Claudel family and purchases, the latest being *The Wave* put *in situ* in February 1995.

CLAUDINE MITCHELL

Collot, Marie-Anne
French sculptor, 1748–1821

Born in Paris, 1748. Studied under Jean-Baptiste Lemoyne, then Etienne-Maurice Falconet. Accompanied Falconet to St Petersburg, Russia, 1766. Married Falconet's son, Pierre-Etienne, 1777; one daughter. Returned to Paris, 1778; brought legal action against her husband for abusive behaviour; remained estranged from him until his death in 1791. Joined her father-in-law in The Hague, Netherlands, 1779. Moved back to Paris, 1782; nursed Falconet after a stroke until his death in 1791. Moved to Lorraine and purchased an estate at Marimont, 1791. Member of the St Petersburg Academy. Died in Nancy, 23 February 1821.

Bibliography

Levesque, *Oeuvres complètes d'Etienne Falconet*, 3 vols, 3rd edition, Paris, 1808; reprinted Geneva: Slatkine, 1970

Antony Valabrègue, *Madame Falconet: Une artiste française en Russie, 1766–1778*, Paris: Rouam, 1898

Louis Réau, ed., *Correspondance de Falconet avec Catherine II*, Paris: Champion, 1921

Louis Réau, "Une femme sculpteur française au XVIIIe siècle: Marie-Anne Collot (1748–1821)", *Bulletin de la Société de l'Histoire de l'Art Français*, 1924, pp.219–29

——, "Les bustes de Marie-Anne Collot", *La Renaissance*, xiv, 1931, pp.306–12

Denis Diderot, *Correspondance*, ed. Georges Roth, 16 vols, Paris: Minuit, 1955–70

——, *Salons*, ed. Jean Seznec and Jean Adhémar, 4 vols, Oxford: Clarendon Press, 1957–67

Hal Opperman, "Marie-Anne Collot in Russia: Two portraits", *Burlington Magazine*, cvii, 1965, pp.408–13 (earlier works containing references to Collot listed in footnote 6)

La Femme artiste d'Elisabeth Vigée-Lebrun à Rosa Bonheur, exh. cat., Musée Despiau-Wlerick, Donjon Lacataye, Mont-de-Marsan, 1981

La France et la Russie au siècle des lumières: Relations culturelles et artistiques, exh. cat., Grand Palais, Paris, 1986

"I do not want to exaggerate her talent, but your Majesty knows that it is singular and that she is the only one of her sex who has devoted herself to the difficult profession of cutting marble and of cutting it successfully." So the sculptor Falconet described his student, Marie-Anne Collot, to Catherine the Great in 1771. Indeed, Collot is one of the few women before 1800 known to have practised sculpture as a profession, and she earned her living by what contemporaries saw as "indefatigable industry".

Born in Paris in 1748, Collot reputedly worked first with Jean-Baptiste Lemoyne, a prominent portraitist and noted teacher. She entered the atelier of Etienne-Maurice Falconet in 1763 when she was 15. Why (and if) Collot changed studios is not certain, nor do we know how as a young woman she came to enter any sculpture studio at all. But by 1766 Collot had made five or six portrait busts, including those of *Grimm*, the actor *Préville*, the Russian minister *Galitzine* and *Denis Diderot* (all untraced). In his *Salon of 1767* Diderot remarked on the portrait of himself, which replaced a less successful piece by Falconet: "When Falconet saw the bust his student had made, he took a hammer and broke his own in front of her. That was truthful and courageous."

Falconet's regard for Collot's talents is well documented, and he entrusted her with making the head of *Peter the Great* for the equestrian monument commissioned by Catherine II (completed 1782; St Petersburg). In 1766 Collot accompanied Falconet to St Petersburg; she was still a minor but apparently had been abandoned by her father. Her travel and work with Falconet predictably provoked gossip, even though her relation to the sculptor seems to have been one of dutiful daughter (and later daughter-in-law).

Falconet arranged for Catherine's patronage of Collot; he brokered her commissions and interceded on her behalf. During the 12 years she spent in Russia, Collot executed various portrait busts and medallions of the Empress, all of which were repeatedly replicated, often by Collot herself. Many of the extant works are now in the Hermitage, St Petersburg. Catherine also commissioned portrait medallions of her son *Paul Petrovich* and his first wife, *Natalya Alexeyevna*, in 1775. In addition, she ordered a medallion of *Count Orlov*, commemorating his relief of the plague-stricken in Moscow. This work suggests something of the collaboration between Collot and Falconet. Having educated himself in the classics, Falconet devised the iconography for the portrait, and wrote to Catherine on 17 November 1771: "This medallion must not only represent M. le Comte, but also characterise his great, memorable and humane act". He goes on to say that the ancients gave the oak crown to a citizen who had saved the life of another, but that Orlov's

generous actions saved many lives. Falconet argued that no attribute could make the tribute clear, and suggested instead the inscription: "to the citizen who saved his country". Two branches of oak entwined in the border would indicate an action worthy of commemoration.

Collot's most famous collaborative work with Falconet is undoubtedly the monument to *Peter the Great*. She was involved with many aspects of the work, as Falconet suggested to Catherine in October 1776:

> Your Majesty knows that it is standard to save a small model of an equestrian statue from which one can make small bronzes. The model that I made to begin my work has been broken, and anyway, its proportions were too large. Mlle Collot has been busy for a long time making studies relative to that object ... I would have liked to make the model myself, if my eyesight still allowed me to model in a small scale, but Mlle Collot who knows my work perfectly, who has followed all its operations, and who will work under my direction, will complete it successfully.

Collot is generally viewed, however, as having made only the portrait head (indeed, the small bronzes of the work, such as that in the Tretyakov Gallery, Moscow, are rarely attributed to her). In modelling the head (bronze cast, 1770; State Russian Museum, St Petersburg) she worked from Rastrelli's mask of the tsar. She idealised the features, but also stressed the intense gaze and furrowed brow, which convey an energetic determination that contributes to the overall effect. In making the head of Peter, Collot followed a procedure that she had used in several other "retrospective" portraits commissioned by Catherine, which included busts of *Henry IV* and *Sully*. In describing the genesis of these works, Falconet referred to Collot "dreaming" them. Although certainly drawing on her imaginative faculties, the artist also depended on portrait masks sent from Paris by Lemoyne.

If Collot dreamed for Catherine the images of past rulers, that of *Falconet* (1773; Hermitage Museum, St Petersburg) she rendered for the Empress from life. The bust shows Collot's teacher informally dressed and wigless and, with high forehead, upturned eyes and deeply drilled pupils, the portrait invokes conventions for depicting the artist. Despite the conventional aspects, Falconet's features appear mobile – the smile is about to break, the eyebrows are lifted slightly – and Collot devised a lively and subtle expression that seems liable to change.

In addition to the portraits produced for Catherine, Collot also worked on private commissions. Her bust of *Mary Cathcart*, daughter of the British ambassador, exists in three examples: a finished work in marble (signed and dated 1772; State Russian Museum), an unfinished marble version (Musée des Beaux-Arts, Nancy) and a plaster bust (signed and dated 1768; Louvre, Paris). An anonymous "Eloge" to Collot praises the bust as "one of the prettiest that you can imagine" and remarks on its modest expression that lends truth and interest to the work. In contrast to the strikingly individual and animated features of her bust of *Falconet*, those of Miss Cathcart establish the contemporary ideal of fragile and vulnerable femininity. That ideal is evident in the perfected, generalised traits and downcast eyes, which allow viewers to look freely, sure that this young girl is not the sort who would brazenly return the gaze. For the same family Collot exercised her talents in retrospective portraiture, executing from memory a posthumous, life-size marble medallion of *Jane Hamilton, Lady Cathcart* (1772; Collection of the Earl Cathcart, Sandridge).

Few known works by Collot are dated after she returned to Paris from Russia in 1778. Those extant or recorded in literary sources include a bust of her husband *Pierre-Etienne Falconet* (Musée des Beaux-Arts, Nancy), that of the *Chevalier d'Eon*, whom she had known in Russia, and a third of *Charles-Godefroy de Villetaneuse*. In 1779 Collot joined her father-in-law in The Hague, leaving Paris after her husband's abusive and irrational behaviour provoked her to file an official complaint. During her sojourn in the Netherlands she executed marble busts of *William V* and his wife (1782; Mauritshuis, The Hague), and one in bronze of the physician *Camper* (1781; destroyed in a fire, 1907), which she gave to him in gratitude for saving her daughter.

It is not clear when and why Collot's production ended, but always the dutiful daughter, she spent the years between 1783 and 1791 in Paris nursing her father-in-law who was partly paralysed from a stroke. Both her husband and father-in-law died in 1791, and Collot retreated to Lorraine. The writer Levesque, an acquaintance of Falconet, went to visit Collot in 1808 and reported: "Madame Falconet,

after having spent eight years in the sad and respectable profession of sick nurse, did not believe she could take up again an art that she had neglected for so long" (Levesque 1808, p.21). Even if she had wanted to return to her work, the problem of seeking out new patrons, as well as both the difficulty and expense of obtaining materials and founding a studio, would have been considerable, especially for a woman past her 50th year. Moreover, with her own earnings and her considerable legacy from Falconet, Marie-Anne Collot was financially secure – so secure that she married her daughter, Marie-Lucie, to the Baron de Jankowitz, a Polish nobleman established in Lorraine. It was Marie-Lucie who preserved the memory of Collot's art in France, donating her works and papers to the State in the hope that her mother might find a place in the national *patrimoine*.

MARY D. SHERIFF

Coster, Anne *see* Vallayer-Coster

Cosway, Maria
British painter, illustrator and printmaker, 1760–1838

Born Maria Louisa Caterina Cecilia Hadfield in Florence, Italy, 1760; father ran fashionable inns. Copied paintings in Florence, 1773–8; elected member of the Accademia del Disegno, Florence, 1778. Visited Rome and Naples, 1778–9. Moved to London with her family, 1779. Married painter Richard Cosway in London, 1781; daughter born 1790 (d. 1796). Visited Paris and toured Flanders with husband, 1786; met Thomas Jefferson. Visited Paris alone, 1787. Lived alone in Venice and Genoa, 1790–94. In London with Richard Cosway, 1794–1801. Close association with the London-based print publisher Rudolph Ackermann, 1800–03. In Paris alone, copying in the Louvre, 1801–3. Established "a college for young ladies" at Lyon under the patronage of Joseph Fesch, Archbishop of Lyon and later Cardinal, 1803–9. Founded school for girls at Lodi, Lombardy, with the support of Francesco Melzi d'Eril, vice-president of the Cisalpine Republic and later Duke of

Lodi, 1812; college re-established under the religious order of the Dame Inglesi, 1830. Visited Richard Cosway in London, 1815; stayed with him from 1817 until his death in 1821; arranged five auctions of his collections. Toured Scotland, 1822. Returned to Lodi, 1822; lived there for the rest of her life. Arranged publication of a selection of Richard Cosway's drawings, engraved by Paolo Lasinio, Florence, 1826. Created a Baroness by the Austrian emperor Francis I, 1834 (group portrait of *Baroness Maria Cosway, Surrounded by Sisters and Pupils, Listening to an Oration by Vittoria Manzoni* painted by Gabriele Rottini *c*.1835; Fondazione Cosway, Lodi). Died in Lodi, 5 January 1838.

Principal Exhibitions
Royal Academy, London: 1781–9, 1796, 1800–01

Bibliography

Anthony Pasquin [John Williams], *The Royal Academicians: A Farce as It Was Performed to the Astonishment of Mankind by His Majesty's Servants, at the Stone House, in Utopia, in the Summer of 1786*, London, 1786

"Cenni biografici sopra la Baronessa Maria Hadfield Cosway …", (a pamphlet inserted in the) *Gazzetta Privilegiata di Milano*, 11 February 1838

Frederick B. Daniell, *A Catalogue Raisonné of the Engraved Works of Richard Cosway, RA*, London: Daniell, 1890

George C. Williamson, *Richard Cosway RA and His Wife and Pupils, Miniaturists of the Eighteenth Century*, London: Bell, 1897; revised as *Richard Cosway RA*, 1905

E. Fletcher, ed., *Conversations of James Northcote RA with James Ward on Art and Artists*, London: Methuen, 1901

Alfred Whitman, *British Mezzotinters: Valentine Green*, 3 vols, London: Bullen, 1902

E.L.G. Charvet, "Enseignement public des arts du dessin à Lyon, 1804", *Bulletin du Comité des Sociétés des Beaux-Arts des Départements (Réunion des Sociétés des Beaux-Arts des Départements)*, xxxv, 1912, pp.79–112

Emma Ferrari, "Di alcuni documenti riguardanti Riccardo Cosway nella biblioteca di Lodi", *Archivio Storico per la Città di Lodi*, xxxii, 1913, pp.171–86; xxxiii, 1914, pp.25–48, 75–93

P. B[arghazi], "Dalla corrispondenza di lettere con Madama Baronessa Maria Hadfield Cosway", *Archivio Storico per la Città e i Comuni del Circondario e della Diocesi di Lodi*, xliv, 1925, pp.109–20

Arthur T. Bolton, ed., *The Portrait of Sir John Soane RA (1753–1837), Set Forth in Letters from His Friends (1775–1837)*, London: Sir John Soane's Museum, 1927

Helen Duprey Bullock, *My Head and My Heart: A Little History of Thomas Jefferson and Maria Cosway*, New York: Putnam, 1945

Fawn M. Brodie, *Thomas Jefferson: An Intimate History*, New York: Norton, and London: Eyre Methuen, 1974

John Ford, *Ackermann, 1783–1983: The Business of Art*, London: Ackermann, 1983

Maurizio Lozzi and Angelo Stroppa, *Il Collegio Cosway ieri e oggi*, Lodi, 1985

John Walker, "Maria Cosway, an undervalued artist", *Apollo*, cxxiii, 1986, pp.318–24

Elena Cazzulani and Angelo Stroppa, *Maria Hadfield Cosway: Biografia, diari e scritti della fondatrice del Collegio delle Dame Inglesi in Lodi*, Orio Litta: L'Immagine, 1989; reviewed by Stephen Lloyd, *Burlington Magazine*, cxxxii, 1990, p.799

Philippe Bordes, "Jacques-Louis David's anglophilia on the eve of the French Revolution", *Burlington Magazine*, cxxxiv, 1992, pp.482–90

Stephen Lloyd, "The accomplished Maria Cosway: Anglo-Italian artist, musician, salon hostess and educationalist (1759–1838)", *Journal of Anglo-Italian Studies*, ii, 1992, pp.108–39

Ann Bermingham, "The aesthetics of ignorance: The accomplished woman in the culture of connoisseurship", *Oxford Art Journal*, xvi/2, 1993, pp.3–20

Richard and Maria Cosway: Regency Artists of Taste and Fashion, exh. cat., Scottish National Portrait Gallery, Edinburgh, and National Portrait Gallery, London, 1995 (contains extensive bibliography)

Maria Cosway was the most significant woman artist to exhibit her work publicly in London during the last two decades of the 18th century, after the departure of Angelica Kauffman (q.v.) for Rome in 1781. The contemporary reputation of her work was based on three factors: the history paintings and portraits shown at the Royal Academy; their reproduction as prints by major engravers such as Valentine Green and Francesco Bartolozzi; and between 1800 and 1803 her close association with the art entrepreneur Rudolph Ackermann, who published a number of prints after her paintings as well as various series of her etchings and illustrations. Until recently Cosway's artistic production and career received little critical study, in contrast with the attention given to her brilliant but eccentric husband Richard Cosway. For instance, it is still commonly assumed that she was a miniaturist, although there is no evidence for this. Cosway has been and will always be best known for her romance with Thomas Jefferson (*Jefferson in Paris*, film by Merchant Ivory Productions, 1995), which was just one of the many intense relationships that marked her fascinating life.

In 1787 one of the three self-portraits (all untraced) that Maria Cosway painted and exhibited at the Royal Academy in the 1780s was engraved in mezzotint by Green. At the time of the print's publication Cosway was in her late twenties, at the height of her success as an artist and between two visits to Paris. This self-portrait, which was titled *Mrs Cosway*, is perhaps the strongest composition of her career, and has a clarity reminiscent of the work of Elisabeth Vigée-Lebrun (q.v.). The artist chose to present herself three-quarter length within a fictive window or picture frame, seated confidently and strongly lit against an open background of sea and dark sky, shown either at sunrise or sunset. The assertive pose adopted is notable for the crossed arms, which while acting as a neat device to conceal the hands, also help lend an air of forthright determination to the image. This aspect of Cosway's character was noted by the painter James Northcote, who cited her as the only individual apart from his master (Reynolds) who was superior to circumstances: "I knew her when she was in the greatest distress; I knew her when she was in high prosperity, and visited by the Prince of Wales, but at both periods her behaviour was exactly the same" (quoted in Fletcher 1901, pp.79–80). In the *Self-Portrait* Cosway turns her head to face the viewer with a gaze of wide-eyed intensity and unaffected seriousness. This is achieved despite her fashionable appearance with puffed and powdered hair, offset by a characteristic turban. She decided against including any props, such as a palette or harp, which might have referred to her activities as an artist or musician. The emphasis is very much on her appearance and presence. She depicted herself wearing a cross at the end of a dark ribbon choker, tied at the front of the neck with a heart-shaped locket. This was both a fashionable piece of decorative jewellery and an overt reference to her strong Catholicism, the deep impact of which is vital for an understanding of her biography and artistic production.

Maria Hadfield's career as an artist was based on her training in Florence during childhood and adolescence. As she recorded in an autobiographical letter to Sir William Cosway (1830; National Art Library, Victoria and Albert Museum, London, MS Eng.L.961–1953), she began drawing at eight years of age; she was trained by Violante Cerroti; and she is known to have copied paintings in the galleries of the Uffizi and Palazzo Pitti in the years 1773–8. Among the works that Maria Hadfield studied were those of Correggio, van Meiris, Trevisani and Reynolds. Copies from this period of Raphael's *Large Cowper Madonna*, Correggio's *Virgin and Child with St Jerome* and Rubens's *Four Philosophers* are still preserved in the Fondazione Cosway, Lodi. Cosway was also taught by Zoffany and received lessons from Wright of Derby. On her visit to Rome in 1778–9 she did not attend formal classes but made sketches from "all that was high in painting and sculpture". She also met a number of the major artists including Batoni, Mengs and Maron, as well as many of those visiting from Britain. She was greatly impressed by Fuseli's "extraordinary visions".

The paintings that Cosway exhibited at the Royal Academy were much influenced by Kauffman and Fuseli in terms of style, handling and range of subject matter. Her interest in spiritual iconography was part of an increasing trend during the 1780s that was dominated by Fuseli, but which received a mixed critical response. Horace Walpole recorded in his Royal Academy catalogue of 1783 that "of late Barry, Romney, Fuseli, Mrs Cosway, and others, have attempted to paint deities, visions, witchcrafts, etc., have only been bombast and extravert, without true dignity" (quoted in Martin Postle, *Sir Joshua Reynolds: The Subject Pictures*, Cambridge, 1995, p.265). Cosway's paintings comprised some notable "in character portraits", but they were principally ambitious subject pictures with mythological, literary and biblical themes drawn from such sources as Homer, Virgil, Diodorus Siculus, Petrarch, Spenser, Shakespeare, Pope, Gray, Rogers, Macpherson (*Works of Ossian*) and Hannah Cowley as well as the Bible. Her most successful work was the portrait of *Georgiana, Duchess of Devonshire as Cynthia* (1782; Duke of Devonshire and Chatsworth Settlement Trustees) based on Spenser's *Faerie Queene*. This dramatic, full-length portrait shows the Duchess flying through the night sky directly towards the viewer. One critic praised the "elegant compliment" paid to the sitter, noting the painting's originality and delicacy, and also asserted that Cosway was "the first of female painters" and among the male sex only inferior to her husband and Reynolds (*Morning Chronicle*, 9 May 1782). Other untraced paintings such as *Eolus Raising a Storm* (exh. Royal Academy 1782), *Samson* (exh.

Royal Academy 1784), *The Deluge* (exh. Royal Academy 1785) and *A Vision* (exh. Royal Academy 1786), stylistically influenced by Fuseli, were generally considered failures by the reviewers. It is notable that all four of these compositions are included in the caricature etching of Cosway entitled *Maria Costive at Her Studies* (1786; British Museum, London). More successful was the painting of *The Hours* (1783; untraced), which was engraved in stipple by Bartolozzi (1788; British Museum) for Thomas Macklin's *British Poets* series. An impression of the print was sent to Jacques-Louis David, who in a letter to Cosway praised both the composition and the artist very warmly.

David's influence can be seen in the arrangement of figures and prominent use of gesture in an unusual painting by Cosway of the *Death of Miss Gardiner* (1789; Musée de la Révolution Française, Vizille), although it also shows handling and lighting characteristic of Reynolds. One of the few signed and dated works by Cosway to survive, this is also one of the finest. The subject is typical of sentimental taste across Europe, and reflects the spiritual interests of Cosway, who, like her husband, was a follower of Swedenborgian doctrines. Miss Gardiner, who is shown dying while being supported by her aunt Lady Townshend, had a vision of her deceased mother, and expressed a desire to join her. In the painting Cosway gave particular emphasis to Miss Gardiner's raised arm. Philippe Bordes (*Revue du Louvre*, v–vi, December 1994, p.102, no.30) has plausibly described this painting as offering a specifically feminine vision of death, where emotional expressiveness contained within a private space may be contrasted with masculine stoic heroism set in public, which for instance Cosway would have seen in David's *Death of Socrates* (1787; Metropolitan Museum of Art, New York).

The following decade was one of disruption and great emotional turmoil for Cosway, and she exhibited only one painting at the Academy, in 1796. In that year the Cosways' only daughter Louisa died of a fever aged six. Cosway became increasingly religious and involved with girls' education, concerns that were eventually to dominate the rest of her life. Among the compositions that survive from this period, a number shows grieving or prostrate women, which suggests that these works may be revealing of her psychological state. The first and most important of these is the image of the dissolving water nymph *Lodona*, taken from Pope's poem *Windsor-Forest*, which was engraved in stipple by Bartolozzi (1792; British Museum) from an untraced oil painted for Macklin's *Poets Gallery*.

At the end of the decade Cosway painted for the Catholic Salvin family a huge altarpiece of the *Exultation of the Virgin Mary, or the Salvation of Mankind, Purchased by the Death of Jesus Christ* (1799; Croxdale Hall, Co. Durham), which was exhibited under that title at the Royal Academy in 1801. A smaller replica exists (c.1799; Fondazione Cosway, Lodi), and it was engraved in mezzotint by Green as the *Descent from the Cross* (1801; British Museum). The intensely emotional treatment of this subject – with its vivid colouring and broad handling – places particular emphasis on the Virgin, who is shown raising both her arms in triumph. This painting heralded a final surge of activity in Maria Cosway's career, which continued until her departure from Paris for Lyon in 1803. Seven paintings were exhibited at the Academy in 1800, with three more shown the following year. The most significant was perhaps the *Birth of the Thames* (c.1800; private collection, Ireland), which was engraved by P.W. Tomkins (1802; British Museum). In this highly unusual and original subject the River Thames is shown as a baby being raised above the bulrushes by a chorus of water nymphs and a swan.

This print was published by Ackermann and his influential print-selling business, *Repository of Arts*. Ackermann went on to publish many more of Cosway's projects, among which were a drawing book of her etchings after a selection of Richard Cosway's drawn sketches, entitled *Imitations in Chalk* (1800; Yale Center for British Art, New Haven); two series of moral illustrations known as the *Progress of Female Progress* and the *Progress of Female Dissipation* (1800; British Museum), which were engraved by A. Cardon; and the series of 12 pen and wash illustrations to Mary "Perdita" Robinson's pathetic autobiographical poem *The Winter Day* (c.1803; New York Public Library), which were etched in aquatint (1803; Courtauld Institute Galleries, London) by Caroline Watson (q.v.). The poem and the accompanying designs contrast "the evils of poverty and the ostentatious enjoyment of opulence". Ackermann in his introduction to the poem aptly described Cosway's style as demonstrated in these illustrations, and his criticism can be taken as referring to much of her other work:

Mrs Cosway's designs, it must be admitted, are sometimes eccentric, but it is the eccentricity of genius, and we have seen instances where she has snatched a grace beyond the reach of art. That extravagance carried to excess is an error, cannot be denied, but we prefer the artist who rather overcharges his figure, to him who touches the canvas with a timid feeble pencil, and leaves the imagination of the spectator to express what he cannot or dare not express. We prefer the extravagance of Michelangelo to the highest finishing of a dull Dutch artist. The horse that outstrips his competitors may be curbed; but the animal who is sluggish and incapabable of exertion cannot be spurred into speed.

Of all the artistic projects in which Cosway was involved around 1800, the most ambitious and demanding was that undertaken in Paris between 1801 and 1803. This was to copy and etch Dominique Vivant-Denon's display of the newly arrived old master paintings in the Musée Central or the Grand Gallery of the Louvre, with descriptive texts being provided by the entrepreneur Julius Griffiths. Eight folio-sized plates of the *Galerie du Louvre* (1802; British Museum) were published in Paris and made available to subscribers either monochrome or coloured. The original presentation volume of coloured etchings with the names of the French and British subscribers survives (1801–3; Fondazione Cosway). Despite signing the volume at the head of the Bonaparte family, Napoleon himself was disparaging about the quality of Cosway's copies, a judgement with which she herself concurred.

In her paintings Cosway wholeheartedly followed the impulse of her imagination, but her career as an artist was encouraged and affected by her husband. Richard Cosway portrayed his wife on many occasions, but in only one portrait drawing of her (*c*.1789; Fondazione Cosway) – shown with a bust of Leonardo da Vinci – did he represent her with palette and brushes. Moreover, he refused to allow her to sell her work, which, as she admitted in the letter of 1830, had a damaging effect on its quality: "had Mr C. permitted me to paint professionally, I should have made a better painter, but left to myself by degrees instead of improving, I lost what I had brought from Italy of my early studies." This honest statement is highly revealing of the problems that talented women artists encountered

in having their activities and production recognised with professional status. This fact should not, however, detract from further study of one of the most accomplished women artists working in Europe in the late 18th century and at the beginning of the 19th.

STEPHEN LLOYD

Cunningham, Imogen
American photographer, 1883–1976

Born in Portland, Oregon, 12 April 1883. Studied chemistry at University of Washington, Seattle, 1903–7. Worked in Seattle studio of photographer Edward S. Curtis, 1907–9. Won scholarship to study photographic chemistry at the Technische Hochshule, Dresden, 1909. Opened portrait studio on return to Seattle, 1910. Married Roi Partridge, February 1915; son born December 1915, twin sons born 1917; divorced 1934. Moved to San Francisco, 1917. Resumed commercial portrait business, 1921; occasionally carried out assignments for *Vanity Fair* magazine, 1931–6. Founder-member, with Edward Weston and Ansel Adams, of Group f/64, San Francisco, 1932–5; participated in *Group f/64* exhibition at M.H. de Young Memorial Museum, San Francisco, 1932. Also included in the exhibitions *Film und Foto*, Deutscher Werkbund, Stuttgart, 1929, and *Photography, 1839–1937*, Museum of Modern Art, New York, 1937. Taught photography at California School of Fine Arts, San Francisco, 1947–50; San Francisco Art Institute, 1965–7 and 1973. Founded Imogen Cunningham Trust, 1975. Recipient of honorary doctorates from California College of Arts and Crafts, Oakland, 1969, and Mills College, Oakland, 1975; Guggenheim fellowship, 1970; Artist of the Year award, San Francisco Art Commission, 1973; Summa Laude Dignatus award, University of Washington, Seattle, 1974. Fellow, American Academy of Arts and Sciences, 1967. Died in San Francisco, 23 June 1976.

Selected Individual Exhibitions
Brooklyn Institute of Arts and Sciences, NY: 1914
Portland Art Museum, Oregon: 1914
M.H. de Young Memorial Museum, San Francisco: 1931, 1970
Los Angeles County Museum of Art: 1932

Dallas Art Museum: 1935
San Francisco Museum of Art: 1951, 1964
Mills College Art Gallery, Oakland: 1953
Cincinnati Museum of Art: 1956
Oakland Art Museum: 1957, 1974
International Museum of Photography, George Eastman
House, Rochester, NY: 1961
Art Institute of Chicago: 1964
Henry Gallery, University of Washington, Seattle: 1965,
1974 (retrospective)
Stanford University Art Gallery, CA: 1967, 1976 (both
retrospectives)
Museum of History and Technology, Smithsonian
Institution, Washington, DC: 1968
California College of Arts and Crafts, Oakland: 1968
Atholl McBean Gallery, San Francisco Art Institute: 1971
Seattle Art Museum: 1971
Metropolitan Museum of Art, New York: 1973
San Francisco Art Commission "Capricorn Asunder"
Gallery: 1973 (*Artist of the Year*)

Selected Writings

"Photography as a profession for women", *Arrow*,
xxix/2, January 1913, pp.203–9

Bibliography

Flora Huntley Maschmedt, "Imogen Cunningham: An
appreciation", *Wilson's Photographic Magazine*, li,
March 1914, pp.96–9, 113–20
Minor White, "An experiment in 'reading' photographs",
Aperture, v, 1957, pp.66–71
Edna Tartaul Daniel, ed., *Imogen Cunningham: Portraits,
Ideas and Design*, Berkeley: University of California
Regional Cultural History Project, 1961
Minor White, ed., *Imogen Cunningham*, Rochester, NY:
Aperture, 1964
Margery Mann, "Imogen Cunningham", *Infinity*, xv,
November 1966, pp.25–8
Imogen Cunningham: Photographs, 1921–1967, exh.
cat., Stanford University Art Gallery, CA, 1967
Elizabeth Borden, "Imogen Cunningham", *US Camera
World Annual*, 1970, pp.60–65, 206
Margery Mann, ed., *Imogen Cunningham: Photographs*,
Seattle: University of Washington Press, 1970
[Bill Jay], "Imogen Cunningham", *Album*, no.5, June
1970, pp.22–38
Imogen! Imogen Cunningham Photographs, 1910–1973,
exh. cat., Henry Gallery, University of Washington,
Seattle, 1974
Imogen Cunningham: A Celebration, exh. cat., Stanford
University Art Gallery, 1976
Margaretta Mitchell, ed., *After Ninety*, Seattle: University
of Washington Press, 1977
Barnaby Conrad III, "An interview with Imogen
Cunningham", *Art in America*, lxv, May–June 1977,
pp.42–7
Thomas Joshua Cooper and Gerry Badger, "Imogen
Cunningham: A celebration", *British Journal of
Photography Annual*, 1978
Judy Dater, *Imogen Cunningham: A Portrait*, Boston:
New York Graphic Society, and London: Gordon
Fraser, 1979
*Reclaiming Paradise: American Women Photograph the
Land*, exh. cat., Tweed Museum of Art, University of
Minnesota, 1987
The Eclectic Spirit: Imogen Cunningham, 1883–1976,
exh. cat., Glasgow Museums and Art Galleries, 1990
Amy Rule, ed., *Imogen Cunningham: Selected Texts and
Bibliography*, Boston: Hall, and Oxford: Clio, 1992
Richard Lorenz, *Imogen Cunningham: Ideas Without
End: A Life in Photographs*, San Francisco: Chronicle,
1993

Unpublished correspondence and writings are in the
Imogen Cunningham Papers, Archives of American Art,
Smithsonian Institution, Washington, DC, and the
Imogen Cunningham Archives, Imogen Cunningham
Trust, Berkeley, CA (the latter also contains
Cunningham's original photographs and negatives).

Imogen Cunningham was one of the pre-eminent
forces in 20th-century photography. Throughout
her long career – she exhibited professionally from
1914 until her death in 1976 – she continued to
expand the boundaries of the medium both technically and aesthetically. Cunningham majored in
chemistry at the University of Washington in Seattle,
where she had lived from the age of six. After graduating, she worked in the portrait studio of Edward
S. Curtis, whose romanticised portrayals of Native
American life had won great renown. In 1909 she
travelled to Dresden to study photographic chemistry with Robert Luther at the Technische
Hochschule and did research on various printing
processes, the results of which she published the
following year. On her trip back to Seattle, she met
Alvin Langdon Coburn in London, and Alfred
Stieglitz and Gertrude Kasebier (q.v.) in New York,
photographers with whom she remained in professional contact for years. Other contemporaries with
whom she had significant artistic dialogue included
Roi Partridge (to whom she was married from 1915
to 1934), Dorothea Lange (q.v.), Beaumont
Newhall, Lisette Model, Edward Weston and Ansel
Adams.

One of Cunningham's first and most daring
contributions to the field of fine art photography
was her exploration of the nude male figure in the
landscape. *The Bather* (1915), a nude image of her
husband contemplating his reflection, Narcissus-

like, at the edge of a pond, created a local scandal. But, as her biographer Richard Lorenz asserted:

> Cunningham's intention to deliberately devise shock value in her art, her willingness to transgress the boundaries of bourgeois morality, indicates a courageous, adventurous talent just beginning to bloom as well as a determination to advance the critical acceptance of photography [Lorenz 1993, p.20].

Although she experimented with "pictorial" photography – the use of the medium to echo conservative academic painting conventions – in such early works as *Marsh, Early Morning (Marsh at Dawn)* (1905–6) and in the hazy focus of *The Bather*, Cunningham was soon drawn to "straight" photography. With Weston and Adams, among others, she founded the influential Group f/64, a name chosen to indicate their shared preference for realistic photography executed with small apertures to achieve detailed images. The *Magnolia Blossom* (1925), which draws the viewer into intimate, erotic encounter with the undulating, fleshy petals of a single white blossom, recalls both Weston's clarity of detail and the vital, luxuriant canvases of sensual flowers by Georgia O'Keeffe (q.v.). (It should be noted that Cunningham did not meet O'Keeffe until a trip to New York in the 1930s.)

In the 1930s Cunningham began to photograph celebrities. She started with Martha Graham, the innovative expressionist dancer and choreographer, who found Cunningham to be the first photographer with whom she could collaborate. Of the two portraits that appeared in *Vanity Fair* magazine in December 1931, *Martha Graham* 44 positions the dancer shadowing her lowered face with raised, bent arms, as brilliant light angles across her bare breasts. Later in the decade, the magazine commissioned Cunningham to photograph such Hollywood stars as James Cagney, Spencer Tracy and Cary Grant. The stark, precise realism of these images stands in marked contradistinction to the idealisation of most studio photographs.

In 1934 the University of California professor Paul Taylor invited Cunningham and Dorothea Lange to provide visual documentation for his research on migrant workers. The invitation led to what Cunningham called her "stolen pictures", images of the disenfranchised in American culture, such as the two troubled youths who loiter in a doorway in *Rebecca's Boys, Hume, Virginia* (1934)

and the *Watchers of the Evangel Meeting, San Francisco* (1936). At the same time, Cunningham began experimenting with double exposures and photomontage. Certainly this was influenced by Cubism and other avant-garde movements in Europe, as evidenced in the overlaid multiple views of the head in *Gertrude Stein, San Francisco 2* (1935).

Although rarely aligned with organised feminist groups, as early as 1913 Cunningham had published an article entitled "Photography as a profession for women" in which she wondered "Why women for so many years should have been supposed to be fitted only to the arts and industries of the home …". Referring to the early years of her marriage, when she brought up her young sons, Cunningham later said of herself:

> she had a skill with the camera, which she was not willing to sacrifice to maternity, so she turned her camera to use and photographed the things she had around her – her own children of course and plants that she cultivated. It is quite easy to do a bit of gardening work and yet attend children. It is not as easy to do good photographic work, but it can be done. She did both [interview with Edna Tartaul Daniel for the Regional Cultural History Project, University of California, Berkeley, June 1959].

Cunningham's letters during the break-up of her marriage indicate that she resented her husband's traditional gender expectations, and she chose to live independent of a male partner for the rest of her life. In her seventies, that is, in the 1950s, the artist joined the San Francisco Society of Women Artists and turned increasingly to women's subjects. As Lorenz noted of her *Pregnant Nude* (1959), which he described as "startling" in its objectivity: "Cunningham's choice of the pregnant nude as a subject – during a decade when the word was not even allowed to be spoken on television – was a refreshingly candid challenge to the societal taboos of the Eisenhower years" (Lorenz 1993, p.50).

Imogen Cunningham continued to create compelling photographs throughout the 1960s and 1970s. Her *Self-Portrait, Denmark* (1961) presents a dark reflection of the aged artist, her face partially obscured by two fashionable girdles displayed in a shop window. A canny commentary on how women's very identities are veiled by the constraints of culturally imposed ideals of beauty, the *Self-Portrait* demonstrates the pertinence of the text on the Chinese chop or seal with which the artist, later in life, described and labelled her oeuvre: "Ideas without End". (Prints of all cited works are in the collection of the Imogen Cunningham Trust, Berkeley, California.)

BETTY ANN BROWN

D

Damer, Anne Seymour

British amateur sculptor, 1748–1828

Born 1748, to Field Marshal Henry Seymour
Conway and Lady Caroline Ailesbury. During her
parents' sojourns abroad, lived under the care of
writer and patron Horace Walpole. Married the
Hon. John Damer, 1767; he committed suicide in
1776, leaving debts of some £7000. Subsequently
began serious study of sculpture, having a jointure
of £2500 a year and no children. Honorary
Exhibitor at the Royal Academy. Lived at
Strawberry Hill, Twickenham, as Walpole's residuary legatee, 1797–1811, also maintaining a town
house in London with studios at both sites.
Supported the Whig cause throughout her life,
canvassing in the Westminster election (1784) for
Charles James Fox. Produced Mary Berry's play
Fashionable Friends, 1801. Visited France with
Berry during the Peace of Amiens (1802) and
presented Napoleon with her bust of *Fox*. Lived at
York House, Twickenham, from 1811, continuing
to work in studio there despite failing health. Died
at London house in Upper Brook Street, 28 May
1828; buried in Sundridge, Kent, with her sculptor's tools and the ashes of her favourite dog.

Principal Exhibitions

Royal Academy, London: 1784–5, 1787–90, 1795,
    1799–1800, 1803–6, 1810, 1813–14, 1816, 1820
Leverean Museum, London: 1794 (statue of George III)

Selected Writings

Belmour, 1801 (novel)

Bibliography

Horace Walpole, *Anecdotes of Painting*, ed. James
    Dallaway, iv, London, 1827

Allan Cunningham, *The Lives of the Most Eminent
    British Painters, Sculptors and Architects*, iv, London:
    Murray, 1830
Mary Berry, *Extracts of the Journals and Correspondence
    of Miss Berry*, ed. Theresa Lewis, 3 vols, London:
    Longman, 1865; reprinted New York: AMS Press,
    1971
Percy Noble, *Anne Seymour Damer: A Woman of Art
    and Fashion, 1748–1828*, London: Kegan Paul Trench
    Trubner, 1908
Mary Berry, *The Berry Papers: Being the Correspondence
    Hitherto Unpublished of Mary and Agnes Berry,
    1763–1852*, ed. Lewis Melville, London: Lane, 1914
Rupert Gunnis, *Dictionary of British Sculptors,
    1660–1851*, 2nd edition, London: Abbey Library,
    1968
Susan Benforado, *Anne Seymour Damer (1748–1828),
    Sculptor*, PhD dissertation, University of New Mexico,
    Albuquerque, 1986
Margaret Whinney, *Sculpture in Britain, 1530–1830*,
    revised edition by John Physick, London and New
    York: Penguin, 1988

Anne Seymour Damer's output of sculpture was
immensely varied but always exemplified her
pursuit of the classical ideal. While her efforts to
pursue this art were lampooned in popular prints
and derided by contemporaries such as Joseph
Farington, she was, nevertheless, the only woman
sculptor to be included in Cunningham's *Lives of
the Most Eminent … British Sculptors …*, published
in 1830. Here she was placed alongside Banks,
Flaxman and others, and although the author criticised her work, hinting that it was often carved by
others and that it lacked "poetic feeling", he singled
out her achievement "as a woman" in this pantheon
of the British school. By her death in 1828 she was
established as the leading woman sculptor of her
day. While there were other women who had
successful professional careers as makers of sculpture in wax or artificial stone, Damer was recognised in Britain for her single-minded pursuit of the

"high" style. She was an Honorary Exhibitor at the Royal Academy exhibitions, where she showed 32 works; the title denoted her "amateur" status, appropriate to her class. There is little evidence that she sold her work for profit or pursued business interests as was the case with other contemporary professional sculptors. She was therefore not constrained by the demands of patrons or by the need to earn a living from her art.

Damer's contributions to the Royal Academy exhibitions included 20 ideal and idealised portrait busts. One of the earliest of these was her marble head of *Lady Melbourne* (1784; private collection), a skilful rendition that was praised by Erasmus Darwin in *The Economy of Vegetation* (1791). Several of her publicly exhibited works represented actors and actresses and included *Mrs Siddons as Melpomene* (before 1794; untraced), *Mrs Elizabeth Farren as Thalia* (c.1788; National Portrait Gallery, London) and *Master Betty* (exh. Royal Academy 1805; untraced). She also sculpted busts of *Admiral Nelson* (1798; several versions, earliest terracotta untraced) and *Joseph Banks* (British Museum, London), the former being taken from life during a stay in Naples. An ideal bust of *Isis* (exh. Royal Academy c.1789; Victoria and Albert Museum, London), which she executed in a severe "Greek" style and carved in Greek marble, is a prime example of her ability to respond to the demands of the true and correct style. An early example of her Neo-classicism is the *Self-Portrait* (1778; Uffizi, Florence) that she gave to the royal gallery in Florence and which was placed in the hall of Ancient and Modern Painters; the sole example of a sculpted self-portrait in this important collection. For Boydell's Shakespeare Gallery she made two terracotta reliefs (untraced) that placed her work in the company of leading British exponents of history painting. Engravings after these lost works show her assimilation of Neo-classicism in their representation of scenes from *Antony and Cleopatra* and *Coriolanus*.

There are few remaining examples of her public sculpture, apart from the statue of *George III* (1794; ht 2.43 m.) made for the Register House, Edinburgh. This severe, almost schematic representation of the monarch was alleviated by the introduction of a metal crown and sceptre. She was reputed to have modelled and cast in bronze a statue of *King Joseph I of Portugal* (1791) in Lisbon. A colossal statue of *Apollo* (c.1792; destroyed 1809),

executed for Drury Lane Theatre, London, is now known only through contemporary prints. Smaller-scale works included terracotta and marble versions of animal sculptures, for which she was over-praised by Walpole and for which she is now chiefly remembered. These are, however, misleading if understood to be representative of Damer's oeuvre as a whole, which is dominated by a more austere response to the classical ideal.

As the only child of an aristocratic family, Damer grew up in a privileged environment that was predominantly Whig. She was reputedly challenged to take up sculpture by her father's secretary, David Hume. Her education as a sculptor was the result of private tuition, notably from Giuseppe Ceracchi, who made a full-length statue of her as the *Muse of Sculpture* (c.1777; British Museum), and John Bacon RA. She also had anatomy lessons from Dr William Cumberland Cruikshank. Her support for Charles James Fox was well known and in 1802 she presented Napoleon with a plaster bust of the hero (untraced), which was followed by a marble version in 1812 (Louvre, Paris). She corresponded with the Empress Josephine, with whom she exchanged botanical specimens. She was friendly with Princess Caroline of Brunswick (who practised sculpture as an accomplishment art), executing a terracotta bust of her in 1814 (Ranger's House, London).

Horace Walpole, one of Damer's most enthusiastic supporters, encouraged her early interest in sculpture and was to make her his residuary executrix. Through Walpole she met Mary Berry with whom she developed a close and passionate friendship, recorded in letters and journals of the 1790s. It is not known that they had a physical relationship, but her reputed lesbianism had been made public in the 1770s by the publication of *A Sapphick Epistle from Jack Cavendish to the Honourable and Most Beautiful Mrs D.* (c.1770).

Damer was well-educated, speaking several languages and, like Mary Berry, was tutored in ancient Greek and Latin. In many ways the range of her intellectual and literary pursuits links her with the Bluestockings. These included: the publication of a novel, *Belmour*; her association with the writer Joanna Baillie as well as with Agnes and Mary Berry; and her friendship with Princess Daschkow, whose salon in Rome attracted several artists including Gavin Hamilton. Damer performed in amateur theatre, both at the Duke of Richmond's private theatre and that at Strawberry Hill,

Twickenham. She made many lengthy trips abroad, travelling in France, Portugal, Spain and Italy. During these she set up studios to continue working on her sculpture. In Naples, as a close friend of Sir William Hamilton, she was able to persuade Nelson to sit for his portrait in 1799, following his victory at the battle of the Nile. This became her best-known work – she presented the City of London with a version (Guildhall, London) following Nelson's death at Trafalgar in 1805 when she took the opportunity of offering to make the Guildhall monument to him at no charge. Thomas Hope, following its inclusion in the Royal Academy exhibition of 1804, praised Damer's achievement in the *Morning Post*. Here he described the bust as having "that very breadth of style ... discarding every incidental minutiae of feature". Casts of Damer's bust of *Nelson* were advertised in the newspapers in November 1805 and he was to be the subject of her last sculpture, a bronze bust (Royal Collection) for the Duke of Clarence, completed shortly before her death.

ALISON YARRINGTON

Dehner, Dorothy
American sculptor and printmaker,
1901–1994

Born in Cleveland, Ohio, 23 December 1901. Studied under Gilmor Brown at the Pasadena Playhouse, 1918–21; drama major at University of California, Los Angeles, 1921–2. Moved to New York, 1922, to study at the American Academy of Dramatic Arts and to pursue a career in theatre, 1922–4. Travelled alone to Europe, 1925, visiting Italy, Switzerland and France; saw the Paris World's Fair of 1925. Enrolled at the Art Students League, New York, September 1925, studying drawing under Kimon Nicolaides and painting under Kenneth Hayes Miller. Married artist David Smith, 1927; separated 1950; divorced 1952. Studied with Smith under Jan Matulka at the Art Students League, 1929–31. Lived in Bolton Landing, New York, 1940–50. Attended Skidmore College, Saratoga Springs, New York, 1951–2 (BA). Began making prints at Stanley William Hayter's Atelier 17, New York, 1952. First sculpture produced in 1955; first solo exhibition of

sculpture at Willard Gallery, New York, 1957; also exhibited in New Sculpture Group with Peter Agostini, Reuben Kadish, Philip Pavia, George Sugarman and others. Invited to become a member of the Federation of Modern Painters and Sculptors, and Sculptors Guild, 1957. Married New York publisher Ferdinand Mann, 1955; he died 1974. Recipient of Yaddo Foundation fellowship, 1970; visiting artist, Tamarind Lithography Workshop, 1971; honorary doctorate, Skidmore College, 1982; Women's Caucus for Art award for outstanding achievement in the visual arts, 1983; award of distinction, National Sculpture Conference: Works by Women, University of Cincinnati, 1987. Died in New York, 22 September 1994.

Selected Individual Exhibitions
Albany Institute of History and Art, NY: 1943 (with David Smith), 1952
Rose Fried Gallery, New York: 1952
Art Institute of Chicago: 1955
Willard Gallery, New York: 1957, 1959, 1960, 1963, 1966, 1970
Columbia University (Avery Hall), New York: 1961
Jewish Museum, New York: 1965 (retrospective)
Hyde Collection, Glens Falls, NY: 1967
City University of New York: 1970, 1991 (retrospective)
Jane Voorhees Zimmerli Art Museum, Rutgers University, New Brunswick: 1984 (with David Smith, touring)
Wichita Art Museum, KA: 1985
Muhlenberg College, Allentown, PA: 1988
Phillips Collection, Washington, DC: 1990
Katonah Museum of Art, NY: 1993–4 (touring retrospective)
Boulder Art Center, Boulder, CO: 1994
Cleveland Museum of Art: 1995 (retrospective)

Selected Writings
"Plexiglas relief for the Great Southwest Industrial Park, Atlanta, Georgia", *Leonardo*, ii, 1969, pp.171–3
"Introduction" in John P. Graham, *Systems and Dialectics of Art*, Baltimore: Johns Hopkins University Press, 1971
"Medals for dishonor: The fifteen medallions of David Smith", *Art Journal*, xxxvii, Winter 1977–8, pp.144–50

Bibliography
Joan Marter, "Dorothy Dehner", *Woman's Art Journal*, i/2, 1980–81, pp.47–50
Judd Tully, "Dorothy Dehner and her life on the farm with David Smith", *American Artist*, xlvii, October 1983, pp.58–61, 99–102

Dorothy Dehner and David Smith: Their Decades of Search and Fulfillment, exh. cat., Jane Voorhees Zimmerli Art Museum, Rutgers University, New Brunswick, and elsewhere, 1984

Charlotte Streifer Rubinstein, *American Women Sculptors*, Boston: Hall, 1990

Dorothy Dehner: Sixty Years of Art, exh. cat., Katonah Museum of Art, NY, and elsewhere, 1993

Between Transcendence and Brutality: American Sculptural Drawings from the 1940s and 1950s, exh. cat., Tampa Museum of Art, FL, 1994

Mara R. Witzling, ed., *Voicing Today's Visions: Writings by Contemporary Women Artists*, New York: Universe, 1994

Dorothy Dehner Papers are in the Archives of American Art, Smithsonian Institution, Washington, DC.

Dorothy Dehner is recognised as one of the few women artists to be associated with the Abstract Expressionist generation. She created innovative abstract drawings and prints, and used wax to form sculptures at a time when most of the male artists were creating direct metal constructions.

From the beginning of her career, Dehner intended to be a sculptor but, as she acknowledged, it was impossible to make sculpture during her marriage to David Smith. In 1931 Dehner and Smith travelled to the Virgin Islands where they both made still-life paintings. Dehner's paintings were accomplished abstractions, still indebted to Synthetic Cubism, but with organic forms predominating – particularly shells and marine life. A trip to Europe in 1935 was to have a lasting impact on her art. She and Smith went to Paris, Brussels, Greece, and later the Soviet Union and Britain. They spent six months in Greece, where Dehner made sketches in black and white. By the late 1930s she had abandoned abstraction for a representational approach, a miniaturist style based on her interest in illuminations in medieval manuscripts. While many of her works of these years were lost, the *Life on the Farm* series survives (Storm King Art Center, Mountainville, NY). These tempera paintings depict Dehner's life at Bolton Landing, including scenes of the daily chores on a farm she and Smith had purchased near Lake George, New York.

Dehner and Smith were closely involved in their creative activities during the 1940s. She gave titles to his sculpture, posed for some of his works and participated in the progress of his welded metal constructions. Both Dehner and Smith were inspired by the same images: the skeleton of a prehistoric bird from the American Museum of Natural History was the basis for Dehner's drawing *Bird of Peace* (1946), Smith's *Royal Bird*, *Jurassic Bird* and several other examples. For both artists the prehistoric creature assumed the appearance of a menacing predator, indicative of their political views in the post-war years. But for Dehner, *Country Living (Bird of Peace)* (1946; Snite Memorial Art Gallery, University of Notre Dame) held personal associations: the spectral presence of the skeletal creature and the barren, jagged peaks below it alluded to the anguish of her private life. The series of dramatic works on paper made in the 1940s are among the most provocative drawings of Dehner's career. The *Damnation Series* (artist's estate) consists of skilfully rendered pen and ink studies of nude figures, accompanied by vultures, bats and other animals. *Suite Moderne* (artist's estate) includes ghoulish figures dancing gigues, fandangos and gavottes, all of which become "dances of Death". Such images relate to post-war tensions, but have more to do with Dehner's state of mind in these final years of her marriage to Smith.

Dehner exhibited her work only a few times in the 1940s. She was in a number of group exhibitions in these years, and in 1946 the Audubon Artists awarded her a first prize for drawing. In this period she found a copy of Ernst Haeckel's seminal study of natural forms, *Kunstformen der Natur* (1904), and embarked on a series of drawings of microscopic organisms. She gained confidence in this new direction for her art, and created many successful abstractions in gouache and ink. In these works on paper Dehner introduced a repertory of biomorphic forms that related to Paul Klee, Joan Miró and Mark Rothko, among others. Unlike the Surrealists, Dehner did not emphasise the disquieting aspects of her imagery, but celebrated the animate energy of these unicellular forms of life. An innovative approach to watercolour can be found in drawings of this period: working wet on wet, the artist allowed for spontaneity and a full range of visual effects by applying water to the paper surface before brushing on colour, and then allowing liquid elements to blend in rich and lively variations.

In 1950 Dehner left Bolton Landing, and she was divorced from Smith two years later. She came to New York, where she taught at various schools, including the Barnard School for Girls, studied engraving at Stanley William Hayter's Atelier 17 and began experimenting in wax, with the intention of making three-dimensional works. Dehner's imagery was derived from her earlier abstract drawings and paintings, even going back to the organic abstractions of the 1930s. Sculpture dominated Dehner's production from 1955 until her death. Her work always emphasised contour rather than mass: she assembled sculptures of disparate parts and approached the use of wax as a constructivist using planar elements. Textural effects were explored: in *Low Landscape Sideways* (1962; Hyde Collection, New York), for example, she braised and drew on the wax slabs, introducing other textures by adding small pieces of metal. To create a lively visual effect, she used faceted elements to form planes that shimmer when reflecting light.

While Dehner's sculptures are abstract, they consistently make reference to the natural world. Vertical compositions evoke a totemic presence, while the horizontal format can be viewed as a landscape. *Encounter* (1969), a work consisting of six separate sculptures, alludes to a chance meeting of people both in composition and in concept. The disparate totemic forms relate to one another, as individuals of varying sizes and proportions. This work and others suggest human gestures or evoke journeys through time. Her abstract sculptures represent a personal iconography that recurs over the decades. Imagery of circles, moons, ellipses, wedges and arcs abound. Like other artists of the New York School, Dehner acknowledges in her art that abstract symbols can communicate content that is private, but with universal implications.

By 1970 both the scale and monumentality of Dehner's sculpture had increased. She evoked architectural forms, and some of the totems became human-scale. In 1974 she changed her medium from cast metal to wood, and made constructed pieces using small wooden elements. While the bronzes have textured surfaces, the wooden constructions rely solely on variations of the graining to create lively surfaces. These wooden constructions have a strong association with architecture, and works that Dehner referred to as "toy-like" can also be considered to include fragments of memory and time. *Gateway* (1979; Metropolitan Museum of Art, New York) includes various woods with different grainings and tonalities. The architectonic structures of her wooden ensembles, with thrusting verticals or stacked elements, resemble the skyline of a fanciful city.

In the early 1980s Dehner began a new series of works of heroic proportions in corten steel. These powerful sculptures were fabricated, and were based on earlier works from the 1960s and 1970s that were originally cast in bronze from wax models. *Demeter's Harrow* (1990; artist's estate) attests to Dehner's long-standing involvement with imagery rich with personal associations. In the corten steel construction, polygonal and circular forms extend outwards in a sculptural composition that suggests a dynamic interplay of space and mass. Dehner's years at Bolton Landing must have offered many opportunities to see fields broken up and levelled by spike-tooth harrows or harrows with sharp-edged discs. With this sculpture she alludes to a farm implement, but also to the Goddess of the Corn, who made the fields rich with fruits, flowers and leaves, and instructed man about the sowing of corn. Demeter was also the sorrowing mother of Persephone, maiden of the spring and summer, who died every year and returned to the underworld. Demeter was therefore associated with the earth's fecundity, but was also a goddess who mourned for her beloved child. Thus, the mythological reference seems fitting for Dehner herself, who had known mourning from her earliest years, and worked as an artist to sustain herself in times of personal anguish. Her sculptures are like silent witnesses, enduring testimony to a life dedicated to art and to the pursuit of a visual equivalent to life's journeys.

JOAN M. MARTER

Delaunay, Sonia (Ilinichna)
Russian painter and designer, 1885–1979

Born Sarah Stern in Gradiesk, Ukraine, 14 November 1885; called Sonia. Moved to St Petersburg to live with her maternal uncle, 1890; adopted his surname Terk. Studied under Ludwig Schmid-Reutter in Karlsruhe, 1903–5. Made her first trip to Paris, 1905; studied at La Palette; met the artists Amédée Ozenfant and Segonzac. Marriage of convenience to German critic and collector Wilhelm Uhde, 1908; divorced 1910. Married French painter Robert Delaunay, 1910; one son, born 1911; husband died 1941. Established studio with Robert on the rue des Grands-Augustins, Paris, working there until 1935. Close friendships with the poets Blaise Cendrars and Guillaume Apollinaire, c.1912–13. Moved to

Madrid at the outbreak of World War I; stayed in Portugal, 1915–16; met Sergei Diaghilev in Madrid, 1917; designed costumes for Diaghilev's production of *Cleopatra* in London, 1918. Back in Paris, 1920; made contact with members of the Dada group and future Surrealist movement. Opened fashion atelier with Jacques Heim, 1924. Concentrated on textile design, 1920s. Member of Abstraction-Création group, 1932. Helped to organise first exhibition of the Réalités Nouvelles group at Galerie Charpentier, Paris, 1939. Moved to Grasse, Provence, after Robert's death, 1941; lived near Jean Arp and Sophie Taeuber-Arp (q.v.); returned to Paris, 1945. Founder-member of Groupe Espace, 1953. Donated works to Musée National d'Art Moderne, Paris, 1963; Musée de l'Impression sur Etoffes, Mulhouse, 1971; Centre Georges Pompidou, Paris, 1976; Bibliothèque Nationale, Paris, 1977. Recipient of Grand Prix de l'Art Féminin, Salon International de la Femme, Cannes, 1969; Grand Prix, Ville de Paris, 1973. Chevalier des Arts et Lettres, 1958; Officier, Légion d'Honneur, 1975. Died in Paris, 5 December 1979.

Principal Exhibitions

Individual

Galerie Notre-Dame-des-Champs, Paris: 1908
Nya Konstgalleriet, Stockholm: 1916 (with Robert Delaunay)
Galerie Fermé la Nuit, Paris: 1929
Galerie des Deux Iles, Paris: 1948 (with Sophie Taeuber-Arp, Jean Arp and Alberto Magnelli)
Galerie Bing, Paris: 1953, 1954 (with Sophie Taeuber-Arp and Alberto Magnelli), 1957 (with Robert Delaunay)
Rose Fried Gallery, New York: 1955
Kunsthaus, Bielefeld: 1958
Musée des Beaux-Arts, Lyon: 1959 (with Robert Delaunay)
Galerie Denise René, Paris: 1962
Musée du Louvre, Paris: 1964 (*Donation Robert et Sonia Delaunay*)
Galerie Minima, Paris: 1964
National Gallery of Canada, Ottawa: 1965 (with Robert Delaunay)
Musée National d'Art Moderne, Paris: 1967 (retrospective), 1975 (*Hommage à Sonia Delaunay*)
La Demeure, Paris: 1970
Fundaçao Calouste Gulbenkian, Lisbon: 1972 (with Robert Delaunay and friends)
Musée d'Art Moderne de la Ville de Paris: 1972 (retrospective)
Galerie Gmurzynska, Cologne: 1975

Bibliothèque Nationale, Paris: 1977 (with Robert Delaunay)

Group

Galerie Der Sturm, Berlin: 1913 (*Erster deutscher Herbstsalon*), 1920
Salon des Indépendants, Paris: 1914, 1922
Salon d'Automne, Paris: 1925, 1939
Exposition Internationale des Arts Décoratifs et Industriels Modernes, Paris: 1925 (with Jacques Heim)
Société des Artistes Indépendants, Grand Palais, Paris: 1926 (*Trente ans d'art indépendant, 1884–1914*)
Union des Artistes Modernes, Musée des Arts Décoratifs, Paris: 1930
Abstraction-Création, Paris: 1932
Exposition Internationale, Paris: 1937 (gold medal, with Robert Delaunay)
Salon des Réalités Nouvelles, Paris: from 1939
Galerie René Drouin, Paris: 1945 (*Art concret*)
Galerie Denise René, Paris: 1947 (*Tendances de l'art abstrait*)
Galerie Maeght, Paris: 1949 (*Premiers maîtres de l'art abstrait*)
Musée National d'Art Moderne, Paris, 1953 (*Cubisme, 1907–1919*)

Selected Writings

"Tissus et tapis", *L'Art International d'Aujourd'hui*, no.15, Paris: Moreau, 1929
Compositions, couleurs, idées, Paris: Moreau, 1930
"Les artistes et l'avenir de la mode", *Revue de Jacques Heim*, no.3, September 1932
"Collages de Sonia et Robert Delaunay", *XXe Siècle*, no.6, January 1956, pp.19–21
The New Art of Color: Writings of Robert and Sonia Delaunay, ed. Arthur A. Cohen and others, New York: Viking, 1978
Nous irons jusqu'au soleil, Paris: Laffont, 1980 (memoirs)

Bibliography

André Lhôte and others, *Sonia Delaunay, ses objets, ses tissus simultanés, ses modes*, Paris: Librairies des Arts Décoratifs, 1925
Jacques Damase, *Sonia Delaunay: Rhythms and Colors*, Greenwich, CT: New York Graphic Society, and London: Thames and Hudson, 1972 (French original, 1971)
Arthur A. Cohen, *Sonia Delaunay*, New York: Abrams, 1975
Sonia Delaunay, exh. cat., Galerie Gmurzynska, Cologne, 1975
Cindy Nemser, *Art Talk: Conversations with 12 Women Artists*, New York: Scribner, 1975
Sonia et Robert Delaunay, exh. cat., Bibliothèque Nationale, Paris, 1977

Künstlerinnen der Russischen Avantgarde/Russian Women Artists of the Avant-Garde, 1910–1930, exh. cat., Galerie Gmurzynska, Cologne, 1979

Joan M. Marter, "Three women artists married to early modernists: Sonia Delaunay-Terk, Sophie Taüber-Arp and Marguerite Thompson Zorach", *Arts Magazine*, liv, September 1979, pp.88–95

Sonia Delaunay: A Retrospective, exh. cat., Albright-Knox Art Gallery, Buffalo, NY, and elsewhere, 1980

Bernard Dorival, *Sonia Delaunay: Sa vie, son oeuvre, 1885–1979*, Paris: Damase, 1980

J.C. Marcadé, ed., "La correspondance d'A.A. Smirnov avec S.I. Terk (Sonia Delaunay), 16 Septembre 1904–8 Avril 1905", *Cahiers du Monde Russe et Soviétique*, July–September 1983, pp.289–327

Isabelle Anscombe, *A Woman's Touch: Women in Design from 1860 to the Present Day*, London: Virago, and New York: Viking, 1984

Annette Malochet, *Atelier Simultané de Sonia Delaunay, 1923–1934*, Milan: Fabbri, 1984

Delaunay (Sonia et Robert), exh. cat., Musée d'Art Moderne de la Ville de Paris, 1985

Peter-Klaus Schuster, *Delaunay und Deutschland*, Cologne: DuMont, 1985

Sonia Delaunay, exh. cat., La Boetie, New York, and elsewhere, 1986

Elizabeth Morano, ed., *Sonia Delaunay: Art into Fashion*, New York: Braziller, 1986

Axel Madsen, *Sonia Delaunay: Artist of the Lost Generation*, New York: McGraw-Hill, 1989

Jacques Damase, *Sonia Delaunay: Fashion and Fabrics*, London: Thames and Hudson, and New York: Abrams, 1991 (French original)

Sonia & Robert Delaunay: Künstlerpaare-Künstlerfreunde/Dialogues d'artistes-résonances, exh. cat., Kunstmuseum, Bern, 1991

Whitney Chadwick, "Living simultaneously: Sonia and Robert Delaunay", *Significant Others: Creativity and Intimate Partnership*, ed. Whitney Chadwick and Isabelle de Courtivron, New York and London: Thames and Hudson, 1993, pp.30–49

Stanley Baron and Jacques Damase, *Sonia Delaunay: The Life of an Artist*, New York, Abrams, and London: Thames and Hudson, 1995

Gill Perry, *Women Artists and the Parisian Avant-Garde*, Manchester: Manchester University Press, and New York: St Martin's Press, 1995

Sonia Delaunay should be remembered in equal measure as a studio artist and as a designer. Throughout her long career, she worked with many media – easel painting, needlework, scenography, industrial design; and, in fact, she came to her mature style of painting around 1910 after concentrating on embroidery (she had earlier painted in a Fauvist manner under the influence of van Gogh and Gauguin). Delaunay's peculiar collocations of bold colours and her repetition of motifs and figures in rhythmic cycles often bring to mind the craft of quilts and plaids – an association that Delaunay herself emphasised and cultivated. Even her confrontations with the written and published word – that is, her visual perception of language – constitute a patchwork of genius. Delaunay's designs for Guillaume Apollinaire's poem *Zone* (1913) and Blaise Cendrars's *La Prose du Transsibérien et de la petite Jehanne de France* (1913), for example, cannot be classified as mere "illustrations", for they are an organic part of the literary whole and continue a synthetic tradition reinforced by the French and Russian Symbolists, in particular. But at the same time, with their borders and sectioning, they also bring to mind the traditional crochet and embroidery of her homeland, the Ukraine.

Delaunay elaborated her Simultanist concept of painting through a variety of engagements: the decorative arts, Fauvism, Cubism, Futurism, the topical fascination with electric illumination, and intense discussions with fellow artists and critics in Paris such as Apollinaire, Cendrars, Marc Chagall and, of course, her husband Robert. Consequently, inspired by many concepts and conditions, Delaunay's paintings sometimes elicit associations with concurrent works by other artists. Her decorative arrangements for the *Bal Bullier* of 1912–13, for example, remind us of Gino Severini's *Bal Tabarin* (1912; Museum of Modern Art, New York), while her compositions of the 1930s such as *Composition No.38* (1938; gouache on paper; 105 × 74.5 cm.; ex-artist's collection) bring to mind certain abstract works of Giacomo Balla and Lyubov Popova (q.v.). Delaunay, however, developed her own special vision, and her exercises in luminosity and refractivity remain unmatched in their vigorous and radical resolutions of colour and movement.

The painting *Electric Prisms* (1914; Centre Georges Pompidou, Paris), shown at the Salon des Indépendants in 1914, is a case in point. Not only did it confirm that Delaunay "liked electricity. Public lighting was a novelty. At night, during our walk, we entered the era of light, arm-in-arm" (*Nous irons jusqu'au soleil* 1980, p.43). But in some sense also, *Electric Prisms* can be regarded as a visual manifesto of intent, for the interpenetrating planes of colour, the evocation of solar and planetary bodies, and the juxtaposition of solidity, translucency and dissolution, are elements identifiable with much of Delaunay's work and with her fundamental conception of rhythm. They recur in other master paintings such as the *Rhythm in Colour* series of the 1960s and provide the driving force behind so much of her design work – for fabrics and textiles, for the stage (e.g. the *Quatre Saisons* ballet of 1928–9) and for interiors (e.g. the projects for the Air Pavilion, Paris, 1936). As she asserted: "Rhythm is based on numbers because colour can be measured by its vibrations. This was a completely new concept that opened infinite horizons for painting and could be used by anyone who felt and understood" (*The New Art of Colour* 1978, p.197).

Although Delaunay left Russia for Paris as a very young woman and never returned there, she – and her husband Robert – maintained close communication with Russian artists, choreographers, impresarios and designers, especially during the 1910s and 1920s. Indeed, a number of Delaunay's experimental undertakings done in Paris found immediate parallels among the avant-garde communities in Moscow and St Petersburg. For example, as early as 1904–5 she was exchanging ideas on sound and colour with the literary historian and musicologist Alexander Smirnov and her Simultanist colour accompaniments to Cendrars's *La Prose du Transsibérien et de la petite Jehanne de France* were held in high regard by both the French and the Russian Cubists. Even her bold fabric designs of the 1920s are curiously similar to those of the Constructivists Popova and Varvara Stepanova (q.v.) done in Moscow – something that became clear from the parallel exhibits at the Paris Exposition of 1925. The connections between the Delaunays in Paris with their theory of Simultanism and the colour theories of Aristarkh Lentulov and Georgy Yakulov in Moscow are also striking, even though the latter maintained that Simultanism was his invention (Lassaigne in Cologne 1979, p.79). In any case, what critics called Orphism in the context of Robert Delaunay's paintings of 1912 and what Sonia then absorbed into her theory of Simultanism is applicable to the work of many artists of the time: "Light in Nature creates color movement. Movement is provided by relationships of uneven measures, of color contrasts among themselves that make up Reality. This reality ... becomes rhythmic simultaneity" (Robert Delaunay, "Uber das Licht" (1913), quoted in Roger Lipsey, *An Art of Our*

Own: The Spiritual in Twentieth-Century Art, Boston: Shambala, 1988, p.97).

Primarily, Sonia Delaunay is now remembered for her clothes and textile designs, although she was also active as a stage designer, especially just before and after 1920. In 1918 she designed the costumes for Sergei Diaghilev's production of *Cleopatra* in London; in 1919 she designed the inaugural revue for the Petit Casino in Madrid; and in 1923 she designed the *Soirée du Coeur à Barbe* directed by Ilya Zdanevich (Ilyadze) and Serge Romoff for the Cherez group in Paris. In this way, Delaunay established a fruitful relationship with the Paris Dada circle, leading, for example, to her fanciful costumes for Tristan Tzara's *Le Coeur à Gaz* in 1924. In these spectacles, Delaunay applied her notion of Simultanism, which one critic has defined succinctly as "based on colour relations that can be observed in their action on one another ... contrasts are completed by harmonies based on dissonances" (Lassaigne in Cologne 1979, p.79). In her fabric designs for *Cleopatra* Delaunay demonstrated her radical position *vis-à-vis* the more conventional patterns in cloth design of her time. Here she substituted traditional ornamentation with geometric motifs and erotic imagery, and her bright, contrasting colour combinations, coupled with graduated tints and harmonies, anticipated a central direction of future fashion. Cyril Beaumont, who attended the production at the Coliseum, recalled:

> There was also a new costume for Cleopatra, designed by Sophie [sic] Delaunay; it was another vivid conception in yellow, red and gold not improved by a segment of mirrorglass affixed to the girdle, which winked like a heliograph every time it caught the light ... [Cyril Beaumont, *The Diaghilev Ballet in London*, London: Maclehose, 1940, pp.109–10].

Like Alexandra Exter (q.v.), Delaunay transferred some of her lessons from stage design directly to fashion design. In this discipline she worked on several levels – providing total, "simultaneous" ensembles (from purse to gown to automobile) for the wealthy Parisienne as well as simple *tissupatrons* or cut-out patterns that the working woman could use. While applying Simultanist devices to her dress creations, as evidenced by her concentration on colour rhythm and rotational pattern, Delaunay concerned herself with "liberating" the female body and she was an enthusiast of the "sack". In the words of André Lhôte (1925), she covered the "sweet undulations of the human body with geometric architectures". With her unabating artistic curiosity and *joie de vivre*, Delaunay continued to elaborate these initial ideas throughout her long and active career. With her bold colour resolutions and emphasis on dynamic interplay of forms, she anticipated – and contributed to – the Op Art and Kinetic movements of the 1960s.

JOHN E. BOWLT

De Morgan, Evelyn

British painter, 1855–1919

Born Mary Evelyn Pickering, 1855; father Percival Pickering QC. Studied at the Slade School of Fine Art, London, under Edward Poynter, 1873–5 (Slade scholarship); studied in Italy, 1875–7. Subsequently established own studio in London. Often visited her uncle, the painter John Roddam Spencer-Stanhope, in Tuscany. Married William Frend De Morgan, art potter and later novelist, 1887; settled in Chelsea, London. Spent winters in Florence on account of husband's health, 1893–1914. Pottery business closed down, 1905. Completed two of husband's novels left unfinished at his death (1917). Died in London, 2 May 1919.

Principal Exhibitions

Grosvenor Gallery, London: 1877–88
Liverpool Autumn Exhibitions: 1884, 1888, 1890–93, 1897–1905, 1908
New Gallery, London: 1888–92, 1900–01, 1908–9
Bruton Galleries, London: 1906 (individual)
Red Cross Benefit, London: 1916 (individual)

Bibliography

The De Morgan Collection of Pictures and Pottery to which are Added a Few Pictures by Roddam Spencer-Stanhope and other Pre-Raphaelite Artists, London: Ryling, n.d.
Walter Shaw Sparrow, "The art of Mrs William De Morgan", *The Studio*, xix, 1900, pp.220–32
Isabel McAllister, "In memoriam: Evelyn de Morgan", *The Studio*, lxxix, 1920, pp.28–33
A.M.W. Stirling, *William De Morgan and His Wife*, London: Thornton Butterworth, and New York: Holt, 1922
Theodore Crombie, "Paintings from the De Morgan Foundation at Cragside", *National Trust Studies*, 1981, pp.17–26
The De Morgan Foundation at Old Battersea House: Paintings and Drawings by Evelyn De Morgan, Roddam Spencer-Stanhope and William De Morgan, Ceramics by William De Morgan, London: Wandsworth Borough Council, 1983
Pamela Gerrish Nunn, *Victorian Women Artists*, London: Women's Press, 1987
Jane Sellars, *Women's Works: Paintings, Drawings, Prints and Sculpture by Women*, Liverpool: National Museums and Galleries on Merseyside, 1988
Jan Marsh and Pamela Gerrish Nunn, *Women Artists and the Pre-Raphaelite Movement*, London: Virago, 1989
The Last Romantics: The Romantic Tradition in British Art: Burne-Jones to Stanley Spencer, exh. cat., Barbican Art Gallery, London, 1989
Deborah Cherry, *Painting Women: Victorian Women Artists*, London and New York: Routledge, 1993
A Struggle for Fame: Victorian Women Artists and Authors, exh. cat., Yale Center for British Art, New Haven, 1994
Catherine Gordon, ed., *Evelyn De Morgan: Oil Paintings*, London: De Morgan Foundation, 1996

Evelyn De Morgan created a strange and beautiful world in her paintings. A brilliantly coloured land peopled by sinewy female figures, often entwined, forming convoluted human friezes, with their bodies shrouded in a swirling arabesque of drapery. The serpentine whorls, the fearful, wistful, sometimes expressionless faces, interpreted her recurrent themes of depression, struggle, darkness and light, regret, yearning, sleeping and dreaming, all derived from literary and mythological subjects. The settings of her pictures describe an enclosed world with a strangely airless quality, often incorporating the drama of the sea, the mountains, vivid sunrise and the impenetrable night sky.

Her compositions are frequently bisected, as if to denote one dreamworld and the next. The scale of her work is large and ambitious; her palette has a Pre-Raphaelite brilliance and her sharply linear draughtsmanship shows a striking debt to Burne-Jones – her painting *Aurora Triumphans* (1886; 116 × 172 cm.; Russell-Cotes Art Gallery, Bournemouth) was for 20 years misattributed to Burne-Jones because of a forged monogram signature – but the greatest influence on her was Italian art, especially that of Botticelli. De Morgan was one of the first generation of women to study at the Slade School of Fine Art, with Mary Huxley, Mary Kingsley, Dorothy Tennant and Mary Stuart Wortley. She was a distinguished pupil, in her first year winning the prize for painting from the antique, and in her second the prize for painting from life and one of the first Slade scholarships to be awarded. She was also taught by her uncle John Roddam Spencer-Stanhope, with whom she spent much productive and inspirational time at his villa near Florence. In 1883 De Morgan was nominated by Charlotte Weeks in her article "The Slade girls" for the *Magazine of Art* (p.329) as having obtained a position of standing among the artists of the day.

All the accounts of De Morgan's life and work mention her tremendous industry, her passion for painting and her joy in her art. Her friend May Morris, for example, wrote:

> Her pictures have an epic quality and are spacious in conception, while [in her later work] showing an almost exaggerated insistence on decorative detail. They are remarkable for the beauty of drapery design, for vigorous and delicate drawing and for sumptuous colour, for great enjoyment of textures. She had astonishing physical endurance and Power of work [quoted in *The De Morgan Foundation ... 1983*].

Yet the pictures themselves seem to speak more of a woman imprisoned.

The artist's long and happy partnership with her husband, the potter William De Morgan, gave her work pragmatic purpose: the income from the sales of her pictures was essential to prop up her husband's uncertain business. She never exhibited at the Royal Academy, but instead at the more avant-garde Grosvenor and New galleries, and in the big provincial shows in Manchester and Liverpool. Some work was sold through the Fine Art Society and on commission. She developed an aversion to showing her work, setting each canvas aside as soon as she had finished it and immediately beginning to paint another.

De Morgan's biographer, her sister Wilhelmina Stirling, gives a full account of the artist's struggles to gain an education and work as a painter (Stirling 1922). De Morgan kept a journal when she was 16, in which she wrote obsessively about her feeling that a moment not spent painting was a part of her life wasted. She bitterly resented the tedious demands made on her time by the petty routines and enforced idleness of daily life. A Sunday entry reads: "Got up late; dawdled over dressing, went to Church; in the afternoon walked. Dawdled, dawdled, dawdled through a great deal of precious time". On her 17th birthday she wrote: "Art is eternal, but life is short, and each minute idly spent will rise, swelled to whole months and years, and hound me in my grave."

De Morgan found her subjects in literary sources, from Classical mythology, the Bible, medieval and contemporary poetry, in verse by Shelley and Tennyson, from Hans Christian Andersen's fairy-tales. She painted for an audience that almost ceased to exist with the end of the Victorian age, one who knew well the stories of Hero and Leander, Cadmus and Harmonia, Boreas and Orithyia, Cassandra and Helen of Troy, and who recognised every biblical reference or a quote from Tennyson's poetry. The 20th-century viewers' bafflement at these unfamiliar themes makes De Morgan's painted world seem yet more remote today: we do not know the stories, and the morals of the tales elude us. To the modern viewer, the subtext of the late Victorian woman artist struggling with her ambition and her dreams is the subject that leaps to the eye.

The largest collection of De Morgan's paintings and drawings belongs to the De Morgan Foundation, established in the early 1930s at Old Battersea House, London, by Wilhelmina Stirling. Substantial parts of the picture collection are on display there and also in appropriate late-Victorian settings at Cardiff Castle and Knightshayes Court, Devon, both houses designed by William Burges, and at Cragside, Northumbria, the house designed for Lord Armstrong by Norman Shaw. This group of works spans De Morgan's lifetime, from the first picture she exhibited, *Ariadne on Naxos*, at the Grosvenor Gallery in 1877, to her war painting *The Red Cross*. An overview of them reveals that De Morgan's compositional range was not great: the single female figure draped horizontally across the picture plane (*Port after Stormy Seas*, 1905), or standing like a sculpture in a vertical niche (*The Dryad*, 1884; *Helen of Troy*, 1898); a frieze-like procession of many figures, linked by gestures of hand and arm (*Grey Sisters*, 1880–81; *St Christina Giving Her Father's Jewels to the Poor*, 1904) and, at her most ambitious, a maelstrom of floating, crouching women (*The Kingdom of Heaven Suffereth Violence, The Captives, Daughters of the Mist*).

All the energy in De Morgan's pictures is

contained in the individual poses of her figures that, despite the ever-linking hands and arms, seem curiously separate from each other. For this reason, De Morgan's most successful works are those of her single female subjects, such as *Medea* (1889; 150 × 89 cm.; Williamson Art Gallery and Museum, Birkenhead), in which the fearsome murderous character of Greek mythology is depicted as a more benign sorceress, standing reed-like within the marbled corridor of a Renaissance palace, and *Flora* (1894; De Morgan Foundation), probably her masterpiece, painted in Florence as a homage to Botticelli's *Primavera* (Uffizi, Florence) and commissioned originally by an enthusiastic patron, the Liverpool shipowner, William Imrie. De Morgan is least successful, but wonderfully ambitious in scale, in such pictures as *Life and Thought Have Gone Away* (1893; 165 × 293 cm.), one of the earliest pictures by a woman artist to be bought by the Walker Art Gallery in Liverpool (1901). The vast canvas depicting lines from Tennyson's poem "The Deserted House" seems to consist, typically, of two unrelated picture planes – the symbolic figures of a knight and his lady in front of a tomb on the left, and the flurry of highly coloured angels on the right, intact in their own Pre-Raphaelite landscape.

De Morgan lived to see the beginnings of modern art and was bewildered by it. On seeing an exhibition of Cubist and Futurist art she commented: "… if that is what people like now, I shall wait for the turn of the tide". By the time of her death in 1919, her elaborate Symbolist pictures (e.g. *The Red Cross*, *Scrap of Paper* and *Coming of Peace*) already seemed to belong to another age. During World War I De Morgan frightened visitors to her studio with the notes of tragedy and evil to be found in her pictures, in which she symbolised the conflict. She willed these works to be auctioned with the rest of her studio contents after her death (the sale never took place) to raise funds for soldiers blinded in action – a fate that to the artist Evelyn De Morgan seemed worse than death.

JANE SELLARS

do Amaral, Tarsila *see* Amaral

Duparc, Françoise   [fig. 20]
French painter, 1726–1778

Baptised in Murcie, Spain, 15 October 1726; daughter of Antoine Duparc, a sculptor from Marseille, and his Spanish wife, Gabrielle Negrela. Moved to Marseille with her family, 1730. Said to have studied under Jean Baptiste van Loo, who was living in nearby Aix-en-Provence in 1735–6 and 1742–5. Moved to Paris with a younger sister, also an artist, who died soon afterwards. Subsequently said to have stayed in London; assumed to be the artist of similar name who exhibited there in the 1760s. Returned to Marseille by 1771; made a member of the local Academy, 1776. Died in Marseille, 11 October 1778.

Principal Exhibitions
Free Society, London: 1763 ("Mrs Dupart")
Society of Artists, London: 1766 ("Duparc")

Bibliography
Philippe Auquier, "An eighteenth-century painter: Françoise Duparc", *Burlington Magazine*, vi, 1904–5, pp.477–8
Joseph Billioud, "Un peintre de types populaires: Françoise Duparc de Marseille (1726–1778)", *Gazette des Beaux-Arts*, 6th series, xx, 1938, pp.173–84
Les Femmes peintres au XVIIIe siècle, exh. cat., Musée Goya, Castres, 1973
Women Artists, 1550–1950, exh. cat., Los Angeles County Museum of Art, and elsewhere, 1976
Nancy G. Heller, *Women Artists: An Illustrated History*, 2nd edition, New York: Abbeville, 1991

It was only at the beginning of the 20th century that Françoise Duparc became known in her own country and started to be included in exhibitions. She received her first public recognition in London in 1763. During her time there she exhibited various works at both the Free Society and the Society of Artists. As she did not sign or date her works, most are unknown today, with the exception of four paintings that she bequeathed to the town hall in Marseille (all now Musée des Beaux-Arts, Marseille), although there were reported to be 41 paintings in her studio at her death. The surviving documented works, usually of working people, "genre portraits", have earned her a comparison with Chardin. Yet, unlike Chardin and Greuze, who both had a tendency to moralise, Duparc's aim appears to have been the simple depiction of people from southern France, her immediate environment.

Coming from an artistic family – her brother and sister were also artistically precocious – Françoise received her early art education from her sculptor father, Antoine Duparc. Undoubtedly, her most formative place of study was the studio of Jean Baptiste van Loo. She is thought to have been in his studio in Aix-en-Provence either before or after his stay in England (1737–42). He insisted that she be quoted as one of his pupils and thus it can be assumed that he was impressed by her talent (Billioud 1938, p.174). Despite the frequent comparisons made between Duparc's work and that of Chardin and Greuze, van Loo was surely the biggest influence on her artistic development.

The sensitivity and humility of Duparc's works suggest a familiarity with either the sitters themselves or their social contexts. It is this focus solely on the figures, rather than objects and interiors, that gives her work its strength. Her work is both simple and direct, it does not shift into the realm of nostalgia. In her works we glimpse a brief moment of working lives, as Ann Sutherland Harris acknowledged: "Duparc had an exceptional gift for capturing a fleeting moment of evocative expression" (Los Angeles 1976, p.173).

Although Duparc did not date her work, which makes it difficult to trace her stylistic development with certainty, there are nevertheless clear distinctions among her surviving paintings. The three portraits, *Man with a Sack*, *Tisane Seller* and *Old Woman*, bear certain common characteristics. All are half-length portraits with minimal backgrounds. Each of the sitters gazes out at the viewer, but their gaze is not challenging; it is almost as if they see through us. In spite of this, the portraits possess a very intimate feel, and, although definitely staged, they preserve a sense of spontaneity. The *Tisane Seller* depicts a woman in grey dress with starched white apron, out of which emerges a blue striped scarf. She carries an urn upon her back, the tap in her right hand and the cup in her left. She makes her living selling her wares on the street and yet she does not look jaded. Her head is slightly tilted as if the weight of the urn is weighing her down. Similarly, the *Old Woman* gazes out at the viewer. Her arms are crossed at her belt, her shoulders covered with a scarf. Although she is called *La Vieille*, her face is neither young nor old (*ibid.*, p.172). Her posture, however, appears to be that of an elderly woman, drawn in on herself. It has been suggested that she is a symbol of after-work rest, for she is still in her work clothes (*idem*). She epitomises the perceived image of working life in the French countryside. Her clothes and the chair on which she rests are the only objects that could possibly distract from the sitter, but they do not do so. Attention focuses entirely on her and all she embodies. Much the same can be said about *Man with a Sack*. All the works share an anonymity reinforced by the nature of their titles.

The fourth work, *La Tricoteuse*, while sharing this sense of anonymity, is markedly different. Unlike the other works, the subject is absorbed. She gazes not at the viewer, but at her knitting. She is a young girl, her head bent down towards the wool resting on her lap. This work has been aptly subtitled "Poésie du travail incarnée", for she is completely engrossed in her work. Duparc focuses little on the actual domestic interior; the sitter remains her main concern. But unlike the other works, the knitter has become the passive object of the viewer's gaze, her space intruded.

Our preoccupation with Duparc's place in art history as a "female Chardin" is symptomatic of a wish to fill in the gaps and make sense of this woman who could so effectively portray unaffected figures. Her works are undated and unsigned: so much in the artistic as well as personal life and career of Françoise Duparc remains a mystery.

UTE KREBS and ESMÉ WARD

E

Eakins, Susan Macdowell

American painter and photographer,
1851–1938

Born Susan Hannah Macdowell in Philadelphia,
Pennsylvania, 21 September 1851; father an
engraver. Studied at the Pennsylvania Academy of
the Fine Arts, Philadelphia, 1876–82. Married
painter Thomas Eakins, 1884; he died 1916.
Member, Philadelphia Photographic Salon, 1898.
Died in Philadelphia, 27 December 1938.

Principal Exhibitions

Pennsylvania Academy of the Fine Arts, Philadelphia:
    1876–9, 1881–2, 1905 (Mary Smith prize 1879,
    Charles Toppan prize 1882)
Philadelphia Photographic Salon: 1898
Philadelphia Art Club: 1936 (works by Susan Macdowell
    Eakins, her sister Elizabeth, Thomas Eakins and
    followers)

Bibliography

Lloyd Goodrich, *Thomas Eakins: His Life and Work*,
    New York: Whitney Museum of American Art, 1933
Susan MacDowell Eakins, 1851–1938, exh. cat.,
    Pennsylvania Academy of the Fine Arts, Philadelphia,
    1973
Lloyd Goodrich, *Thomas Eakins*, 2 vols, Cambridge,
    MA: Harvard University Press, 1982
American Women Artists, 1830–1930, exh. cat., National
    Museum of Women in the Arts, Washington, DC,
    1987

Until the 1970s the artistic accomplishments of
Susan Macdowell Eakins were virtually unknown in
the academic and museum worlds. Before marriage,
Macdowell had studied at the renowned
Pennsylvania Academy of the Fine Arts, which, in
spite of restrictions women faced in the use of the
nude life model, fostered a creative atmosphere that
nurtured the training or careers of various women
artists such as Mary Cassatt (q.v.), Alice Barber
Stephens (q.v.), Cecilia Beaux (q.v.) and Emily
Sartain. She was the daughter of a distinguished
engraver who, with his wife, created a progressive
and artistic home environment for their eight children. Another sister, Elizabeth, also painted, and
Susan Macdowell went to study at the Academy in
1876, first under the conservative tutelage of
Christian Schussele and then with the more radical
Thomas Eakins, whom she met in 1877. Macdowell
attended portrait, life and antique classes and from
the outset was supportive both of Eakins's teaching
abilities and of the need for decent life-class training
for art students. She exhibited intermittently from
1876 at the Academy and in 1879 submitted seven
works, one of which won her the first Mary Smith
prize, given to the best work by a Philadelphia
female artist. This was followed in 1882 by the
Charles Toppan prize, awarded to an outstanding
male or female student at the Academy for the most
accurate drawing.

In her own paintings, especially those executed
during her student years at the Academy, the subject
matter is of a private and domestic nature, with
sitters primarily drawn from the insular world of
family and friends. Both she and her husband
painted her father's strong features on various occasions, and her solid drawing, sombre hues and characterisation in individual portraits were all indebted
partly to Eakins's own aesthetic and techniques.
During this early period Macdowell's talents as a
watercolourist also evinced themselves in examples
such as *Chaperone* (private collection, repr.
Philadelphia 1973, p.17) and *Roseanna Williams*
(private collection), each dated 1879. Both use
Eakinsesque subject matter of a solitary, introverted
figure (often a contemplative female reading or knitting) as well as kindred technique, combining
refined colour harmony, a beautiful range of

textures and sensitive modelling of the face. In oil paintings such as her *Portrait of a Gentleman and Dog* (*c*.1878–9; private collection, *ibid.*, p.9), Macdowell's firm handling and solid anatomical construction are blended with generally dark tonalities. This work was chosen to be engraved for an article by William C. Brownell on Philadelphia art schools ("The art schools of Philadelphia", *Scribner's Monthly Illustrated Magazine*, xviii, 1879, pp.745 and 749), an obvious *coup* for the young artist. Another of her best works of this period, and of her entire career, was *Portrait of a Lady* (1880; private collection, repr. Philadelphia 1973, p.20), a probing, skilfully rendered portrait of an introspective female dressed in shades of pale blue and cream.

Macdowell married Thomas Eakins in January 1884 and thereafter she devoted much of her time to domestic issues and the maintenance of her husband's career over her own artistic pursuits. Apart from her addition of her spouse's portrait to his *Agnew Clinic* (University of Pennsylvania, Philadelphia) in 1889 and her assistance with his portrait of *Dr Spitzka* (1913; private collection), the two were not known to collaborate or interfere with one another's paintings. Portraiture became a main preoccupation in her middle years (after her departure from the Academy until 1916), mostly of friends, relatives and others in their personal circle. Described as a very loyal and generous friend by contemporaries, she was also an accomplished pianist and shared her husband's interest in music as well as photography. She was a photographer even before the time she and Eakins met, and was among the first members of the Philadelphia Photographic Salon, founded in 1898. Occasionally she exhibited her work in this medium: *Child with Doll*, for example, was in the photography salon of 1898 at the Academy. Like her spouse, she is also known to have used photographs as an aid for her own paintings, especially for portraits.

After the death of her husband in 1916 Macdowell Eakins began to paint on a regular, often daily basis and continued doing so until her death in 1938. Her late style generally reflected a weakening solidity of three-dimensional form and more acid, higher-keyed colours, both indicating movement away from a purely Eakinsesque practice and palette. In the 1920s and 1930s her production was erratic in quality, although there was considerable pictorial freshness conveyed, for example, in her portraits of the *Lewis Sisters* and *The Bibliophile* (both 1932; private collections, *ibid.*, pp.32 and 34). Occasionally she produced still lifes that seemed influenced by the example of such artists as Maria Oakey Dewing and J. Alden Weir, but it was her portraiture that was her pre-eminent contribution to American art. The only exhibition of her work in any quantity occurred in 1936, when 20 paintings by the artist, in addition to those by her husband, her sister Elizabeth and various Eakins followers were displayed at the Philadelphia Art Club. In the end, the final phase of her own career coincided with the decreasing power of the Eakins tradition among followers.

Macdowell Eakins also appeared in a number of her husband's paintings as a somewhat haunting, enigmatic figure, testimony to the melancholic mood with which he often imbued his female sitters. In addition to various photographic portraits of her, the artist's best-known images of his wife are found in his *Portrait of a Lady with Setter Dog* (*c*.1885; Metropolitan Museum of Art, New York) and the portrait of *Mrs Thomas Eakins* (*c*.1899; Hirshhorn Museum and Sculpture Garden, Washington, DC). Her posthumous portrait of *Thomas Eakins* (*c*.1920–25; Philadelphia Museum of Art) aged about 45 in a shadowed studio corner mirrors her own adaptation of this theme. Most of Macdowell Eakins's surviving paintings are in private collections in the USA, although scattered examples may be found in a few American museums.

Susan P. Casteras

Ellenrieder, Marie
German painter, 1791–1863

Born in Konstanz (Constance), 20 March 1791. Took lessons with the miniature painter Joseph Einsle, *c*.1810–13. Studied under Johann Peter von Langer at the Munich Academy, the first woman to receive training there, 1813–16. Invited to the Hohenzollern court in Sigmaringen, 1818. Stayed at the Fürstenberg court in Donaueschingen, 1819. Invited to the Baden court in Karlsruhe, 1820. Worked in Rome, 1822–4; associated with Friedrich Overbeck and the Nazarenes. Appointed court painter at Baden by Grand Duke Ludwig I,

1829. Second journey to Italy, 1838–40. Subsequently retired to Konstanz; died there, 5 June 1863.

Bibliography

Cotta's Kunstblatt, Stuttgart and Tübingen, 1820–40, 1845, 1848, 1858

Friedrich Pecht, *Recensionen über bildende Kunst*, 1863, p.159

Hermann Uhde, ed., *Erinnerungen und Leben der Malerin Louise Seidler: Selbstbiographie*, Berlin, 1874; revised editions, 1875 and 1922; abridged edition, Weimar, 1964

Oscar Gehrig, "Maria Ellenrieder", *Die Christliche Kunst*, 1912–13, pp.292ff

Klara Siebert, *Marie Ellenrieder als Künstlerin und Frau*, Freiburg in Breisgau, 1916

Friedrich Noack, *Das Deutschtum in Rom*, i, Stuttgart, 1927; reprinted Aalen: Scientia, 1974

Margarete Zündorff, *Marie Ellenrieder: Ein deutsches Frauen- und Künstlerleben*, Konstanz, 1940

Otto Kähui, "Marie Ellenrieder in der Ortenau", *Ekkhart, Jahrbuch für das Badner Land*, 1959

Friedhelm Wilhelm Fischer and Sigrid von Blanckenhagen, *Marie Ellenrieder: Leben und Werk der Konstanzer Malerin*, Konstanz: Thorbecke, 1963 (contains catalogue raisonné)

Arthur von Schneider, *Badische Malerei des XIX. Jahrhunderts*, Karlsruhe: Muller, 1968

Jan Lauts and Werner Zimmermann, *Katalog neuere Meister 19. und 20. Jahrhundert: Staatliche Kunsthalle Karlsruhe*, 2 vols, Karlsruhe: Staatliche Kunsthalle, 1971

Women Artists, 1550–1950, exh. cat., Los Angeles County Museum of Art, and elsewhere, 1976

Baden und Württemberg im Zeitalter Napoleons, exh. cat., 2 vols, Württembergisches Landesmuseum, Stuttgart, 1987

Das Verborgene Museum I: Dokumentation der Kunst von Frauen in Berliner öffentlichen Sammlungen, exh. cat., Akademie der Künste, Berlin, 1987

Gottfried Sello, *Malerinnen aus fünf Jahrhunderten*, Hamburg: Ellert und Richter, 1988

Kunst in der Residenz, exh. cat., Staatliche Kunsthalle Karlsruhe, Heidelberg, 1990

"… und hat als Weib unglaubliches Talent" (Goethe): Angelika Kauffmann (1741–1807), Marie Ellenrieder (1791–1863), exh. cat., Rosgartenmuseum, Konstanz, 1992

Marie Ellenrieder diaries and archive are in the Rosgartenmuseum, Konstanz.

"All things considered, Marie Ellenrieder must be one of the most important German female artists of modern time", was the judgement of the painter and art writer Friedrich Pecht on her death in 1863. Even in her lifetime Ellenrieder was highly regarded:

she was the first woman to be trained as an artist at a German Academy. The Grand Duke Ludwig von Baden appointed her court painter in 1829 after she had already been awarded a gold medal of art and science by the Baden artists' society – the first woman to be so honoured. Ellenrieder is known as a representative of the Nazarene style. Within this style, which was based on Renaissance and medieval German art, her works show an individual character to which her deep religiosity and sensitive perception strongly contributed. Her excellent painting technique distinguishes her works from those of other Nazarenes. Ellenrieder also left extensive diaries that reveal a sensitive artist who reacted strongly to the contemporary religious morality and its inherent contradictions. Ellenrieder has received only scant attention in art history, which does justice neither to her nor to her work.

Ellenrieder studied for three years under the Konstanz miniature painter Joseph Einsle before beginning her studies at the Munich Academy. In 1813, with the help of her patron and mentor Ignaz Heinrich, Freiherr von Wessenberg, a Konstanz church official, she was accepted into the Munich Academy, where she studied under the classicist painter Johann Peter von Langer. Von Langer recognised her exceptional talent for portrait painting and gave her strong support. Influenced by the Baroque, Ellenrieder's early works show a preference for the deliberate use of light emerging from a dark background. Some studies of male heads executed with a broad brush and lively, strong colours reveal an impressive vividness and force. She created technically excellent etchings – mostly copies of old masters – in the period 1815–16, making use of varied cross-hatching (a method used in Baroque copper engravings), which she also employed in her later pastel works, a genre in which she was especially talented and in which she created her most beautiful and lively works.

The period 1817–22 is now seen as the most productive of Ellenrieder's career. Her works from that time display an enthusiasm and sensitivity that allowed her to capture the particular qualities of the people she painted. Through the deepening of spiritual expression, Ellenrieder was in advance of the realistic portraiture of the second half of the 19th century. Her early portraits, mostly half-length and partly in profile, were created in the middle-class milieu of her family and home on Lake Konstanz. Psychological characterisation is their most important feature. The portraits of her parents (1819; Rosgartenmuseum, Konstanz) are among the best. The portrait of *Baron von Wessenberg* (1819; Wessenberg-Galerie, Konstanz) conveys the sensitive character of the sitter with freshness and immediacy.

For many of her portraits, Ellenrieder prepared pastel drawings, which show an even greater degree of liveliness. She very much enjoyed painting portraits of children. The sketch for the portrait of *Prince Carl von Hohenzollern-Sigmaringen, Heir to the Throne* (c.1818; Wessenberg-Galerie) as well as the portrait of the *Artist's Nephews* (c.1818–19, private collection, repr. Konstanz 1992, ill.3) and the *Daughters Thurn-Valsassina* (1818; private collection, Kunsthaus, Zürich, *ibid.*, ill.23) are among Ellenrieder's most beautiful portraits of children, showing them refreshingly unself-conscious. It is only in the later portraits that she portrayed children as ideals of angelic goodness. She portrayed herself as a vivacious, self-confident and merry young woman in two self-portraits (1818; Staatliche Kunsthalle; Karlsruhe; 1819; Rosgartenmuseum), whereas her later portraits (e.g. *Self-Portrait*, 1827; Staatliche Kunsthalle; *Self-Portrait, Head Study with Bonnet*, 1827; Rosgartenmuseum) document the increasing loss of these characteristics and her retreat to an inner life of self-doubt.

From 1818 onwards Ellenrieder received princely commissions, painting the portraits of *Princess Jablonowska* (1818; Rosgartenmuseum) and *Carl Egon II and Amalie von Fürstenberg* (1819; private collection, *ibid.*, ill.24), and then began to portray the sitters half- and full-length. In 1820 she was called to the Baden court at Karlsruhe to paint the portraits of *Margrave Leopold and Margravine Sophie von Baden* (private collection, *ibid.*, p.193). In these portraits Ellenrieder managed to combine the public with the private, the representation of a public figure with the characteristics of an individual.

Ellenrieder's first religious canvases, *St Cecilia* (1816; Rosgartenmuseum) and *St Jerome* (c.1817; Wessenberg-Galerie), show a strong reliance on Baroque art in content, form and manner of representation. One can see here the excellent results of her academic studies and the flowering of her talent for colour and composition, as well as her sensitivity and liveliness. She used quick and firm brush strokes and light to model the figures and give depth to the surroundings. In 1820 she was the first woman to receive a commission for the decoration of a Catholic church, the Pfarrkirche zu Ichenheim (Baden), for which she painted three altarpieces: the *Virgin Mary Enthroned*, *St Nicholas*, the church's patron saint, and a *Resurrection* (all *in situ*). In these paintings a retreat from the liveliness of her earlier work towards the coldness of Neo-classicism is first apparent. This tendency mirrored her own incessant religious soul searching for purity and idealism.

Ellenrieder left Konstanz in 1822 to travel to Italy, where she stayed for several years. In Rome she stayed with the Weimar artist Louise Seidler, who introduced her to the colony of German artists around Friedrich Overbeck. The art theories of the Nazarenes had an impact on Ellenrieder, a deeply religious woman who had a tendency towards self-denial and asceticism. Her manner of painting changed completely as a result of their influence and her impressions of the art of Raphael and Perugino; at the same time she perfected her technical skills. The paint surface of her works now attains the quality of smooth enamel, the range of colours is lighter, the plasticity of the figures and the sense of depth are gone, and the faces are highly idealised. The luminous enamel of the colouring generates a lyrical continuation of transcendental rapture. The figures move to the foreground of the picture plane as if stepping out of a flood of divine light. With these painterly techniques, Ellenrieder gave her paintings the static timeless quality that is associated with the works of the Nazarenes.

Ellenrieder's drawing technique also changed completely under the influence of the Nazarenes, who saw drawings and cartoons as works of art in themselves, which in their opinion embodied the purest depiction of truth, a notion that Ellenrieder took on board. Whereas she used a mixed and differentiated technique for her early works – soft and fine modelling and open outlines were characteristic of this – she now laid a strong emphasis on contour. Her mixed technique is rectified and large areas of light now contrast with deep shadows.

Her main work of this period is an almost life-size painting of the *Virgin Mary with the Christ Child* (completed 1824; Staatliche Kunsthalle, Karlsruhe). The structure, forms and colouring of the work reveal intensive study of the works of Raphael. The painting was highly praised by contemporary critics. It was of lifelong importance to the artist, who kept it in her studio. The harmony of a mystical radiant power and human closeness is an artistic quality of Ellenrieder's work that makes her paintings stand out from that of the other Nazarenes. There is, however, an inherent danger in such a harmony of sentimentality that Ellenrieder did not always avoid.

Her stay in Italy brought about a break from her former life. Disappointed by the lack of acknowledgement from other German artists in Rome, Ellenrieder returned to Konstanz via Florence, where her tendency towards depression became more prominent. She left Italy with the intention of putting her art in the service of religion and only accepted commissions for portraits if they came from the court of the Grand Duke. In 1827 she painted the *State Portrait of the Grand Duke Ludwig von Baden* (private collection, repr. Konstanz 1992, ill.25), with whose family she enjoyed a friendly relationship. In 1832 Ellenrieder received a commission for a family portrait of the *Grand Duchess Sophie von Baden with Her Five Children* (completed 1834; private collection, ex-Zähringersammlung, Neues Schloss, Baden-Baden). The clarity of drawing, balance of composition and the delicate harmony of the colours make this painting one of the finest family portraits of the 19th century. In these images one can increasingly detect Ellenrieder's efforts to create idealised portraits and bestow upon the sitters an individuality and quasi-religious meaning. Especially in her portraits of children, she attempted to show the pure and childlike "angelic soul" (Ellenrieder) and their proximity to God.

Ellenrieder became the most popular female religious artist in southwest Germany. In 1828 she received the honourable commission of painting an enormous work for the high altar of the Stadtkirche St Stephan in Karlsruhe, the *Martyrdom of St Stephen* (4.7 × 3.2 m.; now Pfarrkirche St Stephan, Konstanz). She was the first and only woman to create a work of such huge dimensions. The structure of the work is reminiscent of Italian Renaissance paintings. She avoided the common but brutal depiction of the stoning of the saint since art was meant to contribute to the "ennobling and edification of the beholder" (Ignaz Heinrich von Wessenberg, *Die christlichen Bilder, ein Beförderungsmittel christlichen Sinnes*, Konstanz, 1827, pp.42, 155, 186 and 201). The work signifies an important step in Ellenrieder's career as well as being of great importance in her oeuvre as a whole. It was decisive in her appointment as court painter.

The largest commission she received from the Grand Duke Ludwig was the decoration of the castle chapel in Langenstein (1828) with life-size biblical scenes, including the *Feeding of the Five Thousand* and the *Blessing of the Children*, a theme that she particularly liked and executed more than once.

Ellenrieder's depression in the years after 1834 was accompanied by a waning in creativity. In 1838 she again went to Italy on a journey from which she hoped to be inspired and encouraged. Despite the praise her work received in these years – especially the *Blessing of the Children* (1839; Rosgartenmuseum) and *Angel with a Bowl of Tears* (second version 1842; Kloster Lichtenthal, Baden-Baden) she returned to Konstanz in 1840 disappointed and depressed. The following years were marked by illness, depression and diminishing creativity. She painted many small, sometimes miniature-like works with religious subjects that were always in demand. She also received some commissions for large-scale works. In 1847 and 1849 she executed two large religious paintings for Queen Victoria (*St Felicitas and Her Sons* and *Christ in the Temple*; Royal Collection, Osborne House, Isle of Wight). In the last decade of her life she had a renewed burst of creativity, painting some altarpieces and at least 23 oil paintings, but the artistic quality of her earlier years seems to have been lost. She created one more masterpiece in the genre of portraiture with the pastel portrait of the *Three Young Countesses Douglas* (private collection, repr. Konstanz 1992, p.200).

Marie Ellenrieder had no artistic successors. She did not have many students because she found them disruptive, and the artistic taste of the second half of the 19th century took a different direction. The continuation of her style led to the sickly sweet devotional art that makes it so difficult to judge Ellenrieder's work justly and without prejudice. Soon after her death she disappeared into increasing obscurity. In three important exhibition catalogues of the art of the Nazarenes (1977, 1981 and 1989) her name is not even mentioned, although many of her technically excellent compositions should be recognised as masterpieces in the Nazarene tradition. In order to award Ellenrieder her just and valid place within art history one should consider especially her early works, which were influenced by the spirit of Romanticism. Ellenrieder must be counted among the best artists of southwest Germany.

KARIN STOBER

Exter, Alexandra

Russian painter and designer, 1882–1949

Born Alexandra Alexandrovna Grigorovich in Belestok, near Kiev, Ukraine, 6 January 1882. Attended Kiev Art Institute, 1901–7. Married lawyer Nikolai Exter, 1908; he died 1918. Frequently visited Paris and other European cities from 1908; studied at Académie de la Grande Chaumière, Paris, under Charles Delval, 1908. Took part in several Kiev exhibitions including David Burlyuk's Zveno (The Link), the first of many involvements with the avant-garde. Moved to St Petersburg, 1912. Began professional theatre work with designs for *Thamira Khytharedes* produced by Alexander Tairov at the Chamber Theatre, Moscow, 1916. Founded her own studio in Kiev, 1918; many artists of later fame, such as Isaak Rabinovich, Alexander Tyshler and Pavel Tchelitchew, studied there. Stage designer at the Theatre of the People's House, Odessa, 1920. Turned to textile and fashion design for the Atelier of Fashions, Moscow, 1923. Emigrated to Paris, 1924; worked for the Ballets Romantiques Russes with Léon Zack and Pavel Tchelitchew; taught stage design and painting at Fernand Léger's Académie d'Art Moderne. Continued to work on stage and interior design, 1920s and 1930s. Died in Fontenay-aux-Roses, near Paris, 17 March 1949.

Principal Exhibitions

Individual

Galerie Der Sturm, Berlin: 1927–8
Galerie Quatre Chemins, Paris: 1929
Prague: 1937

Group

Zveno (The Link), Kiev: 1908
Izdebsky Salon, Odessa: 1909–10 (*International Exhibition*, touring)
Soyuz molodyozhi (Union of Youth): 1910, 1913
Bubnovy valet (Jack/Knave of Diamonds), Moscow: 1910–17
Salon des Indépendants, Paris: 1912, 1914
Moscow: 1914 (*Exhibition of Paintings No.4*), 1916 (*Futurist Exhibition: The Store*), 1918 (*First Exhibition of Paintings of the Professional Association of Artists*), 1921 (5 × 5 = 25, with Rodchenko, Stepanova, Popova and Vesnin)
Koltso (The Ring), Kiev: 1914
Galleria Sprovieri, Rome: 1914 (*Libera mostra internazionale futurista di pittura e scultura*)
Petrograd: 1915 (*Tramway V: First Futurist Exhibition of Paintings*)
Galerie van Diemen, Berlin: 1922–3 (*Erste russische Kunstausstellung*, touring)
Museum of Decorative Painting, Moscow: 1923 (*Moscow's Theatrical and Decorative Art, 1918–1923*)
Venice Biennale: 1924
Exposition Internationale des Arts Décoratifs et Industriels Modernes, Paris: 1925
Cercle et Carré, Paris: 1930

Selected Writings

(as A.E.), "Novoye vo frantsuzskoy zhivopisi" [What's new in French painting], *Iskusstvo*, 1912, no.1–2, p.40

Bibliography

5 × 5 = 25, exh. cat., Moscow, 1921
Yakov Tugendkhold, *Alexandra Exter*, Berlin: Zaria, 1922
Alexander Tairov and others, *Alexandra Exter: Décors de théâtre*, Paris: Quatre Chemins, 1930
Alexandra Exter, exh. cat., Galerie Jean Chauvelin, Paris, 1972
Artist of the Theatre: Alexandra Exter, exh. cat., Center for the Performing Arts, Lincoln Center, New York, 1974
Alexandra Exter: Marionettes, exh. cat., Leonard Hutton Galleries, New York, 1975
Ronny H. Cohen, *Alexandra Exter and Western Europe: An Inquiry into Russian-Western Relations in Art, Theater and Design in the Early Twentieth Century*, PhD dissertation, New York University, 1979
Künstlerinnen der russischen Avantgarde/Russian Women Artists of the Avant-Garde, 1910–1930, exh. cat., Galerie Gmurzynska, Cologne, 1979
Alexandra Exter: Marionettes and Theatrical Designs, exh. cat., Hirshhorn Museum and Sculpture Garden, Washington, DC, 1980
Alexandra Exter, exh. cat., CTM, Moscow, 1988
Alexandra Exter, exh. cat., Odessa Art Museum, 1989
M. Kolesnikov, "Alexandra Exter i Vera Mukhina", *Panorama iskusstv*, no.12, Moscow, 1989, pp.89–110
M.N. Yablonskaya, *Women Artists of Russia's New Age, 1900–1935*, New York: Rizzoli, and London: Thames and Hudson, 1990
Alexandra Exter e il teatro da camera, exh. cat., Museo d'Arte Moderna e Contemporaneo di Trento, Rovereto, 1991 (contains exhibition list and extensive bibliography)
G. Kovalenko, *Alexandra Exter*, Moscow: Galart, 1993
D. Gorbachev, "Exter in Kiev – Kiev in Exter", *Experiment*, no.1, 1995, pp.299–320

Painter, book illustrator, teacher and above all stage designer, Alexandra Exter was a primary member of the international avant-garde and, like many of her colleagues in Russia and the Ukraine, she was in close contact with artists and writers in Kiev, Moscow, St Petersburg, Paris and Milan. But like Kazimir Malevich, Lyubov Popova (q.v.) and Vladimir Tatlin, Exter managed to integrate the principles of Cubism and Futurism with her own indigenous traditions (such as Ukrainian folk art) to produce distinctive interpretations of Cubo-Futurism, Suprematism and Constructivism.

Exter spent long periods in France and Italy, studied Cubism and Futurism, and was especially close to such artists as Robert and Sonia Delaunay (q.v.) and Ardengo Soffici. Robert Delaunay's Orphism also left a permanent imprint on her early work, and in her article on French painting she even promoted his ideas, using a Futurist terminology to explain his system: "instead of one plane he presents simultaneously several constructive planes mutually intersecting at the angle like the sides of a prism" ("Novoye vo frantsuzskoy zhivopisi", 1912). Indeed, Exter might well have been describing her own Cubo-Futurist paintings of 1912–15, for such works as *City at Night* (1913; State Russian Museum, St Petersburg), *Florence* (1914–15; 109 × 144 cm.) and *Composition* (1914; 90.7 × 72.5 cm.; both Tretyakov Gallery, Moscow), all oil on canvas, incorporate recognisable elements of the Delaunays' polychromatic system, evident in the street lamps reverberating as coloured discs. In turn, the refractive and rhythmic concentrations of Exter's paintings recur in those of her Ukrainian colleagues such as Vladimir Baranov-Rossiné and Alexander Bogomazov. Certainly, paintings such as *City at Night* are powerful gestures to the combined forces of French Cubism and Italian Futurism but, for Exter, they were only laboratory experiments that culminated in her non-objective paintings of 1916 onwards. While indebted to her formal training in Paris, such abstract compositions as *Non-Objective Composition* (1917–18; State Russian Museum) derive from many other pictorial sources, not least Kazimir Malevich's Suprematist system (1915 onwards), and some scholars even contend that Exter's move towards abstraction was also stimulated by the rich patterns of Ukrainian decorative arts (e.g. Gorbachev 1995). In any case, by 1915–16 the non-objective aesthetic was of primary importance to Exter; she joined Malevich's Supremus group, and contributed Suprematist works to the *0.10* exhibition in Petrograd. Just before and after the October Revolution of 1917,

with Ivan Klyun, Malevich, Lyubov Popova and Tatlin, Exter was at the forefront of the Russian abstract movement – evidenced by colourful and dynamic canvases such as *Construction of Planes along Movement of Colour* (1918; Wilhelm Hack Museum, Ludwigshafen) and *Colour Construction* (1921; Radishchev Museum, Saratov).

Ultimately, however, Exter achieved an international reputation as a stage designer rather than as an easel painter. While trained as a studio artist, Exter came to the world of the theatre through her deep interest in the applied arts, contributing designs for dresses, scarves and cushions to Moscow design exhibitions in the 1910s. This was an interest that derived from her innate concern with fabric, material, pattern, colour application, sewing and weaving – an aspect of her career that tends to be overshadowed by the more familiar Cubism and abstract paintings. Although of a later generation, Exter was much indebted to the basic theatrical concept formulated by Leon Bakst – that a stage design must transcend the confines of the pictorial surface and organise forms in interaction with space. Exter's awareness of this interaction became especially evident in her first collaborations with Alexander Tairov at the Chamber Theatre in Moscow (where she also collaborated with Vera Mukhina, q.v.): the productions of *Thamira Khytharedes* (1916), *Salome* (1917) and *Romeo and Juliet* (1921). Aware of the principles of Edward Gordon Craig, Adolphe Appia and Sergei Volkonsky (Appia's apologist in Russia), Tairov and Exter conceived of the stage for *Thamira Khytharedes* as a volumetrical, constructive space where actors and scenery had equal roles and where, as Tairov himself recalled, the guiding force of the sets and costumes was "the Apollonian rhythm inherent in the figure of Thamira" (A. Tairov, "Zapiski rezhissyora" [Director's notes], *A.Ya. Tairov o teatre*, ed. P. Markov, Moscow: VTO, 1970, p.163).

Exter's concentration on what her friend the critic Yakov Tugendkhold called an "organic connection between the moving actors and the objects at rest" (Ya. Tugendkhold, "Pismo iz Moskvy" [Letter from Moscow], *Apollon*, 1917, no.1, p.72) pointed to her Constructivist costume designs for ballets performed by Bronislava Nijinska's Théâtre Chorégraphique in Britain and Paris (see *Bronislava Nijinska: A Dancer's Legacy*, exh. cat., Cooper-Hewitt Museum, New York, and elsewhere, 1986) and to her designs for the science-fiction film *Aelita*, released in 1924. Indeed, perhaps Exter attained the high point of her scenic career in the dynamic medium of film, where focus and sequence change constantly, where formal contrast is transmitted by a rapid variability of light, and where light itself plays a constructive role. *Aelita* was Exter's only major commitment to the art of film, although sources mention her involvement in others such as *Daughter of the Sun*, and she also created, with Nechama Szmuszkowicz, marionettes in 1926 for a film projected, but not produced, by Peter Gad in Paris. With *Aelita*'s easy plot, box office stars (Yuliya Solntseva as Aelita and Yury Zavadsky as Gor) and futuristic costumes by Exter, this "cosmic Odyssey" (V. Rakitin, "Marsiane A. Exter", *Dekorativnoye iskusstvo*, 1977, no.4, p.29), anticipated such recent space fantasies as *Star Wars*.

In the 1920s Exter continued to investigate the "dynamic use of immobile form" (Tugendkhold *op. cit.*), filling her Constructivist scenographies with staircases and platforms, manipulating planes and solids, and juxtaposing verticals with diagonals. Exter's experiments with stage lighting and her general emphasis on the dynamic and architectonic possibilities of the stage influenced a number of younger stage designers in Russia and the Ukraine such as Anatoly Petritsky, Isaak Rabinovich and Alexander Tyshler, and even the Surrealist Pavel Tchelitchew, remembered now for his canvas *Hide and Seek* (Museum of Modern Art, New York), started his career as a student of Exter in Kiev.

Exter continued to experiment throughout her Paris years, applying her ideas to ballets, revues and books – she illustrated a number of de luxe limited editions such as Marie Collin-Delavaud's *Panorama de la montagne* and *Panorama de la côte* (both Paris: Flammarion, 1938) and her own *Mon jardin* (Paris: Flammarion, 1936). In 1925 she even invented "epidermic costumes" for a ballet project in which the dancers were painted, not dressed (for a photograph of three performers wearing these costumes, see *Il contributo russo alle avanguardie plastiche*, exh. cat., Galleria del Levante, Milan, 1964, p.31). As Tyshler said: "In her hands, a simple paper lampshade turned into a work of art" (quoted in O. Voronova, *V.I. Mukhina*, Moscow: Iskusstvo, 1976, p.43).

JOHN E. BOWLT

F

Fini, Leonor
Italian painter, 1908–1996

Born in Buenos Aires, 30 August 1908, to parents of mixed European and Argentinian origin. Grew up in mother's home town of Trieste, Italy, from 1920; expelled from every school she attended; moved in intellectual circles, meeting writers James Joyce, Italo Svevo and Umberto Saba. Self-taught in art, studying old and modern masters in museums, and drawing corpses at the morgue. Participated in a group exhibition in Trieste at age 17, earning a commission in Milan. Moved to Paris, 1936. Made friends among the Surrealists, exhibiting with them in London (1936), New York (1936) and Tokyo (1937), but never became an official member of the group. Visited New York, 1939. Lived in Monte Carlo and Rome during World War II, returning to Paris in 1946. Died in Paris, 18 January 1996.

Selected Individual Exhibitions
Julian Levy Gallery, New York: 1939
Palais des Beaux-Arts, Brussels: 1949
Galleria-Galatea d'Arte Contemporanea, Turin: 1957, 1966
Kaplan Gallery, London: 1960
Galerie Iolas, Paris: 1965
Hanover Gallery, London: 1967
Galerie Brockstaedt, Hamburg: 1969
Yomiuri Shimburu, Tokyo: 1972 (touring retrospective)
Galerie Proscenium, Paris: 1978, 1982, 1991
Musée Ingres, Montauban: 1981 (touring retrospective)
Galerie Artcurial, Paris: 1981
Galleria Civica d'Arte Moderna, Ferrara: 1983 (retrospective)
Sago, Yokohama: 1985–6 (touring retrospective)
Musée du Luxembourg and Galerie Proscenium, Paris: 1986
Galerie Guy Pieters, Belgium: 1988
Mussavi Gallery, New York: 1989
Galerie Bosquet, Paris: 1991
Musée St Roch, Issoudun: 1991
CFM, New York: 1992
Galerie Dionne, Paris: 1992, 1993, 1995
Maison du Loir et Cher, Blois: 1992

Selected Writings
Histoire de Vibrissa, Paris: Tchou, 1973
Le Livre de Leonor Fini, Lausanne: Clairefontaine, and Paris: Vilo, 1975; 2nd edition, 1979
"Surtout les puanteurs", *Sorcières*, no.5 [c.1975]
Mourmour, conte pour enfants velus, Paris: Editions de la Différence: 1976
Le Miroir des chats, Lausanne: Guilde du Livre: 1977
L'Onéïropompe, Paris: Editions de la Différence, 1978
Rogomelec, Paris: Stock, 1979
Les Chats de Madame Helvétius, Paris: Navarra, 1985
Chats d'atelier, ed. Guy Pieters, Paris: Trinckvel, 1988; 2nd edition, 1994
Les Passagers, Paris: Dionne, 1992
Entre le Oui et le Non, Paris: Dionne, 1994

Bibliography
Paul Eluard, "Le tableau noir", *Donner à voir*, Paris: Gallimard, 1939 (poem dedicated to Leonor Fini)
Marcel Brion, *Leonor Fini et son oeuvre*, Paris: Pauvert, 1955
Leonor Fini, exh. cat., Kaplan Gallery, London, 1960
Leonor Fini, exh. cat., Casino Communale, Knokke-le-Zoute, 1964
Yves Bonnefoy, *Leonor Fini, ou, La Profondeur délivrée*, Montpellier: Leo, 1965
Leonor Fini, exh. cat., Galleria-Galatea d'Arte Contemporanea, Turin, 1966
Constantin Jelenski, *Leonor Fini*, Lausanne: Clairefontaine, 1968 and 1972
Xavière Gauthier, *Leonor Fini*, Paris: Musée de Poche, 1973
Obliques, no.14–15, 1977 (special issue: *La Femme surréaliste*)
Jean-Claude Dedieu, *Leonor Fini*, Paris: Birr, 1978
Jacques Audiberti and others, *Leonor Fini*, Paris: Hervas, 1981
Pierre Borgue, *Leonor Fini, ou, "Le Théâtre de l'imaginaire"*, Paris: Lettres Modernes, 1983

Leonor Fini, exh. cat., Galleria Civica d'Arte Moderna, Ferrara, 1983

Whitney Chadwick, *Women Artists and the Surrealist Movement*, Boston: Little Brown, and London: Thames and Hudson, 1985

Guy Pieters, ed., *Leonor Fini*, Paris: Trinckvel, 1986

Tiziana Villani, *Parcours dans l'oeuvre de Leonor Fini*, Paris: Trinckvel, 1986

La Femme et le surréalisme, exh. cat., Musée Cantonal des Beaux-Arts, Lausanne, 1987

Martine Antle, "Picto-théâtralité dans les toiles de Leonor Fini", *French Review*, lxii, 1989, pp.640–49

Georgiana M.M. Colvile, "Beauty and/is the beast: Animal symbology in the work of Leonora Carrington, Remedios Varo and Leonor Fini", *Surrealism and Women*, ed. Mary Ann Caws and others, Cambridge: Massachusetts Institute of Technology Press, 1991, pp.159–81

Leonor Fini: The Artist as Designer, exh. cat., CFM, New York, 1992

Leonor Fini peintures, Paris: Trinckvel, 1994

Peter Webb, *Leonor Fini* (in preparation)

Whether or not Leonor Fini should be considered a Surrealist remains an ongoing debate. She herself never wanted to be one, in spite of her friendships with numerous members of the group. She also refused to be isolated as a "woman artist" and was quite convinced that women's art and literature should be integrated with men's rather than constitute a separate corpus. Nevertheless, as Fini has been included in a number of exhibitions and critical volumes on Surrealism, whether on women or both genders, it seems most appropriate to classify her as an individual, independent artist with Surrealist tendencies.

Fini's early paintings tended to be slightly uncanny compositions principally involving female figures (*Black Room*, 1938; private collection, repr. Jelenski 1968) or portraits (*Anna Magnani*, 1949; Collection Anna Magnani, *ibid.*, *Jean Genet*, 1949; private collection, Turin, *ibid.*). She then increasingly represented her favourite mythical monster, the sphinx, and her personal totem creature, the cat, in conjunction with hybrid animal, plant or alchemical female figures, as in *Sphinx Amalburga* (1942; private collection, *ibid.*), *World's End* (1949; private collection, *ibid.*) and *Guardian of Phoenixes* (1954; private collection, *ibid.*), all small-scale oil paintings. Later, Fini experimented more with brighter colours, as in *Heliodora* (1964; private collection, Cannes, *ibid.*), developed the themes of woman as sorceress, often poised as a threat to a weak male, and especially the cat motif in both drawings and paintings (*The Mutants*, 1971; private collection, Paris). Like those of Remedios Varo (q.v.), most of her figures have her own face.

Fini's traditional, carefully crafted and precise draughtmanship (she has been frequently accused of slickness) can be considered as contrary to Surrealism's liberation of form and yet makes her work comparable, at a certain level, to that of Max Ernst, Salvador Dalí, René Magritte and Remedios Varo. Like them, she subverts the content of her compositions, sometimes by means of a single detail, for example, in *La Belle Dame sans merci* (1969), in which a young woman takes a footbath and one of her feet, depicted as a monstrous, bulbous club-foot in dark hues contrasting with the otherwise pastel tones, undercuts the aesthetic harmony of the painting. *Les Invitées* (1971; private collection, New York, *ibid.*) shows two greedy female guests devouring platefuls of a pink substance, while their hostess hides her face: it soon becomes apparent that what they are eating must be her face.

Fini's work is strikingly decorative. She created the sets for more than 20 plays, including Jean Genet's *Les Bonnes* (1961) and *Le Balcon* (1969), and designed the costumes for two films: Renato Castellani's *Romeo and Juliet* (1963) and John Huston's *A Walk with Love and Death* (1969). For many years she loved to dress up in outlandish costumes and masks with her friends. These outfits and the theatrical poses they inspired no doubt provided her with visions of the majestic, either lavishly draped or proudly naked women who inhabit the world of her art. During the 1950s Fini produced an important series of canvases, in which a regally robed woman with shaved head guards a large alchemical egg varying in colour, or displays an ovoidal shape as part of her body (*Silence Enveloped*, 1955; Alexander Iolas Collection, New York; *Guardian with a Red Egg*, 1955; Suzanne Flon Collection, Paris; *Oval Lady*, 1956; private collection, Lausanne, *ibid.*).

During the late 1950s and early to mid-1960s Fini's paintings underwent a radical change: an explosion of colour and a blurring of form are conveyed by extremely delicate brushwork and the elaborate floral backgrounds, sometimes even foregrounds, evoke such Pre-Raphaelite works as John Everett Millais's *Ophelia* (1852; Tate Gallery, London), with discreet human and animal figures emerging from a floral jungle, as in *The Dew* (1963;

private collection, Paris, *ibid.*) and *Trough of Night* (1963; artist's estate). Soon Fini's preference for clear forms and self-imposing personae re-emerged, while she retained the delicate and brightly coloured backgrounds of flowers, greenery or aquatic turquoise. In the late 1960s the dominant beautiful women are often enhanced by the presence of Art Nouveau objects: in *Guardian of the Wells* (1967; private collection, Milan, *ibid.*), a lovely young lady with feline eyes, ivory skin and red hair decked with flowers watches over a set of delicate, multi-coloured Lalique-style vases.

By 1969–70 the lush backgrounds become less frequent and Fini's compositions often stage a strange surreal scene with mythical implications and erotic undertones. In *Capital Punishment* (1969; private collection, *ibid.*) three women make ready for a sinister ritual: one with red hair, wearing nothing but turquoise thigh-boots, sits with legs apart, revealing a red mound of venus, and looks coldly at a half-naked, brown-haired servant kneeling before her, holding a white, limp, sacrificial goose, while a third, fair-haired and straight out of an Impressionist painting, in a high-necked white dress and lacy hat whose broad rim hides her eyes, brandishes a castrating knife. Fini's most mythical canvas, *Narcissus* (1971; private collection, Basel), with a beautiful background of turquoise water and waterlilies, provides a perfect illustration for Pausanias' version of the Narcissus story, in which the young man nourishes an incestuous passion for his twin sister, and after her death mistakes his own image in a pool for hers. To the left of Fini's picture, the young naked Narcissus sits by a pool in which he is clearly reflected, legs apart, genitals displayed; next to him, a standing figure, also naked, has been cut off mid-thigh by the frame, so that the person's sexual identity remains concealed, though the legs look masculine; the corresponding reflection, however, reveals a complete and clearly female body, thus creating a climate of ambiguous androgyny.

Fini's passion for cats and her identification with them inspired much of her writing and other people's writing about her, as well as the most important single motif to appear in her painting from the early days to the mid-1990s. Xavière Gauthier tells a remarkable story, according to which until the age of four Leonor Fini had vertical pupils like a cat! (Gauthier 1973, p.88). *The Mutants* represents three little girls on a swing, with

such feline features that they appear to be turning into cats. As an additional Freudian *Witz*, such as the Surrealists enjoyed, each child is holding a large, live "pussy" (*chatte*) between her legs. Fini represented herself in *Ideal Life* (1950) as sitting on an exotic throne, surrounded by splendid Persian and other rare felines; she and the animals have the same cold, head-on stare. A visitor would find the artist in that same position, surrounded by a dozen similar long-haired cats of different colours. The animals inspired several of her later paintings, such as *Tigrana* (1994) and *Sunday Afternoon* (1980; both artist's estate). Her shows at the Galerie Dionne in Paris in the 1990s included many pen-and-ink drawings of cats, some of which were used to illustrate her feline children's story *Mourmour* (1976). Fini's last work, apart from the numerous cat pictures, consisted of a series of faces (*Passengers*, 1992; Galerie Dionne, Paris), as well as theatrical grotesques. Leonor Fini deservedly achieved considerable fame throughout Europe and continued to lead a very productive, though retired life, near the Palais Royal in Paris until her death.

GEORGIANA M.M. COLVILE

Flack, Audrey

American painter and sculptor, 1931–

Born in Washington Heights, New York, 30 May 1931. Studied at Cooper Union, New York, 1948–51; Yale University, New Haven (BFA 1952); Institute of Fine Arts, New York University, 1953; Art Students League, New York. Subsequently worked as a part-time teacher in New York: at Pratt Institute and New York University, 1960–68; Riverside Museum Master Institute, 1966–7; School of Visual Arts, 1970–74; National Academy of Design, from 1987; also Albert Dorne Professor, University of Bridgeport, Connecticut, 1975, and Mellon Professor, Cooper Union, 1982. Married H. Robert Marcus in 1970 (second marriage); two daughters from previous marriage born 1959 and 1961. Recipient of award of merit, Butler Institute of American Art, Youngstown, Ohio, 1974; Citation and honorary doctorate, Cooper Union, 1977; Saint-Gaudens medal, Cooper Union, 1982; Artist of the Year award, New York City Teachers Association, 1985. Member of the Board of

Directors, College Art Association of America, 1989–94. Lives in New York.

Selected Individual Exhibitions

Roko Gallery, New York: 1959, 1963
French and Co., New York: 1972
Louis K. Meisel Gallery, New York: 1974, 1976, 1978, 1983, 1991, 1995 (retrospective)
Joseloff Gallery, University of Hartford, CT: 1974
Carlson Gallery, University of Bridgeport, CT: 1975
Fine Arts Gallery, University of South Florida, Tampa/Art and Cultural Center, Hollywood, FL: 1981
Armstrong Gallery, New York: 1983
Hewlett Art Gallery, Carnegie-Mellon University, Pittsburgh: 1984
Cooper Union, New York: 1986–8 (*Saints and Other Angels*, touring)
Belk Building, Town Center Mall, Rock Hill, SC: 1990
Parrish Art Museum, Southampton, NY: 1991
Frederick S. Wight Art Gallery, University of California, Los Angeles: 1992–3 (*Breaking the Rules*, touring retrospective)

Selected Writings

"Luisa Ignacia Roldán", *Women's Studies*, vi, 1978, pp.23–33
Audrey Flack on Painting, New York: Abrams, 1981
"On Carlo Crivelli", *Arts Magazine*, lv, June 1981, pp.92–5
Art and Soul: Notes on Creating, New York: Dutton, 1986
Audrey Flack: The Daily Muse, New York: Abrams, 1989

Bibliography

Cindy Nemser, *Art Talk: Conversations with 12 Women Artists*, New York: Scribner, 1975
Audrey Flack: "The Gray Border Series", exh. cat., Louis K. Meisel Gallery, New York, 1976
Louis K. Meisel, *Photorealism*, New York: Abrams, 1980
Eileen Guggenheim-Wilkinson, *Photo-Realist Painting*, PhD dissertation, Princeton University, 1982
Charlotte Streifer Rubinstein, *American Women Artists from Early Times to the Present*, Boston: Hall, 1982
Thalia Gouma-Peterson, "Icons of healing energy: The recent work of Audrey Flack", *Arts Magazine*, lviii, November 1983, pp.136–41
Audrey Flack: A Pantheon of Female Deities, exh. cat., Louis K. Meisel Gallery, New York, 1991
Laurie S. Hurwitz, "A bevy of goddesses: Paintings and sculptures by Audrey Flack", *American Artist*, September 1991, pp.42–7, 85–7
Breaking the Rules: Audrey Flack: A Retrospective, 1950–1990, exh. cat., Frederick S. Wight Art Gallery, University of California, Los Angeles, and elsewhere, 1992 (contains extensive bibliography)
Louis K. Meisel, *Photorealism since 1980*, New York: Abrams, 1993
Mara R. Witzling, ed., *Voicing Today's Visions: Writings by Contemporary Women Artists*, New York: Universe, 1994
Patricia Mathews, "Goddess Redux", *Art in America*, lxxxii, March 1994, pp.88–91, 124–5
David R. Brigham, "The new civic art: An interview with Audrey Flack", *American Art*, ix, Winter 1994, pp.2–21

Audrey Flack was one of the first artists of the 1960s to use photographs as the basis for painting, yet her subject matter differed greatly from that of her male photo-realist colleagues – jewellery and perfume bottles, Hispanic Madonnas and narrative still lifes rather than the shiny surfaces of cars and motorcycles. Over the years she has been interested in imbuing her works – first paintings and then sculpture – with richly resonant layers of symbolic meaning. As a student at Cooper Union, she was recruited by Josef Albers to participate in the fine arts program at Yale University, although in contrast to his purist aesthetic she was captivated by the rich, lush surfaces of Baroque art. After graduation from Yale in 1952, she moved back to New York and studied anatomy with Robert Beverly Hale at the Art Students League, in response to her felt need to paint realistically, a technique that had been ignored in her previous art education.

During the 1950s Flack abandoned the Abstract Expressionist idiom used in her earliest paintings because of her belief that art's purpose was to communicate. Soon after she began her studies with Hale, recognisable imagery appeared in her work. One of a series of still lifes painted during this period, *Still Life with Apples and Teapot* (1955; private collection, repr. Los Angeles 1992, p.15), shows Flack's interest in recording the things of this world while retaining some elements of Abstract Expressionism. She also painted a series of self-portraits, very private images that she did not exhibit and through which she began to work out her conflict regarding both style and content. Beginning with the Abstract Expressionist *Self-Portrait* (1952) and culminating in *Self-Portrait: Dark Face* (1960; both Miami University Art Museum, Oxford, OH), her work shows an increasingly stabilising image of the artist, executed with broad, sometimes dripping, painterly strokes.

The 1960s represented a period of artistic consolidation for Flack. She abandoned her own image as a subject, painting instead those of her daughters, Melissa and Hannah. In the mid-1960s she branched away from the private sphere, basing her compositions on photographs pertaining to documentary news, focusing on such public figures as Roosevelt, Rockefeller, even Hitler. *Kennedy Motorcade* (1964; private collection, *ibid.*, p.53), her first work based on a colour photograph, showed President and Jackie Kennedy and the Texas governor John Connally, just moments before Kennedy was shot. This work confirmed the future direction of her art in terms of subject matter and style, as well as in her working method, which became increasingly based on photographic images.

The most important breakthrough for Flack occurred during the painting of the *Farb Family Portrait* (1969–70; Rose Art Museum, Brandeis University, Waltham, MA), when her impatience to move beyond the preliminary stage of blocking the drawing on to canvas with charcoal led her to project a slide directly on to canvas and to apply colour through the projected image. This technique quickly led to her mature style, in which she applied paint in layers with an airbrush, mixing primary colours directly on the surface of the painting, in order to achieve a more intense luminosity than through conventional means. After the Farb portrait, Flack experimented with this photo-realist technique in works built from easily recognisable imagery. Her complex, monumental still lifes of the 1970s may be seen as the culmination of these endeavours.

In the early 1980s Flack underwent another period of intense self-questioning, which resulted in her changing her primary artistic medium, from painting to sculpture. She describes the change as a response to the felt need for "something solid, real, tangible. Something to hold and to hold on to" (*Art and Soul* 1986, p.26). Her earliest piece was a small bronze putto, *Angel with Heart Shield* (1981; Ari Ron Meisel collection, New York). She soon executed a somewhat larger work in clay, *Black Medicine* (1981–2; Pamela Rosenau collection, New York), whose model was a 75-year-old black woman. This was the first of a series of diverse, heroic women and goddess figures – many of them in bronze – that formed the major part of Flack's output over the next decade, culminating in her commission of 1990–91 for the Rock Hill City Gateway, South Carolina, four "visions" of female strength, each 3.9 metres high. In the early 1990s she was also commissioned to make a colossal statue of *Queen Catherine of Braganza* (the founder of the New York borough of Queens) to stand opposite the United Nations. Flack's women depart from conventional images of femininity in that they are athletic, older, fierce. As Flack describes them: "they are real yet idealized … the 'goddesses in everywoman'" (lecture at the University of New Hampshire, May 1993).

Flack's sculptures bear a deep connection to her earlier work, particularly in their relation to femininity and its construction. The tension between woman as artist and woman as subject was a leitmotif in the series of self-portraits executed during the 1950s, particularly the *Anatomy Lesson* (1953; Miami University Art Museum) – a reference to Rembrandt's *Anatomy Lesson of Dr Tulp* (1632; Mauritshuis, The Hague) – and *Self-Portrait in Underpants* (1958; Miami University Art Museum), in which she stands at the easel, one hand on her tilted hip, confronting the viewer head on. When Flack began painting in a photo-realist style, women were a central subject of her art: Harry Truman's teachers, nuns leading a march, two women grieving over Kennedy, Carroll Baker, Marilyn Monroe. Flack also dealt with the construction of femininity in her monumental still lifes, without painting the actual likeness of a specific woman. A work such as *Jolie Madame* (1972; National Gallery of Australia, Canberra) presents in hot, lush, red tones the accoutrements of self-adornment of the beautiful woman. These works enabled her to explore the reflective surfaces that male photo-realists had found so captivating, yet their subject matter – "women's things" – is one that has been trivialised, seen as less appropriate or valuable, in our culture.

From the time she abandoned Abstract Expressionism, Flack sought a means of communicating expressive content through her work. While other photo-realists claimed that the subjects of their works were irrelevant, Flack chose to base her paintings on photographic imagery that communicated a particular socio-political point of view, culminating in the *Vanitas* series, including *Marilyn* (1977; University of Arizona Art Museum, Tucson) and *Wheel of Fortune* (1977–8; Louis K. Meisel Gallery collection, New York). These works make direct reference in both structure and motif – the candles, the hourglass – to the *vanitas* paintings of the Baroque period, with their didactic, symbolic purpose and engagement with broad philosophical issues, such as the passage of time and the meaning of life. Flack continued to explore "iconic images

for a secularized age" in such works from the early
1980s as *A Course in Miracles* (Linnea S. Dietrich
collection) and *Fruits of the Earth* (private collection, repr. Los Angeles 1992, p.96), in which she
deliberately attempted to create a harmonious integration of paths towards spirituality. Flack's sculptural works fulfil the purpose of her artistic endeavour in that they make a comprehensible statement
through manipulation of "readable" iconographic
elements. Her goddesses are all given symbolic and
mythological attributes – the *Egyptian Rocket
Goddess* (1990; private collection, Ontario, *ibid.*,
p.109) wields a snake, *Islandia* (1987; Samuel P.
Harn Museum of Art, University of Florida,
Gainesville) offers a conch, an eagle perches atop
the head of *American Athena* (1989; Donna and
Neil Weisman collection). Some of these figures, like
the *Rocket Goddess*, are hybrids, synthesised by
Flack; others, like *Athena*, *Diana* and *Medusa* are
reinterpretations of traditional mythological figures,
from a contemporary, feminist perspective.

MARA R. WITZLING

Fontana, Lavinia
Italian painter, 1552–1614

Baptised in Bologna Cathedral, 24 August 1552,
daughter of the painter Prospero Fontana and his
wife Antonia de Bonardis. Married Gian Paolo
Zappi of Imola, 1577; eleven children, 1578–95;
only three children were living in 1607. In Rome
by 28 April 1604. Died in Rome, 11 August 1614;
buried in Santa Maria sopra Minerva.

Bibliography
Raffaello Borghini, *Il Riposo*, Florence, 1584; reprint, ed. Mario Rosci, Milan, 1967

Francesco Cavazzoni, *Pitture et sculture ed altre cose notabili che sono in Bologna e dove si trovano*, Bologna, 1603; ed. Ranieri Varese in "Una guida inedita del seicento bolognese", *Critica d'Arte*, xvi, 1969, no.103, pp.25–38; no.104, pp.31–42; no.108, pp.23–34

Giulio Mancini, *Considerazioni sulla pittura* (c.1617–28), ed. Adriana Marucchi and Luigi Salerno, 2 vols, Rome: Accademia Nazionale dei Lincei, 1956–7

Giovanni Baglione, *Le vite de' pittori, scultori et architetti dal Pontificato di Gregorio XIII del 1572 in fino a' tempi di Papa Urbano Ottavo nel 1642*, Rome: Fei, 1642; reprinted Bologna: Forni, 1975–6

Antonio di Paolo Masini, *Bologna perlustrata*, Bologna, 1666

Carlo Cesare Malvasia, *Felsina pittrice: Vite dei pittori bolognesi*, Bologna, 1678; reprint, Bologna, 1969

—, *Le pitture di Bologna*, Bologna, 1686; reprint, ed. Andrea Emiliani, Bologna: ALFA, 1969

Luigi Lanzi, *Storia pittorica della Italia*, v, Bassano, 1819; as *The History of Painting in Italy*, London, 1828

Giordano Gaetano, *Notizie sulle donne pittrici di Bologna*, Bologna, 1832

Antonio Bolognini Amorini, *Vita de' pittori ed artefici bolognesi*, i/3, Bologna, 1843

Giovanni Gozzadini, "Di alcuni gioelli notati in un libro di ricordi del sec. XVI e di un quadro di Lavinia Fontana", *Atti e memorie della Reale Deputazione di storia patria per le province di Romagna*, i, Bologna, 1883, pp.1–16

Laura M. Ragg, *The Women Artists of Bologna*, London: Methuen, 1907

Tancred Borenius, "A portrait by Lavinia Fontana", *Burlington Magazine*, xli, 1922, pp.41–2

Bice Viallet, *Gli autoritratti femminili delle R. Gallerie degli Uffizi in Firenze*, Rome: Alfieri e Lacroix, 1923

Romeo Galli, *Lavinia Fontana, pittrice, 1552–1614*, Imola: Galeati, 1940

Paolo Della Pergola, "Contributi per la Galleria Borghese", *Bolletino d'Arte*, xxxix, 1954, pp.134–40

Eleanor Tufts, "Ms Lavinia Fontana from Bologna: A successful 16th-century portraitist", *Art News*, lxxiii, February 1974, pp.60–64

Women Artists, 1550–1950, exh. cat., Los Angeles County Museum of Art, and elsewhere, 1976

Eleanor Tufts, "L. Fontana: Bolognese humanist", *Le arti a Bologna e in Emilia dal XVI al XVII secolo: Atti del XXIV congresso internazionale di storia dell'arte: Bologna*, 1982, pp.129–34

Liana Cheney, "Lavinia Fontana: Boston *Holy Family*", *Woman's Art Journal*, v/1, 1984, pp.12–15

Angela Ghirardi, "Una pittrice bolognese nella Roma del primo seicento: Lavinia Fontana", *Carrobbio*, x, 1984, pp.149–61

Jean Owens Schaefer, "A note on the iconography of a portrait medal of Lavinia Fontana", *Journal of the Warburg and Courtauld Institutes*, xlvii, 1984, pp.232–4

The Age of Correggio and the Carracci: Emilian Painting of the Sixteenth and Seventeenth Centuries, exh. cat., Pinacoteca Nazionale, Bologna, and elsewhere, 1986

Vera Fortunati Pietrantonio, *Pittura bolognese del '500*, 2 vols, Bologna: Grafis, 1986

Maria Teresa Cantaro, *Lavinia Fontana bolognese, "pittore singolare", 1552–1614*, Milan: Jandi Sapi, 1989

Myriam Chiozza, *Lavinia Fontana: La rittratistica di committenza bolognese*, tesi di laurea, University of Bologna, 1993–4

Lavinia Fontana, 1552–1614, exh. cat., Museo Civico Archeologico, Bologna, 1994

Caroline P. Murphy, "Lavinia Fontana: The making of a woman artist", *Women of the Golden Age*, ed. Els Kloek and others, Hilversum: Verloren, 1994, pp.171–81

——, *Lavinia Fontana: An Artist and Her Society in Late Sixteenth-Century Bologna*, PhD dissertation, University of London, 1996

——, "Lavinia Fontana and female life-cycle experience in late sixteenth-century Bologna", *Picturing Women in Renaissance and Baroque Italy*, ed. Sara Matthews Grieco and Geraldine Johnson (in preparation)

Lavinia Fontana was the first female painter in Western Europe to have practised professionally not in a court or a convent, but as an equal among men in a city. In her lifetime she acquired an international reputation, and her works were sent to Spain, Germany and Persia. Fontana has the largest remaining oeuvre (more than 100 paintings) of any woman artist before the 18th century, producing small devotional paintings, large-scale altarpieces, portraits and mythological works.

She was the only surviving child of Prospero Fontana, an artist well-known in his day in Bologna, who taught her to paint. No indication has been found that Lavinia Fontana was a member of the painters' guild in Bologna, but her father was elected its head several times and this association may have allowed her to practise in the city without formal membership. Although Vasari knew Prospero, he makes no mention of his daughter in the second edition of his *Lives of the Artists* (1568), although he does mention Fontana's almost exact contemporary Barbara Longhi (q.v.); this would suggest that Fontana was at least in her late teens when she began her artistic education. Prospero ran a workshop frequented by a number of prominent Bolognese painters (Ludovico and Agostino Carracci, Denis Calvaert, Lorenzo Sabbatini and Orazio Sammachini), but it is not known whether Fontana learned and worked alongside them or if her father taught her privately. The difficulty with which she expressed her knowledge of anatomy in her paintings would suggest that anatomical drawing was not the focus of her training. Judging from her earliest works, from the early 1570s, it seems most likely that Prospero taught her to paint by setting her to work on small devotional paintings for domestic use, works for which there was a significant and steady demand in Counter-Reformation Bologna.

Gabriele Paleotti, Bishop of Bologna and a patron of Fontana, stated in *Il discorso intorno alle imagini sacre e profane* (1581), his treatise on sacred images, that religious paintings must be theologically correct, their messages clear and easy to understand. Fontana conformed to these injunctions. The *Mystic Marriage of St Catherine with SS Joseph, John the Baptist and Francis* (signed, c.1574; oil on copper; private collection, New York, repr. Cantaro 1989, p.56) is stylistically imbued with a sweetness and grave simplicity. The *Annunciation* (signed, c.1575; oil on copper; Walters Art Gallery, Baltimore) emphasises Mary's humility by contrasting her simple costume and downcast gaze with a dazzling and exotically clad angel. Both of these works show Fontana's taste at this time for a delicate and jewel-like colouring; she used soft blues, greens and pinkish tones. As she developed her artistic skills, her palette grew richer and her colours bolder. That these early pictures are both on copper, an expensive support, suggests that Fontana had already attracted a well-to-do clientele. She continued to paint such pictures on copper, but most of her subsequent work was on canvas. Her early works also reveal that she was much more influenced by Correggio and painters of the post-Tridentine era such as Federico Barocci and Scipione Pulzone than she was by her own father, who favoured a more acidic palette and grandiose rhetorical style. Clearly her father did not attempt to mould her in his own image.

Fontana also began to work on portraits of children during this period. Her earliest signed and dated work (1575) is a painting of a small boy holding a carnation (untraced, *ibid.*, p.63) which, with its warm tones, the bright orange of the boy's jerkin and his thoughtful, engaged expression, suggests that she may have used Venetian models for portraiture rather than the prevalent, rather chilly Bolognese portrait style typified by Bartolomeo Passerotti. Children's portraiture (including post-mortem portraits) is a genre that Fontana practised throughout her career.

In 1577 Fontana married Gian Paolo Zappi, a member of a minor noble family from Imola (after which she changed the signature on her paintings to Lavinia Fontana de Zappis). The change in marital status allowed her to expand her client base. She became the portrait painter of choice for scholars at the University of Bologna and over the next decade garnered a reputation as a painter of famous intellectuals. She represented these subjects in three-quarter profile, seated at a desk, perhaps in the throes of composition, as in *Portrait of a Scholar* (signed and dated 1581; Pinacoteca Nazionale, Bologna), or with their publications, correspondence and students in the background, as in the portrait of the historian *Carlo Sigonio* (signed, *c.*1578–9; Museo Civico, Modena). These men are given the appearance of being deep in thought, looking beyond the viewer with pensive expressions of psychological depth. The rendering of their academic robes reveals Fontana's great skill in the depiction of fabric, for which the Bolognese held her in great esteem.

Scholars' portraits also helped to establish Fontana's reputation outside Bologna. Men of letters were part of international scholarly networks – Carlo Sigonio had friends such as Fulvio Orsini in Rome, who expressly requested Sigonio's portrait to be painted by Fontana. In 1584 she was described by Borghini in *Il riposo* as a painter of both public and private works, whose paintings had been sent to Rome and elsewhere, where they were greatly prized. About this time Fontana also began to work for the Bolognese nobility and to forge particularly close relationships with Bolognese noblewomen. In 1584 she undertook a commission for a family portrait from Laudomia Gozzadini, a member of a prominent family. The portrait of the *Gozzadini Family* (signed and dated 1584; Pinacoteca Nazionale, Bologna) depicts Laudomia with her dead sister Ginevra with their husbands and dead father. The painting, some 2.1 × 2.4 metres, was innovative in Bologna in terms of size alone. As far as one can tell, no portrait in that city had ever been so large. The figures are life-size and are situated against an architectural background that is perspectivally rendered. It was designed, when hanging on a wall, to give the illusion that the sitters were in the same room as the viewer. The production of the portrait cemented a long-standing relationship between Fontana and Laudomia Gozzadini, who gave her many more commissions and was godmother to her son Severo in 1586.

Laudomia was probably responsible for helping to launch Fontana as the fashionable Bolognese society portraitist and for the next 20 years of her career, the Bolognese nobility, and in particular Bolognese noblewomen, would be the staple of Fontana's income. As in the case of her paintings of scholars, she developed a successful pictorial formula for the depiction of noblewomen. They were usually posed either seated or standing in a

half- or three-quarter-length portrait format, with a three-quarter profile view. They are invariably accompanied by a small dog, a popular companion for Bolognese noblewomen and a symbol of fidelity, a virtue in womanhood. Every detail of lavish, ornate dresses and jewels is recorded by Fontana. The personality of the women is an important feature of these portraits too – their gazes meet that of the viewer, their expressions are lively and intelligent – as can be seen in the portraits of *Costanza Alidosi Isolani* (two versions, both in private collections, *c.*1587, repr. Cantaro 1989, pp.172–3), *Isabella Ruini* (signed and dated 1593; Galleria Palatina, Palazzo Pitti, Florence) and the widowed *Ginevra Aldrovandi Hercolani* (*c.*1595; Walters Art Gallery). All these women were well-known personalities and beauties in their day in Bologna and were part of the same social group, which thus facilitated the creation of a patronage network for Fontana.

Fontana was also employed as a portraitist to visiting dignitaries in Bologna. In 1585 she painted *Francesco Panigarola* (signed and dated 1585; Galleria Palatina), a Franciscan prelate, later Bishop of Asti, who had been invited to preach in the cathedral of San Petronio that year. Her most elaborate work of this type is a picture of the *Queen of Sheba's Visit to Solomon* (National Gallery, Dublin), in which the figures are believed to be the Mantuan duke and duchess Vincenzo and Eleonora Gonzaga with their retinue, whose likenesses were taken by Fontana during one of their visits to Bologna in 1598 and 1600. The portrait-like heads were clearly painted at a different time from the bodies, judging from the uneasy relationship between the two. This disjuncture suggests that Fontana was painting the visiting subjects with the knowledge that they would soon be gone from the city.

Fontana appears to have been the first woman painter to produce a considerable number of large-scale altarpieces. Her first was *Christ in the House of Martha and Mary* (*c.*1580; Conservatorio di Santa Marta, Bologna) for the church of Santa Marta Zitella in Bologna, possibly painted in collaboration with her father (he was most likely responsible for the figure of Christ, while she herself painted the two women). Iconographically it is an unusual rendering of the subject, in part due to its focus on the women, because Mary occupies the centre of the canvas, a space usually reserved for Christ. She is also presented as an earnest young girl, rather than a sensual penitent. Another

Fontana altarpiece in which the female emphasis is striking is the nocturnal *Birth of the Virgin* (signed, *c.*1590; SS Trinità, Bologna). The painting has a genre-like character: the young girls in the foreground are totally occupied in bathing and swaddling the newborn child, while in the background food is given to the new mother.

Some of Fontana's most prestigious commissions were in the form of altarpieces. In 1589 she painted the *Holy Family with Sleeping Christ Child and Infant St John the Baptist* (signed and dated 1589; Escorial, Madrid). Philip II of Spain paid the huge sum of 1000 ducats for this picture, which arrived at the Escorial in 1593 and is now in the burial chapel of the Spanish Infanti. Whether Philip II commissioned this picture, or purchased it on the advice of one of his agents, is not known, but what is documented is Lavinia Fontana's association with the collector Alonso Ciacono, a friend of Francesco Pacheco, painter and artistic adviser to Philip II.

In 1599 Fontana received her first public commission in Rome, when she painted the *Virgin Appearing to St Hyacinth* for Cardinal Ascoli's chapel in Santa Sabina (signed and dated; *in situ*). This commission won her great praise in Rome and probably helped facilitate her move there in 1604, after which she became a portraitist at the Vatican court of Pope Paul V. Among the court dignitaries impressed by her artistic virtuosity was the Persian ambassador, who wrote a madrigal in her honour and claimed that of all the wonders he had seen in Rome, Lavinia Fontana was by far the greatest. In 1611 Fontana received another honour, when an Imolese medallist, Felice Antonio Casoni, cast a bronze portrait medal of her image (Biblioteca Communale, Imola). Its recto shows Fontana in a profile portrait, presented as a respectable matron, while its verso depicts her in a muse-like guise, seated at her easel, her painting instruments around her and her hair tussled, an indication of her inspired creativity.

Fontana also appears to have been the first woman artist to paint female nudes, of which three survive. The earliest of these, *Venus and Cupid* (signed and dated 1585; private collection, Venice, *ibid.*, p.136), has a chaste and moralising quality more usually seen in northern versions of this subject. Venus and Cupid, depicted full length, negate each other's erotic powers: Cupid clasps a pink train over Venus's pudenda, while Venus has taken Cupid's bow away from him. It is, however, still a sensual image: Venus caresses Cupid, the pink cloth and a gold veil contrast with the whiteness of her skin, and the jewels that adorn her body invite comment on the comparison between their hard lustre and the softness of her flesh. Venus is bedecked in a similar fashion in a half-length *Venus and Cupid* (signed and dated 1592; Musée des Beaux-Arts, Rouen). Here she has taken Cupid's arrow away from him, rendering him powerless, but what is most interesting is the Venus's striking similarity to Fontana's portrait of the famous local beauty, *Isabella Ruini*.

The last of her trio of nudes and the last known painting by her is perhaps the most interesting of all: *Minerva in the Act of Dressing* (dated 1613; Galleria Borghese, Rome), which was executed for the Borghese family who had been enthusiastic patrons of Fontana. As with the *Venus and Cupid* of 1585, this work is not an overtly erotic one. The goddess is shown from the side, so her body is visible only in silhouette. Around her lie her shield, cuirass, helmet, her instruments of war, now abandoned for the courtly robe she is about to don. The goddess, perhaps weary of war, invites comparison with Fontana's own state of mind. According to Mancini (*c.*1620, i, p.235), she had never recovered from the death of her only daughter in 1605, whom she had been training as a painter. In 1609 she wrote to a patron declaring that she was overburdened with work and that her hands were "broken" (Cantaro 1989, document 5a 24, p.314), suggesting that now in pain she was weary of the profession she had pursued for more than 40 years. She died the year after *Minerva* was painted. The woman painter, like the woman warrior, had finally laid down her tools.

CAROLINE P. MURPHY

Francis, Mary *see* Thornycroft

Frankenthaler, Helen
American painter and sculptor, 1928–

Born in New York, 12 December 1928. Studied at Bennington College, Vermont, 1946–9 (BA); Graduate School of Fine Arts, Columbia

University, New York, 1949. Married (1) artist
Robert Motherwell, 1958; divorced 1971; (2)
Stephen Dubruel, 1994. Taught at New York
University, 1959–61; Yale University, New Haven,
1966, 1967 and 1970; Hunter College, New York,
1970; Princeton University, 1971; Harvard
University, Cambridge, Massachusetts, 1976.
Represented USA at Venice Biennale, 1966.
Recipient of first prize, Paris Biennale, 1959; gold
medal, Pennsylvania Academy of the Fine Arts,
Philadelphia, 1968; Garrett award, Art Institute of
Chicago, 1972; Arts and Humanities, Yale
University, New Haven, 1976; New York City
Mayor's Award of Honor for Arts and Culture,
1986; Lifetime Achievement award, College Art
Association, 1994; and numerous honorary doctorates. Member, Fulbright Selection Committee,
1963–5; Board of Trustees, Bennington College,
1967–82; National Institute of Arts and Letters,
1974; National Council on the Arts (NEA),
1985–92; American Academy of Arts and Letters,
1990 (Vice-Chancellor 1991); American Academy
of Arts and Sciences, 1991. Lives in New York.

Selected Individual Exhibitions

Tibor de Nagy Gallery, New York: 1951, 1953, 1954,
  1956, 1957, 1958
André Emmerich Gallery, New York: 1959, 1960, 1961,
  1963, 1965, 1966, 1968, 1969, 1971, 1972, 1973,
  1975, 1977, 1978, 1979, 1981, 1982, 1983, 1984,
  1986, 1987, 1988, 1989, 1990, 1991, 1993
Jewish Museum, New York: 1960 (retrospective)
Kasmin Gallery, London: 1964
Whitney Museum of American Art, New York: 1969
  (touring retrospective, organised by International
  Council of Museum of Modern Art)
Janie C. Lee Gallery, Houston: 1975, 1976, 1978, 1980,
  1982
Corcoran Gallery, Washington, DC: 1975 (touring)
Solomon R. Guggenheim Museum, New York: 1975,
  1985–6 (touring)
Jacksonville Art Museum, FL: 1977–8 (touring)
Knoedler Gallery, London: 1978, 1981, 1983, 1985
Sterling and Francine Clark Art Institute, Williamstown,
  MA: 1980–81 (touring)
Rose Art Museum, Brandeis University, Waltham, MA:
  1981
Museum of Modern Art, New York: 1989–90 (touring
  retrospective)
M. Knoedler & Co., New York: 1992, 1994, 1995
National Gallery of Art, Washington, DC: 1993–4
  (touring)

Bibliography

E. C. Goosen, "Helen Frankenthaler", Art International,
  5 October 1961, pp.76–9
Henry Geldzahler, "An interview with Helen
  Frankenthaler", Art Forum, iv, October 1965,
  pp.36–8
Gene Baro, "The achievement of Helen Frankenthaler",
  Art International, xi, September 1967, pp.33–8
Barbara Rose, "Paintings within the tradition: The career
  of Helen Frankenthaler", Art Forum, 7 April 1969,
  pp.28–33
Lawrence Alloway, "Frankenthaler as pastoral", Art
  News, 10 November 1971, pp.67–8, 89–90
Hilton Kramer, "Helen Frankenthaler", New York Times,
  1 December 1973, p.27
E. A. Carmean, Jr, "On five paintings by Helen
  Frankenthaler", Art International, xxii, April–May
  1978, pp.28–32
Irving Sandler, The New York School: The Painters and
  Sculptors of the Fifties, New York: Harper, 1978
Barbara Rose, Frankenthaler, 3rd edition, New York:
  Abrams, 1979
John Russell, "Recent paintings by Helen Frankenthaler",
  New York Times, 13 November 1981, p.C26
Karen Wilkin, Frankenthaler: Works on Paper,
  1949–1984, New York: Braziller, 1984
H. H. Arnason, History of Modern Art: Paintings,
  Sculpture, Architecture, Photography, 3rd edition,
  revised by Daniel Wheeler, New York: Abrams, 1986
John Elderfield, Frankenthaler, New York: Abrams, 1989
Helen Frankenthaler: A Paintings Retrospective, exh. cat.,
  Museum of Modern Art, New York, and elsewhere,
  1989
Helen Frankenthaler: Prints, exh. cat., National Gallery
  of Art, Washington, DC, and elsewhere, 1993
Pegram Harrison and Suzanne Boorsch, Frankenthaler: A
  Catalogue Raisonné: Prints, 1961–1994, New York:
  Abrams, 1996

In 1953 Helen Frankenthaler had a solo exhibition
at the Tibor de Nagy Gallery, an important New
York gallery, featuring a landmark painting,
Mountains and Sea (1952; artist's collection), and a
good review in a major art journal, Art Digest.
Although this was still a coup for a young female
painter in New York – she had just turned 24 –
Frankenthaler was well prepared. The third daughter of New York State Supreme Court Justice Alfred
Frankenthaler and his wife Martha, she had been
educated at Dalton School in New York (where she
studied with Rufino Tamayo) and graduated from
Bennington College in Vermont. By 1950, she had
met the artists Lee Krasner (q.v.), Willem and Elaine
de Kooning, Franz Kline and Barnett Newman, and
the following year visited the studios of David Smith

and Jackson Pollock. In 1952 she travelled to Nova Scotia and Cape Breton in Canada in the summer, and in the autumn turned to paintings based on watercolours from that trip.

One of those autumn works, *Mountains and Sea*, is, historically, the most famous of the artist's works. The imagery, although abstracted, is still present in the composition, with the green and orange wooded peaks of the Nova Scotia mountains placed in contrast to the horizontal blues of the ocean. The palette of the picture is almost Cézanne-like in its pale tones, and reflects her summer watercolours. Most noteworthy – and also probably inspired by watercolours – was the application of paint, thin washes of oil spread on and thus soaking into unprimed canvas. Furthermore, whole areas were left unpainted, leaving even the artist to question when working on the painting: "Is it finished? Is it a complete picture?"

Mountains and Sea soon led to the creation of a whole school of painting, a first, historically speaking, for a female painter. Shortly after its first exhibition, two painters in Washington, DC, Kenneth Noland and Morris Louis, travelled to Frankenthaler's studio to see it, Louis calling it a "revelation". When they returned home, they adopted Frankenthaler's staining technique to more serial-type imagery – Noland's *Targets* and Louis's *Veils and Unfurleds*, and with these works established the so-called Color-Field School.

With this influence, Frankenthaler was considered a key member of the Color-Field School as it was recognised and then widely exhibited during the 1950s and 1960s. Her work, however, was decidedly different from the movement, remaining individual – rather than serial – and less than abstract. In such pictures as *Mother Goose Melody* (Virginia Museum of Fine Arts, Richmond) she used open drawing and stained passages to suggest that she and her sisters were being read to in a nursery, while in *Arden* (1961; Whitney Museum of American Art, New York) she employed an interweaving of areas of colour to suggest the forest in Shakespeare's play *As You Like It*. This latter connotation of an imaginary landscape gave way in the mid-1960s to works such as *The Bay* (1963; Detroit Institute of Arts), where the imagery is reflective of actual environments, in this instance Provincetown Bay where Frankenthaler had a summer studio.

As if in reaction to this direction in her own work, during the later 1960s and early 1970s there was a dramatic change in her painting, towards a nearly total abstraction. Now, simple block-like shapes of colour are abutted, or simple long lines of colour employed, in works whose only reference could be to heraldry or flags, as in *Summer Banner* (1968; collection Mr and Mrs Fayez Sarofim). In the mid-1970s Frankenthaler acquired a new summer/weekend studio and residence in Connecticut, in addition to those maintained in New York. As Frankenthaler worked beside Long Island Sound, the role of nature as seen returned to her work in pictures such as *Ocean Drive West No.1* (1974; private collection), which abstractly captures the sense of water and horizons seen from her studio. This aspect of her works – she also continued making less "relational" paintings – can also be seen in large canvases done in response to her experience of the great American Southwest – pictures such as *Natural Answer* (1976; Art Gallery of Ontario, Toronto), where the earthlike tones and horizontal strata link the work to the 19th-century American tradition of grand landscape painting.

From time to time in her career, Frankenthaler has chosen to paint works that can be seen as variations on those of the old masters. Her early *Las Mavas* (1958; Collection Norman and Irma Braman) is seen as an abstract composition until one realises that it is an inverted variation on Goya's *Mayas on a Balcony* (Metropolitan Museum of Art, New York). In a similar manner, her large abstract painting of 1981, *For E.M.* (private collection), is in fact a response to Edouard Manet's *Still Life with Carp* (Art Institute of Chicago).

Frankenthaler's career is also distinguished by her works in other media besides painting. In 1972, in Anthony Caro's studio in London, she created nine extraordinary works in welded sculpture, an interest she continued in 1975 in ceramic works made at Syracuse University. She has also worked extensively in printmaking and in illustrated books, and in 1985 designed the sets and costumes for the Royal Ballet's production of *Number Three* at Covent Garden, London. Works on paper – drawings and paintings – play the second largest role in her art, beginning in the 1950s and continuing today. Indeed, such recent large sheets as *Aerie* (1995; M. Knoedler & Co., New York) have approached the impact of her works on canvas.

E.A. CARMEAN, JR

Fuller, Meta Vaux Warrick   [fig. 22]

American sculptor, 1877–1968

Born Meta Vaux Warrick in Philadelphia, 9 June 1877. Studied at Pennsylvania School of Industrial Art (later Philadelphia College of Art), 1894–9 (scholarships; George K. Crozier and metalwork prizes 1899); Ecole des Beaux-Arts and Académie Colarossi, Paris, under Jean-Antoine Injalbert and Rollard, 1899–1903; also studied under Rodin in Paris. Attended Pennsylvania Academy of the Fine Arts, Philadelphia, 1907. Married psychiatrist Solomon Carter Fuller, 1909; three sons born 1910, 1911 and 1916; husband died 1953. Lived in Framingham, Massachusetts, after marriage. Most early work destroyed in a fire, 1910. Recipient of second prize, Massachusetts branch of Women's Peace Party, 1915. Fellow, Academy of the Fine Arts, Philadelphia. Member, Boston Art Club; American Federation of Arts; Federation of Women's Clubs, Wellesley Society of Artists; Civic League; Framingham Women's Club; honorary member and chair, Art Committee, Business and Professional Women's Club; chapter president, Zonta; honorary member, Alpha Kappa Alpha and Aristo Club, Boston. Died in Framingham, 13 March 1968.

Principal Exhibitions

Paris Salon: 1898–9, 1903
Pennsylvania Academy of the Fine Arts, Philadelphia: 1906, 1908, 1920, 1928
Jamestown Tercentennial Exposition: 1907 (gold medal)
Emancipation Proclamation Exposition, New York: 1913
New York Public Library: 1921
Boston Public Library: 1922
Art Institute of Chicago: 1927
Harmon Foundation, New York: 1931, 1932, 1933
Augusta Savage Studio, New York: 1939
Chicago: 1940 (*American Negro Exposition*)
Howard University, Washington, DC: 1961 (*New Vistas in American Art*, silver medal and citation)
Framingham Center Library, Framingham, MA: 1964 (individual)
City College of New York: 1967

Bibliography

Lorado Taft, *The History of American Sculpture*, 3rd edition, New York: Macmillan, 1930
Benjamin Brawley, *The Negro Genius: A New Appraisal of the Achievement of the American Negro in Literature and the Fine Arts*, New York: Dodd Mead: 1937
James A. Porter, *Modern Negro Art*, New York: Dryden Press, 1943; reprinted New York: Arno Press, 1969
Sylvia G.L. Dannett, "Meta Warrick Fuller", *Profiles of Negro Womanhood*, ii, Yonkers, NY: Educational Heritage, 1966, pp.31–46
Allan Morrison, "(Black) women in the arts", *Ebony*, August 1966, pp.90–94
The Evolution of Afro-American Artists, 1800–1950, exh. cat., City College of New York, 1967
Ten Afro-American Artists of the Nineteenth Century, exh. cat., Howard University Gallery of Art, Washington, DC, 1967
Ralph L. Harley, Jr, "A checklist of Afro-American art and artists", *Serif*, vii/4, 1970, pp.3–63
Elton Fax, *Seventeen Black Artists*, New York: Dodd Mead, 1971
Eleanor Tufts, *Our Hidden Heritage: Five Centuries of Women Artists*, New York and London: Paddington, 1974
Two Centuries of Black American Art, exh. cat., Los Angeles County Museum of Art and elsewhere, 1976
Samella S. Lewis, *Art: African American*, New York: Harcourt Brace, 1978; revised edition as *African American Art and Artists*, Berkeley: University of California Press, 1990
An Independent Woman: The Life and Art of Meta Warrick Fuller (1877–1968), exh. cat., Danforth Museum of Art, Framingham, and elsewhere, 1984
The Harlem Renaissance: Art of Black America, exh. cat., Studio Museum in Harlem, New York, 1987
Charlotte Streifer Rubinstein, *American Women Sculptors*, Boston: Hall, 1990

A sculptor of the Victorian era whose style ranged from romanticism to realism, Meta Fuller was one of the most prolific precursors of the Harlem Renaissance. Born to a middle-class family in Philadelphia, the daughter of a barber and a hairdresser, she attended the Pennsylvania School of Industrial Art for five years (1894–9), gaining recognition as the "sculptor of horrors" for her clay *Head of Medusa* and a figure of *Christ*. These works already indicate her absorption with heroic themes of sacrifice, slavery and suffering. By 1899 she was in Paris, studying at the Académie Colarossi and the Ecole des Beaux-Arts, and with artists including Rodin. Critics and historians have identified her with an elite group of African-American artists that included Henry Ossawa Tanner, William Edward Scott and May Howard Jackson. An alternative African-American art world was developing at the turn of the 19th and 20th centuries, and Fuller's stay in Paris reflected a pattern among many artists of colour to escape the restrictions of segregated, provincial America and seek training and exhibition opportunities in Europe.

For the Tercentennial Exposition in Jamestown of 1907 Fuller was commissioned to produce a 15-piece sculpture highlighting the history of African Americans. The African-American spokesman W. E. B. Du Bois commissioned a sculpture, *Emancipation Proclamation* (1913; plaster; Museum of the National Center of Afro-American Artists and Museum of Afro-American History, Boston), for the Emancipation Proclamation Exposition in New York of 1913. Fuller explained the subject thus:

> I represented the race by a male and a female figure standing under a tree, the branches of which are the fingers of Fate grasping at them to draw them back into the fateful clutches of hatred ... Humankind [is] weeping over her suddenly freed children who, beneath the gnarled fingers of Fate, step forth into the world, unafraid ... The Negro has been emancipated from slavery but not from the curse of race hatred and prejudice [quoted in Rubinstein 1990, p.202].

Fuller's *Awakening of Ethiopia* (1914; Schomburg Center for Research in Black Culture, New York) is composed of a partially wrapped mummy, bound from the waist down but with the hair and shoulders of a beautiful African woman, wearing the headdress of an ancient Egyptian queen: "in title and spirit ... unquestionably the image of Ethiopia, mythical symbol of Black Africa" (David Driskell in New York 1987, p.108). The work became emblematic of the Harlem Renaissance and the New Negro Movement and was associated with what the historian Alain Locke described as a rebirth of consciousness rooted in African art. Widely exhibited and acclaimed, this shrouded female figure reflected the contemporary obsession with Egyptian culture.

In 1915 Fuller was awarded second prize by the Women's Peace Party for her group sculpture *Peace Halting the Ruthlessness of War*. American racism presented her with the challenge of reconciling aesthetics and social advocacy, as in *Mary Turner (A Silent Protest Against Mob Violence)* (1919; painted plaster; Museum of Afro-American History), which commemorated a silent parade of 10,000 black workers in New York in 1917 to protest against continued violence against blacks. Fuller's piece was prompted by accounts in the *New York Times* and *Crisis* magazine, edited by Du Bois, of the lynching in Georgia of Mary Turner, a black woman accused of planning to murder a white man. Racial violence and the evasion of prosecution by whites was a major theme for UNIA (United Negro Improvement Association) and other political organisations of the period.

Fuller's involvement with the international tendency of the time is reflected in her marriage to the Liberian psychiatrist Dr Solomon Carter Fuller in 1909. The couple settled in Framingham, Massachusetts, and had three sons. She constructed a studio and continued to sculpt, despite a suspicious fire in 1910. Working primarily in plaster and bronze, she paid tribute to distinguished black Americans including *William Monroe Trotter, Samuel Coleridge Taylor, Frederick Douglass* and *Sojourner Truth*. Later works include *Talking Skull* (1937; bronze; Museum of Afro-American History), in which a nude black man kneels on the ground, gazing at a skull in front of him, and *Refugee* (1940; painted plaster; private collection), showing a refugee Jew trudging forward with a walking-stick. Fuller continued to exhibit until her death, and in 1984 the first retrospective exhibition was held at the Danforth Museum of Art in Framingham, curated by Joy L. Gordon, with works from the Meta Warrick Fuller Legacy founded by her family. Her work was also featured in the major exhibition *The Harlem Renaissance: Art of Black America*, held at the Studio Museum in Harlem in 1987.

Fuller's compositional power and aesthetic drive have been praised in many texts on American art, sculpture, women's art and African-American art. She led an active civic life and was a pioneer in combining a family and a career as a professional artist. She and her husband were honoured posthumously by the Framingham City Council and historical society in 1995 with the rededication of a city school as the Solomon and Meta Fuller Middle School.

ROBIN M. CHANDLER

G

Galizia, Fede [fig. 23]

Italian painter, *c.*1578–*c.*1630

Born *c.*1578; father Nunzio Galizia, a miniature painter from Trento who was active in Milan. Last recorded 21 June 1630, the date of her will, made in Milan.

Bibliography

Giovanni Paolo Lomazzo, *Idea del tempio della pittura*, Milan, 1590; reprint, ed. Robert Klein, 2 vols, Florence, 1974

Paolo Morigia, *La nobiltà di Milano*, Milan, 1595, p.282

Stefano Ticozzi, *Dizionario degli architetti, scultori, pittori ...*, 4 vols, Milan, 1830–33

Luigi Malvezzi, *Le glorie dell'arte Lombarda, ossia illustrazione storica delle più belle opere che produssero i lombardi in pittura, scultura ed architettura dal 1590 al 1850*, Milan, 1882, p.212

Gino Fogolari, "Artisti trentini a Milano: Nunzio e Fede Galizia", *Tridentum*, i, 1898, pp.307–18

Curt Benedict, "Osias Beert", *L'Amour de l'Art*, xix, September 1938, pp.307–14

Roberto Longhi, "Un momento importante nella storia della 'natura morta'", *Paragone*, i/1, 1950, pp.34–9

G. De Logu, *Natura morta italiana*, Bergamo, 1962

Stefano Bottari, "Fede Galizia", *Arte Antica e Moderna*, vi/24, 1963, pp.309–18

—, *Fede Galizia pittrice (1578–1630)*, Trent, 1965

Renato Ruotolo, "Un dipinto ignoto di Fede Galizia", *Paragone*, xix/215, 1968, pp.65–6

Dizionario enciclopedico Bolaffi dei pittori e degli incisori italiani, Turin: Bolaffi, 1972–6

Women Artists, 1550–1950, exh. cat., Los Angeles County Museum of Art, and elsewhere, 1976

M. Rosci, "Italia", *Natura in posa: La grande stagione della natura morta europea*, Milan, 1977, pp.83–112

M. Bona Castellotti, "Due aggiunte al catalogo di Fede Galizia", *Arte Lombarda*, no.49, 1978, pp.30–32

Charles Sterling, *Still Life Painting from Antiquity to the Twentieth Century*, revised edition, New York: Harper, 1981 (French original, 1952)

Italian Still-Life Paintings from Three Centuries, exh. cat., Centro Di, New York, and elsewhere, 1983

Natura morta italiana/Italienische Stillebenmalerei aus drei Jahrhunderten: Sammlung Silvano Lodi/Italian Still-Life Painting from Three Centuries: The Silvano Lodi Collection/Tre secoli di natura morta italiana: La raccolta Silvano Lodi, exh. cat., Alte Pinakothek, Munich, and elsewhere, 1984

Luigi Salerno, *La natura morta italiana, 1560–1805/Still Life Painting in Italy, 1560–1805*, Rome: Bozzi, 1984

Giacomo Berra, "Alcune puntualizzazioni sulla pittrice Fede Galizia attraverso le testimonianze del letterato Gherardo Borgogni", *Paragone*, xl/469, 1989, pp.14–29

M. Natale and A. Morandotti, *La natura morta in Lombardia*, i, 1989, pp.196–317

Francesco Porzio, ed., *La natura morta in Italia*, 2 vols, Milan: Electa, 1989

Giacomo Berra, "La natura morta nella bottega di Fede Galizia", *Osservatorio delle Arti*, no.5, 1990, pp.55–62

Flavio Caroli, *Fede Galizia*, 2nd edition, Turin: Allemandi, 1991

—, "Aggiunte a Sofonisba Anguissola e Fede Galizia", *Notizie da Palazzo Albani*, xx/1–2, 1991, pp.143–8

Giacomo Berra, "Appunti per Fede Galizia", *Arte Cristiana*, lxxx/748, 1992, pp.37–44 (with English summary)

It is not certain that Milan was Fede Galizia's city of birth: according to some writers she arrived there as a small child with her father Nunzio Galizia, a miniature painter of some repute from Trento, who was called to the city to execute some works; according to other sources, she was born when her father was already in Milan. What is certain is that her development as a painter took place in Milan and thus in Lombardy, which in this period was under the domination of Spain and the Counter-Reformation, with consequences that in figurative art brought a return to educative and devotional religious painting, to comply with the requirements of the Church. But, paradoxically, some painters abandoned religious painting to take refuge in genre painting, which allowed them to adhere to a realistic vision of life and thus to continue the Lombard pictorial tradition.

Fede Galizia was not a follower of any particular school, but her antecedents are the greatest representatives of the Lombard spirit of realism, such as Moretto da Brescia, Gian Girolamo Savoldo and Vincenzo Campi. She must have turned to Lorenzo Lotto for her introspective portraits, while her theories on the motions of the soul derive from Giovan Paolo Lomazzo. She developed a personal style that nevertheless in her religious pictures reflects the late Mannerism of Emilia and in her portraits the naturalism and interest in psychological analysis typical of Lombardy.

According to a late supposition (Ticozzi 1830), followed by many later 19th-century critics, in the early years of her career Galizia painted miniatures, but nothing is known of these today. In 1590, when the child prodigy was only 12 years old, Lomazzo, the celebrated painter and historian of the period, recorded his admiration for her copies after the best Italian painters. Accomplished equally in painting and in drawing, and considered a most excellent artist, Galizia impressed the critics of the day with her portraits, which were regarded as miraculous for the accuracy of their likeness.

The Jesuit historian Paolo Morigia, who mentioned Galizia in his *Nobiltà di Milano* (1595) as among the most distinguished people of the period, recorded some works by her that are now untraced, including a *Portrait of the Father and Mother of the Painter* and portraits of *Paolo Morigia* (1595), *Maria Giron de Velasca* and *Camilla Ferraro*. Among other documented works, also untraced, were those commissioned from Galizia by the Emperor Rudolph II. Her portraits were never idealised, but resulted from a desire to render reality, the basis of which lay in the studies of physiognomy developed in the 16th century and which revolutionised portraiture. In 1596 she painted another portrait of *Paolo Morigia* (Pinacoteca Ambrosiana, Milan), with an inscription stating that she was 18, from which her date of birth has been deduced. The historian is depicted after having written a poem about the painter and the painting itself. The pensive expression of the sitter is achieved through the reproduction of his characteristic expressions: mouth firmly closed and deep wrinkles on the forehead, lively eyes and the patient expression of someone doing his best to hold a pose; the lenses that reflect the room record the optical experiments

typical of northerners; and the volume of the *Nobiltà di Milano*, on the left of the picture, reflects the fashion for portraying scholars, flanked by a still life of heaped books, an inkstand and a manuscript. The portrait of *Pietro Martire Mascheroni* (1622; Ospedale Maggiore, Milan), the benefactor of the Milan hospital, which is documented in the hospital's register of expenses of 1623 with a note of the artist's remuneration, reveals in the ruff the care that Galizia paid to details. The portrait of *Ludovico Settala* (collection Mina Gregori, Florence, repr. Caroli, *Fede Galizia*, 1991, fig.28), with an old inscription on the back that credits it to the painter, is one of the paintings that Galizia executed for the gallery of the noble Milanese family of Settala. A probable self-portrait is the signed *Woman Dressed as Diana* (c.1590s; private collection, Milan, *ibid.*, fig.l of appendix), in which the embroidery on the dress, the jewels and the smooth face resemble other female figures by Fede. A painting such as *St Carlo in Ecstasy* (San Carlo alle Mortelle, Naples), signed and dated (1611) at the bottom, recalls the moving devotional paintings of Giovanni Battista Crespi in the expressions of the saint, and the Lombard tradition for the background landscape and the angel chorus in the upper right of the canvas, while the saint's cope and the ecclesiastical dress are reproduced with the telling detail typical of the artist.

The Leonardesque landscape and Correggesque Emilian accents that Galizia introduced into her religious painting are found in the *Noli me tangere* (Santo Stefano, Milan), a signed painting executed in 1616 for the high altar of the church of the Maddalena in Milan. The realist tendency of Galizia's portraits was sacrificed in her pictures of religious themes to comply with the moral exigencies of the period and to pursue a model of ideal beauty: the figure of Christ, wrapped in a white cloth, is too rounded in bulk and has a mannered pose; the Magdalene, sinuously kneeling and elegantly dressed, flaunts a flowing blond head of hair. The flowers beside Christ, painted with the precision typical of the artist, form a counterbalance to the background landscape.

Perhaps it was feminine sensibility that caused Galizia to identify herself with the heroine Judith and to paint several versions of *Judith with the Head of Holofernes*. Of these, we know of a painting on canvas (Ringling Museum of Art, Sarasota. FL), which bears, inscribed on the knife in Judith's left fist, the signature and date (1596). Galizia's careful execution of the jewels and fabrics in this work is particularly notable – a precision in the rendering of detail that derives from her probable training as a miniature painter with her father. There is also a version on panel (private collection, Milan, *ibid.*, fig.4), datable to *c.*1620. Another version, executed by Galizia in 1601, is now in the Galleria Borghese, Rome. In this work, echoes of Emilian Late Mannerism are so obvious that until the discovery of the signature and date (1601) the painting was attributed to Lavinia Fontana (q.v.). The style, compared to the Sarasota version, is softer, the jewels and the dress differ subtly, and the whole scene is less disturbing due to the fact that Judith gazes in a different direction in relation to the viewer.

There is little documentation about Galizia, her private life was free from great events, and it is only thanks to 20th-century scholars that she is known as a painter of still lifes. This happened following a discovery, published by Curt Benedict (1938), of a still life signed and dated 1602, the *Tazza with Plums, Pears and a Rose* (ex-Anholt collection, Amsterdam, *ibid.*, fig.5). This is now untraced, but a slightly larger version (private collection, Bassano, *ibid.*, fig.6) is the model for stylistic comparison for other still lifes assigned to the painter. In some cases Galizia's still lifes have been confused with those of Panfilo Nuvolone, a contemporary painter, but closer observation reveals a more sculptural style, more spacious composition and a more meticulous rendering of the modelling. True still lifes, introduced into Italy and Milan at the end of the 16th century, about the time of the one secure still life by Galizia, are few indeed: the *Basket of Fruit* (*c.*1596; Pinacoteca Ambrosiana) by Caravaggio, which marks the difference from the Flemish still lifes executed in Italy by Jan Bruegel, and the *Peaches on a Dish*, dated 1595, the only still life by the Milanese painter Ambrogio Giovanni Figino. Galizia, in this light, can be seen as an artist of the avant-garde, present at the moment in which objects of nature became autonomous subjects in painting.

Simple, balanced compositions, never excessive, few objects depicted, frontal and slightly raised viewpoint, and dark backgrounds characterise her still lifes: above all not analytic nor herbalistic research, but a sensitive representation of the object. A central tazza, of a type common in Lombardy, with few surrounding elements, is frequently repeated by Galizia: the example from the Anholt collection, like the copy in Bassano, is slightly assymmetrical and includes some perfectly formed fruit, almost unreal, and at the bottom a blackened half pear next to another pear that is half bright red and half yellow, counterbalanced with a slightly faded rose, symbol of the transience of beauty.

The *Glass Tazza with Peaches and Apples* (Museo Civico, Cremona), often copied (French and Co., New York, ex-Vitale Bloch collection; private collection, *ibid.*, fig.12; private collection, Bassano, *ibid.*, fig.13; Silvano Lodi collection, Campione d'Italia, *ibid.*, fig.2 of appendix), for which a probable pendant is *Apples, Basket with Chestnuts and a Rabbit* (Museo Civico, Cremona), also copied (private collection, *ibid.*, fig.60; private collection, Milan, *ibid.*, fig.61), has a more monumental setting, but also is lightened by the glass tazza and the delicate jasmine. It is interesting to note, in the *Wicker Basket with Peaches and Jasmine* (private collection, New York, ex-Sperling collection, *ibid.*, fig.23), the absence of the front part of the supporting plane that usually appears in the still lifes of Galizia and the clean cut of the flower on the lower right, suggesting a late reduction in size of the panel to give greater emphasis to the roundness of the fruit. *Peaches in a Ceramic Basket* (Silvano Lodi collection, Campione d'Italia) can be seen as a *vanitas* because of the three stages of fruit represented: to the left the unripe plums, in the centre the mature peaches and to the right the slightly faded plums. The ceramic basket, another motif that occurs frequently in her still lifes, stands out in the centre against a very dark background.

After a period of new experiments with more casual compositions to which she added irregularly formed vegetables, Galizia recovered the balance that had been characteristic of her still lifes, which were now more interesting due to her increased confidence and experience. The forms, constructed by reflections of light, and the composition, balanced yet varied, made even more expressive and intimate the relationship between the painter and her works. Datable to this last period are the *Tazza with Pears* (ex-Lorenzelli collection, Bergamo, *ibid.*, fig.21), in which Galizia used the corner of a table as a support, and *Grapes and Plums in a Ceramic Basket* (private collection, Italy, *ibid.*, fig.34) and its pendant, *Grapes in a White Ceramic Bowl* (private collection, *ibid.*, fig.35). Versions of the two preceding works are *Grapes and Plums in a Ceramic Basket* (private collection, Switzerland, repr. Caroli,

Notizie da Palazzo Albani, 1991, fig.8) and *Grapes in a White Ceramic Bowl* (private collection, Switzerland, *ibid.*, fig.9), discovered a few years ago.

Roberto Longhi (1950) was correct when he defined the still lifes of Fede Galizia as "careful" but "sad"; like the artist, they are pious, balanced and silent. The religious fervour of the painter is also evident from the will she made in 1630, probably when there was an outbreak of plague in Milan: she asked that her bequests, almost exclusively paintings, should be given to the religious order of Theatines, to which she was particularly linked, and to her cousin and nephew, her only relatives.

DOMENICA SPADARO and FLAVIO CAROLI

Garzoni, Giovanna
Italian painter, 1600–1670

Born 1600, probably in Ascoli Piceno, Marche, to Giacomo Garzoni and Isabetta Gaia, who came from a family of artists of Venetian origin. In Venice c.1615–30, perhaps not continuously. In Naples, in the service of the Spanish viceroy, the Duque de Alcalá, 1630. In Turin, in the service of Cristina of France, wife of Vittorio Amedeo I, Duke of Savoy, 1632–7. In Florence, working for the Medici, 1642 and c.1646–51. Settled in Rome permanently, 1651. Made a will in 1666, bequeathing her estate to the painters' guild in Rome, the Accademia di San Luca, on condition that they erect her tomb in their church, SS Luca e Martino. Died in Rome between 10 and 15 February 1670 (monument designed by Mattia de' Rossi, with portrait and inscription by Giuseppe Ghezzi of Ascoli, erected in SS Luca e Martino, 1698).

Bibliography

Lione Pascoli, *Vite de' pittori, scultori et architetti moderni*, 2 vols, Rome: Antonio de' Rossi, 1730–36; ed. Alessandro Marabottini, Perugia: Electa Umbri, 1992

La natura morta italiana, exh. cat., Palazzo Reale, Naples, 1964

Angela Cipriani, "Giovanna Garzoni miniatrice", *Ricerche di Storia dell'Arte*, i, 1976, pp.241–54

Women Artists, 1550–1950, exh. cat., Los Angeles County Museum of Art, and elsewhere, 1976

Italian Still-Life Paintings from Three Centuries, exh. cat., Centro Di, New York, and elsewhere, 1983

Sylvia Meloni, "Giovanna Garzoni miniatora medicea", *FMR*, no.15, 1983, pp.77–96

Immagini anatomiche e naturalistiche nei disegni degli Uffizi sec. XVI e XVII, exh. cat., Galleria degli Uffizi, Florence, 1984

Natura morta italiana/Italienische Stillebenmalerei aus drei Jahrhunderten: Sammlung Silvano Lodi/Italian Still-Life Painting from Three Centuries: The Silvano Lodi Collection/Tre secoli di natura morta italiano: La raccolta Silvano Lodi, exh. cat., Alte Pinakothek, Munich, and elsewhere, 1984

Marco Rosci, "Giovanna Garzoni dal Palazzo Reale di Torino a Superga", *Scritte di storia dell'arte in onore di Federico Zeri*, ii, Milan, 1984, pp.565–7

Luigi Salerno, *La natura morta italiana, 1560–1805/Still Life Painting in Italy, 1560–1805*, Rome: Bozzi, 1984

Silvia Meloni, "The gentle genre: Giovanna Garzoni", *FMR America*, no.11, 1985, pp.105–24

Il seicento fiorentino: Arte a Firenze da Ferdinando I a Cosimo III, exh. cat., 3 vols, Palazzo Strozzi, Florence, 1986

Francesco Porzio, ed., *La natura morta in Italia*, 2 vols, Milan: Electa, 1989

Gerardo Casale, *Giovanna Garzoni, "Insigne miniatrice", 1600–1670*, Milan: Jandi Sapi, 1991 (contains extensive bibliography)

Although the Baroque artist Giovanna Garzoni produced religious, mythological and allegorical paintings in her early years (examples of the latter genres all untraced), from the 1640s she specialised in still life. Little is known of her early artistic training; it is possible that she began her apprenticeship with her maternal uncle, Pietro Gaia, a painter and engraver in her home town of Ascoli Piceno. By c.1620 Garzoni had contributed a *St Andrew* (Accademia, Venice) to a series of the *Apostles* painted for the church of the Ospedale degli Incurabili in Venice, an important commission that suggests that she had been studying there with an influential master, perhaps even Jacopo Negretti, known as Palma il Giovane, whose style permeates the *St Andrew*. Soon afterwards, however, Garzoni abandoned the monumental style and rich colourism of the Venetian manner and began to work on an intimate scale, using water-based paint on parchment.

The *Portrait of a Gentleman* (Stichting Historische Verzamelingen van het Huis Oranje-Nassau, The Hague), signed and dated 1625, Venice, on the reverse, shows Garzoni's delicate stippled technique that, combined with carefully handled gradations of colour, results in an extremely refined and luminous surface. Garzoni's early interest in decorative design and naturalistic motifs can be seen in a book of calligraphic studies (Biblioteca Sarti, Rome), in which she illuminates a capital letter with fruit, flowers, birds and insects. The drawing is executed with graceful, flowing lines, subtle colouration and a fine pointillist technique, all characteristic of her mature style.

Garzoni never married; she pursued her artistic career with intensity, enjoying a life of steady work and constant success. In the few lines devoted to her in the *Vite* (1730–36) Lione Pascoli comments on Garzoni's productivity, and on the fact that she sold her works "for whatever price she wished", counting among her patrons the Medici in Florence and the powerful Barberini family in Rome. In 1632, after a year in Naples in the service of the Spanish viceroy, Garzoni was persuaded by Cristina of France, Duchess of Savoy, to move to Turin, where she came into contact with Netherlandish and northern Italian paintings; the portrait of *Vittorio Amedeo, Duke of Savoy* (Uffizi, Florence) shows Garzoni's preoccupation with the naturalism and meticulous attention to detail of the northern schools, as well as her knowledge of the English portrait tradition.

Between 1646 and 1651 Garzoni resided in Florence. To these years dates the quaint portrait of a *Lap Dog with Biscuits and a Cup* (Galleria Palatina, Palazzo Pitti, Florence), commissioned by Vittoria della Rovere, wife of Grand Duke Ferdinand II de' Medici, a work that attests to Garzoni's familiarity with Dutch painters. For her Florentine patrons she also produced paintings on the popular theme of a vase of flowers; both casual arrangements set in a simple glass vase (*Vase with Tulips and Hyacinths*; Uffizi), in the tradition of the Roman followers of Caravaggio, and much more elaborate bouquets, decorated with butterflies, insects and exotic shells (*Vase with Various Flowers Resting on a Marble Ledge, with a Shell on Either Side and Several Butterflies Above*; Gabinetto Disegni e Stampi degli Uffizi, Florence), reminiscent of compositions by the Dutch painter Ambrosius Bosschaert. In 1651 Garzoni moved to Rome, well-known, wealthy and closely connected with the Accademia di San Luca (opinions vary as to whether she had actually been elected to the Academy, although she did leave her estate to it and was buried in its church; cf. Casale 1991, p.11, with Harris in Los Angeles 1976, p.135).

Garzoni is best known today for the series of 20 small tempera still lifes of fruit and vegetables that she completed for Ferdinand II de' Medici between c.1650 and 1662 (all Galleria Palatina). The illustration of agrarian bounty was a traditional theme for the decoration of country villas, and Garzoni's elegant and refined interpretation of such ordinary subjects was well suited to her aristocratic patrons. *Dish with Plums, Jasmine and Walnuts* shows the characteristic composition of a central dish of fruit, here resting on a stippled, rocklike surface. In the front of the picture plane, to add interest to the composition, the artist introduces another single flower, or split fruit, or sometimes a bird or insect. In this example, jasmine and morning glory are intertwined with the delicately coloured plums, while a cracked walnut decorates the foreground. The composition is sophisticated and deceptively simple. Garzoni skilfully modulates shapes, textures and colours to evoke the sense of smell and touch, as well as vision – a preoccupation with the senses that was characteristic of 17th-century Dutch and Flemish art. The works of such Lombard painters as Fede Galizia (q.v.) and Panfilo Nuvolone, which Garzoni had seen in Turin, were also a strong influence. Galizia's small still lifes of, for example, a dish of peaches, centrally placed and set on a shallow stage, show a similar concern with representing reality through reference to the senses.

Another important model for Garzoni were the natural science illustrations by the Veronese artist Jacopo Ligozzi, who around 1576 was working in Florence for Francesco I de' Medici. Ligozzi's elegant and precise tempera drawings exhibited a refinement and formal clarity evident in Garzoni's later still lifes and botanical drawings; in fact, several of Garzoni's works, including *Still Life with Birds and Fruit* (Cleveland Museum of Art), were thought to be by Ligozzi until Mina Gregori corrected the misattribution (Gregori in Naples 1964, p.28). Although Garzoni was predisposed early on to naturalism and close observation, with the possible exception of a herbal (c.1650–55; Dumbarton Oaks, Washington, DC) containing 49 highly naturalistic botanical drawings, her works do not strictly fit the category of scientific illustration (for a discussion of the herbal, see Paola Lanzara in Casale 1991, pp.34–44). *Hyacinth Plant with Four Cherries, a Lizard and an Artichoke* (Uffizi), one of a series of four botanical studies dating to the end of the 1640s, exemplifies Garzoni's particular talent of combining naturalistic observation with a strong sense of the decorative and the aesthetic. The plant is drawn in minute detail, botanically accurate with flower, stem, bulb and roots, but the combination of the four subjects on the page is purely aesthetic. There is no natural correlation between them; they are a study in shapes and textures. A large fly is posed on the cut stem of the artichoke – reminiscent of Dutch still lifes – and the unnatural position of the lizard's legs suggests that it has been drawn not from life, but from a dead specimen.

Dish with an Open Pomegranate, a Grasshopper, a Snail and Two Chestnuts (Galleria Palatina) shows a variation on the theme that unites the 20 temperas cited above, and further illustrates Garzoni's interest in showing the variety of the natural world in all its precise detail, but only in so far as it suited her artistic aims. With its grainy-textured terrain continued into the background, the unnaturally large grasshopper and the subtly modulated colour contained within crisp outlines, the little picture vibrates with a living energy; the effect is charming and poetic, a fantasy still life, despite microscopic attention to detail. The awkward perspective, which adds to the abstract quality of the picture, may be due to Garzoni's use of the convex mirror, a standard artist's aid of the time. The *Old Man of Artimino* (?1648–9; Galleria Palatina) shows Garzoni's idiosyncratic use of perspective and proportion, as well as her consistently fine technique.

ELIZABETH MULLEY

Geddes, Margaret *see* Carpenter

Geddes, Wilhelmina (Margaret)
Irish stained glass and graphic artist,
1887–1955

Born in Drumreilly, Co. Leitrim, 25 May 1887. Studied at Belfast Municipal Technical Institute, *c.*1901–13; Metropolitan School of Art, Dublin, *c.*1911–12. Joined An Túr Gloine (Tower of Glass), Dublin, 1912; subsequently worked in Dublin and Belfast. Lived in Belfast, 1922–5.

Worked independently in London, based at the Glass House, Fulham, from 1925; taught the technique of stained glass to Evie Hone (q.v.). Member, Belfast Art Society, 1907–10 and 1925–8; Guild of Irish Art Workers, 1917; Ulster Academy, 1932. Died in London, 10 August 1955.

Principal Exhibitions

Arts and Crafts Society of Ireland, Dublin: 1910, 1917, 1921, 1925
Royal Hibernian Academy, Dublin: 1913–14, 1916, 1930
Whitechapel Gallery, London: 1913 (*Irish Art*)
British Empire Exhibition, Wembley, London: 1914
Musée du Louvre, Paris: 1914 (*Arts décoratifs de Grande Bretagne et d'Irlande*)
Royal Dublin Society Art and Industries Show: 1921
Galerie Barbazanges, Paris: 1922 (*L'Art irlandais*)
John Magee's Gallery, Belfast: 1924 (with Rosamond Praeger)
Arts and Crafts Exhibition Society, England: from 1926
Design and Industries Association, Leipzig: 1927
Society of Scottish Artists, Edinburgh: 1929

Selected Writings

"Making stained glass windows", *Belfast News-letter*, 25 September 1930

Bibliography

Stephen Gwynn, "The art of Miss W.M. Geddes", *The Studio*, lxxxiv, 1922, pp.208–13
Charles J. Connick, "Modern glass: A review", *International Studio*, lxxx, October 1924, pp.40–52
Bernard Rackham, "Stained glass windows by Miss W.M. Geddes", *The Studio*, xcviii, 1929, pp.682–3
Joan Howson, "Obituary", *Journal of the British Society of Master Glass Painters*, xii/1, 1955–6, pp.68–70
Anthea Callen, *Angel in the Studio: Women in the Arts and Crafts Movement, 1870–1914*, London: Astragal, 1979; as *Women Artists of the Arts and Crafts Movement, 1870–1914*, New York: Pantheon, 1979
Nicola Gordon Bowe, "Wilhelmina Geddes: Ireland's extraordinary artist", *Quarterly of the Stained Glass Association of America*, lxxvi, Spring 1981, pp.41–3
——, *Irish Stained Glass*, Dublin and Belfast: Arts Councils of Ireland, 1983 (text and fully documented slide pack)
The Dublin Arts and Crafts Movement, 1880–1930, exh. cat., Edinburgh College of Art, 1985
Women Artists of the Arts and Crafts Movement, exh. cat., William Morris Gallery, Walthamstow, 1985
Nicola Gordon Bowe, "Cats are my favourite animals: Wilhelmina Geddes (1887–1955)", *New Perspectives: Studies in Art History in Honour of Anne Crookshank*, ed. Jane Fenlon and others, Dublin: Irish Academic Press, 1987, pp.207–18
——, "Women and the Arts and Crafts revival in Ireland, *c.*1886–1930", *Irish Women Artists from the*

Eighteenth Century to the Present Day, exh. cat., National Gallery of Ireland, Dublin, and elsewhere, 1987, pp.22–7

——, "Wilhelmina Geddes", *Irish Arts Review*, iv/3, Autumn 1987, pp.53–9

Centenary Exhibition of Wilhelmina Geddes, exh. cat., Arts Council of Northern Ireland, Belfast, 1987

Nicola Gordon Bowe, "Wilhelmina Geddes, 1887–1955: Her life and work – a reappraisal", *Journal of Stained Glass*, xviii, 1988, pp.275–301

——, "Wilhelmina Geddes, Harry Clarke and their part in the Arts and Crafts movement in Ireland", *Journal of Decorative and Propaganda Arts*, no.8, Spring 1988, pp.58–79

Nicola Gordon Bowe, David Caron and Michael Wynne, *Gazetteer of Irish Stained Glass*, Dublin: Irish Academic Press, 1988

Nicola Gordon Bowe, "Two early twentieth century Irish Arts and Crafts workshops in context: An Túr Gloine and the Dun Emer Guild and Industries", *Journal of Design History*, ii, 1989, pp.193–206

Katherine Shaw, *Wilhelmina Geddes and Her Laleham Window*, BA thesis, West Glamorgan Institute of Higher Education, 1989

Fiona Ciaran, *Stained Glass in Canterbury, New Zealand, 1860–1988*, PhD dissertation, University of Canterbury, Christchurch, 1992

Nicola Gordon Bowe, "Wilhelmina Geddes (1887–1955): Stained glass designer", *Women Designing: Redefining Design in Britain Between the Wars*, exh. cat., University of Brighton Gallery, 1994, pp.64–70

Shirley Anne Brown, "Wilhelmina Geddes' Ottawa window", *Irish Arts Review* 1994, ix, pp.180–88

When Wilhelmina Geddes was 32, her stained-glass war memorial for the Duke of Connaught, erected in St Bartholomew's, Ottawa, after exhibition in Dublin and London, assured her of an "enviable position among modern artists". Charles Connick, the American stained-glass artist and writer, admired "the spiritual beauty, the poetry and the youthful audacity wrought into … glass, lead and iron". Geddes's unstinting courage, "outstanding artistry and craftsmanship", "strong expressive drawing", sober richness of colour and "power of simplifying without loss of meaning" were qualities that led her contemporaries to see in her work "a revival of the mediaeval genius".

Geddes had a rare ability to synthesise the earthy, smouldering colours and textures she selected in her glass with a uniquely loose, painterly technique and a direct, deeply spiritual integrity of vision. This was all the more remarkable when applied to the demanding architectural context and scale of the traditionally male-oriented craft of stained glass. Her work was consistently figurative throughout her career. She was an avid and sharply intelligent reader (and writer), who easily absorbed the influences of Archaic, Classical, Romanesque and Assyrian sculpture, progressive black-and-white illustration and northern European medieval stained glass. Providentially, the glowing watercolour *Cinderella Dressing the Ugly Sister* (1910; Hugh Lane Municipal Gallery of Modern Art, Dublin) was brought to the attention of Sarah Purser, who had set up a co-operative stained-glass workshop, An Túr Gloine, in Dublin in 1903 and who was to become her lifelong mentor. Founded along progressive Arts and Crafts lines, its aim was to counter inferior foreign imports and to provide a base for Irish artists trained in the newly established stained-glass classes at the Dublin School of Art to work in a fresh, original, evocatively Irish mode in the spirit of the Celtic Revival. The finest materials were to be an intrinsic aspect of style, and commissions were to be undertaken throughout by one artist, according to their own interpretation but in a modern idiom.

Geddes's first stained glass essay for Purser, the anguished El Greco-like triptych, *St Colman MacDuagh* (1911–12; Hugh Lane Municipal Gallery of Modern Art), immediately revealed her aptitude for the medium. In 1912 her first window, the *Angel of Resurrection* (St Ninidh's, Inishmacsaint, Co. Fermanagh), showed that she could sustain dramatic compositions on a large scale, while integrating juxtapositions of inventive decorative detail to enhance the play of light so that it seemed trapped mysteriously within the surface of the glass. Her tightly draped figures, attenuated, lilting and intent, seem lost in meditation, displaying her "gift for the simple rendering of essential action"; this, whether in glass, linocut or pen-and-ink illustration.

The series of Archangel windows, *St Michael* (1918; St Anne's, Dawson Street, Dublin), *St Michael the Archangel and Soldier Saints* (1919; St Bartholomew's, Ottawa) and *SS Michael, Gabriel and Raphael* (1920; destroyed, repr. Bowe in *Irish Arts Review* 1987, p.54) for All Saints', Blackrock, Dublin, mark Geddes's early artistic maturity. Her instinctive choice and use of both glass and lead-lines, her expressionist brushwork and consummate understanding of the limitations and potential of the stained-glass technique were and still are rare. The lithe, almost defiant figures, frozen in angular poses in poignant variations of scale, and the unusual colour combinations give these windows an original, dramatic intensity. The small figures in glowing colours meandering through a stage-set forest in the rich tapestry window, the *Leaves of the Tree Were for the Healing of the Nations* (1920; St John's, Malone Road, Belfast), give only a hint of the metamorphosis evident in her next work, the monumental *Crucifixion* window (1922; St Luke's, Wallsend-on-Tyne), where the full-scale figures seem intent on bursting their architectural confines. In the *SS Patrick and Columba* window (1923; Church of Ireland, Larne, Co. Antrim) the rough-hewn saints are barely contained in each light, as they persevere on their physically tough and spiritually demanding missions.

In 1922 Geddes formally left An Túr, dogged by emotional and artistic misgivings and undermined in health. The ensuing period of self-doubt is reflected in the contortions and introspection of her figures, whether in book illustrations (Harrap's *One Act Plays of Today*, 1924, 1926 and 1927; Harrap's *Essays of Today*, 1923; Bruce Graeme's *The Return of Blackshirt*, 1927) or in linocut portraits of her family and cat. She continued to exhibit with the Arts and Crafts Society of Ireland, for which she designed a fiercely graphic cover, *The Saint* (repr. Bowe in *Irish Arts Review* 1987, p.58), and more occasionally elsewhere, with a joint show in Belfast with Rosamond Praeger, her other mentor and old family friend, of 33 items – drawings, book illustrations, linocut portrait studies, designs for windows, stained glass and embroidered panels.

Geddes left Ireland for good in 1925 and rented a studio in the purpose-built Glass House in Fulham. Here, a growing band of devotees saw the painstakingly slow process of her windows before they were dispatched for installation. She abandoned the *St Brendan* window, the design for which was exhibited in the Basilica of the British Empire Exhibition at Wembley, for completion by her Dublin An Túr colleagues. Before she left, she had continued to design small wooden-framed panels for her sister to embroider; she would make them in glass and they would exhibit together. A version of one of these, somewhat Cubist in treatment, *Rhoda Opening the Door to St Peter* (1934; Ulster Museum, Belfast), is one of her few stained-glass cabinet panels to have survived. The watercolour designs (private collections, *ibid.*, p.57) demonstrate what a loss they are; subjects included Dr Johnson and Boswell, the Scottish Border Ballads and Charles Lamb's *Essays of Elia*. In 1930 the Ulster

Museum commissioned a staircase window illustrating the ancient legend of the *Children of Lir* (1930; in storage, repr. Michael Wynne, *Irish Stained Glass*, Dublin: Eason, 1977, back cover), which consisted of a series of enchanting and dramatic narrative panels. Geddes took with her to London several Ulster commissions, including a second window for Larne, *Christ with Martha and Mary* (1927), where large pieces of ruby, purple and blue glass seem to resonate and the women's gesturing profiles introduce an arresting new element in the iconography of stained glass. Sadly, her four visionary windows of 1929 for Rosemary Street Presbyterian Church, Belfast, were destroyed in 1944.

Geddes's first English window, small but monumental and executed in flaming hues, portrayed a titanic *St Christopher* with a crew-cut St Cecilia flexing her forearms and red-legginged St Hubert looming large above the angling organist commemorated, wearing amber oilskins (1926; All Saints', Laleham, Middlesex). It recalls Raphael's Cartoons (Victoria and Albert Museum, London) and works by Michelangelo in its monumentality, but so disturbed the congregation that it was removed to the back of the church. Critics were stunned by the "virile, almost alarming strength" in Geddes's work, reflecting "the religion of power and fighting", and admired her "fine, bold drawing, afraid of nothing, even brutal at times".

In the 1930s, still varying the scale of her figures within a window and lightly inscribing seemingly incidental notes around the sketched-in, masklike features, Geddes would contrast growing areas of grisaille with gloriously orchestrated gold, pinks, purples, greens and yellows, as in the *Joseph of Arimathea* window (1933; Otterden Place Church, Kent). In *St Francis of Assisi Preaching to the Birds* (1930; Northchapel parish church, near Petworth, Sussex) the little figures seem to float, while in *Psalm 100* (1934; Egremont United Reform Church, Wallasey) the small figures appear suspended against a fishing net that covers the surface of the window.

Geddes was unstinting in her pursuit and acceptance of only the "right" piece of glass for each window. Such dedication cost her her health, particularly in the most demanding of all her commissions, the huge *Te Deum* rose window commissioned by the British Army and Royal Air Force to commemorate the King of the Belgians, finally erected in 1938 in the rebuilt cathedral of St Martin, Ypres. At the end of her life, her sight almost gone but her artistic and technical powers unimpaired, her work was imbued with an elemental gentleness, warmth and deeply moving spiritual quality, seen in the *Virgin and Child* (1952; All Hallows', Greenford, Middlesex) and *St Elizabeth, the Virgin and St Mildred* (1954; St Mildred's, Lee, Kent). It is surely only because Geddes worked in the inaccessible and breakable medium of stained glass that her extraordinary artistic achievement is so little known.

NICOLA GORDON BOWE

Gentileschi, Artemisia   [fig. 24]
Italian painter, 1593–1652/3

Born in Rome, 8 July 1593, to the painter Orazio Gentileschi and Prudentia Montone. In March 1612 Orazio sued the painter Agostino Tasso for the rape of his daughter, initiating a seven-month trial; Artemisia was tortured to verify her testimony; case dismissed October 1612. Married Florentine painter Pietro Antonio di Vincenzo Stiattesi in Rome, 29 November 1612; at least four children, all born in Florence, two sons, born 1613 and 1615, two daughters, born 1617 and 1618; separated from husband c.1626. Member of the Accademia del Disegno, Florence, by 19 July 1616; remained in Florence until February 1620. In Rome, 1620, 1622 and 1624–6; visited Venice by 1627. In Naples by August 1630; left November 1637. In England, in the service of Queen Henrietta Maria, by December 1639. Subsequently in Naples. Died 1652/3.

Bibliography

Giovanni Baglione, *Le vite de' pittori, scultori et architetti dal Pontificato di Gregorio XIII del 1572 in fino a' tempi di Papa Urbano Ottavo nel 1642*, Rome: Fei, 1642; reprinted Bologna: Forni, 1975–6 (life of Orazio Gentileschi)

Joachim von Sandrart, *L'Accademia todesca della architectura, scultura e pittura: Oder Teutsche Academie der edlen Bau-, Bild- und Mahlerey-künste*, 2 vols, Nuremberg, 1675–9; ed. A.R. Peltzer, Munich, 1925; reprinted Farnborough: Gregg, 1971

Filippo Baldinucci, *Notizie de' professori del disegno da Cimabue in qua*, Florence, 1681–1728; reprinted Florence, 1751, and in *Opere di Filippo Baldinucci*, 14 vols, Milan, 1808–12

Giovanni Battista Passeri, *Vite de' pittori, scultori ed architetti che anno lavorato in Roma: Morti dal 1641 fino al 1673*, Rome, 1772; reprinted in *Die Künstlerbiographien von Giovanni Battista Passeri*, ed. Jacob Hess, Leipzig and Vienna, 1934

Roberto Longhi, "Gentileschi padre e figlia", *L'Arte*, xix, 1916, pp.245–314; reprinted in *Scritti giovannili, 1912–1922*, i, Florence: Sansoni, 1961, pp.219–83

Vincenzo Ruffo, "La Galleria Ruffo (appendice)", *Bollettino d'Arte*, xii, 1919, pp.43–56

R. Ward Bissell, "Artemisia Gentileschi: A new documented chronology", *Art Bulletin*, l, 1968, pp.153–68

Eva Menzio, *Artemisia Gentileschi/Agostino Tassi: Atti di un processo per stupro*, Edizione delle Donne, xxxvi, Milan, 1981

Roberto Fuda, "Un'inedita lettera di Artemisia Gentileschi a Ferdinando II de' Medici", *Rivista d'Arte*, xli, 1989, pp.167–71

Mary D. Garrard, *Artemisia Gentileschi: The Image of the Female Hero in Italian Baroque Art*, Princeton: Princeton University Press, 1989

Mina Gregori, "Una nota per Artemisia Gentileschi", *Paragone*, xli/487, 1990, pp.104–6

Artemisia, exh. cat., Casa Buonarroti, Florence, 1991; review by John Spike, *Burlington Magazine*, cxxxiii, 1991, pp.732–4

Susanna Stolzenwald, *Artemisia Gentileschi: Bindung und Befreiung in Leben und Werk einer Malerin*, Stuttgart and Zürich: Belser, 1991

Elizabeth Cropper, "Artemisia Gentileschi, La 'Pittora'", *Barocco al Femminile*, ed. G. Calvi, Rome: Laterza, 1992, pp.191–218

—, "New documents for Artemisia Gentileschi's life in Florence", *Burlington Magazine*, cxxxv, 1993, pp.760–61

Mary D. Garrard, "Artemisia Gentileschi's 'Corisca and the Satyr'", *Burlington Magazine*, cxxxv, 1993, pp.34–8

Artemisia Gentileschi was born in Rome. Her father was the Pisan painter Orazio Gentileschi, who had married a Roman woman, Prudentia Montone. Artemisia was the oldest of three surviving children, but as the only girl it was unlikely that she would become her father's artistic heir. The death of her mother in 1605 changed her life completely. Left alone with her younger brothers, she could no longer rely on the normal protection of family life. Her father seems to have been a solitary man, utterly devoted to his work, and the Gentileschi moved house often in the artists' neighbourhood around the Piazza della Trinità and the Via Margutta. Orazio's most important artistic relationship was with Caravaggio, whose practice of working directly from the model had a profound impact on Orazio's more ideally mannered style, and at the very moment when Artemisia was beginning to take a serious interest in painting.

In 1612 Orazio reported to the Grand Duchess of Tuscany that Artemisia had learned so much in three years that she had no equal. Such recognition, and the public life of a successful painter, presented unusual problems for an unmarried woman whose personal honour was vested in her virginity. When her mother died Artemisia was 12, and could normally have looked forward to contracting a marriage in three or four years. Meanwhile, Orazio taught her to paint. He was able to do this because he worked in the studio at home. In 1610 (or possibly in the early months of 1611, if like many Tuscans the Gentileschi kept to the calendar *ab incarnatione* even in Rome), after working beside her father for several years, Artemisia completed her first known masterpiece, *Susanna and the Elders* (Schloss Weissenstein, Pommersfelden).

Artemisia was 17, and reaching the age when marriage was imperative. At this delicate moment Orazio was embarking on fresco commissions on the Quirinal in collaboration with Agostino Tassi. He was out much of the time, leaving Artemisia without a chaperone. In 1611 Orazio tried to solve this problem by proposing to a woman called Tuzia, who lived opposite, that the two households move into new quarters together. His other proposal that Artemisia become a nun was completely unsuccessful. It was soon after the move, while Artemisia was supposedly under Tuzia's supervision, that she was raped by her father's colleague Agostino Tassi.

Much about Orazio's charges against Tassi almost a year later in 1612 can be understood in terms of legal convention. The suit was delayed in the hope that another way out would be found – the usual solution was marriage to the aggressor, or the latter's provision of a dowry to make possible marriage to another man. Artemisia's claim that she had been deflowered (which was surely true) included the required mention of blood. She testified, as the law expected and as was also surely true, that she had resisted Tassi by attacking him with a knife.

Tassi had promised to marry Artemisia, and consequently they had had regular sexual relations in Gentileschi's house for about eight months. Orazio's decision to go to court was the result of further events that pushed the threat to the family's honour beyond breaking point. Tassi already had a wife when he made his promise to Artemisia, and he almost certainly had her murdered. Events had finally got out of hand during carnival of 1612, when Artemisia and Tassi had sexual relations in the house of friends, making the affair a public scandal. In his petition Orazio cited not only rape and fornication, but also the theft from his daughter of some paintings, and especially a large *Judith*. There is no agreement about which of several versions of the subject this was, or whether it was in fact painted by father or daughter. But Artemisia had almost certainly represented herself either as Judith or as her servant in a scene in which a chaste and powerful virago kills or has just killed the man who has tried to seduce her.

At stake for Orazio was the ability to continue his profession as a painter, for which he needed to keep an open house without sacrificing his reputation. This was also critical for Artemisia. *Susanna and the Elders* was almost certainly completed before the rape; but so much sexually charged gossip circled around her independently of that act of violence that the picture demands to be read as a powerful commentary by the 17-year-old Artemisia on the salacious curiosity she aroused. In her version of the story two whispering and conspiratorial men in modern dress lean over the wall of the pool where the naked Susanna bathes. Her body facing us, she turns away from them and holds up her arms in protection against their voices as much as against their gaze.

Artemisia's apprenticeship to her father caused prurient commentary. In various Roman workshops it was claimed that Orazio did not want her to marry, made her pose in the nude and liked people to look at her. Muse, whore and daughter, Artemisia was the object of such male fantasies because of the extraordinary fact that she was a painter. She was painting when Tassi came to rape her. He snatched away her palette and brushes and threw them away, saying, she reported: "Not so much painting, not so much painting".

In November 1612 Artemisia was married to Pietro Antonio di Vincenzo Stiattesi. The couple's first child was born in Florence in September of the following year, and the family would remain there until February 1620. Aurelio Lomi, Orazio's half-brother, had also returned to Florence in 1613, and Artemisia would adopt the Tuscan family name of Lomi for works executed in her Florentine period. She produced a number of small religious works in

Florence, but the more ambitious group of the *Penitent Magdalene* (c.1618; Palazzo Pitti, Florence), *Jael and Sisera* (signed and dated 1620; Szépművészeti Múzeum, Budapest), and *Judith Beheading Holofernes* (Uffizi, Florence; surely completed before early 1621, but perhaps sent from Rome), all indicate a renewed commitment to the vividly naturalistic portrayal of strong women in morally justified opposition to men that had begun with the *Susanna* and the stolen *Judith*. Their production also reflects Artemisia's reputation for this sort of painting in Florence, where the Caravaggesque manner was still novel and her feminist version of it all the more so.

Artemisia's first known Florentine commission was in a different mode. In 1615 Michelangelo Buonarroti the Younger asked her to paint an *Allegory of Inclination* for the ceiling of the Casa Buonarroti. She produced a luminous fleshy female nude so natural and alluring that Buonarroti's great-nephew would later have Volterrano cover it with painted draperies. That she was paid more than the other artists for allegories of similar size reflects her superior reputation, but also reveals Buonarroti's understanding of her difficulties. In November 1615, for example, Buonarroti's servant delivered money in response to Artemisia's plea that she was in great need because she was in childbed. In fact she produced four children in five years in Florence.

Artemisia was constantly in debt. One tradesman to whom she owed money was the carpenter who produced the furnishings for her studio, whose account began on 24 October 1614. More serious were the debts incurred by her husband without her knowledge. On 5 June 1619 she appealed to the Grand Duke Cosimo II de' Medici through the Accademia del Disegno, explaining that her husband was indebted to a shopkeeper who had obtained a judgement against her that Stiattesi had also concealed. She begged the Academy to reconsider, and to suspend the seizure of her goods on the grounds that a woman could not take on a debt while her husband was living with her.

Artemisia Gentileschi was the first woman member of the Accademia del Disegno, and so the first to pose this problem of responsibility for debts. Her inscription, probably under the sponsorship of her patron the grand duke, passed without comment. She paid her initial matriculation fee on 19 July 1616, but only as her debts mounted did she realise the privileges and responsibilities of membership.

In addition to supporting Artemisia in court, the grand duke also patronised her by buying paintings. In February 1619 a *Bath of Diana* (untraced) entered the Medici collection. She received an advance for another painting, and in January 1620 she requested a supply of ultramarine to use in a *Hercules* (untraced). But the trials of surviving as painter, mother and wife had taken their toll. In February 1620 Artemisia wrote to Cosimo II asking permission to spend some months in Rome.

The *Jael and Sisera* and *Judith Beheading Holofernes* already cited were to be followed by the forceful *Lucretia* (c.1621; Palazzo Cattaneo-Adorno, Genoa), the frankly nude *Cleopatra* (1621–2; Collection Amedeo Morandotti, Milan) and the last great version of *Judith and Her Maidservant* (c.1625; Detroit Institute of Arts). With the exception of the first, all bespeak a renewed contact with the vigorous tradition of Roman painting in the 1620s, and especially the work of Vouet. The signed and dated *Susanna and the Elders* (Burghley House, Stamford) of 1622 also reflects her knowledge of Guercino. But the subjects and the vision of these paintings, with their powerful women so directly described, set them apart.

The portrait of a *Knight of the Order of SS Maurice and Lazarus* (Pinacoteca Nazionale, Bologna), also signed and dated in Rome in 1622, is more indicative of Artemisia's later commissions than are these violent images of strong women. She became famous as a portraitist, and would secure fame through noble patronage. She was befriended by Cassiano dal Pozzo, who in turn brought her work to the attention of the Barberini. Artemisia's decision to go to Naples was probably the result of having sold several paintings in Rome in 1626 to the Duke of Alcalá, who then served as viceroy from 1629 to 1631. In the summer of 1630 she wrote to Dal Pozzo, reporting that she was making some paintings for the sister of the King of Spain. She received important ecclesiastical commissions, such as the *Annunciation*, probably for San Giorgio de' Genovesi, and three large works (Museo di Capodimonte, Naples) for the choir of Pozzuoli Cathedral. But she also painted for the palace of the King of Spain at Buen Retiro, for Charles Lorraine, Duc de Guise, for Cardinal Antonio Barberini and for Francesco I d'Este in Rome, among other princes. Her years under the protection of the grand duke in Florence had prepared her for the ways of the court; most important of all, Artemisia had gained control over her own affairs by learning to write letters.

This skill made it possible for Artemisia to participate in both the world of law and contract and in the culture of courtly artistic diplomacy. She was also skilful in creating her own reputation. In a letter to Galileo dated 9 October 1635 (cited in Garrard 1989, pp.383–4) she refers to her collection of gifts and letters from the kings and rulers of Europe, expressing her displeasure at having received no favour from the Grand Duke Ferdinando II in Florence. Artemisia had learned to play upon the notion of herself as a vassal of princes offering gifts of love and courtesy, a powerless woman who served the greatest powers in Europe.

These skills did not secure Artemisia's hoped-for return to Florence in the mid-1630s, when she began to find Naples unbearably dangerous and expensive; instead, she took up a long-standing royal invitation to join her father in London, where he had been working since 1626. The atmosphere at court was highly charged, as suspicions rose that Queen Henrietta Maria and her advisers were working to convert Charles I and the kingdom to Catholicism (with art and artists not the least of their weapons). Plague was rife. None the less, Artemisia agreed to help Orazio with his commission to decorate the ceiling (now at Marlborough House, London) of the Queen's House at Greenwich.

Artemisia probably arrived in 1638. Within a year of her arrival her father was dead. The queen helped her to re-establish her contacts in Italy by sending a painting to Francesco I d'Este in Modena, but at this point the historical record of Gentileschi's life is broken by a nine-year silence. During most of this time she was probably in Naples, for she was well established there when she struck up her correspondence with Don Antonio Ruffo, the celebrated Messinese collector.

The 13 letters from Artemisia to Ruffo, dating from January 1649 to January 1651, provide a glimpse of the relationship between the painter and her patron. They also reveal tensions inherent in the new market for paintings. In her arguments with Ruffo over prices, Artemisia never hesitated to charge him with underestimating her because she was a woman. "The reputation of a woman stands in doubt until her work is seen", she wrote in 1649

in connection with the *Galatea* (untraced), and in response to her sense that Ruffo felt sympathy rather than admiration for her. Later, writing about the ambitious *Hunt of Diana* (untraced), with its eight figures, two dogs and landscape, she promised that she would make him see "what a woman can do". Her delay in completing the work in the summer's heat led Ruffo to demand a reduction in its price. This aroused Artemisia's fury at having to serve her "noviciate" all over again for a patron to whom she was charging less than she had the chamberlain of the King of Spain. She would rather give her work away, and believed that she had foolishly diminished her own value by asking too low a price because she needed cash.

Artemisia also explained why she had to have some money in advance. For each figure in the *Diana* she needed a model, and female models were especially difficult to find: they were expensive and she found that for every fifty who stripped only one was any good. In this work, she reminded him, she could not use a single model because there were eight figures, which had to be beautiful in different ways. Artemisia's own style had become more idealising, but the mode of production and vision she had learned in Rome had not changed. She still needed models for the paintings of female bodies that had become her speciality.

In addition to her dedication to the natural model, Artemisia took pride in her ability to invent on a given theme. Nicolas Poussin was also famous for this, defining invention in the terms used by Tasso, not as the discovery of wholly new themes, but as the disposition of something already known. Remarkably, Artemisia gave a similar response to the specification by a client that his *Galatea* be different from Ruffo's. In a letter to Ruffo of 13 November 1649 (Garrard 1989, pp.397–8) she replied tersely that he was dealing with a woman who had never repeated so much as a hand. She refused to set a price, and further refused to send a drawing because she had had her ideas stolen in the past. In one case a patron had saved money by giving her composition to another artist to execute. Artemisia claimed that this would never have happened to a man, but in fact several of her male counterparts were engaged in the same dilemma concerning their intellectual property rights.

In the allegorical self-portrait that Artemisia probably painted in London around 1640 (Royal Collection), sometimes dated *c*.1630, she presents herself as the figure of *La Pittura* – immortally young, proudly displaying her snowy breasts at the centre of the canvas, her gold chain a sign of princely honours, and her unruly locks representing her untrammelled thoughts. Painting's right hand is poised to begin the work of execution on the empty canvas, but it pauses there as "Arte-mi-sia" (or "May art be me") turns her gaze expectantly towards the light of the inventive intellect. The artist's colours are earthy, Neapolitan, Caravaggesque; her attitude is rhetorical, inquiring, closer to the world of Cassiano dal Pozzo and Tuscany. The confidence in her claim to fame is her own.

More than any other contemporary woman painter, Artemisia Gentileschi made her own career in the marketplace. But although she protected her daughters by marrying them within the aristocracy (as well as teaching them to paint), her own honour remained fragile, and misogynist anger against her talent persisted. The erotic legend around Artemisia was already being propagated by 1653, when, in a volume of satirical epitaphs (*Cimiterio, epitafi giocossi di Giovan Francesco Loredano e Pietro Michele*, Venice, 1653, cited in translation in Garrard 1989, p.137), she was made to say "Ne l'intagliar le corna a mio marito/Lasciai il pennello, e preso lo scalpello" (or, "To carve my husband's horns I put down my brush and took up a knife"). This satirical joke, which is our only evidence for the date of Artemisia's death, confirms that she invoked fears of castration beyond the grave.

Gentileschi persisted because of her talent, but also because she had the strength and intelligence to adapt to social circumstances, and because she determined to secure the fame reserved for men. Her painting reflects a similar path: the vulnerability of the early *Susanna* was superseded by a manner in which directness was combined with the detailed depiction of rich stuffs and fine jewels; in the end she painted with detachment, giving collectors what they wanted in the form of beautiful female nudes. The distinction between Artemisia's own body and her representations of the female nude necessarily widened with age. The exposed body of the female painter, putting her first foot in the water, is defence-less against gossip in the early *Susanna and the Elders*, whereas the women in the late *Bathsheba* and the *Tarquin and Lucretia* (both Neues Palais, Potsdam; late 1640s; with uncertain attribution) are rhetorical figures derived from the bodies of those

models whom Artemisia accused of fleecing her. In this regard, the self-portrait as *La Pittura* marks a turning point in Artemisia's ability to conceive of herself as subject and object, to fashion a self through metaphor. Although her sexual identity determined everything in her life, Artemisia did not continue to identify with the female bodies she presented to the male gaze. As a result her late work has been quite misunderstood, considered empty, and its authenticity questioned.

ELIZABETH CROPPER

Gérard, Marguerite
French painter and printmaker, 1761–1837

Born in Grasse, Provence, 28 January 1761; father a perfume distiller. Probably moved to Paris after her mother's death in 1775; lived with her sister and brother-in-law, the painter Jean-Honoré Fragonard; looked after nephews after sister's death in 1824. Died in Paris, 18 May 1837.

Principal Exhibitions

Paris Salon: 1799 (prix du 5ème classe), 1801 (prix d'encouragement), 1802, 1804 (gold medal), 1806, 1808, 1810, 1814, 1817, 1822, 1824

Bibliography
Jeanne Doin, "Marguerite Gérard (1761–1837)", *Gazette des Beaux-Arts*, 4th series, viii, 1912, pp.429–52

George Levitine, "Marguerite Gérard and her stylistic significance", *Baltimore Museum of Art Annual*, iii, 1968, pp.21–31

Carol Duncan, "Happy mothers and other new ideas in French art", *Art Bulletin*, lv, 1973, pp.570–83

Women Artists, 1550–1950, exh. cat., Los Angeles County Museum of Art, and elsewhere, 1976

Sally Wells-Robertson, "Marguerite Gérard et les Fragonard", *Bulletin de la Société de l'Histoire de l'Art Français*, 1977, pp.179–89

——, *Marguerite Gérard*, PhD dissertation, New York University, 1978

Alexandre Ananoff, "Propos sur les peintures de Marguerite Gérard", *Gazette des Beaux-Arts*, 6th series, xciv, 1979, pp.211–18

Consulat-Empire-Restauration: Art in Early XIX Century France, exh. cat., Wildenstein and Co., London, 1981

Fragonard, exh. cat., Grand Palais, Paris, and Metropolitan Museum of Art, New York, 1987

Jean-Pierre Cuzin, *Jean-Honoré Fragonard: Life and Works: Complete Catalogue of the Oil Paintings*, New York: Abrams, 1988

Thanks to the research of Sally Wells-Robertson, the works of Marguerite Gérard have been rescued from the obscurity that enshrouded them after the artist's death in 1837. In her own lifetime, Gérard's paintings were anything but obscure, and LeBreton's official report detailing the state of French art (1808) claims that by 1789 Gérard's reputation matched those of Anne Vallayer-Coster (q.v.), Adélaïde Labille-Guiard (q.v.) and Elisabeth Vigée-Lebrun (q.v.). What sets Gérard apart from them is that she was not a member of the Academy, and she first showed her work at the Salon in 1799, six years after the exhibition was opened to all artists. Nothing indicates that Gérard ever sought or desired academic recognition, and her close association with Jean-Honoré Fragonard, himself a renegade from the royal institution, suggests that his support may have compensated for a lack of institutional backing. As part of the Fragonard household, and sister to the painter's wife, Gérard was trained in the family atelier, a circumstance long common to both male and female artists. That Fragonard had entrée to private collections throughout Paris and that his lodgings were located in the Louvre allowed Gérard access to both art works and artistic community. He launched her on a career that brought the proverbial fame and fortune.

Marguerite Gérard came to Paris from Grasse in 1775, and in that year joined the Fragonard household. Only three years later she produced her first etching, the *Swaddled Cat*, made after a drawing by Fragonard and signed "first plate of Mlle Gérard, aged 16, 1778". Two more etchings of children's play followed, and Gérard returned to themes of childhood throughout her career. Indeed, she is best known today for painting mothers and children and depicting joyous family life. Works such as *Beloved Child* (1787–90) and *First Steps of Childhood* (1780–83; both Fogg Museum of Art, Harvard University) have suggested Gérard's role in propagating Rousseauian themes. Such images constitute a sizeable percentage of her production; they hang in public collections and have attracted recent commentary. But equally important are Gérard's depictions of female intimacy, feminine ritual and heterosexual lovemaking, which despite their presence in a few prominent collections (e.g. *Bad News*, c.1804; Louvre, Paris) remain less well known. Moreover, Gérard's range of subjects is not obvious because so many of her works are either lost or in private hands. Particularly keen is the loss of works

that show the artist experimenting with a variety of subjects; her *Clemency of Napoleon*, exhibited in 1808 and bought by the Emperor for Josephine's private collection at Malmaison, is among those paintings whose recovery would give us a more complex picture of Gérard's artistic production.

Although Gérard's representations of motherhood seem to exemplify normative female behaviour, not all are as simple as they appear. One critic's remark points towards other possible readings: "Always a mommy with her little darling, always a dog, a maid, a cat, a cradle, a bird and some dolls" (*Revue du Salon de l'An X*, Paris, 1802, Collection Deloynes, no.1769, p.30). The critic suggests what becomes evident in looking at a selection of these images – cherished children, pampered pets, fetishised objects – all seem to hold the same importance in the visual and emotional world of Gérard's painting. For example, the cuddled babe in *First Caresses of the Day*, engraved by Henri Gérard in the 1780s, seems interchangeable with the Persian cat in *Triumph of Minette*, engraved by Vidal in 1786. The *Triumph of Raton* (1800–04; untraced, known only through reproduction) shows the performing dog as much an object of affection as the children cavorting around it, and the mother, holding centre stage, displays a ring biscuit – the prop that both Fragonard and Clodion rhymed with the female genitals in their overtly erotic images of women playing with lap-dogs. These observations suggest that at least some of Gérard's images critique the conventions and pleasures of elite motherhood. Moreover, the high artifice of Gérard's paintings – their constant referral to other works of art (by herself, Fragonard, Greuze, Dutch genre painters, Prud'hon, Vigée-Lebrun and so forth) – undercuts any attempt to read her images as transparent to life. As much as "real" domesticity, Gérard's images signal artifice and the cabinet piece, the sort of art sought by the collector who valued sensuous surface effects and bravura handling.

It is perhaps for this market that Gérard perfected what has become known as her "Metsu manner", a style reminiscent of the detailed, precisely finished and highly glazed surfaces wrought by that 17th-century Dutch painter. The *Music Lesson* (1782–3), known only through written descriptions and a detailed wash study (private collection), suggests that in the early 1780s Gérard was already producing elegant images of women in activities related to love (here, making music) inspired by such artists as Metsu. Gérard developed this subject and handling in advance of such artists as Boilly, who were credited with originating the neo-Dutch mode. In addition to genre scenes, Gérard made her career by painting portraits and portrait miniatures, and works produced in the 1780s and 1790s (e.g. the portrait miniature of a woman of 1785; Louvre) with their looser and less meticulous paint handling suggest that Gérard had an impressive control over the technical skills of her art.

Although interpreters have readily acknowledged the erotic content of images by Fragonard, Boilly and Schall, Gérard's renderings of love letters (*Billet Doux*, 1795–1800; untraced), music making (*The Concert*, 1800–05; private collection, New York) and female intimacy (*The Reader*, 1783–5; Fitzwilliam Museum, Cambridge; *The Confidantes*, Musée des Beaux-Arts, Bordeaux) are usually considered innocent – or, as the critic Eméric David suggested of *Reading a Letter* (exh. Salon 1817; untraced), as showing a decency in their conception. Yet traditionally the iconography chosen by Gérard carried an erotic charge, sometimes carefully concealed, in the symbolic meaning of accoutrements, in the comparison between musical instruments and the female body, in the lap-dog or cat as surrogate lover. As a woman artist, Gérard's use of erotic subjects and symbols would of necessity be subtle, veiled or distanced through historical disguise. Her setting of love scenes in the courtly Middle Ages (as in the *Art of Love*, 1785–90; engraved by Henri Gérard in 1792) heralds the Troubadour style developed in the first half of the 19th century by such artists as her nephew Evariste Fragonard. Rather than promoting an exact historical reconstruction, Gérard's work is suffused with the theatricality of the Rococo pastoral and often uses the courtly tradition to signify a delicacy of sentiment, and perhaps also an imagined moment of woman's ascendancy.

The proliferation of love themes in Gérard's work and her reliance on well-established conventions of erotic depiction suggest that the thoughts of her women protagonists may not be as "decent" as moralising critics would have it. Recent feminist considerations of painted and textual images of female friendship, as well as recent work on women's literature, also suggest that Gérard's images transgress the decency seen by male Salon writers. Women's literature of the same period often exploited the unacknowledged sexual overtones of female friendship. Such friendships could be looked on with apprehension in the dominant culture, which feared that bad advice and moral corruption could be passed along in the exchange of confidences between women. Even Gérard's images of maternal bliss, as Wells-Robertson perceptively noted, can have erotic overtones. By representing bared breasts and joyful – even ecstatic – mothers, images such as *Nursing Mother* (*c*.1804; Musée Fragonard, Grasse) solicit male voyeurism. They also, however, underwrite the promise of sexual excitation that many writers on breast feeding guaranteed women as a happy by-product of fulfilling their maternal duty. Taking into account the eroticism of Gérard's art, we can more easily understand why she was commissioned to illustrate both Louvet de Couvray's *Les Amours du Chevalier de Faublas* (1798; examples in British Museum, London, and Bibliothèque Nationale, Paris) and Choderlos de Laclos's *Les Liaisons dangereuses* (1796; examples in Bibliothèque Nationale and Musée Fragonard).

It is both ironic and predictable that tradition would cast Marguerite Gérard as lover to the artist who was her teacher and her sister's husband, and at the same time find in her images only virtuous women. Wells-Robertson has shown the affair between Fragonard and Gérard to be pure fantasy; on the other hand, there is reason to suggest that Gérard's art, like that of Fragonard, was invested less in moral example and more in passion, pleasure and sensual appeal. Whereas such "authorities" as Rousseau generally held women susceptible to infatuation and physical stimulation, they also believed them incapable of *representing* love. "I would bet anything", wrote Rousseau, "that the *Lettres portugaises* were authored by a man". He would probably say the same of Gérard's impassioned *Geneviève de Brabant* (engraved by Augustin Le Grand, 1790) and her sensuous *Married Couple Re-reading Their Love Letters*, works that only recently have been recognised as the work of this woman artist.

MARY D. SHERIFF

See also Printmakers survey

Gerowitz, Judy *see* Chicago

Ghisi, Diana *see* Mantuana

Gluck
British painter, 1895–1978

Born Hannah Gluckstein in London, 1895.
Attended classes at St John's Wood School of Art,
1913–16. First visited Lamorna, Cornwall, meeting
Laura Knight (q.v.) and Dod Procter, 1916.
Subsequently left home, called herself Gluck and
worked briefly at Selfridge's department store,
London, painting portraits. Relationship with
decorator Constance Spry, early 1930s, with writer
Nesta Obermer, from 1936. Lived in London, then
at The Chantry House, Steyning, Sussex, early
1940s. Died 10 January 1978.

Selected Individual Exhibitions
Dorien Leigh Galleries, London: 1924
Fine Art Society, London: 1926, 1932, 1937, 1973 (retro-
spective), 1980 (retrospective)

Selected Writings
"The dilemma of the painter and conservator in the
synthetic age", Museum Association Conference,
London, 1954
"The impermanence of paintings in relation to artists'
materials", Royal Society of Arts Lecture, London,
1964
"On the quality of paint", *Tempera: Yearbook of the
Society of Painters in Tempera*, 1969, pp.2–4

Bibliography
Gluck, 1895–1978, exh. cat., Fine Art Society, London,
1980
Painting in Newlyn, 1880–1930, exh. cat., Barbican Art
Gallery, London, 1985
*British Art in the Twentieth Century: The Modern
Movement*, exh. cat., Royal Academy, London, and
elsewhere, 1987
Diana Souhami, *Gluck, 1895–1978: Her Biography*,
London: Pandora, 1988
Emmanuel Cooper, *The Sexual Perspective:
Homosexuality and Art in the last 100 Years in the
West*, 2nd edition, London and New York: Routledge,
1994

Gluck received her only systematic artistic training
during World War I, when she travelled to Lamorna,
Cornwall, to study with the creative community
associated with the so-called Newlyn School. These
artists specialised in idyllic, pastoral and often
meticulously literal landscapes and genre scenes of
the surrounding Cornish life. Gluck's move to
Lamorna was also a retreat from her prominent and
wealthy London family, founders of the caterers J.
Lyons and Co. Refusing her given name, Hannah
Gluckstein, was only the first of many ruptures that
characterised her troubled connection to a social
milieu that she found personally repressive but to
which she remained inextricably linked throughout
her life and career. While her family's name and
reputation guaranteed social acceptance, her lesbian
sexuality and determined self-presentation in
masculine clothing ensured that such acceptance
was always conditional and limited. Gluck's training
in a carefully naturalistic style and her relation to a
sophisticated, wealthy post-Edwardian society are
the crucial elements from which her paintings
emerged. Throughout her career Gluck ignored the
modernist trend towards abstraction and remained
faithful to a naturalistic style that agreed with the
more conservative, traditional tastes of her upper-
class associations. At the same time she permeated
her works with a utopian rhetoric of essences into
which the subject of her lesbian identity occasionally erupted.

In 1926 Gluck had her first major solo exhibition
at the Fine Art Society in London, called *Stage and
Country*. The title and format signified the
dichotomy of her social position, including landscapes and genre scenes of Cornwall, where she
lived as a "rebel", a freely expressive artist, as well
as paintings of the self-consciously sophisticated
and artificial world of the London stage to which
she had privileged access through her family's
commercial venues. The "country" works centred
on local Cornish events such as the Buryan races or
views of the surrounding countryside. *Phoebus
Triumphant* (c.1920; private collection, repr.
Souhami 1988, p.46), with its huge expanse of sky
and low horizon, typifies Gluck's landscapes, always
marked by a pastoral stillness and idealised calm. In
contrast to the idyllic ideology of the countryside,
with her "stage" paintings Gluck underscores the
blurred lines between theatrical performance and
the performative artifice of London's theatre society.
Alongside paintings of individuals of this wealthy
and seemingly carefree world, Gluck exhibited
specific depictions of London stage entertainers,
including 15 images of the famous C.B. Cochran
revues staged at her family's Trocadero Restaurant.

Performers appear either on stage under intense spotlights or in more complex images in which Gluck seemed to be particularly interested in the theatre's interplay of reality and artifice. In such paintings as *Massine Waiting for His Cue* (*c*.1926; Victoria and Albert Museum, London) and *On and Off (Teddie Gerard on Stage at the Duke of York Theatre)* (*c*.1924; private collection, *ibid.*, p.57) Gluck contrasts the dimly lit wings of the theatre with the bright stage lights and includes custodians, actors and patrons engaged in backstage activities. The uncharacteristically complicated spatial arrangements of these works suggest a playful ambiguity and a knowing artifice that enveloped theatrical culture. In these paintings everything and everyone remain behind masks, costumes, screens and props under the harsh glare of public scrutiny.

Despite their diverse subjects, these paintings had a stylistic and conceptual unity to which Gluck adhered throughout her 50-year artistic career. Often small in scale, her paintings have a monumentality, meticulous rendering and sparse, geometrically schematic compositions. Within her closely observed naturalism there is, however, a simultaneous suppression of incidental detail that creates a sense of isolated utopia and suggests a symbolic layering of meanings behind the seemingly scrupulous attention to facts. Her notes on landscape painting signal clearly this dual trajectory:

> The sky is a bowl, not a flat backcloth, and its colour and light reflect in every blade of grass, every twig ... a landscape is chameleon to the light ... Will [the landscape's unique] note have reached you so clearly that no matter what changes and interruptions occur you will, like a good tuning fork, continue to vibrate to that note unerringly? [*ibid.*, p.42].

The duality of purpose between incident and symbol becomes an artistic credo for Gluck, and her writings often repeat this theme in relation to portraiture, genre scenes and flower paintings.

Gluck's portraits of the early 1920s almost immediately established a formula that forever defined her portraiture. Her sitters invariably appear alone, with frank, usually unsmiling faces and direct looks, against minimal backgrounds that sometimes contain objects or patterns that suggest an attribute, symbolic marker or allegorical icon. Her *Self-Portrait* (1942; National Portrait Gallery, London) confirms this formula and also concisely engages the often contradictory aspects of her work: the construction of a defiant and isolated individualism but with the unmistakable marks of social privilege, articulated through a meticulously naturalistic aesthetic. Gluck presents herself with an unflinching look and tightly closed mouth to suggest both rebellion and control. The intensive attention to surfaces and details records each sign of age and passing time. Her severely cropped hair and stiffly binding collars both record her habitual masculine style and echo the unwavering control that pervades her face. Gluck's personal style is one specifically associated with the male British landed gentry of the early 20th century, and her slightly elevated viewpoint, forbidding gaze and clenched jaws suggest a position of superiority, privilege and judgement. The portrait simultaneously implies a potentially subversive sexuality and an aristocratic heritage and address. Thus the hermetic isolation of the artist's face is nevertheless permeated by the intersecting networks of individual agency and social context.

Gluck's other sitters are subjected to the relentless fidelity and intensity of observation with which she treated her own image. Among others, she painted the eminent psychiatrist *Sir James Crichton-Browne* (1930), the art patron *Lady Mount Temple* (*c*.1936), the architect *Sir Edward Maufe* (1940) and *The Rt Hon. Sir Raymond Evershed, Master of the Rolls* (1951; all private collections, *ibid.*, pp.68, 145, 184 and 241 respectively). Together they are a record of Gluck's movements within particular strata of British society throughout her career, facilitated by the financial freedom to choose her sitters. They also reveal a very modern conception of self-sufficient individuality placed within an airless and remote atmosphere that recalls 19th-century Symbolism.

In the early 1930s Gluck's subject matter changed substantially, but the paintings remain intimately linked to her quotidian associations within a British class system. This change coincided with her relationship with the decorator Constance Spry, whose innovative flower arrangements became virtual requirements in the homes of wealthy, upper-class Londoners. Floral still lifes dominated Gluck's work (e.g. *Chromatic*, *ibid.*, p.91) and often she based her compositions on the unique and "modern" arrangements that made Spry famous. At this time, Gluck also developed and patented the three-tiered "Gluck frame" to achieve an integrated effect of picture and decorative scheme. Because it reflected contemporary ideas combining artistic form with practical utility, the Gluck frame became very popular and was used both in fashionable interiors as well as two major British Art in Industry exhibitions in the 1930s.

After her relationship with Constance Spry ended in 1936, Gluck painted fewer flower pictures. She became involved with the writer Nesta Obermer and soon produced two paintings that marked a dramatic departure from her established artistic interest. The two paintings, *Medallion* (1936; private collection, *ibid.*, p.8) and *Noel* (1937; private collection, *ibid.*, p.125), are an interjection of lesbian experience into Gluck's work that is uncommonly explicit and personal, a change perhaps due to the intensity of the relationship. Gluck considered that she and Nesta were married, and painted *Medallion* to commemorate their wedding ceremony in 1936 (Nesta was already involved in a heterosexual marriage of convenience, a common arrangement in early 20th-century European culture that allowed prominent society members to retain the necessary veneer of social respectability while not appearing to sanction homosexual relationships, particularly among women). In this painting Gluck presents her profile matched and surrounded completely by Nesta's; both figures are ambiguously androgynous and idealised. Gluck called the painting "YouWe", signalling her belief in the total merging of two individuals into a single being by an intensity of mutual feeling. This collapsing together of language, of distinct identities, of genders, is part of the larger utopian project that characterises Gluck's work. In *Medallion* she attempts to visualise symbolically a union that was illegible to the dominant British culture in which she and Nesta lived. That the two women continued the heterosexual terms of marriage – referring to each other as husband and wife – while visualising themselves as outside such conventions points to the irreconcilable demands of conformity that pervaded the contemporary British class and gender systems. *Noel* is less provocative but no less a commemorative painting to the women's relationship. The picture is an elaborate still life of decorations and desserts that celebrates the first Christmas they spent together. Through the scrupulously realised textures and surfaces and the solid armature of the composition, Gluck arrests time at a particular moment in their lives, creating a memorial of mundane objects that are infused and coded with the lesbian relationship that stands unseen behind them.

A decade-long gap in Gluck's production resulted from her self-proclaimed "paint war", a crusade against inferior artists' materials that brought her into conflict with the British Board of Trade and commercial paint producers and eventually led to the formation of the British Standards Institution Technical Committee on Artists' Materials, which for the first time published standards for naming and defining pigments. After her return to painting in the 1960s, Gluck became preoccupied with time once again, specifically the passage from life to death and the consolation of the cycle of life. As in her earlier paintings, ordinary objects are suffused with implications of symbolic meanings that cling to the picture's surface and hover just below an explicit reading. The dead bird of *Requiem* (1964; private collection, *ibid.*, p.287), the solitary flight over the landscape in *Homeward* (1964; private collection, *ibid.*, p.286), the decaying fish in the surf from *Rage, Rage Against the Dying of the Light* (1970–73, private collection, *ibid.*, p.295): all are permeated with a mystical sense of the presence of death that Gluck called "beautiful and calming".

JOE LUCCHESI

Golubkina, Anna (Semyonovna)
Russian sculptor, 1864–1927   [fig. 26]

Born in Zaraysk, Ryazan province, 28 January 1864. Studied painting and sculpture in Moscow, 1889–94, and at the Academy of Arts, St Petersburg, under sculptor V.A. Beklemishev, 1894–5. Trip to Paris to study at Académie Colarossi, 1895–6; met and worked with Rodin during second trip to Paris, 1897. Taught sculpture in Moscow, 1901–3. Trip to Paris and London, 1902–4. In Moscow from 1905; active in revolutionary movement; imprisoned, then released on bail, 1907. Taught workers' classes in sculpture, 1913. Held solo exhibition to aid war wounded, 1914. Taught sculpture at Svomas (State Free Art Studios), Moscow, 1918–20; professor at Vkhutemas (Higher State Artistic and Technical Workshops), Moscow 1920. Health declined from 1924, but continued to work and exhibit. Took part in the organisation of the ORS (Society of

Russian Sculptors), 1926. Died in Zaraysk, 7 September 1927.

Principal Exhibitions

Moscow Society of Art Lovers: 1898, 1913
Moscow Association of Artists: 1898
SRKh (Union of Russian Artists), Moscow: 1898
Mir Iskusstva (World of Art), St Petersburg: 1898, 1913
Salon de Printemps, Paris: 1899 (third-class medal)
Moscow: 1913 (*Twentieth Exhibition of Watercolours*), 1925 (*Women in Russian Art*), 1925 (*Drawings by Contemporary Russian Sculptors*), 1944 (retrospective)
Museum of Fine Arts, Moscow: 1914 (individual)
Moscow Salon: 1917, 1923
Grand Central Palace, New York: 1923–4 (*Russian Art*, touring)

Selected Writings

Mastera iskusstva ob iskusstve [Masters of art on art], ed. A. Fyodorov-Davydov and G. Nedoshivin, vii, Moscow: Iskusstvo, 1970 (selections from Golubkina's letters and book)
Pisma. Neskolko slov o remesle skulptora. Vospominaniya sovremennikov [Letters. Some words on the sculptor's craft. Reminiscences of contemporaries], ed. N.A. Korovich, Moscow, 1983 (*Neskolko slov o remesle skulptora* first published 1923)

Bibliography

Boris Nikolayev (Ternovets), "Anna Semyonovna Golubkina", *Iskusstvo*, no.3, 1939, pp.117–21
Anna Golubkina: Yubileynaya vystavka [Anna Golubkina: Jubilee exhibition], exh. cat., Moscow, and elsewhere, 1964
Elena Murina, "Anna Semyonovna Golubkina", *Dekorativnoye iskusstvo*, no.6, 1964
Trois sculpteurs soviétiques: A.S. Goloubkina, V.I. Moukhina, S.D. Lebedeva, exh. cat., Musée Rodin, Paris, 1971
Ksenya V. Ardentova, *Anna Golubkina*, Moscow: Izobrazitelnoye Iskusstvo, 1976
Aleksandr Abramovich Kamensky, *Anna Golubkina: Lichnost, epokha, skulptura* [Anna Golubkina: Her personality, epoch, sculpture], Moscow: Izobrazitelnoye Iskusstvo, 1990
M.N. Yablonskaya, *Women Artists of Russia's New Age, 1900–1935*, New York: Rizzoli, and London: Thames and Hudson, 1990

Anna Golubkina was among the most highly acclaimed sculptors of early 20th-century Russia. From a provincial peasant background, self-taught until she began her artistic training, Golubkina identified strongly with Russia's common people. Politically active, she spent time in prison and was often without food and money, but she gave away large amounts when she could. Her subjects ranged from portraits of major cultural figures to painful images of loneliness and old age. A down-to-earth fascination with the sculptor's materials combined with a bold fantasy gave Golubkina's work an unusually broad stylistic range and wide appeal.

Golubkina was born in 1864 in the town of Zaraysk, south of Moscow. Her grandfather was a serf who purchased his freedom, her father sold produce at the local market and died young, and Golubkina worked in the family garden until she was 25. With no chance of formal education, she read books in the library of a local merchant, and began drawing and modelling clay on her own. She decided to go to Moscow in 1889, with the modest ambition of learning to paint porcelain dishes, but she soon realised that she could do more. At the Moscow School of Painting, Sculpture and Architecture she studied under the painter Sergei Ivanov and the sculptor S.M. Volnukhin, and in 1894 transferred to the Academy of Arts in St Petersburg, where she worked under the sculptor V.A. Beklemishev. Golubkina appreciated Beklemishev's ability to teach without forcing pupils to emulate him, but in 1895 she left for Paris, hoping to work under Auguste Rodin.

Golubkina studied in Paris for more than a year; she did not meet Rodin during this trip, but worked in the studio of Filippo Colarossi. She returned to Paris in 1897 and established her own studio there. She did not study with Rodin formally, but consulted him and later called herself his pupil. Golubkina was not, however, overwhelmed by the master's enormous prestige and authority. When she used models or themes similar to Rodin's, she found emphatically different interpretations. The model who had posed for Rodin's statuette the *Helmet-Maker's Wife* (mid-1880s) became the subject for Golubkina's life-sized figure *Old Age* (1897; Golubkina Studio Museum, Moscow). Rodin's work, based on a ballad by François Villon, expressed a lament for lost beauty. Golubkina avoided this story-telling element: her old woman crouches defensively, an arm barely supporting her heavy head. The artist's empathy with the woman's physical and psychological condition reaches beyond symbolism. Exhibited at the Salon de Printemps in Paris in 1899, the work announced Golubkina's artistic maturity.

A large bronze sculpture, *Walking Man* (1903; Golubkina Studio Museum), recalls Rodin's *Walking Man* (1877–8; Musée Rodin, Paris) and *Age of Bronze* (1875–7; Musée d'Orsay, Paris), but her treatment of the material emphasises potentially explosive strength. To Maxim Gorky and other contemporaries, the figure presaged the proletarian uprising of 1905. A later companion work, *The Slave* (1909; Golubkina Studio Museum), seemed to personify the State's repression of peasants and workers. Such interpretations were entirely in keeping with Golubkina's experience of poverty and commitment to revolutionary goals.

Golubkina accepted a commission for the first Russian bust of *Karl Marx* (1905; Tretyakov Gallery, Moscow), and she donated her fee to a fund for homeless workers. She opened her home as a temporary hospital and distributed revolutionary pamphlets. Arrested in 1907, she argued that urging the peasants to overthrow the tsar was no crime. In prison she went on a hunger strike, and illness resulted in an early release on bail. During this time of intense political involvement, Golubkina acknowledged Rodin's role in liberating her potential as an artist, writing to him:

> I dreamed of creating something good and enduring, and thought that ... I could express my gratitude to you. Now I have no hope of doing this. ... I am writing now because our country is going through alarming times and no-one knows how it will turn out. They are throwing everyone into prison, and I have been in prison once. In the autumn I will have a new trial, and I fear that you will never know how much I venerate you ... While I live I shall always revere you as a great artist and as the person who gave me the possibility of life [Musée Rodin, reprinted in Fyodorov-Davydov and Nedoshivin, eds, 1970, pp.287–8].

A decade after her encounter with Rodin, Golubkina invoked not his stylistic influence but rather his image as a heroic personification of the power of sculpture.

Golubkina's subjects included well-known figures in Russian culture such as the writers *Andrei Bely* (1907; State Russian Museum, St Petersburg), *Alexei Remizov* and *Alexei Tolstoy* (both 1911; Tretyakov Gallery) and the art patrons *Savva Morozov* (1902; Golubkina Studio Museum) and *E.*

Nosova-Ryabushinskaya (1911; State Russian Museum). She also portrayed simple people whose faces express recognisable experiences and feelings: her grandfather *Polikarp Golubkin* (1892), the frail little girl *Manka* (1898) and the *Old Woman* (1907; all Tretyakov Gallery), whose piercing gaze makes her seem like an ancient prophet. Golubkina worked in a range of materials, starting with clay, plaster and bronze, studying techniques of marble sculpture during another trip to Paris in 1902 and exploiting the graining of wood for her portrayal of Remizov. Her book of 1923, *Neskolko slov o remesle skulptora*, discussed both techniques and reasons for working in specific materials. Golubkina understood how to use textures and other physical qualities of material in order to convey atmosphere or mood, and her work is usually identified with impressionism in sculpture. While emphasising the solidity of the underlying structures of the human form, Golubkina was also attuned to the more ephemeral, visionary aspects of symbolism. Her relief panel for the entrance of the Moscow Art Theatre, *In the Waves* (1902; *in situ*), and other, smaller works contain layers of form, human faces and abstract, swirling textures suggesting a cosmic environment.

In 1914–15 Golubkina held a personal exhibition of 150 sculptures in order to raise money for the victims of World War I. Critics compared her to Michelangelo, and rejoiced that Russian sculpture had at last attained independence from painting, had become more than decoration and could express the full range of human experience. Golubkina fell seriously ill in the 1920s; forced to stop working on large-scale sculptures, she executed miniature cameos in highly inventive forms. She also taught (as she had early in her career, and sporadically before and after the Revolution), but she was too exacting to enjoy teaching, and her best service was through her book on the sculptor's craft. During the last five years of her life, Golubkina created her most expressive and spiritually rich works, an imagined portrait of the writer *Lev Tolstoy*, posed as a sage with one finger to his brow, and *Little Birch-tree* (both 1927; Tretyakov Gallery), in which the figure of a young girl stands erect as a brisk wind sweeps her garments diagonally across her body, evoking ancient Russian folk beliefs about the female spirits dwelling in birch-trees. Both works, the spiritual portrait and the animistic fantasy, combine a solid, realist approach to the human figure and the mystical tones of symbolism; they are both a departure from and a culmination of Golubkina's earlier work. After her death in 1927, Golubkina's niece inherited her house and studio, and managed to preserve and restore the buildings as a permanent studio museum.

ALISON HILTON

Goncharova, Natalya (Sergeyevna)
Russian painter, printmaker and stage designer, 1881–1962   [fig. 25]

Born in the village of Negayevo, Tula Province, 21 June (Old Style calendar)/4 July (New Style calendar) 1881. Studied at the Moscow School of Painting, Sculpture and Architecture, c.1898–1910. Initially studied sculpture, but took up painting after meeting Mikhail Larionov, with whom she lived and worked for the rest of her life. Founder-member, Bubnovy valet (Jack/Knave of Diamonds) exhibition society, 1910; seceded with Larionov to found Osliny khvost (Donkey's Tail) group, 1912. Invited by Diaghilev to join the Ballets Russes as a stage designer; visited Paris to supervise designs for the ballet Le Coq d'Or, 1914. Left Russia with Larionov to join Diaghilev in Switzerland, 1915. Toured with the Ballets Russes to France, Spain and Italy, 1916–17. Settled permanently in Paris, working as a painter, stage designer and graphic artist, 1919. Made designs for the ballets Les Noces, 1923, and The Firebird, 1926. Worked as a stage designer for many different ballet companies after Diaghilev's death in 1929. Became a French citizen, 1936. Married Larionov, 1955. Died in Paris, 17 October 1962.

Principal Exhibitions

Individual
Obshchestvo svobodnoye estetiki, Moscow: 1910
Art Salon, Moscow: 1913
Art Bureau Dobychina, St Petersburg: 1914
Galerie Paul Guillaume, Paris: 1914 (with Mikhail Larionov)
Galerie Sauvage, Paris: 1918 (with Mikhail Larionov)
Galerie Barbazanges, Paris: 1919 (with Mikhail Larionov)
Kingore Galleries, New York: 1922 (with Mikhail Larionov)

Galerie Shiseido, Tokyo: 1923 (with Mikhail Larionov)
Galerie des Deux-Iles, Paris: 1948 (with Mikhail Larionov)
Galerie de l'Institut, Paris: 1956 (with Mikhail Larionov)
Arts Council of Great Britain, Leeds: 1961 (with Mikhail Larionov, touring)
Musée d'Art Moderne de la Ville de Paris: 1963 (with Mikhail Larionov, retrospective)

Group
Salon d'Automne, Paris: 1906 (Exposition de l'art russe)
Zveno (The Link), Kiev: 1908
Zolotoye runo (The Golden Fleece), Moscow: 1908–10
Soyuz molodyozhi (Union of Youth), St Petersburg: 1910–12
Bubnovy valet (Jack/Knave of Diamonds), Moscow: 1910–11
Der Blaue Reiter, Munich: 1912
Grafton Galleries, London: 1912 (Second Post-Impressionist Exhibition)
Osliny khvost (Donkey's Tail), Moscow: 1912
Mishen (Target Group of Artists), Moscow: 1913
Galerie Der Sturm, Berlin: 1913 (Erster deutscher Herbstsalon)
Moscow: 1914 (Exhibition of Paintings No.4), 1915 (Exhibition of Paintings, "The Year 1915", "1915 god")
Museum of Modern Art, New York: 1936 (Cubism and Abstract Art)

Selected Writings
"Pismo k redaktsiyu" [Letter to the editor (on Cubism)], Stolichnaya molva, no.230, 20 February 1912, p.5 (English translations in Loguine 1971, pp.21–3, and Bowlt 1988, pp.77–8)
"Indusskiy i persidskiy lubok" [The Hindu and Persian "lubok"], Vystavka ikonopisnykh i podlennikov lubkov [Exhibition of icon paintings and "lubok" woodcuts], exh. cat., Khudozhestvenny Salon, Moscow, 1913, pp.11–12
"Luchisty i budushchniki: Manifest" [Rayists and Futurepeople: Manifesto], Osliny khvost i Mishen [Donkey's Tail and Target], Moscow: Ts. Myunster, 1913, pp.9–48 (English translation in Bowlt 1988, pp.87–91) (with Mikhail Larionov and others)
Radiantismo giudizi raccolti e tradotti dal Francese e dal Russo da N.A., Rome, 1917 (with Mikhail Larionov)
Les Ballets Russes de Serge de Diaghilew: Décors et costumes, Paris: Galerie Billiet, 1930 (with Michel Georges-Michel and Waldemar George)
"The creation of 'Les Noces'", Ballet, viii/3, 1952, pp.22–6
Serge de Diaghilew et la décoration théâtrale, Belvès, Dordogne: Vorms, 1955 (with Mikhail Larionov and Pierre Vorms)

Bibliography

Eli Eganbyuri (pseudonym Ilya Zdanevich), *Natalya Goncharova, Mikhail Larionov*, Moscow: Ts. Myunster, 1913

Osliny khvost i Mishen' [Donkey's Tail and Target], Moscow: Ts. Myunster, 1913 (essays by S. Khudakov, pp.125–53, and Varsanofy Parkin, pp.49–82)

V. Songaillo, *O vystavke kartin N.S. Goncharovoy* [On the exhibition of paintings by N.S. Goncharova], Moscow, 1913

Vystavka kartin Nataliy Sergeyevny Goncharovoy, 1900–1913 [Exhibition of the paintings of Natalya Sergeyevna Goncharova], exh. cat., Khudozhestvenny Salon, Moscow, 1913 (foreword by Goncharova translated in Bowlt 1988, pp.54–60)

Yakov Tugendkhold, "Vystavka kartin Nataliy Goncharovoy" [The exhibition of paintings by Natalya Goncharova], *Apollon*, no.8, October 1913, pp.71–3

Nikolai Khardzhiyev, "Pamyati Nataliy Goncharovoy i Mikhaila Larionova" [To the memory of Natalya Goncharova and Mikhail Larionov], *Iskusstvo knigi, v, 1963–1964*, 1968, pp.306–18

Tatiana Loguine, *Gontcharova et Larionov: Cinquante ans à Saint Germain-des-Prés*, Paris: Klincksieck, 1971

Mary Chamot, *Nathalie Gontcharova*, Paris: Bibliothèque des Arts, 1972

Susan P. Compton, *The World Backwards: Russian Futurist Books, 1912–16*, London: British Museum, 1978

Mary Chamot, *Goncharova: Stage Designs and Paintings*, London: Oresko, 1979

Abstraction: Towards a New Art: Painting, 1910–1920, exh. cat., Tate Gallery, London, 1981

Anthony Parton, "Russian 'Rayism': The work and theory of Mikhail Larionov and Natalya Goncharova, 1912–1914: Ouspensky's four-dimensional super race?", *Leonardo*, xvi, 1983, pp.298–305

—, "'Goncharova and Larionov': Gumilev's pantum to art", *Nikolai Gumilev, 1886–1986*, Oakland, CA: Berkeley Slavic Specialities, 1987, pp.225–42

John E. Bowlt, ed., *Russian Art of the Avant-garde: Theory and Criticism, 1902–1934*, 2nd edition, London and New York: Thames and Hudson, 1988

Alison Hilton, "Natalia Goncharova and the iconography of revelation", *Studies in Iconography*, xiii, 1989–90, pp.232–57

Marina Tsvetaeva, *Nathalie Gontcharova: Sa vie, son oeuvre*, Paris: Hiver, 1990 (Russian original)

M.N. Yablonskaya, *Women Artists of Russia's New Age, 1900–1935*, New York: Rizzoli, and London: Thames and Hudson, 1990

John E. Bowlt, "Natalia Goncharova and futurist theater", *Art Journal*, xlix, Spring 1990, pp.44–51

L'Avant-garde russe, 1905–1925, exh. cat., Musée des Beaux-Arts, Nantes, and elsewhere, 1993

Elena Basner, "Natalya Goncharova i Ilya Zdanevich" [Natalya Goncharova and Ilya Zdanevich], *Iskusstvo avangarda yazyk miravogo obshcheniya* [The universal language of avant-garde art], Ufa, 1993, pp.68–80

Anthony Parton, *Mikhail Larionov and the Russian Avant-Garde*, Princeton: Princeton University Press, 1993

Jane Sharp, "Redrawing the margins of Russian vanguard art: N. Goncharova's trial for pornography in 1910", *Sexuality and the Body in Russian Culture*, ed. Jane T. Costlow and others, Stanford, CA: Stanford University Press, 1993, pp.97–123

Nathalie Gontcharova, Michel Larionov, exh. cat., Musée National d'Art Moderne, Centre Georges Pompidou, Paris, 1995

The work of Natalya Goncharova first received critical attention in 1906 when she exhibited a series of impressionist pastel landscapes at the Salon d'Automne in Paris. Goncharova's work at this time was principally inspired by that of her teachers at the Moscow School of Painting such as Konstantin Korovin, as well as that of members of her peer group, such as Mikhail Larionov and Pavel Kuznetsov. In 1907 Goncharova fell under the influence of Symbolism and became friendly with the painter and financier Nikolai Ryabushinsky, who publicised both the Symbolist poets and the painters in his luxurious art magazine *Zolotoye runo* (Golden Fleece) of 1906–10. This magazine played an important role in the development of Russian art at this time and not least in Goncharova's own development. In 1908 *Zolotoye runo* sponsored a major exhibition of modern and contemporary French art that featured not only the work of French Symbolist painters but also the work of van Gogh, Gauguin, Cézanne, Matisse and the Fauves. The impact of this exhibition upon Goncharova cannot be overstated and during the next two years she began to assimilate these diverse approaches to modernism in her own work. In addition she began to study the impressive collections of French painting that were then being assembled by Ivan Morozov and Sergei Shchukin.

Goncharova's attention was principally attracted by the work of Gauguin, and in 1909 she executed a series of figure paintings entitled *God of Fecundity* (Larionov Goncharova Museum, Moscow) that emulated Gauguin's painting *Blue Idol* (Hermitage, St Petersburg). Several of Goncharova's paintings were exhibited at the Society of Free Aesthetics in March 1910, but the exhibition was criticised in the press as being "pornographic" and Goncharova was subsequently taken to court by the authorities on a charge of indecency. Although she was acquitted, this event was significant not only because it introduced Goncharova and Russian modernism into the public domain, but also because, as Jane Sharp has argued, from a feminist perspective it may be seen as the first response of the male art establishment to the work of a female artist that broke the accepted canons. From this point on Goncharova was to find herself at odds with and lampooned by society not only because of her staunch affiliation to the principles of the avant-garde but also because of her sex. The press, in particular, proved biting in their many caricatures of Goncharova and jibes at her expense (for the question of Goncharova's relationship with the Russian press, see Basner in Paris 1995).

Although these first figure paintings were deliberately calculated to shock the public, Goncharova entertained serious painterly interests at this time. *God of Fecundity* demonstrates not only the impact of Gauguin, but in the overall fracturing of the background plane also reveals a study of early Cubism. Indeed, in an interview with the press Goncharova declared that, in common with Picasso and Braque, she was attempting to find "sculptural distinctiveness" in her work (*Stolichnaya molva*, no.115, 5 April 1910, p.3). Having said this, the example of Gauguin remained important for several years. Like Gauguin, Goncharova associated rural life with moral regeneration, and she frequently returned to the provinces, where she mixed with the peasants on and around her parents' estate. Her first-hand experience of peasant life shaped a strong interest both in the subject of the peasantry and in their innate feeling for colour, composition and decoration, which found expression in her paintings. Works such as *Spring Gardening* (1909; Tate Gallery, London), which portrays the peasant women on the estate as they plant flowers, are characteristic of Goncharova's approach to art at this time. The stylisation of the figures, the Cubist fracturing of surface and the rich colours and garlands of blossom that decorate the surface of the painting idealise the life of the Russian peasantry in a similar way to Gauguin's paintings of the Tahitians among whom he lived.

During 1910, however, one may discern a clear development in Goncharova's peasant paintings. In *Washing Linen* (Tretyakov Gallery, Moscow) she abandoned the stylised forms of the peasant women and the rich colouring that had characterised her earlier work. Here, the figures are more crudely delineated, the colouring is more naturalistic and the rough texture of the paint seems to act as a metaphor for the mean life of provincial peasant women. From a feminist perspective it is interesting to note that during this period Goncharova executed many paintings specifically featuring women at work. Several such as the *Bread Seller* (1911; Musée National d'Art Moderne, Paris) are the more shocking because they represent a critique of the socio-economic circumstances in which the Russian peasantry found themselves. Here, the "picturesque" aspects of peasant life, alluded to in the bright colouring and decorative features of the background, act as a foil against which is set the vacant, lifeless and harrowing face of the bread seller.

While it is difficult to know what was Goncharova's precise political persuasion at this time, she did entertain socialist sympathies. She was friendly, for example, with the Russian socialist poet Mikhail Tsetlin, whose portrait she painted in 1910 (untraced). It seems likely that her political views played an important role in the development of her work since she also painted the "outcasts" of Russian society, in particular the Jews. In this, Goncharova's work must be seen in the context of that of her colleagues: Larionov, for example, who painted the prostitutes, Gypsies and common soldiers of the provinces, and Malevich, who worked closely with Goncharova at this time and stated categorically that the peasant paintings executed by himself and Goncharova were meant to function on a social plane.

Several of Goncharova's peasant paintings were exhibited at the Jack of Diamonds show of 1910–11. Shortly afterwards, however, Goncharova and Larionov seceded from the group on the grounds that it was necessary to break with Western artistic conventions and to develop a truly Russian school of modernist painting. To this end, they adopted what they called a Neo-primitive style, in which the subjects of the Russian peasantry and the urban workforce were expressed in the style of the visual traditions of the Russian people. During the next two years there followed an enormous series of Neo-primitivist paintings. Larionov was particularly inspired by the conventions of the Russian popular print (*lubok*) and whereas this traditional form of popular art impinged upon Goncharova, she turned more towards the conventions of icon painting and the provincial signboard. Goncharova's series of *Evangelists* (State Russian Museum, St Petersburg) are among the best known of her Neo-primitive paintings that emulate the icon tradition, whilst the bright colours and crude forms of her series *The Harvest* (Tretyakov Gallery; State Russian Museum; Musée National d'Art Moderne; and elsewhere) owe an obvious debt to the tradition of hand-painted signboards to be found in the Russian provinces.

Although Goncharova's Neo-primitivism proposed a genuine reinvestigation of the indigenous visual traditions of the Russian people, the style was deliberately calculated to offend, since "cultivated" Russian society found the artefacts of the Russian peasantry boorish and disgusting. Consequently, Goncharova's Neo-primitive work was frequently criticised in the press and her religious paintings were impounded by the police on two occasions. In common with other members of her generation, Goncharova's socialist sympathies were mixed with an interest in religion and mysticism. In the years before World War I, for example, Goncharova was in correspondence with Kandinsky, whose famous series *Compositions* of 1911–13 adopted the theme of judgement as described in the biblical book of Revelation. It is interesting that in 1911 Goncharova executed a series of nine panels entitled the *Grape Harvest* (Tretyakov Gallery; Musée National d'Art Moderne; and elsewhere), which were also based on the divine judgement of society as described in Revelation. Goncharova's panels (assembled for the first time since 1913 in the exhibition *Nathalie Gontcharova, Michel Larionov*, see Paris 1995) are based on the style of signboard painting and seem to narrate a very contemporary judgement on the evils of her own society. Indeed this was a theme that Goncharova adopted again during World War I in a folio of lithographs *Misticheskiye obrazy voyny* (Mystical images of war; Moscow, 1915), when it was possible to identify the war with that of the Last Battle described in Revelation.

During the years 1912–14 Goncharova's interest in mysticism also found expression in a series of abstract and non-objective compositions painted in Larionov's innovative Rayist style, which represented a response to Analytical Cubism, Italian Futurism and Simultanism as practised by Robert and Sonia Delaunay (q.v.) in Paris. According to Larionov's theory of Rayism, which was publicised in several manifestoes during 1913–14, rays of light reflected from three-dimensional objects are able to create spatial forms in the atmosphere that represent a higher reality, identified by Larionov with the fourth dimension of space. It was this higher reality that Larionov attempted to interpret in his Rayist work by fragmenting the picture surface and presenting the spectator with an ambiguous and shifting surface of interconnecting planes. Goncharova undoubtedly played a role in the development of Rayism and, according to her statement in the catalogue to her one-woman exhibition in 1913, she subsequently elaborated the style. Typical of Goncharova's Rayist works is her painting *Cats: Rayist Perception in Rose, Black and Yellow* (1912; Solomon R. Guggenheim Museum, New York), in which the picture surface is shattered by sharp rays and fragmented planes, a formulation that recalls Cubist example. Goncharova's most important series of Rayist paintings, however, is entitled *Rayist Forest* (1912–14; Staatsgalerie, Stuttgart; Thyssen-Bornemisza Collection, Madrid; and elsewhere). It is these that principally express Goncharova's metaphysical and mystical philosophy relating as they do to the Eastern concept of the "world soul" and more specifically to the philosophy of Pyotr Ouspensky who, in his book on the subject of the fourth dimension entitled *Tertium organum* (St Petersburg, 1911), which was popular among the Russian avant-garde, identified the Forest as an example of the "fourth state of life activity". Despite the theoretical and philosophical depth of the Rayist style, which also relied on scientific developments such as the development of X-ray photography and the writings of Marie Curie, the critics invariably described Rayism as a degenerate form of Cubism. Rayism, however, was of historic importance in that several of Larionov's and a few of Goncharova's paintings were completely non-objective and were hence the forerunners of the non-objective tradition in modern Russian art.

In addition to Rayist paintings, Goncharova also practised in what has since become known as a Cubo-Futurist style, which amalgamated the stylistic devices of the French Cubist and Italian Futurist movements. Representative of Goncharova's work in this genre is *Woman in Hat* (1913; Musée National d'Art Moderne). Here, aspects of the portrait such as the nose, mouth and eyes are repeated across the canvas according to Futurist example, while the use of stencilled letters in the composition and the restricted palette testify to Cubist practice. The range of Goncharova's work in

1913 was particularly diverse and her one-woman exhibition in Moscow of that year represented more than 700 works. The exhibition clinched her reputation as one of the leading members of the Russian avant-garde, which was strengthened throughout the year by her lively participation in Russian Futurist activities. She illustrated Russian Futurist books for the poets Alexei Kruchyonykh, Velimir Khlebnikov, Sergei Bobrov and Konstantin Bolshakov, she painted her face and paraded the Moscow streets in the company of Larionov and Ilya Zdanevich, performed in a Futurist theatre called The Pink Lantern, and finally starred in a Russian Futurist film entitled *Drama in the Futurists' Cabaret No.13*.

It was partly due to Goncharova's popular notoriety that the impresario Sergei Diaghilev invited her to make the designs for his forthcoming production of the ballet *Le Coq d'Or*, which was to be staged in Paris in 1914. Goncharova accepted the commission and from 1914 onwards began to practise principally as stage designer for the Ballets Russes. In June 1915 Goncharova and Larionov left Russia to join Diaghilev in Switzerland, where the two artists were engaged to design new ballets for his repertoire. In 1916 Goncharova followed Diaghilev to Spain, which proved an important visit in the development of her work over the next two decades. The inspiration that Goncharova drew from her time there is embodied in a diverse series of *Espagnoles* (Musée National d'Art Moderne). The hieratic figures of Spanish women dressed in elaborate national dress and bedecked with tall mantillas appear in many of Goncharova's easel paintings and painted screens of the period, where they are treated in figurative, stylised and abstracted modes of representation. The *Espagnoles* are related to Goncharova's previous Russian work in that they show a monumental approach to figure painting. The works are often executed on a large scale and the figures almost fill the available picture space. Moreover, their format recalls that of the icon style of the years 1910–12, particularly that of the *Evangelists*. Although the *Espagnoles* represent a new and secular theme of Spanish ladies in their festival finery, they operate on the same principle as some of Goncharova's earlier peasant paintings, which use the monumental scale of the figure and quotations from the icon tradition in order to elevate the humble peasantry to the rank of saints and angels. In this sense the *Espagnoles* represent a reprise, though in different guise, of earlier work.

Unfortunately, Goncharova's painterly work in the West suffered a critical failure. First, she exhibited infrequently, and while exhibitions at the Galerie Sauvage (1918) and the Galerie Barbazanges (1919) established her reputation as a contemporary stage designer, they failed to promote her painterly work. Second, contemporary critical literature was almost exclusively devoted to her theatrical work. Third, from the late 1920s interest was focused principally on Goncharova's paintings from the Russian period at the expense of her contemporary work. Goncharova's initial critical success in the West might have been sustained had she been supported by the dealer system but she shunned any association with dealers, preferring to sell her work either in the Paris Salons or in small Parisian galleries. Despite her aggressive self-promotion during the Futurist years in Moscow, Goncharova was modest in terms of promoting her work. She also had an aversion to selling her work, preferring to give her paintings away. Consequently, it is only comparatively recently that Goncharova's original contribution has been properly assessed and her Russian work singled out as having played a crucial role in the development of Russian modernism.

ANTHONY PARTON

Gonzalès, Eva
French painter, 1849–1883

Born in Paris, 19 April 1849, daughter of the novelist Emmanuel Gonzalès, later honorary president of the Société des Gens de Lettres. Studied in Paris under Charles Chaplin, 1866–7, then in the studio of Edouard Manet. Married engraver Henri Guérard, 1879. Died 6 May 1883, after giving birth to a son. Her sister Jeanne, also a painter, became Guérard's second wife.

Principal Exhibitions
Paris Salon: 1870, 1872, 1874, 1876, 1878–80, 1882–3
Salon des Refusés, Paris: 1873
Cercle Artistique et Littéraire, Paris: 1882 (*Exposition spéciale des oeuvres des artistes femmes*)
Salons de la Vie Moderne, Paris: 1885 (retrospective)

Bibliography

Maria Deraismes, "Une exposition particulière de l'Ecole réaliste", *L'Avenir des femmes*, 5 July 1874

Eva Gonzalès, exh. cat., Salons de la Vie Moderne, Paris, 1885; reprinted in *Modern Art in Paris, 1855–1900*, no.40, New York: Garland, 1981

Eva Gonzalès, exh. cat., Galerie Bernheim-Jeune, Paris, 1914

Etienne Moreau-Nélaton, *Manet raconté par lui-même*, 2 vols, Paris: Laurens, 1926

Eva Gonzalès, exh. cat., Galerie Marcel Bernheim, Paris, 1932

Paule Bayle, "Eva Gonzalès", *La Renaissance*, xv, June 1932, pp.110–15

Eva Gonzalès, exh. cat., Galerie Daber, Paris, 1950

Claude Roger-Marx, *Eva Gonzalès*, Saint-Germain-en-Laye: Neuilly, 1950

François Mathey, *Six femmes peintres*, Paris: Editions du Chêne, 1951

Pierre Courthion and Pierre Cailler, eds, *Portrait of Manet by Himself and His Contemporaries*, London: Cassell, 1960

John Rewald, *The History of Impressionism*, 4th edition, London: Secker and Warburg, 1973

Women Artists, 1550–1950, exh. cat., Los Angeles County Museum of Art, and elsewhere, 1976

Charlotte Yeldham, *Women Artists in Nineteenth-Century France and England*, 2 vols, New York: Garland, 1984

Tamar Garb, *Women Impressionists*, Oxford: Phaidon, 1986

Marie-Caroline Sainsaulieu and Jacques de Mons, *Eva Gonzalès, 1849–1883: Etude critique et catalogue raisonné*, Paris: La Bibliothèque des Arts, 1990

Les Femmes impressionistes: Mary Cassatt, Eva Gonzalès, Berthe Morisot, exh. cat., Musée Marmottan, Paris, 1993

Albert Boime, "Maria Deraismes and Eva Gonzalès: A feminist critique of *Une loge aux Théâtre des Italiens*", *Woman's Art Journal*, xv/2, 1994–5, pp.31–7

Until quite recently, Eva Gonzalès was marginalised by modern scholars as little more than a beautiful model and student of the French realist painter, Edouard Manet. But to many of her peers Gonzalès's position as a woman painter in Paris in the era of the Impressionists was a formidable one.

The daughter of a well-known French novelist, Eva Gonzalès grew up surrounded by illustrious members of Parisian literary and artistic circles. Through Philippe Jourde, publisher of the journal *Le Siècle*, she met Charles Chaplin, a popular academic painter who had instituted a woman's programme in his studio and would later teach Mary Cassatt (q.v.). In 1866, at the age of 17,

Gonzalès began her formal training in Chaplin's studio. *Tea* (private collection, repr. Sainsaulieu and Mons 1990, cat. no.6), an early genre painting executed in a tight realist style, probably dates from her brief tenure as Chaplin's student. Yet the intimate subject, a graceful interior that includes such emblems of gender as the gilded mirror, diminutive tea set, delicate furniture, fan, flowers and pink, unsealed letter, links the painting as well to a larger feminine visual culture that legions of amateur women painters would perpetuate in their work. Berthe Morisot (q.v.) among others would embrace this refined, protected world in her paintings of interiors in the following decade. One of Gonzalès's first pastels, *The Fan* (1869; Minneapolis Institute of Arts), again depicts the "feminised interior", but in the freer technique and lighter palette she would often explore in this more ephemeral medium.

By 1869 Gonzalès had met Manet and started to work in his studio. With his encouragement, she began to submit her work on a regular basis to the annual Salons. Her Salon debut in 1870 (in which she exhibited three works), however, was dramatically overshadowed by her presence at the same Salon as a subject in Manet's portrait of *Mlle E.G.* (National Gallery, London). Suffering a critical fate common to women artists who worked with older, established male painters, Gonzalès's public persona often revolved around critics' perceptions of her as dark-haired and fashionable, a subject and decorative acolyte of Manet's rather than as a professional artist in her own right. In an attempt to combat this perception, Gonzalès listed herself as a student of Chaplin, but few Salon viewers were fooled. Her own major submission, the life-sized *Little Soldier* (Musée Gaston Rapin, Villeneuve-sur-Lot), was an unmistakable reference to Manet's infamous *Fife Player* (1866; Musée d'Orsay, Paris). In her painting, however, Gonzalès subtly transformed Manet's radically two-dimensional figure into a once-more volumetric form, whose slightly turned pose, soft modelling and extended cast shadows re-establish the space and realist figural tradition that Manet had boldly flattened. The few critics who responded to Gonzalès's work recognised only her debt, not her response to Manet. Even they, however, could not separate their assessment of the actual woman painter from the image of elegant dilettante that Manet's portrait had established. As one review wrote condescendingly of *Little Soldier*: "It is an astoundingly strong statement from such a pretty little author" (Louis Leroy, *Le Charivari*, May 1870).

Undaunted, however, Gonzalès continued to work in a sober realist manner reminiscent of Manet's earlier Spanish period and began to enjoy some success. A small circle of critics, several of whom were also loyal admirers of her father, Emmanuel Gonzalès, applauded her efforts, and in particular a series of large genre works for which her sister Jeanne posed. Such paintings as *Indolence* (Sainsaulieu and Mons 1990, cat. no.39) and the smaller pastel *Favourite Plant* (*ibid.*, cat. no.40), both accepted for the Salon of 1872, were lavishly praised by Emile Zola, Jules Castagnary and others in their reviews, and established the subject of the contemplative, self-absorbed modern woman as a focus of Gonzalès's oeuvre. A more formal portrait of her sister from the same period (collection Judith and Alexander M. Laughlin, New York), which the dealer Durand-Ruel held briefly, exhibited the broad, summary handling, flattened space and black-and-white palette that characterise many of her early works and that critics quickly likened to Manet.

Although like Manet Gonzalès chose not to participate in the group exhibitions of the Impressionists, her painting did not escape their influence. Several small landscape studies from the early 1870s already suggest an awareness of the emerging Impressionist style. *Beach at Dieppe* (Musée Château, Dieppe), painted in Normandy in 1870–71, when the Gonzalès family sought refuge there from the Franco-Prussian war, uses the high bird's-eye viewpoint, flattened expanses and sunlit palette that had characterised Monet's views of Sainte-Adresse a decade earlier. Likewise, the luminous green tonality, sketch-like brushwork and motif of a reflective pond in *Osier Beds* (Kunsthistorisches Museum, Vienna) owed much to the plein-air technique and palette of early Impressionist landscapes. Even Gonzalès seemed to sense this new, if momentary affinity. When *Osier Beds* was rejected from the Salon of 1873, she did not hesitate, in this instance, to part company with Manet and to exhibit with Renoir and countless others at the Salon des Refusés, re-instituted that year to compensate for an unusually hostile Salon jury.

The fate of Gonzalès's work at the Salon of 1874, which opened shortly after the first Impressionist show closed, offers a revealing glimpse of the gendered discourse that would become commonplace in Impressionist art criticism. Her small pastel toilette scene *The Nest* (Musée d'Orsay), executed with smooth blended strokes and a muted pastel palette, was accepted as a sketch and widely acclaimed. Critics had previously likened the artist's pastels to those of the noted 18th-century pastellist Rosalba Carriera (q.v.), and in *The Nest*, as in traditional pastels, traces of a thin red line still rim the edges of the figure's hands, the mirror and still life. Gonzalès's fascination here with the fall of light on translucent fabric, conveyed with a subtle mixture of white, pink and soft blue sketch-like strokes, also aligns her work with the Impressionist Edgar Degas's earliest studies in pastel. But in Salon reviews *The Nest* became a paradigm of "feminine technique": Castagnary, for example, lauded its "seductive harmony" and "simple, natural grace" ("Le Salon de 1874", *Le Siècle*, 26 May 1874, p.2). Ironically, although such observations might seem to limit her "public" role as artist, the longstanding belief that the ephemeral medium of pastel was uniquely suited to the assumedly more delicate sensibilities of women artists actually allowed Gonzalès a unique freedom to experiment.

In contrast, Gonzalès's other submission in 1874, the monumental realist painting *Box at the Théâtre des Italiens* (Musée d'Orsay), was rebuffed by the Salon Jury. No doubt its ambitious scale (98 × 130 cm.), deemed more appropriate to the heroic subjects and aspirations of better established (male) painters, would have rendered problematic Gonzalès's elegant modern genre scene of a woman and her male escort at the theatre. The inclusion of a sumptuous floral bouquet – in the eyes of many viewers a pointed allusion to the analogous flowers (and erotic symbolism) in Manet's scandalous *Olympia* (1863; Musée d'Orsay) – only added to the painting's contentiousness. But it was above all her solid and forceful brushwork, in which critics detected a surprisingly "masculine vigour", that led to the work's rejection. As the feminist Maria Deraismes noted in her crucial essay on Gonzalès ("Une exposition particulière de l'Ecole réaliste", 1874), Gonzalès's painting was refused in 1874 not only because of its visible attachment to Manet, who still provoked controversy in some quarters, but also because it boldly defied gender-polarised conceptions of feminine delicacy. The painting seemed strident and defiant, while her more quietly venturesome pastel work appeared to sustain the status quo. When *Box at the Théâtre des Italiens* was finally shown at the Salon of 1879 – at the very moment that Mary Cassatt was exploring the same subject in her work – the skill and power of Gonzalès's painting still surprised her critics (quoted in Bayle 1932).

Several of Gonzalès's subsequent paintings, works that were not exhibited during her lifetime, embraced the kind of intimate genre themes favoured by Cassatt and Morisot and also illustrate a gradual loosening of her technique. In *The Awakening* (Kunsthalle, Bremen), one of two pendant paintings of *c.*1877–8 depicting her sister Jeanne reclining in bed, the potentially erotic subject in this instance provides only a pretext for the artist to respond to the animate surface of the setting, describing a vast range of pale pinks, violets, greys and blues reflected off diaphanous white fabrics. Equally subdued in theme but rich in tonal values is the related sketch-like canvas *The Convalescent* (Ordrupgaardsammlingen, Charlottenlund). In the paintings she produced at this point for public exhibition, however, Gonzalès attempted to reconcile her earlier realism with scattered Impressionist effects, and the results were often less successful. *Miss and Baby* (private collection, repr. Sainsaulieu and Mons 1990, cat. no.41), shown at the Salon of 1878, is her first full-scale landscape painted in plein air, and depicts a fashionable woman and child in a shady garden in Dieppe. But it is also a thinly disguised reworking of Manet's *Railroad* (National Gallery of Art, Washington, DC) and, lacking the spatial and psychological tensions of Manet's masterful prototype, suffers in comparison. More successful is Gonzalès's landscape from Grandcamp, *Brother and Sister* (*c.*1877; National Gallery of Ireland, Dublin). In this painting, the tactile brushwork and axial placement of the foreground still-life recall a favourite spatial ploy of Manet's. But Gonzalès's new attentiveness to surface effects and her depiction of a vast sunlit marine landscape, loosely sketched with a brightened palette, draw her at the same time closer to the Impressionist aesthetic. And in the *Donkey Ride* (*c.*1880; Museum and Art Gallery, Bristol), a small figure painting whose triangular composition and genre format recall the earlier *Box at the Théâtre des Italiens*, Gonzalès displays a combination of disparate techniques – thin oil washes, calligraphic lines and highly finished painterly details – that reveal the

intense experimentation her painting as a whole underwent at this point.

After a decade in public view, Gonzalès seems finally to have hit her full stride in her late work, stepping forth from the shadow of Manet that hovered so long over her art. Her growing sense of self-assertion is especially evident in a series of radiant pastel portraits, including the portrait of *Mademoiselle S.* [Sarrasin] (Wadsworth Atheneum, Hartford, CT), exhibited at the Salon of 1879. A charming image of a young girl in fancy dress, it anticipates Cassatt's many later pastel portraits of well-dressed children. Against a luminous background through which the texture of the paper is allowed to sparkle, Gonzalès built up the child's face and bodice with pastel strokes that augmented the medium's traditional delicacy with a new vigour. Even more assured is the technique in *Woman in Pink* (*c.*1879; private collection, *ibid.* cat. no.99), a profile portrait of her sister. Gonzalès's interspersed hatchings of vibrant pink, blue and salmon overlay vestiges of a red pastel outline in this work, suggesting an intimate knowledge of Degas's work from the same period and drawing attention to its highly animated overall surface with confident self-awareness. In *L'Espagnole* (Eastlake Galleries, New York), a late and particularly dazzling pastel portrait on canvas, the full breadth of Gonzalès's mastery of the medium is evident. She exploits the bare patches to enhance the work's luminosity and texture, and also employs the hatching technique as a vivid compositional element. The downcast line of the model's gaze, the angle of her jawline, the slanted edge of her barely limned fan and the plaited lines of her coiffure all subtly reinforce the diagonal hatchings of the artist's pastel marks.

By the end of her brief career, Gonzalès's kinship with Degas and the Impressionists extended beyond questions of technique. In such works as the large and exquisitely rendered pastel, *A Milliner* (*c.*1882; Art Institute of Chicago), she took up a favourite Degas theme, one in which the worlds of female vanity, commercial display and the urban working woman intersect. Yet in her intimate focus on the milliner, as fashionable herself as the luxurious fabrics and flowers that surround her, Gonzalès paints not an urban type but an elegant modern portrait and thus pointedly avoids the dialectics of class and gender that infuse the work of so many of her Impressionist peers. Perhaps recognising the significance of this work to her woman-centred oeuvre, as well as its highly politic approach to a popular contemporary subject, Gonzalès showed it in 1882 at a special women's exhibition at the Cercle de la rue Volney, frequented by the more conservative painters of the Union des Femmes. In 1883, the year of Gonzalès's death, it represented the artist at the annual Salon.

MARY TOMPKINS LEWIS

Graves, Nancy (Stevenson)
American sculptor and painter, 1940–1995

Born in Pittsfield, Massachusetts, 23 December 1940. Studied at Vassar College, Poughkeepsie, New York, 1957–61 (BA in English Literature); School of Art and Architecture, Yale University, New Haven, 1961–4 (BFA, MFA). Received Fulbright-Hayes grant for study in Paris, 1964. Lived and worked in Florence, Italy, 1965–6. Settled in New York, 1966. Taught at Fairleigh-Dickinson University, Rutherford, New Jersey, 1966–8. Resident, American Academy in Rome, 1979. Recipient of Vassar College fellowship, 1971; National Endowment for the Arts (NEA) grant, 1972; Creative Artists Public Service (CAPS) grant, 1974; Skowhegan medal for drawings/graphics, 1980; Yale University Distinguished Artistic Achievement award, 1985; New York Dance and Performance Bessie award for sets for Trisha Brown's *Lateral Pass*, 1986; Vassar College Distinguished Visitor award, 1986; American Art award, Pennsylvania Academy of the Fine Arts, 1987; honorary doctorates from Skidmore College, Saratoga Springs, 1989; University of Maryland, Baltimore, 1992; Yale University, 1992. Member, American Academy and Institute of Arts and Letters, 1991. Died in New York, 21 October 1995.

Selected Individual Exhibitions
Whitney Museum of American Art, New York: 1969
Museum of Modern Art, New York: 1971
Institute of Contemporary Art, University of Pennsylvania, Philadelphia: 1972–3 (touring), 1979
La Jolla Museum of Contemporary Art, CA: 1973
André Emmerich Gallery, New York: 1974, 1977
Knoedler and Co., New York: 1978, 1979, 1980, 1981, 1982, 1984, 1985, 1986, 1988, 1989, 1991, 1993, 1995

Albright-Knox Art Gallery, Buffalo, NY: 1980–81 (touring)
Vassar College Art Gallery, Poughkeepsie, NY: 1986 (touring)
Hirshhorn Museum and Sculpture Garden, Washington, DC: 1987–8 (touring retrospective, organised by Fort Worth Art Museum, TX)
Fine Arts Gallery, University of Maryland Baltimore County: 1993–4 (touring)

Bibliography
Gregory Battcock, "Camels today", *New York Free Press*, 2 May 1968, pp.8, 11
Nancy Graves: Sculpture, Drawings, Films, 1969–1971, exh. cat., Neue Galerie, Aachen, 1971
Hilton Kramer, "Downtown scene: A display of bones", *New York Times*, 19 January 1971, p.5
Nancy Graves: Sculpture and Drawings, 1970–1972, exh. cat., Institute of Contemporary Art, University of Pennsylvania, Philadelphia, and elsewhere, 1972
Lucy R. Lippard, "Distancing: The films of Nancy Graves", *Art in America*, lxiii, November–December 1975, pp.78–82; reprinted in Lucy R. Lippard, *From the Center: Feminist Essays on Women's Art*, New York: Dutton, 1976
Mimi Crossley, "Nancy Graves: Recent paintings, watercolors and sculptures", *Houston Post*, 24 November 1978, p.9AA
John Russell, "Art people", *New York Times*, 26 January 1979, p.C16
Nancy Graves: A Survey, 1969–1980, exh. cat., Albright-Knox Art Gallery, Buffalo, NY, and elsewhere, 1980
John Russell, "Nancy Graves makes art of science", *New York Times*, 1 June 1980, p.D25
Nancy Graves: Painting and Sculpture, 1978–82, exh. cat., Santa Barbara Contemporary Arts Forum, CA, 1983
Michael Edward Shapiro, "Nature into sculpture: Nancy Graves and the tradition of direct casting", *Arts Magazine*, lix, November 1984, pp.92–6
Nancy Graves: Painting, Sculpture, Drawing, 1980–85, exh. cat., Vassar College Art Gallery, Poughkeepsie, NY, and elsewhere, 1986
Avis Berman, "Nancy Graves' new age of bronze", *Art News*, lxxxv, February 1986, pp.56–64
E.A. Carmean, Jr, and others, *The Sculpture of Nancy Graves: A Catalogue Raisonné*, New York: Hudson Hills Press, 1987
Amy Fine Collins and Bradley Collins, Jr, "The sum of the parts", *Art in America*, lxxvi, June 1988, pp.112–119
Thomas Padon, *Nancy Graves: Excavations in Print: A Catalogue Raisonné*, New York: Abrams, 1996

A descendant of Cotton Mather, a founding New England patriarch, Nancy Stevenson Graves grew up immersed in her father's world of a small western Massachusetts museum that exhibited both art and natural science. This pairing – and the urge to merge them together – marked virtually all of Graves's mature work, following her graduate studies and degrees from Yale University. Highly educated and learned, she began her career in Florence in 1965. Influenced by the wax models of the 18th-century anatomist Clemente Susini, Graves first made two life-sized sculptures of *Camels*, placing pelts over an internal structure of her own design. Although the first pair was destroyed before she left Italy, she resumed the camels when she returned to New York in 1966, eventually creating a total of 25, of which only five remain intact, including *Camels VI, VII* and *VIII* (all National Gallery of Canada, Ottawa). When these three were first shown at the Whitney Museum of American Art in New York in 1969, they quickly established Graves as an important new artist.

From 1969 until 1971 Graves's sculpture focused on bones of animals and on abstract constructions that seemingly recreated ancient rituals, the latter including *Shaman* (1970; Museum Ludwig, Cologne). But after this intensive period of work, she turned to other media, first filmmaking, such as *Izzy Bourir* shot in Morocco in 1971, and then, in 1972, she resumed painting and began making prints. While these two-dimensional works continued to draw upon the natural world, they did so less directly, being based on abstract renderings or topographic maps.

In 1979 and 1980 Graves returned to sculpture in a major fashion, working on a larger scale and in collaboration with fabricators first at the Johnson Atelier in Princeton, New Jersey, and then with Lippincott, in North Haven, Connecticut. Her real breakthrough, and the start of her mature career, came when she began working with Richard Polich and the Talix Foundry in Peekskill, New York. Now using the lost wax technique, she began casting natural forms in bronze, creating elements ranging from leaves and bananas to turkey bones and sardines. Following in the path of the American sculptor David Smith, Graves welded these varying cast materials into open, abstract compositions of increasing complexity and ever-larger physical size, until her untimely death at the age of 54.

As the critic Robert Hughes observed, a key aspect of Graves's sculpture is its "subversiveness". In her art, forms take on unexpected permutations. First, in the material itself, cast bronze, which challenges the identity of many objects and their assumed "natural" weight. Casting also allows for changes in "normal" sizes, while the open, welded structure often affords unusual placements or unexpected rhythms. Colour in the sculpture is also subversive, being "unreal" and created using four different methods: unaltered, natural surfaces; patina; glass enamelling; being painted with polyurethane.

A distinguishing factor about Graves's sculpture was her ability to work at widely different sizes, from small intimate pieces to constructions that tower at heights of 2.4 metres. Medium-size works also began to influence her paintings, and by the mid-1980s she had begun adding flat relief sculptures to her paintings so that they jutted outwards from the two-dimensional surfaces. In turn, in her later works, Graves began making sculptural reliefs proper, through dimensional structures intended to hang on the wall.

Graves's sculpture of the mid-1990s is marked by two fundamental changes – the palette is more restrained, and other new elements are introduced – quotations from other works of art, such as the Venus de Milo and Michelangelo's figure of Adam from the Sistine Chapel ceiling. All of this comes together in Graves's last sculpture, *Metaphore and Melanomy* (1995; Brooks Museum of Art, Memphis). Soaring to 3 metres in height and nearly 3 × 3 metres across, it is the largest of her interior works. The sculpture colour is now subtle, largely a golden bronze patina, with only a hint of colour – pale pink, green and blue. Her cast baseball bat and a cheese grater are joined by the Head of Nefertiti and Venus de Milo and the pointing finger of the Sistine Adam. The title of the work alludes to the shifting references of her sculptured vocabulary and an acknowledgement that this would be her final, heroic work.

E.A. CARMEAN, JR

Greenaway, Kate
British illustrator and painter, 1846–1901

Born Catherine Greenaway in Hoxton, London, 17 March 1846. First trained by her father, a wood engraver. Attended evening classes at Female School of Art, Clerkenwell, 1853–9, then day classes at Finsbury School of Art, under National

Course of Art Instruction scheme; awarded national art competition prizes for drawings. Studied at South Kensington School of Art, 1865–9 (silver medal); subsequently took life classes at Heatherley's; enrolled at Slade School of Fine Art, 1871. Began career as freelance illustrator and painter with studio in Islington, London, 1870; worked for a number of publishers including Marcus Ward, Frederick Warne, Edmund Evans, Macmillan, George Routledge, Chatto and Windus, as well as her father's publishers, Griffith and Farran, Cassell, and Petter and Galpin. Began lifelong correspondence with John Ruskin, 1882. Member of the Royal Institute of Painters in Watercolours, 1889. Died in London, 6 November 1901.

Principal Exhibitions

Dudley Gallery, London: from 1868 (watercolour)
Royal Society of British Artists, London: 1870, 1872–5
Royal Academy, London: 1877–80, 1890, 1895
Fine Art Society, London: 1891, 1894, 1898 (all individual), 1902 (retrospective)
World's Columbian Exposition, Chicago: 1893
Royal Institute of Painters in Watercolours, London: 1893, 1895–7

Bibliography

"Art in the nursery", *Magazine of Art*, vi, 1883, pp.127–32
John Ruskin, "In fairyland", *The Art of England: Lectures Given in Oxford ... During His Second Tenure of the Slade Professorship*, Orpington: Allen, 1883
Austin Dobson, "Kate Greenaway", *Art Journal*, 1902, pp.33–6, 105–9
M.H. Spielmann, "Kate Greenaway: In memoriam", *Magazine of Art*, xxvi, 1902, pp.118–22
M.H. Spielmann and G.S. Layard, *Kate Greenaway*, London: A. & C. Black, 1905; reprinted New York: Blom, 1969
Austin Dobson, *De Libris: Prose and Verse*, London: Macmillan, 1908; New York: Oxford University Press, 1923
Jeanne Doin, "Kate Greenaway et ses livres illustrés", *Gazette des Beaux-Arts*, 4th series, iii, 1910, pp.5–22
Kate Greenaway Pictures, London: Warne, 1921
Anne Carroll Moore, *A Century of Kate Greenaway*, London and New York: Warne, 1946
Frances Paul, "A collection of children's books illustrated by Walter Crane, Kate Greenaway and Randolph Caldecott", *Apollo*, xliii, 1946, pp.141–3
Edward Ernest, ed., *The Kate Greenaway Treasury: An Anthology of the Illustrations and Writings of Kate Greenaway*, Cleveland: World Publishing, 1967; London: Collins, 1968
Kate Greenaway, 1846–1901, exh. cat., Bolton Art Gallery, 1975
Rodney Engen, *Kate Greenaway*, London: Academy Editions, and New York: Harmony Books, 1976
Bryan Holme, ed., *The Kate Greenaway Book*, New York: Viking, and London: Warne, 1976
Susan Ruth Thomson, *A Catalogue of the Kate Greenaway Collection, Rare Book Room, Detroit Public Library*, Detroit: Wayne State University Press, 1977
Kate Greenaway, exh. cat., Hunt Institute for Botanical Documentation, Carnegie Mellon University, Pittsburgh, 1980
Rodney Engen, *Kate Greenaway: A Biography*, London: Macdonald, and New York: Schocken, 1981
Thomas E. Schuster and Rodney Engen, *Printed Kate Greenaway: A Catalogue Raisonné*, London: Schuster, 1986
Ina Taylor, *The Art of Kate Greenaway: A Nostalgic Portrait of Childhood*, Exeter: Webb and Bower, 1991

During a career that spanned three decades, and included illustrations for more than 150 books and 90 periodicals, as well as 49 exhibited paintings, Kate Greenaway founded a tradition of children's illustration that continues even today. The Greenaway style has been reproduced and imitated on merchandise ranging from clothes to tea-sets, playing cards to paper dolls, ceramic tiles to wallpaper (the only product she ever authorised), and she has correctly been described as the most exploited, imitated and promoted artist of the Victorian period. After more than a century of these often saccharine spin-offs, the original strength of Greenaway's work can be difficult to appreciate. But considered within the context of the garishly coloured, over-produced and poorly designed books that dominated the children's market of the 1870s, her appeal regains its forcefulness. With Walter Crane and Randolph Caldecott, she was at the forefront of a movement to supply well-designed and well-produced children's books to a market that was booming under the influence of Forster's Education Act of 1870.

Greenaway was born in northeast London to lower-middle-class parents. During periods of financial hardship the Greenaway children spent time with relatives in the Northamptonshire countryside; her idealised memories of these visits provided her with the material for her first major collection of drawings and verse, *Under the Window* (1879), and continued to serve as a source of inspiration throughout her career. Encouraged by her father, a professional engraver with whom she would later share illustration projects, Greenaway undertook ten years of formal study on the National Course of Art Instruction, eventually attending the South Kensington School of Art, where she shared a studio with Elizabeth Thompson, later Lady Butler (q.v.). Greenaway excelled under the highly structured National Course, and her mature style retained its emphasis on linear draughtsmanship and decorative design, despite additional training at Heatherley's and the Slade School of Fine Art. The South Kensington focus on professional craftsmanship combined with economic necessity to encourage Greenaway to adopt a commercial approach to her career.

Even before she left school Greenaway began to receive illustration commissions. Her specialisation in scenes of childhood was established early, beginning in 1867 with the frontispiece for a nursery guide, *Infant Amusements*, and continuing with a series of fairytale books and numerous drawings of children for magazines such as *Cassell's* (1873–4), *Illustrated London News* (1874–9) and *Little Folks* (1876–9). Similar subjects were undertaken in her exhibited paintings as well. *A Flower Girl* (exh. Royal Society of British Artists, 1874; private collection, repr. Taylor 1991, p.21) and *Misses* (exh. Royal Academy, 1879; Walker Art Gallery, Liverpool) are characteristic of her early finished watercolours in their full-length frontal portrayal of young girls against a shallow background. Illustration and exhibition were linked for Greenaway from her first show at the Dudley Gallery (1868), when the Revd William Loftie purchased a series of fairy paintings for inclusion in his *People's Magazine*. Through Loftie she established a connection with the publisher Marcus Ward, for whom she designed 32 separate sets of greeting cards between 1868 and 1877, when his repeated exploitation of her designs without further payment led her to sever their connection. The cards served a triple purpose for Greenaway: they provided a steady income, they gave her work public visibility, and they furnished a forum in which to develop the "Greenaway child" that would become her hallmark. Despite the rather garish colours employed in Ward's early chromolithographs, samples preserved in the greeting-card collection of the Victoria and Albert Museum, London, show both the evolution of Greenaway's style and its departure from other exceedingly mawkish cards then on the market. The valentine

Disdain is a notable example. An especially popular greeting card, it was repackaged with other designs by Greenaway and Walter Crane and sold as a book, *The Quiver of Love* (1876). Its Pre-Raphaelite tone would resurface more forcefully in much later paintings, such as the *Fable of the Girl and Her Milk Pail* (1893; private collection, repr. Engen 1981, p.176).

The connection with Walter Crane was reinforced in 1878, when Greenaway entered into partnership with the printer Edmund Evans, who was already producing a series of toybooks by Crane and Randolph Caldecott. The collaboration between Greenaway and Evans was auspicious for both of them. His three-colour woodblock printing technique was highly accurate in its reproduction of both the subtle colours and the refined outlines of the original watercolours. The quality of the printing itself contributed to the astounding success of their initial venture, *Under the Window*, which sold more than 100,000 copies. But Evans's impact should not be overstated, as it has sometimes been. Comparison of the paintings for *Mary, Mary Quite Contrary* and *Polly Put the Kettle On* (photographs in Witt Library, Courtauld Institute of Art, London) with the printed versions in *Mother Goose* (1881) reveals an engaging fluidity that Evans could not capture. The *Art Journal* found the prints to be "as moonlight unto sunlight compared with the original drawings" (Dobson 1902, p.109), and the *Illustrated London News* acknowledged in the watercolours a "delicacy and sense of humour which defy reproduction" (1891, p.215).

The publication of *Under the Window* ushered in a decade of intense work. Greenaway's *Birthday Book for Children* (1880) included 382 drawings, and in the same year there were further illustrations in 18 books, eight journals and a calendar. With the exception of *The April Baby's Book of Tunes* (1900), all of Greenaway's major illustration projects were published between 1879 and 1889. She continued to illustrate other authors' writings, most notably Robert Browning's *The Pied Piper of Hamelin* (1888), but gave preference to her own collections of verse and prose. In her annual almanacs and books of songs, games, rhymes and stories she persistently focused on scenes of children's play. There is frequent emphasis on the ceremonial aspects of childhood pursuits, apparent in such pen and watercolour drawings as *May Day* (Huntington Art Gallery, San Marino, CA). While her earlier paintings of flower girls and watercress sellers bore traces of Victorian social realism, her book illustrations were completely devoid of class differences and political concerns. Only in one unusual drawing from 1886, *White Rose and White Lily* (photograph in Witt Library), do we see the transformative social power of the Greenaway pen, as a group of impoverished, ragged children is magically transformed through the agency of two maiden fairies into a stream of gay and gleaming girls and boys.

Stylistically, Greenaway's delicate lines, minimal shading, spare lay-out and pastel colours spoke with a clarity and freshness that captivated a book-buying public newly influenced by the Aesthetic movement. Aesthetic sensibilities were further engaged by details of subject matter such as blue-and-white china, rush-bottom chairs, sunflowers and flowing clothes. The high-waisted dresses and mob-caps coincided with a nascent 18th-century revivalism; the idyllic rural settings resonated with the pastoral nostalgia of industrialised England; the solemn, sexless, pretty children reinforced the cult of childhood innocence. The combination was to prove tremendously appealing. In the estimation of John Ruskin (1883), Greenaway's art had "the radiance and innocence of re-instated infant divinity ... All gold and silver you can dig out of the earth are not worth the kingcups and daisies she gave you of her grace".

Formally, Greenaway's drawing had certain weaknesses. Her scene of the *Four Princesses*, from *Marigold Garden* (1885), reveals a persistent difficulty with perspective. The feet of her figures were often disproportionately large, and their fingers stick-like. Most notably, the limbs of her subjects sometimes seemed detached from their bodies, giving them an awkwardness readily apparent in *Boy and Girl with a Cat* (Lady Lever Gallery, Port Sunlight). Her adviser and fellow artist Henry Stacy Marks admonished Greenaway for the way in which the girl descending *Pippin Hill* (*Mother Goose*, 1881) defied physical laws: "How about the centre of gravity, madam?" (Engen 1981, p.81). Intriguingly, however, these flaws do not seriously detract from the overall effect of her scenes. In this politely ordered world, where children are always good and the hedges are always perfectly trimmed, acceptance of an awkward pose here and there is by no means the greatest suspension of disbelief that viewers are asked to make. Such details may even

contribute to the fantasy quality of "Greenaway land".

Writing in the *Art Journal*, Greenaway's colleague Austin Dobson enumerated the pleasures of this land, where the "most attractive environment of flower-beds or blossoming orchards, and red-roofed cottages with dormer windows" was peopled by children "so gentle, so unaffected in their affectation, so easily pleased, so innocent, so trustful, and so confiding" that no real children could compare (Dobson 1902, pp.33–4). Yet while Dobson readily conceded the unreality of these imaginary beings, many critics and historians have been eager to attribute the personal qualities of these fantasy children to Greenaway herself. "Never was an artist's self more truly reflected on to her paper" wrote her biographer M.H. Spielmann (1902), emphasising Greenaway's modesty, purity, simplicity and grace of mind. More recently, Ina Taylor has suggested that "to understand Kate Greenaway's early life is to understand her art, for she virtually painted her autobiography" (Taylor 1991, p.11). Critical assessment of the work and skills of women artists have often been subsumed within the details of their domestic and emotional lives. In Greenaway's case this approach combined with her focus on children and her unmarried status to create a perception of the artist as essentially childlike. John Ruskin described her as a mixed child and woman, and Greenaway herself encouraged the image, relating how she hated to be grown-up, and cried when she had her first long dress. One of the results of this construction was that it led even such staunch admirers as Spielmann to devalue the intense labour she put into her art, concluding that her talent arose "as much from intuition as from scholarly training" (Spielmann 1902, p.121).

Another biographical detail that Greenaway repeatedly asserted was the happiness of her childhood. In searching for a source of her idealised, idyllic creations, biographers have frequently quoted her account of childhood as "one long continuous joy – filled ... with a strange wonder and beauty" (Greenaway Correspondence, Carnegie Mellon University Library, Pittsburgh). "I had such a happy time when I was a child", she wrote, "and curiously, was so very much happier than my brothers and sisters, with exactly the same surroundings" (Engen 1981, p.15). But, in fact, one aspect that repeatedly troubled critics was the sadness that so often appeared on the faces of Greenaway's children. In *Under the Window* a procession of children files out from school to the rhyme "School is over, oh, what fun!" Yet while the children in the distance fulfil their promise to run and laugh, the expressions of the main figures are unmistakably morose. Though Greenaway acknowledged that this sadness was perceived as a flaw, she was either unable or unwilling to change the tone of her work. It is revealing to note that Edmund Evans sometimes made the changes for her.

In 1890 Kate Greenaway decided to stop illustrating books and to pursue a gallery career. In this decision she was partly influenced by her intimate and often tumultuous friendship with Ruskin, who wished her to "make more serious use of her talent, without any reference to saleableness" (Engen 1981, pp.109–10). In contrast to her other close adviser, the poet Frederick Locker-Lampson, Ruskin felt that Greenaway's ornamental style was a weakness; he urged her to be truer to nature, as he did with all his protégés, and set her technical exercises such as the *Study of Moss, Rock and Ivy* (1885; Ruskin Gallery, Sheffield). Some evidence of an increasing naturalism may be seen in the illustrations of 1886 to Bret Harte's *The Queen of the Pirate Isle*.

Greenaway was also disillusioned by the widespread plagiarism of her work, which led to financial difficulty. Already by the time of *Marigold Garden* (1885) she had tired of the grind of publishing demands. From that point, illustration would be little more than an economic necessity for her. In 1889 she became a member of the Royal Institute of Painters in Watercolours, and renewed her friendship with her former classmate Helen Allingham (q.v.). Their sketching trips into the countryside provided the initial inspiration for an exhibition at the Fine Art Society in 1891, and subsequent one-woman shows were held in 1894 and 1898. Perceiving her own over-dependence on Allingham's style and technique (see the *Old Farm House*, Victoria and Albert Museum) she abandoned their working association, but isolated in her studio she lacked the influx of new ideas that might have facilitated the creative rejuvenation she sought. She exhibited at the Royal Academy and struggled with oil techniques, but such late paintings as *The Muff* (untraced, repr. Engen 1981, p.204) were largely stilted elaborations of themes that she had expressed more convincingly in her earlier illustration.

KRISTINA HUNEAULT

Guiard, Mme *see* Labille-Guiard

H

Hamnett, Nina
British painter, 1890–1956

Born in Tenby, Pembrokeshire, 14 February 1890.
Led an itinerant childhood, attending classes at
Portsmouth School of Art, 1903, and Dublin
School of Art, 1906, until her father, an army
captain, lost his money. Subsequently trained at
Pelham School of Art, South Kensington, under Sir
Alfred Cope, and London School of Art under
Frank Brangwyn, John Swan and William
Nicholson, 1907. First visited Paris, 1912.
Employed in Omega Workshops, London,
1913–19; also taught at Westminster Technical
Institute. Married Norwegian artist Edgar de
Bergen (adopted name Roald Kristian), 1914; son
born prematurely and died, 1915; lost touch with
husband when he was deported as an alien, 1917.
Lived and worked in Paris and London. Exhibited
at Salon d'Automne and Salon des Indépendants in
Paris, and in London with the Allied Artists
Association, 1913–14; Friday Club, 1914–15;
Grafton Group, 1914; Goupil Gallery Salon;
included in *Artists of Fame and Promise* exhibi-
tions at Leicester Galleries, London. Died in
London, after falling from apartment window, 16
December 1956.

Selected Individual Exhibitions
Cambridge Magazine Art Gallery, Cambridge: 1918
Eldar Gallery, London: 1918, 1919
Independent Gallery, London: 1919
Galerie Lucien Vogel, Paris: 1923
Claridge Gallery, London: 1926, 1927 (illustrations for
    Seymour Leslie's *The Silent Queen*)
Tooth Gallery, London: 1928
Prince Vladimir Galitzine's Gallery, London: 1930
Zwemmer Gallery, London: 1932
Redfern Gallery, London: 1948

Selected Writings
Laughing Torso: Reminiscences, London: Constable,
    1932; reprinted London: Virago, 1984
Is She a Lady? A Problem in Autobiography, London:
    Wingate, 1955

Bibliography
Mrs Gordon-Stables, "Nina Hamnett's psychological
    portraiture", *Artwork*, i, 1924, pp.112–15
Judith Collins, *The Omega Workshops*, London: Secker
    and Warburg, 1983; Chicago: University of Chicago
    Press, 1984
Nina Hamnett and Her Circle, exh. cat., Michael Parkin
    Fine Art, London, 1986
Denise Hooker, *Nina Hamnett: Queen of Bohemia*,
    London: Constable, 1986
Teresa Grimes, Judith Collins and Oriana Baddeley, *Five
    Women Painters*, London: Lennard, 1989

Nina Hamnett made a significant contribution to
the modern movement in London in the years
around 1915–32. A self-appointed artistic ambassador between London and Paris, she benefited from
her first-hand knowledge of the avant-garde movements in both cities to develop her own individual
style while remaining independent of the competing
factions that proliferated in those years. Friends and
mentors included Henri Gaudier-Brzeska, Amedeo
Modigliani, Walter Sickert, Roger Fry and Augustus
John.

It was as a draughtswoman that Hamnett
excelled. In his introduction to her first solo exhibition in 1918, Sickert acutely observed: "I cannot see
her drawing not leading her to sustained practice in
sculpture, sculpture being merely the multiplication
by a theoretic infinity of the sharp silhouette that
her uniform and sensitive line defines with such
expressiveness and such startling virtuosity"
(*Cambridge Magazine*, 8 June 1918, pp.770–71).
Sculptors figured prominently among Hamnett's
friends, and she drew from the model alongside

Gaudier-Brzeska and Modigliani. She met Gaudier-Brzeska when they were both exhibiting with the Allied Artists Association in 1913, and they posed naked for each other. The ease and fluidity of Hamnett's line, her pared-down simplification of form, had much in common with Gaudier's style. In Paris in 1914 she admired Modigliani's sculptures and drawings of elongated heads with highly simplified, stylised features. His bold, fluent contour and purity of form had a lasting influence on her. The pronounced sculptural quality of Hamnett's drawings also appeared in her oil paintings. Her portrait of the sculptor *Ossip Zadkine* (1914; private collection, on loan to Cartwright Hall, Bradford) was one of her most accomplished works of this time. Thickly painted in sombre tones, Zadkine's features are solidly modelled with a multitude of subtly differentiated brush strokes. The contrast between his lively, intelligent face and the anguished mood of the sculpture behind him is used to great psychological effect.

At Fry's Omega Workshops, Hamnett carried out decorative work, such as painting designs on candlesticks and a mural on the theme of contemporary London life for the art dealer Arthur Ruck at 4 Berkeley Street in 1916. Apart from portraits, in 1916 she began to depict rooftops and the backs of houses – subjects much favoured by the Camden Town Group. Influenced by Fry and French art, particularly Cézanne, Hamnett's solution to the problem of translating perceived reality into paint was to concentrate on its underlying formal structure. In *Housetops* (*Colour* magazine, January 1917) the view from a window of backyards with washing hanging on a line is seen in terms of severely simplified geometric planes and volumes. Hamnett also painted several strong, spare still lifes in the years 1915–20, emphasising the abstract spatial relationships and volumetric qualities of the objects depicted (e.g. *Der Sturm*; collection Edward Booth-Clibborn, repr. Grimes, Collins and Baddeley 1989, p.90).

Hamnett was not, however, concerned with abstract form for its own sake and declared: "I am more interested in human beings than in landscapes or in still life" (Gordon-Stables 1924). She painted and drew what she saw and felt about the people and scenes around her with a sharp eye for the underlying human comedy. Her subject matter wittily reflected her fascination with life: café and pub scenes, the circus, the boxing ring and the park bench. Fry commented on her "alert and slightly disillusioned, but never ill-natured, awareness of the general character and situation of human beings" (*The Nation & The Atheneum*, 11 May 1926).

Hamnett's ambition was "to paint psychological portraits that shall represent accurately the spirit of the age" (Gordon-Stables 1924). Her sitters included many of the leading artistic personalities of the time, such as *Walter Sickert, Horace Brodzky, Edith Sitwell, Osbert Sitwell* (1918; National Portrait Gallery, London), *W.H. Davies, Rupert Doone* (1922–3; Doncaster Museum and Art Gallery) and *Alvaro Guevaro*. Her portraits are strong, bold statements of character rather than exact likenesses. Features are simplified and exaggerated to express her concise view of the sitter's personality. The combination of fine draughtsmanship with well-defined modelling of forms gives the portraits an almost sculptural solidity. Her richly low-toned palette is relieved by well-placed details of colour.

Hamnett was always attracted to people and places with any kind of oddity value. In 1928 she collaborated with Osbert Sitwell on *The People's Album of London Statues* (London: Duckworth), a book of drawings that are among her best works. She infused even the most solemn official statue with humour, vitality and movement, wittily capturing respected dignitaries from unexpected angles. Augustus John wrote of "her light, savant and malicious touch" and praised "her perfectly original talent which (in the case of her drawings) falls into line with the grand tradition of British humouristics" (*Vogue*, April 1928).

By the mid-1930s Hamnett's talent was in decline and despite a brief revival of artistic energy in the late 1940s and early 1950s, she produced little work beyond quick portrait sketches. Distracted by life, she failed to develop her style and technique. Always willing to tell another anecdote in return for the next drink, gradually Nina Hamnett the celebrated bohemian personality took over from the respected artist she had once been.

DENISE HOOKER

1. **Amaral:** *EFCB (Estrada de Ferro Central do Brasil/Brazilian Central Railway),* 1924; oil on canvas, 142 × 126.8 cm., Museu de Arte Contemporânea da Universidade de São Paulo, Brazil

2. **Ancher:** *Maid in the Kitchen,* 1883–6; oil on canvas; 87.7 × 68.5 cm.; Hirschsprung Collection, Copenhagen

3. **Bashkirtseff:** *The Meeting,* 1884; Musée d'Orsay, Paris

4. **Benoist:** *Portrait of a Negress,* exhibited Salon of 1800; Musée d'Orsay, Paris

5. **Anguissola:** *Bernardino Campi Painting a Portrait of Sofonisba Anguissola*, late 1550s; oil on canvas; Pinacoteca Nazionale, Siena

6. **Bonheur:** *The Horse Fair*, 1853; oil on canvas; 244.5 × 506.7 cm.; Metropolitan Museum of Art, New York: Gift of Cornelius Vanderbilt, 1887 (87.25)

7. **Bourgeois:** *Untitled (With Foot, "Do You Love Me?")*, 1989; pink marble; 76.2 × 66 × 53.3 cm.

8. Bourke-White: Chrysler Building gargoyle, New York, 1930

9. Brandt: *Self-Portrait in Studio, Bauhaus, Dessau*, Winter 1928–9; Bauhaus Archiv, Berlin

10. Butler: *The Roll Call: Calling the Roll after an Engagement, Crimea*, 1874; oil on canvas; Royal Collection © Her Majesty Queen Elizabeth II

11. **Brooks:** *Self-Portrait*, 1923; oil on canvas; 117 × 68.3 cm.; National Museum of American Art, Smithsonian Institution, Washington, DC

12. **Cahun:** *Self-Portrait (Blue-Beard's Wife: Double Portrait)*, 1929; black-and-white photograph; private collection, Musée des Beaux-Arts, Nantes

13. **Cameron:** *Ellen Terry*, c.1864; carbon print; diameter 24 cm.; Royal Photographic Society, Bath

14. Carr: *Gwayasdoms d'Sonoqua*, 1928–30; oil on canvas; 100.3 × 65.4 cm.; Art Gallery of Ontario, Toronto: Gift from the Albert H. Robson Memorial Subscription Fund, 1942

15. Carriera: *Caterina Sagredo Barbarigo*, 1740s; pastel; 42 × 33 cm.; Gemäldegalerie Alte Meister, Staatliche Kunstsammlungen, Dresden

16. Leonora Carrington: *Max Ernst*, 1939; Young-Mallin Archive Collection, New York

17. Cassatt: *The Letter*, 1890–91; drypoint and aquatint on colour, State III; Metropolitan Museum of Art, New York: Gift of Paul J. Sachs, 1916

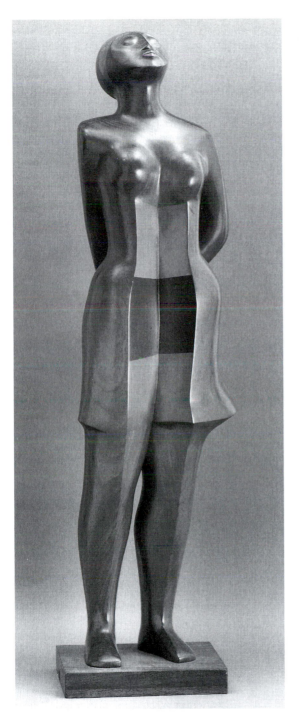

19. **Chicago:** *The Dinner Party*, view from Emily Dickinson's place setting, 1979; artist's collection

18. **Catlett:** *Political Prisoner*, 1971; polychrome sculpture, cedar wood; Art and Artifacts Division, Schomburg Center for Research in Black Culture, New York Public Library-Astor, Lenox and Tilden Foundations

20. **Duparc:** *Old Woman*, oil; Musées des Beaux-Arts, Marseille

21. **Claudel:** *Maturity (L'Age mur)*, Musée Rodin, Paris

23. Galizia: *Peaches in a Ceramic Basket*, oil on panel; 30 × 41.5 cm.; Collection Silvano Lodi, Campione d'Italia, Switzerland

22. Fuller: *Awakening of Ethiopia*, 1914; bronze; Art and Artifacts Division, Schomburg Center for Research in Black Culture, New York Public Library, Astor, Lenox and Tilden Foundations

24. Gentileschi: *Self-Portrait as La Pittura*, *c.*1640; Royal Collection © Her Majesty Queen Elizabeth II

25. **Goncharova:** *Cats: Rayist Perception in Rose, Black and Yellow*, 1912; oil on canvas; 85 × 86 cm.; Solomon R. Guggenheim Museum, New York

26. **Golubkina:** *Old Age*, 1897; bronze;
Golubkina Studio Museum, Moscow

27. **Hepworth:** *Mother and Child*, 1934; grey stone; Tate Gallery, London

28. **Hartigan:** *Hollywood Interior*, 1993; oil on canvas; 167.6 × 198.1 cm.

29. **Hemessen:** *Portrait of a Man*, 1552; National Gallery, London

30. **Höch:** *Cut with the Kitchen Knife Dada, Through the Last Weimar Beer-Belly Cultural Epoch of Germany*, 1919–20; Nationalgalerie, Berlin

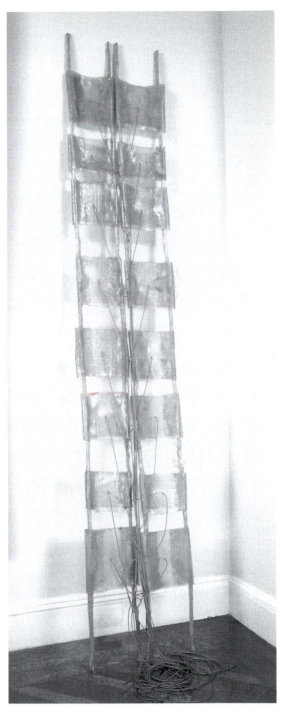

31. **Hesse:** *Vinculum I*, 1969; fibreglass and polyester resin, vinyl tubing and metal screen; each of two units, 264.2 × 21.6 × 5.1cm.; Collection of Mrs Victor W. Ganz

32. Hildegard of Bingen: *The Trinity:* formerly Wiesbaden, Hessisches Landesbibliothek, MS 1, fol.172 (Book III, vision 7)

33. Johnston: *Women Workers Leaving the Lynn Massachusetts Shoe Factory,* 1895; Library of Congress, Washington, DC (neg. LC-USZ-62-81152)

34. John: *Young Woman Holding a Black Cat*, 1914–15; Tate Gallery, London

35. Jones: *Ubi Girl from the Tai Region*, 1972; acrylic on canvas; 110 × 150 cm.; Museum of Fine Arts, Boston, Hayden Collection

36. Kauffman: *Self-Portrait Hesitating Between Music and Painting*, 1794; National Trust, Nostell Priory, Wakefield

37. **Kielland:** *Summer Night*, 1886; oil on canvas; 100.5 × 135.5 cm.; Nasjonalgalleriet, Oslo

38. **Kahlo:** *Self-Portrait with Thorn Necklace and Hummingbird*, 1940; Harry Ransom Humanities Research Center, University of Texas at Austin

39. **Kollwitz:** *The Volunteers, War: Plate 2*, 1922–3; woodcut; National Gallery of Art, Washington, DC, Rosenwald Collection

40. **Laurencin:** *Apollinaire and His Friends*; or, *Country Reunion*, 1908; oil on canvas; 82 × 124 cm.; Musée National d'Art Moderne, Centre Georges Pompidou, Paris

41. Labille-Guiard: *Madame Adélaïde de France*, exhibited 1787; Palais de Versailles, Paris

42. Lama: *Virgin and Child with Saints*, altarpiece, commissioned 1722; Santa Maria Formosa, Venice

43. Leyster: *Man Offering Money to a Young Woman*, 1631; Mauritshuis Museum, The Hague

44. Longhi: *Virgin and Child with St John the Baptist*, c.1598–1600; oil on canvas; 88.5 × 71 cm.

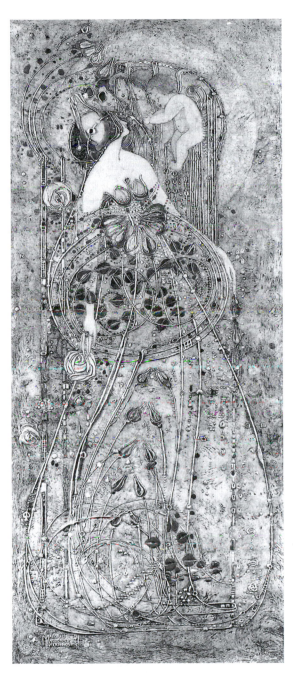

46. Modersohn-Becker: *Self-Portrait with Amber Necklace*, 1906, oil; 61 × 50 cm.; Kunstmuseum, Basel

45. Margaret Macdonald: *Summer*, 1904; National Museum of Antiquities, Edinburgh

47. Maar: *Arums*, 1930; Musée National d'Art Moderne, Centre Georges Pompidou, Paris

50. **Moillon:** *Basket with Peaches and Grapes,* 1631; Staatliche Kunsthalle, Karlsruhe

48. **Marisol:** *Women and Dog,* 1964; wood, plaster, synthetic polymer, taxidermed dog head and miscellaneous items; installed dimensions: 183.5 × 185.4 × 78.6 cm.; Whitney Museum of American Art, New York; purchased with funds from the Friends of the Whitney Museum of American Art

49. **Morisot:** *View of Paris from the Trocadéro,* 1872; oil on canvas; 45.9 × 81.4 cm.; Santa Barbara Museum, California, Gift of Mrs Hugh N. Kirkland

51. **Münter:** *Anna Roslund,* 1917; oil on canvas; 94 × 68 cm.

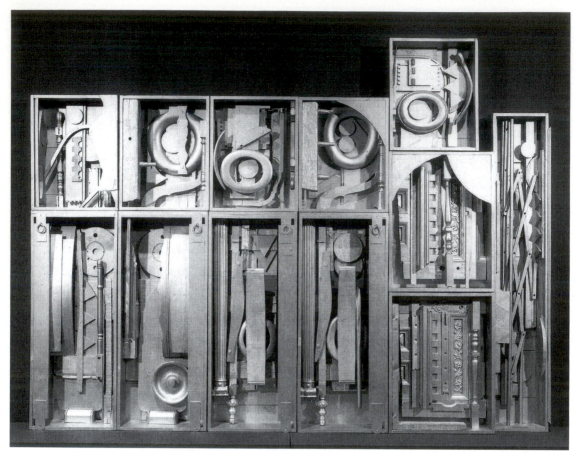

52. Nevelson: *Royal Tide II*, 1962–3; wood painted gold; 240 × 321.3 × 20.3 cm.; Whitney Museum of American Art, New York; gift of the artist

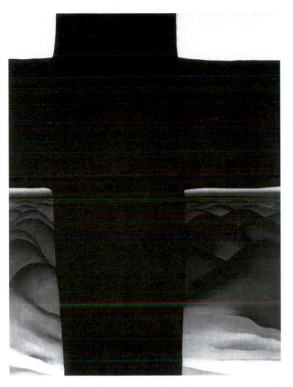

53. O'Keeffe: *Black Cross, New Mexico*, 1929; oil on canvas; 99 × 77.2 cm.; Art Institute of Chicago, Purchase Fund (1943.95)

54. Rego: *Joseph's Dream*, 1990; acrylic on paper on canvas; 183 × 122 cm.; private collection

55. Riley: *Fall*, 1963; emulsion on board; 141 × 140 cm.; Tate Gallery, Liverpool

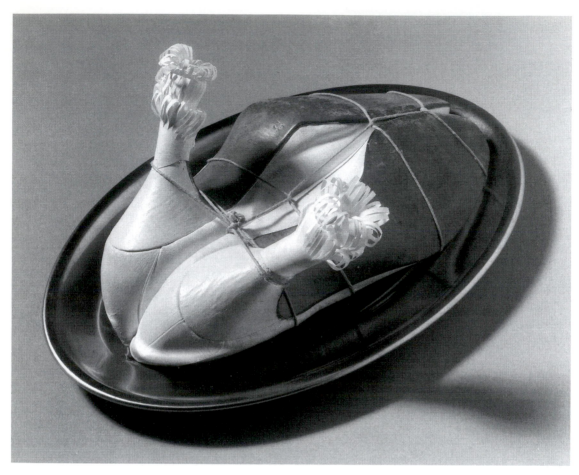

56. **Oppenheim:** *Ma gouvernante*, 1936; 14 × 21 × 33cm.; Moderna Museet, Stockholm

57. **Spero:** *Re-Birth of Venus* (detail), 1989

58. Roghman: *Woman Scouring Metalware,* engraving; Rijksmuseum, Amsterdam

59. Roldán: *Ecce Homo,* 1684; Cádiz Cathedral

60. Ruysch: *Flowers in a Glass Vase,* 1704; oil on canvas; 83 × 66 cm.; Detroit Institute of Arts; Founders Society Purchase, aided by various funds and donors

61. Saint Phalle: *Black Venus,* also titled *Miss Black Power,* 1965–7; painted polyester; 279.4 × 38.9 × 61 cm.; Whitney Museum of American Art, New York; Gift of the Howard and Jean Lipman Foundation Inc.

62. **Rozanova:** *City Landscape*, 1913; lithograph

63. **Salomon:** From *Leben? oder Theater?*, 1940–42; gouache; Collection Jewish Historical Museum, Amsterdam

64. **Serebryakova:** *Self-Portrait at the Dressing Table*, 1909; Tretyakov Gallery, Moscow

65. Schjerfbeck: *Self-Portrait with Palette*, 1937;
Moderna Museet, Stockholm

66. Sirani: *Judith Triumphant*, 1658; Burghley
House Collection, Stamford

67. Alice Barber Stephens: *The Women's Life
Class at the Pennsylvania Academy of the Fine
Arts*, c.1879; oil on cardboard (grisaille); 30.5 ×
35.6 cm.; Pennsylvania Academy of the Fine Arts,
Philadelphia; Gift of the artist

68. Stölzl: *5 Chöre*, 1928; jacquard wall hanging; Museum für Kunst, Lubeck

69. Toorop: *Three Generations*, 1941–50; oil on canvas; 200 × 121 cm.; Museum Boijmans Van Beuningen, Rotterdam

70. Vigée-Lebrun: *Self-Portrait in a Straw Hat*, exhibited Salon of 1783; National Gallery, London

71. **Valadon:** *The Future Unveiled; or, The Fortune-Teller*, 1912; oil on canvas; 130 × 163 cm.; Musée du Petit Palais, Geneva

72. **Werefkin:** *Black Women*, 1909; gouache over graphite on board; 72.5 × 111.5 cm.; Sprengel Museum, Hannover

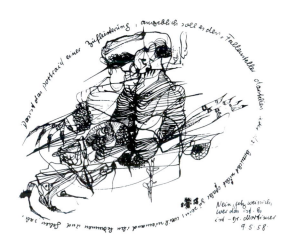

73. **Zürn:** *Portrait of a Whispered Message*, from
The House of Illnesses, 1958

Hartigan, Grace
[fig. 28]

American painter, 1922–

Born in Newark, New Jersey, 28 March 1922.
Married (1) Robert Jachens, 1941; son born 1942;
divorced 1947; (2) artist Harry Jackson (Shapiro),
1949; marriage annulled 1950; (3) Long Island
gallery owner Robert Keene, 1958; divorced 1960;
(4) Dr Winston Price, research scientist at Johns
Hopkins University, Baltimore, 1960; he died
1981. Studied mechanical drawing at Newark
College of Engineering, New Jersey, 1942; subsequently worked as mechanical draughtswoman,
and studied painting privately under Newark artist
Isaac Lane Muse. Moved to New York, 1945; met
Jackson Pollock, Willem de Kooning and other
members of the New York School. Selected by
Clement Greenberg and Meyer Schapiro for *New
Talent* exhibition at Kootz Gallery, New York,
1950; exhibited in avant-garde *Ninth Street Show*,
1951. Moved to Baltimore, 1960. Artist-in-resi-
dence, Maryland Institute College of Art,
Baltimore, from 1965; Avery Chair, Bard College,
Annandale-on-Hudson, 1983. Recipient of
Mademoiselle magazine merit award for art, 1957;
Childe Hassam purchase award, National Institute
of Arts and Letters, 1974; honorary life trustee,
Baltimore Museum of Art; honorary degrees from
Moore College of Art, Philadelphia; Goucher
College, Towson, Maryland, and Maryland
Institute College of Art. Lives in Baltimore.

Selected Individual Exhibitions

Tibor de Nagy Gallery, New York: 1951, 1952, 1953,
    1954, 1955, 1957, 1959
Vassar College, Poughkeepsie, NY: 1954
Gres Gallery, Washington, DC: 1960
Chatham College, Pittsburgh: 1960
Martha Jackson Gallery, New York: 1962, 1964, 1967,
    1970
University of Minnesota, Minneapolis: 1963
Maryland Institute College of Art, Baltimore: 1967, 1990
University of Chicago: 1967
Gertrude Kasle Gallery, Detroit: 1972, 1974, 1976
American University, Washington, DC: 1975, 1987
    (retrospective)
C. Grimaldis Gallery, Baltimore: 1979, 1981, 1982,
    1984, 1986, 1987, 1989, 1990, 1993, 1995
Baltimore Museum of Art: 1980 (touring), 1990
State University of New York, Plattsburgh: 1980
University of Maryland, College Park: 1980
Fort Wayne Museum of Art, IN: 1981 (retrospective)
Lafayette College, Easton, PA: 1983, 1990
Gruenebaum Gallery, New York: 1984, 1986, 1988
Kouros Gallery, New York: 1989 (retrospective)
ACA Galleries, New York: 1991, 1992, 1994
Skidmore College, Saratoga Springs, NY: 1993

Selected Writings

"An artist speaks", *Carnegie Magazine*, February 1961
Statement for exhibition at Martha Jackson Gallery, New
    York, 1964; typescript in Martha Jackson Papers,
    Archives of American Art, Smithsonian Institution,
    Washington, DC

Bibliography

Twelve Americans, exh. cat., Museum of Modern Art,
    New York, 1956; artist's statement reprinted in *The
    New American Painting*, exh. cat., Museum of
    Modern Art, New York, 1959, p.44
"Women artists in ascendance", *Life*, xlii, 13 May 1957,
    pp.75–6
Harold Rosenberg, *The Tradition of the New*, New York:
    Horizon Press, 1959; London: Thames and Hudson,
    1962
Grace Hartigan, exh. cat., Martha Jackson Gallery, New
    York, 1962
Barbara Flanagan, "Lively artist rebels at labeling and
    doesn't like to be lionized", *Minneapolis Tribune*, 24
    September 1963; press clipping in Grace Hartigan
    Papers, George Arents Research Library, Syracuse
    University, Syracuse, NY
Three American Painters, exh. cat., Grand Rapids Art
    Museum, MI, 1968
Allen Barber, "Making some marks", *Arts Magazine*,
    xlviii, June 1974, pp.49–51 (interview)
Cindy Nemser, *Art Talk: Conversations with Twelve
    Women Artists*, New York: Scribner, 1975
Frank O'Hara, *Standing Still and Walking in New York*,
    ed. Donald Allen, Bolinas, CA: Grey Fox Press, 1975
Irving Sandler, *The New York School: The Painters and
    Sculptors of the Fifties*, New York: Harper, 1978
Eleanor Munro, *Originals: American Women Artists*,
    New York: Simon and Schuster, 1979
Laurence Campbell, "To see the world mainly through
    art: Grace Hartigan's *Great Queens and Empresses*
    (1983)", *Arts Magazine*, lviii, January 1984, pp.87–9
Robert S. Mattison, "Grace Hartigan: Painting her own
    history", *Arts Magazine*, lix, January 1985, pp.66–72
Stephen Westfall, "Then and now: Six of the New York
    School painters look back: Grace Hartigan", *Art in
    America*, lxxiii, June 1985, pp.118–20
Ann Schoenfield, "Grace Hartigan in the early 1950s:
    Some sources, influences and the avant-garde", *Arts
    Magazine*, lx, September 1985, pp.84–8
Eleanor Heartney, "How wide is the gender gap?", *Art
    News*, lxxxvi, Summer 1987, pp.139–45
Grace Hartigan: Four Decades of Painting, exh. cat.,
    Kouros Gallery, New York, 1989
Robert S. Mattison, *Grace Hartigan: A Painter's World*,
    New York: Hudson Hills Press, 1990

Terence Diggory, "Questions of identity in *Oranges* by Frank O'Hara and Grace Hartigan", *Art Journal*, lii, Winter 1993, pp.41–50

Frank O'Hara, "Second avenue", *The Collected Poems*, ed. Donald Allen, Berkeley: University of California Press, 1995, pp.139–50

Although she is usually described as a leading representative of the "second generation" of New York School artists, Grace Hartigan has always resisted assimilation to any movement. Despite her love for the abstraction of Jackson Pollock and Willem de Kooning of the late 1940s, she gave up abstraction in 1952 to engage in a "struggle with content" that would test her right to claim the forms of Abstract Expressionism for herself (Sandler 1978, p.113). Then, after returning to abstraction, a decade later she "left expressionism" (New York 1962), although she refused to adopt the dead-pan objectivity of Pop or Minimalism, the emerging alternatives to Expressionism. Painting must have emotion, Hartigan insisted, but it must belong to the painting, not necessarily to the artist. A similar distinction informed her reluctance to enlist in the women's art movement that arose in the 1970s. "To be truthful I didn't much think about being a woman", she explained, "I thought about how difficult it was to paint" (Nemser 1975, p.150). Such an attitude aligns Hartigan most closely with Harold Rosenberg's theory of "action painting" free of all prior commitments: "action painting is painting in the medium of difficulties" (Rosenberg 1959, p.33).

For Hartigan, the New York School was a school in the literal sense of being the site of her education in art. She arrived in New York in 1945 with some experience in mechanical drawing, a sporadic history of evening art classes and a strong creative urge that began to assume definite direction as she visited galleries and museums and met the painters, poets and musicians whose paths criss-crossed the world of the avant-garde as if it were a tiny village. Her membership in that community was confirmed in 1950 when the landmark *New Talent* show, selected by Clement Greenberg and Meyer Schapiro for the Kootz Gallery, exhibited Hartigan's *Secuda Esa Bruja* (1949; artist's collection). This work proves her already committed to the formal ideals of "all over" composition and integrity of surface that Hartigan has upheld ever since. It also points to concerns beyond formalism in its quasi-surrealist, non-representational figuration. White wind-sock shapes seem to ascend in an up draught fanned by a sheet of orange and yellow flame. The title, which Hartigan translates as "The Witch is Flying" (Mattison 1990, p.13), points to a later statement in which she identifies witchcraft with the painter's power to transform what she cannot bear in her environment (Flanagan 1963). Unlike her friend Jackson Pollock, who tended to identify the creative self with nature, Hartigan often claims a demonic power.

Appropriately, in 1952, Hartigan reversed the canvas she had used for *Secuda Esa Bruja* and painted *Frank O'Hara and the Demons* on the other side. While the "demons" in this picture retain some of the abstract quality of the earlier work, the figure of O'Hara is loosely representational in a manner that Hartigan was just beginning to employ. The rebellion against the orthodoxy of abstraction that occurred among a number of "second generation" painters at this time is often traced to the example of de Kooning's *Women* paintings, which Hartigan had seen evolving in his studio before they were first exhibited in 1952. For Hartigan in particular, however, the example of O'Hara's poetry may have been equally important, for in poetry the image served the purpose not only of representation but of transformative "witchcraft", through the device of metaphor (Grand Rapids 1968). In *Oranges No. 6* (1952–3; Gallery K, Washington, DC), one of a series of paintings incorporating text by O'Hara, Hartigan portrays a young girl who appears immobilised by the weight of an absurdly "feminine" bow, while at her feet her dolls stir with a lurid sexuality. Through this demonic twist on the conventional image of woman as doll, the picture acquires a metaphoric density that matches its "packing" of forms, a technique that Hartigan connects both with de Kooning's painting *Excavation* (1950; Art Institute of Chicago) and with O'Hara's poem "Second Avenue" (1953; remarks at a reading from the poetry of Frank O'Hara, Skidmore College, Saratoga Springs, 24 March 1993).

Another lesson for which Hartigan credits O'Hara is the possibility of drawing on popular culture as a source of imagery (Irving Sandler, "Artists talk on art series", public interview with Grace Hartigan, Fulcrum Gallery, New York, 11 November 1994). *Grand Street Brides* (1954; Whitney Museum of American Art, New York), perhaps Hartigan's best-known painting, exemplifies the resulting fusion of "high" and "low", for like many of Hartigan's paintings at this time it has a source in art history, in this instance the court scenes of Velázquez and Goya, but it also responds to the display windows of bridal shops that lined Grand Street on New York's Lower East Side, where Hartigan lived and worked (Mattison 1990, pp.33–4). Perhaps in reaction to the flatness of the figures, viewers have been tempted to read some form of critique into this painting's use of popular imagery. In his influential article, "Nature and new painting" (1954), O'Hara claimed that Hartigan's brides "face without bitterness the glassy shallowness of American life which is their showcase" (O'Hara 1975, p.45). Two decades later Cindy Nemser invited Hartigan to read *Grand Street Brides* in terms of the roles that society imposes on women, but Hartigan demurred (Nemser 1975, pp.157–8). Such interpretations mistakenly emphasise weakness while Hartigan's paintings are primarily about power: an artist's power to give life to shop-window mannequins, or a woman's power to multiply roles and thus extend rather than limit the range of self-expression. For example, throughout 1954 Hartigan exhibited under the name "George"; sometimes describing this practice as a homage to George Sand and George Eliot, Hartigan has always denied that she was conforming to a male-dominated art world. Only recently has she offered the fuller explanation that she was "camping", playfully crossing gender lines in the spirit of the homosexual men she met at the Tibor de Nagy Gallery (Diggory 1993, p.49).

According to Hartigan, gender discrimination became an issue in the New York art world only in the latter half of the 1950s, as the prospect of money and fame began to intensify competition among artists (Heartney 1987, p.141). At first, Hartigan's career seemed to prosper in this new atmosphere. In 1956 Dorothy Miller selected her work for inclusion in the exhibition *Twelve Americans*, spotlighted at the Museum of Modern Art. From this show, Nelson Rockefeller purchased Hartigan's *City Life* (1956; National Trust for Historic Preservation, Nelson A. Rockefeller Collection), a work incited, like *Grand Street Brides*, by "that which is vulgar and vital in American modern life", as Hartigan expressed it in her catalogue statement. In 1957 *Life* magazine placed Hartigan, as the "most celebrated of the young American women painters", at the head of a list that included Nell Blaine, Joan Mitchell (q.v.),

Jane Wilson and Helen Frankenthaler (q.v.) ("Women artists in ascendance"). In 1958 the International Program of the Museum of Modern Art, where O'Hara worked, included Hartigan in the show that defined "The New American Painting" on a tour of eight European countries. Although she benefited from the accompanying media attention, Hartigan began to resent the attempt to define her with her paintings. Marriage (her fourth) to Dr Winston Price in 1960 provided the satisfaction of love untainted by art-world politics as well as the opportunity to put some breathing space between herself and New York. She joined Price in Baltimore, where he pursued medical research at Johns Hopkins University, and where, in 1967, Hartigan began teaching at the Maryland Institute College of Art.

In Hartigan's paintings of the late 1950s the recognisable imagery of the "city life" paintings disappears, while broader planes of colour and more expansive brushwork seem to open up the surface area, an effect reinforced by extending the dimensions of the canvases to as much as 2.4 metres. Hartigan was responding to the landscape of eastern Long Island as well as to the contemporary work of de Kooning and Franz Kline, who reinforced the suggestion of landscape by using place names in their titles, as Hartigan did, for example, in *Montauk Highway* (1957; Sarah Campbell Blaffer Foundation, Houston) and *Interior – "The Creeks"* (1957; Baltimore Museum of Art). Technically, these are gorgeous, often breathtaking paintings, but they capture a moment after the creative struggle has been won, rather than recording the process of that struggle, which has always been Hartigan's chief aim.

To return to that aim, Hartigan began to reintroduce imagery from the visible world. At first, however, in such work as *Phoenix* and *Lily Pond* (both 1962; collection Mr and Mrs H. Perry, Germantown, NY), the mood seemed too "lyrical" – a judgement that for Hartigan implied an acceptance of visible beauty as given rather than achieved through creative transformation (Martha Jackson Gallery statement, 1964). *Marilyn* (1962; collection Mr and Mrs H. Perry) marks a significant turning point. When this work was first shown in 1962 by Martha Jackson, Hartigan's new dealer in New York, some viewers, including Frank O'Hara (O'Hara 1975, p.143), read it as a surrender to the new Pop trend, but in retrospect the mood is clearly different from the contemporary *Marilyns* of Warhol or Rosenquist. Although we see only human fragments – white teeth gleaming through red lips at the top of the canvas, an elegant hand extended at the bottom – the painter's fluid gestures recompose these fragments and assert a life force that Pop's irony drains away. Thematically, the same life force can be traced throughout this period in Hartigan's engagement with a variety of heroic female personae, from the mythical *Dido* (1960; McNay Art Museum, San Antonio) and *Pallas Athena – Earth* (1961; National Museum of American Art, Smithsonian Institution, Washington, DC) to the historical *Duchess of Alba* (1963; Collection Dr and Mrs S.E. Harris, Baltimore) and the archetypal *Mountain Woman* (1964; Huntington Art Gallery, University of Texas, Austin). These works remain essentially abstract, however. Stylistically, the promise of *Marilyn* is not realised until the later 1960s, when recognisable imagery, once again often drawn from popular culture, decisively re-emerges in such paintings as *Modern Cycle* (1967; National Museum of American Art).

At this point, Hartigan seems to have struck the balance that she wanted between image and abstraction. Although the battle still has to be refought in the process of composing each painting, she seems secure in her confidence that the image will emerge in the end without violating the surface. Her subsequent development focuses on expanding her range of techniques for unfurling the surface itself as a space that is not illusionistic, in the sense of suggesting three-dimensional depth, but rather metaphoric, in the way that a poem creates a space in the mind. A first step in this direction, already evident in *Modern Cycle*, was the use of line "like a lasso" to surround and define images as specific yet at the same time as flat (Barber 1974, p.50). A second step, offering a counter-statement to the reassertion of drawing, was the staining of primed canvas by rubbing it down with a sheepskin mitt steeped in pigment. This technique proved especially effective for evoking the quality of remembered images, as in *Black Velvet* (1972; Flint Institute of Art, Michigan), an elegy for Hartigan's father, and *Autumn Shop Window* (1972; Baltimore Museum of Art), which is in part a lament for her husband's slow decline towards his death in 1981 (Mattison 1990, pp.90–93). To pose the tension of drawn line

and stained field within a single work, Hartigan began in the late 1970s to permit line to bleed colour that drips down the canvas in rivulets, partially hiding the images yet making their presence all the more tantalising. The related themes of costume and role-playing, harking back to *Oranges No. 6* and *Grand Street Brides*, resurface in two series of the 1980s that both employ the "drip" technique: the *Paper Dolls* portraying film stars of the past, for instance, *Constance* [Bennett] (1981; collection Dolly Fiterman, Minneapolis), and the *Great Queens and Empresses*, for example, *Theodora* (1983; Solomon R. Guggenheim Museum, New York).

Hartigan's several styles have developed through expansion rather than succession. Rather than one style replacing another, all remain simultaneously available for the artist to call upon in response to the demands of a particular painting, just as she feels free to call upon and combine the images of "high" and "low" culture. Among the works included in her show at the ACA Galleries in New York in 1994, *Hollywood Interior* (1993) gives fullest expression to this complex freedom. Like most of the other works in the exhibition, it employs a technique of overpainting to produce an effect of multiple exposure, as in photography. One of the figures, at the upper right, playfully recalls Caravaggio's *Bacchino Malato* (1593–4; Galleria Borghese, Rome), already the inspiration for Hartigan's *Bacchus* (1985; collection Mick Jagger and Jerry Hall, New York). In *Hollywood Interior* the figure is reversed in lateral position (left to right), in gender (male to female) and in level of iconography (the grapes that the classical god Bacchus holds in his upraised hand are replaced by the starlet's telephone). If the allusion to Hollywood directly refers to role-playing, the presence of multiple figures suggests multiple roles. In an interview, Hartigan proposed that such multiplicity may distinguish her images of women from those of male contemporaries such as de Kooning or Dubuffet, who essentially portray one woman. Explaining that all of the women in her paintings are aspects of her "many selves", she has speculated: "maybe it takes a woman to know the many faces of Eve" (Hartigan interview with Sandler, 1994, *op. cit.*).

TERENCE DIGGORY

Hawarden, Clementina, Viscountess
British photographer, 1822–1865

Born at Cumbernauld House near Glasgow, 1 June 1822, to the Hon. Charles Elphinstone Fleeming, an admiral, and his wife Catalina Paulina Alessandro of Cádiz. Married Cornwallis Maude, 1845; ten children, one son and seven daughters surviving infancy. Husband succeeded to title as 4th Viscount Hawarden, with estate at Dundrum, near Cashel, Co. Tipperary, Ireland, 1856; family moved there, 1857. Started taking photographs at Dundrum, late 1857 or early 1858. Moved to 5 Princes Gardens, South Kensington, London, 1859. Member, Photographic Society of London, 1863. Died of pneumonia, 19 January 1865.

Principal Exhibitions
Photographic Society of London: 1863 (silver medal for best contribution by an amateur), 1864 (silver medal for best composition from a single negative)

Bibliography
British Journal of Photography, x, 1863, pp.69, 79
Journal of the Photographic Society, ix, 1864, p.69
Photographic News, viii, 1864, pp.303, 348
O. G. R[ejlander], "In memoriam", *British Journal of Photography*, xii, 1865, p.38
Helmut Gernsheim, *Lewis Carroll: Photographer*, London: Parrish, and New York: Chanticleer Press, 1949; reprinted New York: Dover, 1969
Charles Lutwidge Dodgson, *The Diaries of Lewis Carroll*, ed. Roger Lancelyn Green, i, London: Cassell, and New York: Oxford University Press, 1954
Helmut Gernsheim, *Creative Photography: Aesthetic Trends, 1839–1960*, London: Faber, and Boston: Boston Book and Art Shop, 1962
"From Today Painting Is Dead": The Beginnings of Photography, exh. cat., Arts Council of Great Britain and Victoria and Albert Museum, London, 1972
Graham Ovenden, ed., *Clementina, Lady Hawarden*, London: Academy Editions, and New York: St Martin's Press, 1974
R. Aspin, "Oh, weary, neutral days: The photographs of Lady Hawarden", *British Journal of Photography*, cxxix, 28 May 1982, pp.564–6
Mark Haworth-Booth, ed., *The Golden Age of British Photography*, Millerton, NY: Aperture, 1984
Michael Bartram, *The Pre-Raphaelite Camera*, London: Weidenfeld and Nicolson, and Boston: Little Brown, 1985
Virginia Dodier, "Haden, photography and salmon fishing", *Print Quarterly*, iii, 1986, pp.34–50
Helmut Gernsheim, *The Rise of Photography, 1850–1880*, 3rd edition, London and New York: Thames and Hudson, 1988
Virginia Dodier, "Clementina, Viscountess Hawarden: Studies from life", *British Photography in the Nineteenth Century: The Fine Art Tradition*, ed. Mike Weaver, Cambridge and New York: Cambridge University Press, 1989, pp.141–50
Michael Hallett, "Lady of noble talents", *British Journal of Photography*, cxxxvi, 21 September 1989, p.25
Domestic Idylls: Photographs by Clementina, Lady Hawarden, exh. cat., J. Paul Getty Museum, Malibu, CA, 1990
Lady Hawarden: Photographe victorienne, exh. cat., Musée d'Orsay, Paris, 1990
Virginia Dodier, "Portraits in the mirror", *Antique Collector*, lxi, July 1990, pp.68–71
——, "From the interior: Photographs by Clementina, Viscountess Hawarden", *Magazine Antiques*, cxxxix, 1991, pp.196–207

In 1939 the descendants of Clementina, Viscountess Hawarden presented 776 of her photographic prints made between 1857 and 1865 to the Victoria and Albert Museum, London. Although recognised for her photographs by awards in 1863 and 1864, Lady Hawarden's early death from pneumonia at the age of 42 terminated a promising career. As most of her photographs were privately held, it was not until the bulk of her work reached a public collection that the extent and quality of it could be assessed, and it was not until the 1990s that individual exhibitions of Lady Hawarden's work were held, in London, Paris, the J. Paul Getty Museum in California and the Museum of Modern Art in New York, among others.

Although her photographs were appreciated in her own time, by awards and by praise from such photographers as Lewis Carroll and O.G. Rejlander, Hawarden's work is in many ways very different from typical Victorian photographs. She did not photograph celebrities or hire models but used her family, especially her two oldest daughters, as her subjects. Instead of proper Victorian young ladies, she revealed adolescent dreams and fantasies. Narrative elements are at a minimum. In her frequent use of mirror and window images, Hawarden's photographs show a preoccupation with the formal possibilities of composition. This is reinforced by her experimentation with variations on a composition, such as her series of her daughter Clementina Maude in vaguely medieval costume standing next to a mirror that reflects profile or full-face poses in different combinations, and also a series of her daughters in oriental dress in a variety of poses (all Victoria and Albert Museum). This interest in mirror imaging was also a preoccupation of 19th-century painters such as Berthe Morisot (q.v.), Mary Cassatt (q.v.) and Edouard Manet, among others.

One of the main elements in Hawarden's work is her use of light. Several studies are taken by windows, and while the concentration of light would obviously aid in the production of the photograph itself, the diffuse lighting often seems to become an element of mood within the composition. In her interest in defining and dissolving objects and scenes through lighting conditions, Hawarden shows obvious parallels with the preoccupations of the Impressionist painters a decade later. Another element in Hawarden's photographs that has parallels in the work of other Victorian photographers is the depiction of subjects in fancy dress or exotic costume. There are a number of period costume pieces, and even a few studies in "beggar rags" with bare feet (Victoria and Albert Museum). Although this delight in dressing up can be found in the photographs of such contemporaries as Lewis Carroll, Julia Margaret Cameron (q.v.), David Wilkie Wynfield and Roger Fenton, with Lady Hawarden, it is just an element in composition rather than a complete tableau or narrative.

Very little is known about Lady Hawarden's formal training as a photographer. It was not until her husband inherited his title and estate in 1856 that she could afford the expense of photographic equipment. Some of the influences on her work may have been the pictorialist photographer O.G. Rejlander and Charles Thurston Thompson, who was the official photographer of the South Kensington Museum and taught photography there. It is possible that she was one of Thompson's students, especially as she showed and sold her photographs at a bazaar in 1864 for the benefit of female artists at the South Kensington Museum school. Her first camera may have been a stereoscopic one, because a number of her early photographs are in stereopticon double image format. She produced albumen prints made from wet collodion on glass negatives, the largest size of her prints being approximately 9. × 11 inches (24 × 38 cm.).

Hawarden's first photographs were stereoscope views of the house and park at Dundrum and of her family and labourers on the Irish estate. Her early studies of trees are particularly striking, although

not unique. In her South Kensington home Hawarden had the use of the first floor with its French windows and terrace for her photographic work. At this time she began to concentrate mainly on studies of her two eldest daughters, either singly or together, usually in interiors, until around 1862. The costume pieces and mirror images date mainly from her late work of 1862–4. Here Hawarden explored such oppositions as inside/outside, back/front images, as in *Study from Life* (1864; Victoria and Albert Museum), in which Isabella Grace Maude and Clementina face each other on two sides of a French window at 5 Princes Gardens. Hawarden also used mirror images reflecting another aspect of the model, and window images with light streaming in, sometimes in the same photograph, suggesting two aspects of women's experience – inner reflection and the exterior world.

One of the questions that arises in connection with Hawarden's work is whether it can be called Pre-Raphaelite. Michael Bartram included Lady Hawarden in his book *The Pre-Raphaelite Camera* (1985) and pointed to such Pre-Raphaelite elements as loosened long hair, flowing gowns, mirror imagery and costume pieces. Contemporaries, however, denied that she was anything but a photographer of natural settings (O.G.R. 1865). Julia Margaret Cameron with her medieval references fits more easily into the Pre-Raphaelite category. It is interesting to note that contemporaries such as Lewis Carroll, commenting on Hawarden's and Cameron's work, vastly preferred Lady Hawarden's; in a diary entry of 23 June 1864 he proclaimed that the best photographs in the Photographic Society exhibition were by Lady Hawarden, and later purchased five of her photographs for his collection (Gernsheim 1949, p.57).

In her brief career Lady Hawarden produced more than 800 photographs. Her mature work reveals a fascination with inner and outer reflections, of light dissolving form and of the dimensions of female experience. Although she shared many interests with her Victorian contemporaries, her photographs with their formal oppositions and suggestions of interior life are timeless and untraditional, haunting in their mystery and their intimations.

ALICIA CRAIG FAXON

Hébert, Hélène *see* Bertaux

Heemskerck, Jacoba van

Dutch painter, printmaker and stained-glass designer, 1876–1923

Born in The Hague, 1 April 1876. Initially taught by her father, Jacob Eduard van Heemskerck van Beest; attended classes in painting at The Hague Academy, 1897–1900; moved to Laren and received training in graphics by F. Hart Nibbrig, 1901–3; visited Paris and trained in the studio of Eugène Carrière, 1904–5. Alternated between The Hague and Domburg; use of studio in the garden of the villa Loverendale, Domburg, owned by art patron Marie Tak van Poortvliet, 1906–14. Visited Berlin with van Poortvliet, 1913; met art dealer and publisher Herwarth Walden. Attended Rudolf Steiner lecture cycle in The Hague, 1913. Corresponded with German Expressionist critic and writer Dr Adolf Behne, who collected her works, 1916. Approximately 14 works destroyed or damaged in a fire at a warehouse of *Der Sturm* in Berlin, 1917. Conducted controlled experiments on children with medical student F.W. Zeylmans van Emmichoven on the psychological and emotional effects of colour, 1918. Commissions for her lead and coloured-glass experiments secured by the architect Jan Buijs, 1919. Died in Domburg, 3 August 1923.

Principal Exhibitions

Salon des Indépendants, Paris: 1911–14
Moderne Kunstkring [Modern Art Circle], Amsterdam: 1911–13
Galerie Der Sturm, Berlin: 1913 (*Erster deutscher Herbstsalon*), 1914 (with Marianne Werefkin), 1915 (individual)
London Salon of the Allied Artists Association: 1913
Der Sturm, Berlin: 1916 (2nd exhibition), 1920 (83rd exhibition), 1921 (102nd exhibition), 1924 (129th exhibition, *Gedächtnis-Ausstellung*)
Kunstzalen d'Audretsch, The Hague: 1916 (*Expressionisten, Kubisten*)

Bibliography

"R", "Kunst te Domburg", *Domburgsch Badnieuws*, xxx/8, 1912
Adolf Behne, *Zur neuen Kunst*, Der Sturm, 1915 (Sturm-Bücher vii), first edition, 1916
F.W. Zeylmans van Emmichoven, "De geestelijke richting in de nieuwe schilderkunst: Jacoba van Heemskerck" [The spiritual direction of the new art: Jacoba van Heemskerck], unpublished article, 1917
Marie Tak van Poortvliet, *Jacoba van Heemskerck*, Sturm Bilderbuch, vii, Berlin, 1924
Nell Walden and Lothar Schreyer, *Der Sturm: Ein Erinnerungsbuch an Herwarth Walden und die Künstler aus dem Sturmkreis*, Baden-Baden: Klein, 1954
A.B. Loosjes-Terpstra, *Moderne Kunst in Nederland, 1900–1914*, Utrecht: Dekker & Gumbert, 1959
Jacoba van Heemskerck, 1876–1923: Kunstenares van het Expressionisme [Jacoba van Heemskerck, 1876–1923: Woman artist of Expressionism], exh. cat., Haags Gemeentemuseum, The Hague, 1982
Georg Brühl, *Herwarth Walden und "Der Sturm"*, Cologne, 1983
Shulamith Behr, *Women Expressionists*, Oxford: Phaidon, and New York: Rizzoli, 1988
K. Winskell, "The art of propaganda: Herwarth Walden and 'Der Sturm', 1914–1919", *Art History*, xviii, 1995, pp.315–44

Jacoba van Heemskerck was one of the few women artists to emerge as a major abstractionist in the second decade of the 20th century. Interaction with avant-garde groups in Paris and Berlin between 1911 and 1923 secured her familiarity with the fundamental tenets of early modernism. Moreover, the impact of the ideas of Rudolf Steiner, who enjoyed a substantial following in the Netherlands during this period, reinforced van Heemskerck's belief in the ability of the work of art to transmit spiritual values.

Her contact with the Berlin-based art dealer and publisher Herwarth Walden and his wife, the Swedish artist Nell Roslund, contributed to her celebrated reception within German Expressionist circles. Above all, however, it was her friendship with the patron Marie Tak van Poortvliet, a major collector and publicist of modern art in Holland, that gave the artist the continued security to pursue an agenda that isolated her from her Dutch contemporaries. Although these features of van Heemskerck's career suggest that she engaged exclusively in activities consistent with male avant-garde practice at the time, it is interesting to note that she exhibited at the Union des Femmes Peintres et Sculpteurs while in Paris and was treasurer for the Sub-committee of Fine Arts that formed to organise the large exhibition *De Vrouw, 1813–1913* (The woman, 1813–1913).

As the daughter of a well-known seascape painter, Jacob Eduard van Heemskerck van Beest, van Heemskerck received a traditional training. Evidence of this can be found in her small-scale character portraits, such as the coloured crayon drawing of the *Old Fisherman* (1906–7; Haags Gemeentemuseum, The Hague), which reveal her forceful command of linear configuration. Experimenting, as well, with graphic techniques, her lithographs of farmers and genre interiors demonstrate a finely tuned handling of realist detail united by a compositional use of chiaroscuro (e.g. *Farmer's Interior*, 1906–7; Haags Gemeentemuseum).

While these works testify to van Heemskerck's identification with the regionalism of the Hague School, it is evident that her acquaintance with the artists' colony at the Domburg coastal retreat turned her attention to landscape painting. Participating in summer exhibitions in Domburg, she was reviewed favourably by a certain "R" in the *Domburgsch Badnieuws* (1912):

> Also, it can be seen that Miss van Heemskerck van Beest leans in the direction of Cubism which, by this time, she can express by preference. The form is already her own, that she handles without much difficulty and, with her diligence and good will, she will also master the exact colour.

In such oil paintings as *Mountain Landscape with Trees* (1912–13; Haags Gemeentemuseum) van Heemskerck exploited geometrical fragmentation while retaining forceful, linear definition of the shapes. Seemingly, however, the reviewer seized on the powerful effects of colour that differentiated her works from the tonal investigations of Analytical Cubism. By exhibiting annually with the Moderne Kunstkring in Amsterdam between 1911 and 1913, the artist firmly associated herself with a form of internationalism currently being promoted by Herwarth Walden. Already in 1912, his Sturm gallery had organised exhibitions in The Hague, Amsterdam and Rotterdam that included works by the Futurists, Wassily Kandinsky and Franz Marc, a pattern that gathered pace due to German Foreign Office approval and Holland's neutrality during World War I.

By 1915 van Heemskerck's technical radicalism became more pronounced; she abandoned the practice of giving titles to her paintings and drawings, preferring to allocate numbers. Her seascape and harbour scenes (e.g. *Painting No.23*, 1915; Haags Gemeentemuseum) were reduced to a rhythmic repetition of quasi-geometric motifs and colours – dark, symmetrically placed trees, inverted white sails on red triangular-shaped bases, pyramidal mountain peaks – enlivened by the contrasting whiplash tendrils of the branches. Her works aroused much interest when exhibited from 1915 in Berlin at the Sturm galleries and, until 1920, her production was exclusively distributed through Walden's dealership. At least 21 of her abstracted woodcuts were illustrated in the journal *Der Sturm* between 1914 and 1921, the dramatic use of the medium suitably reinforcing the emblematic content of the landscape motifs.

Due to her intensified activities in Steiner's anthroposophic movement, van Heemskerck became preoccupied with the mystical and expressive components of colour and, by 1920, this became the most powerful feature of her paintings. In *Painting No.105* (1920; Haags Gemeentemuseum) the reference to residual landscape imagery is almost dissolved as the autonomous painterly surface dominates the composition. Dispensing with the quasi-geometric forms, she explored the values of organic and aura-like shapes of saturated coloration. The artist's interest in colour symbolism received further impetus from her circle of friends in the Netherlands as she turned her attention to creating coloured-glass and lead compositions. Through the agency of the architect Jan Buijs, she received her first commission for the Wulffraat villa in Wassenaar in 1919 (The Hague 1982, cat. no.102). Inspired by her reading of Paul Scheerbart's book *Glasarchitektur* (1914), she aspired to achieve glowing, coloured light consistent with the demand for heightened spirituality in the Expressionist interior.

Following van Heemskerck's untimely death, van Poortvliet secured the artist's reputation by dedicating a book to her in 1924 and by bequeathing 37 of her works to the Haags Gemeentemuseum (1936). Subsequent bequests to this museum, for instance by Jan Buijs (woodcuts, drawings and lithographs), resulted in eventual public recognition of van Heemskerck in the early 1960s and acknowledgement of the crucial role that she played in the history of Dutch modernism.

SHULAMITH BEHR

Hemessen, Catharina [Catherina, Caterina] van [de]   [fig. 29]
South Netherlandish painter, 1528–after 1565

Daughter of the Antwerp painter Jan Sanders van Hemessen. Married the musician Chrétien de Morien, and went with him to Spain in the entourage of Queen Mary of Hungary, 1556.

Bibliography

Lodovico Guicciardini, *Descrittione di tutti i paesi bassi, altrimenti detti Germania Inferiore*, Antwerp, 1567; 2nd edition, 1588

Giorgio Vasari, *Le vite de' più eccellenti pittori, scultori ed architettori*, Florence, 1568; ed. Gaetano Milanesi, vii, Florence: Sansoni, 1881, p.588; as *Lives of the Most Eminent Painters, Sculptors and Architects*, 10 vols, London: Macmillan-Medici Society, 1912–15, ix, p.269; reprinted New York: AMS, 1976

Johan van Beverwyck, *Van de wtnementheyt des vrouwelicken geslachts* [On the excellence of the female sex], Dordrecht, 1639

Christiaan Kramm, *De levens en werken der Hollandsche en Vlaamsche kunstschilders, beeldhouwers, graveurs en bouwmeesters* [The lives and works of the Dutch and Flemish painters, sculptors, engravers and architects], ii, Amsterdam, 1859

Elizabeth F.L. Ellet, *Women Artists in All Ages and Countries*, New York: Harper, 1859

F. Joseph Van den Branden, *Geschiedenis der Antwerpsche Schilderschool* [History of the Antwerp school of painting], Antwerp, 1883

Exposition de la Toison d'or à Bruges, exh. cat., Bruges, 1907

Felix Graefe, *Jan Sanders van Hemessen und seine identification mit dem Braunschweiger monogrammisten ...*, 2 vols, Leipzig, 1908

Kurt Erdmann, "Notizen zu einer Ausstellung flämischer Landschaftmalerei im 16. und 17. Jahrhundert", *Repertorium für Kunstwissenschaft*, xlix, 1928, pp.211–19

Jean Denucé, *Inventare von Kunstsammlungen zu Antwerpen im 16. u. 17. Jahrhundert*, Antwerp: De Sikkel, 1932

Le Portrait dans les Anciens Pays-Bas, exh. cat., Musée Communal des Beaux-Arts (Musée Groeninge), Bruges, 1953

Flandres, Espagne, Portugal du XVe au XVIIe siècle, exh. cat., Galerie des Beaux-Arts, Bordeaux, 1954

Simone Bergmans, "Le problème Jan van Hemessen, monogrammiste de Brunswick: Le Collaborateur de Jan van Hemessen: L'Identité du monogrammiste", *Revue Belge d'Archéologie et d'Histoire de l'Art*, xxiv, 1955, pp.133–57

——, "Note complémentaire à l'étude des De Hemessen, de van Amstel et du monogrammiste de Brunswick", *Revue Belge d'Archéologie et d'Histoire de l'Art*, xxvii, 1958, pp.77–83

Le Siècle de Bruegel: La Peinture en Belgique au XVIe siècle, exh. cat., Musées royaux des Beaux-Arts de Belgique, Brussels, 1963

Simone Bergmans, "Le problème du Monogrammiste de Brunswick", *Bulletin Musées Royaux des Beaux-Arts de Belgique*, xiv, 1965, pp.143–62

Irmgard Hiller and Horst Vey, *Katalog der Deutschen und Niederländischen Gemälde bis 1550 ... im Wallraf-Richartz-Museum und im Kunstgewerbemuseum der Stadt Köln*, Cologne: Wallraf-Richartz-Museum, 1969

Gert von der Osten and Horst Vey, *Painting and Sculpture in Germany and the Netherlands, 1500–1600* (Pelican History of Art), Harmondsworth and Baltimore: Penguin, 1969

Eleanor Tufts, *Our Hidden Heritage: Five Centuries of Women Artists*, London: Paddington Press, 1974

Max J. Friedländer, *Early Netherlandish Painting*, xii, New York: Praeger, and Leyden: Sijthoff, 1975 (German original, 1935)

Arthur van Schendel and others, *All the Paintings of the Rijksmuseum in Amsterdam: A Completely Illustrated Catalogue*, Amsterdam: Rijksmuseum, 1976

Women Artists, 1550–1950, exh. cat., Los Angeles County Museum of Art, and elsewhere, 1976

Jeannine Lambrechts-Douillez, "The Ruckers family and other harpsichord makers in Antwerp in the sixteenth and seventeenth centuries", *Connoisseur*, cxciv, 1977, pp.266–73

Henri Hymans, ed., *Le Livre des peintres de Carel van Mander (1548–1606)*, 2 vols in 1, Amsterdam: Hissink, 1979 (van Mander discusses Jan van Hemessen but not Catharina; Hymans includes her in his commentary, p.77)

The Women's Art Show, 1550–1970, exh. cat., Nottingham Castle Museum, 1982

Burr Wallen, *Jan van Hemessen: An Antwerp Painter Between Reform and Counter-Reform*, Ann Arbor, MI: UMI Research Press, 1983

Martin Davies, *Early Netherlandish School*, National Gallery Catalogues, 4th edition, London, 1987 (revised edition by Lorne Campbell in preparation)

Mary Ann Scott, *Dutch, Flemish and German Paintings in the Cincinnati Art Museum: Fifteenth Through Eighteenth Centuries*, Cincinnati: The Museum, 1987

Catalogus Schilderkunst: Oude Meesters [Catalogue of painting: Old masters], Koninklijk Museum voor Schone Kunsten, Antwerp, 1988

Maria van Hongarije, 1505–1558: Koningin tussen keizers en kunstenaars [Mary of Hungary, 1505–1558: Queen among emperors and artists], exh. cat., Zwolle, 1993

Karolien De Clippel, *Catharina van Hemessen*, PhD dissertation, University of Leuven (in preparation)

Catharina van Hemessen was the daughter of the Antwerp painter Jan Sanders van Hemessen. The earliest reference to her is in Guicciardini's *Descrittione de tutti i paesi bassi*, first published in Antwerp in 1567. She is included among four living women artists considered to be famous not only in the Netherlands, but in much of the world. Guicciardini mentions that she was the wife of the musician Chrétien de Morien, that the couple went to Spain with Queen Mary of Hungary, and were well provided for at her death (1588 edition, pp.130–31). Vasari gives a similar account in the second edition of his *Vite* (1568), although he lists her among miniaturists in his chapter on *Divers Flemings* (Vasari 1976, ix, pp.268–9); based on Vasari, she is sometimes erroneously cited as a miniaturist. Catharina is mentioned also in Johan van Beverwyck's *Wtnementheyt des vrouwelicken geslachts* of 1639. He includes the four artists mentioned by Guicciardini (among others) and much of the same information, but adds that Catharina learned her art from her father (fols 290–91). At least one work by Catharina, a portrait of a man, is recorded in an Antwerp collection in the 17th century (Denucé 1932, p.107).

Specific dates are not given in these early sources. Mary, younger sister of the emperor Charles V and married to Louis II of Hungary, was widowed in She returned to the Netherlands and took over as governor-general in 1531 after the death of her aunt Margaret of Au 1526. stria. Her primary residence was at the palace in Brussels, and a court ordinance of 1555 lists "kleine Catheline" as lady-in-waiting, among other court functionaries (Zwolle 1993, pp.189 and 202). Charles V abdicated in 1555 and the following year Charles, Mary and their sister Eleanor left for Spain, with Catharina and her husband in the entourage. In 1558, after Eleanor's death and at the urging of Charles and the Spanish monarchs, Mary agreed to return to the Netherlands where her expertise was needed in the conflicts with the French. Charles died in September and, as Mary prepared to leave Spain the following month, she too died. At this time we have no documents or sources to indicate exactly what Catharina might have painted while in Spain, and whether she and her husband left immediately after Mary's death for the return trip to the Netherlands. The following year the Cremonese painter Sofonisba Anguissola (q.v.) was invited to join the court of the new Spanish queen Elisabeth (later Isabel) of Valois as lady-in-waiting, but there is no evidence that Catharina was still there or that the two artists met in Spain.

Catharina's date of birth was determined by the inscription and date on the *Self-Portrait* of 1548: EGO CATERINA DE HEMESSEN ME PINXI 1548 ETATIS SVÆ 20 (31 × 25 cm.; Kunstmuseum, Basel). Catharina presents herself here as a serious painter, seated at her easel as she looks out at the viewer while working on a framed panel with a face visible in its upper-left corner. From the same year, the painting of a young woman at the virginal (32.2 × 25.7 cm.; Wallraf-Richartz-Museum, Cologne: CATERINA DE HEMESSEN PINGEBAT 1548 ÆTATIS SVÆ 22) probably represents her sister Christina. As noted in Los Angeles 1976 (p.105), there is a strong resemblance between the two sitters, they face each other and the panels are almost identical in size, suggesting that they may have been intended as pendants. Catharina's father portrayed a young girl playing a clavichord (1534; Worcester Art Museum, Worcester, MA), also about three-quarter length but set in a more elaborate room. The instruments in both are precisely portrayed, and the virginal in Catharina's painting is decorated with a printed dolphin design on paper with a partial inscription that is identical to one on an existing instrument of 1644 (see Lambrechts-Douillez 1977). A slightly smaller portrait of a young woman is sometimes also considered a self-portrait, but the inscription does not establish this and the resemblance is not convincing (24 × 17 cm.; Rijksmuseum, Amsterdam: CATHERINA DE HEMESSEN PINXIT 1548).

The other portraits signed by Catharina van Hemessen or attributed to her are similar in size, with three-quarter-length figures, hands visible, set against plain backgrounds and dressed in fashionable clothes. They accord with the direction that her father's portrait style took in the 1540s, which was to be developed in the work of Antonis Mor in his portraits for Habsburg patrons, including Mary of Hungary. Pendant portraits of 1549 (*Portrait of a Man*: CATHERINA DE HEMESSÉ PINGEBAT 1549 ÆTATIS SVÆ 42; *Portrait of a Woman*: CATHERINA DE HEMESSEN PINGEBAT 1549 ÆTATIS SVÆ 30; both 22 × 17 cm.; Musées royaux des Beaux-Arts de Belgique, Brussels) follow this format. The couple is portrayed with quiet dignity and an easy naturalism; only the hands betray some weakness in drawing. Two separate portraits in the National Gallery, London, are of elegantly dressed sitters, and the anatomy is now somewhat more expertly rendered.

The lady holds an equally elegant dog under her right arm (22.7 × 175 cm.; CATHARINA DE HEMESSEN PINGEBAT 1551), while the man grasps a sword hilt in his right hand (CATHARINA.FILIA IOANNIS DE HEMESSEN PINGEBAT. 1552. "over another, apparently similar inscription or signature", as noted in Davies 1987, p.67). An attributed *Portrait of a Young Woman* (20 × 15 cm.; Koninklijk Museum voor Schone Kunsten, Antwerp) is described as once having the monograms CJgF and CHF visible, but this would seem to be atypical. Another version of this painting was on the art market in 1939 (17.8 × 13.8 cm.; American Art Association sale, Anderson Galleries, Inc., 20 April 1939; listed as Catherina Hemessen and said to be accompanied by a signed certificate of endorsement by Max J. Friedländer). Other attributed portraits include: *A Lady* (36.8 × 27.9 cm.; Holburne Museum and Crafts Study Centre, Bath; attributed to Zucchero in the 19th century), elaborately dressed in what appears to be court costume, *A Young Lady* (30.4 × 22.9 cm.; Baltimore Museum of Art: c.1560 suggested), *A Woman* (33 × 25 cm.; Fitzwilliam Museum, Cambridge) and *A Man* (34 × 25.2 cm.; Rhode Island School of Design, Providence).

Catharina is best known as a portrait painter, and the most frequently reproduced works are the two portraits of 1548. She also painted religious subjects, three of them signed (and possibly one more, the *Crucifixion*). A *Rest on the Flight into Egypt* (74.5 × 64 cm.; Musée de la Vie Montoise, Maison Jean Lescarts, Mons; once mistakenly recorded as signed 1555, see Erdmann 1928, pp.211–12) carries the inscription CATERINA DE HEMESSEN PINGEBAT but no date. The unusually large panel shows the Virgin seated with the Christ Child standing on her lap, situated on a rise in front of a tree with an extensive landscape background. It recalls several compositions attributed to Catharina's father (repr. Friedländer 1975, figs 197–202). *Christ and Veronica* is signed CATHARINA DE HEMESSEN PINGEBAT (30 × 40 cm.; Convent des Pères Redemptoristes, Mons; see Brussels 1963, p.110, cat. no.127, ill.121). Bergmans states here that if a work is not signed as on this painting, it cannot be attributed to the artist. As we have seen, however, the spelling of the name varies, and certainly there may be works that were not signed or with now lost inscriptions. The painting shows a standing Christ carrying the cross followed by a crowd of figures, with the kneeling Veronica at the

lower left. A signed and dated *Flagellation* (21.6 × 34.9 cm.; CATHARINA FILIA IOANNIS DE HEMESSEN PINGEBAT 1555) from a private collection was in a Christie's sale of 20 October 1988 (lot 127). The three main figures are large and set close to the picture plane, their bodies twisted in Mannerist torsion and strongly reminiscent of some of her father's figures. Indeed, in this inscription, Catharina again proudly proclaims herself daughter of Jan.

On the other hand the three figures in the *Crucifixion* are calm in pose and project a quiet sorrow (ex-Palais des Beaux-Arts, Brussels; Brussels Keyaerts sale, 18–19 November 1946, lot 260; according to a photograph in the Rijksbureau voor Kunsthistorische Documentatie, The Hague, the work was signed CATHARINA; no other information available). Other works are sometimes mentioned as all or in part by Catharina, for example a diptych of *SS Peter and Catherine* in the Catharinaconvent, Utrecht, and the *Tendilla Retablo* (open: 3.55 × 4.57 m.; Cincinnati Art Museum: Jan Sanders van Hemessen, studio, with Catharina van Hemessen). In this large altarpiece of *Scenes from the Old and New Testaments*, comprising 13 panels, four different hands can be identified. The panels attributed by the Cincinnati Museum to Hand B are closest to van Hemessen's style in the *Crucifixion* and in the portraits in London and Brussels. While probably painted for a Spanish patron, these panels are considered to date from just before her departure from the Netherlands rather than from the years in Spain, and it is suggested that she may have carried the panels with her when she left (Wallen 1983, pp.123–4; Scott 1987, pp.69–73).

Efforts have been made to detect Catharina's hand in the backgrounds of some of her father's compositions, and to identify the Brunswick Monogrammist as Jan, Catharina or another artist (see Bergmans 1955, 1958 and 1965; von der Osten and Vey 1969, p.199; Friedländer 1975, pp.44–52, 136–8). These questions have hardly been resolved and require further investigation.

Catharina van Hemessen was honoured by mention in her lifetime and by the court position she secured. She left signed and dated works to document her activity. Yet much remains to be done fully to understand her career and her contributions to the art of 16th-century Flanders. Archival research in Habsburg court documents may reveal other references to the artist and her duties for Mary of

Hungary, and records in Spain may also yield information. It is surely premature to say that she did not paint after her marriage, or that her role as lady-in-waiting precluded painting for the queen and her court. The existence of signed and dated works presents the opportunity for scientific examination of the known paintings in order to establish a basis for authenticating attributed works – for example, the new technique of infra-red reflectography could provide the "handwriting" of the artist's underdrawing for comparison purposes.

Van Hemessen's portraits exhibit changes in the 1550s towards a severe yet elegant and sophisticated style, different from the naive and intimate early works, no doubt reflecting the demands of court patronage. The humanistic and artistic atmosphere at the court, and Mary of Hungary's contacts with Erasmus and Luther and the ideas of the Reformation have been documented (Zwolle 1993). Jan van Hemessen's art was affected by the turbulent religious currents of the time, and may have had an impact on his daughter's attitudes and prospects (Wallen 1983). The impact of the painters, architects, sculptors and musicians resident there, as well as the books and manuscripts that were available in the court libraries, should also be evaluated. We would then be able to add valuable evidence for the contributions of women artists in the Netherlands of the 16th century.

LOLA B. GELLMAN

See also Amateur Artists survey

Hepworth, Barbara
[fig. 27]

British sculptor, 1903–1975

Born in Wakefield, Yorkshire, 10 January 1903. Won scholarship to Leeds School of Art, where first met Henry Moore, 1920; studied sculpture at Royal College of Art, London, 1921–4 (diploma). Awarded Yorkshire County Council travelling scholarship, 1924; lived in Florence and Siena. Married sculptor John Skeaping in Florence, 1925; lived in Rome for 18 months before moving to London, where son Paul born 1929 (killed in air crash while serving in the Royal Air Force, 1953); divorced 1933. Triplets, one son, two daughters, by artist Ben Nicholson born 1934; married Nicholson, 1936; separated 1951. Member, Seven and Five Society, London, 1931–6; Abstraction-Création group, Paris, 1933–5; only woman member, Unit One, London, 1934. Visited France frequently, 1932–6; met Picasso, Braque, Mondrian, Brancusi, Gabo, Herbin and Hélion. Moved to Cornwall with her family, 1939; purchased Trewyn Studio, St Ives, 1949. Founder-member, Penwith Society of Arts, Cornwall, 1949. Recipient of gold medal for sculpture, Hoffman Wood Trust, Leeds, 1951; second prize, Unknown Political Prisoner competition, London, 1953; Grand Prix, São Paulo Bienal, 1959; Lion of St Mark plaque, International Festival of Films on Art, Venice, 1962; Foreign Minister's award, Tokyo Biennale, 1963; Grand Prix, Salon International de la Femme, Nice, 1970; honorary doctorates from University of Birmingham, 1960; University of Leeds, 1961; University of Exeter, 1966; University of Oxford, 1968; University of London, 1970; University of Manchester, 1971. Trustee of Tate Gallery, 1965–72. Freedom of Borough of St Ives, 1968; Bard of Cornwall, 1968. Honorary fellow, St Anne's College, Oxford, 1968; senior fellow, Royal College of Art, London, 1970; honorary member, American Academy of Arts and Letters, 1973. Commander (CBE), 1958, and Dame (DBE), 1965, Order of the British Empire. Died in a fire at studio in St Ives, 20 May 1975. Barbara Hepworth Museum opened in St Ives, 1976.

Selected Individual Exhibitions

Beaux Arts Gallery, London: 1928
Arthur Tooth Gallery: 1930 (with John Skeaping), 1932 (with Ben Nicholson)
Reid and Lefevre Gallery: 1933 (with Ben Nicholson), 1937, 1946, 1950, 1952, 1954
Temple Newsam, Leeds: 1943 (retrospective, with Paul Nash)
Wakefield City Art Gallery: 1944, 1951 (both touring retrospectives)
Venice Biennale: 1950 (retrospective)
Whitechapel Art Gallery, London: 1954, 1962 (both retrospectives)
Walker Art Center, Minneapolis: 1955–6 (touring retrospective)
Gimpel Fils, London: 1956, 1958, 1961, 1964, 1966, 1972, 1975
São Paulo Bienal: 1959–60 (touring retrospective)
Moderna Museet, Stockholm: 1964–5 (touring, organised by British Council)
Rijksmuseum Kröller-Müller, Otterlo, Netherlands: 1965–6 (touring retrospective)
Tate Gallery, London: 1968 (retrospective)

Hakone Open-Air Museum, Kyoto: 1970 (touring)

Abbotsholme, Uttoxeter: 1970–71 (touring, organised by Arts Council of Great Britain)

Marlborough Fine Art, London: 1972

Selected Writings

"The sculptor carves because he must", *The Studio*, civ, 1932, pp.332–3

"Sculpture", *Circle*, ed. J.L. Martin, Ben Nicholson and Naum Gabo, London: Faber, 1937, pp.113–16; reprinted 1971 and in Witzling 1991

Statement in *Unit 1*, London, 1943, pp.17–25

"Approach to sculpture", *The Studio*, cxxxii, 1946, pp.100–01

Carving and Drawings, London: Lund Humphries, 1952 (with Herbert Read)

"Greek diary", *J.P. Hodin: European Critic*, ed. Walter Kern, London: Cory, Adams and Mackay, 1965

A Pictorial Autobiography, Bath: Adams and Dart, and New York: Praeger, 1970; 3rd edition, London: Tate Gallery, 1985

Bibliography

Lillian Browse, ed., *Barbara Hepworth: Sculptress*, London: Faber, 1946

A.M. Hammacher, *Barbara Hepworth*, London: Zwemmer, 1958; New York: Universe, 1959 (Dutch original)

Edouard Roditi, *Dialogues on Art*, London: Secker and Warburg, 1960; interview with Hepworth reprinted in Prosyniuk 1992, pp.256–8

J.P. Hodin, *Barbara Hepworth: Life and Work*, London: Lund Humphries, and Boston: Boston Book and Art Shop, 1961

Michael Shepherd, *Barbara Hepworth*, London: Methuen, 1963

Alan Bowness, *Drawings from a Sculptor's Landscape*, London: Cory, Adams and Mackay, and New York: Praeger, 1966

Barbara Hepworth, exh. cat., Tate Gallery, London, 1968

Alan Bowness, ed., *The Complete Sculpture of Barbara Hepworth, 1960–69*, London: Lund Humphries, 1971

A.M. Hammacher, *The Sculpture of Barbara Hepworth*, 2nd edition, London: Thames and Hudson, and New York: Abrams, 1987

Barbara Hepworth: The Art Gallery of Ontario Collection, exh. cat., Art Gallery of Ontario, Toronto, and elsewhere, 1991

Mara R. Witzling, ed., *Voicing Our Visions: Writings by Women Artists*, New York: Universe, 1991; London: Women's Press, 1992

Joann Prosyniuk, ed., *Modern Arts Criticism*, ii, Detroit: Gale Research, 1992

Barbara Hepworth: A Retrospective, exh. cat., Tate Gallery, Liverpool, and elsewhere, 1994

Margaret Gardiner, *Barbara Hepworth: A Memoir*, revised edition, London: Lund Humphries, 1994

Sally Festing, *Barbara Hepworth: A Life of Forms*, New York and London: Viking, 1995

Re-presenting Barbara Hepworth, Liverpool: Tate Gallery and University of Liverpool Press, 1996 (contains extensive bibliography)

Hepworth–Read correspondence is in the Herbert Read Archive, University of Victoria, Canada; some of Barbara Hepworth's files of correspondence with dealers, art galleries and institutions are in the Tate Gallery Archive, London; the rest remain with the Estate.

Barbara Hepworth's working career covered a full 50 years, from 1925 to 1975. Thus, although Hepworth tends to be earmarked for certain contributions, it is important to remember that her career was a long one, and more diverse than is commonly realised. The context in which she is most often placed is that of the group of British and Continental modernists who came together in Hampstead, London, in the decade before World War II. By this time Hepworth was living with her second partner, the painter Ben Nicholson, and they were close to Henry Moore and the critic Herbert Read. Read promoted Hepworth and Moore as the first of a new generation of direct carvers, sculptors who returned to the block of stone in the manner of medieval or non-Western carvers. In fact, Hepworth had been carving direct since the mid-1920s, and with her first husband, John Skeaping, was part of a recognised group of stone carvers by the end of that decade.

Skeaping was an important contact for Hepworth in terms of educating her about carving, because the technique was by no means part of the contemporary syllabus for a fine art training. It may be that Hepworth was able to learn something about carving from the craft teachers at the Royal College of Art, but she was actually enrolled in the sculpture school, whose teachers still believed in modelling from life in clay or plaster before turning over the work to the foundry or the stonemason. An early work such as *Doves* (*c*.1927; Manchester City Art Galleries) typifies the context of the mid-1920s, in which carvers tended to use animal and bird subjects as a way of escaping the constraints of the figurative tradition. It also demonstrates a concern to show the stone from which the carving emerges (in which it probably draws still from the treatment of Rodin's marbles). Hepworth and Skeaping made a series of animal carvings in the late 1920s, and these found favour with a group of patrons in London who were otherwise associated with oriental studies and collections. It would seem that the appreciation of form in the non-Western tradition allowed a greater tolerance of these first steps towards an appreciation of form for form's sake in sculpture. Other works, for example, *Mask* (1928), *Kneeling Figure* (1932; both Wakefield City Art Gallery), *Head* (1930; Leicester Art Gallery) and *Torso* (1932; Aberdeen Art Gallery), show Hepworth's knowledge of and interest in the non-Western traditions of carving that she found in the British Museum.

World War I had caused a significant hiatus in British sculpture, and thus in Hepworth's early works we can see her consolidating some of the steps that had been made earlier by Jacob Epstein and Eric Gill. *Mother and Child* (1927; Art Gallery of Ontario, Toronto), which is actually signed Barbara Skeaping, is of the same date as *Doves* but reveals a greater interest in the block of stone itself. Whereas the concern of the traditional 19th-century or Edwardian sculptor was to create an illusion by setting the carving free of its block, the new creed sought to bring attention to the stone itself, and to the symbiotic relationship between the medium and the image within.

The *Mother and Child* of 1927 should probably be seen as much in the light of Henry Moore's development of this theme as in Hepworth's. It is the first "Maternity" in her work, and prefigures the important series she made from 1932 to 1934. Hepworth's own pregnancies frame, rather than coincide with, her work on the maternity theme. She had her first child in the summer of 1929, and her triplets in the autumn of 1934, and shortly afterwards began to make her first really abstract work. It is through her "Mother and Child" carvings that Hepworth began to work out her tendency to pierce the stone and to group pieces in relation to each other. In many ways the removal of stone at the centre of the figure, and its apparent fashioning into the small dependent form, seem integrally bound up with the development of the hole in modern sculpture. It is somewhat difficult to mark out which of Hepworth's works should be included within this series, partly because of the possibility of including even abstract compositions with larger and smaller components, and also because a number of works from this period are now lost or destroyed. There are eight works from 1932 to 1934 that bear the title, but the only readily accessible example is the carving of 1934 in grey Cumberland stone acquired

by the Tate Gallery, London, in 1993. This piece probably post-dates Hepworth's first pierced work by three years, and shows her instead developing the conceit of the "hole" being the "baby", the form that is removed from the main body of the stone and now balanced precariously on the knee of the parent stone.

Thereafter Hepworth's compositions of two or three forms become less organic and much more regular; they are now spheres or polyhedrons arranged on grounds of the same material. In 1934–5 she made over half a dozen variations on *Two Forms*, and two *Three Forms* compositions (both Tate Gallery). By this point, however, the theme had expanded well beyond that of the mother and child, and should be seen to include also such works as *Discs in Echelon* (1935; Museum of Modern Art, New York) and the more mathematical groupings of segments and spheres. This turn in Hepworth's work can be referred to the increasingly disciplinarian approach taken by the small group of like-minded artists who saw themselves as making concrete abstract art, and the fact that the grouping in Hampstead came to include further continental European immigrants, such as Naum Gabo and Mondrian, who brought with them the more austere approach of Constructivism, in contrast to the organic or Surrealist aspect of Moore's carving. Although the bringing together of forms on one plane was to remain important to Hepworth, another motif, which also first made its appearance in the mid-1930s, is perhaps of greater significance for her later oeuvre. This is that of the "Single Form", which by 1937 had assumed its distinctive role within Hepworth's production (see *Single Form* of 1937–8; holly wood; Leeds City Art Gallery).

Hepworth continued her exploration of the single, double and triple form motifs throughout the 1930s. Reintroducing wood into her range of materials allowed her greater freedom in this exploration, and probably encouraged the trend away from the predominantly horizontal compositions in carved stone towards the verticality of the single form. When World War II broke out in 1939 and Adrian Stokes offered Hepworth, Nicholson and their children accommodation near St Ives in Cornwall, this rhythm was abruptly broken. Although Hepworth never intended to settle there, and at first yearned to return to London, she was to stay in Cornwall for the rest of her life, for the next 35 years. In many ways St Ives marks her gradual separation from Nicholson, who was to spend a good deal of time in London, and by 1950 they had definitely fallen out. The war separated many erstwhile close colleagues, and thus Moore moved to Hertfordshire, and Read to Yorkshire. From now on Hepworth was much more on her own, and developed her own vision more or less in isolation. Though physically isolated, she was not cut off. She not only enjoyed a regular correspondence with Read for the rest of his life, but was also actively in contact with galleries, patrons and commissioners. In St Ives Hepworth steadily developed a business concern that was able to deal with and put out sculptures to any part of the world. This, however, was to evolve gradually, and in many ways only after the 1940s.

The 1940s are a distinctive period in that Hepworth was unable to get to work for much of the war, and when she did, she produced a stunning, but ultimately limited collection of abstract sculptures, which refine her pre-war ideas in combination with the stimulus of the Cornish landscape. This group of works is marked by its spherical or conical tendency, as opposed to the vertical feel of her work thereafter. The sculptures are mainly in wood, and set off by the stringing that Hepworth had introduced to her work in 1940 (which she and Gabo both used at this time) and by their painted interiors. Here Hepworth effectively sets up a sustained discourse between interior and exterior, having artificially created the effect of an interior that is separate from its exterior casing. In this group one might well locate some of Hepworth's greatest achievements: *Oval Sculpture* (1943; Pier Gallery, Stromness), *Wave* (1943–4; on loan to Scottish National Gallery of Modern Art, Edinburgh), *Landscape Sculpture* (1944; Hepworth Museum, St Ives) and *Pelagos* (1946; Tate Gallery).

In many ways, however, one can see this group as the delayed culmination of her earlier work, because it is also clear that while she was living in St Ives, the war and some of the post-war initiatives in the art world set Hepworth on to a new agenda. It is possible to read her reaction to the war as a positive one, which led her to set aside the isolation of the Hampstead group, in the face of her feeling that a collective approach was now not only desirable, but also possible. She understood abstraction as always to have been on the side of socialism, but now she felt herself to be really part of a community (St Ives), and able to respond to the new opportunities for an artist to be part of the reconstruction of society. Hepworth was certainly one of those avant-garde artists espoused by the new bodies set up for the encouragement of the arts in Britain: the Arts Council and the British Council chief among them, but reflected also in the development of the New Towns, educational planning and building, and the schemes of the London County Council.

A new period in Hepworth's career began with her commission in 1949 to make a large outdoor sculpture for the Festival of Britain site of 1951. This work – *Contrapuntal Forms*, 3 metres high, and now in Harlow New Town, Essex – marks the beginning of Hepworth's career as a public sculptor. With this commission came also the beginning of the press and public attention that put Hepworth up alongside (but still, at this point, secondary to) Britain's established public sculptors: Epstein, Moore and Dobson. Her recognition within the new artistic establishment being created by the two Councils is revealed by the fact that, after Moore was shown at the Venice Biennale of 1948, Hepworth was chosen for the Biennale of 1950. What should, however, have been a triumph, turned out badly for her. The 1950 Biennale as a whole was much less well received than that of 1948 (which was the first after World War II), and, for Hepworth, its particular timing meant that she was thereafter seen as Moore's disciple.

It is likely that it was the new interest in the human figure and humanitarian values brought on by the war that encouraged Hepworth to turn back to figuration. This tendency is most overt in her drawings of the period 1947–53, but visible too in her carvings. Those in stone attempt to integrate a human profile into an otherwise abstract whole (*Biolith*, 1948–9, and *The Cosdon Head*, 1949; both Birmingham City Art Gallery; *Hieroglyph*, 1953; Leeds City Art Gallery), while those in wood tend towards a broadly human form in their monolithic disposition (*Rhythmic Form*, 1949; British Council; *Figure (Churinga)*, 1952; Walker Art Center, Minneapolis; *Two Figures*, 1954–5; Art Institute of Chicago).

It was in 1956 that Hepworth first used metal, at first in the form of copper sheet, and thereafter in the more traditional bronze. Because she (like Moore) had previously attacked so fiercely this indirect way of making sculpture, one has to assess what her reasons might have been for this volte-face. It goes without saying that making bronzes not only made the work of a public sculptor more practicable (essentially quicker) but also allowed larger work to be supported through the sale of smaller-scale spin-offs in edition. It is also known from Hepworth's correspondence that in their touring programme the British Council preferred to use bronzes because they were more resistant to damage. It is also clear that she was increasingly aware of how well Moore was doing, and it is likely that she would have identified bronze as a way of giving herself a greater advantage in the competition. But metals were also the materials of post-war sculpture, and by using them Hepworth was also placing herself in a new generation, and a new sensibility. Moreover, bronze offered her creative opportunities in terms of opening up her work. Some of her most significant public commissions, *Meridian* (1958; originally for an office on High Holborn, London; now at Pepsico, USA) and *Winged Figure* (1957–62; John Lewis, Oxford Street, London), show how bronze allowed Hepworth to make stronger, lighter works. Her crowning achievement within the stakes of public sculpture, however, is a monolithic bronze, 6.6 metres high, outside the Secretariat building of the United Nations in New York. This work, *Single Form*, which was unveiled in 1964, reveals its origins instead in an earlier wood-carving. Its significance lies as much in Hepworth's relationship with the man it commemorates – Dag Hammarskjöld, the Secretary General of the UN – and their common concern to make order out of chaos.

For ten years Hepworth's use of bronze mirrors her career as a maker of large-scale works for public sites. During the last decade of her career, however, she returned to carving in marble and slate, and to smaller-scale, grouped compositions along the lines of her pre-war works. She was increasingly ill in this period, and would have been unable to produce these works without her assistants. Nevertheless, it is clear that in such pieces as *Three Part Vertical* (1971), *Two Rocks* (1971; artist's estate) and *Fallen Images* (1974–5; Hepworth Museum) the sculptor is returning not only to the tradition of Brancusi and modernist carving, but also to her own early works, such as the *Doves* of 1927 and *Three Forms* of 1934.

PENELOPE CURTIS

Herrad
Abbess of Hohenbourg, *c*.1178–*c*.1196

Bibliography

Rosalie Green and others, *Herrad of Hohenbourg: Hortus Deliciarum*, 2 vols, London: Warburg Institute, and Leiden: Brill, 1979 (contains bibliography)

B. S. Eastwood, "The diagram *spera celestis* in the *Hortus deliciarum*", *Annali dell'Istituto e Museo di Storia della Scienza di Firenze*, vi/1, 1981, pp.177–86

Robert Will, "La reconstitution des miniatures de l'*Hortus deliciarum*: A la recherche des sources", *Cahiers Alsaciens d'Archéologie, d'Art et d'Histoire*, xxvi, 1983, pp.99–116

M. Curschmann, "Herrad von Hohenburg (Landsberg)", *Theologische Realenzyklopädie*, xv, Berlin and New York: de Gruyter, 1986, pp.162–4 (contains further bibliography)

Robert Will, "La reconstitution des miniatures de l'*Hortus deliciarum*", *Cahiers Alsaciens d'Archéologie, d'Art et d'Histoire*, xxx, 1987, pp.207–10

Thérèse B. McGuire SSJ, "Monastic artists and educators of the Middle Ages", *Woman's Art Journal*, ix/2, 1988–9, pp.3–9

P. C. Mayo, "*Concordia discordantium*: A twelfth-century illustration of time and eternity", *Album Amicorum Kenneth C. Lindsay: Essays in Art and Literature*, ed. Susan Alyson Stein and George D. McKee, Binghamton: State University of New York, 1990, pp.29–56

Herrad was appointed abbess of the Augustinian convent on the Odilienberg (popularly known as Hohenbourg) in Alsatia before or during 1178; she died in or after 1196. Even by medieval standards, this is a life of obscurity. The date and place of her birth are unknown: the legend that she was a member of the aristocratic von Landsberg family and born in the ancestral castle near Strasbourg is late and probably invented by the family itself. All that is known of her early years is that she was brought up in the convent by her predecessor, the abbess Relindis. There is fragmentary documentation of her administrative abilities, and circumstantial evidence of the high reputation of her house: when the Emperor Henry VI exiled Queen Sibylla of Sicily and her daughters in 1195, it was in Herrad's convent that they took refuge. But it is not as an administrator that Herrad is remembered; it is as the compiler of one of the most celebrated illuminated manuscripts of the Middle Ages: the *Hortus deliciarum*.

A large book (nearly 700 pages over 50 cm. high), the *Garden of Delights* is a retelling of the biblical story of salvation, from the fall of Lucifer to the last judgement. It is told in Latin prose, in verse, in song and in pictures; Herrad's intention, stated on the title-page, was that "the little group of young women should be continually delighted" by her work, and the nuns, as well as reading the book and singing the songs, will have enjoyed exploring the intricate pictures – especially the last, which is a group portrait of all of them, each identified by name. This is a charming, if somewhat self-indulgent painting; the others are of a different and quite unusual character. They are not simply illustrations to the text, but restatements of it in visual form. Often passages from the main text are repeated on the pictures, so the reader has the choice of being informed by word alone, or by word and image. The use of visual aids for teaching was common in the Middle Ages; what is uncommon here is the high quality of the art work, the novelty of the designs and the relative complexity of the ideas represented.

The text is not an original composition, but a collection chosen by Herrad from the work of other writers. Its originality resides in the way it is organised: while the historical narrative provides a solid framework, it is told from various points of view, and Herrad digresses freely into other subjects whenever appropriate. Thus the Genesis account of the creation of the heavenly bodies leads to a discourse on astronomy, which in turn leads to geography before getting back to Genesis and the story of Adam and Eve. In this way the volume acquires some of the qualities of an encyclopedia, and would have provided Herrad's community with a good all-round education.

There is no precedent for a book like this; others had assembled illustrated anthologies; none had done so with Herrad's clear sense of structure, nor with the assistance of such outstanding artists as those she employed. It is not known if these were men or women; the poets of the verses that were specially written for the book were men. Nor is it clear what Herrad's role in the design of the imagery was; in her preface she says only that she was responsible for the text, but it is hard to believe that she was not also involved in what is such a vital part of the *Hortus deliciarum*.

The pictures are of two kinds, narrative and dogmatic. The dogmatic ones are overtly the more remarkable: they present in pictorial form the Church's teaching on such matters as sin, redemption, the Eucharist, and the Christian's proper attitude to classical learning and literature. The illustrations employ symbols, especially symbolic animals, and are often laid out in the circular format that was characteristic of classroom visual aids. The most elaborate of these designs epitomises contemporary ethical teaching as a battle for the soul between medieval knights, and combines dogma with a pictorial chivalric narrative.

Most of the narrative pictures are of biblical subjects, usually arranged in three zones and illustrating the Old Testament selectively and the New Testament exhaustively. Compared with the dogmatic pictures, this may seem like a conservative pictorial programme; but when medieval artists illustrated the Bible, they generally chose from a restricted repertory of familiar subjects: the beginning and the end of Christ's life, for instance, received much more attention than his ministry. Herrad's artists were innovative, depicting the miracles and parables in as much detail as the infancy and passion. The artists must have gone to considerable trouble to find prototypes for these pictures, searching through Greek as well as Latin manuscripts to build up an unrivalled collection of New Testament scenes; and what they could not find, they invented. Such topics as the parable of the houses built on rock and sand and St Peter healing with his shadow are otherwise unknown in medieval iconography.

The arrangement in three zones is not invariable; particularly towards the end of the book there are single scenes filling the whole page, and it is these that demonstrate best the quality that, with iconographic originality, characterises Herrad's book: a monumentality that evokes wall-painting or even sculpture. Both qualities are evident in the painting of the overthrow of the whore of Babylon (fol.258v). At the top, the whore's devotees lament her downfall. They face two burly angels with well-developed wings, who thrust the whore, and the beast with seven heads on which she rides, into the pit of hell, where she is engulfed in almost palpable tongues of fire. The figure of the whore falling headlong in her finery is an extraordinary invention, at once fantastic and convincing.

This account of Herrad's work has been misleading in using the present tense. The book was burned in Strasbourg in 1870; all that remains are 19th-century copies of varying quality: fortunately the finest copyist recorded the page described above.

MICHAEL EVANS

Hesse, Eva [fig. 31]
American sculptor, painter and graphic artist, 1936–1970

Born in Hamburg, Germany, 11 January 1936, into a Jewish family. Left Germany with elder sister Helen, 1938; joined parents and emigrated to New York, 1939 (later naturalised). Mother committed suicide, 1946. Studied at Pratt Institute (advertising design course), 1952–4; Art Students League, 1953; and Cooper Union, 1954–7, all in New York; at Yale Summer School, Norfolk, Connecticut, 1957; Yale School of Art and Architecture, New Haven, under Josef Albers, Rico Lebrun and Bernard Chaet, 1957–9 (BFA). Moved back to New York, 1959. Married sculptor Tom Doyle, 1961; separated 1966. Lived in Kettwig-am-Ruhr, West Germany, 1964–5; returned to New York, 1965. Began teaching at School of Visual Arts, New York, 1968. Died of a brain tumour in New York, 29 May 1970.

Selected Individual Exhibitions
Allan Stone Gallery, New York: 1963
Kunsthalle, Düsseldorf: 1965
Fischbach Gallery, New York: 1968, 1970
Solomon R. Guggenheim Museum, New York: 1972
    (retrospective)

Bibliography
Robert Pincus-Witten, "Eva Hesse: Post-Minimalism into sublime", Artforum, x, November 1971, pp.32–44
Eva Hesse: A Memorial Exhibition, exh. cat., Solomon R. Guggenheim Museum, New York, 1972
Robert Pincus-Witten, ed., "Eva Hesse: Last words", Artforum, xi, November 1972, pp.74–6
David Shapiro, "The random forms in soft materials and string by the late young innovator Eva Hesse", Craft Horizons, xxxiii, February 1973, pp.40–45, 77
Cindy Nemser, Art Talk: Conversations with 12 Women Artists, New York: Scribner, 1975
Lucy R. Lippard, Eva Hesse, New York: New York University Press, 1976 (contains bibliography)
——, From the Center: Feminist Essays on Women's Art, New York: Dutton, 1976
Eva Hesse: Sculpture, exh. cat., Whitechapel Art Gallery, London, and elsewhere, 1979
Eva Hesse: A Retrospective of the Drawings, exh. cat., Allen Memorial Art Museum, Oberlin College, OH, and elsewhere, 1982
Marytha Smith-Allen, The Art of Eva Hesse, Mel Bochner and Vito Acconci as Indicative of Shifts in Mainstream Art Between 1966 and 1973, PhD dissertation, New York University, 1983
Ellen H. Johnson, "Order and chaos: From the diaries of Eva Hesse", Art in America, lxxi, Summer 1983, pp.110–18
Eva Hesse: The Early Drawings and Selected Sculpture, exh. cat., Rose Art Museum, Brandeis University, Waltham, 1985
Bill Barrette, Eva Hesse: Sculpture: A Catalogue Raisonné, New York: Timken, 1989
Charlotte Streifer Rubinstein, American Women Sculptors, Boston: Hall, 1990
Eva Hesse: A Retrospective, exh. cat., Yale University Art Gallery, New Haven, and elsewhere, 1992
Eva Hesse, exh. cat., IVAM Centre Julio González, Valencia, and Galerie Nationale du Jeu de Paume, Paris, 1993
Robert Taplin, "Vital parts", Art in America, lxxxi, February 1993, pp.70–75
Eva Hesse: Drawing in Space/Bilder und Reliefs, exh. cat., Ulmer Museum, Ulm, and elsewhere, 1994
Anne M. Wagner, "Another Hesse", October, no.69, Summer 1994, pp.49–84
Mara R. Witzling, ed., Voicing Today's Visions: Writings by Contemporary Women Artists, New York: Universe, 1994
Anne M. Wagner, Three Artists (Three Women): Modernism and the Art of Hesse, Krasner and O'Keeffe, Berkeley: University of California Press, 1996

Eva Hesse Archives are in the Allen Memorial Art Museum, Oberlin College; Hesse's diaries and Papers, 1955–1970, are in the Archives of American Art, Washington, DC.

Eva Hesse's career is distinguished not only by the innovative work that she produced between 1960 and her untimely death ten years later, but by an equally impressive mythology that now seems inseparable from it. Labelled an "Abstract Inflationist", "Stuffed Expressionist" and "Eccentric Abstractionist", Hesse never occupied stylistic niches comfortably. Like any discourse developing in a non-defined gap, her work fought against easy classification. While navigating within the formal boundaries of Minimalism, she veered towards extremes that transfigured the minimal object. It is impossible to dissociate the work she did – paintings, painted constructions, sculptures and works on paper – from its critical milieu; her receptiveness to work by Sol LeWitt, Mel Bochner, Donald Judd, Carl André and Agnes Martin (q.v.) was balanced by a deep respect for the work of Jackson Pollock, Willem de Kooning, Claes Oldenburg, Lee Bontecou (q.v.) and Lucas Samaras. Her uneasiness about the cool constraint of the former was tempered by the (sometimes fetishistic) exuberance of the latter. Her own work evolved through empirical processes yet still maintained, as its generative basis, a rigorous order. Courting the notion of absurdity through repetition and the marriage of bipolar tendencies, Hesse's art occupies an important place within the greater history of art of the 1960s; at the same time it continues to influence subsequent generations of sculptors. That she was also a woman who died tragically young, leaving behind candid diaries that reveal her personal trials, adds yet another dimension to the story.

Early on Hesse decided to become an artist. Given the circumstances leading up to this decision – her family's flight from Nazi Germany, her father's remarriage and mother's subsequent suicide – it is not surprising that she gravitated towards a profession that indulged cathartic self-expression. By the time she entered Yale School of Art and Architecture at the age of 21, she was determined to paint, as though painting, rather than sculpture, was a discipline of the highest calling. But from the beginning she struggled with the medium, which seemed to resist her best intentions. And still she persisted. Time and time again she wrote in her diary about "wanting to paint", "needing to paint", "fighting to paint" (New Haven 1992, pp.21 and 22). Apparently, painting was the one thing she felt she had to master, even though at times the task seemed daunting. Her role models then were the first-generation Abstract Expressionists – Jackson Pollock and Willem de Kooning – and in both her painted abstractions and works on paper she emulated their activated surfaces and bravura. Some of the most intriguing pictures from Hesse's postgraduate period (1960–63) are a series of introverted, frontal self-portraits, several of which – *Untitled* (1960; Museum of Modern Art, New York), *Untitled* (1960; Collection Galerie Sophia Ungers, Cologne) and *Self-Portrait* (1961; Collection Ruth and Samuel Dunkell) – were included in the Yale retrospective of 1992. In each of these small-scale pictures, the head dominates the composition. Its features are distorted; eyes are rendered askew, mouths as a bright patch of colour or eliminated entirely. These are troubled images not only for their confrontational distortion but for the struggle with paint that seems to characterise their making. Hesse truly wanted to find her own voice through painting. "I should like to achieve free, spontaneous painting", she wrote, "delineating a powerful, strong, structured image. One must be possible with the other"

(*ibid.*, p.23). But her tendency to belabour execution, to rework an idea until structure superseded spontaneity, sometimes compromised the integrity of the image and ultimately made painting a frustrating endeavour.

A combination of spontaneity and structure was more possible with drawing, which became Hesse's breakthrough medium, even though for years she considered it preliminary to painting. Drawing allowed for more process-oriented images. It was fluid, like paint, but capable of greater delicacy and nuance; it allowed the artist's subconscious to bleed through. And Hesse was burdened by it, probably because, in her mind, it did not carry the same historical weight. She could afford to take chances with drawing, and did. More like writing, drawing was a natural extension of her diaristic tendencies, an imagistic counterpart to her ongoing self-analysis.

The drawings reveal a great deal about the origin of many of Hesse's ideas. Ellen H. Johnson, the first person comprehensively to assess Hesse's preoccupation with drawing, noted:

> From the beginning, drawing was close to the centre of Hesse's creativity. It was in her drawings that she first achieved a personal style – and recognition of it. From start to finish, she was a better painter in her drawings than in her work on canvas; and it was finally through her use of line that she discovered she was a sculptor [Oberlin 1982, p.9].

Many of the works on paper executed between 1960 and 1962 are unpretentious studies, whose diminutive scale (one of the largest sheets measures only 27 × 22 cm.) in no way diminishes their importance. Conceived in ink, wash and, in some cases, gouache, some of these images, such as *Untitled* (1960; private collection, repr. New Haven 1992, p.151) and *Untitled* (1961; private collection, *ibid.*, p.153), recall a similar figuration found in Hesse's contemporaneous painting; others, including *Untitled* (1961; Lucy R. Lippard) and *Untitled* (1961; Ellen H. Johnson), explore motifs that later became sculpture.

In 1964 Hesse accompanied Tom Doyle, then her husband, to Kettwig-am-Ruhr, Germany, where they stayed for 15 months as guests of F. Arnhard Scheidt, a German textile manufacturer and art collector interested in Doyle's work. It was a difficult period for Hesse, whose apprehension about returning to a Germany she was forced to leave as a young child, and intermittent bouts of pain at the time, made working difficult. When painting once again seemed impossible, she drew. This time the results were revelatory. About a year before going to Germany, she had been given a solo drawings exhibition at the Allan Stone Gallery, New York. Stylistically, these works ranged from a free-form abstraction – sheets filled with graffiti-like scrawls, patches of colour and, sometimes, geometric forms and arrows – and sparser images in which the repetition of various motifs, mostly boxes and circles, created a more ordered progression. She seemed to be investigating a personalised abstraction, marking more expansive sheets with colour washes, dense linear patterns or crisp outlines, as though they were symbolic microcosms, an arena for enacting scenes of struggle, confrontation and dialogue.

In Germany Hesse explored several graphic styles simultaneously. Drawing liberated her at this juncture, as a catalyst beyond painting. She wrote to her good friend Sol LeWitt back in New York:

> I have done drawings. Seems like hundreds, although much less in numbers. There have been a few stages. First kind of like what was in past, free crazy forms – well done and so on. They had wild space, not constant, fluctuating and variety of forms, etc ... 2nd Stage. Contained forms somewhat harder often in boxes and forms become machine like, real like, and as if to tell a story in that they are contained ... 3rd Stage. Drawings – clean, clear – but crazy like machines, forms larger and bolder, articulately described. So it is weird. They become real nonsense [*ibid.*, p.33].

A recurring motif in the German drawings is the square or rectangle – what Hesse later described as a "box" or "window". It appears in many variations and contexts (in some cases only implied through the inherent dimensions of the actual sheet) and becomes a leitmotif in both her works on paper and sculptures. Several writers have discussed the significance of this motif (Lippard, *Eva Hesse*, 1976, p.158; Ellen Johnson in Oberlin 1982, p.22; Anna Chave in New Haven 1992, pp.110–12; Wagner 1994, pp.71–5), whose multivalent associations Hesse mined. In one well-known drawing from this period, *And He Sat in a Box* (1964; Barbara Gross Galerie, Munich), the box functions literally as

metaphor for self-imposed isolation. This drawing, and others like it, has a diagrammatic quality, like a flow chart with a personal story to tell. In another, *Untitled* (1965; Wiesbaden Museum), the partitioning of the sheet into frames filled with fantastic biomorphic shapes suggests the narrative sequence of a story-board.

The box or window signified many things for Hesse: a frame through which to self-project; an image that may have symbolised her mother's suicide and Doyle's residual presence in her life; a comfort zone; and a continued reference to painting. But other associations are possible as well. Considering Hesse's early training with and admiration for Josef Albers, it is probably no coincidence that the square vehicle for Albers's colour theories became central to her own work. Hesse described herself as "Albers's little color studyist" (New Haven 1992, p.20), and her persistent use of the box (or, for that matter, any variation on the square) would seem inseparable from this formative encounter.

Hesse's interpretations, however, are both a homage and a violation. Her forms are far from perfect. Drawn freehand, stretched and warped, they resonate eccentrically. The box, like the circle, offered Hesse a formal starting point for her own variations and, ultimately, a departure from Minimalism's more austere incarnations. Although formal perfection was compatible with her aesthetic, as some of her exquisitely executed "target" drawings from 1966–7 attest, it was the notion of imperfection, what she later referred to as the "ugly zone", that preoccupied her. Courting the absurd meant avoiding the beautiful and decorative for something clumsy, unresolved, even chaotic.

Hesse returned from Germany to New York in 1965 having produced an impressive number of drawings, as well as 14 wood-and-masonite reliefs, many of which remained with F. Arnhard Scheidt. These painted constructions, first assembled with cord, plaster and, in some cases, discarded machine parts, are technically her first sculptures. Many evolved out of a series of bold contour drawings that recall Francis Picabia's and Marcel Duchamp's biomechanistic morphologies of the 1910s. In their quirky constitution, unlikely combination of organic and geometric forms and labour-intensive execution, works such as *Ringaround Arosie* (1965; Martin Bernstein), *Tomorrow's Apples* (or *5 in White*) (1965; Tate Gallery, London) and *Cool Zone*

(1965; Audrey and Sidney Irmas, Los Angeles) set the tenor for subsequent sculptures.

From 1965 until her death Hesse worked primarily as a sculptor. With the confidence of someone who had finally found her calling, she began a protean production, experimenting with new materials such as fibreglass, latex, sculptmetal and polyester resin and stretching the formal limits of Minimalism. Merging oppositional principle – male/female, resilience/vulnerability, hard/soft, perfect/imperfect – was important to her. So was working the gap between painting and sculpture. She explored a range of images. Some – *Untitled* ("Bochner Compact") (1966; Mel Bochner, New York), *Untitled* ("Vollmer Balloon") (1966; Museum of Modern Art, New York), *Compass* (1967; Marilyn Cole Fischbach, New York) and *Iterate* (1966–7; Dr Robert Pincus-Witten, New York) – breastlike and phallic, are smaller scaled and intimate, in some cases studies for larger variations. Others were conceived as more monumental installations. Hesse probed the viability of an idea through what she called "test pieces". Independent works in their own right, and akin to the traditional maquette or bozetto, these preliminary experiments with materials and process initiated some of her most ambitious projects: *Accretion* (1968; Rijksmuseum Kröller-Möller, Otterlo), *Expanded Expansion* (1969; Solomon R. Guggenheim Museum, New York), *Right After* (1969; Milwaukee Art Center), *Contingent* (1969; National Gallery of Australia, Canberra) and *Seven Poles* (1970; Centre Georges Pompidou, Musée National d'Art Moderne, Paris).

There is nothing tentative about Hesse's sculptural statements. And yet a strange fragility permeates much of the work. This sense of vulnerability, due in part to the materials she used, also has to do with the way in which many pieces suspend and extend physically and emotionally. Hesse never intended her sculptures to appear dematerialised or inert, as objects transcending their environment. *Vinculum I* (1969; Collection of Mrs Victor W. Ganz) requires a wall to lean against; its origin on the wall and termination on the floor, where rubber tubing falls helter-skelter, highlights the ambiguity between painting and sculpture and plots a progression from order to disorder. *Metronomic Irregularity I* (1966; Wiesbaden Museum) addresses similar issues: two painted panels systematically pierced and gridded are overlaid with skeins of

sculptmetal and wire that randomly interconnect the diptych.

Towards the end of her life Hesse investigated a less structured, more amorphous image. In some of her last works on paper – *Untitled* (1969; Gioia Timpanelli) and *Untitled* (1969–70; private collection, Germany, repr. New Haven 1992, p.203) – luminous passages of gouache and watercolour hover within a shifting frame of activated ink lines and shadings. And an untitled rope piece (1970; Whitney Museum of American Art, New York) is the sculptural analogue for controlled chaos. In her last works Hesse moved beyond a discernible motif, what had always been her base ground, a formal and psychological centre. Her late drawings transcended the box by dissolving its borders; a sculpture such as *Right After* (1969; Milwaukee Art Museum), with its skeins of fibreglass cord suspended from the ceiling, yields a different configuration with each installation. It was Robert Pincus-Witten who first noted Hesse's reclamation of an earlier Abstract Expressionist tenet and her transition to another place altogether. "In her last year Eva Hesse discovered the sublime", he wrote, "another place and time at which the critic only guesses and of which the historian maps only these superficial paths" (Pincus-Witten 1971, p.43). That Hesse achieved this state as a sculptor rather than as a painter makes her accomplishment all the more poignant.

DOUGLAS DREISHPOON

Hildegard of Bingen   [fig. 32]

German illustrator, writer and musical composer, 1098–1179

Born near Mainz, 1098, the tenth child of a noble couple, Hildebert von Bermersheim and Mechthild. Presented by her parents at the age of eight as an oblate to a cell attached to the Benedictine monastery of Disibodenberg in the basin of the Nahe and Glan, southern tributaries of the Rhine. Brought up there by an anchoress, Jutta of Sponheim, who gradually attracted more daughters of nobility as followers. Became leader of this community after Jutta's death in 1136. Continued her studies in Latin under a monk, Volmar, who encouraged her to write a book recording her visions; illustrations to this work, the *Scivias*, were at some time completed under her direction; the unfinished text was shown to Pope Eugenius III and St Bernard of Clairvaux at the Synod of Trier in 1147–8, and they endorsed her continuation of it; Volmar acted as her mentor and scribe until his death in 1173. Other preserved writings include a book on the rewards and punishments of good and evil (1158–63), a treatise on the workings of God in the universe (*Liber divinorum operum*, completed 1174), a medical treatise and one on natural science, two saints' lives, the first known morality play (with music), about 400 letters, and a commentary on the Rule of St Benedict. Also invented a language with its own alphabet. Founded two Benedictine houses for women, one in 1150 at Rupertsberg near Bingen on the Rhine, where she served as *Magistra* (Mother Superior) until her death, and another in 1165 at Eibingen. Biography written by Gottfried, a monk of Disibodenberg and her secretary at Rupertsberg until his death in 1175/6; completed by Theodorich, a monk of Echternach. Died 1179, at the age of 81. Often called a saint, but never officially canonised.

Manuscripts and Reproductions

Scivias (lost), formerly Wiesbaden, Hessisches Landesbibliothek, MS 1; attributed to Rubertsberg, *c.*1165

Louis Baillet, "Les miniatures du 'Scivias' de Sainte Hildegarde conservé à la bibliothèque de Wiesbaden", *Académie des Inscriptions et Belles Lettres, Monuments et Mémoires*, xix, 1911, pp.49–149 (reproductions of the lost *Scivias* illuminations)

Rheinisches Bildarchiv, Cologne; complete set of black-and-white negatives of the illustrations in the lost Rupertsberg manuscript, taken about 1925

Complete copy of the Rupertsberg *Scivias*, made under the direction of Josepha Knips, 1927–33, Abtei St Hildegard, Eibingen, Codex 1

Maura Böckler, *Hildegard of Bingen, Wisse die Wege, Scivias*, Salzburg, 1928 (with photographs of the original *Scivias* manuscript; unfortunately, the later editions of 1954 and 1963 use the modern copy)

Adelgundis Führkötter, *The Miniatures from the Book Scivias – Know the Ways – of St Hildegard of Bingen from the Illuminated Rupertsberg Codex*, Turnhout, 1977 (facsimile of the Knips copy of the *Scivias*)

Liber divinorum operum, Biblioteca Governativa, Lucca, MS 1942, *c.*1220–30 (black-and-white photographs and slides available from the library)

Calderoni Masetti, Anna Rosa Calderoni and Gigetta dalli Regoli, *Sanctae Hildegardis revelationes mano-*

scritto 1942, Lucca: Case di Risparmio di Lucca, 1973 (facsimile of illuminated pages from the Lucca manuscript and introductions)

Matthew Fox, tr., *Hildegard of Bingen's Book of Divine Works*, Santa Fe: Bear, 1987 (with drawings after the Lucca manuscript by Angela Werneke)

Liber divinorum operum, ed. Albert Derolez and Peter Dronke, Corpus Christianorum Continuatio Mediaevalis, 92, Turnhout: Brepols, 1996 (complete text and colour illustrations)

Selected Writings

"Sanctae Hildegardis Abbitissae opera omnia" in *Patrologia Latina*, ed. J.-P. Migne, cxcvii, Paris, 1855; reprinted Turnhout: Brepols, 1976

Hildegardis Scivias, ed. Adelgundis Führkötter and Angela Carlevaris, Corpus Christianorum Continuatio Mediaevalis, 43 and 43a, Turnhout: Brepols, 1978 (with plates from the modern copy of the Rupertsberg manuscript)

Ordo virtutum, ed. Audrey Ekdahl Davidson, Kalamazoo, MI: Medieval Institute Publications, 1984 (performance edition, with English translation)

Symphonia: A Critical Edition of the Symphonia Armonie Celestium Revelationum, ed. Barbara Newman, Ithaca, NY: Cornell University Press, 1988

Scivias, ed. Mother Columba Hart and Jane Bishop, New York: Paulist Press, 1990 (with plates by Placid Dempsey redrawn from the copy of the Rupertsberg manuscript)

Epistolarium, ed. Lieven van Acker, Corpus Christianorum Continuatio Mediaevalis, 91 and 91a, Turnhout: Brepols, 1993

The Letters of Hildegard of Bingen, ed. Joseph L. Baird and Radd K. Ehrman, i, Oxford and New York: Oxford University Press, 1994

Liber vitae meritorum, ed. Angela Carlevaris, Corpus Christianorum Continuatio Mediaevalis, 90, Turnhout: Brepols, 1995

Physica, ed. Irmgard Müller, Corpus Christianorum Continuatio Mediaevalis (in preparation)

Bibliography

Primary sources

Anna Silvas, "Saint Hildegard of Bingen and the *Vita Sanctae Hildegardis*", *Tjurunga*, xxix, 1985, pp.4–25; xxx, 1986, pp.63–73; xxxi, 1986, pp.32–41; xxxii, 1987, pp.46–59

Monika Klaes, ed., *Vita Hildegardis*, Corpus Christianorum Continuatio Mediaevalis, 126, Turnhout: Brepols, 1993

Secondary sources that discuss Hildegard's artistic involvement

Charles Singer, "The visions of Hildegard of Bingen", *From Magic to Science: Essays on the Scientific Twilight*, London: Benn, and New York: Boni and Liveright, 1928, pp.199–239

Rita Otto, "Zu den gotischen Miniaturen einer Hildegardhandschrift in Lucca", *Mainzer Zeitschrift*, lxxi–lxxii, 1976–7, pp.110–26

Christel Meier, "Zum Verhältnis von Text und Illustration im überlieferten Werk Hildegards von Bingen", *Hildegard von Bingen, 1179–1979: Festschrift zum 800. Todestag der Heiligen*, ed. Anton P. Brück, Mainz: Mittelrheinische Kirchengeschichte, 1979, pp.159–69

Karl Clausberg, "Mittelalterliche Weltanschauung im Bild, z.b. die Visionen de Hildegard von Bingen, oder: Mikrokosmos-Makrokosmos 'reconsidered' und auf den neuesten (Ver-)Stand gebracht", *Bauwerk und Bildwerk im Hochmittelalter*, ed. Karl Clausberg and others, Giessen: Anabas, 1981, pp.236–58

Otto Pächt, *Book Illumination in the Middle Ages: An Introduction*, London: Harvey Miller, 1986

Marilyn R. Mumford, "A feminist prolegomenon for the study of Hildegard of Bingen", *Gender, Culture and the Arts*, ed. Ronald Dotterer and Susan Bowers, Selinsgrove, PA: Susquehanna University Press, 1993, pp.44–53

Carolyn Wörman Sur, *The Feminine Images of God in the Visions of Saint Hildegard of Bingen's Scivias*, Lewiston, NY: Mellen Press, 1993

Madeline H. Caviness, "Anchoress, abbess and queen: Donors and patrons or intercessors and matrons?", *Women's Literary and Artistic Patronage in the Middle Ages*, ed. June Hall McCash, Athens: University of Georgia Press, 1996, pp.113–17

——, "Gender symbolism and text image relationships: Hildegard of Bingen's *Scivias*", *Translation Theory and Practice in the Middle Ages*, ed. Jeanette Beer, Kalamazoo, MI: Medieval Institute Publications, 1997, pp.81–123

Other useful sources

Werner Lauter, *Hildegard-Bibliographie: Wegweiser zur Hildegard-Literatur*, 2 vols, Alzey: Rheinhessischen Druckwerkstätte, 1970–84

Albert Derolez, "Deux notes concernant Hildegarde de Bingen", *Scriptorium*, xxvii, 1973, pp.291–5 (on the *Scivias* portrait)

Peter Dronke, *Women Writers of the Middle Ages: A Critical Study of Texts from Perpetua to Marguerite Porete*, Cambridge and New York: Cambridge University Press, 1984

Bernhard W. Scholz, "Hildegard von Bingen on the nature of woman", *American Benedictine Review*, xxxi, 1984, pp.361–83

Prudence Allen, *The Concept of Woman: The Aristotelian Revolution, 750 BC–AD 1250*, Montreal: Eden Press, 1985

Janet Martin and Greta Mary Hair, "*O Ecclesia*: The text and music of Hildegard of Bingen's sequence for St Ursula", *Tjurunga*, xxx, 1986, pp.3–60

Barbara Newman, "Divine power made perfect in weakness: Hildegard on the frail sex", *Medieval Religious Women, ii: Peaceweavers*, ed. Lillian Thomas Shank and John A. Nichols, Kalamazoo, MI: Cistercian Publications, 1987, pp.103–21

——, *Sister of Wisdom: St Hildegard's Theology of the Feminine*, Aldershot: Scolar Press, 1987; Berkeley: University of California Press, 1989

Elisabeth Gössmann, "Hildegard of Bingen", *A History of Women Philosophers*, ed. Mary Ellen Waithe, ii, Dordrecht: Kluwer, 1989, pp.27–65

Kathryn Kerby-Fulton, *Reformist Apocalypticism and Piers Plowman*, New York: Cambridge University Press, 1990

Anne Clark Bartlett, "Miraculous literacy and textual communities in Hildegard of Bingen's Scivias", *Mystics Quarterly*, xviii, 1992, pp.43–55

Audrey Ekdahl Davidson, *The Ordo Virtutum of Hildegard of Bingen: Critical Studies in Early Drama, Art and Music*, Kalamazoo: Medieval Institute, 1992

Helen J. John, "Hildegard of Bingen: A new twelfth-century woman philosopher?", *Hypatia*, vii/1, Winter 1992, pp.115–23

Laurence Moulinier, *Le Manuscrit perdu à Strasbourg: Enquête sur l'oeuvre scientifique de Hildegarde*, Paris: Presses Universitaires de Vincennes, 1996

Hildegard's inclusion in a dictionary of artists depends on my firm attribution to her of the designs for the illuminations in the lost Rupertsberg *Scivias* (Caviness 1996). Most recent authors had prevaricated on this issue, suggesting that she played some more distant role (Pächt 1986, pp.159–60; Newman, *Sister of Wisdom*, 1987, pp.17–18; Sur 1993, pp.17–19). I also contend that the Lucca manuscript of the *Liber divinorum operum* has illuminations copied from a recension that Hildegard designed (Caviness, work in progress). Once her artistic role is accepted, she becomes the only "great master" of the Middle Ages, comparable to such Renaissance figures as Leonardo da Vinci in the breadth of her achievements and in the originality of her images. Unlike the 12th-century metalworkers Godefroid de Claire of Huy and Nicholas of Verdun, her only rivals for fame and production, she was responsible for a very significant corpus of writings and musical compositions, and her life is closely documented not only by a contemporary biography, but also through letters and mentions in chronicles. Although highly appreciated as a German mystic and even as an artist earlier in the 20th century, it is only during a recent 40-year campaign of rigorously editing, studying and translating her writings that she has emerged as a medical scientist, philosopher and theologian (Allen 1985; Gössmann 1989; Bartlett 1992; John 1992). Making pictures is now definitively added to those logocentric activities.

And her musical works are increasingly available on compact disc.

In such a brief article, it will be useful to examine one of Hildegard's original compositions for the way in which the text mediates the visionary image, particularly in relation to its authority in matters of the highest theological import. The illustration for Book III vision 7 in the lost *Scivias* manuscript of *c.*1165 depicts the *Trinity*. It is of particular interest because it demonstrates the non-figural mode of Hildegard's visions; in most other cases, although the primary visual experience she describes is non-figural, these dynamic schematas incorporate figures at a later stage in the text, as part of her explanation of their metaphorical meanings. In this case, a vast seamless column at one corner of a building has three sharp metallic ridges, and she explains the configuration as the Trinity: "Thus the Father, the Son and the Holy Spirit testify that they are in no way disunited in power, even though they are distinguished in Persons, because they work together in the unity of the simple and immutable substance".

Hildegard did not image the Trinity in any of the standard 12th-century ways, which included the identical bearded pair with a dove that Christina of Markyate had seen in a vision some 25 years earlier, even though she refers several times to Christ's becoming human, and once to the Holy Spirit as a dove (*Scivias*, ed. Hart and Bishop 1990, pp.411–21). She construed her vision as having a particular relationship to non-Christians: the straw scattered to the southwest (our right) represents heretics, the severed wings (or feathers as drawn) to the northwest (left) are Jews, and the excised dead branches in the west (centre) are pagans. She finishes with a long passage describing the punishment of one who "obstinately sought out what he should not have sought out", indicating her awareness of heretical beliefs concerning the Trinity, probably including those of the famous theologian, Abelard. She had submitted her own text to St Bernard of Clairvaux, who was well known to have judged Abelard. She also preached against the Cathars (a heretical dualistic sect), yet the non-figural rendering of the Godhead might have fitted their precepts as well as those of the Cistercians. Lest we doubt her authority (and her text provides the usual humility *topoi*), a reference here to the Holy Spirit coming to the Apostles "openly in tongues of fire" resonates with the author portrait at the beginning of the work, in which Hildegard herself is shown receiving tongues of flame from heaven and making a record on tablets like those of Moses.

Many of the lost *Scivias* compositions are characterised not only by irregular, non-representational forms (Book I, vision 3; Book III, vision 1), but also by a variety of human figures. Some gigantic, majestic, frontal figures may hold diminutive humans in their arms (e.g. Ecclesia, Book II, visions 3 and 4, and Synagogia, Book I, vision 5). When these are half-length, the suggestion of immense size is all the greater – like the column of the Trinity that disappears out of sight above and below. Other humans are reduced to truncated heads (Book I, visions 1, 4–6; Book III, vision 11), or even a headless body (Book I, vision 1). Architectural motifs, especially common in Book III, are drawn at unusual angles, conveying something like a cornerwise bird's-eye view. Bright elements in silver or gold (whether stars or fragmentary people) are counter-changed black or purple, and tiny white dots on the contours make them shimmer. Most of these effects mimic the scintillating scotomas experienced by patients before the onset of a migraine headache (Singer 1928; Caviness 1997). This confirms Hildegard's hand in the first stage of design, since autobiographical and biographical accounts of her sickness and pain accord well with a migraine disorder of early onset (at three or four) that was particularly severe in her forties, presumably around menopause, at the time she was composing the *Scivias*. Her ability to jot down the compositions and colours of these visual disturbances accords with her claim: "My outward eyes are open. So I have never fallen prey to ecstasy in the visions, but I see them wide awake, day and night. And I am constantly fettered by sickness, and often in the grip of pain so intense that it threatens to kill me" (Newman, *Sister of Wisdom*, 1987, p.6). Her images in the lost *Scivias* are unlike any others in the visionary tradition, such as Apocalypse or Beatus illustrations, or 12th-century images of divine order that have regular geometries.

The illuminations in the Lucca manuscript of the *Liber divinorum operum* are somewhat more conventional, whether because they were "normalised" in the course of posthumous copying from a recension made under Hildegard's direction, or because she (en)visioned the microcosm and macrocosm in somewhat traditional terms. Yet the disjunctures of human scale, fragmentation, oddly angled architecture, androgynous nudes and specific motifs such as a profile head with large wings suggest common authorship. As if to reinforce her agency in the design of the illuminations, Hildegard appears below most of the cosmic spheres, her eyes open to the flaming light that descends on her, her tablets in hand. It is excellent that the Corpus Christianorum text edition also includes the images that are integral to it. Although modernist categories and definitions tended to exclude Hildegard from all the canons, she may fare better in the postmodern era.

MADELINE H. CAVINESS

Hjertén, Sigrid
Swedish painter, 1885–1948

Born in Sundsvall, 27 October 1885; father a vice-district judge; mother died when Hjertén was aged two. Sent to school in Stockholm, 1897. Graduated as a drawing teacher from the Advanced School for Arts and Crafts, Stockholm, 1908; initially specialised in textile art. In Paris, autumn 1909–spring 1911; studied at the Académie Matisse; belonged to a group of Swedish painters in Paris, including Isaac Grünewald, who also trained at the Académie Matisse. Returned to Stockholm, and married Grünewald, 1911; son Iván, also a painter, born November 1911; divorced 1937. Only female member, De Åtta (the Eight) group, 1912. Trips to Gilleleje, 1917, and Fanø, 1918, both in Denmark; Italy, Austria and Germany, 1920. Lived in Paris with son, 1920–32, then returned to Sweden because of signs of mental illness; recovered temporarily, and went to France, 1933, and Sicily, 1934. Ceased painting, and admitted to Beckomberga Mental Hospital, 1938. Died after brain surgery, 24 March 1948.

Principal Exhibitions

Individual
Hallins Konsthandel: 1913 (with Isaac Grünewald and Einar Jolin)
Stadsgårdsateljén, Stockholm and Oslo: 1913 (with Isaac Grünewald)
Valand Academy, Göteborg: 1916 (with Isaac Grünewald)
Galleri Ny Konst, Göteborg: 1918 (with Nils Dardel)
Konsthallen, Göteborg: 1935 (with Isaac and Iván Grünewald)
Malmö Museum: 1935 (with Isaac Grünewald)
Royal Academy of Fine Arts, Stockholm: 1936 (retrospective)
Skånska Konstmuseet, Lund: 1938
Galerie Moderne, Stockholm: 1940 (with Iván Grünewald)
Nationalmuseum, Stockholm: 1949 (touring retrospective)

Group
Salong Joel, Stockholm: 1912 (De Åtta [the Eight])
Malmö: 1914 (Baltiska utställningen [Baltic exposition])
Galerie der Sturm, Berlin: 1915 (Schwedische Expressionisten)
Den frie udstillingsbygning, Copenhagen: 1916 (Moderne svensk kunst [Swedish modernism])
Liljevalchs Konsthall, Stockholm: 1917 (Föreningen Svenska konstnärinnor [Association of Swedish women artists]), 1918 (Expressionistutställningen [Expressionist exhibition]), 1919 (Stockholm i bild [Stockholm in pictures]), 1921 (Aprilutställningen [April exhibition]), 1927 (Unionalen), 1948 (Nordiska konstnärinnor [Nordic women artists])
Göteborg: 1923 (Nordisk konst [Nordic art])
Nordiska Museet, Stockholm: 1941 (Barnet i konsten [The child in art])
Nationalmuseum, Stockholm: 1944 (Den unga expressionismen [Young Expressionism])

Selected Writings
"Modern och österländsk konst" [Modern and oriental art], Svenska Dagbladet, 24 February 1911
"Paul Cézanne: Något om hans lif och verk" [Paul Cézanne: Something about his life and work], Svenska Dagbladet, 24 September 1911

Bibliography
"Intervju med Sigrid Hjertén" [Interview with Sigrid Hjertén]", Idun, 23 November 1924
Célie Brunius, "Jag målar mitt livs bilderbok" [I paint my life's picture book], Bonniers Månadstidning, no.4, 1934
Carl Palme, Sigrid Hjertén, Stockholm, 1936
Ingrid Rydbeck, "Sigrid Hjertén", Konstrevy, xii/3, 1936
Lars-Erik Åström, "Sigrid Hjertén: Randanteckningar till en minnesutställning" [Sigrid Hjertén: Annotations to a commemorative exhibition], Konstrevy, xxv/2 1949
Tor Bjurström, "Sigrid Hjertén", Paletten, x/2, 1949
Sigrid Hjertén: Minnesutställning [Sigrid Hjertén: Commemorative exhibition], exh. cat., Nationalmuseum, Stockholm, and elsewhere, 1949
Gösta Lilja, Det moderna måleriet i svensk kritik, 1905–1914 [Modern painting in Swedish criticism, 1905–1914], dissertation, Malmö, 1955
Maj Bring, Motljus [Against the light], 1960
Sigrid Hjertén, 1885–1948, exh. cat., Moderna Museet, Stockholm, 1964

L'altra metà dell'avanguardia, 1910–1940: Pittrici e scultrici nei movimenti delle avanguardie storiche, exh. cat., Palazzo Reale, Milan, and elsewhere, 1980

Elisabet Haglund, "Kvinnan i den röda rullgardinen" [The woman in the red roller blind], *Moderna Museet*, no.4, 1982

Marit Werenskiold, "Sigrid Hjertén som ekspresjonist: En analyse av 'Självporträtt' 1914" [Sigrid Hjertén as an expressionist: Analysis of the self-portrait of 1914], *Konsthistorisk Tidskrift*, lii/1, 1983, pp.31–43

Elisabet Haglund, *Sigrid Hjertén*, Stockholm: 1985; revised edition, Stockholm: Raster, 1991

Nina Weibull, "Sigrid Hjertén eller en annan bild av människan" [Sigrid Hjertén or another picture of man], *Liv*, no.4, 1985

Shulamith Behr, *Women Expressionists*, London: Phaidon, and New York: Rizzoli, 1988

Folke Lalander, "Sverige och modernismen: 10-talets konst" [Sweden and modernism: The art of the 1910s], *Modernismens genombrott* [The breakthrough of modernism], exh. cat., Nordiska Ministerrådet, Copenhagen, 1989

Scandinavian Modernism: Painting in Denmark, Finland, Iceland, Norway and Sweden, 1910–1920, exh. cat., Göteborgs Konstmuseum, Göteborg, and elsewhere, 1989

Anita Goldman, *I själen alltid ren: Om Sigrid Hjertén* [In the ever-pure soul: About Sigrid Hjertén], Stockholm: Natur & Kultur, 1995

Maria Lind, "Sigrid Hjertén och Isaac Grünewald: Melankoli och virtuositet" [Sigrid Hjertén and Isaac Grünewald: Melancholy and virtuosity], *Dubbelporträtt: Konstnärspar i seklets början* [Double portrait: Artist couples at the beginning of the century], ed. Ingamaj Beck and Barbro Waldenström, Stockholm: Natur & Kultur, 1995

Sigrid Hjertén, exh. cat., Liljevalchs Konsthall, Stockholm, 1995 (contains extensive bibliography)

When Sigrid Hjertén entered the Académie Matisse in 1909 she was already trained as a designer of tapestries. It was only during her years of study in Paris that she received a proper education in painting and aesthetics. Some of her fellow students have given evidence of Henri Matisse's high appreciation of her painting, especially her independent attitude: "She was very gifted" (Bring 1960, p.125). *Still Life with Ginger Jar* (1910–11; private collection, repr. Stockholm 1995, pl.1 and p.154), a composition representing a private rather than a traditional choice of objects and painted in brilliant, light colours, bears witness to the strong impression that Cézanne's method of combining and analysing objects in a restricted space had made on Hjertén. Following Cézanne she combined jars and fruit with statuettes, but chose women nudes in contrast to

Cézanne's plaster cast of *Cupid*. A sensuous humour prevails in her *Female Nude* (1910; Moderna Museet, Stockholm, *ibid.*, pl.1).

On a small scale Hjertén continued to design tapestries, such as *Adam and Eve* (1912; long-pile rug; Sveriges Radio, *ibid.*, pl.23), and furniture and to decorate ceramics, but she was never engaged by the art industry. Her verbal-analytical competence, held back in favour of her painterly-intuitive activity, was expressed in two articles published in *Svenska Dagbladet* in February and September 1911. Here she introduced the life and art of Cézanne to the Swedish public, and further presented her reflections on principles of composition in old Oriental as compared to modern French painting. She articulated her observations of "elementary laws" in Chinese religious painting, thereby declaring her own aesthetic programme and bearing witness to Matisse's strong influence:

> Some of these laws are: the consistent simplification of lines in order to obtain the greatest possible expressiveness, the subordination of proportion to the demands of the composition, concentration on the strongest moments of a movement on the part of the figure performing the movement, the supremacy of colour over tone. The movement of the figure is now compressed within the curve of one single line. The curve is the tune of the work, and its consistency must in no way be disturbed by the figure ["Modern och österländsk konst", 1911].

Such paintings as *Brunette and Blonde* (1912; Sundsvalls Museum, Sundsvall, repr. Stockholm 1995, pl.7), *Dora and Iván* and *Elder Tree* (both 1913; private collection, *ibid.*, pls 11 and 8) follow this aesthetic programme. The elastic outline is accentuated and brought into a full, rhythmic effect. The weight and volume of a dominating figure are set to play against a secondary one, added at an angle to the first as an element acting with alternative effects within the confined space. The subject matter in Hjertén's painting of the 1910s often combines, as rivalling principles, modernism's interest in depicting the model as an impersonal arrangement of volume, line and colour, and the traditional genre of middle-class home interiors filled with an emotionally condensed content. *Brunette and Blonde* is a good example of a modernist subject. The "Brunette", dressed in bright green, is engaged in sewing or reading. Her large but intimate figure is pushed into the background by the dominating "Blonde", characterised by golden hair, sensuously naked shoulders and arms, and heavy legs clad in sky-blue stockings. Draperies of ruby red and black, pale purple and white fill the surrounding space. Two later paintings, *Iván Sitting in an Armchair* (1915; private collection, *ibid.*, pl.19) and *Iván Asleep, or, The Balcony* (1915; Svenska Handelsbanken, *ibid.*, pl.12), may well illustrate the traditional genre. The room is a nicely furnished interior, dominated by warm red and yellow, but opening up to a cool and remote exterior seen through a large window. The small, solitary figure of Iván, Hjertén's four-year-old son, is made the very focus of the room, but he has powerful competitors for our attention, in the bric-à-brac and energetically patterned drapery that lines the living-room window.

Hjertén has been said to "anticipate the home ideal of our time, with the window wide open to society" (Carlo Derkert, *Nordisk Målarkonst*, Stockholm, 1951). But the relationship between her studio/living room and the vast room of society glimpsed through her window was one of tense contrast rather than of ideal harmony. In *View of the Locks* (1919; Moderna Museet, Stockholm; repr. Behr 1988, pl.24) Hjertén grasps the panoramic view from her studio overlooking the Old Town of Stockholm north of the locks, transforming its dynamic forces represented by pointed church towers, edgy buildings, steamers, trains and tram-cars, into a decorative zigzag pattern. The spectacle to be seen outside the low balcony railing is converted into a flat screen invaded by constant movement and a pulsating interplay of hot red-yellow tones and cold blue-green. A small doll on the balcony in the foreground has her back turned to the shallow space of the city behind her. Hjertén's singular choice of colours was described by the art critic August Brunius in 1918: "Her signature is a dry, hot nuance of red combined with a cool, moist one, the colours approaching each other with dangerous refinement". Recurring combinations of colour in the 1910s are pale purple, vermilion, bright pink, rose terra, golden ochre, ultramarine and cobalt blue and turquoise green, all colours often blended with white.

In 1913 a competition was held for the decoration of the Wedding Room in the Stockholm City Law Courts. Hjertén painted four sketches for which she, in a style close to a parody of Cézanne, chose three themes: the wedding ceremony, modern city and nakedness (Skissernas Museum, Lund, repr. Stockholm 1995, pls 91–3). But unlike Isaac Grünewald she never participated in the contest. With an ambiguous effect Hjertén places her husband's sketch as a halo to her face in her large *Self-Portrait* (1914; Malmö Konstmuseum, repr. Haglund 1985, pl.8). A drawing of the composition was published as cover picture of *Der Sturm*, no.7–8, 1915, in connection with the exhibition *Schwedische Expressionisten*. Little Iván acts as a link between his father's project behind him and the frail and extremely elongated figure of his mother, who is seated on a chair to work on an unseen canvas. Her face is white with a disquieting expression of painful abandon under the plumed hat. She wears an ice-green blouse and a vermilion red skirt, and on her breast a red bow of conspicuous size. In this large and important self-portrait Hjertén seems to confront her growing difficulties of being an artist, a wife and the mother of an unplanned child.

The dynamic, diagonal scheme of the *Self-Portrait* recurs in a number of large paintings depicting family and social life, such as *Tea Time* (1915; sold Sotheby's 1989, private collection, *ibid.*, p.17) and *At the Theatre* (1915; private collection, repr. Stockholm 1995, pl.24), a playfully naïve portrait of the dreaming, effeminate and orientalised Grünewald, and behind him Hjertén, confronting the passionate drama performed on the brightly illuminated stage. *Interior/Black Boot* (1917; sold Bukowski, 26 October 1995, lot 497, *ibid.*, pl.35) depicts a "chez-nous" of both intimacy and tension. Child and husband turn their backs on the slender, barely dressed Hjertén. Compositionally her high-heeled black boot extends Grünewald's figure; Iván's blue toy trailer and its counterpart, the grapes in the drapery pattern behind Hjertén, form a second focal point. The arrangement of dynamically opposed figures is brought to a climax in the important *Studio Interior* (1917; Moderna Museet). Is the subject to be understood as an ironic depiction of artistic social life, as a mythologising, split self-portrait, or as a bold expressionist arrangement of curved lines, flattened volumes and opposed colours in a room defined by planes, not by perspective? Hjertén sits by the large window in the company of her husband and the painter Einar Jolin; behind them is a sculptured nude woman and a painted Gypsy mother and child. A glamorous, anonymous woman, dressed in black and accompanied by the painter Nils Dardel, whose colour is pale mauve, dominates the foreground and the entire room. She has been interpreted as Hjertén's other self (Haglund 1985), but also as a figuration of "the Other", an impersonal imaginary representation of Hjertén's extreme opposite, perhaps experienced as a threat to her own self by the artist (Weibull 1985).

In 1916 Wassily Kandinsky wrote in a letter to Gabriele Münter (q.v.): "You must not envy Mme Grünewald on account of her talent for composition – the lady's paintings are beautiful, but not sufficiently powerful. Your paintings are much more serious, deep, enduring." Hjertén and Münter met as artists and friends in Stockholm in 1917, and in Copenhagen in 1918–19. Münter described Hjertén's painting as "harder" than that of her husband's, showing "a cool Nordic and naïvist tendency". Münter may allude to the degree of distortion of the body that Hjertén allowed herself in her search for decorative qualities, as in her arrangement of swinging dancers in *The Masquerade* (1916; private collection, repr. Stockholm 1995, pl.28). In *Red Blind* (1916; Moderna Museet, *ibid.*, pl.26) the element of distortion is brought to an extreme and even parodic expression (Behr 1988, p.54). The aggressively twisted position of the stiff, tanned body of a nude reclining on a chaise longue in a cramped bedroom, the atmosphere of which is heightened by an exploding table lamp, suggests a site of desperately blocked sexual energy rather than an intimate chamber promising erotic pleasures. The brass bedpost resembles a boxing glove raised to crush the red blind that closes the window. Only the cool, silver-blue tones of the bedcover and the model's hair offer some relief from the claustrophobic atmosphere. It has been suggested that the red colour of the blind is metonymically identical to the red of the Matisse-looking *Turkish Drapery* (1923; private collection, repr. Stockholm 1995, pl.57), indicating female sexuality, here kept in place by a pale turquoise-green framework (Tom Sandqvist in *ibid.*, p.178).

Blocked sexuality is the manifest subject of the almost surrealistic *Harlequin* (1928; private collection, *ibid.*, pl.60). Brought together in an easy chair, a large female plaster torso, a squint-eyed male doll and a folded umbrella form a composition of undeniably symbolic dimension. The close background shows a harlequin-patterned drapery, softly painted in grey, green, pale purple and blue, rich red and

bright yellow, as a striking contrast to the rigidity of the objects. The picture may well be seen as an expression of a situation of disharmony and lack, but its painterly qualities and sad, uncanny mood lift it above the private level. In a letter of 1927 to Grünewald, still formally her husband, Hjertén wrote: "I understand that you accept the *artistic* erotic feeling that is mine, but that you confuse it with the feeling that you experience yourself and which does not spring from the same source". A few years earlier she had commented on her situation: "I do not work much nowadays, I am absorbed in the work of my husband. His success, adversities, dreams and aspirations are mine, and then I also have the boy and the housekeeping. That is enough, and I take pleasure in it. I now paint only for my pleasure" (*Idun*, 1924). Significant paintings from the Paris years are *Berthe Darning Socks* (1922; private collection, repr. Haglund 1985, pl.39), *In the Garden* (1922; private collection, repr. Stockholm 1995, pl.49), both scenes of domestic intimacy reminiscent of the art of "Les Nabis", and *The Nunnery* (1922; Göteborgs Konstmuseum, Göteborg, repr. Haglund 1985, pl.36).

A fine expression of Hjertén's "artistic erotic feeling" is *The Beach* (1917; Göteborgs Konstmuseum, repr. Stockholm 1995, pl.31), one of a number of spontaneous, sensual studies of sunbathers. In a later version she drew a sharp line splitting the scene in two, one part glowing with golden sunlight, the other chilled with blue shadow (*Beach and Shadow*, 1918; private collection, *ibid.*, pl.44). In the *Chalk Cliff, St Aubin* (1921; private collection, *ibid.*, pl.46) she contrasted the luminous monumentality of the cliff wall and the cool, cloudy sky with the small boats and human figures. Twelve years later she painted the subject anew, but as a screen of glowing, contrasting colours, the intensity of which seems to reveal a mental state of anguish rather than of pleasure (*Chalk Cliffs in Brittany*, 1933; private collection, *ibid.*, pl.67).

The playfully futuristic *Harvesting Machines in Stadsgården* (1915; *ibid.*, pl.18) can be instructively compared to a number of paintings dating from 1934, such as *Large Red Crane* (private collection, repr. Haglund 1985, pl.58), *Steamers in Stadsgården* (private collection, *ibid.*, pl.62) and *Wooden Horses and Cock* (1934; Stockholms Konstråd, *ibid.*, pl.65). Through her work Hjertén privileges the vermilion, cadmium and red-lead tones, in the 1910s using it as a signifier of intense, often sexually connoted, disciplined energy, in the 1930s loading it with an unconscious, anguished meaning. Her painting manifests a gradual shift from the communication of symbolic language to the dissolved flow of materialised colour that refers to nothing but itself.

From the very beginning Hjertén's art was treated with an almost entire lack of understanding, not to say frank disdain, by most Swedish art critics. In 1912 even Brunius, who was to become one of her few supporters, wrote: "The paintings by Mrs Grünewald have a mild and amiable clang of echo." The critique aimed at her art can be summarised in three points: her work was compared to that of her husband and considered a weak and affected copy; when her art was described as "feminine" or "primitive" it was always in a derogatory sense; her paintings were attacked as perverse and even insane. It was not until the large exhibition of 1935 in Göteborg and her first solo exhibition, in 1936, at the Royal Academy of Fine Arts in Stockholm that her art was recognised as being deeply original, securing her a distinguished position in her generation of artists. Today the work of Sigrid Hjertén is greatly appreciated in Sweden, and regarded as an uncompromising, vigorous, sensitive and very bold expression of her time and being.

NINA WEIBULL

Höch, Hannah
[fig. 30]

German artist, 1889–1978

Born Johanne Höch in Gotha, Thuringia, 1 November 1889. Enrolled at the Kunstgewerbeschule, Berlin, and studied glass design under Harold Bengen, 1912. Travelled to Cologne to see the Werkbund exhibition, 1914. Studied graphic art at the Staatliche Lehranstalt des Kunstgewerbemuseum (State School of the Arts and Crafts Museum) under Emil Orlik, 1915. Affair with artist Raoul Hausmann, 1915–22. Worked three days a week as a designer of handiwork patterns at the Ullstein Verlag, Berlin, 1916–26. Associated with the Berlin Dada circle from 1917. Met and collaborated with Kurt Schwitters, 1919. Visited Venice and Rome, 1920. Accompanied Hausmann and Schwitters on their performance tour "Anti-Dada-Merz-Tournee" to Prague, 1921. Travelled to Paris for the first time, 1924; met Mondrian. Lived with Til Brugman in The Hague, Netherlands, 1926–9; contact with De Stijl group. Moved back to Berlin with Brugman, 1929. Married Kurt Matthies, 1938; separated 1942; divorced 1944. Forbidden to exhibit by the National Socialists. Moved to Heiligensee in north Berlin, 1939. Guest at Villa Massimo, Rome, 1962. Died in Berlin-Heiligensee, 31 May 1978.

Principal Exhibitions

Individual

Kunsthuis de Bron, The Hague: 1929 (touring)
Kunstzaal d'Audretsch, The Hague: 1934, 1935
Brno, Czechoslovakia: 1934
Galerie Gerd Rosen, Berlin: 1946, 1957
Galerie Nierendorf, Berlin: 1964
Marlborough Gallery, London: 1966
Berlin Academy: 1971 (retrospective)
National Museum of Modern Art, Kyoto: 1974
Musée d'Art Moderne de la Ville de Paris: 1976 (touring retrospective)

Group

Graphisches Kabinett I.B. Neumann, Berlin: 1919 (*Dada*)
Novembergruppe, Berlin: 1920–23, 1925–6, 1930–31
Kunsthandlung Dr Otto Burchard, Berlin: 1920 (*Erste Internationale Dada-Messe*)
Moscow: 1924 (*Allgemeine deutsche Kunstausstellung*)
Onafhankelijken group, Netherlands: 1928–9
Deutscher Werkbund, Stuttgart: 1929 (*Film und Foto*, touring)
Grosse Berliner Kunstausstellung: 1930–31
Staatliche Kunstbibliothek, Berlin: 1931 (*Fotomontage*)
Haus der Juryfreien, Berlin: 1931 (*Frauen in Not*, touring)
Palais des Beaux-Arts, Brussels: 1932–3 (*Exposition internationale de la photographie*, touring)

Bibliography

Dada – Hannah Höch – Dada, exh. cat., Galleria del Levante, Milan and Munich [1963]
Hannah Höch, exh. cat., Marlborough Gallery, London, 1966
Heinz Ohff, *Hannah Höch*, Berlin: Mann, 1968
Hannah Höch: Collagen aus den Jahren 1916–1971, exh. cat., Akademie der Künste, Berlin, 1971
Hannah Höch Fotomontagen und Gemälde, exh. cat., Kunsthalle, Bielefeld, 1973
Suzanne Pagé, "Interview mit Hannah Höch", *Hannah Höch: Collages, peintures, aquarelles, gouaches, dessins*, exh. cat., Musée d'Art Moderne de la Ville de Paris, and elsewhere, 1976, pp.23–32
Hannah Höch zum Neunzigsten Geburtstag, exh. cat., Galerie Nierendorf, Berlin, 1979
Götz Adriani, ed., *Hannah Höch*, Cologne: DuMont, 1980

Jula Dech, *Schnitt mit dem Küchenmesser DADA durch die letzte Weimarer Bierbauchkulturepoche Deutschlands: Untersuchungen zur Fotomontage bei Hannah Höch*, Münster, 1981

Hannah Höch, 1889–1978, exh. cat., Fischer Fine Art, London, 1983

Helen Serger, *Hannah Höch, 1889–1978*, New York: La Boetie, 1983

Hannah Höch, 1889–1978: Collagen, exh. cat., Institut für Auslandsbeziehungen, Stuttgart, 1984 (with English text)

Hannah Höch, 1889–1978: Ihr Werk, Ihr Leben, Ihre Freunde, exh. cat., Berlinische Galerie, Berlin, 1989

Hannah Höch: Eine Lebenscollage, 2 vols, Berlin: Berlinische Galerie, 1989

Jula Dech and Ellen Maurer, *Da-da zwischen Reden zu Hannah Höch*, Berlin: Orlanda-Frauenverlag, 1991

Maud Lavin, *Cut with the Kitchen Knife: The Weimar Photomontages of Hannah Höch*, New Haven and London: Yale University Press, 1993 (contains extensive bibliography)

Marsha Meskimmon, *The Art of Reflection: Women Artists' Self-Portraiture in the Twentieth Century*, London: Scarlet Press, and New York: Columbia University Press, 1996

Hannah Höch had a long and varied career from the time of her association with the Berlin Dada group to the end of her life in 1978. She was a pioneer of photomontage, worked with graphics, photography, painting, collage and even produced puppets (Dada dolls). She was also responsible, during the Nazi period, for salvaging the work and papers of the Berlin Dada group that would have been confiscated and destroyed by the Reichskulturkammer because of their subversive political content. Despite the fact that she was forbidden to exhibit during the Third Reich, she remained in Berlin throughout the war years. Her position as a woman artist in the period makes her works fascinating studies of the gender politics of the day, and her development throughout her career of the themes of gender and racial boundaries and their disruption marks her out as an artist whose contemporary relevance is only beginning to be recognised fully.

Höch began her art training in 1912 at the Kunstgewerbeschule in Berlin. Her early training was decidedly that of a craftswoman; within the arts and crafts school, she studied glass painting. The outbreak of World War I spelt a break in her training and in 1915 she entered the graphics class of Emil Orlik at the Kunstgewerbemuseum school. Again, although this was not a fine art background *per se*, she would exploit the graphics training

successfully in her Dada years. By 1919 she was active within the Berlin Dada group, whose membership included Raoul Hausmann, Johannes Baader, Hans Richter, George Grosz, John Heartfield and Wieland Herzfelde.

This politicised group formed the core of an anarchic practice that centred on the use of mass media and montage; both of these forms suited Höch's own aesthetics perfectly. However, the subtle themes in Höch's work differentiated her from the rest of the group, who mainly produced blatant forms of political propaganda and social criticism. Such subtle differences are apparent in such works as *Cut with the Kitchen Knife Dada, Through the Last Weimar Beer-Belly Cultural Epoch of Germany* (1919–20; Nationalgalerie, Berlin) and *Da Dandy* (1919; private collection, repr. Lavin 1993). In these works Höch used the photomontage common to the Dada group in order to explore particular ideas of gender politics within the wider socio-political realm. In *Cut with the Kitchen Knife*, for example, she included a variety of male politicians from the government of the Weimar Republic, such as President Ebert, Reichswehrminister Noske and General von Pflazer-Baltin, but placed them with reference to a host of images concerned with the phenomenon of the *neue Frau* (New Woman). On one level, the work associated the right-wing and moderate politicians with "anti-Dada"; the social criticism of this placement is explicit and over-determined. Ebert and the others share space with Kaiser Wilhelm II and Friedrich von Hindenberg at the upper right of the work, while the Dadaists sit at the lower right with Karl Marx.

On another level, however, Höch's juxtapositions of these politicians and male artists with popular icons of the New Woman, such as Niddy Impekoven, Asta Nielsen and Pola Negri as well as the head of the well-known woman artist Käthe Kollwitz (q.v.), take this photomontage out of the simple realms of party politics and critique. Such popular images of female dancers and artists represented the possible liberation of women in the period through their newly acquired access to the public sphere. As Maud Lavin has noted: "Women occupy the principal revolutionary roles in *Cut with the Kitchen Knife*, often signified by dramatic or assertive physical movement, such as dancing or ice skating" (1993, p.23). The "kitchen knife" of the title further suggests the way in which the domestic, feminine sphere could enact the decisive cutting through of sterile, masculine party politics.

Höch's use of mass-media images derived from journals particularly concerned with a female audience (that new phenomenon, the "woman's magazine", exemplified by *Die Dame*) also heightened the gender implications of her recontextualising montages. It is not insignificant that between 1916 and 1926 she worked at the Ullstein Verlag, one of whose main publication interests was the woman's magazine. Her graphics background and knowledge of photographic technique meant that she was well suited to her work at Ullstein, while their publications were clearly of great interest to her. Throughout her life, Höch collected mass-media images, which she kept in journals and scrapbooks. Her scrapbooks from the Weimar Republic practically document the publications aimed at a female audience.

Da Dandy examined these images further. In this work Höch montaged a series of fashion plates of the New Woman into a work that both critically examines and celebrates this image. The way in which the figures of the women are composed of a number of isolated sections drawn from photographs of women parodies the fetishisation of women in mass-media advertising and exposes the mythical nature of the "ideal" woman. But this work also experiments with recombinations that are aesthetically pleasing in their own right and address the spectator in a very direct manner. Such multivalent uses of popular imagery were to characterise Höch's oeuvre throughout her life.

Höch's reputation during the Dada years was overshadowed by those of her male contemporaries and especially by the fact that she was romantically linked to Hausmann. In Hans Richter's memoirs of the Berlin Dada group, for example, Höch is consistently referred to as peripheral to the group, despite her activities within it. Most of the literature on Dada has tended until recently to marginalise Höch's contribution and ignore her integral participation in such events as the infamous *Erste Internationale Dada-Messe* of 1920 in Berlin and her collaborations with the Hannoverian Dadaist Kurt Schwitters. Höch produced photomontages and dolls that were displayed alongside works by the male members of the Berlin Dada group and, in a form of three-dimensional montage, Höch added two "grottoes" to the now-destroyed *Merzbau* that Schwitters produced during the 1920s.

Clearly, the emphasis on women's roles and the domestic sphere in Höch's Dada works also served to distance her from the centre until recent feminist re-evaluations of the period sought to explore these themes. Works such as the watercolour *Bourgeois Bridal Couple* (1920; private collection) and *My House-Sayings* (1922; Galerie Nierendorf, Berlin) are particularly concerned with the domestic roles performed by middle-class women in the period. While they provide brilliant critiques of these roles, their very domesticity in content marked Höch's distinction from the rest of the Berlin set. *Bourgeois Bridal Couple* uses the image of the bride as a mannequin, so commonplace in advertising images of women in the period, to suggest the mindlessness and emptiness of the role of the wife in contemporary society. This is represented by a large church, a series of houses and a huge coffee grinder in addition to the figure of the groom, in order to play out the masquerade. *My House Sayings* takes the form of the guest book kept by middle-class housewives for their visitors to write in. Höch's guest book parodies this trite convention by having Dada sayings written all over it, such as "Death is a thoroughly Dadaist affair" by Richard Huelsenbeck. Furthermore, the montaged images, which include a self-portrait of Höch and ball bearings next to bits of lace and needlepoint diagrams, underlie the critical eye with which the artist approached such domestic fancies.

By the mid-1920s Höch's associations with the members of the Berlin Dada group had mainly ended, as had her relationship with Hausmann. She was far more involved artistically during this period with Kurt Schwitters in Hannover and with Jean Arp and Sophie Taeuber-Arp (q.v.), Theo and Nelly van Doesburg and Til Brugman in the Netherlands. From 1926 until 1929 Höch lived with Brugman in Holland and worked closely with the Bauhaus and De Stijl circles. Again, these ties were with the part of the avant-garde that most thoroughly integrated fine and mass production, the arts and the crafts. Höch's work continued to be conceived from this very union between fine art and mass media. From this point, the more subtle themes of androgyny and ethnicity that would characterise her late work entered into her production.

In such works as *The Coquette I* (1923–5) and *Half-Caste* (1924; both Institut für Auslandsbeziehungen, Stuttgart) Höch manipulated the conventions of gender and race in order to produce works that explored the boundaries of those concepts and their social and political meanings. *The Coquette I* shows the stylish body of a woman being fêted by a "man-bear" and "man-dog", two composite representations derived from images of humans and animals. The fashionable female figure is surmounted by a man's head. Hence, the very standard poses of the coquette and her suitors are turned back upon themselves and confounded by the viewer's inability to fix any gender or biological identities to the figures. *Half-Caste* suspends our ability to determine racial identity in much the same way. Placed in the centre of an Asian female face is a pair of "Clara Bow" lips, a white woman's lips in the fashionable red lipstick of the period. Such imagery not only points to the construction of gender and racial identity as mere image, but parodies our attempts to fix these and mediate between people based on such false constructs. Given the period in which these were produced, when the politics of fixed gender and racial identity were so critical to power relations, Höch's work can be seen to be decidedly anarchic and subversive.

These themes were also explored as a means towards redefining canons of beauty and aesthetics. Looking at the two works *Strange Beauty* (1929; private collection, *ibid.*) and *Strange Beauty II* (1966; private collection, repr. Stuttgart 1984), the production of which was separated by almost four decades, reveals the way in which such multiplication of meaning remained a constant source of inspiration to Höch in her work. *Strange Beauty* placed a reclining, white female nude body into communion with a montaged African "fetish" head; both blurred gender and racial boundaries are again suggested in the piece. The work, however, also queries beauty itself as an operative visual category. By indicating estrangement, Höch was able, like Brecht, to distance the viewer critically and insist that new strategies of looking be defined. The sheer appeal of this work and its counterpart, *Strange Beauty II*, with its voluptuous colours and textures, confronts us with an alternative space for pleasure.

Such subtle refinements in concepts of seeing and reading work have made Hannah Höch one of the best-known and most discussed women artists of the last two decades. She has been subject to a number of outstanding critical reviews and her works have been shown widely. Her training, association with the avant-garde and sophisticated questioning of gender stereotypes all make her an ideal topic for feminist re-evaluations of the art produced by women in the 20th century.

MARSHA MESKIMMON

Hodgkins, Frances
New Zealand painter, 1869–1947

Born in Dunedin, South Island, 28 April 1869; father a solicitor and amateur painter. Took classes with visiting Italian painter Girolamo Pieri Nerli, 1893. Attended Dunedin School of Art, 1895–6. First visited Europe, 1901, travelling in England, France, Italy, Morocco and the Netherlands; attended Norman Garstin's sketching classes at Caudebec and Dinan, France, summers 1901 and 1902. Returned to New Zealand, 1903, opening studio in Wellington. Second visit to Europe, 1906; stayed in the Netherlands, 1907–8, before settling in Paris; first woman teacher at Académie Colarossi, 1910. Returned to New Zealand for the last time, 1912–13, then settled permanently in Europe. Lived in St Ives, Cornwall, during World War I, then divided time between Britain and France, painting in Spain, 1932–3 and 1935–6. Died at Herrison House, a psychiatric hospital near Dorchester, Dorset, 13 May 1947.

Principal Exhibitions

Individual
Claridge Gallery, London: 1928
Bloomsbury Gallery, London: 1929 (with Vera Cunningham)
St George's Gallery, London: 1930, 1948 (retrospective)
Lefevre Gallery, London: 1933, 1937, 1940, 1943, 1946 (retrospective)
Leicester Galleries, London: 1935, 1941
Wertheim Gallery, London: 1936
Manchester City Art Gallery: 1947

Group
New Zealand Academy of Fine Arts, Wellington: 1892, 1898, 1900
Otago Art Society, Dunedin: 1890, 1895–6, 1898, 1900–02
Doré Gallery, London: 1902
Royal Academy, London: 1903–5, 1915–16
Fine Art Society, London: 1903
Paris Salon: 1909
Société Nationale des Beaux-Arts, Paris: 1911–12
International Society, Grosvenor Gallery, London: 1915–19

Women's International Art Club, London: 1919, 1924

London Salon of the Allied Artists Association: 1920–21

Salon d'Automne, Paris: 1924, 1938

London Group: 1927, 1929

New English Art Club, London: 1927–8, 1932–3

Seven and Five Society, London: 1929, 1931, 1932, 1933, 1934

Lefevre Gallery, London: 1938 (*New Paintings*), 1945 (with Francis Bacon, Henry Moore, Matthew Smith and Graham Sutherland), 1946 (*British Painters Past and Present*)

London Gallery, London: 1939 (*Living Art in England*)

National Gallery, Wellington: 1939 (*Centennial Exhibition of International and New Zealand Art*)

Hertford House, London: 1940 (*Paintings Selected for Inclusion in the 22nd Biennale di Venezia*)

Musée du Jeu de Paume, Paris: 1946 (*Tableaux britanniques modernes appartenant à la Tate Gallery*, organised by British Council)

Albright Art Gallery, Buffalo: 1946 (*British Contemporary Painters*)

Selected Writings

Letters of Frances Hodgkins, ed. Linda Gill, Auckland: Auckland University Press, 1993

Bibliography

John Piper, "Frances Hodgkins", *Horizon*, iv/24, 1941, pp.413–16

Eardley Knollys, "Obituaries: Frances Hodgkins", *Burlington Magazine*, lxxxix, 1947, pp.197–8

Geoffrey Gorer, "Remembering Frances Hodgkins", *The Listener*, 19 June 1947, p.968

Myfanwy Evans, *Frances Hodgkins*, Harmondsworth: Penguin, 1948

Arthur Rowland Howell, *Frances Hodgkins: Four Vital Years*, London: Rockliff, 1951

Ethel Walker, Frances Hodgkins, Gwen John: A Memorial Exhibition, exh. cat., Tate Gallery and Arts Council, London, 1952

E. H. McCormick, *The Expatriate: A Study of Frances Hodgkins*, Wellington: New Zealand University Press, 1954

——, *Works of Frances Hodgkins in New Zealand*, Auckland: Auckland City Art Gallery, 1954

Ascent, 1969 (Frances Hodgkins commemorative issue)

Charles Brasch, "Frances Hodgkins at one hundred", *Landfall*, no.92, 1969, pp.265–76

Frances Hodgkins, 1869–1947: A Centenary Exhibition, exh. cat., Auckland Art Gallery, and elsewhere, 1969

J. Rothenstein, *Modern English Painters: Sickert to Smith*, 2nd edition, London: Macdonald and Jane's, 1976

E. H. McCormick, *Portrait of Frances Hodgkins*, Auckland: Auckland University Press, 1981

Katy Deepwell, "Women in the Seven and Five Society", *Women Artists Slide Library Journal*, no.22, April–May 1988, pp.10–12

Frances Hodgkins, 1869–1947, exh. cat., Whitford and Hughes, London, 1990

Michael Dunn, *A Concise History of New Zealand Painting*, Sydney: Craftsman House, 1991

Frances Hodgkins: The Late Work, exh. cat., Minories Art Gallery, Colchester, and elsewhere, 1991

Anne Kirker, *New Zealand Women Artists: A Survey of 150 Years*, 2nd edition, Tortola, BVI: Craftsman House, 1993

Iain Buchanan, "Frances Hodgkins and Neo-romanticism", *Writing a New Country: A Collection of Essays Presented to E. H. McCormick in his 88th Year*, ed. James Ross, Linda Gill and Stuart McRae, Auckland, 1993, pp.155–64

R. D. J. Collins, "A long attachment: Frances Hodgkins in France", *ibid.*, pp.84–95

Women's Suffrage Exhibition, exh. cat., Museum of New Zealand, Te Papa Tongarewa, Wellington, 1993

Iain Buchanan, Elizabeth Eastmond and Michael Dunn, *Frances Hodgkins: Paintings and Drawings*, Auckland: Auckland University Press, 1994; London: Thames and Hudson, 1995

Pamela Gerrish Nunn, "Frances Hodgkins: A question of identity", *Woman's Art Journal*, xv/5, 1994–5, pp.9–13

Influence and Originality: Ivon Hitchens, Frances Hodgkins, Winifred Nicholson: Landscapes, c.1920–1950, exh. cat., Djanogly Art Gallery, University of Nottingham, and elsewhere, 1996

Unpublished correspondence, 1875–1946, is in the Alexander Turnbull Library, Wellington; Frances Hodgkins Papers are in the Tate Gallery Archives, London.

Frances Hodgkins was a key figure in the context of British art of the 1930s and 1940s. Her early career developed with the support of her father, the watercolourist William Matthew Hodgkins, and alongside that of her initially more successful sister Isabel. Her great achievement, after absorbing the possibilities available in New Zealand's then provincial and colonial situation, and after several decades of persistent work, travel and experimentation in Europe and Britain, was to contribute significantly to British modernism. From about the age of 60 until the year before her death she held numerous solo exhibitions in London and exhibited with such avant-garde groups as the Seven and Five Society. She was invited to join Unit One (but withdrew), was one of the artists chosen to represent Britain at the Venice Biennale of 1940, exhibited at the Lefevre Gallery with Francis Bacon, Henry Moore, Matthew Smith and Graham Sutherland in 1945, and took part in a number of Neo-romantic group exhibitions and other international exhibitions.

Hodgkins's career can be roughly divided into three main phases: the period up to 1913, when she left New Zealand for the last time; the period from 1914 to c.1929; and the period from c.1929, when she first exhibited with the Seven and Five Society, until 1946, the year before her death. Her early works of the 1890s in New Zealand show the influence of her father, but figure subjects, not landscapes, predominate. The teaching of an Italian expatriate, Girolamo Pieri Nerli, was an important influence at this stage. The intimate qualities and loose watercolour technique of such portraits as the *Girl with the Flaxen Hair* (1893; Museum of New Zealand, Te Papa Tongarewa) can be linked to Nerli's portraiture of young women. Her genre scenes, such as *A Goose Girl* (1893; private collection, New Zealand, repr. McCormick 1981, p.22), show the artist adopting a conventionally sentimental approach to rural activity of the kind common in the work of certain late 19th-century European and European-influenced artists such as Helen Allingham. Hodgkins also produced a number of works based on Maori subjects, mainly studies of women and children. *Maori Girl* (1896; Dunedin Public Art Gallery), which displays her proficiency at laying on wet-on-wet watercolour washes, has the girl's head isolated against the ground; the treatment of the subject again somewhat romanticises and arguably decontextualises (as with other artists' treatment of related subjects) Maori in terms of their then marginal and underprivileged social status. Depicting Maori as "exotic" connects works of this kind with the practice of such European artists as Jules Bastien-Lepage (whose work was known in New Zealand) in his paintings of peasants and peasant labour.

From 1901 to 1912 Hodgkins's work became, through her travels, more directly inspired by European art, although this inspiration was still Impressionist-based rather than a response to the European avant-garde of the first decade of the 20th century. She spent several years in France and in 1910 taught a class in watercolours at the Académie Colarossi. Paintings from this period, such as *Orange Sellers, Tangier* (1903; Olveston, Dunedin), can be related to similar subjects by Frank Brangwyn and Arthur Melville, while the breezy plein-air spirit of *Hill Top* (c.1908; Museum of New Zealand), with its group of women interacting with relaxed intimacy, its windswept outdoor setting and the spontaneous, vigorous brushwork, can be read as signifying something of the atmosphere of contemporary emancipation. The theme of women together, or of women with children, often treated in a way that iconographically and stylistically explores notions of intimacy, is a feature of several works throughout Hodgkins's career, and is an emphasis that connects some of her more Impressionist-related works of the pre-1920s with the women Impressionists Berthe Morisot (q.v.) and Mary Cassatt (q.v.). One of her last works in this style is *At the Window* (c.1912; Art Gallery of South Australia, Adelaide), which prefigures a major thematic preoccupation of her late phase: the still-life landscape.

The war years of 1914–18, when Hodgkins was based in St Ives, corresponded to a major shift in her practice. She moved away from watercolour, Impressionist-influenced plein-air paintings to a series of often large-scale figurative works in oil. In *Loveday and Anne* (1916; Tate Gallery, London) the figures are posed informally in an interior domestic setting. Stylistically there is now more in common with the Post-Impressionists and with such Intimists as Bonnard and Vuillard, while Hodgkins conveys her increasingly individual painterly approach by engagingly free brushwork and a subtle and witty response to the different personalities of the figures. She links them in a formal and symbolic sense in terms of their relationship and femininity by the dominant motif and vivid colours of the foreground basket of flowers. Hodgkins was friendly with the older members of the Cornish School (Norman Garstin, Moffat Lindner, Stanhope Forbes), although her art was far less conservative. Later, as a result of the visit of Cedric Morris and Lett Haines in 1919–20, she probably came into contact with younger, rather more progressive artists such as Laura Knight (q.v.). The themes of Sickert's work appear to have exerted an influence in the choice of some of her subjects around 1919–20 (e.g. *My Landlady*, c.1920; Auckland City Art Gallery), while during the early to mid-1920s, when she was often based in France, she experimented with Post-Impressionism (portrait of *Lett Haines*, c.1920; untraced, repr. Buchanan, Eastmond and Dunn 1994, fig.21) and Cubism (*Red Cockerel*, 1924; Dunedin Public Art Gallery), and produced a dynamic series of black chalk drawings of the Provençal landscape (*Olives, St Tropez*, c.1921; Hocken Library, Dunedin).

The years 1925–7 were spent in Manchester, where Hodgkins worked for a time for the Calico Printers' Association. Little is known of her work for them, although the Association sent her to the Exposition Internationale des Arts Décoratifs et Industriels Modernes in Paris (1925), where she would have seen the work of such artist-designers as Dufy and Sonia Delaunay (q.v.). *Double Portrait* (1922–5; Hocken Library) displays rich, Matissean decorative effects that probably reflect her textile work. A spectacular, large-scale drawing of this time, *Seated Woman* (c.1926; Tate Gallery), also displays a brilliant handling of both bold and subtle decorative effects. While in Manchester Hodgkins met one of her most important collectors, Lucy Wertheim, a gallery owner who also frequently exhibited Hodgkins's work of the later 1920s.

From 1928 to 1930 Hodgkins developed a strong, consistent personal style, focused on figure and landscape subjects. She began to experiment with what was to become a frequent theme in her art into the 1940s: the still-life landscape. In 1929 she exhibited for the first time with the Seven and Five Society, and in 1930 her crucial solo exhibition at St George's Gallery established her as an important British modernist whose sensuous French School-inspired colour was her strong suit. The *White House* (c.1930; Art Gallery of New South Wales, Sydney) is an early example of the still-life landscape combination. Painted in France, it demonstrates Hodgkins's rich, fluid paintwork and sensuous colour typical of this period. A little later, outstanding works such as *Wings over Water* (1931–2; Tate Gallery), *Arum Lilies* (c.1931; private collection, Britain; repr. Buchanan, Eastmond and Dunn 1994, pl.26), which was much reproduced in the 1930s, *Spanish Still Life and Landscape* (1932–3; Robert McDougall Art Gallery, Christchurch) and the watercolour *Enchanted Garden*, also known as *Cornish Garden* (1932; Sheffield City Art Galleries), continue to explore this conflation of genres in diverse ways.

From the early 1930s until her death Hodgkins was based in Britain, with much of the last ten years spent in or near Corfe Castle in Dorset. The period included sojourns at Bradford-on-Tone, Somerset, trips to Wales and two significant periods of work in Spain: 1932–3 in Ibiza and 1935–6 in Tossa de Mar. Her work, with its highly individual approach to colour and continual exploration of new kinds of increasingly calligraphic brushwork, moved through a succession of phases of selective and intelligent response to current movements in the arts: from the lyrical naturalism and *faux-naïveté* associated with the Seven and Five Society, to New Classicism of the 1920s, to Surrealism, through to Neo-romanticism, always tempered by her interest in major artists of the French School such as Matisse, Picasso and Dufy. The aesthetics of other cultures and times were also important to her: Chinese art, medieval art and child art, for instance, while her paintings of the 1940s show concerns similar to those of Paul Nash and John Piper.

While the combination of the still-life and landscape genres is not confined to Hodgkins, her persistent and individual exploration of variations on this theme is unique. Her still-life landscapes demonstrate a concern for transgressing boundaries of genre and setting in their varied plays on interior/exterior spaces, and her selection of still-life motifs is often strongly suggestive and with clearly symbolic overtones. Early examples such as *Wings over Water* (1931–2; Tate Gallery) have the still-life elements (here lushly painted large-scale shells) set on a ledge overlooking a coastal view, while a later example such as *Walled Garden with Convolvulus* (1942–3; private collection, New Zealand, *ibid.*, pl.21) places the still life within a landscape setting and merges the two elements by adopting an overall calligraphic painterly approach bordering on abstraction. Still-life-related motifs are also a feature of one of the few large-scale figure compositions of Hodgkins's late work: *Spanish Shrine* (1933–4; Auckland City Art Gallery). Eric Newton praised the balance achieved here between "the world of her eye and the world of her mind's eye … The picture is both a symbol and a description and the two are interwoven" (Eric Newton, "Frances Hodgkins", *The Listener*, 2 October 1941, p.473). Begun, if not completed in Ibiza in 1933, the painting's two neo-primitivising figures of women carrying on their heads, respectively, a barrel and a basket of fruit flank a mysterious, grisaille depiction of a statue of a woman with closed eyes. There are echoes of Rouault and Picasso, while the dynamic achieved between the three iconic, frontally positioned figures and the marvellously subtle array of shifting patches of salmon pinks, pale aquamarines and bronzes contributes to the painting's unique quality.

In the mid-1930s Hodgkins produced two innovative paintings that combine the genres of still life and self-portraiture. In one, *Self-Portrait: Still Life* (c.1935; Auckland City Art Gallery), a table-top is tilted vertically to frame various objects chosen by the artist to speak for her presence: a central bowl and pink rose, symbols of femininity; a belt, suggestive of the absent body; an amusingly frivolous pink high-heeled shoe and a mass of patterned scarves. This painting makes an intriguing addition to the range of self-representations made by women artists in the inter-war period.

Works of the later 1930s painted in Spain, such as the gouache *Pumpkins and Pimenti* (c.1935–6; Fletcher Challenge Art Collection, New Zealand; once owned by Sir Kenneth Clark), show that the artist was alert to Surrealism – distant mountains appear to erupt through the table and around the effectively sombre greys, sharp blues and reds of this Mediterranean still-life landscape. Hodgkins's one major experiment in printmaking was also produced in these years: the buoyant and boldly designed *Arrangement of Jugs* (1938), which was published by Contemporary Lithographs Ltd and printed at the Curwen Press. Hodgkins's last major figure painting was also done at this time: the Picassoesque *Double Portrait No.2 (Katharine and Anthony West)* (1937–9; oil; Museum of New Zealand). Hodgkins, a close friend of the Wests, here produced a variant on her longstanding interest in the double portrait by focusing on a male/female couple rather than her customary double portraits of women.

A significant number of Hodgkins's works of the war period, mostly highly individual and superbly painterly transformations of specific landscapes, show her connections with the Neo-romantics. She exhibited frequently both with established Neo-romantics such as Moore, Nash, Sutherland and Piper and also with the younger group, including John Minton, and the "two Roberts", Colquhoun and McBryde. But while the connections in terms of subject (e.g. *Broken Tractor*, 1942; gouache; Tate Gallery) and colour are clear, what set Frances Hodgkins apart from her colleagues (apart from gender and age) was the individual painterliness of her approach, with its continuing allegiance to the French School. As she herself put it, it was "that universality I ever strive after ... between the Ecole de Paris & FH" (letter from Frances Hodgkins to Duncan Macdonald, 11 April 1943). Many of Hodgkins's works from 1935 onwards are in gouache, a medium she exploited successfully in her increasingly free approach to colour, line and form.

Church and Castle, Corfe (1942; Ferens Art Gallery, Hull City Museums and Art Galleries) includes typically Neo-romantic motifs of ruined castle and local church amidst an overall free surface play of ambiguous graphic effects, which renders these sites barely recognisable as a result of her increasingly abstract approach. A small group of major late works were, however, done in oil. These include the series based on the courtyard outside her studio at Corfe Castle, of which the darkly dramatic *Courtyard in Wartime* (1944; University of Auckland Art Collection) is one important version. Another outstanding late oil is *Spanish Well, Purbeck* (1945; Auckland City Art Gallery). Both works combine a highly personal response to the idiosyncrasies of place with a freely inventive formal approach verging on abstraction. The rather more highly keyed colouring of *Spanish Well, Purbeck* links it with her last post-war works, ebullient gouaches such as *Cherry Tree at the Croft* (1946; private collection, Britain, repr. London 1990, pl.32), painted at the age of 77.

Frances Hodgkins's important late work was generally highly regarded in her lifetime: besides representation in the exhibitions cited above, she was favourably reviewed by the critics Eric Newton, Raymond Mortimer and John Piper; she was included in John Piper's *British Romantic Artists* (London, 1947), and Myfanwy Evans's *Frances Hodgkins* (Harmondsworth, 1948) in the Penguin Modern Painters series was underway before her death. But the subsequent evaluation of her art has been somewhat uneven: she is widely recognised in New Zealand as one of the country's most important expatriate artists, and a major retrospective was held there in 1969, followed by several smaller exhibitions. But little of substance, until recently, has been written on her work (see Buchanan, Eastmond and Dunn 1994). In common with some other women artists, her situation as an "exceptional" woman has resulted in a focus on her life (McCormick 1981) and, as a successful expatriate New Zealander, as an exemplar of the complexities associated with expatriatism (McCormick 1954). The publication of Linda Gill's *Letters of Frances Hodgkins* (1993) has provided further invaluable material for both biographical and art historical study on this artist. In Britain, while some small recent exhibitions have signalled renewed interest in Hodgkins, and while she is covered in Frances Spalding's *British Art since 1900* (1989), such exhibitions as *British Art in the 20th Century* at the Royal Academy (1987) and *A Paradise Lost: The Neo-Romantic Imagination in Britain, 1935–55* at the Barbican, London (1987), did not include her. Neither did such major feminist resources on women artists as Germaine Greer's *The Obstacle Race* (1979) and *Women Artists, 1550–1950*, the catalogue of an exhibition held at the Los Angeles County Museum of Art in 1976.

ELIZABETH EASTMOND

Hosmer, Harriet (Goodhue)
American sculptor, 1830–1908

Born in Watertown, Massachusetts, 9 October 1830; father a physician. Educated as a boarder at Mrs Charles Sedgwick's School for Girls in Lenox, Massachusetts, 1846–9. Had a private studio at the family home and studied under the Boston sculptor Peter Stephenson. Took lessons in anatomy at Missouri Medical College, St Louis, 1850. Lived in Rome, 1852–1900; pupil of John Gibson, the leading British sculptor there, 1852–c.1859; established own studio at 116 Via Margutta, early 1860s. Defended status as a professional sculptor with regard to her authorship of *Zenobia*, 1863–5. Production of sculpture declined from the 1880s; became involved in scientific experimentation. Close link with the feminist movement in USA, 1890s. Returned to her home town of Watertown, 1900. Member, Accademia, Rome, 1858. Died of pneumonia in Watertown, 1908.

Principal Exhibitions

Royal Academy, London: 1857
International Exhibition, London: 1862
New York, Boston and Chicago: 1864–5 (*Zenobia*, touring)
International Exhibition, Dublin: 1865
Colnaghi's Gallery, London: 1878
World's Columbian Exposition, Chicago: 1893
California Midwinter International Exposition, San Francisco: 1894

Selected Writings

Letter in *Art Journal*, new series, iii, 1 January 1864, p.27
"The process of sculpture", *Atlantic Monthly*, xiv, December 1864, pp.734–7
Harriet Hosmer: Letters and Memories, ed. Cornelia Crow Carr, New York: Moffat Yard, 1912

Bibliography

Elizabeth Fries Ellet, *Women Artists in All Ages and Countries*, New York: Harper, 1859
Lorado Taft, *The History of American Sculpture*, 3rd edition, New York: Macmillan, 1930
Van Wyck Brooks, *The Dream of Arcadia: American Artists and Writers in Italy, 1760–1915*, New York: Dutton, and London: Dent, 1958
The White Marmorean Flock: Nineteenth-Century American Women Neoclassical Sculptors, exh. cat., Vassar College Art Gallery, Poughkeepsie, 1972
Joseph Leo Curran, ed., *Harriet Goodhue Hosmer: Collected Sources*, 7 vols, 1974, Watertown Free Public Library Collection, Massachusetts, microfilm, Archives of American Art, Smithsonian Institution, Washington, DC
Andrea Hoffman, *Harriet Hosmer's Life and Work*, PhD dissertation, University of Southern California, Los Angeles, 1979
Barbara S. Groseclose, "Harriet Hosmer's tomb to Judith Falconnet: Death and the maiden", *American Art Journal*, xii, Spring 1980, pp.78–89
Alicia Faxon, "Images of women in the sculpture of Harriet Hosmer", *Woman's Art Journal*, ii/1, 1981, pp.25–9
Philipp P. Fehl, "A tomb in Rome by Harriet Hosmer: Notes on the rejection of gesture in the rhetoric of funerary art", *Ars auro prior: Studia Ioanni Białostocki sexagenerio dicata*, ed. Juliusz A. Chrościcki and others, Warsaw: Państwowe Wydawnictwo Naukowe, 1981, pp.639–49
Andrea Mariani, "Sleeping and waking fauns: Harriet Goodhue Hosmer's experience of Italy, 1852–1870", *The Italian Presence in American Art, 1760–1860*, ed. Irma Jaffe, New York: Fordham University Press, 1989, pp.66–81
Carol Zastoupil, "Creativity, inspiration and scandal: Harriet Hosmer and *Zenobia*", *ibid.*, pp.195–207
Joy S. Kasson, *Marble Queens and Captives: Women in Nineteenth-Century American Sculpture*, New Haven and London: Yale University Press, 1990
Charlotte Streifer Rubinstein, *American Women Sculptors*, Boston: Hall, 1990
Dolly Sherwood, *Harriet Hosmer: American Sculptor, 1830–1908*, Columbia: University of Missouri Press, 1991
Mara R. Witzling, ed., *Voicing Our Visions: Writings by Women Artists*, New York: Universe, 1991; London: Women's Press, 1992
The Lure of Italy: American Artists and the Italian Experience, 1760–1914, exh. cat., Museum of Fine Arts, Boston, 1992
Wendy Slatkin, *The Voices of Women Artists*, Englewood Cliffs, NJ: Prentice Hall, 1993

Harriet Hosmer's career as a sculptor is notable for her single-minded adherence to the classical ideal. Her first major works produced in the 1850s established her international reputation as a maker of ideal sculpture and gallery pieces. In the main these took up themes of women, noble in their suffering and differing from other interpretations of similar subjects in their dignity and chaste decorum. *Oeone* (c.1855), *Beatrice Cenci* (1853–7; both St Louis Mercantile Library) and *Zenobia, Queen of Palmyra* (1859; original untraced; reduced marble version, Wadsworth Atheneum, Hartford, CT) are major examples of her high style which was popular both with British and American patrons until the 1880s. Her oeuvre also included commissions for public sculpture, notably the statue of *Thomas Hart Benton* (1860–68; Lafayette Park, St Louis, MI), fountains and busts, as well as smaller-scale gallery pieces, such as the popular *Puck* (1856; Wadsworth Atheneum) and *Will-o'-the Wisp* (1858; Chrysler Museum, Norfolk, VA). Her sculpture for the tomb of *Judith Falconnet* (1857; Sant'Andrea delle Fratte, Rome) is a notable interpretation of the popular form of 19th-century church monument in which the deceased is shown as though sleeping. Hosmer's portrait statue conveys the fragility and the pathos of the subject with its references to 15th-century Italian tomb sculpture. When unveiled it was the only example of a church monument in Rome executed by an American sculptor. Hosmer's works were often reproduced in reduced form, including small replicas in terracotta, which were popular in America.

Unusually for a woman of her generation, Hosmer's education as a sculptor included anatomy lessons and the study of the life model. Her first lessons in sculpture, which began around 1849, were from Peter Stephenson and she also took modelling classes in Boston. At this time she worked from her own studio in the family home in Watertown. In her ambition to become a professional sculptor she was encouraged by the British actress Fanny Kemble, whom she had first met while at Mrs Sedgwick's school. In the autumn of 1850 her father (a doctor) asked the Boston Medical Society that Hosmer be allowed to study anatomy, a vital element in any sculptor's training. This request was refused, and as a result she left her home town in order to study under the direction of Dr Joseph Nash McDowell at the Missouri Medical College, St Louis. Evidence of her anatomical studies is found in surviving drawings. In St Louis she lived with her school friend Cornelia Crow Carr, who was later to become her biographer. Cornelia's father, Wayman

Crow, was to be one of Hosmer's first and most loyal patrons, subsidising her career by providing her with money after her father's financial crisis of 1854 seemed to threaten her attempts to establish her own sculptural practice in Rome. His financial support continued until his death in 1885.

Hosmer's lifelong adherence to the Neo-classical idiom was first fostered by the sculptor John Gibson, whose promotion of this "true" and "correct" style continued while many of his British contemporaries were moving towards a more natural interpretation of the human form. For a period of some seven years dating from 1852, when she was admitted as a pupil in his Via Fontanella studio in Rome, she gained technical expertise in modelling and carving under his direction, as well as being able to pursue her own study of ancient sculpture at first hand. This continuing close attention to canonical works from antiquity is most overt in a work such as the *Sleeping Faun* (1865; Forbes Collection, New York). This modern interpretation of the Barberini *Faun* was shown at the Dublin International Exhibition of 1865, where it excited positive critical responses, some of which pointed to connections with Nathaniel Hawthorne's novel *The Marble Faun* (1860).

Hosmer's natural talent and her passionate enthusiasm for sculpture were nurtured by Gibson who promoted her career well beyond any training in sculptural method. He introduced her to influential figures in the art world and was responsible for showing some of her early sketch models to Christian Rauch. (He had earlier helped Mary Thornycroft, q.v., by recommending her to Queen Victoria.) In Gibson's studio Hosmer was able to study from the life model, which she relished. Her interest in studying the human form at first hand included taking casts from the entire body of a woman model. In July 1854 her compatriot, the sculptor Thomas Crawford, reacted to the inappropriateness of such study, primarily on the grounds of gender: "Miss H[osmer's] want of modesty is enough to disgust a dog" (cited in Sherwood 1991, p.346, note 18).

Hosmer's lack of feminine decorum reaped its rewards. Her sculpture shows control of the medium as well as an in-depth knowledge of the human form. In her sculpture, although she was interested in decorative and poetic elements, she was never distracted by the minutiae of surface detail. She always reduced this to a minimum in order to create an overall harmony through the use of expressive contour. She maintained her preference for the calm grandeur and noble simplicity of the Neo-classical ideal throughout her career and, later in life, she openly criticised the naturalism evident in much late 19th-century sculpture. She is thought to have "tinted" some of her sculptures, following the example of Gibson. The *Sleeping Faun* and *Zenobia* both had a discreet, creamy, fleshlike tint, less overtly stated than in Gibson's polychromed works.

Hosmer's reputation as a professional sculptor came under public scrutiny in 1863 with the questioning of her authorship of *Zenobia*, the 2.43-metre-high statue that had been a major success at the London International Exhibition of 1862 and subsequently toured to New York, Boston and Chicago. The mostly positive critical response to *Zenobia* and the popularity of copies and reductions of the work, including that in Parian ware, confirm that she was establishing her professional status in Europe and America. A defamatory challenge to this was first raised publicly in the *Art Journal* (new series, II, 1 September 1863, p.181) and *The Queen*. At this time Hosmer was in the process of setting up her own studio at 116 Via Margutta, where in future years she was to employ up to 24 studio assistants. She responded to the accusation that *Zenobia* was the work of her assistants in a letter to the *Art Journal* (1864). This provides important details of Hosmer's working methods on this statue, not least that she spent eight months perfecting the half-size clay model before it was transferred to marble. In her claims to authorship she was backed by Gibson, William Wetmore Story and Hiram Powers. She then published a detailed account of her working practice in "The process of sculpture" (1864), which demonstrates that her working methods were similar to those then employed by the majority of sculptors. Like them she concentrated most upon the creation of the original model, leaving the transfer and working of the marble to her studio assistants. In this sense the accusations against her had some foundation, but applied equally to the established studio practices of her contemporaries. Hosmer used her article as publicity for her case when *Zenobia* was exhibited in New York and Boston. She remained convinced that the attack upon her was prompted by her gender, and there is evidence that this was partly the case. She identified her fellow American sculptor Joseph Mozier as the perpetrator of the slander against her and was

supported in her position by Gibson, Story and Powers. Later she was to support Vinnie Ream, who in 1871 was similarly accused of over-reliance upon studio assistants in her sculpture. In 1874 she also became peripherally involved in retaliating to a more general attack – raised by Stephen Weston Healy – relating to the authenticity of sculpture emanating from Italian studios at that time. In the 1860s her reputation was further enhanced by the success of her bronze statue of *Thomas Hart Benton*, unveiled in 1868. A portrait statue of *Maria Sophia, Queen of Naples*, exiled to Rome after the fall of Gaeta, was another major commission on which she was working around 1868–9, all visual records of which are now lost. In many ways this work seems to have formed the modern counterpart to the heroism encapsulated in the figure of *Zenobia*.

In the early years in Rome Hosmer attracted a circle of men and women who were involved in the arts. From 1853 she developed a close friendship with Elizabeth Barrett Browning and Robert Browning, making a life cast of their joined hands (1853). The friendship with Robert waned after Elizabeth's death in 1861. Sophia and Nathaniel Hawthorn were other acquaintances and she also formed a lifelong friendship with Frederic Leighton. Her aristocratic British patrons included Lady Marian Alford and Lady Louisa Ashburton.

Hosmer became identified with the women's rights movement in later life as an example of a successful woman with a professional practice and international reputation. She supported women's suffrage and was particularly closely connected with the feminist movement in Chicago during the early 1890s. She was commissioned to execute a statue of *Queen Isabella of Castile* by the Daughters of Isabella, a Chicago suffragist group, but opposed the placement of her (plaster?) statue in the Woman's Building of the World's Columbian Exposition, preferring instead that it be located outside the California Pavilion (Sherwood 1991, p.325; repr. p.326). A version of the statue (destroyed *c*.1906) was exhibited at the California Midwinter Exposition in 1894. *Queen Isabella* shows the extent to which Hosmer absorbed the more decorative and imaginative surface prevalent in *fin-de-siècle* sculpture by the end of her career. Her last years were spent in scientific investigations. She returned to her home town in 1900, remaining there until her death.

ALISON YARRINGTON

J

Jellett, Mainie
Irish painter, 1897–1944

Born Mary Harriet Jellett in Dublin, 20 April 1897. Enrolled at the Metropolitan School of Art, Dublin, 1915. Studied under Walter Sickert at the Westminster School of Art, London, 1917–19. Awarded two prizes in Dublin, enabling her to study in Paris; joined Evie Hone at Académie Lhôte, then studied with Hone in the studio of Albert Gleizes, 1921–2; again in Paris, winter 1922–3. Lived in Dublin from 1923, but visited Gleizes each summer in France until 1932. Visited the Baltic States and Germany, 1931; Amsterdam, 1933. Member, Society of Dublin Painters, 1920; founder-member, Abstraction-Création group, Paris, 1931; associate member, White Stag Group, 1940. First Chair, Irish Exhibition of Living Art, 1943. Died in Dublin, February 1944.

Principal Exhibitions

Individual
Mills Hall, Dublin: 1920 (with Lilian Davidson)
Dublin Painters' Gallery, Dublin: 1924 (with Evie Hone), 1925, 1926, 1927, 1928, 1929, 1931, 1933, 1935, 1937, 1939, 1941, 1944 (retrospective)
Waddington Gallery, Dublin: 1944 (retrospective)

Group
Royal Hibernian Academy: 1918–21, 1930–37
Salon des Indépendants, Paris: 1922
Society of Dublin Painters: from 1923
L'Art d'Aujourd'hui, Paris: 1925
London Group, London: 1925–6
Seven and Five Society, London: 1926
Palais des Beaux-Arts, Brussels: 1930 (*L'Art irlandais*)
Salon des Surindépendants, Paris: 1930–38
Abstraction-Création, Paris: 1931–6
New York World's Fair: 1939
Contemporary Picture Galleries, Dublin: 1940 (*Académie Lhôte Irish Students*), 1943 (*Watercolours*)

Selected Writings
"An approach to painting", *Irish Art Handbook*, Dublin: Cahill, 1943, pp.17–18
The Artist's Vision: Lectures and Essays on Art, ed. Eileen MacCarvill, Dundalk: Dundalgan Press, 1959

Bibliography
James White, "The art of Mainie Jellett", *The Studio*, cxxix, 1945, pp.192–3
Stella Frost, ed., *A Tribute to Evie Hone and Mainie Jellett*, Dublin: Browne and Nolan, 1957
Mainie Jellett, 1897–1944: A Retrospective Exhibition of Paintings and Drawings, exh. cat., Municipal Gallery, Dublin, 1962
Mainie Jellett, 1897–1944, Neptune Gallery, Dublin, 1974
Irish Art, 1900–50, exh. cat., Municipal Art Gallery, Crawford, 1975
Abstraction-Création, 1931–1936, exh. cat., Westfälisches Landesmuseum für Kunst und Kulturgeschichte, Münster, and elsewhere, 1978
Mainie Jellett: Abstracts, exh. cat., Neptune Gallery, Dublin, 1980
Irish Women Artists from the Eighteenth Century to the Present Day, exh. cat., National Gallery of Ireland, Dublin, and elsewhere, 1987
S.B. Kennedy, *Irish Art and Modernism, 1880–1950*, Belfast: Institute of Irish Studies, 1991
Bruce Arnold, *Mainie Jellett and the Modern Movement in Ireland*, New Haven and London: Yale University Press, 1991
Mainie Jellett, exh. cat., Irish Museum of Modern Art, Dublin, 1991

Mainie Jellett is the leading modernist Irish painter of the 20th century, and a significant figure in the international movement of pure abstract art that was led by the French painter Albert Gleizes. She worked closely with Gleizes during the crucial years of 1921–4, during which he formulated his principles and ideas on pure abstract painting and wrote his seminal works on the subject. She remained in close contact with him thereafter, and with others associated with the movement, including Robert and Sonia Delaunay (q.v.), Robert Pouyaud and her compatriot Evie Hone. But in 1923 she returned to Dublin, exhibiting her first pure abstract works, and followed this in 1924 with a solo exhibition of abstract painting, provoking an artistic controversy that pushed her to the forefront of the modern movement in Ireland. She led it, and was its most outspoken proponent from then until her death. She influenced many younger artists, and she taught painting, but she did not develop any school of abstraction, though she lectured widely on the subject.

Jellett's work went through several stages of development. Her background was the conventional one of the eldest child in a prominent Unionist and Protestant family in Dublin. Her ancestors, on both sides of the family, had distinguished forebears tracing their involvement in Dublin life back to the 17th century. Her father, a successful barrister, was also a Unionist Member of Parliament, representing Trinity College. She was given an education entirely at home, and was a remarkably gifted musician. She was a pupil, in her childhood, of Elizabeth Yeats, the sister of the painter Jack Yeats and the writer W.B. Yeats. She studied at art school in Dublin, and briefly under William Orpen, before going to London, where she became a star pupil of Walter Sickert. She was, and is, much admired for her drawings, watercolours and oils in his manner. She was the leading figure of her time at the Westminster School, and won the Taylor and other prizes in Dublin after her return.

In 1920 she went to Paris, and was a pupil of André Lhôte for almost a year, producing a surprisingly large body of Cubist work, including landscapes, nudes and classical studies based on Poussin and other artists. Towards the end of the following year she and Evie Hone called on Albert Gleizes and, against his will – which was not strong – persuaded him that they had to become pupils. The association led to regular visits to France from Dublin, and direct involvement in the Gleizes-inspired experiment in artistic commune-living, at Moly Sabata in the 1930s. But both women were dedicated to their own city of Dublin and to the development of modern methods and beliefs among Irish artists. Jellett was successful in this. Ten years before Ben Nicholson introduced abstraction to an English public, Jellett had established a following for such work in Dublin, and had steadily developed

the theories of "translation" and "rotation" and the later theories of colour in abstract art that were central to the methods of the followers of Gleizes. They have since become fundamental to abstract theory, and are widely and increasingly recognised for their central importance in 20th-century art.

Jellett was a founder-member of Abstraction-Création, and exhibited in a number of European cities with other modernist painters, as well as being represented in the early shows of that movement. There were notable stylistic developments during the 1920s. Her earliest abstract works had great simplicity and purity, leading to comparisons with Juan Gris and the Delaunays. A more decorative style followed, and dominated her earliest public exhibitions in Dublin, which began after her return to the city in 1923, and continued, usually at two-year intervals, throughout the 1920s and 1930s. Greater expression of rational and structured composition is evident in her paintings into the 1930s, and in 1936 she moved towards a form of semi-abstract realism and produced a succession of great canvases on religious themes, including several Pietàs, Crucifixions, and representations of the Virgin and of Christ on the Cross. It is difficult to cite individual works by name, since she eschewed titles and often used only such words as Abstract Study or Abstract Painting. But the *Ninth Hour* (1941; Hugh Lane Municipal Gallery of Modern Art, Dublin) and *Madonna of Spring* (1939; private collection, Ireland, repr. Arnold 1991, fig.224) are notable examples of the later manner.

Jellett befriended many refugee artists at the beginning of World War II, and became an increasingly influential figure during the war years, when artistic life flourished in neutral Ireland. She was associated with one of the dominant groups of the period, the White Stag Group, and in 1943 she was a leading activist in setting up the Irish Exhibition of Living Art, a modernist forum that quickly became the main rival to the academic school of the Royal Hibernian Academy. In the autumn of that year she contracted cancer of the pancreas, and died early in 1944. A full retrospective was not held until 1962. There were several shows of her work put on in Dublin in the 1960s and 1970s by a private gallery, and in 1991 a major solo exhibition was held at the Irish Museum of Modern Art.

Mainie Jellett is widely regarded as the leading Irish woman artist of the 20th century, if not of all centuries. Her command of colour and composition is outstanding. Her courage, in facing early indifference and then the ignorant disdain of critics in Dublin, paid off handsomely, and largely through the strong support and encouragement of other women, including both painters and women working in other fields of art. She had a natural sympathy with all the arts, and believed in their collective promotion and in the common bond of understanding required by the theory and practice of modernist beliefs.

BRUCE ARNOLD

John, Gwen [fig. 34]
British painter, 1876–1939

Born Gwendolen Mary John in Haverfordwest, Wales, 22 June 1876; older sister of the painter Augustus John. Grew up in Tenby, Wales, from 1884. Studied at Slade School of Fine Art, London, under Frederick Brown and Henry Tonks, 1895–8 (won Melvill Nettleship prize, 1897); Académie Carmen, Paris, under James McNeill Whistler, 1898–9. Lived in London, 1899–1903; Paris 1904–11 (worked as artist's model); Meudon, near Paris, 1911–39. Converted to Catholicism, 1913. Died in Dieppe, France, 18 September 1939.

Principal Exhibitions
New English Art Club, London: 1900–03, 1908–11
Carfax & Co., London: 1903 (with Augustus John)
International Exhibition of Modern Art, "Armory Show", New York: 1913
Penguin Club, New York: 1918
Salon d'Automne, Paris: 1919–20, 1923
Société Nationale des Beaux-Arts, Paris: 1920, 1924–5
Paris Salon: 1920
Sculptors Gallery, New York: 1922
Salon des Tuileries, Paris: 1924
New Chenil Galleries, London: 1926 (individual)
Art Center, New York: 1926 (*Representative Works Selected from the John Quinn Collection*)
Carnegie Institute, Pittsburgh: 1930
Deffett Francis Art Gallery, Swansea: 1935
National Eisteddfod, Fishguard: 1936
Matthiesen Ltd, London: 1946 (retrospective)
Arts Council of Great Britain, London: 1946 (touring retrospective)

Bibliography
Anthony Bertram, "The Johns", *Saturday Review*, cxli, 5 June 1926, pp.676–7

M. Chamot, "Gwen and Augustus John", *Country Life*, lix, 5 June 1926, pp.771–3
——, "An undiscovered artist: Gwen John", *ibid*, 19 June 1926, pp.884–5
William Rothenstein, *Men and Memories: Recollections of William Rothenstein*, 3 vols, London: Faber, 1931–9; New York: Coward McCann, 1931–40; revised edition, ed. Mary Lago, Columbia: University of Missouri Press, 1978
Augustus John, "Gwendolen John", *Burlington Magazine*, lxxxi, 1942, pp.236–40
Gwen John Memorial Exhibition, exh. cat., Matthiesen Ltd, London, 1946
Gwen John, exh. cat., Arts Council of Great Britain, London, 1946
Wyndham Lewis, "The art of Gwen John", *The Listener*, xxxvi, 1946, p.484
Denys Sutton, "Gwen John", *Country Life*, c, 25 October 1946, p.762
J. Wood Palmer, "Gwen John", *The Studio*, cxxxiv, 1947, pp.138–9
Augustus John, *Chiaroscuro: Fragments of Autobiography: First Series*, London: Cape, 1952
Ethel Walker, Frances Hodgkins, Gwen John: A Memorial Exhibition, exh. cat., Tate Gallery, London, 1952
J. Wood Palmer, "Gwen John", *Connoisseur*, cli, October 1962, pp.88–92
Jacques Maritain, *Carnet des notes*, Paris: De Brouwer, 1965
Gwen John: A Retrospective Exhibition, exh. cat., Arts Council of Great Britain, London, 1968
B.L. Reid, *The Man from New York: John Quinn and His Friends*, New York: Oxford University Press, 1968
Annela Twitchin, *Gwen John: Her Art and Her Religion*, MA thesis, Courtauld Institute of Art, University of London, 1972
Gwen John: A Retrospective Exhibition, exh. cat., Davis & Long Co., New York, 1975
Raïssa Maritain, *Raïssa's Journal*, ed. Jacques Maritain, Albany, NY: Magi, 1975
Michael Holroyd, *Augustus John*, 2 vols, 2nd edition, London: Penguin, 1976
Richard Shone, "Gwen John at Anthony d'Offay", *Burlington Magazine*, cxviii, 1976, pp.175–6
Christopher Neve, "In empty rooms: Gwen John (1876–1939)", *Country Life*, clix, 11 March 1976, pp.620–21
"The Noble Buyer": John Quinn: Patron of the Avant-Garde, exh. cat., Hirshhorn Museum and Sculpture Garden, Washington, DC, 1978
Susan Chitty, *Gwen John, 1876–1939*, London: Hodder and Stoughton, 1981
Gwen John, exh. cat., Anthony d'Offay, London, 1982
Gwen John: Paintings and Drawings from the Collection of John Quinn and Others, exh. cat., Stanford University Museum of Art, CA, 1982

Sara John, "Shades of meaning: Gwen John (1876–1939)", *Country Life*, clxxii, 12 August 1982, pp.462–4

A Very Private View, film, BBC Wales, 25 April 1984 (repeat), written and produced by Herbert Williams

Journey into the Shadows: A Portrait of Gwen John, 1876–1939, film, BBC2, 27 May 1984, written by Elaine Morgan, produced and directed by Anna Benson-Gyles

Cecily Langdale and David Fraser Jenkins, *Gwen John: An Interior Life*, Oxford: Phaidon, 1985; New York: Rizzoli, 1986

Mary Taubman, *Gwen John: The Artist and Her Work*, London: Scolar Press, and Ithaca, NY: Cornell University Press, 1985

Cecily Langdale, *Gwen John: With a Catalogue Raisonné of the Paintings and a Selection of the Drawings*, New Haven and London: Yale University Press, 1987

Ceridwen Lloyd-Morgan, *Gwen John Papers at the National Library of Wales*, Aberystwyth: National Library of Wales, 1988

Alicia Foster, "She shopped at the Bon Marché", *Women's Art Magazine*, no.65, July–August 1995, pp.10–14

Gwen John Papers are in the National Library of Wales, Aberystwyth; her correspondence with John Quinn is in the John Quinn Collection, New York Public Library; her letters to Auguste Rodin are in the Musée Rodin, Paris.

Gwen John did fewer than 200 paintings, and some several thousand drawings. From first to last, her pictures appear modest and unassuming. The pictures are invariably muted in palette, small in size and restrained in mood. The repertoire of subject matter is extremely limited: an impassive woman or girl; small groups of children and nuns viewed from behind; the occasional austere interior or still-life arrangement; an infrequent landscape. None the less, they evoke from the viewer a powerful emotional response out of all proportion to their reticence.

Again and again John's art is described as "reticent", "private", "quiet". She herself wrote: "As to whether I have anything worth expressing ... I may never have anything to express except this desire for a more interior life" (letter of 4 September 1912(?) to Ursula Tyrwhitt). The viewer is drawn into that interior life, into an intensely private communion with the artist. Because of the intimacy of that communion, one forgets how public her art has become. More than a third of John's paintings are now in public collections; more than 1000 of her drawings belong to the National Museum of Wales in Cardiff; most of her letters and papers are preserved in various public collections. Her following is large and passionately devoted to her art. Once known primarily as the sister of the celebrated painter and flamboyant personality Augustus John, Gwen John is now widely recognised as one of the most important British artists of the 20th century. Augustus's own prophecy, "Fifty years after my death I shall be remembered as Gwen John's brother" (Holroyd 1976, p.61), has been fulfilled.

To understand John's art, one must remember that she was Anglo-French. Brought up in Wales, she lived in London until the age of 27. She then went to France, where she lived until her death 36 years later. She consciously distanced herself from her family and background, returning to Britain only very rarely, declaring it "quite a foreign country" (letter postmarked 3 December 1914 to Ursula Tyrwhitt). Nevertheless, her art always retained certain British traits. Its tonalism and intimist subject matter are legacies of her Slade School training and New English Art Club associations, while the patterned brushwork, dry surfaces and subdued colour of her mature paintings recall the work of such Camden Town contemporaries as Walter Sickert, Frederick Spencer Gore, Malcolm Drummond and Robert Bevan. Yet John had a vivid appreciation of avant-garde Parisian art and was by no means untouched by her French experience; her mature work also shows hints of affinities with Cézanne, Modigliani, Picasso, Puvis de Chavannes and Rouault, among others.

John's instruction at the Slade School was in the academic tradition; her teachers there, Frederick Brown and Henry Tonks, painted somewhat Victorian intimist views. James McNeill Whistler, her teacher during her brief studies at the Académie Carmen in Paris, commented that her work had "a fine sense of *tone*" (John 1952, p.48). Her first mature oil compositions reflect this training. The portrait of *Mrs Atkinson* (Metropolitan Museum of Art, New York), *Landscape at Tenby, with Figures* (private collection, USA, repr. Langdale 1987, pl.6) and *Interior with Figures* (National Gallery of Victoria, Melbourne) are carefully executed tonal paintings of rather detailed genre subjects.

After the Académie Carmen, the artist returned to London for several years of "subterranean life" (Augustus John, "Introduction", London, Arts Council, 1946, p.7). In 1904 she left Britain permanently for an independent and comparatively isolated existence in Paris. Living in a series of modest Montparnasse rooms, she painted, supporting herself by working as an artist's model. It was then that she met the great sculptor Auguste Rodin, for whom she posed, and with whom she immediately fell profoundly in love. Like her pictures, John herself appeared self-effacing; but her quiet exterior hid enormous passion, a passion she fixed upon Rodin obsessively for nearly a decade. Although she now complained that "everything interests me more than painting" (letter of 4 February (1910?) to Ursula Tyrwhitt), she did continue to work, and some of her best-known paintings date from this period. They include *La Chambre sur la cour* (collection of Mr and Mrs Paul Mellon, repr. Langdale 1987, pl.47), *A Corner of the Artist's Room in Paris* (Sheffield City Art Galleries) and *Girl Reading at the Window* (Museum of Modern Art, New York), all meticulously rendered interiors still in the Slade tradition. In two other paintings, both monochromatic and both entitled *Woman Sewing* (both private collection, *ibid.*, pls 57 and 184), the emaciated, stylised figures clearly reveal a familiarity with Picasso's Blue Period pictures. Equally celebrated are certain drawings of this time: her watercolours of a tortoiseshell cat (e.g. *Cat*; Tate Gallery, London) and her eloquent and assured pencil and wash drawings of Chloë Boughton-Leigh (e.g. *Bust of a Woman*; Albright-Knox Art Gallery, Buffalo, NY), and of "a lady" (e.g. *Portrait of a Lady*; Borough of Thamesdown-Swindon Permanent Art Collection). The ease and spontaneity of these sheets are reminiscent of Rodin's drawings of much the same time.

During the early 1910s several significant changes occurred in John's life. Her obsession with Rodin waned, freeing her to turn more fully to her art. In 1910 she met John Quinn, the distinguished American lawyer and collector. Their relationship endured until his death in 1924, and precisely paralleled her time of greatest artistic productivity, a productivity due in no small part to his influence. Quinn became her patron and most enthusiastic supporter. He ultimately acquired about a dozen of her paintings, and numerous drawings. His provision of a stipend gave her a modest financial security; his attention and encouragement stimulated her to work.

In 1911 John moved to the Paris suburb of Meudon (where Rodin also lived), where she was to stay for the rest of her life. Her studio at 29 rue Terre Neuve is the subject of a number of paintings, including *Interior, Rue Terre Neuve* (Manchester City Art Galleries). As her relationship with Rodin diminished, she found comfort in religion, and was received into the Catholic Church in early 1913. She spent considerable time in the local church, where she saw the children and nuns who appear in hundreds of her watercolours (e.g. *Nun with a Group of Orphans*; collection of Mr and Mrs Paul Mellon, *ibid.*, pl.83). For those Dominican nuns, she did a famous series of paintings of their order's founder (e.g. *Mère Poussepin*; Southampton Art Gallery).

By the end of the decade, John's style had reached full maturity. Most of her paintings are of female sitters, usually anonymous, most often of the woman known as "the convalescent" (e.g. *Young Woman Holding a Black Cat*, Tate Gallery; *Seated Girl Holding a Piece of Sewing*, Aberdeen Art Gallery and Museums). For the artist, the model was not of interest as an individual, but as "an affair of volumes" (undated letter of 1936 to Ursula Tyrwhitt). These paintings are rigorously edited: detail is suppressed both in the monumental, impassive figure and in the background. Surfaces are chalky and opaque; pigment is applied in small rhythmic strokes to a thinly primed canvas; and the predominantly cool-grey palette and range of tonal values are severely limited. John's often-expressed admiration for Cézanne is evident in these pictures; the compositions and proportions of the figures – small heads set on massive, pyramidal bodies – are akin to those in his late portraits. Also from this time is a series of eleven paintings of a convalescent (e.g. *Convalescent*, Tate Gallery; *The Letter*, Manchester City Art Galleries), which exemplify a curious feature of John's art: the repetition again and again of a composition with very little change indeed. Although not evident to the viewer, presumably a process of refinement was occurring for the artist; the repetition is surely also an expression of the obsessiveness that was such a notable attribute of John's character.

After about 1923 John's paintings change subtly but distinctly. They are still usually portraits of women in simple interiors, but the palette, proportions and silhouettes change. Paint application is bolder and more vigorous; the palette is more varied, with a new mauvish cast; and there are stronger contrasts between light and dark. Forms are now sometimes reduced to flat patterned passages. The figures are more slender, their silhouettes more irregular, their features more stylised (e.g. *Girl with a Blue Scarf*; Museum of Modern Art, New York). There is a resemblance to the women in Modigliani's portraits of the late 1910s: the proportions and simple poses are similar; the sitters' eccentric features (for which Modigliani was indebted to African masks) are strikingly alike.

Of John's drawings, among the most moving are a group of charcoal and wash studies of children done during the late 1910s (e.g. *Elisabeth de Willman Grabowska*; Victoria and Albert Museum, London). They are clearly done from life, and the draughtsmanship is fluid and economical. The same sitters appear repeatedly, but always in slightly altered poses; this is the one area of her mature work in which there are no repetitions.

From the early 1910s until the end of her working life most of John's watercolours are of women and children in church. These intimate, reticent studies typically show figures seen from the rear, and their setting is summarily indicated by an occasional prie-dieu. Compositions are repeated again and again, sometimes with alterations in palette or size. The earlier watercolours tend to be muted and translucent (e.g. *Seated Woman*; Stanford University Museum of Art, CA); the later ones are increasingly colourful and opaque (e.g. *A Girl Wearing a Hat and Coat with a Fur Collar, Seated in Church*; National Museum of Wales, Cardiff).

The portrait of *Miss Bridget Sarah Bishop* (1929; Johannesburg Art Gallery) is John's last known finished oil, but she continued to work in watercolour and gouache for several more years. Her last works on paper are opaque, brightly coloured and increasingly abstract; these stylised decorative images (e.g. *Seated Girl Holding a Child*; private collection, *ibid.*, pl.377) have real similarities to the art of Chagall and Rouault. She also made vast numbers of tiny ink sketches, often a dozen to a page; these nervous, angular drawings seem almost like unconscious jottings. There is no evidence that she did anything at all after about 1933.

Quinn's death in 1924 broke John's strongest connection to the art world, and in her later years she became increasingly solitary. She did maintain certain old friendships, and she formed one final passionate attachment to Véra Oumancoff, sister-in-law of the eminent neo-Thomist philosopher Jacques Maritain, and her neighbour in Meudon. This attachment was entirely one-sided, and was ended by Véra around 1930, when she found the artist's attentions unbearable. John's last decade was marked by growing self-neglect. A visitor in 1937 described her as living "like a feminine St Gerome" (letter of 6 May 1946 from Maynard Walker to Edwin John), and her niece believed that she "gave up ... (it) may have been her unconscious that was trying to get her to die" (Vivien John in *A Very Private View* 1984). In September 1939 John drew up her will before travelling to Dieppe where she died eight days later, at the age of 63.

The idea that before her final years John lived in isolation is a mistaken one. Rodin, John Quinn, Rainer Maria Rilke and Arthur Symons were all close friends; and at one time or another she also met Picasso, Braque, Wyndham Lewis, Brancusi, de Segonzac, Ezra Pound, Lady Gregory, Maud Gonne and Henri-Pierre Roche. Nor did she refuse to exhibit or sell her work. Although she had only one large exhibition during her lifetime, in London at the New Chenil Galleries in 1926 (a show that was notably well received), she showed in London from 1900 until before World War I, once at Carfax & Co. and a number of times at the New English Art Club. In 1913 she was included in the famous "Armory Show" in New York. After the war, until 1924, she exhibited repeatedly at various Paris salons. Her pictures received considerable attention and were frequently sold out at these shows. In 1919 *Nude Girl* (Tate Gallery) became the first of John's pictures to enter a public collection. By 1930 there were several works at the Tate, several at the City of Manchester Art Galleries and others at the Whitworth Art Gallery, University of Manchester; Hugh Lane Municipal Gallery of Modern Art, Dublin; Albright-Knox Art Gallery, Buffalo, New York; and the Art Institute of Chicago. The first major exhibition after her death was a retrospective at Matthiesen in London; since that time her reputation has steadily grown, and she is now one of the most profoundly admired of all British artists.

Gwen John is a particular feminist heroine. It must be said, however, that she was probably far less constrained by her gender than most women of her generation or, indeed, later. It is true that, as a girl, she was kept at home while her younger brother was allowed to attend a Tenby art school, but from the time she entered the Slade she lived as independently as she wished. Because of her unhappy relationship with Rodin, she is often viewed as a victim, but in fact she was ruthlessly self-willed. She once said: "I think if we are to do beautiful pictures we ought to be free from family conventions & ties ... I think the family has had its day. We don't go to Heaven in families now but one by one" (undated letter of about 1910 to Ursula Tyrwhitt), and she lived by that belief.

CECILY LANGDALE

Johnston, Frances Benjamin [fig. 33]
American photographer, 1864–1952

Born in Grafton, West Virginia, 15 January 1864. Graduated from Notre Dame of Maryland Collegiate Division, Govanston, 1883; studied art at Académie Julian, Paris, 1883–5; Art Students League, Washington, DC, 1885–8; studied photography under Thomas William Smillie, Smithsonian Institution Division of Photography, Washington, DC, 1890. Opened professional studio in Washington, 1890; specialised in documentary work and portraiture of political and society celebrities. Served as member of jury for Philadelphia Photographic Society annual exhibition, 1899. Championed photography as a career for women. Organised exhibition of prints by 28 American women photographers for the Exposition Universelle, Paris, 1900; the display was also seen in St Petersburg and Moscow (autumn 1900) and at the Photo Club of Paris (1901). Received first architectural commission to photograph the New Theatre, New York, 1909. Studio on Fifth Avenue, New York, with Mattie Edwards Hewitt, 1913–17; specialised in architectural commissions. Took photographs of gardens and estates from 1917. Received seven consecutive grants from the Carnegie Corporation to photograph American colonial architecture in nine southern states, 1933–40. Moved to New Orleans, 1940. Associate member, Photo-Secession, 1904; member, New York Camera Club; honorary member, American Institute of Architects, 1945. Donated prints, negatives and correspondence to Library of Congress, 1947. Died in New Orleans, 1952.

Principal Exhibitions
New York Camera Club: 1898
Exposition Universelle, Paris: 1900 (gold medal)

Library of Congress, Washington, DC: 1929, 1947 (both individual)

Selected Writings
"What a woman can do with a camera", *Ladies Home Journal*, September 1897, pp.6–7
"The foremost women photographers in America", *Ladies Home Journal*, May 1901–January 1902 (series of seven articles)

Bibliography
Mammoth Cave by Flash-Light, Washington, DC: Gibson, 1893
The White House, Washington, DC: Gibson, 1893
Jaun Abel, "Women photographers and their work", *Delineator*, October 1901, pp.574–9
Henry Irving Brock, *Colonial Churches in Virginia*, Richmond: Dale Press, 1930; reprinted Port Washington, NY: Kennikat Press, 1972 (photographs)
Thomas Tileston Waterman, *The Early Architecture of North Carolina: A Pictorial Survey*, Chapel Hill: University of North Carolina Press, 1941
Samuel Gaillard Stoney, *Plantations of the Carolina Low Country*, Charleston, SC: Carolina Art Association, 1945
Paul Vanderbilt, "Frances Benjamin Johnston, 1864–1952", *Journal of American Institute of Architects*, xviii, 1952, pp.224–8
Frederick Doveton Nichols, *The Early Architecture of Georgia*, Chapel Hill: University of North Carolina Press, 1957
Lincoln Kirstein, ed., *The Hampton Album: 44 Photographs from an Album of Hampton Institute*, New York: Museum of Modern Art, 1966
Pete Daniel and Raymond Smock, *A Talent for Detail: The Photographs of Miss Frances Benjamin Johnston, 1889–1910*, New York: Harmony, 1974
Frances Benjamin Johnston: Women of Class and Station, exh. cat., University Art Museum and Galleries, California State University, Long Beach, 1979
Toby Quitslund, "Her feminine colleagues: Photographs and letters collected by Frances Benjamin Johnston in 1900", *Women Artists in Washington Collections*, exh. cat., University of Maryland Art Gallery, College Park, 1979
Amy S. Doherty, "Frances Benjamin Johnston, 1864–1952", *History of Photography*, iv, 1980, pp.97–111
Frances Benjamin Johnston: What a Woman Can Do with a Camera, exh. cat., Impressions Gallery of Photography, York, 1984
C. Jane Gover, *The Positive Image: Women Photographers in Turn of the Century America*, Albany: State University of New York Press, 1988
Lamia Doumato, *Frances Benjamin Johnston, Architectural Photographer: A Bibliography*, Monticello, IL: Vance, 1990

Dolores Mitchell, "The 'new woman' as Prometheus: Women artists depict women smoking", *Woman's Art Journal*, xii/1, 1991, pp.3–9

Naomi Rosenblum, *A History of Women Photographers*, London and New York: Abbeville, 1994

Frances Benjamin Johnston is best known for her documentary photographs of the American Scene of the turn of the century, but she also earned renown for her portraits, landscapes and architectural work. An advocate of photography as a career for women of her generation, Johnston wrote articles for the *Ladies Home Journal* in which she offered practical advice and encouragement to novices ("What a woman can do with a camera") and highlighted and promoted the work of prominent women colleagues both by writing about them ("The foremost women photographers in America") and by organising an important exhibition of their prints as part of the US Government exhibit for the Paris Exposition Universelle of 1900.

Like many women photographers, Johnston began as a student of drawing and painting, at the Académie Julian in Paris and at the Art Students League of Washington, DC (later part of the Corcoran Gallery School). She planned to become an illustrator, but after briefly working in that career, realised that the photograph would soon replace illustration in newspapers and magazines, and decided to become a professional photographer. She learned her craft as an apprentice to commercial photographers and later to Thomas William Smillie, head of the Division of Photography at the Smithsonian Institution. She later admitted candidly: "I entered upon my new vocation with an ignorance of photography that was as dense as my self-confidence was unbounded" (Long Beach 1979, p.11). Johnston "seems to have enjoyed immediate success, artistically and financially" (Kirstein 1966, p.53). Social position, family connections and parental encouragement no doubt helped. Her father worked for the US Treasury Department, she was distantly related to Frances Folsom, the wife of President Grover Cleveland, and her parents not only built a studio for her located – with Victorian propriety – in the rose garden behind their Washington home, but also helped to manage her business correspondence as well as supervise the work of her darkroom assistant (Gover 1988, p.38).

Johnston set high professional standards for herself and had an independent spirit: "I've learned not to depend on the Lord, I'll make the changes myself" (Daniel and Smock 1974, p.34), which enabled her to accept several daunting assignments requiring not only an adventurous nature but also physical stamina. Johnston was to photography what Ida Tarbell was to reference journalism. For *Demorest's Family Magazine* (March 1892), she did photographic essays of Pennsylvania coalfields, which entailed going down into mineshafts with heavy photographic equipment. She also gamely photographed America's natural wonders: *Mammoth Cave by Flashlight* (1892) and *Yellowstone by Stagecoach* (1903; both Library of Congress, Washington, DC). Writing the accompanying explanatory text, Johnston did several notable series focusing on American workers: in the United States Mint in Philadelphia; in the Bureau of engraving and printing in Washington (*Demorest's Family Magazine*, 1889); on Iron Workers; and also on women workers (*Women Workers at the Lynn Massachusetts Shoe Factory*, 1895; Library of Congress), their private lives and standards of living.

By the 1890s Johnston had become known as the "photographer of the American Court" (Daniel and Smock 1974, p.5); she had easy access to the White House and photographed the administrations of presidents Cleveland, Harrison, McKinley, Theodore Roosevelt and Taft. Mrs Cleveland, Mrs McKinley and the wives of Cabinet members posed for Johnston in her studio. With the help of Roosevelt (then Secretary of the Navy) and on commission from a news syndicate, she got permission to photograph Admiral George Dewey on his flagship, the *USS Olympia* (1899), while it was anchored in the Bay of Naples soon after his triumphant victory in Manila Bay during the Spanish-American war (1898). She also recorded several world's fairs: the World's Columbian Exposition in Chicago (1893), the Pan-American Exposition in Buffalo (1901) and the Louisiana Purchase Exposition in St Louis (1904).

Johnston's photographic essay on the public school system of Washington, DC, attracted considerable attention and led to what is probably her most famous body of work: a suite of photographs of the Hampton Institute, Virginia (1899). A progressive and experimental institution, Hampton was founded in 1868 "to train selected Negro youth who should go out and teach and lead their people" (Kirstein 1966, p.6). In the hope of interesting patrons in the work of the Institute, a bound presentation album of Johnston's prints was prepared, and was part of the Negro exhibit at the Paris Exposition of 1900.

Johnston found her personal vision and style early and rarely deviated from it. Her work is generally sober, austere, static and quiet. Her images are always thoughtfully composed – little is left to chance – and the carefully arranged figures that inhabit them seem hypnotically frozen in time and possess a monumental dignity. The photographer may well have found inspiration in the work of the American painters William Sidney Mount and Thomas Eakins, both for her compositions and for the solemn and respectful treatment of her subjects (see the Hampton Album studies *Poor Black Family at Mealtime*, *Black Farm Hands: Tending the Horse* and *Stacking Pumpkins in Barn*, 1899). The occasional Impressionist influence can also be found in the photographer's work (*Rainy Day, the Pan-American Exposition*, 1901). One of Johnston's most interesting and provocative photographs is a *Self-Portrait* (c.1896; Library of Congress), in which the photographer sits in a no-nonsense and, for the time, shocking manner – her legs are crossed and her skirts hiked up to reveal not only a petticoat but also well-turned calves and ankles. By holding a cigarette in one hand and a large beer stein in the other, the young woman flaunts typically masculine attributes outrageously, thereby proclaiming her status as an independent "New Woman", albeit in the safety and seclusion of her properly Victorian and artfully appointed "bohemian" studio.

HELEN GOODMAN

Jones, Lois Mailou [fig. 35]
American painter and designer, 1905–1998

Born in Boston, Massachusetts, 3 November 1905. Apprenticed to Grace Riley, costume designer and professor of Rhode Island School of Design, then employed by Ripley Studios to make costumes and masks for Ted Shawn School of Dance. Studied at School of the Museum of Fine Arts, Boston, 1923–7 (diploma in design); Boston Normal Art School, 1926–7 (certificate); Designers Art School of Boston, 1927–8 (diploma); Harvard University, 1927; Columbia University, New York, 1934–6; Howard University, Washington, DC (AB in art

education 1945). Freelance textile designer, especially for F.A. Foster Company, Boston, and Schumacher Company, New York, 1927–8. Chair and instructor, Palmer Memorial Institute, Sedalia, North Carolina, 1928–30; instructor and professor of art, Howard University, Washington, DC, 1930–77. Studied at Académie Julian during sabbatical year in Paris, 1937–8; exhibited at Société des Artistes Français and Salon des Indépendants, 1938. Married Haitian graphic designer Louis Vergniaud Pierre-Noël in Cabris, France, 1953; he died 1982. Taught at Centre d'Art and Foyer des Arts Plastiques, Port-au-Prince, Haiti, 1954. Worked on Howard University Black Visual Arts project, travelling widely to collect data on Haitian, African and African-American art and artists, 1968–71; lectured on African-American art in several African countries as cultural ambassador for the United States Information Service, 1970. Recipient of numerous honours and awards, including diplôme and décoration, Ordre National d'Honneur et Mérite, Haitian government, 1954; Candace award, Metropolitan Museum of Art, New York, 1983; Outstanding Achievement in the Visual Arts award, Women's Caucus for Art, 1986; honorary doctorates from Colorado Christian College, Lakewood, 1973; Suffolk University, Boston, 1981; Massachusetts College of Art, Boston, 1986; Howard University, 1987; Findlay University, Ohio, 1993; Tougaloo College, Mississippi, 1994. First African-American artist to be elected honorary member of Society of Washington Artists, 1954; fellow, Royal Society of Arts, London, 1962; honorary member, Art Association, Washington, DC, 1972. Died in Washington, DC, 9 June 1998.

Selected Individual Exhibitions
Hampton University, Hampton, VA: 1935
Howard University Gallery of Art, Washington, DC: 1937, 1948, 1972 (retrospective), 1987, 1988, 1989
Robert C. Vose Galleries, Boston: 1939
Barnett-Aden Gallery, Washington, DC: 1946
Centre d'Art, Port-au-Prince, Haiti: 1954
Pan-America Union Building, Washington, DC: 1955
Galerie International, New York: 1961, 1968
Galerie Soulanges, Paris: 1966
Association for the Presentation and Preservation of the Arts, Washington, DC: 1968 (retrospective)
Museum of Fine Arts, Boston: 1973 (retrospective)
Phillips Collection, Washington, DC: 1979

Harbor Gallery, University of Massachusetts, Boston: 1985
Musée d'Art Haitien, Port-au-Prince, Haiti: 1986
Brody Gallery of Art, Washington, DC: 1988
Meridian House International, Washington, DC: 1990–94 (touring)

Selected Writings
Lois Mailou Jones: Peintures, 1937–1951, Tourcoing: Presses Georges Frère, 1952

Bibliography
Alain Locke, *The Negro in Art*, Washington, DC: Associates in Negro Folk Education, 1940; reprinted New York: Hacker, 1968
James A. Porter, *Modern Negro Art*, New York: Dryden Press, 1943; reprinted New York: Arno, 1969
Samella S. Lewis and Ruth G. Waddy, *Black Artists on Art*, i, Los Angeles: Contemporary Crafts, 1969
J. Edward Atkinson, ed., *Black Dimensions in Contemporary American Art*, New York: New American Library, 1971
Lois Mailou Jones: Retrospective Exhibition, 1932–1972, exh. cat., Howard University Art Gallery, Washington, DC, 1972
Elsa Honig Fine, *The Afro-American Artist: A Search for Identity*, New York: Holt, Rinehart and Winston, 1973
Reflective Moments: Lois Mailou Jones: Retrospective, 1930–1972, exh. cat., Museum of Fine Arts, Boston, 1973
Robert Taylor, "Lois Jones achieves identity in retrospective art show", *Boston Globe*, 26 March 1973
Juliette H. Bowles, "Lois Mailou Jones: Portrait of an artist", *New Directions* (Howard University), iv/3, July 1977, pp.4–23
Women Artists in Washington Collections, exh. cat., University of Maryland Art Gallery, College Park, 1979
Forever Free: Art by African-American Women, 1862–1980, exh. cat., Illinois State University, Normal, 1980
Lois and Pierre: Two Master Artists, exh. cat., Museum of the National Center of Afro-American Artists, Boston, 1983
Keith Morrison, *Art in Washington and Its Afro-American Presence, 1940–1970*, Washington, DC: Washington Project for the Arts, 1985
Betty LaDuke, "Lois Mailou Jones: The grande dame of African-American art", *Woman's Art Journal*, viii/2, 1987–8, pp.28–32
American Women Artists: The 20th Century, in Celebration of Woman's Art Journal's 10th Anniversary, exh. cat., Knoxville Museum of Art, 1989
Romare Beardon and H.A. Henderson, *A History of African-American Art from 1792 to the Present*, New York: Pantheon, 1993
Tritobia Hayes Benjamin, *The Life and Art of Lois Mailou Jones*, San Francisco: Pomegranate, 1994 (contains extensive bibliography)
—, "Lois Mailou Jones", *Gumbo ya ya: Anthology of Contemporary African-American Women Artists*, ed. Leslie King-Hammond, New York: Midmarch Arts Press, 1995, pp.126–9

Lois Mailou Jones had a long and productive career as painter, educator, designer and illustrator. Her influence as an artist and teacher was felt by several generations of African-American students and colleagues in the USA, and also in Haiti and Africa where she exhibited, taught and lectured. She was a shining example of an artist who successfully followed an original talent and vision, undeterred by issues of prejudice against women artists or those of African-American descent. Throughout her career Jones found new subjects in African, Haitian and African-American themes and expressed her perceptions in bold and unique ways.

Jones was influenced in the choice of career by her friendship with the African-American sculptor Meta Vaux Warrick Fuller (q.v.), whom she met at Martha's Vineyard where Jones's family owned property and spent their summers. In 1923 she won a four-year scholarship to the School of the Museum of Fine Arts, Boston, where she was the only black student. After graduating from the Designers Art School of Boston she became a successful freelance designer, but decided to become a painter because her work would then be recognised as her own. At the same time she developed her career as a teacher, first at the Palmer Memorial Institute, a junior college in Sedalia, North Carolina, and then from 1930 at Howard University in Washington, DC. While teaching painting, Jones was also a freelance illustrator for Associated Publishers of Washington, DC, from 1936 to 1963.

The breakthrough in Jones's painting came in 1937 when she was awarded an Education Board Fellowship to study at the Académie Julian in Paris for the next academic year. In her education and new-found freedom abroad she was following the steps of illustrious African-American artists such as Fuller, who had lived in Paris and studied with Rodin, and Henry Ossawa Tanner, a distinguished expatriate who lived and exhibited his paintings in Paris during most of his career. Sharing a studio at 23 rue Campaigne Première with Céline Tabary, who became a valued friend, Jones adopted plein-air painting, which she continued all her life. Her early still-life paintings such as *Cauliflower and Pumpkin, Paris* (1938; Metropolitan Museum of Art, New York) show a thorough understanding of academic technique, combined with fluid brush strokes and vibrant colour. Jones's mastery of volumetric form is frequently displayed in a number of Paris street scenes, such as *Rue St Michel* (1938; artist's collection) and *Place du Tertre* (1938; Phillips Collection, Washington, DC). Here the underlying structure of the buildings reveals her interest in Cézanne's techniques. She exhibited her works at the Salon de Printemps of the Société des Artistes Français and also at the Salon des Indépendants in Paris in 1938.

Another important revelation of her Paris period was the interest in African art, dance and music. "When I arrived in Paris, African art was just the thing. All the galleries and museums were featuring African sculptures, African designs, and I sketched, sketched everything", Jones recounted (Benjamin 1994, pp.ix–x). Her response to this stimulus was *Les Fétiches* (1938; National Museum of American Art, Smithsonian Institution, Washington, DC), a painting that interprets the dynamic rhythms of African culture in an angular, semi-abstract collage of masks, both completely modern and in the tradition of African culture.

Jones returned to Howard University to resume her teaching there in 1938. Her friend Céline Tabary came to Washington for a visit in 1940, and stayed with Jones in the USA for seven years. Tabary would often deliver Jones's paintings to museum and gallery competitions where they would not have been accepted or won prizes if they were known to have been painted by an African-American artist. During the 1940s Alain Locke encouraged Jones to use African-American experience as subject matter. Her most moving painting of this period is *Mob Victim (Meditation)* (1944; artist's collection). This three-quarter view of a bearded, grey-headed African-American man with bound hands done with a muted palette of browns and greys is an eloquent testimony to fortitude in the face of racial violence.

Jones's marriage to Louis Vergniaud Pierre-Noël, a Haitian citizen and graphic designer, in 1953 opened a new chapter in her artistic as well as her personal life. Her annual trips to Haiti from 1954 onwards resulted in a period of Haitian subject matter with new locales, flattened forms and brilliant colour. In 1954 she was invited by the President of Haiti to teach at the Centre d'Art and at the Foyer des Arts Plastiques. This produced such paintings as *Peasant Girl, Haiti* (1954; Wadsworth Atheneum, Hartford, CT), a brilliant study of a seated girl in orange, brown and green in which the coiled energy of the girl's body contrasts with the cubic volume of the block against which she rests. In a later Haiti painting, *Les Vendeuses de tissus* (1961; Johnson Publishing Company Art Collection), forms have become more abstract, spread out in a long horizontal line.

In 1970 Jones visited eleven African countries on a grant from Howard University to research African art and culture. Her experiences ignited a series of paintings on African themes between 1971 and 1989, her most original contributions to American art. In these large-scale acrylic paintings on canvas Jones juxtaposed three-dimensional African figures on a flat background of native patterns, masks, carvings and textiles. She combined art forms from different regions to suggest the underlying unity of the African continent. An example of this is *Ubi Girl from the Tai Region* (1972; Museum of Fine Arts, Boston), which was in her solo exhibition in Boston in 1973. Here masks from Zaïre and a heddle pulley from the Ivory Coast are combined with the three-dimensional portrait head of the Ubi girl silhouetted against an African textile, creating tensions of form versus colour and Western-style portraiture versus African symbols and designs. This breakthrough in style, subject matter and design moved Jones's paintings into a new stage and resulted in new recognition of her art in solo exhibitions and honorary degrees.

Lois Mailou Jones worked in a wide array of media and subject matter. Although social comment can be found in such paintings as *Mob Victim (Meditation)* (1944) and *We Shall Overcome* (1988; commissioned by the *Washington Post*), Jones's primary concern was to use her African and Western heritage to create original works on African, Haitian, American and European themes in which women often play a prominent role. Her superb technique and imaginative juxtapositions, especially in her Haitian and African works, show an artist creatively combining new themes and styles in a vision sensitive to the unique aspects of place, persons and culture on an international scale.

ALICIA CRAIG FAXON

K

Kahlo, Frida

[fig. 38]

Mexican painter, 1907–1954

Born in Coyoacán, a suburb of Mexico City, 6 July
1907. Permanently injured after a streetcar accident, 1925; taught herself to paint during convales-
cence. Joined Young Communist League, 1927.
Married mural painter Diego Rivera, 1929;
divorced 1939; remarried 1940. With Rivera travelled to USA, living in San Francisco, Detroit and
New York, 1930–33. Met André Breton in
Mexico, 1938. Trip to New York, 1938; to Paris,
1939. Appointed painting professor, La Esmeralda,
the Education Ministry's School of Painting and
Sculpture, 1943. Began diary, charting her physical
decline, c.1945. Recipient of National Prize of Arts
and Sciences, Education Ministry, Mexico, 1946.
Hospitalised for several months after a spine operation, 1950; gangrenous right leg amputated,
1953. Died in the Casa Azul, Coyoacán, 13 July
1954.

Principal Exhibitions

Julien Levy Gallery, New York: 1938 (individual)
Galerie Renau et Colle, Paris: 1939 (*Mexique*)
Galería de Arte Mexicano, Mexico City: 1940
    (*Exposición internacional del surrealismo*, touring)
Galería de Arte Contemporáneo, Mexico City: 1953
    (individual)

Selected Writings

"Portrait of Diego", *Calyx*, v/2–3, October 1980,
    pp.93–107 (Spanish original in *Hoy*, xxii, January
    1949)
The Diary of Frida Kahlo: An Intimate Self-Portrait, ed.
    Carlos Fuentes and Sarah M. Lowe, New York:
    Abrams, 1995

Bibliography

Bertram D. Wolfe, "Rise of another Rivera", *Vogue*, xcii,
    October–November 1938, pp.64, 131

W[alter] P[ach], "Frida Rivera: Gifted canvases by an
    unselfconscious Surrealist", *Art News*, xxxvii, 12
    November 1938, p.13
Frida Kahlo: Exposición nacional de homenaje, exh. cat.,
    Palacio de Bellas Artes, Mexico City, 1977
Raquel Tibol, *Frida Kahlo: Crónica, Testimonios y
    Aproximaciones*, Mexico City: Ediciones de Cultura
    Popular, 1977
Frida Kahlo and Tina Modotti, exh. cat., Whitechapel Art
    Gallery, London, and elsewhere, 1982
Rupert Garcia, *Frida Kahlo: A Bibliography*, Berkeley:
    University of California Chicano Studies Library
    Publications Unit, 1983
Hayden Herrera, *Frida: A Biography of Frida Kahlo*,
    New York: Harper, 1983; London: Bloomsbury, 1989
Terry Smith, "From the margins: Modernity and the case
    of Frida Kahlo", *Block*, no.8, 1983, pp.11–23
—, "Further thoughts on Frida Kahlo", *Block*, no.9,
    1983, pp.34–7
Susan B. Laufer, "Kahlo's gaze", *Poetics Journal*, iv, May
    1984, pp.124–9
Whitney Chadwick, *Women Artists and the Surrealist
    Movement*, Boston: Little Brown, and London:
    Thames and Hudson, 1985
Helga Prignitz-Poda, Salomón Grimberg and Andrea
    Kettenmann, eds, *Frida Kahlo: Das Gesamtwerk*,
    Frankfurt: Neue Kritik, 1988
The Art of Frida Kahlo, exh. cat., Art Gallery of South
    Australia, Adelaide, and elsewhere, 1990
Joan Borsa, "Frida Kahlo: Marginalization and the criti-
    cal female subject", *Third Text*, no.12, 1990,
    pp.21–40
Martha Zamora, *Frida Kahlo: The Brush of Anguish*, San
    Francisco: Chronicle, 1990 (Spanish original, 1987)
Janice Helland, "Aztec imagery in Frida Kahlo's paint-
    ings: Indigenity and political commitment", *Woman's
    Art Journal*, xi/2, 1990–91, pp.8–13
Oriana Baddeley, "'Her dress hangs here': De-frocking
    the Kahlo cult", *Oxford Art Journal*, xiv, 1991,
    pp.10–17
Hayden Herrera, *Frida Kahlo: The Paintings*, New York:
    HarperCollins, and London: Bloomsbury, 1991
Sarah M. Lowe, *Frida Kahlo*, New York: Universe, 1991
Janice Helland, "Frida Kahlo: The politics of confession",
    Latin American Art, iii, December 1991, pp.31–4

Edward J. Sullivan, "Frida Kahlo", *ibid.*, pp.34–6

David Lomas, "Body languages: Kahlo and medical imagery", *Body Imaged: The Human Form and Visual Culture since the Renaissance*, ed. Marcia Pointon and Kathleen Adler, Cambridge and New York: Cambridge University Press, 1993, pp.5–19, 191–2

Raquel Tibol, *Frida Kahlo: An Open Life*, Albuquerque: University of New Mexico Press, 1993 (Spanish original, 1983)

Paula M. Cooey, *Religious Imagination and the Body: A Feminist Analysis*, New York: Oxford University Press, 1994

Renée Riese Hubert, *Magnifying Mirrors: Women, Surrealism and Partnership*, Lincoln: University of Nebraska Press, 1994

Frida Kahlo's career spanned less than three decades, from 1926 when she painted *Self-Portrait Wearing a Velvet Dress*, until 1954, the year of her death and the date of *Marxism will Heal the Sick*. She produced about 130 paintings, some 30 drawings and a handful of watercolours; she made around 30 portraits and as many still-life paintings. The balance of her oeuvre is marked by a preponderance of images in which she appears – either in formal, bust-length self-portraits or larger, tableau images. Kahlo is primarily remembered for her obsessive rendering of herself, a preoccupation that achieved worldwide recognition decades after her death. The feminist movement of the 1980s was largely responsible for her sudden burst on to an international scene, specifically, the publication of her biography (Herrera 1989).

Kahlo worked in the years following the Mexican Revolution, a period of cultural renaissance when the visual arts were in ascendancy, enlisted as a tool in the government's massive social reforms.. Thus although Kahlo's paintings are seen as highly personal, in part because the literature on Kahlo focuses on her dramatic and traumatic life, her work resonates with international and national artistic concerns and styles of the time. She was skilled at fusing an astounding variety of visual forms – many of them Mexican in origin – with her own symbolism, and her oeuvre establishes her as an inventive and effective artist.

Kahlo encouraged the perception that she was *sui generis*, a notion strengthened by her naive painting style. She had limited artistic training, beginning in the studio of her father Guillermo Kahlo, a successful photographer, who taught her the painstaking technique of touching up hand-coloured photographs. One characteristic of her own work are tiny, indivisible brush strokes. Kahlo attended the prestigious National Preparatory School in Mexico City from 1922 until 1925, following a course of study that would have led to a medical career. There she took two required art classes: two-dimensional drawing and three-dimensional clay modelling. During the first half of 1925 Kahlo studied drawing with Fernando Fernández, a commercial engraver, who had her copy reproductions of etchings by Anders Zorn, nudes and portraits of *fin-de-siècle* intellectuals. She performed the task easily with free-hand replication. A number of watercolours from the 1920s indicate Kahlo's innate ability for verisimilitude, and she considered using this aptitude for a profession in scientific illustration.

Later, after they married in 1929, Kahlo's husband, Diego Rivera, was an influence on her art-making. He was a passionate, dedicated and driven artist. Rivera was a prominent player in Mexico's mural movement and a proponent of using Mexican culture and history as both source and subject in his art, and Kahlo saw him as a painter of his time and of his country. She followed his example of rejecting European abstraction and adapting a descriptive realism, although she favoured the intimate rather than the large-scale style that was the hallmark of muralism. Both artists turned to Mexico's rich artistic heritage as a visual resource. Kahlo followed a road independent of Rivera, however; whereas he peopled his frescoes with anonymous masses who symbolised the material condition of "humanity", Kahlo concentrated on images of herself, which transcend her personal story and speak of the emotional and spiritual aspects of the human condition.

Kahlo's focus on her own body and the vivid, sometimes gruesome imagery of many of her self-portraits are understandable in the light of a series of physical misfortunes she endured. She contracted polio as a child, and in 1925 nearly died in a horrendous traffic accident. By her own count, she underwent at least 22 operations (some therapeutic abortions). Her inability to bear a child was a continual torment to her, and a leitmotif in her work. In her unremitting preoccupation with her body and "selves", Kahlo undertook to position herself at various levels of being, exploring her condition as Mexican, as woman and as artist.

Kahlo's earliest works were self-portraits and portraits of friends, in which the figures are presented in a shallow space, sometimes with a token signifying an interest of theirs. These works are reminiscent of Italian Renaissance portraiture, a source evident in Kahlo's first painting, *Self-Portrait Wearing a Velvet Dress* (1926; private collection, repr. Herrera 1991, p.43), which is modelled after a work by the 16th-century Mannerist painter Bronzino. A year after her marriage, Kahlo travelled with Rivera to the USA where they lived in San Francisco, Detroit and New York. They moved in art circles and Kahlo met a number of artists, among them Edward Weston, Imogen Cunningham (q.v.), Georgia O'Keeffe (q.v.) and Louise Nevelson (q.v.), and had the opportunity to visit a great many museums. Her reaction to America, which she called "Gringolandia", was largely negative and fuelled her already heightened nationalism.

Following a miscarriage in 1932, Kahlo painted *Henry Ford Hospital* (1932; Fundación Dolores Olmedo, Mexico), a painting that marks the beginning of the style and content she would develop over the next 20 years. Here she fuses her own experience with a formal construction based on the specifically Mexican conventions found in the tiny ex-voto paintings done on tin. Kahlo made use of an extensive variety of visual references, culled from a myriad of sources. In particular, art forms distinctive to Mexico are expressly evident in much of her work, and add a powerful dimension to her autobiographical oeuvre. Elements of Aztec culture are conspicuous in a number of paintings, for example, *My Nurse and I* (1937; Fundación Dolores Olmedo). Kahlo paints the face of her wet nurse as a mask resembling the stone heads from Pre-Columbian Teotihuacán culture, while the figure itself is copied from a Jalisco funerary figure of a nursing mother in Kahlo's collection (Helland 1990–91). Kahlo thus makes visible her Mexican ancestry.

Kahlo's self-conscious disregard of traditional rules of academic painting, especially of linear perspective, allies her with a number of visual traditions in Mexico. She admired the provincial painters of Mexico's colonial period, such as José Maria Estrada, José Agustín Arrieta and Hermenegildo Bustos. Child mortuary portraiture, for example, was a genre that provided income to itinerant artists, and is the macabre subject matter of the *Deceased Dimas* (1937; Fundación Dolores Olmedo). Kahlo's hyper-realist approach gives the image a somewhat surreal appearance, but the subject itself was also taken up by her contempo-

raries, among them David Alfaro Siqueiros, María Izquierdo and Juan Soriano.

Another source of inspiration for Kahlo was the work of the turn-of-the-century printmaker José Guadalupe Posada, whose political prints were peopled by *calaveras* (skeletons), the ever-present Mexican symbol of death. Many of Kahlo's paintings share with his prints the mingling of the grotesque with the ordinary, as, for example, Kahlo's *A Few Small Nips* (1935; Fundación Dolores Olmedo). The muralists also championed Posada as a home-grown source who developed independent of European influence.

Kahlo consciously emulated the style of unschooled retablo or ex-voto painters. She collected hundreds of these tiny images rendered to commemorate some divine intervention in the lives of individuals who, having experienced a miraculous recovery from an accident or illness, would commission a local artist to execute a votive offering. The coexistence of fact and fantasy – the journalistic verity of the incident with the patron saint's intercession – is a prominent feature of many of Kahlo's paintings, for example, *Henry Ford Hospital*. Kahlo found this blending of the visible and the invisible a useful means to express the physical manifestations of feelings and of sensation, a bio-psychological mapping that merges the scientific with the emotional. In *The Broken Column* (1944; Fundación Dolores Olmedo) Kahlo depicts her pain using X-ray vision, showing the viewer where she hurts, and underscoring her agony with pins as large as nails pricking her entire naked body.

In her visualisation of experience, the painting of feelings not otherwise articulable, Kahlo's approach resembles that of the Surrealist René Magritte. Kahlo has been linked to the Surrealist movement, in part because its leader André Breton championed her work. Breton and his wife, the painter Jacqueline Lamba, visited Mexico in 1938. Breton wrote an enthusiastic essay to accompany Kahlo's first one-person show, held at the Julien Levy Gallery in New York (English translation in London 1982, p.36), and then arranged for her to exhibit her work in Paris early the following year. Breton also had a hand in the organisation of the International Surrealist Exhibition in Mexico City in 1940, in which Kahlo showed her two largest canvases.

Kahlo travelled to New York in October 1938 to help organise her November show, and sailed for

Europe in January, staying with the Bretons in Paris. There she met many of the Surrealists, all of whom, with the exception of Marcel Duchamp, she disdained. After her sojourn in Paris, Kahlo was ambivalent about being labelled a Surrealist, even though her work, in some respects, shares many of its aspects. While her paintings most resemble such imagists as Magritte and Salvador Dalí, Kahlo's diary demonstrates her use of automatic drawing, a method advocated in the Manifesto of Surrealism (1924). Its proponents – Max Ernst, André Masson and Joan Miró – relied on automatism, accident and biomorphism as means of expression (see *The Diary of Frida Kahlo* 1995). Kahlo's formal innovations, like her subject matter, sprang from Mexican sources, however, and not the intellectual constructions that motivated Breton and his circle.

During the 1940s Kahlo enjoyed a good deal of professional success. Her work was shown steadily in numerous exhibitions internationally and her signature self-portraits were much sought after. *Self-Portrait with Thorn Necklace and Hummingbird* (1940; Harry Ransom Humanities Research Center, University of Texas at Austin) is an especially deft example of Kahlo's ability to merge various artistic sources. Here she draws from native sources and imported Catholic symbolism to create a truly syncretic image. The severe frontality of the pose casts the portrait as a secular icon, while her pets, a monkey and black cat, act as religious attributes. In Aztec belief, however, animals were thought to be alter egos for their owners. The necklace of thorns refers most obviously to Christ's crown, but the humming-bird, as well as the butterflies, are Aztec symbols.

In 1943 Kahlo was appointed a painting professor at the Education Ministry's La Esmeralda art school, where she was extremely popular. Four students with whom she worked especially closely – Fanny Rabel, Arturo García Bustos, Guillermo Monroy and Arturo Estrada – became known as "Los Fridos". The decade was also one of personal loss and physical decline, and Kahlo charted the last years of her life in a diary she began in the mid-1940s, shortly after her father's death and her divorce and remarriage to Rivera. Over the next 12 years she endured numerous tests and medical procedures, including confinement in a series of 30 plaster and steel corsets and countless operations on her back and leg, as well as lengthy hospital stays.

As Kahlo's health deteriorated, her production of self-portraits subsided, and she began to make still lifes, a subject that had interested her since the 1930s. Between 1951 and 1954, the years immediately preceding her death, Kahlo painted 13 extremely disturbing works in this genre. There is a quality about these pictures that suggests Kahlo has replaced her obsession with her own visage with images of strange fruits, some deteriorating, and that this new preoccupation parallels her own disintegration. At the same time she both displaced her own image and anthropomorphised inanimate objects, as in *Looks – Still Life – Coconuts* (1951; Museo de Arte Moderna, Mexico City), where the coconut has tears rolling down its "face".

Kahlo's last work, *Marxism will Heal the Sick* (1954; Museo de Frida Kahlo, Mexico City), brings together several themes that are evident throughout her work. The image amounts to a political ex-voto, Marx functioning as the divine being, intervening to protect and strengthen her. Throughout her life Kahlo was politically active. She joined the Young Communist League in 1927; ten years later, she worked in support of Mexicans fighting on the side of the Spanish Loyalists during the Spanish Civil War; and she gave Leon Trotsky and his wife refuge in her home when the exiled leader found asylum in Mexico in 1938. Later, Kahlo disavowed her association with Trotsky, opting instead to put her faith in Marx and his dream of a political utopia, a deliverance depicted in this last painting.

SARAH M. LOWE

Käsebier, Gertrude
American photographer, 1852–1934

Born Gertrude Stanton in Fort Des Moines (now Des Moines), Iowa, 18 May 1852; grew up in Colorado; moved to Brooklyn, New York, 1864. Married Eduard Käsebier, a shellac importer from Germany, 1874; three children (one son, two daughters), born 1875, 1878 and 1880; husband died 1909. Studied at Pratt Institute, Brooklyn, 1889–96; taught photography by a priest, Father Wenzel, late 1880s. First visited Europe, 1894; studied under Frank Vincent Dumond at Crécy-en-Brie, near Paris, and at Académie Julian; apprenticed to a photographic chemist in Germany. Began career as commercial portrait photographer, 1896; opened first New York studio, winter 1897–8; new studio at 273 Fifth Avenue, 1899; students included Alice Austin and Alvin Langdon Coburn. Met Alfred Stieglitz, 1898. Joined Camera Club of New York, 1899; Alfred Stieglitz's Photo-Secession, 1902 (resigned 1912); Professional Photographers of New York, 1906. Co-founder, Women's Federation of the Photographers' Association of America; taught women photographers under its auspices, 1909–10. Honorary vice president, Pictorial Photographers of America (PPA), 1915. Died in New York, 13 October 1934.

Principal Exhibitions

Individual
Boston Camera Club: 1896, 1900
Camera Club of New York: 1899 (organised by Alfred Stieglitz)
Little Galleries of the Photo-Secession, New York: 1906 (with Clarence H. White)
Brooklyn Institute of Arts and Sciences (now Brooklyn Museum), NY: 1929 (retrospective)

Group
Philadelphia Photographic Salon: 1898–1900
Exposition Universelle, Paris: 1900 (display of prints by American women photographers organised by Frances Benjamin Johnston; also shown in St Petersburg, Moscow and Photo-Club de Paris)
Royal Photographic Society, London: 1900–01 (New School of American Photography, touring, organised by F. Holland Day)
National Arts Club, New York: 1902 (American Pictorial Photography Arranged by the Photo-Secession)
International Photography Exhibition, Dresden: 1909
Albright Art Gallery (now Albright-Knox Art Gallery), Buffalo, NY: 1910 (International Exhibition of Pictorial Photography)

Selected Writings
"Studies in photography", Photographic Times, xxx, June 1898, pp.269–72; reprinted in A Photographic Vision: Pictorial Photography, 1889–1923, ed. Peter C. Bunnell, Salt Lake City: Peregrine Smith, 1980

Bibliography
Joseph T. Keiley, "Mrs Käsebier's prints", Camera Notes, iii, July 1899, p.34
"Some Indian portraits", Everybody's Magazine, iv, 1901, pp.3–24
Charles H. Caffin, "Mrs Käsebier and the artistic-commercial portrait", Everybody's Magazine, iv, 1901, pp.480–95; included in Photography as Fine Art, New York: Doubleday, 1901; reprinted Hastings-on-Hudson, NY: Morgan and Morgan, 1971, and New York: Amphoto, 1972
Frances Benjamin Johnston, "Gertrude Käsebier: Professional photographer", Camera Work, no.1, January 1903, p.20
Mary Fanton Roberts [Giles Edgerton], "Photography as an emotional art: A study of the work of Gertrude Käsebier", Craftsman, xii, April 1907, pp.80–93; reprinted in Image, xv, December 1972, pp.9–12
"Threescore years and sixteen is ardent exponent of photography", New York Sun, 5 January 1929, p.21; reprinted as "Gertrude Käsebier is interviewed", Photo-Era, lxii, March 1929, pp.129–30
A Pictorial Heritage: The Photographs of Gertrude Käsebier, exh. cat., Delaware Art Museum, Wilmington, and elsewhere, 1979
Barbara L. Michaels, Gertrude Käsebier: The Photographer and Her Photographs, New York: Abrams, 1992 (contains extensive bibliography)
Naomi Rosenblum, A History of Women Photographers, New York: Abbeville, 1994

Gertrude Käsebier's correspondence is in the Alfred Stieglitz Archive, Collection of American Literature, Beinecke Rare Book and Manuscript Library, Yale University, New Haven.

From the late 1890s until the 1920s Gertrude Käsebier was the pre-eminent woman among the international group of pictorial photographers who considered photography to be a fine art. Her portraits, as well as expressive scenes on themes of womanhood, motherhood and family life, inspired other photographers, including Edward Steichen and Imogen Cunningham (q.v.).

Around 1900 Käsebier's sensitive portraits helped her to reach the highest levels of the photographic world, both as a founding member of Alfred Stieglitz's Photo-Secession and as a commercial photographer on Fifth Avenue, New York. In taking likenesses of celebrities, including Mark Twain, Booker T. Washington, Jacob Riis (published in the magazine World's Work, 1900–01) and the French sculptor Auguste Rodin (1905; Musée Rodin, Paris), Käsebier endeavoured to capture each sitter's temperament or personality. By dispensing with the fancy backdrops and furnishings that conventional photographers considered de rigueur, Käsebier concentrated attention on the sitter. Her plain backgrounds are especially effective in the many portraits of Sioux men (1898–1901; Division of Photographic History, National Museum of American History, Smithsonian Institution, Washington, DC) who toured with Buffalo Bill's "Wild West" show. They posed in Käsebier's studio during several visits that Buffalo Bill's troupe made to New York. Most of the pictures show them in full regalia with feathered head-dresses, but Käsebier prized the few pictures in which she was able to show the men in simpler garb, as she remembered the Indians she had known during her childhood in Colorado.

The photographer's informal and conversational manner helped her to achieve the relaxed poses for which she was noted. In 1899 Alfred Stieglitz, the noted American photographer and tastemaker, called her "beyond dispute the leading portrait photographer in this country" (*Camera Notes*, July 1899, p.24). Käsebier's ideas about individualised portraiture came from her painting studies at Pratt Institute in Brooklyn, which she began after her son and two daughters were past primary school. She studied photography on her own and as a studio apprentice, adapting concepts of composition that she had learned from Arthur W. Dow and others during her years at Pratt.

Many of her portraits illustrate her friendships with other advanced photographers of her era, including *Fred Holland Day* (c.1900; Metropolitan Museum of Art, New York), *Alvin Langdon Coburn* (c.1902) and *Baron de Meyer* (1903; both International Museum of Photography at George Eastman House, Rochester, NY), *Edward Steichen* ([1901]) and *Alfred Stieglitz* (1902; both Museum of Modern Art, New York). Some of these pictures were taken out of doors, during holidays in Newport, Rhode Island, and in France. Even when working away from her studio, however, Käsebier tended to support her camera on a tripod and to use $6^{1}/_{2} \times 8^{1}/_{2}$-inch (16.5 × 21.5 cm.) glass plate negatives. Her prints were usually about that size or enlarged to about 9 × 12 inches (23 × 30cm.).

Two portraits of her colleague Clarence H. White and his family demonstrate Käsebier's skill at group portraiture, as well as her stylistic development. In the earlier portrait she depicted the Whites and their sons at home, in evenly lit shallow space (*Clarence H. White and Family*, 1908; print from negative of 1902; Metropolitan Museum of Art). *Sunshine in the House* (1913; Museum of Modern Art, New York) portrays the Whites in a furnished, sun-streaked room, using a composition typical of the deeper, light-accented formats that Käsebier adopted around 1909 in scenes of her own family, including one of her daughter, *Gertrude Käsebier O'Malley* (c.1909; J. Paul Getty Museum, Malibu),

shown playing billiards at the Käsebier home in Oceanside, Long Island.

Beginning at the Philadelphia Photographic Salons in 1898 and 1899, Käsebier won acclaim for her tender representations of motherhood, especially *The Manger* (1899; Museum of Modern Art, New York) and *"Blessed Art Thou Among Women"* (1899; Metropolitan Museum of Art), both of which Stieglitz reproduced in the first issue of *Camera Work* (January 1903), which featured Käsebier's photographs. *"Blessed Art Thou Among Women"* remains a prime example of Käsebier's imagery, as it is an environmental portrait of her friend Agnes Lee, the poet and author of children's books, as well as a memorable depiction of motherhood. The photograph's title derives from the biblical inscription surrounding Selwyn Image's print of the *Annunciation* hanging behind the figures. The photograph, which was taken at the Lee home in Boston, stands for the Lee family's dedication to both Christianity and the Arts and Crafts movement. In *The Sketch* and *The Picture-Book* (both 1903; Metropolitan Museum of Art) Käsebier alludes to another friend's career as an artist and illustrator, by showing Beatrice Baxter (Ruyl) drawing or helping Käsebier's grandson, Charles O'Malley, to draw. On the other hand, in *Miss N.* ([1902]; National Gallery of Canada, Ottawa) the photographer portrayed the well-known model and showgirl, Evelyn Nesbit, as a temptress in an off-the-shoulder gown.

Although Käsebier played down the importance of technique to her work, many of her platinum prints (her most usual medium) are now considered exemplary for their velvety quality and subtle tonalities. From around 1901 she also began to use the gum-bichromate process to create pictures with a more textured or painterly appearance. She often used whatever combination of media seemed to suit her expressive needs. For instance, in two versions of the *Road to Rome*, a picture of her three-year-old grandson, Charles O'Malley, approaching a long, winding path, she painted over parts of a gelatin silver print, re-photographed it on to a new glass plate negative and made a gum-bichromate exhibition print from that negative (both prints 1903; Art Museum, Princeton University). The picture is a metaphor for a child's – and an artist's – imagination and creativity. Käsebier also used gum bichromate effectively to simulate the grainy intensity of charcoal in *Labor* (c.1902), a scene of men shovelling, and in the poster-like landscape, *Bungalows* (*c*.1907; both Museum of Modern Art, New York). Towards the end of her career (and as an aftermath to her own unhappy marriage and the break-up of her daughter Hermine Turner's marriage) she turned a country scene of a boy and girl gazing at yoked oxen into an ironical commentary on wedlock by darkening the original version with handwork, printing the picture in gum bichromate and titling the completed image *Yoked and Muzzled – Marriage* (1915 or earlier; Library of Congress, Washington, DC).

Käsebier never became a modernist photographer, but the landscapes she took during a visit to Newfoundland in 1912 (International Museum of Photography) show a responsiveness to geometric forms that may have been influenced directly or indirectly by Cubism. Although her work fell out of critical favour during the period of high modernism, the revival of interest in Käsebier's images since the 1970s confirms her belief that: "The key to artistic photography is to work out your own thoughts, by yourselves ... New ideas are always antagonized. Do not mind that. If a thing is good it will survive" ("Studies in photography", 1898).

BARBARA L. MICHAELS

Kauffman [Kauffmann], Angelica
Swiss painter, printmaker and designer, 1741–1807   [fig. 36]

Born in Chur (Coire), 30 October 1741, to Johann Josef Kauffman, a painter from Bregenz, Austria, and his wife Cleofa Lucin (d. 1757). Living with her family in Como, north Italy, 1752; in Milan, 1754. Travelled with her father to Modena and Parma, 1759. Elected member of Accademia Clementina, Bologna, and Accademia del Disegno, Florence, 1762. Moved to Rome, 1763; stayed in Naples, 1763–4; in Rome, 1764–5. Elected member of Accademia di San Luca, Rome, 1765. Travelled to England via Bologna, Venice and Paris, arriving in London in June 1766. Married an impostor, the "Count de Horn", 1767; marriage annulled 1768. Founder-member of Royal Academy, London, 1768. Began collaborating with printmaker W.W. Ryland, 1770. Spent six months in Ireland, 1771. Married painter Antonio Zucchi,

1781; he died 1795. Left England for Italy, 1781. Settled in Rome, 1782; toured Italy, 1805. Died in Rome, 5 November 1807; buried in Sant'Andrea delle Fratte.

Principal Exhibitions
Free Society of Artists, London: 1765–6, 1783
Society of Artists of Great Britain, London: 1768 (special exhibition for King Christian VII of Denmark)
Royal Academy, London: 1769–82, 1786, 1788, 1791, 1796–7

Bibliography
Giovanni Gherardo De Rossi, *Vita di Angelica Kauffmann, pittrice*, Florence: Molini Landi, 1810; reprinted London: Cornmarket, 1970

Frances A. Gerard, *Angelica Kauffmann: A Biography*, London: Ward and Downey, and New York: Macmillan, 1893

Lady Victoria Manners and G.C. Williamson, *Angelica Kauffmann RA: Her Life and Her Works*, London: Bodley Head, 1924; reprinted New York: Hacker, 1976

Adeline Hartcup, *Angelica: The Portrait of an Eighteenth-Century Artist*, London: Heinemann, 1954

Eugen Thurnher, *Angelika Kauffmann und die deutsche Dichtung*, Bregenz: Vorarlberger, 1966

Claudia Helbok, *Miss Angel: Angelika Kauffmann: Eine Biographie*, Vienna: Rosenbaum, 1968

Angelika Kauffmann und ihr Zeitgenossen, exh. cat., Vorarlberger Landesmuseum, Bregenz, and elsewhere, 1968

Peter Walch, *Angelica Kauffman*, Ph.D. dissertation, Princeton University, 1969

Women Artists, 1550–1950, exh. cat., Los Angeles County Museum of Art, and elsewhere, 1976

Peter Walch, "An early Neoclassical sketchbook by Angelica Kauffman", *Burlington Magazine*, cxix, 1977, pp.98–111

Angelika Kauffmann und ihre Zeit: Graphik und Zeichnungen von 1760–1810, exh. cat., C.G. Boerner, Düsseldorf, 1979

Arthur S. Marks, "Angelica Kauffman and some Americans on the Grand Tour", *American Art Journal*, xii/2, 1980, pp.5–24

Anthony Clark, "'Roma mi è sempre in pensiero'", *Studies in Roman Eighteenth-Century Painting*, ed. E.P. Bowron, Washington, DC: Decatur House Press, 1981, pp.125–38

Wendy Wassyng Roworth, "The gentle art of persuasion: Angelica Kauffman's *Praxiteles and Phryne*", *Art Bulletin*, lxv, 1983, pp.488–92

—, "Angelica Kauffman's 'Memorandum of Paintings'", *Burlington Magazine*, cxxvi, 1984, pp.629–30

Ellen Spickernagel, "'Helden wie zarte Knaben oder verkleidete Mädchen': Zum Begriff der Androgynität bei Johann Joachim Winckelmann und Angelika Kauffmann", *Frauen-Weiblichkeit-Schrift*, new series, xiv, ed. Renate Berger and others, Berlin: Argument, 1985, pp.99–118

Ellis Waterhouse, "Reynolds, Angelica Kauffmann and Lord Boringdon", *Apollo*, cxxii, 1985, pp.270–74

Sabine Hammer, *Angelica Kauffman*, Vaduz: Haas, 1987

Wendy Wassyng Roworth, "Artist/model/patron in Antiquity: Interpreting Ansiaux's *Alexander, Apelles and Campaspe*", *Muse*, xxii, 1988, pp.92–106

——, "Biography, criticism, art history: Angelica Kauffman in context", *Eighteenth-Century Women and the Arts*, ed. Frederick M. Keener and Susan E. Lorsch, New York: Greenwood, 1988, pp.209–23

Bettina Baumgärtel, "Freiheit-Gleichkeit-Schwesterkeit: Der Freundschaftskult der Malerin Angelika Kauffmann", *Sklavin oder Bürgerin Französische Revolution und Neue Weiblichkeit, 1760–1838*, exh. cat., Historisches Museum, Frankfurt am Main, 1989, pp.325–39

——, *Angelika Kauffmann (1741–1807): Bedingungen weiblicher Kreativität in der Malerei des 18. Jahrhunderts*, Weinheim and Basel, 1990

Angela Rosenthal, "Die Zeichnungen der Angelika Kauffmann im Vorarlberger Landesmuseum, Bregenz", *Jahrbuch der Vorarlberger Landesmuseumsvereins. 1990*, Bregenz, 1990, pp.139–81

Bettina Baumgärtel, "'Ich zeichne beständig …': Unbekannte Zeichnungen und Olskizzen von Angelika Kauffmann (1741–1807)", *Weltkunst*, no.19, 1991, pp.2832–4; no.22, 1991, pp.3542–4

Malise Forbes Adam and Mary Mauchline, "*Ut Pictura Poesis*: Angelica Kauffmann's literary sources", *Apollo*, cxxxii, 1992, pp.345–9

Hommage au Angelika Kauffmann, exh. cat., Liechtensteinische Staatliche Kunstsammlung, Vaduz, and Palazzo della Permanente, Milan, 1992

Angelika Kauffmann (1741–1807)/Marie Ellenrieder (1791–1863), exh. cat., Rosengartenmuseum, Konstanz, 1992

Angela Rosenthal, "Angelika Kauffman ma(s)king claims", *Art History*, xv, 1992, pp.38–59

Wendy Wassyng Roworth, ed., *Angelica Kauffman: A Continental Artist in Georgian England*, London: Reaktion, 1992

"… ihr werten Frauenzimmer, auf!": Malerinnen der Aufklärung, exh. cat., Roselius Haus, Bremen, 1993

Angela Rosenthal, "Double-writing in painting: Strategien der Selbstdarstellung von Künstlerinnen im 18. Jahrhundert", *Kritische Berichte: Zeitschrift für Kunst- und Kulturwissenschaften*, iii/3, 1993, pp.21–36

Wendy Wassyng Roworth, "Anatomy is destiny: Regarding the body in the art of Angelica Kauffman", *Femininity and Masculinity in Eighteenth-Century Art and Culture*, ed. Gill Perry and Michael Rossington, Manchester: Manchester University Press, 1994, pp.41–62

——, "Painting for profit and pleasure: Angelica Kauffman and the art business in Rome", *Eighteenth-Century Studies*, xxix, 1995–6, pp.225–8

Angela Rosenthal, *Angelika Kauffmann: Bildnismalerei im 18. Jahrhundert*, Berlin: Reimer, 1996

Throughout her life Angelica Kauffman enjoyed admiration for her considerable talents and acclaim for her professional accomplishments. This exceptionally prolific artist earned large sums of money from the sale of pictures, commissions and the reproduction of her compositions in a variety of media. These included etchings, engravings, book illustrations and designs for ceramics, fans, textiles and furniture. She painted fashionable oil portraits for a large international clientele and created a broad range of mythological, religious and literary paintings. Kauffman's delicate Neo-classical compositions were especially suitable for the interior designs of the architect Robert Adam, and while she provided drawings for some of his projects, recent research has shown that almost all the decorative compositions attributed to her were executed after her designs by copyists (Forbes Adam and Mauchline in Roworth 1992).

Kauffman's ability to please a varied audience from aristocratic patrons to such intellectuals as the German antiquarian Johann Joachim Winckelmann (*Winckelmann*, 1764; Kunsthaus, Zürich), her friend during her early years in Rome, and the poet Johann Wolfgang von Goethe (*Goethe*, 1787; Goethe-Wohnhaus, Weimar), whom she met during his travels in Italy in the late 1780s, to the wider public taste for her decorative work secured her a place within the mainstream of artistic developments during the latter half of the 18th century. As a result of her extensive activities and critical acclaim, Kauffman stands out as one of the few female artists whose name never entirely disappeared from the history of art and design.

Kauffman first made her name as a portrait painter, but some of her most popular pictures were Classical allegories (*Beauty Directed by Prudence Rejects with Scorn the Solicitations of Folly* and *Cupid Bound by the Graces*, repr. Roworth 1992, pp.130 and 160) and versions of sentimental scenes from Shakespeare, Homer, Ovid and other literary sources such as *Rinaldo and Armida* (Iveagh Bequest, Kenwood) from Tasso's *Gerusalemme liberata*, *Poor Maria* (1777; Burghley House, Stamford) from Laurence Sterne's *Sentimental Journey* and Alexander Pope's *Eloisa to Abelard* (*c.*1778; Burghley House).

While Kauffman produced many types of art, she identified herself primarily as a history painter, an unusual designation for a woman artist in the 18th century when portraiture and flower painting were still considered more appropriate for women. History painting, as defined in academic art theory, was classified as the most elevated category. Its subject matter, the representation of human actions based on themes from history, mythology, literature and scripture, required extensive learning in biblical and Classical literature, knowledge of art theory and a practical training that included the study of anatomy from the male nude. Most women were denied access to such training, especially the opportunity to draw from nude models; yet Kauffman managed to cross the gender boundary to acquire the necessary skills to build a reputation as a successful history painter who was admired by colleagues and eagerly sought by patrons.

Several factors contributed to Kauffman's success. One was her arrival in England in 1766 shortly before the establishment of the Royal Academy of Arts. During the 1760s British artists had been trying to cultivate a public taste and potential patrons for historical and mythological subjects. Kauffman originally came to England because of the well-established market for portraits, but she also had experience as a history painter. That background, combined with a clever business sense and winning personality, paved the way for professional recognition. The fact that she was a woman probably helped, for she was less likely to be seen as a serious rival by British artists. Kauffman found a receptive public, admiring friends of both sexes and the support of influential figures among artists and patrons such as Joshua Reynolds, one of the strongest advocates for history painting, Lady Spencer and Lord Exeter, for whom she made a number of important pictures (*Cleopatra Adorning the Tomb of Mark Antony*, 1770; Burghley House).

Kauffman and Reynolds became close friends. Her engaging portrait of *Reynolds* (1767; National Trust, Saltram), made within a year of her arrival, was well received, and soon Kauffman was in great demand for portraits of men, women and children. One of her popular portrait types depicted aristocratic women dressed in pseudo-Turkish dress (*Mary, 3rd Duchess of Richmond*, 1775; Goodwood House, Sussex) and engaged in solitary domestic pursuits such as needlework. Other portraits from the 1770s include *John, Lord Althorp, with His Sisters* (1774; Spencer Collection, Althorp) and *Frances Anne Hoare with a Bust of Clio* (*c.*1770–75; National Trust, Stourhead). Kauffman's six months in Ireland in 1771 resulted in a number of large family portraits (*Henry Loftus, Earl of Ely, His Wife and Nieces*, 1771; National Gallery of Ireland, Dublin).

Kauffman's remarkable popularity does not mean that she was universally admired or without detractors. Some contemporaries criticised the "effeminacy" of her male figures and other deficiencies. Her relationship with Reynolds was mocked in a painted satire by Nathaniel Hone (*The Conjuror*, 1775; National Gallery of Ireland), which she succeeded in having removed from public display. After her death, as the taste for Neo-classicism and allegorical subjects declined during the 19th century, her work fell out of fashion. In more recent histories of art she has often been dismissed as a mere "decorative" painter of lesser stature than her celebrated contemporaries Jacques-Louis David, Joshua Reynolds and Benjamin West. Nevertheless, her influence has persisted.

Kauffman's keen practical sense of how to succeed as a woman artist within the male art establishment served her well. As revealed in correspondence, financial records, biographies and the observations of her contemporaries, she worked hard at promoting her career. This evidence suggests that she supervised most aspects of her professional life and arranged her studios, both in London where she lived from 1766 to 1781 and in Rome where she settled in 1782, to show herself and her work to the greatest advantage. She was aided by her father, whom she supported through her work, and when at the age of 40 she married the older artist Antonio Zucchi, her husband took over the day-to-day management of her business affairs. On the occasion of this marriage they signed an agreement that ensured Kauffman's continuing control of her own considerable wealth. David Alexander's research has shown that she was directly involved in the production and marketing of prints after her work and the selling of compositions for mechanical paintings ("Kauffman and the print market in eighteenth-century England" in Roworth 1992). Throughout her years in England she collaborated with engravers and publishers in the production and sale of stipple prints and mezzotints after her paintings and drawings. She was one of the few contemporary artists whose works were used in the production of "mechanical paintings", a new process of colour reproduction invented in the mid-1770s. Kauffman's profitable involvement in what were considered the "minor" arts, as well as the higher categories of portraiture and grand-style history painting, reveals an important aspect of her shrewd and practical nature. She did not affect the temperament that had come to be associated with the idea of artistic genius, that heroic, masculine quality, cultivated by most academicians, and which Kauffman, as a woman, could not adopt. Instead she managed a successful balance between the desirable feminine traits of modesty and charm, polite society's ideal of an 18th-century woman of accomplishment, and her ambition to be accepted at the highest level of academic achievement.

Kauffman's awareness of the constraints on women artists may have contributed to her motivation to provide generous financial as well as moral support to younger women artists. She assisted Maria Cosway (q.v.) in her career, encouraged the talent of Georgiana Keate, the daughter of her friend the poet George Keate, and her own cousin Rosa Florini, who married the architect Joseph Bonomi.

According to her biographer and friend, Giovanni Gherardo De Rossi (1810), as a young woman Kauffman was equally talented as a painter and musician, and she faced the hard choice of which career to pursue. Thirty years later she commemorated this choice in a well-known allegorical portrait, which exists in two versions (1791; Pushkin Museum, Moscow; 1794; National Trust, Nostell Priory, Wakefield). She portrayed herself as a youthful woman between female personifications of the sister arts, Music and Painting. The composition was based on the Classical story of "The Choice or Judgement of Hercules" (Xenophon, *Memorabilia*, II, i, 22). Hercules, an exemplar of heroic virtue, had to choose between the easy joys of Pleasure and the hard, rocky path of Virtue that led to the Temple of Fame. In a deliberate gender shift, Kauffman played the role of the mythical hero and portrayed herself hesitating between gentle Music and powerful Painting. This story of Kauffman's decision to follow what was considered to be the more rigorous and intellectually challenging art must be based on some truth, but the fact that her biographer chose to relate it at length and the artist herself to memorialise it in a major self-portrait is

noteworthy. This characterisation of Kauffman in both biography and portrait ensured that she would be recognised as not only intelligent, hard-working and ambitious, but also remembered as a proper woman of virtue, the female equivalent of the masculine hero.

In addition, Kauffman's abandonment of Music represented a deliberate departure from a tradition of Italian Renaissance self-portraits of women artists, such as those by Lavinia Fontana (1578), Sofonisba Anguissola (1561) and Marietta Robusti (c.1580) (all q.v.), who had portrayed themselves with keyboard instruments, which associated them with Music, an art considered a proper feminine accomplishment (although this had more to do with class and decorum than their status as either musicians or painters). Kauffman, despite the coy playfulness of her self-portrait, demonstrated through the rejection of Music her desire to be recognised within the noble tradition of history painting, the most public and "masculine" of all genres. Her knowledge of history and literature was obtained, according to her biographer, through extensive reading. Instead of attending to amusements or the distractions of love, she devoted herself studiously to reading history, as well as the Italian, French and German poets. These sources provided ideas for painting and stimulated her lively imagination (De Rossi 1810, pp.14–15).

After her initial training with her father, a provincial painter, Kauffman followed the established practice for artistic education by travelling throughout Italy. She copied paintings by the Renaissance and 17th-century masters in the galleries of Milan, Parma, Bologna, Rome, Florence and Naples, and drew from the great works of Classical antiquity. It was through studies of statues and paintings that she learned human anatomy and the representation of figures in action. According to De Rossi, she sometimes worked from live male models, but her father was present and they were always properly covered except for their limbs. Kauffman was accepted as a member of the Accademia Clementina in Bologna (1762), the Accademia del Disegno in Florence (1762) and the Accademia di San Luca in Rome (1765). As a female prodigy, she attracted attention and received many visitors to her studio. By the mid-1760s she was producing large history paintings of Classical subjects (*Penelope at Her Loom*, 1764; Hove Museum and Art Gallery; *Bacchus and Ariadne*, 1764; Rathaus, Bregenz) and portraits for British visitors on the Grand Tour, such as the actor *David Garrick* (1764; Burghley House). She became friends with many artists who were involved in the development of the Neo-classical style such as the American Benjamin West, the Scotsman Gavin Hamilton, and Nathaniel Dance, to whom she was briefly engaged.

Soon after her arrival in England Kauffman nearly ruined her developing career when in 1767 she married a man who turned out to be an impostor, the Swedish "Count de Horn". This very brief and apparently unconsummated marriage ended when the truth came to light – he had at least one other wife – and Kauffman paid him to leave. It is remarkable that what could have been a disaster and was certainly the subject for much gossip did not affect her career. Ironically, it may have been this illegal marriage that allowed her to maintain her freedom and control of her career. Whether through poor judgement, rashness or innocence, Kauffman in effect exempted herself from the traditional expectation of marriage and motherhood, a situation that would probably have curtailed the high aspirations and heavy workload she maintained. After this episode she retained a peculiar status: neither spinster nor virgin, widow nor wife, and not quite a fallen woman, a situation that seems to have kept further suitors at bay and turned attention to her work rather than her person.

In 1768 Kauffman became one of the founding members of the Royal Academy of Arts, one of two women – Mary Moser was the other – within that elite group. Her earliest history paintings exhibited at the Royal Academy in 1769 were among the first Classical subjects shown in public by any artist in England: *Penelope Taking Down the Bow of Ulysses*, *Hector Taking Leave of His wife Andromache*, *Aeneas and Achates Meeting Venus Disguised as a Hunting Maiden* and *Achilles among the Daughters of Lycomedes* (National Trust, Saltram Park). All four subjects from the Trojan legend were bought by Reynolds's old friend John Parker for his country seat at Saltram, Devon, to be installed in the Grand Saloon designed by Robert Adam. As a group they represented the conflicts between love and war, personal desire and civic duty, male and female roles, and employed gender reversals and disguises. Kauffman frequently chose subjects that allowed for the treatment of women in prominent roles as a way to draw attention to her unique status as a female history painter and in

order to attract patronage, especially from a female clientele. In fact, she received support from Queen Charlotte (*Queen Charlotte Raising the Genius of the Fine Arts*, engraved by Burke, 1772) in England, and in her later years she counted the Empress Catherine of Russia, Maria Theresa of Austria and her daughter Queen Carolina of Naples (*King Ferdinand IV and Queen Carolina of Naples and His Family*, 1783; Capodimonte, Naples) among her most important patrons.

Most notable of Kauffman's female subjects is Penelope, the crafty and wise heroine of the Odyssey, the embodiment of feminine virtue under the guidance of Minerva: patient, faithful, devoted to husband and son, and adept at the female art of weaving. Kauffman was the first artist to exploit the image of Penelope, and the subject became something of a speciality. Some were shown at the Royal Academy exhibitions and many were reproduced as popular engravings: *Penelope Sacrificing to Minerva for the Safe Return of Telemachus* (1774; National Trust, Stourhead), *Penelope Awakened by Euryclea with the News of Ulysses' Return* (engraved by Burke, 1773), *Return of Telemachus* (1775; Lord Derby, Knowsley) and *Penelope Weeping over the Bow of Ulysses* (1777; Burghley House).

The choice of female characters was practical in terms of the moralising purpose of history painting and her own strategies for success, but it also allowed her to avoid the depiction of active nude or semi-nude male figures. In fact, Kauffman's paintings were more likely to represent subjects in which gender roles are ambiguous, reversed, masked or disguised, such as *Achilles Disguised as a Maiden Discovered by Ulysses* (1768; Saltram), the young *Telemachus at the Court of Sparta Weeping for the Loss of His Father* (engraved by Ryland, 1773) and *Imbaca Disguised as a Warrior, Revealing Herself as a Maiden to Trenmor from "Ossian"* (1773; private collection, repr. Bregenz 1968, fig.30).

Two other large history paintings (also at Saltram) were the first subjects from British history exhibited at the Royal Academy: *Vortigern, King of Britain Enamoured of Rowena at the Banquet of Hengist* (1770) and *Interview of King Edgar and Elfrida after Her Marriage with Aethelwold* (1771), the first known pictorial representation of this subject. Kauffman continued to exhibit regularly at the annual Royal Academy exhibitions. Other important paintings of Classical and historical subjects from this period include *Sappho and Cupid*

(1775; John and Mable Ringling Museum, Sarasota), *Andromache Fainting at the Unexpected Sight of Aeneas* (1775; Walker Art Gallery, Liverpool), *Tender Eleanora Sucking the Venom out of the Wound of Edward I* (1776; engraved by Ryland, 1780) and *Lady Elizabeth Grey Imploring Edward IV for the Restitution of Her Deceased Husband's Lands* (engraved by Ryland, 1780). These are treated in similar Neo-classical fashion with figures arranged near the picture plane in eloquent interaction of gestures and expressions based on Classical reliefs and Renaissance paintings. The sources for Kauffman's British subjects are David Hume's and Nicholas Rapin's histories of England, although Reynolds or someone else may have suggested some of the specific subjects. Many of her Classical scenes, but not all, were taken from the Comte de Caylus's book *Tableaux tirés de l'Iliade, de l'Odyssée d'Homère et de l'Enéide de Virgile* (Paris, 1757).

In 1773 Kauffman was one of five painters commissioned to paint the dome of St Paul's Cathedral in London with historical subjects, although this project was never carried out. When the Royal Academy moved into new premises at Somerset House in 1780, Kauffman made four oval ceiling paintings of allegorical subjects (now Burlington House, London) as part of the didactic decoration for the Council Chamber. These represented the four parts of the art of painting: *Invention, Composition, Drawing* (Design) and *Colouring*.

After a highly successful career in England, Kauffman returned to Italy to take advantage of the wider and more sophisticated Continental market. She and Zucchi, her husband, were soon established in a large house in Rome with their impressive collection of paintings, engravings and books by Classical and modern authors, and she quickly became one of the stars of the international community. In 1788 she was honoured by the acceptance of her self-portrait into the Medici collection of artists' portraits (Uffizi, Florence). Her studio became a popular stop on the Grand Tour for fashionable visitors and clients, agents and dealers, painters and engravers, poets and princes from Britain, Germany, Russia and Poland who wished to have their portraits made, to order history paintings or simply to participate in the evenings of conversation, poetry reading and music. Her work of this period

is recorded in the *Memorandum of Paintings* kept by Zucchi until his death in 1795.

Kauffman also continued to produce pictures for British patrons, most notably George Bowles, who owned many of her most interesting Classical and allegorical works. These included *Zeuxis and the Maidens of Crotona* (c.1778; Annmary Brown Collection, Brown University, Providence), which contained a cleverly masked self-portrait, and *Self-Portrait in the Character of Design Embraced by Poetry* (1782; Iveagh Bequest). Three of her most severely Neo-classical and serious moralising paintings for Bowles were exhibited at the Royal Academy in 1786. These represent *Cornelia, Mother of the Gracchi Showing Her Sons as Her Treasures* (Virginia Museum of Fine Arts, Richmond), *Pliny the Younger with His Mother at Misenum* (Art Museum, Princeton) and *Vergil Writing His Own Epitaph at Brundisium* (private collection, repr. Los Angeles 1976, p.177).

Despite the turmoil that engulfed Europe during the French Revolution and its aftermath, and her failing health in later years, Kauffman remained busy making paintings for such patrons as the King of Poland, Prince Poniatowski, the Emperor Franz Joseph and Frederick, Prince of Wales. Among works of this period are portraits of *Lady Hamilton*, the novelist *Cornelia Knight* (1793; Manchester City Art Galleries), *Thomas Noel Hill, 2nd Lord Berwick* (1793; National Trust, Attingham) and *Ludwig I of Bavaria* (1805–7; Bayerische Staatsgemaldesammlungen, Munich). She turned increasingly to religious subjects, for example the *Holy Family*, the *Annunciation, Christ and the Woman of Samaria* (1795; Bayerische Staatsgemaldesammlungen) and *David Reproached by Nathan* (1797; untraced, engraved by Ryland, 1773). The last two pictures were carried in the elaborate funeral procession held in Rome at her death in 1807. Her will records that she left considerable wealth and property to her family and to the poor of her father's home parish in Bregenz, Austria, but Kauffman left an even greater legacy in her role as one of the most successful and influential women artists, whose image continued to inspire later generations of women painters.

WENDY WASSYNG ROWORTH

See also Academies of Art and Printmakers surveys

Kelly, Mary
American artist, 1941–

Born in Minneapolis, Minnesota, 1941. Studied at College of St Teresa, Winona (BA 1963); Pius XII Institute, Florence, Italy, 1963–5 (MA); St Martin's School of Art, London, 1968–70 (diploma). Taught at American University of Beirut, 1965–8. Married British artist Ray Barrie; son born, 1973. Joined editorial board of *Screen* magazine, 1979. Returned to New York to teach on Independent Study Program, Whitney Museum of American Art, New York, 1989, and became Director of Studios. Artist-in-residence, New Hall, Cambridge University, England, 1985–6. Recipient of Arts Council of Great Britain award, 1977; Lina Garnade Memorial Foundation award, 1978; National Endowment for the Arts (NEA) fellowship, 1987. Lives in New York.

Selected Individual Exhibitions
South London Art Gallery: 1975 (*Women and Work*, with Kay Hunt and Margaret Harrison)
Institute of Contemporary Arts, London: 1976
Museum of Modern Art, Oxford: 1977
Fruitmarket Gallery, Edinburgh: 1985 (*Interim*, touring)
New Museum of Contemporary Art, New York: 1990–91 (*Interim*, touring)
Herbert F. Johnson Museum of Art, Ithaca, NY: 1992 (*Gloria Patri*, touring)

Selected Writings
"Re-viewing modernist criticism", *Screen*, no.22, Autumn 1981, pp.41–62
Post-Partum Document, London: Routledge, 1983
"Desiring images/imaging desire", *Wedge*, vi, Winter 1984, pp.4–9
"Beyond the purloined image", *Framing Feminism: Art and the Women's Movement, 1970–1985*, ed. Rozsika Parker and Griselda Pollock, London: Pandora, 1987, pp.249–53
"On sexual politics and art", *ibid.*, pp.303–12
"On representation, sexuality and sameness: Reflections on the 'Difference Show'", *Screen*, no.28, Winter 1987, pp.102–7
"From Corpus", *Taking Our Time: Feminist Perspectives on Temporality*, ed. Frieda Forman, Oxford: Pergamon, 1989, pp.153–9
"Re-presenting the body", *Psychoanalysis and Cultural Theory: Thresholds*, ed. James Donald, London: Macmillan, and New York: St Martin's Press, 1991
"(P)age 49: on the *subject* of history", *New Feminist Art Criticism: Critical Strategies*, ed. Katy Deepwell, Manchester: Manchester University Press, 1995, pp.147–52

Imaging Desire, Cambridge: Massachusetts Institute of Technology Press, 1997

Bibliography
Hayward Annual '78, exh. cat., Arts Council of Great Britain, London, 1978
Griselda Pollock and Rozsika Parker, *Old Mistresses: Women, Art and Ideology*, London: Routledge, and New York: Pantheon, 1981
Jo-Anna Isaak, "Our mother tongue: The *Post-Partum Document*", *Vanguard*, xi, April 1982, pp.14–17
Mary Kelly: Interim, exh. cat., Fruitmarket Gallery, Edinburgh, and elsewhere, 1985
"Mary Kelly and Laura Mulvey in conversation", *Afterimage*, xiii, March 1986, pp.6–8
Griselda Pollock, *Vision and Difference: Femininity, Feminism and the Histories of Art*, London and New York: Routledge, 1988
Laura Mulvey, *Visual and Other Pleasures*, Bloomington: Indiana University Press, and London: Macmillan, 1989
Mary Kelly: Interim, exh. cat., New Museum of Contemporary Art, New York, and elsewhere, 1990
John Roberts, *Postmodernism, Politics and Art*, Manchester: Manchester University Press, 1990
Charlotte Streifer Rubinstein, *American Women Sculptors*, Boston: Hall, 1990
Parveen Adams, "The art of analysis: Mary Kelly's *Interim* and the discourse of the analyst", *October*, no.58, 1991, pp.81–96
Emily Apter, "Fetishism and visual seduction in Mary Kelly's *Interim*", *ibid.*, pp.97–108
Cassandra Langer, "Mary Kelly's *Interim*", *Woman's Art Journal*, xiii/1, 1992, pp.41–5
Judith Mastai, ed., *Mary Kelly and Griselda Pollock in Conversation at the Vancouver Art Gallery, June 1989*, Vancouver: Vancouver Art Gallery, 1992
"Mary Kelly and Margaret Iversen in conversation", *Talking Art I*, ed. Adrian Searle, London: Institute of Contemporary Arts, 1993
Mara R. Witzling, ed., *Voicing Today's Visions: Writings by Contemporary Women Artists*, New York: Universe, 1994
Helaine Posner, "The masculine masquerade: Masculinity represented in recent art", *The Masculine Masquerade: Masculinity and Representation*, ed. Andrew Perchuk and Helaine Posner, Cambridge: Massachusetts Institute of Technology Press, 1995, pp.21–30

Mary Kelly's entrance into the international art scene of the mid-1970s was nothing short of audacious. The first three sections of *Post-Partum Document* were exhibited at the London Institute of Contemporary Arts in 1976 and were given a noisy reception by the tabloid press: "Dirty nappies!", they shrieked. In fact, Part I of the *Document*, which is concerned with the mother's anxieties over the months of weaning her baby from the breast, consists of analysed faecal stains (or their simulation) on nappy liners and are exhibited with pristine elegance. The liners are fixed flat within recessed frames like precious prints on some rare, hand-made paper and the stains themselves form shadowy images reminiscent of the Shroud of Turin. An obsessively careful daily diary of the infant's solid food intake is printed at the bottom of each liner.

The tabloid press represents one extreme reaction to the work that deemed it scatological. But Kelly's work met with another negative reaction, which judged it to be too cerebral and obscure. This split response is eloquent testimony to a deep ambivalence that inhabits all her work. Her "style" evokes the precision and restraint of Minimalism and her use of language and diagrams that record and analyse the results of extended research projects links her to the strategies of Conceptualism. But what Conceptualist would have thought of inserting a mother and baby into that art discourse? Even some feminists were a bit surprised since they were busy asserting their right to be free from the demands of reproduction, which was thought to hamper women's creative production. The mother-artist was an oxymoron both within Patriarchy and within the movements that sought to challenge it.

Kelly's work shares with Conceptualism a political commitment to reflect on cultural discourses, but she exchanges the tools of linguistic analysis for those of psychoanalysis. Her "content" or raw material is subjectivity, the body, fears and desires, and the cultural forms that condition them. The systematic lucidity of Kelly's art is set against powerful emotion and it sometimes tips over into anxious repetition. *Post-Partum Document* marks a highly significant turn towards the subject in art practice and theory prompted mainly by feminists. Kelly was well placed to take the lead. Although born in the USA and now returned there, she spent formative years in the 1960s and 1970s in London in close contact with Juliet Mitchell (*Psychoanalysis and Feminism*, New York: Pantheon, and London: Allen Lane, 1974) and Laura Mulvey ("Visual pleasure and narrative cinema", 1975; reprinted in Mulvey 1989, pp.14–26). She has maintained this incisive cutting-edge. In the following discussion of this great installation work, made readily available in book form, and the two other major works to date, *Interim* and *Gloria Patri*, the three terms – art

practice, feminism and psychoanalysis – must be kept in play if the full measure of Kelly's astuteness, inventiveness and audacity is to be appreciated.

The tension or ambivalence at the heart of *Post-Partum Document* (1973–8) is summed up succinctly by Kelly's statement that it concerns "my lived experience as a mother and my analysis of that experience". In it she explores, with the aid of psychoanalysis, the way biological sex difference is made to conform to patriarchal social norms of gender difference that are "sealed", so to speak, in the woman's experience of maternity. Her status as the gender that lacks a penis is momentarily absolved by the birth of a baby. But separation, anxiety and loss mark even the early months of motherhood. She re-experiences the symbolic castration she underwent as a little girl. Understanding these psychic processes through which women internalise their oppression was thought to be a crucial first step towards liberation.

How are these processes to be represented? Actual pictures of mother and child, an icon of love and tenderness in the history of art, could now only be sentimental and kitsch and, in any case, would lack explanatory power. Kelly's "modernist" eschewal of figurative representation is also motivated by the vulnerability of the woman's body to appropriation and exploitation within patriarchal culture. Instead, one finds a division in the work between gestural marks, traces, moulds (what C.S. Peirce called indexical signs) and writing, diagrams, symbols. The index, to some extent, resists verbalisation and is related to the sense of touch, so these signs invoke the sensuous, emotive quality of the mother's lived experience. The mute immediacy of this experience is relieved through the other register of Lacanian theory and diagrams in which these experiences are situated and put in perspective. These antagonistic registers of signification are used very effectively in the pre-document series that consists of four tiny undershirts in a row, each one adding a line to complete a Lacanian diagram. The piece suggests that the mother's intense attachment to these objects is now mediated by an explanatory theory.

The "beauty" of the undershirts or of the plaster casts of the child's hand in Documentation IV raises another issue explored in the work: maternal fetishism. According to psychoanalytic theory, fetishism is an exclusively male perversion, but Kelly suggests that if a baby fulfils in fantasy the lack carved out in the woman by a phallo-centric society, then the loss of the maturing child must represent a castration threat. As a consequence, the mother preserves little fetishes – shoes, photographs, locks of hair, school reports – that both memorialise the loss and defend against it. The small scale and box-like dimensions of the individually framed units allude to this fetishisation, yet they also combine to form "cinematic" frames recording the passage of time and the changes occurring in the mother's relationship with her child. Kelly calls this latter strategy "the narrativization of space" (Kelly and Iversen 1993, p.103) and it is crucial to her ongoing explorations of complex social realities and theories.

With *Post-Partum Document* Kelly broke the taboo surrounding maternity in contemporary critical art practice. She followed this up with an equally provocative topic: women and middle age. *Interim* (1984–9) explores the crisis of identity experienced by the older, post-maternal woman. What are the social roles, the self-images, the expectations in circulation for her? The work is truly monumental in scale: it filled the New Museum of Contemporary Art in New York when it was exhibited there in 1990. But it might also be considered monumental in other senses since it is so reflexive about the past and concerned with memory, both personal and collective. It has been suggested that "middle age" is also metaphorically the position of the women's movement itself, which is in the process of redefining itself.

The work consists of four parts that focus on the Body, Money, History and Power (with the Latin titles *Corpus, Pecunia, Historia* and *Potestas*). In the same way that the earlier work proposed maternal fetishism as a specifically feminine "aesthetic", *Interim* turns on the issue of identification and disidentification in relation to representations as well as to other people. Kelly began her project by sifting through pop-cultural artefacts (such as women's magazines) and by recording conversations with many women in order to find out what positions they habitually take up or what ones are fantasised. Part I, *Corpus*, consists of photographs of garments arranged in different postures: Menacé, Erotisme, Extase – which are paired with first person, anecdotal text panels. Charcot's practice of documenting photographically his hysterical patients and his classification of *attitudes passionelles* are invoked here but not uncritically. In an interview with Hal Foster, Kelly remarked that "*Interim* proposes not one body but many bodies, shaped within a lot of different discourses. It doesn't refer to an anatomical fact or to a perceptual entity, but to the dispersed body of desire" (quoted in New York 1990, p.55). The absence of iconic images of the woman's body in Kelly's work is in response to the special requirements of the female spectator: it prevents her "hysterical" identification with the male voyeur and the use of writing helps to open up a gap: "to distance the spectator from the anxious proximity of her body" (*idem*).

Interim is addressed to a female spectator as the subject of desire. How does it propose to do this? By representing the maternal body as lost and therefore as an object of desire. The "middle-aged" or post-maternal woman is ideally placed to make this transition to sublimated pleasure, for at that moment the stability and pleasure of identification with the mother's body in maternity give way to shifting instability that can be experienced as pleasurable loss. Perhaps this is why the garments in *Corpus* have a ghostly presence – they are semi-transparent photo-laminates affixed to sheets of raised Perspex so that they "float" and cast a shadow. The beautiful image of a summer dress, for example, with its tiny waist was apparently inspired by shop-window displays that frequently show impossible anatomies. But, through the text panel, Kelly links the image to the fantasies of romantic fiction with their excess of desire and straining for release from normative strictures.

Although Part II is called *Pecunia* (Latin: money), it is less about money than the way that a culture dominated by commodities and the imperative of professional or business success inflects our most intimate desires. We see these desires in turn refracted through four social positions – mother, daughter, sister and wife. The series is made up of cleverly folded "pop-up" pieces of galvanised steel, treated in such a way that they have the glitzy iridescence of greeting cards. The narratives printed inside the "cards" are scenes from the everyday life of everywoman. Some of them are horribly familiar: there is the self-sacrificing mother who has "postponed her life" and the housewife whose idea of happiness is a perfectly clean toilet bowl, emblem of her independent identity – "Now everything would be her way".

The first-person fictional narratives of *Corpus* contrast with the "true stories" of *Historia*. Identification in the latter case is about the assumption of a political identity in the women's movement. Here, again, Kelly presents not a monolith of the collectivity of women, but four consecutive and parallel personal histories told by four generations of feminists since 1968. The texts in this section offer a utopian vision of political, ethnic and age differences subsumed within a jubilant common gender identity, and they also question this aspiration. Formally, the *Historia* series looks like open books and newspaper galleys recording what might otherwise have been hidden from history, and also like tombstones, monuments to the courage of those who have gone before. The last Part, *Potestas* or Power, is made up of contrasting metal bars that evoke, for men, the work of the Abstract Expressionist sculptor David Smith and, for women, the rusted surfaces of Richard Serra's much-maligned minimalist prop pieces. Although the work as a whole is deeply informed by psychoanalytic and Foucauldian theory, it does not rest content with representing the circumstances of women's oppression. Self-transcendence is presented as a possibility within the history of the women's movement.

One of the most striking images of *Corpus* is a glossy black leather jacket, the artist's equivalent of the businesswoman's tailored suit, which mimes male attire and points to the importance of identification with the father. One of the paths through the Oedipal complex in girls as described by Freud is the "masculinity complex" in which she stubbornly resists the imputation that she has not got the Phallus. In fantasy, she does and so presumably do men whose penis inevitably falls far short of the Phallus.

In *Gloria Patri* (1992) Kelly analyses the masculinity complex in men and women. The work was also sparked by the media coverage of the Gulf War and the quite sinister spectacle of violent aggression set against a weakened national position following the end of the Cold War. The polished aluminium shields that make up part of the installation are meant, first, to evoke a pathological, armoured, masculine ideal and, second, to show this up as a façade. The narratives printed on the shields do the same; they are scenarios of failed masculinity taken, not from war, but from everyday life.

The other elements of the installation, all in polished aluminium, are 20 discs silk-screened with re-configured military logos and two-dimensional trophies topped by male figurines in an archaic

"deco" style. Its forbidding visual quality, heightened by "search-beam" up-lighting, is in fact counterpointed by the narratives themselves, which are sympathetic. There are ironic rhymes between the snatches of Gulf War rhetoric printed on the trophies and the downbeat stories – for example, Schwarzkopf's stated strategy for liquidating the Iraqi army, "cut it off and kill it", is echoed in the reflections of a lone fisherman stalking a brook trout: "He could do whatever he wanted: cut it up and eat it or throw it back". The common element of sadistic pleasure is underscored in both. Yet the fisherman's puffed-up, confident mastery is punctured at the end of the story by the mere quizzical gaze of a Great Blue heron; the man suddenly sees his own muddled reflection in the water. The other stories concern different fantasies of mastery: a man witnesses his son's birth with mixed emotions; an adolescent boy's nascent masculinity rebels at the sight of greens on his plate, emblem of the mother and of femininity generally. The last story is about a woman on a body-building machine attacking her soft feminine flesh: if only she could "cut off her sequacity and kill it". In each case an armour-like shell of an ego defends against a sense of bodily fragmentation and the distress of helplessness. Have women unconsciously incorporated a masculine ego ideal? And if so, what price Glory?

Works by the artist in public collections are to be found at the Arts Council of Great Britain; Tate Gallery, London; Vancouver Art Gallery; New Museum of Contemporary Art, New York; Kunsthaus, Zürich; Helsinki City Museum; and the National Gallery of Australia, Canberra.

MARGARET IVERSEN

Kielland, (Christine) Kitty (Lange)
Norwegian painter, 1843–1914   [fig. 37]

Born in Stavanger, 8 October 1843. Studied under Fanny Zeuthen in Stavanger, 1860s; under Morten Müller in Christiania (Oslo), c.1870. Studied in Karlsruhe, at the Kunstschule and under Norwegian painter Hans Gude, 1873–5; in Munich under Norwegian painter Eilif Peterssen, 1875–8, and Hermann Baisch, c.1876. Usually spent summers in Jären, Norway, after 1876. Lived in Paris, 1878–89; studied at Académie Julian, under

Tony Robert-Fleury, 1879; private studies under Léon Pelouse in Cernay-la-Ville and Brittany, intermittently 1880–86; attended Académie Colarossi, 1883 and 1886–7. Member of Norwegian art committee for Exposition Universelle, Paris, 1889. Lived in Christiania from 1889, with frequent trips abroad, often with Harriet Backer (q.v.). Active participant in Norwegian debates on art and the women's movement, late 1880s. Recipient of King's gold medal of merit, 1908. Honorary member, Norwegian Students Society. Died in Oslo, 1 October 1914.

Principal Exhibitions

Individual

Blomqvist, Christiania: 1899
Christiania Kunstforening: 1904
Trondheim Kunstforening: 1904
Diorama Gallery, Christiania: 1911

Group

Drammens Kunstforening (Art Association), Christiania: from 1878
Paris Salon: 1879–83, 1887
Christiania Kunstforening (Art Association): from 1880
Göteborg: 1881 (*Nordisk konstutställningen* [Nordic exhibition])
Høstutstillingen (Autumn Salon), Christiania: 1882–92, 1894–1908
Charlottenborg, Copenhagen: 1883 (*Den Nordiske udstilling* [Nordic exhibition]), 1888 (*Den Nordiske udstilling* [Nordic exhibition])
Exposition Universelle d'Anvers, Antwerp: 1885
Valand, Göteborg: 1886 (*Nordisk konstutställningen* [Nordic exhibition])
Exposition Universelle, Paris: 1889 (silver medal), 1900
World's Columbian Exposition, Chicago: 1893
Venice Biennale: 1897, 1899, 1907
Blomqvist, Christiania: 1910 (*Malerindeforbundets utstilling* [Society of Women Painters exhibition])

Selected Writings

"Et indlæg i kvindesagen" [A plea for the women's movement], *Luthersk Ugeskrift*, 1885, pp.209–15
"Mors kjæledægge" [Mother's pet], *Nyt Tidsskrift*, 1885, pp.282–99
Kvindespørgsmaalet [The woman question], Christiania, 1886
"Et par ord i diskussionen" [A few words in the discussion], *Nyt Tidsskrift*, 1887, pp.714–20
"Svar til Gina Krog" [Reply to Gina Krog], *Nylænde*, 1887, pp.341–6
"Kunstkritik" [Art criticism], *Dagbladet*, 1 May 1887 (signed "en maler", "a painter")
"Nogle betragtninger over stiftsmødets forhandlinger angaaende kvindens deltagelse i Guds ords forkyn-delse" [Some thoughts on the diocesan meeting's negotiations regarding women's participation in the spreading of God's word], *Morgenbladet*, 12 December 1888
"Lidt om norsk kunst" [Something about Norwegian art], *Samtiden*, 1890, pp.223–8
"Svar til Andreas Aubert" [Reply to Andreas Aubert], *Dagbladet*, 17 November 1890
"Lidt om eller mod Le Bons artikel" [Something about or against Le Bon's article], *Samtiden*, 1891, pp.161–7
"Hafdan Egedius", *Samtiden*, 1899, pp.83–7
"Jæderen", *Norge i det nittende aarhundrede* [Norway in the 19th century], ii, Christiania, 1900, pp.158–65

Bibliography

Andreas Aubert, *Det nye Norges malerkunst* [Painting of the new Norway], Christiania, 1904
Jen Thiis, *Norske malere og billedhuggere* [Norwegian painters and sculptors], Bergen, i, 1904, pp.185, 311; ii, 1907, pp.311–16
E. Lone, *Harriet Backer*, Oslo, 1924
B. Kielland, *Min far Alexander L. Kielland* [My father Alexander L. Kielland], Oslo, 1929
H. Aars, "På Fleskum i Bærum" [At Fleskum in Bærum], *Kunst og Kultur*, 1941, pp.93–110
A. Durban, *Malerskikkelser fra 80-årene* [Figures in painting from the 1880s], Trondheim, 1943
E. Christie Kielland, "Kitty L. Kielland", *Urd*, 1943, pp.376–8
G.S. Hidle, *Profiler og paletter i Rogalands kunst* [Profiles and palettes in Rogland's art], Stavanger, 1965
U. Hamran, "Harriet Backer og Kitty L. Kielland på Bosvik sommeren 1885" [Harriet Backer and Kitty L. Kielland in Bosvik in the summer of 1885], *Aust-Agder arv: Aust-Agder Museum Årbok*, 1977, pp.117–26
Marit Lange, "Fra den hellige lund til Fleskum: Kitty L. Kielland og den nordiske sommernatt" [From the holy grove to Fleskum: Kitty L. Kielland and the Nordic summer night], *Kunst og Kultur*, 1977, pp.69–92
——, "Kitty Lange Kielland", *Norske mesterverker i Nasjonalgalleriet* [Norwegian masterpieces in the National Gallery], Oslo, 1981, pp.56–8
Anne Wichstrøm, "Blant likemenn: Søkelys på Harriet Backers og Kitty L. Kiellands karrierer" [Among equals: Spotlight on the careers of Harriet Backer and Kitty L. Kielland], *Den skjulte tradisjon* [The hidden tradition], Bergen, 1982, pp.172–91
Harriet Backer, 1845–1932, Kitty L. Kielland, 1843–1914, exh. cat., Stiftelsen Modums Blaafarvevaerk, Drammen, 1983
Anne Wichstrøm, *Kvinner ved staffeliet: Kvinnelige malere i Norge før 1900* [Women at the easel: Women painters in Norway before 1900], Oslo: Universitetsforlaget, 1983 (revised edition in preparation)

1880-årene i nordisk maleri [The 1880s in Nordic paint-
ing], exh. cat., Nasjonalgalleriet, Oslo, and elsewhere,
1985

*Dreams of a Summer Night: Scandinavian Painting at the
Turn of the Century*, exh. cat., Arts Council of Great
Britain, London, 1986

De drogo till Paris: Nordiska konstnärinnor på 1880-talet
[They went to Paris: Nordic women artists in the
1880s], exh. cat., Liljevalchs Konsthall, Stockholm,
1988

Kirk Varnedoe, *Northern Light: Nordic Art at the Turn
of the Century*, New Haven and London: Yale
University Press, 1988

Alessandra Comini, "Nordic luminism and the
Scandinavian recasting of Impressionism", *World
Impressionism: The International Movement,
1860–1920*, ed. Norma Broude, New York: Abrams,
1992, pp.274–313

Knut Berg, "Naturalisme og nyromanrikk" [Naturalism
and Neo-romanticism], *Norges Malerkunst*, ed. Knut
Berg, Oslo: Gyldendal, 1993

Tradisjon og fornyelse [Tradition and innovation], exh.
cat., Nasjonalgalleriet, Oslo, 1994

Anne Wichstrøm, "At century's end: Harriet Backer, Kitty
Kielland, Asta Nørregaard", *At Century's End:
Norwegian Artists and the Figurative Tradition,
1880/1990*, exh. cat, Henie-Onstad Art Center,
Høvikodden, and National Museum of Women in the
Arts, Washington, DC, 1995, pp.21–67

Best known for her landscapes of the Jæren region,
Kitty Kielland was an integral member of Norway's
National Romantic generation of painters. There
were several women in this group, and they worked
with their male colleagues as peers and equals,
developing a distinctive group style that won them
immediate and continuing popularity. While the
urge to define a national identity distinct from
Denmark (which had ruled Norway prior to 1815)
and Sweden (which ruled Norway until 1906) had
fuelled ethnographic pursuits and permeated literature and music since the beginning of the century, it
was not until the 1880s that the impulse to manifest
a Norwegian identity in painting appeared.
Kielland, always devoted to an exacting observation
and experience of nature as part of the creative
process, was an important link between Naturalism
and Nordic Symbolism.

Kielland was the only member of this group
trained by a woman; her first studies in her home
town of Stavanger were given by Fanny Zeuthen.
While Zeuthen was a painter of purely local significance, the fact that women painters functioned as
teachers in the 1850s and 1860s indicates the relatively high stature of women artists in the Nordic

countries. Kielland spent most of the 1870s in
Germany, primarily in Munich, where she pursued
plein-air landscape painting. Rather than studying
with a local artist, she relied on the critique of
fellow Norwegian artist Eilif Peterssen, who began
his career as a history painter, turning to landscape
only in the 1880s during his residence in Paris. Since
Kielland was a leading proponent of Naturalistic
landscape painting from the very beginning, she
exerted an influence on Peterssen and other
Norwegians who turned to landscape painting as
the National Romantic movement escalated.

Kielland's small-format compositions typically
involved a detailed foreground and a broadly delineated background. In the Naturalist tradition, her
images were unpretentious. Narrative was reduced
to a minimum, forcing the viewer's concentration on
subtleties of light, shadow and atmosphere. Often
the only figure in her landscapes is a lone woman,
quietly engaged in a leisure activity, as in *After
Sunset* (1885; Slottet, Oslo), where a woman rows
on a placid lake in front of a manor house, and
Jærtun, Kvalbein (1904; Breidablikk Foundation,
Stavanger), where a peasant woman draws water
from a well on a rural Norwegian farm. While
Kielland's sketchy brushwork conveys the impression of an image executed in plein air, there is a
methodical and unhurried quality about it that
conveys a sense of tranquillity rather than agitation.

One of Kielland's best known-works, *Summer
Night* (1886; Nasjonalgalleriet, Oslo), was
produced during her residence at the summer artists'
colony flourishing at Fleskum Farm, near Oslo.
Amidst the invigorating company of more than a
half dozen Norwegian National Romantic painters,
all of whom had resided in Munich and Paris during
the previous decade, Kielland painted one of her
largest landscapes (1 × 1.35 m.), which must be
understood as a major declaration of her artistic
intentions. Here the pervasive sense of tranquillity
in nature found in much of Kielland's production
attains its most emphatic expression. She chose as
her subject the unusual atmospheric conditions of
summer nights in the northernmost latitudes, where,
for a brief period, darkness never falls. The darkness
of the earth contrasts dramatically with the silvery
blue sky, reflected on the water, but the dominance
of a cool palette restrains the emotional tenor to one
of quiet contemplation. A lone figures rows towards
the distant shore, creating a slight ripple in the
otherwise static surface. Conceptualising this paint-

ing as a kind of visual "tone poem" makes explicit the urge of National Romantic painters to achieve a form of musical harmony in their works. They were interested in producing paintings that had the evocative potential of music in order to create an emotional bridge between the artist and the viewer.

In *Summer Night* Kielland places the viewer among the reeds near, but not on, the shore. The low vantage point suggests that the artist/viewer is situated on a boat (it is too low to be a dock), furthering the sense of immersion in and identity with the landscape that National Romantic painters sought to convey. Their intent was to create a pictorial analogue for the symbiotic relationship they felt existed between Norwegians and Nordic nature. The decorative patterning of the lily pads evidences the simplification and stylisation utilised by Kielland to represent her subject more emphatically, and points towards the evolution of a highly stylised, Art Nouveau style that would emerge in other Norwegian painters (particularly Gerhard Munthe) towards the end of the 19th century. *Summer Night* was immediately acclaimed a key National Romantic work, and appeared at the Paris Salon of 1887, the Nordic exhibition in Copenhagen in 1888 and at the Paris Exposition Universelle of 1889 before being purchased by the Norwegian government in 1890. While most of Kielland's works remain in private collections in Norway, examples can also be found in the Nasjonalgalleriet, Oslo, the Faste Galleri, Stavanger, and the Lillehammer Bys Malerisamling.

MICHELLE FACOS

af Klint, Hilma
Swedish painter, 1862–1944

Born in Stockholm, 26 October 1862. Attended the Technical School, Stockholm, and studied privately under portrait painter Kerstin Cardon, c.1880; studied at the Royal Academy of Fine Arts, Stockholm, 1882–7. Professional portrait and landscape painter, 1887–1908. Seriously involved in spiritualism by 1879. Formed a spiritualist group with four other women, called the Friday Group or The Five, 1890s. Met social philosopher Rudolf Steiner, 1908. Ceased painting, 1908–12. Moved to Helsingborg, southern Sweden, and made first of many visits to Steiner in Dornach, Switzerland, 1920. Became increasingly interested in theosophy and anthroposophy after 1922. Died in Djursholm, 21 October 1944.

Selected Writings
"Anteckningsböcker" [Notebooks], manuscript, 1882–1944, Hilma af Klint Foundation, Stockholm
"Avskrifter ur föredrag av Rudolf Steiner" [Transcripts of speeches by Rudolf Steiner], manuscript, Hilma af Klint Foundation, Stockholm
"Studier över själslivet" [Soul studies], manuscript dictated by Hilma af Klint to Dr Anna Ljungberg, 1917–18, typed in 1941–2, Hilma af Klint Foundation, Stockholm

Bibliography
Åke Fant, "Synpunkter på Hilma af Klints måleri" [Points of view about Hilma af Klint's painting], *Studier i konstvetenskap tillägnade Brita Linde* [Studies in art history dedicated to Brita Linde], Stockholm: Konstvetenskapliga Institutionen, 1985, pp.45–54
——, *Kring Hilma af Klints sekelskiftesmåleri* [Around Hilma af Klint's turn-of-the century paintings], Helsinki, 1986
The Spiritual in Art: Abstract Painting, 1890–1985, exh. cat., Los Angeles County Museum of Art, and elsewhere, 1986
T. Dijkhuis and others, *Het mysterie van de abstracten: Het onzichtbare zichtbaar gemakt* [The mystery of the Abstracts: The invisible made visible], Utrecht, 1987
T. Ekbom, *Bildstorm* [Picture storm], Uppsala, 1987
Het Mystere van de Abstracten, 1890–1985 [The mystery of the Abstracts, 1890–1985], exh. cat., Haags Gemeentemuseum, The Hague, 1987
Hilma af Klints hemliga bilder [Hilma af Klint's secret pictures], exh. cat., Nordiskt Konstcentrums, 1988
Konkret i Norden/Scandinavian Concrete Art, exh. cat., Amos Andersson Museum, Helsinki, and elsewhere, 1988
Brooks Adams, "Contemplating the rose hip", *Art in America*, lxxvii, December 1989, pp.164–7
J. Clair and others, *Wunderblock: Eine Geschichte der modernen Seele*, Vienna: Messepalast, 1989
Hilma af Klint: Ockult målarinna och abstrakt pionjär [Hilma af Klint: Occult painter and abstract pioneer], exh. cat., Museum Moderna Kunst, Stockholm, 1989 (contains extensive bibliography)
Nancy G. Heller, *Women Artists: An Illustrated History*, 2nd edition, New York: Abbeville, 1991
Okkultismus und Abstraktion: Die Malerin Hilma af Klint (1862–1944), exh. cat., Graphische Sammlung Albertina, Vienna, and elsewhere, 1991

The oeuvre of the Swedish painter Hilma af Klint can be divided into two distinct groups. During her studies at the Royal Academy of Fine Arts in Stockholm in the 1880s and just after, she devoted herself to landscape and portrait painting. In their fresh, naturalistic rendering of nature and great sensitivity to colour and light, such works as *View over Mälaren* (1903; Hilma af Klint Foundation, Stockholm) are linked to the practice of the time. Although af Klint continued to produce this type of naturalistic painting throughout her artistic career, it was the second and very extensive group of works, begun in earnest in 1906, that was to be of much greater significance. A secret occupation that was made known to the public only in the 1980s, this group of works moves away completely from contemporary forms of expression, and is of particular interest for its originality. The style of painting is strange, full of symbols that can be difficult to interpret. The high degree of abstraction in the paintings aroused great interest when the works were first exhibited. Under the influence of a sort of inner spiritual guide, af Klint executed such paintings as *Swan No.16* and *Swan No.17* (both 1914–15; Hilma af Klint Foundation), both of which went far in their exquisite reduction of colour and form. Yet such pictures were already emerging in the *Urkaos* series of 1906 (Hilma af Klint Foundation). In these af Klint abolished natural forms, thereby anticipating some of modernism's great male artists in abandoning the representation of external reality. Af Klint executed this work secretly within a small circle of women, and apparently without any influence from the nascent Scandinavian modernism.

In her autobiographical notes or "Soul studies" ("Studier över själslivet", 1917–18) af Klint wrote:

> In order to execute work that is extremely important I have been obliged to give up that which during my youth my heart yearned for: to be able to represent external forms and colours. In other words, I have frankly been held back from a sphere of activity, and laboriously clambered up the steps …

This task, which came from a spirit named Amaliel by af Klint in her notes, resulted in a series of works emerging from processes that occasionally overlap one another chronologically. In 1905 "Amaliel" gave her a commission that resulted in the *WU Series/The Rose* (1906–7), the *WUS Series/Seven Stars* (1908), the *SUW Series/The Swan*, the *UW Series/The Dove* and *Altar Pictures* (1915) and finished with the summary painting *Human Chastity* (1915; all Hilma af Klint Foundation). The next period began with the *Parsifal* series (1916) and continued until 1920 with another series *The Atom: Series II–VIII* (all Hilma af Klint Foundation). Thereafter there was some reduction in af Klint's productivity, but up to her death she executed works that can be linked as much to the naturalistic as to the abstract part of her artistic make-up.

The first series, from 1906, the *WU Series/The Rose*, are small-format paintings (50 × 38 cm.) on the theme of Urkaos (Original chaos). They are all executed with expressive brushwork contrasting with more massed shapes: embryo, star or snail forms. The paintings are completely free of the careful representation of nature that distinguishes af Klint's earlier paintings, and seem to derive their form from apparently uncontrolled hand movements on a canvas only partially visible. Af Klint characterises these as an exercise in anticipation of future commissions. After a series of smaller paintings, the *Series II*, in which, against an overall light background, she executed forms with marked contours and combinations of letters and symbols that are difficult to interpret, she began to paint in much larger formats.

Human figures appear in the *Large Figure Paintings* of 1907. These were made while af Klint "was without consciousness", according to her notes. In several of them (such as nos 3, 4, 6 and 7A) the figure of a man or woman occurs in different symbolic compositions, not infrequently accompanied by a third, prophet-like figure. In her notebooks af Klint writes about the *Large Figure Painting No.3*: "Devan (natural spirit) is represented as a middle-aged man. Free from karma he supports humankind's imprisoned children." In the picture the prophet-like man sits in a yellow cloak, with a female figure kneeling beside him and a standing male figure turning towards him, his hands clasped behind his back. The figures are painted here without great attention to proportions and angles, against a ground that is reminiscent of the *Urkaos Series*: the gesticulating paint strokes against a black background create a cell-like double form. In the next series, *Ten Largest*, which are as large as 328 × 240 centimetres, the lines become more loaded, the forms ever larger and flower-like, with some of them even completely geometrical. According to af Klint these forms represent evolution: "It was the leader's intention to give the world an insight into the systematisation of the four departments of people's lives. Ardent childhood, adolescence as well as old age". Here the colours are clear, and unified in fields of blue, green, orange and red-pink as backgrounds.

The *Swan* series dates from after the completion of the *Ten Largest* series. *Swan No.24* is typical in the way in which the picture is built up from symmetries, or occasionally in geometrical planes divided in four. Here a white and a black swan are joined in an embrace. Their beaks meet in a kiss, also comprising a hook and eye, which according to af Klint are the symbols for woman and man respectively. The background is made up of four square fields. The degree of abstraction culminates, as mentioned above, in the beautiful *Swan No.16* and *Swan No.17* (1914–15). In these paintings the divided circular form rests against a monochrome background, with a triangle in the centre. The compositional austerity and use of colour are very sophisticated. Within the limits of the secret commissions that af Klint received, *The Dove* and *Altar Pictures* stand out as high points in conveying religious meaning.

In order to get closer to an understanding of af Klint's work, one can regard her painting and the texts she and her female friends wrote as two aspects of the same oeuvre, although the writings are insufficient tools for the interpretation of the pictures. The texts register the creation of the pictures: she formulated the spiritual guide's commission as it appeared to her, describing her own emotions during its execution.

Throughout her career af Klint appears to have strongly identified with the female sex. She grew up during a time and in a social milieu – she came from a prominent naval family – when a clear distinction between the characteristics and areas of activity of the two genders was constantly maintained. Af Klint experienced love during her youth but remained unmarried. Throughout her life she sought solidarity exclusively with women, in groups in which she was often the central figure. She was a strong believer, but also enterprising, an organiser who inspired confidence. From 1879 to 1882 she participated in organised seances. She appears not to have been interested in either the Swedish opponent movement or later in the dawning modernism of the 1910s. She joined the Association of Swedish Women Artists when it was founded in 1910.

Af Klint was well acquainted with the ideas of the period's theosophical and spiritual teachers.

Rudolf Steiner, whom she met in Stockholm, was a great role-model for her. She visited him in Dornach, hoping to gain acknowledgement and an explanation of her life's work. But Steiner, who stressed the importance of the conscious development of the soul, considered her working methods unsuitable. This became a conflict for af Klint, and she was disappointed by his lack of appreciation of her work. Her own working method was spiritual; during the working process she experienced the fact that her work was conceived and directed by external intelligences.

Af Klint's world of thought and conception of life was constructed dualistically. She had experience of a male opposite, Gidro, whom she never met in her real life. She saw her life's task as being the intermediary between what she called "dual knowledge", a platonically coloured understanding emanating from the fact that each person belongs with a particular individual of the opposite sex. In her "Studier över själslivet", dictated in 1917–18 and recorded in a typescript of 2058 pages in 1941–2, she returns repeatedly to the dual thought. It is a detailed vision of the different functions of the souls of men and women and of the positive strength contained in the struggle between them.

It is possible to interpret the abstract qualities of Hilma af Klint's paintings as resting on a dichotomy. The symmetry or the divided halves are the recurring compositional models, which point towards a correspondence between her understanding of the world and her painting. Through her extensive and innovative life's work she was to overcome the gender order of her period, at the same time as having a deep conviction of this order's fundamental significance. Af Klint allowed no-one outside a small circle of women to see this part of her work. She stated in her will that her paintings should be kept together, and not be exhibited publicly for 20 years after her death.

ANNIKA ÖHRNER

Knight, Laura

British painter and graphic artist, 1877–1970

Born Laura Johnson in Long Eaton, Derbyshire, 4 August 1877. Studied at Nottingham School of Art, 1891–7 (several awards). Exhibited at Royal

Academy from 1903. Married portrait painter Harold Knight, 1903; he died 1961. Lived in Staithes on the Yorkshire coast and in Laren, Netherlands, before settling in Cornwall, 1907, in Newlyn then Lamorna. Moved to London after World War I, but retained studios in Cornwall. Stayed in USA, 1922 and 1926–7; acted as judge for international art exhibition at Carnegie Institute, Pittsburgh, 1922. Commissioned by the War Artists' Advisory Committee during World War II; painted Nuremberg trials, 1946. Recipient of honorary doctorates from University of St Andrews, 1931; University of Nottingham, 1951. Member, Royal Watercolour Society, 1928; Royal Society of Painter-Etchers and Engravers, 1932; President, Society of Women Artists. Associate, 1927, and member, 1936 (the first woman since the 18th century), Royal Academy. Dame Commander of the British Empire (DBE), 1929. Died in London, 7 July 1970.

Selected Individual Exhibitions

Leicester Galleries, London: 1906, 1907, 1912 (all with Harold Knight), 1918, 1920, 1926, 1928 (with Mark Gertler), 1932, 1934, 1939
Alpine Club Galleries, London: 1922, 1930
Cleveland Art Institute, Chicago: 1931 (touring)
Usher Art Gallery, Lincoln: 1931
Laing Art Gallery, Newcastle upon Tyne: 1933
Museum and Art Gallery, Leicester: 1934 (with Harold Knight)
Castle Museum, Nottingham: 1934 (with Harold Knight), 1970 (retrospective)
Ian MacNichol's Galleries, Glasgow: 1946
Worthing Art Gallery, Sussex: 1963
Upper Grosvenor Galleries, London: 1963, 1967 (with Harold Knight), 1968, 1969 (retrospective)
Royal Academy, London: 1965 (retrospective)
Aquascutum Ltd, London: 1970

Selected Writings

Oil Paint and Grease Paint: Autobiography of Laura Knight, London: Nicholson and Watson, and New York: Macmillan, 1936
"Nuremberg diary", manuscript, 1947, Nottingham Record Office
"An artist's experience", *The Studio*, cxlviii, 1954, pp.129–35
A Proper Circus Omie, London: Davies, 1962
The Magic of a Line: The Autobiography of Laura Knight, London: Kimber, 1965

Bibliography

Norman Garstin, "The art of Harold and Laura Knight", *The Studio*, lvii, 1913, pp.183–200
Charles Marriott, ed., *A Book of Drawings*, London: Lane, 1923
M.C. Salaman, *Laura Knight*, London: Studio, and New York: Rudge, 1932
Janet Dunbar, *Laura Knight*, London: Collins, 1975
Meirion and Susie Harries, *The War Artists*, London: Joseph, 1983
Painting in Newlyn, 1880–1930, exh. cat., Barbican Art Gallery, London, 1985
Caroline Fox, *Dame Laura Knight*, Oxford: Phaidon, 1988
On with the Show: Drawings by Dame Laura Knight (1877–1970), exh. cat., David Messum, London, 1988
Teresa Grimes, Judith Collins and Oriana Baddeley, *Five Women Painters*, London: Lennard, 1989
The Staithes Group, exh. cat., Nottingham Castle Museum, and elsewhere, 1993
G. Fredric Bolling and Valerie A. Withington, *The Graphic Work of Laura Knight Including a Catalogue Raisonné of Her Prints*, Aldershot: Scolar Press, 1993

Laura Knight's artistic career spanned some 70 years and was in many respects exceptional. The scope of her subject matter displays enormous versatility, although the portrayal of women and their lives is a recurring motif. During the late 1920s and early 1930s she achieved great popular success with her ballet and circus paintings and, in 1927, was only the second woman, after Annie Swynnerton, to be elected an Associate of the Royal Academy since its foundation. Her election was probably due to the efforts of her friend Alfred Munnings, who had submitted her name several times before 1927 without success, but her autobiography also acknowledges the part played by Swynnerton in breaking down prejudice against women painters within the Academy. She became a full member in 1936 and served on the council for the following two years. Thirty years later she was the first woman to be honoured with a solo exhibition at the Royal Academy Diploma Gallery. Ironically it was her allegiance to the Royal Academy and the conservative, academic tradition that led to critical attacks on her lack of emotional and intellectual rigour and to the decline of her reputation since her death.

Laura Johnson received her training at the Nottingham School of Art, where she met her future husband, Harold Knight. Under the life master, Wilson Foster, teaching at the school emphasised an exact understanding of the model and little beyond. Several of her charcoal portrait studies submitted for the annual South Kensington examinations are in the collection of Nottingham Castle Museum and Art Gallery. They reveal a precocious technical proficiency and confidence in line drawing. According to the artist, she was continually upbraided for making her lines too heavy and for "drawing like a man" – from the shoulder rather than the wrist – and encouraged to develop her "feminine" side, something she felt unable to do. She was critical of the limitations of her art-school training and particularly of the fact that women were barred from working from the nude model. None the less, she was a successful student and won several awards, including, in 1894, the Princess of Wales scholarship for the female student with the most awards, and the Queen's prize in 1896.

Around 1898 Laura and Harold left Nottingham and settled in the north Yorkshire fishing village of Staithes, which had been recommended to them by a master at the School of Art. Since the 1880s Staithes and the neighbouring village of Runswick had been the focus for a growing colony of artists, drawn largely from the Midlands and the North, attracted there by the unspoilt lifestyle of the local fishing communities. Laura had been deeply impressed by an exhibition of Newlyn School artists held at Nottingham Castle Museum in 1894, and her early pictures painted at Staithes reflect her allegiance to the tenets of plein-air realism. She made numerous watercolour studies of children playing on the beach that display an increasing spontaneity in her figure painting. It was a period of enthusiastic experimentation, and much of the work was subsequently destroyed.

Knight's most ambitious painting to survive from the early years at Staithes, and signed with her maiden name, is the *Fishing Fleet* (Bolton Museum and Art Gallery). Painted in a muted palette of grey and brown that also characterised Harold's work at this time, it exemplifies a preoccupation in both artists' work with the harsh and tragic lifestyle of the local fishing community and, in mood, is reminiscent of some of the Newlyn paintings of Walter Langley and Frank Bramley. Laura had particularly admired Bramley's *A Hopeless Dawn* at the Nottingham exhibition of Cornish painters in 1894. While at Staithes Laura received some instruction in colour theory from the Scottish painter Charles Hodge Mackie, who taught her the laws of complementary colours and how, by using a restricted palette of earth pigments, a colour might be suggested in a neutral grey through the presence of its complementary.

Between 1904 and 1907 the Knights (who had married in 1903) made three visits to the Netherlands to work amid a colony of artists at Laren, a location popularised by the Dutch realist painter Anton Mauve. Laura painted almost exclusively genre subjects of peasant interiors in a limited range of predominantly grey tones that perhaps owed something to the influence of the Hague school artists (e.g. *Peeling Potatoes*, c.1904–7; Castle Museum and Art Gallery, Nottingham). These were shown alongside those of Harold at their first London exhibition, *Dutch Life and Landscape*, held at the Leicester Galleries in 1906. They had first met Ernest Brown of the Leicester Galleries in 1904 and were to exhibit there together again in 1907 and 1912; Laura had several further exhibitions at the galleries before World War II.

The artist achieved something of a breakthrough with her painting *Dressing the Children* (Ferens Art Gallery, Hull), exhibited at the Royal Academy in 1906. Although painted at Staithes, it shares many of the preoccupations of contemporary Dutch works. She painted many such domestic scenes of mothers and their children in dimly lit interiors illuminated by a single window. Avoiding Harold's dramatic use of light and silhouette, she concentrates instead on the unremarkable action of a daily chore. Her paintwork is animated by a swift outlining of contour and drapery folds, a characteristic more pronounced in her watercolour work.

In 1907 the Knights moved to Newlyn in Cornwall, where Stanhope Forbes had founded a School of Painting, and were introduced to his pupils Dod Shaw (later Dod Procter), Ernest Procter and Charles Simpson, who formed part of a thriving artists' community. In Cornwall Laura continued painting children as she had done in Staithes, but the canvases exhibited at the Royal Academy in 1909 (*The Beach*; Laing Art Gallery, Newcastle upon Tyne) and 1910 reveal a marked change of direction. She was now working on a much larger scale with broad, confident brushwork and a lighter, more colourful palette that captured the fall of the bright Cornish sunlight on her subjects. The angst and grim realism of the Staithes work is replaced by a vigour and *joie de vivre* that reflects the Knights' new-found pleasure in their carefree, bohemian lifestyle in Cornwall.

In 1911 Laura Knight's subject matter changed and she began painting hired models, both clothed and naked, in the open air at Lamorna, again observing the fall of natural light on flesh. Her willingness to flout convention is poignantly expressed in *Self-Portrait with Nude* (1913; National Portrait Gallery, London) where she portrays herself, brush in hand, before a posed naked female model, subverting the traditional iconography of the male artist and his muse. The subject of women posed in the open air and on cliff tops culminated around 1917 in a group of paintings that were characterised by high horizons, a certain flattening of illusionistic space and broad, unmodulated blocks of bright colour (e.g. *Lamorna Cave, c.*1917; private collection, Sotheby's, repr. Fox 1988, pl.30). Similarities were drawn with the work of Augustus John, to whom she had been introduced by Munnings in 1913. As the art critic Paul Konody pointed out, however (*Country Life*, February 1918), Knight's intention was fundamentally different to John's and she remained essentially attached to a realist tradition, absorbed by effects of light and atmosphere.

The Knights' move to London after World War I occasioned another change in Laura's subject matter, when she gained permission to work backstage with Diaghilev's Ballets Russes. Whereas Sickert and Gore, in their music-hall paintings, had focused attention on what was happening on the stage and in the audience, Knight's interest lay in the more informal moments of theatre that she witnessed in the dressing rooms or waiting in the wings, both at the ballet and at the productions of the Birmingham Repertory Theatre. She made studies of the famous ballerinas Lydia Lopokova and, later, Anna Pavlova, but perhaps the most significant introduction for the development of her work was to the Maestro, Cecchetti, at whose dance classes she learned to execute swift, economic line drawings at great speed to capture the movement and stance of her models.

A new emphasis on line is also evident in the etchings and aquatints she began to produce in 1923, apparently working directly on to the plate with no preliminary drawings or tracing. She received much technical help from an artist friend, John Everett, and also took advice from Gerald Brockhurst. The subjects of her printed works mirrored her obsessions during the 1920s and early 1930s with the ballet, theatre and circus; the years 1923 and 1925–6 were particularly productive. Despite Brockhurst's advice to concentrate on pure line, she preferred the combination of etching and aquatint. In two aquatints of Diaghilev's Spanish dancers, produced in 1923 (repr. Bolling and Withington 1993, nos 8 and 19), and much indebted to Goya's *Los caprichos*, she created highly decorative surfaces using a three-tone ground. The rhythmic use of line and dramatic silhouette were entirely new to her work but very much in keeping with the medium and subject. She experimented later with drypoint, engraving and soft ground etching. In the early 1930s the market for prints slumped and her printmaking activities largely ceased around 1935.

A number of nudes and ballet subjects, exhibited at the Royal Academy in the late 1920s and featuring strong, solid-limbed women, reveal something of the influence of Dod Procter and the spirit of new realism on Knight's work at that time. In these works a cool studio light gives strong, sculptural form and an impressive, physical presence to the model even when in an outdoor setting. The artist Eileen Mayo, who was a favourite model of both Laura and Harold, posed for several of her nudes but it is in an uncharacteristically restrained portrayal of a young girl in *Susie and the Washbasin* (1929; Harris Museum and Art Gallery, Preston) that she is perhaps closest in spirit to Dod Procter's work.

The circus paintings for which Knight became best known and loved by the British public were exhibited at the Royal Academy between 1928 and 1938. She sketched backstage at Fossett's "old-fashioned" circus in Islington and with Bertram Mills's circus at Olympia in the early 1920s, capturing the movement and agility of the performers as she had those of the corps de ballet. The life of the circus was to become an obsession, and in the early 1930s she joined Carmo's on two separate tours of the country. Although popular, her circus pictures did not meet with critical success, and she herself admitted that she had probably found the whole experience too entertaining to produce her best work. Too often the spectacle of costume and circus paraphernalia dominate at the expense of any deeper feeling for her subjects, and we are rarely given any insight into the personalities behind the grease paint. *Charivari; or, Grand Parade* (1928; Newport Museum and Art Gallery, Gwent), exhibited at the Royal Academy in 1929 and parodied in *Punch*, is perhaps an extreme example of this tendency and was significantly excluded from her choice of pictures for her retrospective exhibition in Nottingham in 1970.

Executed in the late 1930s and early 1940s and rather more successful in their depth of characterisation were her portraits of Gypsies. At Munnings's suggestion she went to the horse races at Epsom and Ascot and several spirited crowd scenes resulted from these visits. It was the Gypsies "working the crowd", however, who really engaged her attention, and her best work was produced at the Gypsy camp at Iver, Buckinghamshire, following an invitation there from one of her models. The enigmatic features of a Gypsy girl called Beulah, of whom she made several portraits, and the proud bearing of a beplumed doyenne in *Fine Feathers (Gypsy Splendour)* (1939; Castle Museum and Art Gallery, Nottingham) reveal the very real talent Knight possessed for portraiture. In 1938, in some particularly prickly correspondence regarding his resignation from the Royal Academy and in which he accused Knight of siding with the forces of conservatism, Augustus John, another great devotee of Gypsy life, complimented her on her portraits of Romany girls exhibited that year. Knight appears to have preferred painting women and children – she made a number of sensitive portraits of black children in a Baltimore hospital in 1927 (e.g. *The Piccaninny*, c.1927; private collection, Pyms Gallery, London, repr. Fox 1988, pl.49) – and her Gypsy work is unusual in that it includes several revealing paintings and studies of a Gypsy man on his sick bed (e.g. *A Gypsy*, 1938–9; Tate Gallery, London).

Knight's popular success and objective, academic style of painting were no doubt what commended her to the propagandist ends of the War Artists' Advisory Committee chaired by Kenneth Clark during World War II. She was commissioned to paint several portraits of women with distinguished service in the Women's Auxiliary Air Force (WAAF), and a number of paintings emphasising the importance of women workers to the war effort. A portrait of a young munitions factory worker, *Ruby Loftus Screwing a Breech-ring* (1943; Imperial War Museum, London), was exhibited at the Royal Academy to particular acclaim. In 1946, at her own suggestion, she flew to Germany to record the trial of Nazi war criminals at Nuremberg. Given the unpromising subject matter, the resulting canvas, *The Dock, Nuremberg* (1946; Imperial War Museum), manages to achieve both a factual account of the courtroom with an imaginative composition incorporating scenes of the concentration camp atrocities and the destruction of Nuremberg.

Despite the gradual eclipse of Laura Knight's reputation in the post-war period, there has been a re-evaluation of her early paintings made at Staithes and Newlyn within the context of exhibitions surveying English Impressionism, notably *Painting in Newlyn* (Barbican Art Gallery, London, 1985) and *The Staithes Group* (Castle Museum and Art Gallery, Nottingham, 1993).

NEIL WALKER

Kollwitz, Käthe   [fig. 39 and cover]

German graphic artist and sculptor, 1867–1945

Born Käthe Schmidt in Königsberg (now Kaliningrad, Russia), 8 July 1867. First art lessons with engraver Rudolf Maurer in Königsberg, 1881–2. Visited Switzerland, Berlin and Munich with mother and sister Lise, 1884. Studied painting under Karl Stauffer-Bern at the Zeichen- und Malschule des Vereins der Künstlerinnen und Kunstfreundinnen zu Berlin, 1885–6; taught etching and painting there from 1898. Studied under Emil Neide in Königsberg, 1886, then under Ludwig Herterich in Munich, 1888–9. Rented a studio in Königsberg, 1890. Settled in Berlin after marriage to physician Karl Kollwitz, 1891; two sons, born 1892 and 1896; husband died 1942. Member of Berlin Secession, 1899. Studied sculpture at Académie Julian and met Rodin during stay in Paris, 1904. Studied in Florence after winning the Villa Romana prize, established by Max Klinger, 1907. Elected member of the Prussian Academy and named professor, 1919; director of the master studio for graphic arts, 1928; forced to resign by National Socialists, 1933. Visited Moscow with husband, 1927. Recipient of Ordre pour le Mérite for peace work, 1929. Unofficially forbidden to exhibit by the National Socialists, 1936. Evacuated to Nordhausen to escape bombing, 1943; much of her work destroyed in an air raid in Berlin later that year. Died in Moritzburg, near Dresden, 22 April 1945.

Principal Exhibitions

Individual

Galerie Cassirer, Berlin: 1917
Kunsthalle, Bremen: 1917
Berlin Secession: 1917
Civic Club, New York: 1925
Kupferstichkabinett, Basel: 1929
Moscow and Leningrad: 1932
Jake Zeitlin Bookshop and Galleries, Los Angeles: 1937
Kleemann Galleries, New York: 1938
Berner Kunstmuseum, Bern: 1946 (retrospective)

Group

Freie Kunstausstellung, Berlin: 1893
Galerie Gurlitt, Berlin: 1897 (*Kunstlerinnen Ausstellung*)
Grosse Berliner Kunstausstellung, Berlin: 1898
Dresden: 1899 (*Deutsche Kunstausstellung*, small gold medal)
Freie Secession, Berlin: 1916

Selected Writings

Ich will wirken in dieser Zeit, ed. Friedrich Ahhlers-Hestermann, Frankfurt am Main, 1952; 2nd edition, edited by Hans Kollwitz, 1981
The Diary and Letters of Käthe Kollwitz, ed. Hans Kollwitz, Chicago, 1955; 2nd edition, Evanston, IL: Northwestern University Press, 1988 (German original, 1948)
Briefe der Freundschaft und Begegnungen, ed. Hans Kollwitz, Munich, 1966
Bekenntnisse, Leipzig, 1981 (with appendix by Volker Frank)
Ich sah die Welt mit liebevollen Blicken: Käthe Kollwitz, Ein Leben in Selbstzeugnissen, ed. Hans Kollwitz, Wiesbaden: Fourier, 1988
Die Tagebücher, ed. Jutta Bohnke-Kollwitz, Berlin, 1989
Briefe an den Sohn, 1904 bis 1945, ed. Jutta Bohnke-Kollwitz, Berlin, 1992

Bibliography

Julius Elias, "Käthe Kollwitz", *Kunst und Künstler*, xvi, 1917, pp.540–49
Alfred Kuhn, *Käthe Kollwitz: Graphiker der Gegenwart*, vi, Berlin, 1921
Kurt Glaser, "Käthe Kollwitz", *Die Graphik der Neuzeit vom Anfang des 19. Jahrhunderts bis zur Gegenwart*, Berlin, 1923, pp.466–70
Arthur Bonus, *Das Käthe-Kollwitz-Werk*, Dresden, 1925
Elizabeth McCausland, "Käthe Kollwitz", *Parnassus*, ix, February 1937, pp.20–25
Carl Zigrosser, *Käthe Kollwitz*, New York: Bittner, 1946; reprinted 1961
Beate Bonus-Jeep, *Sechzig Jahre Freundschaft mit Käthe Kollwitz*, Boppard: Rauch, 1948; reprinted 1963
August Klipstein, *The Graphic Work of Käthe Kollwitz: Complete Illustrated Catalogue*, Bern: Klipstein, and New York: Galerie St Etienne, 1955 (catalogue raisonné of prints; German original)
Glaubrecht Friedrich, "Käthe Kollwitz als Zeichnerin", *Dresdner Kunstblätter*, iv, 1960, pp.148–50
Harri Nündel, *Käthe Kollwitz*, Leipzig, 1964
Otto Nagel, *Die Selbstbildnisse der Käthe Kollwitz*, Berlin, 1965
Käthe Kollwitz, exh. cat., Akademie der Künste, Berlin, 1967
Leopold Reidemeister, *Käthe Kollwitz: Das plastische Werk*, Hamburg, 1967
Carl Zigrosser, *Prints and Drawings of Käthe Kollwitz*, New York: Dover, 1969
Otto Nagel, *Käthe Kollwitz*, London: Studio Vista, and Greenwich, CT: New York Graphic Society, 1971 (German original, 1963)
Otto Nagel and Werner Timm, *Käthe Kollwitz: Die Handzeichnungen*, Berlin and Stuttgart, 2 vols, 1972–80 (catalogue raisonné of drawings)
Käthe Kollwitz, exh. cat., Frankfurter Kunstverein, Frankfurt am Main, 1973
Werner Timm, *Käthe Kollwitz*, Welt der Kunst, Berlin, 1974
Mina C. Klein and H. Arthur Klein, *Käthe Kollwitz: Life in Art*, New York: Holt Rinehart, 1975
Martha Kearns, *Käthe Kollwitz: Woman and Artist*, Old Westbury, NY: Feminist Press, 1976
Käthe Kollwitz, exh. cat., Galerie St Etienne and Kennedy Galleries, New York, 1976
John A. Walker, "Art and the peasantry 2", *Art and Artists*, xiii, February 1979, pp.14–17
Alessandra Comini, "State of the field, 1980: The women artists of German Expressionism", *Arts Magazine*, November 1980, pp.147–53
Ilse Kleberger, *"Eine Gabe ist eine Aufgabe": Käthe Kollwitz*, Berlin: Klopp, 1980
Renate Hinz, ed., *Käthe Kollwitz: Graphics, Posters, Drawings*, New York: Pantheon, and London: Writers and Readers, 1981 (German original, 1980)
Käthe Kollwitz, 1867–1945: The Graphic Works, exh. cat., Kettle's Yard, Cambridge, 1981
Catherine Krahmer, *Käthe Kollwitz in Selbstzeugnissen und Bilddokumenten*, Reinbek bei Hamburg: Rowohlt, 1981
German Expressionist Sculpture, exh. cat., Los Angeles County Museum of Art, 1983
France Roussillon, *La Sculpture de Käthe Kollwitz*, PhD dissertation, Paris-Sorbonne, 1983
The Print in Germany, 1880–1933: The Age of Expressionism, exh. cat., British Museum, London, 1984
Käthe Kollwitz Handzeichnungen, Cologne: Käthe Kollwitz Museum, 1985
Ateliergemeinschaft Klosterstrasse: Vom Stillen Kampf der Künstler, exh. cat., Galerie Mitte, Berlin, 1988
Tom Fecht, ed., *Käthe Kollwitz: Works in Color*, New York: Schocken, 1988 (German original, 1987)
Elmar Jansen, *Ernst Barlach – Käthe Kollwitz: Die Geschichte einer verborgenen Nähe*, Berlin, 1988

Die Kollwitz-Sammlung des Dresdner Kupferstich-Kabinettes: Graphik und Zeichnungen, 1890–1912, exh. cat., Käthe Kollwitz Museum, Cologne, 1988

Alexandra von dem Knesebeck, "Die Bedeutung von Zolas Roman 'Germinal' für den Zyklus 'Ein Weberaufstand' von Käthe Kollwitz", *Zeitschrift für Kunstgeschichte*, iii, 1989, pp.402–22

Zwischen den Kriegen: Druckgraphische Zyklen von Kollwitz, Dix, Pechstein, Masereel u.a., exh. cat., Käthe Kollwitz Museum, Berlin, 1989

"Käthe Kollwitz Museum Köln", *Kölner Museums-Bulletin*, i–ii, 1991 (special issue)

Mara R. Witzling, ed., *Voicing Our Visions: Writings by Women Artists*, New York: Universe, 1991; London: Women's Press, 1992

Käthe Kollwitz, exh. cat., National Gallery of Art, Washington, DC, 1992

Angela Moorjani, *The Aesthetics of Loss and Lessness*, New York: St Martin's Press, 1992

Käthe Kollwitz, exh. cat., Fondation Neumann, Gingins, 1994

Käthe Kollwitz: Artist of the People, exh. cat., South Bank Centre, London, and elsewhere, 1995

Schmerz und Schuld, exh. cat., Käthe Kollwitz Museum, Berlin, 1995

Celebrated and beloved throughout the world, the graphic artist and sculptor Käthe Kollwitz (*Self-Portrait in Profile Facing Left, Drawing*, 1933; National Gallery of Art, Washington, DC) is known for her powerful treatment of the themes of mothers and children, of solidarity among human beings, and of protest against suffering and social injustice. Spanning the turn of a century, two world wars and the turbulent Weimar Republic, Kollwitz's life was as rich as her art and is well documented in letters, in accounts by friends and family and in the extensive diaries she kept from 1910 to 1943.

Critics and the public appreciated Kollwitz's art from the time it was first exhibited in 1893; its accessible style and humanitarian subject matter ensured a wide audience both during her lifetime and to this day. Yet Kollwitz is a somewhat anomalous figure of the modern period because she was a woman working in a male-dominated field, because she depicted socially engaged subjects when this was unfashionable and because she steadfastly adhered to a figurative style in the era of abstraction. For these reasons, Kollwitz and her work (which includes five published graphic cycles and numerous single-sheet prints, as well as sculptures) have always been studied from the perspectives of politics and feminism (understood from a late 20th-century viewpoint) and this during an age when formalism dominated critical discourse. The newest scholarship, by contrast, has devoted attention to the technical and aesthetic aspects of her oeuvre, because too little has been known about Kollwitz as a technically brilliant graphic artist as well as a virtuosic visual rhetorician.

Kollwitz's preoccupation with socially engaged subjects grew out of her family background. She was born in Königsberg to a solidly middle-class, highly cultivated family, in which the tone was set by her maternal grandfather Julius Rupp, a dissident Protestant minister who founded a Free Congregation emphasising morality, duty and the intellect. Her family was supportive of her artistic ambitions and sent her to art classes both in her home town and in Berlin. In the Prussian capital, she studied under the Swiss artist Karl Stauffer-Bern, who encouraged her to pursue drawing; she also encountered the work of Stauffer-Bern's friend Max Klinger, whose etched cycle, *A Life*, and treatise *Malerei und Zeichnung* of 1891 would deeply influence her eventual decision to abandon painting in favour of the graphic arts. Klinger believed that the graphic arts, far more than painting, were capable of exploring ideas and social issues, partly because they were, according to his definition, executed exclusively in black and white and therefore not subject to the "pure enjoyment" that colour provided. He also valued the reproducible quality of the print and saw it as a more democratic art.

Kollwitz perfected her drawing skills in Berlin, and then in Munich under the direction of Ludwig Herterich, frequently using herself as a model, something she would do throughout her life (*Self-Portrait en face, Laughing*, c.1888–9; Käthe-Kollwitz-Museum Berlin; *Self-Portrait*, 1891; Art Institute of Chicago). She gradually began to synthesise her interest in socially engaged subject matter with the notion of graphic media as understood by Klinger. Kollwitz had long been attracted to what she perceived as the beauty and romance of the lives of workers as opposed to the middle classes; only later would she depict the poor and suffering out of direct observation and social conviction. In Munich she decided to create a visual narrative based on Emile Zola's naturalist mining novel, *Germinal*, which had appeared in 1885. Her *Scene from Germinal* (1891; private collection, repr. Washington 1992, p.20), which depicts the character of Catherine being fought over by two men, was much praised by her art school classmates and

Kollwitz felt that with this work her career had taken a definitive turn. In 1893, in Berlin, she attended a performance of Gerhart Hauptmann's play *The Weavers*. This was such a transformative experience for the young woman that she immediately abandoned the Zola novel as the subject of her proposed graphic cycle and began work on the series that she would entitle *A Weavers' Rebellion* (*Ein Weberaufstand*).

As Kollwitz began work on the cycle that would win her both critical and popular success nationally, her circumstances were much changed. No longer a free young art student, she had married Dr Karl Kollwitz, a friend of her brother Conrad, and had moved with him to the working-class Prenzlauer Berg district of Berlin where her husband set up a practice caring for the industrial poor. Her first son, Hans, was born in 1892; her second, Peter, would be born four years later. The artist faced a challenging moment as she confronted the dual responsibilities of family and career.

At the beginning of the 1890s Kollwitz began to pursue the graphic arts seriously. Given her technical and expressive brilliance, it is remarkable to realise that she was virtually self-taught as a print-maker. She had received some training in Königsberg from a copper engraver and then in Berlin laboured to teach herself how to etch. Her letters of the early 1890s document her experiments with the difficult intaglio media. Yet with the firm foundation of her drawing talent (and her protests to the contrary), the artist soon became familiar with the graphic techniques, and her first etched self-portrait of 1891 (Klipstein 1955, no.8) reveals her increasing ambition and mastery. Kollwitz also learned lithography, a more straightforward process. With these tools, she was ready to embark upon *A Weavers' Rebellion*.

In 1893 Kollwitz began work on the six images of the series: *Poverty, Death, Council, March of the Weavers, Storming the Gate* and *End*. Unusually, the cycle combined different media: the first three images were lithographs, the last three were etchings. These six prints comprise a loose narrative that only roughly relates to Hauptmann's play. The product of extensive preliminary studies in different media and different compositional formats (*Storming the Gate*, 1897; private collection, courtesy Galerie St Etienne, New York, repr. Washington 1992, p.143; *End*, 1897; Staatliche Kunstsammlungen, Dresden), they recount the miserable conditions of cottage industry weavers who rise up against the boss and are slaughtered. In the dense, often claustrophobic images, Kollwitz eloquently yet unsentimentally communicated the plight of these people: a mother mourns her dead child; men and women rip up cobblestones to fling through the ornate gate of the boss's estate; and the dead are ignominiously carried back to the dark huts where the looms take up more space than the people.

The cycle received great attention and praise when it was exhibited in 1897 at the *Kunstlerinnen Ausstellung* at the Galerie Gurlitt and then at the Grosse Berliner Kunstausstellung. It was also a *succès de scandale*: in the cycle, the artist succeeded in combining an essentially academic style with a topic that was considered so unconventional and subversive in the repressive, philistine Prussian era that Kaiser Wilhelm II was advised by his ministers to prevent the artist from receiving the Berlin Salon's small gold medal. He is said to have remarked: "I beg you, gentlemen, a medal for a woman, that would really be going too far ... Orders and medals of honor belong on the breasts of worthy men!" (Alessandra Comini in *ibid.*, p.100).

Kollwitz was nevertheless greatly encouraged by the reception of *A Weavers' Rebellion*, and in the ensuing 15-year period she created some of her finest images, including the *Peasants' War* cycle and the series of images of *Woman with Dead Child*. In them, she experimented with increasingly inventive graphic techniques, including complex soft-ground etching processes. Kollwitz also made her images larger; the scale of the motifs grew along with the artist's ambition and desire to convey important messages. This was true for her more socially oriented subjects as well as for her more symbolic images; indeed, Kollwitz was as interested in the ideal as the real (*From Many Wounds You Bleed, O People*, 1896; Städelsches Kunstinstitut, Frankfurt am Main; *The Downtrodden*, 1900; Staatliche Kunstsammlungen, Dresden). This creative period coincided with a love affair (roughly 1905–9) between the artist and the Viennese publisher Hugo Heller. Probably related to this affair is a series of some ten erotic drawings executed by the artist and entitled the *Sekreta* (*c*.1910; Käthe-Kollwitz-Museum Berlin). At this time, too, Kollwitz began to place her art at the service of society in such posters as the *Poster for the German Home Workers Exhibition* (1906; National Gallery of Art, Washington, DC). Kollwitz also explored the use of colour in her prints: in *Female Nude with Green Shawl Seen from Behind* (1903; Kunsthalle, Bremen; Staatliche Kunsthalle, Dresden) and *Woman Arranging Her Hair* (1900; Staatliche Kunstsammlungen, Dresden) the artist moved away from social and emotional themes to indulge herself in some isolated, and non-recurring, moments of lyrical aestheticism.

One of the most compelling motifs of this period is that of the *Woman with Dead Child*. The artist was always influenced by Renaissance art and by traditional Christian iconography, and with her interest in mothers and children it is no surprise that she should have concentrated on that theme. After executing a series of large drawings and lithographs of a theme she called *Pietà* (1903; Käthe Kollwitz Museum, Cologne; Staatliche Museen zu Berlin; National Gallery of Art), which focused on a seated mother bent over and clasping a dead child, Kollwitz slightly altered the motif. In *Woman with Dead Child* (1903; National Gallery of Art) she used the process of direct and soft-ground etching to create, through rough, passionately scratched lines, the highly simplified scene of a naked woman who, seated cross-legged in an indeterminate space, sinks her head into the lifeless body of her child. The image was of such raw grief that it terrified her best friend, who immediately recognised the child as Kollwitz's son Peter (who indeed had been the model) and thought that he must actually have died. Kollwitz printed many versions of this motif, so revelatory of her sense of tragedy and empathy, and of her gift for conveying deep emotions in visual form. Among them are experimental impressions that she hand-coloured and printed with gold backgrounds (1903; British Museum, London).

Around 1903 Kollwitz undertook her second graphic cycle. *Peasants' War* was based on a historical event, the peasants' revolt of 1522–5, which Kollwitz had read about in an account of 1841–2 by the Swabian theologian and historian Wilhelm Zimmermann. The seven large images of the cycle – they are the size of small easel paintings – were made out of order and later arranged to fashion a rough narrative continuity. The artist depicted humans ploughing the land as if they were animals (*The Ploughers*, 1906); a peasant woman raped by a feudal lord (*Raped*, 1907); the peasants preparing for revolt (*Whetting the Scythe*, 1905; *Arming in a Vault*, 1906); charging into battle (*Outbreak*, 1903); their defeat (*Battlefield*, 1907); and the taking of prisoners (*The Prisoners*, 1908; all Staatliche Kunstsammlungen, Dresden). Typical of the artist's approach, she never once portrayed the perpetrators of injustice, preferring to give voice to the suffering of the victims. Further, she avoided specifying a particular time or place for the events, aiming for the expression of human universals.

The plates of *Peasants' War* are among the most technically unusual of her works. She explored new surface textures through the use of soft-ground etching, sometimes placing a cloth over the plates to create a canvas-like background on the print (*Outbreak*). The scope of her invention may be witnessed in the numerous states of each motif, created as the artist searched for the most expressive configurations. With the *Woman with Dead Child* and the colour lithographs, the sheets of the *Peasants' War* represent one of the most creative moments in Kollwitz's career, from the perspective of technique as well as compositional power. This was the last time she worked so intensely with intaglio methods. The technical complexity of the copper-plate images would no longer seem suitable for her goals of the succeeding decades, which required a poster-like immediacy and accessibility. Later, other media such as woodcut and sculpture would challenge as well as trouble her, but never again did the artist pursue technique with the same joy in materials and pure experimentation.

As Kollwitz became increasingly committed to using her art for social ends, she turned to lithography, and particularly transfer lithography, as her medium of choice, rather than etching. The more spontaneous handling evident in her work after 1908 may be seen in the drawings she contributed for reproduction in the political-satirical magazine *Simplicissimus*, such as *Out of Work* (1909; National Gallery of Art, Washington, DC), which portrays an unemployed man sitting dejectedly beside the sick-bed of his wife and children. At this time the artist also abandoned the practice of making studies from life; her simplified and concentrated images were now often made from memory and imagination.

The commitment that Kollwitz had always felt to social causes became urgent with the onset of World War I. A turning point was the death in combat of her younger son Peter at the age of 18 in October 1914. Like many young men across Europe, Peter Kollwitz had enlisted in the army as a volunteer, and Kollwitz's diaries chronicle her dilemma between disgust for the endless fighting and numerous casualties, and the fear that her son's death was meaningless. The death cast a pall over the artist's life; from then on much of her work, especially in sculpture, was an attempt to come to terms with the notions of sacrifice and loss. The war and the violent establishment of the Weimar Republic also precipitated a shift in Kollwitz's attitude towards the function of art. In 1922, in a now-famous diary entry, she observed: "Actually my art is not *pure* art … But still art. Each works as he can … my art has *purpose. I want to have an effect on this time*, in which human beings are so much at a loss and so in need of help" (4 December 1922).

Kollwitz's more political orientation may be seen in the *Memorial Sheet to Karl Liebknecht* (1919; National Gallery of Art, Washington, DC), which commemorated the Spartacist leader who was assassinated on 15 January 1919 in the midst of the juggling for power as the Weimar Republic was formed. An acquaintance of the Liebknecht family, the artist visited the morgue and made drawings of the dead man. After many unsatisfactory drawings, trial etchings and lithographs depicting Liebknecht surrounded by mourners (1920; Käthe-Kollwitz-Museum, Berlin), Kollwitz, inspired by her recent viewing of woodcuts by the sculptor and printmaker Ernst Barlach, decided that woodcut was the very medium in which to realise her idea. Woodcut had been a popular medium in Germany since c.1905, when Die Brücke group, especially Ernst Ludwig Kirchner, adopted it to achieve a new primitive and expressive language. Although the loose, somewhat abstract handling of the woodcut, with its broad planes of black and white, might initially seem unsuited to Kollwitz's far more naturalistic style, throughout the 1920s she exploited its qualities in her rendering of more universal themes as well as for some of her self-portraits (*Self-Portrait*, 1924; National Gallery of Art). By contrast, she continued to make her anecdotal images and posters in the more narrative medium of lithography. When the *Memorial Sheet* was completed, its stark monumentality accounted for its success; the woodcut went into two editions and was sold very cheaply at an Arbeiter Kunstausstellung in Berlin in 1920.

This was a wrenching time for Kollwitz. She had never before been programmatically political but soon felt that the chaotic events at the end of the war and the beginning of the Weimar Republic were forcing her into a role that she hesitated to fill. In a diary entry of October 1920 she noted that, because of her previous work, she was being praised as an artist of the proletariat and of the November Revolution, but that in fact, out of cowardice, she did not belong to any political party, and certainly not to the Communist Party. Yet at the same time, she did wish her art to serve a social function. Her stance was further complicated by the fact that in 1919 she was appointed the first woman professor at the Prussian Academy, an establishment position. The artist was torn between her wish for social reform and her deployment of her work to that end, and the forces of the establishment art world. Although she was committed to engaged art, she felt that the role of "standard bearer" had been thrust upon her at the price of some of her artistic freedom and of much personal ambivalence.

Recognising that the simplicity and readability of the expressionist woodcut style had a unique potential to convey ideas quickly and powerfully, Kollwitz chose it for her third graphic cycle, *War* (1922–3). This seven-sheet portfolio comprises *The Sacrifice, The Volunteers, The Parents, The Widow I, Widow II, The Mothers* and *The People* (published 1924; National Gallery of Art). As with *Peasants' War*, and unlike any other war portfolios such as Otto Dix's, Kollwitz portrayed no scenes of combat, only images of mothers and children, widows, parents and volunteers. Drastically reductive, transcending time and place, the *War* series, in its iconic abstraction, captures the full horror of loss and the equivocal nature of sacrifice.

In the years between the wars, Kollwitz was occupied with teaching at the Academy, with her family (her remaining son Hans married in 1920 and he and his wife had four children between 1921 and 1930) and with social concerns. She lithographed many posters such as *Never Again War!* (1924), executed for a pacifist organisation, and images such as *Municipal Shelter* (1926; both National Gallery of Art), in which a homeless mother bearing Kollwitz's own features huddles over her two sleeping children. In 1925 she made a three-sheet woodcut cycle called *Proletariat*; the eight sheets of her last series, entitled *Death*, were lithographed in 1934–5. In the most famous of the *Death* images, *Call of Death* (1934; National Gallery of Art), the artist herself receives the touch of a disembodied hand, calling her away from earthly existence. A concrete expression of Kollwitz's lifelong dialogue with death, the lithograph reveals the artist's mastery of expressive draughtsmanship and her astonishing economy of means.

Although Kollwitz continued to pursue her graphic work until 1942, three years before her death, sculpture was her main interest in the last decades of her life. It is surprising how little is known about this aspect of her oeuvre. For example, one account lists 25 works; another lists 19. Not all of their dates are known. The artist received her first introduction to the medium during a sojourn in Paris in 1904; she visited Rodin's studio and took some sculpture lessons at the Académie Julian. She returned to sculpture in 1909. Kollwitz was a modeller, working in clay and plaster, as in *Lovers* (1913; Museum of Fine Arts, Boston), leaving the bronze casting or stone cutting to other hands. Kollwitz made most of her sculptures during the 1930s and early 1940s after she signed an appeal to unify leftist party candidates against the Nazis and was dismissed from her professorship and directorship of the master studio for graphic arts at the Prussian Academy. In that year, 1933, Kollwitz joined a number of young artists in a communal studio building in the Klosterstrasse and, unofficially forbidden to exhibit her work, found solace during her internal exile, as she called it, in working in three dimensions. The artist's longest ongoing project was the two figures of the mourning father and mother, her monument to her son Peter. She discussed it at length in her diaries and agonised over it for some two decades before the finished plasters were translated into granite and finally put into place in 1932 in the military cemetery at Dixmuiden, Belgium, where Peter was buried. In their enclosed, inward-looking, blocky forms, these works convey a simplicity, self-contained apartness and quiet pathos that may be seen as well in some of the bronze relief sculptures, such as her plaque for her family grave *Rest in the Peace of His Hands* (1935; National Gallery of Art) and *Lamentation: In Memory of Ernst Barlach, Who Died in 1938* (1938; Hirshhorn Museum and Sculpture Garden, Washington, DC).

Kollwitz was devastated when World War II broke out in 1939. Her husband Karl died in 1942, the same year that her grandson Peter was killed on the Eastern Front. In response, Kollwitz made her last lithograph, an anti-war statement entitled *Seed Corn Must Not Be Ground* (1942; Staatliche Museen zu Berlin), after a phrase from Goethe, in which a mother encircles her children protectively. In the summer of 1943 the artist was evacuated to escape the bombing of Berlin; later that year her home was destroyed. In 1944 Kollwitz accepted the invitation of Prince Ernst Heinrich of Saxony to live on the grounds of his Schloss Moritzburg outside Dresden. She died the following year and was ultimately buried in the Central Cemetery in Berlin.

By the time Kollwitz died at the age of 78, she was already one of the best-known German artists. Her work had been sought after since the 1890s by major figures of the art world such as Max Lehrs, director of the world-famous Dresden Kupferstichkabinett, as well as by numerous German private collectors. The prints gained an even wider audience through the inexpensive reproductions that were published from 1913 onwards. By the 1920s, one could find reproductions, if not original examples of her images, in millions of homes throughout Germany. In 1927 she visited the Soviet Union, where she was already well-known and appreciated. Since then, her fame has spread throughout the world. By the late 1950s and 1960s, the German Art Council was sending exhibitions of her work to cities as distant as Paris and Cape Town, South Africa. During and after World War II, German refugees brought Kollwitz prints to America and elsewhere. More recently, with the aid of the artist's grandchildren, two museums entirely devoted to her art have been established in Berlin and Cologne, and a new one has opened in Moritzburg.

Kollwitz's art has not always been admired, however. Critics, especially modernists, have objected to its retardatory naturalism, its privileging of theme over style, and what some view as its bathetic sentimentalism. Käthe Kollwitz, however, who in many ways was far more a 19th-century naturalist than a 20th-century modernist, on the whole considered that she had served the world by fulfilling her grandfather Rupp's dictum "a talent is a duty" ("Eine Gabe ist eine Aufgabe"). Because of the accessibility of her style and the universal humanitarianism of her imagery, her art can be understood by all. Indeed, Kollwitz has come to be regarded by Germans as well as by other citizens of the world as a "symbol of [that] nation's 'good conscience in its darkest times', and 'the embodiment of the good Germany'" (Gunther Thiem, quoted by Hildegard Bachert in Washington 1992, p.125). More than any of her contemporaries, she was, as individual and as artist, truly the conscience of her age.

ELIZABETH PRELINGER

Kozloff, Joyce

American painter and public artist, 1942–

Born Joyce Blumberg in Somerville, New Jersey, 14 December 1942. Studied at Art Students League, New York, 1959; Rutgers University, New Brunswick, New Jersey, 1962; Università di Firenze, Italy, 1963; Carnegie Institute of Technology, Pittsburgh (BFA 1964); Columbia University, New York (MFA 1967). Married Max Kozloff, 1967; one son. Held teaching positions in elementary and secondary schools, then at Queens College, New York, 1972–3; School of Visual Arts, New York, 1973–4; Art Institute, Chicago, 1975; Syracuse University, New York, 1977; University of New Mexico, Albuquerque, 1978; Brooklyn Museum Art School, New York, 1978–9; Washington University, St Louis, 1986; Cooper Union, New York, 1990; International Art Workshop, Teschemakers, New Zealand, 1991; Rutgers University, 1992. Recipient of Tamarind Lithography Institute grant, Albuquerque, 1972; Creative Artists Public Service (CAPS) grants, 1972 (New York State Council on the Arts) and 1975; National Endowment for the Arts (NEA) grant, 1977. Member of the Board of Directors, College Art Association, 1985–9. Lives in New York.

Selected Individual Exhibitions

Tibor de Nagy Gallery, New York: 1970, 1971, 1973, 1974, 1976, 1977
Mabel Smith Douglass Library, Rutgers University, New Brunswick: 1973
Everson Museum, Syracuse, NY: 1979–81 (*An Interior Decorated*, touring)
Joslyn Art Museum, Omaha, NE: 1982
Institute of Contemporary Art, University of Pennsylvania, Philadelphia: 1983 (with Keith Haring, Jenny Holzer and Rich Paul)
Lincoln Center for the Performing Arts, New York: 1983 (with Judith Murray and Elizabeth Murray)
Boston University Art Gallery: 1986–7 (*Visionary Ornament*, touring retrospective)
Lorence-Monk Gallery, New York: 1990–93 (*Patterns of Desire*, touring)
Tile Guild, Los Angeles: 1995

Selected Writings

"The Women's Movement: Still a 'source of strength' or 'one big bore'?", *Art News*, lxxv, April 1976, pp.49–50 (with Barbara Zucker)
"Art hysterical notions of art history", *Heresies*, no.4, Winter 1978, pp.38–42 (with Valerie Jaudon); reprinted in *Theories and Documents of Contemporary Art: A Sourcebook of Artists Writings*, ed. Kristine Stiles and Peter Selz, Berkeley: University of California Press, 1996
Patterns of Desire, New York: Hudson Hills Press, 1990 (introduction by Linda Nochlin)

Bibliography

Joseph Masheck, "Joyce Kozloff", *Artforum*, xii, September 1973, pp.76–7
Nancy Foote, "Joyce Kozloff at de Nagy", *Art in America*, lxiii, May 1975, pp.88–9
John Perreault, "Issues in pattern painting", *Artforum*, xvi, November 1977, pp.32–6
Amy Goldin, "Pattern and print", *Print Collector's Newsletter*, ix, 1978, pp.10–13
Carrie Rickey, "Joyce Kozloff", *Arts Magazine*, lii, January 1978, pp.2, 29
Joyce Kozloff: An Interior Decorated, exh. cat., Everson Museum, Syracuse, NY, and elsewhere, 1979
Jeff Perrone, "Joyce Kozloff", *Artforum,* xviii, November 1979, pp.78–9
Robin White, "Joyce Kozloff", *View*, Oakland, CA: Crown Point Press, 1981 (interview)
Jeff Perrone, "Two ethnics sitting around talking about Wasp culture", *Arts Magazine*, lix, March 1985, pp.78–83 (interview)
Joyce Kozloff: Visionary Ornament, exh. cat., Boston University Art Gallery, and elsewhere, 1986
Sally Webster, "Pattern and decoration in the public eye", *Art in America*, lxxv, February 1987, pp.118–25
Peggy Phelan, "Crimes of passion", *Artforum*, xxviii, May 1990, pp.173–7
Charlotte Streifer Rubinstein, *American Women Sculptors*, Boston: Hall, 1990
Hermine Freed, *Joyce Kozloff: Public Art Works*, video, New York, 1996

Joyce Kozloff creates walls of decorative colour. Trained in the Hard Edge minimalist vocabulary that dominated the eastern seaboard of the USA in the 1960s, she was inspired by her feminist studies to fuse geometric compositions with specific historical content that honours the ethnically and racially diverse, often female makers. Kozloff's first solo exhibition (New York, 1970) featured large acrylics of rectilinear patterns derived from Greek temple façades. By the mid-1970s, after having spent time in Mexico and the American Southwest, she began to look to native textile and architectural designs for inspiration. *Mitla* (1974; Massachusetts Institute of Technology, Cambridge) is a gouache and coloured pencil recollection of the fine stone mosaic façades of the stunning Zapotec Indian site in Oaxaca, Mexico. Six horizontal bands animate the composition, each a brilliant ribbon of colour marked with a variation of the Zapotec step-fret pattern. Although Kozloff derived the *Mitla* image from architectural sources, the stone mosaics themselves were originally derived from Zapotec textile patterns. Aware of this, Kozloff realised that many of the fabric, ceramic and basketry forms she admired had been made by women, and that most of these women had been lost to anonymity in the dominant historical discourse. The artist then determined to use her painting and pattern-making to honour such "disappeared" artists and their art forms.

When Kozloff exhibited such Mexican works as *Mitla*, she was praised for the rich elaboration of colour and pattern, but criticised for the "literalism" of her work. As, however, Patricia Johnston, curator of Kozloff's retrospective at the Boston University Art Gallery, asserted:

> Kozloff's fidelity to her sources may be the most radical aspect of her art. Pattern is not secondary ... [it] functions as both the form and the subject matter of her painting; its associations constitute its meaning. The specificity of her motifs forces the viewer to confront its content: the aesthetic strength and cultural value of the decorative arts [Boston 1986, p.4].

Since the 1970s Kozloff has travelled the planet (both literally and figuratively) to mine a multitude of artistic traditions for decorative sources. She has explored these sources in formats that range from intimate watercolours to immense public works, but she has remained consistent in her "literal" interpretations and in her assertion that decorative and popular art traditions are worthy of aesthetic investigation.

In the late 1970s Kozloff worked on a large installation that she entitled *An Interior Decorated*. First exhibited at the Everson Museum, Syracuse, in the autumn of 1979 and later at the Renwick Gallery of the National Museum of American Art, Smithsonian Institution, Washington, DC (August 1980), *An Interior Decorated* marks Kozloff's move from painted canvas to work applied directly to the wall. An elaborate environment combining ceramic tile "rugs" with silkscreened and lithographed fabric wall works, *An Interior Decorated* embodies what Kozloff called her

> personal anthology of the decorative arts [with motifs derived from] American Indian pottery, Moroccan ceramics, Viennese Art Nouveau book ornament, American quilts, Berber carpets, Caucasian kilims, Egyptian wall paintings, Iznik and Catalan tiles, Islamic calligraphy, Art Deco design, Sumerian and Romanesque carvings, Pennsylvania Dutch designs, Chinese painted porcelain, French lace patterns, Celtic illuminations, Turkish woven and brocaded silks, Seljuk brickwork, Persian miniatures and Coptic textiles [Syracuse 1979, p.8].

It is, as the critic Carrie Rickey wrote in the catalogue: "where painting meets architecture, where art meets craft, where personal commitment meets public art" (*ibid.*).

Even as she was working on *An Interior Decorated*, Kozloff was also beginning her foray into public art. Each of her public art projects has been initiated by research into the popular and folk art traditions germane to the site and each has placed locally relevant decorative motifs in architectural arenas, often the large walls that commuters see as they hurry from one train or subway stop to another. Kozloff intends the complexity of her compositions to allow multiple "reads" to be "discovered" over time, as viewers pass her work repeatedly. To date, she has completed 12 major public art commissions: Harvard Square Subway Station, Boston, and Amtrak Station, Wilmington (both 1979–85); California Airport, San Francisco (1982–3); Humboldt-Hospital Subway Station, Buffalo (1983–4); Suburban Train Station, Philadelphia (1985); Financial Station, Detroit, Michigan (1985); Home Savings Tower, Los Angeles (1989); Home Savings of America Headquarters, Irwindale (1989); Plaza Las Fuentes, Pasadena (1990); Intermediate School 218, New York (1991); Seventh & Flower Metro Station, Los Angeles, (1993); and Memorial Library foyer, Mankato State University (1995).

Kozloff's Mankato project is one of her most complex and successful. She entitled it *Around the World on the 44th Parallel*, because she began with the library's latitudinal position and circled the globe to locate other cities on the same parallel, selecting Nice, Ravenna, Florence and Sarajevo from Europe; Urumqi, Changchun, Sapporo and Vladivostok from Asia; and Burlington, Eugene, Toronto and, of course, Mankato from North America. Her compositions began with strips from each city map, over which she laid patterns derived from the local art traditions. There were Northwest coast Native American images for Eugene, golden mosaics for Ravenna, tile work and carpets from the Ottoman Empire for Sarajevo. All these images were painted on majolica ceramic tiles made at the Tile Guild in Los Angeles. The tile panels encircle large open bays in the library, inviting viewers to consider the confluence of architecture and geography that produces the patterns of maps and the smaller folk and popular art patterns created by the inhabitants of those cities. A scintillating kaleidoscope of visionary decoration, Kozloff's Mankato project reveals the consistency and validity of her compelling patchworks of colour, design, image and pattern.

BETTY ANN BROWN

Krasner, Lee
American painter, 1908–1984

Born Lena Krassner in Brooklyn, New York, 27 October 1908. Studied in New York at Women's Art School of Cooper Union, 1926–8; Art Students League, 1928; National Academy of Design, 1928–32; City College and Greenwich House, 1933; Hans Hofmann's School of Fine Arts, 1937–40. Employed on Public Works of Art Project (PWAP), 1934; Temporary Emergency Relief Administration, 1934–5; Mural Division of Works Progress Administration Federal Arts Project (WPA/FAP), 1935–43, all in New York. Member of American Abstract Artists (AAA) from 1939. Married painter Jackson Pollock, 1945; he died 1956. Moved to The Springs, East Hampton, New York, 1945. Recipient of Augustus Saint-Gaudens medal, Cooper Union Alumni Association, 1974; Lowe Fellowship for Distinction, Barnard College, New York, 1974; Outstanding Achievement in the Visual Arts award, Women's Caucus for Art, 1980. Died in New York, 19 June 1984.

Selected Individual Exhibitions

Betty Parsons Gallery, New York: 1951
Stable Gallery, New York: 1955
Martha Jackson Gallery, New York: 1958
Signa Gallery, East Hampton, NY: 1959
Howard Wise Gallery, New York: 1960, 1962
Whitechapel Art Gallery, London: 1965–6 (touring, organised by Arts Council of Great Britain)
University Art Gallery, University of Alabama, Tuscaloosa: 1967
Marlborough Gallery, New York: 1968, 1969, 1973
Whitney Museum of American Art, New York: 1973
Corcoran Gallery of Art, Washington, DC: 1975 (touring)
Pace Gallery, New York: 1977, 1979, 1981
Janie C. Lee Gallery, Houston: 1978, 1981
Guild Hall Museum, East Hampton, NY: 1981 (with Jackson Pollock)
Grey Art Gallery and Study Center, New York University: 1981 (*A Working Relationship*, with Jackson Pollock)
Robert Miller Gallery, New York: 1982
Museum of Fine Arts, Houston: 1983–5 (touring retrospective, accompanied by *The Education of an Artist*)

Bibliography

Paintings, Drawings and Collages, exh. cat., Whitechapel Art Gallery, London, and elsewhere, 1965
Lawrence Campbell, "Of Lilith and lettuce", *Art News*, lxvii, March 1968, pp.42–3, 61–4
Emily Wasserman, "Lee Krasner in mid-career", *Artforum*, vi, March 1968, pp.38–43
Lee Krasner: Large Paintings, exh. cat., Whitney Museum of American Art, New York, 1973
Bryan Robertson, "The nature of Lee Krasner", *Art in America*, lxi, November–December 1973, pp.83–7
Cindy Nemser, "Lee Krasner's paintings, 1946–49", *Artforum*, xii, December 1973, pp.61–5
——, *Art Talk: Conversations with 12 Women Artists*, New York: Scribner, 1975
——, "The indomitable Lee Krasner", *Feminist Art Journal*, iv, Spring 1975, pp.4–9
Barbara Rose, "Lee Krasner and the origins of Abstract Expressionism", *Arts Magazine*, li, February 1977, pp.96–100
Abstract Expressionism: The Formative Years, exh. cat., Herbert F. Johnson Museum of Art, Ithaca, NY, and elsewhere, 1978
Elsa Honig Fine, *Women and Art*, Montclair, NJ: Allenheld and Schram, and London: Prior, 1978
Eleanor Munro, *Originals: American Women Artists*, New York: Simon and Schuster, 1979
Barbara Cavaliere, "An interview with Lee Krasner", *Flash Art*, no.94–5, January–February 1980, pp.14–16
The Abstract Expressionists and Their Precursors, exh. cat., Nassau County Museum of Fine Arts, Roslyn Harbor, NY, 1981

Amei Wallach, "Lee Krasner out of Jackson Pollock's shadow", *Newsday*, 23 August 1981, pp.10–15, 29–31, 33–4

Ellen G. Landau, "Lee Krasner's early career", *Arts Magazine*, lvi, October 1981, pp.110–22; November 1981, pp.80–89

Charlotte Streifer Rubinstein, *American Women Artists from Early Times to the Present*, Boston: Hall, 1982

Lee Krasner: A Retrospective, exh. cat., Museum of Fine Arts, Houston, and elsewhere, 1983

Ellen G. Landau, "Lee Krasner's past continuous", *Art News*, lxxxiii, February 1984, pp.68–76

Marcia E. Vetrocq, "An independent tack: Lee Krasner", *Art in America*, lxxii, May 1984, pp.136–45

Michael Cannell, "An interview with Lee Krasner", *Arts Magazine*, lix, September 1984, pp.87–9

John Bernard Myers, "Naming pictures: Conversations between Lee Krasner and John Bernard Myers", *Artforum*, xxiii, November 1984, pp.69–73

Lee Krasner: Collages, 1939–1984, exh. cat., Robert Miller Gallery, New York, 1986

Abstract Expressionism: The Critical Developments, exh. cat., Albright-Knox Art Gallery, Buffalo, NY, 1987

Robert Hobbs, "Lee Krasner: A retrospective", *Woman's Art Journal*, viii/1, 1987, pp.42–5

Lee Krasner, Jackson Pollock: Künstlerpaare-Künstlerfreunde/Dialogues d'artistes-résonances, exh. cat., Kunstmuseum, Bern, 1989

Steven Naifeh and Gregory White Smith, *Jackson Pollock: An American Saga*, New York: Potter, 1989; London: Barrie and Jenkins, 1990

Anne M. Wagner, "Lee Krasner as L.K.", *Representations*, no.25, Winter 1989, pp.42–57; reprinted in Norma Broude and Mary D. Garrard, eds, *The Expanding Discourse: Feminism and Art History*, New York: Icon, 1992, pp.425–36

Stephen Polcari, "In the shadow of an innovator", *Art International*, August 1990, pp.105–7

——, *Abstract Expressionism and the Modern Experience*, Cambridge and New York: Cambridge University Press, 1991

Robert Hobbs, *Lee Krasner*, New York and London: Abbeville, 1993

Lee Krasner: Umber Paintings, 1959–1962, exh. cat., Robert Miller Gallery, New York, 1993

Anne M. Wagner, "Fictions: Krasner's presence, Pollock's absence", *Significant Others: Creativity and Intimate Partnership*, ed. Whitney Chadwick and Isabelle de Courtivron, New York and London: Thames and Hudson, 1993, pp.222–43

Ellen G. Landau and Jeffrey D. Grove, *Lee Krasner: A Catalogue Raisonné*, New York: Abrams, 1995

Anne M. Wagner, *Three Artists (Three Women): Modernism and the Art of Hesse, Krasner and O'Keeffe*, Berkeley: University of California Press, 1996

Recognised at the time of her death in 1984 as a "pioneering Abstract Expressionist", "a major force in the art world" and "an artist's artist", Lee Krasner is today viewed as a visionary Abstract Expressionist painter. However, the dual stigma that she bore both as a female artist and as the wife and widow of one of the 20th century's most infamous painters, Jackson Pollock, led to an "odd mixture of fame and obscurity" (London 1965, p.5) that plagued Krasner's own development and reception as an independent artist during most of her life.

Pursuing her vocation with unwavering dedication (her nephew stated that she believed in art the way other people believed in God), as a teenager Krasner commuted daily from Brooklyn to Manhattan to study at Washington Irving High School (1922–6), the only public high school where a girl could study art. She then graduated to the Women's Art School of the Cooper Union and the National Academy of Design. Her work from this period is discursive, embracing developments in Social Realism, Surrealism and Cubism, arriving ultimately at a reverence for Picasso and Matisse. While working as an artist for the Public Works of Art Project in 1937, Krasner joined Hans Hofmann's School of Fine Arts, an experience she described as "opening a new world for me". Working from the model, Krasner created figure studies that echo the structure of still-life arrangements and developed a private language of cubo-abstraction stressing spatial relationships of colour and structure. *Composition* (c.1940–43; National Museum of American Art, Smithsonian Institution, Washington, DC) illustrates her quest at this time to follow Matisse by eliminating ordinary perspective, creating an illusion of depth through colour and formal organisation.

In 1939 Krasner joined the American Abstract Artists (AAA), a group of politically concerned artists dedicated to the principles of non-objective painting. While involved with the group, Krasner painted several canvases influenced by her hero Piet Mondrian's Neo-Plasticism (repr. Laudau 1981, fig.23). Concurrently, Krasner was employed by the Mural Division of the Federal Arts Project of the Works Progress Administration, and much of her output between 1940 and 1943 grew out of ideas for mural projects. Becoming progressively more abstract, these biomorphic and geometric designs still belie their derivation from the still-life arrangements that Krasner first drew at the Hofmann school.

In 1942 Krasner became involved with Pollock and for the next three years virtually abandoned her own art-making, stymied by her admitted struggle to "lose Cubism" and "absorb Pollock". Shortly after their marriage in late 1945 and move to rural East Hampton, Krasner commandeered the living room of their rustic home as a studio where she began turning out her signature "Little Images". Purely abstract, the Little Images took three typical forms: thickly impastoed dabs (*Shattered Color*, 1947; Guild Hall Museum, East Hampton, NY), thin skeins with an all-over patterning (*Untitled*, 1948; Metropolitan Museum of Art, New York) and serial hieroglyphs (*Untitled*, 1949; Museum of Modern Art, New York). These discreetly proportioned paintings allowed Krasner to develop a typology of devices that she reiterated in larger paintings throughout her career.

In 1950, moving her studio to the upstairs bedroom, Krasner broke the Little Image cycle and created her first large-scale works: a series of automist-inspired, quasi-figural works dubbed the "personage paintings". These large-scale, thickly painted canvases prefigured the strong verticality manifested in Krasner's canvases of the mid-1950s (see Nemser 1975). Now destroyed, they are known only through photographs taken by Hans Namuth (repr. Rose 1977, fig.64). In a now characteristic move, Krasner radically shifted styles to create next a series of thinly painted canvases concerned with "holding the vertical" (Nemser 1975). Although only two paintings remain intact (*Number 3 [Untitled]*, 1951; Museum of Modern Art), the rest served as backdrops for collages shown at the Stable Gallery in 1955. Clearly, their tonal, reductive surfaces had more in common with the colour field abstractions of later Rothko, Still and Newman than with Pollock's own frenzied skeins of paint.

In 1953, as the conflicts in their relationship increased, Krasner began creating large-scale collages reflecting a renewed attention to natural elements rather than academic styles. Using fragments of drawings and canvas, torn and shorn from her own as well as Pollock's rejected works, Krasner's art began to disclose a new confidence and mastery of form. 1955 was a break-out year. The large, stylistically sophisticated collages Krasner showed that year at the Stable Gallery constituted a revolutionary development in her career: not only a unique recontextualisation of old paintings, new materials, cloth, canvas and paint, these surfaces seemed to function as a direct outlet for the friction Krasner was experiencing with Pollock at this time. Perceiving the organic metaphors embedded in Krasner's materials, Fairfield Porter compared the surface of one painting to a "messed-up beach of pebbles" and noted that such works as *Milkweed* (1955; Albright-Knox Art Gallery, Buffalo, NY) resembled "nature photographs magnified" (Fairfield Porter, "Art news of one year: November, Lee Krasner", *Art News*, November 1955, pp.66–7).

After Pollock's death in 1956, Krasner, refocusing on her own creativity and ambition, worked on an escalated scale and with increased ferocity. Taking over Pollock's large studio, she created her first series of large, Abstract Expressionist canvases. An early example from this group, *The Seasons* (1957; Whitney Museum of American Art, New York), is one of the largest she ever painted. In this work Krasner developed an exuberantly expressionistic composition dominated by rhythmically interactive, sexually suggestive organic forms; allusions to specific anatomical parts (heart, buttocks, penis, eyes, mouths, labia) are cleverly combined with other natural forms (leaves, fruit, etc.). Natural processes of growth and change are suggested through her gestural and painterly technique, through emphasis on the spherical and curvilinear, and through the use of fresh greens and bright pinks modulated by cream and black. In 1981 John Russell of the *New York Times* declared *The Seasons* "one of the most remarkable American paintings of its date" ("Delights, surprises – and gaps", 8 March 1981, section 2, p.D31).

In the early 1960s Krasner created the *Umber and White* series, a group of more than 30 enormous canvases characterised by the poet Richard Howard as psychoanalytically motivated "mourning" pictures of which *Gothic Landscape* (1961; Tate Gallery, London) is a prime example (see Howard in New York 1993). Ferocious and lyrical, these canvases disclose Krasner's investigation of Jungian precepts that she had previously held in suspicion. These tumultuous canvases, worked from left to right in violent, slashlike rhythms, seem to express turmoil and rage, perhaps over Pollock's or her mother's death.

It was during the late 1960s to mid-1970s that feminist-oriented art historians and critics first began to take note of Krasner and re-evaluate her position within the history of modern art, particularly the Abstract Expressionist movement. In the late 1960s Krasner returned to more foliate schemes in which she experimented with highly keyed colour and regenerative, biotic forms. Interestingly, works like these, exemplified by *Pollination* (1968; Dallas Museum of Art), were the first to be interpreted along the lines of feminist rhetoric. Describing *Pollination*, Cindy Nemser remarked on its "thrusting phallic, pistil-like shapes, ejecting fructifying splinters of paint, evok[ing] the plant, animal, and human processes of regeneration" ("In the galleries: Lee Krasner", *Arts Magazine*, April 1968, p.59). Although Krasner once claimed: "I have very little patience with clubby attitudes toward it [feminism]", she approved of and encouraged the movement's role in elevating consciousness of female artists, and in late 1972 she even joined the group Women in the Arts to picket the Museum of Modern Art for its neglect of female artists. Newly "radicalised", and an example to a new generation of "feminist" artists, Krasner again made an abrupt switch in both scale and form in her art of the 1970s. From 1970 to 1973, to a certain degree recapitulating and magnifying the vocabulary of marks and gestures initiated in the "Little Images", Krasner created a group of large paintings that embraced concurrent developments in Color Field and Op Art. Such works as *Rising Green* (1972; Metropolitan Museum of Art) demonstrate that at the age of 62 Krasner was clearly intent on positioning herself as a forward-looking artist.

Krasner's most significant late-career contribution came in 1976 when she once again chose to cannibalise her own past, cutting up her own Hofmann School charcoal drawings from the 1930s and 1940s and recontextualising them into eleven stunning collages based on a linguistic system suggesting time and its conditions. The group, entitled *Eleven Ways to Use the Words to See*, was characterised by Grace Glueck as "the present ingesting the past" ("How to recycle your drawings", *New York Times*, 25 February 1977, p.C18). Indeed, such works as *Past Continuous* (1976; Solomon R. Guggenheim Museum, New York), with its repetition of expressionistically deformed female figures, signifies Krasner's quest to explore in this series "in what ways I, as an artist, differed now from then" (Myers 1984). Underlying Krasner's re-evaluation of her own career was her inclusion as the sole female artist in two important revisionist studies of Abstract Expressionism's early years: *Abstract Expressionism: The Formative Years* (Ithaca, NY, 1978) and *The Abstract Expressionists and Their Precursors* (Roslyn Harbor, NY, 1981). Krasner once claimed: "I certainly was there through the formative years of Abstract Expressionism and I have been treated like I wasn't", and it took shows like these, her retrospective of more than 150 works in 1983–4 and her rediscovery by feminist writers and art historians to ensure her position today as "one of the handful of important abstract expressionists" (Mark Stevens, "The American masters", *Newsweek*, 2 January 1984).

JEFFREY D. GROVE

See also Training and Professionalism survey 5

Kruger, Barbara

American photographer and artist, 1945–

Born in Newark, New Jersey, 26 January 1945. Studied at Syracuse University, New York, 1964–5; Parsons School of Design, New York, under Diane Arbus (q.v.) and Marvin Israel, 1965–6. Subsequently designer for *Mademoiselle* magazine, Condé Nast Publications; also freelance graphic designer. Independent artist and photographer from 1972. Visiting artist, California Institute of the Arts, Valencia; Art Institute of Chicago; University of California, Berkeley. One of the few women to be included in Documenta VII art fair, Kassel, 1982. Recipient of Creative Artists Public Service (CAPS) grant, 1976; National Endowment for the Arts (NEA) grant, 1982. Lives in New York.

Selected Individual Exhibitions

Artists Space, New York: 1974
Fischbach Gallery, New York: 1975
PS 1, Long Island City, NY: 1980
Institute of Contemporary Arts, London: 1983–4
   (touring)
Kunsthalle, Basel: 1984
Rhona Hoffman Gallery, Chicago: 1984, 1986, 1990
Los Angeles County Museum of Art: 1985
Krannert Art Museum, University of Illinois, Urbana:
   1986
Mary Boone Gallery, New York: 1987, 1989, 1991, 1994
National Art Gallery, Wellington, New Zealand: 1988
Kölnischer Kunstverein, Cologne: 1994

Selected Writings

Editor, *TV Guides: A Collection of Thoughts about Television*, New York: Kuklapolitan Press, 1987

My Pretty Pony, New York: Knopf, 1989 (with Stephen King)

Editor, *Remaking History*, Albany, CA: Bay Press, 1989 (with Phil Mariani)

Remote Control: Power, Cultures and the World of Appearances, Cambridge: Massachusetts Institute of Technology Press, 1993 (collected essays)

Bibliography

Hal Foster, "Subversive signs", *Art in America*, lxx, November 1982, pp.88–92

Craig Owens, "The discourse of others: Feminists and postmodernism", *The Anti-Aesthetic: Essays on Postmodern Culture*, ed. Hal Foster, Port Townsend, WA: Bay Press, 1983; London: Pluto, 1985, pp.57–77

We Won't Play Nature to Your Culture: Works by Barbara Kruger, exh. cat., Institute of Contemporary Arts, London, and elsewhere, 1983

Howard N. Fox, Miranda McClintic and Phyllis Rosenzweig, *Content: A Contemporary Focus, 1974–1984*, Washington, DC: Smithsonian Institution Press, 1984

Kunst mit Eigen-Sinn: Aktuelle Kunst von Frauen, Vienna and Munich: Locher, 1985

Kate Linker, "Barbara Kruger", *Flash Art*, no.121, 1985, pp.36–7 (interview)

Slices of Life, exh. cat., Krannert Art Museum, University of Illinois, Urbana, 1986

Anders Stephanson, "Barbara Kruger", *Flash Art*, no.136, 1987, pp.55–9 (interview)

Carol Squiers, "Diversionary (syn)tactics: Barbara Kruger has her way with words", *Art News*, lxxxvi, February 1987, pp.76–85

Jeanne Siegel, "Barbara Kruger: Pictures and words", *Arts Magazine*, lxi, Summer 1987, pp.17–21; reprinted in *Art Talk: The Early 80s*, New York: Da Capo Press, 1990, pp.299–312

Anne Le Schreiber, "You can look at Oliver North and listen to him speak and wonder how a nation doesn't know a sociopath when it sees one", *Vogue*, October 1987, pp.260–62

Nancy D. Campbell, "The oscillating embrace: Subjection and interapellation in Barbara Kruger's art", *Genders*, no.1, 1988, pp.56–74

Barbara Kruger, exh. cat., National Art Gallery, Wellington, 1988

Laura Mulvey, *Visual and Other Pleasures*, Bloomington: Indiana University Press, and London: Macmillan, 1989

Kate Linker, *Love for Sale: The Words and Pictures of Barbara Kruger*, New York: Abrams, 1990

W. J. T. Mitchell, "An interview with Barbara Kruger", *Critical Inquiry*, xvii, 1991, pp.434–48

David Deitcher, "Barbara Kruger: Resisting arrest", *Artforum*, xxix, February 1991, pp.84–92

Mignon Nixon, "You thrive on mistaken identity", *October*, no.60, 1992, pp.58–81

Mara R. Witzling, ed., *Voicing Today's Visions: Writings by Contemporary Women Artists*, New York: Universe, 1994

Jill Diane Ball, *The Effects of Public Representation upon the Identity of the Subject: Two Case Studies in Public Art*, PhD dissertation, University of California at Los Angeles, 1995

Melissa Harris, ed., *On Location with Henri Cartier-Bresson, Graciela Iturbide, Barbara Kruger, Sally Mann, Andres Serrano, Clarissa Sligh*, New York: Aperture Foundation, 1995

Eleven years' work as a graphic designer for Condé Nast publications and as a free-lance picture editor taught Barbara Kruger that if the viewer did not look at the design: "you were fired". Before her commercial career, Kruger spent a year at Syracuse University and a year at Parsons School of Design, where she studied under Marvin Israel and the photographer Diane Arbus (q.v.), who once assigned her to photograph the exterior of buildings and to imagine the lives lived inside. Her first solo show at Artists Space in New York in 1974 did not, however, feature photography, but abstract painting and fibre work (*Two A.M. Cookie*, 1973), reflecting the then-prevalent taste for both abstraction and the fibre arts on the New York art scene. The decorative style of these pieces coincided with the Pattern and Decoration movement that flourished in California during the mid-1970s. In these years, Kruger was active with Artists for Cultural Change, which strengthened her personal interest in feminism and its criticism, and in the relationship between art and politics, pivotal issues in her later work.

In 1976 Kruger began using language in a performance piece – for her a major shift in style and content. The *Hospital Series* followed in 1977. Combining photographs taken in New York hospitals with patients' voices ("No don't/Not now/Go away/Not that") and other texts ("The technology of early death/The providing of consumer goods to a dying populace"), Kruger began to probe social ideology through the incisive juxtaposition of image and text. A self-published collection of photographs paired with invented narratives entitled *Picture/Readings* followed in 1978. Since then she has marshalled the skills of the graphic designer and advertiser to deconstruct media culture through black-and-white photographs paired with short, evocative texts. Together they become insidious critiques of the established cultural narrative.

Echoes of the early modernists' exploration of poster design and the photo-montages of the Dadaists Hannah Höch (q.v.) and John Heartfield underlie her work, although as Kruger emphasises, their impact on advertising and graphic art were her direct sources of influence; she did not discover Heartfield's work until 1981.

Kruger's subjects range from stereotypes of social roles to feminist deconstructive criticism of the gaze, as in *Untitled (Your Gaze Hits the Side of My Face)* (1981). Her use of text resonates with the linguistic theory of the French Post-structuralist philosopher Roland Barthes and his analysis of "language as legislation", and also the writings of Jean Baudrillard, such as his essays on fashion and its territorial scope, "Design and environment", and other essays on the commodification of the art object: "The art auction" and "Gesture and signature". Discovered by artists of the later 1970s, these writings were also widely discussed by avant-garde critics. Congruent with her generation's concern with art in the public sphere, Kruger dispersed her works on matchbooks, T-shirts, postcards and billboards, echoing the strategies used by her contemporary and friend, Jenny Holzer. Under the auspices of the US Public Art Fund, in 1983 she produced *I AM NOT TRYING TO SELL YOU ANYTHING* for the Spectacolor board in Times Square, New York, which was followed that year by the *Sign on a Truck* project to coincide with the re-election campaign of President Ronald Reagan. In 1985 she began producing public billboards: in the USA they appeared in Minneapolis, Berkeley, Chicago and Los Angeles, and 30 billboards were designed for Las Vegas. She designed more than 80 others in England, Scotland and Northern Ireland.

Stylistically, the art that Kruger created during the early 1980s was dominated by black-and-white media photographs from the post-war years, often culled from the photo archives of the New York Public Library, paired with short phrases or narrative texts, and framed by a trademark red border. Such works, which were transferred to paper and sometimes to vinyl or mirrored glass through photo-silkscreen, reflect the dominance of photography and absence of expressionistic handling that typified the "image scavenger" artists who came to dominate the New York scene in the early 1980s, including Ross Bleckner, Sherrie Levine and Richard Prince, as well as the Neo-expressionist David Salle. These friends shared with Kruger a fascination with the photographic and cinemagraphic dimensions of contemporary media culture, as well as its social impact, its structures of representation and codes of public speech. Kruger's concern with such issues also finds an outlet in the film and television criticism she first began writing in 1976, while teaching at the University of California, Berkeley, and which she continues to contribute to such magazines as *Artforum*.

In 1986 she began experimenting with colour photography, as in *Untitled (Give Me All You've Got)* (1986; Dennis and Ellen Schweber Collection), and also with innovative techniques, such as lenticular imagery. This process – popular in the USA during the 1950s for gifts distributed in boxes of cereal – consists of dual pictures covered by a lenticular lens. Tilting the picture brings the secondary image into focus. In *Untitled (Read My Lips: My Tongue is in Your Cheek)* (1986; repr. Wellington 1988, cat.19) Kruger combines a photographic image with an insidious and haunting sub-text. More recently, she has used 19th-century photo-engraved plates for her works. Perhaps due to her experience as a graphic artist, Kruger has often worked collaboratively, with Jenny Holzer, Keith Haring and other artists for the *Sign on a Truck* project, and published illustrated books (with Stephen King, *My Pretty Pony*, 1989). Her recent projects have included installations, such as *Untitled (Pledge)* (1989) for the Museum of Contemporary Art, Los Angeles, curating exhibitions, such as *Picturing Greatness* for the Museum of Modern Art, New York, in 1988, and also organising critical symposia, such as *Remaking History* for the Dia Art Foundation in 1989, whose proceedings she also edited.

"I'm interested in making art that displaces the powers that tell us who we can be and who we can't be", she observed in an interview in 1989 (Deitcher 1991, p.90). Barbara Kruger continues to challenge the role that women play in society through her photographic imagery, her billboards, her film and television criticism, and her exhibitions.

PHYLIS FLOYD

L

Labille-Guiard, Adélaïde [fig. 40]

French painter, 1749–1803

Born Adélaïde Labille in Paris, 11 April 1749; father a haberdasher. Trained by the miniaturist François-Elie Vincent, by the pastellist Maurice Quentin de la Tour, and subsequently by the academician François-André Vincent. Taught art, c.1779–93. Admitted to the Académie Royale des Beaux-Arts, 1783. Awarded the title of Peintre de Mesdames (the king's aunts), 1787. Married (1) financial clerk Louis-Nicolas Guiard, 1769; legally separated, 1779; divorced 1793; (2) François-André Vincent, 1800. Died in Paris, 24 April 1803.

Principal Exhibitions

Académie de Saint-Luc, Paris: 1774
Salon de la Correspondance, Paris: 1782–3
Paris Salon: 1783, 1785, 1787, 1789, 1791, 1795, 1798–1800

Bibliography

Roger Portalis, "Adélaïde Labille-Guiard (1749–1803)", *Gazette des Beaux-Arts*, 3rd series, xxvi, 1901, pp.353–67, 477–94; xxvii, 1902, pp.100–18, 325–47
Les Femmes peintres au XVIIIe siècle, exh. cat., Musée Goya, Castres, 1973
Anne-Marie Passez, *Adélaïde Labille-Guiard (1749–1803): Biographie et catalogue raisonné de son oeuvre*, Paris: Arts et Métiers Graphiques, 1973
Women Artists, 1550–1950, exh. cat., Los Angeles County Museum of Art, and elsewhere, 1976
Elsa Honig Fine, *Women and Art: A History of Women Painters and Sculptors from the Renaissance to the 20th Century*, Montclair, NJ: Allanheld and Schram, and London: Prior, 1978
Germaine Greer, *The Obstacle Race: The Fortunes of Women Painters and Their Work*, London: Secker and Warburg, and New York: Farrar Straus, 1979
La Femme artiste d'Elisabeth Vigée-Lebrun à Rosa Bonheur, exh. cat., Musée Despiau-Wlerick, Donjon Lacataye, Mont-de-Marsan, 1981
Vivian Cameron, *Woman as Image and Image-Maker in Paris During the French Revolution*, PhD dissertation, Yale University, 1983
Danielle Rice, "Vigée-Lebrun vs Labille-Guiard: A rivalry in context", *Proceedings of the XIth Annual Meeting of the Western Society for French History: Riverside, 1983*, pp.130–38
Diaconoff Suellen, "Ambition, politics and professionalism: Two women painters", *Eighteenth-Century Women and the Arts*, ed. Frederick M. Keener and Susan E. Lorsch, New York: Greenwood, 1988, pp.201–8
Viktoria Schmidt-Linsenhoff, "Gleichheit für Künstlerinnen?", *Sklavin oder Bürgerin? Französische Revolution und Neue Weiblichkeit, 1760–1830*, exh. cat., Historisches Museum, Frankfurt am Main, 1989, pp.114–32
Marie-Jo Bonnet, "La révolution d'Adélaïde Labille-Guiard et Elisabeth Vigée-Lebrun ou deux femmes en quête d'un espace dans la société", *Les Femmes et la Révolution française*, ed. Marie-France Brive, Toulouse: Presses Universitaires du Mirail, 1991, pp.337–44

As one of four female members of the French Académie Royale des Beaux-Arts, Adélaïde Labille-Guiard is famous for her accomplished portraits in pastels and oils. In her teens she was trained by the miniaturist François-Elie Vincent. One of her first known works, a *Self-Portrait* in miniature (untraced, repr. Passez 1973, pl.I), which was exhibited at the Académie de Saint-Luc in 1774, demonstrates a fairly finicky, nervous touch, with a concern for the details of setting and dress that would remain with Labille-Guiard throughout her life. After her marriage in 1769, and before 1774, she became a student of Maurice Quentin de la Tour for instruction in the technique of pastels. The attention to veracity in representing both the character of the sitter as well as the details of costume and surroundings, so characteristic of Quentin de la Tour's work, was also a hallmark of Labille-Guiard's, as in the portrait of the *Marquise de Montciel* (untraced, *ibid.*, pl.XVII). Ever ambitious, she decided to study oil painting after 1777 and became an apprentice of François-André Vincent, *agrée* at the Academy in 1777 and eldest son of her first teacher. During her training she continued to execute pastels and miniatures. She also separated from her husband, and shortly thereafter opened an atelier for students to supplement her income. Teaching had a high priority in her life, and she continued instruction until 1793.

After the Académie de Saint-Luc had been dissolved in 1776, Labille-Guiard found a new site to exhibit at the Salon de la Correspondance, first showing numerous works there in June 1782, including her portrait of the *Comte de Clermont-Tonnerre* (Anzy-le-France, *ibid.*, pl.XIX, oil replica), dressed in the costume of a "Dragon de la Reine", which shows a skilful rendering of costume and sensitivity to different textures, as well as the accomplished placement of the figure in space. Also exhibited there was a *Head of Cleopatra* (untraced, *ibid.*, pl.XXIII), which depicts the heroine in the style of Guido Reni, eyes raised to the skies, left breast exposed to receive the bite of the asp, and which shows Labille-Guiard's early interest in history painting. She was exceptionally productive during this year and the next, creating numerous pastels of various members of the Academy, including those of *Voiriot* (private collection, Brussels, *ibid.*, pl.XXII), *Bachelier* (Louvre, Paris), *Vien* (Musée Fabré, Montpellier), *Pajou* and *Beaufort* (both Louvre). Exhibited first during various months at the Salon de la Correspondance, most of these pastels were re-exhibited at the Salon of 1783 after her acceptance into the Academy on 31 May 1783. For her reception pieces, she submitted the portrait of *Pajou* as well as an oil painting of the sculptor *Gois* (untraced). She also exhibited a sensitive portrayal of maternity in the group picture of *Madame Mitoire and Her Children* (private collection, Paris, *ibid.*, pl.XXXIII), representing the granddaughter of Carle van Loo nursing a baby, with her young son. With the accessories of the small round table, the painting formally balances the round form of the mother, the heads of the two children and the oval of the table top. Socially, the work documents a contemporary fashionable attitude about nursing promoted earlier by Rousseau (see Carol Duncan, "Happy mothers and other new ideas in French art", *Art Bulletin*, lv, 1973,

pp.470–83). It may well have been this work that attracted the notice of the Comtesse de Flahaut, sister-in-law to d'Angiviller, Directeur Général des Bâtiments, who commissioned her own portrait with her young son gazing at a medallion representing d'Angiviller's wife, an oil painting exhibited at the Salon of 1785 (private collection, Jersey, repr. Passez 1973, pl.XLIV). Indeed, Madame d'Angiviller herself had earlier commissioned a portrait of the poet *Ducis* (Comédie Française, Paris, *ibid.*, pl.XXXVII) from the new academician. Other commissions from nobility, such as the *Princesse de la Trémoïlle* (private collection, France, *ibid.*, pl.XLI), followed.

It was at the Salon of 1785 that Labille-Guiard exhibited her brilliant *Self-Portrait with Two Students* (Metropolitan Museum of Art, New York), a work possibly inspired by Vigée-Lebrun's *Self-Portrait with a Straw Hat* (private collection, Switzerland). The names of Elisabeth Vigée-Lebrun (q.v.) and Labille-Guiard were frequently paired by the critics, starting with their first exhibition at the Académie de Saint-Luc (*ibid.*, pp.12–13). Both women were accepted into the Academy on the same day, and both exhibited at the Salon in 1783. Reviewers of that Salon generally favoured Vigée-Lebrun with lengthier and more laudatory reviews, which must have caused particular dismay to Labille-Guiard, who was sometimes even ignored. Such evaluations may well have spurred her to reassess her production critically, with the *Self-Portrait with Two Students* as a result. It was her most complex effort to date. On the one hand, she demonstrated her virtuosity as a technician in the fine rendering of textures (she had copied ter Borch, for instance). On the other, while the painting is part of the tradition of the artist and his family, Labille-Guiard, through her rich costume, elevated herself above the class of ordinary academician, showing an ambition to rise in social status. At the same time she affirmed that she was a producer of paintings, depicting herself absorbed in the act of creating, gazing at her model (the viewer). Further, the presence of the statue of a Vestal Virgin alludes to her role as a teacher, keeping the flames of creativity burning. The work won much critical acclaim, and also earned her the admiration of Madame Adélaïde, aunt to Louis XVI. Indeed, this interest helped Labille-Guiard in her straitened circumstances in 1785 to obtain a government pension of 1000 livres.

Both aunts, Mesdames Adélaïde and Victoire, as well as the king's sister, Madame Elisabeth, subsequently commissioned portraits. That of *Madame Adélaïde de France* (Palais de Versailles), exhibited in 1787, was intended to be more than a capturing of the physiognomy of the sitter. Labille-Guiard's largest and most complicated portrait to date, the work represented the life-sized figure of Madame Adélaïde standing in front of an easel, on which rests a composite portrait in profile of her father Louis XV, her mother and brother, the dauphin, all deceased. Decorating the architectural background is a relief showing the presence of the Princess at her father's deathbed, when he was ill with smallpox. Filial piety, loyalty and devoutness (a plan of a convent rests on a stool) are conveyed in the painting, which is intended not only to indicate qualities of this princess, but also meant to be part of royalist propaganda to support the weakened throne of Louis XVI. The attention to the rendering of specific textures is even more refined here, as Labille-Guiard captured everything from gilded wood to marble, paper to satin, painted bronze to flesh. The pendant to the work, *Madame Victoire* (Château, Versailles), exhibited at the following Salon of 1789, was equally meticulously painted, showing the Aunt on the terrace of the property at Bellevue. Like many of the Vestals seen in earlier French paintings, the virginal aunt pays homage to a sculpture of Friendship. A vase of lilies gave Labille-Guiard the opportunity to demonstrate her talents as a still-life painter, while the background, claimed by one critic to be by a M. Hue not by her (*ibid.*, p.210), gave her a chance to show her skills as a landscapist.

Labille-Guiard's opportunity to win acclaim as a history painter came in 1788 when she was commissioned by the king's brother, the Comte de Provence, to paint a large work (4.26 × 5.18 m.) depicting the *Reception of a Chevalier de Saint-Lazare by Monsieur, Grand Master of the Order*, on which she worked for two and a half years before the emigration of the count in June 1791. The incomplete painting was rolled up; in 1793 she received the order to destroy the work.

While Labille-Guiard was labouring on this large painting, she was also active in the reforms of the Academy. Attempting to throw open the doors of the Academy to women and gain status for her students, in September 1790 she proposed that the number of women accepted into the Academy be indeterminate and that those who were accepted be given an honorary academic distinction of Conseiller only. Although the proposal was passed by the moderates, the conservative academicians turned it down and called her a "Jeanne d'Arc", "a hen amongst roosters", spreading dissension among them (see Cameron 1983, pp.86–8). The radicals, who formed the Commune des Arts, equally condemned   her.

Ever pragmatic, with the loss of her royalist patrons, Labille-Guiard continued to paint portraits, first that of her friend *Madame Genlis* (Bethesda, MD, repr. Passez 1973, pl.LXXXIX), through whose salon she was probably introduced to various political members. At the Salon of 1791, she exhibited portrait busts, some in pastel, some in oil, of deputies of various political persuasions of the National Assembly, from Robespierre to the Duc d'Aiguillon. She was equally active as an advocate for women, presenting the National Assembly with a mémoire about the education of young women deprived of fortune (now lost), to which Talleyrand referred as a model. Indeed, although the Academy may not have been amenable to the rights of female artists, the government commissioned Labille-Guiard, as well as Jacques-Louis David, to paint a work representing the king giving the Constitution to the dauphin. All sketches for this work have been lost.

During the Terror, Labille-Guiard obtained a divorce. She remained installed in a country home in Pontault-en-Brie with François-André Vincent (whom she married in 1800), but in 1795, with the support of Joachim Lebreton, chief of the bureaux of the Museums of Public Instruction, she obtained a lodging at the Louvre as well as a pension of 2000 livres. She continued to exhibit portraits at the Salons until 1800. In such works as the portrait of her student, *Gabrielle Capet* (private collection, Paris, *ibid.*, pl.CVII), exhibited in 1798, she maintained her high technical standards and also offered a sensitive portrayal of another serious woman artist.

VIVIAN P. CAMERON

See also Academies of Art survey

Lama, Giulia

[fig. 41]

Italian painter, 1681–1747

Born in the parish of Santa Maria Formosa, Venice, 1 October 1681, to Agostino Lama, painter, and his wife Valentina (not surnamed Jugali, as sometimes stated). Died in Venice, 7 October 1747.

Bibliography

Antonio Maria Zanetti, *Descrizione di tutte le pubbliche pitture della città di Venezia*, Venice, 1733; reprinted Bologna: Forni, 1980

Giuseppe Fiocco, "Il ritratto di Giulia Lama agli Uffizi", *Rivista d'Arte*, xi, 1929, pp.113–17

Ugo Ruggeri, *Disegni Piazzetteschi ... di raccolte bergamasche*, Bergamo: Monumenta Bergomensia, 1967

Rodolfo Pallucchini, "Per la conoscenza di Giulia Lama", *Arte Veneta*, xxiv, 1970, pp.161–72

Don Gino Bortolan, "Per una 'più completa' conoscenza di Giulia Lama", *Ateneo Veneto*, ii/2, 1973, pp.183–9

——, "S. Maria Formosa nel '700", *Bollettino dei Musei Civici Veneziani*, xviii, 1973, pp.10–17

Ugo Ruggeri, *Dipinti e disegni di Giulia Lama*, Bergamo: Monumenta Bergomensia, 1973

Leslie Jones, *The Paintings of Giovanni Battista Piazzetta*, PhD dissertation, Institute of Fine Arts, New York, 1981

Adriano Mariuz, *L'opera completa del Piazzetta*, Milan: Rizzoli, 1982

Ugo Ruggeri, "Giulia Lama", *Giambattista Piazzetta: Il suo tempo, la sua scuola*, exh. cat., Palazzo Vendramin-Calergi, Venice, 1983, pp.119–29

Peter Krückmann, *Federico Bencovich, 1677–1753*, Hildesheim: Olms, 1988

George Knox, *Giambattista Piazzetta, 1682–1754*, Oxford: Clarendon Press, 1992

Giulia Lama is known principally for her two large altarpieces in the Venetian churches of Santa Maria Formosa and San Vidal, both of the 1720s. Since Fiocco published her *Self-Portrait* (1725; Uffizi, Florence) in 1929, and identified the celebrated Piazzetta in the Thyssen collection as a portrait of *Giulia Lama as "Painting"*, her name has been linked, even mildly romantically, with the Venetian artist Piazzetta: it was once even suggested that they were cousins, on the basis of an error in the interpretation of documents. Since Don Gino Bortolan established the date of her birth and death in the registers of Santa Maria Formosa, it has become clear that she was some four and a half months older than Piazzetta, and a contemporary rather than a pupil or follower of his.

A unique contemporary description of the painter survives, contained in a letter from the Abate Conti to Mme de Caylus, dated 1 March 1728:

> I have just found here a woman who paints better than Rosalba [Carriera], so far as large compositions are concerned ... this woman excels as much in (poetry) as in painting, and I find in her poems the turn of phrase of Petrarch: she is named Giulia Lama, and in her youth she studied mathematics under the celebrated p. Maffei: the poor girl is persecuted by the painters, but her virtue triumphs over her enemies. It is true that she is as ugly as she is witty but she speaks with grace and precision, so one easily forgives her her face. She works in lace ... [quoted in Ruggeri 1983, p.120].

Sadly, we have no further evidence of Lama's skills as a mathematician and her gifts as a poet, nor do we know anything further of the hostility of her male fellow artists, except to note that she does not appear to figure in the guild lists of the "Fraglia dei pittori", as is also the case with the celebrated Rosalba Carriera (q.v.), some five years her senior. As for her appearance, to which Conti ungallantly refers, the Uffizi portrait, which of itself testifies to her professional standing in 1725, depicts a woman of 45, while the Piazzetta portrait, a passionate and sensuous study, now generally thought to be at least ten years earlier in date, shows a woman far from ugly.

As children of artists, Piazzetta and Lama probably knew each other from childhood, and by the time of his marriage in 1724 he was known as a resident of the parish of San Lio, adjacent to Giulia's parish of Santa Maria Formosa. It is possible that she shared in some degree his education in the school of Antonio Molinari. Around 1715, the supposed date of Piazzetta's portrait of her, she appears to have been closely associated with him and with Federico Bencovich in the production of a series of small canvases on the theme of *St Mary Magdalene in the Desert*, all closely related in style and character, which must have been executed before Bencovich went to Vienna in 1716. A painting from this series attributed to Lama, the *Penitent Magdalene*, appeared on the Milan art market in 1970 (Finarte sale, Milan, 21 May 1970; see Knox 1992, p.71, note 18). The first secure date for

Lama's work, 1719, marks the publication of a portrait of *Pietro Grimani*, engraved by Andrea Zucchi after a drawing by Lama. In 1722 she secured the important commission to paint the high altarpiece for her parish church, the beautiful and prominent Santa Maria Formosa in the Sestiere of Castello. This now hangs on the back wall of the church, where it can be seen through the arch of the high altar that originally contained it, in better light but in a rather cramped space. The painting depicts the Virgin and Child above, St Matthew below to the left, his attribute, an angel, in the centre and St Joseph on the right. In the lower foreground on the left is a richly dressed woman, sometimes identified as Ecclesia (Church). The composition, which appears to be highly original, has dignity and assurance; the paint surface is boldly handled, with the touch that will become characteristic of the artist, and one feels that her fellow parishioners must have been more than satisfied with this important addition to their church.

The *Crucifixion*, painted for the central altar on the left side of San Vidal, facing a sculptured altar of the *Annunciation* by Antonio Tarsia on the right, indicates that Lama played a leading role in a scheme of decoration in which she was surrounded by a group of distinguished painters. Over the high altar hangs a great work by Carpaccio; to the left hangs the *Immaculate Conception* by Sebastiano Ricci, opposite is the *Guardian Angel with SS Anthony of Padua and Gaetano Thiene* by Piazzetta; by the door, on the left, *SS Sebastian and Roch* by Angelo Trevisan, and on the right, the *Trinity with SS Joseph and Francis of Paola* by Antonio Pellegrini, documented to 1727, giving an approximate date for the whole scheme. Again, the *Crucifixion* is a work of astonishing originality, the figure of Christ offcentre to the right, balanced by two weeping putti; the Almighty and the Holy Dove above, almost suggesting (so invisible is the Cross) an Assumption rather than a Crucifixion. The off-centre axis of the picture is taken up in the fine figure of St John, lower left, with his right hand circling the Cross by the terrible nail piercing Christ's feet, while the Virgin swoons (lower right) into a luminescent mass of drapery with two gesticulating Apostles above her. This is one of the great paintings of its time, and one of the most neglected.

It is perhaps less surprising that Lama's third great religious work in the vicinity of Venice should also be neglected and completely misunderstood, for the parish church at Malamocco on the Lido is well off the beaten track. It was first noticed by Fiocco in 1927, and since then has always been referred to as *A Saint in Glory*. So bold and original is the conception of this painting that no-one has noticed that it in fact represents the *Assumption of the Virgin*. The canvas is almost square, and has probably lost the lower half of the composition, with the Twelve Apostles and the empty Tomb. The Virgin is shown kneeling on a cloud (as canonical usage requires), slightly off-centre, in the upper half of the canvas. She is supported by three angels: one steadies her with outstretched arm as she gazes up to heaven; one supports the cloud with back and another outstretched arm; a third strikes a balletic pose on the right. The work is generally dated to the 1730s, which appears to be right, but if it is compared with the great monumental versions of this theme by Ricci in Vienna, and by Piazzetta in Paris and in Parma, the extraordinarily vivid and personal quality of Giulia Lama's achievement is immediately and brilliantly manifest. Other works attributed to Giulia Lama are *Judith and Holofernes* (Accademia, Venice), the *Martyrdom of St John the Evangelist* (Musée des Beaux-Arts, Quimper) and *Christ on the Road to Calvary* (Eremo Camaldolesi, Monte Rua).

GEORGE KNOX

Lange, Dorothea
American photographer, 1895–1965

Born Dorothea Margaretha Nutzhorn in Hoboken, New Jersey, 25 May 1895; took mother's family name of Lange, 1918. Moved to New York with her family as a child. Attended New York Training School for Teachers, 1914–17; during this period was also apprenticed to photographers Arnold Genthe and Charles H. Davis; studied under Clarence H. White at Columbia University, New York, 1917–18. Settled in San Francisco, 1918. Opened own portrait studio after working as a photo finisher, 1919. Married (1) painter Maynard Dixon, 1920; two sons, born 1925 and 1928; divorced 1935; (2) Paul Schuster Taylor, an agricultural economist at the University of California, 1935. Began taking documentary photographs of conditions resulting from the Depression, 1933. Worked for various state and federal agencies, including the State Emergency Relief Administration, Federal Emergency Relief Administration, Resettlement Administration, Farm Security Administration, Bureau of Agricultural Economics, War Relocation Authority and Office of War Information, 1935–45. Resumed photography after a five-year break due to illness, 1951. Subsequent work included photo-essays on Mormon towns in Utah (1953–4), on Ireland (1954–5), and the Public Defender (1955). Travelled extensively with Taylor to Asia, South America and the Middle East, 1958–63. Recipient of Guggenheim fellowship, 1941. Died of cancer in Marin County, California, 11 October 1965.

Principal Exhibitions

Willard Van Dyke studio, 683 Brockhurst Street, Oakland, CA: 1934 (individual)
Museum of Modern Art, New York: 1955 (*Family of Man*, touring), 1962 (*The Bitter Years: FSA Photographs, 1935–41*, touring), 1966 (touring retrospective)

Selected Writings

An American Exodus: A Record of Human Erosion, New York: Reynal and Hitchcock, 1939 (with Paul Schuster Taylor)
"Fortune's wheel", *Fortune*, xxxi/2, 1945 (with Ansel Adams)
"Miss Lange's counsel: Photographer advises use of picture themes", *New York Times*, 7 December 1952
"Photographing the familiar", *Aperture*, i, 1952, pp.4–15, 68–72 (with Daniel Dixon)
Death of a Valley, Rochester, NY: Aperture, 1960 (with Pirkle Jones)

Bibliography

Dorothea Lange, exh. cat., Museum of Modern Art, New York, and elsewhere, 1966
Suzanne Riess, *The Making of a Documentary Photographer*, Berkeley: Bancroft Library Regional Oral History Office, 1969 (interview)
Celebrating a Collection: The Work of Dorothea Lange, exh. cat., Oakland Museum, CA, 1978
Milton Meltzer, *Dorothea Lange: A Photographer's Life*, New York: Farrar Straus and Giroux, 1978
Howard M. Levin and Katherine Northrop, eds, *Dorothea Lange: Farm Security Administration Photographs, 1935–1939*, 2 vols, Glencoe, IL: Texte-Fiche Press, 1980
Karin Becker Ohrn, *Dorothea Lange and the Documentary Tradition*, Baton Rouge: Louisiana State University Press, 1980
Robert Coles, *Dorothea Lange: Photographs of a Lifetime*, Millerton, NY: Aperture, and Oxford: Phaidon, 1982
Penelope Dixon, *Photographers of the Farm Security Administration: An Annotated Bibliography, 1930–1980*, New York: Garland, 1983
John Rogers Puckett, *Five Photo-Textual Documentaries from the Great Depression*, Ann Arbor: UMI Research Press, 1984
Jan Arrow, *Dorothea Lange*, London: Macdonald, 1985
Christopher Cox, ed., *Dorothea Lange*, Millerton, NY: Aperture, 1987
James Curtis, *Mind's Eye, Mind's Truth: FSA Photography Reconsidered*, Philadelphia: Temple University Press, 1989
Dorothea Lange: American Photographs, exh. cat., San Francisco Museum of Modern Art, and elsewhere, 1994
Elizabeth Partridge, ed., *Dorothea Lange: A Visual Life*, Washington, DC: Smithsonian Institution Press, 1994
Karen Tsujimoto, *Dorothea Lange: Archive of an Artist*, Oakland, CA: Oakland Museum, 1995
Charles Wollenberg, *Photographing the Second Gold Rush: Dorothea Lange and the East Bay at War, 1941–1945*, Berkeley, CA: Heyday, 1995
Keith F. Davis, *The Photographs of Dorothea Lange*, New York: Abrams, 1996
Gerry Mullins and Daniel Dixon, *Dorothea Lange's Ireland*, Washington, DC: Elliott and Clark, and London: Aurum Press, 1996
Betsy Fahlman, "Cotton culture: Dorothea Lange in Arizona", *Southeastern College Art Conference Review*, xiii/1, 1996, pp.32–41

One of the most important documentary photographers of the 20th century, Dorothea Lange made images during the years of the American Depression that remain emblematic of that era. She was part of a group of photographers employed by Roy Stryker to make a historical record of the work of several government agencies: the Resettlement Administration (RA, 1935–7), the Farm Security Administration (FSA, 1937–42) and the Office of War Information (OWI, 1942–3). While these photographers were hired to make official records, their considerable skills as artists brought a high level of aesthetic quality to their work. Lange's strong humanitarian concerns, which are evidenced in her photographs, were deeply rooted in her personal history.

Lange's childhood was not an easy one. Her father's desertion of his family when she was 12 was traumatic, and resulted in her parents' divorce in 1907. A bout with polio at the age of seven left her with a permanent limp. These events had a strong emotional impact on her, though she rarely discussed them, even with those closest to her. By her late teens she had determined to become a photographer. With a friend, she left New York in 1918 with the intention of travelling around the world. But when her funds were stolen in San Francisco she decided to settle there, and for the remainder of her career established herself as one of California's leading photographers. Opening her own portrait studio in 1919, she embarked on what would be a successful 14-year career in commercial work. Working in a pictorialist style and favouring imaginative poses, she photographed many prominent residents of the community, and was also part of a lively group of artists and writers, many of whom visited her studio, including the painter Maynard Dixon, who became her first husband. Travelling together throughout the Southwest, he sketched subjects for later canvases and she took her first photographs outside the studio, making prints of the Native Americans she saw and the environment in which they lived. Her work in this period is rather stereotypical and romantic, and contrasts both with her portraiture and her later documentary work.

The beginning of the Depression in 1929 brought widespread unemployment and plunged America into economic crisis. In 1933, no longer able to ignore the conditions of dislocation she witnessed just outside her fashionable studio, Lange turned from portraiture to subjects of strong social content. Emblematic of the shift in her work is *White Angel Breadline* (1933), one of her most powerful photographs. Here she drew on a long art-historical tradition of image-making, as she isolates a single figure from a crowd of men who face in the other direction; his eyes are shielded by his hat, his hands folded as if in prayer. She first exhibited her new documentary photographs in 1934, when they were seen by Paul Schuster Taylor, an agricultural economist from the University of California whose speciality was migrant labour. They soon married and embarked on a productive intellectual collaboration that continued for the rest of Lange's career. Their work for state agencies came to the attention of Roy Stryker, the head of the Resettlement Administration's Historical Section, who employed Lange in 1935. Remaining based in California, she continued her government-sponsored work under several other agencies, including the Farm Security Administration and the Bureau of Agricultural Economics. Although she photographed a wide range of conditions suffered by the rural poor, many driven west by Dust Bowl conditions, migrant

labour was a particular focus, and she travelled widely around the country on assignments, producing a series of memorable images, of which *Migrant Mother* (1936), taken in Nipomo, California, remains the most famous. Flanked by two of her children, and holding a third, this destitute 32-year-old woman in a squatter camp vividly evokes iconography of the Virgin and Child. The image *Migratory Cotton Picker, Eloy, Arizona* (1940) was part of a study undertaken for the Bureau of Agricultural Economics. While the identity of the figure remains anonymous, he is emblematic of many such workers. Lange frames her shot up close, recording the subject as he pauses for a moment. The labour in which he is engaged is exhausting and his economic situation unpromising; his hand shields him from the hot sun as well as from the intrusive camera.

At the outbreak of World War II Lange worked for the War Relocation Authority (photographs in National Archives), recording the forcible removal of Japanese-Americans from the San Francisco Bay area to internment camps away from the coast, and she photographed them once resettled at Manzanar, one of the California camps. Work for the Office of War Information permitted her to record changed conditions during the war years. Although almost all of the work she did for this agency has been lost, with Ansel Adams she recorded wartime shipbuilding industries in Richmond (just north of her Berkeley home) on assignment for *Fortune* magazine.

With the end of the World War II in 1945, serious illness made Lange inactive as a photographer. She did not resume work again until 1951, and did not travel until 1953. An assignment from *Life* in 1953 permitted her to collaborate with her old friend Ansel Adams to produce a series on several Mormon towns in Utah. This and her photographic essays on *The Public Defender* (1954) and *Death of a Valley* (1956) are among her best work of the 1950s. Although she took pictures throughout her travels with Taylor to developing countries, they lack the sensibility of deeply personal experience and the humanitarian grounding in difficult social conditions in need of change that marked her work of the 1930s and 1940s. Among the strongest work of her later years is a highly personal visual diary of the activities of family (especially grandchildren) and friends at her home in Berkeley and at a cabin she and Taylor acquired in 1955 at Steep Ravine in

Marin County about 32 kilometres north of San Francisco. Although continuing health problems (ulcers, esophagitis, malaria, chronic fatigue) reduced Lange's productivity during the last two decades of her life, the keen visual intelligence that informs her most perceptive work remained alert to the end, even as she was working on the retrospective of her work at the Museum of Modern Art, which opened after her death.

Lange's work for the FSA is in the Prints and Photographs Division of the Library of Congress; that for the Bureau of Agricultural Economics is in the National Archives. Most of her non-governmental photographs are in the Dorothea Lange Collection, Oakland Museum, California.

BETSY FAHLMAN

Laurencin, Marie [fig. 40]
French painter and designer, 1883–1956

Born in Paris, 31 October 1883; mother from a Creole family, father unknown. Started training as a porcelain painter at Ecole de Sèvres, 1902; studied art at the Académie Humbert, Paris, from 1904; met Georges Braque, who introduced her to Picasso and his circle. Exhibited at Salon des Indépendants from 1907. Lived with writer and critic Guillaume Apollinaire, 1907–12. Included in *Section d'Or* exhibition at Galerie La Boétie, Paris, 1912. Married German artist Otto van Wätjen, 1914; divorced 1921. Lived in Spain during World War I; while in Madrid, co-edited the Dada magazine *391* with Picabia, Gleizes and Arthur Cravan. Spent a year in Düsseldorf at end of war, returning to Paris in 1920. Designed costumes and décor for Francis Poulenc's ballet *Les Biches*, commissioned by Diaghilev, 1923. Visited Italy, 1928. Taught at Académie du XVIe, Paris, founded by Laboureur, 1933. Died in Paris after a heart attack, 8 June 1956.

Selected Individual Exhibitions
Galerie Berthe Weill, Paris: 1908 (with Jacqueline Marval)
Galeries Paul Rosenberg, Paris: 1921, 1936
Galerie Alfred Flechtheim, Berlin: 1925 (with Renée Sintenis)
Galerie H. Clovis Sagot, Paris: 1944
Gimpel Fils, London: 1947

Librairie Paul Morihien Paris: 1949
Kunsthalle, Düsseldorf: 1957 (retrospective)

Selected Writings
Les Carnets des nuits, Brussels: Nouvelle Revue Belgique, 1942; revised Geneva: Cailler, 1956

Bibliography
Roger Allard, *Marie Laurencin*, Paris: Nouvelle Revue Française, 1921
Marcel Jouhandeau, *Marie Laurencin*, Paris: Quatre Chemins, 1928
George Day, *Marie Laurencin*, Paris: Dauphin, 1947
René Gimpel, *Diary of an Art Dealer*, New York: Farrar Straus, and London: Hodder and Stoughton, 1966 (French original)
Charlotte Gere, *Marie Laurencin*, London: Academy, and New York: Rizzoli, 1977
Daniel Marchesseau, *Catalogue raisonné de l'oeuvre gravé de Marie Laurencin*, Tokyo: Kyuryodo, and San Francisco: Alan Wofsy Fine Arts, 1981
——, *Catalogue Raisonné of the Paintings of Marie Laurencin*, San Francisco: Alan Wofsy Fine Arts, 1986 (French original)
Flora Groult, *Marie Laurencin*, Paris: Mercure de France, 1987
Julia Fagan-King, "United on the threshold of the twentieth-century mystical ideal: Marie Laurencin's integral involvement with Guillaume Apollinaire and the inmates of the Bateau Lavoir", *Art History*, xi, March 1988, pp.88–114
Marie Laurencin: Artist and Muse, exh. cat., Birmingham Museum of Art, AL, and elsewhere, 1989 (contains extensive bibliography)
Ute Brandenburger and Petra Welzel, "Marie Laurencin (1883–1956): Die 'Dernière femme des 18. Jahrhunderts' und die 'Frau von heute'", *Profession ohne Tradition*, exh. cat., Berlinische Galerie, Berlin, 1992, pp.249–58
Marie Laurencin: Cent oeuvres des collections du Musée Marie Laurencin au Japon, exh. cat., Fondation Pierre Gianadda, Martigny, 1993
Elisabeth Couturier, "Marie Laurencin: Mémoires d'une jeune fille rangée", *Beaux Arts*, no.118, December 1993, pp.96–101
Gill Perry, *Women Artists and the Parisian Avant-Garde*, Manchester: Manchester University Press, and New York: St Martin's Press, 1995
Diane Radycki, "Pretty/ugly: Morphing Paula Modersohn-Becker and Marie Laurencin", *Make: The Magazine of Women's Art*, no.72, 1996, pp.19–21

Of all the women artists associated with the Cubist movement, it is Marie Laurencin whose name is now best known, and whose work is best documented. Her (marginal) position in many histories of the movement was encouraged by the support of the critic Guillaume Apollinaire, who described her works in the Salon des Indépendants of 1910 as *cubiste*. While studying art at the Académie Humbert, a private Parisian art school, Laurencin became friendly with the Cubist painter Georges Braque. In 1907 he introduced her to the circle of artists and writers who gathered regularly in Picasso's studio, the Bateau Lavoir on the rue Ravignon. This group is commemorated by Laurencin in two versions of the painting *Apollinaire and His Friends* of 1908. In the first version, titled *Group of Artists* (Baltimore Museum of Art), Laurencin places herself between the two male protagonists, Picasso and Apollinaire, as if to suggest some comparable status. However, in the larger version, *Apollinaire and His Friends* or *Country Reunion* (Centre Georges Pompidou, Paris), Laurencin is dressed in a pale blue dress and is seated to the far right, conspicuously separated off from the central group of artists around Apollinaire and Picasso. This self-representation on the margins of the avant-garde may partly reflect Laurencin's view of herself as a separate "feminine" artist, practising a quintessentially "feminine" art. It has also been suggested that this work is steeped in quasi-religious ideas about the roles of art and artists that were fashionable at the time. According to Julia Fagan-King (1988, p.88), Apollinaire, with whom Laurencin was having a relationship at the time, pursued such ideas with a characteristic missionary zeal. Fagan-King has suggested that Laurencin may have cast her protagonists in ambitious symbolic roles in this painting, echoing the mystical ideology with which some members of the group identified. Thus the central figure of Apollinaire, crowned with a halo-like shape, may represent Christ; Picasso may be symbolically cast as John the Baptist, and Laurencin, dressed in blue, as the Virgin Mary.

Laurencin's peripheral involvement with Cubism continued during the years leading up to the outbreak of World War I, when her work was included in several Cubist shows, and in 1914 she contributed to the decorations for the Maison Cubiste, an experiment in interior design led by Raymond Duchamp-Villon and André Mare. Throughout her career she continued to work on decorative and applied designs and book illustration, a division of labour often associated in contemporary criticism with "feminine" artistic pursuits.

Laurencin is perhaps best known for her work from the 1920s and 1930s, when her paintings sold well and she benefited from a business relationship with the dealer Paul Rosenberg. Her work from this period, examples of which can now be found in French public collections, included many portraits and portrait commissions of women and children, painted in soft pastel tones with delicate features. Her delicately painted, fashionably dressed adolescent women provided contemporary critics with an idealised image of contemporary femininity, or what the critic Louis Vauxcelles called "un Marie Laurencin". This feminine type proved highly marketable, and was itself appropriated as an image of fashionable modernity. In 1924, after seeing the ballet *Les Biches*, for which Laurencin had designed the sets, the art dealer René Gimpel wrote:

> the whole ballet comes to look like the figures she paints. In the corridor I heard a woman say to a man: "Look around the house, all the women look as though they were by Marie Laurencin; she has fashioned a type just as Boldini created the eel look fifteen years ago" [Gimpel 1966, entry for 17 May 1924].

Moreover, such images of women were often identified by contemporary critics as mirror images of the artist herself, thus helping to establish a contemporary notion of a woman artist narcissistically reproducing an idealised image of her own femininity (see also entry on Jacqueline Marval). Laurencin welcomed such popular interpretations of her imagery of women, and encouraged critical representations of her work as quintessentially feminine. In the 1920s and 1930s such images were also claimed by critics such as Vauxcelles and André Salmon as revealing a national identity. In his *L'Histoire générale de l'art histoire français de la Révolution à nos jours* (vol.ii, Paris, 1922, p.321), Vauxcelles described Laurencin's ideal feminine type as revealing "une sensibilité racée" (a thoroughbred sensibility) – an essential Frenchness. While such associations may be more troubling to a modern audience, during the inter-war period Laurencin's fashionably dressed adolescent women were easily appropriated as marketable symbols of modernity and desirable French femininity.

GILL PERRY

Lempicka, Tamara de

Polish painter, 1898–1980

Born Tamara Gorska in Warsaw, 16 May 1898. Travelled to Italy with her grandmother, 1911; educated in Lausanne; went to live with an aunt in Petrograd, Russia, 1914. Married lawyer Tadeusz Lempicki in Petrograd, 1916; one daughter; divorced 1928. Emigrated to Paris via Copenhagen, 1918. Studied painting at Académie de la Grande Chaumière and Académie Ranson, Paris; instructors included Maurice Denis and André Lhôte. Exhibited at Salon des Indépendants and Salon d'Automne, Paris, from 1923; at Salon des Femmes Artistes Modernes, Paris, 1924. Visited Italy, 1925; met poet Gabriele D'Annunzio. Married Hungarian Baron Raoul Kuffner, 1933; he died 1962. Emigrated to USA, 1939, settling in Beverly Hills, California. Moved to New York, 1943; Houston, Texas, to live near her daughter Kizette, 1963; Cuernavaca, Mexico, 1974. Recipient of first prize, Exposition Internationale, Bordeaux, 1927; bronze medal, International Exhibition, Poznań, 1929. Died in Cuernavaca, 18 March 1980.

Selected Individual Exhibitions

Galerie Colette Weill, Paris: 1923
Bottega di Poesia, Milan: 1925
Galeria Zacheta, Warsaw: 1928
Galerie Zak, Paris: 1928
Carnegie Institute, Pittsburgh: 1929
Galerie du Cygne, Paris: 1934
Galerie Charpentier, Paris: 1938
Julien Levy Gallery, New York: 1941
Galerie du Luxembourg, Paris: 1972 (retrospective)

Bibliography

Tamara de Lempicka, exh. cat., Galerie du Luxembourg, Paris, 1972
Giancarlo Marmori, *Tamara de Lempicka* [with] *The Journal of Aelis Mazoyer, Gabriele D'Annunzio's Housekeeper*, Milan: Ricci, 1977
Tendenzen der Zwanziger Jahre: 15 Europäische Kunstaustellung, exh. cat., Neuen Nationalgalerie, Akademie der Künste and Grossen Orangerie des Schlosses Charlottenburg, Berlin, 1977
Giancarlo Marmori, *The Major Works of Tamara de Lempicka, 1925–1935*, Milan: Idea, 1978
Szymon Bojko, "Tamara de Lempicka", *Art and Artists*, xv, June 1980, pp.6–9
Geneviève Bréerette, "The strange life and work of Tamara de Lempicka", *The Guardian*, 12 October 1980
Françoise Gilot, "Tamara: The mystery of a great artist, and perhaps a greater tease", *Art and Antiques*, January 1986, pp.64–9, 88
Alberto Arbasino, "Tamara in Hollywood", *FMR*, no.18, February–March 1986, pp.99–100
Giancarlo Marmori, "Tamara: Painting the beau monde", *ibid.*, pp.77–97
Baroness Kizette de Lempicka-Foxhall and Charles Phillips, *Passion by Design: The Art and Times of Tamara de Lempicka*, New York: Abbeville, and Oxford: Phaidon, 1987
Vivienne Heines, "My mother the artist: Houstonian recalls life of Tamara de Lempicka", *Houston Chronicle*, 22 September 1987
Szymon Bojko, "Tamara de Lempicka, 1898–1980", *Pro Arte*, Winter 1987, pp.84–97
Agnieszka Morawińska, *Autoportret w zielonym Bugatti* [Self-portrait in Green Bugatti], Warsaw: Centrum Sztuki STUDIO, 1990 (published to accompany performance of the play *Tamara*, written by John Krizanc and directed by Richard Rose)
—, "Tamara Lempicka, 1927", *Dialog*, nos 5–6, 1991, pp.158–61
Artystki polskie [Polish artists], exh. cat., National Museum, Warsaw, 1991
Voices of Freedom: Polish Women Artists and the Avant-Garde, 1880–1990, exh. cat., National Museum of Women in the Arts, Washington, DC, 1991
Gilles Néret, *Tamara de Lempicka, 1898–1980*, Cologne: Taschen, 1992
Ellen Thormann, *Tamara de Lempicka: Kunstkritik und Künstlerinnen in Paris*, Berlin: Reimer, 1993
Maurizio Calvesi and Alessandra Borghese, *Tamara de Lempicka: Tra eleganza e trasgressione*, 4th edition, Milan: Arte, 1994

Above all other artists, Tamara de Lempicka has come to symbolise the painting style of Art Deco in the inter-war period. Hard-edged and controlled, de Lempicka's art was that of gesture and theatrical display rather than emotional statement, decorative rather than profound, reflecting the often desperate, frantic spirit of the times. In 1925, the year that the Exposition Internationale des Arts Décoratifs et Industriels Modernes – popularly known as Art Deco – opened in Paris, a self-portrait, *Tamara in the Green Bugatti* (1925; private collection), appeared on the cover of the magazine *Die Dame*, the caption describing her as a "symbol of women's liberation 1925". The tight, precise composition of the painting, the carefully selected range of colours, the inscrutable look of the artist viewing the world from beneath lowered eyelids and the racy, expensive sports car were all vital elements of the art and image of de Lempicka. *Tamara in the Green Bugatti* is also a ruthless portrait of an independent woman, self-possessed and self-assured, symbolising the move towards female emancipation.

Born in Warsaw at the turn of the century to well-to-do parents, at the age of 14 she declared her passion for Count Lempicki, a handsome aristocrat, and married him two years later in Petrograd. In 1917 Count Lempicki was arrested in the city by the Bolsheviks, but the resourceful and determined Tamara de Lempicka succeeded in securing his release. After a visit to London, she and her husband followed her parents to Paris, and though she gave birth to a daughter, Kizette, the romance of the marriage was over, and de Lempicka sought to establish her career as an artist. She enrolled at the Académie de la Grande Chaumière and also studied the work of the old masters, in particular the paintings of such Mannerists as Bronzino and Pontormo. Later she studied in the studio of the successful Symbolist artist Maurice Denis, who taught her to simplify line and colour. More significantly, she worked in the atelier of the Cubist artist and theoretician André Lhôte, who in his own paintings sought to combine Cubism with the avant-garde experiments of Juan Gris and Georges Braque. Through Lhôte she also learned to appreciate the precise and sensuous work of Ingres, which later inspired her to paint seductive harem compositions of voluptuous naked women.

By 1923 Tamara de Lempicka was showing paintings in galleries in Paris, including Galerie Colette Weill, the Salon des Indépendants, the Salon d'Automne and the Salon des Mins de Trente Ans. The de Lempicka style of the inter-war years is characterised by a hard, enamel-like handling of paint, the use of a loosely Cubist approach of small planes to build up the composition – identified as Synthetic Cubism – a controlled palette that restricted the range of colours to achieve maximum visual impact rather than convey a sense of naturalism, and tight, often photographically inspired compositions.

Tamara de Lempicka's paintings, both in their choice of subject matter – single and double portraits and flower paintings – and in their ordered compositions, epitomise the style, mood and excitement of the inter-war years in cities such as Paris and Berlin. They also reflected an interest in the sort of authoritarian control offered by Fascist ideology, which was welcomed by many as a resolution to escalating inflation and apparent aimlessness. In tune with her own acquired aristocratic background, de Lempicka took her family and friends as her subject matter, portraying them to suggest wealth, glamour and sophistication. Sitters also included deposed Russian nobility, aristocrats, famous writers, distinguished scientists and industrialists, as well as male and female lovers. Notable examples are *Portrait of a Man (Baron Kuffner)* (1929; Musée National d'Art Moderne, Paris) and *Adam and Eve* (1932; Musée du Petit Palais, Geneva). As a successful and fashionable portrait painter, de Lempicka painted, among others, the *Duchesse de la Salle* (1925; Galerie du Luxembourg, Paris), *Young Girl in Green* (c.1928; Centre Georges Pompidou, Paris), *Queen Elizabeth of Greece* (private collection), *Suzy Solidor* (1922; Musée de Cagnes sur Mer), the owner of a lesbian nightclub, and the eminent chemist and his wife, *Dr and Mme Boucard* (1931; Collection Boucard, Paris).

In 1929 de Lempicka visited New York to carry out a commission, and while in the USA arranged an exhibition of her work at the Carnegie Institute, Pittsburgh. In 1933 she married Baron Raoul Kuffner, and six years later, as the German armies rolled across Europe, they moved to America, settling first in Hollywood and then New York. With the change of country and the outbreak of war, the persona of Tamara de Lempicka, the Parisian artist, was abandoned in favour of the more subdued Baroness Kuffner.

Although for a time she continued to paint in the familiar hard-edged style, with the subject matter of figures from high society replaced by still lifes (examples in Centre Georges Pompidou), stilted portraits (*Mexican Girl*, Musée des Beaux-Arts, Nice) and mythical and religious figures (examples in Musée de l'Oise, Beauvais), the life and vigour in her art had gone, and her work seemed dated and irrelevant in a climate in which Abstract Expressionism was the favoured style. Experiments with abstraction in the 1950s fail to carry conviction. In the 1960s she adopted a freer, more relaxed style, characterised by closely toned pastel colours and the dry use of paint applied with a palette knife, taking as her subject matter cityscapes, figure studies and flower arrangements. Again they failed to carry the conviction and assurance of the paintings from the inter-war period, and attempts to exhibit them met with little success. (While most of her paintings remain in private collections, public collections not already referred to include the Metropolitan Museum of Art, New York, and Musée des Beaux-Arts, Le Havre.) Out of favour and out of fashion, Tamara de Lempicka's work was all but forgotten until the success of a retrospective exhibition at the Galerie du Luxembourg in 1972 introduced her work to a new generation. She remains an artist quintessentially associated with Art Deco, with all its excess, theatricality and power.

EMMANUEL COOPER

Leroulx-Delaville, Marie Guillemine

see Benoist

Lewis, Edmonia
American sculptor, *c.*1844–after 1911

Probably born in Ohio or New York State, *c.*1844, of mixed African-American and Chippewa Indian parentage. Entered Oberlin College, Ohio, 1859; left before graduation after being accused of poisoning two white room-mates and of theft. Moved to Boston, 1863; became involved with abolitionists and began to study sculpture under Edward Brackett. Sailed to Europe, 1865, visiting London, Paris and Florence; established studio in Rome, winter 1865–6. Occasionally revisited USA. Converted to Catholicism, *c.*1868. Last recorded living in Rome in 1911.

Principal Exhibitions
San Francisco Art Association: 1873
Memorial Hall, Centennial Exposition, Philadelphia: 1876
World's Columbian Exposition, Chicago: 1893

Bibliography
Henry T. Tuckerman, *Book of the Artists: American Artists Life*, New York: Putnam, 1867; reprinted New York: Carr, 1966
Clara Erskine Clement and Laurence Hutton, *Artists of the Nineteenth Century*, 2 vols, Boston: Houghton Osgood, 1879; reprinted New York: Arno Press, 1969
Lorado Taft, *The History of American Sculpture*, 3rd edition, New York: Macmillan, 1930
James A. Porter, *Modern Negro Art*, New York: Dryden Press, 1943; reprinted New York: Arno, 1969
Van Wyck Brooks, *The Dream of Arcadia: American Artists and Writers in Italy, 1760–1915*, New York: Dutton, and London: Dent, 1958
Margaret Farrand Thorp, *The Literary Sculptors*, Durham, NC: Duke University Press, 1965
The White Marmorean Flock: Nineteenth Century American Women Neoclassical Sculptors, exh. cat., Vassar College Art Gallery, Poughkeepsie, 1972
William H. Gerdts, *American Neo-Classic Sculpture: The Marble Resurrection*, New York: Viking, 1973
Marcia Goldberg, "A drawing by Edmonia Lewis", *American Art Journal*, ix, November 1977, p.104
J.T., "More information on the Edmonia Lewis drawing", *American Art Journal*, x, May 1978, p.112
John S. Crawford, "The classical tradition in American sculpture: Structure and surface", *American Art Journal*, xi, July 1979, pp.38–52
Forever Free: Art by African-American Women, 1862–1980, exh. cat., Illinois State University, Normal, 1980 (includes extensive bibliography and lists of collections and exhibitions)
Wayne Craven, *Sculpture in America*, 2nd edition, Newark: University of Delaware Press, 1984
Cynthia D. Nickerson, "Artistic interpretations of Henry Wadsworth Longfellow's *The Song of Hiawatha*, 1855–1900", *American Art Journal*, xvi, Summer 1984, pp.49–77
Sharing Traditions: Five Black Artists in Nineteenth-Century America, exh. cat., National Museum of American Art, Smithsonian Institution, Washington, DC, and elsewhere, 1985
Marilyn Richardson, "Vita. Edmonia Lewis: A brief life of a neo-classical sculptor", *Harvard Magazine*, March–April 1986, p.40
American Women Artists, 1830–1930, exh. cat., National Museum of Women in the Arts, Washington, DC, 1987
Ron Grossman, "Two savoirs vie for 'Cleopatra'", *Chicago Tribune*, 20 June 1988
Charlotte Streifer Rubinstein, *American Women Sculptors*, Boston: Hall, 1990
The Lure of Italy: American Artists and the Italian Experience, 1760–1914, exh. cat., Museum of Fine Arts, Boston, 1992
Romare Bearden and Harry Henderson, *A History of African-American Artists from 1792 to the Present*, New York: Pantheon, 1993
L. Frapiselli, "Una scultrice afro-indiana dall'America a Roma al tempo di Pio IX", *Strenna dei Romanisti*, 18 April 1994, pp.213–22

Edmonia Lewis was the first professional American sculptor of colour, and was quickly identified with the conditions of her societal marginalisation by contemporary critics. Henry James noted that one of the "white, marmorean flock" of American women sculptors in Rome "was a negress, whose colour, picturesquely contrasting with that of her plastic material, was the pleading agent of her fame" (*William Wetmore Story and His Friends*, 1903). Henry Tuckerman described Lewis "[i]n her coarse but appropriate attire, with her black hair loose, and grasping in her tiny hand the chisel with which she does not disdain – perhaps with which she is obliged – to work", and suggested that "with her large, black, sympathetic eyes brimful of simple, unaffected enthusiasm, Miss Lewis is unquestionably the most interesting representative of our country in Europe" (Tuckerman 1867, pp.603–4). As Lynda Roscoe Hartigan remarked, however, Lewis was seen as "triply disadvantaged as a black, Indian woman" and "offered a tempting opportunity to those eager to demonstrate their support of human rights" (Hartigan in Washington 1985, p.88). Accordingly, her works have typically been read through a "trivialising elision" with both her racial background and her gender (a phenomenon in art criticism of women artists elucidated by Claudine Mitchell in "Intellectuality and sexuality: Camille Claudel, the *fin de siècle* sculptress", *Art History*, xii, 1989, pp.419–47).

Lewis's first works, of 1864–5 – portrait busts of abolitionist leaders such as *William Lloyd Garrison*, *Senator Charles Sumner*, *Wendell Phillips* (president of the Anti-Slavery Society in America) and *Colonel Robert Gould Shaw*, leader of a black regiment in the Civil War – were well received among progressive New Englanders who hoped to assist the cause of emancipation by supporting the emerging artist (later abolitionist portraits included *Abraham Lincoln*, Municipal Library, San Jose, CA; *Ulysses S. Grant* and *Maria Weston Chapman*, head of the Boston Female Anti-Slavery Society). Lewis, however, initially seems to have identified herself more with her mother's Indian heritage than with her father's African-American one, perhaps a response to the ranking of Native Americans over African Americans in the American racial hierarchy, where African Americans were perceived as inferior for having "submitted" to slavery, while Native Americans had the dubious distinction of representing the "Noble Savage".

While tracing the roots of her creativity to her Chippewa mother's inventive embroidery patterns, Lewis qualified this heritage by suggesting: "perhaps the same thing is coming out in me in a more civilized form" (Lydia Maria Child, "Edmonia Lewis", *Broken Fetter*, 3 March 1865, p.25, quoted in Washington 1985, p.88). She described her first work made in Italy, the *Freed Woman and Her Child* (1866; untraced), as "a humble one, but my first thought was for my poor father's people, how I could do them good in my small way" (*The Revolution*, 20 April 1871). Thus Lewis simultaneously claimed and rejected her racial identity, an ambivalence further evidenced by her early busts of white – rather than of black – abolitionist men.

There was also ambivalence among Lewis's supporters, who frequently perceived her as impetuous and lacking in good business judgement. While Lewis was sculpting the portrait bust of *Colonel Robert Gould Shaw* (marble copy of 1867 made in Rome; Museum of Afro-American History in Boston), the sale of which funded her trip to Rome, the abolitionist Lydia Maria Child, sceptical of Lewis's ability to model the Boston hero's features adequately, neglected to show the photographs she owned of Shaw to the artist in an attempt to dissuade her from what she considered an overly ambitious undertaking. Only the actress Charlotte Cushman, herself a maverick, expatriate in Rome, and particular patron of the pioneering women sculptors there, seems to have recognised the "fight" in Lewis's character as a determination to succeed in her career (see Rubinstein 1990).

Lewis completed the necessary Neo-classical apprenticeship by studying with the sculptor Edward Augustus (also known as Edwin C. or E.) Brackett in Boston, but neither these credentials nor the pathos of her racial and economic position paved the way for easy integration into the Roman artistic community. Despite a warm reception by Harriet Hosmer (q.v.) and Charlotte Cushman, among others, Lewis was all too aware of her vulnerability to prejudices against her gender and colour. She reportedly refused to employ artisans to carve her works according to the accepted practice of the day for fear of being accused of not producing her own work – charges that had been levelled against Harriet Hosmer and Vinnie Ream. The sculptor Anne Whitney related that for the same reason Lewis rejected recourse to the instruction and criticism of her peers. It should be noted that early American sculptors, with no true art Academy available at home, frequently pursued and succeeded in their profession with little or no formal instruction. Thus Lewis's choice to remain outside the "Academy" was neither uncommon nor a sign of amateurism.

Lewis seems to have decided soon after her arrival in Rome that it was to be her permanent home. Around 1868 she was received into the Catholic Church and shortly thereafter executed a marble altarpiece of the *Virgin and Child with Angels* for the Marquis of Bute and, in 1883, an *Adoration of the Magi* for a church in Baltimore (both works untraced). As was the case with many 19th-century women sculptors, the Classical and classicising works on view in Rome were sources for both art and anatomy instruction. Among Lewis's study copies was a marble *Moses* (1875; National Museum of American Art, Smithsonian Institution, Washington, DC), a small-scale version of the *Moses* of Michelangelo. Another copy, the bust of *Young Octavian* (*c.*1873; National Museum of American Art) after the ancient original in the Capitoline Museums, had great success with a visiting American tourist, Elisabeth Buffum Chase. Chase purchased the head, pronouncing it the "best reproduction of the original then offered by any artist in Rome" (Porter 1943, pp.60–61).

Lewis's faithful study of Michelangelo's *Moses* may have inspired the long, twisting curls of another life-sized figure of the same year, *Hagar* (1875; National Museum of American Art). Although there is nothing in the rendering of Hagar's features to associate her with an African slave, she is represented after her expulsion into the wilderness by her jealous mistress, Sarah. Hagar is represented as looking up in mid-stride with her hands clasped in prayer, and the agitated movement of her drapery and the overturned pitcher at her feet testify to her desperation. Long, coarse locks of hair repeat the highly textured patterns of light and shadow in her gown and lend the whole figure a sense of movement that defies both the rigidly vertical Neo-classical pose of the body and the Neo-classical preference for figures in idealised, "transcendental" repose.

Critics have frequently identified Lewis's Native American background as the reason for her affinity with the story of *Hiawatha*, from which, in 1865, she modelled three small groups in clay – the *Wooing of Hiawatha* (untraced), *Marriage of Hiawatha* (destroyed) and *Departure of Hiawatha and Minnehaha* (untraced) – which bear a strong resemblance in size and sentiment to the celebrated small anecdotal "parlour groups" of her contemporary John Rogers, and small busts of *Minnehaha* (Detroit Institute of Arts; Kennedy Galleries, New

York) and *Hiawatha* (Kennedy Galleries), executed in marble in 1866–7. Her versions were, however, mediated by the poem *The Song of Hiawatha* (1855) by H. W. Longfellow, whom she sculpted in 1871 during a visit to Rome (bust in Harvard University Portrait Collection, Cambridge, MA). A later group, the *Old Arrow Maker*, also known as *"Old Indian Arrow Maker and His Daughter"* (two copies, dated 1872 and *c.*1872; National Museum of American Art), also recalls stories that Lewis told of a nomadic childhood spent with her mother's tribe, making baskets and embroidering moccasins. Many contradictory stories have been reported about Lewis's childhood that have obfuscated her origins, but what has emerged consistently from these tales has been an affectionate and proud, though problematically picturesque view of the Native American (the most deeply researched account of Lewis's background to date is given in Bearden and Henderson 1993). Perhaps the Indian cycle works represent a further move by the artist to identify herself with a Native American ancestry that was to be read as admirable and artistic, not as savage or dangerous.

While Lewis's selection of these subjects seems to have followed many of the sentimental conventions of the period, her renderings of the *Old Arrow Maker* and, to a lesser extent, of *Minnehaha* are unusual in that their facial features do not repeat the European ideal preferred by the Neo-classical style. Laura Curtis Bullard praised this realism in Lewis's treatment of these figures in a letter to the *New National Era* in May 1871, reporting:

> In both, the Indian type of feature is carefully preserved, and every detail of dress, etc., is true to nature; the sentiment is equal to the execution. They are charming bits, poetic, simple and natural, and no happier illustrations of Longfellow's most original poem were ever made than these by the Indian sculptor [quoted in Craven 1984, p.334].

Crawford (1979) has related Lewis's developing realism to "structural classicism", a willingness to experiment with the Neo-classical idiom in freely adapting its traditional poses and forms to non-European figural types. The strength, and indeed the appeal, of structurally classical works lay in their "democratic, *American* spirit" of independence and innovation with respect to their European roots. Without much exposure to the European cultural vocabulary, Americans could appreciate structurally classical works as addressing themes and representing people of importance to them.

Crawford identified Lewis's representation of the freed man in her life-sized marble group *Forever Free* (1867; Howard University Gallery of Art, Washington, DC) as a reference to the Montorsoli restoration of the *Laocoön*, and the kneeling female figure as a possible adaptation of Doidalsas's *Crouching Aphrodite* (*ibid.*, pp.46–8). The basic forms of these ancient works have been made contemporary by the use of modern dress, unclassical racial types, unidealised proportions and reference to contemporary events. As Crawford observed, Lewis made the bold move of rewriting the captive Trojan priest as a modern African-American slave, finally "forever free" (*ibid.*, p.46). Indeed, Lewis seems more willing here to re-fashion the classical tradition than to question modern gender iconographies in the two figures of *Forever Free*. The contrast between the erect, active male figure, triumphant in having broken his fetters, and the passive female figure, kneeling in prayerful gratitude for having been liberated, is as much a representation of 19th-century concepts of sexual difference as it is of racial emancipation. Freeman Murray, the first African-American art historian, sent a photograph of Lewis's *Forever Free* to the contemporary African-American woman sculptor, Meta Vaux Warrick Fuller (q.v.), who interpreted the piece thus: "The man accepts it [freedom] as a glorious victory, while the woman looks upon it as a precious gift" (Freeman H.M. Murray, *Emancipation and the Freed in American Sculpture: A Study in Interpretation*, Washington, DC: privately printed, 1916, p.225).

Another gender distinction in *Forever Free* as well as in the *Hagar* and, to a lesser extent, in the Indian cycle works, is made according to the convention seen in Greek vase paintings, Etruscan tomb paintings and the like, whereby females are painted in a lighter colour than males. Lewis reproduced the painterly effect in marble by making her male figures noticeably more "ethnic" in their facial features than their female counterparts. As her studies of Michelangelo, the *Laocoön* and the *Octavian*, among others, indicate, Lewis gave particular attention to the historical and art-historical research of her works (her first known work was a pencil drawing of the *Muse Urania* done as a wedding present for a classmate at Oberlin College,

1862; Oberlin College Archives) and could probably have learned of this convention from Roman art collections such as the celebrated Albani collection of Greek vases, held in the Capitoline Museums in the 19th century.

Lewis did try her hand at three works in the popular "conceit" mode, treating light-hearted themes from popular literature, legend and mythology. Lewis's "conceits" or "fancy-pieces" directly reference successful works on the same theme by contemporaries. Her *Poor Cupid* (1876; National Museum of American Art) recalls in particular Horatio Greenough's *Love Prisoner to Wisdom* (1836; Museum of Fine Arts, Boston). The companion pieces of infants *Asleep* (1871) and *Awake* (1872; both San Jose Public Library) evoke both Harriet Hosmer's impish putti, the *Puck* (1856) and *Will-o'-the-Wisp* (1858; copies of both in Watertown Free Public Library and National Museum of American Art), and sleeping figures of children by William Rinehart and Thomas Crawford.

The Classical world provided Lewis with the subjects for two more of her most important works, the marble *Death of Cleopatra* (Historical Society of Forest Park, IL), exhibited at the Philadelphia Centennial Exposition in 1876, and *Hygeia*, a monument for the grave of Dr Hariot Kezia Hunt in Mount Auburn Cemetery, Cambridge, Massachusetts. Of the *Cleopatra*, William J. Clark wrote:

This was not a beautiful work, but it was a very original and striking one, and it deserved particular comment, as its ideals were so radically different from those adopted by Story and Gould in their statues of the Egyptian Queen. ... The effects of death are represented with such skill as to be absolutely repellent. Apart from all questions of taste, however, the striking qualities of the work are undeniable, and it could only have been reproduced by a sculptor of genuine endowments [*Great American Sculptures*, Philadelphia: Gebbie and Barrie, 1878; reprinted New York: Garland, 1977, pp.141–2].

While Lewis's *Cleopatra* has fortunately been brought back to light, the *Hygeia*, monument to one of America's first female physicians, is slowly eroding in Mount Auburn Cemetery. Despite the obviously lamentable damage, the weather has given the marble *Hygeia* a strikingly ancient-looking patina and surface texture that reveals, perhaps just as well as its pristine state, Lewis's classicising touch.

NANCY PROCTOR

Leyster, Judith   [fig. 43]
Dutch painter, 1609–1660

Baptised in the Grote Kerk, Haarlem, 28 July 1609, the eighth child of Jan Willemsz and his wife Trijn Jaspers. Enrolled in the guild of St Luke, Haarlem, 1633; had three pupils in 1635. Moved to Amsterdam after marriage to painter Jan Miense Molenaer, 1636; at least five children (three sons, two daughters), born 1637, 1639, 1643, 1646 and 1650. Moved back to Haarlem by 1649. Buried in nearby Heemstede, 10 February 1660.

Bibliography

Samuel van Ampzing, *Beschrijvinge ende Lof der stad Haerlem in Holland* [Description and praise of the town of Haarlem in Holland], Haarlem, 1628

Theodorus Schrevelius, *Harlemias, Ofte, om beter te seggen, De eerste stichtinghe der Stadt Haerlem* [Harlemias; or, that is to say, the first foundation of the town of Haarlem], Haarlem, 1648

Cornelis Hofstede de Groot, "Judith Leyster", *Jahrbuch der Königlich Preussischen Kunstsammlungen*, xiv, 1893, pp.190–98, 232

Juliane Harms, "Judith Leyster: Ihr Leben und ihr Werk", *Oud Holland*, xliv, 1927, pp.88–96, 112–26, 145–54, 221–42, 275–9

Frima Fox Hofrichter, *Judith Leyster: A Woman Painter in Holland's Golden Age*, Doornspijk: Davaco, 1989

Judith Leyster: A Dutch Master and Her World, exh. cat., Frans Halsmuseum, Haarlem, and Worcester Art Museum, MA, 1993 (contains extensive bibliography)

Judith Leyster was one of the few master women painters of Holland's golden age and the only female member of the painters' guild known to have had a workshop. Her work, which consists primarily of scenes from daily life, reflects the interest of ordinary Dutch citizens who at the time were replacing the Church and State as the chief client of artists.

Leyster had a remarkable career in a male-dominated profession. Unlike most women artists of her day, she was not born into an artistic family. Her father was involved in both cloth manufacturing and brewing, two of the major industries in Haarlem, her home town. It is not certain with whom Leyster studied, though she may have first trained in the studio of Frans Pieter de Grebber, a well-established Haarlem master who specialised in portrait and history painting in a traditional manner. It is in connection with the de Grebber family that Leyster was first cited in 1628 – when she was still a teenager – as one who painted with "a good, keen sense" (Ampzing 1628, p.370). Yet, by 1629, the date of her earliest known signed paintings, *Jolly Toper* (Rijksmuseum, Amsterdam; on loan to Frans Halsmuseum, Haarlem) and *Serenade* (Rijksmuseum), Leyster was clearly influenced by Haarlem's most innovative painter, Frans Hals. Like Hals, she incorporated spontaneous poses and bold brushwork to impart a lifelike quality to contemporary subjects. Recent technical examination of Leyster's work suggests that, like Hals, she sketched the composition directly on the primed panel or canvas and often revised it in the painting process. If Leyster was associated with Hals's workshop early in her career, she was already asserting her independence by signing her paintings with her monogram, which features a star, a reference to her family name, which translates as "lodestar" or "leading star".

Leyster was also attracted to the work of Frans Hals's younger brother Dirck, who was the leading exponent of small-scale genre scenes of full-length figures. Another artist who influenced Leyster and who was also influenced by Dirck Hals was Jan Miense Molenaer, the man she eventually married. Leyster appears to have been in close contact with both of these artists, even sharing studio props with Molenaer long before their marriage. Although she was clearly influenced by several of her male colleagues, Leyster developed her own style that was crystallised in small, intimate scenes such as *Man Offering Money to a Young Woman* (Mauritshuis Museum, The Hague), *Young Woman with a Lute* (private collection, London, repr. Haarlem and Worcester 1993, p.83) and *A Game of Tric-Trac* (Worcester Art Museum, MA). In these works Leyster focuses on one or only a few figures with little attention to the interior setting. By carefully orchestrating the artificial light on the figures, who are set against a dark, shadowy background, she creates an intimate mood and an air of mystery.

Leyster's oeuvre is small – only about 20 works are attributed to her – yet in subject and style her captivating scenes of everyday life compose a microcosm of Haarlem genre painting at its height. These so-called realistic scenes, which at the time were referred to as "modern figures" (*moderne beelden*), often incorporate symbolic elements that reflect the moral values of 17th-century Dutch society. For example, in Leyster's *Last Drop* (Philadelphia Museum of Art), two young men are joined by a skeleton holding an hourglass to demonstrate the dire consequences of excessive drinking.

Leyster's focus on paintings of moderate scale and price suggests that she was responding to popular taste. She was among the majority of Haarlem artists who made their living by painting primarily for the open market, then a relatively new form of art patronage that was to transform the art world. In fact, only two of Leyster's surviving works, *Portrait of a Woman* of 1635 and a watercolour of a tulip dated 1643 (both Frans Halsmuseum), may have been commissions.

Leyster's acceptance into the Guild of St Luke in 1633 confirmed her status as a professional artist. Because her father was not a member of the painters' guild, nor was she married to a guild member at the time, she had to join it to receive its benefits, which included the right to sell art in the local market. Guild membership also enabled Leyster to establish a workshop and take on students. She is known to have had at least three male pupils.

Leyster appears to have painted most of her pictures between 1629 and 1635 when she was single. After her marriage to Molenaer in 1636 she appears to have spent her time bringing up their children and helping with her husband's business, which included both painting and art dealing. Only one of her known works, the watercolour of a tulip, bears a date after her marriage. And yet in 1648, just before she and Molenaer settled back in Haarlem after spending a decade in Amsterdam, she was still referred to in her home town as "the true leading star in art" (Schrevel 1648, pp.384–5), which suggests the community's pride in its women artists.

In spite of her fame during her lifetime, Leyster was virtually forgotten from the time of her death until the end of the 19th century. During this time many of her works were attributed to Frans Hals, including two of her most celebrated paintings, *Self-Portrait* (National Gallery of Art, Washington, DC) and *Young Flute Player* (Nationalmuseum, Stockholm). It was the discovery of Leyster's mono-gram on her *Carousing Couple* (Louvre, Paris) that led to the first study on her in 1893 written by Cornelis Hofstede de Groot. One hundred years later, in 1993, the Frans Halsmuseum and the Worcester Art Museum co-organised the first retrospective exhibition of Leyster's work.

JAMES A. WELU

Liebe, Marianne *see* Brandt

Lisiewska-Therbusch, Anna Dorothea
German painter, 1721–1782

Born Anna Dorothea Lisiewska in Berlin, 23 July 1721, into a Polish family of artists; younger sister of Anna Rosina Lisiewska. Pupil of her father, Georg Lisiewski. Married Berlin inn proprietor Ernst Friedrich Therbusch, 1742; at least three children; husband died 1772. Ceased working professionally after her marriage until 1760. Invited to the court of Duke Karl Eugen von Württemberg in Stuttgart, 1761. Appointed court painter to Elector Palatine Karl Theodor in Mannheim, 1763. Returned to Berlin, 1764. Travelled to Paris, 1765; elected member of the Académie Royale, 1767. Left Paris, 1768, returning to Berlin via Brussels and the Netherlands. Member, Vienna Academy, 1776. Died in Berlin, 9 November 1782.

Principal Exhibitions
Paris Salon: 1767

Bibliography
Johann Georg Meusel, "Lebensumstände der im Jahre 1782 zu Berlin verstorbenen Madame Therbusch", *Miscellaneen artistischen Inhalts*, Erfurt, 1783, pp.266–7

Leopold Reidemeister, *Anna Dorothea Therbusch: Ihr Leben und ihr Werk*, PhD dissertation, Berlin, 1924

Ludwig Goldscheider, *Five Hundred Self-Portraits from Antique Times to the Present Day*, Vienna: Phaidon, and London: Allen and Unwin, 1937 (German original, 1934)

Jean Adhémar and Jean Seznac, eds, *Diderot Salons (1759–1779)*, iii, Oxford: Clarendon Press, 1963

Höfische Bildnisse des Spätbarock, exh. cat., Schloss
  Charlottenburg, Berlin, 1966
Anna-Dorothea Therbusch, 1721–1782, exh. cat.,
  Kulturhaus Hans Marchwitza, Potsdam-Sanssouci,
  1971
Women Artists, 1550–1950, exh. cat., Los Angeles
  County Museum of Art, and elsewhere, 1976
Germaine Greer, *The Obstacle Race: The Fortunes of
  Women Painters and Their Work*, London: Secker and
  Warburg, and New York: Farrar Straus, 1979
Helmut Börsch-Supan, *Die Kunst in Brandenburg-
  Preussen*, Berlin: Mann, 1980
Ekhart Berckenhagen, "Anna Dorothea Therbusch",
  *Zeitschrift des Deutschen Vereins für
  Kunstwissenschaft*, xli, 1987, pp.118–60
Ekhart Berckenhagen and others, *Antoine Pesne*, Munich,
  1987
*Das Verborgene Museum I: Dokumente von Frauen in
  Berliner öffentlichen Sammlungen*, exh. cat.,
  Akademie der Künste, Berlin, 1987
Die deutschen Gemälde des 17. und 18. Jahrhunderts,
  exh. cat., Herzog Anton Ulrich Museum,
  Braunschweig, 1989
*"… Ihr werten Frauenzimmer auf!" Malerinnen der
  Aufklärung*, exh. cat., Roselius-Haus, Bremen, 1993

Anna Dorothea Lisiewska-Therbusch was the
seventh child of the portrait painter Georg Lisiewski
from Olesko in Poland and his wife Maria
Elisabetha (née Kahlow). Besides Anna Dorothea,
two more of the nine children from this marriage
became artists: Anna Rosina Lisiewska and
Christian Friedrich Reinhold. Christian's activities
in Berlin in the years 1772–9 were of great importance for Anna Dorothea's work. Like her siblings,
she was first a pupil of her father. This is apparent
in the graphic elements in her work, which are characteristic of Lisiewski's painting technique. She
counteracted the characteristic stiffness of
Lisiewski's portraits, however, with a sometimes
seemingly exaggerated agility, thus showing her
interest in figurative compositions. His oeuvre of
realistic and conventional portraits of members of
the princely family of Anhalt Dessau, Prussian officers and civil servants is influenced by Adam
Manjoki and especially Antoine Pesne, whose works
Anna Dorothea initially copied, as well as those of
Watteau. Whether she actually had access to Pesne's
Berlin studio is not known, although the relationship to his work is unmistakable. Like Pesne, she
tried to probe as deeply as possible into the sitter's
personality. It was the emphasis on the individual
that was important to her; she achieved this through
a differing density of painting in the figure and the
surroundings, as well as by striving to convey the
face and hands in three dimensions by modelling.
She also achieved a fine representation of the different materials (e.g. *Anna Elisabeth von Arnim*,
c.1741; Neues Palais, Potsdam).

Her first period of work can be identified by two
conversation pieces that form a pair: *The Swing* and
Game of Shuttlecock (Neues Palais, Potsdam), the
latter being signed and dated 1741. Watteau was
clearly the model for these two park scenes. It is not
only the subjects that are similar to his, but the
figures on the swing are almost identical to those in
his paintings and the works of his follower, Nicolas
Lancret. The subjects are taken from paintings that
were in the collection of Frederick II. It can thus not
be ruled out that she was able to copy from the originals, as was common for prospective artists in the
18th century, and which was permitted in the royal
collections as part of training. It is, however, more
likely that the artist knew of Watteau's work and
that of his followers through engravings, which
were widely available.

Anna Dorothea's first period of work came
before her marriage to the Berlin inn proprietor
Ernst Friedrich Therbusch in 1742. He is sometimes
described as a painter as well, but this has not yet
been substantiated. Her marriage and the birth of
her children initially limited her artistic activity. It
was not until 1760 that she returned to her career,
with a more vigorous style, after a period in which
she taught herself. In 1761 she was called to the
court of Duke Karl Eugen von Württemberg in
Stuttgart, where she painted 18 decorative works
for the hall of mirrors and a series of decorative wall
paintings above doors. It was in Stuttgart that an
important phase of her development started. The
study of Pesne and perhaps also the influence of
Lesueur and van Loo led her to a softer and more
sketchy manner of painting. In 1763 she was called
to Mannheim, where she painted portraits of the
Elector Palatine Karl Theodor and was promoted to
court painter. She soon returned to Berlin, and from
there set off to Paris, where she managed to be
elected a member of the Académie Royale. She sent
several works to the Salon, including her reception
piece for the Academy, *The Drinker* (Ecole
Nationale des Beaux-Arts, Paris), which shows a
young man sitting at a table, holding a glass of wine
in his left hand, lit by candlelight. The portrait of
the painter *Jacob Philipp Hackert* (1768;
Gemäldegalerie, Vienna), painted in Paris, also

brought her the membership of the Vienna Academy (1776).

Despite these successes and her acquaintance with Diderot, her stay in Paris was rather unpleasant. The French public – used to the sophisticated courtly taste of the Rococo – found her works too realistic and she did not receive large commissions. She left Paris as early as 1768, and returned to Berlin via Brussels and the Netherlands.

The artistic advantages of these travels became apparent in her final and most prolific period of work. Since her husband died in 1772, it is likely that economic reasons lay behind her productivity. From this time on she signed her works "Peintre du Roi de France". Lisiewka-Therbusch probably began to conduct colour experiments at this time, possibly with her brother, with whom she shared a studio. The essential result of these experiments was the invention of a glossy red paint, which, when made lighter only with the addition of white, she thought perfect for flesh colours. This unbroken pink is the surest sign for the attribution of paintings to her.

Besides commissions for mythological scenes for Frederick II (e.g. *Anakreon*, 1771; *Toilet of Venus*, 1772; *Diana and Her Nymphs*, 1772; all Neues Palais, Potsdam), Anna Dorothea also painted portraits of Frederick and of other members of the royal family, but these did not lead to an appointment as court painter. In 1772 she received a commission from the Tsar's family to paint eight life-size portraits of the royal family (portrait of *Princess Friederike von Preussen*, Neues Palais, Potsdam; others in Hermitage, St Petersburg). For this commission there is evidence of her brother's collaboration. Her manner of painting had become lighter; a few brush strokes and areas of light would often be enough to characterise a certain material. Her realistic portraits of middle-class sitters are excellent and advanced for their time, but her outstanding achievements in both colour and ideas can also be seen in her large paintings.

Anna Dorothea's self-portraits should surely be counted among her best works. Two years before her death she painted a *Self-Portrait with Eyeglass* (1780; Germanisches Nationalmuseum, Nuremberg), in which she rejected the traditional role of the beautiful and desirable woman – depicted again and again by the French painters of the Rococo – and created instead an image of a distinguished woman. The full-length portrait shows her sitting at a table reading. She looks up incidentally, but still seems to be deep in thought. A monocle held on a leather cord can be seen as an attribute of her rationality and at the same time as a reference to the importance of sight and recognition for her artistic work. It obscures her face and thus intentionally creates a moment of irritation for the viewer. Lisiewska-Therbusch describes her own mature and intellectually alert personality in a rational and sober way. Her self-portrait symbolises and foretells the step for women across the boundaries from the simply beautiful to the intellectual. The combination of the splendour of the Rococo with conscious self-reflection creates a tension, apparent in the figure of this admirable woman, who managed to overcome the barriers set for her person and sex.

EDITH SCHOENECK

See also Training and Professionalism survey 3

Lizarraga, Remedios *see* Varo

Longhi, Barbara [fig. 44]

Italian painter, 1552–1638

Born in Ravenna, 1552; father the painter Luca Longhi, brother the painter and poet Francesco Longhi. Died in Ravenna, 1638.

Bibliography

Giorgio Vasari, *Le vite de' più eccellenti pittori, scultori ed architettori*, Florence, 1568; ed. Gaetano Milanesi, vii, Florence: Sansoni, 1881; as *Lives of the Most Eminent Painters, Sculptors and Architects*, 10 vols, London: Macmillan-Medici Society, 1912–15; reprinted New York: AMS, 1976 (life of Luca Longhi)

Francesco Beltrami, "Il forestiere instruito delle cose notabili della città di Ravenna e suburbane della medesima", Ravenna, 1791; Archivio di Stato, Bologna, MS A91

F. Nanni, *Il forestiero in Ravenna*, Ravenna, 1821

Gaspare Ributti, *Guida di Ravenna*, 1835, 1866 and 1885

Jadranka Bentini, ed., *Luca Longhi e la pittura su tavola in Romagna nel '500*, Bologna: Alfa, 1982

Liana De Girolami Cheney, "Barbara Longhi of Ravenna", *Woman's Art Journal*, ix/1, 1988, pp.16–21

The daughter of Luca Longhi, a provincial Mannerist painter, Barbara Longhi trained with her father and assisted him on his large altarpieces. She was also inspired by the Emilian painters Correggio and Parmigianino, the Roman engravers Marcantonio Raimondi and Agostino Veneziano, and Raphael, particularly his Florentine period (1506–8), when he registered the impact of the works of Leonardo and Fra Bartolommeo. Assimilating these influences, she developed her own recognisable style: in the delicate modelling of the arms and necks of her madonnas, the saints who are no more corporeal than their rippling garments, and her warm and subtle golden palette. Her works won the esteem of contemporary connoisseurs such as Giorgio Vasari and Munzio Manfredi.

Although Longhi was especially admired for her portraits, only one is certainly known. The *Camaldolese Monk* (1570 or 1573; Pinacoteca, Ravenna), one of her few paintings to bear a date, though the last digit is unclear, is also the only one to depict a male subject. The pose of the figure, seated at a table, suggests a Raphaelesque model such as *Leo X and His Nephews* (c.1515; Palazzo Pitti, Florence); the books in the background emphasise the sitter's learning. On the basis of its resemblance to the probable depiction of Longhi as St Barbara in her father's *Virgin and Child Enthroned with Saints* (1570), the *St Catherine of Alexandria* (1589; both Pinacoteca, Ravenna), painted for the monastery of Classe in Ravenna, has been identified as a self-portrait. Several copies are known.

Longhi's paintings reflect the authoritarian ideas of the Counter Reformation, according to which religious images should be simple and unambiguous to elicit a devotional response from the viewer. The element of empathy was crucial. Of the 15 paintings by her that have been identified, 12 depict the Virgin and Child. As the chronology is unclear, they are organised here according to stylistic development. In her earliest works (c.1570–90) Longhi simplified the composition, limited modelling to emphasise linearity of design, used a limited palette and gave her themes a lyrical, intimate treatment, for example in two versions of the *Virgin with Sleeping Child* (both c.1570; Pinacoteca, Ravenna; Grohs-Collison

Collection, Birmingham, AL). The *Madonna del Baldacchino* (c.1570–73; Pinacoteca, Ravenna) has an elaborate canopy and floating angels recalling Raphael's painting of this subject (1506–7; Palazzo Pitti), which Longhi may have known from engravings.

The muted palette and gentle rhythms of the *Reading Madonna* (c.1570–75; Pinacoteca, Ravenna) reveal what Vasari called Longhi's "grace and style". It is signed with her initials B.L.F. (Barbara Longhi Fecit). The pose of the Christ Child, resting on a globe, is reminiscent of works by Mannerist painters such as Parmigianino. Inspiration from another Emilian Mannerist, Correggio, is suggested by her *Virgin and Child with St John the Baptist* (c.1589–90; private collection, repr. Cheney 1988, fig.3), in which the family scene is set off from the landscape by dramatic drapery.

The period c.1590 to c.1605 must be considered Longhi's maturity, as no work that can be attributed to a later period has been discovered. Here her compositional devices include a draped column and a background view showing a scene from nature. The figures have a monumental quality, and the colour is more brilliant. A deeper devotional element is added to the lyrical treatment of the theme. In the *Virgin and Child with SS Agatha and Catherine* (c.1590–95; Pinacoteca, Ravenna) the Virgin is depicted as aloof, in a formal, frontal pose. Longhi depicted these saints in other altarpieces, for example, the *Healing of St Agatha,* painted for San Vitale, Ravenna (c.1595; now Santa Maria Maggiore, Ravenna).

Her *Cappuccini Altarpiece* (c.1595; Brera, Milan), a "sacra conversazione" in an elaborate architectural setting, shows Venetian influence, particularly of Giovanni Bellini's altarpiece for San Zaccaria, Venice (1505). As there is no documentation about Longhi's patrons, the identification of saints in her pictures is often speculative. For example, in the *Virgin and Child with Saint* (c.1590–95; Louvre, Paris) the Franciscan habit of the figure being crowned by Christ suggests she may be St Elizabeth of Hungary, who belonged to the order.

Counter-Reformation themes are evident in the *Virgin and Child with St John the Baptist* (c.1598–1600; Pinacoteca, Ravenna): in the foreground, a small cross at the feet of the Baptist recalls his role forecasting the coming of Christ and is also a reminder of Christ's fate. The painting, which shows the brilliance and variety of her colour, is signed B.L.F. Another version of the same subject (*c.*1595–1600) represents the culmination of Longhi's style: the tender expressions and soft modelling of the children; the *sfumato* treatment of the landscape in the tradition of Leonardo; and the Emilian Mannerist motif of the draped column. In these two works Longhi assimilated the dominant styles of the mid-16th century and added her own intimate and gentle touch.

Longhi's mature style emphasised grace and softness of contour, as in the *Mystical Marriage of St Catherine, with St John the Baptist* (*c.*1600; Museo Biblioteca, Bassano del Grappa). The scene exemplifies Counter Reformation ideas about Christ as an active participant in the lives of saints and about the importance of presenting saints' lives as models for the faithful to emulate. In this picture Longhi visually integrated these didactic religious elements with the artistic quest of Mannerism.

Of the latest-known examples of Longhi's paintings of the Virgin and Infant Christ, the *Virgin with Sleeping Child* (*c.*1600–05; Walters Art Gallery, Baltimore) is perhaps the most intensely devotional. The figures occupy an extremely confined interior space, with a draped column and a window view of heavenly clouds. Mary gazes in adoration at the Child, whose sleep also presages his death. Although the composition recalls works by Bellini (*c.*1505; Isabella Stewart Gardner Museum, Boston) and Lavinia Fontana, q.v. (1603; Prado, Madrid), Longhi has moved away from Bellini's classicism and the Mannerist elaboration of Fontana to focus instead on the intimate spiritual relationship between mother and viewer, both adoring the divine Child. The monumentality of the forms is an analogue for the directness and mysticism expressed in the painting. The *Nursing Madonna* (*c.*1600–05; Brera, Milan) depicts a theme derived from Early Christian art that became particularly popular in Italy in the 14th century. During the Counter-Reformation, however, nudity in sacred figures was not acceptable, and Longhi's Madonna only partially reveals her breast, while Christ gently embraces his mother. The unity of femininity and motherly love expressed in the image are characteristic of her mature style.

Like Fede Galizia (q.v.), Elisabetta Sirani (q.v.) and Artemisia Gentileschi (q.v.), Longhi painted *Judith with the Head of Holofernes* (*c.*1570–75; Pinacoteca, Ravenna). Her Judith shows none of the violence of Gentileschi's versions, however, but looks to heaven as if seeking forgiveness. The acceptance of guilt and faith in divine absolution reflect Counter-Reformation ideas. In her lifetime Longhi's fame did not extend beyond Ravenna, which may be why little is known of her life, and few of her works have been identified. Nevertheless, she was a productive member of the family workshop, and her paintings give some idea of the regional expression of the artistic aims of the Counter-Reformation.

LIANA DE GIROLAMI CHENEY

M

Maar, Dora [fig. 47]
French photographer and painter, 1907–1997

Born Henrietta Théodora Markovič in Tours, 22 November 1907; changed name to Dora Maar early in life. Studied painting in Paris, at the Ecole des Arts Décoratifs, Académie de Passy, Académie Julian and under André Lhôte; also attended Ecole de Photographie. Lived with the writer Georges Bataille, early 1930s. Shared photographic studio with Pierre Keffer in Neuilly, 1931–4, then temporarily one with Brassaï. Introduced to the Surrealists by Paul Eluard, 1934; exhibited with them in Tenerife (1935), London (1936), New York (1936), Tokyo (1937) and Amsterdam (1938). Met Picasso and joined him at Mougins, 1936; suffered nervous collapse after the affair ended in 1945; ceased working for 10 years. Died 16 July 1997.

Selected Individual Exhibitions
Galerie Vanderberg, Paris: 1932
Galerie de Beaune, Paris: 1934
Galerie Jeanne Bucher, Paris: 1944
Galerie René Drouin, Paris: 1945
Galerie Pierre Loeb, Paris: 1946
Galerie Berggruen, Paris: 1957
Leicester Galleries, London: 1958
Standler Gallery, Paris: 1983
Galerie 1900–2000, Paris: 1990
Centre Cultural Bancaixa, Barcelona: 1995

Bibliography
Salvador Dalí, "Objets psycho-atmosphériques-anamorphiques", *Le Surréalisme au service de la Révolution*, no.5, May 1933, pp.45–8
Fantastic Art, Dada, Surrealism, exh. cat., Museum of Modern Art, New York, 1936
Dora Maar, exh. cat., Leicester Galleries, London, 1958
Jean-Paul Crespelle, *Picasso and His Women*, London: Hodder and Stoughton, 1969 (French original)
Roland Barthes, "The photographic message", *Image, Music, Text*, ed. Stephen Heath, London: Fontana, and New York: Hill and Wang, 1977
Walter Benjamin, "A small history of photography" (1931), *One-Way Street*, London: New Left, 1979, pp.240–57 (German original)
L'Amour fou: Photography and Surrealism, exh. cat., Corcoran Gallery of Art, Washington, DC, and elsewhere, 1985
Whitney Chadwick, *Women Artists and the Surrealist Movement*, Boston: Little Brown, and London: Thames and Hudson, 1985
Roy MacGregor-Hastie, *Picasso's Women*, Luton: Lennard, 1988
Dora Maar: Oeuvres anciennes, exh. cat., Galerie 1900–2000, Paris, 1990
Ginger Danto, "Dora Maar: Galerie 1900", *Art News*, lxxxix, November 1990, pp.183–5
James Lord, *Picasso and Dora: A Personal Memoir*, London: Weidenfeld and Nicolson, and New York: Farrar Straus, 1993
Picasso and the Weeping Women: The Years of Marie-Thérèse Walter and Dora Maar, exh. cat., Los Angeles County Museum of Art, and elsewhere, 1994
Dora Maar: Fotógrafa, exh. cat., Centre Cultural Bancaixa, Barcelona, 1995 (with English translation)
Julie L'Enfant, "Dora Maar and the art of mystery", *Woman's Art Journal*, xvii/2, 1996–7, pp.15–20

The artistic career of Théodora Markovič, or Dora Maar as she is better known, was overshadowed by her personal life. As the model for Pablo Picasso's *Weeping Woman* (Tate Gallery, London), her iconic face masked an artistic career that was both varied and fruitful, beginning and ending with painting but being most notable for photography.

Maar took classes in both painting and photography as a student in Paris in the 1920s. Establishing herself as a photographer in 1931 in her own studio at Neuilly with Pierre Keffer, she quickly earned fame with her photographic portraits, still lifes and advertisements. Her talents extended to the film camera, for she worked with Louis Chavance in

1930 and with Jean Renoir in 1935 on his film *Le Crime de Monsieur Lange*. She also produced archaeological photographs in collaboration with Germain Bazin, and after the closure of her studio in 1934, she temporarily shared a studio with another eminent artist – Brassaï.

Maar's studies of Arums (*Arums*, 1930; *Bouquet d'Arums*, 1933; both Centre Georges Pompidou, Paris) are not merely still lifes, they must be viewed – in the light of Roland Barthes's terminology – as "photogenia", that is, embellished images wherein reality is sublimated by techniques of lighting, exposure and printing. It is this quality that brings photography into the realm of aesthetics. Transposing petals and stalks into voluptuous compositions, using light to create a painterly chiaroscuro, juxtaposing fleshy petals with powdery stamens, her *Arums* are posed so that they imply "signifieds of connotation" – namely spirituality, fragility, eroticism.

A comparison of Man Ray's portrait of *Dora Maar* (1936) and her portrait of *Nusch Eluard* (1935; Centre Georges Pompidou) highlights the exciting development of photography as an artistic medium in Paris in the 1930s. While Man Ray's image reduces Maar to a mask-like fetish, Maar's study of Nusch Eluard is seductive, but actively so. While fellow male Surrealists removed woman or the *femme-enfant* from the real, logical world, Maar rejected this mythologising of woman and presented Nusch as an autonomous being, emphasising her strongly lit hands in such a way as to reinforce her concreteness.

It was through Paul Eluard that Maar was first introduced to the Surrealists in 1934. Her composition *29 rue d'Astorg* of 1936 was reproduced in the Surrealist publication *Cartes postales surréalistes* (1937), and her photographs were exhibited in the *Fantastic Art, Dada, Surrealism* exhibition of that year at the Museum of Modern Art, New York. *The Simulator* (1936; Centre Georges Pompidou) exemplifies her surreal blend of eroticism and collage-like juxtapositions, creating a dislocation of meaning. This photomontage challenges the distinction between the real and the feigned in a Freudian scene of a wanderer rapt in a Tower-of-Babel-like turret: lacking fixity, he sways before his unconscious imagination. Maar's image of Alfred Jarry's *Père Ubu* (1936; Collection Arturo Schwarz, Milan) is even more nightmarish. Here she uses virtuoso techniques to distort reality so that the blurring of lines

and close-up of surface create a monstrous image in a Poe-like manner. It is also reminiscent of Salvador Dalí's "psycho-atmospheric-anamorphic object".

Maar's relationship with Picasso from 1936 to 1945 marked a traumatic turn in her artistic and mental well-being. Artistically it heralded a turn to reportage photography with her lengthy documentation of Picasso's *Guernica* in its evolving stages, her study of Giacometti's *La Femme invisible* and of the fur-lined *Objet* by Meret Oppenheim (q.v.), capturing it from a Freudian-womb angle to emphasise its erotic potency. Maar did not merely capture these art works on film, she contributed to their historical production by re-presenting them. She was the catalyst behind Picasso's rare venture into political imagery, suggesting symbols for *Guernica* and inspiring the wailing woman figure bearing her dead child.

For Picasso she was always the weeping woman. In an interview with James Lord, Picasso claimed: "I gave her a tortured appearance, not out of Sadism ... but in obedience to a vision that had imposed itself upon me ... She was anything you wanted, a dog, a mouse, a bird, an idea, a thunderstorm" (quoted in Lord 1993). Evidently her peculiar (for the time and for a lover of Picasso) blend of femininity and intellectuality threatened Picasso, who admitted: "she made my brain work, it was sometimes very tiring". Maar saw that with each lover came a new period in his oeuvre, a new colour scheme, a new self-portrait. She would parody this artist-model relationship in her own Cubist portrait of the master: *Picasso* of 1938 (repr. Paris 1990). Their relationship ended with the arrival of Françoise Gilet, the "Florentine Virgin" in 1945. Maar suffered a nervous breakdown, and was reported to have been found naked in the stairway of her apartment building, hysterical. She was committed to the psychiatric hospital of Sainte-Anne in Paris where she was subjected to electric shock therapy. Eluard was appalled at such treatment – there is no mention of Picasso – and ensured that she was placed under the private analysis of Jacques Lacan instead. This led to mental recovery but her self-image had suffered a heavy blow. She would not produce art for another ten years.

Maar's subsequent move from photography to painting has been attributed to her involvement with Picasso. Her still-life exhibition of 1945 in Paris marked a turn towards bleak palettes and macabre juxtapositions that seemed to match her black-clad image. By 1957 a move from Paris to sunny Provence inspired a series of landscapes that combined her new-found Catholicism with a Buddhist approach to nature. Her *Paysage* (1957; *ibid*), exhibited in Paris and London, marks a renewed confidence in its translation of photographic lyricism into paint. A rolling mountainside, which evokes depth through flat brush strokes and bands of earthy hues, this image is majestic in its worship of nature and yet ominous in its marked lack of human life. In the accompanying catalogue Douglas Cooper noted the influence of Turner and Courbet (London 1958). Apart from vague links with the sublime and the rural this is a tenuous if not mistaken comparison. Maar's dramatic use of colour, surface play and denial of symbolism are better viewed in the light of contemporary Abstract Expressionism.

The lyrical but economic style of Maar's art permeated her exhibition at the Galerie 1900–2000 in 1990. In his catalogue entry Edouard Jaguer described her landscapes as "automatic landscapes", and quoted the artist's artistic intention to "say what I say with authenticity" (Paris 1990). This Surrealist automatism permeates all her art: the orientation of art away from the pictorial, the framed world, and towards the poetic, the indulgence in what Walter Benjamin termed the "optical unconscious". In an interview with James Lord, Maar stated in true Surrealist language, endorsing Barthes's theory of photogenia: "Art after all only embellishes truth. It is not truth itself" (Lord 1993). This conviction was the constant principle on which all her work was based.

ALYCE MAHON

Macdonald, Margaret [fig. 45]
British painter and designer, 1864–1933

Born in Tipton, near Wolverhampton, Staffordshire, 5 November 1864; older sister of Frances Macdonald. Studied at the Glasgow School of Art under Francis Newbery. Set up studio in Glasgow with Frances by 1896. Worked with the group that became known as "The Four": Frances and Margaret Macdonald, architect Charles Rennie Mackintosh and designer James Herbert McNair. Married Mackintosh, 1900; he died 1928.

Lived in Chelsea, London, 1914–23. Moved to the south of France, 1923; lived in Collioure in the French Pyrenees, then in Port Vendres, Provence. Stayed in London while Mackintosh received treatment for cancer, 1927–8; settled in England after his death. Member, Royal Scottish Society of Painters in Watercolours, 1898 (served on Council, 1907–13). Died in Chelsea studio, London, 7 January 1933.

Principal Exhibitions
Arts and Crafts Exhibition Society, London: 1896, 1899, 1916
Royal Scottish Society of Painters in Watercolours: occasionally 1898–1922
International Society of Sculptors, Painters and Gravers, London: 1899, 1909 (special *Fair Women* exhibition)
Esposizione Internazionale d'Arte, Venice: 1899
Vienna Secession: 1900
Esposizione Internazionale d'Arte Decorativa Moderna, Turin: 1902 (diploma of honour, with Charles Rennie Mackintosh)

Bibliography
The Studio, ix, 1896, pp.202–3
Gleeson White, "Some Glasgow designers and their work", *The Studio*, xi, 1897, pp.86–100
Anthea Callen, *Angel in the Studio: Women in the Arts and Crafts Movement, 1870–1914*, London: Astragal, 1979; as *Women Artists of the Arts and Crafts Movement, 1870–1914*, New York: Pantheon, 1979
Margaret Macdonald Mackintosh, 1864–1933, exh. cat., Hunterian Art Gallery, University of Glasgow, 1983
Jude Burkhauser, ed., *Glasgow Girls: Women in Art and Design, 1880–1920*, 2nd edition, Edinburgh: Canongate, and Cape May, NJ: Red Ochre, 1993
Janice Helland, "The critics and the Arts and Crafts: The instance of Margaret Macdonald and Charles Rennie Mackintosh", *Art History*, xvii, 1994, pp.205–23
——, *The Studios of Frances and Margaret Macdonald*, Manchester: Manchester University Press, 1996

In the autumn of 1890 Margaret Macdonald and her younger sister Frances Macdonald enrolled as students at the progressive Glasgow School of Art. The securely middle-class Macdonald sisters studied as day students at the school; young women studying in the evening classes tended to be from working-class homes and followed courses that would lead to careers in teaching or industrial design. The sisters, however, followed courses in drawing, design, metalwork and modelling, and by the beginning of their second year of study registered themselves as design students, thus preparing themselves for careers as decorative artists as well as exhibitors of watercolour paintings.

Margaret Macdonald's career included the production of collaborative art (first with her sister and James Herbert McNair, then with her husband, Charles Rennie Mackintosh), as well as the production of her own decorative art and the making of watercolour pictures. The bold and striking design made to advertise Joseph Wright's umbrella manufacture, *Drooko* (1895; repr. *Dekorative Kunst*, 1899), represents the first commissioned work that the sisters made from their studio in Hope Street. Although the poster was criticised in the *Glasgow Evening News* (February 1895), it established the sisters' reputations as "the only 'new' poster designers" working in Glasgow, and by the spring of the same year their "clever" metalwork was commended by the press when it appeared in a Glasgow Arts and Crafts exhibition.

Following successes in Glasgow, the group of artists who came to be known as "The Four" (Margaret and Frances Macdonald, Mackintosh and McNair) achieved critical acclaim in Europe with their contributions to the Vienna Secession (1900) and the Esposizione Internazionale d'Arte Decorativa Moderna in Turin (1902). In both exhibitions the four artists were responsible for the unusual decoration of spaces set aside as "rooms", considered by German critics to be elegant, magical and bizarre (*Dekorative Kunst*, vii, 1901, p.171). The Scottish section at the Turin exhibition was called "quaint and curious" and Margaret Macdonald's panels were singled out for their elongation and "chimerical character" (*Journal of Decorative Art and British Decorator*, July 1902, p.195).

Macdonald's gesso panels are most representative of her production and bring together the imagery that she used repeatedly in design projects as well as in watercolour painting. A panel made for Kate Cranston's Ingram Street tea rooms, the *May Queen* (Glasgow Museums and Art Galleries), which was also exhibited at the Vienna Secession, is characteristic. Woman becomes a round, enclosed shape, a head emerging from a large blossom, or a narrow, armless and footless shape. Like almost all of Macdonald's representations of women, these figures are decorative, confined and denied movement. The two panels that she exhibited at Turin, *Heart of the Rose* and *The White Rose and the Red Rose*, both of which were purchased by the Viennese

art patron Fritz Wärndorfer, are typical of Macdonald's production in two ways: they depict women and they are not one-of-a-kind productions.

Macdonald continually represented a restricted and limited woman in her gessos and watercolours. In 1901 she made a duplicate *Heart of the Rose* panel for R. Wylie Hill, which was incorporated into a fireplace designed by Mackintosh. The commission probably came to Macdonald through her friend Jessie Newbery. The panel takes as its theme the female experience of childbirth (nativity) shared with another woman. Thus the rose motif, favoured by Newbery, becomes the foil around which to build an image of motherhood and childbirth and, given the time the design for the panel was first made (c.1900), it might represent Frances Macdonald's recent nativity (she gave birth to her only child, Sylvan, in 1900). During the 19th and early 20th centuries sisters often aided each other during childbirth as well as during the subsequent recovery period. In the panel, responsibility for the infant is shared by two women; there is no man present. And while the luxurious surface and sensuous line transfer the image from the material world into the ideal, the sharing of the "rose child" pulls the viewer back into an environment of kinship, support and harmony.

The exquisite panels *Heart of the Rose* and *The White Rose and the Red Rose* represent a decorative motif that Macdonald used as a trademark during the early years of the century. Thus, as with earlier work from the sisters' studio in Hope Street, these two works can be read as highly developed, thought-out designs, recognisable as Margaret's and usually made to interact with commissioned interiors. While reading them hermetically for meanings that might be ascribed to women, one must also read them practically as decorative work made to harmonise with and beautify specific environments. The design prototype or "signature stamp" for the completed projects can be found on the cover of *Deutsche Kunst und Dekoration* (May 1902). The drawing represents woman as rose in full bloom. The three white roses near the top of the drawing, one of which is in the woman's hair, the seven red roses in the composition, the peacock in the upper right-hand corner and the two round purple shapes signal Macdonald's design pattern. The pattern appeared first in her gesso panel *May Queen* and was subsequently repeated in her commissions. This design is not meant as a precious and one-of-a-kind piece but rather as an individualised kind of work-shop production in which the hand of a particular author can be read clearly.

Macdonald's long discussed but "missing" panel of the *Seven Princesses*, which was commissioned by Wärndorfer for the Music Room of his Viennese home around 1900, was recently found locked away in a wooden crate behind a partition wall in the Österreichisches Museum für angewandte Kunst, Vienna. It reveals, as do her other panels, the exquisite sense of detail and elegantly textured surface that characterise the work she did for interiors ("A lost masterpiece is found in Vienna: Margaret Macdonald's triptych resurfaces after fifty years", *Architectural Digest*, October 1995, pp.66–72). This panel was inspired by Maeterlinck's play *The Seven Princesses* (probably at Wärndorfer's request) and, like earlier panels, helped to compose a total environment, a room or rooms designed by Mackintosh and Margaret Macdonald.

In 1909 Macdonald exhibited three of these gesso panels at the International Society of Sculptors, Painters and Gravers' special exhibition of *Fair Women*; they were *In Willow Wood* (1903; Glasgow Art Gallery and Museum), *Summer* (1904) and *The White Rose and the Red Rose* (c.1909; Hunterian Art Gallery, University of Glasgow). According to *Building News*, a "good deal of attention" was claimed by these "three large exhibits in gesso". The critic saw them as "studies of fine-line decoration" in which the female figure had been "introduced merely as something round with which to weave these decorated forms" (*Building News*, 26 February 1909, p.4). The figure in *The White Rose and the Red Rose*, however, is not "something round" but is enveloped in the same tear-drop-shaped shroud that enclosed the women in a set of embroidered panels that Macdonald had designed for the Vienna Secession. *The White Rose and the Red Rose* had hung above the studio fireplace in her own home, and was a duplicate of the panel that had been part of the *Rose Boudoir* at the Turin exhibition of 1902. *Summer* (1904; National Museum of Antiquities, Edinburgh) was probably similar to two earlier pieces: a metal-framed watercolour of the same name from 1897 (Glasgow Art Gallery and Museums) and her watercolour picture, *June Roses* (1898; Neue Galerie in der Stallburg, Vienna); *In Willow Wood* had been lent by Cranston from the Sauchiehall Tea Rooms. The *Building News* selected for discussion the two panels in which the female

figure is more obviously female and implicitly "fair", and ignored the narrow, oblong figure in *The White Rose and the Red Rose*, which, while perhaps less fair than the other representations, does represent a consistent aspect of Macdonald's work – a woman unable to move, restricted and bound. Her watercolour pictures presented the same image of women to their viewers and although her watercolour production represents a smaller part of her work than does her decorative art, it enhances an understanding of it and elaborates upon the theme of all her images: women.

Three watercolour pictures, all exhibited with the Royal Scottish Society of Painters in Watercolours, clearly represent her oeuvre: *Mysterious Garden*, (1911; private collection, repr. Helland 1996, p.150), *Pool of Silence* (1913; private collection, ibid., p.153) and *Legend of the Blackthorns* (1922; Hunterian Art Gallery). All three pictures depict solemn, introspective women who represent a kind of shrouded stillness. Contemporary critics read these pictures as mysterious, strange and decorative (*The Times*, 6 April 1911, p.10; *Glasgow Herald*, 31 March 1911, p.9); to a present-day viewer they might be considered as images that eschew sexual subservience by eradicating desire. Whatever meaning they represent for a viewer they are technically exquisite.

All Macdonald's projects, whether collaboratively made with her sister or her husband, or made alone, speak of intelligence, thoughtfulness and craftsmanship. They represent a caring about her subject matter and a concern for an elegant and precise presentation that has continuing power to fascinate viewers.

JANICE HELLAND

Macdowell, Susan *see* Eakins

Mackintosh, Margaret *see* Macdonald, Margaret

M[a]cPherson, Margaret Rose *see* Preston

Mailou, Lois *see* Jones

Malfatti, Anita
Brazilian painter, 1889–1964

Born in São Paulo, 2 December 1889. Educated at Mackenzie College, São Paulo, 1904–6. Went to Berlin, 1910; studied at the Berlin Academy and under Fritz Burger and Expressionist painter Lovis Corinth, 1913. Returned to Brazil via Paris, 1914, leaving for New York later that year. Studied briefly at the Art Students League, New York, then under Homer Boss at the Independent School of Art; began to produce illustrations for *Vogue*, *Vanity Fair* and other magazines. Returned to Brazil, 1916. Founder member, Grupo dos Cinco, São Paulo, 1922. Lived in Paris, 1923–8; visited Italy, 1924. Returned to São Paulo, 1928. President, Sindicato dos Artístas Plásticos, 1940. Contributed articles to the journal *Deutsche Nachrichten*, São Paulo, from 1955. Died in São Paulo, 6 November 1964.

Principal Exhibitions

Individual
26 rua 15 de Novembró, São Paulo: 1914
111 rua Líbero Badaró, São Paulo: 1917
Galerie André, Paris: 1926
Museu de Arte, São Paulo: 1949 (retrospective), 1955
Clubinho, São Paulo: 1957
São Paulo Bienal: 1963 (retrospective)
Museu de Arte Brasileira, São Paulo: 1971 (retrospective)

Group
Teatro Municipal, São Paulo: 1922 (*Semana de arte moderna*)
Maison de l'Amérique Latine, Paris: 1923
Salon d'Automne, Paris: 1924, 1926–7
Salon des Indépendants, Paris: 1926–8
Roerich Museum, New York: 1930 (*First Representative Collection of Paintings by Contemporary Brazilian Artists*)
Exposição Geral de Belas Artes, Rio de Janeiro: 1931
Exposiçao de Arte Moderna da SPAM, São Paulo: 1933
Salão Paulista de Belas Artes, São Paulo: 1934–6
Salão da Familia Artística Paulista, São Paulo: 1937, 1939–40
Salão do Sindicato dos Artístas Plásticos (SPBA), São Paulo: 1938–9, 1941, 1944, 1946
Galeria Itá, São Paulo: 1946 (*Exposição de pintura moderna em homenagem póstuma a Mário de Andrade*)

São Paulo Bienal: 1951
Museu de Arte Moderne de São Paulo: 1952 (*Exposição comemorativa da Semana de Arte Moderna de 1922*)
Museo Nacional de Bellas Artes, Buenos Aires: 1957 (*Arte moderno en Brasil*)

Bibliography
Monteiro Lobato, "A propósito da exposição Anita Malfatti", *O estado de São Paulo*, 20 December 1917
Oswald de Andrade, "A exposição Anita Malfatti", *Jornal do Comércio*, 11 January 1918
Aracy Amaral, *Artes plasticas na Semana de 22*, São Paulo: Perspectiva, 1970
Paulo Mendes de Almeida, *De Anita ao Museu*, São Paulo: Perspectiva, 1976
Anita Malfatti, 1889–1964, exh. cat., Museu de Arte Contemporãnea, Universidade de São Paulo, 1977 (contains bibliography and full exhibition list)
Marta Rossetti Batista, *Anita Malfatti no tempo e no espaco*, São Paulo: IBM, 1985
Modernidade: Art brésilien du 20e siècle, exh. cat., Musée d'Art Moderne de la Ville de Paris, 1987
Mario de Andrade, *Cartas a Anita Malfatti*, Rio de Janeiro: Forense Universitaria, 1989
Art in Latin America, exh. cat., Hayward Gallery, London, 1989
Edward Lucie-Smith, *Latin American Art of the 20th Century*, London and New York: Thames and Hudson, 1993

The role of Anita Malfatti as the absolute pioneer of Brazilian modern art marked both her career and her work. The artist was 28 years old when her solo show of modern paintings in São Paulo in 1917 provoked the furore of the press and the public in the cosmopolitan, and yet in many ways provincial, state capital. In the early decades of the 20th century São Paulo was a rapidly developing industrial city and the most important business centre of Brazil. In one sense Malfatti's early works reflected the spiritual energies of the place. She was the daughter of immigrants in a city marked by large-scale immigration – her father was Italian, an engineer by profession, her mother, a North American of German descent, was an amateur painter. Of a relatively stable, middle-class family, Malfatti followed the traditional educational path of aspiring artists in Brazil that included a period of study in Europe, whether funded by public grants through annual competitions or by private patronage. The specific difference in her case was not only her young age at the time of her departure to Europe but the fact that the trip, a personal and familial enterprise, combined an educational and professional goal with the private aspect of a visit to the continent of her ancestors. In 1910 she went to Germany, the country of her maternal forebears, to study painting at the Berlin Academy, and at the end of 1914, after a brief period back in São Paulo, she departed for New York.

Her formative years as a young artist, therefore, were spent outside Brazil, and nothing, apart from her own personal sensibility and initiative, and especially nothing in her previous educational experience, prepared her for the artistic choices she made while in Germany, which determined the path of development of her art. In Berlin she felt dissatisfied with the rigidity of the traditional instruction at the Academy and gravitated towards the experimental and innovative works of the German avant-garde. She studied under Lovis Corinth and something of the influence of the German painter, a search for immediacy of form and colour, could be seen in her first (and rather inconspicuous) solo exhibition in São Paulo in 1914, aspects of which were identified by contemporary critics as a lack of mastery and technical crudeness. Uncompromisingly, she reaffirmed her avant-garde leanings in New York, where she studied for a brief period at the Art Students League and with more concentration at the Independent School of Art under the American painter Homer Boss. During her period in New York she met, among other American and European avant-garde artists, Francis Picabia and Marcel Duchamp, and produced the greater part of her works for her exhibition of 1917 in São Paulo. Her New York period was indeed a confirmation of the expressionist disposition she had defined in direct contact with the works of the German avant-garde artists in Europe.

The most effective works of Malfatti's New York period concentrated on the isolated human figure painted directly, emotionally, emphatically, with a firm, vigorous delineation of form and a use of colour that reverberated the subjective tones, the emotional energies of the encounter of artist and sitter in the space of the canvas. In *Yellow Man* and *The Japanese* painted in 1915–16, and in *The Idiot* of 1917, the half-figure confronts the viewer against a background of broken diagonals or of raw surfaces of colour created with rapid, energetic brush strokes. These concentrated and self-absorbed individuals are the masks of the artist's subjectivity.

These were the very works that at first met with incomprehension in São Paulo and then with universal condemnation and ridicule after the show was harshly criticised by the writer Monteiro Lobato in a newspaper article whose title, "Paranoia or hoax?", intended to define not only Malfatti's works but modern art in general as the natural product of a deranged mind or, in the absence of a mental condition, the fruit of a malicious intent to deceive the credulous. The immediate result of Lobato's attack was an atmosphere of public scandal surrounding the exhibition and the sudden notoriety of the young painter. To others, however, the initial feelings of discomfort in front of those "distorted" images and unusual colour harmonies gave way to interest and soon to the positive evaluation of the quality and the importance of the paintings. Such was the case of the writer and poet Mario de Andrade, later one of the leading figures of modern Brazilian literature, for whom the works of Malfatti had the effect of a sudden revelation, of a new artistic universe in the making. Andrade was part of a group of (mostly young) artists and writers that congregated informally in defence of Malfatti's works and of modern art – a group that was to give impulse to the celebrations of the *Semana de Arte Moderna* in São Paulo in 1922. The *Semana* repeated in a larger dimension the scandals associated with modern art in the mind of the Brazilian public since Malfatti's show, but this time as a collective and organised effort of the artists with the deliberate aim of "upsetting the bourgeois". The *Semana* consolidated Modernismo (modernism) as a growing and vital movement in Brazilian art, in a sense bringing to realisation what Malfatti started on a purely individual basis in 1917.

To Malfatti, however, the immediate results of her exhibition were isolation, the loss of sales and the loss of students, a solitary struggle for professional and artistic survival in which the confident experimental character and subjective emotional dimension of her expressionist paintings gave way gradually to an eclecticism of pure aesthetic experimentation on the one hand and the search for stylistic "syntheses" between modern and traditional concepts on the other. Her contact with modern French art in Paris from 1923 to 1928 also contributed to this synthesis. After 1922 the consolidation of Brazilian modernism occurred in the creation of a modern and national art thanks to the efforts of painters such as Tarsila do Amaral (q.v.), Rego Monteiro and Di Cavalcanti and writers such as Mario de Andrade and Oswald de Andrade. The writers developed the ideological basis and theoretical foundations of the Movimento Modernista in manifestoes and critical works as well as fiction and poetry.

The contributions of Anita Malfatti to modern Brazilian art never attained the intensity of the heroic years. At times her later paintings alluded to the achievements of the early years. In a general way, however, Malfatti tended towards an individualised thematic elaboration of, or a response to, some of the nationalist and popular preoccupations of the modernists and their successors in the 1930s and 1940s. Without achieving either the formal or the ideological impact of the avant-garde artists, her works tended more and more towards a somewhat idiosyncratic "return to innocence", a sort of artistic quietism, exemplified in some of the paintings of landscapes of rural Brazil and the depictions of peasant life of her later years.

MARCELO LIMA

Mallo, Maruja

Spanish painter, 1902–1995

Born in Vigo, Galicia, 5 January 1902. Moved to Madrid with her family in 1922, and entered the Academia de Bellas Artes de San Fernando alongside her brother Cristino, a sculptor. Attended the drawing classes of Julio Moisés, where she met Salvador Dalí, José Moreno Villa and others, 1924. Worked in Paris and met André Breton, 1931–2. Taught drawing at Instituto de Arévalo, Instituto Escuela de Madrid and Escuela de Cerámica, early 1930s; taught at Escuela de Artes y Oficios, Vigo, 1936. Left Spain at outbreak of Civil War due to political convictions; lived in Buenos Aires, Argentina, with stays in Chile and Uruguay, until 1961. Returned to Madrid, 1962. Recipient of Estrada Saladrich prize, Barcelona, 1967; gold medal in fine arts, Ministry of Culture, 1982; gold medal, County of Madrid, 1990; gold medal, Council of Galicia, 1991. Died in Madrid, February 1995.

Principal Exhibitions

Individual
Galería de la *Revista de Occidente*, Madrid: 1928
Galerie Pierre, Paris: 1932

Salas Adlan, Centro de la Construcción, Madrid: 1936
Carroll Carstairs Gallery, New York: 1948
Galerie Silvagni, Paris: 1950
Galería del Este, Punta del Este, Uruguay: 1952
Galería Compte, Buenos Aires: 1955
Galería Ruiz Castillo, Madrid: 1979
Galería Guillermo de Osma, Madrid: 1992
Centro de Arte Contemporáneo de Galicia, Santiago de Compostela: 1993–4 (touring retrospective)

Group
Sociedad de Artistas Ibéricos, San Sebastián: 1931
Salón de Otoño, Madrid: 1933 (*Grupo constructivo*)
Musée du Jeu de Paume, Paris: 1936 (*L'Art espagnol contemporain*)
Galería D'Art Catalonia, Barcelona: 1936 (*Exposición Lógicofobista*, organised by ADLAN, Barcelona)
Galería Multitud, Madrid: 1975 (*El surrealismo en España*)

Selected Writings

"Plástica escenográfica", *Gaceta de Arte* (Tenerife), March 1935
"La plástica", *U.O. Revista de Cultura Moderna* (Mexico), August–September 1936
"Proceso histórico de la forma en las artes plásticas", *Grafos* (Havana), November–December 1937; reprinted in *Maruja Mallo*, Buenos Aires: Losada, 1942
"Lo popular en la plástica española a través de mi obra", *Sur* (Buenos Aires), April 1938
"Integración de la forma en las artes plásticas", *Sur* (Buenos Aires), February 1939
"Una sala cinematográfica", *Arquitectura* (Buenos Aires), March 1946
"La ciencia de la medida", *Nuevo Continente*, i, 1947 (signed Buenos Aires, April 1946)
"El surrealismo a través de mi obra", *El surrealismo*, ed. Antonio Bonet Correa, Madrid: Cátedra, 1983 (text of lecture given at Santander University, September 1981)

Bibliography

Ernesto Giménez Caballero, "Notre Dame de la Aleluya", *Papel de Aleluyas* (Seville), March 1928
Melchor Fernández Almagro, "María Mallo", *Verso y Prosa* (Murcia), June 1928
Francisco Alcántara, "María Mallo en la *Revista de Occidente*", *El Sol* (Madrid), 13 June 1928
Antonio Espina, "Arte 'Nova Novorum': Maruja Mallo", *La Gaceta Literaria* (Madrid), 15 June 1928
Manuel Abril, "María Mallo", *Revista de Occidente* (Madrid), July 1928
Sebastián Gasch, "Els pintors nous: Maruja Mallo", *L'Amie de les Arts* (Sitges), 31 September 1928
Rafael Alberti, "La primera ascensión de Maruja Mallo al subsuelo", *La Gaceta Literaria* (Madrid), 1 July 1929

Luis Gómez Mesa, "Cinema y arte nuevo: Originalidad de Maruja Mallo", *Popular Film* (Barcelona), 15 May 1930

Benjamín Jarnes, "Sobre una definición pictórica del hombre", *La Vanguardia*, 12 April 1931

Jean Cassou, "Maruja Mallo", *Revue Hebdomadaire*, May 1932

Maruja Mallo, exh. cat., Salas Adlan, Centro de la Construcción, Madrid, 1936

Margarita Nelken, "La vida artística: Exposición Maruja Mallo", *Claridad* (Madrid), 11 June 1936

Ernesto Giménez Caballero, "El arte y la guerra", *Levante*, 21 July 1939

Alfonso de Sayons, "Maruja Mallo y lo popular en la plástica española", *Conducta al servicio del pueblo* (Buenos Aires), September–October 1939

Ramón Gómez de la Serna, *Maruja Mallo*, Buenos Aires: Losada, 1942

—, "Nueva actualidad de Maruja Mallo", *Atlántida* (Buenos Aires), May 1956

Francisco Rivas, "Homenaje de Maruja Mallo a *Revista de Occidente*", *El País*, 12 April 1976

Maria Escribano, "Las fantásticas criaturas de Maruja Mallo", *Arteguia*, Madrid, 1979

Juan Manuel Bonet, "Maruja Mallo: Pura y genial paradoja", *El País*, 25 October 1979

Consuelo de la Gandara, "Maruja Mallo en la *Revista de Occidente*", *Ya* (Madrid), 4 November 1979

Francisco Calvo Serraller, "Maruja Mallo: Invencible en su sueño", *El Pais*, 25 September 1983

Estrella de Diego, "Los paisajes del límite: Frida Kahlo y Maruja Mallo a partir de un retrato", *La balsa de la Medusa*, Madrid, 1991

Maruja Mallo, exh. cat., Galería Guillermo de Osma, Madrid, 1992

Maruja Mallo, exh. cat., Centro de Arte Contemporáneo de Galicia, Santiago de Compostela, and elsewhere, 1993

Estrella de Diego, "María, Maruja, Mallo", *Revista de Occidente*, May 1995

Maruja Mallo is perhaps one of the most interesting female painters of the Spanish avant-garde, both in terms of her pictorial contribution and because of her personality, which was very unusual within the somewhat closed Spanish society of the 1930s, particularly as regards female behaviour. From many points of view she is the type of artist who falls within the definition of the avant-garde; in fact, her most interesting work was produced during the 1920s and 1930s. The friend of, among others, Salvador Dalí, Benjamín Palencia, Federico García Lorca, Miguel Hernández, Rafael Alberti, Pablo Neruda and Rafael Barradas, she represents the ideal of the modern woman, which was frequently opposed to the more restrictive expectations of a "middle-class young lady".

Mallo moved from Galicia to Madrid with her family in 1922, when she was 20. There she met the philosopher and writer José Ortega y Gasset, founder of the magazine *Revista de Occidente*, who would affect her career in many ways. When he saw her paintings, Ortega decided to support her by means of an exhibition in the magazine's gallery in 1928 as well as by commissioning a series of cover illustrations for the magazine, which reveal the geometric style that would characterise Mallo's work throughout her career.

Mallo showed about 30 works in this exhibition – both oil paintings and coloured prints – which attracted the interest and admiration of Madrid intellectuals. The city was then living through the final years of the collapsing dictatorship of Primo de Rivera and was enjoying a period of intensely animated cultural activity. Mallo's work at this time centred on two series which denote a passion for modernity very much in keeping with the spirit of the time and with that of Mallo herself: the *Fairs* and *Sporting Elements*. The first series comprises four large paintings in which parts of the city and its leisure activities are depicted in a vertiginous manner within the picture space. Without abandoning a certain kind of realism that predominates throughout Mallo's work, the style of these pictures uses futuristic, almost *simultaneist* devices in a manner similar to that of Barradas to create the idea of speed, fragmentation and simultaneously occurring events. *The Fair* (1928; Museo Nacional Centro de Arte Reina Sofía, Madrid) portrays two Amazonian women characteristic of Mallo's work, together with sailors, puppets, civil guards, magicians – and everything that years later in a lecture given by the artist in Santander in 1981 she defined as an allegory of popular and pagan leisure. The universe that she presents in this series is the world of her journeys through the city – soldiers, maids, policemen, shawls, along the lines of popular cinematographic productions such as those of the writer Ernesto Giménez Caballero – and at the same time a territory of subverted values, as shown by the Three Magi – one white and two black – in *Easter Procession* (1927; private collection, New York, repr. Santiago de Compostela 1993, p.62) or the pigs replacing the fairground horses in *The Fair* (1928; Centre Georges Pompidou, Paris, *ibid.*, p.65). It may have been these unexpected associations that have led to the frequent use of the label Surrealist to describe the painter.

The same type of strange associations and taste for urban life is evident in some of the works belonging to the second series referred to above, *Sporting Elements* (1926-7), in which Mallo uses her typical style, at once realist and fragmented. The paintings depict objects related to a kind of open-air life. *Sporting Elements* (1927; private collection, Madrid, *ibid.*, p.61), in which a racquet, a fan, a chess board and a miniature aeroplane share the picture space with other artefacts, may speak, like the woman in a bathing costume cycling on the beach in *Cyclist* (1927; untraced, repr. Gómez de la Serna 1942), of some of the photographs of modern life that fascinated the entire Art Deco generation.

Another series dating from 1927 is *Kinetic Prints*, in which angels and mannequins, skyscrapers and businessmen in top hats and suits live together in the recurring theme of the metropolis, as in perhaps the most popular of these works *Print* (1927; private collection, Barcelona, repr. Santiago de Compostela 1993, p.68). The most striking aspect of this series is the almost total absence of colour and the use of mannequins, a favourite pictorial motif of the Surrealists. This may in part be explained by Mallo's meeting Dalí at the Residencia de Estudiantes in Madrid during these years; he had already become very familiar with André Breton's definition of Surrealism through his trips to Paris. Be that as it may, and despite the use of mannequins, the Surrealist elements here are isolated traits. The cut legs, feet, torsos, wigs and long hair that define the world of Mallo's cities in the late 1920s are painted in an identical, fragmented style. Besides, in contrast to the work of some of the women artists associated with Surrealism, such as Claude Cahun (q.v.) and Ithell Colquhoun, Mallo's work of these years reveals no attempt to revise the Surrealist vocabulary from a female point of view.

Mallo also met Federico García Lorca and Rafael Alberti at the Residencia de Estudiantes. She worked with Alberti on a production of *La pajara pinta*, producing figurines and decorations for the scenery, as well as on other projects, also unrealised but which nevertheless demonstrated her passionate search for other forms of artistic expression beyond strictly pictorial ones. In fact, in the early 1930s, Mallo strengthened her interest in stage design through a project to execute the theatrical decorations for a play about García Lorca's bullfighter friend Ignacio Sánchez Mejía; the Ampliación de Estudios, associated with the same Residencia de Estudiantes and the Institución Libre de Enseñanza, progressive bodies of the period, awarded her a grant to study scenography.

In 1931, shortly before leaving for Paris for several months with her father, Mallo took part in the II Exposición de los Ibéricos in San Sebastián, in which a good selection of Spain's avant-garde artists were included. Mallo's style underwent a radical transformation during her stay in Paris, becoming more dramatic and less vital. The world of fairs was replaced by horrifying visions of a world submerged in catastrophe. Bones and dead birds, as in *Rooks and Excrements* (1931; private collection, Madrid, *ibid.*, p.74), and devastated lands, as in *Land and Excrements* (1932; Museo Nacional Centro de Arte Reina Sofía, *ibid.*, p.81) are among the works of this period in which the colours are also darker, closer to earth pigments. The 16 works that Mallo exhibited in the Galerie Pierre in Paris in 1932 form part of this series. Some of the most celebrated international artists of the time visited the show, which again aroused great interest; not only did Picasso and Jean Cassou see the exhibition, but Breton himself seems to have bought a work, *Scarecrow*, reproduced in the book that Ramón Gómez de la Serna wrote during his exile in Argentina in the 1940s (Gómez de la Serna 1942).

Breton's fascination may have been the cause of Mallo's slightly forced inclusion among the Surrealists, added to the isolated elements in her work previously mentioned. Whatever the reasons, the series *Sewers and Bell Towers* is usually considered to be the most Surrealist of her works, partly due to its reception by Breton and partly due to Mallo's lecture of 1981 in which the painter acknowledged the series as Surrealist. In any case, if these works are compared with Mallo's later interests, her growing fascination with nature and its internal order made visible in such series as *Mineral Architectures* and *Vegetal Architectures*, dating from these same years, it is perhaps possible to read *Sewers and Bell Towers* from a perspective that is not strictly, or at least not only, Surrealist. In fact, this period also coincides with Mallo's friendship with some of the painters of the so-called Vallecas School, outstanding among whose members were Benjamín Palencia and Alberto Sánchez. Seen from this perspective, *Sewers and Bell Towers* inserts itself within her interest in nature and the changes that occur within it, while also bearing a relationship to Dalí's "putrefactions", if one recalls the photograph in which Mallo is represented as the high priestess of a cult of rubbish (date unknown; repr. Madrid 1992, p.110). The materials used for the colour and the texture itself, compared with *Architectures*, enable reference to be made to the influence of Alberto and Palencia in journeys through the south of Madrid rather than to that of Surrealism itself. On the other hand, some of these works, such as *Vegetal Architectures* (1933; private collection, Madrid), testify to the painter's growing interest in geometry with her adoption of the golden section and the meticulous study of mathematics that she undertook in 1933 in the little-known Madrid circle of Torres García, who included her in the *Grupo Constructivo* that he showed at the XVI Salón de Otoño in Madrid.

Following her passion for artistic forms other than painting, Mallo continued to execute some of her scenographic experiments, most of which are preserved only through reproductions in magazines of the period, such as the *Gaceta de Arte* (Canary Islands). In the mid-1930s she executed some ceramics that, together with geometric designs, used humorous figures belonging to popular Spanish traditions as shown by a cartoon representing a bullfighter (1935; private collection, Madrid).

Mallo's inclusion in the exhibition *L'Art espagnol contemporain* at the Musée du Jeu Paume in Paris, as well as her participation in the *Exposición Lógicofobista* in Barcelona, reveal an increasingly mature artist who presents herself as such in one of her most spectacular works, the *Wheat's Surprise* (1936; private collection, Madrid, repr. Santiago de Compostela 1993, p.105). The impressive painting manifest in Mallo's best pieces appears here united with a metamorphic passion – evident in the hands from which the wheat springs – that the artist always related to the Castilian landscapes through which she had travelled with the poet Miguel Hernández.

This work was one of the last paintings she executed in Spain; when the Spanish Civil War erupted in July 1936, Mallo was teaching at the Escuela de Artes y Oficios in Galicia and, given her political convictions, she left for Argentina via Portugal, thanks to an invitation from the Amigos del Arte of Buenos Aires. During the ensuing years in the Americas, Mallo alternated her activities as a lecturer with working on her series *Work*, in which elements of the sea are united with those of the land. In this series executed between 1936 and 1938,

Mallo returned to the Amazonian type of woman first seen in such early works as *Cyclist*, and which may be analysed from a feminist perspective: doubles (mirror images), metamorphosis. A second glance also makes it possible to connect Mallo's passion for strong women manifested in her particular taste for convincing, solid forms with the geometries in which the "doubles" can also be included, such as *Song to the Ear of Grain* (1939; Museo Nacional Centro de Arte Reina Sofía).

Mallo's portraits from the early 1940s can be included within this same line and perhaps constitute the last truly interesting works by the artist. Some of the paintings in this series – feminine full-face and profile portraits of white and black women, generally preserved in Argentinian museums or private collections, such as *Woman's Head* (1941; Museo Provincial de Bellas Artes, Santa Fé) – precede mysterious and lively works such as *Human Hind* (1948; private collection, Buenos Aires, *ibid.*, pp.134–5), in which Mallo's taste for metamorphosis and forms generating forms reappears.

Mallo also executed works such as the series *Still/Moving Life* and *The Grapes* (1944; whereabouts unknown, repr. Madrid 1992) during her exile in Argentina, which she interspersed with journeys to Chile and Uruguay and with meetings with such Latin American intellectuals as Pablo Neruda. A preparatory drawing for *The Grapes* reveals the geometric process the artist used. The *Mask* series, in which geometric masks alternate with fashionable beaches where bathers play with sunshades or dance, dates from these same years.

While in Buenos Aires Mallo received a commission to paint a mural in the Los Angeles Cinema. She also received other offers to paint murals during her visit to New York in 1947 – the Rockefeller Foundation and the Metro-Goldwyn-Mayer Studios – although none was executed. Three years later she held another exhibition in Paris, at the Galerie Silvagni. In 1951 *Human Hind* was shown in Madrid at the Primera Bienal Hispano-Americana de Arte. During these years she began several studies of dancers that testify to Mallo at her most vital.

After spending several years withdrawn from the world, in 1961 Mallo decided to return to Spain. Several exhibitions were organised on her return in various cities, and she received awards and prizes. She again produced illustrations for the *Revista de Occidente* and began the series *Inhabitants of*

Space, totally submerged in a type of composition without reference to anything beyond pure geometric forms, and fascinated by word play, as shown by *Geonautic Almotron* (1975; Guillermo de Osma Collection, Madrid). In the early 1980s Mallo became ill and remained in a clinic until her death in 1995. In one way, until very recently Mallo remained one of the great forgotten figures of Spanish art and it is only in the last few years that retrospective exhibitions of her work have been mounted: at the Galería Guillermo de Osma in Madrid in 1992 and the retrospective held in Galicia in 1993.

ESTRELLA DE DIEGO

Mantuana [Mantovana; Ghisi; Scultori], Diana

Italian printmaker, *c*.1547–1612

Born in Mantua, *c*.1547, to the engraver and stucco-worker Giovanni Battista Mantuano and his wife Osanna de Aquanegra; younger sister of the engraver and print publisher Adamo Scultori. Moved to Rome at the time of her marriage to the architect Francesco Capriani da Volterra, 1575; one son, Giovanni Battista Capriani, born 2 September 1578; husband died 1594. Received honorary Volterran citizenship with her husband, 1579. Joined the religious confraternity of Roman artists and craftworkers, the Compagnia di San Giuseppe di Terra Santa, 10 April 1580. Married the architect Giulio Pelosi, 1596. Buried in San Lorenzo in Lucina, Rome, 5 April 1612.

Bibliography

Giorgio Vasari, *Le vite de' più eccellenti pittori, scultori ed architettori*, Florence, 1568; ed. Gaetano Milanesi, vi, Florence: Sansoni, 1881; as *Lives of the Most Eminent Painters, Sculptors and Architects*, 10 vols, London: Macmillan-Medici Society, 1912–15; reprinted New York: AMS, 1976 (lives of Benvenuto Garofalo and Girolamo da Carpi)

Giovanni Francesco Peranda, *Lettere del Signor Gio. Francesco Peranda*, Venice, 1621

Giovanni Baglione, *Le vite de' pittori, scultori et architetti dal Pontificato di Gregorio XIII del 1572 in fino a' tempi di Papa Urbano Ottavo nel 1642*, Rome: Fei, 1642; reprinted Bologna: Forni, 1975–6

Carlo D'Arco, *Di cinque valenti incisori mantovani*, Mantua, 1840 (as Diana Ghisi)

A. Cinci, "Francesco Capriano e Diana Mantovana", *Dall'Archivio di Volterra, memorie e documenti*, Volterra, 1885

G.F. Hill, *Portrait Medals of Italian Artists of the Renaissance*, London: Warner, 1912

J.A.F. Orbaan, "Virtuosi al Pantheon: Archivalische Beitrag zur römischen Kunstgeschichte", *Repertorium für Kunstwissenschaft*, xxxvii, 1914, pp.17–52

Adam von Bartsch, *Le Peintre-graveur*, xv, Würzburg, 1920 (as Diana Ghisi)

Incisori mantovani del '500, exh. cat., Istituto Nazionale per la Grafica-Calcografia, Rome, 1980 (as Diana Scultori)

Loránd Zentai, "Portrait inconnu de Diana Scultori", *Bulletin du Musée Hongrois des Beaux-Arts*, no.62–3, 1984, pp.43–51

Suzanne Boorsch and J.T. Spike, *Italian Artists of the Sixteenth Century* (Illustrated Bartsch, xxxi), New York: Abaris, 1986 (as Diana Scultori)

Paolo Bellini, *L'opera incisa di Adamo e Diana Scultori*, Vincenza: Pozza, 1991

Laura Marcucci, *Francesco da Volterra*, Rome: Multigrafica, 1991

Valeria Pagani, "A *lunario* for the years 1584–1586 by Francesco da Volterra and Diana Mantovana", *Print Quarterly*, viii, 1991, pp.140–45

——, "Adamo Scultori and Diana Mantuana", *Print Quarterly*, ix, 1992, pp.72–87

Evelyn Lincoln, *Printing and Visual Culture in Italy, 1470–1575*, PhD dissertation, University of California, Berkeley, 1994

——, "Making a good impression: Diana Mantuana's printmaking career", *Renaissance Quarterly* (in preparation)

Diana Mantuana was the only female engraver of the 16th century who signed her prints with her own name. She was also, possibly not coincidentally, one of only five professional craftswomen mentioned by name in the second edition (1568) of Vasari's *Vite* (the other four are Properzia de' Rossi, Sofonisba Anguissola, Suor Plautilla Nelli, all q.v., and Lucrezia Quistelli). He noted that Diana "engraves so well that it is a wonderful thing and ... is a very well-bred and charming young lady", having met her on a trip to Mantua in 1566. Like many Renaissance artists and almost every Renaissance woman in the arts, Diana learned her trade from her father and brother. For her father, a draughtsman and decorator working for the Gonzaga court from designs by Giulio Romano and Giovanni Battista Bertani, printmaking represented a much-needed independent income for his family (*Lettere di artisti italiani ad Antonio Perrenot di Granvelle*, Madrid: Istituto Italiano di Cultura di Madrid, 1977, and Lincoln 1994). Diana's brother Adamo preceded her to Rome where he engraved for several publishers and tried publishing himself (G.L. Masetti-Zannini, *Stampatori e librai a Roma nella seconda metà del cinquecento*, Rome, 1980). Diana followed him there in 1575 after the death of her father and her marriage to the architect Francesco da Volterra, but there is no record of professional links between Diana's printing and that of her brother.

In Rome, in June 1575, Diana requested and obtained a papal privilege that protected her rights to print and market images from the copper plates that she had brought from Mantua. She was then able to operate freely, signing her prints Diana Mantuana (or Mantovana), a form of her name that identified her with the Mantuan court and with a printing tradition that had begun with Andrea Mantegna and continued through her family. This kind of signature, consisting of a first name with a surname that identified the provenance or profession of the bearer, was a common form of self-identification for people of non-noble birth. Diana's father used the name Giovanni Battista Mantuano, Scultor (Giovanni Battista, Mantuan sculptor); her brother adopted Scultori as a surname, although it was professionally descriptive as well. Diana never used that name, but identified herself on her earliest prints by first name only, then after arriving in Rome usually as "Diana Mantuana", often appending some written connection identifying herself as the wife of Francesco da Volterra. After her husband obtained honorary Volterran citizenship in 1579 which extended to her (Cinci 1885), she often signed her prints "Diana Mantovana, civis volaterrana". She never used the surname "Scultori", which was assumed for her by art historians of the 19th century (for a fuller discussion of Diana's name, see Ugo Bazzotti and M.G. Savoia, "Uno scritto del giugno 1592", *La Gazzetta di Mantova*, 24 November 1981, and for a discussion of the significance of signing, Lincoln 1994). Diana's first dated engraving is marked 1575 and the last is marked 1588, but since she did not always date her prints the exact time-span of her engraving career is not certain. She was already engraving well before Vasari's visit to Mantua in 1566, and there is no reason to believe that she did not produce undated engravings after 1588. During her lifetime her prints were published by herself, Antonio Lafreri, Claudio Duchet and Orazio Pacifico. Some of the plates later entered the stock of the de' Rossi family, and from there passed into the collection that became the core

of the Calcografia Nazionale in Rome (some of her plates still exist at the Calcografia, see Bellini 1991). Other publishers who printed her plates include Antonio Carenzano (possibly working during Diana's lifetime), Carlo Losi, Calisto Ferranti, Vincente Billy, Hendrick van Schoel and Giovanni Orlandi. (A complete list of her known engravings may be found by consulting Bellini 1991 with the addition of Pagani 1991.)

The Roman market for engravings after inventions by other artists provided Diana with many opportunities to make prints. She engraved several drawings by her father and Giulio Romano, and continued with decorative architectural drawings by her husband. She also collaborated with Francesco on a calendar, or "Lunario", illustrated with motifs from the painted rooms of the Mantuan palaces on which Diana's father worked, and presumably for which she had access to drawings (for a recently discovered impression of this print, see Pagani 1991). She also made engravings after the works of such earlier artists as Correggio and Salviati, and copied an engraving by Marcantonio Raimondi. Likewise, her own engraving after Daniele da Volterra (Bellini 1991, p.25) was used for a painting by Lavinia Fontana (q.v.; see also M.T. Cantaro, *Lavinia Fontana bolognese*, Rome, 1989, cat. 4a.30, and Lincoln 1994).

It is unlikely that Diana had much formal training in drawing, but it seems on the evidence of the prints that she was trained to engrave drawings on to copper plates with a good deal of fidelity. She based her engraving technique on the later 16th-century Roman school, incorporating a northern style much like that of Cornelis Cort or her fellow Mantuan, Giorgio Ghisi, but with less emphasis on chiaroscuro and texture and more on clarity of subject matter. She was also adept at elegant forms of address, and several of her earlier Roman engravings bear long, complicated and courtly dedications designed to win favour for her work and, used as gifts, to obtain employment for her husband in Rome (Lincoln 1994).

Although she became well known in the 19th and 20th centuries as one of the few Renaissance female artists to sign her work, in the 16th century she seemed to enjoy a certain amount of fame both in her own right and as a member of a successful artistic family. Besides being mentioned by Vasari, her work was noted with praise during her lifetime by Giovanni Francesco Peranda, the secretary to the

Caetani family who employed Diana's husband. Among his published letters is one in which he thanks Francesco for the gift of Diana's engraving of the *Feast of the Gods* after Giulio Romano. Both socially and professionally she was part of an active artistic circle in Rome: the painter Durante Alberti was her son's godfather, and portrait medals were made of both her and Francesco da Volterra by the Medallist T.R. (repr. Hill 1912 and Pagani 1991). Diana's portrait was also engraved by Cherubino Alberti and drawn by Federico Zuccaro (repr. Zentai 1984).

Neither Diana's social connections nor her entry into the artists' confraternity of San Giuseppe provided her with a public voice on the Roman art scene, however. Women were recruited to enlarge the pool of dues-paying members, active mainly in choosing brides to be dowered on the confraternity feast day. They had no say in confraternity government and did not attend the plenary meetings. Neither could she belong to Federico Zuccaro's newly re-formed Accademia di San Luca, of which her husband was a founding member (R. Alberti, *Origine e progresso dell'Accademia del disegno de' pittori, scultori e architetti in Roma*, Pavia, 1604). Here again she was excluded because of her sex. As a printmaker, however, Diana mobilised her name, her position and her access first to the Mantuan images of Giulio Romano, then to the wider circle of her Roman friends (including Durante and Cherubino Alberti, Federico Zuccaro, Raffaellino da Reggio and others) in order to publicise her own and her husband's presence in Rome, his skill as an architect and the willingness of both of them to work in their adoptive city.

EVELYN LINCOLN

Marisol   [fig. 48]
Venezuelan sculptor and graphic artist, 1930–

Born Marisol Escobar in Paris, 22 May 1930, to Venezuelan parents. Grew up in Europe, the USA and Caracas. Studied at Ecole des Beaux-Arts and Académie Julian, Paris, 1949–50; Art Students League, New York, 1950; New School for Social Research and Hans Hofmann School, New York, 1951–4. Subsequently travelled widely. Represented Venezuela at Venice Biennale, 1968.

Recipient of honorary doctorates from Moore College of Art, Philadelphia, 1969; Rhode Island School of Design, Providence, 1986; State University of New York, Buffalo, 1992. Member, American Academy of Arts and Letters, 1978. Lives in New York.

Selected Individual Exhibitions
Leo Castelli Gallery, New York: 1958
Stable Gallery, New York: 1962, 1964
Arts Club of Chicago: 1965
Sidney Janis Gallery, New York: 1966, 1967, 1973, 1975, 1981, 1984, 1989
Hanover Gallery, London: 1967
Museum Boymans-van Beuningen, Rotterdam: 1968
Moore College of Art, Philadelphia: 1970 (retrospective)
Worcester Art Museum, MA: 1971 (retrospective)
New York Cultural Center: 1973
Estudio Actual, Caracas: 1974
Contemporary Arts Museum, Houston: 1977
Boca Raton Museum of Art, FL: 1988
Galerie Tokoro, Tokyo: 1989
National Portrait Gallery, Smithsonian Institution, Washington, DC: 1991 (retrospective)

Bibliography
Lawrence Campbell, "Marisol's magic mixtures", *Art News*, lxiii, March 1964, pp.38–41, 64–5
Marisol, exh. cat., Arts Club of Chicago, 1965
Grace Glueck, "It's not Pop, it's not Op – it's Marisol", *New York Times Magazine*, 7 March 1965, pp.34–5, 45–9
Lucy R. Lippard, *Pop Art*, New York: Praeger, and London: Thames and Hudson, 1966
José Ramon Medina, *Marisol*, Caracas: Armitano, 1968
Marisol, exh. cat., Moore College of Art, Philadelphia, 1970
Marisol, exh. cat., Worcester Art Museum, MA, 1971
Marisol: Prints, 1961–1973, exh. cat., New York Cultural Center, 1973
Cindy Nemser, *Art Talk: Conversations with 12 Women Artists*, New York: Scribner, 1975
Jeff Goldberg, "Pop artist Marisol – 20 years after her first fame – recalls her life and loves", *People*, 24 March 1975, pp.40–43
Robert Creeley, *Presences: A Text for Marisol*, New York: Scribner, 1976
Roberta Bernstein, "Marisol as portraitist: Artists and artistes", *Arts Magazine*, lv, May 1981, pp.112–15
——, "Marisol's self-portraits: The dream and the dreamer", *Arts Magazine*, lix, March 1985, pp.86–9
Paul Gardner, "Who is Marisol?", *Art News*, lxxxviii, 1989, pp.146–51
Carol Anne Mahsun, ed., *Pop Art: The Critical Dialogue*, Ann Arbor: UMI Research Press, 1989
Marisol: Recent Sculpture, exh. cat., Galerie Tokoro, Tokyo, 1989

Charlotte Streifer Rubinstein, *American Women Sculptors*, Boston: Hall, 1990

Magical Mixtures: Marisol Portrait Sculpture, exh. cat., National Portrait Gallery, Smithsonian Institution, Washington, DC, 1991 (contains extensive bibliography)

Born of Venezuelan parents in Paris, the artist known since the 1950s as Marisol (meaning "sea and sun" in Spanish) decided to become an artist by the age of 16. During her childhood her family lived in Europe and then commuted between the USA and Caracas. In 1946 her family moved to Los Angeles, where her father supported her desire to study art with Howard Warshaw at the Jepson School. In 1949 Marisol returned to Paris to study at the Ecole des Beaux-Arts, but remained there only a year before returning to the USA, where she has subsequently resided apart from periods spent travelling or living abroad (e.g. in Rome from 1958 to 1960 and to Asia and elsewhere in 1968). In New York she studied at the Art Students League, the New School for Social Research, then worked with the noted abstract German expressionist Hans Hofmann at the school he founded.

From the outset, Marisol received some favourable attention from the art world. Her work was included in many group shows of the 1950s, and her first solo exhibition was held in New York in 1958 at the Castelli Gallery. She also contributed to the Venice Biennale in 1968 as well as many group shows at the Museum of Modern Art and the Whitney Museum of American Art in New York, the Los Angeles County Museum, innumerable private galleries, the Tate Gallery, London, and elsewhere. A full-scale retrospective was mounted in 1971 by the Worcester Art Museum and in the Moore College of Art, Philadelphia, the previous year, although earlier, smaller exhibitions of her work had also been shown at the Arts Club in Chicago in 1965. Currently her works can be found in many private as well as public collections, from the Museum of Modern Art in New York to the Hadone Open-Air Museum in Japan and the Wallraf-Richartz Museum in Cologne, Germany.

In the early 1950s, inspired by Pre-Columbian art as well as South American folk art, Marisol turned her attention from painting to sculpture. In 1961 she began to create life-size wooden constructions (to which plaster casts and real objects were sometimes affixed) with provocative titles such as *The Family*, *The Generals*, *The Wedding*, *The Party*, *Dinner Date*, *The Kennedys*, *The Royal Family*, *Women and Dog* and *The Dealers*. This artist's unique, mostly figurative sculpture uses diverse materials and techniques and blends highly illusionistic images with often two-dimensional surfaces such as wood (often pine or mahogany). Marisol also incorporates Plexiglas, plastic, steel, bronze and other materials alongside ready-made objects such as a car, a sofa or a rug. By her own admission, her unique interpretation of "realism" is also indebted to important American painters such as Jasper Johns and Robert Rauschenberg. In the early 1960s Marisol's unique imagery was associated with Pop Art, mostly because her subjects – like those of Andy Warhol and others – often derived from mass-media images of contemporary society, popular celebrities and everyday objects or activities such as sunbathing, bicycle riding, riding in a car and enjoying a party. Works such as *The Family* (1963; Milwaukee Art Museum) also wittily parody the middle-class concept of the family, its function and its individual members.

Marisol's singular style of sculpture also created a new direction for modern sculpture; like Warhol, she drew many of her sitters from the realms of entertainment and the mass media. Her portraits from the late 1960s include those of *Bob Hope*, *Mao Tse-tung*, *Harold Wilson*, *Generalissimo Francisco Franco*, *Hugh Hefner*, *John Wayne*, *Charles de Gaulle* and *Lyndon B. Johnson*. Members of the British royal family in her "figures of state" sculpture, for example, elicited some indignation from critics and viewers when it was exhibited at the Hanover Gallery in London in 1967. In such assemblages she forged a new modernist aesthetic for the heroic and political potential of sculpture. There is also a highly personal element in many works, since she frequently used herself as a model (her face, hands or body parts) for convenience as well as artistic reasons. For example, in *The Party*, a large work with 13 figures and two servants, all the figures derive from Marisol's own features.

In appearance, her inventive, highly original images evoke multiple associations with Gothic wooden saints, early American folk art and Surrealist imagery. In addition, her multi-figure assemblages combine autobiography with sometimes revealing commentary on gender roles and issues, notably in her group constructions of families and also her works of 1965–6 dealing almost exclusively with females and their features.

Following her travels to Asia, South America and Europe in 1968, Marisol returned to New York in 1970 and discovered a changing art scene no longer dominated by Pop Art. The artist shifted her focus from cultural icons to organic subjects such as fish, although she occasionally produced a portrait (such as a cover for *Time* magazine in 1972). In 1975 her new graphic art was on view at the Sidney Janis Gallery, with various wall pieces such as *I Have Been Here 24 Years*. At about this time she ceased using her face as part of her sculpture. Instead she produced a series of roughly carved portraits of "artists and artistes" (as she called them), older artists whom she personally respected. The resulting rather hieratic figures paid homage to *Picasso*, *Georgia O'Keeffe*, *Louise Nevelson* and *Marcel Duchamp*. Marisol also returned somewhat to the theme of the family, transformed, however, by a new use of rough carving, uncoloured wood and occasional religious allusions. In the early 1980s she explored other avenues of portraiture in images of *Mark Twain*, *Abraham Lincoln* and other important figures from American history and literature. Later in the decade she produced powerful portrait sculptures of *Bishop Desmond Tutu* and the *Emperor Hirohito with Empress Nagako*.

SUSAN P. CASTERAS

Martin, Agnes
Canadian painter, 1912–

Born in Maklin, Saskatchewan, 22 March 1912; grew up in Vancouver. Emigrated to USA, 1931; naturalised 1950. Studied at Western Washington College of Education, Bellingham, 1934–7 (teaching certificate); Teachers College, Columbia University, New York, 1941–2 (BS), 1951–2 (MA); University of New Mexico, Albuquerque, 1946–8. Painting instructor, University of New Mexico, 1947–8; Eastern Oregon College, La Grande, 1952–3. Lived in Taos, New Mexico, 1954–7; returned to New York, 1957; settled in New Mexico, 1967. Abandoned painting for seven years, 1967–74. Recipient of Alexej von Jawlensky prize, Wiesbaden, Germany, 1991; Oskar Kokoschka prize from Austrian government, 1992.

Presented work to Taos Museum, 1993. Member, American Academy and Institute of Arts and Letters, New York, 1989. Lives in New Mexico.

Selected Individual Exhibitions

Betty Parsons Gallery, New York: 1958, 1959, 1961
Robert Elkon Gallery, New York: 1962, 1963, 1965, 1966, 1970, 1972, 1974, 1976, 1978
Institute of Contemporary Art, University of Pennsylvania, Philadelphia: 1973 (touring retrospective)
Galerie Yvon Lambert, Paris: 1973, 1987
Kunstraum, Munich: 1973–4 (touring)
Museum of Fine Arts, Santa Fe: 1974, 1979, 1994
Pace Gallery, New York: 1975, 1976, 1977, 1978, 1979, 1980, 1981, 1982, 1984, 1985, 1986, 1989, 1990, 1991, 1995 (Pace Wildenstein)
Hayward Gallery, London: 1977 (touring retrospective, organised by Arts Council of Great Britain)
Wichita State University, Wichita, KS: 1980–81 (touring, organised by Pace Gallery, New York)
Waddington Galleries, London: 1986, 1990
Annemarie Verna Galerie, Zürich: 1986
Akira Ikada Gallery, Tokyo: 1989
Stedelijk Museum, Amsterdam: 1991–2 (touring retrospective)
Whitney Museum of American Art, New York: 1992–4 (touring retrospective)
Serpentine Gallery, London: 1993

Selected Writings

"On the perfection underlying life", lecture given at Institute of Contemporary Art, Philadelphia, 14 February 1972; published in Munich 1973
"Untroubled mind", ed. Ann Wilson, *Studio International*, clxxxvi, 1973, pp.63–4
We Are in the Midst of Reality Responding with Joy, Santa Fe: Museum of New Mexico, 1979 (lecture)
"Beauty is the mystery of life", *El Palacio*, xcv/1, Fall–Winter 1989 (lecture given in April 1989 at the Museum of Fine Arts, Santa Fe)
Hiljaisuus Taloni Lattialla [The silence on the floor of my house], Helsinki: Vapaa Taidekoulu, 1990 (in Finnish and English)
Writings/Schriften, ed. Dieter Schwarz, Winterthur: Kunstmuseum, 1991
La Perfection inhérente à la vie, ed. Dieter Schwarz, Paris: Ecole Nationale Supérieure des Beaux-Arts, 1993

Bibliography

Dore Ashton, "Agnes Martin", *Quadrum* 20, 1966, pp.148–9
Ann Wilson, "Linear webs", *Art and Artists*, i, October 1966, pp.46–9
Lucy R. Lippard, "The silent art", *Art in America*, lv, January–February 1967, p.61

——, "Diversity in unity: Recent geometricizing styles in America", *Art since Mid-Century*, i, ed. Jean Leymarie, Greenwich, CT: New York Graphic Society, 1971, pp.231–3

Agnes Martin, exh. cat., Institute of Contemporary Art, University of Pennsylvania, Philadelphia, 1973

Agnes Martin, exh. cat., Kunstraum, Munich, and elsewhere, 1973

Lawrence Alloway, "Formlessness breaking down form: The paintings of Agnes Martin", *Studio International*, clxxxv, 1973, pp.61–3

——, "Agnes Martin", *Artforum*, xi, April 1973, pp.32–7

Lizzie Borden, "Early work", *Artforum*, xi, April 1973, pp.39–44

Carter Ratcliff, "Agnes Martin and the 'artificial infinite'", *Art News*, lxxii, May 1973, pp.26–7

Susan Moss Galloway, "Agnes Martin: Master artist", *Womanspace Journal*, Summer 1973

Douglas Crimp, "Agnes Martin: Numero, misura, apporto", *Data*, iii, Winter 1973, p.83

John Gruen, "Agnes Martin: 'Everything, everything is about feeling ... feeling and recognition'", *Art News*, lxxv, September 1976, pp.91–4

Agnes Martin: Paintings and Drawings, 1957–1975, exh. cat., Arts Council of Great Britain, London, 1977

William Peterson, "Agnes Martin: The islands", *Artspace*, Summer 1979, pp.36–41

Kate Horsfield, "On art and artists: Agnes Martin", *Profile*, i, March 1981, pp.1–24

Dore Ashton, *American Art since 1945*, New York: Oxford University Press, 1982

Thomas McEvilley, "'Grey Geese Descending': The art of Agnes Martin", *Artforum*, xxv, Summer 1987, pp.94–9

Mark Stevens, "Thin gray line", *Vanity Fair*, March 1989, pp.50–56

Agnes Martin: Paintings and Drawings/Schilderijen en Tekeningen/Gemälde und Zeichnungen/Peintures et Dessins, 1974–1990, exh. cat., Stedelijk Museum, Amsterdam, and elsewhere, 1991

Eva Schmidt, "Agnes Martin", *Kunstforum International*, no.114, 1991, pp.316–25

Marja Bloem, "Agnes Martin: The late works", *Forum International*, no.7, March–April 1991

Agnes Martin, exh. cat., Whitney Museum of American Art, New York, and elsewhere, 1992

Holland Cotter, "Agnes Martin: All the way to heaven", *Art in America*, lxxxi, April 1993, pp.88–97, 149

Mara R. Witzling, ed., *Voicing Today's Visions: Writings by Contemporary Women Artists*, New York: Universe, 1994

Joan Simon, "Perfection is in the mind: An interview with Agnes Martin", *Art in America*, lxxxiv, May 1996, pp.82–9, 124

During the late 1950s, at a time when painting was very much involved with the gestural and representational, Agnes Martin developed an intuitive type of painting that can be characterised as "mental". The intentions behind Martin's work, which draws on resources within herself and not on outside impressions, is to develop an "awareness of a perfection, that which is forever known in the mind". She would like her work to be recognised as being in the "classic" tradition (Coptic, Egyptian, Greek, Chinese), it being not based on the observation of nature but on the representation of the Ideal in the mind ("On the perfection underlying life", 1972). Her thinking is influenced by the Chinese philosophers Chuang-tzu and Lao-tzu, who exalt an ego-less abstraction, preach detachment, humility and the need to listen to one's own mind, and the Buddhist doctrine of the wheel of life.

Martin belongs to the generation of the Abstract Expressionists to whom she feels kinship because of their shared spiritual values. They also have in common the holistic character of the composition and the idea of originality. But because she was a woman she was not taken as seriously as her male contemporaries. And although she was highly respected, she had to wait until late in life for recognition in terms of major museum exhibitions. Because of her later work, with its geometrical, repetitive structures, Martin is also compared to Minimalist artists. Although she reduces her means to attain the essence of painting, however, there is no relation to Minimalist art because her paintings are more emotional and expressionistic and are not machine-made.

Martin began to paint seriously when she was 25. Most of the early work grew from realistic, Rouault-inspired portraits and landscapes, into a kind of surrealistic painting with biomorphic or flat geometrical forms and, later, to a more abstract style. She destroyed all these works because for her they only represented stages along the way to discovering her own form and content. *Landscape-Taos* (1947; watercolour on paper; 29.9×38.6 cm.; Jonson Gallery, University of New Mexico, Albuquerque) shows a strong linearity, simple forms and strong contrast between shadow and light. *Untitled* (1955; oil on canvas; 83.8×134.6 cm.; whereabouts unknown), a surrealistic painting with linear, vaguely descriptive forms floating in a weightless, frontally conceived space, still seems to contain a horizon line. The work reminds one of Ashile Gorky. *Drift of Summer* (1957; oil on canvas; $c.160 \times 100$ cm.; private collection) is a more abstract painting in matching tones of sienna and ochre.

In her search for simplicity and the non-representational Martin became involved in systems, repetition and the suppressing of hierarchical order. Around 1960 she arrived at her characteristic form: the grid. The grid is flat, anti-nature and anti-reality, a result of aesthetic considerations, not of observation. In *Untitled* (1962; gesso, graphite and brass nails on canvas; 30.4 × 30.4 cm.; San Diego Museum of Contemporary Art, La Jolla) the horizontal and vertical lines of the grid continue to the edge of the canvas, but the point of focus is formed by the regularity of the nails. The work is very literal and does not allude to something outside itself. The eye and mind grasp at the same time the ground and the image. The image occupies the entire surface, is totally frontal and is void of a hierarchic order.

After living for about 10 years in New York – where she had moved at the request of Betty Parsons who showed her work regularly with that of other Abstract Expressionist artists, Martin left the city in 1967 and stopped painting until 1974. During this period she re-thought her work and spent time travelling and living in primitive conditions in the American Southwest. This self-imposed exile contributed to her becoming a kind of legendary figure. When she started painting again in 1974 – the only work she had produced in the interim was a series of prints in 1971 – she continued where she had left off in 1967. The format that she chose when she started painting again is similar to a work of 1967, *Grass* (acrylic, pencil, canvas; 180 × 180 cm.; Stedelijk Museum, Amsterdam), a grid on square canvas. From 1974 onwards the format is always square, on a human scale of 1.8 × 1.8 metres (although when she was in her eighties the format became smaller, 1.5 × 1.5 m.). Her works are no longer painted in oil paint, but in gesso, acrylics, Indian ink and pencil. Her grids are never absolutely square, they are rectangles, as she says: "in order to lighten the weight of the square, to destroy its power" ("Homage to the square", *Art in America*, July–August 1967, p.55).

Martin's work, although there is a preconceived plan for every painting which is jotted down with numbers, is not at all mechanical, for any irregularity in the canvas, a trembling of her hand, the pressure of pencil, brush or knife and ruler are all visible; measure and order, scale and colour, proportions and rhythms, the atmospheric oscillating between ground and lines, are important for the impact of the image, but at the same time they also express something about process, time and concentration. In order to see the work, to see the illusions of changing textures, the viewer has to come close and then increase the distance.

Martin accepts the canvas as the bounds of the image; there is indeed neither a beginning nor an end – what matters is the tension between the square canvas and the lines traced on it. The pencil lines determine where the colour is found and indicate divisions, but it is not clear if they confine the colour or merely provide an indication for the paint strokes. The lines sometimes continue right up to the edge of the canvas and sometimes end several centimetres short of the edge, thereby creating a floating effect. Through the length of the lines aspects of time and space figure in the content of the work.

The works from the 1970s on have mostly horizontal divisions – vertical lines no longer appear – and the colours are soft, with a frequent use of grey and white. The paint is invariably applied in one direction. *Untitled No.9* (1990; acrylic and graphite on canvas; Whitney Museum of American Art, New York) is built up from three different tones of grey in horizontal bands of different height. An exceptional group of works of this late period, the *Black Paintings* (Pace Gallery, New York), are canvases thickly painted in dark grey acrylic, which seem weightless.

Even though in certain periods works have been given titles that refer to nature, the paintings are not abstractions from nature. The titles, which come later through looking at the work, are not descriptions or allusions. The paintings are reflections of Martin's desire for, and of her actual experience of, the potential peace, rhythm and beauty of the universe. It is this universal quality that makes her paintings feel familiar, thereby evoking a sense of nature.

In her texts and lectures, which parallel her paintings, Martin makes her position as an artist clear by going her own way and sticking to her own concerns. She is not involved in feminist issues; her artistic language is modernistic if one assumes that geometry is a typical male vocabulary; and she feels that it is important to give the young artist advice about the morality of painting. Martin is as unambiguous about the theme of her work as she is about its form:

Art without a theme is meaningless ... I think I will say my oldest paintings are about joy. And the middle ones I did in 1974 and 1975 were about happiness and innocence ... But now [c.1990] I know what I am going to paint about and I discovered it when I was making a print. I am going to be painting a lot about praise ["Art as art", *Art International*, December 1992, p.37].

Her whole oeuvre in fact is, as she says, "a celebration of life".

MARJA BLOEM

Matthiasdóttir, Louisa
Icelandic painter and sculptor, 1917–2000

Born in Reykjavik, 1917. Studied at the College of Industrial Design, Copenhagen, 1934–7; studied under Marcel Gromaire in Paris, 1938–9. Returned to Iceland, 1939. Moved to New York, 1941, to study under Hans Hofmann, 1942–4. Married painter Leland Bell, 1943; one daughter, Temma, also a painter. Died in New York, 26 February 2000.

Selected Individual Exhibitions

Jane Street Gallery, New York: 1948
Tanager Gallery, New York: 1958
University of Connecticut, Storrs: 1960
Robert Schoelkopf Gallery, New York: 1964, 1966, 1968, 1969, 1972, 1974, 1976, 1978, 1980, 1982, 1984, 1987, 1989, 1991
Litchfield Art Center, CT: 1972
Windham College, Putney, VT: 1972
University of New Hampshire, Durham: 1978
Mount Holyoke College Art Museum, South Hadley, MA: 1982
Bryggens Museum, Norway: 1987
Meredith Long, Houston: 1988
Donald Morris Gallery, Birmingham, MI: 1988, 1994
Municipal Art Museum, Reykjavik: 1993
Salander-O'Reilly Galleries, New York: 1994

Bibliography

Martica Sawin, "Louisa Matthiasdóttir: A painter of the figure", *Arts Magazine*, November 1961, pp.26–33
Hilton Kramer, "Realists and others", *Arts Magazine*, xxxviii, January 1964, pp.18–23
Leland Bell, Louisa Matthiasdóttir, exh. cat., Austin Art Center, Trinity College, Hartford, CT, 1969
John Ashbery, "North light", *Art News*, lxx, February 1972, pp.44–5
Leland Bell, Louisa Matthiasdóttir, Temma Bell: A Family of Painters, exh. cat., Canton Art Institute, OH, 1973
Deborah Rosenthal, "Louisa Matthiasdóttir", *Arts Magazine*, l, April 1976, p.12
Ruth Gilbert Bass, *Five Realist Painters*, PhD dissertation, New York University, 1978
Gerrit Henry, "Louisa Matthiasdóttir", *Art News*, lxxvii, April 1978, p.149
Harry Rand, "Louisa Matthiasdóttir", *Arts Magazine*, lii, April 1978, p.4
Janet Hobhouse, "Independent Icelander", *Quest*, April 1979, pp.98–100
Jim Monte, "Louisa Matthiasdóttir at Schoelkopf", *Art in America*, lxviii, May 1980, p.156
Deborah Rosenthal and Jed Perl, "Louisa Matthiasdóttir", *Arts Magazine*, liv, May 1980, p.4
Louisa Matthiasdóttir, exh. cat., Robert Schoelkopf Gallery, New York, 1982
"Louisa Matthiasdóttir", *Art News*, lxxxi, January 1982, p.170
Mark Strand, ed., *Art of the Real: Nine American Figurative Painters*, New York: Potter, 1983; as *Art of the Real: Nine Figurative Painters*, London: Aurum Press, 1984
Adalsteinn Ingolfsson, "A solid and serene world", *Iceland Review 3*, xxiii, 1984, pp.18–24
Hearne Pardee, "The new American landscape", *Arts Magazine*, lviii, April 1984, pp.116–17
Deborah Rosenthal, "Louisa Matthiasdóttir at Robert Schoelkopf", *Art in America*, lxxii, November 1984, pp.164–5
Jed Perl, Deborah Rosenthal and Nicholas Fox Weber, *Louisa Matthiasdóttir: Small Paintings*, New York: Hudson Hills Press, 1986 (contains bibliography)
Jed Perl, "Art", *New Criterion*, v, March 1987, pp.60–61
Scandinavian Review, lxxv, Spring 1987, pp.61–5
Becky Brimacombe in *Arts Magazine*, lxiii, Summer 1989, p.78
G. Laderman, "In the galleries", *Art and Antiques*, vi, Summer 1989, p.37
Jed Perl, "Art", *New Criterion*, ix, November 1990, pp.66–7
John Russell, "An artist looks at other people's paintings: Art view", *New York Times*, 9 August 1992

On the surface, Louisa Matthiasdóttir's paintings are reticent and unadorned – silent landscapes inhabited only by the occasional figure, farm animal or horse and rider; empty cityscapes that have been compared to the work of both Giorgio de Chirico and Edward Hopper; sparse arrangements of still-life elements; faceless portraits and strong, unyielding self-portraits. They are also astonishingly consistent paintings. Neither the subjects nor their presentation changed much over 50 years. Where there is change, it is in the direction of ever greater simplicity and economy: fewer colours and broader brush strokes. The key to Matthiasdóttir's work lies in her decision, whether conscious or not, to confine herself to these few, apparently mundane subjects. When linked to her preferred method of working – she seldom, if ever, reworked a painting, but moved on readily to re-examine (but not repeat) the same subject on a fresh canvas – the result is a grasp of content and form that is intimate and sure. The subjects were so well known, the process so regularly rehearsed, that they became second nature. The magic is that each remaking is a new birth – spontaneous, fresh and full of wonder.

The constancy of her work was mirrored in Matthiasdóttir's life. She lived in New York, at the same address, and painted in the same studio there, from 1954. Yet there are no traces of the life of the metropolis in her work. The landscapes are rooted firmly in memories (renewed through regular visits) of Iceland, a land of such singular beauty and character as to provide inexhaustible inspiration. Sometimes they bear specific place names, like *Olafsvik* or *View from Hverfisgata*, but these are merely points of reference and most titles are spare and descriptive: *Three Sheep*, *Black Horse* or *Red Roof, Yellow House*. Over and over again the basic elements – sky, mountains, lakes and treeless meadows – are deftly arranged and rearranged in carefully overlapped planes. Painted in brilliant colours with lush brush strokes, they are simultaneously both completely unaffected renderings of the real world and skilful painterly abstractions.

In *House and Sheep* (1982) blue mountains extend into the upper corners of the picture format on either side, creating bands of intense, barely modulated colour. In the centre their contours slope down to meet gently and overlap. The inverted triangle thus formed between the two overlapping mountain masses is painted a lighter shade of blue and broken by a few brush strokes that signal white clouds. With this restrained gesture, the sky ceases to be an abstraction and becomes a completely convincing, infinitely receding space. Below, or in front of the mountains, a broad horizontal band of dark olive green is tipped by delicate yellow and reddish brush strokes. Paint becomes tangible reality as the viewer senses the sun casting a glow over the meadow through a break in the cloudy sky. Such effects of light and dark, the result of the most skilful manipulations and colour juxtaposition,

continue towards the foreground through a stretch of water, past simplified and colourful pink and green, yellow and red, windowless "Monopoly houses", over gently rolling hills and around the stolid forms of one black and two white sheep. A whole world, all at once crystal clear yet silent and mysterious, animated yet frozen, is made visible. Tensions like these, set up between the real and the painted forms, the obvious and the hidden content, give Matthiasdóttir's work its arresting power. Spread around her studio, a group of canvases produced a linked sequence, like the frames of a film. Disclaiming, however, the grandiose scale of a cinema screen, many of these panoramas compressed vast stretches of landscape into formats that are often quite small – no more than 25 or 30 centimetres in both dimensions. At other times the scale is expanded to five or six times this size. Some have wide, low, frieze-like formats, others are more regularly rectangular. Seen as a group, the shifts and manipulations of scale and format demand a constant adjustment of eye and mind, so that the viewer is prevented from settling into a complacent and repetitive mode. As the eye moves from canvas to canvas, the spaces between and beyond the paintings dissolve, and the fresh, pulsating Icelandic landscape becomes a tangible presence on a New York street.

As the landscapes are reduced in size and compressed, so the still lifes (by convention usually quiet and intimate subjects) are astonishingly and provocatively exploded in canvases of up to 1.5 or 1.8 metres wide. These still lifes were set up by Matthiasdóttir in the studio. Characteristically they contain a tabletop, wholly or partially covered by a cloth, on which are placed, at strategic intervals, vegetables and occasionally fruits – squashes of all shapes and colours, eggplants and peppers seem most favoured – and often a bottle or other glass or ceramic vessel. Separated from one another, marking out the space, the objects are so vividly painted that they appear not so much real, as *present*, in a most compelling and tangible way. Matisse's statement "Exactitude is not truth", intended to explicate his own work, equally elucidates the realism of Matthiasdóttir's paintings. Matisse eloquently pointed out that truth in painting does not "... depend on the exact copying of natural forms, nor on the patient assembling of exact details, but on the profound feeling of the artist before the objects which he has chosen, on which his attention is focused, and the spirit of which he has penetrated" (Alfred H. Barr, Jr, *Matisse: His Art and His Public*, New York, 1951, p.561).

Although she was almost exclusively recognised as a painter, Louisa Matthiasdóttir also produced some remarkable, though seldom seen sculptures. These were worked in plaster over rough metal or wire armatures and have an unfinished quality, as though created as aids to realising three-dimensional form in her paintings. The unstudied immediacy of these works – mostly heads or partial torsos, but including at least one life-size female figure – their rough surfaces enlivened by traces of the artist's shaping hands, are revelations. They reiterate in a most persistent way the complex understanding of reality that underlies all of this artist's work.

BRENDA DANILOWITZ

Mayer (de la Martinière), (Marie Françoise) Constance
French painter, 1775–1821

Born in Paris, 1775; father a customs official. Convent education in Paris. Studied under Jean-Baptiste Greuze and Joseph-Benoît Suvée, then for a brief period in 1801 under Jacques-Louis David. Became pupil of Pierre-Paul Prud'hon, 1802; collaborated with him, and shared care of his children and helped to run household after his wife's mental collapse. Given lodgings in the Louvre in recognition of achievement as an artist, 1816. Committed suicide in Paris, 26 May 1821.

Principal Exhibitions

Paris Salon: 1796, 1798–1802, 1804, 1806, 1808, 1810, 1812, 1814, 1817, 1819
Paris: 1822 (memorial, organised by Prud'hon)

Bibliography
Charles Clément, *Prud'hon: Sa vie, ses oeuvres et sa correspondance*, Paris: Didier, 1872
Charles Guellette, "Mademoiselle Constance Mayer et Prud'hon", *Gazette des Beaux-Arts*, 2nd series, xix, 1879, pp.476–90; xx, 1879, pp.337–57, 525–38
Jeanne Doin, "Constance Mayer", *Revue de l'Art Ancien et Moderne*, xxix, 1911, pp.49–60, 139–50
Edmond Pilon, *Constance Mayer (1775–1821)*, Paris: Delpleuch, 1927
Carol Duncan, "Happy mothers and other new ideas in French art", *Art Bulletin*, lv, 1973, pp.570–83
Women Artists, 1550–1950, exh. cat., Los Angeles County Museum of Art, and elsewhere, 1976
Helen Weston, "The case for Constance Mayer", *Oxford Art Journal*, iii/1, 1980, pp.14–19
La Femme artiste d'Elisabeth Vigée-Lebrun à Rosa Bonheur, exh. cat., Musée Despiau-Wlerick, Donjon Lacataye, Mont-de-Marsan, 1981

At the end of the reign of Terror, a return to family values under the bourgeois French republic brought a demand in the late 1790s for portraits and miniatures. Constance Mayer was then in her early twenties and converting a hobby of painting portraits and genre scenes into a profession. She was one of an increasing number of women artists who found new opportunities to exhibit work in the Paris Salons. She exhibited at every Salon from 1796, including miniatures of her father, large self-portraits, portraits of women and children and domestic genre scenes. These showed the influence of her first teachers, Joseph-Benoît Suvée and Jean-Baptiste Greuze, in the choice of themes and the use of soft brushwork. They represented popular sentimental subjects of young girls holding pigeons, being caught in a storm and children with portfolios of drawings. Two portraits, however, were of herself as an artist, and these indicated the interest that was developing among women artists from the studios of David, Elisabeth Vigée-Lebrun (q.v.) and Adélaïde Labille-Guiard (q.v.) to assert professional identity. The first represented a *Self-Portrait of Citizenness Mayer Pointing to a Sketch for a Portrait of Her Mother* (exh. 1796 Salon; untraced) and the second a full-length *Self-Portrait with Artist's Father: He Points to a Bust of Raphael, Inviting Her to Take This Celebrated Painter as a Model* (exh. 1801 Salon; Wadsworth Atheneum, Hartford, CT). In common with other women artists of her time, Mayer found strategies for ensuring that her work would be acceptable, by masking this public self-assertion and professional aspiration with an acceptance of parental protection and control within the image, and by submitting this work as by a pupil of Suvée and Greuze. She could thus be seen as dutiful daughter and subordinate pupil. In fact, in 1801 she worked briefly in David's studio and this may account for the new simplicity, incisiveness and the reference to Raphael and the antique to be seen in this self-portrait. On the other hand, David's women pupils were often expected to emphasise their dependence on the master by including in their self-portraits copies after David's works which they were seen to be copying. By avoiding this configuration of the master-pupil relationship and by placing herself standing with her own portfolio of works, Mayer expressed a sense of ambition and separateness as an artistic identity.

Although she attempted allegorical subjects after this date, which would come into the category of history painting, these still bore the imprint of Greuze's sentimentalism. In 1802 she became a pupil of Prud'hon, and this quickly developed into friendship and mutual devotion, as Mayer took on the roles of housekeeper and child-minder, following Mme Prud'hon's mental breakdown and transfer to a nursing home in 1803. From this point Mayer and Prud'hon worked collaboratively, Prud'hon producing the early drawings and sketches and Mayer working them up into paintings with his assistance. A case in point is *Innocence Preferring Love to Wealth* (exh. 1804 Salon; Hermitage, St Petersburg), finally exhibited under her name. *Innocence Drawn by Love and Followed by Regret* (exh. 1810 Salon; private collection), for which Prud'hon had done studies in Rome in the 1780s, was a reprise of a Greuzian subject, begun by Mayer but finished by Prud'hon and catalogued under his name. This collaborative process has led to many confusions. The *Sleep of Venus and Cupid, Disturbed by Zephyrs* (Wallace Collection, London), for example, was commissioned from Mayer by Empress Josephine and exhibited under Mayer's name in the Salon of 1806. With its pendant it was sold as a Mayer for a modest sum but later attributed to Prud'hon and sold for a grossly inflated price. Catalogued by the Goncourts as a Prud'hon and displayed in the Wallace Collection until 1911 as a Prud'hon, this work has suffered the fate of many at the hands of dealers and misogynist historians, and Mayer's reputation with it.

During her lifetime Mayer's Salon submissions of genre scenes and mythologies incurred the familiar scorn of critics who saw them as a violation of nature and of "all the laws of modesty (*pudeur*)". She and her female colleagues were advised to limit themselves to flower painting and family portraits. What many of them in fact took up was the subject of motherhood, which had been popularised by the *philosophes* of the 18th century and by politicians of the Revolution. In the early 19th century there was continuing interest in painting the joys of breast

feeding, observing the child's first steps, the importance of inoculations and the grief at the loss of a child. Mayer produced the *Happy Mother* (exh. 1810 Salon) and the *Unfortunate Mother* (exh. 1812 Salon; both Louvre, Paris), the latter in the tradition of personifications of Melancholia and sepulchral gloom that women artists, in particular, had produced in the wake of the revolutionary and Napoleonic wars. The *Unfortunate Mother* shows a solitary, luminous figure in a mysterious moonlit landscape, of a type that had gained currency in the work of Girodet-Trioson, Gros and Prud'hon.

Mayer continued to paint portraits, mostly of her circle of female artists and friends (*Mme Voïart*, exh. 1814 Salon; Musée des Beaux-Arts, Nancy), in a style that was softer and less dramatic than Prud'hon's, but she persisted with more ambitious genre and allegorical works despite adverse critical comment, focusing on subjects of poverty and wretchedness, such as the *Unfortunate Family* (begun 1821; private collection) and *Dream of Happiness* (exh. 1819 Salon; Louvre). These lugubrious subjects are again close to those of Greuze, but have nothing of the melodramatic appeal and theatricality of his works, nor the overt moralising nature. The *Unfortunate Family* does not preach filial duty in a rustic family, and the happiness in the *Dream of Happiness* is not that of the village bride. The mood is sinister and the happiness threatened. Mayer's work has a seriousness, an inwardness, that locate it firmly within the early Romantic tradition of the 19th century. She was becoming increasingly melancholic herself even though she had gained a reputation as an artist and had been given lodgings in the Louvre in 1816. Unhappy with her personal life, and the more so when Prud'hon refused to remarry in the event of his wife's death, Mayer committed suicide, using his razor to cut her throat, in 1821. The following year Prud'hon organised an exhibition of her works in tribute to her talent.

HELEN WESTON

Merian, Maria Sibylla
German painter, 1647–1717

Born in Frankfurt am Main, 2 April 1647, youngest daughter of the draughtsman, printmaker and publisher Matthäus Merian the Elder (d. 1650). Taught the art of flower painting by her stepfather, the still-life painter Jacob Marell, and his assistants Johann Andreas Graff and Abraham Mignon. Married Graff, 16 May 1665; two daughters, Johanna Helena, baptised in Frankfurt, 5 May 1668, and Dorothea Maria, baptised in Nuremberg, 2 February 1678. Moved to Nuremberg, 1670; taught the art of flower painting to unmarried women. Returned to Frankfurt, 1682. Separated from husband in 1685; with her daughters and mother joined half-brother Caspar Merian in the Labadist community of Den Bosch castle in Wieuwerd, West Friesland, Netherlands, 1685–6. Settled in Amsterdam with her daughters, 1691; lived by selling natural history paintings, colouring copies of the caterpillar book and providing illustrations for books, including Agnes Block's *Groot Konst Boek* and Georg Everhard Rumpf's *D'Amboinsche Rariteitkamer*, Amsterdam, 1705. Sailed with Dorothea Maria to Dutch colony of Surinam, South America, where they studied the metamorphoses of tropical insects on their fodder plants, June 1699–September 1701. Died in Amsterdam, 13 January 1717.

Selected Writings

Neues Blumenbuch, 3 vols, Nuremberg, 1675–80; facsimile edition with text by Helmut Deckert, Leipzig, 1966

Der Raupen wunderbare Verwandelung und sonderbare Blumennahrung, 3 vols, 1679–1717; part facsimile edition with text by Armin Geus, Dortmund, 1982

Metamorphosis insectorum surinamensium, Amsterdam: G. Valk, 1705; facsimile editions, Leipzig, 1975 (commentary by Helmut Deckert); 2 vols, London: Pion, 1980–82 (commentary by Elisabeth Rücker); Frankfurt am Main: Insel, 1991

Erucarum ortus: Alimentum et paradoxa metamorphosis ..., Amsterdam, 1718

Butterflies, Beetles and Other Insects: The Leningrad Book of Notes and Studies, ed. Wolf-Dietrich Beer and others, New York: McGraw Hill, 1976 (German original)

Bibliography

Joachim von Sandrart, *L'Academia todesca della architectura, scultura e pittura: Oder Teutsche Academie der edlen Bau-, Bild- und Mahlerey-künste*, Nuremberg, i, 1675, p.339; ii, 1679, p.85; ed. A.R. Peltzer, Munich, 1925; reprinted Farnborough: Gregg, 1971

Arnold Houbraken, *De groote Schouburgh der Nederlantsche Konstschilders en Schilderessen*, iii, Amsterdam, 1721, pp.173–6

Johann Gabriel Doppelmayr, *Historische Nachricht von den Nürnbergischen Mathematicis und Künstlern*, Nuremberg, 1730, pp.255, 268–70

Heinrich Sebastian Hüsgen, *Artistisches Magazin*, Frankfurt am Main, 1790, pp.263–73

Friedrich Carl Gottlob Hirsching, *Historisch-Literarisches Handbuch berühmter und denkwürdiger Personen*, v, Leipzig, 1800–01, pp.271–8

Philipp Friedrich Gwinner, *Kunst und Künstler in Frankfurt am Main*, Frankfurt am Main, 1862, pp.168–74

Max Adolf Pfeiffer, "Das neue Blumenbuch der M.S. Merian", *Philiobiblon*, ix, 1936, pp.97–102

Jantje Stuldreher-Nienhuis, *Verborgen Paradijzen: Het leven en de werken van Maria Sibylla Merian, 1647–1717*, Arnhem, 1944; 2nd edition, 1945; abridged edition, Arnhem and Amsterdam, 1952

Margarete Pfister-Burkhalter, "Florum Fasciculi Tres", *Stultifera Navis*, iv, 1947, pp.114–25

"A Surinam portfolio", *Natural History*, lxxi/10, 1962, pp.30–41

Maria Sibylla Merian, 1647–1717, exh. cat., Germanisches Nationalmuseum, Nuremberg, 1967

Ernst Ullmann and others, eds, *Maria Sibylla Merian: Leningrad Watercolors*, 2 vols, New York: Harcourt Brace, 1974 (German original)

William T. Stearn, ed., *The Wondrous Transformation of Caterpillars: Fifty Engravings Selected from Erucarum Ortus*, London: Scolar Press, 1978

A. Tatiana Lukina, *Maria Sibylla Merian, 1647–1717*, Leningrad: Nauka, 1980

Margarete Pfister-Burkhalter, *Maria Sibylla Merian: Leben und Werk, 1647–1717*, Basel: GS Verlag, 1980

Maria Sibylla Merian (1647–1717), exh. cat., Rosenborg Slot, Copenhagen, 1983

Ingrid Guentherodt, "Maria Cunitz und Maria Sibylla Merian: Pionierinnen der deutschen Wissenschaftssprache im 17. Jahrhundert", *Zeitschrift für Germanistische Linguistik*, xiv/1, 1986, pp.23–49

Charlotte Kerner, *Seidenraupe, Dschungelblüte: Die Lebensgeschichte der Maria Sibylla Merian*, Basel: Weinheim, 1988

Flowers, Butterflies and Insects, New York: Dover, and London: Constable, 1991

Natalie Zemon Davis, *Women on the Margins: Three Seventeenth-Century Lives*, Cambridge, MA: Harvard University Press, 1995

Heidrun Ludwig, "Von der Betrachtung zur Beobachtung: Die künstlerische Entwicklung der Blumen- und Insektenmalerin M.S. Merian in Nürnberg (1670–1682)", *Der Franken Rom*, ed. John Roger Paas, Wiesbaden, 1995, pp.95–113

The importance of Maria Sibylla Merian is based on a specific, perhaps feminine synthesis of natural history and art, of an observant and at the same time contemplative view of nature. During her years in Amsterdam and in the course of the 18th century,

Merian's accomplishments were seen mainly as contributing to the field of entomology. In the 19th and early 20th centuries her discoveries no longer attracted attention, and the interest in her shifted from science to art. The image of a harmless and gentle flower painter, absorbed in the meditation of butterflies and flowers, concealed her merits as a natural historian. More recently, historians, natural scientists and linguists have tried to see Merian in her historical context and have rediscovered her achievements in the field of natural history as well as in the history of art of the second half of the 17th century.

As a member of a family of artists, Merian had access to a workshop where she received basic training as a painter – although as a woman she was severely restricted in her education by guild regulations. Joachim von Sandrart mentioned oil paintings by Merian but none has as yet come to light. Since only licensed painters were allowed to paint in oil, it is probable that Merian was restricted to body- and watercolour painting, a technique that was then regarded as appropriate for amateur painters and for women who were not able to receive an official training. Like her stepfather, Jacob Marell, Merian specialised in still lifes. That she was also an expert in the textile arts, in painted and embroidered fabrics with designs of flowers and the metamorphoses of insects, sheds light on her early work. In the manner of embroiderers she composed her pictures by adding and arranging motifs that she had copied from engravings or drawn from life; as a result, motifs are often repeated in her early works. The close affinity that Merian saw between painting and embroidery is expressed in her first publication, the *Neues Blumenbuch*, a pattern book containing 36 engravings of flowers.

Merian painted pictures of flowers and fruits, enlivening them with butterflies and insects, as was customary in Dutch and German still-life painting. In Nuremberg she started to develop the art of natural history painting. It now seemed insufficient merely to copy natural objects and to place them into artificially composed art works. Like the Dutch still-life painter Otto Marseus van Schrieck, she started to breed her models. With the assistance of her husband Johann Andreas Graff she collected native insects, fed them and observed their metamorphoses. In 1679 she published some of her observations in the first part of the caterpillar book, *Der Raupen wunderbare Verwandelung und sonde-*

bare Blumennahrung, which contains 50 plates with descriptions. The phenomena of metamorphosis had already been discovered and explored, but Merian's book for the first time showed the metamorphoses on those plants from which caterpillars drew their nourishment. By depicting plants and insects, Merian was able to combine her experience as a flower painter with her interest in natural history. Her approach to the observation of nature was not limited to the single phenomenon or to dried specimens. Instead, she tried to understand the overall correlation of living nature and its relation to God.

Scholars received Merian's caterpillar book and her insect and flower paintings favourably. Although the extraordinary beauty and the careful rendering of nature in her works attracted admiration, they were far from causing a sensation. Merian's international reputation as a learned woman and as a natural historian was founded largely on her expedition to Surinam, a Dutch colony in South America. Many European collectors owned dried specimens from Surinam, but the fauna and flora of this tropical country were barely explored. Merian and her younger daughter Dorothea Maria took the risk of the voyage and used the opportunity to observe the beautiful exotic insects and their fodder plants. Furthermore, they studied the customs of the native people, and tried to improve their conditions by looking at their plants and finding an economic use for them. After two years Merian, who suffered from malaria, had to return to Amsterdam. There she started to work on a book about the metamorphoses of the Surinam insects. Investing large amounts of money in the publication, she employed professional engravers for the large-sized plates done after her paintings. She wrote the descriptions herself, but the director of the Amsterdam botanical garden, Caspar Commelin, determined the species of the plants. The appearance of the *Metamorphosis insectorum surinamensium* in 1705 caused a sensation. The beautiful, life-size plates showed the exotic insects in previously unpublished states and in their natural surroundings. The 62 plates and the careful descriptions kindled the imagination of natural history collectors, who knew the species only from dried specimens.

As an artist and as a natural historian, Merian devoted her art and experience to an aim that she shared with many artists and scientists of the time. She believed that natural phenomena could only be understood with regard to God. While she observed nature, admired its beauty and was astonished by its wonders, she always set her observations in relation to men and to God. She shared the Protestant view of her time that God had created the beauties of nature not only for its reproduction, but also for humankind, in order to make men respect and praise him. From this point of view Merian's paintings might be considered Protestant adoration pictures.

Early flower pieces by Merian are kept in the Kupferstichkabinett, Staatliche Preussischer Kulturbesitz, Berlin, and in Rosenborg Castle, Copenhagen. The Academy of Sciences in St Petersburg possesses Merian's entomological study book, as well as a large collection of her flower paintings. There are insect pieces by her and by her daughter Johanna Helena Graff in the British Museum, London. Paintings from Surinam that relate to the published book can be found in the British Museum and in the Royal Collection, Windsor Castle. The Fitzwilliam Museum, Cambridge, the Städelsches Kunstinstitut, Frankfurt am Main, and the Albertina, Vienna, own smaller collections of her gouaches.

HEIDRUN LUDWIG

Messager, Annette

French artist, 1943–

Born in Berck-sur-Mer, 30 November 1943. Studied at the Ecole Nationale Supérieure des Arts Décoratifs, Paris, 1962–6. Recipient of first prize, Kodak Photography International, 1964; Grand Prix, Ville de Paris, and Grand Prix des Arts Plastiques, 1994. Teaches at Ecole Nationale des Beaux-Arts, Paris. Lives in Paris.

Selected Individual Exhibitions

Musée de Peinture et de Sculpture, Grenoble: 1973, 1989–90 (touring retrospective)
Musée d'Art Moderne de la Ville de Paris: 1974, 1984 , 1995
Rheinisches Landesmuseum, Bonn: 1976, 1978
Holly Solomon Gallery, New York: 1978
Galerie Gillespie-Laage Salomon, Paris: 1979, 1985
Fine Arts Gallery, University of California, Berkeley: 1981
PS 1, Long Island City, NY: 1981
Artists' Space, New York: 1981

Musée des Beaux-Arts, Calais: 1983
Riverside Studios, London: 1985
Artspace Visual Arts Centre, Surrey Hills, Australia: 1986
Vancouver Art Gallery, Vancouver: 1987, 1991
Centre d'Art Contemporain, Dijon: 1988
Galerie Crousel-Robelin Bama, Paris: 1990
Mercer Union, Toronto: 1991 (*Making Up Stories/Faire des histoires*, touring)
Arnolfini, Bristol: 1992 (*Telling Tales*, touring)
Josh Baer Gallery, New York: 1992, 1993
Monika Sprüth Galerie, Cologne: 1992, 1994
Foksal Gallery, Warsaw: 1995
Los Angeles County Museum of Art: 1995 (touring)

Bibliography

Barbara Radice, "Annette Messager", *Flash Art*, June 1974 (interview)
Annette Messager: Chimères, 1982–1983, exh. cat., Musée des Beaux-Arts, Calais, 1983
Annette Messager: Les Pièges à chimères, exh. cat., Musée d'Art Moderne de la Ville de Paris, 1984
Annette Messager: Comédie, Tragédie, 1971–1989, exh. cat., Musée de Peinture et de Sculpture, Grenoble, and elsewhere, 1989
Mona Thomas, "Les ficelles d'Annette", *Beaux Arts Magazine*, no.74, 1989, pp.58–63
Lynn Gumpert, "Annette Messager: Comédie, tragédie", *Galeries Magazine*, no.35, 1990, pp.86–9
Annelie Pohlen, "The utopian adventures of Annette Messager", *Artforum*, xxix, September 1990, pp.111–16
Mo Gourmelon, "Arbitrated dissections: The art of Annette Messager", *Arts Magazine*, lxv, November 1990, pp.66–71
Gianni Romano, "Talk dirt: Interview with Annette Messager", *Flash Art*, no.159, 1991, p.102
Eric Troncy, "Annette Messager", *ibid.*, pp.103–5
Annette Messager: Telling Tales, exh. cat., Arnolfini, Bristol, and elsewhere, 1992
Annette Messager, exh. cat., Los Angeles County Museum of Art and elsewhere, 1995
Penelope Rowlands, "Art that annoys", *Art News*, xciv, October 1995, pp.132–5

Self-confessed collector, artist, handy-woman, trickster and peddler, Annette Messager has emerged as the chameleon of French contemporary art over the past 20 years. When in 1989 the newspaper *Le Monde* declared her a "sensational new discovery", Messager had been exhibiting nationally and internationally for more than 15 years. Her oeuvre reflects a compelling, sometimes morbid, fascination with the fragmented or absent body and a rejection of painting and sculpture in favour of "bricolage". Due to the resurgence of interest in artists concerned with the body (such as Kiki Smith, Robert Gober and Geneviève Cadieux) in the 1990s, Messager's work has been identified as a significant contribution to recent debates on the body as the site of struggle over identity, gender and race.

Messager studied traditional fine art in Paris during the turbulent years of the late 1960s, a period of intense reconsideration of political, social and cultural beliefs, epitomised in the work of French post-modern thinkers such as Lyotard and Foucault and feminist philosophers such as Hélène Cixous, Julia Kristeva and Luce Irigaray. It was this social and political climate that formed the critical context for Messager's developing creative imagination.

Rejecting traditional high art values, Messager first became an avid collector. During the 1970s she produced a plethora of albums, sketchbooks and boxes, designed to be hand-held for intimate viewing. In these works she combined the media of painting, drawing and photography with those skills traditionally ascribed to a so-called feminine sensibility – needlework, knitting and collage. *My Collection of Proverbs* (1974; private collection, repr. Grenoble 1989, pp.26–7), for example, comprises a set of tissues embroidered with homilies. While North American and British women artists such as Miriam Schapiro (q.v.) and Joyce Kozloff (q.v.) were criticised for essentialising "women's art", in France Messager was also reproached for reinforcing the notion of women's art as merely "decorative". It is possible, however, to read her collections as intentionally deconstructive in their dissection and examination of established visual languages and codes.

In more than 56 albums comprising two years' work, Messager sought to document, categorise and display the everyday. What emerges is a fascination with 19th-century methods of taxonomy and the study of physiognomical features, seen in the collection of 86 photographs, *Voluntary Tortures* (1972; Fonds Régional d'Art Contemporain de Rhône-Alpes, Dijon). Here, by isolating images of masochistic beauty treatments through which women seek to transform their bodies into the socially acceptable ideal, Messager refuses to supply a celebratory, positive image of female power. Rather she confronts the viewer with meanings that oscillate between the grotesque and the beautiful, between death and desire, and she sets in motion an unnerving and equivocal voyeurism that is found throughout her career. This work also marks her subversion of the sign of the female body as the cipher of desire epitomised in Surrealist works (see René Magritte's *L'Evidence éternelle*, 1930; Menil collection, Houston).

During the 1970s Messager expanded and developed this "taxidermy of desire". In *Happiness Illustrated* (1975–6; Musée Departmental d'Art Contemporain de Rochechouart) she drew together miniature paintings and drawings based on the clichéd images in tourist brochures; in *My Clichés* (1976–7, private collection, *ibid.*, p.59) she used reproductions of film stills to explore further the spaces between fiction and reality into which viewers project their own fantasies.

Photography, historically bound to criminal anthropology, became for Messager the primary medium through which to immobilise and isolate the objects of her fascination. Her *Chimèras* (1982–4; Fonds National d'Art Contemporain, Paris), for example, were shaped from torn photographs of enlarged body parts into monstrous shapes – spiders, knives and dragons – and then mounted on to canvas. The colouring of these motifs served to heighten their haunting quality, rendering them bewitching shadows of the everyday. Messager developed this iconography in *Mounted Piece* (1986). The screaming mouth of *Mounted Piece*, from which fragmented limbs descend, draws strongly on Charcot's study (and construction) of female hysteria at the Salpêtrière hospital in the late 1880s, which had a profound effect on Messager's artistic sensibility.

What emerges in Messager's practice during the mid- to late 1980s is a funereal mood epitomised in *My Little Effigies* (1988; Musée National d'Art Moderne, Centre Georges Pompidou, Paris). Strongly influenced by the custom of pilgrimage offerings, Messager pinned cuddly toys to the wall of the gallery, hanging pictures of bodily parts around their necks. Not only do these objects seem like ex-voto offerings, they also take on the violent associations of trophies. They recall the unnerving impact of the *Sleep of the Boarders* (1971–2; Musée National d'Art Moderne), in which Messager displayed a collection of dead sparrows in baby clothes. These haunting and repulsive configurations reflect Messager's continuing fascination with childhood fears and taboos, but also mark the expansion of her work into the gallery space in the form of installation, relating to the work of Mike Kelly.

Histories of Dresses (1991; Fond Regional d'Art Contemporain de Languedoc-Roussillon) were composed of a series of glass coffins in which the remnants of a life – clothes pinned with charms and tokens – narrate the absence of their female owners. They are testimonies to the rites of passage for women in society and expose the hollowness of exterior appendages and adornments. In particular they relate to the narrative process of Messager's contemporary Sophie Calle and to the Catholicism of Messager's earlier veneration pieces. Messager's feminist consciousness can be seen to develop further in *My Wishes* (1988–91; Fonds Regional d'Art Contemporain de Corse), in which the body is reconstituted into a cluster of images hung from the ceiling. As tongue is juxtaposed with belly button and female mouths with male hands, this body is rendered non-hierarchical and disintegrates. The polished, complete female body of consumer culture is smashed by this work into tiny pieces and the objectification of the female body is destroyed through the denial of the mastery of the viewer's gaze.

The idea that began with the glimpse of private albums and developed through the fragmented forms of the body and the disturbing juxtapositions of cuddly toys and dead birds culminates in an exploration of the relationship between fetish object and voyeur. "I still find myself working on the same idea of hiding while showing, stimulating curiosity, suggesting that what lies underneath is more important than what you actually see", Messager says. "In this way, there is always the idea of secrecy even if it is a false secrecy because it ends up being put on exhibition" (Romano 1991).

CLAIRE DOHERTY

Miller, Lee

American photographer, 1907–1977

Born in Poughkeepsie, New York, 23 April 1907. Travelled to Europe on a school trip, staying on alone in Paris to study art, 1925; forced home by her father, and enrolled in Art Students League, New York, 1926. Pursued a successful career as a fashion model in New York, 1927–9. Worked with the photographer Man Ray in Paris, and associated with the Surrealists, 1929–32. Opened own studio in New York, 1932. Married Egyptian businessman Aziz Eloui Bey, 1934; lived in Egypt until separation in 1937; divorced 1947. Returned to Paris, 1937; travelled extensively with old Surrealist friends and met painter and art critic Roland Penrose. Settled in London with Penrose and began work as staff photographer for *Vogue*, 1940; war correspondent for US Armed Forces during World War II. Married Penrose, 1947; son born later that year. Moved to Farley Farm, Sussex, 1949. Died there of cancer, 27 July 1977.

Principal Exhibitions

Galerie de la Pléiade, Paris: 1931 (*Groupe annuel des photographes*)
Julien Levy Gallery, New York: 1932 (*Modern European Photography*), 1933 (individual)
Museum of Modern Art, New York: 1955 (*The Family of Man*, touring)

Selected Writings

Grim Glory: Pictures of Britain under Fire, ed. Ernestine Carter, London: Lund Humphries, 1941
Wrens in Camera, London: Hollis and Carter, 1945
Lee Miller's War: Photographer and Correspondent with the Allies in Europe, 1944–45, ed. Antony Penrose, Boston: Little Brown, and London: Condé Nast, 1992

Bibliography

Mario Amaya, "My Man Ray: An interview with Lee Miller Penrose", *Art in America*, lxiii, May–June 1975, pp.54–61
Roland Penrose, *Scrap Book, 1900–1981*, London: Thames and Hudson, and New York: Rizzoli, 1981
Atelier Man Ray, Berenice Abbott, Jacques-André Boiffard, Bill Brandt, Lee Miller, 1920–1935, exh. cat., Centre Georges Pompidou, Paris, 1982
L'Amour Fou: Photography and Surrealism, exh. cat., Corcoran Gallery of Art, Washington, DC, and elsewhere, 1985
Whitney Chadwick, *Women Artists and the Surrealist Movement*, Boston: Little Brown, and London: Thames and Hudson, 1985
Antony Penrose, ed., *The Lives of Lee Miller*, London: Thames and Hudson, and New York: Holt Rinehart, 1985
La Femme et le surréalisme, exh. cat., Musée Cantonal des Beaux-Arts, Lausanne, 1987
Jane Livingston, *Lee Miller: Photographer*, London and New York: Thames and Hudson, 1989
Renée Riese Hubert, *Magnifying Mirrors: Women, Surrealism and Partnership*, Lincoln: University of Nebraska Press, 1994
Val Williams, *Warworks: Women, Photography and the Iconography of War*, London: Virago, 1994

Unpublished material, prints and negatives are in the Lee Miller Archive, Chiddingly, Sussex.

To examine Lee Miller's photography is to examine Lee Miller's history, because her biography is bound to the striking images that divulge her talent and the tales of her varied life as a model, a muse, a Surrealist, a fashion photographer and a photojournalist.

Miller's artistic career is often described through photographs of her rather than by her, perhaps because she took up photography while modelling. After leaving her home town of Poughkeepsie, she lived in New York and attended the Art Students League, studying theatrical design and lighting. In 1927 she was befriended by the magazine publishing magnate Condé Nast, who offered her modelling work; soon, Miller had a successful career as a high fashion model. Photographers such as Edward Steichen, Arnold Genthe and Horst P. Horst frequently photographed Miller, and her image was often featured in *Vogue*.

Miller's first work as a photographer came in 1929 when a *Vogue* designer sent her to Europe to make detailed drawings of Renaissance ornamentation. Rather than drawing them, Miller experimented with capturing the details on film. Her photographic interest came not only from modelling, but also from her father, Theodore Miller, an avid amateur photographer. Her past experiences, as well as her exposure to European art and culture, motivated Miller to pursue a career as a professional photographer. Armed with a letter of introduction from Edward Steichen and determined to learn photography, Miller made her way to the Paris studio of Man Ray, the American Surrealist.

Miller worked with Man Ray and the Surrealist circle from 1929 to 1932. Ultimately, she became Man Ray's student, model, muse, lover and collaborator. Since Surrealist photography often employed depictions of the female body, Miller appears frequently in the canon of Surrealist art, as in Man Ray's *Neck* (1929; Lee Miller Archives, Sussex). This photograph shows only the smooth curves of Miller's neck and cheek, demonstrating the Surrealists' fetishistic visual representation of the female body. Although she submitted her body to Man Ray's dissecting camera lens, Miller appears to have been the first woman to enter the Surrealist circle with the aim of receiving an aesthetic education and producing her own art. Although the visual language of Surrealism informs her photography, Miller developed her own distinctive style. Using simple techniques of "straight" photography (photographically unaltered negatives and prints that are not subjected to double exposure or montage), such as camera angle and lens framing capacity, Miller achieved the Surrealist idea of "convulsive beauty" (André Breton's notion that a shocking sense of beauty is inherent in the accidental or decontextualised). Her photograph *Exploding Hand* (1930; Lee Miller Archives) uses these techniques to create an image that looks like a woman's hand smashing through a glass door. In *Untitled (Hand Reaching for Umbrella Fringe)* (1929; Art Institute of Chicago) Miller makes a simple subject haunting with her use of framing, angle and light. Miller's collaboration with Man Ray led to her accidental discovery of "solarisation" (the practice of exposing negatives to sharp bursts of light to achieve heightened contrast between subject and background). Man Ray later refined this darkroom process to use as his own signature technique. Miller continued to implement solarisation as well in such images as *Dorothy Hill, Solarized Portrait* (1933; Lee Miller Archives). In this extreme close-up, the solarisation creates a distinct, almost glowing boundary between the subject's translucent skin and the dark background.

Miller severed her romantic ties with Man Ray and returned to New York in 1932. Here she opened her own studio with her younger brother, Erik, as assistant. From 1932 to 1934 she maintained her studio with fashion, advertising and portrait shoots. *Scent Bottles* (1933; Lee Miller Archives), which shows a row of perfume bottles perfectly doubled by their mirrored reflection, exemplifies Miller's ability to enhance ordinary subject matter with her unique vision. Her most creative work appears in her portrait photography of clientèle consisting mostly of New York actors, artists and socialites. The portrait of *Joseph Cornell* (1933; Lee Miller Archives) typifies her interesting style of portraiture, depicting the artist's profile emerging from one of his whimsical, three-dimensional creations.

Miller left New York and her studio on her marriage to Aziz Eloui Bey in 1934. After moving to Egypt, she ceased photographing until 1936, when she began shooting desert landscapes. *Portrait of Space, Near Siwa* (1937; Lee Miller Archives) shows a very deep dimensional view of the desert plains through a ripped screen. This photograph of the open desert paradoxically creates a sense of claustrophobia, perhaps representing Miller's own feelings about Egypt. Unhappy and bored by her life as a businessman's wife, she separated from her husband in 1937 to rejoin her Surrealist friends in Europe. Her photography from this period consists mostly of snapshots of her travelling companions, as in *Picnic* (1937; Lee Miller Archives), which portrays Paul and Nusch Eluard, Man Ray and his lover Ady, and Roland Penrose (whom Miller would later marry) lounging decadently at a picnic in Mougins, France.

Miller's return to professional photography came with the outbreak of World War II. In 1940 she settled in London with Roland Penrose. As a staff photographer for British *Vogue*, she initially carried out routine fashion assignments. On her own, Miller began shooting the devastating effects of the blitz on London. These photographs became part of a book project entitled *Grim Glory: Pictures of Britain under Fire*, which Miller co-produced with American journalists Ernestine Carter and Edward R. Murrow. Her photographs disturb powerfully and beautifully. In *Revenge on Culture* (1940), for instance, Miller photographed the image of a fallen, Venus-like statue whose broken, upper torso is obscured by debris and seemingly dismembered by a fallen power line that brutally marks the statue's marble skin. Eventually *Vogue* began publishing Miller's war coverage in addition to her fashion photography. In 1942 her accreditation as an official US Forces War Correspondent enabled her to pursue photo-journalism actively.

Miller landed in France shortly after D-Day in 1944. Following the Allied advance until the American forces connected with the Russians, she was the only woman photographer on this front. Her written texts and photographs documenting such events as the siege of St Malo, the liberation of Paris and the concentration camps were published in both American and British *Vogue*. Miller's coverage of the concentration camps especially reflects her keen Surrealist eye. *Murdered Prison Guard, Dachau* (1945; Lee Miller Archives) shows a dead SS guard clearly visible in his rippled, sun-dappled watery grave. The photograph simultaneously horrifies and tantalises the viewer.

Miller essentially gave up professional photography after marrying Roland Penrose and giving birth to her son Antony in 1947. After Miller's death, her son and husband found thousands of negatives and prints that she had packed away from her brief photographic career. As a result, Lee Miller's family established an archive to house and collect her photography, enabling a rediscovery of her work and her talent.

JEANA K. FOLEY

Mitchell, Joan
American painter, 1926–1992

Born in Chicago, Illinois, February 1926. Studied at Smith College, Northampton, Massachusetts, 1942–4; Art Institute of Chicago, 1944–7 (BFA) and 1950 (MFA); Columbia University, New York, 1950. Lived in France on Edward L. Ryerson fellowship, 1948–9. Married publisher Barney Rosset, 1950; divorced 1952. Returned to New York, 1950; established studio at St Mark's Place; invited by members of Artists' Club and by dealer Leo Castelli to exhibit in *Ninth Street Show*, 1951. Met Canadian painter Jean-Paul Riopelle in Paris, 1955; lived with him until 1979. Settled in Paris, 1959; moved to Vétheuil, 1968. Recipient of Premio Lissone, Milan, 1961; Brandeis University Creative Arts medal, 1973; Grand Prix National de Peinture, French Ministry of Culture, 1989; Grand Prix des Arts (Peinture) of the city of Paris, 1991; honorary doctorates from Miami University, Oxford, Ohio, 1971; School of the Art Institute of Chicago, 1987; Rhode Island School of Design, Providence, 1992. Member, American Institute of Arts and Letters. Died in Paris, 30 October 1992.

Selected Individual Exhibitions
Saint Paul Gallery, St Paul, MN: 1950
New Gallery, New York: 1952
Stable Gallery, New York: 1953, 1954, 1955, 1957, 1958, 1961, 1965
Southern Illinois University, Carbondale: 1961
New Gallery, Massachusetts Institute of Technology, Cambridge: 1962
Galerie Jean Fournier, Paris: 1967, 1969, 1971, 1978, 1980, 1984, 1987, 1990, 1992
Martha Jackson Gallery, New York: 1968, 1971, 1972
Everson Museum of Art, Syracuse, NY: 1972
Arts Club of Chicago: 1974
Whitney Museum of American Art, New York: 1974 (retrospective), 1992

Xavier Fourcade Inc., New York: 1976, 1977, 1980, 1981, 1983, 1985, 1986
Musée d'Art Moderne de la Ville de Paris: 1982
Herbert F. Johnson Museum of Art, Cornell University, Ithaca, NY: 1988–9 (touring retrospective)
Robert Miller Gallery, New York: 1989, 1991, 1993, 1994
Musée des Beaux-Arts, Nantes, and Galerie Nationale du Jeu de Paume, Paris: 1994 (retrospective)

Bibliography

Irving Sandler, "Mitchell paints a picture", *Art News*, lvi, October 1957, pp.44–7, 69–70
"My Five Years in the Country": An Exhibition of Forty-Nine Paintings by Joan Mitchell, exh. cat., Everson Museum of Art, Syracuse, NY, 1972
James Harithas, "Weather paint", *Art News*, lxxi, May 1972, pp.40–43, 63
Joan Mitchell, exh. cat., Whitney Museum of American Art, New York, 1974
Cindy Nemser, "An afternoon with Joan Mitchell", *Feminist Art Journal*, Spring 1974, pp.5–6, 24
Lucy R. Lippard, *From the Center: Feminist Essays on Women's Art*, New York: Dutton, 1976
Eleanor Munro, *Originals: American Women Artists*, New York: Simon and Schuster, 1979
Barbara Rose, ed., *Bedford Series: A Group of Ten Color Lithographs*, Bedford, NY: Tyler Graphics, 1981
Joan Mitchell: Choix de peintures, 1970–1982, exh. cat., Musée d'Art Moderne de la Ville de Paris, 1982
Charlotte Streifer Rubinstein, *American Women Artists from Early Times to the Present*, Boston: Hall, 1982
Linda Nochlin, "Joan Mitchell: Art and life at Vétheuil", *House and Garden* (USA), clvi, November 1984
Stephen Westfall, "Then and now: Six of the New York School look back", *Art in America,* lxxiii, June 1985, pp.112–21
Joan Mitchell: New Paintings, exh. cat., Xavier Fourcade Inc., New York, 1986
Judith E. Bernstock, *Joan Mitchell*, New York: Hudson Hills Press, 1988 (contains bibliography)
Martica Sawin, "A stretch of the Seine: Joan Mitchell's paintings", *Arts Magazine*, lxii, March 1988, pp.29–31
Harry Gaugh, "Dark victories", *Art News*, lxxxvii, Summer 1988, pp.154–9
Ora Lerman, "The elusive subject: Joan Mitchell's reflections on van Gogh", *Arts Magazine*, lxv, September 1990, pp.42–6
Joan Mitchell: A Portrait of an Abstract Painter, film by Marion Cajori, New York: Christian Blackwood Productions, 1992
Michel Waldberg, *Joan Mitchell*, Paris: Editions de la Différence, 1992
Klaus Kertess, "Joan Mitchell: The last decade", *Art in America*, lxxx, December 1992, pp.94–101
Joan Mitchell: Prints and Illustrated Books: A Retrospective, exh. cat., Susan Sheehan Gallery, New York, 1993
Joan Mitchell, exh. cat., Musée des Beaux-Arts, Nantes, and Galerie Nationale du Jeu de Paume, Paris, 1994 (with English translation)
Joan Mitchell: "My Black Paintings ...", exh. cat., Robert Miller Gallery, New York, 1994
Bill Scott, "In the eye of the tiger", *Art in America*, lxxxiii, March 1995, pp.70–77

Joan Mitchell first received critical acclaim during the 1950s as one of the second generation of Abstract Expressionists. Like her contemporaries Helen Frankenthaler (q.v.), Grace Hartigan (q.v.) and Alfred Leslie, Mitchell sought to extend and develop the abstract language of the older generation. A major aspect of Abstract Expressionism that became central to Mitchell's work was an exploration of the relationship between man and nature. Landscapes, in particular fields, water, land, trees and flowers, were the main inspiration for her paintings. Mitchell drew on her experience both of actual landscapes and of representations of nature in lyrical poetry, notably the work of William Wordsworth and Rainer Maria Rilke as well as contemporary verse by Frank O'Hara and Samuel Beckett, both of whom were her close friends. Although many of her images seem joyful, the predominant themes are death, loss and solitariness. Mitchell's work is distinctly autobiographical in the way in which it is invested with personal significance. Mitchell considered her painting as a dialogue between herself, the canvas and remembered sensations. Thus Mitchell's art is concerned with her "feelings" towards the subject and her memories of past experiences. The titles of the paintings, often given after the works were completed, allude to remembered experiences, people and places.

In 1950, after a year's stay in France, Mitchell returned to New York, where she met Franz Kline and Willem de Kooning, both of whom influenced her subsequent work. At the time Mitchell thought that being a female artist meant that it was unlikely that her work would be taken seriously. It is noteworthy, however, that she was one of the few women members of the exclusive Artists' Club, with Frankenthaler, Elaine de Kooning and Lee Krasner (q.v.). Although some of her work of this period reflected the urban environment in which she worked, there is an overriding preoccupation with what she has described as "remembered landscapes that I carry with me and remembered feelings of them" (Mitchell in Bernstock 1988, p.31). Characteristic of such work is *To the Harbormaster*

(1957; Graham Gund Charitable Trust, Cambridge, MA), which was named after a poem of that title by Frank O'Hara. Mitchell associated large areas of water with Lake Michigan in Chicago where she had spent her childhood. The harbour represented security and calm, but also danger in a storm. The painting consists of short brush strokes that create a criss-cross web of thick impasto marks and drips. As in much of Mitchell's early work, the centre of the image is densely worked with a gradual thinning out towards the margins of the canvas. The contrasting colours, blue, cadmium red, green and crimson, are separated by blank canvas or overpainted in white. Mitchell painted in oil on canvas and although the surface seems frenetic, the way in which the painting was made reveals the deliberation in her technique. In an interview with Irving Sandler, Mitchell described how she worked: "I paint from a distance. I decide what I'm going to do from a distance. The freedom in my work is quite controlled. I don't close my eyes and hope for the best ... I want to know what my brush is doing" (Sandler 1957, pp.46 and 69).

While on a trip to Paris in the summer of 1955, Mitchell met the painter Jean-Paul Riopelle, who was to be her companion until 1979. She divided her time between New York and Paris, and in 1959 acquired a studio on the rue Frémicourt. Mitchell described the subsequent images made in the early 1960s as "very violent and angry paintings" (Bernstock 1988, p.60). The cause of these feelings was complex, but centred on the death of her father in 1963 and her mother's prolonged illness with cancer from 1960 to 1967. Typical of such work is *Calvi* (1964; Robert Miller Gallery and Bernard Lennon Inc., New York), in which a central dark green mass dominates the image and alludes to organic forms, and the large surrounding area is blank or roughly painted in white with traces of colour underneath. The title refers to a place near Juan-les-Pins that Mitchell had visited on a sailing trip. In 1968 she settled permanently at the house she had purchased in the countryside at Vétheuil, north of Paris. She responded to her new environment by introducing intense and brilliant colours to her work. In *Sans neige* (1969; Carnegie Museum of Art, Pittsburgh) the surface of the painting is heavily worked, emphasising the different paint texture in yellows, reds, greens and blues, with white impasto creating a diffused light.

Mitchell always worked on a grand scale using large, individual canvases and multiple canvases (*To the Harbormaster*, for instance, measures 193 × 299 cm.). During the early 1970s she embarked on a series of major triptychs. Typical of these works are the rectangular areas of saturated colour juxtaposed against veils of brushed and dripped paint that create an ambiguous space. Mitchell's use of the rectangle was influenced by the work of Hans Hofmann. In 1947 she had intended to study with Hofmann, but changed her mind after attending one of his classes, although she remained an admirer of his work. The three main themes of these works are beaches, fields and territories. The triptych *Field for Skyes* (1973; Hirshhorn Museum and Sculpture Garden, Smithsonian Institution, Washington, DC) contains green rectangles that both emphasise the flatness of the canvas surface and refer to the fields alongside the Seine at Vétheuil. The oppressive green and the title, however, refer to the death of one of her dogs, a Skye terrier.

Between late 1975 and 1984 Mitchell adopted a more all-over composition and her painting became increasingly lyrical in character. The rectangular shapes are gradually eliminated and replaced by short vertical or loosely criss-crossing marks. The work of this period has been compared to Monet's late images of waterlilies. Although Mitchell rejected any such similarity, her house at Vétheuil was situated on a hill overlooking a house in which Monet had lived and painted between 1878 and 1881. *Goodbye Door* (1980; Musée National d'Art Moderne, Centre Georges Pompidou, Paris) is a quadriptych in which a uniform thickness of paint covers the canvases in blues, greens and white. The title suggests Mitchell's continual preoccupation with the theme of death.

From 1985 onwards Mitchell struggled with mortality, both the prospect of her own death and the deaths of a number of close friends. Flowers, in particular sunflowers, and water are themes that are re-examined in her late work. In 1986 Mitchell explained to Yves Michaud: "Sunflowers are something I feel very intensely. They look so wonderful when young and they are so very moving when they are dying" (New York 1986, p.3). Mitchell's sombre images inspired by sunflowers are redolent with memories of the flowers she grew in her garden and those painted by van Gogh that she greatly admired. As Klaus Kertess observed: "in Mitchell's hands the very subject of sunflowers becomes a stunning *memento mori*" (Kertess 1992, p.100).

ROSEMARY HARRIS

Modersohn-Becker, Paula   [fig. 46]

German painter, 1876–1907

Born Paula Becker in Dresden, 8 February 1876. Moved with her family to Bremen, 1888. Took drawing lessons with the Bremen artist Wiegand, and attended classes at a London art school while staying with a relation, 1892. Teacher-training course at the Bremen Lehrerinnenseminar, 1893–5. Studied at the Zeichen- und Malschule des Vereins der Künstlerinnen und Kunstfreundinnen zu Berlin, Berlin, 1896–8. First visited Worpswede art colony, 1897; settled there, autumn 1898; met painter Otto Modersohn and Clara Rilke-Westhoff. First trip to Paris, 1900; studied at Académie Colarossi and Ecole des Beaux-Arts; subsequent visits to Paris in 1903, 1905 and 1906. Married Modersohn, 1901; lived in Worpswede. Died in Worpswede of a heart attack, 21 November 1907, shortly after giving birth to a daughter.

Principal Exhibitions

Kunsthalle, Bremen: 1899, 1906 (both Worpswede artists exhibitions), 1908 (retrospective)

Selected Writings

Paula Modersohn-Becker in Briefen und Tagebüchern, ed. Günter Busch and Liselotte von Reinken, Frankfurt am Main: Fischer, 1979; as *Paula Modersohn-Becker: The Letters and Journals*, ed. Arthur S. Wensinger and Carole Clew Hoey, New York: Taplinger, 1983; revised edition, Evanston, IL: Northwestern University Press, 1990

The Letters and Journals of Paula Modersohn-Becker, ed. J. Diane Radycki, Metuchen, NJ: Scarecrow Press, 1980

"Lettres choisies (1900–1907), *Cahiers du Musée National d'Art Moderne*, no.10, 1982, pp.196–207

Bibliography

Gustav Pauli, *Paula Modersohn-Becker*, Berlin: Wolff, 1919; 3rd edition, 1934

Waldemar Augustiny, *Paula Modersohn-Becker*, Gütersloh: Mohn, 1960

——, *Paula Modersohn-Becker*, Hildesheim, 1971

Ellen C. Oppler, "Paula Modersohn-Becker: Some facts and legends", *Art Journal*, xxxv, Summer 1976, pp.364–9

Gillian Perry, *Paula Modersohn-Becker: Her Life and Work*, London: Women's Press, 1979

Christa Murken-Altrogge, *Paula Modersohn-Becker: Leben und Werk*, Cologne: DuMont, 1980

Günter Busch, *Paula Modersohn-Becker: Malerin, Zeichnerin*, Frankfurt am Main: Fischer, 1981

Griselda Pollock, "What's wrong with 'images of women'"?, *Framing Feminism*, ed. Rozsika Parker and Griselda Pollock, London and New York: Pandora, 1987

Christa Murken-Altrogge, *Paula Modersohn-Becker*, Cologne: DuMont, 1991

Mara R. Witzling, ed., *Voicing Our Visions: Writings by Women Artists*, New York: Universe, 1991; London: Women's Press, 1992

Diane Radycki, "Pretty/ugly: Morphing Paula Modersohn-Becker and Marie Laurencin", *Make: Magazine of Women's Art*, no.72, 1996, pp.19–21

Paula Modersohn-Becker is now perhaps best known for her powerful, monumental images of motherhood, painted in a style often closely associated with developments in early 20th-century French, rather than with contemporary German, modernism. Before her premature death in 1907 she made four trips to Paris, where she lived and worked for extended periods and became absorbed in the work of such Post-Impressionist painters as Gauguin and the Nabis, van Gogh and Cézanne. But Modersohn-Becker's aesthetic, iconographical and cultural interests also remained firmly rooted in the German environment in which she had lived and studied, especially the north German artists' colony of Worpswede, near Bremen.

In the 1890s a group of former art students from the Düsseldorf and Munich academies had settled in the village of Worpswede, then inhabited by peasant farmers and turf-cutters. In keeping with many other artistic movements flourishing in Germany at the time, this group of artists saw themselves as daring neo-romantics, seeking out "natural" subjects in the form of the indigenous peasant *Volk* in the local landscape. By the late 1890s, when Paula Becker first visited the village, these artists were mostly painting peasant and landscape subjects influenced by the work of Gustave Courbet and the French Barbizon painters. After establishing herself in the village in 1898 she studied under Fritz Mackensen, then well-known for his Courbet-influenced scenes of local peasant life. Partly under his influence, she became absorbed in the local imagery, drawing and painting many images of peasant women nursing their babies. Much of her work from this early period is characterised by a dark-toned, realistic technique, designed to evoke the harshness and poignancy of the "primitive" sources she was depicting. Modersohn-Becker's primitivism, her sense of this subject matter as somehow "other" in relation to her own sophisticated life, also involved a neo-romantic idealisation of the heroic purity of these peasant figures. In a diary entry for 25 October 1898 she wrote:

> I sketched a young mother with her child at her breast, sitting in a smoky hut. If only I could someday paint what I felt then! A sweet woman, an image of charity. She was nursing her big, year-old bambino, when with defiant eyes her four-year-old daughter snatched for her breast until she was given it. And the woman gave her life and her youth and her power to the child in utter simplicity, unaware that she was a heroine [quoted in Witzling 1991, p.193].

The cultural and artistic context provided by the artists colony of Worpswede was fraught with contradictions. Although some of the artistic interests that emerged (particularly in the work of Fritz Mackensen) encouraged a somewhat reactionary form of primitivism that exalted an essentially German peasant culture as a main source of artistic inspiration, there were other artists within the community whose less inward-looking ideas helped to nurture those of Modersohn-Becker. She developed a close friendship with Heinrich Vogeler, whose paintings and works in the applied arts were heavily influenced by the utopian socialist ideals of William Morris and the Arts and Crafts movement. In 1901 she married Otto Modersohn, a Worpswede landscape painter influenced by late 19th-century French landscape painting, in particular the legacy of the Barbizon painters, and who encouraged her own interest in developing a style of landscape painting loosely indebted to Impressionist techniques. At the end of the 19th century rural artists' communities (many of which were formed outside large German towns) provided women with a relatively tolerant social and professional atmosphere in which to work. While aspiring women artists were still handicapped by restricted access to educational opportunities and studio facilities in urban academic circles, within the less formal, generally more liberal environment of the artists' colony they were able to work and study alongside male artists.

However, Modersohn-Becker's letters and diary entries suggest that she felt increasingly stifled by the personal and artistic relationships that she had formed in Worpswede, and yearned for the artistic stimulus of Paris. After her first two trips to Paris in 1900 and 1903, she sought increasingly to reduce her images to more monumental and simplified shapes, using flattened areas of bright colour. In 1903 she wrote in her diary: "A great simplicity of form is something marvelous. As far back as I can remember, I have tried to put the simplicity of nature into the heads that I was painting or drawing. Now I have a real sense of being able to learn from the heads of ancient sculpture" (ibid., p.198). In her works from the period 1903 onwards Modersohn-Becker sought to put such ideas into practice, developing a form of primitivism derived from complex sources. In her *Poorhouse Woman in the Garden*, also titled *Poorhouse Woman with Glass Bowl* (repr. Perry 1979, pl.XV) she applies these techniques to a local Worpswede peasant subject. But her interpretation avoids the idealised, pseudo-religious earth mothers to be found in the work of some other Worpswede artists, notably Fritz Mackensen. She employs Gauguinesque simplifications, reducing the old woman's broad dimensions to flat areas of bright colour. As a result the figure appears both monumentalised and distorted, and is set against a decorative frieze of vertical flowers, giving the image a pattern-like quality. This peasant figure is thus removed from the realities of the local poor house (where Modersohn-Becker found many of her subjects) and has an ornamental, static appearance. In her attempt to combine a supposedly "primitive" subject matter with "primitive" techniques Modersohn-Becker created an ambiguous image of peasant life as remote and unworldly.

Modersohn-Becker's images of motherhood, particularly those produced during the last two years of her life, reveal a woman artist seeking to resolve some of the aesthetic, social and cultural contradictions that she confronted in her personal and professional life. The theme of the peasant woman was well established in European art as a whole, and in the work of the Worpswede group in particular, as a symbolic image for the representation of a "primitive" or natural life. Images of breast-feeding mothers recur in the work of such Worpswede artists as Mackensen, where they stand as potent metaphors for the "primitive" cycle of nature. Modersohn-Becker reworks these traditional symbolic associations in some of her images of peasant mothers, although she rejects the anecdotal realism and Impressionist-influenced styles of her Worpswede colleagues, and often combines the theme with that of the female nude. In her *Kneeling*

Mother with Child (1907; Staatliche Museen Preussischer Kulturbesitz, Nationalgalerie, Berlin) a kneeling, breast-feeding mother is surrounded by fruit and plants, symbols of her fecundity. Although this work is also clearly influenced by Gauguinesque representations of the female nude that she had seen in Paris, this is not a sensual or erotic nude reminiscent of Gauguin's Tahitian works. Modersohn-Becker's figure has a heavily proportioned, monumental form with primitivised features; she suggests a powerful fecundity free of any suggestion of sexual availability. Her interest in this theme, and its monumental implications, are also related to more personal longings and fantasies. Her letters and diary entries reveal a woman who both grew increasingly disillusioned with her marriage, and who also yearned for a somewhat idealised state of motherhood. In her *Self-Portrait on Her Wedding Anniversary* (1906; Sammlung Böttcherstrasse, Bremen) she portrays herself nude with a distended stomach as if pregnant. The work was painted many months before the conception of her only child, and represents a projection of her fantasy of herself as a fertile mother. While the fantasy was fulfilled with the birth of her daughter in November 1907, Modersohn-Becker's tragic death three weeks later has helped to give her interpretations of the theme of motherhood a poignant, almost mythical status.

Images of women, including the female nude, mother and child groups, portraits of women and self-portraits, feature prominently in Modersohn-Becker's work. While this choice of imagery may reveal the artist's preoccupation with the creative self as a woman, the predominance of certain images was also to do with the accessibility of subjects and models. Studies from the female nude formed an important part of the curriculum in the various French and German academies at which she studied. In Worpswede the models most readily available to her were the local women and their children, for most of the male community were working in the fields during the day.

Many of her mother and child compositions include still-life groups of fruit and flowers, where they are resonant with symbolic connotations of natural fecundity. But the still life became increasingly important as a genre in its own right in her work from 1903 onwards. Influenced by interpretations of the theme in the work of Post-Impressionist artists such as Cézanne, Emile Bernard and van Gogh, she became involved with the possibilities for

formal expression that still-life subjects offered. She saw inanimate objects, such as fruit, flowers and jugs, as vehicles for her pursuit of "simplicity of form", for developing simplified compositional structures. In her writings she expresses a desire somehow to penetrate the inner qualities of an object through close observation. Such attitudes may have been informed by the ideas of the German poet Rainer Maria Rilke, with whom Modersohn-Becker became friendly. Influenced by Neo-romantic ideas, and by the work of Rodin (for whom Modersohn-Becker worked briefly as a secretary), Rilke evolved a theory of representation based on the notion of the intrinsic or "inner" meaning of objects, which could be revealed through the careful craftsmanship of the artist.

Modersohn-Becker's letters and diary entries have been seen as a kind of "confessional" within which she could make intimate disclosures about her personal struggles; they provided a space in which she could express her frustration in the face of conflicting demands of being a "woman" and an "artist" seeking a professional career. And the personal and aesthetic struggles that she describes are, of course, mediated by the different cultural contexts and discourses (both French and German) in which she participated. Her self-image as an artist (as expressed in her writings) is both steeped in Neo-romantic ideas about the artist's mission to reveal something deeper beneath the visible surfaces of objects and reveals an increasing concern with her need to study and learn from the work of modernist French painters. Her painted self-images suggest, however, a more ambivalent and even diffident approach to her status as a woman artist. In several self-portraits she paints herself nude with heavy dimensions and simplified forms, and places the figure boldly across the foreground space to suggest a monumental and powerful human presence, as in *Self-Portrait with Amber Necklace* (1906; Kunstmuseum, Basel). But these heroic, unerotic self-images are usually devoid of references to her role as artist, and may reveal the same conflict that she expressed in her writings. During her lifetime Modersohn-Becker sold only two or three paintings, a lack of professional success that must have affected her confidence and her self-image as an artist. In her *Self-Portrait with Amber Necklace*, then, the positive image that she projects is that of "woman" rather than "woman artist".

GILL PERRY

Moillon, Louise

[fig. 50]

French painter, 1609 or 1610–1696

Born in Paris, 1609 or 1610, to Nicolas Moillon (d. 1619), a painter and picture dealer, and his wife Marie Gilbert, the daughter of a goldsmith; Protestant family. In 1720 her mother married François Garnier, also a painter and picture dealer. Married Etienne Girardot de Chancourt, a Parisian wood merchant and Calvinist, 1640; three children; husband died before 23 January 1680. Died aged 86 in Paris, 1696.

Bibliography

Georges de Scudéry, *Le Cabinet de Mr de Scudéri gouverneur de Notre-Dame de la Garde*, 1646

E. Coyecque, "Notes sur divers peintres du XVIIe siècle", *Bulletin de la Société de l'Histoire de l'Art Français*, 1940, pp.76–82

Jacques Wilhelm, "Louise Moillon", *L'Oeil*, no.21, September 1956, pp.6–13

Michel Faré, *La Nature morte en France: Son histoire et son évolution du XVIIe au XXe siècle*, 2 vols, Geneva, 1962

——, *Le Grand Siècle de la nature morte en France: Le XVIIe siècle*, Fribourg: Office du Livre, and Paris: Société Française du Livre, 1974

——, "Trois peintres de fruits du temps de Louis XIII", *Connaissance des Arts*, cclxxii, October 1974, pp.88–95

Women Artists, 1550–1950, exh. cat., Los Angeles County Museum of Art, and elsewhere, 1976

Charles Sterling, *Still Life Painting from Antiquity to the Twentieth Century*, revised edition, New York: Harper, 1981 (French original, 1952)

France in the Golden Age: Seventeenth-Century French Paintings in North American Collections, exh. cat., Grand Palais, Paris, and elsewhere, 1982

Christopher Wright, *The French Painters of the Seventeenth Century*, London: Orbis, and Boston: Little Brown, 1985

Michel and Fabrice Faré, "Louise Moillon, Les Girardot, marchands de bois parisiens et une oeuvre inédite de Louise Moillon", *Gazette des Beaux-Arts*, 6th series, cviii, 1986, pp.49–65

Grand Siècle: Peintures françaises du XVIIe siècle dans les collections publiques françaises, exh. cat., Musée des Beaux-Arts, Montreal, and elsewhere, 1993

Although Louise Moillon painted still lifes exclusively, her work cannot be associated with the humble subject matter that the French Académie Royale confined to the bottom of the artistic hierarchy, nor is it comparable to those paintings by young lady amateurs who became notorious in the 19th century for their still lifes. Instead, Moillon belonged to a circle of painters working in the Saint-Germain-des-Prés area of Paris that provided refuge for those from the southern Netherlands fleeing religious persecution. Both her father and her stepfather and several of her brothers and sisters were painters, and her work belonged to a recognisable artisanal tradition of still life. That is, it was produced for economic reasons and was not the "accomplishment" art that is often identified with women practitioners of the genre.

Stylistically, Moillon's work belongs to the convention of the "table-top" still life that was developed in the Saint-Germain-des-Prés quarter. *Still Life with Fruit and Asparagus* (Art Institute of Chicago), signed and dated 1630, is depicted as if seen from above, sloping towards the viewer and against an indistinct background. The fruit, basket and leaves are meticulously painted with great attention paid to the delineation of different textures. *Basket with Peaches and Grapes* (1631; Staatliche Kunsthalle, Karlsruhe) follows the same formula, with jewel-like fruits glowing against a murky background, and *trompe-l'oeil* elements such as the leaves hanging over the edge of the table and the cut flesh of the peach revealing its inner texture. Combined with their small size, their simplicity and harmony, these works have been seen by some commentators as indicative of Moillon's Protestant faith and her celebration of *la vie silencieuse*. But the intimacy, the domestic subject matter and the absence of human models may be due as much to her gender and the craft tradition within which she worked. Although there are fewer works dating from after her marriage in 1640, the still life was the perfect subject for a woman with other domestic duties to practise at home, being small and needing no models. Other works, however, were larger and more clearly virtuoso demonstrations. *Still Life with Fruit and Vegetables* (Thyssen-Bornemisza Collection) is well over a metre in width and the customary apricots and plums in the basket on a stone shelf are joined by asparagus, artichokes and strawberries in a blue and white porcelain dish. As in all her works, the fruit is perfect, with none of the blemished, over-ripe fruit that Netherlandish artists depicted. Consequently, in Moillon's work there is little suggestion of any symbolic allusion to the frailty of human existence or of time passing: her still lifes embody perpetual present. If anything, Moillon's work suggests bourgeois comfort and plenty and there is little suggestion of frugality.

That Moillon was regarded as the equal of her male peers is demonstrated by Georges de Scudéry (1646), who placed her alongside the still-life painters Linard and Pierre van Boucle and compared all three with Michelangelo, Raphael and Titian. Clearly hyperbolic in tone, Scudéry's analogy highlights the distinction between the very public art of the Italian Renaissance that was to provide the model for the French Académie Royale and the private art of Moillon and those around her in the Saint-Germain-des-Prés area. After Jean François Félibien codified the hierarchy of the genres in the 1660s, still life was increasingly marginalised and seen as the perfect subject for the aspiring female artist, who was denied access to the higher genres because of their dependence on study from the model. Cathérine Duchemin, the first woman member of the Academy, was accepted in 1663 with a reception piece of flowers, and six years later Geneviève and Madeleine Boullogne were accepted with a collaborative still life that included an architectural backdrop and musical trophies. Well into the 19th century, women who wished for any success within the Academic system were more likely to be accepted if they produced still lifes or flower paintings. The stranglehold that the Académie Royale exercised on French artistic life and the constraint of the hierarchy of the genres meant, however, that the tradition of the perfectly crafted, intimate still life was replaced by much more literary and decorative works.

LESLEY STEVENSON

Morgan, Evelyn De *see* De Morgan

Morisot, Berthe   [fig. 49]
French painter, 1841–1895

Born in Bourges, 14 January 1841; father a government official. Settled in the Parisian suburb of Passy with her family, *c*.1852. Took drawing lessons from the academic painter Geoffroy Alphonse Chocarne, 1857, then studied under Joseph-Benoît Guichard of Lyons, a pupil of Ingres and Delacroix. Taught by Camille Corot, then by his pupil Achille-François Oudinot; also took

lessons in sculpture from Aimé Millet. Introduced to Edouard Manet by Henri Fantin-Latour, *c*.1867–8. Travelled to the Pyrenees, 1862, to Normandy 1864; visited Madrid, 1872, England, 1875; spent summers in Pontoise and Brittany. Married Manet's brother Eugène, 1874; daughter born 1878; husband died 1892. Died in Passy, 2 March 1895.

Principal Exhibitions
Paris Salon: 1864–6, 1868, 1870, 1872–3
Impressionist group, Paris: 1874, 1876–7, 1880–82, 1886
Durand-Ruel Gallery, London: 1883
National Academy of Design, New York: 1886 (Impressionist group, special exhibition), 1887 (Impressionist group, organised by Paul Durand-Ruel)
Salon des XX, Brussels: 1887
Galerie Georges Petit, Paris: 1887 (*Exposition Internationale*)
Galerie Boussod et Valadon, Paris: 1892 (individual)
Salon de la Libre Esthétique, Brussels: 1894
Galerie Durand-Ruel, Paris: 1896 (retrospective)

Selected Writings
Correspondance de Berthe Morisot avec sa famille et ses amis, ed. Denis Rouart, Paris, 1950; as *The Correspondence of Berthe Morisot with Her Family and Friends: Manet, Puvis de Chavannes, Degas, Monet, Renoir and Mallarmé*, London, 1957; 2nd edition, 1959; with new introduction and notes by Kathleen Adler and Tamar Garb, London: Camden, 1986

Bibliography
Berthe Morisot (Mme Eugène Manet), 1841–1895, exh. cat., Paris, Galerie Durand-Ruel, 1896
Roger Marx, "Les femmes peintres et l'impressionisme: Berthe Morisot", *Gazette des Beaux-Arts*, 3rd series, xxxviii, 1907, pp.491–508
Armand Fourreau, *Berthe Morisot*, Paris: Rieder, 1925
Monique Angoulvent, *Berthe Morisot*, Paris: Morancé [1933]
Louis Rouart, *Berthe Morisot*, Paris, 1941
Rosamond Bernier, "Dans la lumière impressioniste", *L'Oeil*, no.53, May 1959, pp.38–47
Paul Valéry, *Degas, Manet, Morisot*, London: Routledge, and New York: Pantheon, 1960 (French original)
M.-L. Bataille and G. Wildenstein, *Berthe Morisot: Catalogue des peintures, pastels et aquarelles*, Paris: Les Beaux Arts, 1961
Philippe Huisman, *Morisot: Charmes*, Lausanne: International Art Books, 1962
John Rewald, *The History of Impressionism*, 4th edition, New York: Museum of Modern Art, and London: Secker and Warburg, 1973

Janine Bailly-Herzberg, "Les estampes de Berthe Morisot", *Gazette des Beaux-Arts*, 6th series, xciii, 1979, pp.215–27

Julie Manet, *Journal (1893–1899): Sa jeunesse parmi les peintres impressionistes et les hommes de lettres*, Paris: Klincksieck, 1979; as *Growing Up with the Impressionists: The Diary of Julie Manet*, London: Sotheby's Publications, 1987

Charlotte Yeldham, *Women Artists in Nineteenth-Century France and England*, 2 vols, New York: Garland, 1984

Alain Clairet, "'Le Cerisier' de Mézy", *L'Oeil*, no.358, May 1985, pp.48–51

Tamar Garb, *Women Impressionists*, Oxford: Phaidon, and New York: Rizzoli, 1986

The New Painting: Impressionism, 1874–1886, exh. cat., National Gallery of Art, Washington, DC, and elsewhere, 1986

Kathleen Adler and Tamar Garb, *Berthe Morisot*, Oxford: Phaidon, and Ithaca, NY: Cornell University Press, 1987

Beth Genné, "Two self-portraits by Berthe Morisot", *Psychoanalytic Perspectives on Art*, ed. Mary Mathews Gedo, ii, Hillsdale, NJ: Analytic Press, 1987, pp.133–70

Berthe Morisot: Impressionist, exh. cat., National Gallery of Art, Washington, DC, 1987

Robert L. Herbert, *Impressionism: Art, Leisure and Parisian Society*, New Haven and London: Yale University Press, 1988

Suzanne G. Lindsay, "Berthe Morisot and the poets: The visual language of woman", *Helicon Nine*, no.19, 1988, pp.8–17

Kathleen Adler, "The suburban, the modern and 'une dame de Passy'", *Oxford Art Journal*, xii/1, 1989, pp.3–13

Jean-Dominique Rey, *Berthe Morisot*, 2nd edition, Paris: Flammarion, 1989

T.J. Edelstein, ed., *Perspectives on Morisot*, New York: Hudson Hills Press, 1990

Anne Higonnet, *Berthe Morisot: A Biography*, New York: Harper, and London: Collins, 1990

Berthe Morisot (1841–1895), exh. cat., JPL Fine Arts, London, 1990

Anne Higonnet, *Berthe Morisot's Images of Women*, Cambridge, MA: Harvard University Press, 1992

Wendy Slatkin, ed., *The Voices of Women Artists*, Englewood Cliffs, NJ: Prentice Hall, 1993

Berthe Morisot's critical reputation has always been linked with Impressionism. Not only was she one of the founding and most consistent members of this exhibiting organisation in Paris in the 1870s and 1880s, her work came in the 1890s and subsequent French accounts of the period to stand for the purest and most essential embodiment of the Impressionist aesthetic. While British and American histories of the period all but ignored her contribution to Impressionism until the 1970s, when she was "rediscovered" in the wake of the feminist quest for "lost women artists", French accounts, from the 19th century onwards, afforded her a central place, but one that was circumscribed in highly gendered ways. Morisot came to stand as the quintessential "feminine" painter, one whose adherence to the "spontaneous", "superficial" art of "sensation" that Impressionism was seen to represent fulfilled the demands for the delicate, feminine sensibility deemed appropriate by 19th-century and subsequent French commentators. Unlike her "manly" contemporaries such as Rosa Bonheur (q.v.) and Suzanne Valadon (q.v.), widely seen to have reneged on their intuitive, feminine sensibilities, Morisot fulfilled these in her commitment to an art that celebrated physical sensation, spontaneity and unmediated response. Impressionism was seen as a feminine art, and a skilled woman artist such as Morisot was its most legitimate exponent. Morisot's reputation, although considerable in French art-historical accounts therefore, is based both upon a 19th century notion of "femininity", and a particularly circumscribed understanding of Impressionism.

Morisot's fate in standard anglophone accounts of Impressionism was markedly different. If featured at all, she was most usually referred to as the pupil of Corot (with whom she briefly studied in 1862) or Manet (who was never in fact her teacher), and represented as a marginal if at all visible presence. John Rewald, the standard authority on Impressionism for decades, did not count her among the important "gang of four" – Monet, Renoir, Pissarro and Degas – who constituted, for him, the core Impressionist group. Such an exclusion is hard to justify, especially as Morisot was one of the most consistent participants in the Impressionist exhibitions and was included in seven out of the eight group shows organised between 1874 and 1886. What was more, Morisot, an independently wealthy woman, helped to finance these ventures and was a key personality among the central participants in the group. Married to Eugène Manet, brother of Edouard Manet, the acknowledged mentor to all the younger Impressionists, friend and confidante of Renoir and Degas, referred to by Pissarro as "our old comrade" at the time of her death, and close friend of Stéphane Mallarmé, the Symbolist writer who wrote some of the most important 19th-century art criticism, Morisot was at the heart of progressive artistic and intellectual circles. An examination of her work reveals an artist committed to the naturalist principles of her cohort and a key player in the formation of a plein-air practice based upon the invention of a pictorial language that would be adequate to the recording of visual sensation and commensurate with a modern sensibility and modernist material self-consciousness.

Morisot was born in Bourges in 1841, the youngest of three sisters. Yves, the eldest, was born in 1838, and Edma, who also became an artist, was two years older than Berthe. She also had a younger brother, Tiburce. Their father was a high-ranking civil servant who moved the family to Passy, then still a village just outside Paris, later to become Paris's 16th *arrondissement*, when Morisot was eleven. She remained within the boundaries of Passy from then on for the remainder of her life. She was destined to live the life of any upper-middle-class French woman. Her early education followed the pattern set for young women of her class, and the painting lessons that she and her two sisters took formed part of the accepted grounding in the accomplishment arts without which no *bourgeoise* could be groomed and capable of making an eligible match. The young Morisot sisters were required to dabble in watercolours and sketching as they were required to learn to sew, play the piano and take an interest in fashion and personal adornment. To this end they were enrolled with an art master, Père Chocarne, who undertook to teach them drawing, an experience that they seem to have found dull and onerous. The oldest Morisot sister, Yves, was so put off by the experience that she gave up art altogether, but the two younger sisters were able to change teacher and became the pupils of the conservative painter and teacher, Joseph-Benoît Guichard. Horrified to find that he was dealing with two young ladies of talent, Guichard wrote to their mother:

> Considering the character of your daughters, my teaching will not endow them with minor drawing room accomplishments; they will become painters. Do you realize what this means? In the upper-class milieu to which you belong, this will be revolutionary, I might almost say catastrophic [*Correspondance*, Adler and Garb 1986, p.19].

To her credit, Mme Morisot was undaunted by this prospect and the Morisot girls were able to undertake a relatively serious training in the arts of painting and drawing.

All the official art schools were closed to women at this time, but wealthy women such as the Morisot sisters – unlike the majority of women – could benefit from private tuition. Privileged both materially and through the fact that they had enlightened parents, Berthe and Edma were afforded an unusually serious art education for their time, although they would never be given rigorous training in life drawing or classical culture as would have been the norm for contemporary male students. Like all ambitious young artists, though, they were enrolled as copyists in the Louvre, where many aspirant women artists earned their living by copying famous works for provincial collections. It was here, too, that they made the acquaintance of many of the important younger generation of French artists such as Carolus-Duran (the fashionable portraitist whose wife was an accomplished painter and pastellist), Henri Fantin-Latour (painter and husband of the still-life painter Victoria Dubourg) and Félix Bracquemond (engraver and future husband of the Impressionist painter Marie Bracquemond, q.v.) and began to imagine themselves as potential professional artists rather than as lady amateurs. Morisot was by now aware of the new, naturalist trends in contemporary art and intent on identifying herself with them. She had tired of her teacher Guichard whose teaching could not satisfy her new interests. Camille Corot, the most famous living naturalist landscapist had become a friend of the Morisot family and in 1862 gave Edma and Berthe some art lessons, fully initiating them into the rigours and procedures of plein-air painting. On Corot's recommendation, the sisters were taught by the landscapist Achille-François Oudinot. By the mid-1860s Morisot's apprenticeship was over and, like all young artists, she drew from her contemporaries and predecessors, learning from her peers and influencing them in turn. Probably the most important figure for her during the 1860s was the family friend Edouard Manet with whom she developed a close professional relationship, learning from him at the same time as developing her own painterly and light-filled style that would, in turn, influence the older artist and urge him in the direction of plein-air painting.

In 1864 both Berthe and Edma had works accepted at the Paris Salon, the most important annual exhibition of contemporary work, and they continued to exhibit regularly throughout the 1860s. Edma became engaged to a naval officer, Adolphe Pontillon, in 1867, and when she married him two years later she gave up painting, finding it impossible to combine the roles of professional artist and conventional wife. After the Franco-Prussian war and the Commune (1870–71), Berthe resumed her painting, and continued to submit works to the Salon. She was invited to join the artists planning a group exhibition, independent of the Salon, and in April 1874 her work was on view at the exhibition of the Société Anonyme des Artistes-Peintres, Sculpteurs, Graveurs etc., in the premises of the photographer Nadar on the boulevard des Capucines. This show became known as the first Impressionist exhibition. Morisot married Manet's brother Eugène in December 1874, and their only child, Julie, frequently the subject of her mother's paintings, was born on 14 November 1878.

Morisot remained loyal to the independent exhibitions, and never returned to the Salon. In 1887 her work was included in an International Exhibition organised by the dealer Georges Petit, as well as in his rival Paul Durand-Ruel's Impressionist exhibition in New York. Her first solo exhibition was held in 1892 at the premises of Boussod et Valadon. In 1894 the State made its first purchase of her work, *Jeune femme en toilette de bal* (Musée d'Orsay, Paris). This, like many of Morisot's works, was modelled in the family home. The model is depicted dressed in evening wear, but remains within the confines of the domestic interior. Many of Morisot's works use members of her family as models, and deal with the refined leisure pursuits of upper-middle-class women, their children and the domestic servants on whose labour this class depended. Morisot documented the phases of women's lives, starting with the infancy of her daughter, Julie, and showing her development as a young girl and an adolescent. She also represented her sisters during their confinements, producing some of the few portraits of pregnant women in 19th-century art. Her pastel portrait of Edma (*Mme Pontillon*, 1871; Courtauld Institute Galleries, London), her erstwhile companion and fellow painter, depicts her sister with arms characteristically resting on her swollen belly, once again ensconced within the family interior.

Morisot remained close to her Impressionist colleagues, particularly to Renoir, in the later years of her life. After her death in 1895, Camille Pissarro wrote to his son Lucien:

> You can hardly conceive how surprised we all were and how moved, too, by the disappearance of this distinguished woman, who had such a splendid feminine talent and who brought honour to our impressionist group which is vanishing – like all things. Poor Mme Morisot, the public hardly knows her!

The *View of Paris from the Trocadéro* (Santa Barbara Museum, CA), probably painted in the summer of 1872, provides a useful example of Morisot's practice in both subject matter and technique. The view was one recommended in tourist guides, and very familiar to her, for the Morisot family home at this time was on the rue Franklin, adjacent to the gardens. The painting represents two women and a child on a path separated from the remainder of the grounds by a wooden barrier. Neither of the women is shown looking at the view of the city beyond. This view stretches beyond the immaculate lawns of the Trocadéro to the Seine and the Pont d'Iéna. Immediately beyond the river, to the right of the painting, is the empty space of the Champ de Mars, and beyond, on the horizon, various Paris landmarks can be identified, among them the Palais de l'Industrie, site of the annual Paris Salon, Sainte-Clotilde, Notre-Dame, Saint-Sulpice, the gilded dome of Les Invalides and, in the far distance, the dome of the Pantheon. The gardens of the Tuileries are visible on the extreme left of the painting.

The painting is unusual in its format, being almost twice as wide as it is high. The composition is a variant on one familiar in landscape painting, not only in the work of Corot but in 17th-century precedents, such as Claude and Poussin, with the figures on an elevated section in the foreground and a river leading the eye into the background. But Morisot makes this formula unrecognisable by the freedom with which the middle ground is painted, so that the effect is of a horizontal band, difficult to interpret, running across the painting. Details such as the carriages and figures are sketchily indicated, with no sense of preliminary drawing. Touches of colour – such as the red in the flower-beds to the right and the pink in the buildings on the far bank of the Seine – counter the sense of perspectival distance implied by the distant building, and emphasise the surface of the canvas.

Morisot painted a view of Paris restored to order after the events of the Franco-Prussian War, and especially of the Commune. In mid-May 1871, the year before the painting was executed, the Communards were in charge of the Trocadéro and the Versailles troops had commandeered most of Passy, including the Morisots' home. Constant fire was exchanged between the Communards and the Versaillaises positioned in the Bois de Boulogne, and anyone standing in the position of the figures in this painting would have been caught in the crossfire. At the end of May, many of the public buildings in Paris were destroyed in fires, making the city appear, as Morisot's mother described it, "like a volcanic eruption". Nothing of this is visible in Morisot's painting, which represents Paris returned to order, all scars hidden. In this choice of subject matter, she shared a position with her fellow Impressionists, who also avoided any sites that bore visible traces of the events of the war and the Commune.

Morisot's choice of subject and vantage point is one that occurs frequently in her work. Most of her work represents the lives of women and children in the home, in areas such as Passy, or in places along the Normandy coast frequented by Parisians at leisure. Passy was the most village-like of the areas incorporated by Baron Haussmann in 1860 into the 20 *arrondissements* that make up Paris's administrative structure, and its residents clung to that village-like quality well into the 20th century, seeing their part of Paris as separate from the tumult of the city. This sense of separation is conveyed in Morisot's painting by the barrier of the fence and the sweep of the green lawns. Passy was by this date a suburb, growing rapidly in size, and emulating such London suburbs as Hampstead. It was differentiated from the centre of the city by being, during the day at least, largely a place for women and children, a place from which bourgeois men left to go to work in the heart of Paris. Morisot's painting shows this area as a woman's territory, a space in which women enjoyed a degree of freedom to visit friends and to walk with children. The literature on this painting continues to contrast it with Manet's earlier *View of the Exposition Universelle* (1867; Nasjonalgalleriet, Oslo), a painting to which it is related only by virtue of the fact that both are painted from the Trocadéro gardens. The repetition of this comparison indicates how difficult it is to evaluate Morisot, for she is constantly positioned in the literature of Impressionism in relation to her

male colleagues, invariably in such a way as to diminish her achievement.

This painting was one of several that the dealer Paul Durand-Ruel bought from Morisot on consignment in February 1873. He paid 500 francs for it, and sold it, apparently on the same day, to the collector Ernest Hoschedé, one of the most committed collectors of Impressionist paintings at this date. Hoschedé paid Durand-Ruel 750 francs for the painting. It was then sold to the Romanian collector Georges de Bellio in 1876, immediately after the second independent group show, at the auction of Hoschedé's collection following the crash of his business.

In 1987 Mount Holyoke College Art Museum in association with the National Gallery of Art, Washington, DC, organised the exhibition *Berthe Morisot: Impressionist*. This exhibition, together with revisionist feminist scholarship of the period, made Morisot's oeuvre visible to an English-speaking public for the first time. During the past decade Morisot's achievement not only as an Impressionist but as a major woman artist of the modern period has been reassessed.

KATHLEEN ADLER and TAMAR GARB

Mukhina, Vera (Ignatiyevna)
Russian sculptor, 1889–1953

Born in Riga, Latvia, 19 June 1889. Educated in Feodosiya in the Crimea, where she took lessons in drawing and landscape. Attended Konstantin Yuon's private art school in Moscow, c.1905; started courses in sculpture at Sinitsyna's studio, c.1908; worked in Ilya Mashkov's studio, 1911–12. Travelled to Paris, 1912; studied at Académie de la Grande Chaumière; took lessons from Emile-Antoine Bourdelle; met Ossip Zadkine and Jacques Lipchitz. Travelled with Lyubov Popova (q.v.) to Italy, 1914; returned to Russia at outbreak of World War I. Assistant to Alexandra Exter (q.v.) at the Chamber Theatre, Moscow, 1915–16. Worked on posters, magazine designs and monuments, increasingly turning to monumental sculpture, 1918–20s. Founder member, Monolit (Monolith) group of sculptors, 1919–20. Worked with Exter at the Atelier of Fashions, Moscow, 1923. Taught at Vkhutemas (Higher State Artistic and Technical Workshops), 1926–7; at Vkhutein (Higher State Artistic and Technical Institute), 1926–30. Designed porcelain and glassware, monuments and interiors, 1930s–1940s. Member, Chetyre Iskusstva (Four Arts Society), 1925; ORS (Society of Russian Sculptors), 1926. Academician of the USSR. Died in Moscow, 6 October 1953.

Principal Exhibitions

Monolit (Monolith) group: from 1919
Mir Iskusstva (World of Art), Moscow: 1921
Chetyre Iskusstva (Four Arts Society), Moscow: from 1925
Exposition Internationale des Arts Décoratifs et Industriels Modernes, Paris: 1925
Moscow: 1927 (*Jubilee Exhibition of the Arts of the Peoples of the USSR*), 1943 (with Lebedeva, Gerasimov, Deineka, Konchalovsky and Shmarinov)
Venice Biennale: 1928
State Russian Museum, Leningrad and Moscow: 1932–3 (*Artists of the RSFSR over 15 Years, 1917–1932*)
Exposition Internationale, Paris: 1937

Selected Writings

A Sculptor's Thoughts, Moscow: Foreign Languages Publishing House, n.d. (after 1953)

Bibliography

B. Ternovets, *V.I. Mukhina*, Moscow: Ogiz, 1937
R. Klimov, ed., *Mukhina*, 3 vols, Moscow: Iskusstvo, 1960
Trois sculpteurs soviétiques: A.S. Goloubkina, V.I. Moukhina, S.D. Lebedeva, exh. cat., Musée Rodin, Paris, 1971
O.P. Voronova, *V.I. Mukhina*, Moscow: Iskusstvo, 1976
Pyotr Suzdalev, *Vera Ignatiyevna Mukhina*, Moscow: Iskusstvo, 1981
I.A. Bashinskaya, *Vera Ignatiyevna Mukhina, 1889–1953*, Leningrad: Khudozhnik RSFSR, 1987
M. Kolesnikov, "Alexandra Exter i Vera Mukhina", *Panorama Iskusstv*, 1989, no.12, pp.89–110
Vera Ignatiyevna Mukhina, exh. cat., Tretyakov Gallery, Moscow, 1989
N.V. Voronov, *Vera Mukhina*, Moscow: Izobrazitelnoye iskusstvo, 1989
M.N. Yablonskaya, *Women Artists of Russia's New Age, 1900–1935*, New York: Rizzoli, and London: Thames and Hudson, 1990
Agitation zum Glück: Sowjetische Kunst der Stalinzeit, exh. cat., Documenta-Halle, Kassel, and elsewhere, 1993
Art and Power: Europe under the Dictators, 1930–1945, exh. cat., Hayward Gallery, London, 1995

With Anna Golubkina (q.v.) and Vera Isayeva, Mukhina was one of Russia's greatest sculptors and her influence on the course of Soviet sculpture was profound and permanent. While neither avant-garde nor highly experimental, Mukhina's sculpture demonstrates a strong confidence in the classical tradition and an artistic vitality that became especially appropriate to her interpretations of Socialist Realism. True, Mukhina's admiration of Rodin and Emile-Antoine Bourdelle left an imprint on her early figures, such as her cement portrait of *Alexander Vertepov* (1914; 32 × 18 × 33 cm.; Tretyakov Gallery, Moscow). With her friend Lyubov Popova (q.v.), Mukhina also investigated French Cubism in Paris, extending the new formal principles to sculptures such as *Pietà* (1916; destroyed) and to her dynamic costume designs (not realised) for several plays that Alexander Tairov prepared at his Chamber Theatre in the mid-1910s, such as *La Cena delle Beffe* and *The Rose and the Cross*. An assistant there to Alexandra Exter (q.v.), Mukhina took particular note of her subtle conception of volume and construction, mentioning later that "Exter exerted a deep influence on my entire life" (quoted in Voronova 1976, p.42). Later, in 1923, she worked with Exter and others at the Atelier of Fashions, Moscow, on dress designs and helped Exter with designs for the film *Aelita*, released in 1924.

Mukhina adjusted quickly to the demands of the October Revolution of 1917, producing relevant works such as her project for the *Flame of the Revolution* (1922–3; bronze; 104 × 60 × 60 cm.) and *Peasant Woman* (1927; bronze; 190 × 79 × 70 cm.; both Tretyakov Gallery, Moscow). Mukhina is now remembered for her documentary and often tendentious sculpture, reflecting her commitment to the new political ideology and to the fundamental tenets of Socialist Realism that required the artist to "depict reality in its revolutionary development" (extract from Andrei Zhdanov's speech at the First Congress of Soviet Writers, Moscow, 1934; translation in John E. Bowlt, ed., *Russian Art of the Avant-garde: Theory and Criticism, 1902–1934*, 2nd edition, London and New York: Thames and Hudson, 1988, p.293). Concealing her Cubo-Futurist flirtation, Mukhina brought an energy and clarity of message to her evocations of the Revolution and the Civil War. The grandeur of Mukhina's artistic vision appealed to both the Party and the masses alike, ensuring her prestigious political commissions in the 1930s–50s, such as her figures for the Hotel Moscow (1930s), the buxom harvesters for the New Moscow River

Bridge (1938) and her several responses to World War II, such as the bronze bust of *General Boris Yusupov* (1942; Tretyakov Gallery) and the group *We Demand Peace* (1950–51). Mukhina adjusted her artistic vision to the conventions of the Stalin style unabashedly, extending her love of the histrionic to her monumental busts and statues such as the famous *Industrial Worker and Collective Farm Girl*, erected for the Exposition Internationale, Paris, in 1937. Towering above Boris Iofan's monumental Soviet Pavilion, the new Soviet man and woman, rendered in stainless steel, strode towards the bright future – and towards the Nazi eagle atop the German Pavilion directly opposite. Immediately, *Industrial Worker and Collective Farm Girl*, now in front of the permanent Exhibition of Economic Achievements in Moscow, became one of the most widely recognised symbols of the USSR and a model for many subsequent Soviet monuments.

But Mukhina conveyed individual moods and emotions as well as obvious political statements. Her statues of cultural heroes, from *Peter Tchaikovsky* (1945–53) to *Maxim Gorky* (1952) and the ballerina *Galina Ulanova* (1941; bronze; State Russian Museum, St Petersburg), testifying to an unhesitating mastery of volumetrical form, often show the sitter in a moment of deep concentration or lyrical inspiration; and Mukhina could also produce intimate and pensive sculpture such as her renderings of relatives and friends, including several heads of her husband, *Alexander Zamkov* (e.g. the bronze of 1918; State Russian Museum) and her son. Moreover, her interest in unexpected media such as glass and her numerous pencil and charcoal drawings show an aesthetic diversity and flexibility that are not always apparent from her more familiar public sculpture. Mukhina combined the need for historical accuracy with an impetuous fantasy, prompting the critic Boris Ternovets, Mukhina's old friend, to speak of her "vividness and expressivity of decorative invention" (Ternovets 1937, p.24).

JOHN E. BOWLT

Münter, Gabriele [fig. 51]
German painter and printmaker, 1877–1962

Born in Berlin, 19 February 1877. Settled in Herford with her family, 1878; in Koblenz, 1884.

Received first training in Düsseldorf in the studio of Ernst Bosch and later in the Damenschule (Ladies' School) of Willy Platz, 1897. Visited relatives in USA, 1898–1900. Attended beginners' classes of Maximilian Dasio at the Damenakademie des Münchener Künstlerinnenvereins, Munich, 1901; attended sculpture course under Wilhelm Hüsgen at the newly formed Phalanx school, 1901–2; established contact with the director, Wassily Kandinsky; attended a woodcut course with the graphic artist, Ernst Neumann, 1902–3. Start of intimate relationship with Kandinsky, 1902; travelled with him in Germany and abroad, to the Netherlands, North Africa, Italy and Brussels, 1904–5; resided with him in Paris and Sèvres, attending drawing classes at the Académie de la Grande Chaumière under Théophile Steinlen, 1906–7. Returned to Berlin and thereafter Munich, establishing contact with Russian artists Marianne Werefkin (q.v.) and Alexej Jawlensky, 1908. Founder member, Neue Künstlervereinigung München, 1909; seceded from the association, with Kandinsky and Franz Marc, to initiate Der Blaue Reiter, 1911. Increasing contact with art dealer Herwarth Walden, 1912–13. Travelled to Goldach in Switzerland at outbreak of World War I, and remained in Zürich when Kandinsky returned to Moscow, 1914. Established residence in Stockholm, 1915. Final visit of Kandinsky to Münter before his second marriage to Nina Andreyevskaya, 1916. Moved to Copenhagen, 1917. Returned to Germany, as artistic production continued to dwindle, 1920–22; made numerous short trips in Germany; in Cologne, started text "Beichte und Anklage" (completed 1928); settled in Berlin (until 1929) and joined the Reichsverband Bildender Künstler Deutschlands (German National Federation of Fine Artists), 1925. Made contact with the poet Eleonore Kalkowska and a circle from the Verein der Künstlerinnen zu Berlin, 1926. Trip to Paris, where she was joined by art historian Dr Johannes Eichner, 1929–30. Resided in Murnau with Eichner, 1933. Became a member of the newly formed Reichskammer der bildenden Künste (National Chamber of Visual Arts), 1934. Economic austerity and limited exhibiting outlets through association with "Degenerate Art", 1937–46. Recipient of Munich art prize for painting, 1956. Presented Kandinsky's early works and 25 of her own paintings to the Städtische Galerie im Lenbachhaus, Munich, 1957. Died in Murnau,

19 May 1962. Estate of writings, correspondence and works formed the Gabriele Münter- und Johannes Eichner-Stiftung at the Lenbachhaus, 1966.

Principal Exhibitions

Individual

Kunstsalon Lenoble, Cologne: 1908

Galerie Der Sturm, Berlin: 1913 (touring retrospective), 1915, 1917 (with Gösta Adrian-Nilsson and Paul Klee)

Carl Gummesons Konsthandel, Stockholm: 1916

Nya Konstgalleriet Ciacelli, Stockholm: 1917 (with Georg Pauli)

Den frie udstilling, Copenhagen: 1918

Ny Kunstsal, Copenhagen: 1919

Bremen: 1933–5 (touring retrospective)

Kunstverein Braunschweig: 1949–53 (touring)

Kestner-Gesellschaft, Hannover: 1951 (with Paula Modersohn-Becker)

Moderne Galerie Otto Stangl, Munich: 1954 (with Wassily Kandinsky and Franz Marc)

Städtische Galerie im Lenbachhaus, Munich: 1957 (with Wassily Kandinsky), 1962 (retrospective)

Dalzell Hatfield Galleries, Los Angeles: 1960 (with Wassily Kandinsky), 1963 (retrospective)

Marlborough Fine Art, London: 1960

Leonard Hutton Galleries, New York: 1961

Group

Salon des Indépendants, Paris: 1907–8, 1911–12

Salon d'Automne, Paris: 1907–10

Neue Künstlervereinigung München, Galerie Thannhauser, Munich: 1909, 1910

Isdebsky Salon, Odessa: 1910

Bubnovy valet (Jack/Knave of Diamonds), Moscow: 1910, 1912

Der Blaue Reiter, Galerie Thannhauser, Munich: 1911

Der Blaue Reiter, Kunsthandlung Hans Goltz, Munich, and Galerie Der Sturm, Berlin: 1912

Galerie Der Sturm, Berlin: 1913 (Erster Deutscher Herbstsalon)

Galerie Nierendorf, Berlin: 1927 (Die schaffende Frau in der bildenden Kunst)

Galerie Rudolf Wiltschek, Berlin: 1930

Selected Writings

"Gabriele Münter über sich selbst", Das Kunstwerk, ii/7, 1948, p.25

"Bekenntnisse und Erinnerungen", Menschenbilder in Zeichnungen, ed. G.F. Hartlaub, Berlin, 1952

"Mein Bild Mann im Sessel", Die Kunst und das schöne Heim, li/2, 1953, p.53

Wassily Kandinsky and Gabriele Münter: Letters and Reminiscences, 1902–1914, ed. Annegret Hoberg, Munich: Prestel, 1994

Bibliography

Rheinisch-Westfälische Zeitung, 8 May 1910

Johannes Eichner, "Gabriele Münter: Das Werk von 1908–1933", Die Weltkunst, ix/22, 1935, p.2

Paul Ferdinand Schmidt, "Entdeckung einer Künstlerin", Wiesbadener Kurier, 4 October 1947

Hans Reetz, "Gabriele Münter: Eine Bahnbrecherin in moderner Kunst", Die Welt der Frau, April 1950, pp.4–5

Lilly Rydström-Wickelberg, "Gabriele Münter", Konstrevy, xxviii, 1952, pp.216–20

Johannes Eichner, Kandinsky und Gabriele Münter: Von Ursprüngen moderner Kunst, Munich: Bruckmann, 1957

Hans Konrad Roethel, Gabriele Münter, Munich: Bruckmann, 1957

Maria-Dorothea Beck, "Vom frohen Tun: Die Malerin Gabriele Münter", Mädchenbildung und Frauenschaffen, ix, 1959, pp.1–10

Edouard Roditi, Dialogues on Art, London: Secker and Warburg, 1960; New York: Horizon, 1961

Sabine Helms, Gabriele Münter: Das druckgraphische Werk, Sammlungskatalog 2, Städtische Galerie im Lenbachhaus, Munich, 1967

Peter Lahnstein, Gabriele Münter, Ettal: Buch Kunstverlag, 1971

Liselotte Erlanger, "Gabriele Münter: A lesser life?", Feminist Art Journal, iii/4, 1974–5, pp.11ff

Ursula Glatzel, Zur Bedeutung der Volkskunst beim Blauen Reiter, dissertation, Ludwig-Maximilians-Universität, Munich, 1975

Rosel Gollek, "Murnau im Voralpenland", Deutsche Künstlerkolonien und Künstlerorte, ed. Gerhard Wietek, Munich: Theimig, 1976, pp.178–87

Paul Vogt, Geschichte der deutschen Malerei im 20. Jahrhundert, Cologne: DuMont Schauberg, 1976

Anne Mochon, Gabriele Münter: Still-life, Folk Art and the Blaue Reiter, University of Massachusetts, Amherst, 1977

Erich Pfeiffer-Belli, Gabriele Münter: Zeichnungen und Aquarelle, Berlin: Mann, 1979

Brigitte M. Cole, Gabriele Münter and the Development of Her Early Murnau Style, dissertation, University of Texas, Arlington, 1980

Alessandra Comini, "State of the field, 1980: The woman artists of German Expressionism", Arts Magazine, lv, November 1980, pp.147–53

Gabriele Münter: Between Munich and Murnau, exh. cat., Busch-Reisinger Museum, Harvard University, Cambridge, MA, and elsewhere, 1980

Susan P. Bachrach, "A comparison of the early landscapes of Münter and Kandinsky, 1902–1910", Woman's Art Journal, ii/1, 1981, pp.21–4

Sara H. Gregg, "Gabriele Münter and Sweden: Interlude and separation", Arts Magazine, lv, May 1981, pp.116–19

Kenneth Lindsay, "Gabriele Münter and Wassily Kandinsky: What they meant to each other", Arts Magazine, lvi, December 1981, pp.56–62

Ellen Klausch, *Frauenbilder im Werk Gabriele Münters*, research paper, Berlin, 1987

Shulamith Behr, *Women Expressionists*, Oxford: Phaidon, and New York: Rizzoli, 1988

Gabriele Münter, exh. cat., Kunstverein Hamburg, and elsewhere, 1988

Vivian Endicott Barnett, *Kandinsky and Sweden*, Malmö: Konsthall, and Stockholm: Moderna Museet, 1989

S. Heinlein, *Gabriele Münter und Marianne Werefkin: Die Rollen zweier Frauen im "Blauen Reiter"*, MA thesis, Hamburg University, 1989

Johanna Werckmeister, "'Blauer Reiter' im Damensattel: Rezeptionsraster für eine Künstlerin", *Kritische Berichte*, xvii, 1989, pp.70–77

Gisela Kleine, *Gabriele Münter und Wassily Kandinsky: Biographie eines Paares*, Frankfurt am Main: Insel, 1990

Andreas Hüneke, ed., *Der Blaue Reiter: Dokumente einer geistigen Bewegung*, Leipzig: Reclam, 1991

Sabine Windecker, *Gabriele Münter: Eine Künstlerin aus dem Kreis des "Blauen Reiters"*, Berlin: Reimer, 1991

Shulamith Behr, "Leicestershire's new acquisition: Gabriele Münter's portrait of Anna [Roslund-]Aagaard", *National Arts Collections Fund Review*, London, 1992

Gabriele Münter, 1877–1962: Retrospektive, exh. cat., Städtische Galerie im Lenbachhaus, Munich, and elsewhere, 1992

Writings, correspondence and works are in the Gabriele Münter- und Johannes Eichner-Stiftung, Städtische Galerie im Lenbachhaus, Munich.

Gabriele Münter's contribution to early modernism has received serious academic attention only in the last decade. Moreover, art-historical narratives that have traditionally consigned her role to that of "muse" or companion of Wassily Kandinsky were clearly brought into question by the large retrospective exhibition of 1992–3 that toured to Munich, Frankfurt am Main, Stockholm and Berlin. The overall impact of this spectacle of 160 paintings, 30 graphics and 60 drawings allowed Münter's oeuvre to emerge forcefully from the shadow of Kandinsky, who had been her tutor and lover between the years 1902 and 1916.

As with most women practitioners, Münter's status was problematic in relation to society in general and to the avant-garde communities in which she worked. Münter was descended from an upper-middle-class, Protestant background, and the fact that she lived with a married, albeit separated man, eleven years her senior, was distinctly unconventional for the time. Moreover, she remained childless and career-orientated, refusing to subordinate her aims to the success of the relationship. In

Münter's various self-portraits, the manner in which she negotiated her self-identity testifies to the conflicts engendered between societal constructions of the terms "woman" and "artist" (see Behr in Munich 1992, pp.85–90). Although she was an active contributor to and promoter of the Neue Künstlervereinigung München (1909–12) and Blaue Reiter (1912–14), the artist's ban on the publication of her writings until 50 years after her death have made it difficult to reconstruct her theoretical preoccupations. Abridged versions of her correspondence and journals have recently been published but, on the whole, art historians have assumed that the lack of written testimony accounts for Münter's supposed simplicity of character and intuitive directions in art.

On the whole, it is to Johannes Eichner that we owe the dubious heritage of the elision between psychological character and artistic production, between Münter's so-called naive temperament and "truly primitive" (*echte Primitive*) artistic statement, defined in opposition to Kandinsky's intellectual and spiritual contribution to the origins of modern art (Eichner 1957, pp.22 and 282). Münter herself contributed to this legend in her reminiscences ("Bekenntnisse und Erinnerungen", 1952) which recorded Kandinsky's observation:

> You are hopeless as a pupil. One cannot teach you anything. You can only do what you have inside you. You have everything instinctively [*alles von Natur*]. All I can do for you is to protect and cultivate your talent so that nothing false intervenes.

This must be one of the most frequently derided statements in the annals of feminist criticism due its patronising tone and determinist endorsement of the metaphors of woman as nature and instinct. Yet the myths of the "untutored", the "spontaneous" and "authentic" remained the hallmarks of Münter's reception, a state of affairs that continued unabated well into the 1970s (e.g. Vogt 1976, p.58; for a historiographic survey, see Windecker 1991). These values have to be assessed critically in relation to Münter's oeuvre and interpreted contextually, since such vitalist aspirations were important preoccupations of Expressionist artists at the time.

While anti-academicism may have been a feature of her mature works, this does not necessarily imply that Münter was unskilled; indeed, five sets of remarkable profile-head drawings, in pencil, survive from her school days. The six American sketch-books, containing depictions of people, landscape and plants, reveal her ability to capture likeness and to distil the components of a scene with deft linear strokes and a minimum of subtle shading (e.g. *Aunt Lou in Plainview*, 1899; graphite on white paper; Städtische Galerie im Lenbachhaus, Munich, repr. Cambridge 1980, no.2). Interestingly, even when drawing from the nude model, Münter was far more comfortable when focusing on the salient contours of the pose than on the academic processes of shading and hatching (*Studies from the Model*, c.1902; Städtische Galerie im Lenbachhaus, repr. Munich 1992, fig.4).

Evidently, these skills were appropriate to her exploration of wood- and linocut technique, the processes of which received renewed attention and a growth in demand at the turn of the 19th and 20th centuries. As in the German Arts and Crafts move-ment (Jugendstil), which was particularly forceful in Munich, Münter endorsed the erosion between the fine and applied arts and a stylistic return to the handmade and non-mechanical rhythms of nature. Her colour linoleum print, the portrait of *Kandinsky* (1906; Leonard Hutton Galleries, New York, repr. Cambridge 1980, no.9), offsets a crisp bold silhou-ette against a background of simplified, organic shapes, delineated by contour. Already, during her stay in Paris, her woodcuts were deemed suitable for reproduction in the symbolist magazine *Les Tendances Nouvelles* (1906) and one of Münter's launching exhibitions in 1908 – at Friedrich Cohen's bookstore in Bonn – was exclusively devoted to her print production.

Although the mere existence of innumerable sketchbooks from all periods testifies to the artist's systematic reliance on preliminary studies for her final paintings, it is evident that Münter painted very quickly, often completing one or more large-format pictures in a single afternoon (see Hoberg 1994, letters dated 8 December 1910 and 12–13 December 1910, pp.97–9). Her initial training in the Phalanx school encouraged an interest in *in situ* landscape painting; on Kandinsky's advice, her early works (*Kandinsky Painting in the Landscape*, 1903; oil on canvas; Städtische Galerie im Lenbachhaus, repr. Munich 1992, no.5) rely on a limited colour range of yellows, greens and browns with extensive use of the palette knife. Her interpretation of this genre reached a climax in the Murnau period (see Hoberg in *ibid.*, pp.27–46) when, in the company of

Kandinsky, Marianne Werefkin (q.v.) and Jawlensky, Münter's works abandoned the plein-air, Impressionist qualities of her Sèvres sojourn (*View from the Window in Sèvres*, 1906; oil on canvas; Städtische Galerie im Lenbachhaus, *ibid.*, no.18) to assume the values of synthetism. With their unusual palette of blue, green, yellow, pink with red for emphasis, the diverse surfaces and facture of Münter's Murnau vistas are bound together by strong contour, as in *Landscape with Hut in the Sunset* (1908; private collection, *ibid.*, no.47).

These small-scale oils on board, roughly 33 × 41 centimetres, served as an increasing stimulus for technical radicalism as the artist sought to negotiate a path between Jawlensky's Matisse-linked modernism and the inspiration of folk art. It is testi-mony to Münter's inventiveness that, even when interpreting similar motifs, the landscapes produced throughout her career – as when she returned to Murnau in the 1930s – always retain a freshness of the visual encounter and elements of surprise and pleasure for the viewer (*Street in Murnau*, 1931; private collection, *ibid.*, no.203). Less convincing, however, is the industrial landscape *Blue Excavator* (1935–6; oil on canvas; 60 × 90 cm.; Städtische Galerie im Lenbachhaus, *ibid.*, no.223), which arose from numerous sketches made of urban develop-ment at Olympiastrasse near Garmisch during the early years of the Third Reich. As part of a group of contributions to the travelling exhibition the *Streets of Adolf Hitler in Art* in 1936, these works testify to the invasiveness of official culture in prescribing stylistic limits and reducing the outlets for modern art.

According to Münter, it was Jawlensky who first drew her attention to Bavarian and Bohemian glass painting and the technique known as *Hinterglasmalerei* (painting behind glass). A substantial collection was owned by a local brewer in Murnau, Johann Kroetz (see Hoberg 1994, p.16, now in the town museum at Oberammergau). Münter started her own collection and copied tradi-tional examples of this genre (e.g. *St Florian*, c.1909; repr. Munich 1992, p.253), acquiring the technique from Heinrich Rambold, a glass painter still active in Murnau. Notwithstanding the fact that the production of folk art had long been part of a thriving industry – stimulated by an expanding tourist economy in the region – the members of the Blaue Reiter group cherished the Neo-romantic

belief in the innocent religiosity and naive originality of the artists.

In her *Still Life with St George* (1911; oil on
board; Städtische Galerie im Lenbachhaus, *ibid.*,
no.106) Münter combined a motley assortment of
images: a statue of the Virgin, small crèche figurines
from Oberammergau, a ceramic hen, a vase of
flowers and, on the left-hand side, painted in a hazy
aura, the glass-painting of St George. Divorced from
their original location or narrative sequences, the
votive objects are animated by inconsistent effects of
lighting and invested with new mythic associations.
Hence, in her appropriation of the methods and
motifs of folk art, Münter implicated herself in the
Western-based phenomenon of "modernist primitivism", a trend that transformed the inspiration of
artefacts from so-called primitive societies into the
departure for autonomous art.

In view of the perception of her work as aligned
with nature, how could Münter's production escape
critical understanding of women's creativity as
remaining in the realm of matter, never capable of
approaching male artists' sublimation of the "primitive" into high art? Invariably, she deployed such
referents in ironic and potentially subversive depictions of the domestic, the private spheres of womanhood appropriated by male artists for modern
subject matter. This is most apparent in Münter's
more monumental works that portrayed her
colleagues from the circles of the Neue
Künstlervereinigung München and Blaue Reiter in
rustic interiors, providing a subtle resonance
between the rarefied atmosphere of intellectual
discourse and the leisure activities of avant-garde
communities. In works such as *Kandinsky at the
Tea-Table* (1910; oil on board; Israel Museum,
Jerusalem, *ibid.*, no.74) and *Kandinsky and Erma
Bossi at the Table* (1912; oil on canvas; Städtische
Galerie im Lenbachhaus, *ibid.*, no.113) Münter
demonstrated her interest in juxtaposing animated
still-life objects with figures, frozen in action, radically compressed in a two-dimensionalised space.

In *Man in Chair* (1913; oil on canvas; Bayerische
Staatsgemäldessammlungen, Munich, *ibid.*, no.133)
Paul Klee is portrayed wedged into an armchair set
against an emerald-green rear wall of the Kandinsky
and Münter apartment in Ainmillerstrasse, Munich.
While his legs in white shimmering trousers are
depicted folded sideways, the upper torso in a stiff
black jacket is displayed frontally and comically. On
the same level as his intense gaze, the dramatic

arrangements of Bavarian *Hinterglasbilder* and folk-
art figurines vie for the spectator's attention.
Whether or not Münter was conscious of such infer-
ences, the awkwardness of her sitters' countenances
questions and subverts the assumption of masculine
control of domestic and private spaces. It is interesting to note that Münter's correspondence reveals
this paradoxical tension: an awareness of feminist
ideas counteracted by an apparent obsession with
domesticity: "Wanted to read in the afternoon – the
philosophy of the feminist Lessing – a new book
'Weib, Frau, Dame' but the phonograph was going
across the street ... – so I did some sewing and
ironing – I always have my things quite tidy" (letter
of 12–13 December 1910, Hoberg 1994, p.99).

Significantly, the women in her circle are interpreted far more sympathetically. This was particularly evident during the Scandinavian period
(Annika Öhrner in Munich 1992, pp.67–84) when
Münter depicted a series of women in interiors,
focusing on the themes of isolation, illness and
reverie. Unlike the primitivist and mystical undertones of her earlier compositions, these Swedish
portraits focus attention on the contemplative
mood, short hair-styles and reform dress of early
20th-century womanhood. Münter's friend
Gertrude Holz served as the model for the pendant
pieces *Reflection* (1917; oil on canvas; Städtische
Galerie im Lenbachhaus, *ibid.*, no.154) and *Future
(Woman in Stockholm)* (1917; Frank. E. Taplin, Jr,
USA, *ibid.*, no.155). In both paintings the bust-
length figure is posed in front of a window, reinforcing the contrast between the external world and
the confinement or seclusion of the interior setting.
Strategic use of black and white contrasts with variations of the primary colours – red, yellow and blue
– applied in broad, powerful strokes. Still-life
objects are markedly more delineated than during
the Murnau period but their forceful presence does
not detract from the meditative atmosphere.

While these works were destined for the open
market, Münter consistently sought portraiture
commissions (see Behr 1992, pp.56–9). In the
portrait of *Anna Roslund*, painted in Copenhagen in
1917, Münter adopted a potent, three-quarter-
length composition. Anna Roslund, the youngest
sister of Nell Walden, was a writer and musician,
and Münter represents her as a pipe-smoking,
musing figure, an unconventional metaphor for
creative womanhood. In declaring the confident
independence of the "new woman", the bravura

displayed in this work totally belies the biographical events of Münter's life at the time and alerts one to the dangers of assuming a conflation between the two.

During the 1920s Münter's ability to capture the essential features of a scene with immense economy of line coincided with the values of clarity given priority in Neue Sachlichkeit circles and in the advice offered by her mentor Johannes Eichner (see his letter of 29 September 1928 in Kleine 1990, p.563). In a work painted in Berlin entitled *Reflection II* (1928; oil on canvas; Städtische Galerie im Lenbachhaus, repr. Munich 1992, no.187) the full-length, seated figure is portrayed with crossed legs in profile while the upper part of the body faces the viewer, the head resting on her hands. Though there is an emphasis on two-dimensionality, the chair casts shadows within the shallow space as Münter explores the cubic volumes of the sitter in a range of red and ochre tonalities. This distillation of her painterly abilities needs to be viewed in the context of the crisis of Expressionism rather than as a withdrawal from the intensity of the earlier periods.

Although her works of the post-World War II period remained within the confines of the "lesser" genres – landscape, still life, interior scenes – it is necessary to reappraise Münter's transformation or disruption of figural and narrative material across the span of her oeuvre. Even her abstractions are quite remarkable for their independence from Kandinsky's methods, proclaiming distinctive gender differences with regard to their iconographic departure (see Heller in *ibid.*, pp.47–66). Methodologies that glibly assert the simplicity and "primitive" qualities of her production fail to do justice to their contingent and specific circumstances. Indeed, it is possible to observe that her images of the domestic and private realms were invested with the significance of contemporaneity, representing the equations between modern art and life.

SHULAMITH BEHR

N

Neel, Alice
American painter, 1900–1984

Born in Merion Square, Pennsylvania, 28 January 1900; grew up in Colwyn. Studied at Philadelphia School of Design for Women (now Moore College of Art), Philadelphia, 1921–5; attended Chester Springs summer school of the Pennsylvania Academy of the Fine Arts, 1924. Married Cuban artist Carlos Enriquez, and moved to Havana, Cuba, 1925; two daughters, born 1926 (d. 1927) and 1928; returned to New York, 1927; separated from husband, 1930; nervous breakdown, 1930–31. Moved to Greenwich Village, New York, with Kenneth Doolittle, 1932; he destroyed much of her work, 1934. Son by nightclub entertainer José Santiago born 1939. Met Marxist film-maker Sam Brody, 1940; separated soon after birth of son in 1941. Enrolled on Public Works of Art Project (PWAP), 1933; Works Progress Administration Federal Art Project (WPA/FAP) easel division, 1935. Recipient of Arts and Letters award, American Academy and Institute of Arts and Letters, 1969; honorary doctorate, Moore College of Art, 1971; National Women's Caucus for Art outstanding achievement award, 1979. Member, American Academy and Institute of Arts and Letters, 1976. Died 13 October 1984.

Selected Individual Exhibitions
Contemporary Arts Gallery, New York: 1938
Pinacotheca Gallery, New York: 1944
ACA Gallery, New York: 1950, 1954
New Playwrights Theater, New York: 1951
Graham Gallery, New York: 1963, 1966, 1968, 1970, 1973, 1976, 1977, 1978, 1980
Whitney Museum of American Art, New York: 1974 (retrospective)
Georgia Museum of Art, Athens: 1975 (retrospective)
Artemisia Gallery, Chicago: 1978
University of Bridgeport, CT, and Silvermine Guild of Artists: 1979 (retrospective)
Boston University Art Gallery: 1980
Artists Union, Moscow: 1981
Robert Miller Gallery, New York: 1982

Bibliography
Linda Nochlin, "Some women realist painters of the figure", *Arts Magazine*, xlviii, May 1974, pp.29–33; reprinted in *Women, Art and Power and Other Essays*, New York: Harper, 1988
Cindy Nemser, *Alice Neel: The Woman and Her Work*, Athens: Georgia Museum of Art, 1975
——, *Art Talk: Conversations with 12 Women Artists*, New York: Scribner, 1975
May Stevens, "The non-portraits of Alice Neel", *Women's Studies*, vi, 1978, pp.61–73
Barbaralee Diamonstein, *Inside New York's Art World*, New York: Rizzoli, 1979
Eleanor Munro, *Originals: American Women Artists*, New York: Simon and Schuster, 1979
Rita Mercedes, "Alice Neel", *Connoisseur*, ccviii, September 1981, pp.2–3 (interview)
Charlotte Streifer Rubinstein, *American Women Artists from Early Times to the Present*, Boston: Hall, 1982
Patricia Hills, *Alice Neel*, New York: Abrams, 1983
Alice Neel: Paintings, 1933–1982, exh. cat., Malone Art Gallery, Loyola Marymount University, Los Angeles, 1983
Ted Castle, "Alice Neel", *Artforum*, xxii, October 1983, pp.36–41 (interview)
Judith Higgins, "Alice Neel and the human comedy", *Art News*, lxxxiii, October 1984, pp.70–79
——, "Alice Neel, 1900–1984", *Art News*, lxxxiii, December 1984, p.14 (obituary)
Exterior/Interior: Alice Neel, exh. cat., Tufts University Art Gallery, Medford, MA, 1991
Marilyn Lincoln Board, "The legend of Alice Neel: Re-envisioning the Cinderella story", *Images of the Self as Female: The Achievement of Women Artists in Re-envisioning Feminine Identity*, ed. Kathryn N. Benzel and Lauren Pringle de la Vars, Lewiston, NY: Edwin Mellen Press, 1992
Pamela Allara, *Pictures of People: Alice Neel's American Portrait Gallery* (in preparation)

Alice Neel's career as a painter of portraits, still lifes, cityscapes and narrative scenes spanned over half a century. During that time she emerged from the fringes of the New York avant-garde of the 1920s and participated with other left-wing artists who worked on government projects during the Depression of the 1930s, while at the same time protesting against social conditions and the spread of international fascism. During World War II, struggling to get by in an apartment in Spanish Harlem, New York, and raising her two sons, she still continued to paint. She rarely exhibited during the 1940s and 1950s, but her career picked up as she was rediscovered, first by the Beat Generation of poets in the late 1950s, and later, in the 1970s, by the Women's Movement. When she died in 1984 she was riding the crest of interest in international neo-expressionism.

Neel was brought up in Colwyn, Pennsylvania, a small town that she found stifling. After holding down mundane clerical jobs as a teenager in Philadelphia, she determined to become an artist. Four years at the Philadelphia School of Design for Women (now Moore College of Art) solidified her ambitions and provided her with the solid techniques to produce portraits and other pictures. At a summer school run by the Pennsylvania Academy of the Fine Arts she met and later married Carlos Enriquez, an upper-class Cuban painter. The young couple travelled to Havana in 1925 and spent two years there, where Neel exhibited with the Cuban avant-garde (Allara, book in preparation) and gave birth to her first daughter, Santillana. In 1927 Neel and Enriquez returned to New York to forge their painting careers. Santillana died that December from diphtheria, but another daughter, Isabella, was born the following November. In May 1930 Enriquez left with Isabella for Havana to raise funds from his family for a trip to Paris where they planned to live and paint. Instead, he left their daughter with Cuban relatives and went on alone to Paris. Virtually abandoned, Neel was torn by the contradictions in her life and suffered a nervous breakdown in August 1930. Briefly hospitalised, she was back home in Colwyn that winter and attempted suicide. Institutionalised in hospitals and a sanatorium for over six months, she gradually recovered her equilibrium and was released in September 1931.

In 1932 Neel moved to Greenwich Village with a sailor, Kenneth Doolittle, a jealous lover who later slashed many of her paintings. In contrast to Doolittle, another suitor, John Rothschild, lent her financial support and encouraged her art. She did a series of witty watercolours of herself and Rothschild in the hotel where they stayed on West 42nd Street, for example *Joie de Vivre* (1935; Yale University Art Gallery, New Haven).

During the early Depression years of the 1930s Neel, like many other out-of-work New York artists, signed up to work on the government art projects – first the Public Works of Art Project (PWAP) and later the Federal Art Project of the Works Progress Administration (WPA/FAP). During these years she painted unconventional portraits: *Joe Gould* (1933; artist's estate), in which the eccentric Gould is painted nude with five sets of genitals; *Kenneth Fearing* (1935; Museum of Modern Art, New York), with the poet surrounded by symbols of the Depression; and *Pat Whalen* (1935; Whitney Museum of American Art), in which the Communist labour organiser pounds his fist on a table upon which rests an issue of the *Daily Worker*, the newspaper of the Communist Party. Although unique in American painting, such portraits as *Max White* (1935; National Museum of American Art, Washington, DC) have a stylistic kinship to German portrait painters of the Neue Sachlichkeit (New Objectivity) of the 1920s.

In 1935 Neel met José Santiago, a charming Puerto Rican who played the guitar. She moved with him to Spanish Harlem in 1938 and a year later their son, Richard Neel, was born. Santiago moved out, and Neel became involved with Sam Brody, an intellectual and Communist documentary film-maker. Her son Hartley Stockton Neel was born in September 1941. Neel hung on to her government art job until 1943, when the WPA folded. During the 1940s and 1950s she painted her neighbours in Spanish Harlem and raised her two sons. Throughout this time she maintained her ties with left-wing artists and intellectuals. In 1949 Communist Party members were put on trial for violating the Smith Act, an act (later declared unconstitutional) that made it a crime merely to use the rhetoric of revolution against the US government. Neel attended the sessions of the trial and made drawings of the conservative Judge Medina and the State's star witness, Angela Calomaris. She also painted portraits of Communist Party organisers, such as *Mike Gold* and *Bill McKie*.

In December 1950 Neel had a major solo exhibition at the ACA Gallery in New York, and another in April 1951 at the New Playwrights Theatre. Mike Gold, editor of *Masses and Mainstream*, wrote a foreword for the catalogue of 1951 which said in part:

Alice has for years lived with her children in a Harlem tenement. Her studio is the kitchen and her models the neighbors and the streets. She comes from an old Philadelphia family dating back to the Revolution. But her paintings reveal that here is her true family. In solitude and poverty, Alice has developed like a blade of grass between two city stones. She has become a superb craftsman, and the first clear and beautiful voice of Spanish Harlem. She reveals not only its desperate poverty, but its rich and generous soul ... ALICE NEEL is a pioneer of socialist realism in American painting.

The 24 paintings in the show included *Spanish Family*, *Investigation of Poverty of the Russell Sage Foundation* and *T.B. Harlem* (National Museum of Women in the Arts, Washington, DC). In 1954 Neel held a second exhibition at the ACA Gallery.

A turning point in her career occurred at the end of the 1950s. She began to see a psychologist who encouraged her to be more aggressive in advancing her own career and sending pictures to exhibitions. Encouraged, she contacted the poet Frank O'Hara and persuaded him to pose for her. In 1959 she was asked to play a part in the improvised avant-garde film made by Robert Frank and Al Leslie, *Pull My Daisy*, which also included the Beat Generation writers Allen Ginsberg, Gregory Corso and Jack Kerouac, and the artist Larry Rivers. At this time, her sons were off at college, and all her lovers had departed. Moreover, a woman friend, Muriel Bettancourt, offered to give her an annual stipend so that she would be free of financial worries. She then moved out of Spanish Harlem to 300 West 107th Street.

Neel's career blossomed during the 1960s and 1970s. In 1960 a reproduction of *Frank O'Hara, No.2* (1960; artist's estate) was published in *Art News*. The Graham Gallery, on Madison Avenue where other chic galleries were located, began to show her work in 1963. During the 1960s she painted portraits of art world personalities, such as the collectors *Stewart Mott*, *Arthur Bullowa* and *Walter Gutman*, the critics *Herbert Crehan* and *Henry Geldzahler*, the art dealer *Ellie Poindexter* and the artists *Robert Smithson*, *Milton Resnick*, *Pat Pasloff*, *Red Grooms*, *Mimi Gross* and *Geoffrey Hendricks*. She also turned her attention to her own sons – Richard and Hartley, their girlfriends and, later, their wives.

Neel's gallery of notables grew to include the Nobel Prize winner *Linus Pauling*, the composer *Aaron Copland*, the theatre producer *Joseph Papp*, the art historian *Linda Nochlin*, and further artists: *Duane Hanson*, *Andy Warhol*, *Marisol*, *Faith Ringgold* and *Benny Andrews*. But she also continued to paint neighbourhood people: the taxicab driver and black nationalist *Abdul Rahman*, the *Fuller Brush Man* and her cleaning woman, *Carmen*. Some of these portraits are sympathetically rendered (especially the portrayals of artists, art students and neighbourhood people), others are satirical (particularly the portraits of dealers, patrons, art critics and art historians), but all are painted with expressive candour. Like other artists, she needed, but often resented, the financial and psychological support of private patrons, dealers, art critics, curators, art historians and museum directors. Her ambivalence gave many of these portraits a power and tension, a love/hate nervousness.

One of her favourite ploys consisted in inviting art-world personalities into her studio and then asking them to disrobe so that she could paint them nude. Disarmed by her disingenuousness, they usually complied. Among her most notable nude portraits are those of the art critic *John Perreault*, painted as a frontal nude (1972; Whitney Museum of American Art, New York), and the critic *Cindy Nemser*, demurely covering her exposed breasts with her arms as she clasps the naked knee of her husband Chuck. Neel painted herself nude in 1980 (National Portrait Gallery, Washington, DC), with her flaccid body rolling out of a chair in which she sits, gripping brush with one hand and painting rag with another as she scrutinises the viewer and/or the mirror in which her image is reflected.

The sitters would make their own choices about clothes and body pose. But typically Neel would take over and rearrange them in order to heighten their expressive potential. Whether they timidly display their dimpled nude bodies or shroud themselves in protective layers of leather, wool and fur, Neel made certain that their hands, body pose and facial expression all contributed to the totality of the image – an image both specific and typical of their social class. From her brushes people emerged who seemed to reveal their inner lives through their self-posturing, their relationship to each other, either touching or separated in the double portraits, and their self-consciousness of the painter, staring back at Neel aggressively or pensively dreaming.

Her portraits of her own family members chart their emotional growth and the dynamics of family life. *Richard Neel* (1963) and *Hartley Neel* (1965) depict her two sons in the early years of manhood, direct and open to the viewer's observations. Some 15 years later – in *Hartley* of 1978 and *Richard in the Era of the Corporation* of 1979 – they had changed into professionals in mid-career, with Hartley going into radiology and Richard into corporate law. Neel commented that Richard's portrait of 1979 made her realise that the essence of the 1970s was the domination of American culture by business corporations. The bohemian mother had become ambivalent about the successes of her own sons.

Neel's paintings of Richard's wife, Nancy, are both specific portraits and expressive of women's lives in general. *Pregnant Woman* (1971; artist's estate) reveals Nancy swollen with the twins she will soon deliver. The masklike, expectant face stares impassively; her hands, irrelevant to her state of being, are hidden. Prominent are the rounded, brown-lined belly that contains the children, the buttocks that will release them to the world and the erect nipples ready to nurture them. Anticipation pervades the painting and points to its real subject – the process of human succession from generation to generation, Neel's own continuity with the future.

As early as the 1930s Neel had decided to paint the "human comedy", as Balzac had in his novels. By the 1970s she had a full cast of fascinating urban characters, to which she added in the early 1980s. She went on the lecture circuit with slides of her portraits. Looking like a bespectacled, kindly, white-haired grandmother, she amused her audience with outrageous remarks about her sitters' alleged sexual proclivities. In spite of Neel's own barely veiled misogyny, women art historians and critics enthusiastically organised shows of her work, invited her to campus art schools to speak and promoted her in the art magazines. She had become the paradigmatic "survivor" of the art world – a woman who had managed to achieve fame while raising children and

enduring fickle men. And she did indeed achieve fame – finally, in her seventies. In 1976 Neel was elected to the prestigious American Academy and Institute of Arts and Letters; and in 1979 she was honoured by the National Women's Caucus for Art for outstanding achievement in art and received her award from none other than the President, Jimmy Carter, in the Oval Room of the White House. In 1984, only months before her death from cancer, she appeared on the Johnny Carson television show, regaling audiences across the nation with her stories, her portraits and her ambition to leave to posterity a gallery of American types from the late 20th century.

PATRICIA HILLS

Nelli, Plautilla
Italian painter, 1523–1588

Born Polissena Nelli, 1523, to Pietro di Luca Nelli, a Florentine patrician, and Maria di Biagio di Cristofano. Became a Dominican tertiary, as Suora Plautilla, at the convent of Santa Caterina di Siena, Florence, 1537; elected prioress by 1568. Died 1588.

Bibliography

Giorgio Vasari, *Le vite de' più eccellenti pittori, scultori ed architettori*, Florence, 1568; ed. Gaetano Milanesi, v, Florence: Sansoni, 1880, pp.79–80 (life of Properzia de' Rossi); as *Lives of the Most Eminent Painters, Sculptors and Architects*, 10 vols, London: Macmillan-Medici Society, 1912–15; reprinted New York: AMS, 1976

Ulrich Thieme and Felix Becker, *Allgemeines Lexikon der bildenden Künstler von der Antike bis zur Gegenwart*, xxv, Leipzig: Seeman, 1931

Giovanna Pierattini, "Suor Plautilla Nelli, pittrice domenicana", *Memorie Domenicane*, lv, 1938, pp.82–7, 168–71, 221–7, 292–7

Dizionario biografico italiano, vi, Rome: Istituto dell'Enciclopedia Italiana, 1964 (life of Camilla Bartolini-Rucellai)

Women Artists, 1550–1950, exh. cat., Los Angeles County Museum of Art, and elsewhere, 1976

Plautilla Nelli became a Dominican nun, as Suora Plautilla, at the convent of Santa Caterina di Siena, Florence, in 1537, and was elected prioress by 1568. This convent had been founded and built beside the male Dominican community of San Marco by

Camilla Bartolini-Rucellai, called Suora Lucia, a passionate adherent of the Dominican friar Savonarola. The ethos of this community provided a nurturing environment for a woman with some artistic talent, because at its foundation Savonarola had recommended that the nuns should dedicate themselves to the arts of design, painting and modelling in order to be worthy of their keep and to encourage almsgiving. The fact that Plautilla's sister Costanza (Suor Petronella, another nun in the convent) composed a life of Savonarola suggests that the community maintained his ideals.

It has been speculated that Nelli was trained by male painters at San Marco, among whom was Fra Paolino da Pistoia, who had been an assistant to the Dominican painter Fra Bartolommeo (V. Marchese, *Memorie dei più insigni pittori scultori e architetti domenicani*, 2 vols, Bologna, 1878–9, ii, p.330). The methods of composition used by Fra Bartolommeo, which relied extensively on employing wax and plaster casts, and wax, wood and plaster figurines rather than live models would have suited Plautilla's training conditions. Since Vasari was able to list the contents of the convent's refectory, workroom and choir, it seems likely that Suor Plautilla's community, like many other Third Order convents dedicated to good works, was one that permitted some relaxation of the rules of enclosure – in contrast to the stricter vows of the Second Orders – until 1575, when according to the *Memorie* of the convent and following the Tridentine decrees, complete enclosure was enforced. And while it is customary to single out Plautilla Nelli as a lone woman artist, her near-contemporary Serafino Razzi, writing in 1590, listed her pupils as Suore Prudenzia Cambi, Agata Traballesi and Maria Ruggeri, and Suora Veronica. He also described the sculpture of Suora Maurizia Niccolini and of his own sister, Suora Angelica Razzi.

Lay-women artists seem generally to have been restricted to portraiture, perhaps because in terms of early 16th-century Italian aesthetics portraits were considered as merely imitative of external reality, and therefore subordinate to the religious or historical narrative thought to require the highest creative and imaginative powers. In contrast, Plautilla's confinement in the convent meant that this type of secular representation was inappropriate. Instead, the Savonarolan injunction encouraged her to make large religious narrative paintings, while her own

community exhibited her altarpieces in the public side of their church, guarded her reputation as a woman by the rules of enclosure, and dealt with her clients since all payments were made to the convent, rather than to the artist personally. In this unusually protective and encouraging environment, Plautilla Nelli produced a group of large altarpieces, as well as some small devotional pieces and illuminations.

According to Vasari she painted the following works: *Taking the Body of Christ for Burial with the Virgin Mary, the Three Marys, SS John the Evangelist and Peter, Nicodemus and Joseph of Arimathea*, formerly an altarpiece in the public area of the church of Santa Caterina di Siena, and now in San Marco, Florence (repr. *La chiesa e convento di San Marco a Firenze*, 2 vols, Florence, 1990, p.209, pl.38; the unusual inclusion of Peter in the scene suggests that this may have been a funerary altar for Nelli's father (Pietro) and mother (Maria), since the altar also honours Mary); the *Adoration of the Magi* (Regia Galleria, Parma; see Armando Quintavalle, *La Regia Galleria di Parma*, Rome, 1939, pp.318–19, no.158), also formerly an altarpiece in the public part of the church of Santa Caterina di Siena; and a *Last Supper*, "with life-size figures", for the refectory of Santa Caterina di Siena, Florence, now on deposit in the cloister of Santa Maria Novella, Florence (recorded as untraced in Los Angeles 1976, p.21, note 44, where it is also reported that the painting had been photographed, Alinari 31081, in the Spanish Chapel of Santa Maria Novella).

Vasari lists further works, none of which has been identified: a *Madonna and Child with SS Thomas, Augustine, Mary Magdalene, Catherine of Siena, Agnes, Catherine of Alexandria and Lucy* in the nuns' choir of Santa Lucia, Pistoia; an *Annunciation* in the house of the wife of Signor Mondragone, Florence; an *Annunciation* in the house of Madonna Marietta de' Fedini, Florence; a *Madonna* in San Giovannino, Florence; predella scenes of the *Life of St Zenobius* in the Duomo (Santa Maria del Fiore), Florence; paintings for the workroom of the convent, and also for the director of the hospital of Lelmo di Balduccio; and a copy of Agnolo Bronzino's *Nativity of Christ*.

Padre Serafini Siepi (*Descrizione topologico-istorica della città di Perugia*, ii, Perugia, 1822, pp.516–17) records a *Pentecost* commissioned in 1554 by Guglielmo Pontano, a professor of law, as his funerary altarpiece, which is still in its original location in the left transept, beneath the organ, of San Domenico, Perugia – the patron's memorial is over the door to the left of the altar. This splendid large altarpiece includes two Dominican nuns, placed in the background in the centre, directly behind the Virgin Mary. Nelli further feminised the scene by the unusual inclusion of Mary Magdalene and another Mary on either side of the Virgin. Pentecost, the foundation of the Church's ministry to the world, was often shown as an all-male, apostolic event, but Plautilla put five women in the centre stage and placed the Apostles at the side, in two groups of six. She employed an austere architectural setting, reminiscent of Roman baths, with a barrel vault and a Tuscan order. The attribution of this painting to Nelli is confirmed in her contemporary obituary, written by Padre Modesto Biliotti.

[My thanks to Simon Tugwell of the Historical Institute, Rome, for his help in providing information for this article.]

CATHERINE KING

Nevelson, Louise   [fig. 51]
American sculptor, 1900–1988

Born Leah Berliawsky in Kiev, Russia, 23 September 1900, into a liberal Jewish family. Emigrated to USA with her family, settling in Rockland, Maine, 1905. Married ship owner Charles Nevelson and moved to New York, 1920; son born 1922; separated from husband 1931; later divorced. Studied painting and drawing under Theresa Bernstein and William Meyerowitz in New York, 1920; acting under Princess Norina Matchabelli at International Theater Arts Institute, 1926 (met Frederick Kiesler through Matchabelli). Studied under Kenneth Hayes Miller at the Art Students League, New York, 1929–30; under Hans Hofmann in Munich, 1931–2; also worked as a film extra in Vienna and Berlin, and spent time in Paris and Italy. Returned to New York, 1932; studied modern dance under Ellen Kearns, and worked briefly as assistant to Diego Rivera; studied sculpture with Chaim Gross, 1933. Included in *Young Sculptors* exhibition, arranged by the Secession Gallery at the Brooklyn Museum, New York, 1935. As part of the Works Progress Administration (WPA), taught art at the Educational Alliance School of Art, New York, 1937. Trips to Mexico, late 1940s. Studied printmaking at Stanley William Hayter's Atelier 17, New York, 1949; fellowships to Tamarind Workshop, Los Angeles, 1963 and 1967. Participated in National Council on Arts and Government, Washington, DC, 1965. Recipient of medal, MacDowell Colony, Peterborough, New Hampshire, 1969; Brandeis University Creative Arts award in sculpture, 1971; Skowhegan medal for sculpture, 1971; American Institute of Architects award, 1977; honorary doctorates from Western College for Women, Oxford, Ohio, 1966; Rutgers University, New Brunswick, 1972; Smith College, Northampton, Massachusetts, 1973; Hobart and William Smith Colleges, Geneva, New York, 1971; Columbia University, New York, 1977; Boston University, 1978. Chapter President, New York, 1957–9, and National President, 1962–4, Artists' Equity; first Vice-President, Federation of Modern Painters and Sculptors, 1962–4; Member, National Association of Women Artists and Sculptors' Guild. Died in New York, 17 April 1988.

Selected Individual Exhibitions
Karl Nierendorf Gallery, New York: 1941, 1942, 1944, 1946
Norlyst Gallery, New York: 1943
Grand Central Moderns Gallery, New York: 1956, 1958
Martha Jackson Gallery, New York: 1959, 1961, 1970
Galerie Daniel Cordier, Paris: 1960, 1961
Pace Gallery, New York: 1964, 1965, 1968, 1969, 1971, 1972, 1974, 1976, 1978, 1980, 1981, 1983, 1985, 1986, 1989
Kunsthalle, Bern: 1964
Galleria d'Arte Contemporanea, Turin: 1964
Whitney Museum of American Art, New York: 1967 (retrospective), 1970, 1980 (retrospective)
Rijksmuseum Kröller-Müller, Otterlo: 1969
Museum of Fine Arts, Houston: 1969 (retrospective)
University Art Museum, University of Texas at Austin: 1970
Walker Art Center, Minneapolis: 1973–5 (touring retrospective)
Musée d'Art Moderne de la Ville de Paris: 1974
Neue Nationalgalerie, Berlin: 1974
Storm King Art Center, Mountainville, NY: 1978
Phoenix Art Museum: 1980 (touring)
Galerie Claude Bernard, Paris: 1986
Solomon R. Guggenheim Museum, New York: 1986
List Visual Arts Center, Massachusetts Institute of Technology, Cambridge: 1986

Selected Writings

"Queen of the Black Black", *Art News*, lx, September 1961, pp.45ff

Dawns and Dusks, New York: Scribner, 1976 (with Diana MacKown)

Bibliography

"Louise Nevelson's debut", *Art Digest*, 1 October 1941, p.7

Hilton Kramer, "The sculpture of Louise Nevelson", *Arts Magazine*, June 1958, pp.26–9

Robert Rosenblum, "Louise Nevelson", *Artist's Yearbook*, Paris and New York, 1959, pp.136–9

Sixteen Americans, exh. cat., Museum of Modern Art, New York, 1959

Dore Ashton, "USA: Louise Nevelson", *Cimaise*, April–June 1960, pp.26–36

The Art of Assemblage, exh. cat., Museum of Modern Art, New York, 1961

Cleve Gray, "Tamarind workshop", *Art in America*, li, October 1963, p.98

John Canaday, "Art: Sculptures by Louise Nevelson", *New Yorker*, December 1964, pp.160–62

Louise Nevelson, exh. cat., Whitney Museum of American Art, New York, 1967

Robert Coates, "The art galleries: Sculpture at the Whitney", *New Yorker*, 7 January 1967, pp.84–6

Max Kozloff, "Art", *The Nation*, 10 April 1967, pp.477–88

Grégoire Müller, "A plastic presence", *Arts Magazine*, xliv, November 1969, pp.36–7

Germano Celant, *Louise Nevelson*, Milan: Fabbri, 1973

Nevelson Wood Sculpture, exh. cat., Walker Art Center, Minneapolis, 1973

Arnold B. Glimcher, *Louise Nevelson*, 2nd edition, New York: Dutton, 1976

Louise Nevelson: Atmospheres and Environments, exh. cat., Whitney Museum of American Art, New York, 1980

Laurie Wilson, "Bride of the black moon: An iconographic study of the work of Louise Nevelson", *Arts Magazine*, liv, May 1980, pp.140–48

Robert Hughes, "Sculpture's queen bee", *Time*, 12 January 1981, pp.66–72

Jean Lipman, *Nevelson's World*, New York: Hudson Hills Press, 1983

John Russell, "Louise Nevelson dies at 88: Enduring force in art world", *New York Times*, 18 April 1988

Amei Wallach, "I wanted the whole show: An appreciation of sculptor Louise Nevelson", *New York Newsday*, 19 April 1988

Louise Nevelson Remembered, exh. cat., Pace Gallery, New York, 1989

Laurie Lisle, *Louise Nevelson: A Passionate Life*, New York: Summit, 1990

Louise Nevelson, exh. cat., Palazzo delle Esposizioni, Rome, 1994

By the time Louise Nevelson became a recognised sculptor in New York, she was 60 years old. She struggled to enter the New York art world at a time when few women artists were acknowledged, and none considered equal to men. Nevelson, determined to make a name for herself, created an original body of work and a career that made her one of the most renowned artists of the 20th century.

A Russian Jew, Leah Berliawsky came to the USA at the age of five, and was given a new name and forced to learn a new language. Although she excelled in art classes early on, she had a difficult childhood in Maine where anti-Semitism was prevalent. In 1920, to escape this provincial environment, she married Charles Nevelson, a wealthy ship owner's son almost 15 years her senior. Her son Myron, known as Mike, was born two years later. During the 1920s Nevelson lived as a wealthy married woman in New York, taking art, voice, dance and drama classes.

In Maine her father, who had owned a lumber business in Russia, worked for a time as a junk peddler; later, when he began to sell real estate, Louise would often accompany him, discussing the architecture they encountered. Nevelson began her art career as a painter, making forays into sculpture with a variety of materials, preferring those such as clay that allowed her to work quickly and spontaneously. But she was essentially a collagist and continued to have the greatest affinity for wood. Her large-scale walls reflect the teachings of Kenneth Hayes Miller at the Art Students League, Hans Hofmann's school in Munich, the murals of Diego Rivera at the New School, New York, and the ideas of Frederick Kiesler. She was also influenced by the Pre-Columbian art and architecture that she saw on trips to Central and South America and by Noguchi's theatre designs and lunar landscapes.

Nevelson had her first solo show in New York at the Nierendorf Gallery in 1941. Her individual works, such as *First Personage* (1956; Brooklyn Museum, NY), a two-part wood sculpture painted black, adopted the common Surrealist vocabulary for sculpture that suggested figures without being realistic. Nevelson's early personages owe much to the work of Louise Bourgeois (q.v.). Other Surrealist-related titles refer to kings, queens and moon gardens, themes found in the work of Max Ernst and Alberto Giacometti, among others.

Nevelson developed her signature style in the years 1954–60 during the time when her house on

30th Street was scheduled for demolition and after she moved downtown to Spring Street in 1958. While scavenging the neighbourhood that was being torn down to make way for a housing development (Kips Bay Plaza) she accumulated a mass of junk(ed) materials and began filling boxes with her found objects. She then stacked them against the walls of her studio in a manner reminiscent of Kurt Schwitters.

Moon Garden + One, exhibited at the Grand Central Moderns Gallery in 1958, was lit only by a few blue lights, emphasising its uniform colour and theme. It was immediately called an environment. *Sky Cathedral* (1958; Museum of Modern Art, New York), originally part of this larger work, is typical of Nevelson's best-known and most original sculpture. The painted black structure with its various rectangular boxes at first glance resembles a mysterious closet. Filled with objects that appear both familiar and strange, it suggests a treasure trove with a secret life of its own. Nevelson transformed both her found objects (many pertaining to furniture) and the modernist grid that contains them into a theatrical structure that seems to emit a perpetually cryptic invitation to decipher its enigmatic contents.

She went on to create room-size white environments, such as *Dawn's Wedding Feast* (1959), first exhibited in the *Sixteen Americans* exhibition at the Museum of Modern Art curated by Dorothy Miller, and gold assembled sculptures such as the *Royal Tides* series, first exhibited at the Martha Jackson Gallery in 1961. The white works create an atmosphere of glaring stark purity, reflecting light rather than absorbing it as the black structures do. The gold pieces suggest ancient treasures, altars of some unspecified religion. Themes of royalty, death and marriage predominate, expressed most powerfully in the black wood environments that continue to evoke the strongest fascination, the deepest sense of mystery. Her friend, the artist Lucas Samaras, alluded to their covert sensual presence when he wrote at the time of her death: "The deep dark stark dangerous aroma of your work and passions continue to bedevil and caress me".

Nevelson was featured prominently in *The Art of Assemblage* at the Museum of Modern Art in 1961. This exhibition, according to its curator William Seitz, focused on objects that were "primarily assembled rather than painted, drawn, modeled, or carved" and composed entirely or in part of "preformed natural or manufactured materials, objects, or fragments not intended as art materials" (New York 1961). Nevelson was thus officially contextualised in a history of modern art that encompassed significant works by Picasso, the Italian Futurists, the Russian Constructivists, a number of Dada and Surrealist artists including Duchamp, as well as by 19th-century American *trompe-l'oeil* painters such asJohn Haberle. Her place in the canon of modernism was assured.

In an interview of 1967 she expressed the hope that she might one day have enough money to build a museum for herself (as Noguchi and Warhol subsequently did). Although she never realised that ambition, she succeeded in a way that few women have. Nevelson was represented in the Whitney's American Art Annuals throughout the 1950s and 1960s, and in 1962 she was chosen to participate in the Venice Biennale. Her first major museum retrospective was held at the Whitney in 1967. Subsequent retrospectives were held at the Museum of Fine Arts in Houston (1969–70), the Walker Art Center in Minneapolis (1973–5) and again at the Whitney (1980).

Already in the mid-1950s when Nevelson began to exhibit her assemblages at Grand Central Moderns Gallery, she used unifying themes as well as colours, thereby pioneering the practice of gallery installations that would become the norm for Minimalist artists in the next decade and for others in the decades to come. *Mrs N's Palace* (1964–77) was a self-contained black wooden structure with a black mirror floor that expressed the sculptor's environmental sensibility. The viewer, always reflected back on herself, becomes a stand-in for the artist, for Nevelson implicitly was always at the centre of her work. But this walk-in palace, like Giacometti's tiny *Palace at 4 A.M.* (1932–3; Museum of Modern Art, New York) remains an enigma of mysterious reflections and shadows.

Nevelson also experimented with industrial materials. Her Plexiglas structures such as *Transparent Sculpture I* (1967–8; Albright-Knox Gallery, Buffalo) create a high-tech grid, suggestive of anonymous power stations. She was encouraged and sponsored by Arnold Glimcher, her dealer from 1961, to experiment with more permanent materials that would establish a place for her (and other Pace Gallery artists) in the growing field of public art. Nevelson worked with welders at the Lippincott foundry in Connecticut in a collage-like way, much as she did with her studio assistants using pieces of wood.

Her first public commission in Cor-ten steel was *Atmosphere and Environment X* (1969–70) for Princeton University. Among the first seven works purchased for the university's John B. Putnam, Jr, Memorial Collection, and the only work by a woman, it was sited adjacent to Firestone Library near the town's main street, ensuring public visibility within and outside the campus. The repetition of geometric shapes within a three-dimensional grid has a strong graphic presence but only hints at the depth and formal qualities of her wooden walls without their mystery.

The Princeton piece was the first of many public commissions for a variety of spaces. In 1977 she created a white wood installation at St Peter's Lutheran Church, Citicorp Center, Manhattan, and designed the vestments as well, making Nevelson one of the few 20th-century artists to design an entire chapel. Louise Nevelson Plaza in lower Manhattan, dedicated a year later in 1978 by Mayor Koch and David Rockefeller, chairman of the nearby Chase Manhattan Bank, reflected the degree of her success. When Nevelson viewed the site from above, she decided that she wanted to create sculptures to "appear to float like flags". *Shadows and Flags* includes seven welded black steel pieces, with vertical shafts as high as 21.3 metres.

Nevelson's striking appearance in her later years was as much a personal creation as her work, both concealing as much as they revealed. Her monumental sculpture, built of carefully selected and transformed scraps, suggested a secret language, a layered depth beneath an impenetrable surface. Painted black, sometimes reflected in mirrors, they suggested the darker side of life, the elusiveness of language and the power of scale and composition. Imposing order while suggesting chaos and mystery, Nevelson built her work as she had structured her life, with great drama, originality and determination. It was not by accident that her fame and reputation matched that of such renowned male 20th-century sculptors as Alexander Calder, Henry Moore and Noguchi. Late in life when an interviewer (Charles Kuralt) asked her how she maintained her pace and the quality of her work, Nevelson replied: "Look, dear, if you can walk you can dance".

HARRIET F. SENIE

Nilsson, Vera
Swedish painter, 1888–1979

Born in Jönköping, 1 June 1888. Trained as a drawing teacher at the Technical School, Stockholm, 1906–9; studied under Carl Wilhelmson at Valand Art School, Göteborg, 1910; under Henri Le Fauconnier at La Palette, Paris, 1911–12. In Paris, Brittany and Öland, Sweden, 1913–14; in Stockholm and Öland, 1914–16. Spent nine months in Spain, 1919–20. Worked in Paris, 1921–2 and winters 1922–5; daughter born there, 1922. Spent 1927–8 in Italy as recipient of Ester Lindahl travel award. Settled in Stockholm, 1928; usually spent summers in Öland. Trips to the USSR, 1933; Estonia, 1937. Returned to Paris, 1948–9, 1962, 1971 and 1976; made extended visit to Senegal, 1949–50; trips to New York and Martinique, 1966. Rarely exhibited or sold work. Recipient of Prins Eugen medal, 1948. Only woman member of the group Färg och Form (Colour and Form), constituted in 1932. Only woman member, Royal Academy of Fine Arts, Stockholm, 1954. Died in Stockholm, 13 May 1979.

Principal Exhibitions

Individual
Ovenlyssalen, Copenhagen: 1917 (with Mollie Faustman)
Konstnärhuset, Stockholm: 1933, 1948
Konsthallen, Göteborg: 1934
Göteborgs Konstmuseum, Göteborg: 1943 (with Mollie Faustman and Sigrid Hjertén)
Jönköpings Läns Museum, Jönköping: 1949
Royal Academy of Fine Arts, Stockholm: 1968, 1975 (touring retrospective)

Group
Liljevalchs Konsthall, Stockholm: 1918 (*Yngre svenska konstnärer* [Younger Swedish artists])
Flangen (Phalanx) group, Stockholm: 1922, 1925

Bibliography
Ingrid Rydbeck, "Vera Nilsson", *Konstrevy*, 1933
Erik Blomberg, "Nordisk konst i Mässhallen" [Nordic art in Mässhallen]", *Konstrevy*, 1939, pp.61–8 (special issue)
J.P. Hodin, "Vera Nilsson", *Paletten*, i, 1947
Karl Axel Arvidsson, "Mycket händer i Eskilstuna" [A lot happens in Eskilstuna], *Konstrevy*, 1955, pp.86–7
Elisabeth Lidén, *Expressionismen och Sverige* [Expressionism and Sweden], Lund, 1974

Catharina Nilsson, "Vera Nilsson och hennes fredssträ-vanden" [Vera Nilsson and her peace efforts], *Fred och Frihet*, iv, 1979

Beate Sydhoff, "De slutna rummen: Vera Nilsson's 'Händer' i Djurgårdsskolan, Eskilstuna" [The closed rooms: Vera Nilsson's "Hands" in school of Djurgården, Eskilstuna], *Konstverkens liv i offentlig miljö* [The art work in the public environment], Uddevalla: Sveriges Allmänna Konstförening, 1982, pp.83–7

Catharina Nilsson, *Vera Nilssons blad ur skissböcker, 1911–1979* [Sheets from Vera Nilsson's sketchbooks, 1911–1979], Stockholm, 1983

Ingrid Ingelman, "Women artists in Sweden: A two-front struggle", *Woman's Art Journal*, v/1, 1984, pp.1–7

Marit Werenskiold, *The Concept of Expressionism*, Oslo, 1984

Göran M. Silfverstolpe, *Vera Nilsson*, Uddevalla: Sveriges Allmänna Konstförening, 1986

Shulamith Behr, *Women Expressionists*, Oxford: Phaidon, and New York: Rizzoli, 1988

Marianne Nanne-Bråhammar, "Vera Nilsson: En bild måste vara sägande" [Vera Nilsson: A picture must be expressive], *Konstperspektiv*, no.4, 1990, pp.22–5

"Den otroliga verkligheten": 13 kvinnliga pionjärer ["The incredible reality": 13 women pioneers], exh. cat., Prins Eugens Waldermarsudde, Stockholm, and elsewhere, 1994

Only a few weeks before Vera Nilsson's death, at the age of 91, her last artistic work, *Fredskortet* (Card of Peace), was printed. On the card the text "KVINNOR" (Women) is printed in red, and "Stoppa upprustningarna" (Stop the re-armament) in black against a white background. Three large-scale women are placed frontally, their arms raised to complete a circle made up of similar female figures on a smaller scale. Moreover, the card was printed in Swedish, English and French. Nilsson personally travelled around in a taxi to distribute a number of the edition to museums. The rest were sold on behalf of the International Women's Association for Peace and Freedom.

It was symptomatic that Nilsson's last artistic involvement was concerned with peace, a subject that had preoccupied her deeply throughout her life. Yet she executed very few works with political and social subjects. It was not the choice of subject that determined the degree of involvement in Nilsson's art.

Nilsson was one of the many female artists who, often after pressure at home, trained as a teacher of drawing "for safety's sake". This training, together with a year in Göteborg, was her only formal artistic education in Sweden. It was therefore an even greater honour for Nilsson when she was chosen as the first woman member of the Royal Academy of Fine Arts. For her, this meant that she had the opportunity of influencing and fighting for the acceptance of more women at the Academy, as well as in other male-dominated artists' associations.

In 1911 Nilsson went to France, where she remained until the outbreak of World War I in 1914. She spent the war years in Copenhagen, where she made her exhibition debut in 1917. The French stay was the first of numerous longer foreign trips to continental Europe and Africa. During her travels she met many local people. They made a great impression on her and can be recognised as models for her art. In Paris she also met Nordic artists, many of whom were pupils at the Académie Matisse. Matisse himself did not teach at the school at the time Nilsson arrived in the city, but she nevertheless visited the school and never forgot the experience. She remembered a "'violet-pink studio', bright green doors and an Abyssinian model. God! How beautiful it was!" She chose instead to study with Henri Le Fauconnier at La Palette. The fact that she was trained by a Cubist and not by Matisse was very significant for her art. Only drawings survive from these first years (she had left paintings behind at the outbreak of war, and when she returned to Paris after the war these had been lost). The drawings are executed in a Cubist spirit, both in the representation of space and in the treatment of form. But in her compositions and choice of subject – figures, street-scenes, landscapes – these drawings show that she had found her artistic identity.

One of Nilsson's earliest surviving paintings is *Street in Malaga* (1920–21; Norrköpings Konstmuseum, Sweden), which she executed in Paris on her return from a trip to Spain. The subject matter refers to something that she had herself witnessed, her usual practice. She described the work as follows: "The painting represents three homeless girls. The two faceless, elegant men who pass by represent people who passed by without bothering themselves about the children" (orally to the author). Nilsson depicted the girls in strong contrast to the men. The girls stand out like individuals, the men like anonymous figures who in shape and bearing lean more towards the city than towards the girls. In contrast, both compositionally and in their shape, the girls correspond more closely to the clouds of the background than to the men. In composition, as much as in the formal language and the handling of colour, Nilsson is here connected in a general way with Cubism. The classical spatial composition is abolished and, as in Cubism, the space shown is ambiguous and the depth of the painting is questioned. The strongly turned bodies of the dancing girls create a rhythm on the painting's surface. The colour scale throughout is warm, dominated by red and pink tones as well as black; elements of yellow and white are directly correlated to sources of light outside the painting.

Nilsson's artistry found its shape in the field of tension between Cubism and Expressionism. Works of both these movements as well as of El Greco, one of the old masters who enjoyed a revival during the 1910s, were on view at the *Sonderbund* exhibition in Cologne in 1912. Nilsson, a great admirer of El Greco's art, made sure that she went to this exhibition and, when visiting Spain a few years later, to Toledo. Even if *Street in Malaga* can be said to be a child of its time, it is significant for Nilsson's artistry. Its content and formal richness show an artistic maturity, whose fruits she was to reap at her first solo exhibition in Sweden in 1933; she was then 45 years old.

The 1920s were to be a rich decade for Nilsson. In 1922 her daughter Catharina was born in Paris, and she became a cherished and frequent subject. Nilsson's paintings of children have nothing sentimental about them. The portraits of her daughter say a lot not only about her, but also about children in general, for instance about moments of concentration or new achievements. Several of these paintings are in public collections, for example *The First Step* (1923; Prins Eugens Waldemarsudde, Stockholm), *Playmates* (1926; Göteborgs Konstmuseum, Göteborg) and *Soap Bubbles* (1927; Moderna Museet, Stockholm). Catharina's importance as a model diminished with the years, and thus also Nilsson's paintings of children.

At the beginning of the 1930s Nilsson worked intensively with colours. The year 1932 was a breakthrough one for her with colour: "I was aware myself of not having succeeded in making the chords of colour shine sufficiently" (orally to author). So she painted, for example, some versions of her daughter in front of a window, as in *Blue and Red* (1932–3; Malmö Konstmuseum). In order to achieve this, she chose as her base colours red, blue and yellow as well as green. Black and white were not abolished from her palette, but had less priority during these years.

For an intellectual and radical person such as Nilsson, the 1930s was a decade of much anxiety and disappointment. Hitler's take-over of power in 1933, Italy's annexation of Abyssinia in 1936 and the Spanish Civil War led to a few different and strong paintings by her. The most interesting is *Money Against Life* (1938; Skövde Kulturhus), in which she attacks the capitalists, military and clergy who brought Franco and the Falangists to power. As an old friend of the "Spanish people", for whom she felt a great sympathy, she considered travelling to Spain as a free-lance correspondent, but this did not happen. She was moved by Picasso's *Guernica* when it was shown in Stockholm in 1938, but she missed the colour, stating in this context: "For me colour is expression". Although in a purely artistic way *Money Against Life* is not linked with *Guernica*, both are strongly expressive protest paintings directed against Franco's regime.

Nilsson's fear of an atomic war grew ever stronger over the years. During the latter part of the 1960s she executed a series of paintings, *In Error's Time* (one in Riksdagshuset, Stockholm; another in Eskilstuna Konstmuseum), which show our planet after an atomic war: the earth has cracked and is uninhabitable. Painted in rich colours, mainly in yellow, green, lilac, red, blue and various black tones, Nilsson here stretched the limits of the figurative towards a more abstract formal language.

Vera Nilsson's involvement with people and their condition was deep. She shared this with the central European Expressionists of the 1910s. Like them she wished to make paintings that were "more dynamic, more expressive" (told to author), a driving force that led her along new artistic paths throughout her life. (Examples of her work may be found in the Moderna Museet, Stockholm; Göteborgs Konstmuseum, Göteborg; Malmö Konstmuseum; and the Statens Museum for Kunst, Copenhagen.)

ELISABETH LIDÉN

Normand, Mrs Ernest *see* Rae

Nyström, Jenny
Swedish painter and illustrator, 1854–1946

Born in Kalmar, 13 June 1854. Studied at the Museum Design and Art School, Göteborg, 1868–70; Royal Academy of Fine Arts, Stockholm, 1873–81; Académie Julian and Académie Colarossi, Paris, 1882–6. Married Daniel Stoopendaal, 1887; son born 1893. Lived in Stockholm from 1886. Member, Konstnärsförbundet (Artist's Association), 1886–96. Died in Stockholm, 1946.

Principal Exhibitions
Student exhibition, Royal Academy of Fine Arts, Stockholm: 1881–2 (royal medal, with Richard Hall, 1881)
Sundsvall: 1882 (Konstutställning, industriutställningen [Art exhibition, industrial exhibition])
Paris Salon: 1884–5
Stockholm: 1885 (Från Seinens strand [From the shores of the Seine]), 1885 (Opponenternas utställning [Opponents' exhibition])
Valand, Göteborg: 1886 (Nordisk konstutställningen [Nordic art exhibition])
Blanchs konstsalong, Stockholm: 1886 (Konstnärsförbundets utställning [Artists' Association exhibition])
Konstföreningen för Södra Sverige (Art Society of Southern Sweden), Malmö: 1886, 1888, 1890, 1893, 1896
Konstnärsförbundet (Artists' Association), Stockholm: 1887
Sveriges allmänna konstförening (Sweden's Public Art Society), Stockholm: 1891, 1892 (both touring)
Artist's studio, Stockholm: 1896 (individual)

Selected Writings
"En Kalmarflicka" [A Kalmar girl], Barndomslandet: Barndomsminnen av Jultomtens författare och konstnärer [The land of childhood: Childhood memories by authors and artists of Father Christmas], Barnbiblioteket Saga, no.35, Stockholm, 1918
Några minnen [Some memories], Göteborg: Gamla Majpojkars, 1937

Bibliography
Ulla Ehrensvärd, Gamla vykort: En bok för samlare [Old picture postcards: A book for collectors], Stockholm: Bonnier, 1972
Karl Jäder and Astrid Jäder, Jenny Nyström, den folkkära: En livsskildring [Jenny Nyström, beloved by the people: Picture of a life], Stockholm: Gummesson, 1975
Barbro Werkmäster, "Barnkammarens konstnärer" [Artists of the nursery], Kvinnor som konstnärer [Women as artists], ed. Anna Lena Lindberg and Barbro Werkmäster, Stockholm: Liber, 1975
Ulla Ehrensvärd, Den svenska tomten [The Swedish brownie], Stockholm: Svenska Turistföreningens Publikation, 1979
Anders Neumüller, God Jul: Svenska jultraditioner på helgkort från förr [Happy Christmas: Swedish Christmas traditions on Christmas cards from earlier on], Stockholm: Bonnier, 1980
Ralph Herrmanns, Ett år i Jenny Nyströms Sverige [A year in Jenny Nyström's Sweden], Köping: Lindfors, 1983
Barbro Werkmäster, "'Gebietet barnaverlden' [The province of childhood]: The modern breakthrough in Scandinavian literature, 1870–1905", IASS 1986, ed. Bertil Nolin and Peter Forsgren, Göteborg, 1988
De drogo till Paris: Nordiska konstnärinnor på 1880-talet [They went to Paris: Nordic women artists in the 1880s], exh. cat., Liljevalchs Konsthall, Stockholm, 1988
Gunnel Forsberg Warringer, Jenny Nyström: Konstnärinna [Jenny Nyström: Artist], Kalmar: Kalmar Läns Museum, 1992

Jenny Nyström is one of the best known and beloved of Swedish artists. Her popularity is based primarily on her Christmas cards and her illustrations for children. Many of her cards are still in production and her illustrations are frequently reproduced both as postcards and in advertisements. From the turn of the 19th and 20th centuries, her artistic reputation among critics and artists gradually declined, mostly because of these countless cards, but since the 1970s her work has been increasingly appreciated and has risen in value. This is the result of many factors: the "discovery" of her watercolours and her early paintings and illustrations; a general interest in such realms as mass-media pictures, children's literature and folklore; and the expanding focus on the art of the 19th century and on women artists in general.

Nyström's family background influenced her career. She was born into a middle-class family – her father was a schoolteacher and choir-master – and lived from the age of eight in Sweden's second town, Göteborg. Her artistic talent was noticed early and encouraged; patrons helped to promote her studies at the Royal Academy of Fine Arts in Stockholm, which had held a female class since 1864. At the Academy both teachers and colleagues regarded Nyström as one of the most gifted students. When she left Stockholm for further studies in Paris her decision was to be a painter, and during the next two decades she painted portraits, genre scenes and landscapes. She exhibited a self-portrait and a watercolour at the Paris Salon of 1884, and in 1885 a pastel of an old woman. During the 1880s she participated in several exhibitions in Sweden. At the Academy, Nyström had already reached maturity in the dominating academic style of classicism. Unlike many of her contemporary Swedish colleagues in Paris, she never gave up this style or developed it into other new styles, not even to Art Nouveau, a style that from the 1890s was frequently used in book illustration. Only her landscapes in watercolours give the impression of plein-air painting. Instead, she created a style of her own, based on traditional academic values such as perspective, solid form and outline drawing. Jenny Nyström became an illustrator, a Swedish pioneer in more than one sense. Altogether, she illustrated more than 1000 books and magazines.

Two self-portraits, from 1884 and 1895, can be interpreted as reflecting her choice of artistic career and its development. The first portrait differs in a significant way from other self-portraits of contemporary women artists. Although like many others Nyström depicted herself without artistic milieu or attributes, she added an unusual gesture and glance, and included contrary elements, although without any sense of conflict – the ambivalence of the portrait lies in the eyes of the beholder, not the painter's. The black silk dress is a sign of a middle-class woman, the ring on the bare left hand denotes an engaged woman. Contrarily, the fringe indicates freedom and modernity, and the hat and gloves the outdoors. The woman in the painting looks straight at the beholder with a slight mocking smile, her left hand on her hip in the position of a man of power; for a woman it can represent the pose of a variety singer. Thus the portrait shows the image of a respectable woman, and at the same time a woman on the stage attracting her audience. This audience was a new one historically, a mixture of the traditional cultivated *haute bourgeoisie* and the broad middle classes, both purchasers of public entertainment and, in Nyström's case, not only purchasers of easel paintings, but also buyers of illustrated publications for family reading. Nyström was one of the few artists who understood, accepted and exploited the new situation.

Coming from a non-affluent family, she had to earn her own living early on, which gave her a rather unusual characteristic for an artist – a go-ahead or entrepreneurial spirit. Her marriage to Daniel Stoopendaal was a step upwards socially, but it did not change her economic situation. Her husband never finished his medical studies, and she had to support him – and his life of pleasure. In 1884 she was unaware of these future problems; she painted herself in the guise of a successful painter, an established illustrator and a future doctor's wife, firmly intending to continue her artistic career. As can be seen in a gouache of 1887, she equipped her studio in Stockholm with all the props needed by a portraitist, genre painter and illustrator, such as palms, fans, draperies and a polar-bear-skin rug.

In 1895 Nyström portrayed herself close to her two-year-old son against a green background with flowers – an idealistic mother-and-child image from her own pictorial world, to be compared with the self-portraits of Elisabeth Vigée-Lebrun (q.v.) with her daughter of a century earlier. During the decade between these two self-portraits, Nyström had established herself, describing herself as a person who "successfully specialised in the realm of childhood".

Her career as an illustrator had already started when she was an art student in Stockholm. In 1875, on her own initiative, she illustrated her first book, *Lille Viggs äfventyr på julafton* (Little Vigg's adventure on Christmas Eve), written by the Swedish author Viktor Rydberg and previously published in serial form for a Göteborg newspaper. From 1880 to 1888 she was a contributor to the respected magazine *Ny Illustrerad Tidning*. Besides the many full-page genre pictures in this magazine she also drew report pictures, which was unusual for a woman. Perhaps to avoid the difficulty of being a woman working in a public milieu, some of these pictures were produced in collaboration with a female colleague, Ingeborg Westfelt, a unique co-operation at this time. In 1881, on Rydberg's request, Nyström illustrated his poem about an old goblin, a good-natured man with a long beard dressed in a grey costume of rough homespun cloth, who in the dark of the midwinter night gives a long philosophic monologue. In this illustration, Nyström formed the image of the Swedish *jultomten* (Father Christmas), half a wild goblin, half a domesticated brownie, figured as an old man – an image that she would popularise in numerous pictures.

From the beginning, Nyström was a very clever illustrator, and fully aware of the technical requirements of book reproduction, and eager to learn about new inventions. She was also aware of her public, and letters document how, introducing herself to a new publisher, she would stress those skills that were best suited to the taste of a particular audience. In some of her illustrated works intended for the drawing-room table, for example three collections of poems by C.D. Wirsén (1887–9), the motif, the pictures and the typographical composition form an aesthetic whole. In works for the general public, she stressed clarity of form and the emotionalism of the content.

Her most important achievement as an artist is in the sphere of children's literature. Together with Ottilia Adelborg, who made her debut in 1885, she was often referred to as the "children's artist". The 1880s were the breakthrough years in Sweden for children's literature. Women writers, many of them teachers, formed a new professional group, and Nyström illustrated a large number of their books. In 1882 she created the first Swedish picture book worth its name, *Barnkammarens bok* (Book of the nursery), with lithographic pictures in ten colours, and in 1886–7 she illustrated Johan Nordlander's *Svenska barnboken 1–2* (Swedish children's book), perhaps her most charming work.

Another important medium for illustrators was the many Christmas magazines, which were first published in the early 1890s. During her lifetime Nyström was responsible for the covers of about 250 magazines, and she also contributed full-page colour pictures and illustrations in black and white. It is possible to say that with her Christmas pictures Jenny Nyström helped to form the Swedish way of celebrating Christmas, with her images of sweet children dancing around a Christmas tree, gifts distributed by Father Christmas emerging from the depths of the forest, indoor and outdoor Christmas decorations, and so on. Her conception of Christmas also included Christmas cards, which she introduced into Sweden, paper decorations and tablecloths.

Nyström's best illustrations, especially those in black and white, date from the 1880s and 1890s. She applied her skill as an academically trained painter and draughtswoman on historical, anecdotal, landscape and portrait illustrations for a wide variety of literature. The 1880s mode of collage-formed illustrations also led her to combine elements from different genres in one picture, while the strict wood-engraving technique gave her pictures a distinct and authoritative form. As early as the 1880s, she combined her classicism with the harmony and idealism of such Renaissance painters as Raphael and the sentiment of 19th-century Romanticism. Again and again, Jenny Nyström depicted the ideal child and the ideal world, in many cases without being either sentimental or banal, which unfortunately the large number of commissions often pressurised her to be. Moreover, in her pictures, especially for the Christmas magazines, she also mixed elements from the whole gallery of art history without inhibition. On one example, the cover of a jubilee number of the Christmas magazine for children, *Jultomten*, in 1910, she placed a Father Christmas dressed in blue, with a pink Christian rose wreath around his red hood, on a golden throne decorated with Viking ornaments, a king's crown, Odin's ravens, a sunflower and lions – and the reader finds it quite in order.

With her middle-class background and being both a woman and an illustrator, Nyström belonged to the margins of the discourse of art history. This position can be of advantage, giving greater freedom to play and cross borders. She never became a modernist in a traditional sense, but she can be seen as an agent for modernity in her acceptance of the rules of the commercial mass-media world. In her illustrations, the sign of modern times lies in her way of borrowing and mixing elements from other pictures, even from her own, but also in her pictorial use of such inventions as telephones, cars and aeroplanes. Her classicism and the pictorial content of happy families, family feasts, agricultural life and nature scenes evoke good old times. This combination of modernity and traditionalism attracted – and still attracts – a broad audience. Jenny Nyström's pictures were accessible to all groups of society. Before World War II they were for many people in Sweden their main experience of art.

BARBRO WERKMÄSTER

O

Óbidos, Josefa de *see* Ayala

O'Keeffe, Georgia [fig. 52]
American painter, 1887–1986

Born on a farm near Sun Prairie, Wisconsin, 15 November 1887. Studied at the School of the Art Institute of Chicago under John Vanderpoel, 1905–6; Art Students League, New York, under William Merritt Chase, F. Luis Mora and Kenyon Cox, 1907–8; Alon Bement's summer school at University of Virginia, Charlottesville, 1912 (assisted him in summers of 1913–16); Columbia University Teachers' College, New York, under Arthur Wesley Dow, 1914–16. Freelance commercial artist in Chicago, 1908–10. Taught art at Chatham Episcopal Institute, 1911–12; high school, Amarillo, Texas, 1912–14; Columbia College, South Carolina, 1915–16; West Texas State Normal College, Canyon, 1916–18. Met photographer Alfred Stieglitz in New York, 1916. Left teaching to pursue professional career as an artist in New York, 1918. Lived with Stieglitz from 1918; married him, 1924; he died 1946. Included in *Seven Americans* exhibition organised by Stieglitz, New York, 1925; *Paintings by Nineteen Living Americans*, the second exhibition at the newly opened Museum of Modern Art, New York, 1929. Settled in New Mexico, dividing time between Abiquiu and Ghost Ranch, 1949; subsequently also travelled widely. Lost central vision, 1970. Recipient of numerous awards and honours, including Creative Arts award, Brandeis University, 1963; gold medal for painting, National Institute of Arts and Letters, 1970; Medal of Freedom presented by President Gerald Ford, 1977;

National Medal of Arts presented by President Ronald Reagan, 1985; honorary doctorates from College of William and Mary, Williamsburg, 1938; University of Wisconsin, Madison, 1942; Mount Holyoke College, South Hadley, Massachusetts, 1952; Mills College, Oakland, 1952; University of New Mexico, Albuquerque, 1964; Columbia University, New York, 1971; Brown University, Providence, Rhode Island, 1971; Minneapolis College of Art and Design, 1972; Harvard University, Cambridge, 1973; College of Santa Fe, 1977. Member, National Institute of Arts and Letters, 1949; American Academy of Arts and Letters, 1962; American Academy of Arts and Sciences, 1963; Benjamin Franklin fellow, Royal Society of Arts, London, 1969. Died in Santa Fe, New Mexico, 6 March 1986.

Selected Individual Exhibitions
291 Gallery, New York: 1917
Anderson Galleries, New York: 1923, 1924 (both organised by Alfred Stieglitz)
Intimate Gallery, New York: 1926, 1927, 1928, 1929
An American Place, New York: 1930, 1931, 1932, 1933, 1934, 1935, 1936, 1937, 1938, 1939, 1940, 1941, 1942, 1943, 1944, 1945, 1946, 1950
University of Minnesota, Minneapolis: 1937
College of William and Mary, Williamsburg, VA: 1938
Art Institute of Chicago: 1943 (retrospective)
Museum of Modern Art, New York: 1946 (retrospective)
Downtown Gallery, New York: 1952, 1955, 1957, 1958, 1961
Museum of Fine Arts, Dallas: 1953 (retrospective)
Worcester Art Museum, MA: 1960 (touring retrospective)
Amon Carter Museum of Western Art, Fort Worth, TX: 1966 (touring retrospective)
Whitney Museum of American Art, New York: 1970–71 (touring retrospective)
National Gallery of Art, Washington, DC: 1987 (touring retrospective)

Selected Writings

Some Memories of Drawings, ed. Doris Bry, Albuquerque: University of New Mexico Press, 1974

Georgia O'Keeffe, New York: Viking, 1976

"Introduction", *Georgia O'Keeffe: A Portrait by Alfred Stieglitz*, exh. cat., Metropolitan Museum of Art, New York, 1978

Bibliography

Georgia O'Keeffe, exh. cat., Art Institute of Chicago, 1943

Georgia O'Keeffe: Forty Years of Her Art, exh. cat., Worcester Art Museum, MA, 1960

Georgia O'Keeffe, exh. cat., Amon Carter Museum of Western Art, Fort Worth, 1966

Lisa Mintz Messinger, "Georgia O'Keeffe", *Metropolitan Museum of Art Bulletin*, xlii, Fall 1984 (entire issue)

Jan Garden Castro, *The Art and Life of Georgia O'Keeffe*, New York: Crown, 1985; London: Virago, 1986

Sasha Newman, *Georgia O'Keeffe*, Washington, DC: Phillips Collection, 1985

Georgia O'Keeffe: Works on Paper, exh. cat., Museum of New Mexico, Santa Fe, 1985

Laurie Lisle, *Portrait of an Artist: A Biography of Georgia O'Keeffe*, 2nd edition, Albuquerque: University of New Mexico Press, 1986; London: Heinemann, 1987

Georgia O'Keeffe: Art and Letters, exh. cat., National Gallery of Art, Washington, DC, and elsewhere, 1987 (contains extensive bibliography)

Lisa Mintz Messinger, *Georgia O'Keeffe*, New York: Thames and Hudson, 1988; London: Thames and Hudson, 1989

Anita Pollitzer, *A Woman on Paper: Georgia O'Keeffe*, New York: Simon and Schuster, 1988

Barbara Buhler Lynes, *O'Keeffe, Stieglitz and the Critics, 1916–1929*, Ann Arbor: University of Michigan Research Press, 1989 (contains extensive bibliography)

Roxana Robinson, *Georgia O'Keeffe: A Life*, New York: Harper, 1989; London: Bloomsbury, 1990

Georgia O'Keeffe: Paintings of Hawai'i, exh. cat., Honolulu Academy of Arts, 1990

Charles C. Eldredge, *Georgia O'Keeffe*, New York: Abrams, 1991

Sarah Whitaker Peters, *Becoming O'Keeffe: The Early Years*, New York: Abbeville, 1991 (contains extensive bibliography)

Mara R. Witzling, ed., *Voicing Our Visions: Writings by Women Artists*, New York: Universe, 1991; London: Women's Press, 1992

Alexandra Arrowsmith and Thomas West, eds, *Two Lives: Georgia O'Keeffe and Alfred Stieglitz: A Conversation in Paintings and Photographs*, New York: HarperCollins, 1992

Christopher Merrill and Ellen Bradbury, eds, *Georgia O'Keeffe as Icon*, Reading, MA: Addison Wesley, 1992

Christine Taylor Patten and Alvaro Cardona-Hine, *Miss O'Keeffe*, Albuquerque: University of New Mexico Press, 1992

Charles C. Eldredge, *Georgia O'Keeffe: American and Modern*, New Haven and London: Yale University Press, 1993

Barbara Buhler Lynes, *Georgia O'Keeffe*, New York: Rizzoli, 1993

——, *Georgia O'Keeffe: Catalogue Raisonné* (in preparation)

Georgia O'Keeffe first emerged as an innovative presence in 1916, when her charcoal drawings and watercolours were shown in New York. These abstractions drew on the natural world for their subjects, suggesting botanical forms, geological formations and fluid currents. The primary importance of the works, however, lay not in their images, or in the bold use of abstraction, but in their remarkable intimacy and emotion. O'Keeffe's ability to portray a private sensibility, one both vivid and powerful, would prove one of her greatest strengths and most important contributions.

O'Keeffe was one of the American modernists. Though based in New York, these painters were participants in the aesthetic revolution that began in Germany, with Kandinsky's call to abstraction. John Marin, Marsden Hartley, Arthur Dove, Charles Sheeler and O'Keeffe were all part of a circle dominated by the pioneering photographer and art dealer Alfred Stieglitz, who became O'Keeffe's husband.

O'Keeffe received a conservative education in art. She began at the Art Institute of Chicago in 1905, and went on to the Art Students League in New York two years later. These institutions taught through the imitation of classical and European masters. O'Keeffe became accomplished in the style of her teachers, but could see her way no further. "I began to realise that a lot of people had done this same kind of painting before I came along", she said, "I didn't think I could do it any better" (Katherine Kuh, *The Artist's Voice*, New York: Harper, 1962, p.189). Around 1910 she gave up painting altogether, and resumed it only in 1912, when she encountered the theories of Arthur Wesley Dow, an influential teacher at Columbia University in New York. His approach, based on Oriental principles, required the creative participation of the student, instead of dutiful imitation.

In Europe, pictorial art had traditionally attempted to replicate the three-dimensional world through the use of modelling and perspective. Dow placed little value on the replication of three-dimensional reality, or on the separation between fine and decorative art. He held that pictorial art should create its own two-dimensional reality, and that this should be based on purely aesthetic principles. His approach to composition was abstract, and based on the use of three formal components – line, colour and *notan* (light and dark masses) – and five active principles, including repetition and symmetry. Dow's principles liberated O'Keeffe from conscientious imitation; they also gave her a theoretical basis for the emotional content in her work. In his textbook, *Composition*, Dow wrote: "It is not the province of the landscape painter, for example, to represent so much topography, but to express an emotion, and this he must do by art."

In 1915 O'Keeffe was teaching in South Carolina, isolated from the aesthetic ferment of New York. In late November she received a visit from Arthur Macmahon, the man at the centre of her emotional life. After this encounter, she worked for the next four weeks in a state of nearly ecstatic intensity. The combination of cultural isolation, emotional ferment and solitude produced a profound response. For the first time she was able to move beyond the conventions that had shaped her, and to translate her experience into what was finally and entirely her own work. The drawings of 1915–16 are charcoal abstractions. Typical of this series is *Special No.13* (Metropolitan Museum of Art, New York), in which rounded, bud-like forms nestle between a jagged silhouette and an undulating ripple. The work reveals both O'Keeffe's remarkable control of the medium and her highly personal approach to abstraction. The drawing is powerful in its confident line and its bold masses; it is also feminine, in its delicate forms, subtle undulations and sense of great and immanent tenderness. This paradoxical combination of power and femininity would reappear in O'Keeffe's work.

In 1916 O'Keeffe moved to Texas. In cultural isolation once again, she produced a powerful series in response to the wide-open prairie landscape. She continued to work in charcoal, but also began bold experiments in colour. The oils and watercolours of this period are small and semi-abstract. They are vividly hued, spatially disorienting, and pulsing with a sense of exultant liberation. In glowing, radiant colours O'Keeffe portrayed the Texas sky and its dramatic atmospherics: starlight, sunsets, sunrise. In these works she was experimenting with perspective

and design, line and volume. In some of them the sophisticated manipulation of space makes it possible to read the works both as three-dimensional landscapes and as flat patterned abstractions. *Light Coming on the Plains III* (1917; Amon Carter Museum, Fort Worth) is a small watercolour from this period. A blue dome, its colour deepening upwards, arches nearly to the top of the paper. Below a low horizon lies a strip of blue darkness. From the centre of the horizon spreads a glow, a pale radiance. Here O'Keeffe's control of the medium is extraordinary. In this series the works are liquid, brilliant and fresh, done with great freedom and energy. With complete confidence the artist exploits the transparency and immediacy of watercolour, its potential for luminosity, its liquid, fluid qualities. Lucid, vivid and hauntingly pure, these works are direct translations of the landscape into O'Keeffe's aesthetic lexicon, as well as powerful renderings of the artist's emotional response to her subject.

In 1918 O'Keeffe returned to New York and began to investigate the possibilities of pure abstraction. Dow's approach made little distinction between objective and non-objective art, and O'Keeffe moved easily between the two. During the late 1910s and early 1920s she produced a number of large abstract oils. *Music – Pink and Blue I* (private collection, repr. *Georgia O'Keeffe* 1976), a large oil of 1919, consists of a trembling, lyrical arch of living tissue, formed by layers of rose and creams and giving on to a blue, limitless and ethereal space. O'Keeffe was profoundly engaged by colour, which was a crucial component of her work. She defied the convention that limited serious art to harsh or sombre palettes. On occasion, she revelled in warm, luscious, romantic hues, and the colours in this work are radiant and high-keyed. She did not confine herself to these colours, however: in *Red and Orange Streak* (1919; artist's estate, repr. Washington 1987, no.33) both the palette and the mood are different. Here the tones are rich and sombre, low-keyed and muted. A black background and sleek racing curve produce a futuristic vision of speed and space.

The early exhibitions of O'Keeffe's work (a group show at the 291 Gallery in 1916, and a solo one there in 1917) had commanded critical interest, and in 1921 both she and her work were on exhibition as subjects of Stieglitz's photographs. The sensuality of her work had not escaped notice. Now

Stieglitz's photographs presented her both as an artist, with her work on display in the background, and also as a sensuous young woman, nude, her body on display. To her chagrin, O'Keeffe's sexuality became a matter of public speculation, a situation that would persist throughout her life.

In the early 1920s O'Keeffe executed a series of small experimental still lifes. These were based on Dow exercises, exploring the problems of mass, line and colour. The subjects were fruits, vegetables and leaves. The images were representational, though often the colours were not naturalistic. The forms were simplified, detail eliminated. Perspective was manipulated: depth was flattened and space compressed. Two-dimensional design took precedence over three-dimensional realism, and the result was clean stylised shapes and flat, unshaded masses in strong colour dynamics. In these works O'Keeffe revealed the influence of another member of the Stieglitz circle: the photographer Paul Strand, who had produced a series of brilliant abstract photographs in 1915. He exploited the mechanical manipulation that the camera lens makes possible, and through focusing, cropping, tilting and magnification, he transformed realistic subjects into pure abstractions. O'Keeffe had been struck by this approach, and now began to explore its possibilities. The process of magnification would become a brilliant and powerful component of her work. Whereas Strand had used this device to strip his subjects of identity, rendering their enlarged images as unidentifiable abstractions, O'Keeffe's use of magnification was entirely her own: she enlarged her subjects to intensify their specific identity, to increase their importance and to dramatise their emotional power. The subjects that she chose for this process were plant forms. Although she painted other botanical examples, the one she portrayed over and over again for more than a decade was the flower.

The series of magnified flowers is one of O'Keeffe's most powerful and perhaps the one for which she is best known. By her own account, this resulted from the consideration of two things: a small flower still life by Fantin-Latour, and the mood of speed and technological excitement that permeated New York at the time. Technology was the movement of the age, an exciting, limitless force based on logic. Its manifestations were dazzling: huge structures, blinding speed, unimaginable potency. By contrast, the small Fantin-Latour flower

represented the force of nature: quiet, instinctive and intimate. O'Keeffe believed that nature was the equal of technology and made her flowers into potent presences: "I thought I'd make them big like the huge buildings going up. People will be startled – they'll *have* to look at them and they did" (Kuh *op. cit.* quoted in Robinson 1989).

O'Keeffe's statement resulted in a series of vivid and arresting pictures. *Black Iris III* (1926; Metropolitan Museum of Art) and *Red Poppy* (1927; private collection, repr. Washington 1987) are representative. In both these paintings, a voluptuous amplitude joins with a sense of overwhelming intimacy. The soft, yielding surfaces, the rapturous colours of the poppy, the subtle translucent veils of the iris and the hidden, vulnerable heart of both infuse these paintings with great dramatic depth. Again O'Keeffe produced images that were at once explicitly feminine and explicitly powerful.

The critical response to the flower paintings focused on sexuality. "The show", one critic wrote of her 1939 exhibition, "is one long, loud blast of sex..." (Lewis Mumford, quoted in Robinson 1989, p.282). The images of flowers, with their trembling, fragile layers of tissue, leading to a central, secret heart, were perceived as obvious references to female genitalia. This response was inevitable: Freud's theories of sexuality were popular topics in the artistic community, and O'Keeffe's work was a perfect target. Sex, like beauty, is in the eye of the beholder; the critic finished by admitting that "...perhaps only half the sex is on the walls; the rest is probably in me" (*idem*). He was right: in fact, O'Keeffe's flowers are botanically quite precise, and her pictures are no more prurient than the plants themselves. She used the flower as a metaphor for the emotional world, not the physical one. The statement they made was one of unsettling intimacy, powerful, bold and enchantingly beautiful. The notion of such an intimacy was disturbing to many viewers, and the insistent declaration of sexuality can be read as an attempt to deny the more profound, and truly unsettling nature of the work.

O'Keeffe and Stieglitz spent winters in Manhattan and summers at the Stieglitz family house in upstate New York. Increasingly, O'Keeffe felt stifled among the large clan, and in the summer of 1926 she left for four weeks alone in Maine. The result was a series of subdued but potent paintings, the most powerful of which are *Closed Clam Shell* and *Open Clam Shell* (private collections, repr.

Washington 1987). In both these paintings the single magnified form, dignified and monumental, nearly fills the small rectangular canvas. The enlarged form in the modest space gives the subject a quiet and resonant presence. The power is emotional, as in the flower paintings, but the tone of the *Clam Shells* is very different. The palette is cool and muted, restricted entirely to neutral greys and whites. The shells themselves are smooth and hard, their surfaces impenetrable. In one the revealed opening is barely there; in the other it is inexorably shut in a cool line of denial. If the flower paintings suggest passionate vulnerability, the clam shells imply containment and prohibition, the closed and coupled self.

In 1926 O'Keeffe showed her first urban landscape. Previously, she had drawn exclusively on the natural world for subject matter; now she began to celebrate the smooth towering forms of the new skyscrapers (e.g. *City Night*, 1926; Minneapolis Institute of Arts). The simplification of the shapes and the sophisticated manipulation of perspective emphasise height and distance, giving the buildings dramatic monumentality. In these works atmospherics are as important as the buildings themselves: light, sky, wind, weather and darkness are all powerful compositional elements. O'Keeffe's reductive approach included not only the forms of the buildings but the idea of the city itself. The paintings contain no hint of the actual, messy, active life of the metropolis. They show only the sleek geometric buildings: no cars, no street life and, most strikingly, no people. This is true of almost the entire body of O'Keeffe's work: seldom did she portray a living creature. The animation is interior, however. Most of her works can be read as analogues of the human form or of the human heart; they body forth a powerful emotional state.

O'Keeffe spent the summer of 1929 in New Mexico, near Santa Fe, where she began to record the dry magical landscape. In *Black Cross, New Mexico* (1929; Art Institute of Chicago) the huge shape presses against the picture plane, sombre and threatening, a black symbol of prohibition. Oppressive, severe, it dominates the composition, nearly obliterating the earth and sky beyond it. The painting derives its formal strength from the powerful cruciform shape. Behind the inexorable black geometry of the cross, however, lies a countering force: voluptuous turbulence in the ripple of purple-red hills stretching out to the horizon. This is a recurrent theme in O'Keeffe's work: the dynamic juxtaposition of stern order and riotous passion.

In the early 1930s O'Keeffe began another great series: animal bones. "The bones seem to cut sharply to the center of something that is keenly alive on the desert even tho' it is vast and empty and untouchable – and knows no kindness with all its beauty" (*Georgia O'Keeffe*, exh. cat., An American Place, New York, 1939). In terms of composition, the bones are treated like the flowers: they are enlarged, centred, simplified, sometimes cropped. The mood and the palette are different, however: the bones are far cooler presences than the radiant flowers, more meditative, less demonstrative. They are closer in palette and mood to the muted, contained shells. The smooth osseous shapes, in O'Keeffe's hands, take on a mythic resonance. They suggest an interior strength, tranquil, remote and enduring. Their pearly forms gleam against flat fields of colour – sometimes the sky, sometimes the red hills, sometimes both, enigmatic and beautiful.

In late 1932 O'Keeffe developed severe psychological symptoms, and was hospitalised for a nervous breakdown in early 1933. She did not work again until early 1934. That year she returned to New Mexico, discovering the Abiquiu area, with its astonishing colours. The Abiquiu paintings are of mesas, cliffs and hills: soft collapsing forms, voluptuous run-offs of pink sandstone beneath high bluffs, round mounds of red silt-stone. With their smooth curving forms, soft yielding sensuous shapes, lapped and folded layers and radiant rosy hues, they are strongly suggestive of the female body. The landscapes themselves seem animated, glowing with the artist's radiant response to this new world. From 1935 to 1946 O'Keeffe painted this lyrical landscape, celebrating the rich glowing colours, the pellucid light, the tender rounded hills and the endless and crystalline space (e.g. *Cliffs Beyond Abiquiu*, 1943; repr. *Georgia O'Keeffe* 1976).

O'Keeffe continued to paint animal skulls, their dry porous surfaces polished and smoothed by her brush. Calm, mystical and symmetrical, their shining iconic presences hang clean and centred against the picture plane, before the vast radiant space of New Mexico. In *From the Faraway Nearby* (1937; Metropolitan Museum of Art) a deer skull hangs serenely and mysteriously in the clear air, above a distant line of soft, pale, dreamlike hills. The antlers have been magically augmented; three tiers of them curve against the deepening blue of the sky. The painting reverberates with the combination of beauty, intimacy and haunting distance that characterises some of O'Keeffe's best work.

In the early 1940s O'Keeffe began a new bone series, focusing on the pelvis. This signalled a return to orificial imagery: "I like empty spaces", she said. "Holes can be very expressive" (Calvin Tomkins, "The rose in the eye looked pretty fine", *New Yorker*, 4 March 1974). In this series the bone is suspended against the sky, the ovoid shape central and dominant. The smooth white form is stark, at once abstract and realistic, set against a deep blue space. The paintings combine echoes of both birth and infinity; the sky behind the bones is clear and endless.

In 1946 Stieglitz died. O'Keeffe spent the next three years in New York, settling his estate and painting very little. In 1949 she moved to New Mexico for good and began painting again, but a change had taken place. After Stieglitz's death, O'Keeffe's work lost emotional content. Absent now were those qualities – yielding tenderness, turbulent passion, cold rage – that gave her earlier work such strength. During the 1950s she produced an austere series based on a rectangular wooden door in an adobe wall at Abiquiu. Large, handsome and implacable, the paintings contain a certain majesty, but little emotional power. What strength they have is purely formal. The moods and subjects of the works became increasingly remote. In 1958 she painted the beguiling *Ladder to the Moon* (artist's estate, repr. *Georgia O'Keeffe*, 1976), in which a ladder hangs diagonally and mysteriously against the deepening evening sky. This is an image of transition: the ladder is suspended half-way between earth and air, under a half-moon, at twilight. This strongly suggests the journey from earth to heaven; its psychological content is more spiritual than emotional.

O'Keeffe's last important works are the *Sky above Clouds* series of 1963–5. These enormous canvases are based on the view from an aeroplane. In *Sky above Clouds IV* (1965; Art Institute of Chicago) rows of small puffy white clouds are laid out schematically, in neat horizontal layers, beneath a tranquil sky. The shapes are rhythmic and repetitive, part of a strong decorative pattern. The scale is majestic. Ordered, peaceful and serene, the paintings suggest a sublime removal: there is no earth here, only sky. O'Keeffe lost her central vision in the early 1970s, and died in 1986.

Georgia O'Keeffe is one of the great artists of the 20th century. An early abstractionist, she explored formal and modernist concerns through her imaginative use of focus, scale and perspective. She was a breathtaking colourist, with a rich and vivid range of resonant hues. The greatest strength of O'Keeffe's work, however, lies in its emotional power. At a time when rage and coldness were fashionable, she was not afraid to paint passion, rapture and joy, as well as anger, resentment and withdrawal. The real subject of her paintings is the wide, intense, highly charged spectrum of emotion itself. It is for this remarkable contribution that we are most deeply indebted to her.

ROXANA ROBINSON

See also Training and Professionalism survey 5

Oosterwijck, Maria van
Dutch painter, 1630–1693

Born in Nootdorp, near Delft, 27 August 1630; father and grandfather both ministers in the Dutch Reformed Church. Moved to Amsterdam, 1672 or 1673. Never married, but brought up her orphaned nephew. Died in Uitdam, north of Amsterdam, 12 November 1693.

Bibliography

Jacob Campo Weyerman, *De levens-beschryvingen der Nederlantsche konstschilders en schilderessen* [Lives of the Netherlandish male and female painters], The Hague, 1729–69, ii, pp.262–5

Gerard de Lairesse, *Groot schilderboek* [Great book of painting], ii, 1740, p.360

Arnold Houbraken, *De groote schouburgh der Nederlantsche konstschilders en schilderessen* [The great theatre of Dutch male and female painters], 2nd edition, Amsterdam, 1753, ii, pp.214–18

Jean-Baptiste Descamps, "Marie van Oosterwyck/Eleve de David de Heem", *Vie des peintres flamands et hollandais*, ii, Marseille, 1842, pp.166–8

Johannes Immerzeel, "Oosterwijk, Maria van", *De levens en werken der Hollandische en Vlaamsche kunstschilders, beeldhouwers, graveurs en bouwmeesters, van het begin der vijftiende eeuw tot heden* [The lives and works of the Dutch and Flemish painters, sculptors, engravers and architects, from the beginning of the 15th century to the present], 3 vols, Amsterdam, 1842–3, ii, pp.280–28

Christiaan Kramm, *De levens en werken der Hollandsche en Vlaamsche kunstschilders, beeldhouwers, graveurs en bouwmeesters* [The lives and works of the Dutch and Flemish painters, sculptors, engravers and architects], iv, Amsterdam, 1859

A.L.G. Bosboom-Toussaint, *De bloemschilderes Maria van Oosterwijck* [The flower painter Maria van Oosterwijck], Leiden, 1862; reprinted in *Verzamelde werken van A.L.G. Bosboom-Toussaint* [Collected works of A.L.G. Bosboom-Toussaint], Rotterdam, 1899, pp.289–418

J.A. Worp, *De gedichten van Constantijn Huygens* [The poems of Constantijn Huygens], viii, Groningen, 1898 (contains poems relating to van Oosterwijck, pp.137 and 163)

Abraham Bredius, "Das Nachlass-Inventare von Juriaen Pool", *Künstler-Inventare: Urkunden zur Geschichte der holländischen kunst de XVIten, XVIIten und XVIIIten Jahrhunderts*, 8 vols, The Hague: Nijhoff, 1915–22, iv, p.1257

——, "Archiefsprokkelingen: Een en ander over Maria van Oosterwyck 'vermart Konstschilderesse'" [Gleanings from the archives: Assorted findings on Maria van Oosterwijck, "famous woman painter"], *Oud-Holland*, lii, 1935, pp.180–82

Remmit van Luttervelt, *Schilders van het stilleven* [Painters of still life], Naarden, 1947

Laurens J. Bol, *Holländische Maler des 17. Jahrhunderts nahe den Grossen Meistern: Landschaften und Stilleben*, Braunschweig: Klinkhardt und Biermann, 1969

Women Artists, 1550–1950, exh. cat., Los Angeles County Museum of Art, and elsewhere, 1976

Rosa Lindenburg, "Maria van Oosterwijck, 17th-century Dutch painter", *Woman Art*, ii/1, Fall 1977, p.17

Mary Ann Scott, *Dutch, Flemish and German Paintings in the Cincinnati Art Museum*, Cincinnati: Cincinnati Art Museum, 1987

Flowers and Nature: Netherlandish Flower Painting of Four Centuries, exh. cat., Nabio Museum of Art, Osaka, and elsewhere, 1990

Jan Davidsz. de Heem en zijn Kring [Jan Davidsz. de Heem and his circle], exh. cat., Centraal Museum, Utrecht, and Herzog Anton Ulrich-Museum, Braunschweig, 1991

Die Karl und Magdalene Haberstock-Stiftung, exh. cat., Munich and Augsburg, 1991

Paul Taylor, *Dutch Flower Painting*, New Haven and London: Yale University Press, 1995

Maria van Oosterwijck, the most highly esteemed Dutch woman artist before Rachel Ruysch (q.v.), was Holland's first internationally recognised woman artist. She painted still lifes exclusively. Her earliest-known dated work is from 1667, and her latest, 1689. According to Arnold Houbraken, her first biographer, she received painting instruction from "Jan Davidsz. de Heem of Utrecht", a crucial figure in the evolution of flower painting because of the way in which he combined the exuberance of Flemish still life with the naturalism of Dutch flower painting. Recent scholars have questioned Houbraken's statement since de Heem was residing in Antwerp during van Oosterwijck's youth. They have doubted that she ever actually had contact with him. Her understanding of his particular painterly conventions and techniques, however, suggests that she did study directly under him. De Heem probably began visiting the northern Netherlands again on a frequent basis around 1658, which seems to be the most logical time of contact with van Oosterwijck, particularly since de Heem did not develop the type of flower piece that influenced her until about 1650. In 1658 van Oosterwijck would have been 28, admittedly a late start for a painter, but presumably she would have studied with another master before de Heem. Houbraken stated that she showed talent at an early age, but provided no particulars.

Van Oosterwijck kept a painting studio in Delft until she moved to Amsterdam in 1672 or 1673. According to Houbraken, the flower painter Willem van Aelst visited her Delft studio and proposed marriage to her there. Not wanting to marry, but not wanting to hurt van Aelst's feelings by rejecting him outright, van Oosterwijck devised an agreement with her suitor, knowing that his restless temperament would prevent him from living up to it: if he painted every day for a year she would marry him. Since van Aelst's studio window was directly across the street from hers, van Oosterwijck, who worked religiously each day, was able to see whether or not he was at the easel. At the end of the year, when van Aelst came to claim her hand, she pointed out the large number of marks she had made on her window ledge, each one representing a day he had missed work. The tale appealed to the 19th-century novelist Bosboom-Toussaint, who transformed it into a theatrical historical romance with accompanying sketches by Willem Steelink. One illustration shows van Aelst on his knees in van Oosterwijck's studio, pleading with her as she turns away. Houbraken placed the marriage proposal episode in Delft, but it may well have occurred in Amsterdam where by 1676 the two painters lived opposite each other on the Nieuwe Keizersgracht (the reflection of a gabled house across the street in two of van

Oosterwijck's paintings, in Städtische Kunstsammlungen, Augsburg, and Palazzo Pitti, Florence, may be a reference to van Aelst).

Curiously, the only contemporary documents that connect the two households record a conflict between them. The dispute arose when van Oosterwijck's housemaid, Geertje Pieters, went to van Aelst's house to retrieve a raincoat that her mistress had left there. Van Aelst's maid, Grietge, refused to hand over the coat and showered Pieters and van Oosterwijck with insults, calling them "beasts", "fat cows" and "sows", until a deputy sheriff arrived to break up the disturbance. Van Oosterwijck subsequently lodged formal complaints to the city when she and Pieters were threatened with physical assault by this same servant. From various sources we know that van Oosterwijck's relationship with her maid was unusually close. She even taught Pieters to paint in her manner, an act that became the subject of a poem by Constantijn Huygens in 1677. Pieters's only known flower-piece, featuring van Oosterwijck's trademark sunflower, is in the Fitzwilliam Museum, Cambridge.

Some writers have suggested that van Oosterwijck had some formal training with van Aelst, but this is unlikely. His work is more sumptuous than hers, with such props as silver vases and gold-fringed drapery, rather than the simple glass containers on naked stone or cold marble that van Oosterwijck preferred. What is more, the two artists knew each other at the point when they were already mature painters.

Van Oosterwijck's move to Amsterdam coincided with her increasing success in finding an international circle of wealthy, royal patrons. From the late 1660s until the 1680s, royal art collectors sought to include examples of her work in their galleries. After Louis XIV of France purchased one of her paintings, several other monarchs followed suit: William of Orange and Queen Mary (900 florins for one painting), Jan Sobieski known as August II, King of Poland (2400 Dordrecht guilders for three paintings), and the Elector of Saxony (two flower-pieces and one festoon for 1500 florins). Emperor Leopold of Austria and his wife were so delighted with the painting they purchased from her that they sent her portraits of themselves in frames encrusted with diamonds as a token of their esteem. Van Oosterwijck's success was rivalled by only one other female Dutch painter, Rachel Ruysch, but although van Oosterwijck worked for a greater number of monarchs, she never attained a formal court appointment. Houbraken described van Oosterwijck as unusually devout. She spent large amounts of money on charitable gestures. For example, on several occasions she purchased the freedom of Dutch soldiers who had been captured by Algerian pirates (as recorded in Amsterdam archival documents). The ransom she paid per person was fl. 750 – a considerable sum, equivalent to more than two years' salary of a tradesman in the period.

Houbraken reported that because Maria van Oosterwijck was an exceedingly slow, meticulous painter, works by her were rare. Today only about 20 are known, and most are flower (or flower with fruit) pieces. The lists of her works published in Thieme-Becker and Wurzbach are unreliable, as Ann Sutherland Harris has pointed out (Los Angeles 1976). Autograph paintings are housed in public collections at Augsburg (Städtische Kunstsammlungen), Cincinnati (Cincinnati Art Museum), Copenhagen (Statens Museum for Kunst), Dresden (Gemäldegalerie Alte Meister), Florence (Palazzo Pitti), The Hague (Mauritshuis), London (Kensington Palace, formerly in Hampton Court), Prague (National Gallery), Sacramento (Crocker Art Museum) and Vienna (Kunsthistorisches Museum).

In her work, van Oosterwijck used the artistic conventions developed by de Heem to achieve maximum naturalistic effect. She placed brightly illuminated floral arrangements against dark backgrounds, often within shallow stone niches, so that the shapes would stand in highest possible relief. She included a profusion of incidental insects and shiny water droplets among a great variety of flowers and leaves, to call attention to the carefully crafted spatial relationships existing between the individual elements. In contrast to de Heem, however, van Oosterwijck preferred a colour scheme of juxtaposed warm hues – reds, pinks, ochres, yellowwhites and, particularly, acidic yellow-oranges that would be highly discordant if they were not placed so artfully within her designs. Another preference was a heavy sunflower at the apex of a bouquet (Dresden and The Hague), as well as striped ribbon grasses hanging down in forked patterns to the left or right of a vase.

Van Oosterwijck painted on canvas, copper and panel, and usually signed her paintings with her full name on the edges of painted table tops. Her signatures are made to look as though they have been chiselled into the stone or marble. Perhaps the most memorable and poetic personal trademark in her still lifes is a butterfly – the *Vanessa atalanta*. It can be found in most of her major works, with its wings half spread, resting gently on a book (Kunsthistorisches Museum, Vienna), a ledge (Cincinnati Art Museum and Palazzo Pitti, Florence) or on a stem within a bouquet. Van Oosterwijck employed the "character" of the butterfly to lead the viewer into her paintings, and to direct attention to the heart of her artistic intention.

Van Oosterwijck's paintings seem to be particularly thoughtful and precise expressions of her deep religious beliefs. In the tradition of 17th-century Dutch still life, her works contain symbolic references to the vanity of earthly existence, the transience of all material things, and the need to attend to one's soul by dedicating one's life to God, for only through God can one's soul transcend the perishable world. Without labouring the point, van Oosterwijck would judiciously place an animated element or "protagonist" within the composition, which would then direct the gaze of the viewer to the heart of her message.

Two works stand out as particularly refined examples of these moral messages. The *Vanitas* painting dated 1668 (Kunsthistorisches Museum, Vienna), which Harris identified as the work purchased by Leopold I (*ibid.*), depicts a thick, dog-eared tome entitled *Rekeningh* ("reckoning") surrounded by examples of earthly vanity and transience: a skull, a bag of money, a half-eaten ear of corn, a globe, an hour-glass, books, flowers and a glass flask of *aqua vitae* reflecting a self-portrait of the artist at her easel. The Dutch word *Rekeningh* refers to the settling of an account, but in the context of this painting, the account is one's earthly life. The butterfly, the protagonist in the picture, rests on the title page of the book at the centre of the painting; it appears to be so light that it barely weighs down the sheet of paper it rests upon. Directly above its wing-tips are the words: *Wy Leeúen om te sterúen/En /Sterúen om te leeúen* ("We live to die and die to live"). They underline the fact that the butterfly symbolises both the Resurrection of Christ and that of the human soul on Judgement Day. This bitter-sweet quality found in van Oosterwijck's best works is seldom found in *vanitas* paintings by other artists of the period, who

might pile mountains of skulls on a table in an effort to drive home their message.

The second work, a bouquet of flowers in a carved ivory vase (*c.*1670; Mauritshuis, The Hague), is crowned by a conspicuous sunflower in full bloom. The flower is so named because it turns its face towards the sun, a symbol for Christ or God. On the table next to the bouquet is the lid of the beaker, which has, as its finial, a striking figure of Venus, the pagan goddess of physical love. She seems to have been sharply interrupted while in the process of bathing. Her arm is still raised and her gaze is frozen on the head of the sunflower above, as though she has discovered a beauty that is much greater than her own. This interpretation is reinforced by the putti and satyrs at her feet and on the nearby vase who continue to play with a goat (Bacchus's mount) because they cannot see the divine light above.

The fact that van Oosterwijck remained unmarried without children, choosing instead to lead a quiet life painting highly finished floral bouquets, attracted attention. Early writers, who were struggling to find a way of dealing with the emerging phenomenon of the professional woman artist, generally did so by drawing moral parallels between traditional female virtues and the paintings that women produced. Being unmarried, however, van Oosterwijck did not neatly fit the model of devoted wife and mother. As a result, she never seems to emerge from these accounts as a truly three-dimensional personality; likewise, the very personal qualities of her work are, for the most part, left unexamined. (Those who wrote about Rachel Ruysch a generation later, on the other hand, had an easier time reconciling the artist's profession with her role as a wife and mother: Ruysch emerged as a delightful "Lady Bountiful" who painted cornucopias of fruit and flowers while producing ten children.) A great admirer of van Oosterwijck, the poet Dirk Schelte, for example, wrote a verse celebrating the incredible beauty both of the artist's painted bouquets and her personal character (i.e. chastity and religiosity) in 1673. An unusual double portrait attributed to Gerard de Lairesse (with Gooden and Fox Ltd, London, in 1958) pairs van Oosterwijck with Schelte and seems to illustrate the poem. Van Oosterwijck is posed rather awkwardly in the guise of a painter-muse, gazing at the poet with her brushes and palette in hand, inspiring him to write. The choice to show the unmarried van Oosterwijck with the married Schelte, in the intimate double portrait format usually reserved for married couples, was extremely bold. A more traditional portrait of the artist seated alone with her two interests, the Bible in her right hand and her palette in her left, was painted by Wallerant Vaillant in 1671 (Rijksmuseum, Amsterdam).

MARIANNE BERARDI

Oppenheim, Meret   [fig. 56]

Swiss multi-media artist, 1913–1985

Born in Berlin-Charlottenburg, Germany, 6 October 1913; grew up in the Bernese part of the Canton Jura, and educated at various German and Swiss schools. Studied at the Kunstgewerbeschule, Basel, 1929–30; briefly attended the Académie de la Grande Chaumière, Paris, 1932. Met Jean Arp and Alberto Giacometti, and invited to exhibit with the Surrealists at the Salon des Surindépendants, Paris, 1933; participated in international Surrealist exhibitions in Copenhagen and Tenerife (1935), London and New York (1936) and Amsterdam (1938), and in the exhibition of fantastic furniture with Max Ernst, Leonor Fini and others at Galerie René Drouin et Leo Castelli, Paris, 1939. Returned to Basel, 1937; attended the Allgemeine Gewerbeschule for two years, supporting herself by restoring paintings. Entered a long depression. Associated with the Swiss Gruppe 33, and later Allianz (Union of Swiss Painters), officially becoming a member in 1948. Married Wolfgang la Roche, 1949; he died 1967. Entered a new phase of creativity in the mid-1950s, increasingly expanding her oeuvre to include writing. Recipient of Art Award, city of Basel, 1974; Grand art prize, city of Berlin, 1982. Died in Basel, 15 November 1985.

Selected Individual Exhibitions

Galerie Schulthess, Basel: 1936
Galerie d'Art Moderne, Basel: 1952
A l'étoile scellée, Paris: 1956
Galerie Riehentor, Basel: 1957, 1959
Galleria Schwarz, Milan: 1960
Galerie Gimpel und Hanover, Zürich: 1965
Moderna Museet, Stockholm: 1967 (retrospective)
Galerie Krebs, Bern: 1968
Wilhelm-Lehmbruck-Museum, Duisburg: 1972
Galerie Suzanne Visat, Paris: 1973

Galerie Renée Ziegler, Zürich: 1974
Museum der Stadt, Solothurn: 1974–5 (touring retrospective)
Galerie Levy, Hamburg: 1978
Galerie Edition Claude Givaudon, Geneva: 1981
Galerie nächst St Stephan, Vienna: 1982
Nantenshi Gallery, Tokyo: 1984
Musée d'Art Moderne de la Ville de Paris: 1984
Galerie Oestermalen, Stockholm: 1985
Institute of Contemporary Arts, London: 1989 (retrospective)

Selected Writings

"Enquêtes", *Le Surréalisme même*, no.3, 1957, pp.77, 82
"Enquêtes (le striptease)", *Le Surréalisme même*, no.5, 1959, p.58
"Meret Oppenheim spricht Meret Oppenheim: Man könnte sagen etwas stimme nicht", *Gedichte, 1933–1969*, tape recording, Cologne, 1973; 2nd edition, 1986
Speech given in Basel, 16 January 1975, on receiving the Art Award of the city of Basel, *Kunst-Bulletin des Schweizerischen Kunstvereins*, no.2, February 1975
"Entretien avec Daniel Boone", *L'Humidité*, no.23, 1976, pp.26–7
Sansibar, Basel: Fanal, 1981 (contains poems)
Caroline, Basel: Fanal, 1984
"Das Ende kann nur der Anfang sein", *Wissenschaft und Kunst*, ed. Paul Feyerabend and Christian Thomas, Zürich: Fachvereine, 1984, pp.243–50
Husch, husch, der schönste Vokal entleert sich: Gedichte, Zeichnungen, ed. Christiane Meyer-Thoss, Frankfurt am Main: Suhrkamp, 1984
Aufzeichnungen, 1928–1985: Träume, Bern and Berlin: Gachnang and Springer, 1986
Kaspar Hauser oder die Goldene Freiheit: Textvorlage für ein Drehbuch, Bern and Berlin: Gachnang und Springer, 1987

Bibliography

Lynne M. Tillmann, "'Don't cry...work'", *Art and Artists*, viii, October 1973, pp.22–7 (interview)
Valie Export, "Mögliche Fragen an Meret Oppenheim", *Magna: Feminismus, Kunst und Kreativität*, exh. cat., Galerie nächst St Stephan, Vienna, 1975
Josephine Withers, "The famous fur-lined teacup and the anonymous Meret Oppenheim", *Arts Magazine*, lii, November 1977, pp.88–93
Nicolas Calas, "Meret Oppenheim: Confrontations", *Artforum*, x, Summer 1978, pp.24–5
Ruth Henry, "Meret Oppenheim zum 70. Geburtstag", *Du: Die Kunstzeitschrift*, no.10, October 1983, pp.82–4 (interview)
Liliane Thorn, *Porträt der Künstlerin Meret Oppenheim*, video, RTL, 1984
Jaqueline Burckhardt, "The semantics of antics", *Parkett*, no.4, 1985, pp.22–33

Christiane Meyer-Thoss, "Poetry at work", *ibid.*,
  pp.34–45
Mary Ann Caws, "Ladies shot and painted: Female
  embodiment in Surrealist art", *The Female Body in
  Western Culture*, ed. Susan Rubin Suleiman,
  Cambridge, MA: Harvard University Press, 1986,
  pp.262–87
Meret Oppenheim: Legat an das Kunstmuseum Bern,
  exh. cat., Kunstmuseum, Bern, 1987
Pamela Robertson and Anselm Spoerri, *Imago: Meret
  Oppenheim*, film, 1988
Bice Curiger and others, *Meret Oppenheim: Defiance in
  the Face of Freedom*, Cambridge: Massachusetts
  Institute of Technology Press, 1989 (German original,
  1982)
Stuart Morgan, *Meret Oppenheim: An Essay*, text
  published with 16 postcards of Meret Oppenheim's
  work in a velvet pocket on the occasion of an individ-
  ual exhibition at the Institute of Contemporary Arts,
  London, 1989
Renée Riese Hubert, "From 'Déjeuner en Fourrure' to
  'Caroline': Meret Oppenheim's chronicle of
  Surrealism", *Surrealism and Women*, ed. Mary Ann
  Caws and others, Cambridge: Massachusetts Institute
  of Technology Press, 1991, pp.37–49
Bettina Brandt, *The Coming of Age of the Child-Woman:
  Meret Oppenheim, Surrealism and Beyond*, PhD
  dissertation, Harvard University, 1993
Josef Helfenstein, *Meret Oppenheim und der
  Surrealismus*, Stuttgart: Hatje, 1993
Isabel Schulz, *Edelfuchs und Morgenrot: Studien zum
  Werk von Meret Oppenheim*, Munich: Silke Schreiber,
  1993
Renée Riese Hubert, *Magnifying Mirrors: Women,
  Surrealism and Partnership*, Lincoln: University of
  Nebraska Press, 1994
Bettina Brandt, "Meret Oppenheims Inkognito:
  (De)maskierung und Reflexion in Meret Oppenheims
  Filmskript *Kaspar Hauser oder die Goldene Freiheit*",
  *Der Imaginierte Findling Studien zur Kaspar-Hauser
  Rezeption*, ed. Ulrich Struve, Heidelberg:
  Universitätsverlag C. Winter, 1995, pp.144–62

Meret Oppenheim's most frequently reproduced
work, *A Demi-Tasse, Saucer and Spoon Covered in
Chinese Gazelle Fur* (1936; Museum of Modern
Art, New York), was the young artist's contribution
to Alfred Barr's exhibition *Fantastic Art, Dada,
Surrealism*, the first Surrealist show in the USA. The
hairy lining transformed the ordinary teacup
purchased at a Parisian department store into an
exquisite Surrealist object; the unspoken invitation
to bring one's lips to the fetishised vessel immediately provoked unfamiliar gastronomic and erotic
associations. It was not until 1938 that André
Breton christened the object *Le Déjeuner en fourrure* ("Luncheon in fur"). He chose the object's title

as a play on Manet's famous painting *Le Déjeuner
sur l'herbe* (1863; Musée d'Orsay, Paris), where
fully clad male students lunch on the grass in the
company of female nudes, and Sacher-Masoch's
Venus im Pelz (1869), a *Bildungsroman* about a fur-
wearing, whip-bearing woman, Wanda, and her
slave, the narrator Severin. Treated increasingly
cruelly, Severin finally loses his fascination with the
submissive role when he is almost killed by Wanda
and her latest conquest. Now opting for the domi-
nator's role himself, he understands that "woman,
as nature created her, is his enemy and can only be
his slave or his dominatrix but never his companion". From the beginning, Oppenheim rejected
Breton's title with its inherent repetition of unequal,
patriarchal relations between the sexes, but the
clever object, nevertheless, became canonised under
the Surrealist leader's heading.

The most widely disseminated image of
Oppenheim herself is not one of her own painted
self-portraits but a famous Man Ray photograph
entitled *Erotique voilée*, originally published in the
Surrealist journal *Minotaure* in May 1934. Here the
20-year-old artist, standing nude behind a printing
wheel, which simultaneously hides and covers her
striking, partly blackened physique, is cast as
Surrealism's latest muse: as *femme-enfant* or "child-
woman" who enables the older, male Surrealist
artists to go beyond the constraints of their bourgeois society. This particular Surrealist muse, a type
predominant in the 1930s, was equipped with the
power to transform sight into artistic vision, providing the male Surrealist artist with a convulsive image
from which he subsequently constructed his work of
art. She was the creative medium through which he
channelled his own, otherwise difficult to access,
artistic unconscious. In his riddle-ridden, often
quoted invitation to Oppenheim's first solo exhibition in 1936, her former lover Max Ernst purposefully reinforced this child-woman image: "WOMAN IS
A SANDWICH COVERED IN WHITE MARBLE. Who covers
a soup spoon in precious fur? Little Meret. Who has
outpaced us? Little Meret."

Initially, Oppenheim certainly profited from
these personal and artistic connections with the
more established Surrealist artists, but ultimately
her uninhibited personality and the dramatic success
of one particular work – the scandalous fur-lined
teacup – created a persistent but all too narrow basis
for her international fame.

Shortly before the outbreak of World War II, when a large number of Surrealists were getting ready to leave Paris, Oppenheim returned to Switzerland, where she soon lost faith in herself. She experienced an artistic and human crisis that lasted for almost 18 years. The artist herself once explicitly described this state of shattered self: "I felt as if millennia of discrimination against women were resting on my shoulders, as if embodied in my feelings of inferiority" (Curiger 1989). Oppenheim, who did not want to become known as the artist who lines things, progressed only slowly from enchanting muse and instant Surrealist hit to mature artist in her own right. Many of the works she created during her depression were destroyed by Oppenheim herself, reworked later or simply not shown to the public at all. Two of these works in particular show an increasingly de-stabilising, de-individualised image of the artist. Her oil painting *Stone-Woman* (1938; private collection, Bern, repr. Curiger 1989) depicts a female figure, made out of large boulders, resting at a stream with only her legs immersed in water, and in her drawing *Future Self-Portrait as an Old Woman* (1938; private collection, Basel, *ibid.*) the artist, at the age of 25, aged her features relentlessly to reflect accurately her inner state of mind. Oppenheim's self-questioning regarding the tension between woman as creative artist and woman as subject on whose youthful body others had projected powerful and provocative images continued throughout her work. During these difficult years, Oppenheim studied the writings of Carl Gustav Jung intensively. His article "Woman in Europa" (1924) was especially influential on her artistic philosophy. Regretfully, this Jungian influence has led to certain simplified views on Oppenheim's works that unduly limit the perspective on her varied oeuvre.

Once her depression subsided, the artist, now in her early forties, rented a studio in Bern and designed masks and costumes for Picasso's *How to Catch Wishes by the Tail*. That same year she also created *Le Couple*, a pair of partially laced brown boots, grown together at the toes, with their leather tongues showing. Her work from this period is deeply connected to her earlier work, particularly in its relation to femininity and its constructions. In 1959 Oppenheim organised a banquet, served on the naked body of a female acquaintance and entitled *Spring-Feast*, for several of her intimate friends. Later that same year Breton asked the artist to contribute the *Feast* to the eighth *Exposition InteRnatiOnale du Surréalisme* (EROS) at the Galerie Cordier in Paris. For an enthusiastic public, Oppenheim's *tableau vivant* best captured the spirit of the shocking Surrealist exhibition as a whole. But Oppenheim, apprehensive about her participation early on, was annoyed when her private "feast for both men and women" was reduced to a voyeuristic spectacle where men once again could feast on the female body as a passive object of desire. This was the last time that the artist exhibited with the Surrealists; Oppenheim's work no longer had much in common with the latest generation of Surrealists.

A retrospective at the Moderna Museet in Stockholm in 1967 marked the beginning of the revival of interest in Oppenheim's work. A year or two later, she even made fun of her own "Luncheon in fur". She created the *Souvenir du Déjeuner en fourrure* (Museum of Modern Art, New York), a small, kitsch version of the famous original, explicitly undermining and cashing in on the continued marketability of her early signature work. By now her art had found a new public. At the age of 70 she was asked to participate in the Documenta at Kassel, the most significant European exhibition for contemporary art, organised every five years. There she displayed her latest works among those of 167, often significantly younger, post-modern colleagues. Meret Oppenheim's skilful undermining and ironic fetishisation of precisely those elements that have traditionally contributed to notions of "femininity" in art and society eventually gained the attention of such up-and-coming women artists as Valie Export, who recognised her as a role-model.

BETTINA BRANDT

P

Peale, Anna Claypoole, 1791–1878, and Sarah Miriam, 1800–1885

American painters

Daughters of Mary Claypoole, and of James Peale of Philadelphia, a miniature, still-life and portrait painter; uncle was the painter Charles Willson Peale. Other siblings, including sisters Margaretta Angelica (1795–1882) and Maria (1787–1866), were also painters.

Anna Claypoole Peale Born in Philadelphia, 6 March 1791. Trained by her father. Attended lectures on anatomy for artists at the College of Physicians, Philadelphia, 1819. Lived in Philadelphia, but painted in Washington, DC, late 1818–spring 1819; visited Washington again, 1820; also made annual trips to Baltimore, and painted briefly in Boston, 1821 and 1827, and New York. Married (1) Revd William Staughton, 27 August 1829; he died December 1829; (2) General William Duncan, 1841; he died 1864. Ceased professional activities after second marriage. Member, Pennsylvania Academy of the Fine Arts, Philadelphia, 1824. Died in Philadelphia, 25 December 1878.

Principal Exhibitions

Pennsylvania Academy of the Fine Arts, Philadelphia:
    1811, 1814, 1817–32, 1835–8, 1840–42
Boston Athenaeum: 1828, 1831

Sarah Miriam Peale Born in Philadelphia, 19 May 1800. Trained by her father. Attended anatomy classes at College of Physicians, Philadelphia, with sister Anna, 1819. Travelled between Philadelphia and Baltimore with Anna, 1818–25, working in cousin Rembrandt Peale's Baltimore studio until 1822, and exhibiting work in his Museum. Lived in Baltimore, 1825–46, taking occasional trips to Washington, DC, to paint public figures. Resided in St Louis, 1847–77. Returned to Philadelphia, 1878. Member, Pennsylvania Academy of the Fine Arts, Philadelphia, 1824. Died in Philadelphia, 4 February 1885.

Principal Exhibitions

Pennsylvania Academy of the Fine Arts, Philadelphia:
    1817–22, 1824–31
St Louis Agricultural and Mechanical Association: 1856 (diploma and prize), 1858, 1859 (first prize), 1860 (first prize), 1864 (first and second prizes), 1866, 1867 (two second prizes)
Missouri Historical Society, St Louis: 1872

Bibliography

Elizabeth Fries Ellet, *Women Artists in All Ages and Countries*, New York: Harper, 1859; London: Bentley, 1860

Anna Wells Rutledge, *Cumulative Record of Exhibition Catalogues: The Pennsylvania Academy of the Fine Arts, 1807–1870 ...*, Philadelphia: American Philosophical Society, 1955

Rendezvous for Taste: Peale's Baltimore Museum, 1814 to 1830, exh. cat., Municipal Museum of the City of Baltimore, 1956

The Peale Family and Peale's Baltimore Museum, 1814–1830, exh. cat., Municipal Museum, Baltimore, 1965

Miss Sarah Miriam Peale, 1800–1885: Portraits and Still Life, exh. cat., Peale Museum, Baltimore, 1967

Lillian B. Miller, ed., *The Collected Papers of Charles Willson Peale and His Family*, microfiche, Millwood, NY: KTC Microform, 1980

Charlotte Streifer Rubinstein, *American Women Artists from Early Times to the Present*, Boston: Hall, 1982

Karen McCoskey Goering, "St Louis women artists, 1818–1945: An exhibition", *Gateway Heritage*, iii/1, Summer 1982, pp.14–21

Lincoln Bunce Spiess, "St Louis women artists in the mid-19th century", *Gateway Heritage*, iii/4, Spring 1983, pp.10–23

James L. Yarnall and William H. Gerdts, *The National Museum of American Art's Index to American Art*

Exhibition Catalogs from the Beginning through the 1876 Centennial Year, Boston: Hall, 1987

Anne Sue Hirshorn, "Modes of accomplishment and fortune: Anna Claypoole, Margaretta and Sarah Miriam Peale", *Creation of a Legacy: The Peale Family, 1770–1870*, ed. Lillian B. Miller, New York: Abbeville, 1996

——, *Anna Claypoole Peale* (in preparation)

Unpublished correspondence, papers and catalogues of paintings are in the American Philosophical Society, Philadelphia (Peale-Sellers Papers); Archives of the Municipal Museum of the City of Baltimore (Peale Museum); Catalogue of American Portraits and Peale Family Papers office, National Portrait Gallery, Smithsonian Institution, Washington, DC; and Frick Art Reference Library, New York.

Born into a family of artists, Sarah Miriam Peale and her sister Anna Claypoole were introduced to painting at an early age by their father James Peale, a portraitist and still-life painter, whom they assisted with backgrounds and costume details. Anna reported that she would stand behind her father's chair "for hours and hours at a time watching James progress. He took great pains", she recalled, "in teaching her, pointing out the peculiar touches that produced his best effects by giving a charm to the expression" (Ellet 1859, p.290). They were probably given the usual course of instruction for artists at the time, with emphasis on drawing, the painting of still lifes and copying. The James Peale family lived on an extremely limited income, and at a young age Anna Claypoole worked at filling in outlines of maps with delicate watercolour paint, colouring engravings and, between 1805 and 1807, making an occasional copy of her father's miniature portraits at the request of his patrons. With her sister Maria, she launched her public career in 1811 with the exhibition of a painting of flowers at the Pennsylvania Academy of the Fine Arts. However, it was the delicate art of miniature painting – an art that was considered suitable for a genteel woman – that drew her to the life of an artist; under her father's tutelage and assisted by her uncle, Charles Willson Peale, Anna Claypoole began accepting commissions for such portraits from 1814 on, her father relinquishing the market to her. Although still-life painting continued to command the attention of her older sister Maria and the younger Margaretta (who occasionally exhibited still lifes – or, infrequently, portraits – at the Pennsylvania Academy between 1828 and 1837, but who was essentially an amateur), from this time Anna Claypoole concentrated her artistic attention on miniature work.

Anna's miniatures followed her father's Federal style; lighter in colour, more fluidly painted, her small watercolour portraits on ivory were graceful and elegant. Praised for their "accuracy and truth", clear and precise drawing, minute details of costume and lively expression, such miniatures as *Miss Susannah Williams* (1825; Maryland Historical Society, Baltimore) responded directly to the position of her sitters, in both their public and private lives. Her miniature of *Major General Andrew Jackson* (1819; Yale University Art Gallery, New Haven), for example, places the soldier in a heroic setting, in recognition of his controversial but successful expedition in Florida against the Seminole Indians, but Jackson as an individual remains remote and cold, his gaze turned away from the viewer and his eyes veiled as he contemplates a distant scene. Painted at the same time, her miniature of *Senator Richard Mentor Johnson* (1819; Museum of Fine Arts, Boston) is warmer, more informal, suggestive of a close intimacy between the artist and the Kentucky colonel and statesman, who was a friend of her family and, it would appear, a suitor for a brief time during her Washington visit in 1819.

With the only interruption the brief interlude of her marriage in 1829, Anna Claypoole Peale pursued an ambitious artistic career. Her work reflected changing tastes in the miniature, which were manifested in particular in the work of such Boston artists as Pamela Hill, Sarah Goodridge and her sister Eliza Goodridge. From small delicately painted oval ivories, framed in precious metals or stones, that could be carried or worn, these artists, including Anna, began to favour larger rectangular cabinet miniatures set in leather cases suitable for display on a table top or for hanging on a wall. Instead of presenting the sitter bust-size, her subjects, like others painted in miniature during the 1820s and 1830s, began to be shown in half-length, standing or sitting next to a table and framed by draperies. As taste in the early Victorian period turned to darker palettes, Anna also experimented with a richer, deeper colouring. In response to the early Victorian interest in European old masters and in art as an indication of cultivated taste, she, too, turned to the making of copies, in watercolour on ivory, of European works. Her copy of Guido Reni's *Beatrice Cenci* (1829; untraced) suggests an ambition to create imaginative art beyond the conventional portrait. During these decades, Reni was one of the most popular 17th-century artists in the USA, his *Sibyl* becoming the source of many a Victorian "fancy piece". The story of Beatrice Cenci was also a popular legend; it became the subject of Shelley's tragedy, *The Cenci* (1819), of a painting by Thomas Sully in 1825 after Reni, and of a sculpture by Harriet Hosmer (q.v.). Anna's choice of this tragic heroine as a subject for a miniature suggests a deeper side to the artist than is manifested in her charming, somewhat shallow family miniatures, especially since it was painted soon after the unhappy ending of her short marriage.

Like her sisters, Sarah Miriam Peale also began her artistic career painting still life, but almost immediately turned to portraiture. At the age of 17 she painted her first formal portrait – a *Self-Portrait* (National Portrait Gallery, Washington, DC) – which she exhibited in 1818 at the Pennsylvania Academy to her uncle Charles Willson Peale's praise that it was "wonderfully like". Although her uncle reported in 1818 that Sarah was more interested in breaking hearts than painting portraits, unlike her sister she did not interrupt her career with marriage; instead, she remained, as the *Missouri Republican* noted in 1877, "wedded to her art".

Sarah Miriam Peale is generally associated with Baltimore. Here, she successfully competed for commissions with some of the leading male artists of the time, and included among her patrons members of the city's prosperous middle class – entire families such as the William Jessops and visiting dignitaries such as the first Brazilian Chargé d'Affaires in the USA, *José Sylvestre Rabello* (1826; Brazilian Embassy, Washington, DC). Occasionally, she travelled to Washington, DC, to paint such public figures as the *Marquis de Lafayette* (1824–5; private collection) and, between 1841 and 1843, *Daniel Webster* (Mercantile Library, St Louis), *Abel P. Upshur* (Maryland Historical Society, Baltimore), *Congressman Henry Wise of Virginia* (Virginia Museum of Fine Arts, Richmond), *Congressman Caleb Cushing of Massachusetts* (untraced), *President John Tyler* (Historical Society of Pennsylvania, Philadelphia) and *Senator Thomas Hart Benton of Missouri* (Missouri Historical Society, St Louis). In 1847 Sarah Miriam accepted the invitation of some Missouri social and political leaders, including Nathaniel Childs, Trusten Polk and Senator L.F. Linn, to visit St Louis, where she remained for 30 years. Little is known about her life

during this period, except that she was warmly welcomed in St Louis, a thriving community with a great interest in cultural activities and host to a number of artists. As in Baltimore, Sarah Miriam's patrons consisted of entire families, such as the Edward Armistead Owens family (three portraits, c.1857; private collection). In 1860 her portrait of *Edward William Johnston* (Mercantile Library of St Louis), a colonel in the Mexican War, was awarded the first premium at the St Louis Agricultural and Mechanical Association's fair. From 1859 Sarah Miriam painted primarily still lifes, exhibiting them successfully in the annual St Louis fairs and winning premiums. She returned to Philadelphia in 1878 and died there in 1885, the last member of the second generation of her painting family. One of America's first woman artists to earn professional recognition, she was also one of the first to maintain herself as an artist through a long lifetime.

As a result of her residency in Baltimore, many of Sarah Miriam Peale's Baltimore portraits have been mistakenly attributed to her cousin Rembrandt Peale, although her work is easily distinguished from his. Her portraits are firmly drawn, somewhat linear, and painted with a minimum of shadowing or chiaroscuro. She revelled in finely painted details of lace and fabrics, the use of accessories such as books, flowers or objects pertinent to the sitter's position, and rich colour and glazing that result in translucent, almost oily skin tones. Her sitters look lively and pleasant, and highly naturalistic. An occasional newspaper review of portraits painted in St Louis praised the "accuracy" of her likenesses and their "life like expression". Her portraits of children, such as *Charles Lavallen Jessop (Boy on a Rocking-Horse)* (c.1840; private collection), are imaginatively and charmingly composed. Portraits of women painted during the 1820s and 1830s are enhanced by either a foreground still life or a landscape background; the subjects are elegantly costumed and wear beautifully painted shawls or transparent organdie bonnets. Sarah Miriam delighted in ornament, rich textures and elaborate patterns, as may be seen in the wedding portrait of her cousin, *Charlotte Ramsay Robinson* (c.1840; Peale Museum, Municipal Museum of Baltimore). Her male subjects appear dignified, intelligent and cheerful in simpler portraits that were considered more appropriate to their gender. Conservative and traditional, her portraits only occasionally suggest the spritely and independent personality described in her letters; one that does is *Veil of Mystery* (*c.*1830; Peale Museum), a romantic, sensuous and suggestive image composed around the same time that her sister Anna Claypoole was painting *Beatrice Cenci.*

During her lifetime Sarah Miriam painted at least 50 still lifes, not all of which have been located. Her earlier still lifes reflect the influence of her father James and cousin Raphaelle Peale; primarily depicting fruit composed on a strong diagonal and spilling out of a bowl on to a polished table top, they convey the luxuriance of American nature (e.g. *Still Life*, 1822; Richard York Gallery, New York). Her later still lifes are painted with a looser hand and stylistically reflect the changes that occurred in paintings of this genre in the mid-19th century under the influence of the American Pre-Raphaelites, who depicted flowers or fruit growing in their natural out-of-doors setting rather than artificially collected in containers indoors (e.g. *Cherries*, *c.*1860; private collection).

LILLIAN B. MILLER

Peeters, Clara

Flemish painter, active 1611–21

No certain details of her life are known. Possibly she was the Clara Peeters, daughter of Jan Peeters, who was baptised in St Walburgs, Antwerp, 15 May 1594. The same or another Clara Peeters married Hendrick Joossen in St Walburgs, 31 May 1639.

Bibliography

Women Artists, 1550–1950, exh. cat., Los Angeles County Museum of Art, and elsewhere, 1976

N. R. A. Vroom, *A Modest Message as Intimated by the Painters of the "Monochrome Banketje"*, 2 vols, Schiedam: Interbook International, 1980 (Dutch original, 1945)

Still-life in the Age of Rembrandt, exh. cat., Auckland City Art Gallery, 1982

De Rijkdom Verbeeld: Schatkamer van de Gouden Eeuw/A Prosperous Past: The Sumptuous Still Life in the Netherlands, 1600–1700, exh. cat., Stedelijk Museum Het Prinsenhof, Delft, and elsewhere, 1988

Celeste Brusati, "Stilled lives: Self-portraiture and self-reflection in seventeenth-century Netherlandish still-life painting", *Simiolus*, xx, 1990–91, pp.168–82

Pamela Hibbs Decoteau, *Clara Peeters, 1594–ca 1640, and the Development of Still-Life Painting in Northern Europe*, Lingen: Luca, 1992

Julie Berger Hochstrasser, *Life and Still Life: A Cultural Inquiry into Seventeenth-Century Dutch Still-Life Painting*, PhD dissertation, University of California, Berkeley, 1995

At the beginning of the 17th century in Europe, still life was just emerging as an independent genre in its own right, and Clara Peeters was playing a formative role in its development. Painting in the Netherlands, Peeters was among the originators of the finely detailed oil paintings of flowers, breakfasts and banquets, fish and game that proved so popular over the course of the century. Her earliest dated paintings, with the dates reading most probably 1607 and 1608, are small, intimate still lifes that set the tone for her production (repr. Decoteau 1992, pls 1 and 2). The motifs they present would recur in her work: glasses of wine, biscuits and sweets, oysters and shrimp, bread and fruit. The earlier picture (private collection, England) contains a biscuit in the shape of a *P* that may be self-referential; it is the first of many expressions of a subtle self-consciousness that distinguishes Peeters's art. Most notably, these compact compositions already differ from the more scattered lay-out and more distant, elevated viewpoint characteristic of other early still lifes of the laid table, such as those by the older Antwerp painter Osias Beert. Other early affinities of subject and technique suggest that Peeters may have studied under Beert, although surviving records do not list her as his pupil. But Beert's compositions were soon to appear old-fashioned, whereas Peeters's novel compositional instincts were borne out in the subsequent evolution of 17th-century Netherlandish still life.

Four larger, more elaborate paintings (*Game*, 51 × 71 cm.; *Dainties*, 52 × 73 cm.; *Fish*, 50 × 72 cm.; *Pie*, 55 × 73 cm.; all Prado, Madrid) masterfully summarise themes to which Peeters would return throughout her career. All signed and of nearly identical dimensions, they seem to have been produced as a group; three are dated, all 1611. One featuring a variety of dead birds is the earliest dated example of a "game piece" (unless one counts Jacopo de Barbari's Munich panel of 1504 which stands quite apart). Another focusing on freshly caught fish, shrimp, crabs and a strainer of artichokes presages numerous fish studies by Dutch painters. Peeters's characteristic linear articulation and hair-breadth brushwork detail every scale on the fish, every feather on the birds; in both pictures, closely clustered objects, viewed from a low vantage point, overlap to enhance the impression of depth, marking Peeters's innovative approach to composition. The third Prado painting depicts a banquet laid on a fine damask tablecloth: delicacies such as an elaborate pie, citrus fruits, olives and boiled partridges are served up with fine tableware of silver and porcelain. In a central position at the front of the picture is a silver knife with adornments typical of the *bruidsmessen* (brides' knives) made by Antwerp goldsmiths between 1595 and 1600; along its edge the artist's name is clearly legible, depicted as if engraved there. Whether this was only a pictorial invention (Segal in Delft 1988) or a real object made and personalised for Peeters (Decoteau 1992) – a possibility supported by the fact that she depicted the same knife on several other occasions over a period of 20 years – the artist deploys it here as a distinctive means for signing her work. But a still more remarkable flourish of self-reflection appears in the fourth Prado painting. It combines a vase of flowers with a spread of costly tableware and dainty foods, centring on a finely wrought gilt goblet. Mirrored in the smooth nodes of the gold cup, Peeters has registered the reflection of herself at her easel. Her youthful face appears several times more on the polished surface of the pewter pitcher in the background on the right – and yet again on the lid of the stoneware jug in the fish piece.

These tiny reflections constitute an unusual kind of self-portrait: scarcely visible except under close scrutiny, they incorporate the working artist right into the still-life scenes she depicts. Heir to the sharply honed skills of her earlier Netherlandish predecessors, Peeters painted with oils to an intense level of illusionism. Jan van Eyck had similarly captured his reflection in miniature in the armour of St George in his *Virgin and Child with Canon van der Paele* (1436; Musée Communal, Bruges) – an image that Peeters may have seen (Brusati 1990–91). Her use of the device seems to invoke this heritage, claiming a place for herself within it. But Peeters was among the first painters to integrate such self-portraiture into the realm of still life – only one known example predates hers, an anonymous still life of 1538 (Kröller-Müller Museum, Otterlo) that she had probably not seen. Many other Netherlandish painters were later to incorporate reflected self-portraits into still lifes – Pieter Claesz, Jan de Heem, Abraham van Beyeren and others – often depicting one, occasionally two faces in a picture. But of the surviving examples, Peeters seems to have been the only one to repeat her likeness over and over within one image in this way, as if silently but perseveringly insisting that we cannot overlook the young woman who wields the brush. Rightly so: although in the 18th century still life became known as a woman's genre (a pejorative association reflecting unfavourable estimations of both women and still life), at this early juncture Peeters was the only Netherlandish woman whose name survives among a cast of men at work in this genre. Others followed later in the century – Margaretha de Heer, Maria van Oosterwijck (q.v.), Rachel Ruysch (q.v.) – but Peeters had a seminal role.

From the prolific year of 1612 there are at least ten paintings from her hand, five of them dated; their innovations place Peeters at the forefront of the evolution of the genre. Most are flower paintings (all in private collections or untraced), in which Peeters begins to depart from the conventions of her contemporaries by trying out a more sparse, asymmetrical arrangement with fewer different species. Two of her three food paintings in this year are also signed and dated. Whether focusing on seafood and wine (Poltava Art Museum, Russia), herring, cherries and an artichoke (Richard Green Gallery, London), or gilt cup, sweets and a pomegranate (Richard Green Gallery), all intensify the compressed arrangement of her earliest "banquets". The latter two, of identical dimensions, may form pendants contrasting poor versus rich meals, or perhaps simply everyday versus festive fare; Peeters's face is vaguely visible again on the lid of the stoneware jug of the more "common" still life.

A masterpiece inscribed *CLARA P. ANNO 1612* (Staatliche Kunsthalle, Karlsruhe) revisits the self-reflection exercise in a testimony both to Peeters's prodigious painterly skills and her irrepressible creative personality. It depicts an array of valuable things: gold coins and a golden chain, two extraordinary covered gilt goblets, a Chinese celadon bowl, exotic shells and a vase of rare flowers. The scene has been associated with *Wunderkammer* collections of rare and precious objects: even the blossoms, such as the tulip and the checkered fritillary, were coveted collectibles. Others have interpreted the fragile blooms and expensive display as a *vanitas* admonishing the ephemerality of worldly riches. But Peeters's reflected self-portraits add a unique twist to this image: on the smooth spots of the gilt goblet in the background, we detect again – and again and again, some eight times over – the tiny figure, seated at her easel, palette and brushes in hand, her position adjusted slightly each time for the angle of view. It is a record of patient observation that rewards careful looking, a display of meticulous crafting that rivals the skilful production of the precious objects she depicts (Brusati 1990–91). Peeters informs us in no uncertain terms who has produced the value of this painting. But more than mere self-promotion, these repeated self-reflections challenge the *vanitas* notion by reminding us that it is the unique ability of the artist to overcome the transience of fragile flowers, of earthly wealth, even of this youthful visage – by fixing them, triumphant against the ravages of time, in paint. It is all the more dramatic for the astonishing accomplishment displayed by this painter who, by all the accounts of the uncertain documentation, at the time was only 18 years old.

That scanty documentation is another element in the drama played out in these tiny self-portraits. We do not find Peeters inscribed into the Antwerp guild, though records for many applicable years are lost. Nor did art biographers of the period tell us of her life, despite the part her work clearly played in the course of Netherlandish painting. The only documents we have, about the Antwerp baptism of 1594 and the Antwerp marriage of 1639 of one Clara Peeters, are not even certainly about *this* Clara Peeters. If they are, they establish that her talents were precocious; yet a girl would have had to be exceptional to secure training at all in those days, and these youthful self-portraits do seem to correlate the age these documents indicate. Left as we are with little more than these pictures to inform us about their creator, the insistent painterly presence of these diminutive self-portraits becomes especially poignant.

To survey Peeters's oeuvre is to observe the careful arrangement and rearrangement of certain favoured subjects, masterfully rendered: a stack of cheeses, sometimes topped by a plate of butter pats, an artichoke halved to reveal the delicate patterns of its leaves and centre, whole shrimp with their hair-like antennae, plump red cherries, brittle pretzels, a plate of almonds and figs and raisins. Even the tableware becomes familiar; like many still-life colleagues during this period, Peeters studies the same objects over and over again, sometimes with slight variations. Her choices occasion virtuoso rendering of a wide variety of materials and textures: besides the faithful knife, the gilt goblets and the pewter pitcher, other repeated objects are too numerous to list exhaustively: a cylindrical silver salt-cellar, a certain stoneware jug, a patterned porcelain plate, a particular wicker basket, various distinctive wine-glasses. Her latest surviving dated work stands as an exception to this pattern: a painting on copper of the *Virgin and Child* within a floral wreath (1621; private collection, repr. Decoteau 1992). More representative is a large picture that inventories many of her chosen themes, combining flowers and fruit and other familiar subjects with the pitcher reflecting her face and the knife bearing her name (Ashmolean Museum, Oxford). Other undated paintings attributed to this decade for stylistic reasons include several more food paintings with cheeses or artichokes, and some variations on the theme of a pile of fresh fish eyed by a cat (one in the National Museum of Women in the Arts, Washington, DC). Four signed works probably from the 1630s consolidate the themes already put forward: a "cheesestack" that re-enlists the bridal knife, two fruit baskets with the nibbling monkeys popular in Flemish still life and another fish painting (all untraced). The panel-maker's initials marked on the back of this final piece date it probably after 1637, making it very likely the last of Peeters's surviving signed works.

Clara Peeters's influence was felt well beyond Antwerp, beyond the Southern Netherlands, in the Dutch Republic (the Northern Netherlands) and Germany. The several trips she was thought to have made from Antwerp north into Holland were an important bridge between the two creative centres. Her reduced format, low viewpoint and restricted palette provided impetus towards the monochrome style of such Haarlem painters as Nicolaes Gillis and Pieter Claesz. Peeters's hand is especially evident in Claesz's linear depictions of a few objects on a bare wood table in his "close-up" paintings of the 1620s – so much so that many attributions are disputed between the two artists. This situation is aggravated by their shared initials, as many paintings are monogrammed in ligature (C and P intertwined). In flower painting, her simplified bouquets predated Ambrosius Bosschaert's own adoption of more spacious arrangements, just as her work often anticipated that of Bosschaert's brother-in-law and follower Balthasar van der Ast early in his career. Banquet paintings by both the German Peter Binoit and the Fleming Artus Claessen directly echoed her work in style and motifs. Judging from the large number of paintings that have been attributed to her (particularly by Vroom) and the considerable circle of her influence (19 works have more recently been relegated to the "circle of Peeters" by Decoteau, with many more showing affinities), Clara Peeters was clearly neither minor nor unknown in her time. Decoteau pointed to the need to re-evaluate the extent of her influence and consider the possibility that she headed a small school. Her work demonstrates not only stylistic independence and painstaking technical achievement, but also a vital artistic personality. Besides putting forward her own visions of the possibilities of a new genre, Peeters devised ways to claim them as her own, leaving her mark on the history of still-life painting in the West.

JULIE BERGER HOCHSTRASSER

Pereira, I(rene) Rice
American painter, 1902–1971

Born Irene M. Rice in Chelsea, Massachusetts, 5 August 1902. Attended evening classes at Art Students League, New York, studying under Richard Lahey and Jan Matulka, 1927–31. Travelled to Europe and Africa, 1931–2; possibly studied under Amédée Ozenfant at Académie Moderne, Paris. Taught painting and design synthesis for Design Laboratory, New York, 1936–9 (originally part of the Works Progress Administration Federal Art Project, WPA/FAP). Museum assistant, Museum of Non-Objective Painting, 1940–42. Taught design at Pratt Institute, Brooklyn, 1942–3. Began Jungian psychoanalysis, 1948. Travelled to France, 1949. Moved to Salford, England, 1950. Returned to USA and taught at Ball State University, Muncie, Indiana, 1951. Spent time at MacDowell Colony, Peterborough, New Hampshire, 1953. Made frequent visits to Europe after 1960. Converted to Catholicism, 1963. Established I. Rice Pereira Foundation in New York, 1968. Moved to Spain after eviction from New York apartment, 1970. Married (1) painter and commercial artist Humberto Pereira, 1929; divorced 1938; (2) engineer and amateur photographer George Wellington Brown, 1942; divorced 1950; (3) Irish poet George Reavey, 1950; divorced 1959. Elected Life fellow, International Institute of Arts and Letters, Lindau-

Bodensee, Germany, 1959. Recipient of honorary doctorate, L'Université Libre (Asie), Karachi, Pakistan, and International Federation of Scientific Research Societies of Europe, Asia, Africa and America, 1969. Died of emphysema in Marbella, Spain, 11 January 1971.

Principal Exhibitions

Individual
American Contemporary Arts (ACA) Gallery, New York: 1933, 1934, 1935, 1946, 1949
East River Gallery, New York: 1937
Howard University, Washington, DC: 1938
Julien Levy Gallery, New York: 1939
Museum of Non-Objective Painting, New York: 1940, 1942
Art of This Century Gallery, New York: 1944
San Francisco Museum of Art: 1947
Barnett Aden Gallery, Washington, DC: 1948
Whitney Museum of American Art, New York: 1953 (touring retrospective, with Loren MacIver)
Corcoran Gallery of Art, Washington, DC: 1956
Andrew Crispo Gallery, New York: 1976 (retrospective)

Group
Whitney Museum of American Art, New York: 1935 (Abstract Art in America)
Museum of Modern Art, New York: 1946 (Fourteen Americans, touring)
Metropolitan Museum of Art, New York: 1946 (Advancing American Art, touring)

Selected Writings
"Light and the new reality: A treatise on the metaphysics of light with a new aesthetic", New York, 1951; expanded and reprinted in Palette, Spring 1952, pp.2–11
The Transformation of "Nothing" and the Paradox of Space, New York: I. Rice Pereira, 1953
The Nature of Space: A Metaphysical and Aesthetic Inquiry, New York: I. Rice Pereira, 1956; reprinted Washington, DC: Corcoran Gallery of Art, 1968
The Lapis, New York: Wittenborn, 1957; reprinted Washington, DC: Corcoran Gallery of Art, 1970
Crystal of the Rose, New York: Nordness Gallery, 1959 (poems, with introductions by Lee Nordness and Ranjee Shahani)
The Finite Versus the Infinite, New York: I. Rice Pereira, 1959
The Transcendental Formal Logic of the Infinite: The Evolution of Cultural Forms, New York: I. Rice Pereira, 1966
The Poetics of the Form of Space, Light and the Infinite, New York: I. Rice Pereira, 1969

Bibliography

Elizabeth McCausland, "Alchemy and the artist: I. Rice Pereira", *Art in America*, xxxv, July 1947, pp.177–86

Loren MacIver/I. Rice Pereira, exh. cat., Whitney Museum of American Art, New York, and elsewhere, 1953

James Harithas, "I. Rice Pereira: American painter-writer with bold solutions to old problems", *Vogue*, June 1970

I. Rice Pereira, exh. cat., Andrew Crispo Gallery, New York, 1976

Donald Miller, "The timeless landscape of I. Rice Pereira", *Arts Magazine*, liii, October 1978, pp.132–3

Therese Schwartz, "Demystifying Pereira", *Art in America*, lxvii, October 1979, pp.114–19

Judith K. Van Wagner, "I. Rice Pereira: Vision superseding style", *Woman's Art Journal*, i/1, 1980, pp.33–8

Irene Rice Pereira's Library: A Metaphysical Journey, exh. cat., National Museum of Women in the Arts, Washington, DC, 1988

Mara R. Witzling, ed., *Voicing Our Visions: Writings by Women Artists*, New York: Universe, 1991; London: Women's Press, 1992

Karen A. Bearor, *Irene Rice Pereira: Her Paintings and Philosophy*, Austin: University of Texas Press, 1993 (contains extensive bibliography and full exhibition list)

Irene Rice Pereira's Early Work: Embarking on an Eastward Journey, exh. cat., Lowe Art Museum, University of Miami, Coral Gables, 1994

In 1953 Irene Rice Pereira shared with Loren MacIver the honour of being the first living American woman to be given a retrospective at the Whitney Museum of American Art. Coming at the mid-point of a career spanning four decades, this show testified to her prominence in vanguard art movements of the time and capped a distinguished exhibition record that included solo and group shows at several of the most prominent Manhattan museums and galleries. Pereira became a pioneer in the use of glass as a painting support. Her most impressive works in this medium include *Shooting Stars* (1952; Metropolitan Museum of Art, New York), which is formed by two panes of corrugated glass suspended in a shadow-box frame over a panel. Each visual level is painted with opaque and translucent rectilinear forms that allow shadows and light to be cast into and reflected from the depths of the construction. The resulting effect is one of fugues of radiating colour and light, with geometric shapes appearing to surface within a rippling, aqueous matrix. Well-read in popular science and pseudo-science, idealist philosophy and Jungian psychology, the artist frequently related her

works to the concept of a fluid and relational space-time continuum. She believed this cosmic continuum and the human psyche to be structurally isomorphic; thus these paintings also become metaphoric of the stratiform Jungian psyche. The visual synthesis of the physically discrete levels in these constructions is analogous to the process of individuation, which involves integrating the conscious, personal unconscious and collective unconscious of Jungian psychoanalysis. The mutable forms appearing to ascend from the interiors of paintings can then be interpreted as archetypes emerging from the depths of the collective unconscious.

If Pereira's geometric abstractions seemingly place her within a different artistic tradition from that of her Abstract Expressionist counterparts, her lifelong interest in subjectivity certainly places her within a similar philosophic one. While it is unclear when she became aware of Jung's writings (the earliest confirmed date is 1937), in the early 1930s she shared with her first husband, Humberto Pereira, an interest in the Faust legend – the structure of which Jung related to the process of individuation – and other mythical tales of spiritual quest and transformation. Such tales inform her paintings of machine and marine paraphernalia throughout this decade. These works are stylistically indebted to Synthetic Cubism; many of them are located in the Lowe Art Museum, University of Miami, Coral Gables, Florida, the largest single institutional holding of Pereira's paintings. Dabbling in social critique in 1936, when she became associated with leftist artist organisations in New York, Pereira offered an indictment of the impact of the machine on society in *Man and Machine* (first version, Lowe Art Museum; second version, University of Arizona Museum of Art).

The following year Pereira created her first abstractions, in which she explored the tactile and reflective properties of various materials, her investigations inspired by László Moholy-Nagy's book *The New Vision* (1930), based on Bauhaus studio practices. The Dessau Bauhaus was the pedagogical model for the Design Laboratory, a school of industrial design sponsored by the Works Progress Administration Federal Art Project in New York. Pereira was a member of the original faculty when it opened in 1936, and it was during her tenure there that she was also introduced to writings by Adolf von Hildebrand, Wilhelm Worringer, C. Howard

Hinton and Sigfried Giedion. Texture and light are her main concerns in the abstract painting *White Rectangle No.1* (1938; Lowe Art Museum), which prefigures her first glass paintings of 1939 and 1940, the most successful of which is *Shadows with Painting* (1940; Museum of Modern Art, New York). Her earliest glass paintings are simple in construction, with only a single pane of flat window glass – painted in a style reminiscent of Josef Albers's abstract stained-glass designs of the Bauhaus era – suspended over a panel. These gradually evolved into the more complex glass paintings described above, which Pereira began to create during the mid-1940s.

In 1951 the artist began to publish philosophical essays infused with a light mysticism derived from her reading in 1950 of Richard Wilhelm's *The Secret of the Golden Flower*, a translation of an 8th-century Taoist-alchemical tract. With its introductory commentary written by Jung, this book is crucial to an understanding of Pereira's attempts to develop a philosophy reconciling the temporal and spiritual realms of existence with a system of graphic representation articulating a "circulation" of light. The circular path of light Pereira described in her first essay, "Light and the new reality" (1951), is metaphoric of Faust's chthonic descent and ascent and hence is also metaphoric of psychic individuation. Her third husband George Reavey, a poet and translator of Russian Symbolist literature who had been closely associated with Surrealist movements in London and Paris, encouraged her subsequent investigations into alchemy, mysticism and the occult. These interests are perhaps most evident in *The Lapis* (1957), which provides clues to understanding the angular U- and Z-shaped motifs appearing in canvases from the last two decades of her life, such as *Pillar of Fire* (1955; San Antonio Museum of Art, TX) and *Sphering the Turn* (1962; André Zarré Gallery, New York). Alchemical symbolism figures prominently in the poetry she wrote and published during these last two decades. It appears as well in the figurative gouache and ink drawings she created in leisure hours or as gifts for friends during the same period.

KAREN A. BEAROR

Phalle, Niki de Saint *see* Saint Phalle

Pickering, Evelyn *see* De Morgan

Popova, Lyubov (Sergeyevna)
Russian painter and designer, 1889–1924

Born on the family estate at Krasnovidova, near the village of Ivanovskoye, Moscow province, 24 April (Old Style calendar)/7 May (New Style calendar) 1889. Studied at the Yalta gymnasium, 1902–6; Arsenev gymnasium, Moscow, 1906; A.S. Alferov's School, Moscow, 1906–8 (degree in literature); studied in studio of Impressionist painter Stanislav Zhukovsky, 1907; studios of Konstantin Yuon and Ivan Dudin, Moscow, 1908–9; "The Tower" studio, Moscow, 1912; La Palette, Paris, 1912–13; studio of Vladimir Tatlin, Moscow, 1914–16. Visited Italy, 1910; France and Italy with Vera Mukhina (q.v.), 1914. Taught at Svomas (State Free Art Studios), Moscow, 1918–20; Vkhutemas (Higher State Artistic and Technical Workshops), Moscow, 1920–24; GVTM (Higher State Theatrical Workshops), 1921–2; also taught a course for Proletkult, Moscow, 1924. Member, Inkhuk (Institute of Artistic Culture), 1920–24. Married art historian Boris von Eding, March 1918; son born November 1918; husband died of typhus, 1919. Died in Moscow, 25 May 1924.

Principal Exhibitions
Bubnovy valet (Jack/Knave of Diamonds), Moscow: 1914, 1916
Petrograd: 1915 (*Tramway V: First Futurist Exhibition of Paintings*), 1915 (*0.10 [Zero-Ten]: Last Futurist Exhibition of Paintings*)
Moscow: 1916 (*Futurist Exhibition: The Store*), 1918 (*First Exhibition of Paintings by the Professional Union of Artists in Moscow*), 1918 (*Fifth State Exhibition*), 1919 (*Tenth State Exhibition: Non-Objective Creation and Suprematism*), 1921 (*5 × 5 = 25*, with Rodchenko, Stepanova, Exter and Vesnin)
Galerie van Diemen, Berlin: 1922–3 (*Erste russische Kunstausstellung*, touring)
Museum of Decorative Painting, Moscow: 1923 (*Moscow's Theatrical and Decorative Art, 1918–1923*)
Stroganov Institute, Moscow: 1924 (retrospective)

Selected Writings
Untitled text in *Katalog desyatoy gosudarstvennoy vystavki* [Catalogue of the Tenth State Exhibition], exh. cat., VTsVB IZO Narkompros, Moscow, 1919, p.22
Untitled text in *5 × 5 = 25*, exh. cat., Moscow, 1921

"Poyasnitelnaya zapiska k postanovke 'Zemlya dybom' v teatre Meyerkholda" [Explanatory note on the production of "The Earth in Turmoil at Meyerkhold's Theatre"], *Lef*, no.4, 1924, p.44

Bibliography

Katalog posmertnoy vystavki khudozhnika konstruktora L.S. Popovoy, 1889–1924 [Catalogue of posthumous exhibition of the artist-constructor L.S. Popova, 1889–1924], exh. cat., Stroganov Institute, Moscow, 1924

Künstlerinnen der russischen Avantgarde/Women Artists of the Russian Avant-Garde, 1910–1930, exh. cat., Galerie Gmurzynska, Cologne, 1979

Angelica Zander Rudenstine, ed., *The George Costakis Collection: Russian Avant-Garde Art*, New York: Abrams, and London: Thames and Hudson, 1981

Christina Lodder, *Russian Constructivism*, New Haven and London: Yale University Press, 1983

Liubov Popova: Spatial Force Constructions, 1921–1922, exh. cat., Rachel Adler Gallery, New York, 1985

Art into Life: Russian Constructivism, 1914–1932, New York: Rizzoli, 1990

Briony Fer, "What's in a line? Gender and modernity", *Oxford Art Journal*, xiii, 1990, pp.77–88

L.S. Popova, 1889–1924: Katalog vystavki proizvedeniy k stoletiyu so dnya rozhdeniya [L.S. Popova, 1889–1924: Catalogue of the exhibition of works marking the centenary of her birth], exh. cat., Tretyakov Gallery, Moscow, 1990

Dmitri V. Sarabianov and Natalia L. Adaskina, *Popova*, New York, Abrams, and London: Thames and Hudson, 1990 (Russian original)

M.N. Yablonskaya, *Women Artists of Russia's New Age, 1900–1935*, New York: Rizzoli, and London: Thames and Hudson, 1990

Liubov Popova, exh. cat., Museum of Modern Art, New York, and elsewhere, 1991

Dmitry Sarabyanov, *Lyubov Popova: Zhivopis–Novaya Galereya XX veka* [Lyubov Popova: New Gallery paintings of the 20th century], Moscow: Galart, 1994

Lyubov Popova first came to prominence in the mid-1910s as an artist within the Russian Cubo-Futurist movement, exploring the potential overlay between the ideas of Futurism and the formal language of Cubism. She subsequently played an important role in elaborating the non-objective language of Suprematism and in developing the theory and practice of Constructivism. In 1924 her artistic evolution was summarised:

A Cubist period (the problem of form) was followed by a Futurist period (the problem of movement and colour) and the principle of abstracting the parts of an object was followed logically and inevitably by the abstraction of the object itself. The problem of representation was replaced by the problem of the construction of form and line (Post-Cubism) and colour (Suprematism). In 1917 her revolutionary tendencies came to the fore ... The most productive period of Popova's career took place in the years 1921–24 [Moscow 1924, p.6].

Popova's early training was rooted in Impressionism, Post-Impressionism and the work of Cézanne, as can be seen in such paintings as *Still Life* (1907–8; George Costakis Collection). She also admired the innovative works of Mikhail Vrubel, which she saw in Kiev in 1909, and Giotto's frescoes, which she studied in Italy in 1910. Like many of her generation, she was inspired by the traditional arts and architecture of her homeland and between 1910 and 1911 visited important ancient cities such as Novgorod, Pskov, Yaroslavl and Suzdal. In the early 1910s she produced several drawings in the spirit and style of Neo-primitivism, using motifs and stylistic features derived from ancient Russian icon painting (e.g. *Adoration of the Infant Christ*, early 1910s; Tretyakov Gallery, Moscow).

Although Popova was aware of modern Western developments through journals, temporary exhibitions and permanent collections such as that of Shchukin in Moscow, she became more familiar with contemporary ideas when she spent the winter of 1912–13 in Paris. There she worked at La Palette under the direction of Jean Metzinger and Henri Le Fauconnier and visited the studios of Alexander Archipenko and Ossip Zadkine. This close contact with Cubism was matched by a growing knowledge of Futurist theory and practice, and it seems likely that she saw Umberto Boccioni's Parisian exhibition of July 1913. In Popova's figure paintings of 1913–14, such as *Figure + House + Space* (State Russian Museum, St Petersburg), the various parts of the female body are translated into cuboid and conical elements, while the joints are rendered as open circular forms. Lines extend from these shapes to relate them to the surrounding spatial environment. While the formal language is indebted to Analytical Cubism, Popova's title pays homage to Umberto Boccioni's painting *Head + House + Light* of 1912. In early 1914 her brightly coloured compositions became flatter, the objects became more fragmented, and a greater unity was established between the dislocated elements and the grounds (e.g.

Objects from a Dyer's Shop (Early Morning), 1914; Museum of Modern Art, New York).

After Popova studied at "The Tower" in 1912, she became associated with such artists as Vladimir Tatlin and Nadezhda Udaltsova (q.v.) and in January 1914 she made her exhibition debut with the Knave (or Jack) of Diamonds group. She revisited France and Italy in the summer of 1914. During 1914–15 Popova experimented intensely with the possibilities of the Cubo-Futurist idiom and produced her own personal variations. In *Travelling Woman* (1915; Costakis Collection) Futurist devices, such as lines of force and sequential repetition of elements, are combined with features derived from Cubism, such as dislocation, restrained tonalities and lettering, to evoke the sensation of movement and the experience of travelling through time and geographical space.

In 1915 Popova also started to experiment with collage and to produce three-dimensional reliefs (in her terms "plastic paintings"), such as *Jug on a Table, Relief* (Tretyakov Gallery). This comprises found elements (the table leg), lettering ("2 lir") and heavily worked textures. The forms of the jug are translated into boldly curving sheets of card which are heavily painted and protrude dramatically from the ground plane while evoking the forms of the jug as seen from various viewpoints. Although Popova's reliefs were undoubtedly inspired by Tatlin's example and display a similar interest in textures and the spatial extension of the object, they are clearly distinct from the "culture of materials" that Tatlin developed and according to which the material determines the form. Even Popova's most abstract relief (repr. Moscow 1924) suggests that she was more interested in painted texture (and such pictorial elements as wallpaper) than in the sculptural potential and surface qualities of materials such as wood, metal and glass. Popova showed *Jug* and other reliefs at the *0.10* exhibition (December 1915, Petrograd), where Kazimir Malevich launched his Suprematist paintings of coloured geometric forms on white grounds.

Subsequently, in November 1916, Popova exhibited six non-objective paintings under the title of *Zhivopisnaya arkhitektonika*, which has been translated variously as *Pictorial* or *Painterly Architectonic* or *Architectonics*. These works consisted of coloured planes overlaid in fairly dense, centralised compositions against plain grounds. These retained some relationship to collage, but were evidently also influenced by Suprematism. During the winter of 1916–17 Popova belonged to Malevich's circle and was involved in creating various designs for the group's magazine *Supremus*, which was never published. In 1917 and 1918 she continued to develop her *Pictorial Architectonics*, producing paintings that evoke a greater sense of spatial dynamism by concentrating on large, diagonally intersecting planes of modulated colour (e.g. *Painterly Architectonic*, 1918; Yale University Art Gallery, New Haven). In March 1918 she married the art historian Boris von Eding and in November gave birth to a son. While staying at Rostov on Don during the summer and autumn of 1919, her husband died of typhus and Popova became seriously ill. Not surprisingly, Popova did not produce many paintings between late 1918 and late 1919.

During the Civil War (1918–20) Popova executed some work for the Fine Arts Section (IZO) within the People's Commissariat of Enlightenment (Narkompros), designing propaganda posters (for campaigns such as that against illiteracy) and producing decorations for the revolutionary festivals. In April 1919 she collaborated with the artist and architect Alexander Vesnin on decorating the building of the Moscow Soviet for May Day. Two years later, in May 1921, they worked together with the writer Ivan Aksyonov and the producer Vsevolod Meyerkhold on the staging of a mass festival to be held in Moscow in honour of the Third International. The cast of thousands was to have moved from the "Capitalist Fortress", the city of the past, which was rendered predominantly as a conglomeration of closed cuboid volumes, towards the "City of the Future". The latter was built of far more curving and transparent, open-work constructions, reminiscent of advanced engineering structures such as bridges and cranes and echoing the technological language of iron girders and glazed volumes, which Tatlin had celebrated in his *Model for a Monument to the Third International* of 1920. Popova and Vesnin produced models, but the project was cancelled at a late stage for financial reasons.

In 1918 Popova joined the staff of the Svomas (State Free Art Studios) and she continued to teach there when it changed into the Vkhutemas. She helped to organise the structure of the Basic Course and taught a course on colour construction that formed part of its syllabus. A member of the Inkhuk (Institute of Artistic Culture) from May 1920,

Popova initially worked with Wassily Kandinsky in the Section of Monumental Art. She then helped to formulate the programme of the General Working Group of Objective Analysis, participating actively in the discussions of spring 1921 that sought to define the distinction between concepts of composition and construction. This important debate led to the formation of the Working Group of Constructivists (also known as the First Working Group of Constructivists) in March 1921. These artists denied the validity of art as an autonomous activity and instead wished to participate in the construction of the new socialist society by designing everyday objects, which could be mass-produced by industry. Popova did not join this group initially, but allied herself with the Working Group of Objectivists which included Vesnin, Udaltsova and Alexander Drevin and which met for the first time on 15 April 1921. Popova continued to contribute to Inkhuk meetings and in September 1922 she presented a paper concerning her design for Meyerkhold's production of Fernand Crommelynck's farce, *The Magnanimous Cuckold* of April 1922. She also participated in the debate concerning how art should be taught, producing a paper "Toward the question of the new methods in our art school", which was clearly based on her own pedagogical experience.

In September 1921 Popova collaborated with Alexander Rodchenko and Varvara Stepanova (q.v.), founder members of the Constructivist group, Vesnin and Alexandra Exter (q.v.) in the important exhibition 5 × 5 = 25 in Moscow. The five artists each contributed five works. Popova's exhibits were entitled *Experiments with Pictorial Force Structures*. This marks the first appearance of Popova's *Space-Force Constructions* or *Prostranstvenno-silovoye postroyeniye*, which she continued to produce until 1922. These were often drawn in paint directly on to unsized wood. The compositions were built up of intersecting and overlapping lines of varying thicknesses which created structural and spatial tensions (e.g. *Space-Force Construction*, 1921; Tretyakov Gallery). The title was also applied to works that incorporated arcing or circular lines and were more obviously dynamic in intention (e.g. *Space-Force Construction*, 1921; Costakis Collection). The statement that Popova produced in the 5 x 5 = 25 catalogue indicated that she had rejected easel painting as the ultimate aim of artistic activity and that henceforth she intended to direct her artistic skills towards more immediately

utilitarian objectives. She wrote that the paintings exhibited "are to be regarded only as series of preparatory experiments towards concrete material constructions." From this point onwards Popova became directly involved with more functional design work.

In 1921 Meyerkhold invited Popova to teach a course on the "Analysis of the elements of material design" at his Higher State Theatrical Workshops (or GVTM) in Moscow. Building on this experience, in 1922 she designed the sets and costumes for Meyerkhold's production of *The Magnanimous Cuckold*, transforming the watermill of the action into a multi-levelled, skeletal machine that consisted of staircases, shoots and rotating wheels. She dressed the actors in plain coloured overalls (production clothing or *prozodezhda*), which, she explained, were conceived as prototypes for industrial or working clothing in the real world. This treatment complemented Meyerkhold's acting style, which combined mechanised movements with the gestures of the *commedia dell'arte*. The production was widely regarded as the first application of Constructivist principles to theatrical design. In 1923 her set for Sergei Tretyakov's reworking of Marcel Martinet's play *The Earth in Turmoil* approached the industrial object from a rather more pragmatic standpoint. The set was based on a gantry crane and the costumes and properties were not new artistic prototypes devised by the artist, but were selected from already existing mass-produced objects. Popova also devised a large number of political slogans for the production.

In early 1924 Popova and Stepanova started to work as fabric designers at the First Textile Print Factory in Moscow, which had previously been known as the Emil Tsindel Factory. In accordance with the machine aesthetic that the Constructivists embraced and the mechanical nature of industrial manufacture, Popova and Stepanova considered that the replacement of traditional floral and plant patterns with geometrically based designs was an essential pre-requisite for the rationalisation of textile production and clothing design. By manipulating a small number of simple geometric forms and primary colours, they produced a vast array of exciting designs, some of which went into mass production. At this time Popova also worked on dress designs, sometimes using her own fabrics, so that the pattern emphasised the dress's functional and structural elements.

Popova contributed texts and reproductions to the avant-garde magazine *Lef* (Left Front of the Arts), which was founded by Vladimir Mayakovsky in 1923. She also produced a large number of graphic designs for various projects, including banners, wall labels, musical scores and journals (e.g. *The Cinema* (*Kino*), *c.*1922; Costakis Collection). In spring 1924 she started teaching courses on stage design at Proletkult; a few months later, Popova caught scarlet fever from her son and died on 25 May.

CHRISTINA LODDER

Preston, Margaret

Australian painter and printmaker,
1875–1963

Born Margaret Rose McPherson (later also used spelling MacPherson) in Port Adelaide, 29 April 1875. Attended classes in W. Lister Lister's Angel Place studio, Sydney, 1888. Studied at the National Gallery School, Melbourne, under Frederick McCubbin, 1893–4, and Bernard Hall, 1896–7 (honourable mention, painting and life school, and one year studentship); Adelaide School of Design under H. P. Gill, and Hans Heysen's life drawing class, 1898. Taught at studio in Adelaide, 1899–1912, except for a trip to Europe after mother's death, 1904–6 (attended classes at the Damenakademie des Münchener Künstlerinnenvereins, Munich, studied in Paris and visited Spain). Visited Europe again, 1912–19, staying in France and Britain; studied pottery at Camberwell School of Arts and Crafts, London, and taught crafts at Seale-Hayne Neurological Military Hospital, Devon. Married company director William G. Preston in Adelaide, 1919; moved to Mosman, Sydney, 1920. Subsequently travelled widely, both in Australia and abroad, visiting the Far East, New Zealand, Pacific Islands, North and South America, Middle East and Europe. Fellow, South Australian Society of Arts, 1911; Royal Art Society, 1923. Died in Mosman, 28 May 1963.

Principal Exhibitions

Individual
Preece's Gallery, Adelaide: 1919 (with Gladys Reynell)

Grosvenor Galleries, Sydney: 1925 (with Thea Proctor), 1929
Macquarie Galleries, Sydney: 1936, 1953
Art Gallery of New South Wales, Sydney: 1942 (retrospective, with William Dobell), 1959 (retrospective)

Group
South Australian Society of Arts, Adelaide: 1895–1914, 1936, 1951, 1956
Société Nationale des Beaux-Arts, Paris: 1905–6, 1913–14
Royal Art Society of New South Wales, Sydney: 1910–22, 1951
New English Art Club, London: 1913–18
Society of Women Artists, London: 1913–18
Society of Artists of New South Wales, Sydney: 1922–60
Royal Academy, London: 1923 (*Works by Australian Artists*)
Australian Art Association, Melbourne: 1923–33
Contemporary Group, Sydney: 1924–36
Roerich Museum, New York: 1930 (*First Contemporary All Australian Art Exhibition*)
Australian Pavilion, Exposition Internationale, Paris: 1937 (silver medal)
Art Gallery of New South Wales, Sydney: 1938 (*150 Years of Australian Art*), 1946 (*Exhibition of Australian Women Artists*)
Australian Academy of the Arts: 1938–43
Yale University Art Museum, New Haven: 1941–2 (*Art of Australia, 1788–1941*, touring)
Contemporary Art Society (Australia): 1942–55
Musée d'Art Moderne, Paris: 1946 (*UNESCO, Exposition internationale d'art moderne*)

Selected Writings

Letter to Norman Carter, 18 August 1913, Norman Carter Papers, Mitchell Library, Sydney, MS 471/1
"Why I became a convert to modern art", *Home* (Sydney), iv/2, June 1923, p.20
"Away with poker-worked kookaburras and gumleaves", *Sunday Pictorial* (Sydney), 6 April 1930, p.22
"New developments in Australian art", *Australia National Journal*, ii/6, 1941, pp.12–13
"The orientation of art in the post-war Pacific", *Society of Artists Book 1942*, Sydney: Ure Smith, 1942, pp.7–9

Bibliography

"The art of Margaret Preston", *Art in Australia*, 3rd series, no.22, December 1927 (special issue; includes Preston's autobiography, "From eggs to electrolux")
Sydney Ure Smith and Leon Gellert, *Margaret Preston's Recent Works*, Sydney: Art in Australia, 1929
Basil Burdett, "Australian art today", *The Studio*, cxv, 1938, pp.3–18
Exhibition of Australian Women Artists, exh. cat., Art Gallery of New South Wales, Sydney, 1946
Sydney Ure Smith, ed., *Margaret Preston's Monotypes*, Sydney: Ure Smith, 1949

Joyce Burn Glen, "Outback yields art: Preston painting famous", *Christian Science Monitor*, January 1954, p.6

Leon Gellert, "Margaret Preston was one of the greats", *Daily Telegraph* (Sydney), 8 January 1967, p.14

Humphrey McQueen, *The Black Swan of Trespass: The Emergence of Modernist Painting in Australia to 1944*, Sydney: Alternative Publishing, 1979

The Art of Margaret Preston, exh. cat., Art Gallery of South Australia, Adelaide, and elsewhere, 1980

Janine Burke, *Australian Women Artists, 1840–1940*, Collingwood, Victoria: Greenhouse, 1980

Margaret Preston: The Art of Constant Rearrangement, exh. cat., Art Gallery of New South Wales, Sydney, 1985

Roger Butler, *The Prints of Margaret Preston: A Catalogue Raisonné*, Canberra: Australian National Gallery/Melbourne: Oxford University Press, 1987 (includes extensive bibliography and reprints of articles by Margaret Preston)

Ian North, "Aboriginal orientation", *Creating Australia: 200 Years of Art*, exh. cat., Art Gallery of South Australia, Adelaide, 1988, pp.142–3

Jeanette Hoorn, "Women make Modernism", *Strange Women: Essays in Art and Gender*, ed. Jeanette Hoorn, Melbourne: Melbourne University Press, 1994, pp.9–27

Anne Stephens, "Margaret Preston", *Heritage: The National Women's Art Book*, ed. Joan Kerr, Sydney: Dictionary of Australian Artists/Craftsman House, 1995

As a modernist innovator in Sydney, Margaret Preston enjoyed a degree of influence often denied to female contemporaries in Europe. The magazine *Art in Australia* devoted a special issue to her in 1927, two monographs were published in her lifetime (1929 and 1949) and two retrospective exhibitions were held at the Art Gallery of New South Wales, Sydney (1942 and 1959). She was the first woman to be included in the Art Gallery's collection of self-portraits commissioned from distinguished Australian artists. Her *Self-Portrait* (1930; Art Gallery of New South Wales) shows a woman with a sober, astute gaze, sporting a fashionable hairstyle and a 1920s shift dress; beside her are Australian wildflowers, her favoured subject at this time.

Characteristically, she did not disguise the narcissistic aspects of her early artistic ambitions. In her autobiography "From eggs to electrolux" she describes how she watched students painting at the Art Gallery and wanted to become herself a focus of the visitors' gaze. Male contemporaries complained bitterly about her "vanity" and "jealousy". Some colleagues, the writer Ian Mudie and his circle, attempted to exploit her self-regard by enlisting her in various projects in order to tap into her popularity with critics and the public. An alternative reading is that Preston's confidence in her abilities disturbed male artists, who comforted themselves by invoking stereotypical female qualities of vanity and foolishness. Yet many of the conservative artists who objected to her assertiveness also owned works by her. Her acute consciousness of professionalism as a central issue, beyond gender, derived from her training with Bernard Hall at the National Gallery School in Melbourne. Other female students, including Alice Bale, shared this confidence without, however, responding to modernism.

Preston's studies in Melbourne were interrupted by her father's terminal illness. She returned to Adelaide and supported her mother for nearly two years, before re-enrolling in 1896. Perhaps this early experience of the uncertainty of Victorian middle-class life, when the breadwinner was incapacitated, impressed upon her the necessity of self-reliance. After completing art school, she tried to establish herself in Adelaide, where she was considered prickly and unconventional, and in 1911 was expelled from the Art Society of South Australia by eminent male artists. She did, however, receive important commissions, such as a portrait of the political reformer *Catherine Helen Spence*, and was employed to buy art for the Art Gallery of South Australia. The early figurative works she exhibited in Adelaide, documented in photographs, appear to be deliberately ungainly and un-dainty. Most notable were a portrait filled with the vast hips and stomach of an old man and a study of a girl in a white dress, in which the physical clumsiness of the child was emphasised rather than the romantic clichés usually associated with such images. Preston taught to raise money for study overseas, and for two extended periods she lived abroad with female companions: Bessie Davidson in 1904–6 and Gladys Reynell in 1912–19. During her studies in Munich, on her first trip to Europe, she was disconcerted to encounter contemporary art. Decades later, her writings vividly express her confusion and shock at seeing the works of Theodor Heine at the Secession of 1904.

Rumours that Preston was a lesbian were particularly persistent, but they may reflect the standard Australian response to strong, competent, independent women. She presented herself as very happily married and extremely dependent in an interview (*Sunday Herald*, Sydney, 20 September 1953). Marriage gave her the financial security to take up a central position in Sydney art circles. It freed her from the pressures of the marketplace and enabled her to travel frequently, to South and North America, Africa, Asia and Europe, creating a glamorous media persona for herself.

During World War I Preston gained attention from British critics when she exhibited, as Margaret MacPherson, with the Society of Women Artists. Her works were described as "the chief feature of the exhibition ... delicate colour and well balanced design" (Frank Rutter, *Sunday Times*, 6 February 1916, p.4). Elements later identified with her printmaking appeared in wartime still lifes such as *Flowers* (1917; National Gallery of Australia, Canberra): the rigid design with each petal a cog or ratchet in an intersecting framework; the cloisonnist colour shining out from black line work. Even the gleaming silver and steel industrial surfaces of her Léger-inspired still-lifes of the late 1920s are prefigured in her English flower-pieces: note the handling of the coffee pot in the right of *Still Life No.2* (1915; repr. Sotheby's Melbourne, May 1991), especially the abstraction of the reflections through grey tones.

Preston's detailed letters praise artists she admired in this period (*c.*1910–20), including Matisse, Gauguin and Stanley Spencer, but their influence is not discernible in her slightly decorative Impressionism. Pale tonality, bravura handling of white-on-white in sunlight, was her preoccupation (*Still Life with Teapot and Daisies, c.*1915; Art Gallery of New South Wales). This interest continued until the late 1920s, when she turned briefly to streamlining and industrialisation. She soon returned to themes from nature, specifically Australian flowers, using a more restricted palette and a looser plein-air style in certain flower-pieces of the mid-1930s. Other works, such as *West Australian Gum Blossoms* (1928; Art Gallery of New South Wales) and *Eucalyptus* (1928; Art Gallery of West Australia) were as stark as her outstanding crockery still life *Implement Blue* (1927; Art Gallery of New South Wales). In the later 1930s the influence of aboriginal rock art and bark painting brought a new sense of linear formality to her work.

A small corpus of etchings was produced around 1916. Conventional, picturesque rural scenes, they are among Preston's rare lapses in originality during her prolific career. Etching was not a congenial medium, unlike the woodblock print with which she is so associated in Australia. She claimed to have made wood engravings as early as 1904 in Munich,

although no documentation has been found. Her woodcuts included landscapes, still lifes and figurative subjects, ranging from traditional floral styles, European and Australian, to Art Deco, Primitivism and Expressionism. Her skill with the woodcut is equally evident in decorative alphabets or large, flamboyant compositions such as *Wheelflowers* (1929) and *Bird of Paradise* (1925; both National Gallery of Australia and other collections). By the early 1940s muscle strain forced her to abandon woodcut and she turned to masonite cuts, monotyping and screen printing, including designs for commercial textiles, before settling on stencil prints for the last two decades of her life.

Preston's writings are a significant oeuvre; few Australian artists mapped the intellectual framework of their art with such lucid and far-ranging texts. Consistent themes are nationalism in art and the development of an indigenous Australian style. Her writings on travel, design and fashion, witty and provocative, intensified her artistic and social influence in Sydney before World War II. She lectured frequently, and in 1938 presented an art history course at the Art Gallery of New South Wales, sponsored by the Carnegie Corporation.

In the late 1930s Preston discussed Surrealism in her lectures. She later repudiated the engaging, somewhat camp Sydney Surrealism, the "charm school", in favour of left-wing Sydney modernist factions of the 1940s. Similarly, she moved in the 1940s from the right-wing nationalism of the "Jindyworobak" intellectuals to the writings of the left-wing Australian art historian Bernard Smith, attracted by his *Place, Taste and Tradition* (1945). However, she found in Surrealism keys to an appropriate response to wartime Australia: *Japanese Submarine Exhibition* (1942; Art Gallery of New South Wales), *Tank Traps* (1943; Mornington Peninsula Arts Centre) and the *Children's Corner at the Zoo* (*c.*1944; Art Gallery of New South Wales; all oil on canvas). The last, almost whimsical and childlike, is undercut by a consciousness of the grotesque treatment of performing animals. *Tank Traps*, inspired by the stark geometrical outlines of concrete defence works on a beach, is perhaps her closest approach to pure abstraction.

Chinese art inspired Preston's outstanding landscapes of the early 1940s, linking the viewpoint from an aeroplane with the use of a rising perspective from Chinese landscape painting. The Chinese use of schemas and representative formulae in traditional landscape painting seemed to fascinate her, as did the importance of perception rather than direct representation. Her "Chinese" landscapes still display the earths and ochres of her "Australian" palette and the "Aboriginal" rhythmic patterning within clearly articulated areas of the compositions. These landscapes were structured, while her still lifes became ragged, casual in their design, until the 1950s, when both stencil prints and oils depict diverse objects scattered across table tops: *Sea Shells and Bowl of Flowers* (1955; oil on canvas; Cruthers Collection, Perth), *Sea Flowers* (1953; stencil print; Christie's Melbourne, April 1994). The overall compositions, with their loose horizontal spread, recall her paintings from World War I; some of the objects may be identical. The randomness of these 1950s still lifes represents the purging of "period style" and a degree of "feminine" decoration from the early compositions.

Preston achieved some international exposure in the late 1930s and early 1940s. A landscape featured on the cover of *The Studio* (October 1942). In 1937 she won a silver medal at the Paris Exposition Internationale. In 1939 a series of wild-flower paintings was featured on Australia's "moderne" exhibition stand at the New York World's Fair, and the pictures remained in American public collections. A similar series was commissioned for the P&O liner *Orcades*. Arnold Haskell and Somerset Maugham were impressed by the work of the "unfamiliar" artist. She wrote on Aboriginal art for the exhibition *Art of Australia, 1788–1941*, which toured North America, and a major landscape from the exhibition was bought for the Yale University Art Gallery, New Haven. Her international status suffered subsequently, as outstanding works by her in overseas collections were de-accessioned and sent back to Australia.

Informed by early 20th-century Primitivism, Preston was largely responsible for introducing the influence of Aboriginal art to contemporary design, just as her floral woodcuts allied hard-edge 1920s modernism and Australian flora. Until the late 1920s, Australian Aboriginal art and craft tended to be regarded by whites as anthropological detritus. By the 1930s Aboriginal motifs proliferated in graphic arts, porcelain and fabric designs, in an Australian version of Art Deco, while Aboriginal residents were still denied the vote.

Preston's Aboriginal themes must be assessed in terms of this cultural morality. According to some writers, it is naive to regard white women as tactful colonisers in contrast to insensitive, rapacious male settlers. Roger Butler suggests, however, that Preston, through extensive field trips and consultation with anthropologists, approached a subtler understanding of Aboriginal social, ritual and spiritual values in art. Issues of colonisation and cultural assimilation are touched on in *Aboriginal Flowers* (1928; oil on canvas; Art Gallery of South Australia), which depicts not real flowers but anemones made from feathers by Aboriginal women. This craft, like shell work an adaptation by Aboriginal women of Victorian fancywork, offered a neat conceit for Preston, as the stylisation of the artificial flowers was akin to the ordered geometry she imposed on flowers in paintings and prints. She appreciated the creativity of Aboriginal women, and she raised their status by donating carvings by two Aboriginal women to the Art Gallery of New South Wales. Her late treatments of biblical themes, personified by Aboriginal Australians, can be seen as politically provocative in the context of the widespread racism of the 1950s.

Preston's essay "New developments in Australian art" (1941) idealises Australian Aboriginals as avant-garde-literate noble savages. A "fine simple art" was produced by the intuitive natural modernist "with his mind's eye … A camera-mind produced a camera picture, and this type of mentality has never belonged to the aboriginal". She discusses astutely the symbolic and totemic nature of representation in Aboriginal art. While decrying plagiarism, she advised white artists to emulate the aims and outlook of Aboriginal artists. Her innocent advocacy of Aboriginal art is alien to contemporary post-colonialism, but it has not diminished regard for her. A singular status was first posited for her by Humphrey MacQueen in *The Black Swan of Trespass* (1979). Three other major monographs on her art make her the best-documented Australian woman artist. Research, particularly by Roger Butler, has established a complex outline of her personality and achievements. Margaret Preston is undoubtedly the one Australian woman artist who is widely recognised by the general public.

JULIET PEERS

Properzia de' Rossi *see* Rossi

Q–R

Quick-to-See Smith, Jaune *see* Smith

Rae, Henrietta
British painter, 1859–1928

Born in Hammersmith, London, 30 December 1859; father a civil servant, mother a gifted amateur musician. Studied at Queen's Square (later Female) School of Art, London, 1871–3; studied independently in British Museum and attended evening classes at Heatherly's School of Art, 1874–7; attended Royal Academy Schools, 1877–84. Exhibited widely in London and the provinces, 1879–1922. Married the artist Ernest Normand, 1884; son born 1886, daughter born 1893; husband died 1923. Lived in Kensington, London; studio in Norwood from 1893. Studied in Paris at Académie Julian under Benjamin-Constant and Jules Lefèbvre, and in Grez-par-Nemours, 1890. Visited Italy, 1896. Supported the campaign for women's suffrage. First woman to serve as member of hanging committee, Liverpool Autumn Exhibition, 1893; president, Women's Art Section, *Victorian Exhibition*, 1897. Member, Society of Women Artists, 1905. Died 26 March 1928.

Principal Exhibitions
Society of British Artists, London: 1879–82
Royal Academy, London: 1880–1919
Grosvenor Gallery, London: 1885, 1888–9
Exposition Universelle, Paris: 1889 (honourable mention)
Institute of Painters in Oil, London: 1891–5
World's Columbian Exposition, Chicago: 1893 (medal)
Doré Gallery, London: 1895 (with Ernest Normand)
Earl's Court, London: 1897 (*Victorian Exhibition*)
Louisiana Purchase Exposition, St Louis: 1904

Bibliography
Frank Rinder, "Henrietta Rae – Mrs Ernest Normand", *Art Journal*, 1901, pp.303–7
Arthur Fish, *Henrietta Rae (Mrs Ernest Normand)*, London: Cassell, 1905
Great Victorian Pictures: Their Paths to Fame, exh. cat., Arts Council of Great Britain, London, 1978
Deborah Cherry, *Painting Women: Victorian Women Artists*, London and New York: Routledge, 1993
Pamela Gerrish Nunn, *Problem Pictures: Women and Men in Victorian Painting*, Aldershot: Scolar Press, 1995

Henrietta Rae (later Mrs Normand) was one of the foremost female artists of late Victorian and Edwardian Britain. She was the most prominent woman artist in the classical revival that dominated British art in the last two decades of the 19th century, and the most important female painter of the nude in the pre-modern period. Rae's oeuvre exemplifies the opportunity and the ambition characteristic of the second generation of Victorian women artists, who, after 1860, enjoyed access to the Royal Academy Schools and acceptance as a fact of British cultural life, albeit a still controversial one.

Rae was intended by her mother for a musical career, and thus was a late starter in painting. Her career was marked from the beginning by determination: she was the first female student to be accepted at Heatherly's, the foremost preparatory school for the Royal Academy Schools, and she was accepted into the Schools on her sixth attempt. From her earliest exhibited works, shown while she was still attending the Schools, she painted on a large scale, taking the full-length female figure as her primary motif and the highest genres as her arena: literature, mythology, history. Her subjects ranged from Tennyson, Shakespeare (*Ophelia*, 1890; Walker Art Gallery, Liverpool) and Keats through Greek mythology (*Eurydice Sinking back to*

Hades, 1887; untraced, repr. Fish 1905) to imaginative, pseudo-literary or pseudo-classical figures (*Spring Blossoms*, 1893; David Messum Gallery, London). She was greatly influenced in her participation in the classical revival by the most successful of her male contemporaries and President of the Royal Academy, Frederic Leighton, and her work was often said to be a weak imitation of his. Although her principal works often used the female nude, as did Leighton's, her typical work compares more nearly with less distinguished men of her time, such as Arthur Hacker.

A study trip to France with her husband in 1890, spent at the Académie Julian and other Paris studios and in the rural colony of Grez-par-Nemours, resulted in a new painterliness that moderated the previous academicism of Rae's work, attracting criticism from conservatives for slovenliness. While she continued to mine evergreen literary sources for heroines such as *Ophelia*, *Mariana* (1892; untraced) and *Isabella* (1896; untraced, *ibid.*), the themes and motifs that Rae took from classicism's repertoire were given poetical and rhetorical rather than dramatic treatment, and her occasional attempts to incorporate action, as in *Apollo and Daphne* (1895; untraced, repr. *Royal Academy Pictures*), were not critically successful. Her depiction of men was also particularly rebuffed. Her most ambitious mythological composition, the huge *Psyche Before the Throne of Venus* (1894; untraced, repr. London 1978), represented a passage in William Morris's version of the nymph's story that necessitated more than a dozen full-length figures. Although dismissed by critics as pretty and therefore effete, it entered one of the most important collections of contemporary art (McCulloch). Despite critical carping, Rae consistently sold her paintings – *Ophelia* was purchased by the Liverpool Corporation in 1890. Although many works have now disappeared from view, inhibiting an appraisal of her technical excellence, many are known in engraved or photographic form through Fish's biography published with the artist's co-operation in 1905.

As the first female artist to represent the naked body regularly, Rae – known generally by her maiden name throughout her career – was often cited in the controversy about the nude in art that raged in Britain from 1885 to the end of the 19th century. Much of her use of the female nude looks naive to a 20th-century feminist eye in its acceptance of the erotic strategies of the work of her male

contemporaries. Some of her images have a conspicuously lubricious character (*Loot*, 1903–4; untraced, repr. Fish 1905) and in this respect are indistinguishable from the more offensive nudes of her mentors.

Rae's only piece of public art, the fresco in the Richard Whittington cycle at the Royal Exchange, London, which she completed in 1900, was untypical of her oeuvre and, after the turn of the century, portraits of aristocrats and public servants leavened her output of subject pictures. She continued to exhibit at the Royal Academy and in provincial cities until 1922.

PAMELA GERRISH NUNN

Rainer, Yvonne

American choreographer and film-maker, 1934–

Born in San Francisco, California, 1934. Moved to New York, 1956; trained as a modern dancer from 1957; studied under Martha Graham and Merce Cunningham, 1960–67. Began to choreograph her own work, 1960. Founder-member, Judson Dance Theater, New York, 1962. Presented choreography throughout the USA and Europe, 1962–75, notably on Broadway, 1969, in Scandinavia, London, Germany and Italy, 1964–72, and at the Festival d'Automne, Paris, 1972. Began to integrate short films into her performances, 1968; made complete transition to film-making by 1975. Recipient of Guggenheim fellowships, 1969 and 1988; National Endowment for the Arts (NEA) grants, 1972, 1974, 1983, 1985, 1988, 1990 and 1995; Creative Artist Public Service (CAPS) grants, 1973 and 1975; Deutscher Akademischer Austauschdienst (DAAD) grant, 1976; Rockefeller Foundation grant, 1988 and 1990; Special Achievement award, Los Angeles Film Critics Association, for *Journeys from Berlin/1971* (1980, co-produced with the British Film Institute); James D. Phelan award in Filmmaking, 1990; Geyer Werke prize at the International Documentary Film Festival, Munich, for *Privilege* (1990), 1991; honorary doctorates from Massachusetts College of Art, Boston, 1988; Rhode Island School of Design, Providence, 1988; School of the Art Institute of Chicago, 1993; California Institute of the Arts, Valencia, 1993.

Member, American Film Institute, 1995. Lives in New York.

Selected Writings

"Don't give the game away", *Arts*, xli, April 1967, pp.44–5

Yvonne Rainer: Work, 1961–1973, Halifax: Press of Nova Scotia College of Art and Design, and New York: New York University Press, 1974

"More kicking and screaming from the narrative front/backwater", *Wide-Angle*, vii/1–2, 1985, pp.8–12

The Films of Yvonne Rainer, Bloomington: Indiana University Press, 1989

"Narrative in the (dis)service of identity: Fragments toward a performed lecture dealing with menopause, race, gender and other uneasy bedfellows in the cinematic sheets: Or, how do you begin to think of yourself as a lesbian-and-white when you had just about gotten used to the idea of being an 'A-woman'", *Review of Japanese Culture and Society*, iv, December 1991, pp.46–52

Bibliography

Willoughby Sharp and Liza Bear, "The performer as a persona: An interview with Yvonne Rainer", *Avalanche*, no.5, Summer 1972, pp.46–59

Stephen Koch, "Performance: A conversation", *Artforum*, xi, December 1972, pp.53–8

Annette Michelson, "Yvonne Rainer", *Artforum*, xii, January 1974, pp.57–63; February 1974, pp.30–35

Lucy R. Lippard, "Yvonne Rainer on feminism and her film", *Feminist Art Journal*, iv, Summer 1975, pp.5–11; reprinted in Lucy R. Lippard, *From the Center*, New York: Dutton, 1976

——, "Talking pictures, silent words: Yvonne Rainer's recent movies", *Art in America*, lxv, May–June 1977, pp.86–90

Sally Banes, *Terpsichore in Sneakers: Post-Modern Dance*, Boston: Houghton Mifflin, 1980

Profile, iv/5, Fall 1984 (entire issue)

Robert Storr, "The theoretical come-on", *Art in America*, lxxiv, April 1986, pp.158–65

Ginette Vincendeau, "The man who envied women: Interview with Yvonne Rainer", *Screen*, xxviii, Autumn 1987, pp.54–6

Marianne Goldberg, "The body, discourse and *The Man Who Envied Women*", *Women and Performance*, iii/2, 1987–8, pp.97–102

Peggy Phelan, "Feminist theory, poststructuralism and performance", *Drama Review*, xxxii, Spring 1988, pp.107–27

Berenice Raynaud, "L'ancien et le nouveau (le romantisme de toujours chez les indépendants)", *Cahiers du Cinema*, no.437, November 1990, pp.4–6

Connie Richards, "Films of Yvonne Rainer: Approaches to feminine filmmaking", *Feminisms*, iv, March 1991, pp.17–19

Michele Wallace, "Multiculturalism and oppositionality", *Afterimage*, xix, October 1991, pp.6–9

Scott MacDonald, "Demystifying the female body", *Film Quarterly*, xlv, Fall 1991, pp.18–32

Shelley Green, *Radical Juxtaposition: The Films of Yvonne Rainer*, Metuchen, NJ: Scarecrow, 1994

"Questions of feminism: 25 responses", *October*, no.71, Winter 1995, p.37

Yvonne Rainer's career as a dancer and choreographer began in the early 1960s in New York, where she contributed to the development of a radical modern dance at once analytic, objective and aleatory. She studied with Merce Cunningham from 1960 to 1967, and worked with Robert Dunn, Trisha Brown, Simone Forti and others at what became the Judson Dance Theater between 1961 and 1963. Her *Terrain* (Judson Memorial Church, 28–9 April 1963) was a controlled improvisation in five sections for six performers, lasting one and a half hours. In the first section, "Diagonal", the dancers moved through the performance space using prescribed movements executed according to a complex set of rules; the order in which the activities would occur was contingent upon choices made by the performers during the piece. Some sections were set to music, such as "Duet", performed by Trisha Brown and Rainer, while others were played out against recited texts, as in "Solo Section". *Terrain* emphasised the process of the dance performance and signalled Rainer's concern to question the relationship between performer, performance and audience.

Like Brown and Forti, Rainer critically examined the traditional language of modern dance by using vernacular movement as the basis of her choreography. Rainer's *Trio A*, originally the first part of a larger composition, *The Mind Is a Muscle* (Judson Church, 10 January 1966), consisted of a series of movements, equally weighted and performed without affect by three people simultaneously. The gestures are matter-of-fact, rather than illusionistic or miming, and because none is highlighted by an excess of energy, there is no sense of narrative. The viewer's desire to look at and identify with the dancers is frustrated by the performers, who avert their gazes from the audience. Rainer contributed *Trio A* to the Judson Flag Show, an exhibition organised by the Guerrilla Art Action Group at the Judson Church in November 1970, to protest against the arrests of people accused of desecrating the American flag, under the Flag Desecration Law of 1967. The performers tied flags around their necks and disrobed to dance in the nude, making of the highly abstract and self-reflexive piece a statement against repression and censorship.

The three issues central to *Trio A*, illusion, narrative and the relationship of performer and audience, are articulated in the films Rainer made beginning in 1972. Because dance exists in real time and space, demonstrating its literalness by emphasising duration, gesture is ultimately limited. Film permits space and time to be manipulated and offers more room to explore the complexities of the issues that Rainer finds compelling.

Lives of Performers (1972; all films distributed by Zeitgeist Films, New York) opens with a sequence of dancers in rehearsal, executing movements according to the directions of the off-screen choreographer; the film's roots are in another dance, *Grand Union Dreams* (Emmanuel Midtown YM-YWHA, New York, 16 May 1971). Rainer seems at pains not to seduce the viewer: the close framing of the performers and the choreographer's equivocation make it difficult to decipher the meaning of the scene. The gender differences of the dancers are down-played, which will undercut the emotional content of the apparent narrative. That story about the off-stage romances of the performers is further subverted by the use of voice-overs of the performers and Rainer commenting on the action on screen, often in self-conscious or uninflected voices. The film ends as abruptly and arbitrarily as it began, with a series of tableaux that mimic film stills from G. W. Pabst's *Pandora's Box* (1928). The reference to this film, which starred Louise Brooks as a *femme fatale* who meets her end at the hands of Jack the Ripper, makes clear that Rainer is critically examining the representation of women in film by denying the viewer the visual pleasure he or she expects from narrative cinema.

Rainer's *This Is the Story of a Woman Who ...* (1974) deconstructs narrative strategies by multiplying them. The narrative is acted out, or adumbrated through inter-titles. Two male-female pairs of actors play the main roles, making it difficult to decide whether one or two stories are being told. In a central sequence, Rainer appropriates stills from Alfred Hitchcock's *Psycho* (1960), the shower scene in which the character played by Janet Leigh is murdered. B. Ruby Rich points out that Hitchcock's film transgressed the rules of the suspense genre in killing off a leading character before the end of the

film, and that by making reference to it Rainer legitimises her subversion of narrative (*The Films of Yvonne Rainer* 1989, p.8). That narrative conventions and the denial of subjectivity to women in film go hand in hand is reiterated in a long, discomforting scene in which the camera slowly zooms in on the pubic region of one of the female leads as a man slowly pulls down her undergarments, then tracks back as the garments are replaced. Throughout, the man holds the camera/viewer's gaze unwaveringly, implicating the audience in the objectification of the woman's body.

Rainer made two more films in the 1970s: *Kristina Talking Pictures* (1976) and *Journeys from Berlin/1971* (1980). She said of her first four films that she focused on the production and frustration of narrative at the expense of plot and character development, but that as she became more interested in political and theoretical texts as material, it seemed necessary to couch those interests in a clearer narrative structure. For her political message to come across, she translates it into personal terms by permitting the viewer to identify somehow with the film.

In *The Man Who Envied Women* (1985) Michel Foucault's theory of power and feminist film theories are critically examined. The central character, Jack, is played by two actors. His ex-lover, Trisha, never appears on screen but is present on the soundtrack commenting on the action, invisible to the gaze that is central to so many feminist analyses of film. The central scene occurs between Jack and Jackie (a *femme fatale* figure) in a hallway during a party. Their movements articulate a seduction, but their words are at cross-purposes: his speech quotes Foucault, hers a feminist text by the Australian Meaghan Morris. At the same time, however, Marianne Goldberg argues that the viewer's gaze is finally satisfied with Jackie's appearance, which figures the attraction and repulsion of sexual difference embodied in the woman.

Feminist theory, articulated in the mainstream by white, middle-class women, is questioned in Rainer's film *Privilege* (1990), by her incorporation of issues touching on race, class, age and sexuality. Rainer's *alter ego* is a black woman, Yvonne Washington, who interviews Jenny about her experience with menopause for a documentary. In the course of the interview, Jenny relates her memories of living in a lower-class, racially-mixed neighbourhood, including an incident in which one of her neighbours is raped. Jenny's intervention in the subsequent events, in which she identifies the attacker as black and exaggerates what she knows in order to incriminate him, is exposed through Yvonne's interrogation as determined by her race and class. This is a feminist film in the best sense, at once politically engaged and self-critical.

MARGO HOBBS THOMPSON

Read, Katharine
British painter, 1723–1778

Born in Dundee, Scotland, 1723, to Alexander Read and his wife Elizabeth, daughter of Sir John Wedderburn Bt. Studied pastel painting under Maurice Quentin de la Tour in Paris after 1745; stayed in Rome, 1751–3. Set up studio in London, 1753. Elected honorary member, Incorporated Society, 1769. Sailed for Madras, India, with her niece Helena Beatson, 1777. Made a will, 29 June 1778; left for England and died on board ship, 13 or 15 December 1778.

Principal Exhibitions

Society of Artists of Great Britain, London: 1760, 1766–72
Free Society of Artists, London: 1761–5, 1768–9, 1779
Royal Academy, London: 1773–4, 1776

Bibliography

Edward Edwards, *Anecdotes of Painters*, London: Leigh and Sotheby, 1808
Elizabeth Fries Ellet, *Women Artists in All Ages and Countries*, New York: Harper, 1859; 2nd edition, London: Bentley, 1860
Ellen C. Clayton, *English Female Artists*, 2 vols, London: Tinsley, 1876
A.R. Ellis, ed., *The Early Diary of Frances Burney, 1768–78*, 2 vols, London: Bell, 1889
A.F. Steaurt, "Miss Katherine [sic] Read: Court paintress", *Scottish Historical Review*, ii, 1904, pp.38–46
R.M. Sée, *English Pastels, 1750–1830*, London: Bell, 1911
Sir William Foster, "British artists in India, 1760–1820", *Walpole Society*, xix, 1930–31, pp.1–88
Lady Victoria Manners, "Catherine [sic] Read: The 'English Rosalba'", *Connoisseur*, lxxxviii, 1931, pp.376–86; lxxxix, 1932, pp.35–40, 171–8
Mildred Archer, *India and British Portraiture, 1770–1825*, London and New York: Sotheby Parke Bernet, 1979

Katharine Read was the fifth of 13 children of a merchant from Dundee, Alexander Read, who had joined the land-owning classes on his marriage to Elizabeth Wedderburn. The family were both financially secure and had strong Jacobite connections, two contributing factors that made it possible for Katharine to become an artist. The transition from middle-class "young lady" to trainee professional artist is not documented. However, as drawing lessons formed an important part of the training for "young ladies", it seems likely that Read must have demonstrated strong abilities, and her subsequent contact with the engraver Robert Strange suggests that she may have shared with him the same art teacher in Edinburgh. Thus, in 1745 (the year of the failed Jacobite Rebellion), Katharine Read was still unmarried – and at the age of 22 was no doubt considered a confirmed spinster by society's standards – but she showed considerable artistic talent. It was therefore expedient to send her to Paris to train under the artist Maurice Quentin de la Tour.

The pastel medium came into fashion in Paris with the arrival of Rosalba Carriera (q.v.) in 1720. Her success encouraged La Tour to take up the technique, and by the time of Read's apprenticeship he had become the leading pastel painter of the day and portraitist to the royal family of France. Read's selection of the pastel medium was probably a case of social necessity and financial astuteness. Pastel painting, or crayon painting as it was known in Britain, was considered a "feminine" medium, due to the often cited "delicacy" of touch required when applying the pigment, and the general smallness of scale of works due partly to the medium's inherent fragility. In terms of financial astuteness, while London abounded in portrait painters in oil, pastel – or crayon – painters were much rarer, thus suggesting a market waiting to be exploited. As Read said in a letter from Italy to her brother, Alexander, in 1751: "I hear my old master La Tour is in London where I don't doubt of his getting money by his great merit and great price … however I could have wished he had staid at home."

From 1751 to 1753 Katharine Read stayed in Rome, hopeful that her training in France would enable her to consolidate her position as a professional artist back in Britain. In 1752 she wrote to her brother Alexander: "… as I have staid one year in Rome for Improvement, I must certainly stay in it another for Name, and then you'll see I'll top it with the best of them." She used her time in Rome to establish a clientele not only from the Italian aristocracy, but also from the British nobility visiting Rome on the Grand Tour. On her return to Britain in 1753, Read set up her studio in London. For the next 20 years she was one of the most fashionable crayon painters in the city, painting not only members of the royal family (such as *Queen Charlotte*, in 1761 and 1763), but also members of the aristocracy and Scottish nobility as well as famous people of the day, such as the actor *David Garrick* and his wife *Eva*. Eva is portrayed vividly in one portrait (Victoria and Albert Museum, London), dressed in a Gypsy-style costume, staring confidently out of the picture, her face turned in a typical three-quarter view towards the viewer.

Her success as a crayon painter did not confine Read to this medium. She also painted in oil, as can be seen in her portrait of the *Countess of Sussex* (Ranger's House, London). This three-quarter-length portrait shows the sitter posing in an ermine cloak, against a background of classical pillar and velvet curtain. The casualness of the pose and the inclusion of a pillar – a decorative element usually ascribed to grand-manner portraits of men – gives the work a slightly stronger edge than the figure-hugging clothes and languorously draped arms suggest.

Read's sitters were essentially women and children. The translucent, smudged effect of the crayon medium was considered to suit the subject matter, and the small scale of crayon paintings gave a suggestion of intimacy and informality. Crayon was a modest medium, not for grand-scale portraits and thus deemed well suited to women, as can be seen in Read's portrait of *Lady Shelbourne and Her Son, Lord Fitzmaurice* (Bowood House, Wiltshire). Although Read is often referred to as the "English Rosalba", the comparison is misleading and limiting. She did copy works after Rosalba Carriera, but she cited La Tour as her "model among all portrait painters" and described the Italian artist Guido Reni as "my favourite master". Carriera was a figurehead for all crayon painters of the period, not just Katharine Read.

Read's studio appears to have functioned in a similar way to those of other fashionable artists of the time, who often held "open house" to clients and potential clients from the respectable to the not-so-respectable, providing a spectacle not unlike a visit to the theatre. Fanny Burney (*Early Diary of Frances Burney, 1768–78*) cites a visit to Read's studio directly after a visit to Sir Joshua Reynolds's. Studio visits were a social activity; it was, for example, through illicit meetings at Read's studio that Lady Susan Fox-Strangways was able to cultivate her romance with the actor William O'Brien.

Read's trip to India in 1777 at the age of 54 was a search for a new, and less competitive market, as well as the opportunity to find a suitable match for her niece, Helena Beatson. It appears that her popularity was waning at this time, although Burney described her in 1774 as "Miss Reid [sic], the celebrated paintress". She continued in a less flattering vein, however: "... she is so very deaf, that it is a fatigue to attempt [conversing] with her. She is most exceedingly ugly, and of a very melancholy, or rather discontented humour ..." (*ibid.*). This flippancy does not do justice to the overwhelming achievement of a woman who spent at least 20 years as a professional artist and whose artistic output amounts to more than 200 attributed works, nearly all of which are in private collections.

DORCAS TAYLOR

Redpath, Anne
British painter, 1895–1965

Born in Hawick, Galashiels, 29 March 1895; father the tweed designer Thomas Redpath. Studied at Edinburgh College of Art, 1913–19 (diploma and postgraduate year); trained as an art teacher at Moray House College of Education, Edinburgh, 1913–17. Visited Brussels, Bruges, Paris, Siena and Florence on a travelling scholarship, 1919. Lived in France after marriage to James Beattie Michie, an architect with the War Graves Commission, 1920; three sons; husband died 1958. Returned home to Hawick, 1934. Settled in Edinburgh, 1949; often travelled abroad. Recipient of honorary doctorate, University of Edinburgh, 1955. Professional member, Society of Scottish Artists, 1934; member, 1939, and president, 1944–7, Scottish Society of Women Artists; member, Royal Society of British Artists, 1946–53; Royal Institute of Oil Painters, 1948; associate member, Royal Society of Painters in Watercolour, 1962. Associate member, 1947, and member, 1952, Royal Scottish Academy; member, Royal West of England Academy, Bristol, 1957; Associate, Royal

Academy, 1960. Officer, Order of the British Empire (OBE), 1955. Died in Edinburgh, 7 January 1965.

Selected Individual Exhibitions

Saint-Omer, France: 1921
Casino, Saint-Raphaël: 1928
Gordon Small Gallery, Edinburgh: 1947
Scottish Gallery, Edinburgh: 1950, 1953, 1957, 1960, 1963
Lefevre Gallery, London: 1952, 1959, 1962, 1964
Royal West of England Academy, Bristol: 1956
Danish Institute, Edinburgh: 1958
Stone Gallery, Newcastle upon Tyne: 1961
Festival Exhibition, Edinburgh: 1963 (*Four Scottish Painters*, with William MacTaggart, Robin Philipson and Joan Eardley, organised by Arts Council of Great Britain, Scottish Committee)
Arts Council of Great Britain, Scottish Committee, Edinburgh: 1965 (touring retrospective)

Bibliography

R. H. Westwater, "Anne Redpath", *Scottish Art Review*, v/3, 1955, pp.11–14, 33
T. Elder Dickson, "Anne Redpath", *The Studio*, clix, 1960, pp.86–9
Felix McCullough, "Anne Redpath", *Scottish Art Review*, ix/2, 1963, pp.15–18
Anne Redpath: Memorial Exhibition, exh. cat., Scottish Committee of the Arts Council of Great Britain, 1965
George Bruce, *Anne Redpath*, Edinburgh: Edinburgh University Press, 1974
Anne Redpath, 1895–1965: All the Works in the Collection, exh. cat., Scottish National Gallery of Modern Art, Edinburgh, 1975
Anne Redpath, 1895–1965: Her Life and Work, exh. cat., Bourne Fine Art, Edinburgh, 1989 (contains bibliography)
Scottish Art since 1900, exh. cat., Scottish National Gallery of Modern Art, Edinburgh, and elsewhere, 1989

Anne Redpath was the eldest of a triumvirate of Scottish women artists who were at the forefront of post-war Scottish painting, the others being Joan Eardley and Elizabeth Blackadder. She was born in the Scottish Borders, which, while they have a rich literary tradition, have not produced many well-known painters. Her father was a textile designer in Hawick, and Redpath in later life said: "I do with a spot of red or yellow in a harmony of grey what my father did in his tweeds". She flourished at the Edinburgh College of Art, where she enrolled in 1913 despite parental opposition. Her reputation as the most promising student of her year was confirmed when she won a major travelling scholarship in her final year (1919). She set off for the Continent and was much influenced by the 14th-century frescoes of the Lorenzetti brothers in the Palazzo Pubblico, Siena, where sophisticated and exquisite technique is allied to a simple, powerful vision. Thirty years later she was to acknowledge early Italian painting as the greatest single influence on her work. Her ability mentally to file away visual experiences for indefinite periods was one of the strengths of her artistic sensibility.

She married the architect James Michie and his work took them in 1920 to northern France. This area had been the painting ground where S. J. Peploe and J. D. Fergusson, the Scottish Colourists, found so much inspiration. In the 15 years that she lived there, however, Redpath became thoroughly immersed in the responsibilities of bringing up her three children and found no time and perhaps little inclination for painting. It was not until her family's return to Scotland in 1934, her marriage effectively over, that she returned to full-time painting. In 1961, referring to her time in France, Redpath said:

> Whatever I did for my home was creative but I never ceased to be a painter – I have a painter's mind. Were the choice to be made again, there would not be any division in my mind: my family would come first. However, I always had a rather guilty conscience. I always knew I would come back to painting.

It was not until 1942 that the painter found the confidence that her brilliant student days had promised. It was at this time that she painted what is probably her masterpiece, *Indian Rug (Red Slippers)* (1942; Scottish National Gallery of Modern Art, Edinburgh). While indebted to Matisse for the Fauvist red of the chair and the slippers and the flat patterns of the rug, the painterly enjoyment of pigment and impasto and the use of whites and greys as a contrast to the strong colours are characteristic of Redpath's work.

In 1944 Redpath was elected president of the Scottish Society of Women Artists. Founded in Edinburgh in the 1920s, the Society gave women painters the showcase they felt they were being denied by the Royal Scottish Academy. During Redpath's presidency, younger painters were encouraged and members' paintings were no longer accepted automatically but were judged against the standards set by a nucleus of artists. In later years Redpath changed her opinion about the practice of women exhibiting collectively. She told Sydney Goodsir Smith that it was as silly "as would be a special exhibition by men over six feet tall taking size fourteen shoes". She held strong, reasoned opinions on other painters and could express her views in an articulate and unpretentious manner. Her admiration for such contemporaries as Joan Eardley, Robin Philipson and Willie Gillies was not uncritical. She was uneasy with Eardley's use of materials such as sand, newspaper and grasses; this offended her own belief in truth to materials and she doubted its long-term value. The approach of Redpath, the intellectual, contemplative artist, who created a work of art to be treasured, is in marked contrast to that of Eardley, the highly charged expressionist artist, who employed whatever materials were to hand, and painted for the here and now.

During the 1950s Redpath took several trips abroad. New and exotic surroundings became the source of her inspiration and a catalyst for the development of both technique and subject matter. Although Redpath returned from her continental expeditions brimming with ideas for landscapes, street scenes and church interiors, as many as half the paintings that she exhibited throughout the 1950s were still lifes, featuring objects on a table, plants and flowers. Redpath arranged her still lifes on the floor, making the viewer more aware of the form of the objects – a vase or a teacup appear much rounder when viewed from above. Instead of ellipses, one sees circles. This is an exploration of form and not merely a mannerism. Redpath was able to paint a perfectly modelled object with no trace of highlights or exaggerated shadows.

On painting trips to Fife in the late 1950s she used to curse the bright sunny days, declaring that strong sunlight destroyed form and local colour. She preferred dull weather with no shadows, when colour becomes a property of form and not of light. She was developing an essentially intellectual approach to painting. A great deal more thought than actual activity was going into her oil paintings. The gouaches and colour notes would be executed quickly, on the spot, in order to capture the "essentials", but the painting of the oil itself is reminiscent of the description of Cézanne at work – several minutes between each brush stroke, occupied by the painter staring at his subject.

Further confirmation of this contemplative approach is found in the short film of Redpath produced by the BBC in 1963: "... sometimes I just simply see the picture without having anything actual in front of me. I see it as a completed picture and that means that half the picture is done for me. I see it in colour and shape." Redpath worried that she would become old-fashioned. She witnessed a "happening" in Edinburgh in the late 1950s, where an artist was doing some action painting that included all sorts of random ways of putting paint on canvas short of riding a bicycle over it. According to friends, the subsequent loosening of her technique was not unconnected with that experience. Her concern with keeping up to date with the latest techniques did not mean that she was prepared to compromise on sound and correct methods. She used "degreasing", which involved putting the paint on blotting-paper to drain out the poppy oil and give it a dry, chalky appearance. She hardly ever varnished her oil paintings, preferring to see them "in the raw". For this reason the exhibition oils were always under glass. Another of her methods for getting texture and rough surface was to scour the paint with what was described as a small piece of chain-mail. Individual, adventurous, colourful and independent, Redpath's art was an extension of her personality and the same descriptions apply to both. When she died, at the age of 69, her painting was as fresh and inventive as ever.

PATRICK BOURNE

Rego, Paula (Figueiroa)   [fig. 54]
Portuguese painter and printmaker, 1935–

Born in Lisbon, 26 January 1935. Extra-mural student at Slade School of Fine Art, London, 1952–6. Lived in Ericeira, Portugal, with painter Victor Willing, 1957–62; married him, 1959; three children (one son, two daughters) born 1956, 1959 and 1961; husband died 1988. Divided time between London and Portugal, 1962–75; settled in London, 1976. Selected by Roland Penrose for inclusion in *Six Artists* exhibition at Institute of Contemporary Arts, London, 1965. Represented Portugal, 1969 and 1976, and Britain, 1985, São Paulo Bienal. Visiting lecturer in painting, Slade School of Fine Art, 1983; Senior fellow, Royal College of Art, London, 1989; first National Gallery Associate Artist, 1990. Recipient of honorary degree, Winchester School of Art, 1992. Lives in London.

Selected Individual Exhibitions

Sociedade Nacional de Belas-Artes, Lisbon: 1965
Galeria III, Lisbon: 1978, 1989, 1990
AIR Gallery, London: 1981
Edward Totah Gallery, London: 1982–3 (*Girl and Dog*, touring), 1984, 1985, 1987
Art Palace, New York: 1985
Fundação Calouste Gulbenkian, Lisbon, and Serpentine Gallery, London: 1988 (retrospective)
Marlborough Graphics Gallery, London: 1989, 1992
Galeria III, ARCO, Madrid: 1989
British Council touring exhibition in Europe: 1990–91 (*Nursery Rhymes*)
South Bank Centre, London: 1990–92 (*Nursery Rhymes*, touring)
National Gallery, London: 1991–2 (*Tales from the National Gallery*, touring)
Marlborough Fine Art, London: 1992, 1994

Bibliography

Andrea Hill, "Paula Rego", *Artscribe*, no.37, October 1982, pp.33–7
Paula Rego: Paintings, 1984–5, exh. cat., Edward Totah Gallery, London, 1985
Paula Rego, exh. cat., Fundação Calouste Gulbenkian, Lisbon, and Serpentine Gallery, London, 1988
Sarah Kent, "Rego's girls", *Art in America*, lxxvii, 1989, pp.158–63, 205
Alberto de Lacerda, "Paula Rego e Londres", *Colóquio, Artes*, no.83, 1989, pp.18–23
Paula Rego: The Nursery Rhymes, exh. cat., South Bank Centre, London, and elsewhere, 1990
Sanda Miller, "Paula Rego's *Nursery Rhymes*", *Print Quarterly*, viii, 1991, pp.53–60
Hector Obalk, *Paula Rego*, Kyoto: Kyoto Shoin, 1991
Paula Rego: Tales from the National Gallery, exh. cat., National Gallery, London, and elsewhere, 1991
John McEwen, *Paula Rego*, New York: Rizzoli, 1992; London: Phaidon, 1993 (contains bibliography)
Paula Rego: Peter Pan and Other Stories, exh. cat., Marlborough Fine Art, London, 1992
Ruth Rosengarten, "Tales from the National Gallery: A reading of four recent works by Paula Rego", *London Magazine*, xxxii/9–10, 1992–3, pp.62–76
Paula Rego: Dog Woman, exh. cat., Marlborough Fine Art, London, 1994
Marina Warner, ed., *Nursery Rhymes*, London: Thames and Hudson, 1994
—, ed., *Wonder Tales*, London: Chatto and Windus, 1994

Paula Rego first received widespread critical attention at the time of her first important solo exhibition in London, held at the Serpentine Gallery in 1988.

Most comment was because her paintings were uncompromisingly figurative, not simply in a representational sense, but also in a narrative one. For decades, the idea that paintings could be used to tell stories had been seen as a kind of treason against the modernist cause, yet this exhibition included large-scale works with a traditional illusionistic picture space, which represented characters who were taking part in a story. This was at a time when painting was dominated by the so-called Neo-expressionists, such as Georg Baselitz and Jack Clemente, who were being seen as the successors to the "old guard", those figurative painters grouped around the senior figure of Francis Bacon. Compared to these artists, the spatial and narrative clarity of Rego's work was as unexpected as it was impressive, demonstrating that an artist was under no obligation to be constrained by fashionable dictates.

Rego was born into an affluent Portuguese family in Lisbon. Memories of her childhood, of being brought up as a girl in a male-dominated Roman Catholic society, and of being looked after by servants, were to be of crucial importance to her work. She attended an English school in Portugal, after which she was sent to a finishing school in Kent, England, from which she discharged herself at the age of 17. That same year, 1952, she became a student at the Slade School of Fine Art, where she met and fell in love with fellow student Victor Willing, who was married, and in 1956 their first child was born. After Willing obtained a divorce, they married in 1959. Her work at this time shows strong affinities with Picasso, Joan Miró and especially Jean Dubuffet, whose Art Brut she found particularly exciting. *Salazar Vomiting the Homeland* (Fundação Calouste Gulbenkian, Lisbon) of 1960 has similarities with Picasso's *Dream and Lie of Franco*, with scrawly and expressive biomorphic figures in a political allegory (Salazar was Portugal's right-wing dictator, who was to be overthrown in a bloodless revolution in 1975).

In 1961 Rego had her first professional success. The Gulbenkian Foundation in Lisbon selected three collages for their exhibition *Segunda exposição de artes plásticas*. Collage was an important technique for her at this time: the artist would cut up her own drawings and paintings and rearrange them to make new work. In 1962 she was awarded a two-year Gulbenkian scholarship, living with her husband in Portugal during the summer and in London for the rest of the year. In 1965 she had her first solo exhibition, at the Sociedade Nacional de Belas-Artes, Lisbon, where she was recognised as being one of Portugal's most important artists. *Stray Dogs (The Dogs of Barcelona)* (repr. McEwen 1992, pl.67) was a central work, inspired by a report that the authorities of Barcelona had decided to rid the city of its stray dogs by feeding them with poisoned meat. Executed in collage and oil on canvas, the picture writhes with action, with shapes and forms that evoke grotesquely distorted animals and giant flies. At 1.85 metres across, the work has the scale of a mural. The coarseness and rawness of its appearance owes more to graffiti than to any fine art tradition. Asked in an interview to explain her artistic line of descent, she replied that she could see none: "The reason is perhaps that I get inspiration from things that have nothing to do with painting: caricatures, items from newspapers, sights in the street, proverbs, nursery rhymes, children's games and songs, nightmares, desires, terrors."

In 1969, when she represented Portugal at the São Paolo Bienal, collage was still her favoured way of working. By the early 1970s she had begun to work in the more direct medium of gouache, producing a series of works entitled *Contos populares portuguêsas*, which were inspired by Portuguese folk-tales. The most notable development is that the figures and characters, rather than deriving from Dubuffet or Miró, are now immediately accessible to an audience unfamiliar with the artistic conventions of the 20th century. For example, *Two Men Separated by a River of Blood* (1975; *ibid.*, pl.85) shows two tall cliffs. On top of each sits a man, one of whom is blindfolded. Beneath them and between them a red river flows towards a distant horizon. The picture space perhaps owes something to Salvador Dalí, with Rego turning her back on the pictorial conventions of modernism that had dictated the appearance of her earlier work.

The break was not immediate, however, for several powerful collages were produced during the late 1970s and early 1980s, among them the *Annunciation* of 1981 (*ibid.*, pl.90), a traditional theme that has the archangel Gabriel pieced together as a nightmarish monster. The much smaller *Red Monkey* paintings, which were started in the same year, were of much greater significance. Made in acrylic on paper, they show a series of animals, including a lion, a bear, a rabbit and the red monkey himself, who enact a series of stories, with titles such as the *Red Monkey Beats His Wife* and *Wife Cuts Off Red Monkey's Tail* (*ibid.*, pls 96 and 97). The animals take on human characteristics, combining comic behaviour with alarming violence.

A series of much larger sized works followed, made in acrylic on paper laid down on canvas. These included the *Opera* series, where stories from the opera provided subjects of conflict, desire and human emotions, which were represented with caricatured animals and humans. Finally, there is the *Proles' Wall* (1984; Fundação Calouste Gulbenkian), over 12 m. long and covered with literally hundreds of characters, including dogs, bears, camels and flamingos, acting out comedies and tragedies, including rape, murder and decapitation. Rego's fascination with complex, even chaotic compositions continued with the *Vivian Girls* paintings of 1984 (*ibid.*, pls 126–8, 130). The idea came from her interest in the work of Henry Darger, a Chicago hospital orderly, whose "outsider" novel about a gang of unruly and subversive girls living on a planet ruled by soldiers had been recently discovered after his death.

Tragically, Rego's husband Vic had been diagnosed in 1967 as suffering from multiple sclerosis. During the mid-1980s he became progressively more disabled and Rego spent more and more time nursing him. This period in her life is represented by a series of extremely personal works, with the group title of *Girl and Dog* (*ibid.*). These are acrylic paintings on paper that show a young girl looking after a dog, feeding it, washing it, shaving it. Vic died in 1988, earlier in the year of the Serpentine exhibition, which finally established Rego's reputation as an artist of great originality, conviction and force. The *Red Monkey* and *Girl and Dog* series were shown, as well as several powerful and large-scale works, such as *Little Murderess* (1987; *ibid.*, pl.154), the *Cadet and His Sister* (1988; *ibid.*, pl.160) and *Soldier's Daughter* (1987; *ibid.*, pl.159). These showed a move away from the caricature style of the *Proles' Wall* and the *Vivian Girls* by featuring figures that had all been drawn from life in the studio. The drawings were then used to make the final paintings, where the figures engage with one another in complex and subtle dramas. The theme of powerful women is common to them all. The soldier's daughter plucks a dead goose, the cadet's sister ties his shoe-lace for him, a policeman's daughter cleans her father's boot with her arm thrust symbolically inside it. The figures are squat and stocky, suggestive of physical, sexual and psychological power.

Rego's continuing success was marked by the purchase of *The Dance* (1989) by the Tate Gallery, London. This painting, romantic, wistful and nostalgic, was started before her husband's death and completed afterwards. She was then invited by the National Gallery in London to become its first Associate Artist, with the brief of making work directly inspired by the old masters in the Gallery's collection. Given a studio on the premises, she at first found this a daunting prospect, not least of being a woman suddenly placed among an almost exclusively masculine tradition, but the works produced during this time confirmed her ever-growing status. *Joseph's Dream* (1990; private collection), for example, is a reworking of a 17th-century altarpiece, the *Vision of St Joseph* by Philippe de Champaigne, and can be interpreted as an allegory of a female artist in a man's world. A version of Champaigne's painting is on an easel, in an unfinished state, only now being painted by a female artist, who has firmly blocked in the archangel Gabriel and lightly indicated the Virgin Mary. Rego replaced the Joseph of the original picture by the heavy form of a sleeping man. The small image behind his head shows a rhino with its horn removed, symbolic of his powerlessness. The woman artist seems to receive her inspiration and power from the angel she has just painted and is completely in control, having claimed as her own the production of a man and repainted it for her own purposes.

Also resulting from Rego's time as the National Gallery Associate Artist is a three-part work, displayed as a mural, entitled *Crivelli's Garden*. This was painted for the Gallery's new Sainsbury Wing Restaurant, which opened in 1991. The three paintings hang together and appear to be one continuous work. A traditional Renaissance perspective scheme is used, into which are placed many of the characters who may be found in Italian Renaissance altarpieces, notably those by Carlo Crivelli. Rego playfully imagined them as existing in Crivelli's garden, where he could go and find the ones that he needed to paint in his pictures. Some of these figures are depicted as real, some exist as sculptures in the garden and others are represented on illusionistically painted tiles. These *azulejos* are a popular and ancient Portuguese folk art. Portugal has no "high art" tradition but is rich in folk art, the directness and immediacy of which has always been an important influence on Rego. The common theme that Rego depicts in *Crivelli's Garden* is that of the triumphant woman. St Catherine triumphs over the man who persecuted her, a heavy figure of Delilah crouches over the defeated Samson, a young Judith drops what the viewer imagines to be the severed head of Holofernes into a bag held by her maid. Images from Classical mythology also appear. Diana has transformed Actaeon into a stag, and Odysseus' men have been turned into pigs by the enchantress Circe. One whole panel is devoted to the Virgin Mary. A modern version of the Visitation is painted, as the young Virgin is whispered to by St Elizabeth. Behind them, on the blue *azulejos*, are shown many other traditional scenes from the life of the Virgin. But perhaps the point of these scenes is that Christ is nowhere represented. Mary, the virgin mother, is the crucial figure. After the clarity of the National Gallery work, Rego experienced the desire to regain some of the disjointed and chaotic qualities of her earlier work. Pictures such as *Caritas* are once again jammed with incident but now the figures originate in drawings made from models.

Rego is also highly active as a printmaker. Her *Nursery Rhymes* series reinterpreted traditional English children's themes such as *Baa Baa Black Sheep* and *Little Miss Muffet* into scenes of sinister and frightening implications, and after she finished her time at the National Gallery, she produced a series of etchings on the subject of *Peter Pan*. A change in medium resulted in a set of large drawings in coloured pastel, entitled *Dog Woman*, which were shown in 1994. This is a series of individual studies, made from life, with the model acting in various roles: for example, scavenging or preening. Many are deeply disturbing and can be understood as studies in mental illness that have a precedent in the work of Géricault; others are symbolic of the everyday lives of women, and although no men are seen, their presence and the effect they can have on women's lives are strongly implied.

COLIN WIGGINS

Remedios *see* Varo

Richier, Germaine

French sculptor, 1902–1959

Born in Grans, Bouches-du-Rhône, 16 September 1902. Entered the Ecole des Beaux-Arts, Montpellier, studying under Guigues, a former pupil of Rodin, 1920. Moved to Paris and became sole student of the sculptor Emile Bourdelle, 1926. Married (1) Swiss sculptor Otto Bänninger, 1926; divorced 1954; (2) poet René de Solier, 1954. Studio in Paris from 1930. Trips to Pompeii, 1935; Czechoslovakia, 1938. In Zürich at outbreak of World War II; decided to stay in Switzerland for the duration of the war, supporting herself by teaching. Divided time between France and Switzerland, 1946; then returned to Paris. Exhibited at New York World's Fair, 1939; Salon de Mai, Paris, 1947; Venice Biennale, 1950, 1952 and 1954. Recipient of Prix Blumenthal, 1936; medal of honour, Exposition Internationale, Paris, 1937; first prize for sculpture, São Paulo Bienal, 1951; Grand Prix, Exposition Universelle et Internationale, Brussels, 1958. Died in Montpellier, 31 July 1959.

Selected Individual Exhibitions

Galerie Max Kaganovitch, Paris: 1934
Kunstmuseum, Winterthur: 1942
Anglo-French Art Centre, London: 1947 (retrospective)
Galerie Maeght, Paris: 1948
Hanover Gallery, London: 1955
Musée National d'Art Moderne, Paris: 1956 (retrospective)
Martha Jackson Gallery, New York: 1957
Musée Picasso, Antibes: 1959 (retrospective)

Bibliography

Germaine Richier, exh. cat., Musée National d'Art Moderne, Paris, 1956
Aftermath: New Images of Man, 1945–1954, exh. cat., Barbican Art Gallery, London, 1982
Paris Post-War: Art and Existentialism, 1945–1955, exh. cat., Tate Gallery, London, 1993
Germaine Richier: Rétrospective, exh. cat., Fondation Maeght, Saint-Paul de Vence, 1996 (contains extensive bibliography)

Germaine Richier is perhaps the most powerful French sculptor in bronze of the 20th century. Astonishingly, after her retrospective of 1959 at the Musée Picasso, Antibes, her work was not revealed in full to an international public until the major retrospective of 1996 at the Fondation Maeght, Saint-Paul.

Richier insisted on a traditional training in a métier where her great precursor was Camille Claudel (q.v.); at first, at the Ecole de Beaux-Arts in Montpellier, she worked under Rodin's disciple and assistant Guigues; then in 1926 she went to Paris, and, through sheer perseverance and strength of character, insisted on becoming the only student of Rodin's successor, Emile Bourdelle – a man with links to Provence. During the pre-war period, already acknowleged as a successful professional artist, she made many talented portrait busts including that of *Françoise Cachin-Signac*, granddaughter of Paul Signac and later director of the Musées de France. None was so surprising, however, as a bust of *c*.1934 (repr. Saint-Paul 1996, no.1), in which all personal traits are masked with insect-like scales, anticipating not only her metamorphic mode of the 1940s but a fencer's mask (see *Woman Fencer*, 1943; *ibid.*, no.10).

The pure traditions of monumental sculpture with which she wished to be affiliated, in the line of Rodin and Bourdelle, was modified, in Richier's case, through her anti-Parisian, Provençal link with nature. This became particularly pronounced in her mature work, after World War II, in great contrast to her contemporary Alberto Giacometti, retrospectively the rival whose fame has unjustly eclipsed her reputation. His art, originating in Surrealism, was poised in the 1940s between existentialist tragedy and a sophisticated, urban absurd. His work of this period represented the body as attentuated almost to nothing – a thread of upright metal; or, to read his work more topically, a concentration camp survivor. In contrast, the most powerful – and fleshy – of Richier's male figures, *The Storm* (1948; Louisiana Museum of Modern Art, Humlebaek), used the very model, Nardone, now an old man, who had posed in his youth for Rodin's nude *Balzac* – the very paradigm of male potency and creativity. His female complement, *Hurricane Woman* (*L'Ouragane*) (1948–9; Louisiana Museum of Modern Art), actually subverted the gender of the masculine word "l'ouragan" in French, so that despite the show of strength and equality in Richier's work, its "femaleness" was often directly challenging. Just as Richier would work with Rodin's models, she also worked with his foundries, Rodier, Valsuani and Susse, and embraced both the hard physical labour and the Vulcanic imagery of worker with metal and fire. While the imagery of death in Giacometti's emaciated figures was perhaps starker than Richier's, her relationship to the male and female body and to issues of sexuality and death is equally fascinating. It is to Richier, rather than to Giacometti, that the tradition of post-war sculpture owes its characteristically "brutalised" surfaces, along with the configurations that would be baptised in Britain, after her London retrospective of 1947, as "the geometry of fear". Her scarified surfaces and the deathlike ugliness of some of her female creations countered notions of sculptural beauty with intimations of deformity and mutilation. Yet a unifying totality in tension with a totalising sense of desire in her work conformed perfectly to Sartre's later definition of the Beautiful.

Richier created explicit metaphors of nature's physical invasion of sculpture. In *The Forest* (1946; Fondation Marguerite et Aimé Maeght, Saint-Paul) a disturbing metamorphosis occurs: Richier cast twigs and branches as arms and limbs; leaves were pressed into the wet clay to leave their silhouettes prior to casting. Nature invaded the monument – and the monument would find its home in nature, leaving Giacometti's city square. *Praying Mantis* (1946) represents, upright and deathlike, the insect celebrated by the Surrealists as a token of female sexual power: she devours the male after copulation. Figures such as *The Ant* (1953) evoke both creativity and entrapment with their weblike imagery – ambivalently always, because the spinner, one of the three Fates, is a primeval image of female power. In the aftermath of the death camps and Hiroshima, the idea of a reversal of evolution, the degenerating of the human through mammal and bat to bird and insect forms, was a powerful metaphor in Richier's work, not only of nature, but of regression to a more bestial universe.

It was this element of regression and decay that caused fear and repulsion in Richier's *Crucifix* for the church of Assy in 1950. The Dominicans created a modern, ecumenical church for this sanatorium village in the Haute-Savoie, which involved courageous avant-garde commissions for church decoration from a spectrum of modern artists. On a poetic and etymological level, the fusion of body and bark in Richier's *Crucifix* evoked the metamorphosis of event to symbol. Yet Fernand Léger's magnificent mosaic portals were dubbed a blasphemy; Richier's *Crucifix* caused a riot. The so-called Angers tract was issued by the right-wing Integrists entitled

"God shall not thus be mocked". It juxtaposed Richier's work with a typical head of Christ captioned "The Face of Christ? No!" "A scandal for Christian piety". The work was finally removed by the Bishop of Annecy. The Vatican launched an explicit attack in 1951.

After the Assy scandal Richier continued to work and exhibit through the 1950s. In contrast with the spikiness of the insect women, certain works achieved a solemn and monumental dignity. They remained deeply rooted in Richier's homeland of Provence, using objects found on the land and the seashore: *Shepherd of the Lands* (1951; Louisiana Museum of Modern Art) has his face made from a brick pierced and rubbed smooth by the sea. Richier's collaborations, with Hans Hartung, Zao Wou-ki, and in particular with Maria Elena Vieira da Silva (q.v.), the most important woman painter in the School of Paris, gave her work a new dimension, in which the notion of sculptural patina and base extended to embrace a painted enamel background. *Spinning Top/La Toupie*, which she made with Vieira da Silva, means equally in French "old frump" – the "woman" issue was never far away, despite Richier's evident prowess in her arduous and masculine métier. An expensive métier, too, but Richier was fiercely independent, and throughout her career supported herself by teaching when necessary. "Equality of achievement" was the yardstick for the talented woman in the early 1940s: for Simone Weil as farmworker, member of the Resistance and religious mystic, for Simone de Beauvoir in her novels, travelogues and scholarship, notably *The Second Sex* (1949), as for Richier in sculpture. Richier's sexuality in conjunction with her work challenged and disturbed conventional notions. Francis Ponge, the critic of Fautrier and Dubuffet, wrote in the special number of *Derrière le Miroir* (no.13, 1948) that accompanied Richier's show at the Galerie Maeght: "I dare not pronounce the word 'virility' as regards her work, although that's the most appropriate term." "Le sculpteur", "L'artiste" (both masculine nouns) and Richier's "unfeminine" working ski outfit are balanced against "this universe, where woman is sovereign, which returns to origins", a clear case of confusion surrounding the classical dichotomy: male creativity versus female nature. André Pieyre de Mandiargues, the Provence-based, Surrealist-affiliated writer and follower of the Marquis de Sade, used sadism as a metaphor for Richier the sculptor, who kneads, twists, breaks, pokes and scratches prior to the "orgasm" of consummation between artist and sculpture as the work is deemed finished. He invoked Otto Weiniger's theories of the sadist who ornaments and then strips sculptures to humiliate them – but then hastened to make a compensatory statement: "I've never known a woman so good, so discreet, full of spiritual bounty, a force of nature" ("La main déchaînée", *Le Disque Vert*, no.3, 1953).

Richier's lack of the reputation she deserves beyond France (although complicated by litigation after her death) is not unconnected with the ambiguous reactions that her oeuvre provoked in critics. In contrast to Giacometti, whose works were not shown to a French public until 1951, Richier had become, by 1950, the focus of national controversy with her scarred, eroded *Crucifix* for the church of Assy. A comparison of the exhibiting history of the two artists between 1935 and 1955 would establish Richier's greater contemporary reputation without doubt. Her work never became a commodity, a matter for financial speculation. To what extent was the contrary true of Giacometti, precisely because of the myth-making process that would link him so inextricably with the existentialist writings of Sartre? The fact that, unlike Giacometti, Richier had an immediate posterity in the School of London sculptors, and in the work of César in France, bears a more eloquent witness to her fecundity than any uncomfortable contemporary praise.

The awkward, scratched surfaces of Richier's *Young Girl with a Diabolo*, the informal nudes, together with work by her contemporaries – Jean Fautrier's scarred and iridescent *Hostage* paintings and sculptures or Jean Dubuffet's females such as *Olympia*, literally gouged into the *matière* of his canvases – must read "against" the frou-frou of the New Look, the "Miss Tabou" beauty contests in Saint-Germain-des-Prés, the historical costume dramas in the theatres and the cinema, the taste for a "fantastic forties", all of which played their role in characterising the reborn *Femme française*. Richier's uncompromising toughness and her disturbingly hard, spiky, metamorphic imagery contrasts with the extreme delicacy of the much smaller-scale work she made at the end of her life – possibly when she knew that she had cancer and was unable to continue working on large pieces at the foundry – the tiny figures based on cuttlefish carving, often with a golden finish; the sacred works, such as the model for cathedral doors, which aligns her work

with such Catholic contemporaries as Lucio Fontana; the tremendous exuberance of the polychromed works, kept a secret for so many years, which, surprisingly, look forward to the colourful sculpture of Niki de Saint-Phalle (q.v.). The exhaustive history of Germaine Richier's life and work presented in the Fondation Maeght catalogue of 1996 at last reveals the true stature of this major woman artist.

SARAH WILSON

Rie, Lucie
British potter, 1902–1995

Born Lucie Gompertz in Vienna, 16 March 1902. Studied ceramics at the Kunstgewerbeschule, Vienna, under Michael Powolny, 1922–6. Married Hans Rie, 1926; divorced 1940. Emigrated to Britain, settling in London, 1938; later naturalised. Visited Bernard Leach at Shinner's Bridge Pottery, Dartington, Devon, 1939. Worked for the Bimini glass jewellery and button workshop during World War II. Operated own button-making business and pottery in London, 1945. Shared workshop in Albion Mews, London, with Hans Coper, 1947–58. Taught part-time at Camberwell School of Arts and Crafts, London, 1960–71; also visiting lecturer at Royal College of Art, London, and Bristol College of Art. Recipient of gold medals at Exposition Universelle, Brussels, 1935, Milan Triennale, 1936, and International Exhibition, Munich, 1954; honorary doctorates from Royal College of Art, London, 1969, and Heriot-Watt University, Edinburgh, 1992. Officer (OBE), 1968, Commander, 1981 (CBE), and Dame Commander (DBE), 1991, Order of the British Empire. Died in London, 1 April 1995.

Selected Individual Exhibitions

Berkeley Galleries, London: 1949, 1950 (with Hans Coper), 1951 (with Hans Coper), 1953 (with Hans Coper), 1956 (with Hans Coper), 1960, 1966
Bonnier's Gallery, New York: 1954
Röhsska Konstslöjdmuseet, Göteborg: 1955 (with Hans Coper)
University of Minnesota, Minneapolis: 1957 (with Hans Coper)
Museum Boymans-van Beuningen, Rotterdam: 1967 (with Hans Coper, touring)

Arts Council Gallery, London: 1967 (touring retrospective)

Museum für Kunst und Gewerbe, Hamburg: 1972 (with Hans Coper)

Hetjens Museum, Düsseldorf: 1979

Sainsbury Centre for Visual Arts, Norwich: 1981–2 (touring retrospective)

Peter Dingley Gallery, Stratford-upon-Avon: 1983

Fischer Fine Art, London: 1984 (with Hans Coper)

Galerie Besson, London: 1988 (retrospective), 1990, 1991 (with Hans Coper)

Sogetsu-Kai Foundation, Tokyo: 1989 (*Issey Miyake Meets Lucie Rie*, touring)

Crafts Council Gallery, London: 1992 (retrospective)

Metropolitan Museum of Art, New York: 1994 (with Hans Coper)

Barbican Art Gallery, London: 1997 (retrospective, with Hans Coper)

Bibliography

George Wingfield Digby, *The Work of the Modern Potter in England*, London: Murray, 1952

Dora Billington, "The younger English potters", *The Studio*, cxlv, 1953, pp.78–85

Michael Casson, *Pottery in Britain Today*, London: Tiranti, and New York: Transatlantic Arts, 1967

Lucie Rie, exh. cat., Arts Council Gallery, London, and elsewhere, 1967 (contains bibliography)

Muriel Rose, *Artist Potters in England*, 2nd edition, London: Faber, 1970

Lucie Rie–Hans Coper: Keramik, exh. cat., Museum für Kunst und Gewerbe, Hamburg, 1972

Tony Birks, *The Art of the Modern Potter*, 2nd edition, London: Country Life, 1976; New York: Van Nostrand Reinhold, 1977

British 20th-Century Studio Ceramics, exh. cat., Christopher Wood Gallery, London, 1980

Emmanuel Cooper, "Lucie Rie: Potter", *Ceramic Review*, no.72, 1981, pp.4–9

John Houston, ed., *Lucie Rie: A Survey of Her Life and Work*, London: Crafts Council, 1981 (contains extensive bibliography)

Sheila Hale, "Simple genius: Lucie Rie's pots are high art", *Connoisseur*, cxxv, June 1985, pp.126–30

Issey Miyake Meets Lucie Rie, exh. cat., Sogetsu-Kai Foundation, Tokyo, and elsewhere, 1989

Emmanuel Cooper, "Lucie Rie", *Ceramic Review*, no.134, 1992, pp.26–31

Lucie Rie, exh. cat., Crafts Council Gallery, London, 1992

Oliver Watson, *Studio Pottery: Twentieth-Century British Ceramics in the Victoria and Albert Museum Collection*, London: Phaidon, 1993 (originally published as *British Studio Pottery*, Oxford: Phaidon, 1990)

Tony Birks, *Lucie Rie: An Illustrated Biography*, 2nd edition, Marston Magna: Marston House, 1994 (contains bibliography)

Emmanuel Cooper, "Lucie Rie's notebooks", *Ceramic Review*, no.150, 1994, pp.28–37

Amy Shelton, "Lucie Rie", *Studio Pottery*, no.7, 1994, pp.30–35

"Dame Lucie Rie: Tributes", *Ceramic Review*, no.154, 1995, pp.8–21

Obituaries in *Daily Telegraph*, 3 April 1995; *The Independent*, 3 April 1995; *The Times*, 3 April 1995; *Crafts*, no.134, May–June 1995

Tanya Harrod and others, "Dame Lucie Rie, 1902–1995", *Crafts*, no.135, July–August 1995, pp.42–7

Lucie Rie and Hans Coper: Potters in Parallel, exh. cat., Barbican Art Gallery, London, 1997

Born into an upper-middle-class Viennese family with intellectual interests, Lucie Rie toured Europe with her antiquarian uncle Alexander Wolf before entering the Kunstgewerbeschule, Vienna, at the age of 20. Her studies under Michael Powolny involved exhaustive glaze trials that were to prove the foundation of her later reputation as an exciting potter in control of fantastic colours and textures. As a young woman, married in 1926 to Hans Rie (a manager in a hat factory), Lucie Rie made pots on a wheel set up in her immaculate architect-designed apartment in Vienna (examples from this period may be seen in the Victoria and Albert Museum, London). In 1938 she and her husband came to Britain with very few possessions – refugees from Nazi domination. Hans Rie left for the USA, but Lucie was determined to stay in London, renting a small mews house near Hyde Park in which to recreate her workshop and home. At the outset she asked Bernard Leach (then potting at Dartington in Devon) for advice, and visited him for four days' "tuition". Irrespective of the obvious differences in their work, their subsequent friendship and mutual admiration became an important factor in Rie's development in England.

During the war years Rie was forced to abandon pottery for work in a glass studio, followed by the manufacture of clay buttons and accessories for the clothing trade, in her own workshop. It was not until 1947 that she was able to devote herself to her chosen craft, working long hours in her studio and rarely leaving London. At first the workshop produced thrown earthenware cups and saucers, stylish and simple, glazed in black on the outside and white on the inside. From 1946 she was assisted by the young German refugee, Hans Coper, and from late 1948, as a result of the installation of a reliable new kiln, they worked together on a range of stoneware pots for the table. Rie also introduced porcelain to her workshop for the first time at this date.

Exhibitions in London followed swiftly; the first shows were held at the Berkeley Galleries and pots could always be purchased from the select craft shop Primavera. Throughout the 1950s and 1960s output was made up of tea, coffee and breakfast sets, cleanly thrown and coloured in monochrome, and individual porcelain bowls and bottles, often exploiting *sgraffito* (scratched) decoration in radiating lines. The strong graphic sensibility of Rie's work can be seen at its best in pots from these two decades, when her physical skill and strength were at their zenith.

In her maturity, during the 1970s and early 1980s, abstract elements of colour and texture dominated Rie's work, although she continued to make forms that were essentially useful containers, such as vases and bowls. Glazes of piercingly bright colours, or of bubbling, erupting and pitted surfaces, were combined with shiny, matt or even metallic finishes in a group of clearly identifiable "Rie" shapes. These include the bottle-vase with its tall, flared neck, shaped like a trumpet, the conical bowl, the footed bowl and the essential cylinder or beaker. The work was not without grit: rugged furrowed and flattened-sided pots, and those deeply colour-stained or scored into are also prized; they show Rie in command of a battery of clays, body stains and glazes that she enjoyed manipulating.

The inspiration for Rie's pots came from the process of their making and the results were often much more flamboyant than these processes, the rigorous persona of the maker or her meticulously kept environment would suggest. Her reputation was constantly high, as witnessed by regular showings in Britain and abroad. Recognition by major bodies came first in 1967, when the Arts Council of Great Britain organised a solo retrospective show at its London gallery. This was followed by another in 1981 at the Sainsbury Centre for Visual Arts, Norwich, which toured to the Victoria and Albert Museum, London. In 1991 Lucie Rie was created a DBE, an honour never before granted to a potter.

Although Rie had many imitators, especially potters emulating her glazes, for which they regularly sought the recipes, she had no pupil-followers as such. She did not find teaching a rewarding experience. Working in solitude, as she did for most of her career, or seeing friends in very small groups, suited Lucie Rie best. The major collections of Rie's work are at the Crafts Council, London; Highcross House, Dartington, Devon; Holburne Museum and Crafts Study Centre, Bath; Paisley Museum and Art Gallery, Scotland; and the Victoria and Albert Museum, London. After her death, Stoke-on-Trent City Museum and Art Gallery was given the contents of Rie's studio, including potter's wheels, tools, aprons, a small kiln, tables, chairs and shelving; the intention is to install the studio permanently in the ceramics gallery.

MARGOT COATTS

Riley, Bridget   [fig. 55]
British painter, 1931–

Born in London, 25 April 1931. Studied at Goldsmiths' College School of Art, London, under Sam Rabin, 1949–52; Royal College of Art, London, 1952–5 (ARCA); Thubron's summer school, Norfolk, under Maurice de Sausmarez, 1959. Travelled to Italy with de Sausmarez, summer 1960. Worked for J. Walter Thompson Advertising Agency, 1958–9; part-time lecturer at Loughborough College of Art, Leicestershire, 1959–61, Hornsey College of Art, London, 1960, and Croydon School of Art, Surrey, 1962–4. Spent time in Vaucluse, France, from 1961, building a studio there in 1970s. Travelled widely, making frequent trips to continental Europe with Robert Kudielka, 1971–5, and visiting USA, India, Far East and Australasia. Included in *The Responsive Eye* exhibition, Museum of Modern Art, New York, 1965. Co-founder, with Peter Sedgley, of SPACE, a scheme for the organisation of studios for artists, 1969. Trustee of National Gallery, London, 1981–8. Recipient of prize, John Moore's Exhibition, Liverpool, 1963; International prize for painting (the first woman), Venice Biennale, 1968; Ohara Museum prize, International Prints Biennale, Tokyo, 1972; gold medal, Grafik Biennale, Norway, 1980; honorary doctorates from University of Manchester, 1976; University of Ulster, 1986; University of Oxford, 1993. Commander, Order of the British Empire (CBE), 1972. Lives in London and Cornwall.

Selected Individual Exhibitions

Gallery One, London: 1962, 1963

Richard Feigen Gallery, New York: 1965, 1966, 1967, 1968

British Pavilion, Venice Biennale: 1968 (with Phillip King, touring)

Rowan Gallery, London: 1969, 1971, 1972, 1975, 1976, 1981

Kunstverein Hannover: 1970–71 (touring retrospective)

Arts Council of Great Britain, 1973 (touring), 1980–82 (touring), 1984–5 (*Working with Colour*, touring)

Sidney Janis Gallery, New York: 1975, 1978, 1990

Coventry Gallery, Sydney: 1976

Minami Gallery, Tokyo: 1977

Albright-Knox Art Gallery, Buffalo, NY: 1978–80 (touring retrospective, organised by British Council)

Australian Galleries, Melbourne: 1979

Nishimura Gallery, Tokyo: 1983, 1990

Juda Rowan Gallery, London: 1983

Royal Institute of British Architects, London: 1984

Galerie Reckermann, Cologne: 1984

Galerie und Edition Schegl, Zürich: 1987, 1989

Mayor Rowan Gallery, London: 1987, 1989

Kunsthalle, Nuremberg: 1992–3 (touring)

Karsten Schubert, London: 1992, 1993, 1994, 1996

Tate Gallery, London: 1994

Selected Writings

"The hermaphrodite", *Art and Sexual Politics*, ed. Thomas B. Hess and Elizabeth C. Baker, New York: Macmillan, 1973

"A decoration for the Royal Liverpool Hospital", *Transactions 7*, Royal Institute of Architects, iv/1, 20th Century Series, 1985

"The artist's eye: Seurat", *Modern Painters*, iv/2, 1991, pp.10–14

"Continuing", *Ready Steady Go: Paintings of the Sixties from the Arts Council Collection*, exh. cat., South Bank Centre, London, 1992

Bibliography

Michael Compton, *Optical and Kinetic Art*, London: Tate Gallery, 1967

David Sylvester, "Bridget Riley interviewed", *Studio International*, clxxiii, 1967, pp.132–5

Bridget Riley, exh. cat., Kunstverein Hannover, 1970

Maurice de Sausmarez, *Bridget Riley*, London: Studio Vista, and Greenwich, CT: New York Graphic Society, 1970

Robert Melville. "An art without accidents", *New Statesman*, 23 July 1971

Bridget Riley: Paintings and Drawings, 1961–73, exh. cat., Arts Council of Great Britain, London, 1973

John Rothenstein, *Modern English Painters: Wood to Hockney*, London: Macdonald, 1974

John A. Walker, *Art since Pop*, London: Thames and Hudson, 1975; Woodbury, NY: Barron's, 1978

Hugh Adams, *Art of the Sixties*, Oxford: Phaidon, 1978

Bridget Riley: Works, 1959–78, exh. cat., Albright-Knox Art Gallery, Buffalo, NY, and elsewhere, 1978 (contains bibliography)

J.G. Harper, *Product and Response: The Painting of Bridget Riley*, PhD dissertation, University of London, Courtauld Institute of Art, 1982

Working with Colour: Recent Paintings and Studies by Bridget Riley, exh. cat., Arts Council of Great Britain, London, 1984

"Bridget Riley", *The Great Artists: Their Lives, Works and Inspiration*, iv: *20th century*, London, 1986

Karina Türr, "Jenseits von Op Art? Überlegungen zu Farbstreifen Bridget Rileys", *Pantheon*, xliv, 1986, pp.157–63, 204–5 (with English summary)

The Artist's Eye: Bridget Riley: An Exhibition of National Gallery Paintings Selected by the Artist, exh. cat., National Gallery, London, 1989

The Experience of Painting: Eight Modern Artists, exh. cat., South Bank Centre, London, 1989

Bridget Riley, exh. cat., Sidney Janis Gallery, New York, 1990

Robert Hughes, *The Shock of the New*, 2nd edition, London: Thames and Hudson, and New York: Knopf, 1991

Bridget Riley: Painting, 1982–92, exh. cat., Kunsthalle, Nuremberg, and elsewhere, 1992 (contains bibliography)

The Sixties Art Scene in London, exh. cat., Barbican Art Gallery, London, 1993

Robert Kudielka, ed., *Bridget Riley: Dialogues on Art*, London: Zwemmer, 1995

Edward Lucie-Smith, *Movements in Art since 1945*, 4th edition, London: Thames and Hudson, 1995

Bridget Riley's work is routinely but somewhat narrowly characterised as Op Art; although she would not disclaim such a label for her early work, she has resisted the limitations it would impose on her, laying claim instead to an art that "engages the whole personality" and expects a similar total response from its audience. Certainly the linking thread that runs through from the earliest black-and-white pieces to the coloured syncopations of the 1980s and 1990s is one of perception and the sensations of seeing. As the critic Robert Melville wrote in 1971: "No painter, dead or alive, has ever made us more aware of our eyes than Bridget Riley". Riley has never studied optics, and her works are not optically mechanical. Rather they are dramatic exercises in generating visual sensations, though as she says: "not to the exclusion of emotion". Indeed she has said that one of her aims is that these two responses – the visual and the emotional – "shall be experienced as *one and the same*". More than most, her work is diminished and distorted by reproduction because the sensation it delivers is dependent on an exact concatenation of elements that must be experienced full-scale.

Despite their precision and geometric formality, the compositional structures of her work, and the tonal relationships within them, are not arrived at solely by logic or calculation; intuition plays an important role in ensuring a free play of elements, and a resistance to predictable sequences, logical progressions. Musical analogies are often aptly used to describe and explain her work: from the first she has been concerned with modulation, progression, rhythm, changes in tempo, consonance and dissonance, pause and flow. Throughout her career Riley has eschewed the autographic mark and the distraction of extraneous allusion by employing assistants to paint the final work on canvas following her precise instructions. She composes by means of drawings and watercolours, including full-size cartoons, and latterly by organising cut-out coloured shapes in infinitely variable "patterns". This method of working has the effect of distancing her from the physical character of the work, while not reducing the process to the purely mechanical. Every decision with regard to scale, interval, colour and format is hers alone. Like an architect, she designs every detail of the whole and then directs its realisation.

A student at Goldsmiths' College, and then at the Royal College of Art, it took Riley a long time to find her direction as a painter. The experiments with perception that characterise Futurism and Divisionism interested her to the extent that she sought out works by Gino Severini and Giacomo Balla and copied works by Georges Seurat. She also experimented with a Neo-impressionist style, culminating in *Pink Landscape* (private collection, London), a subject drawn in the hills around Siena during an Italian tour with the painter and art scholar Maurice de Sausmarez in 1960. Of this painting David Thompson later wrote:

> [it is] already concerned with a kind of optical situation which constantly recurs in her later work – that of a dominant formal pattern under pressure of disintegration ... As a painting about making pure colour convey visual shimmer, it is a direct precursor of *Late Morning* (1967–8) [quoted in de Sausmarez 1970].

A personal and artistic crisis later that year led her to repeated attempts to paint one last, black picture; from this originate her first black-and-white works, which are clearly related to contemporary Hard Edge painting (e.g. *Kiss*, 1960–61; Bryan Robertson, London), but rapidly developed into a personal pictorial language. These pictures of the early 1960s have titles such as *Shift* (1963), *Shiver* (1964) and *Static I* (1966) that announce quite directly a concern with visual sensation, but imply too a physical dimension to the passive act of seeing. These apparently simple compositions are a remarkably sophisticated synthesis of mathematical concepts.

Riley's work has always drawn much of its strength from her deliberate economy of means. The paintings of the early 1960s use relatively few structural ideas, such as modulation of contrasted forms, displacement in an otherwise rhythmical progression, a shifting centre within a circular form and dramatic tensions in zigzag patterns. A pivotal work in Riley's development is *Fall* (1963; Tate Gallery, Liverpool). The sense of movement here derives not from a shifting progression of forms but from the cumulative repetition of a single curving line. Repetition and reiteration become the dominant structural devices by which Riley organises her canvases. It is in these black-and-white paintings, and notably in *Fall*, that a particular visual phenomenon becomes apparent. Anton Ehrenzweig, well-known for his work on the psychoanalysis of aural and visual perception, observed of Riley's pictures of this period that "strangely iridescent disembodied colours ... begin to play around the centres of maximum tension".

Riley's "star" status was established with the exhibition *The Responsive Eye* at the Museum of Modern Art in New York, in January 1965. It included two works, *Current*, which was used for the cover of the catalogue, and *Hesitate*. Concurrently she had a sell-out show at the Richard Feigen Gallery, also in New York. The "Op Art" pictures became synonymous with 1960s style and were ruthlessly plagiarised by fashion and advertising.

A period of transition from 1965 to 1967 was marked by the introduction of "coloured" greys into her paintings; polarities of "warm" and "cold" in these greys herald the eventual adoption of colour. Titles, in Riley's work, are always pertinent – the process of composition in these paintings, and their effects on the viewer, are signalled by such titles as *Arrest*, *Drift* and *Deny*. Of *Deny II* (Chase

Manhattan Bank, New York), Riley has said she intended: "To oppose a structural movement with a tonal movement, to release increased colour through reducing the tonal contrast" (Sylvester 1967). In fact the picture sets up a remarkably complex sequence of oppositional forces, subtly deployed: warm is pitched against cold, fast against slow, as the grid of forms rises and falls, ebbs and flows, diagonally left to right and from top to bottom.

A move into pure colour occurred in 1967 with *Chant* (Collection Hoh, Germany) and *Late Morning* (Tate Gallery, London). Red and blue replace the warm and cold greys. *Chant* is a seminal example of Riley's spare use of pure colour to create complex visual effects. Red and blue stripes – red surrounding blue, blue surrounding red – alternate across the canvas; the width of the bands increases and decreases while the white intervals between them remain constant. The picture seems to radiate coloured light, an effect that arises from the fact that colours bordering white may either fuse or induce contrasting colours. This spilling-over of colour is known as adjacent colour-spread. Much of Riley's work has explored this propensity, with her choice of colours designed to induce these effects, for example, the orange, violet and green of *Orient I*. Less dominant colours – cerise, turquoise, olive – can be exploited for their susceptibility to a shifting identity. Many of the gouache studies of 1969–70 use the stripe format to explore the potential of such colour combinations.

Chant was one of the pictures shown at the Venice Biennale in 1968 when Riley was one of the two artists chosen to represent Britain; she became the first woman ever to win the International prize for painting. During this period, continuing until the early 1970s, she produced those works for which she is perhaps best known: the "stripe" paintings, which use a classically simple form to explore colour relationships. She has described the rationale behind the structures of her work and the relation between form and colour. The complex forms and energies of the earlier work could be fully expressed only by simplifying colour to black and white, with occasional grey sequences, whereas "colour energies need a virtually neutral vehicle if they are to develop uninhibited" (London 1973, p.10). She found this vehicle in the repeated stripe. The vertical stripe continued to be the organising element of Riley's compositions, though in the early 1970s she

extended her formal means with such devices as the "twisted" stripes in *Zing I* (1971; private collection, Switzerland) and the undulating curves of *Gala* (1974; private collection, Barbados) and *Rill* (1976; private collection, Cincinnati). In the late 1970s Riley progressively eliminated the white ground, as in *Aurulum* (1977; private collection), with its sequence of five pale colours – blue, pink, yellow, violet, green. The apotheosis of this is reached in the *Song of Orpheus* series of 1978 in which the colours seem almost to disappear.

Subsequent work continued to explore the problem of how to approach colour. A major touring retrospective took place in 1978–80, taking in the USA, Australia and Japan. Riley herself travelled extensively at this time, working meanwhile on a sequence of lyrical "curve" paintings. The next stage was inspired by the remembered colours seen during a visit to Egypt in 1979–80. Freely reconstructing the strong colours of this "Egyptian palette", Riley resumed the simple formal structure of the earlier "stripe" paintings in order to focus on the density of the colours themselves. Other sources in European, and especially Venetian painting became the object of study for colour theory and practice. In 1981 she was appointed a Trustee of the National Gallery, London, where in 1989 she curated one in the series of shows *The Artist's Eye*, which was pertinently subtitled "The Colour Connection". Riley's career has been single-minded in its devotion to painting. Although she has also made prints, her work outside the studio and the gallery has been infrequent: it includes a mural for the Royal Liverpool Hospital in 1983, and stage-set designs for the Ballet Rambert's *Colour Moves* at the Edinburgh Festival the same year.

Sensation became the basis for Riley's changes in the pictorial structure in the years 1980 to 1985: initially black bands articulate the colour orchestration in such works as *Luxor* (1982; Glasgow Art Gallery and Museum), *Summer's Field* (1982; Kunsthalle, Nuremberg) and *Serenissima* (1982; private collection); this device is then discarded for *Greensleeves* (1983) and *Cherry Autumn* (1983; private collection); in *Coxcomb* (1984) lilac is substituted for white; and finally such structural supports are abandoned altogether in *Saraband* (1985) and *Burnished Sky* (1985; private collection). Colour is finally released from the control exerted by the armature of pauses and intervals of black or white. *Cherry Autumn* is the key picture of this period because it predicts a later re-orientation. Riley's initial interest in the chromatic aspect of colour's energy was superseded by the realisation that colour's true potential, for painting, was spatial, or as she prefers to call it, "plastic". In other words, it is not an illusionistic pictorial space in the usual sense, but an unstable and shifting property of colours that fluctuates between them. Experiments in 1984 and 1985 at her studio in Vaucluse made it clear that this "plasticity" could not be developed by means of vertical stripes; thus in 1986 her work took a radical new direction with the balance of the pictorial space disrupted by the introduction of a dynamic diagonal. The building block of the paintings is no longer the stripe but a slanted rectangle. By using these interlocking shapes she was able to subvert the insistent vertical of the stripe while not wholly abandoning it as a compositional device. Although still concerned with sensation, these paintings allow themselves the luxury of a referential dimension, to emotion and to landscape. Colour and form in these latest works offer an expressive complexity that Riley experiences as positive and forward-looking but also open-ended: *From Here* (1994) is both a confident assertion of arrival and vantage, and an honest admission of uncertainty as in "where do we go ...?"

GILL SAUNDERS

Ringgold, Faith

American mixed-media artist and writer, 1930–

Born Faith Jones in Harlem, New York, 8 October 1930. Studied at City College of New York (BS 1955; MA in art 1959). Married (1) jazz pianist Robert Earl Wallace, 1950; two daughters, born 1950; divorced 1956; (2) Burdette Ringgold, 1962. Travelled to Europe for the first time, 1961, to Africa, 1976. Art teacher in New York City public schools, 1955–73; lecturer, Bank Street College Graduate School, New York, 1970–80; visiting professor, 1984, and professor of art, from 1985, University of California, San Diego; subsequently divided time between California and New York. Recipient of Creative Artists Public Service (CAPS) grant, 1971; National Endowment for the Arts (NEA) grants, 1978 and 1989; Wonder Woman award, Warner Communications, 1983; Guggenheim fellowship, 1987; Napouli Foundation award, France, 1990; Artist of the Year, Studio Museum in Harlem, 1991; Coretta Scott King award, for children's book, 1991; Arts International award, 1992; honorary doctorates from Moore College of Art, Philadelphia, 1986; College of Wooster, Ohio, 1987; Massachusetts College of Art, Boston, 1991; City College of New York, 1991; Brockport State University, New York, 1992; California College of Arts and Crafts, Oakland, 1993; Rhode Island School of Design, Providence, 1994. Lives in Englewood, New Jersey.

Selected Individual Exhibitions

Spectrum Gallery, New York: 1967, 1970
Jane Voorhees Zimmerli Gallery, Rutgers University, NJ: 1973 (retrospective)
Summit Gallery, New York: 1979
Museum of African and African-American Art, Buffalo, NY: 1980
Studio Museum in Harlem, New York: 1984 (retrospective)
College of Wooster Art Museum, OH: 1985
Baltimore Museum of Art: 1987
Bernice Steinbaum Gallery, New York: 1987, 1988
Fine Arts Museum of Long Island, Hempstead, NY: 1990–93 (touring retrospective)
Saint Louis Art Museum, MO: 1994, 1995

Selected Writings

"The politics of culture: Black, white, male, female", *Women Artists' News*, vi, Summer 1980, pp.20–19, 13
"Being my own woman", *Confirmation: An Anthology of Africanamerican Women*, ed. Amiri and Amina Baraka, New York: Morrow, 1983
Tar Beach, New York: Crown, 1991 (for children)
"Those cookin' up ideas for freedom take heed: Only a watched pot boils", *Art Journal*, l, Fall 1991, pp.84–6
Aunt Harriet's Underground Railroad in the Sky, New York: Crown, 1992 (for children)
The French Collection, Part 1, New York: Being My Own Woman Press, 1992
Dinner at Aunt Connie's House, New York: Hyperion, 1993 (for children)
We Flew Over the Bridge: The Memoirs of Faith Ringgold, Boston: Little Brown, 1995

Bibliography

Elton C. Fax, *Seventeen Black Artists*, New York: Dodd Mead, 1971
Lucy R. Lippard, "Faith Ringgold flying her own flag", *Ms*, v, July 1976, pp.34–9
Eleanor Munro, *Originals: American Women Artists*, New York: Simon and Schuster, 1979

Faith Ringgold: Twenty Years of Painting, Sculpture and
    Performance (1963–1983), exh. cat., Studio Museum
    in Harlem, New York, 1984
Faith Ringgold: Painting, Sculpture and Performance, exh.
    cat., College of Wooster Art Museum, OH, 1985
Faith Ringgold, Change: Painted Story Quilts, exh. cat.,
    Bernice Steinbaum Gallery, New York, 1987
Thalia Gouma-Peterson, "Faith Ringgold's narrative
    quilts", Arts Magazine, lxi, January 1987, pp.64–9
Freida High Tesfagiorgis, "Afrofemcentrism and its
    fruition in the art of Elizabeth Catlett and Faith
    Ringgold", SAGE, iv, Spring 1987, pp.25–32
Lowery Sims, "Aspects of performance in the works of
    Black American women artists", Feminist Art
    Criticism, ed. Arlene Raven, Cassandra L. Langer and
    Joanna Frueh, Ann Arbor: UMI Research Press, 1988,
    pp.207–25
Judy Seigel, "Faith Ringgold: What do black women
    want?", Women Artists' News, xiii, Summer 1988,
    pp.5–6
Lucy R. Lippard, Mixed Blessings: New Art in a
    Multicultural America, New York: Pantheon, 1990
Faith Ringgold: A 25 Year Survey, exh. cat., Fine Arts
    Museum of Long Island, Hempstead, NY, and else-
    where, 1990
Faith Ringgold: The Last Story Quilt, created and
    produced by Linda Freeman, L and S Video
    Enterprises, Inc., 1991 (video)
Mara R. Witzling, ed., Voicing Our Visions: Writings by
    Women Artists, New York: Universe, 1991; London:
    Women's Press, 1992
Wendy Slatkin, ed., The Voices of Women Artists,
    Englewood Cliffs, NJ: Prentice Hall, 1993
Norma Broude and Mary D. Garrard, eds, The Power of
    Feminist Art: The American Movement of the 1970s,
    New York: Abrams, and London: Thames and
    Hudson, 1994
Melody Graulich and Mara R. Witzling, "The freedom to
    say what she pleases: A conversation with Faith
    Ringgold", NWSA Journal, vi, Spring 1994, pp.1–27

Faith Ringgold successfully merges the Western art tradition in which she was trained with the pictorial and narrative traditions of her African-American heritage. Ringgold has asserted that she did not want to achieve artistic success at the expense of "one iota of my blackness, or my femaleness, or my humanity" (Hempstead 1990, p.23), a goal that she has met successfully. First trained as a painter, Ringgold began using stitched fabric to make figures, which she then engaged in performances. Over the years, her need to articulate her stories expanded, resulting in her creation of text-and-image "story quilts" for which she writes original narratives. Ringgold is also noted as a writer. In 1977 she began writing her autobiography, "Being my own woman", which was published in 1995 as

We Flew Over the Bridge and, since 1989, she has written and illustrated several children's books.

Ringgold remembers the Harlem of her childhood as a culturally rich community. Living close to her extended family, she heard fascinating stories and reminiscences that they traded back and forth. Their neighbours and friends in the elegant Sugar Hill section of Harlem were among the most distinguished black political and cultural figures of the generation. As a child, Ringgold was frequently bedridden with asthma, and artistic creation became one of her favourite escapes from the boredom of illness. She was aware in her early teens of her special talent, and by her senior year in high school had decided that she wanted to become an artist.

Ringgold's formal study of art began in 1948 when she enrolled in the City College of New York as an art education major, specialising in painting. In 1950 she married the jazz pianist Robert Earl Wallace and had two daughters, eleven months apart, before the year was out. She graduated from City College in 1955 with a degree in art education and began an 18-year career teaching art in the New York public schools. Ringgold did not begin to define herself as an artist, however, until the early 1960s. She completed her master's degree in 1959, and in 1961 she took an important trip to Europe to see the art that she had studied. On her return to the USA, she claimed her former dining room as studio space, an important gesture that established artmaking as a major priority in her life. Shortly thereafter, her first marriage having ended, she married Burdette Ringgold, in 1962.

It was at this time that Ringgold began to work towards finding a way to create images of black people that were acceptable to her. She felt that she had to go beyond her education, which taught art through copying the "masters" of the Western tradition. She began to seek models that would allow her to create more vital images, and found inspiration in Cubism and African art. "Instead of looking to Greece, I looked to Africa", she once said. By the later 1960s Ringgold had developed a mature style characterised by bold, flat colours and abstracted forms. This style is evident in works belonging to her American People series and most particularly in such paintings as the Flag Is Bleeding (1967; Bernice Steinbaum Gallery, New York) and Die (1967). In their accessible imagery, the American flag, for instance, these works bear a resemblance to works of the Pop Art movement that was in its heyday at that time, but Ringgold imbued the popular icons with political meaning, commenting on the violence of race relations in the USA. In 1971 she helped to found Where We At, an organisation of black artists.

During the next decade Ringgold began to work with three-dimensional forms executed in fabric. After seeing an exhibition of Tibetan *tankas* in Amsterdam, she decided to mount her paintings on "soft frames" to make them easier to transport. She also began a series called the *Family of Woman*, fiercely haunting masks, their mouths open to allow them to speak, of mixed media, animated with fabric bodies. While working on these pieces she collaborated with her mother, Willi Posey, a seamstress who had by then become a fabric designer. Ringgold recounts that she had taught such African crafts as beading and mask-making for some time before she realised that she could use these techniques in her own work. Giving herself permission to deviate from Western traditions, by incorporating in her own work elements from her African cultural heritage and her mother's art, Ringgold was able to take an important step closer to her goal of expressing her inner vision. By the mid-1970s Ringgold was animating the characters she created, at first stuffing the bodies to give them greater dimension, as in her "bag" couple, Zora and Fish. She then moved to making environmental performance pieces, employing characters she created. The *Wake and Resurrection of the Bi-Centennial Negro* (1976; Bernice Steinbaum Gallery), for example, dealt with the devastating impact of drugs on the lives of black people. In these performances she also collaborated with her daughter, the writer Michele Wallace. Ringgold took a further significant step in 1973 when she resigned from her teaching position in the New York schools in order to devote her energies exclusively to her artistic career.

In the 1980s Ringgold achieved a breakthrough to her greatest artistic achievement to date, in the conception of the "story quilt". She created her first quilt for a project conceived by Charlotte Robinson, entitled *The Artist and the Quilt*, which brought together quilts made by 18 women artists who usually worked in "high art" media. Ringgold collaborated with her mother on *Echoes of Harlem* (1980; Philip Morris Companies, Inc.), portraying in paint the faces of people she had known, while Posey used traditional quilting techniques to sew the finished piece. Although this was their last collaboration (Posey died in 1981), the work provided the catalyst for Ringgold's subsequent artistic development. During the next decade Ringgold executed numerous story quilts: at first, she made single works, such as *Who's Afraid of Aunt Jemima?* (1983; Fred Collins, Brooklyn, NY), but later went on to make multiple-quilt series that elaborated intricately plotted stories, such as her five-quilt sequence, the *Bitter Nest* (1988; Bernice Steinbaum Gallery). While the first quilts were built from individually painted "pieces", her subsequent quilts were made by framing a central painted panel with quilted fabric. As she herself has noted, the story quilts were a vehicle for bringing together the characters she had created in her earlier masks and performance pieces. Each quilt is narrated by a woman, articulating a point of view that is decidedly female. Their scenarios and characters are diverse – a slave born on the crossing from Africa to America, a pious woman from the South, an affluent black alumna of Williams College in Massachusetts, as well as many voices from Harlem. Ringgold wrote all the stories for her quilts herself, with the exception of the narrative material on the *Purple Quilt* (1986; Bernice Steinbaum Gallery), which is derived from Alice Walker's book *The Color Purple*. Their narrative structure derives from her family's oral tradition of story-telling, which Ringgold has claimed as a major influence in her life. Thalia Gouma-Peterson has suggested that some of Ringgold's quilt stories are related to the African "dilemma tale" in which a problem is posed but inconclusively resolved, forcing the viewer/reader to confront ambiguity ("Modern dilemma tales" in Hempstead 1990).

With eight quilts in Part I and four in Part II, the *French Collection* (begun 1991) is her most complex and ambitious work to date, a *Kunstlerroman* in quilts in which Ringgold inserts an African-American presence into the tradition of Parisian modernism in which she was trained. Her protagonist is a young African-American woman, Willia Marie Simone, who goes to Paris to study art in the 1920s. Each quilt presents a fictional gathering of a cast of characters interpolated with at least one "masterpiece" of the Euro-centric tradition. In the first quilt of the series, the three daughters of Willia's friend go dancing at the Louvre (also the name of the quilt) in front of the *Mona Lisa*. In the *Picnic at Giverny* Willia paints a group of contemporary feminists who sit in Monet's famous garden.

The series explores themes related to being a woman artist, especially one of African-American heritage, in the bastion of male artistic hegemony. Through Willia, Ringgold asserts that, rather than being models and muses, women can be the speaking subjects of their lives. In *Sunflower Quilting Bee at Arles* (private collection) the National Sunflower Quilters, female African-American freedom fighters, gather in van Gogh's sunflower fields, saying: "Now we can do our real quilting, our real art – making this world piece up right" (*The French Collection* 1992, p.24).

Ringgold's use of the quilting medium shows her awareness of traditional African quilting methods and her sensitivity to the significance that quilts have had in women's lives. She allows black women to speak with authority in their own voices, to tell their own stories, bypassing the stereotypes of the dominant culture, thus giving them power and centrality. Freida High Tesfagiorgis has described Ringgold as an "Afrofemcentrist", because her art consistently and centrally shows black, female subjects and conveys black women's realities. Perhaps the greatest significance of the story quilts is the challenge that they present to the assumptions regarding the traditionally separate realms of crafts and fine art. Since the 19th century, women have used quilts to express the truths about their lives, whether through the vaguely referential symbolic language of pattern or through more directly representative means. The very fabrics used for quilts often have meaning to their makers, and quilts are used to mark events of importance, such as engagements and births. Like those quilts produced from within the crafts tradition, Ringgold's quilts maintain those connections to women's lives. Yet Ringgold is an artist trained in the fine art tradition; she exhibits her quilts in art galleries, not at craft fairs, and they are bought by museums. The quilts thus cross the borders between cultural and artistic traditions; as objects and in the stories they tell, they have many meanings.

Ringgold has also reiterated her affirmative vision in several award-winning books which she both wrote and illustrated. The first, *Tar Beach* (1991), based on her story quilt *Tar Beach* (1988; Solomon R. Guggenheim Museum, New York), shows tenement dwellers on a hot summer night picnicking on the roof, the only "beach" they can afford to visit. It echoes African folk stories about people who fly, with its protagonist, eight-year-old

Cassie Louise Lightfoot, flying over the George Washington Bridge and claiming it as her own, and concludes: "anyone can fly". In Ringgold's second book, *Aunt Harriet's Underground Railroad in the Sky* (1992), the first written especially for children, Cassie and her little brother Bebe encounter Harriet Tubman. Her third book, *Dinner at Aunt Connie's House* (1993), a revision of another story quilt, *Dinner Quilt*, introduces children to other heroic African-American women, "sheroes" as Ringgold calls them.

MARA R. WITZLING

See also Training and Professionalism survey 5

Rivera, Frida *see* Kahlo

Robineau, Adelaide Alsop
American ceramist, 1865–1929

Born Adelaide Beers Alsop in Middletown, Connecticut, 9 April 1865. Married Frenchman Samuel Robineau in New York, 1899; one son, born 1900, two daughters, born 1902 and 1906. Co-founder, with her husband, 1899, and editor, 1899–1928, of the Arts and Crafts magazine *Keramic Studio* (title changed to *Design*, 1924). Moved to Syracuse, New York, 1901. Began making art porcelains in her pottery in Syracuse, 1903. Worked with the French ceramist Taxile Doat at the Art Academy (part of the American Woman's League), University City, Missouri, 1909–10. Returned to Syracuse, 1911; ran Arts and Crafts summer schools at her home, 1912–14. Recipient of honorary doctorate in ceramic science, Syracuse University, 1917. Joined the staff of Syracuse University, 1921. Died of cancer in Syracuse, 18 February 1929.

Principal Exhibitions

Esposizione Internazionale, Turin: 1911 (with American Woman's League; grand prix)
Panama-Pacific International Exposition, San Francisco: 1915 (Grand prize)
Metropolitan Museum of Art, New York: 1929 (retrospective)

Bibliography

Irene Sargent, "An American maker of hard porcelain: Adelaide Alsop Robineau", *Keystone*, xxvii, June 1906, pp.921–4

Frederick H. Rhead, "Adelaide Alsop Robineau, maker of porcelains", *Potter*, i, February 1917, pp.81–8

A Memorial Exhibition of Porcelain and Stoneware by Adelaide Alsop Robineau, exh. cat., Metropolitan Museum of Art, New York, 1929

Frederick Hurten Rhead, "Chats on pottery", *Potters Herald* (East Liverpool, OH), 1934–5, passim

Carlton Atherton, "Adelaide Alsop Robineau", unpublished memoir, *c.*1935; Robineau Archive, Everson Museum of Art, Syracuse, NY

Robert W. Blasberg, "American art porcelain: The work of Adelaide Alsop Robineau", *Spinning Wheel*, April 1971, pp.40–42

Anthea Callen, *Angel in the Studio: Women in the Arts and Crafts Movement, 1870–1914*, London: Astragal, 1979; as *Women Artists of the Arts and Crafts Movement*, New York: Pantheon, 1979

Peg Weiss, ed., *Adelaide Alsop Robineau: Glory in Porcelain*, Syracuse, NY: Syracuse University Press, 1981 (contains extensive bibliography)

Martin Eidelberg, "Apotheosis of the toiler", *American Craft*, xli, December 1981–January 1982, pp.2–5

Jane Perkins Claney, "Edwin Atlee Barber and the Robineaus: Correspondence, 1901–1916", *Tiller*, November–December 1982, pp.31–54

Barbara Perry, ed., *American Ceramics: The Collection of the Everson Museum of Art*, New York: Rizzoli, 1989

When she died in 1929 Adelaide Alsop Robineau was regarded as one of America's most distinguished ceramists, her art porcelains evoking, in the words of her assistant Carlton Atherton, "a feeling of awe and wonder". Initially a watercolourist and miniaturist, she turned to china painting and then, around 1903, she began making art porcelains. Robineau was largely self-taught, but her work developed rapidly and her incised and glazed wares were considered among the most beautiful pieces ever produced.

Robineau had taught herself china painting in the 1880s to provide additional income for her family. Although she worked successfully in this competitive field for some 20 years, she never achieved any particular prominence. Then in 1899 she married Samuel Robineau, a Frenchman living in New York, and within weeks they had launched *Keramic Studio*, an Arts and Crafts orientated monthly intended "for the designer, potter, decorator, firer". This magazine was to provide the Robineaus with an income for years to come. Robineau herself took on the editorship, contributing written material and publishing many of her own designs, which often reflected the current vogue for Art Nouveau. These were frequently adapted from such European publications as *The Studio*, *Art et Décoration* and *Dekorative Vorbilder*.

Robineau, encouraged by her husband, now became interested in making porcelains. Her new ambition may have been stimulated by an article she had published in *Keramic Studio* on the Paris Exposition Universelle of 1900, where the Scandinavian potteries in particular had put on notable shows of porcelain, and where there had been striking displays of crystalline glazes. In 1901 the Robineaus moved to Syracuse, a centre of the American Arts and Crafts movement and an ideal environment for the development of Robineau's ideas. She still practised her china painting, but in 1903, in search of instruction on the making of porcelains, she attended the short summer course at Alfred University run by a British potter, Charles Binns. That same year Samuel Robineau obtained a treatise on porcelain-making from the Sèvres ceramist Taxile Doat. Translated by Robineau himself, it appeared in *Keramic Studio* as a series of didactic articles under the title "*Grand feu* ceramics".

Adelaide Robineau now began to make porcelains in earnest, undertaking all the processes herself – designing, making the pots, choosing the composition of the bodies and the glazes, carrying out the decorations and overseeing the firing. Switching from china painting to making porcelains was not an easy option and was "about as rational and as possible as a vocational change ... from dentistry to cello playing", as her friend the Anglo-American potter Frederick Hurten Rhead observed (*Potters Herald*, 9 May 1935). Robineau was able to meet this challenge because she was "the possessor of a remarkably placid and tranquil mind together with a patient and gentle obstinacy or determination which no influence could affect" (*idem*). She made rapid progress and by 1904 had produced her first successful crystalline glaze.

The next year Robineau began carving, or excising, the porcelain. It is for this decorative method that she is best known. An excised design is formed on the ware by gradually scraping away the background until the ornament stands out in relief, a particularly difficult operation on porcelain, which has to be worked when dry. Robineau used only one tool, a very sharp point, which also made the work extremely slow, requiring "inexhaustible, consistent and tranquil patience" (Rhead 1917, p.87). She seems to have positively welcomed the difficulties, as excising was the method that pleased and suited her best. She even preferred excising to another highly skilled decorative process, *pâte-sur-pâte*, "not only", as she explained, "because it is more artistic, but also because it is more difficult" (*Panama-Pacific Exposition, Robineau Porcelains*, 1915, n.p.).

Robineau's early carved, as well as her rare incised designs, relied heavily on motifs from her pottery painting days. A vase decorated in 1905 with carved dragonflies (private collection, New Brunswick), for instance, was based on a design that had appeared in *Art et Décoration*, and the ships she excised on another piece made the same year, the *Viking Ship Vase* (Everson Museum of Art, Syracuse), were adapted from a *Dekorative Vorbilder* design of 1901. Standing 18.4 centimetres high, this piece was decorated in blue, green and brown glazes. Incised decoration appears on another work in the Everson Museum, the *Poppy Vase* of 1910. This has inlaid slips of blue, pink and olive and a white crystalline glaze and may owe something to Japanese prints.

In 1909 the Robineaus and Frederick Hurten Rhead joined the Ceramics Division of the Art Academy at the People's University, Missouri. The University, a part of the American Woman's League, was the brain child of the entrepreneur Edward G. Lewis and he had persuaded the Sèvres ceramist Taxile Doat to head the Division. The project was fatally flawed, but for a period in 1910 some prestigious work was produced. It was here that Robineau made her most famous piece, the *Scarab Vase* (Everson Museum of Art), the excised work taking her 1000 hours and the glazing a further week. Its motif was the sacred Egyptian beetle, and on the underside she cut the words "Apotheosis of the Toiler". The "Toiler" here referred not only to her own labours on the vase but to the scarab as a symbol of rebirth and resurrection. Another work completed in 1910, the *Pastoral Vase* (National Museum of American History, Smithsonian Institution, Washington, DC), was made by Robineau for her daughter Priscilla. The pastoral theme combined an overall pattern of excised daisies with satyr masks executed in *pâte-sur-pâte*, a rare instance of her use of this technique.

After World War I, Robineau was invited to join the staff of Syracuse University, where her teaching inspired a generation of students. During the last decade of her life she also produced some of her most original work. She was, for instance, intent on reproducing works and glazes that had been perfected by the Chinese. Among these glazes were flambés that have been compared with the finest Chinese oxbloods. She also developed some unusual crystalline glazes, ranging from pale pinks and lavenders to a deep rose red, colours considered by some to be almost impossible to achieve (Weiss 1981, p.151). Other notable achievements were her eggshell bowls, made to what Atherton described as "an unbelievable thinness". These were extremely difficult to work and in the event only three were completed, one of which, the largest and best, was broken when Robineau allowed it to drop. Asked by Rhead how long it would take her to replace it, she replied "that she had no intention of ever attempting another eggshell piece of that size. She had succeeded in making a perfect piece of this type and that was that!" (*Potters Herald*, 24 October 1935). The Metropolitan Museum of Art in New York owns one of the two survivors, a piece completed in 1924 with pierced and excised floral decoration.

Robineau herself knew the value of her work, though during her lifetime it never fetched its true worth. After her death the Metropolitan Museum paid her the tribute of mounting a retrospective exhibition "to the memory of one who may with every reason be called a master craftsman".

BERNARD BUMPUS

Robusti, Marietta

Italian painter, *c*.1552 or 1560–1590

Born in Venice, *c*.1552 or 1560; father the painter Jacopo Robusti, known as Tintoretto. Married a goldsmith, Mario Augusta. Died in Venice, 1590; buried in Santa Maria dell'Orto.

Bibliography

Carlo Ridolfi, *Vita de G. Robusti, detto il Tintoretto*, Venice, 1642; as *The Life of Tintoretto and of His Children Domenico and Marietta*, University Park and London: Pennsylvania State University Press, 1984

Adolfo Venturi, *Storia dell'arte italiana*, ix, Milan: Electa, 1901

Evelyn Phillipps, *Tintoretto*, London: Methuen, 1911

E. Tietze-Conrat, "Marietta, fille du Tintoret: Peintre de portraits", *Gazette des Beaux-Arts*, 6th series, xii, 1934, pp.258–62

Hans Tietze, *Tintoretto: The Paintings and Drawings*, London: Phaidon, 1948

Eric Newton, *Tintoretto*, London: Longman, 1952

Rodolfo Pallucchini and Paola Rossi, *Tintoretto: L'opera completa*, 2 vols, Venice: Alfieri, 1974–82

Francesco Valcanover, *Tintoretto*, New York: Abrams, 1985

Whitney Chadwick, *Women, Art and Society*, New York and London: Thames and Hudson, 1990; revised edition, 1996

Only a handful of women artists had successful careers during the Renaissance. These women were either born into noble families, and had the means and social connections to pursue careers in the arts, or, as demonstrated in the case of the 16th-century Venetian painter Marietta Robusti, they were born into the family trade. Marietta was an active contributor throughout her lifetime in the workshop of her father, Jacopo Robusti (known as Tintoretto), and was renowned in her own right for her work as a portraitist. According to her 17th-century biographer, Carlo Ridolfi, she was trained by Tintoretto in "design and colour, whence later she painted such works that men were amazed by her lively talent"; her "special gift" was "knowing how to paint portraits well". Ridolfi records that she portrayed many noble Venetian men and women, as well as the goldsmith friends of her husband. He noted her portrait of the long-bearded *Marco dei Vescovi*, which was still in the possession of the Tintoretto family, along with that of his son, Pietro, and also mentions a portrait of *Jacopo Strada* (untraced), the antiquarian of the Emperor Maximilian, who presented it to his patron. To date, however, only one work has been attributed to Robusti alone, the portrait of an *Old Man with Boy* (c.1585; Kunsthistorisches Museum, Vienna). For years the work was considered to be one of Tintoretto's finest portraits, but according to Tietze-Conrat (1934) it bears Robusti's monogram, and should be considered as autograph (some subsequent scholars, however, have questioned his reading of the monogram). A high level of training is evident in the sophisticated handling of the paint, the keenly observed characterisation and the contrast of the two states of youth and old age.

Unfortunately, to date no documentation has emerged to clarify the various roles played by family members in Tintoretto's workshop; any attempt to create an artistic identity for Robusti has rested exclusively on stylistic evidence. It is known that she worked for her father for about 15 years, and that her fame as a portraitist spread as far afield as Spain and Austria. She was invited first to the court of Emperor Maximilian, and later to work for Philip II of Spain. Her father, however, refused to allow her to leave his workshop, and she remained in Venice until her death in 1590.

The first attempt to identify works that might have been produced by her was undertaken by Adolfo Venturi (1901); he considered her work to display a "sentimental femininity, a womanly grace that is strained and resolute". His views are not generally accepted by modern scholars. In the 1940s Hans Tietze created the art-historical category of the "Tintorettesque style", in an attempt to reconcile the tremendously varied output of Tintoretto's studio. He chose not to identify specific works, which might have been created by different individuals in the workshop; instead, he promoted the belief that Tintoretto "used his own works to educate his assistants, until their manner of seeing and depicting approximated to his own". Thus, the artistic identities of individual contributors to Tintoretto's works were subsumed within a larger, corporate whole ruled by the master.

Later in the 20th century, such scholars as Valcanover, Pallucchini and Rossi continued to follow this hierarchical and conservative view of Tintoretto's workshop, relying on traditional art-historical constructions of artistic genius. For instance, it is reasonable to assume that Marietta contributed to the creation of large altarpieces, as well as being a skilled portraitist: this was normal practice in Renaissance family workshops. It is assumed by these scholars that she and her brother Domenico would have been assigned the less important parts of the painting, leaving the more important parts of the work to the master, her father. Such a hierarchical view of artistic production has been criticised by more recent scholars, however. It seems evident that the notion of the genius of her father Tintoretto, who is claimed to have done the highest quality work and left the more mundane areas to the lesser individuals in his workshop, has tended to obscure Marietta's contribution to Venetian painting; however, more work remains to be done on this subject.

According to Ridolfi, Marietta also displayed excellent skills in music and deportment; he placed her among the most illustrious women of all time, comparing her to famous women in antiquity. His work is indebted to earlier debates on the ideal of femininity during the Renaissance. This debate had begun in earnest around 1528, in Baldassare Castiglione's *Book of the Courtier*; according to such writers as Castiglione and the Florentine artist Giorgio Vasari, women artists were considered to be exceptional within society, their talent legitimised because of its combination with other, "feminine" virtues. Ridolfi's life of Marietta continues this tradition into the next century: she is especially praised by him for her virtuous conduct and unusually brilliant mind. Although impossible to verify, Ridolfi also mentions that she dressed as a boy and accompanied her father everywhere, suggesting that she had to flout social conventions to succeed in her art.

During the 19th century, the biography of Marietta Robusti inspired Romantic painters and authors to create paintings, a novel and several plays based on her life, which focused on her presumed filial devotion and tragic early death: she became a model of the demure, long-suffering heroine, who inspires the men in her life – first, her father Tintoretto, and later, in the play by Luigi Marta, the 16th-century Venetian painter Paolo Veronese – to new creative heights. As Chadwick has indicated (1990), this treatment of her life diminished her role as an artistic producer in her own right, by denying her individuality and treating her only in relation to male creativity. Hopefully, continued research on this artist will extend the rather limited view we currently have of her achievements.

CATHERINE HARDING

Roeder, Emy

German sculptor and draughtswoman, 1890–1971

Born in Würzburg, 30 January 1890. Studied under the sculptor Arthur Schleglmünig in Würzburg, 1908–10; studied at the Munich Academy, 1910–11, then in Darmstadt under Bernhard Hoetger, 1912–14. Moved to Berlin, 1915; member of Freie Secession, 1918; founder member, Novembergruppe zu Berlin, 1919. Married sculptor Herbert Garbe, 1920; he died 1945. First woman Meisterschülerin (master student) of sculpture at Berlin Academy, under Hugo Lederer, 1920–25. Learned woodcarving in Oberammergau, c.1920–21. Stayed in Paris, 1923; Rome and Paris, 1933–5. Moved to Florence, Italy, 1937. Banned from exhibiting under the National Socialists, 1937–45. Arrested in Italy as a German national and interned, 1944–5. Lived in Rome and surrounding area, 1945–9. Returned to Germany, July 1949. Taught at Landeskunstschule, Mainz, 1950–53. Studio in Aibling, Bavaria, from 1959. Frequent travels abroad, 1954–67. Recipient of numerous awards including Rohr prize, Berlin Academy, 1920; prize of the city of Cologne, 1929; Villa Romana prize, 1936; prize of the city of Berlin, 1953; art prize, state of Rheinland-Pfalz, 1956; art prize, state of Nordrhein-Westfalen, 1960; Great Distinguished Service Cross, Federal Republic of Germany, 1960; art prize, city of Würzburg, 1966. Member, Verein der Berliner Künstlerinnen, 1927–30. Died in Mainz, 7 February 1971.

Principal Exhibitions

Individual

Galerie Goldschmidt und Wallerstein, Berlin: 1922, 1925
Galerie Möller and Galerie Nierendorf, Berlin: 1927
Berlin Secession: 1931
Städtische Kunsthalle, Mannheim: 1950
Kestner-Gesellschaft, Hannover: 1953
Hessisches Landesmuseum, Darmstadt: 1958
Städtisches Kunstmuseum, Duisburg: 1958 (with Marg Moll and Johanna Schütz-Wolff)
Singener Kunstausstellung, Singen: 1962 (special exhibition, with H. Purrmann)
Kunstkabinett Hannah Bekker vom Rath, Frankfurt am Main: 1965
Städtische Galerie, Würzburg: 1969 (touring)

Group

Freie Secession, Berlin: 1918–19, 1923
Novembergruppe, Berlin: 1919–21, 1929
Anderson Galleries, New York: 1923 (*A Collection of Modern German Art*)
Juryfreie Kunstschau, Berlin: 1929
Haus der Juryfreien, Berlin: 1931 (*Frauen in Not*, touring)
Munich: 1937 (*Entartete Kunst*)
Deutscher Künstlerbund, Berlin: 1951
Kestner-Gesellschaft, Hannover: 1951 (*Deutsche Bildhauer der Gegenwart*), 1954

Bibliography

Adolf Behne, "Graphik und Plastik von Mitgliedern der Novembergruppe Berlin", *Menschen*, ii/14, December 1919, pp.1–2, 48–9

Alfred Kuhn, "Emy Roeder: Über das Formproblem der Plastik", *Der Cicerone*, xii, 1920, pp.423–35

Peter Leu, *Führer durch die Abteilung der Novembergruppe: Kunstausstellung, Berlin, 1920*, Berlin-Friedenau: Novembergruppe [1920]

Alfred Kuhn, *Emy Roeder*, Junge Kunst, xviii, Leipzig: Klinkardt und Biermann, 1921

——, *Die neuere Plastik von Achtzehnhundert bis zur Gegenwart*, Munich: Delphin, 1921

K[arl] Sch[effler], "Ausstellungen Berlin", *Kunst und Künstler*, xxi/2, 1922, p.68

Willi Wolfradt, "Umschau-Ausstellungen", *Das Kunstblatt*, vi, 1922, p.503

A[lfred] K[uhn], "Berliner Ausstellungen", *Der Cicerone*, xix, 1927, pp.676, 705–7

Hans Hildebrandt, *Die Frau als Künstlerin*, Berlin: Rudolf Mosse, 1928

Viktor Wallerstein, "Zeichnungen der Bildhauerin Emy Roeder", *Das Kunstblatt*, xiv, 1930, pp.205–7

"Zwei Bildnerinnen über ihr Schaffen", *Koralle*, new series, iv, 31 January 1936, pp.156–7 (includes statement by Roeder)

Alfred Hentzen, *Deutsche Bildhauer der Gegenwart*, 2nd edition, Berlin: Rembrandt, 1937

Friedrich Gerke, *Emy Roeder: Werkbiographie (mit Gesamtkatalog der Bildwerke und Zeichnungen)*, Wiesbaden: Steiner, 1963 (catalogue raisonné of sculptures and drawings)

Helga Kliemann, *Die Novembergruppe*, Berlin: Mann, 1969

Emy Roeder: Bildwerke, Handzeichnungen, exh. cat., Städtische Galerie, Würzburg, 1981

Ulrike Evers, *Deutsche Künstlerinnen des 20. Jahrhunderts: Malerei, Bildhauerei, Tapisserie*, Hamburg: Schultheis, 1983 (contains extensive bibliography)

Das Verborgene Museum I: Dokumentation der Kunst von Frauen in Berliner öffentlichen Sammlungen, exh. cat., Akademie der Künste, Berlin, 1987

Emy Roeder, 1890–1971: Akzente, exh. cat., Städtische Galerie, Würzburg, and elsewhere, 1989

Entartete Beeldhouwkunst: Duitse Beeldhouwers, 1900–1945 [Degenerate sculpture: German sculptors, 1900–1945], exh. cat., Commanderie van St Jan, Nijmegen, and elsewhere, 1991

Magdalena Bushart, "Der Formsinn des Weibes: Bildhauerinnen in den zwanziger und dreißiger Jahren", *Profession ohne Tradition: 125 Jahre Verein der Berliner Künstlerinnen*, exh. cat., Berlinische Galerie, Berlin, 1992, pp.135–50

Erich Ranfft, "Expressionist sculpture, *c*.1910–30, and the significance of its dual architectural/ideological frame", *Expressionism Reassessed*, ed. Shulamith Behr and others, Manchester: Manchester University Press, 1993, pp.65–79

——, "German women sculptors, 1918–1936: Gender differences and status", *Visions of the "Neue Frau": Women and the Visual Arts in Weimar Germany*, ed. Marsha Meskimmon and Shearer West, Aldershot: Scolar Press, 1995, pp.42–61

Elizabeth Tumasonis, "The sculpture of Emy Roeder: Expressionism and beyond", *Woman's Art Journal*, xviii/1, 1997, pp.20–25

Emy Roeder was one of Germany's most important modern sculptors of the 20th century. Her production of more than 100 sculptures was complemented by an output of several hundred finished drawings. Her artistic career spanned more than five decades, beginning with her growing prominence while based in Berlin during the Weimar Republic, from 1919 until the early 1930s. Roeder's status placed her in the company of the most famous Weimar women sculptors – Milly Steger (q.v.), Renée Sintenis and Käthe Kollwitz (q.v.).

Central to Roeder's sculptures and drawings were the female figure and themes of childhood, adolescence, pregnancy and motherhood. Also significant were her depictions of animals and her portraits. Her sculptural production consisted mainly of free-standing pieces under 50 centimetres in height, reliefs of an area under 35×35 centimetres, and portrait busts in life-size proportions. After 1930 most of her works were cast in bronze (unless otherwise indicated, all works listed below are of this medium). The finished drawings, begun as a main preoccupation after 1925, were made from black or red chalk or pencil. They are typically line drawings with shading along the contours. The Städtische Galerie in Würzburg possesses the most comprehensive collection of sculptures and drawings by Roeder.

Roeder's first years as a professional artist were marked by her evocative contributions to German Expressionist sculpture before *c*.1923. Early on she was heavily influenced by Bernhard Hoetger, her former teacher. His eclectic use of historicising and exotic motifs was echoed, for example, in Roeder's set of five figural groups comprising the *Manger* (1916; terracotta; private collection, Mainz, repr. Kuhn 1920, p.431), which synthesises Egyptian, Near Eastern and Oriental sources into a Christian theme. Roeder's Expressionism after 1918 was motivated by her involvement in the Berlin Novembergruppe and by the post-war "ecstasy" of Christian religious and spiritual expression. In this milieu she worked closely with the sculptor Herbert Garbe, whom she married in 1920.

Roeder's pivotal sculpture was the frontally posed, half-figure of *Pregnant Woman* (1919; terracotta; 80.5 cm.?; repr. Ranfft 1993, p.72, and Ranfft 1995, pl.6, front and side views), which she produced in the village of Fischerhude, near Bremen. Roeder wrote that she felt "the cosmic of all being" (quoted in Kuhn, *Emy Roeder*, 1921, p.15) in the experience of pregnancy and motherhood among the peasant women and animals. Roeder's romanticisation of Fischerhude was not unlike the sentiments of Paula Modersohn-Becker (q.v.) for Worpswede. Within Expressionist ideology, *Pregnant Woman* had a spatial and ritualistic presence: "Her hands lie protecting the cathedral body which carries a Saviour" (Kuhn, *Die neuere Plastik ...*, 1921, p.105). Roeder's communion with Fischerhude also inspired her first animal sculptures, such as *Mare and Foal* (1919; Nationalgalerie, Staatliche Museen zu Berlin).

Pregnant Woman was followed by a "life-cycle" of female figures, such as *Embryo* (1919; artificial stone; repr. Kuhn, *Emy Roeder*, 1921, pl.22) and *Family* (1920; wood; repr. Tumasonis 1997, fig.4), which strongly suggests the matriarchal grouping of a grandmother holding her pregnant daughter and infant. These figures are delineated in reductivist and angular shapes that are compressed into an overall relief-like surface. In its showing at the Novembergruppe exhibition of 1920, it was described as "the very embodiment of the spiritual" (Leu [1920], p.17). *Family* was also an example of Roeder's participation in the Expressionist vogue for carving in wood, which she learned in 1920 in Oberammergau from Bavarian artisans: for instance, *Manger Relief* (1920; Robert Gore Rifkind Collection, Beverly Hills, CA), whose angularity and harsh diagonals (akin to Expressionist woodcuts) imbue the religious scene with "ecstatic" resonance, while *Praying Boy* (1921; 98.5 cm.; Städtische Galerie, Würzburg) presents solidity of form and smoothened surfaces, under the influence of Ernst Barlach.

From 1925 until the late 1930s Roeder continued to preoccupy herself with the female figure and portray those individuals with whom she shared a close connection, especially the poorest of the city and country (such as farmers and Gypsies). Unlike Käthe Kollwitz or Katharina Heise, she did not seek to make social or political statements. Her sculp-

tures during the late 1920s did, however, express degrees of pathos and empathy. These works were marked by more naturalistic handling of form and detail, such as *Head of the Girl Else* (1929–30; artificial stone; Städtische Galerie, Würzburg) and the highly emotive *Heads of Children* (1928; artificial stone; Nationalgalerie, Staatliche Museen zu Berlin), which depicts the upper torso of a boy holding the head of his sister in his arms. Thereafter Roeder simplified her sculptures and concentrated on rounded contours, which were indebted to the classicising influence of Aristide Maillol (e.g. *Seated Young Woman with Towel*, 1937; *Girl Friends*, 1940–41; both Städtische Galerie, Würzburg).

Roeder enjoyed far greater support than her husband during the Weimar years, which had much to do with the assertion of her feminine identity in the critical reception: "the man [Garbe], the larger intellect, the woman, the even deeper artist" (Kuhn 1927, p.676). The sincerity of her conviction was often noted, as she is "the intense woman who works seriously" (1927) and "belongs to the most endearing of creative female personalities in the world" (1936; both quoted in Ranfft 1995, p.50). Hers was a maternal image conflated by the early 1930s with women's dominant media image of domesticity. In contrast, Roeder's "sensitivity" was seen as a disadvantage when compared to the "masculine strength" of Milly Steger.

After World War II Roeder drew inspiration from her period of internment at Padula (1944–5): each of the four reliefs of *Padula* (I, II and III of 1945–6, V of 1949; all Städtische Galerie, Würzburg) depicts three young nude women in the camp's showers, their bodies and arms moving gracefully under the downpour of water. Roeder then undertook numerous two- and three-dimensional representations of animals, such as the sculptures *Two Sheep with Lamb Resting* (1946–7) and *Pair of Resting Goats* (1958; both Städtische Galerie, Würzburg). These works are characterised by reductive, planar forms with angular contours. Such qualities were taken to an extreme flatness in the relief *Cows in the Rain* (1962; 47 × 34.5 cm.; Städtische Galerie, Würzburg), in which Roeder has simply "etched" the design on to the surface.

In the 1960s Roeder began anew to sculpt and draw representations of women, especially Moslem women. Her sculpted figures featured elongated bodies with slender limbs and a simplification of form and detail through the suggestion of their enveloping clothing (e.g. *Tunisian Women Beggars*, 1971; Städtische Galerie, Würzburg). This period was also marked by two monumental, over-life-size sculptures: the seated woman of *Tripoli III* (1963) and the *Standing Woman from Tripoli* (1967; both Städtische Galerie, Würzburg).

Portrait busts continued to be an important preoccupation; the best known are those of Roeder's old artist friends, *Erich Heckel* (1951–2), *Hans Purrmann* (1950–1; both Städtische Galerie, Würzburg) and *Karl Schmidt-Rottluff* (1955–6, Brücke Museum, Berlin; Städtische Galerie, Würzburg). More remarkable were Roeder's self-portraits, in two busts of 1958 and 1964 (both Städtische Galerie, Würzburg) and in more than ten drawings in black chalk, beginning in 1965 (average size 47 × 35 cm.; all Städtische Galerie, Würzburg). Inviting comparisons to the sculpted self-portrait (1926–36; bronze) by Käthe Kollwitz, Roeder's bust of 1964

> is a powerfully honest statement of old age and physical decay. Roeder did not shrink from the depiction of the wrinkles lining her forehead, cheeks, and the papery flesh of her throat. Yet it is clear that they were made by laughter as well as by care. The corners of the eyes are crinkled; the mouth is curved in a faint smile, wry and self-mocking [Tumasonis 1997].

ERICH RANFFT

Roghman, Geertruydt [Giertje]

Dutch printmaker, 1625–after 1651   [fig. 58]

Baptised in the Nieuwe Kerk, Amsterdam, 19 October 1625, eldest child of Hendrik Lambertsz. Roghman, engraver and apprentice of Harmen Jansz. Muller, and Maritje Saverij, who came from a family of artists in Courtrai. Worked in the family workshop in Amsterdam with her father, brother Roelant and sister Magdalena. Never married. Last documented March 1651; deceased by December 1657.

Bibliography

Arnold Houbraken, *De Groote Schouburgh der neder-lantsche konstschilders en schilderessen* [The great theatre of Dutch male and female painters], iii, Amsterdam, 1721

F. W. H. Hollstein, *Dutch and Flemish Etchings, Engravings and Woodcuts*, xx, Amsterdam: van Gendt, 1949

Margarita Russell, "The women painters in Houbraken's Groote Schouburgh", *Woman's Art Journal*, ii/1, 1981, pp.7–11

W. T. Kloek, *De Kasteeltekeningen van Roeland Roghman* [The Castle drawings of Roeland Roghman], ii, Canaletto: Alphen aan den Rijn, 1990

Martha Moffitt Peacock, "Geertruydt Roghman and the female perspective in 17th-century Dutch genre imagery", *Woman's Art Journal*, xiv/2, 1993–4, pp.3–10

Like many female artists of the 17th century, Geertruydt Roghman was born into an artistic heritage. With her father, her brother Roelant and sister Magdalena, she was part of a family workshop whose major production was in the field of printmaking. In connection with this role, Roghman spent much of her time engraving or etching the designs of other artists. In particular, she made a number of prints after the landscape drawings of her brother. While these images gave her little chance for experimentation, a series of domestic genre scenes that she designed and engraved demonstrates her unique approach, in both composition and mood, to a ubiquitous 17th-century Dutch subject.

It is likely that Roghman's earliest extant work is an engraved portrait (1647; Rijksprentenkabinet, Amsterdam) after a lost painting by Paulus Moreelse of her great-uncle Roelant Saverij, painter to Emperor Rudolph II. It is a portrait in the manner of her father's work, and is accompanied by a eulogising verse signed by him. Although no other works by Roghman are dated, it may be that an engraved copy (Rijksprentenkabinet) in reverse of Aegidius Sadeler's print after Tintoretto's *Massacre of the Innocents* also belongs to this early period, in which she copied the works of other artists. The copy is quite accurately handled, but she makes the significant alteration of writing out the biblical text in Dutch rather than Latin. This penchant for the common and ordinary permeates all of Roghman's works.

This characteristic is very evident in a series of 14 landscape prints done after drawings by her brother. The series, *Plaisante lantschappen ofte vermakelijcke gesichten na t'leven* (Pleasant landscapes or entertaining/enjoyable views after life/nature; c.1645–8; Rijksprentenkabinet), is typical of a formula developed earlier on by the artist and publisher Claes Jansz. Visscher (who also published this series). After the title plate, which indicates Roelant as the inventor of the scenes, views from the districts around Amsterdam are depicted with identifying inscriptions. In addition to landmarks such as churches, these prints contain many commonplace genre activities and details. While there is some question regarding the etching of these prints, most scholars attribute it to Roghman, due to the careful technique, resembling engraving. This is supported by the existence of one other landscape etching, *House [Castle] at Zuylen* (after 1652; Rijksprentenkabinet), in which the inscription identifies Roghman as the etcher after a design by Roelant. As in the previous series, a number of genre details – figures gathered around a sketching artist and water fowl – have been added to the foreground. In this particular case (and perhaps by association with the previous series) we can assume that these humanising details were added by Roghman, because of their absence in the still-extant preliminary drawing by Roelant.

It is possible that Roghman was given more significant credit in the *Zuylen* print than in the earlier landscape series because she had established, by then, an artistic reputation of her own, through her domestic series. These prints, designed and engraved by Roghman, were published twice, and are unique as subjects in printmaking. Although the engravings depict well-known conventions in contemporary painting – *Two Women Sewing*, *Woman with Vanitas Objects*, *Pancake Baker*, *Woman Spinning*, *Woman Scouring Metalware* (*c*.1650; Rijksprentenkabinet) – they portray the women in a much less anecdotal or didactic fashion than other depictions of the themes.

The final print in the series, *Woman Scouring Metalware*, demonstrates Roghman's distinctly different interpretation of the subject. Dutch images of the 17th century depicting women scouring metalware in the kitchen almost always contained sexual innuendo. At times the erotic anecdote was acted out in theatrical fashion (usually between a maid and her master), while elsewhere it was only humorously indicated through the use of sexual metaphors handled by bawdy, grinning females. In contrast to such images, Roghman's maidservant is decidedly non-sexual. From a surprising and innovative back view (common to three of the prints), she does not tempt the viewer with her gaze, smile

or décolletage. She scrubs away vigorously at her burdensome task, creating an unposed slice-of-life effect. As in the other scenes, Roghman concentrates exclusively on the common yet monumental figure, her work and the tools specific to it.

Such an altering of artistic conventions suggests that Roghman saw these domestic images in a different light from many of her male predecessors. It appears that she viewed such scenes as reflections of a new interest in women and their domain that bestowed a greater importance on the roles of women. One other work that indicates the significance Roghman attributed to these figures is her only extant drawing. It depicts a *Female Artist* (*c*.1650; private collection, repr. *Bernard Houthakker, Old Master Drawings*, sale cat. 253, 1975), drawing with charcoal in the same (reversed) pose of the profile needlewoman in the first scene of the print series. Both females, whether sewing or drawing, are intent on their work, as if they are tasks of great significance. Just as Roghman gained a certain amount of power and reputation through her skill as an artist, other women in this middle-class society achieved status through their skilful management of home, children and servants.

Although recently the trend in feminist studies has been to treat women artists in a gender-less fashion, the art of Roghman indicates that abandonment of a gendered approach altogether is problematic. Roghman's images demonstrate how significant the female experience was to these innovative views of a 17th-century woman's world. Post-structuralist methods, however, are also necessary in order to understand fully Roghman and the role her art played in gender relationships of the 17th century. Not all male artists of the period, for example, treated women in a moralising or titillating fashion. Like Roghman, many males treat the depicted women in domestic genre sympathetically – as subjects busy with their own pursuits, rather than as objects for the male gaze. Many male artists seem to have been influenced towards this more sympathetic view in part because of their contact with Roghman's prints, and the opportunity they provided to view women through the eyes of a woman. The several back and lost-profile views of women at fireplaces or windows in barren settings by Jacobus Vrel and Esaias Boursse post-date and are obviously influenced by Roghman's scenes. Specifically, Caspar Netscher's *Lacemaker* (1662; Wallace Collection, London) with its barren setting, sparse still-life objects and seated, lost-profile figure appears indebted to Roghman's *Woman Spinning*. And, finally, it might be suggested that either directly or indirectly the domestic images of Johannes Vermeer, Pieter de Hooch and Pieter Janssens Elinga that concentrate on singular females busy at their domestic tasks owe something to the quiet, dignified and powerful females of Geertruydt Roghman's vision.

MARTHA MOFFITT PEACOCK

Roldán, Luisa (Ignacia)
Spanish sculptor, 1652–1706

[fig. 59]

Born in Seville, 1652, to the sculptor Pedro Roldán and his wife Teresa de Ortega y Villavicencio; at least two of her siblings, María Josefa and Francisca, mother of the sculptor Pedro Duque Cornejo, were also sculptors. Trained by her father; married, against his wishes, a sculptor, Luis Antonio de los Arcos Navarro, 1671; seven children, of whom at least two survived infancy. In Cádiz, 1684–7. Moved to Madrid, 1688/9; named "Sculptor to the Bedchamber" (*Escultora de Cámara*) by Charles II, 1692; appointed "Sculptor to the King" by Philip V, 1701; subsequently signed herself "escultora de su Magestad". Accademica di Merito, Accademia di San Luca, Rome, 1706. Died in Madrid, 10 January 1706.

Bibliography
Juan Agustín Ceán Bermúdez, *Diccionario histórico de los más illustres profesores de las bellas artes en España*, 6 vols, Madrid, 1800

María Elena Gómez Moreno, *Escultura del siglo XVII*, xvi of *Ars Hispaniae: Historia universal del arte Hispánica*, 22 vols, Madrid: Plus-Ultra, 1947–77

E. Sánchez Corbacho, *Pedro Roldán y sus discípulos*, Seville, 1950

Beatrice Gilman Proske, "Luisa Roldán at Madrid", *Connoisseur*, clv, 1964, pp.126–32, 199–203, 269–73

Domingo Sánchez-Mesa Martin, "Nuevas obras de Luisa Roldán y José Risueño en Londres y Granada", *Archivo Español de Arte*, xl, 1967, pp.325–31

Jorge Bernales Bellesteros, *Pedro Roldán: Maestro de escultura (1624–1699)*, Seville: Arte Hispalense, 1973

María Victoria Garciá Olloqui, *La Roldana: Escultora de Cámara*, Seville: Arte Hispalense, 1977

Antonio Palomino, *Lives of the Eminent Spanish Painters and Sculptors*, Cambridge and New York: Cambridge University Press, 1987 (Spanish original, 1724)

Catherine Hall-van den Elsen, "Una valoración de dos obras en terracota de Luisa Roldán", *Goya*, no.209, 1989, pp.291–5

——, "Una obra inédita de Luisa Roldán", *Archivo Hispalense*, no.221, 1989, pp.205–8

Domingo Sánchez-Mesa Martin, *El arte del barroco*, vii of *Historia del arte en Andalucia*, Seville: Gever, 1991

Catherine Hall-van den Elsen, *The Life and Work of the Sevillian Sculptor Luisa Roldán, with a Catalogue Raisonné*, PhD dissertation, La Trobe University, Melbourne, 1992

Very little is known about Luisa Roldán's life and work, and many details of her life remain obscured beneath a mist of conjecture. Identification of her early work, done while she was attached to her father's studio, has been hindered by the enormous output of her father's workshop, one of the largest in Seville during the second half of the 17th century.

After her marriage to Luis Antonio de los Arcos in 1671, Roldán began to work independently of her father, completing life-sized figures in polychromed wood for the commissions for multi-figure processional Holy Week floats representing the *Passion*, which her husband received from Sevillian brotherhoods. These were initially inspired by her training in her father's studio but reveal her steady progression from his didactic approach to the single standing figure towards a more dynamic, High Baroque sentiment, perhaps under the influence of Juan de Valdes Leal, her sister's godfather. Two early figures, the thieves from the float of the *Exaltation of the Cross* (1678–9; Santa Catalina, Seville), reveal Roldán's mastery of the male nude – an exceptional skill for a female in 17th-century Spain – which must have been acquired in her father's studio. As with a number of works included in commissions signed by Roldán's husband, attribution of these figures is based on stylistic evidence, since she rarely signed a wooden sculpture.

Recognition of her independence from her famous father was confirmed when she spent time in the city of Cádiz from 1684 to 1687. The free-standing *Ecce Homo* (1684), a recently identified sculpture in Cádiz Cathedral, is a typical example of her work of this period. The moment portrayed is immediately after the scourging and mocking of Christ by the Roman soldiers. The body of Christ is very slender, with the bones appearing to press almost through the skin. This is most noticeable at the collar-bone, the upper ribs and the left hip, seen beneath the abdominal cavity. The veins of the arms, forearms and hands are emphasised and the hands are finely sculpted and appear almost skeletal. Christ's face is gaunt, his mouth half open with exhaustion. Delicately traced eyebrows emphasise translucent eyelids and an elongated nose. The neck is slender, revealing veins beneath the surface of the skin. This innovative work foreshadows the advances Roldán would make during her next period, where rather than being content with modest success close to her home town, she would reveal both the complexity and individuality of her talents. Sometime in 1689 Roldán travelled to Madrid with her husband and the two or three surviving children of the seven she bore. After establishing herself in the court city, possibly with the assistance of a Sevillian noble, in 1692 she received the title of Sculptor to the Bedchamber of King Charles II.

The most significant difference between the market for sculpture in Seville and that in Madrid was the less prestigious role accorded in the capital to sculptors, who still retained the rank of tradesmen. Royal taste in public sculpture, influenced by Italian theorists, favoured marble over wood. There were fewer opportunities open to sculptors in Madrid to display their work. The importance of processional images to Sevillian religious life guaranteed their authors publicity. Madrid society, however, placed less importance on sculpture as a vehicle for disclosing the mysteries of faith, and painting remained the preferred medium for many patrons.

As a sculptor at the Spanish court, Roldán was one of a number of artists and writers whose work reflects the struggle to maintain confidence in Spain, when the political and social currents in Madrid were anything but reassuring. In a court full of political and moral uncertainties, great reliance was placed on the Church for assurances of the righteousness of basic articles of faith. Together with the glorification of the Virgin Mary and reminders of the inescapable presence of death, they occupied an important place in Spanish culture as stimuli for artistic endeavour. Roldán interpreted the themes of the day with an immediacy conveyed by the three-dimensionality of her medium that was unavailable to court painters, limited by the surfaces of their canvases. The first work in wood that she executed specifically for King Charles in 1692 was the over-life-size *St Michael and the Devil* (1692; El Escorial Monastery, Madrid). The figure of St Michael continues the pattern of innovation initiated by

Roldán four years earlier in Cádiz. Added to this is a new, vital sense of movement intrinsic to Madrid art of the period that was often ignored by sculptors of her father's school, where sculpture served a didactic rather than a rhetorical purpose. The work is signed by both Roldán and her husband's younger brother Tomás Antonio de los Arcos, a painter of sculpture who regularly worked with Roldán.

In the same year as the *St Michael* Roldán sculpted in wood the head and hands of a *St Clare* for a royal convent in Murcia. Now lost, the figure was designed to hold a monstrance in accordance with the saint's traditional iconography. Like St Michael, St Clare was an important figure in late 17th-century Spain, famed for her legendary use of the Eucharist in the defence of the city of Assisi when it was under attack by the Saracens. For the anxious Spaniards of the late 17th century, St Clare's victory was a commentary on the triumph of Catholicism over Protestantism.

Despite her membership of one of Seville's most prolific families of sculptors in wood, and continuing to produce wooden sculptures throughout her life, Roldán is now known principally for her work in terracotta. She began producing terracotta sculptures – images of the Virgin Mary and the Christ Child, measuring approximately 40×50 centimetres – soon after her arrival in Madrid. These intimate works are characterised by simplicity and warmth, which are conveyed by the cherubs, animals and plants that adorn the scenes. One of her earliest works in terracotta, the *Virgin and Child with St John the Baptist* (1691; Martin D'Arcy Gallery, Loyola University, Chicago) is a typical example of Roldán's iconographically simple works, which associate an intimate familial scene and an admonition of its sanctity by its reference to the Holy Family.

Many of her more elaborate terracotta works are more iconographically complex than is generally acknowledged. When read in the light of the 17th-century Spanish literary tradition, in which image and symbol are interpreted as a single unit, these sculptures present a compelling reaffirmation of the strength of the Catholic faith. One of the most iconographically complex of all of Roldán's terracotta groups is the work known as the *Death of Mary Magdalene* (c.1697; Hispanic Society, New York). The work is composed of the reclining figure of the Magdalene attended by angels and cherubs. Among the animals and plants depicted are an owl, a rabbit nibbling at a clump of blue and white irises, a scourge, a skull resting on a book and below that a salamander and a snake. The salamander and the snake placed beneath the Magdalene suggest a more significant iconological role than has previously been attributed to them. The salamander is a symbol of chastity and among its mythical powers is the ability to withstand and even to extinguish fire. The placing of these two animals beneath the figure of the Magdalene is indicative of their relevance to the theme of repentance. The snake, symbol of the fires of Hell, is placed next to the animal capable of withstanding the flames. The salamander here symbolises spiritual salvation, as recounted in Isaiah 43:1–3. The conflict between sin and salvation represented by the snake and the salamander can be related to the conflict between lust and chastity that is symbolised in this work by the rabbit and the irises. By placing the symbols relating to the life of the penitent saint directly beneath her reclining body, Roldán reminds us that the Magdalene has triumphed over lust and the flames of passion. Her salvation has been achieved through withdrawal from society (the owl) and repentance (the scourge, the skull and the book).

The power with which Roldán was able to convey the strength of Spain's religious conviction in over-life-size sculptures belies the tendency of writers to cast her in a mould of helpless subservience. Like Ceán Bermúdez, who in 1800 saw Roldán's terracotta works as appropriate to the delicacy of her gender (*delicadeza de su sexo*), some have had difficulty in reconciling their image of a female artist with the force of her work in wood. It is, however, not surprising that until the age of 40 Roldán confined her artistic output to a medium with which she had grown up. Her family, her friends and the godparents of her children were all involved in different stages of the production of wooden figures as sculptors, joiners, painters and gilders. While those sculptures reflect both her roots in the Sevillian Holy Week tradition and, in her later work, the ethos of Madrid's golden age of painting, her terracotta groups respond to a quieter faith, where miracles reward the saintly deeds of the protagonists. Delicate workmanship attracts the lingering gaze of the viewer, who must contemplate the image for protracted periods of time in order to comprehend the often complex message contained within the group. The intimate contact the viewer is required to have with the works recalls immediately the art of Murillo and Zurbarán in Seville, as well as that of Claudio Coello and Mateo Cerezo in Madrid. The elaborate details reveal Roldán's affinity with contemporary painting rather than wooden sculpture, which as a medium was still confined to the representation of grandiloquent figures of saints and kings. The pastel colours employed in the polychromy of her terracotta works reflect a concern for subtle harmonies of tone that were not adopted in Spain until the establishment of porcelain factories in the second quarter of the 18th century.

Luisa Roldán sought and received recognition in her home town, in the important cathedral city of Cádiz, in the Royal Palace, in the household of at least one noble patron and, on the day she died, from the Roman Accademia di San Luca, which honoured her with the title of Accademica di Merito on 10 January 1706. This final honour was substantially more than any received from the prestigious academy by contemporary Spanish painters. Roldán's place in history should not be confined to a final paragraph of a book on the golden age of Spanish sculpture. Her work is the manifestation of a truly Spanish tradition, and she should be accorded a place among the leading artists of her time.

CATHERINE HALL-VAN DEN ELSEN

Rosalba *see* Carriera

Rossi, Properzia de'
Italian sculptor, active 1514–29

Born in Bologna, *c.*1490 (cited as aged 25 in a document of 1515); father a Bolognese citizen and the son of a notary. Brought before the Bologna tribunal on several occasions to answer charges of disorderly conduct, 1520–21; again in 1525, accused of throwing paint in the face of another artist. Employed by the Fabbrica di San Petronio, Bologna, 1525–6. Patient in the Ospedale di San Giobbe, Bologna, April 1529. Dead by February 1530 (Vasari).

Bibliography

Giorgio Vasari, *Le vite de' più eccellenti architettori, pittori et scultori italiani, da Cimabue insine à tempi nostri*, 1550, ed. Luciano Bellosi and Also Rossi, Turin: Einaudi, 1986, pp.728–31

——, *Le vite de' più eccellenti pittori et scultori ed architettori*, Florence, 1568; ed. Gaetano Milanesi, v, Florence: Sansoni, 1880, pp.73–81; as *Lives of the Most Eminent Painters, Sculptors and Architects*, 10 vols, London: Macmillan-Medici Society, 1912–15; reprinted New York: AMS, 1976

Antonio Saffi, *Della vita e delle opere di Maria de' Russi scultrice bolognese: Discorso all'Accademia di Belle Arti in Bologna, detto il 22 giugno 1830*, Bologna, 1832

Michelangelo Gualandi, "Memorie intorno a Properzia de' Rossi scultrice bolognese", *L'Osservatorio*, nos 33, 34 and 35, Bologna, 1851

Ottavio Mazzoni-Toselli, *Racconti storici estratti dall'Archivio Criminale di Bologna*, ii, Bologna: Chierici, 1868

Laura M. Ragg, *The Women Artists of Bologna*, London: Methuen, 1907

I.B. Supino, *Le sculture delle porte di S. Petronio in Bologna*, Florence: Istituto Micrografico Italiano, 1914

Vera Fortunati Pietrantonio, "Per una storia della presenza femminile nella vita artistica del cinquecento bolognese: Properzia De Rossi, 'schultrice'", *Carrobbio*, vii, 1981, pp.167–77

Fredrika H. Jacobs, "The construction of a life: Madonna Properzia De' Rossi 'schultrice bolognese'", *Word & Image*, ix, 1993, pp.122–32

With the exception of several payment records and some documents in the Archivio Criminale, Bologna, few facts are known about Properzia de' Rossi. The principal source of information about the sculptor comes from the first and second editions of Giorgio Vasari's *Vite* (1550 and 1568). Subsequent writers, such as Raffaello Borghini (*Il Riposo*, 1584) and Antonio Saffi (1832), did little more than to repeat information stated by Vasari.

Vasari reported that de' Rossi's earliest works were carvings of peach stones. The one described by him, a cluster of eleven stones intricately carved with scenes of the *Passion* and images of martyrs, all of which were set within a silver filigree coat-of-arms of the Grassi family of Bologna, is still extant (Museo Civico Medievale, Bologna). A similar carving, but rendered from a cherry stone (Museo degli Argenti, Palazzo Pitti, Florence), was first attributed to de' Rossi by Gaetano Milanesi in his edition of Vasari's *Vite*. Such carvings reflect the popularity of objects deemed "marvels" for their

artistic virtuosity that were being assembled in *Kunst- und Wunderkammern* throughout 16th-century Europe.

The Grassi heraldic device was not de' Rossi's only commission from Bolognese nobility. Vasari reported that she carved in marble a portrait bust of *Conte Guido Peppoli* (Museo di San Petronio, Bologna) to demonstrate her mastery of the medium in the hope of securing work on the decorative project for the church of San Petronio. Given the influential role played by Guido's son Alessandro Peppoli in the awarding of commissions for this project, and considering the appearance of de' Rossi's name in Fabbrica records from 1525, there is little reason to question Vasari on this point.

On 15 January and 5 April 1526 two other sculptors engaged on the San Petronio façade, Tribolo and Alfonso Lombardi, were paid for "models made by Propertia". Several months later, on 4 August, the balance of her account for carvings of two sibyls, at least two angels and a "panel" (*quadro*) was settled for 40 lire. While the earlier payment records indicate that de' Rossi was not paid directly, the amount she received is commensurate with the compensation given to her male peers. Vasari is responsible for identifying the *quadro* in question, a relief depicting *Joseph Fleeing Potiphar's Wife* (Museo di San Petronio, Bologna). The muscular figure types and classicising profiles bear a striking resemblance to Raphael's rendition of the story in the Vatican Logge, Rome, an image subsequently engraved by Marcantonio Raimondi (c.1517; National Gallery of Art, Washington, DC). Since in the second edition of the *Vite* Vasari notes his acquisition of "some very good [pen] drawings" by de' Rossi's hand "copied from works by Raphael", it is likely that her conception of classical form owes a debt to artistic developments in Rome during the 1510s. Accepted as an autograph work, *Joseph Fleeing Potiphar's Wife* is the measure for identifying de' Rossi's hand elsewhere on San Petronio's façade. *Potiphar's Wife Accusing Joseph* seems a plausible candidate. It is not clear which of the many sibyls and angels flanking and surrounding the portals might be attributed to her. What, if any, effect de' Rossi's confrontations with Bologna's civil and criminal justice authorities in 1525 had on her relationship with the Fabbrica is uncertain, but her name disappears from the records after the payment of 4 August 1526, with the sole exception of being listed as a patient in the Ospedale di San Giobbe, a hospital reserved for indigents, in April 1529. Although Vasari says that she spent her last years working in engraving, no works in this medium have been attributed to her.

FREDRIKA H. JACOBS

Rozanova, Olga (Vladimirovna)

Russian painter, printmaker, designer and poet, 1886–1918   [fig. 62]

Born in Melenki, near Vladimir, 22 June (Old Style calendar)/4 July (New Style calendar) 1886; father police chief Vladimir Rozanov. Studied art in Moscow at the private Bolshakov School of Painting and Sculpture, 1904–9; also took classes in Konstantin Yuon's studio. Joined Soyuz molodyozhi (Union of Youth), and moved to St Petersburg, 1911; began to participate regularly in their half-yearly exhibitions and to contribute to the journal of the same name; wrote Union of Youth manifesto, 1913. From 1913 worked on many book-design projects with Futurist poet Alexei Kruchyonykh, who became her companion; they never married, due to their anarchic beliefs. Member of Kazimir Malevich's group Supremus, 1916–17. Active after the Revolution in the organisation of the first professional union of Russian artists, 1917–18, and joined IZO, Narkompros (Fine Arts Section, People's Commissariat of Enlightenment). Died from diphtheria in Moscow, 7 November 1918.

Principal Exhibitions

Soyuz molodyozhi (Union of Youth), St Petersburg: 1911–13

Galleria Sprovieri, Roma: 1914 (*Libera mostra internazionale futurista di pittura e scultura*)

Petrograd: 1915 (*Tramway V: First Futurist Exhibition of Paintings*), 1915 (*0.10 [Zero-Ten]: Last Futurist Exhibition of Paintings*)

Bubnovy valet (Jack/Knave of Diamonds), Moscow: 1917

Moscow: 1917 (*Verbovka: Contemporary Applied Art*), 1918 (*First Exhibition of Paintings by the Professional Union of Artists of Moscow*), 1918 (retrospective)

Selected Writings

"Cubism, Futurism, Suprematism", *Von der Malerei zum Design*, exh. cat., Cologne, 1981

"The bases of the New Creation", *Russian Art of the Avant-garde: Theory and Criticism, 1902–1934*, ed.

John E. Bowlt, 2nd edition, London and New York: Thames and Hudson, 1988

"Manifest soyuza molodyozhi" [Manifesto of the Union of Youth] and "Kubizm, Futurizm, Suprematizm", *Neizvestniy Russkiy Avangard* [The unknown Russian avant-garde], ed. A. Sarabyanov and Nina Guryanova. Moscow, 1992

Bibliography

Pervaya gosudarstvennaya vystavka: Posmertnaya vystavka kartin, etyudov, eskizov i risunkov O.V. Rozanovoy [First State exhibition: Posthumous exhibition of paintings, studies, sketches and drawings by O.V. Rozanova], exh. cat., Moscow, 1918

Varst (V. Stepanova), "O vystavke Rozanovoy" [On Rozanova's exhibition], *Iskusstvo*, no.4, 22 February 1919

A. Efros, "O. Rozanova", *Profili*, Moscow, 1930, pp.228–9

Camilla Gray, *The Great Experiment: Russian Art, 1863–1922*, London: Thames and Hudson, and New York: Abrams, 1962

Nikolai Khardzhiyev, ed., *K istoriy russkogo avangarda/The Russian Avant-Garde*, Stockholm: Hylaea, 1976

Künstlerinnen der russischen Avantgarde/Women Artists of the Russian Avant-Garde, 1910–1930, exh. cat., Galerie Gmurzynska, Cologne, 1979

Angelica Zander Rudenstine, ed., *The George Costakis Collection: Russian Avant-Garde Art*, New York: Abrams, and London: Thames and Hudson, 1981

Gerald Janacek, *The Look of Russian Literature: Avant-Garde Visual Experiments, 1900–1930*, Princeton: Princeton University Press, 1984

Vera Terechina, "Majakowski und Rosanowa", *Bildende Kunst*, no.11, 1988, pp.499–501

Nina Guryanova, "Na puti k novomu iskusstvu: Olga Rozanova" [Towards the new art: Olga Rozanova], *Iskusstvo*, no.1, 1989

Charlotte Humphreys, *Cubo-Futurism in Russia, 1912–1922: The Transformation of a Painterly Style*, PhD dissertation, University of St Andrews, 1989

E.F. Kovtun, *Russkaya futuristicheskaya kniga* [The Russian Futurist book], Moscow: Kniga, 1989

V. Terekhina, "O.V. Rozanova", *Panorama iskusstv*, xi, Moscow, 1989, pp.38–62

M.N. Yablonskaya, *Women Artists of Russia's New Age, 1900–1935*, New York: Rizzoli, and London: Thames and Hudson, 1990

Olga Rozanova, exh. cat., Moscow, 1992

John E. Bowlt and N. Misler, *The Thyssen-Bornemisza Collection: Twentieth-Century Russian and East European Painting*, New York, 1993

L'Avant-garde russe, 1905–1925, exh. cat., Musée des Beaux-Arts, Nantes, and elsewhere, 1993

Nina Guryanova, "Olga Rozanova: Colore libero", *Art e Dossier*, no.85, December 1993, pp.37–43

——, "Suprematism and transrational poetry", *Elementa*, i, 1994, pp.369–83

The direction of Russian avant-garde art – with its characteristic traits of constant renewal, bold experimentation and negation of previous traditions – was fully reflected in Rozanova's painting, poetry and theoretical articles. Her complicated daily life hurtled through war, revolution, disorder, poverty and, at times, extreme isolation and incomprehension. During her artistic training in Konstantin Yuon's studio, she created several works in Post-Impressionist and Neo-primitivist styles, but soon went over to the Cubist and Futurist trends. From the very beginning of her mature artistic career (which lasted only eight years) Rozanova preferred abstract compositions, based on dynamics, interactions of colour and discordant linear rhythms, which were created, as it were, "in a single breath", in contrast to the plot-oriented scenes and "literariness" of traditional Russian art. She often experimented with new painterly techniques and genres. Futuristic works by Rozanova (who never travelled outside Russia) were so unusual and innovative that they were introduced in the Russian section of the first Futurist exhibition in Rome in 1914 alongside paintings by Alexandra Exter (q.v.) and sculpture by Alexander Archipenko, who were both already well known in Europe. During the next four years Kazimir Malevich, Mayakovsky, Khlebnikov, Rodchenko and Lyubov Popova (q.v.) were among Rozanova's friends and collaborators.

From 1911 to 1914 Rozanova was a leading member of the Union of Youth, one of the first associations of avant-garde artists in Russia, located in St Petersburg. Among the participants were Pavel Filonov, Malevich and David Burlyuk, who worked in the so-called Cubo-Futurist style. During these years, the most fruitful of her career, Rozanova moved gradually from early Neo-primitivist still lifes and portraits, such as *Still Life* (1912–13; Saratov State Art Museum), *Blue Vase with Flowers* (1912; State Russian Museum, St Petersburg) and *Woman in a Pink Dress (Portrait of A.V. Rozanova, Sister of the Artist)* (1911–12; Ekaterinburg Museum of Fine Arts; all oil on canvas), towards the new Futurist dynamism and expressiveness of abstraction with scenes of the industrial city and its spiritual disharmony. Her best compositions in this genre – *Embankment* (Thyssen-Bornemisza Collection), *City (Industrial Landscape)* (Historical Museum, Slobodskoy), *The Port* (untraced), *Man in the Street* (Thyssen-Bornemisza Collection), *Construction Work* (Samara Art Museum; all 1913;

oil on canvas) and *Fire in the City* (1914; oil on tinplate; Samara Art Museum) – are characterised by rich surface texture, a combination of a light point touch with an energetic, wide brush stroke, and the striking application of a black line or contour, creating a strong feeling of dissonance.

Suprematist abstraction was already anticipated in Rozanova's canvases of 1914–15, such as *Playing Cards (Series)* (1915), *Metronome* (1915; Tretyakov Gallery, Moscow), *Writing Desk* (1915; State Russian Museum, St Petersburg; all oil on canvas) and *Workbox* (1915; oil and collage with lace on canvas; Tretyakov Gallery). These works display a painterly construction composed of colour planes that served as a background for "random" highlighted objects or details. The purely Cubo-Futurist "intonation" of the street scene, which stressed dynamism and simultaneity, is no longer present. On the contrary, these constructions can be seen as a kind of hypothetical "picture" or rebus offered to the viewer. As a rule, the isolated sign, or object, or signboard, etc., "torn off" from its usual context, becomes a requisite attribute of such compositions, and the irrational laws of construction for such painterly texts were in many ways identical to the laws governing the construction of the new transrational poetry, created by the Russian Futurists.

Rozanova's powerful lyrical sense and ability to improvise marked her out from the start as an independent talent. As Alexei Kruchyonykh noted in one of his books: "Rozanova knows how to introduce feminine cunning into all the 'horrors of Cubism', which is so startlingly unexpected that it confuses many people." Rozanova's graphic work suited itself perfectly to the style, intonation and internal logic of verse by Kruchyonykh, who was also the inventor and theoretician of the transrational (*zaum*) language. In 1913 he published his famous manifesto *The Word as Such*, in which he proclaimed "a new verbal form", "a language lacking a determinate rational meaning". The artistic and personal ties between Rozanova and Kruchyonykh were most fruitful, and resulted in the creation of the unique style of Russian Futurist books. *Vzorval* (Explodity), in which Rozanova's lithographs appear alongside works by Malevich and Natalya Goncharova (q.v.), *Utinoye gnezdyshko … durnykh slov* (A duck's nest … of dirty words), *Igra v adu* (A game in hell), *Te li le* (Te li le) and others were produced in 1913–14. *Te li le* was made in the genre of "colourful auto-writing" invented by Rozanova, an early virtuoso demonstration of visual poetry, in which line was the equivalent of the word, and colour the equivalent of sound.

In 1915–16 Rozanova and Kruchyonykh created a new version of the Futurist book by using collages made from coloured paper. Rozanova employed this technique in designing a book by Kruchyonykh and Alyagrov (pseudonym for Roman Jakobson), *Zaumnaya Gniga* (Transrational book; 1915), and a portfolio of verse by Kruchyonykh entitled *Voyna* (War; 1916), which contained colour linocuts and collages. Rozanova was so enthusiastic about transrational poetry that she began to compose verse influenced by Kruchyonykh's work. Kruchyonykh, in his turn, applied himself to visual art, and under Rozanova's guidance created some collages, publishing them in his album *Vselenskaya voyna* (Universal war; 1916). In the preface to this edition he declared "transrational" (here in the sense of abstract) painting to be the winner, and wrote: "it was Rozanova, who first gave examples of the style that now is given the inexpressive name of Suprematism by other artists … Transrational language, of which I am the first representative, gives its hand to transrational painting." During this period, Rozanova arrived at abstraction: through the medium of coloured-paper collage she was able to solve purely painterly issues, similar to those with which Malevich was dealing in his Suprematist compositions.

Malevich greatly appreciated Rozanova's painting of this period, and in a polemic recognised her as "the only true Suprematist". In such sophisticated abstract paintings as *Suprematism* (State Russian Museum), *Suprematism* (Tretyakov Gallery) and *Suprematism: Flight of the Aeroplane* (Samara Art Museum; all 1916; oil on canvas) Rozanova reveals the discordant concordance of coloured planes through the effects of their interaction and the rhythm that had been liberated from objectivity. In 1916–18 she worked in close collaboration with Malevich, as a member of his group Supremus and secretary-editor of their magazine.

From the beginning of her artistic career, colour was Rozanova's main concern – in theory, and in practical experimentation with new ideas of colour schemes. In 1916–17 she tried to formulate her own concept on this matter in the article "Kubizm, Futurizm, Suprematizm". She created her own variant of Suprematism (defined as *tsvetopis*), in which the emphasis moved from form and painterly texture to the spiritual, mystical qualities of colour and its interconnection with light. One of the best examples of this style is *Green Stripe* (1917; Costakis Collection; another version of the same title in Rostov Museum), once part of triptych (the other two canvases, *Purple Stripe* and *Yellow Stripe*, are untraced and probably destroyed), as well as *Non-Objective Composition* (1917; Simbirsk Art Museum). At the same time Rozanova was considering some of the projects involving the projection of strong light into the open space of the Moscow stadium. Her ideas influenced Rodchenko, who created a whole series of compositions named *tsvetopis* in 1918–19.

The last year of Rozanova's life, 1918, was dedicated not only to painting but also to social action: she wrote several polemical articles on the poetics of anarchy in art in the newspaper *Anarkhiya* (Anarchy), closed by the Bolsheviks at the end of that year.

One of the most original, fascinating and distinguished artists of the Russian avant-garde of the 1910s, Rozanova is still not well known. Her premature death in 1918 prevented her from receiving the place in history that belongs to her: after her death, her paintings shared the fate of avant-garde art after the Revolution, when masterpieces by Kandinsky, Malevich and Chagall were sent to provincial museums, many of them to be destroyed in the 1930s. Almost all of Rozanova's archive was destroyed during the Russian Civil War. As a result, for many years her name was a mere "legend" for scholars. It was only in the 1970s that her "rebirth" began: some of her articles on art were translated into English for the first time, and her paintings began to be shown in various exhibitions of the Russian avant-garde. The Futurist books and paintings by Rozanova have found their places in such world-famous collections as the State Russian Museum, St Petersburg; Tretyakov Gallery, Moscow; Thyssen-Bornemisza Collection; Galerie Gmurzynska and Ludwig Museum, Germany; Marinetti Collection, Rome; and the Russian avant-garde collection of the late George Costakis, to whom belongs the following words about Rozanova's work:

Shortly after the end of the Second World War, by accident, I encountered some avant-garde art. The painting I saw first was done in 1917, yet it might easily have been a revolutionary work of about 1950. Indeed it might almost have been mistaken for a canvas by Barnett Newman, who, to be sure, had no knowledge of its existence. Olga Rozanova was the artist, and she died in 1918. It was her work that opened my eyes to the existence and compelling power of the avant-garde [Rudenstine 1981].

NINA GURYANOVA

Ruysch, Rachel

[fig. 60]

Dutch painter, 1664–1750

Born in The Hague; baptised in the Groote Kerk, 3 June 1664; father the eminent scientist Frederik Ruysch; maternal grandfather Pieter Post, architect to the Dutch stadhouder. Moved to Amsterdam with her family, 1667. Studied under the flower painter Willem van Aelst. Married portrait painter Juriaen Pool II, 1693; ten children, none of whom became painters, born 1695–1711. Both Ruysch and her husband became guild members in The Hague. Court painter to the Elector Palatine, Johann Wilhelm, in Düsseldorf, 1708–16. Died in Amsterdam, 12 October 1750.

Bibliography

Jan van Gool, *De nieuwe schouburg der Nederlandsche kunstschilders en schilderessen* [The new theatre of Netherlandish male and female painters], i, The Hague, 1750; reprinted Soest, 1971, pp.210–33

Jean-Baptiste Descamps, *La Vie des peintres flamands, allemands et hollandais*, iii, Paris, 1760

John Smith, *A Catalogue Raisonné of the Works of the Most Eminent Dutch, Flemish and French Painters*, vi, London, 1835; reprinted 1908

Abraham Bredius, "Das Nachlass-Inventare von Juriaen Pool", *Künstler-Inventare: Urkunden zur Geschichte der holländischen Kunst des XVIten, XVIIten und XVIIIten Jahrhunderts*, 8 vols, The Hague: Nijhoff, 1915–22, v, pp.1203–9

Cornelis Hofstede de Groot, *Beschreibendes und kritisches Verzeichnis der Werke des hervorragensten holländischen Maler des XVII. Jahrhunderts*, x, Esslingen, 1928, pp.309–31

Maurice H. Grant, *Rachel Ruysch, 1664–1750*, Leigh-on-Sea: Lewis, 1956

Werner Timm, "Bemerkungen zu einem Stilleben von Rachel Ruysch" [Remarks on a still life by Rachel Ruysch], *Oud-Holland*, lxxvii, 1962, pp.137–8

Jaromir Síp, "Notities bij het stilleven van Rachel Ruysch" [Notes on the still life by Rachel Ruysch], *Nederlands Kunsthistorisch Jaarboek*, xix, 1968, pp.157–70

Peter Mitchell, *European Flower Painters*, London: A. & C. Black, 1973

Women Artists, 1550–1950, exh. cat., Los Angeles County Museum of Art, and elsewhere, 1976

A Flowery Past: A Survey of Dutch and Flemish Painting from 1600 until the Present, exh. cat., Kunsthandel P. de Boer, Amsterdam, and Noordbrabants Museum, 's-Hertogenbosch, 1982

Yvonne Friedrichs, "Adriaen van der Werff und Rachel Ruysch: Zwei Hofmaler des Kürfursten Johann Wilhelm von der Pfalz in Düsseldorf", *Weltkunst*, vi, 1984, pp.712–15

Marianne Berardi, "The nature pieces of Rachel Ruysch", *Porticus*, x–xi, 1987–8, pp.2–15

Stillevens uit de Gouden Eeuw/Still Life Paintings from the Golden Age, exh. cat., Museum Boymans-van Beuningen, Rotterdam, 1989

Jan Davidsz. de Heem en zijn Kring [Jan Davidsz. de Heem and his circle], exh. cat., Centraal Museum, Utrecht, and Herzog Anton Ulrich-Museum, Braunschweig, 1991

Die Karl und Magdalene Haberstock-Stiftung, exh. cat., Munich and Augsburg, 1991

Mauritshuis in Bloei: Boeketten uit de Gouden Eeuw/Mauritshuis in Bloom: Bouquets from the Golden Age, exh. cat., Zwolle and The Hague, 1992

Renate Trnek, "Ruysch, Rachel," *Die holländischen Gemälde des 17. Jahrhunderts in der Gemälde-Galerie der Akademie der Bildenden Künste in Wien*, Vienna: Bohlau, 1992, pp.333–42

Erika Gemar-Koeltzsch, *Luca Bild-Lexikon: Holländische Stillebenmaler des 17. Jahrhundert*, iii, Lingen: Luca, 1995

Wiepke Loos and others, *The Age of Elegance: Paintings from the Rijksmuseum in Amsterdam, 1700–1800*, Amsterdam: Rijksmuseum, 1995

Paul Taylor, *Dutch Flower Painting, 1600–1720*, New Haven and London: Yale University Press, 1995

Rachel Ruysch was the most celebrated Dutch woman artist of the 17th and 18th centuries, and enjoyed a long and prosperous life as one of Holland's most esteemed flower painters (her main artistic rival was Jan van Huysum). Her career intersected with the lives of scientists, artists, wealthy Dutch merchants, powerful politicians and an international group of aristocratic patrons, creating a fascinating web of cross-disciplinary influences.

Archival records suggest that Ruysch lived in Amsterdam, the commercial capital of Holland, for all but the first three years of her life – initially in her parents' house on the Bloemgracht (flower canal), and from the time of her marriage until her death on the nearby Wolvenstraat. Her lucrative artistic career spanned more than 65 years, and she continued to paint well into her eighties. Her earliest dated work, a floral festoon (private collection, New York), is from 1681; her latest, companion paintings of nosegays (Musée des Beaux-Arts, Lille) are dated 1747.

Ruysch owed part of her professional success to her father, a man of astonishing energy and one of the most remarkable scientists of his time. Over a 90-year lifespan, Frederik Ruysch catalogued the Amsterdam botanical garden, which he expanded to the richest in the world; developed new techniques of obstetrics; invented an improved embalming fluid and method of surgical injection; and created the first natural history museum in Europe in a few rented rooms on the Nieuwezijds Achterburgwal – while simultaneously engaging in heated disputes with hostile religious figures and rival scientists, and corresponding with Sir Isaac Newton and Marcello Malpighi, among others. Like his daughter, he was also a shrewd entrepreneur, amassing a sizeable fortune from his scientific work, and gaining patrons from as far away as Russia, where he drew support from Peter the Great. Contemporary sources show that Dr Ruysch drew his family into his scientific adventures, particularly the preservation and display of rare specimens – a new art form of its own. In his cabinets, embalmed hydrocephalic children, wrapped in their own intestines, and other such wonders were arranged like *tableaux vivants* – playing instruments and engaging in other lifelike activities. Rachel Ruysch's woodland still-life paintings of *c*.1683–9, in which fire-breathing lizards are juxtaposed with accurately observed grasses and bindweeds, exhibit a similar mixture of science and fantasy, didacticism and entertainment. Clearly, Rachel's childhood experience in preparing specimens schooled her in the theatrics of visual arrangement.

At the age of 15, Ruysch studied with the noted flower painter Willem van Aelst. Once launched, her career followed a logical course. She seems to have set clearly defined artistic problems for herself, mastered them with a single-minded focus and then moved on to a new set of challenges. Generally, she tended to concentrate on a particular type of still life, or a specific way of composing it, for a period of five to seven years before shifting to something new. Throughout her career, however, she remained focused on fruit, flowers and nature pieces, never seeming to deviate from that speciality into other genres of still life, such as breakfast, *vanitas*,

banquet, kitchen and hunting pieces. It is particularly interesting that she seems to have had no interest in painting game pieces despite her familiarity with zoology and her teacher van Aelst's reputation for painting exquisite trophies of the hunt. Her nature pieces differ from those of her male contemporaries because the violent encounters she depicts between insects and reptiles never seem to result in dead animals.

Ruysch spent approximately the first decade of her career (*c*.1679–91) painting a wider variety of still life than she did at any other point in her life. She painted floral garlands and flower and fruit festoons against dark backgrounds and shallow niches (National Gallery, Prague); nature pieces with mossy banks, caves and dark woodland pools in the manner of both Otto Marseus van Schrieck (Glasgow Art Gallery and Museum; University of Rostock; Fitzwilliam Museum, Cambridge; Gemäldegalerie Alte Meister, Dresden; National Gallery, Prague) and Jan Davidsz. de Heem (Schloss Wilhelmshöhe, Kassel; Memorial Art Gallery, University of Rochester, NY; Museum Boijmans Van Beuningen, Rotterdam); fruit still lifes with peaches and grapes on a simple marble ledge (ex-Christie's, New York, 12 January 1996, lot 96); and small bouquets of flowers in blown-glass goblets or vases placed on a ledge (Hamburger Kunsthalle, Hamburg), sometimes with gold-fringed velvet cloths nearby. These paintings imitated the work of van Aelst and his colleagues quite closely, but showed Ruysch's great skill in designing a range of compositions and rendering a wide variety of textures. She also learned to paint landscape as a back-drop for her outdoor still lifes, but these glimpses of scenery are seldom as convincing as the still lifes in front of them, and often have the feeling of a natural history diorama.

Being a woman presented serious obstacles to the next phase of Ruysch's career. She was not admitted to the Amsterdam painters' guild, which did not accept women to its membership, and consequently she could not sell her works as an independent artist. This probably explains why, for approximately five years from 1690 to 1695, her paintings were quite modest in scale and in subject. In this period, Ruysch seems to have devoted her efforts to painting small-scale nosegays, which often contain about a dozen varieties of common garden flowers. She presented these intimate bouquets rather casually on a marble or stone ledge, against plain dark backgrounds (Fitzwilliam Museum; Gemäldegalerie Alte Meister, Dresden; Hamburger Kunsthalle; Victoria and Albert Museum, London; Norton Simon Museum, Pasadena). Van Aelst also painted this type of composition, but chose larger, more formal flowers such as roses for his bouquets, and rendered them in a harder manner with cooler hues. By contrast, Ruysch's nosegays include not only roses but columbine and snapdragons, and often use field grasses and garden herbs (ribbon grass and rue are favourites) to create a web of graceful linear rhythms that soften the edges of the bouquet. The overall effect is wistfully romantic. Her bouquets appear to have been discarded absent-mindedly, the stems of the flowers often falling in all directions, since the string that bound them has slipped away. During the last half of the 1690s Ruysch painted traditional arrangements of flowers in a glass vase, but designed them along an S-curve from lower left to upper right (Städelsches Kunstinstitut und Städtische Galerie, Frankfurt am Main) and suffused them in a smoky atmosphere. Sometimes Ruysch introduced a landscape element or glimpse of sky into the dark backgrounds, which recalled her work with nature pieces from the previous decade (Musée Thomas Henry, Cherbourg). The asymmetry of these bouquets, with their snipped-off central blossom, also had its roots in van Aelst's floral arrangements.

In 1701 Ruysch and her husband became members of the painters' guild in The Hague, where women were welcome. Interestingly, at this point Ruysch's sex became an asset rather than a detriment to her career. Having been not only much better trained and educated than most women artists of the period – who seldom rose above the rank of amateur – but also more thoroughly schooled in flower painting than many men, she became a "celebrity". In less flattering terms, she was a "curiosity", who reached the pinnacle of success in a discipline in which there were no models for women. During her years in the guild at The Hague, Ruysch began to paint her first major flower-pieces, which she sold to an international group of patrons. These paintings feature spectacular horticultural specimens, including varieties that the Dutch had only recently begun to hybridise. Ruysch organised the flowers comprising these bouquets within a pronounced triangular geometry. The largest, most striking blossoms are pushed forward to define the surface of the triangle and are painted as though under a spotlight. During this period, Ruysch frequently placed a piece of fruit, and sometimes a fallen blossom, on the table top beside the vase. Perhaps her most exquisite work from the guild years, and unquestionably her finest painting in an American museum, is the flower-piece with an aubergine on a ledge (1704), recently acquired by the Detroit Institute of Arts.

From 1707 Ruysch began to paint ambitious outdoor fruit pieces as pendants to her prize floral bouquets, and such pendants became one of her specialities after she gained court patronage. She invariably placed a bounty of cultivated fruit in a setting rather incongruous for such unnaturally occurring produce – in deep woodlands usually in front of a cave. The idea for this subject derives from paintings by Abraham Mignon, which are in turn derived from compositions by Jan Davidsz. de Heem. Although Ruysch adapted Mignon's general subject matter, probably from first-hand knowledge of his paintings, her displays are none the less significantly different in appearance and probably in intention. Mignon, a devoutly religious man, described each piece of fruit with strong outline and full illumination, as if each specimen rested clearly in the light of religious truth. In Ruysch's work, by contrast, the fruit seems to be a more ambiguous emblem of the overwhelming variety, abundance and mystery of nature. Consequently, her fruit scenes exist in a kind of murky, somewhat forbidding half-light. In a painting of 1714 (Städtische Kunstsammlungen, Augsburg) she combined both a harvest of fruit and an overflowing basket of flowers within a single canvas, creating one of her most sumptuous outdoor compositions.

Ruysch's skill was such that in 1708 she was offered an appointment as court painter in Düsseldorf by the Elector Palatine, Johann Wilhelm, an admirer of the *fijnschilder* technique (a detailed and polished method of painting). The Elector bought everything that Ruysch produced over a four-year period (1710–13), and sent two of her paintings (Uffizi, Florence) to his Medici in-laws in Florence as a gift.

Ruysch's flower-pieces of the Düsseldorf period maintain the dark backgrounds of her earlier work. She moved away from bouquets of triangular shape, however, preferring rounder arrangements centred on a bright triad of blossoms, usually roses. In an effort to create more graceful, natural-looking compositions, she often surrounded her bright centres with smaller, more delicate flowers that let the darkness sift through them to form a rather ambiguous perimeter to the arrangement. Ruysch would then place a few large dramatic blossoms at the outer edge. These perimeter accents vary from painting to painting, but generally consist of African marigolds, flamed tulips, sunflowers, a cluster of primroses, a cabbage rose and a passion flower (Alte Pinakothek, Munich; Rijksmuseum, Amsterdam).

After the death of the Elector (1716) until 1723, Ruysch continued to paint fruit and flower pieces, often on a somewhat less grand scale, for patrons in the Netherlands and abroad. Her work became increasingly refined, with the central core of the bouquet growing in density and becoming a more sculptural mass of blossoms. In 1723 Ruysch, her husband and their son Georgio won the Holland jackpot of 60,000 florins, a windfall that seems to have led to a substantial drop in Ruysch's productivity as a painter for approximately one decade. From the mid-1720s to 1730s no known works survive, although there are several paintings from these years attributed to Ruysch in old sale catalogues and inventories.

By the 1720s the trend in flower painting had begun to shift away from the darker backgrounds favoured by Ruysch, which ultimately depend upon the work of painters from the previous generation, such as Jan Davidsz. de Heem and Willem van Aelst. Taste began to favour lighter backgrounds and more pastel hues, a trend that Ruysch herself never entirely followed, although her few surviving works from the years 1739, 1741, 1742 and 1743 show a tentative move in that direction. Jan van Huysum set the model for this brighter style, which carried flower painting into the late 18th century. During the last five years of her life, from 1745 onwards, although her eyesight and steadiness of hand were clearly failing, Ruysch again began to produce paintings with some frequency. These nosegays are similiar in composition to those that she produced in the 1690s but with much less sure draughtsmanship.

By the time of her death, Ruysch's career had been celebrated in published biographies and poems and her paintings sold for prices in excess of 1000 guilders, equalled by only half a dozen other Dutch painters. Her first biographer, Jan van Gool, visited the elderly Ruysch for an interview in her home two years before her death and found it remarkable that she was still at work. Impressed with Ruysch as both a personality and artist of great achievement, van Gool devoted one of the longest biographies in *De nieuwe schouburg* to her. The *bloemschilderesse* herself was memorialised in several portraits by other artists, including works by Juriaen Pool II (Stadtmuseum, Düsseldorf; Museum Boijmans Van Beuningen; Stedelijk Museum "De Lakenhal", Leiden), Aert Schouman (Rijksmuseum), Arnold Houbraken (etching after Schouman published in van Gool's biography of her), Godfried Schalcken (Cheltenham Art Gallery and Museums), Ludolf Bakhuysen (Hermitage, St Petersburg) and Michiel van Musscher (private collection, London). Ruysch's fame remained unparalleled by any woman artist until Elisabeth Vigée-Lebrun (q.v.).

Approximately 100 paintings by Ruysch are known to survive today, although records of paintings sold during her lifetime suggest that she produced nearly twice that number, averaging about three per year. She worked primarily on canvas, but occasionally produced works on panel and copper. Throughout her career, Ruysch maintained her maiden name and usually signed her paintings in full in the lower right or left corner, often dating them as well. Her signature changed over the years, from a large, highly calligraphic script with strong flourishes to one that was increasingly smaller and simplified. The signatures on her late works from the 1740s are an exception, for they are proportionally quite large for the paintings, and often include the artist's age – almost as a symbol of pride that she was still at the easel.

Many of Ruysch's finest and most ambitious paintings are preserved in German museums, having come from the collection of her work in the Elector Palatine's Düsseldorf gallery. No drawings by Ruysch's hand have yet been securely identified, although like many other flower painters of the period she doubtless kept sketchbooks containing studies of individual blossoms. Michiel van Musscher's portrait of Rachel Ruysch from 1692 (noted above), which depicts the artist in her studio preparing to paint a flower-piece, implies just this. Before her are a bouquet of live flowers as well as three pattern or sketchbooks – suggesting that she worked both from nature and from reference drawings made after nature. On 25 January 1751, three months after Ruysch's death, an anonymous collection of prints, drawings and rarities was sold through a book dealer in Amsterdam. The sale included 12 sheets of flower drawings described as being by Ruysch. These items may well have included some of Ruysch's own artistic reference material that her descendants (who were not painters) disposed of after her death.

Like numerous Dutch artists of the period, Ruysch may have occasionally collaborated with other painters. She is known to have contributed the floral bouquet to her husband's painting of their family group in 1716 (Stadtmuseum, Düsseldorf). She apparently had no students outside her family. She probably taught her sister Anna Elisabeth (1666–after 1741) as well as her father to paint. Recent scholarship suggests that Anna Ruysch was probably more prolific than previously supposed, and may well have studied directly with van Aelst, and Ernst Stuven, a German painter who trained with van Aelst, though these facts are not recorded. A nature piece bearing her signature (Staatliche Kunsthalle, Karlsruhe) copies a composition by Mignon (Musées royaux des Beaux-Arts de Belgique, Brussels). A bouquet of flowers in a footed vase in the Musée des Beaux-Arts, Rouen, which has a false Rachel Ruysch signature, is probably also by Anna Ruysch.

Ruysch's highly refined technique and the linear grace of her arrangements continued to be prized by collectors long after her death. Artists working in Germany, where Ruysch's best works were most numerous, often copied and mimicked her style well into the 18th century, even though the blonder tonalities were in vogue at the time. Her work seems to have had a particular attraction for other women flower painters. Jacobea Nikkelen, a pupil of Herman van der Mijn, who also worked at the court in Düsseldorf, produced bouquets with rather compact arrangements and low centres of gravity, reflecting Ruysch's manner. Interestingly, Ruysch's particular aesthetic seems to have skipped a generation, resurfacing in the mid-19th century. At that point, Victorian still-life painters began to employ many of her motifs: discarded nosegays on a slab, a bouquet of flowers left negligently in a wood, or a drama between weak and strong creatures (a theme that took on new meanings in the light of Darwinian theory). It is also striking that Ruysch's paintings entered British collections in great quantity during the Victorian period.

MARIANNE BERARDI

S

Saar, Betye

American sculptor, 1926–

Born Betye Irene Maze in Los Angeles, 30 July 1926; grew up in Pasadena, California. Studied at University of California, Los Angeles (BA 1949); California State University, Long Beach, 1958–62; University of Southern California, Los Angeles, 1962; California State University, Northridge, 1966; American Film Institute, Los Angeles, 1972. Married artist Richard W. Saar, 1952; three daughters (one the artist Alison Saar born 1956); divorced 1968. Instructor in art, California State University, Hayward, 1971, Northridge, 1973–4; Otis Art Institute, Los Angeles, 1976–83; lecturer and freelance designer for films, 1970–75; costume designer, Inner City Cultural Center, Napa Valley Theatre Company, 1968–73. Recipient of National Endowment for the Arts (NEA) grants, 1974 and 1984; J. Paul Getty fellowship, 1990; Guggenheim fellowship, 1991; James Van Der Zee grant, 1992; Fresno Art Museum Distinguished Artist award, California, 1993. Member, Los Angeles Institute of Contemporary Art. Lives in Los Angeles.

Selected Individual Exhibitions

Multi-Cul Gallery, Los Angeles: 1972
Berkeley Art Center, CA: 1973
Fine Arts Gallery, California State University, Los Angeles: 1973
Whitney Museum of American Art, New York: 1975
Wadsworth Atheneum, Hartford, CT: 1976
San Francisco Museum of Modern Art: 1977 (with Marie Johnson)
Studio Museum in Harlem, New York: 1980
Museum of Contemporary Art, Los Angeles: 1984, 1990
List Visual Arts Center, Massachusetts Institute of Technology, Cambridge: 1987
Wight Art Gallery, University of California, Los Angeles: 1990–91 (with Alison Saar, touring)
Objects Gallery, Chicago: 1991
Joseloff Gallery, University of Hartford, CT: 1992
University of Colorado Art Galleries, Boulder: 1992
Fresno Art Museum, CA: 1993
Santa Monica Museum of Art, CA: 1994
Exhibits USA: 1995 (*Personal Icons*, touring)

Bibliography

Betye Saar, exh. cat., Whitney Museum of American Art, New York, 1975
Cindy Nemser, "Conversation with Betye Saar", *Feminist Art Journal*, iv, Winter 1975–6, pp.19–24
Channing Johnson, "Betye Saar's 'Hoodoo' World of Art", *Essence*, March 1976, pp.84–5
Ishmael Reed, *Shrovetide in Old New Orleans*, New York: Doubleday, 1978
Phylis Floyd, "An interview with Betye Saar", *Kresge Art Museum Bulletin*, vii, 1979, pp.1–11
Eleanor Munro, *Originals: American Women Artists*, New York: Simon and Schuster, 1979
Houston Conwill, "Interview with Betye Saar", *Black Art: An International Quarterly*, iii/1, 1980, pp.4–15
Rituals: The Art of Betye Saar, exh. cat., Studio Museum in Harlem, New York, 1980
Crystal Britton, "Interview: Betye Saar", *Art Papers*, v, September–October 1981, pp.8–9
Gretchen Erskine Woelfle, "On the edge: Betye Saar, personal time travels", *Fiberarts*, ix, July–August 1982, pp.56–60
Betye Saar, exh. cat., Museum of Contemporary Art, Los Angeles, 1984
Betye Saar: Resurrection: Site Installations, 1977 to 1987, exh. cat., Art Gallery, California State University, Fullerton, 1988
Making Their Mark: Women Artists Move into the Mainstream, exh. cat., Cincinnati Art Museum, and elsewhere, 1989
Lilly Wei, "The peripatetic artist: 14 statements: Betye Saar", *Art in America*, lxxvii, July 1989, p.135
Lucy R. Lippard, *Mixed Blessings: New Art in a Multicultural America*, New York: Pantheon, 1990
Charlotte Streifer Rubinstein, *American Women Sculptors*, Boston: Hall, 1990
Secrets, Dialogues, Revelations: The Art of Betye and Alison Saar, exh. cat., Wight Art Gallery, University of California, Los Angeles, and elsewhere, 1990

Jon Etra, "Family ties", *Art News*, xc, May 1991, pp.128–33

M.J. Hewitt, "Betye Saar: An interview", *International African American Artist*, x/2, 1993, pp.7–15

Betye Saar: Secret Heart, exh. cat., Fresno Art Museum, CA, 1993

Lizzetta LeFalle-Collins, *The Art of Betye Saar and John Outtenbridge: The Poetics of Politics, Iconography and Spirituality*, Washington, DC: United States Information Agency, 1994

Betye Saar: Personal Icons, exh. cat., Exhibits USA, 1995

Growing up in Pasadena during the 1930s, Betye Saar often walked with her grandmother to see Simon Rodia craft mosaic and wire, broken bottles, mirrors and shells into his famous Watts Towers in Los Angeles. The experience sensitised her to the transformative power of artefacts, which, thanks to the ingenuity of folk artists, can become mysterious and magical works of art. Saar was first trained as a commercial artist and graphic designer, and she enjoyed a successful career in these fields while bringing up her three children. (Her daughter Alison is also a renowned artist, and once took a seminar that her mother taught at the Otis Art Institute.) Although she thought of herself as a painter, in 1966 Betye saw a retrospective exhibition of Joseph Cornell and was struck by the possibilities of assemblage. She was also spurred to experiment with mixed-media, perhaps unconsciously influenced by the southern California art scene, where assemblage dominated the art of the 1960s, best represented by the work of Ed Kienholz. Frequent excursions to natural history museums also fortified Saar's interest in the expressive language of artefacts.

In 1966 she created *Mystic Window for Leo* (artist's collection), the first of her so-called window assemblages, which reveal her ongoing concerns with history – here family history – and with the type of seeing that art makes possible. "The window", says Saar, "is a way of traveling from one level of consciousness to another, like the physical looking into the spiritual" (Los Angeles 1984, p.11). Betye studied diverse occult and spiritual traditions – voodoo and shamanism, phrenology and palmistry – and their symbols regularly appear in her work.

During the later 1960s and early 1970s, as the cries of the Civil Rights movement resonated in the background, Saar answered by again recalling history, this time the history of African-Americans, whose stereotypical images had been woven into the fabric of the majority culture. (Extensive and thought-provoking evaluation by both women and artists of colour, their place in art, culture and society, took centre stage in critical discussions of American art during these years. In southern California, projects such as Womanhouse in central Los Angeles and reformations in art instruction and criticism, as reflected in the program at the California Institute of the Arts in Valencia, resulted from such discussions. Although Saar was not directly involved with these groups, she felt their impact.) The assassination of Martin Luther King in 1968 convinced her to forgo the more autobiographical "windows" to produce boxes or "coffins", such as the *Liberation of Aunt Jemima* (1972; University of California Art Museum, Berkeley) and *Is Jim Crow Really Dead?* (1972; Dr Janice C. Johnson Collection, Los Angeles), which she acknowledges reflected the anger she felt at having been excluded from the political realm as well as the art world: "When I look back on it, I think I was angry" (Nemser 1975, p.20).

Although she softened her tone in the mid-1970s and the message seemingly became more subtle, Saar's later assemblages bespoke ongoing concerns with content and with history. "The content of my art", Saar wrote, "has progressed from ancestral history (ritual works), to family history (nostalgic works) to personal history ... My concerns, however, remain the same: the recycling and transformation of materials, the quality of texture, form, pattern, a sense of beauty, and mystery" (Los Angeles 1984, p.8). In the series entitled *Mojotech*, a centrepiece in her more recent work, symbols, artefacts and stories from both the mainstream Western culture as well as ancient traditions, such as those of Africa, Egypt and Mexico, express her fascination with systems of spirituality and technology, as well as the conflicts that invariably arise between them. Inspiration to pursue the theme came in part from a residency at the Massachusetts Institute of Technology in 1987, but the immediate trigger was the film *The Gods Must Be Crazy*. One can imagine that the sight of Simon Rodia using mirror, glass and wire to create his "fairy tale palace" in Watts also had a nascent impact. "Mojos combine mystical symbols with natural objects ... Each Mojo is constructed with a particular essence to act as its protective charm" (Johnson 1976, p.85). *Cryptic Confession: The Question* (1988; private collection), which is nearly identical to its counterpart *Cryptic Confessions: The Answer*

(1988; Kresge Art Museum, East Lansing), both belong to this group. Resembling ancient Persian miniatures, *Cryptic Confessions* are dominated by scarabs, *milagros*, Egyptian figurines and computer boards – prevalent in the second-hand shops of southern California where Saar seeks her source materials and which she first used for an assemblage in 1975 (*Samadhi*; High Museum, Atlanta). A rich blue ground, nearly universally associated with spirituality, she notes, dominates the two assemblages.

Throughout her career, Saar has resurrected found materials for altars (*Indigo Mercy*, 1976; Studio Museum in Harlem, New York), collages, murals and, since the late 1970s, installations. Among these, the *House of Gris Gris* (1988) was conceived in collaboration with her daughter, Alison, for a joint exhibition curated by the Wight Art Gallery of the University of California, Los Angeles, whose tour included a showing at the Museum of Contemporary Art in Chicago. While Saar uses found objects, each element, she explains, is selected for its "ancestral, ritual, autobiographical, nostalgic and historical aura". Individual elements embody their own histories, but they also take on a life and metaphysical meaning in combination with other materials. This resurrection and transformation, the mystery and magic they evoke, form the basis of Betye Saar's work.

PHYLIS FLOYD

Sage, Kay
American painter, 1898–1963

Born Katherine Linn Sage in Albany, New York, 25 June 1898; father a wealthy senator. Lived with her mother after parents' separation in 1900, attending a variety of schools in Europe and USA. Attended classes at Corcoran School of Art, Washington, DC, and worked as translator for Censorship Bureau, New York, during World War I. Studied painting and drawing at British School and Scuola Libera delle Belle Arti, Rome, 1920. Married Prince Ranieri di San Faustino, 1925; lived in Rome and Rapallo until divorce, 1935. Moved to Paris, 1937; discovered by the Surrealists after exhibiting a single painting at the Salon des Surindépendants. Returned to New York after outbreak of World War II and helped a number of Surrealists to escape there. Exhibited with the Surrealists in New York (1942) and Paris (1947). Married painter Yves Tanguy, 1940. Moved to Woodbury, Connecticut, 1941. Became reclusive after Tanguy's death in 1955. Stopped painting due to failing eyesight, 1958. Attempted suicide, 1959. Shot herself in Woodbury, 8 January 1963.

Selected Individual Exhibitions
Galleria del Milione, Milan: 1936
Pierre Matisse Gallery, New York: 1940
San Francisco Museum of Art: 1941
Julien Levy Gallery, New York: 1944, 1947
Catherine Viviano Gallery, New York: 1950, 1952, 1956, 1958, 1960 (retrospective), 1961
Galleria dell'Obelisco, Rome: 1953
Galerie Nina Dausset, Paris: 1953
Wadsworth Atheneum, Hartford, CT: 1954 (with Yves Tanguy)
Herbert F. Johnson Museum of Art, Cornell University, Ithaca, NY: 1977 (touring retrospective)

Selected Writings
"China eggs", manuscript, 1955, Archives of American Art, Washington, DC (autobiography)
Demain, Monsieur Silber, Paris: Seghers, 1957 (collected poems)
The More I Wonder, New York: Bookman, 1957 (poems)
Faut dire c'qui est, Paris: Debresse-Poésie, 1959 (poems)
Mordicus, Paris: Benoît, 1962
Yves Tanguy: Un recueil de ses oeuvres, New York: Matisse, 1963

Bibliography
Yves Tanguy, Kay Sage, exh. cat., Wadsworth Atheneum, Hartford, CT, 1954
Kay Sage: Retrospective Exhibition, 1937–1958, exh. cat., Catherine Viviano Gallery, New York, 1960
Kay Sage, 1898–1963, exh. cat., Herbert F. Johnson Museum of Art, Cornell University, Ithaca, NY, and elsewhere, 1977
Charlotte Streifer Rubinstein, *American Women Artists from Early Times to the Present*, Boston: Hall, 1982
Stephen R. Miller, "The Surrealist imagery of Kay Sage", *Art International*, xxvi, September–October 1983, pp.32–47, 54–6
Whitney Chadwick, *Women Artists and the Surrealist Movement*, Boston: Little Brown, and London: Thames and Hudson, 1985
La Femme et le surréalisme, exh. cat., Musée Cantonal des Beaux-Arts, Lausanne, 1987
Mary Ann Caws, Rudolf E. Kuenzli and Gwen Raaberg, eds, *Surrealism and Women*, Cambridge: Massachusetts Institute of Technology Press, 1991
Mara R. Witzling, ed., *Voicing Our Visions: Writings by Women Artists*, New York: Universe, 1991; London: Women's Press, 1992

Judith D. Suther, "Separate studios: Kay Sage and Yves Tanguy", *Significant Others: Creativity and Intimate Partnership*, ed. Whitney Chadwick and Isabelle de Courtivron, New York and London: Thames and Hudson, 1993, pp.136–53

Renée Riese Hubert, *Magnifying Mirrors: Women, Surrealism and Partnership*, Lincoln: University of Nebraska Press, 1994

Judith D. Suther, *Kay Sage: Solitary Surrealist* (in preparation)

Kay Sage was one of the few women artists to be officially designated as a participant in the Surrealist movement by André Breton, the group's leader (Charles Henri Ford, "Interview with André Breton", *View*, no.7–8, October–November 1941). However, her association with the Surrealists and marriage to the painter Yves Tanguy occurred well after the collective formulation of Surrealist doctrines. The influences of Giorgio de Chirico and Tanguy are immediately identifiable in her paintings, yet Sage's mature vocabulary of architectural scaffolding set in barren landscapes infused with a disquieting melancholy is intensely personal and entirely her own.

Sage studied drawing briefly at the Corcoran School of Art in 1919 before moving to Italy the following year. In Rome she enrolled in classes at the British School and Scuola Libera delle Belle Arti but took little interest in formal training. *Young Girl in Orange Dress* (c.1920; Mattatuck Museum, Waterbury, CT), one of the few known paintings from this period, is a standard academic portrait bearing a marked resemblance to the artist. Certainly the girl's sad, pensive expression conjures the psychological discomfort and loneliness expressed so forcefully in Sage's later imagined landscapes and poetry. Sage soon joined Onorato Carlandi, an older artist, on his weekly informal painting excursions to the countryside, producing realistic views of rolling hillsides (*Landscape with Poplar*, 1923; *Landscape with Five Trees*, 1923; both Mattatuck Museum). She considered the expansive horizons envisioned in her Surrealist canvases as originating from these early experiences: "I think my perspective idea of distance and going away is from my formative years in the Roman Campagna. There is always that long road and the feeling it gives that it goes a long way, and living near the Mediterranean, the sea and boats, the feeling of the sun" (Julien Levy, "Tanguy, Connecticut, Sage", *Art News*, liii, September 1954, p.27).

Sage rarely painted during the years of her marriage to an Italian prince, but in 1936, only one year after separating from her husband, she held her first solo exhibition at the Galleria del Milione in Milan. It included geometric abstract paintings, of which few survive. One transitional work, *Untitled* (c.1930; Collection Daniel Filipacchi), marks a significant departure from the landscapes of the early 1920s, with its Cubist rooftops composed of jutting diagonals and horizontals. In place of the conventional device of trees uniting fore- and background, a monolithic building rises incongruously from amidst the low houses; the mountains are reduced to an undulating line across a blank sky. A non-representational idiom of overlapping geometric forms is adopted in *Vorticist* (c.1935; Mattatuck Museum), a small oil on panel. Ezra Pound, a friend of Sage's, may have introduced her to Vorticism, and perhaps even encouraged her to resume painting (Miller 1983, p.33).

Following Sage's move to Paris in 1937, the considerable impact of de Chirico is evident in the gradual evolution from abstraction to dreamscapes occupied by mysterious objects with elusive meanings. This shift is illustrated in *Afterwards* (1937; Colorado Springs Fine Arts Center), in which slatted shapes of varying sizes appear stacked haphazardly at an exaggeratedly tilted perspective. Slight shadows, a muted palette and minute, precise brushwork together lend a connotation of eerie stillness to what is still an abstract composition. Further configurations of geometric forms are placed in undefined settings with greater contrasts of light and dark (*Untitled*, c.1938, Collection Herbert B. Palmer; *Sempre*, 1938; repr. New York 1960, no.2). As a result, the objects exist in a space that seems simultaneously recognisable and ambiguous. Around 1940, Sage bought de Chirico's *Torment of the Poet* (1940). Her iconography of the late 1930s–early 1940s is primarily borrowed, though altered, from the Italian metaphysical painter, as Sage sought her own distinctive voice. It includes the egg, sloping ramp and arched doorway (*A Little Later*, 1938; Denver Art Museum; *My Room Has Two Doors*, 1939; Mattatuck Museum), distant diagonally cast shadows (*I Have No Shadow*, 1940; Worcester Art Museum, MA) and figures shrouded in drapery (*Near the Five Corners*, 1943; *ibid*, no.13; *The Hidden Letter*, 1944; Fine Arts Museums of San

Francisco; *I Saw Three Cities*, 1944; Princeton University Art Museum).

During her first year in Paris, Sage became acquainted with Surrealism and was especially impressed by the work of Tanguy. She met Tanguy, as well as Breton and other Surrealist colleagues, in the autumn of 1938. With the outbreak of World War II, Sage returned to New York, followed by Tanguy, and they married. These developments in Sage's personal life pertain directly to the formal path taken in her art, since Tanguy's stylistic influence would prove crucial both as inspiration and as catalyst for determining an individualistic course. Her concern that her work should not be perceived as derivative even made her reluctant to exhibit with Tanguy. In a joint interview in 1954, Sage remarked: "We are really concealed from each other in our work. He doesn't know what picture I am painting – although I take more interest in his than he does in mine – naturally" (Hartford 1954, pp.24–5).

Sage's paintings of the mid-1940s until Tanguy's death in 1955 are ultimately her strongest, for in them she realised her signature imagery. Already in works such as *Danger, Construction Ahead* (1940; Yale University Art Gallery, New Haven), *At the Appointed Time* (1942; Newark Museum) and *In the Third Sleep* (1944; Art Institute of Chicago) she created desolate vistas inhabited by angular, unidentifiable shapes concealed beneath drapery. While possessing similarities to Tanguy's meticulous depictions of vast plains peopled with imaginary forms, where Tanguy's figuration is biomorphic, Sage's remains decidedly non-organic, differentiating it from popular Surrealist imagery. Beginning with *Bounded on the West by the Land under Water* (1946; University of Michigan Museum of Art), scaffolding appears in her pictures; subsequently, architectural structures become a constant theme. These constructions are rearranged in a multitude of ways, but the external attributes of each silent landscape – parched beneath a blank sky illuminated by an unseen source, and painted in cool tones of silvery blue, ochre, grey and pale green – express an interior mental state of bleak isolation. An underlying sense of tragedy prevails throughout. In *All Soundings Are Referred to High Water* (1947; Davison Art Center, Wesleyan University), *The Instant* (1949; Mattatuck Museum) and *Unusual Thursday* (1951; repr. New York 1960, no.35) the scaffolding lies dismantled in the foreground, both leading the viewer in and acting as barrier.

Intermittently, drapery softens the harsh edges of forms. Interlocking slats obliterate all traces of the human face in *Small Portrait* (1950; Vassar College Art Gallery, Poughkeepsie, NY), with only reddish blond hair hinting at a female identity. In fact, this is one of two rare self-portraits. The thin latticework might combine with heavy upright boards (*Third Paragraph*, 1953; Mattatuck Museum), rest against a receding line of massive blocks (*No Passing*, 1954; Whitney Museum of American Art, New York) or be erected as a tower (*Hyphen*, 1954; *Tomorrow Is Never*, 1955; both Metropolitan Museum of Art, New York). Close-range perspectives from within the scaffolding in *Day Without Name* (1955; Collection Mr and Mrs Lee Ault, New York) and *A Bird in the Room* (1955; Cleveland Museum of Art) exude a particularly haunting element of confrontation. Unusually, both depict night scenes, which adds to the sinister effect; in the former, two rows of white cloths sway slightly; in the latter, rocks drip from vines like dead foliage. *Le Passage* (1956; Collection Mrs Wirt Davis II, Dallas), the second self-portrait, is anomalous within this period because it conveys the human figure and lacks scaffolding. The figure, shown from behind, hides her face and naked breasts as she pulls her hair forward, thereby denying typical aspects of feminine portraiture. Removed beyond a border of razor-like rocks, she connects with the distant faceted terrain, avoiding the observer's scrutiny and indicating the artist's barred encounter with her self.

Sage was diagnosed with cataracts in 1956, and her late works reflect her fear of no longer being able to paint. Titles become more literal and associative. A succession of empty frames or easels in *The Answer Is No* (1958; Collection Alexandra Darrow) evoke a mournful gathering of canvases never to be realised. Viewed from above, the stacked easels in *Watching the Clock* (1958; Museum of Modern Art, New York) fill the entire picture plane. On its completion, Sage had two bullet holes shot through this canvas, inviting speculation over the meaning of this gesture as Surrealist irreverence for the work of art or a chilling premonition of her suicide by gunshot to the heart. Among Sage's last works are small watercolour collages resembling rock formations, suggesting that her failing vision prompted a more intimate examination of landscape (*Blue Wind*, 1958; Collection Alexandra Darrow; *The Great Impossible*, 1961; Museum of Modern Art).

After Tanguy's death, Sage published four volumes of poetry characterised by a detached fatalism that not only mirrors the depression to which she had succumbed, but also parallels the harsh, disturbing world represented in her paintings of the previous 15 years. Writing "I have built a tower on despair/You hear nothing in it, there is nothing to see" (from "Tower", 1957), Sage could be describing her spare structures devoid of human presence.

When Breton first saw Sage's painting in 1938 he assumed its tense, calculated air must have been created by a man. Indeed, her work opposes the Surrealist analogy of the fertile earth to the nurturing, life-affirming female nature. Unlike other women artists associated with Surrealism, she avoided autobiographical and organic content, preferring the cryptic. Sage came into her own as a painter relatively late, drawing upon the language of Surrealism only in her forties. Although she embraced its penchant for enigmatic titles and the dislocation of dreams, the austerity of Sage's vision corresponds powerfully to her own feelings of alienation, setting her apart from her contemporaries.

MARY CHAN

Saint Phalle, Niki de [fig. 61]
French painter and sculptor, 1930–

Born Catherine Marie-Agnès Fal de Saint Phalle in Neuilly-sur-Seine, 29 October 1930. Worked as a fashion model, appearing in *Vogue*, *Harper's Bazaar* and *Life* magazines, 1948–9. Married US marine Harry Mathews (later a novelist and poet), 1950; daughter born 1951, son born 1955; divorced 1960. Lived in Cambridge, Massachusetts, 1950–52, then returned to Paris. Studied drama at Ecole de la rue Blanche, 1952–3. Hospitalised after a nervous breakdown, 1953. Lived with Nouveau Réaliste artist Jean Tinguely from 1960; married him, 1971; he died 1991. Joined Nouveaux Réalistes group, Paris, 1961. Suffered a pulmonary abscess, which led to hospitalisation, 1974; ill for four years after an attack of rheumatoid arthritis in 1982. Lives in France and USA.

Selected Individual Exhibitions
Galerie J, Paris: 1961

Galerie Rive Droite, Paris: 1962
Alexander Iolas Gallery, New York: 1962 (with Jean Larcade), 1965, 1966, 1967
Hanover Gallery, London: 1964, 1968, 1969
Stedelijk Museum, Amsterdam: 1967 (*Les Nanas au pouvoir*, touring)
Gimpel Fils, London: 1972, 1982, 1985, 1988, 1991
Gimpel and Weitzenhoffer Gallery, New York: 1973, 1977, 1979–82 (*Monumental Projects*, touring), 1982, 1985, 1990
Musée National d'Art Moderne, Centre Georges Pompidou, Paris: 1980–81 (touring retrospective)
Kunsthalle der Hypo-Kulturstiftung, Munich: 1987
Nassau County Museum of Fine Art, Roslyn, NY: 1987 (retrospective)
Galerie de France and JGM Galerie, Paris: 1989, 1990
Kunst- und Ausstellungshalle der Bundesrepublik Deutschland, Bonn: 1992–3 (touring retrospective)

Bibliography
Richard Roud, "Taboo or not Taboo", *The Guardian*, 6 April 1973 (Arts section)
Niki de Saint Phalle: Exposition retrospective, exh. cat., Musée National d'Art Moderne, Centre Georges Pompidou, Paris, and elsewhere, 1980
1960: Les Nouveaux Réalistes, exh. cat., Musée d'Art Moderne de la Ville de Paris, 1986
Les Années 60: L'Object – sculpture, exh. cat., JGM Galerie, Paris, 1990
Jean-Paul Ameline, *Les Nouveaux Réalistes*, Paris: Centre Georges Pompidou, 1992
Niki de Saint Phalle, exh. cat., Kunst- und Ausstellungshalle der Bundesrepublik Deutschland, Bonn, and elsewhere, 1992 (contains extensive bibliography)
Phyllis Braff, "Nanas, guns and gardens", *Art in America*, lxxx, December 1992, pp.102–7
Mary Blum, "Niki de Saint Phalle: Bursting out of the frame", *International Herald Tribune*, 21 June 1993
Barbara Jones, *Images of the Body*, MA thesis, University of East London, 1994
Joanna Thornberry, *Niki de Saint Phalle: Tirs and Trangressions*, MA thesis, Courtauld Institute of Art, University of London, 1995

Niki de Saint Phalle has produced a prolific body of work that spans oil painting, assemblage, performance art, film, sculpture and even architecture. Her art, in its diversity, thus defies easy categorisation. Saint Phalle turned to art after a nervous breakdown that led to hospitalisation and electro-shock treatment in 1953. She has never received any form of artistic training and as an auto-didact she likens herself to primitive man who was also unable to draw in three dimensions. Although she identifies herself with "outsider art" such as Art Brut, she does not associate herself directly with any sort of movement and is instead desirous to remain outside the realms of high art tradition.

Her early oil paintings, for example *Round Room* (1956; repr. Bonn 1992, p.191), illustrate this primitive quality. They are garishly coloured and executed with childlike simplicity. Despite their fairy-tale subject matter, their fragmented surfaces and thick impasto brushwork create a sense of disorder and confusion. They can be considered as a visual expression of the mental turmoil that led to her nervous breakdown. The fragmentation of these oil paintings became three dimensional in Saint Phalle's first assemblages. Influenced by the international emergence of Neo-dadaism, an art form that appropriated and extended the metaphor of Marcel Duchamp's ready-made, Saint Phalle began to fix real objects such as knives, scissors and guns to the surface of the canvas embedding them in thick, uneven plaster; the result: bleak, threatening and surreal landscapes exemplified by *Bouche d'incendie* (1959; ibid., p.195).

In 1961 the inherent violence of the oil paintings and assemblages became explicit when Saint Phalle created her first "tirs" or shooting paintings (1961–3). For these "tirs" Saint Phalle constructed reliefs with a profusion of different found objects and sealed sachets containing paints of different colours, or sometimes food such as eggs and spaghetti, and then painted the whole thing white. The finished assemblage was then hung and bullets fired into it, bursting the sachets, which would splatter and seep paint over the work. Despite this aggressive and apparently nihilistic gesture, Saint Phalle's purpose was in fact positive; the gun shot did not symbolise death but instead a point of departure. Her ultimate message, implicit within the "tirs", was creation through destruction. Saint Phalle's "tirs", although initially abstract, gradually became more explicitly religious and political, illustrated by the works *Khrushchev and Kennedy* (1962; JGM Galerie, Paris) and *Autel, noir et blanc* (1962; Collection Alexandre Iolas, Athens).

It was Saint Phalle's use of the found object and her Neo-dadaist tendencies that brought her to the attention of Pierre Restany, the art critic and leader of the Nouveaux Réalistes, who asked her to join the group in 1961. Saint Phalle's profound exploration of contemporary society differs, however, from the group's concern with an art form that communicated the look of contemporary society often without questioning its basis. Perhaps as a consequence Saint Phalle has remained a somewhat marginal figure within the group.

In 1963 Saint Phalle began making relief assemblages and free-standing sculptures that focused upon women's roles in contemporary society. Subjects such as brides, mothers and whores recurred. These works, constructed with chicken wire, papier-mâché, textiles, plastic dolls and animals, represent the female body in a form of grotesque realism. In creating these works Saint Phalle aimed to expose the horror of the roles that a patriarchal society demanded of women. This is clearly illustrated by the horrific birthing scene *L'Accouchement en rose* (1963–4; Moderna Museet, Stockholm) and *La Mariée et le cheval* (1963–4; ibid., p.219).

The disappearance of the more gruesome assemblages from Saint Phalle's oeuvre marked the arrival of the "nanas" in 1965 and a more optimistic phase in her work. The "nana", from Parisian slang for "chick" or "babe", was inspired by Larry Rivers's drawings of his pregnant wife. These three-dimensional sculptures are large, round and fun, for example, *Upside-Down Nana* (1967; Clarice Rivers Collection) and *Black Venus*, also titled *Miss Black Power* (1965–7; Whitney Museum of American Art, New York). Unlike the amputated forms of Saint Phalle's earlier female assemblages, the "nanas" are whole, smooth and brightly painted; they glory in their feminine bodies, in their sexuality and physicality. The "nanas" marked a new period of contentment for Saint Phalle who described them as a way "of 'blowing out' into my own feminity and liberation which was suppressed for so many years" (unpublished interview). The "nana" also inspired Saint Phalle's first architectural venture, a collaborative piece entitled *La Hon* (which means "she" in Swedish), which was constructed in the Moderna Museet, Stockholm, in 1966 (ibid., pp.60–71). Unlike the earlier "nanas", which merely suggested sexual penetration, this monumental "nana" (24.9 × 9.1 × 6 m.) was literally penetrable through a vaginal portal. Features inside the huge reclining figure included a planetarium in the left breast and a milk bar in the right.

Saint Phalle's interest in building and shaping space evinced by *La Hon* is further exemplified by her numerous architectural projects, which include for example *Golem* (1972; Jerusalem), a children's playhouse, and *Le Temple idéal* (1990; Nîmes), a house of worship for all denominations. Marking the world with a place of her own had been an obsession of Saint Phalle's since seeing Antonio Gaudí's Parc Güell in Barcelona in 1955 and finds its fullest realisation in her monumental Giardino del Tarocchi (1978–94; *ibid.*, pp.108–23) in Tuscany. This sculpture park or garden takes the 22 major Arcana of the tarot pack as its theme. Each tarot card is represented by an individual sculpture/building constructed in metal, concrete and ceramics and decorated with mosaics of mirrored glass, which, in reflecting the light and the landscape, unite the sculpture with its surroundings. The garden thus functions as a continual dialogue between architecture and nature, a place of escape and calm meditation.

Although the Giardino del Tarocchi has occupied much of Saint Phalle's time and energy since the late 1970s, she has continued to produce numerous individual pieces. For example the "skinny" sculptures that she started in 1979 are figures that, as the name suggests, literally exist as lines in space, exemplified by *La Déesse de la lumière* (1980; *ibid.*, p.248). They contrast dramatically with the solidity and corporeality of works such as the "nanas", expressing their life force not through weighty flesh but instead through space. As Saint Phalle emphasises: "The skinnys breathe. They are air sculptures" (exh. cat., Gimpel Fils, London, 1982). Saint Phalle's highly finished bronze sculptures of the 1990s, based on Egyptian gods and goddesses such as *Anubis* (1990; JGM Galerie), not only demonstrate the diversity of her materials but also her artistic development from the aggressive, crude debris constructions of the early 1960s. Saint Phalle's most recent artistic ventures are the "Tableaux éclatées", for example *Méta-Tinguely* (1992; artist's collection), created as a homage to her late husband, the artist and designer Jean Tinguely. The collage elements on these canvases are operated by photo-electric cells that break apart as the spectator approaches and then regroup. They symbolise the movement from chaos to order, from destruction to creation, echoing the ideas initially explored in the "tirs".

It is through film that Saint Phalle has created some of her most controversial work, developing the socially exploratory nature of the "tirs". For example, her film *Daddy – A Bedtime Story* (1972–3) is a subversive and pornographic work that explores incest, transvestism, lesbianism and patricide. Like the "tirs" the film functions as an exhortation, revealing human evil in order to effect its positive transformation (see Thornberry 1995).

JOANNA THORNBERRY

Salomon, Charlotte [fig. 63]
German painter and graphic artist, 1917–1943

Born in Berlin-Charlottenburg, 16 April 1917. Studied applied art under Erich Böhm at Vereinigte Staatsschulen für freie und angewandte Kunst (United State Schools for Free and Applied Art), Berlin; studied illustration and drawing under Ludwig Bartning, 1936–8. Emigrated to Villefranche-sur-Mer, France, 1939. Interned for one month in a camp for the imprisonment of foreign Jews in Gurs, Pyrenees, 1940. Married Austrian-Jewish emigrant Alexander Nagler, May 1943. Deported to Auschwitz, 21 September 1943; last recorded on arrival there, 7 October 1943.

Selected Writings

Leben? oder Theater? Ein autobiographisches Singspiel in 769 Bildern, ed. Judith Herzberg, Cologne, 1981; as *Charlotte: Life? or Theater?*, New York: Viking, and London: Allen Lane, 1981

Bibliography

Paul Tillich and Emil Straus, *Charlotte: A Diary in Pictures*, New York: Harcourt Brace, and London: Collins, 1963
Susanne Hassenkamp, "Das Leben malen, um es zu bewahren", *Art*, no.6, 1981, pp.70–85
Katja Reichenfeld, "Leben? oder Theater? Regie: Charlotte Salomon", *Jong Holland*, iv, 1981, pp.20–29
Dalia Elbaum, "Esthetische analyse van het werk van Charlotte Salomon: Leben? oder Theater?" in exh. cat., Bibliothèque royale Albert 1er, Brussels, 1982, pp.24–33
Susanna Partsch, "Charlotte Salomon: Anmerkungen zu einem Zyklus", *Kritische Berichte*, x/4, 1982, pp.49–56
Christine Fischer-Defoy, ed., *Charlotte Salomon: Leben? oder Theater? Das "Lebensbild" einer jüdischen Malerin aus Berlin, 1917–1943: Bilder und Spuren, Notizen, Gespräche, Dokumente*, Schriftenreihe der Akademie der Künste, xviii, Berlin, 1986
Mary Lowenthal Felstiner, "Engendering an autobiography in art: Charlotte Salomon's 'Life? or Theater?'", *Revealing Lives: Autobiography, Biography and Gender*, ed. Susan Groag Bell and Marilyn Yalom,

Albany: State University of New York Press, 1990,
pp.183–92
Charlotte Salomon: Life? or Theatre?, exh. cat., Joods
Historisch Museum, Amsterdam, 1992
Charlotte Salomon: Vie? ou théatre?, exh. cat., Musée
National d'Art Moderne, Centre Georges Pompidou,
Paris, 1992
Friedrich Rothe, "Lotte Laserstein und Charlotte
Salomon: Zwei künstlerische Entwicklungen unter den
Bedingungen der NS-Zeit", *Profession ohne Tradition:
125 Jahre Verein der Berliner Künstlerinnen*, exh. cat.,
Berlinische Galerie, Berlin, 1992, pp.151–8
Sabine Dahmen, *Bilder von Liebe und Tod in Charlotte
Salomons "Leben? oder Theater?"*, MA thesis,
Universität Bonn, 1994
Mary Lowenthal Felstiner, *To Paint Her Life: Charlotte
Solomon in the Nazi Era*, New York: HarperCollins,
1994

In addition to self-portraits, landscape studies and graphic works, Charlotte Salomon left a work that is unique in the history of painting. Created at night during her exile in France, *Leben? oder Theater?* is a series of 769 gouaches synthesising painting, literature and music in a range of styles from medieval manuscript illumination to Expressionist elements and cinematographic techniques. In the first third she wrote the texts in pencil on parchment paper and placed them over the matching gouaches. These texts consist of dialogues and comments as well as musical quotations from popular operas and songs, which intensify the already dense narrative atmosphere of the gouaches. References to an aria from *Carmen* or *Orpheus and Eurydice* or a line from Rilke or Goethe's *Faust* convey the artist's unspoken thoughts or feelings. From the second third onwards the texts are written directly on the gouaches and thus become an integral part. A few weeks after its completion and shortly before she was deported to Auschwitz, Salomon gave the work to the doctor of Villefranche-sur-Mer, reportedly saying: "Take good care of it. It is my whole life …".

Leben? oder Theater? does have pronounced autobiographical features, although its division into acts and scenes like a classical play distances it from the artist. She described and painted her life in retrospect: the childhood in Berlin dominated by the loss of her mother, her intense, secret love for her father's second wife, Paula Lindberg, a famous opera singer whom he married in 1930. She depicted the seizure of power by the National Socialists on 30 January 1933 in impressive compositions, while in the same period she covered several hundred pages with images of her second intense insecure love, for her

stepmother's singing teacher, Alfred Wolfsohn, who was also a passionate admirer of the singer. Everybody who appears in the play was given a name imitative of sound: the diva is "Paulinka Bimbam", the ever-penniless Wolfsohn is "Amadeus Daberlohn", a German term referring to his financial misery.

In January 1939 Salomon left Germany to join her grandparents in the south of France. The following year her grandmother committed suicide, and only after this event did she learn that her mother had not in fact died of influenza, but that she too had killed herself. This traumatic news gave her the urge either to take her own life "or to undertake something extraordinarily crazy" (*Leben? oder Theater?*, p.777). This explanation for the "crazy undertaking" is given on one of the last sheets of the cycle, at the end of which the viewer/reader is asked to return to the beginning. Here again, the third gouache shows a stage with the curtain up, introduces the figures, and the tragic "play" of persecution, love and death can start anew.

Leben? oder Theater? is of singular importance because at that time all art in Germany was censored by the National Socialist regime. Yet, in the face of this terror, the loss of so many loved ones and the knowledge that her own death was imminent, the young artist created a life's work in a very brief period. In 769 sheets she moved from a detailed narrative to an extremely gestural, expressive, even forceful and liberating pictorial language with which she challenged all the injustice she had endured and all that awaited her.

As the epilogue of the work is roughly foreshadowed in its prologue – the transformation of her experience of the fear of death and suicide, the conscious will to create – it can be assumed that a concept informed the creation of all the parts. This is shown by the numerous cross-connections evident to the attentive viewer in sheets from different parts of the work: for example, the depiction of a woman lying on the floor in a pool of blood refers to the suicide of her mother (p.32) and her grandmother (p.748).

In the isolation of exile, Salomon cast off the academic norms she had been taught at art school and created an individual style of great authenticity, which in its combination of writing and pictures seems immensely modern. The work depicts interiors, streets, sometimes landscapes, but mainly people in their complicated entanglements of life and love. Although the pictures are figurative, they are never realistic; on the contrary, the sheets of the epilogue tend towards abstraction, when for example the cross-hatched blue lines and brown dots represent planes dropping bombs and the horror of war.

Leben? oder Theater? was created in the exceptional situation of exile, when in two years of intensive, even manic work Salomon struggled to produce a painted autobiography. Its quality and fascination stem from the tension of the different styles, the dynamic relationship of text and picture and the great variety of themes with which she treated openly and sensitively subjects that are often taboo in art, such as female homosexuality and suicide. Her exemplary depiction of the systematic destruction of Jewish culture is important not least because it prevents viewers from suppressing, or even forgetting, the Holocaust.

Salomon always remembered Wolfsohn's farewell words to her, in her play attributed to Amadeus Daberlohn: he begged her "not to forget that I love life and have a very positive attitude to it. To love life completely, it may be necessary to encompass and understand its other side, death, as well. Never forget that I believe in you" (*ibid.*, pp.665–6). These words became a magic formula for the artist, lending her the strength to overcome the thought of suicide and to venture without compromise into the depths of her life: despite all the pain and loss, to paint and write of her childhood and years as a young Jew in a time of racial hatred. At the end of *Leben? oder Theater?* she wrote: "And she saw with daydreaming eyes all the beauty surrounding her, saw the sea, felt the sun and knew: she had to disappear for some time from the human surface and to sacrifice much for it – in order to create her world anew from the depth" (*ibid.*, pp.782–3).

SABINE DAHMEN

Savage, Augusta
American sculptor, 1892–1962

Born Augusta Christine Fells in Green Cove Springs, Florida, 29 February 1892. Married (1) John T. Moore, 1907; daughter born 1908; husband died a few years later; (2) James Savage *c.*1915; divorced early 1920s; (3) Robert L. Poston, 1923; he died 1924. Moved to West Palm Beach with her family, 1915. Moved to Jacksonville, Florida, 1919; to New York, 1921. Studied at Cooper Union, New York, 1921–3; also attended Women's Art School. Studied in Paris, funded by two Julius Rosenwald fellowships, 1930–32; studied at Académie de la Grande Chaumière under Félix Benneteau-Desgrois and later Charles Despiau; then eight-month study tour in France, Belgium and Germany funded by Carnegie Foundation grant. Established Savage Studio of Arts and Crafts, New York, 1932. Organised a group of young intellectuals, the Vanguard, 1933. First black member, National Association of Women Painters and Sculptors, 1934. Assistant supervisor, Works Progress Administration Federal Art Projects (WPA/FAP), 1936. First director, Harlem Community Art Center, 1937. Director, Salon of Contemporary Negro Art in Harlem, 1939. Recipient of silver medal, Women's Service League of Brooklyn, 1939. Retired to Saugerties in the Catskill Mountains, New York, 1945. Died in the Bronx, New York, 26 March 1962.

Principal Exhibitions
Douglas High School, Baltimore: 1926
Salon d'Automne, Paris: 1930–31
Spring Salon, American Art Anderson Galleries, New York: 1932
Argent Galleries, New York: 1934, 1938 (both group), 1939 (individual)
New York World's Fair: 1939
Tanner Art Galleries, Chicago: 1940 (*American Negro Exposition*)

Selected Writings
"An autobiography", *The Crisis*, xxxvi, August 1929, p.257

Bibliography
Maxine Block, ed., "Augusta Savage", *Current Biography*, New York: Wilson, 1941
De Witt S. Dykes, Jr, "Augusta Christine Savage", *Notable American Women, the Modern Period: A Biographical Dictionary*, ed. Barbara Sicherman and Carol Hurd Green, Cambridge, MA: Harvard University Press, 1980, pp.627–9
Augusta Savage and the Art Schools of Harlem, exh. cat., Schomburg Center for Research in Black Culture, New York Public Library, 1988

Against the Odds: African-American Artists and the Harmon Foundation, exh. cat., Newark Museum, NJ, 1990

Charlotte Streifer Rubinstein, *American Women Sculptors*, Boston: Hall, 1990

Romare Bearden and Harry Henderson, *A History of African-American Artists from 1792 to the Present*, New York: Pantheon, 1993

Deirdre Bibby, "Augusta Savage", *Black Women in America: An Historical Encyclopedia*, ii, ed. Darlene Clark Hine, Elsa Barkley Brown and Rosalyn Terborg-Penn, New York: Carlson, 1993

Three Generations of African-American Women Sculptors: A Study in Paradox, exh. cat., Afro-American Historical and Cultural Museum, Philadelphia, 1996

The standing of Augusta Savage in the world of 20th-century American art rests as much on the role she played during the 1930s in teaching young African-American artists, promoting their art, fighting racism in the art world and being a forceful presence in the Harlem community of New York as on her actual sculptural production which, although often beautifully conceived and executed, never exceeded more than a few dozen pieces. Specific information about Savage's early marriages and her primary school and art education are sketchy at best, and brief biographies written during her own lifetime, while stressing her triumphs over adversity, often contradict one another. De Witt S. Dykes, Jr (1980) made the first attempt to sort through the rich archives at the Schomburg Center for Research in Black Culture, a branch of the New York Public Library, and to use the files of Savage's daughter to establish the actual birth date. And when Deirdre L. Bibby organised the exhibition *Augusta Savage and the Art Schools of Harlem* (1988) for the Schomburg Center, further biographical puzzles became untangled, with Bibby's essay and the chronology prepared by Juanita Marie Holland, based on scrapbooks held by Savage's family. The essay that best captures the personality and fighting spirit of Savage was written by the artist Romare Bearden and completed by Harry Henderson after Bearden's death in 1988. As a close friend of her students during the 1930s, Bearden appreciated the very real struggles that Savage confronted as she developed from a poor, black Southern child into the dynamic presence that dominated the Harlem art world.

The incidents that recur in the early biographies and newspaper stories emphasise the poverty and racism that she continuously had to overcome, her perseverance and the instant recognition of her talent by people with the means to help her. Born the seventh child in a poor, African-American family of 14 children, at the age of 15 Savage married John T. Moore and gave birth to her only child, Irene Connie Moore. When her husband died, she rejoined her family with her child; and in 1915 they all moved to West Palm Beach. In one account Savage recalled that her religious father, a part-time Methodist preacher who supported the large family with carpentry, fishing and farming, "almost whipped all the art" out of her, because he disapproved of the "graven images" she had created as a child from the clay she found near her home (Bearden and Henderson 1993, p.168). Another tells how a high school principal introduced her to a local potter, who gave her 25 pounds of clay. Thus encouraged, she modelled an image of the Virgin Mary and a horse, which won the admiration of the principal and prompted him to employ her to teach a class in modelling for a dollar a day (New York 1988, p.12). Another opportunity came when George Graham Currie, superintendent of the West Palm Beach County Fair in 1919, urged her to enter her work. Her sculpture met with enthusiasm, and she received a special prize of $25, as well as $175 from the fair-going public eager to help her budding career (Dykes 1980, p.627). After a brief sojourn in Jacksonville, Florida, where she had unrealistically hoped to earn a living with portrait commissions from the black middle class, she moved on to New York in 1921. She left behind her second husband, James Savage, a carpenter, whom she subsequently divorced (New York 1988, p.12). Like many young African-American women with single-minded ambitions and a supportive family, she left her daughter behind with her parents when she moved to New York to make her fortune.

Possessing a letter of introduction from Currie, Savage called on the sculptor Solon Borglum, a founder of the School of American Sculpture in New York. Realising that her poverty precluded her paying the tuition fees, he directed her to Kate Reynolds, the director of Cooper Union, an endowed art school without fees to students (*ibid.*, p.13). Once enrolled at Cooper Union, Savage studied under George Brewster and moved rapidly through her studies, while supporting herself with part-time jobs (Bearden and Henderson 1993, p.169). But racism impeded her opportunities. In

1923 she entered a competition for a summer scholarship to an art school located at Fontainebleau, outside Paris. Although accepted, her scholarship was withdrawn by the judges to appease white Southern girls who also planned to attend the school. Savage challenged the judges; she told the *New York World* (20 May 1923):

> My brother was good enough to be accepted in one of the regiments that saw service in France during the war, but it seems his sister is not good enough to be a guest of the country for which he fought ... How am I to compete with other American artists if I am not to be given the same opportunity? [quoted in Bearden and Henderson 1993, p.170].

Although both black and white intellectuals mounted a protest against the racist decision, the judges would not waver, with the exception of the sculptor Hermon A. MacNeil, who promptly invited Savage to study with him that summer.

Savage's assertiveness was not surprising, given her personality as well as the climate of quiet but firm protest then developing among the black intelligentsia. Many of them, like Savage, had moved to New York in the early 1920s as part of the "great migration" – a voluntary relocation of two million African Americans during and after World War I from the South in search of well-paid jobs and opportunities in the northern cities of Chicago, Detroit and New York. Harlem – that area of Manhattan north of Central Park – became one of the destinations of these migrants. In the 1920s Marcus Garvey and his Universal Negro Improvement Association preached self-esteem and independence for blacks. W. E. B. Du Bois, editor of *The Crisis*, the journal of the National Association for the Advancement of Colored People, urged young writers and artists to develop their minds; he felt that the "talented tenth" would counter racist stereotypes. By the mid-1920s musicians, poets, novelists and other intellectuals had created what came to be known as the New Negro Movement, or the Harlem Renaissance. Savage quickly found a place in these circles. The branch library in Harlem commissioned her to model a portrait bust of *Du Bois* (untraced); another commission set her to work on a bust of *Garvey* (repr. Bearden and Henderson 1993, p.171). Through this commission she met and married one of Garvey's chief lieu-

tenants, Robert L. Poston. Although Poston died a few months later, she remained a lifelong black nationalist.

In 1925 Du Bois attempted to raise funds for Savage to study in Rome, but the funds fell short of realistic living expenses. Her own earnings went to support her parents, who eventually moved in with her. Four years later, however, the directors of the Julius Rosenwald Fund were so impressed with *Gamin* (1929; Schomburg Center for Research in Black Culture, New York), a sculptured bust of her nephew as a cocky African-American street kid, that they awarded her a year-long fellowship (renewed for a second year) for study in France.

On her return to New York in 1932, she was confronted with the economic Depression that had gripped the country. Both the Argent Galleries and the Art-Anderson Galleries accepted her work, and she secured some portrait commissions, but she felt that young black artists needed her help. She opened the Savage Studio of Arts and Crafts, in a basement apartment on West 143rd Street, and obtained a grant of $1500 from the Carnegie Foundation to teach art to children. Her adult students included Norman Lewis, William Artis, Ernest Crichlow, Elton C. Fax and later Gwendolyn Knight. In 1934 her exhibition at the Argent Galleries led to an invitation to join the National Association of Women Painters and Sculptors, the first African American to be so honoured.

In 1933 Savage organised a group, the Vanguard, which supported progressive causes (*ibid.*, p.15), and also participated with her colleagues in creating the Harlem Artists Guild, which held exhibitions at the Harlem branch of the Young Men's Christian Association (YMCA). She pressed the government to support the arts, and in 1936 she became an assistant supervisor for the Federal Art Project of the Works Progress Administration, which employed destitute artists in exchange for their participating on mural projects, painting easel pictures for schools and hospitals, producing posters and teaching at community centres. In this position she made sure that young black artists, such as Jacob Lawrence, were taken on. When in December 1937 the WPA's Harlem Community Art Center opened with great fanfare (which included an official visit from Eleanor Roosevelt), Savage became its first director.

That same month she received the commission from the board of design of the New York World's Fair to sculpt a work "symbolic of the unique contribution made by the American Negro to the world's music, particularly in song" (*New York Times*, 9 December 1937). Taking a leave of absence from the Harlem Community Art Center, she worked on *The Harp*, which was installed in the courtyard of the Contemporary Arts Building for the duration of the Fair (1939–40). More than 4.87 metres tall, made of plaster painted black, *The Harp* depicted African-American singers in choir robes as the strings of a harp, while the forearm and cupped hand of the Creator formed its base. Kneeling in front, an African-American man stretches out his arms as he holds a plaque inscribed with musical notes from James Weldon Johnson's famous anthem "Lift Every Voice and Sing". Because funds for bronze casting could not be raised, *The Harp* was destroyed at the conclusion of the Fair; but a small bronze replica, *Lift Every Voice and Sing* (1939; Schomburg Center), survives.

Savage continued to be active in artists' organisations and for a brief period ran a private art gallery, the Salon of Contemporary Negro Art, but her own artistic output was slim. The expense of bronze casting no doubt held her back. She eschewed the innovations of modernism (including modernism's indebtedness to African art forms) in favour of a soft naturalistic style, particularly for her portraits. *Gamin* is considered her *chef d'oeuvre*, because it ushered in a period when the frank portrayal of African-American physiognomy spurred other artists to infuse racial pride into their own work.

During the late 1930s, when private patronage barely existed, and when exhibitions of her work did not bring her the critical acclaim she felt she deserved, Savage decided to leave Harlem. In the early 1940s she moved to Saugerties, and lived in isolation from the New York art world for most of the last 17 years of her life. During the 1930s, however, there was probably no other artist in Harlem with quite the single-minded force of Savage. Because of her and the young artists she mentored, the Harlem Renaissance of the visual arts, unlike the literary arts, can be said to have flourished well into the 1940s.

PATRICIA HILLS

Schapiro, Miriam
American multi-media artist, 1923–

Born in Toronto, Canada, 15 November 1923; grew up in New York. Studied at Museum of Modern Art and attended Federal Art Project classes, 1937–41; studied at Hunter College, New York, 1943; University of Iowa, Iowa City, 1943–9 (BA 1945; MA 1947, MFA 1949). Married artist Paul Brach, 1946; son born 1955. Lived in Columbia, Missouri, working as children's art teacher, 1950–52; in New York, 1952–67. Instructor, Parsons School of Design, New York, and visiting lecturer, Connecticut College for Women, New London, 1966–7. Moved to La Jolla, California, with family, 1967; taught at University of California, San Diego, 1967–9. Faculty member, California Institute of the Arts, Valencia, 1970; co-director, with Judy Chicago (q.v.), Feminist Art Program, 1971 (sole director 1973). Co-founder, Los Angeles Institute of Contemporary Art, 1974. Returned to New York, 1975. Co-founder of the feminist journal *Heresies*, 1976; founder-member of Feminist Art Institute, New York, 1977. Recipient of Ford Foundation grant for printmaking, Tamarind Lithography Workshop, 1964 (with Paul Brach); National Endowment for the Arts (NEA) grant, 1976; Guggenheim fellowship, 1987; honors award, Women's Caucus for Art, 1988; honors award, National Association of Schools of Art and Design (NASAD), 1992; honorary doctorates from College of Wooster, Ohio, 1983; California College of Arts and Crafts, Oakland, 1989; Minneapolis College of Art and Design, 1994. Member of advisory board, Women's Caucus for Art; College Art Association (former director); associate member, Heresies Collective. Lives in New York.

Selected Individual Exhibitions
André Emmerich Gallery, New York: 1958, 1960, 1961, 1963, 1967, 1969, 1971, 1973, 1976, 1977
Skidmore College, Saratoga Springs, NY: 1964
Lyman Allen Museum, New London, CT: 1966 (touring retrospective)
Newport Harbor Art Museum, CA: 1969 (retrospective, with Paul Brach)
Comsky Gallery, Los Angeles: 1974, 1975
Mandeville Art Gallery, University of California at San Diego: 1975
Allen Memorial Art Museum, Oberlin College, Oberlin, OH: 1977–9 (*Femmages*, touring)
Lerner-Heller Gallery, New York: 1979, 1980

Galerie Marcel Liatowitsch, Basel: 1979
Barbara Gladstone Gallery, New York: 1980, 1981, 1982
College of Wooster Art Museum, Wooster, OH: 1980–82
(touring retrospective)
Galerie Rudolf Zwirner, Cologne: 1981
Dart Gallery, Chicago: 1984
Bernice Steinbaum Gallery, New York: 1986, 1988, 1990,
1991
Guild Hall Museum, East Hampton, NY: 1992
ARC Gallery, Chicago: 1993
Steinbaum Krauss Gallery, New York: 1994

Selected Writings

"The education of women as artists: Project
Womanhouse", Art Journal, xxxi, 1972, pp.268–70
"Female imagery", Womanspace Journal, i/1, Summer
1973, pp.11–17 (with Judy Chicago)
Editor, Anonymous Was a Woman, Valencia: California
Institute of the Arts, 1974
"Notes from a conversation on art, feminism and work",
Working It Out, ed. Sara Ruddick and Pamela
Daniels, New York: Pantheon, 1977, pp.283–305
"Waste not/want not: Femmage", Heresies, no.4, Winter
1978, pp.66–9 (with Melissa Meyer); reprinted in
Collage: Critical Views, ed. Katherine Hoffman, Ann
Arbor: UMI Research Press, 1989, pp.295–315
"Recalling Womanhouse", Women's Studies Quarterly,
xv, Spring–Summer 1987, pp.25–30
"Cunts/quilts/consciousness", Heresies, no.24, 1989,
pp.6–13 (with Faith Wilding)
Rondo: An Artist Book, San Francisco: Bedford Arts
Press, 1990

Bibliography

Paul Brach and Miriam Schapiro: Paintings and Graphic
Works, exh. cat., Newport Harbor Art Museum,
Newport Beach, CA, 1969
Linda Nochlin, "Miriam Schapiro: Recent work", Arts
Magazine, xlviii, November 1973, pp.38–41
Miriam Schapiro: The Shrine, the Computer and the
Dollhouse, exh. cat., Mandeville Art Gallery,
University of California at San Diego, La Jolla, 1975
Jeff Perrone, "Approaching the decorative", Artforum,
xv, December 1976, pp.26–30
Mary Stofflet, "Miriam Schapiro", Arts Magazine, li,
May 1977, p.12
Donald Kuspit, "Interview with Miriam Schapiro", Art in
America, lxv, September 1977, p.83
Eleanor Munro, Originals: American Women Artists,
New York: Simon and Schuster, 1979
John Perreault, "The new decorativeness", Portfolio,
June–July 1979, pp.46–51
Jim Collins and Glenn B. Opitz, eds, Women Artists in
America, revised edition, Poughkeepsie, NY: Apollo,
1980
Miriam Schapiro: A Retrospective, 1953-1980, exh. cat.,
College of Wooster Art Museum, Wooster, OH, and
elsewhere, 1980
Norma Broude, "Miriam Schapiro and 'femmage':
Reflections on the conflict between decoration and
abstraction in twentieth-century art", Arts Magazine,
liv, February 1980, pp.83–7; reprinted in Feminism
and Art History: Questioning the Litany, ed. Norma
Broude and Mary D. Garrard, New York: Harper,
1982, pp.315–29
Charlotte Streifer Rubinstein, American Women Artists
from Early Times to the Present, Boston: Hall, 1982
Elizabeth Frank, "Miriam Schapiro: Formal sentiments",
Art in America, lxx, May 1982, pp.106–11
Paula Bradley, Miriam Schapiro: The Feminist
Transformation of an Avant-Garde Artist, PhD disser-
tation, University of North Carolina, Chapel Hill,
1983
Charlotte Robinson, ed., The Artist and the Quilt, New
York: Knopf, 1983
Miriam Schapiro: Femmages, 1971–1985, exh. cat.,
Brentwood Gallery, St Louis, 1985
Katherine M. Duncan, "The early work of Miriam
Schapiro: The beginnings of reconciliation between
the artist and the woman", Athanor, v, 1986,
pp.43–51
"I'm Dancing as Fast as I Can": New Paintings by
Miriam Schapiro, exh. cat., Bernice Steinbaum
Gallery, New York, 1986
Thalia Gouma-Peterson, "The theater of life and illusion
in Miriam Schapiro's recent work", Arts Magazine, lx,
March 1986, pp.38–43
Susan Gill, "From 'femmage' to figuration", Art News,
lxxxv, April 1986, pp.94–101
Christy Sheffield Sanford and Enid Shomer, "An inter-
view with Miriam Schapiro", Women Artists News,
xi, Spring 1986, pp.22–6
Daniel Wheeler, Art since Mid-Century: 1945 to the
Present, Englewood Cliffs, NJ: Prentice Hall, and
London: Thames and Hudson, 1991
Norma Broude and Mary D. Garrard, eds, The Power of
Feminist Art: The American Movement of the 1970s,
New York: Abrams, and London: Thames and
Hudson, 1994
Miriam Schapiro's Collaboration Series: "Mother
Russia", exh. cat., Steinbaum Krauss Gallery, New
York, 1994
Lucy R. Lippard, The Pink Glass Swan: Selected Essays
on Feminist Art, New York: New Press, 1995
Wendy Slatkin, Women Artists in History: From
Antiquity to the Present, 3rd edition, Englewood
Cliffs, NJ: Prentice Hall, 1997

Typically identified as a feminist artist whose art is
described as "decorative", Miriam Schapiro's recent
work has concentrated on explorations of larger
questions of how artists relate to their immediate
society. One of the first artists to investigate the
potential of non-traditional materials, she adapted
the visual language of Abstract Expressionism to her
increasingly strong statements about issues of

particular concern to women artists working in an artistic tradition established by men. Schapiro's art offers a profoundly human social statement that inevitably raises it above the level of mere feminist expression.

Beginning her career during the 1950s when Abstract Expressionism dominated Western art, Schapiro explored both figural and landscape themes in the context of this avant-garde style. She was an acknowledged member of the "second generation" of the New York School, and her paintings *Bouquet*, *Idyll No.1* and *Idyll No.2* were included in the *New Talent* exhibition in 1957 at the Museum of Modern Art, New York. At her first solo show at the prestigious André Emmerich Gallery in 1958, she exhibited *By the Sea*, *Nightwood* and *Fanfare*. This was followed in 1960 by a second solo show of Abstract Expressionist paintings of film stars and tropical gardens at the same gallery. That same year she was included in the *Woman Artists* exhibition at Dord Fitz Gallery, Texas, with 19 artists including Helen Frankenthaler (q.v.) and Louise Nevelson (q.v.).

During the late 1960s, and coinciding with the early stages of the women's movement, Schapiro immersed herself and her art in feminist purpose. Her large painting *OX* (1967; Museum of Contemporary Art, Los Angeles) became the banner for the Women's Movement in California where she and her husband were teaching at the University of San Diego. Thalia Gouma-Peterson explained that the "O", the nucleus of *OX*, is the egg transformed into an octagon, exposing its own cavity and extending dynamically outwards in the outstretched limbs of the "X" (Wooster 1980). Schapiro herself considered this painting to be the final resolution of her identity crisis and formal proclamation that a woman is capable of male-associated assertiveness and logical reasoning in a woman's body.

Schapiro was among the first artists to recognise the artistic potential of the computer, producing Hard Edge computerised paintings that communicated her newly awakened feminist intentions effectively. In 1970 she collaborated with the physicist David Nalibof to program perspective images into a computer, creating forms reminiscent of *OX* and later described by Barbara Rose as "abstract illusionism". The result was a series of large (1.02 × 1.27 m.) computerised images painted in enamel on magna on canvas.

In 1971 Schapiro was appointed, with Judy Chicago, to teach at the California Institute of the Arts where the two artists exchanged ideas, initiated the Feminist Art Program and collaborated with students and several other Los Angeles artists to produce *Womanhouse* (1972; Institute of the Arts, Valencia). This project consisted of converting an abandoned house into a space in which feelings, fantasies and fears about being women who were also artists could be expressed in visual terms. The house was designed to embody all the diverse ideas of the artists who worked on it, and it included works in the tradition of crafts, quilts and other examples of the anonymous expressions created by women throughout history. The challenge for women artists during this period of embryonic feminism was to expand the definitions of art by exploring alternative approaches and by experimenting with materials from the domestic realm instead of traditional oil paint on canvas or bronze sculpture. She asserted that feminism had taught her not to worry about what she was "allowed" or "not allowed" to do.

Aligned with the *Womanhouse* project, Schapiro and Sherry Brody worked on the *Dollhouse* (1972; artist's collection), a miniature three-dimensional construction with six rooms, each of which contained a specific political message. The form of the dollhouse, chosen for its insignificance, provided an arena in which to explore the symbol of house as woman and to connect the triviality of interior decoration with artistic purposes. The *Dollhouse*, too, was a mixed-media construction that included a variety of non-art materials. In her unabashed use of fabric, wood and paper, and techniques that included stitching and pasting, Schapiro contributed to the ever-widening range of artistic approaches.

In 1975 Schapiro returned to New York where she continued to make statements about women's issues with complex collages in which she included a wide range of materials. The large *Anatomy of a Kimono* (1975–6) is an example of the bold imagery that came out of her association with West Coast artists with feminist concerns. *Anatomy of a Kimono*, an architectural construction combining fabric collage and painting, developed from the earlier "Femmages" that emphasised themes and materials associated primarily with women.

Schapiro defined collage, explored during the early 20th century by Pablo Picasso, Wassily Kandinsky and Henri Matisse, as "pictures assembled from assorted materials". Femmage, she asserted, described the activity, appropriated by modernist artists, that women had practised for centuries as quilting, brocade, appliqué and embroidery. By working with fabric swatches and embroidery techniques, Schapiro established a connection with a tradition that preceded modernist collage and one that is more authentic to purposes shared by many contemporary women artists. In *Anatomy of a Kimono*, for example, she employed monumental scale to emphasise ideas previously dismissed as irrelevant to mainstream artistic developments. Women, Schapiro believes, have always been creative and able to "make something out of nothing", but the results of their efforts have rarely been valued. Schapiro's femmage aesthetic is demonstrated in the large *Barcelona Fan* (1979; 1.83 × 3.66 m.; Howard Kalka and Stephen M. Jacobson), a fan-shaped canvas as support for acrylic paint and sheer fabric. *Wonderland* (1983; 2.5 × 4 m.; Bernice Steinbaum Gallery, New York) is an even more complex acrylic and fabric collage on canvas that combines old Australian needlework, crocheted aprons and embroidered handkerchiefs.

When a search for reproductions of the work of women artists in history for her *Collaboration* series (1974) yielded only a few examples by artists such as Angelica Kauffman (q.v.), Mary Cassatt (q.v.) and Berthe Morisot (q.v.), Schapiro realised that most women artists had been excluded from the art-historical record. Textbooks used for survey classes in art history rarely, if ever, introduced women artists to beginning students. Infuriated, she raised the issue with the board of the College Art Association, of which she was a member, arguing effectively for awareness of the need for wider historical coverage. She has also served on the governing board of the Women's Caucus for Art, is a founding member of the Feminist Art Institute in New York, and has lectured widely on feminist issues and feminist education at conferences, colleges, universities and for various professional associations. Later work includes *Wonderland* (1983; Bernice Steinbaum Gallery), an acrylic and fabric collage on canvas. In this, and other works, she continues to explore the additive and inclusive methods that emerged during the collaborations of the 1970s but that became cool and austere in works such as *Heartland* (1985; Bernice Steinbaum Gallery). During her career, Miriam Schapiro has successfully synthesised abstraction and feminist

iconography to comment on the history of civilisation from a fresh perspective.

MARY F. FRANCEY

Schjerfbeck, Helene [fig. 65]
Finnish painter, 1862–1946

Born Helena Sofia Schjerfbeck in Helsinki, 10 July 1862; later changed the spelling of her name from Helena to Helene. Hip injury at the age of four; suffered from ill health for the rest of her life. Studied at the Finnish Art Society drawing school, Helsinki, 1873–7 (scholarship 1877); Adolf von Becker's private art academy, Helsinki, 1877–9. Recipient of Finnish Imperial Senate travel grant, 1880; scholarship, 1881. Studied at Académie Colarossi, Paris, under Gustave Courtois and others, 1881–4; copied paintings in the Louvre, particularly works by Velázquez; lived and studied in France and Britain during most of the 1880s, spending time at the artists' colonies at Concarneau and Pont-Aven, Brittany, and St Ives, Cornwall; also visited Italy and St Petersburg. Taught painting at the Finnish Art Society drawing school, Helsinki, 1892–1902 (resigned because of failing health). Stayed in Florence, Italy, 1894. Lived in Hyvinkää, 1902–25; Tammisaari, 1925–41. Between 1939 and 1944 moved to several different places in southern Finland due to the Winter War and World War II. Moved to Saltsjöbaden, near Stockholm, February 1944. Recipient of Finnish State second prize in genre painting, 1882 and 1886; Order of the White Rose of Finland, 1920; Artists and Writers Foundation pension, 1921. Foreign member of the Academy of Free Arts, Royal Academy of Fine Arts, Stockholm, 1942. Died at Saltsjöbaden, 23 January 1946; buried in Helsinki.

Principal Exhibitions

Individual
Stenman Gallery, Helsinki: 1917
Liljevalchs Konsthall, Stockholm: 1934 (with Hannes Autere, Marcus Collin and T.K. Sallinen)
Stenmans Galleri, Stockholm: 1937, 1938, 1939, 1940, 1942, 1944, 1946 (touring retrospective)

Group

Finnish Art Society, Helsinki: occasionally 1879–1946
(third prize 1879)
Paris Salon: 1883–4, 1888
Exposition Universelle, Paris: 1889 (first-class bronze
medal)
Institute of Painters in Oils, London: 1889
Turku Art Society: occasionally 1891–1941
Ateneum, Helsinki: 1905 (women artists)
Friends of Finnish Handicraft: 1905, 1908–9, 1911
Malmö: 1914 (*Baltiska utställningen* [Baltic exposition])
Liljevalchs Konsthall, Stockholm: 1916 (*Finsk konst*
[Finnish art]), 1929 (*Finlands nutida konst*
[Contemporary Finnish art])

Selected Writings

"Helene Schjerfbeck: Seitsemän kirjettä Maria Wiikille"
[Helene Schjerfbeck: Seven letters to Maria Wiik], ed.
Kaarina Calonius, *Suomen taiteen vuosikirja 1946*
[Yearbook of Finnish Art 1946], Poorvoo, 1946,
pp.48–69

Bibliography

H. Ahtela [Einar Reuter], *Helena Schjerfbeck*, Helsinki,
1917
Helena Schjerfbeck, 1879–1917, exh. cat., Stenman
Gallery, Helsinki, 1917
Helena Westermarck, *Mina levnadsminnen* [My
memoirs], Åbo, 1941
Hanna and Eilif Appelberg, *Helene Schjerfbeck: En
biografisk konturteckning* [Helene Schjerfbeck: A
biographical outline], Helsinki, 1949
H. Ahtela [Einar Reuter], *Helena Schjerfbeck: Kamppailu
kauneudesta* [Helena Schjerfbeck: The struggle for
beauty], Porvoo: Söderström, 1951; Swedish edition,
Stockholm: Rabén & Sjögren, 1953
John Boulton Smith, *The Golden Age of Finnish Art: Art
Nouveau and the National Spirit*, 2nd edition,
Helsinki: Otava, 1985
*Dreams of a Summer Night: Scandinavian Painting at the
Turn of the Century*, exh. cat., Arts Council of Great
Britain, London, 1986
Lena Holger, *Helene Schjerfbeck: Liv och konstnärskap*
[Helene Schjerfbeck: Life and art], Stockholm: Ekdahl,
Pettersson & Winbladh, 1987
Riitta Konttinen, "Finska konstnärinnors, 1880-tal: Ljus,
luft och färg" [Finnish women artists in the 1880s:
Light, air and colour], *De drogo till Paris: Nordiska
konstnärinnor på 1880-talet* [They went to Paris:
Nordic women artists in the 1880s], exh. cat.,
Liljevalchs Konsthall, Stockholm, 1988, pp.220–53
——, *Suomalaisia naistaiteilijointa 1880-luvulta* [Finnish
women artists in the 1880s], Helsinki, 1988
Kirk Varnedoe, *Northern Light: Nordic Art at the Turn
of the Century*, New Haven and London: Yale
University Press, 1988
Denise Delouche, "Helene Schjerfbeck: Les funérailles à
Pont-Aven, 1884", *Artistes étrangers à Pont-Aven,
Concarneau et autres lieux de Bretagne*, Rennes, 1989
Helene Schjerfbeck: Finland's Modernist Rediscovered,
exh. cat., Finnish National Gallery Ateneum, Helsinki,
Phillips Collection, Washington, DC, and elsewhere,
1992
Lena Holger, *Helene Schjerfbeck: Teckningar och
akvareller* [Helene Schjerfbeck: Drawings and water-
colours], Stockholm, 1994
Michelle Facos, "Helene Schjerfbeck's self-portraits:
Revelation and dissimulation", *Woman's Art Journal*,
xvi/1, 1995, pp.12–17

The Finnish artist Helene Schjerfbeck is one of the
links in the enormous transformation that took
place in art at the turn of the 19th and 20th
centuries, from realism to modernism and abstraction. She started her training as an artist at a very
early age. In 1873 she entered the drawing school in
Helsinki aged eleven, some six or seven years
younger than the other pupils, and soon became the
best of them. Her family could not afford her education, but she received a grant. At the age of 16 she
won a prize at the annual exhibition. Her first
known *Self-Portrait* (Museet Ett Hem, Turku), a
black-and-white crayon drawing of 1878, belongs
to this period. It shows a curly-haired, good-looking
girl. Schjerfbeck's talented and strong pencil work is
already apparent.

Schjerfbeck shows how art can be non-realistic
without compromising naturalism. Beginning in the
1880s, using French subjects, Schjerfbeck followed
naturalism, which focuses on the personal rather
than the general, but she tempered it with the
outlines of modern art. In all her portraits the spiritual dimensions of the human mind are made
visible, as in the boy *Woodcutter II* (1911; Turun
Taidemuseo, Turku) and *Stubborn Girl* of 1939.
Schjerfbeck painted her sitters as if the light were
coming from inside them, as if they were their own
lamps. Her technique minimalises. She takes more
and more details away, yet there is still a sense of
growth in what is left. The series of self-portraits
painted between 1942 and 1945, when she was in
her old age, is particularly raw and gripping – she
painted these images as if to surprise even herself.

With the economic development and internation-
alisation of the Nordic countries at the turn of the
19th and 20th centuries, art and women's education
became acceptable, and Finnish women were the
first in Europe to be enfranchised (1906). This was
accompanied by a demand for freedom in all areas

of life – in society, in religion and in dress. Women cut their hair, shortened their skirts to the knee and even wore trousers. This is not to say that everyone did, nor that Schjerfbeck did – she was brought up two generations earlier – but these things now became possible, and gave both society and art a certain freedom. In Nordic literature these social changes first became apparent in works by the Danish literary critic Georg Brandes and by his friend the Swedish writer Ernst Ahlgren, a pseudonym for Victoria Benedictsson, in her novels *Pengar* (Money; 1885) and *Fru Marianne* (Mrs Marianne; 1887); in Norway by Henrik Ibsen's *Et dukkehjem* (A doll's house; 1879) and in Sweden by August Strindberg's *Ett drömspel* (A dream play; 1902). They all discussed the status of women in society, fought against conservatism and declared that women had a right to their own intellectual opinions and, at least in theory, to work with equal status to men, especially in the arts.

Schjerfbeck read these books and started a series of portraits of working women, with whom she wished to identify. The first of these, *The Seamstress* (1903–5; Ateneum, Helsinki), shows a seated woman, painted in sharp profile, taking a rest from her work. She is dressed in black, in contrast to the red of the rocking chair. The pause from work is almost over, and the figure is preparing to rise. Schjerfbeck's concept of modernism was simplicity. She formed no details if her eye did not register them when she first conceived of her idea. She focused on her subject, saw the basic concept of the form and noticed the crucial details – which is why her model here is equipped with a pair of scissors, the seamstress's tool, hanging on a green band from her waist. Later, in 1927, when she made a second free version of *The Seamstress* (private collection, Finland), Schjerfbeck narrowed her interest to the sitter's face and upper body, painting a half-length portrait. Her focus had changed, and women had obtained some rights in society as well. She concentrated her attention on problems of form, as Picasso, for example, had done ten years earlier, showing that she was well aware of the discourses in European art. The same process, focused on line and form, is also apparent when in 1927 she made a second version of her colouristic and sensitive *Convalescent* (first version, 1888; Ateneum; second version, private collection, Sweden). The first version, her best-known painting from her realist period, was exhibited at the Paris Salon of 1888 and

the Exposition Universelle of 1889. By the time she made the second version, she was more than 60 years old, free in her mind and at last accepted as an artist by the art world. When her mother died in 1923 Schjerfbeck was also free to move, and from 1925 lived by the sea in the small town of Tammisaari (Ekenäs); for the first time she had her own studio.

Schjerfbeck is best known for her self-portraits, her still lifes and to some extent for her landscape paintings. These were all ordinary subjects for an artist of the time, but are different when interpreted by Schjerfbeck's sensitive talent. She would use still-life motifs to find out what time did to the shape and colour of a fruit or a flower. In *Market Apple* (1927; private collection, Finland) she painted a red volume on a green surface, two complementary colours, so that the apple looks as if it is flying. In *Lemons in a Wooden Bowl* (1934–44; private collection, Sweden) the motifs appear to be suspended on the canvas, while in *Still Life in Green* (1932; Ateneum) some pears are turning black because the painting took too long – the putrefaction process had already started. Schjerfbeck's still lifes are sensual, fresh and exquisite.

In the years around 1900 Finland was struggling for autonomy in the face of pressure from the Russian government. In countries with low populations women as well as men are resources in the fight for independence. Strong women artists, such as Schjerfbeck's closest friend Helena Westermarck, also a writer and champion of women's rights, played a prominent role. In Brittany Schjerfbeck captured the sitter's strong character in the expressionistic *Helena Westermarck in Profile* (1884; Gösta Serlachiuksen Taidemuseo, Mänttä), painted in plein air. In 1907 Westermarck bought Schjerfbeck's painting of an *Old Woman* (1905; private collection, Finland), in which the artist gave a personal face to the fighting spirit of a proud Finnish woman, a mother and grandmother, sitting upright in front of the woods. But Schjerfbeck herself was not active in the women's rights movement. Her letters show that although she did have some reflections on the subject, what she wanted most was to be accepted as an independent artist by her family, her friends and the Finnish art world. But it was not until 1915 that the Finnish Art Society commissioned her self-portrait for their collection (*Self-Portrait with Black Background*, 1915; Ateneum; repr. Facos 1995, cover).

Schjerfbeck had close friendships with three women artists, whom she called "my painting sisters". All three – Maria Wiik, Ada Thilén and Westermarck – had Swedish as their mother tongue, and they derived strength from each other. They met at the Finnish Art Society drawing school and from time to time a pair of them would share a studio in France or Finland and make study trips together. None of them was married. It was not that Schjerfbeck did not like men – in her twenties she had been engaged to a British painter, and there were later two other serious relationships with men – but she decided to live alone, even if this decision was not entirely her own. In 1918, when she was 54, she painted in light colours a portrait of *The Sailor*, a young, muscular and good-looking man wearing a tight shirt and bearing a cautious smile. The model was the writer and artist Einar Reuter, with whom she stayed friends all her life. As early as 1888 she had written to Wiik about being an artist and being married: "They say she had to marry because she did not get on with her painting. If only being alone would help!" (Åbo Akademi, Turku). Schjerfbeck could not compromise, and her love for art dictated her priorities.

The painting sisters got to know other women artists, particularly in Paris, and visited them in their home countries, which introduced them to new ideas. Thilén, for example, painted in Norway with the Norwegian artist Kitty Kielland (q.v.), and Schjerfbeck went to England with the Austrian painter Marianne Stokes. She also portrayed Stokes at the Académie Colarossi in Paris, with the light on her back and her hair formed into a halo (1881; *Two Profiles*; Ateneum). In 1889 Wiik followed Schjerfbeck to England, where they used the same old woman as a model, Schjerfbeck in *Autumn Rose* and Wiik in *Out in the World* (both Ateneum). The women all travelled a great deal, and in 1894 Schjerfbeck stayed in Florence, where she studied the work of Italian Renaissance painters and of Titian, and shared a studio for some months with another Finnish painter, Ellen Thesleff (q.v.), in the cloister of San Marco. They studied Fra Angelico's frescoes and were both influenced by the Symbolist movement. Schjerfbeck's awareness of the special Italian silver light is seen in *Fiesole Landscape* (private collection, Finland).

Some years later Schjerfbeck painted *Old Manor House* (1901; Åbo Konstmuseum, Turku), one of her few paintings in the Symbolist style. By that time she had nearly finished her teaching career at her old drawing school in Helsinki, which had reduced her own painting opportunities. She meant a great deal to some of her pupils, notably Sigrid Schauman, but she had little influence on the younger generation until after the 1930s.

From 1900 Schjerfbeck stayed in Finland, until she was forced to go to Sweden in 1944, as a result of World War II. In 1913 she was visited by the Finnish-Swedish art dealer Gösta Stenman, who organised her first solo exhibition in 1917 in Helsinki, but she was not well known until he presented her work to a wider public, starting in Sweden in 1937. In 1938–9, on Stenman's initiative, she made six lithographic prints, her only ones, incorporating motifs from her paintings.

Schjerfbeck developed an ascetic and almost abstract style in contact with the traditions of European modernism, known to her after the turn of the century only through magazines, art books and the reports of friends. She painted mostly in a soft and temperate, but fastidious, colouring, with a strong outline, pointing to the essentials in the work. During her lifetime Schjerfbeck was overshadowed by such male artists as the Finnish painters Albert Edelfelt, for a time also her teacher, and Akseli Gallen-Kallela, whose work was more nationalistic in character. Today her work, with that of the Norwegian Expressionist artist Edvard Munch, is considered to be the most important in Nordic art. Schjerfbeck is represented in a number of Finnish museums, as well as, in Scandinavia, the Nasjonalgalleriet, Oslo; Göteborgs Konstmuseum, Göteborg; Malmö Museum; Moderna Museet and Nationalmuseum, Stockholm.

LENA HOLGER

Schneemann, Carolee
American artist, 1939–

Born in Fox Chase, Pennsylvania, 12 October 1939. Studied at Universidad de Puebla, Mexico; New School for Social Research, New York; Columbia University School of Painting and Sculpture, New York; Bard College, Annandale-on-Hudson (BA); University of Illinois, Urbana (MFA). Settled in New York, 1962. Founder-director, Kinetic Theater movement and design workshops, New York, 1963–8; founder-member, International-Local group, New York, 1976. Taught at University of Illinois, Urbana, 1961–2; artist-in-residence, Colby College, Waterville, Maine, 1968; Dartington College, Totnes, Devon, 1972. Recipient of National Endowment for the Arts (NEA) grants, 1974, 1977, 1978 and 1983; Creative Artists Public Service (CAPS) grant, 1978; Guggenheim fellowship, 1993. Lives in New York.

Principal Exhibitions

Individual

Artist's Studio, New York: 1962, 1963, 1964
University Art Museum, University of California, Berkeley: 1974
Galerie De Appel, Amsterdam: 1979
Real Art Ways, Hartford, CT: 1981
Max Hutchinson Gallery, New York: 1982, 1983, 1985
New Music America, Miami: 1988
Emily Harvey Gallery, New York: 1990
Penine Hart Gallery, New York: 1994
Kunstraum, Vienna: 1995
New Museum of Contemporary Art, New York: 1996 (retrospective)

Group

Sculpture Center, New York: 1984 (*Sound Art*)
Milwaukee Art Museum: 1995 (*Neo-Dada: Redefining Art*, touring)

Selected Writings

Parts of a Body House Book, Cullompton, Devon: Beau Geste Press, 1972
Cézanne: She Was a Great Painter: Essays on History, Sexuality and Naming: Unbroken Words to Women, New Paltz, NY: Trespuss Press, 1975
Cézanne: She Was a Great Painter: The Second Book, January 1975: Unbroken Words to Women, Sexuality Creativity Language Art History, New Paltz, NY: Trespuss Press, 1975
Up To and Including Her Limits, privately printed, 1978
More than Meat Joy: Complete Performance Works and Selected Writings, ed. Bruce McPherson, New Paltz, NY: Documentext, 1979
The Recent History and Destruction of Lebanon: A Research Extract, privately printed, 1983
Carolee Schneemann: Early and Recent Work, New Paltz, NY: Documentext, 1983
"The obscene body/politic", *Art Journal*, l, Winter 1991, pp.28–35

Bibliography

Ann Sargent-Wooster, "Carolee Schneemann", *Artforum*, xiv, May 1976, pp.73–4

Ted Castle, "Carolee Schneemann: The woman who uses her body as her art", *Artforum*, xix, November 1980, pp.64–70
Daniel Cameron, "Object vs. persona: The early work of Carolee Schneemann", *Arts Magazine*, lvii, May 1983, pp.122–5
Scott Macdonald, "The men cooperated", *Afterimage*, xii, April 1985, pp.12–15
Udo Kultermann, "Die Performance-Art von Carolee Schneemann", *Idea: Jahrbuch der Hamburger Kunsthalle*, vi, 1987, pp.141–51
Barbara Smith, "On the body as material", *Artweek*, xxi, 4 October 1990, pp.24–5 (interview)
Andrea Juro and V. Vale, eds, *Angry Women*, San Francisco: Re/Search, 1991
Johannes Birringer, "Imprints and re-visions: Carolee Schneemann's visual archeology", *Performance Art Journal*, June 1993, pp.31–46
Norma Broude and Mary D. Garrard, eds, *The Power of Feminist Art: The American Movement of the 1970s*, New York: Abrams, and London: Thames and Hudson, 1994
Joanna Frueh, "The erotic as social security", *Art Journal*, liii/1, 1994, pp.66–72
Jay Murphy, *Imaging Erotics: The Body Politics of Carolee Schneemann* (in preparation)

A few memorable images from Carolee Schneemann's work of the 1960s and 1970s normally represent her oeuvre in overviews of the avant-garde work of that time: a naked, body-painted Schneemann boldly staring into the camera, ensconced in a multi-media environment, in *Eye Body* (1963); Schneemann and other barely clad performers rolling about with chicken carcasses in *Meat Joy* (1964); Schneemann, again naked and body-painted, gradually un-twining a delicate paper scroll from her vagina, in *Interior Scroll* (1975). These and other works assure her place as a pioneering and influential figure in body art, performance art and experimental film.

Schneemann had been painting in a loosely expressionistic style before arriving in New York in 1962. Through the mid-1960s her paintings evolved into painted collages, boxed constructions and even kinetic works, whose complex surfaces have been compared to contemporary work by Robert Rauschenberg. They also bear the imprint of Joseph Cornell, whom she eventually met. The representative *Native Beauties* (1962–4; artist's collection), a collaged and constructed diptych, juxtaposes images of a Senegalese woman and Schneemann on a beach towel, with bits of driftwood, pebbles, glass and painted areas added.

Schneemann's breakthrough work *Eye Body* (1963) occurred when she felt the need to add her own body to an extensive loft environment of mirrors, rope, plastic and other materials, in a private performance recorded by a photographer. Of her painted body, she later wrote that it was both "erotic, sexual, desired, desiring" and also "written over in a text of stroke and gesture discovered by my creative female will" (*More than Meat Joy* 1979, p.52). The work's title, "Eye Body", nicely condenses a sense, running through much of her work, of the importance of a (specifically female) sensuous self-awareness as an instrument of knowing.

Meanwhile, Schneemann had already begun taking part in the fertile performance experimentation centred on the Judson Dance Theater. She participated in works with Robert Morris and Claes Oldenberg, and was choreographing works for groups of performers, including Yvonne Rainer (q.v.), Deborah Hay, Dorothea Rockburne and others, as early as 1962 (*Glass Environment for Sound and Motion*, Living Theater). *Meat Joy* (1964), the most shocking and ambitious of her large performances, was performed in Paris, London (its only all-nude performance) and New York. Conceived as having "the character of an erotic rite: excessive, indulgent, a celebration of flesh as material" (*ibid.*, p.63), the work involved its nine performers in planned but improvisational encounters with piles of shredded paper, flashlights, dead fish, chickens, chains of sausages and buckets of paint.

Schneemann began making films during this time, as well as incorporating film in some performances. *Viet-Flakes* (1965; distributed by Film-Makers Cooperative, New York) montaged and altered photographs from the Vietnam War; the performance *Snows* (New York, 1967) combined film clips, music and performers on a bright white stage to explore again the costs of that war. *Fuses* (1967; distributed by Film-Makers Cooperative) is a landmark erotic film by a woman artist. Observer and participant, Schneemann used a hand-held camera to film herself and her then-husband, James Tenney, making love; she then subjected the film to heat, acid, paint and scratching, a disordering and dismemberment analogous to the intensity of subjective sexual experience.

Two major performance works involved suspended bodies. In *Water Light/Water Needle* (1966) Schneemann and several other performers travelled along ropes suspended across the performance space. In *Up To And Including Her Limits* (first performed in New York, 1973) Schneemann dangled and swung, nude, in a leather harness, creating random markings on a papered stage. Daniel Cameron's observations apply well to such works: "She projects toward the viewer an intensely intimate persona, and then intercepts it with a formalized and/or chance activity that allows one to see the artist, as it were, through a screen of materiality" (Cameron 1983, p.125). *Interior Scroll* (1975), in which Schneemann read from a scroll while pulling it from her vagina, engaged a number of concepts: her own theory of "vulvic space", the sense of knowledge emerging from the body, and the symbology of the serpent.

Although Schneemann associated and performed with participants in the major performance movements of that time – Alan Kaprow and other makers of Happenings, the Vienna Group and Fluxus – she often felt isolated, unsupported in her own work, even rebuffed. Her relationship with Fluxus was particularly rocky. A work that she directed for Kaprow, part of Charlotte Moorman's New York Avant Garde Festival (*Push and Pull*, 1965), degenerated into chaos, damaging the theatre and ending with police intervention. Shortly after *Meat Joy* was performed, the Fluxus founder George Maciunas circulated a letter, warning that Schneemann was not to be considered a Fluxus artist, because of her eroticism and baroque tendencies. The unacknowledged sexism underlying such difficulties has been partly redressed by her inclusion in numerous recent retrospectives and anthologies devoted to Fluxus activity.

Although she abandoned large-scale performance in the mid-1970s, Schneemann has continued to produce mixed-media environmental works and performances that expand on her continuing themes. *Fresh Blood – A Dream Morphology* (1981–7) offered, through live performance and slide images, an exploration of menstruation, as multi-layered symbol and experience. *War Mop* (1986; artist's collection) responded to the civil war in Lebanon, with a motorised mop striking a television monitor playing images from the war. In *Cycladic Imprints* (1988; artist's collection, repr. David Joselit, "Projected identities", *Art in America*, lxxix, November 1991, p.120), with motorised violins and projected images of stringed instruments, Cycladic sculptures, hourglass-shaped objects, female bodies and genitals, Schneemann ironically reclaimed the Surrealist icon of woman-as-instrument. Her *Mortal Coils* (1994; artist's collection, repr. *Artforum*, xxxiii, September 1994, p.109), a kinetic and projected environment of similar scope, acted as a memorial, with images and written reminiscences of dead friends and colleagues, slithering motorised ropes as mortal coils and images of her own body.

Schneemann has written extensively and articulately about her work and other issues, notably in her compilation *More than Meat Joy* (1979). Her insistence on the interconnected validity of her "creative female will" and sexuality as a mode of perception and experience has under-girded a body of work that remains both disturbing and powerful.

MIRIAM SEIDEL

Schurman, Anna Maria van

Netherlandish amateur artist, 1607–1678

Born in Cologne, 1607, to Frederik van Schurman of Antwerp and his wife Eva von Harff de Dreiborn. Moved to Utrecht with her family, *c.*1616. Included in the register of the Guild of St Luke in Utrecht, 1643. Lived in Cologne, 1653–*c.*1655, then in the countryside near Vianen. Back in Utrecht by 1660; became a follower of the Protestant preacher Jean de Labadie; joined the Labadist community in Amsterdam, *c.*1669; moved with the community to Herford in Westphalia, then Altona and later Wieuwerd in Friesland. Died in Wieuwerd, 4 May 1678.

Selected Writings

De vitae humanae termino, Leiden, 1639; Paris, 1646

Dissertatio de ingenii muliebris ad doctrinam et meliores litteras aptitudine, Leiden: Elzevir, 1641; English edition as *The Learned Maid; or, Whether a Maid May Be a Scholar?*, London, 1659

Opuscula hebraeca, graeca, latina, gallica: Prosaica et metrica, Leiden: Elzevir, 1642; Utrecht, 1652; London, 1649; revised edition ed. Dorothea Loeber, Leipzig, 1749

Eukleria, seu melioris partis electio, Altona, 1673; Amsterdam: Van de Velde, 1684; reprinted Leeuwarden: De Tille, 1978

Bibliography

Una Birch, *Anna van Schurman: Artist, Scholar, Saint*, London: Longman, 1909

Katlijne Van der Stighelen, *Anna Maria van Schurman (1607–1678) of "Hoe hooge dat een maeght kan in de konsten stijgen"* [Anna Maria van Schurman (1607–1678) or "How high a maid may rise in art"], Louvain: Universitaire Pers Leuven, 1987

Mirjam de Baar and others, eds, *Choosing the Better Part: Anna Maria van Schurman, 1607–1678*, Dordrecht: Kluwer Academic Publishers, 1996 (Dutch original, 1992)

Commanding in her lifetime such titles as "Wonder of the Upper World", "The Tenth Muse", "Gabenzelt" and "La Célèbre", Anna Maria van Schurman enjoyed a Europe-wide reputation as a phenomenon of female talent. Besides her proficiency in a range of artistic media and her musical and poetic abilities, she was renowned for her knowledge of ancient and modern languages and for her scholarship in general, numbering among her acquaintance such intellectuals as Constantijn Huygens and Descartes. Her artistic output is perhaps best understood as one aspect of this many-sided virtuosity. Despite a brief period of training, she seems never to have worked as a professional artist. Instead her art functioned as part of a complex construction of herself as multi-talented, a construction that may be seen as a deliberate assertion of the possibility of female equality in all branches of the arts and sciences, and which reflects the arguments of her treatise, the *Dissertatio* (1641), for the inclusion of women in higher education and for their suitability for scientific study. This multiplicity also extended to her artistic oeuvre as a single element within that self-construction: although it consists almost entirely of portraits and self-portraits, of similar format, these are executed in a spectacular variety of media.

In *Eukleria*, a kind of "spiritual autobiography" written late in life, van Schurman claims to have had no artistic training. It seems, however, that in her youth she was apprenticed for a time to the engraver Magdalena van der Passe. Despite her description in the *Eukleria* of the admiration shown her work by Gerrit van Honthorst, and the suggestion by subsequent writers that she may have studied at his Utrecht academy, which, according to Roger de Piles, accepted women students, there is no evidence of any direct contact between Honthorst and van Schurman.

Her earliest dated works, two small portraits in oil on panel ('t Coopmanshûs, Franeker), probably of her brothers Hendrik Frederik and Johan Gotschalk van Schurman, are of 1623 and 1624 respectively. Her most productive period, however, was the 1630s and 1640s. Her inclusion in the members' register of the Utrecht Guild of St Luke in 1643 as "artist, sculptor and engraver" thus comes near the end of her artistic career. Although it would seem to imply that she was then working professionally, she appears to have had no other links with the guild and did not pay yearly contributions. It is therefore more than likely that this registration was honorary, reflecting her position of esteem within the city – a position that van Schurman herself cultivated. Known as the "Star of Utrecht", she characterised herself as one of its wonders. The anonymous engraved portrait of her in Jacob Cats's *Werelts begin midden en eynde, besloten in den trou-ringh, met den proef-steen van den selven* (The beginning, middle and end of the world, contained in the wedding ring, with the proving-stone of the selves; Dordrecht, 1637), which he dedicated to her, follows her own design and shows her in front of a window through which may be seen the tower of Utrecht's famous cathedral. This juxtaposition both posits her as an equivalent attraction and advertises her presence in the city – with topographical accuracy, since the van Schurman house was in the Domskerkhof.

Prestigious visitors to this house, including Louise-Maria de Gonzaga, Queen of Poland (1645), and Christina of Sweden (*c.*1651), testify to van Schurman's contemporary fame. During these visits to the "Pinacoteca Schurmannae" they witnessed the Tenth Muse herself, admired the fruits of her talents and saw those talents in action: contemporary sources confirm that it was her custom to make portraits of visitors. Besides such visitors, family and friends were both the viewers and the subjects of her works, almost all of which are portraits. Her etched portrait of *Gisbert Voet* (1647; Rijksprentenkabinet, Rijksmuseum, Amsterdam; Historisch Museum, Rotterdam) is characteristic of her works, being modest in scale and format, with the subject shown bust-length and in three-quarter profile, without hands. This practice of using associates as models may be partly ascribed to convenience. It is also possible, however, to see van Schurman's decision to represent individuals with whom she enjoyed a familial or amicable, rather than a merely commercial relationship as a deliberate attempt to emphasise her artistic activity as the exercise of a liberal art, not just the fulfilment of a financial contract.

Van Schurman's many self-portraits may be placed within a tradition of self-portraiture by women artists that included, in the Netherlands, Catharina van Hemessen (q.v.) and Judith Leyster (q.v.). This tradition may have depended in part on the prototype of Iaia, one of the women artists named by Pliny, who describes her as painting her own portrait with the aid of a mirror. In this context, van Schurman's self-portrayal, for example the signed and dated etching, *Self-Portrait at 25* (1633), the inscription of which refers pointedly to its own making, may be seen as the defining gesture of the woman artist. At a period when only certain human qualities were considered to justify portrayal, it also constitutes a repeated assertion of herself as a woman of exceptional knowledge and talent.

Van Schurman was proficient in an extraordinary variety of media, producing portraits in oil, gouache, graphite and pastel, engraved and etched portraits and portraits modelled in wax and carved in ivory and boxwood. Her pastel *Self-Portrait* of 1640 ('t Coopmanshûs, Franeker) is the earliest known example of this technique in the Netherlands. She was also skilled in activities more commonly practised by women of good family: embroidery, calligraphy, paper cut-outs and glass engraving. These forays into an unusually broad range of techniques may be interpreted as an attempt to demonstrate a many-sided virtuosity, and as a way of claiming some kind of mastery over the world. In the 1640s van Schurman's artistic output declined considerably, probably as a result of her developing interest in theological issues and her commitment to a religious life.

KATE BOMFORD

See also Amateur Artists survey

Scultori, Diana *see* Mantuana

Serebryakova, Zinaida (Evgenevna)
Russian painter, 1884–1967   [fig. 64]

Born Zinaida Evgenevna Lansere on the family estate of Neskuchnoye, near Kharkov, 28

November (Old Style calendar)/10 December (New Style calendar) 1884; grew up in St Petersburg. Studied at Tenisheva School under Ilya Repin, 1901; visited Italy, 1902–3; studied under the portrait painter Osip Braz, 1903–5; studied at the Académie de la Grande Chaumière, Paris, 1905–6. Married writer and railway engineer Boris Serebryakov, 1905; four children, born 1906, 1907, 1912 and 1915. Lived at Neskuchnoye. Joined Mir Iskusstva (World of Art) group, 1906. Nominated for rank of Academician, Petrograd Academy of Arts, 1916. Left Neskuchnoye after home burned (1918) and husband died of typhus (1919); moved to Petrograd and worked in IZO (Fine Arts Section) of Narkompros (People's Commissariat of Enlightenment), 1920. Went to Paris to fulfil a commission, 1924; never returned to Russia. Travelled and painted in England, Brittany and North Africa. Lived in Paris until her death, 19 September 1967.

Principal Exhibitions

SRKh (Union of Russian Artists), St Petersburg: 1910
St Petersburg/Petrograd: 1910 (*The Contemporary Female Portrait*), 1918 (*Russian Countryside*)
Mir Iskusstva (World of Art): 1910–13, 1922, 1924
Kharkov Soviet Worker Deputies, Kharkov: 1919 (*First Exhibition of the Arts*)
House of Arts, Petrograd: 1920
Tretyakov Gallery, Moscow: 1924 (*The Peasant in Russian Painting*)
Galerie Charpentier, Paris: 1927 (individual)
Union of Artists of the USSR, Moscow: 1965–6 (touring retrospective)

Bibliography

V. Dmitriyev, "Khudozhnitsy" [Women artists], *Apollon*, 1917, nos 8–10
Sergei Ernst, *Z.E. Serebryakova*, Petrograd: Akvilon, 1922
Zinaida Serebryakova: Vystavka proizvedeniy iz muzeyev i chastnykh sobraniy [Zinaida Serebryakova: Exhibition of works from museums and private collections], exh. cat., Union of Artists of the USSR, Moscow, and elsewhere, 1965
Alexandre Benois, "Zinaida Serebryakova", *Aleksandr Benua razmyshlayet* [Alexandre Benois reflects], Moscow: Nauka, 1968, pp.219–22
V. Lapshin, *Serebryakova*, Moscow: Sovetsky Khudozhnik, 1969
Aleksei Savinov, *Zinaida Serebryakova*, Leningrad: Khudozhnik RSFSR, 1973
V.P. Knyazeva, *Zinaida Evgenevna Serebryakova*, Moscow: Izobrazitelnoye Iskusstvo, 1979
Alison Hilton, "Zinaida Serebriakova", *Woman's Art Journal*, iii/2, 1982–3, pp.32–5
M.N. Yablonskaya, *Women Artists of Russia's New Age, 1900–1935*, New York: Rizzoli, and London: Thames and Hudson, 1990
Vsevolod Petrov and Alexander Kamensky, *The World of Art Movement in Early 20th-Century Russia*, Leningrad: Aurora, 1991

Zinaida Serebryakova's paintings reflect none of the tumult of the Russian avant-garde era. Fascinated with the human figure and dedicated to careful observation and fresh rendering of her perceptions, before the Bolshevik Revolution of 1917 she was acclaimed for her portraits and her large-scale paintings of nudes and of peasants at work or at rest. After leaving the country to pursue career prospects, she became a reluctant exile in Paris for almost half her life, but she always identified her art as Russian. Neither allied with avant-garde abstraction nor with Socialist Realism, Serebryakova worked in near isolation, concentrating on a limited range of subjects and formal problems.

She was born on the estate of Neskuchnoye, near the provincial city of Kharkov. Her father Evgeny Lansere was a sculptor known for lively bronze figures of Cossack horsemen; one brother became a painter and graphic artist, the other an architect. Her mother Ekaterina Lansere, a painter, came from the Benua (Benois) family, whose members included an architect, a composer and the artist Alexandre Benois, a founder of the World of Art group. After her father's death in 1886, her mother took the young children to live in the Benois household in St Petersburg, where they all began to draw and grew accustomed to the presence of painters, musicians, writers and other figures in the art world.

At the age of 17 Zinaida Lansere began her formal art training at the school founded by Princess Marya Tenisheva and directed by the realist painter Ilya Repin; she studied with the portraitist Osip Braz for two years, and spent several months in Italy. After her marriage to Boris Serebryakov in 1905, she went to Paris to study at the Académie de la Grande Chaumière. Her notes and copies of paintings show an interest in the works of Titian, Rubens and Rembrandt, Watteau and Fragonard, Renoir, Monet and Degas. When she returned to St Petersburg in 1906, she joined the cosmopolitan World of Art group. Benois, Sergei Diaghilev, Leon Bakst, Konstantin Somov, her brother Evgeny Lansere and other founders of the World of Art believed that direct interaction between Russian and European artists was essential to break down provincialism and invigorate contemporary art. Their journal, exhibitions and Diaghilev's opera and ballet productions emphasised aesthetic values rather than content; international in spirit, they also fostered appreciation of the distinctiveness of Russian culture. Serebryakova shared the group's standards of artistic quality and admiration for a timeless concept of beauty, but she was not interested in the historicism and stylisation of much of their work. She decided to live at Neskuchnoye, and to bring up her four children in the country while focusing her art on the activities of rural life. She corresponded with her brother and uncle, made several trips to St Petersburg and abroad, and generally stayed in touch with artistic events, but her paintings display a serenity that might have been hard to achieve in the capital.

Her portraits, landscapes and studies of peasants show Serebryakova's ability to clarify the chief features of a place or a person and to integrate figures with their settings. Her best-known work, *Self-Portrait at the Dressing Table* (1909; Tretyakov Gallery, Moscow), was admired for its originality and lack of pretension. It came about casually, when the artist was snowed-in at Neskuchnoye with no other models, and began painting her reflection along with all the trifles, as she said, that made up her intimate environment. The painting is structured so that every part of the composition contains elements that parallel those in other sections: the delicate toiletries in the foreground have simpler echoes in the wash-basin, jug and mirror in the background, and the lace-trimmed dresser-scarf picks up the textures of the pillow-case and the nightshirt. The creamy tint of the walls, bedspread and chemise draws the scene together, while the verticals of the candle and its reflection reinforce the painted frame of the mirror, just inside the edge of the canvas. In contrast, the action of the arms brushing the thick dark hair and the parallel diagonals of the hat-pins create an energetic hub at the very centre of the picture, drawing the viewer's eyes to the oblique glance of the reflected artist. In 1910 Serebryakova sent the painting to the Union of Russian Artists' exhibition in St Petersburg, where it was purchased by the Tretyakov Gallery, a remarkable success for a young artist's first show.

At the Table (1914; Tretyakov Gallery) combines the strong framework of the table with the apparent spontaneity of the children, who seem to look up questioningly at an adult. A close viewpoint and lack of horizon also convey a sense of familiarity in *Peasants at Dinner* (1914; State Russian Museum, St Petersburg), showing a woman and a man preparing for their noon meal. The large-scale figure composition *In the Bathhouse* (1913; Tretyakov Gallery) could be classified as genre, but it comes closer to a rhythmic choreography of nude bodies arranged in distinct planes across the composition. The steamy atmosphere and natural postures in the study (1913; State Russian Museum) are absent in the almost manneristic final version. In two large outdoor scenes, *Harvest* (1915; Art Gallery, Odessa) and *Bleaching Linen* (1917; Tretyakov Gallery), the statuesque figures of peasant women seem stilled in a moment of purely aesthetic balance, rather than captured in the midst of activity. These works, with their low viewpoints, monumentality and harmony, testify to Serebryakova's productive study of High Renaissance art. Her affinity for the Renaissance was most apparent in a mural project for the Kazan Railway Station in Moscow. The project was not realised, but her tempera studies for the lunettes survive (1916; Tretyakov Gallery). Four female nudes personifying Persia, Siam, Turkey and India and two odalisques exemplify the decorative tendency of her work, while their complex crouching poses are reminiscent of Michelangelo's *ignudi*.

Within a decade of finishing her studies, Serebryakova had achieved success and recognition by her peers. In the autumn of 1916 the council of the Academy of Arts took the first step in recognising the achievements of women by recommending that the title of Academician be awarded to Serebryakova and three other women artists, Anna Ostroumova-Lebedeva, Olga Della-vos Kardovskaya and A.P. Shneyder (hitherto, Artist of the Third Rank was the highest title that women could earn). Ironically, the session of the Academy at which the final vote would take place was cancelled because of the outbreak of the February Revolution in 1917.

Soon after the October Revolution, Serebryakova's life changed abruptly. A fire destroyed her house and many of her paintings in 1918, and a year later her husband died of typhus. She found a temporary job at the Kharkov Archaeological Museum, but it was a difficult time, and a painting of her children entitled *House of Cards* (1919; State Russian Museum) conveys the family's uncertainty. They moved to the Benua home in 1920, and

Serebryakova found new subjects in the theatre and ballet. She watched rehearsals and drew pencil and pastel studies of dancers, emphasising the difficult poses of trained bodies and playing with the effects of mirror reflections, oblique angles and the interactions of figures with the surrounding space.

Serebryakova worked in the IZO (Fine Arts Section) of Narkompros (People's Commissariat of Enlightenment), but she did not expect regular employment, and in 1924 she decided to accept a commission in Paris. Circumstances forced her to remain abroad, but she made no effort to become part of the Russian émigré circle in Paris, a group that included Natalya Goncharova (q.v.), Larionov and other members of the former avant-garde. She took part in few exhibitions and felt alienated from the arguments of the contemporary art world. She travelled to Morocco and Algeria, to Britain and Brittany, and continued to paint landscapes, portraits and decorative compositions, with a strong feeling for visual rhythm. In 1955 she sent some of her best works to Soviet museums, and in 1965–6 a retrospective exhibition of her work was held in Moscow, Kiev and Leningrad. A year later she died in Paris.

Serebryakova remained a figurative artist throughout her life. She never felt that she was limited in copying nature, and did not question the validity of realism. Like her World of Art colleagues, she emphasised aesthetic values, and she regarded the extreme formalist experiments of Goncharova, Lyubov Popova (q.v.), Kazimir Malevich and other avant-garde contemporaries as a denial of those values. Although she experienced privations during the Revolution and Civil War, and in the long years of isolation abroad, Serebryakova did not allow the circumstances to disturb the essential harmony of her art.

ALISON HILTON

Sirani, Elisabetta [fig. 66]
Italian painter and printmaker, 1638–1665

Born in Bologna, 8 January 1638, daughter of the painter Giovan Andrea Sirani, assistant to Guido Reni; her two sisters Barbara and Anna Maria were also painters. Trained by her father. Lived in Bologna all her life. Member of Accademia di San Luca, Rome. Buried in San Domenico, Bologna, 29 August 1665 (maid accused of poisoning her, but autopsy revealed perforated stomach ulcers).

Bibliography
Luigi Picinardi, *La poesia muta celebrata della pittrice loquaci applausi di nobili ingegneri al pinnello immortale della Signorina Elisabetta Sirani pittrice bolognese*, Bologna, 1666 (funeral oration, as "Il pennello lagrimato ...", 1665, reprinted in Malvasia 1678)

Carlo Cesare Malvasia, *Felsina pittrice: Vite de' pittori bolognesi*, ii, Bologna, 1678, pp.385–407 (contains "Nota delle pitture fatte da me, Elisabetta Sirani", pp.393–6)

Luigi Crespi, *Vite de' pittori bolognese*, Rome, 1769 (as third volume of Malvasia 1678)

G. Giordani, *Notizie delle donne pittrici di Bologna*, Bologna, 1832

Ottavio Mazzoni-Toselli, *Di Elisabetta Sirani pittrice bolognese e del supposto veneficazione credeesi morta*, Bologna, 1833

Domenico Vaccolini, *Biografia di Elis. Sirani scritta dal Prof. D. Vaccolini*, Rome, 1844

Carolina Bonafede, *Cenni biografici e ritratti d'insigni donne bolognese raccolti dagli storici più accreditati*, Bologna, 1845

Andrea Bianchini, *Prove legali sull'avvelenamente della celebre pittrice bolognese, Elisabetta Sirani, emergenti dal relativo processo*, Bologna, 1854

——, *Il processo di avvelenamento fatto 1665–66 in Bologna contro Lucia Tolomelli per la morte di Elisabetta Sirani*, Bologna, 1904

Laura M. Ragg, *The Women Artists of Bologna*, London: Methuen, 1907

Evelyn Foster Edwards, "Elisabetta Sirani", *Art in America*, xvii, August 1929, pp.242–6

Otto Kurz, *Bolognese Drawings in the Royal Library at Windsor Castle*, London, 1955

G. Baldi, *La farmacia nella breve mortale malattia della pittrice bolognese Elisabetta Sirani*, Pisa, 1958

Andrea Emiliani, "Giovan Andrea ed Elisabetta Sirani", *Maestri della pittura del Seicento emiliano*, exh. cat., Palazzo dell'Archiginnasio, Bologna, 1959, pp.140–45

Women Artists, 1550–1950, exh. cat., Los Angeles County Museum of Art, and elsewhere, 1976

P. Bellini, "Elisabetta Sirani: Catalogue des gravures", *Nouvelles de L'Estampe*, November–December 1976, pp.7–12

Fiorella Frisoni, "La vera Sirani", *Paragone*, xxix/335, 1978, pp.3–18

Germaine Greer, *The Obstacle Race: The Fortunes of Women Painters and Their Work*, London: Secker and Warburg, and New York: Farrar Straus, 1979

Edward Goldberg, *Patterns in Late Medici Art Patronage*, Princeton: Princeton University Press, 1983

Elisabetta Landi and Massimo Pirondini, "Elisabetta Sirani", *Arte emiliana dalle raccolte storiche al nuovo collezionismo*, ed. G. Manni, E. Negro and M. Pirondini, Modena: Artioli, 1989, pp.108–11

Fiorella Frisoni, "Elisabetta Sirani", *La Scuola di Guido Reni*, ed. Emilio Negro and Massimo Pirondini, Modena, 1992

Adelina Modesti, "Elisabetta Sirani 'Pittrice eroina': A portrait of the artist as a young woman", *Identità ed appartenza: Donne e relazioni di genere dal mondo classico all'età contemporanea. Acts of the First International Congress of the Italian Society of Women Historians: Rimini, 1995*

In Counter- and post-Reformation Bologna an unprecedented number of women became professional artists; among these, Elisabetta Sirani, like Lavinia Fontana (q.v.), gained international recognition. As a young girl, Sirani was apprenticed to her father Giovan Andrea Sirani at the insistence of the critic Malvasia, who noticed her precocious drawing talent. She is often regarded as a mere imitator of her father's master, Guido Reni, but she produced more than 200 works in a career of only 13 years, and her achievements deserve closer attention. She was a full member of the Accademia di San Luca in Rome, although she never left her home town of Bologna, where she was the centre of an artistic circle. A master by the age of 19, she ran the Sirani workshop, which included her sisters Barbara and Anna Maria, and supported the whole family when her father was no longer able to paint. She also established an art school for young girls and, in addition to her sisters, her pupils are said to have included Teresa Muratori, Vincenza Franchi, Lucrezia Bianchi, Antonia Pinelli, Maria Oriana Galli Bibiena, Veronica Fontana, Lucrezia Scarfaglia, Camilla Lanteri, Caterina Mongardi, Teresa Maria Coriolani, Ginevra Cantofoli, Vincenza Fabbri and Giovan Battista Zanichelli (most from artists' families), as well as the noblewomen Caterina Pepoli and Maria Elena Panzacchi, all of whom worked professionally at some point.

The literature about Sirani is extensive but largely hagiographic, depicting her as a romantic heroine. Typical of this mythologising tendency is Luigi Picinardi's oration at her state funeral, in which he referred to her as "the glory of the female sex"; while Malvasia praised her "extraordinary moral virtue ... modesty and inimitable goodness". Her attested beauty and "femininity" ensured that Sirani conformed to the female ideal specified in Renaissance treatises. As a professional painter, unmarried and childless, she also fitted the model of the virtuous noble artist described by Leon Battista Alberti and Giorgio Vasari and epitomised by Raphael. Her works, like Raphael's, were believed to reflect the beauty of her character. Since both the muse of painting and its allegorical personification were female, Sirani could represent both the beauty of womanhood and the perfection of art (see her self-portraits, e.g. as *La Pittura*; Pinacoteca Nazionale, Bologna).

Unlike the paintings of her near contemporary Artemisia Gentileschi (q.v.), which often subvert traditional notions of femininity, Sirani's works do not challenge the male symbolic order, a factor that undoubtedly contributed considerably to her popularity and critical success. Interpreting established artistic models and iconographic traditions in a more personal and intimate manner, she executed mythological works, allegorical scenes and *vanitas*, portraits and large-scale history paintings, both religious and classical (e.g. *Judith Triumphant*, 1658; Burghley House, Stamford; *Portia Wounding Her Thigh*, signed and dated 1664; ex-Wildenstein Collection, New York). The main subjects of her oeuvre, however, are the Holy Family and the Virgin and Child, from one of her earliest public commissions, the *Madonna of the Rosary* (1657; Parish Church, Coscogno), to the numerous small paintings on canvas and copper she produced for private devotional use (e.g. *Madonna of the Girdle* for the Marchese Cospi, 1663; Parish Church, Bagnarola di Budrio). In her last painting, a portrait of *Anna Maria Ranuzzi as Charity* (signed and dated 1665; Cassa di Risparmio, Bologna), the relationship between mother and children is presented in the refined manner of Reni, but with a greater naturalism typical of Emilia, the half-length figures filling the composition and emphasising the closeness of the family group. The representation of maternal love as the Christian virtue of charity gives a spiritual dimension to this secular portrait. A sense of immediacy and intimacy is also seen in Sirani's depictions of the Holy Family in everyday domestic situations to accord with Counter-Reformation devotional requirements (*Madonna of the Swaddling Clothes*, signed and dated 1665; private collection, Madrid, repr. Frisoni 1978, fig.26).

In particular Sirani developed a new iconography of the Virgin and Child with St John the Baptist, presenting the cousins as ordinary playful children (e.g. *Christ Child and Young St John the Baptist*, signed and dated 1661; private collection, repr. Manni, Negro and Pirondini 1989, fig.79), with the

Virgin as a more accessible earthly figure wearing the turban of Bolognese peasant women rather than the traditional veil (e.g. two versions of *Virgin and Child with the Young St John*, both 1664; Cassa di Risparmio, Cesena; Museo Civico, Pesaro). Her depictions of children are especially notable: *Vincenzo Ranuzzi as Cupid* (signed and dated 1663; National Gallery, Warsaw), *Sleeping Infant Christ* (Fondazione Querini-Stampalia, Venice) and the cherubs and angels of numerous altarpieces (e.g. *St Antony with the Christ Child*, 1662; Pinacoteca Nazionale, Bologna). The sentimentality and soft *colorito* of these images recall the work of Sirani's Spanish contemporary Murillo. Another favoured subject was the *Penitent Magdalene* (e.g. signed and dated 1660; Pinacoteca Nazionale, Bologna), associated with Guido Reni.

The most important sources for Sirani's life and work are the writings of the critic and historian Conte Carlo Cesare Malvasia, who was a close family friend. In his famous two-volume work, *Felsina pittrice: Vite de' pittori bolognesi* (1678), he included "Nota delle pitture fatte da me Elisabetta Sirani", an incomplete inventory list of *c*.182 works painted by Elisabetta between the age of 17 and her death, as well as a eulogy to her, the "Pittrice Eroina" of Bolognese painting. In this first text promoting a Bolognese school of painting, Malvasia aimed to redress the central Italian bias of Vasari's *Lives* (1550 and 1568), presenting Reni as Bologna's most important and influential artist. It is in this context of the articulation of a specifically Bolognese artistic identity (that was increasingly identified with the school of Reni), which challenged the hegemony of the central Italian art promoted by Vasari, that Sirani's work should be considered. Having learned the elegant Renian classical *maniera* from her father, Reni's foremost assistant, Sirani was primarily responsible for passing on Reni's legacy to the latter half of the 17th century.

An extremely fashionable artist, Sirani had a coterie of aristocratic patrons cultivated by her protective father and influential family friends. Documents indicate that her patrons and collectors included many of the most prominent Bolognese families as well as representatives of other social levels: friends, the fishmonger, her music teacher and doctor, clergymen and members of the nobility and royalty, such as the King of Poland. Although she never travelled, her reputation and fame spread far beyond Bologna, with nobility from all over Europe coming to watch her work, as noted by Sirani in her diary entries and confirmed by early sources.

Her fame was based on her prodigious talent, her deft touch and masterly handling of paint, and her skill as a portraitist, especially of women. Contemporaries often stressed her painterly skills and virtuoso brushwork, associating her with Venetian *colorito* rather than central Italian *disegno*. In her drawing style as well she rejected the Vasarian model of finely studied preliminary drawings for paintings, preferring the Venetian use of wash sketches made with a few quick brush strokes. Such a bold, freely sketched drawing style, which differs from 17th-century Bolognese practice (usually more detailed and linear, in pen and black chalk), seems to have been her own invention and was used only by artists she influenced, such as Zani. The apparent effortlessness of her *maniera*, akin to the studied spontaneity of Rubens, can be seen for example in such passages as Anna Maria Ranuzzi's sleeve, the opalescent flesh of her favoured subjects, young children, and the fine modelling and delicate facial features of her madonnas, saints and sibyls.

According to Malvasia, Sirani aimed at developing an individual style, and he cited her largest and most important public commission, the *Baptism of Christ* (signed and dated 1657; La Certosa, Bologna) as evidence of her "genius/invenzione". He claims that immediately on receiving the commission, Sirani, then age 19, dashed off her "concetto" for the composition in a brush-wash sketch (Albertina, Vienna). This confirms that she created her own designs and did not merely copy the compositions of others, a criticism often directed against women artists. Because of her painterly skills and invention she was said to have "acquired the virile sex" (Picinardi); this is also demonstrated by the association of her work with traditionally male artistic concepts such as "genius" and "invention". Considered the equal of any male artist, she was compared with masculine ideals and judged by male aesthetic standards.

More recent writers have rightly attempted to extract the "true" Sirani from her identity as a follower of Reni, arguing that she developed a distinct personal style independent of his, in order to give her work credibility. Yet it also must be remembered that her professional standing and popularity were due precisely to the fact that she was considered the "second Guido". Unlike her father, Sirani consciously modelled herself on Reni: her appropriation of his style and iconography, which she transformed in her original compositions into a warmer and more intimate and naturalistic form of his academic classicism, appears to have been a carefully considered career choice. Malvasia lamented that her father, in his determination to develop a distinctive style of his own, lost an opportunity to share in Reni's glory and remained a mediocre artist.

Although her work is now less valued than that of the great Guido, Sirani was perhaps more marketable to the majority of collectors. Many of her patrons were members of the Bolognese middle class, who could not afford an original Reni and wished to possess the next best thing: a copy or a work in a similar style inspired by his iconography of swooning saints and beautiful madonnas. Current research confirms Sirani as one of the most commissioned and collected artists among Reni's followers. According to archival sources, many Bolognese collections included at least one work by her, which was often the only painting listed by title and singled out for comment, and among the highest valued (c.300–500 lira, as opposed to 100 lira for the majority of works cited in inventories).

To own a "Sirana" was highly prized until the late 19th century, when the Bolognese school fell out of favour with critics such as Ruskin and Baudelaire and her works were regarded as typifying the school's less glorious aspects: its lack of perfection in design and its vigorous new deep colouring. By the early 20th century her work – and by implication Reni's – was considered of little artistic value, judging by an exhibition catalogue entry of 1924 in which it was dismissed as "tired and pallid imitations of the most tired and pallid manner of Guido Reni" (*La pittura italiana del Seicento e del Settecento alla mostra di Palazzo Pitti*, Milan-Rome, 1924, p.81).

While some of Sirani's paintings are of extremely high quality (*Anna Maria Ranuzzi*, *St Antony with the Infant Christ*, *Portia*, *Baptism of Christ*) and show her compositional skill in dealing with crowd scenes on a grand scale, with an appropriate variety of gestures, poses and emotions, her oeuvre is inconsistent in quality, style and type. Her popularity and fame may seem incomprehensible, since collectively the work does not represent a "great" talent, yet many are probably workshop pieces, produced by her assistants to satisfy high public demand. In 17th-century workshops, copying the master's work was one method of training apprentices. It was normal practice for the master to create the concept and design and for assistants either to work on sections of the painting, leaving important areas such as the figures and faces to be completed by the master (considered an "original"), or to complete the whole painting themselves (a work of the pupil "after" the master, for example Ginevra Cantofoli's altarpiece of the *Last Supper* for San Procolo, based on a design by her teacher Sirani). Artistic collaboration appears to have been quite common: Sirani is known to have worked with her father, with Lorenzo Loli, and with Teresa Maria Coriolani.

While contemporaries were sometimes critical of Sirani, they did value her as an artist in her own right: her portrait was painted a number of times (e.g. by her sister Barbara Borgognoli and Lorenzo Loli) and her paintings were copied and reproduced as prints by other artists (e.g. Bartolommeo Zanichelli and Loli). The cycle of copying extended from Reni to his students and followers, of whom a select few were themselves copied, with Sirani the principal disseminator of his style. From Malvasia onwards, in critical attempts to establish an artistic identity and cultural authority for the Bolognese school of painting Sirani has been cited as exemplifying its particular qualities: sweetness, naturalism, refined and erudite elegance, virtuoso brushwork, subtlety of expression and sensual colour. Both in artistic discourse and in the popular imagination Sirani represented the success that women could achieve with natural talent, diligence and skills cultivated through sound workshop training (albeit without life drawing).

ADELINA MODESTI

See also Printmakers survey

Sleigh, Sylvia
British painter, 1916–

Born in Llandudno, Wales, 8 May 1916. Studied at Brighton School of Art, Sussex, 1933–7; University of London Extra-Mural Department (diploma 1947). Married art critic Lawrence Alloway, 1954; he died 1990. Moved to USA, 1961. Edith Kreeger Wolf distinguished professor, Northwestern University, Evanston, Illinois, 1977; visiting assistant professor, State University of New York, Stony

Brook, 1978; instructor, New School of Social
Research, New York, 1974–7 and 1978–80; visiting artist, Baldwin Seminar, Oberlin College, Ohio,
1982. Recipient of National Endowment for the
Arts (NEA) grant, 1982; Pollock-Krasner
Foundation award, 1985. Lives in New York.

Selected Individual Exhibitions
Bennington College, Bennington, VT: 1963
SoHo 20 Gallery, New York: 1973, 1980, 1985
AIR Gallery, New York: 1974, 1976, 1978
Mabel Smith Douglass Library, Rutgers University, New
    Brunswick, NJ: 1974
Wadsworth Atheneum, Hartford, CT: 1976
Zaks Gallery, Chicago: 1976, 1985
Ohio State University, Columbus: 1976
Everson Museum of Art, Syracuse, NY: 1976 (*Paintings
    by Three American Realists*, with Alice Neel and May
    Stevens)
G.W. Einstein Co. Inc., New York: 1980, 1983, 1985
Gallery 210, University of Missouri, St Louis: 1981
Milwaukee Art Museum: 1990 (*Invitation to a Voyage
    and Other Works*, touring)
Stiebel Modern, New York: 1992 (retrospective), 1994

Bibliography
Linda Nochlin, "Some women realists: Painters of the
    figure", *Arts Magazine*, xlviii, May 1974, pp.29–33
Gerrit Henry, "The artist and the face: A modern
    American sampling", *Art in America*, lxiii,
    January–February 1975, pp.34–41
Lisa Tickner, "The body politic: Female sexuality and
    women artists since 1970", *Art History*, i, 1978,
    pp.237–51
Margaret Walters, *The Nude Male: A New Perspective*,
    New York and London: Paddington, 1978
Deborah Schwartz, "An interview with Sylvia Sleigh",
    Arts and Sciences, Spring 1978, pp.11–15
Kevin Eckstrom, *Images of Men in the Paintings of Sylvia
    Sleigh*, MA thesis, Indiana University, 1980
Sylvia Sleigh: Recent Paintings, exh. cat., G.W. Einstein
    Co. Inc., New York, 1980
Alessandra Comini, "Art history, revisionism and some
    holy cows", *Arts Magazine*, liv, June 1980, pp.96–100
Charlotte Streifer Rubinstein, *American Women Artists
    from Early Times to the Present*, Boston: Hall, 1982
Gerrit Henry, "Sylvia Sleigh at G.W. Einstein", *Art in
    America*, lxxi, Summer 1983, pp.158–9
Joanna Frueh, "Chicago: Sylvia Sleigh at Zaks", *Art in
    America*, lxxiv, January 1986, pp.143–5
Betty Ann Brown and Arlene Raven, *Exposures: Women
    and Their Art*, Pasadena, CA: New Sage Press, 1989
Sylvia Sleigh: Invitation to a Voyage and Other Works,
    exh. cat., Milwaukee Art Museum, and elsewhere,
    1990
John Loughery, "Sylvia Sleigh: Invitation to a voyage and
    other works", *Woman's Art Journal*, xii/1, 1991,
    pp.69–71
The Sixties Art Scene in London, exh. cat., Barbican Art
    Gallery, London, 1993
Ken Johnson, "Sylvia Sleigh at Stiebel Modern", *Art in
    America*, xii, December 1994, p.98

Sylvia Sleigh is a portrait painter. "Even if I paint a
leaf, it should be a portrait", she once asserted to
Arlene Raven, "It is my belief that if we could all
appreciate every living thing in detail, we would be
kinder and better to one another" (Brown and
Raven 1989, p.68). Sleigh is perhaps best known for
her nude portraits of men. Many of these are single
figure studies. *Philip Golub Reclining* (1971;
Milwaukee Art Museum), which quotes the *Toilet
of Venus* (1651; National Gallery, London) by
Velázquez, is remarkable because of its gender inversion, that is, its unsettling presentation of a male
figure laid out on a bed to receive the erotic gaze our
culture has usually directed at women. It is also
remarkable in its studied refusal of prettied idealisation. While nude females are often distanced and
objectified in order to receive the gaze (to become
sex "objects", as it were), Golub, the son of the
artists Nancy Spero (q.v.) and Leon Golub, is
presented as a unique and known individual, fully
human and fully vulnerable. In 1973 Sleigh painted
the *Turkish Bath* (artist's collection), a large group
portrait inspired by Ingres's depiction of harem
women (1863; Louvre, Paris). Again, Sleigh not
only reversed gender, thus challenging the cultural
expectations of the eroticised gaze, she also
presented known individuals rather than idealised
or stereotyped "objects". One of the men in the
Turkish Bath is Lawrence Alloway, a renowned
critic and the artist's husband.

Alloway and Sleigh emigrated from Britain to the
USA in 1961. Sleigh was soon swept into the feminist art movement. She founded, joined and became
active in several artists' groups, including the Ad
Hoc Women Artists Committee, Women in the Arts,
SoHo 20 and the AIR Cooperative Gallery. Sleigh's
portraits of the members of SoHo 20 (1974;
University of Missouri at St. Louis) and of the AIR
Gallery (1977; artist's collection) remain important
documents of the New York women's art movement. The 20 women of the AIR Gallery are clustered in a three-tiered composition that unfolds
towards the viewer. The women settle into comfortable and companionable conversation among them-

selves and, it seems, with the viewer, in a manner reminiscent of Rembrandt's group portraits.

Sleigh's group portraits are, in a sense, her rewriting of art history. For centuries, European academies valued history painting above all other genres. Barred from anatomy classes, women could not receive the training necessary for complex compositions involving numerous human figures. To develop her own history paintings, and to work directly with nude models, is to assert that women certainly have the capacity – the vision and the skills – to produce the art that history denied them. Sleigh never merely quotes the works of old masters, but always transforms them into contemporary terms that are idiosyncratically her own. *Venus and Mars* (1976; Milwaukee Museum of Art) presents portraits of Maureen Connor and Paul Rosano (one of Sleigh's favourite sitters) in positions that echo Botticelli's early Renaissance painting of the Classical gods (National Gallery, London). The specificity of Connor's fashionable attire, carefully painted features and alert expression lift her out of allegory into individuality. Rosano, on the other hand, is nude except for cut-off jeans and appears to sleep while the artist immortalises him. Here Sleigh inverts the traditional bipolar opposition that links male with active (which has been valued historically) and female with passive (devalued historically). In grappling with archetypes and challenging the unexamined assumptions on which we all too often build our identities, Sleigh uses portraiture to explore the meaning of human subjectivity.

While Sleigh has often worked on a large scale – many of her nudes are somewhat larger than life-size – her largest work is *Invitation to a Voyage* (1984; artist's collection), an immense mural consisting of 14 oil-on-canvas panels, each 2.4 × 1.5 metres, which wraps around a room and was originally exhibited at the Milwaukee Museum of Art. Inspired by the French writer Baudelaire's poem, Sleigh depicted a group of her contemporaries picnicking at the edge of the Hudson River. Behind them stands Bannerman's Island Arsenal, which Sleigh romanticises as a Claudian "enchanted castle". Artists, writers and other friends stroll through the radiant landscape, frozen by the time-lessness of paint into what the art critic Ken Johnson has referred to as Sleigh's "persuasive marriage of the actual and the numinous" (Johnson 1994).

BETTY ANN BROWN

Sleigh, Clarissa
American photographer and installation artist, 1939–

Born in Washington, DC, 30 August 1939. Studied at Hampton Institute, Virginia (BS 1961); Howard University, Washington, DC (BFA 1972); Skowhegan School of Art, Maine, 1972; University of Pennsylvania, Philadelphia (MBA 1973); International Center of Photography, New York, 1979–80. Part-time research assistant, Philadelphia Federal Reserve Bank and Wharton Entrepreneurial Center, 1972–3; financial analyst, Mobil Oil Corporation, New York, 1974–5, and Goldman, Sachs and Company, New York, 1975–84; computer programmer, National Aeronautics and Space Administration's Manned Space Flight Program, Maryland, and Price Williams and Associates, 1962–72. Visual arts instructor, City College of New York, 1986–7; visiting artist faculty, Minneapolis College of Art and Design, 1988–9; arts instructor, Lower Eastside Printshop, New York, 1988–90; Dayton Hudson distinguished visiting artist and teacher, Carleton College, Northfield, Minnesota, 1992. Recipient of National Endowment for the Arts (NEA) grant, 1988; New York State Council on the Arts Visual Artists Sponsored Work Project award, 1990; Artiste en France fellowship, Greater New York Links and French Government, 1992; International Center of Photography Annual Infinity award, 1995. Board member, National Women's Caucus for Art of the College Art Association, 1991–2; Printed Matter and Visual Studies Workshop, 1991–4. Has one daughter. Lives in New York.

Selected Individual Exhibitions
CEPA Satellite Space, Buffalo, NY: 1987
White Columns, New York: 1990
Washington Project for the Arts, Washington, DC: 1991
Center for Photography in Woodstock, NY: 1992
Art in General, New York: 1992
Afro-American Historical and Cultural Museum, Philadelphia: 1993
Toronto Photographers Workshop, Toronto: 1994
Galerie Junge Kunst, Trier: 1995

Selected Writings
Reading Dick and Jane with Me, New York: privately printed, 1989

"On being an American black student", *Heresies*, vii/1, 1990

"Witness to dissent: It wasn't Little Rock", *Ikon*, no.12–13, 1992

"Home truths", *What Can a Woman Do with a Camera?*, ed. Jo Spence and Joan Solomon, London: Scarlet Press, 1995

"Reliving my mother's struggle", *Liberating Memory: Our Work and Our Working-Class Consciousness*, ed. Janet Zandy, New Brunswick: Rutgers University Press, 1995

Bibliography

Constructed Images: New Photography, exh. cat., Schomburg Center, New York Public Library, and elsewhere, 1989

Naomi Rosenblum, *World History of Photography*, 2nd edition, New York: Abbeville, 1989

Deborah Willis-Thomas, *An Illustrated Bio-Bibliography of Black Photographers, 1940–1988*, New York: Garland, 1989

Convergence: 8 Photographers, exh. cat., Photographic Resource Center and Visual Studies Workshop, 1990

Ann R. Langdon, *Women Visual Artists You Might Like to Know*, New Haven: Women in the Arts, 1990

Lucy R. Lippard, *Mixed Blessings: New Art in a Multicultural America*, New York: Pantheon, 1990

Words and Images with a Message, exh. cat., Women's Studio Workshop, Rosendale, NY, 1990

Clarissa Sligh: The Presence of Memory, exh. cat., Robert B. Menschel Photography Gallery, Syracuse University, NY, 1991

Clarissa Sligh: Witness to Dissent: Remembrance and Struggle, installation brochure, Washington Project for the Arts, Washington, DC, 1991

Crossing Over/Changing Places, exh. cat., Print Club, Philadelphia, and elsewhere, 1991

Bridges and Boundaries: African Americans and American Jews, exh. cat., Jewish Museum at New York Historical Society, and elsewhere, 1992

Alice R. George and others, *Flesh and Blood: Photographers' Images of Their Own Families*, New York: Picture Project, and Manchester: Cornerhouse, 1992

Malcolm X: Man, Ideal, Icon, installation brochure, Walker Art Center, Minneapolis, 1992

Prisoners of War: In My Native Land/On Foreign Soil, exh. cat., Parsons School of Design, New York, 1992

Personal Narratives: Women Photographers of Color, exh. cat., Southeastern Center for Contemporary Art, Winston-Salem, NC, 1993

The Subject of Rape, exh. cat., Whitney Museum of American Art, New York, 1993

Imagining Families: Images and Voices, exh. cat., National African American Museum Project, Smithsonian Institution, Washington, DC, 1994

Multiple World: An International Survey of Artists' Books, exh. cat., Atlanta College of Art Gallery, 1994

Naomi Rosenblum, *A History of Women Photographers*, New York: Abbeville, 1994

Melissa Harris, ed., *On Location with Henri Cartier-Bresson, Graciela Iturbide, Barbara Kruger, Sally Mann, Andres Serrano, Clarissa Sligh*, New York: Aperture Foundation, 1995

Make Yourself at Home: Race, Ethnicity and the American Family, exh. cat., Atlanta College of Art Gallery, 1995

In the brief period from 1984, Clarissa Sligh has amassed a body of photographic collage constructions whose content bears witness to the confrontation between American democratic ideals and the history of enslavement. During the turbulent era of the American civil rights movement, she was one of many black children involved in the school desegregation crisis of the 1950s. Memory and the child's voice reverberate in her photographic collages, artist books and installations. In her early works of the 1980s she combined negatives to create works that include writing ("mark-making") and drawing with a centrepiece of the photograph-as-artefact (interview with artist, 21 June 1995). Using the text – visual and written – as a forum for shattering taboos and silences about the commodification of the black and/or female body, she made a personal and historical inquiry into the affective domain where such dramatic events as abuse, racism and sexism are treated courageously in *Witness to Dissent: Memory, Yearning and Struggle*, a series of site-specific installations at the Washington Project for the Arts (1991) and Art in General in New York (1992). She expresses memories of terror and powerlessness in assembling and re-framing photographs of desegregation in Virginia in the 1960s ("Witness to dissent", 1992, p.115).

With a photographic palette limited to black, white and van-dyke brown, Sligh experimented with methods of photography and printing to perfect a documentary technique to fit the epic form of her dense narratives on African-American cultural life and the American political landscape. During a residency at Pyramid Atlantic in Maryland, she collaborated with the master printer Susan Rostow on *What's Happening with Momma?* (1988), an artist's book of interconnected paper row houses with triangular roofs containing family photographs and commentary. An attempt "to connect to who she was" in the photographs, the work represents the interface between myth and public opinion as a site of self-censorship (see artist's commentary in

Philadelphia 1991). By the late 1980s, when field research was popularised by artists of colour to formulate ideas and images, Sligh used conversation, reading and questionnaires to collect data for the content of her works. She employed this scrapbook approach in *Momma*, a photographic technique in which reshoots, reprints and rewrites are a means for self-reconstruction, healing and discovery about experiences unique to the Black tradition. Portions of the *Witness* series (*Untitled, Witness to Dissent: Remembrance and Struggle*) were also produced at Pyramid Atlantic in collaboration with the master printer and paper maker Helen C. Frederick. The work is a pulp painting on handmade cotton and abaca paper, executed by pouring liquid pulp on to wet paper, creating the effect of a print. The series toured the USA and Europe under the 1992 Arts in America Program of the United States Information Agency.

Sligh's works have become integral to the lived histories of women who have experienced abuse, as in her cyanotypes *Seeking Comfort, I Suck My Thumb* (1989) and *Wonderful Uncle* (1988), the latter a van-dyke brown print in which text surrounds a girl alienated by sexuality, hypocrisy and power within the presumed safety of the family. She revisited these disjunctive emotions in *Seeking Comfort*, retreating to a metaphor of juvenile security in the visual space while her mind journeys to the dangerous and fearsome moments of childhood.

The late 1980s were a turning point for Sligh, marking a transition from her career as a financial analyst and computer programmer. Her work with the Women's Caucus for Art introduced her to exhibition organising in 1986, initially as East Coast coordinator and co-curator of the *Coast to Coast: National Women Artists of Color Book Project* and exhibition. In 1988 she was national co-ordinator and co-curator of the *Coast to Coast* initiative, which opened at Diverse Works in Houston in conjunction with the Women's Caucus for Art annual national conference, and toured to nine sites nationally. Two commissions established her as an installation artist. In 1992 she collaborated with the artist Carole Byard on the Walker Art Center group exhibition *Malcolm X: Man, Ideal, Icon*, which travelled to the Institute of Contemporary Art in Boston in 1993. Their *EHM (El-Haj Malik)* was a site-specific work in which images and artefacts associated with the assassinated American hero addressed both the spiritual and materialist

commercialisation of Malcolm X. At the end of the 1980s Sligh was occupied with lectures and panel discussions, and in 1995 she was the keynote speaker at the annual conference of the Society for Photographic Education in Atlanta, which established her as a spokesperson for the use of photography as interactive narrative documentary art. Her work is in major private and public collections including the Museum of Modern Art and Schomburg Center for Research in Black Culture, New York Public Library, New York; National Museum of Women in the Arts and Corcoran Gallery of Art, Washington, DC; Museum of Fine Arts, Boston; George Eastman House, Rochester, New York; and the National Gallery of Australia, Canberra.

Sligh's work exemplifies and parallels late 20th-century debates on the role of the arts in the formation of cultural identity and its relationship to nationalism, gender and politics. Riding this wave, she employed an artistic practice that weaves the personal, the political, the public and the private, using the photograph as a means of indictment and liberation. In both technique and imagery Sligh surpasses the photo-realist tradition, featuring autobiography and sacrificing personal privacy as a way into the collective unconscious of civil rights activism and feminist social action, and as a way out of personal isolation.

ROBIN M. CHANDLER

Smith, Jaune Quick-to-See

American painter and mixed-media artist, 1940–

Born in St Ignatius, Flathead Indian Reservation, Montana, 15 January 1940, a Native American of Salish, French-Cree and Shoshone heritage. Studied at Framingham State College, Massachusetts (BA in art education 1976); University of New Mexico, Albuquerque (MFA 1980). Recipient of Purchase award, Academy of Arts and Letters, New York, 1987; Fellowship award, Western States Art Foundation, 1988; Association of American Cultures Arts Service award, 1990; honorary doctorate, Minneapolis College of Art and Design, 1992. Honorary professor, Beaumont Chair,

Washington University, St Louis, 1989. Lives in Corrales, New Mexico.

Selected Individual Exhibitions

Kornblee Gallery, New York: 1979
University of Pittsburgh: 1980
Marilyn Butler Gallery, Santa Fe: 1983, 1985, 1987, 1988
Galerie Akmak, Berlin: 1983
Bernice Steinbaum Gallery, New York: 1983, 1985, 1987, 1990
Washington State Arts Commission: 1984 (*Flathead Wellspring*, touring)
Peter Stremmel Gallery, Reno, NV: 1985
Yellowstone Art Center, Billings, MT: 1986
Cambridge Multi-Cultural Art Center, MA: 1989
California State University, Long Beach: 1989
Anne Reed Gallery, Sun Valley, ID: 1991
Steinbaum Krauss Gallery, New York: 1992
Chrysler Museum, Norfolk, VA: 1993 (touring)

Bibliography

Jamake Highwater, *The Sweet Grass Lives On: Fifty Contemporary North American Indian Artists*, New York: Crowell, 1980
Laurel Reuter, "Jaune Quick-to-See Smith", *Artspace*, June 1980
Ronny Cohen, "Jaune Quick-to-See Smith at Kornblee", *Art in America*, March 1980, pp.116–17
Edwin C. Wade and Rennard Strickland, *Magic Images: Contemporary Native American Art*, Norman: University of Oklahoma Press, 1981
Deborah C. Phillips, "Jaune Quick-to-See Smith", *Art News*, lxxxii, October 1983, p.93
Ruth Bass, "Jaune Quick-to-See Smith", *Art News*, lxxxiii, March 1984, p.224
Women of Sweetgrass, Cedar and Sage, exh. cat., Gallery of the American Indian Community House, New York, 1985
Gregory Galligan, "Jaune Quick-to-See Smith: Crossing the great divide", *Arts Magazine*, lx, January 1986, pp.54–5
—, "Jaune Quick-to-See Smith: Racing with the moon", *Arts Magazine*, lxi, January 1987, pp.82–3
Committed to Print: Social and Political Themes in Recent American Printed Art, exh. cat., Museum of Modern Art, New York, 1988
Betty Ann Brown, "Review shorts", *Artweek*, xx, 21 October 1989, pp.11–12
The Decade Show, exh. cat., The New Museum, New York, 1990
Lucy R. Lippard, *Mixed Blessings: New Art in a Multicultural America*, New York: Pantheon, 1990
Shared Visions: Native American Painters and Sculptors in the Twentieth Century, exh. cat., Heard Museum, Phoenix, and elsewhere, 1991
Melanie Herzog, "Building bridges across cultures: Jaune Quick-to-See Smith", *School Arts*, xcii, October 1992, pp.31–4
Jenifer P. Borum, "Jaune Quick-to-See Smith: Steinbaum Krauss Gallery", *Artforum*, xxxi, January 1993, pp.87–8
Lawrence Abbott, ed., *I Stand in the Center of the Good: Interviews with Contemporary Native American Artists*, Lincoln: University of Nebraska Press, 1994

Over the past 20 years, Jaune Quick-to-See Smith has earned a position as one of the best known Native American artists of her generation. She enjoys a substantial international reputation not only for her well-honed and powerful art but also for her work as a curator, lecturer and environmental activist. Her wide-reaching career has established Smith as an eloquent and effective spokesperson for contemporary Native American perspectives and values in a world that is increasingly aware of its multi-cultural base.

Smith's journey to her achievements might well be termed an odyssey in which the time frame shifts back and forth. Hers was a childhood that established a firm hold on traditional Native American values; it was followed by a formal Euro-American art education that engaged her for 22 years, and a belated art career that places her between modernism and post-modernism. Smith's essential identity and consistent point of reference is her childhood experience on the Flathead Reservation of the Confederated Salish and Kootenai tribes of southwestern Montana, where she acquired a traditional sensitivity to the land and the animals and people who are one with it. Smith aspired to be an artist from early childhood, and her education was spread across a generation of dramatic change in Native American art. When she studied art in the 1960s and 1970s, her role models were such artists as Oscar Howe, Allan Houser and Fritz Scholder, who took their native heritage into the mainstream. By the time Smith received her MFA degree from the University of New Mexico in 1980, she was a member of a substantial group of Native American artists with university educations, strong personal styles and increasing access to the art establishment. Artists such as Smith, George Longfish and Hachivi Edgar Heap of Birds have been aggressive on political issues ranging from social conditions on the reservation to the exploitation of the environment. Accordingly, Smith and others have been characterised as post-modern both for their political content, coming as it does from a minority cultural perspective, and formally because of the ease with which they appropriate the modernist idiom and merge it with their native tradition and intent.

Early in her studies, Smith faced discouragement when advised by a teacher not to consider an art career because that was only for men. The pain of this comment struck deeply, but she eventually found encouragement through women teachers and students as the women's movement grew in the 1970s. Smith was likewise frustrated by a lack of critical responsiveness to Native American artists who were dismissed for mixing abstraction with tribal motifs, even though this was an accepted vocabulary for other modernists. In fact, she states that throughout her years of college education "it wasn't acceptable to show any ethnicity in my work" and that her professors "taught from a perspective that was all white, Eurocentric, and male" (Abbott 1994, p.216). These experiences helped to galvanise Smith's outspoken activism on women's and Native American issues. She began drawing as a child, an activity encouraged by her father, and she began formal art education in 1958.

From the beginning Smith had a strong interest in the environment, and landscape became a consistent feature of her work. Her view of the land was a gentle one, a land inhabited by plants, insects, animals and people, a perspective that she considers to be inherently Native American and highly positive. In the mid-1970s she painted on unstretched canvases loosely resembling hides in a style marked by muted colour and minimal design (e.g. *Ronan Robe* series). Her career took off in 1979 when she participated in two exhibitions in New York: a group show at the Droll/Kolbert Gallery and a two-artist show at the Kornblee Gallery. The works in these exhibitions were from her *Wallowa Waterhole* series inspired by readings about Chief Joseph (e.g. *Kalispell No.2*, 1979; pastel on paper; repr. Cohen 1980). Smith says that in this series she "developed a language that has sustained me to this day. Picto figures of humans and animals emerged" (Abbott 1994, p.213). Works of this period are lyrical, combining figurative and abstract images in a fragmented narrative. Pictograph-like outlines of horses and stick-figure men are given a modernist feeling through compositional devices reminiscent of such modern artists as Paul Klee and Joan Miró. An example of work in this style is the pastel *Porcupine Ridge Series, No.35* (1979; Laurel Reuter Collection, ND). In the early 1980s Smith continued working on landscapes with animals in series such as *Red Lake*. Soon she had developed a sophisticated and integrated style merging landscapes with pictographic symbolism with a powerful personal expressiveness and modern quality, well represented by *Herding* (1985; Bernice Steinbaum Gallery, New York).

A series of paintings executed in 1986–7 and inspired by efforts to save the petrographics on a lava escarpment west of Albuquerque, New Mexico, propelled Smith into greater environmental activism. Works in this series became bolder with strong movement and large shapes based on pictographs. In 1989 she began a series of paintings based on Chief Seattle's environmental speech of 1854. In these paintings she incorporated words and attached objects – small found materials such as tin cans – to the painted surface. This trend towards a stronger mixed-media approach continued into the 1990s with increasingly direct messages about threats to the environment, for example, *Rain* (1991; Heard Museum, Phoenix, AZ). Smith's response to the Columbus Quincentenary produced such works as *Trade (Gifts for Trading Land with White People)* (1992; Chrysler Museum of Art, Norfolk, VA). Of this strongly political piece, which features a row of items such as Washington Redskin caps and plastic tomahawks, Smith said that if it could speak, it might say "why won't you consider trading the land we handed over to you for these silly trinkets that so honor us? Sound like a bad deal? Well, that's the deal you gave us" (Arlene Hirschfelder, *Artists and Craftspeople*, New York: Facts on File, 1994, p.115).

Critical response to Smith has been fairly consistent and generally quite positive. From the earliest reviews of her work, authors have made the most of Smith's self-proclaimed goal to bridge the Native American and Euro-American cultures. Like other artists before her, she is positive about connecting the traditional and contemporary worlds. Much was made by commentators in the early and mid-1980s of Smith's synthesis of Euro-American art education and her American Indian heritage. Critics found in her affinity with Willem de Kooning, Miró, Klee, Franz Marc and Robert Rauschenberg a reaffirmation of the mainstream. They made much of the compatibility of traditional Native American art and modern abstraction, and to be sure, the similarity is not missed on the artist. By the late 1980s, such terms as neo-expressionist were left behind when referring to Smith, and she is increasingly discussed in terms of how she fits with post-modernism. Her overt and aggressive political messages and the directness of her mixed-media technique place her squarely in the forefront of Native American post-modernism.

JOHN A. DAY

Snyder, Joan

American painter and mixed-media artist, 1940–

Born in Highland Park, New Jersey, 16 April 1940. Studied at Douglass College (AB in sociology 1962) and Rutgers University (MFA 1966), both in New Brunswick. Moved to New York, 1967; to Eastport, New York, 1985. Taught at State University of New York, Stony Brook, 1967–9; Yale University, New Haven, 1974; University of California, Irvine, 1975; San Francisco Art Institute, 1976; Princeton University, 1975–7; Parsons School of Design, New York, 1992–3. Married Laurence Fink, 1969; daughter born 1979; divorced. Recipient of National Endowment for the Arts (NEA) grant, 1974; Guggenheim fellowship, 1981. Lives in Brooklyn, New York.

Selected Individual Exhibitions

Paley & Lowe, New York: 1970, 1971, 1973
Los Angeles Institute of Contemporary Art: 1976
Neuberger Museum, State University of New York at Purchase: 1978
Hamilton Gallery of Contemporary Art, New York: 1978, 1982
WARM, Minneapolis: 1979 (touring)
San Francisco Art Institute: 1979–80 (touring)
Wadsworth Atheneum, Hartford, CT: 1981
Nielsen Gallery, Boston: 1981, 1983, 1986, 1991, 1992, 1993, 1994
Hirschl and Adler Modern, New York: 1985, 1988, 1990, 1992, 1994
David Winton Bell Gallery, Brown University, Providence, RI: 1988–9 (*Joan Snyder Collects Joan Snyder*, touring)
Allentown Art Museum, PA: 1993
Rose Art Museum, Brandeis University, Waltham, MA: 1994 (retrospective)

Selected Writings

"Passages", *Modern Painters*, iv, Autumn 1991, pp.48–9

Bibliography

Marcia Tucker, "The anatomy of a stroke: Recent paintings by Joan Snyder", *Artforum*, ix, May 1971, pp.42–5
Joan Snyder: Seven Years of Work, exh. cat., Neuberger Museum, State University of New York at Purchase, 1978
Joan Snyder at WARM: A Women's Collective Art Space, exh. cat., Women's Art Registry of Minnesota, Minneapolis, and elsewhere, 1979
Gerrit Henry, "Joan Snyder", *Art in America*, lxx, Summer 1982, pp.141–2
Carter Ratcliff and others, "Expressionism today: An artists' symposium", *Art in America*, lxx, December 1982, pp.58–75, 139
Joan Snyder, exh. cat., Hirschl and Adler Modern, New York, 1985
Paul Gardner, "When is a painting finished?", *Art News*, lxxxiv, November 1985, pp.89–100
Gerrit Henry, "Joan Snyder: True grit", *Art in America*, lxxiv, February 1986, pp.96–101
Jed Perl, "Houses, fields, gardens, hills", *New Criterion*, February 1986
Susan Gill, "Painting from the heart", *Art News*, lxxxvi, April 1987, pp.128–35
Joan Snyder Collects Joan Snyder, exh. cat., David Winton Bell Gallery, Brown University, Providence, RI, and elsewhere, 1988
Joan Snyder, exh. cat., Hirschl and Adler Modern, New York, 1990
Joan Snyder, exh. cat., Nielsen Gallery, Boston, 1991
Joan Snyder: Works with Paper, exh. cat., Allentown Art Museum, PA, 1993
Joan Snyder: Painter, 1969 to Now, exh. cat., Rose Art Museum, Brandeis University, Waltham, MA, 1994
Donald Kuspit, "Joan Snyder", *Artforum*, xxxii, Summer 1994, pp.92–3
Bill Jones, "Painting the haunted pool", *Art in America*, lxxxii, October 1994, pp.120–23, 157

Joan Snyder discovered painting in 1962 while she was a student at Douglass College in New Brunswick, New Jersey. It was an epiphanous experience: "… when I started to paint, it was like speaking for the first time. I mean, I felt like my whole life, I had never spoken. I had never been heard. I had never said anything that had any meaning. When I started painting, it was like I was speaking for the first time" (Minneapolis 1979, p.16). The discovery also entailed what might be called a spiritual conversion, as the following statement indicates: "…my painting is my religion. It's the altar that I go to and it's where I face myself and find out who I am … And you make offerings at the altar. At some level you give generously" (Boston 1991, n.p.).

Snyder realised her initial maturity at the end of the 1960s in a series of pictures that became known as her stroke paintings, the first of which was *Lines and Strokes* (1969; artist's collection). It consists of eight horizontal swathes of colour, each spreading more than less from one side of the canvas support to the other, each resembling the horizon line in a landscape image. But landscape is not what the picture is about. Stacked as they are, each laden with a distinctly expressive energy, the lines and strokes refer to nothing outside themselves, nothing, that is, except the fundamental urge to make an expressive mark and thereby take possession of a space. Thick and thin, large and small, transparent, opaque, elegant, rough-hewn, brushed on, squeezed from the tube, carefully controlled and impulsively splotched, the strokes deconstruct the medium, resulting in an impressive painting primer that reveals Snyder personalising her medium and finding her voice. In the stroke paintings, we see her learning to speak visually.

The stroke paintings were well received and deeply satisfying, but Snyder herself was not finally satisfied by them: "They were easy, I could do them in two days ... Everybody loved them, and I stopped doing them. I had to change ... I had nowhere to go but into my own past, into my own iconography ... and that is what I did" (Purchase 1978, pp.2 and 20). In paintings such as *Flesh/Art* (1973–4; artist's collection) and *Heart-On* (1975; Metropolitan Museum of Art, New York) she began to explore that personal iconography, which consisted of images of the female body, childlike drawings of houses and landscape spaces, hand-written diaristic notes and a wide range of challenging and funky collage elements such as fabric, papier-mâché, wallpaper and linoleum. In addition, she adopted new and unconventional techniques that entailed slashing, stuffing and sewing the canvas, engaging it as an active and physical entity instead of a merely passive and accommodating support. In emphasising her experience of being in the world, Snyder's work became personal in a new way, the way not of a reductive abstraction but of an embracing feminism that she was instrumental in forging. She thus became in the 1970s a model for ambitious women artists of her generation and a leading example of their innovative approaches to thinking about and making art.

Expressive landscapes were among the images that Snyder produced when she began painting, and she often returned to landscape in her paintings of the 1980s. Pictures such as *Beanfield with Music*

(1984; First Church of Christ Scientist, Boston), *Waiting for a Miracle (for John and Nina)* (1986; Collection Mr and Mrs Gifford Phillips, New York) and *Ode to the Pumpkin Field* (1986–7; Twin Farms Collection, Barnard, VT) are typically expansive and physical, incorporating a variety of materials and offering a wide range of feelings associated with space and light and colour, the changing seasons, dormancy, rebirth, flowering, abundance. More often than not the images ascend and spread across the entire surface, rising before us without horizons, as if limitless, their presentation suggesting that we might be lying face down in these landscapes, embracing them, one with them. The erotic equation of landscape and the human body represents a theme that Snyder first entertained as a young artist in the 1960s and occasionally explored from a feminist perspective, graphically, with frustration and anger, during the decade that followed (e.g. *Nude in Landscape*, 1977; Parrish Art Museum, Southampton, NY). When she returned to it in the 1980s, she did so with the full powers of a mature painter and with a clearly more resolved and optimistic vision: "I painted sacred fields, serene fields, fields of moons, moons in mud, and cantatas. This work reflects all of my moods, my sorrows, losses and struggles, and a peace that has finally come into my life" (New York 1990, p.5).

In more recent works Snyder's concerns have broadened further. *Women in Camps* (1988; Collection Mr and Mrs Richard Albright, Wayland, MA) summons the grim memory of the Holocaust through haunting photographs of its victims, while *Journey of the Souls* (1993; private collection, Boston), its centre black and vast and impenetrable, refers to the frightening tragedy of AIDS. Such pictures take us to a new level of global concern, and in this they embody the values and aims of a second generation of feminist artists, a generation for whom Snyder's vision is as much a model today as it was for her contemporaries more than two decades ago.

CARL BELZ

Solomon, Rebecca
British painter, 1832–1886

Born in London, 26 September 1832, into a large Jewish family. Attended Spitalfields School of

Design with older brother Abraham. Exhibited widely in London and the provinces, 1850–74. Assisted painters Thomas Faed, William Frith, John Phillip and John Everett Millais, 1850s–60s. Travelled abroad with younger brother Simeon, c.1857; to Italy with him, 1865–6. Worked as a graphic artist for illustrated papers, 1860s. Died after being run over by a hansom cab in the Euston Road, London, 20 November 1886.

Principal Exhibitions
British Institution, London: 1850–54, 1866
Royal Academy, London: 1852, 1854–65, 1867, 1869
International Exhibition, London: 1862
Dudley Gallery, London: 1865–9, 1871
Society of Lady Artists, London: 1874

Bibliography
Ellen C. Clayton, *English Female Artists*, 2 vols, London: Tinsley, 1876
Pamela Gerrish Nunn, "Rebecca Solomon: Painting and drama", *Theatrephile*, ii/8, 1985, pp.3–4
Solomon: A Family of Painters, exh. cat., Geffrye Museum, London, and elsewhere, 1985
Lynda Nead, *Myths of Sexuality: Representations of Women in Victorian Britain*, Oxford: Blackwell, 1988
Pamela Gerrish Nunn, "Rebecca Solomon's 'A Young Teacher'", *Burlington Magazine*, cxxx, 1988, pp.769–70
Deborah Cherry, *Painting Women: Victorian Women Artists*, London and New York: Routledge, 1993

Rebecca Solomon is one of a handful of successful Jewish artists to practise in Victorian Britain, and the middle member of a unique trio of sibling artists: her older brother Abraham and her younger brother Simeon were also professional painters. Her career shows that by the middle of the 19th century it had become possible for women to carry on a professional painting practice, earning a living and making a name, though not necessarily breaking new ground or allying themselves with any particular school or style.

Like Abraham, in whose home she lived and by whom she was partially trained, Rebecca Solomon served the mainstream public with medium-size paintings of moral and sentimental themes with figures in modern or historical dress. Essaying subjects of interest to the contemporary middle class, such as *The Governess* (1854; Yale Center for British Art, New Haven) and the *Story of Balaclava* (1855; ex-Leicester Galleries, London), though with a keen eye for a female point of view of those topics, she produced paintings that did the rounds of the London and provincial exhibitions. Her subject matter reflects the range of mainstream taste, though her work was frequently accused, with Abraham's, of vulgarity, and her technical excellence was uneven. Her biggest successes were with paintings that fell within the higher genres of history or literature, *Peg Woffington's First Visit to Triplet* (1860; untraced, repr. London 1985) and *Fugitive Royalists* (1862; untraced, *ibid.*). Both works use ingredients – several figures in an interior, connected by a presumed narrative of some complexity and shown in a moment of emotional drama – that the artist employed successfully on several other occasions, as in *Behind the Curtain* (1858; private collection, *ibid.*) and *A Plea for Mercy* (*Sweet Mercy Is Nobility's True Badge*) (1865; Geffrye Museum, London).

Financial difficulties in the mid-1860s after Abraham's unexpected death in 1862 led to her having to supplement her original work with assisting several popular painters known to her through Abraham and with illustrations for middle-class periodicals such as *London Society* and *Churchman's Family Magazine*. She may have worked also as an artist's model at this time, and began to produce and exhibit watercolours as well as oil paintings. She took up residence with her younger brother Simeon, whose wild social life was in marked contrast to her alleged religious observance. Simeon's connections with the circle of Dante Gabriel Rossetti brought both siblings in touch with second-wave Pre-Raphaelitism and Aestheticism, stylistic trends that can be seen in *Primavera* (1864; private collection, Japan) and *Wounded Dove* (1866; University College of Wales, Aberystwyth). Since none of the artist's late work is presently traced, it is difficult to know if she persisted in this vein.

It is possible that Simeon's covert homosexuality, which led eventually to his prosecution and ostracism from artistic circles, hampered Rebecca's professional standing from the late 1860s. Equally, it was suggested after her death that she became an alcoholic in her mature years. Like Abraham but in marked contrast to Simeon, Rebecca made little reference to her Jewishness in her painting. Titles of works exhibited after 1866 (e.g. *Giovannina, Rome*, 1867; untraced) indicate a body of work resulting from the artist's travels in Italy as well as a continued appeal to the literary element of mainstream taste (e.g. *Helena and Hermia*, 1869; untraced)

Overall, Solomon's œuvre represents vividly the struggle of a working woman artist of the mid-19th century to compete with her male contemporaries in an increasingly commodified art market.

PAMELA GERRISH NUNN

Spence, Jo
British photographer, 1934–1992

Born in South Woodford, Essex, 15 June 1934. Attended secretarial college, 1948–50. Secretary and assistant in PhotoCoverage commercial studio, 1951–62; assistant, secretary and printer to Canadian advertising photographer Walter Curtin, 1962–4; farm secretary, 1965. Own photographic studio, Joanne Spence Associates, in Hampstead, London, 1967–74. Abandoned commercial work for radical documentary photography, 1973. Co-founder, with photographer Terry Dennett, of Photography Workshop, 1974. Subsequently helped to set up photography collective, the Hackney Flashers, 1975, and started *Camerawork* magazine, 1976. Degree course in film and photographic arts at Polytechnic of Central London (now University of Westminster), attending classes with Victor Burgin, 1979–82 (BA). Breast cancer diagnosed, 1982; with Rosy Martin and others, developed photo therapy, an alternative treatment of the emotional aspects of cancer, 1984–9. Toured Australia, Canada and USA, 1990. Chronic lymphatic leukaemia diagnosed, 1990. Married David Roberts (second marriage), 1992. Died in London, 24 June 1992.

Principal Exhibitions

Shaw Theatre, London: 1976 (*Children Photographed*, touring)
Massachusetts Institute of Technology, Cambridge: 1983 (*Re-modelling Photohistory*, with Terry Dennett, touring)
Cockpit Gallery, London: 1985 (*The Picture of Health?*, organised by Photography Workshop, touring)
Photography Workshop, London: 1985 (*Photo Therapy Road Show*, with Rosy Martin, touring)
Cambridge Darkroom, Cambridge: 1985 (touring retrospective)
National Portrait Gallery, London: 1987 (*Staging the Self: Self-Portrait Photography, 1840–1980s*)

Miriam and Ira Wallach Art Gallery, Columbia University, New York: 1988 (*Sexual Difference: Both Sides of the Camera*, with Terry Dennett)
Metropolitan Museum of Photography, Tokyo: 1990 (*Exploring the Unknown Self*)
Australia and USA: 1990–91 (*Jo Spence: Collaborative Works*, touring)
McLellan Galleries, Glasgow: 1991 (*Narratives of Disease: Ritualised Procedures*, with Tim Sheard; touring, organised by Photography Workshop)
Leeds City Art Gallery: 1991 (*Missing Persons/Damaged Lives*, touring)
Museet for Fotokunst, Odense: 1992 (*Real Stories: The Crisis Project: Scenes of the Crime*, with Terry Dennett, touring)
South Bank Centre, London, and Impressions Gallery, York: 1994–5 (touring retrospective)

Selected Writings

"The politics of photography", *Camerawork*, no.1, 1976; reprinted in *British Journal of Photography*, 26 March 1976
Photography, London: Macdonald, 1977 (with Richard Greenhill and Maggie Murray)
"Photography, ideology and education", *Screen Education*, no.21, 1977 (with Terry Dennett)
"What do people do all day? Class and gender in images of women", *Screen Education*, no.29, Winter 1978–9; reprinted in *In Whose Image? Writings on Media Sexism*, ed. Kath Davies and Julienne Dickey, London: Women's Press, 1986
Editor, *Photography/Politics: One*, London: Photography Workshop, 1979 (with Terry Dennett, David Evars and Sylvia Gohl)
"Remodelling photo-history: A collaboration between two photographers", *Ten 8*, no.9, 1982 (with Terry Dennett)
Editor, *Photography/Politics: Two*, London: Comedia, 1986 (with Patricia Holland and Simon Watney)
Putting Myself in the Picture: A Political, Personal and Photographic Autobiography, London: Camden Press, 1986; Seattle: Real Comet, 1988
"The picture of health", *Spare Rib*, no.163, February 1986; no.165, April 1986
"Re-working the family album", *Media Education*, no.12, 1990
Editor, *Family Snaps: The Meanings of Domestic Photography*, London: Virago, 1991 (with Patricia Holland)
The Creatures Time Forgot: Photography and Disability Imagery, London and New York: Routledge, 1992 (with David Hevey and Jessica Evans)
Cultural Sniping: The Art of Transgression, ed. Jo Stanley, London and New York: Routledge, 1995 (anthology of writings)
What Can a Woman Do with a Camera? London: Scarlet Press, 1995 (with Joan Solomon)

Bibliography

Three Perspectives on Photography, exh. cat., Hayward
    Gallery, London, 1979
John Roberts, "Jo Spence", *Art Monthly*, no.87, June
    1985, pp.6–8
*Matter of Facts: Photographie art contemporain en
    Grande-Bretagne*, exh. cat., Musée des Beaux-Arts,
    Nantes, and elsewhere, 1988
John Roberts, *Postmodernism, Politics and Art*,
    Manchester: Manchester University Press, 1990
Jan Zita Grover, "Photo therapy: Shame and the mine-
    fields of memory", *Afterimage*, xviii, Summer 1990,
    pp.14–18
——, "The artist and illness", *Artpaper*, xi, January 1992,
    pp.11–13 (interview)
David Hevey, "Marks of struggle", *Women's Art
    Magazine*, no.47, July–August 1992, pp.8–11 (inter-
    view)
Jane Brettle, Val Williams and Rosy Martin, "Putting us
    all in the picture: Jo Spence", *Women's Art Magazine*,
    no.48, September–October 1992, pp.14–15
Hilary Robinson, "Jo Spence, 1934–1992", *Portfolio
    Magazine*, no.15, Winter 1992, pp.15–16
Rosy Martin, "Putting us all in the picture: The work of
    Jo Spence", *Camera Austria*, no.43–4, 1993, pp.42–55
——, "Home truths? Phototherapy, memory and iden-
    tity", *Artpaper*, xii, March 1993, pp.7–9
*Jo Spence: Matters of Concern: Collaborative Images,
    1982–1992*, exh. cat., South Bank Centre, London,
    Impressions Gallery, York, and elsewhere, 1994

The Jo Spence Memorial Archive is c/o Terry Dennett,
152 Upper Street (Rear Entrance), London N1 1RA; tele-
phone/fax 020 7359-9064.

Jo Spence was a feminist photographer, writer and
theorist. She was born in London in 1934 and her
childhood was marked by her experience of evacua-
tion during World War II and a transient early existence: she had moved home eleven times and been to
six different schools by the time she was ten. In later
years much of her photographic work reflected
upon the role that these early experiences had had
on the formation of her subjectivity and identity as
a working-class woman. She left school at the age of
13, and trained to become a secretary. Her first
encounter with photography was while she was
employed as a shorthand typist and bookkeeper in a
small commercial photographers in London. She
soon purchased her own camera and began on the
career that was to mark her as one of the most
important and influential photographers of her
time.

Initially she started with small commissions,
weddings and portraits, for family and friends, but
moved on to develop a professional commercial
career, specialising at one stage in the production of
portfolios for actors and models. She also cited her
year as assistant to the Canadian advertising
photographer Walter Curtin and her work for a
Fleet Street photographer, where she was taught
picture editing skills, as influential on her developing career and later work. These formative years in
commercial photography were to have a profound
effect and influence on her later experimental and
artistic photographic work. Her later work returns
to these earlier commercial experiences to interro-
gate the conventions and hidden meanings involved
within traditional commercial images.

Spence's transition away from commercial
photography began in the early 1970s when she
became involved in the vibrant socialist and feminist
movements of the period, and her photographic
style changed dramatically. She destroyed most of
her earlier commercial work, explaining later that
she was ashamed "ideologically speaking" of what
she had been doing. Her work now took on the
campaigning and tendentious style of the documentary photograph. She became involved in a number
of campaigns ranging from a photographic exhibition on children's rights to documenting a Gypsy
literacy project. As her experience of documentary
photography developed, however, she found herself
increasingly questioning the power relationship
involved in the taking of such photographs and the
ways in which those depicted were shown. It was
during this time that she met her fellow photographer and lifelong friend Terry Dennett. In the mid-
1970s Jo Spence's work began to take up clearly
identifiable feminist politics and concerns. She
began to show her photographs in the feminist
publication *Spare Rib* and to work on her contribution for a feminist photographic exhibition that
documented the invisible and hidden work of
working-class women, titled *Women and Work*.

In 1974, with Terry Dennett, she helped to found
the photographic project Photography Workshop.
This became an important educational, research,
publishing and resource centre for many photographers, photographic groups and projects. Spence
became a member of one such group initiated by the
Photography Workshop, the Hackney Flashers
Collective. The Hackney Flashers was a socialist,
feminist group that employed photography to
campaign on issues of importance for working-class
women. During this time Spence also became interested in radical anti-realist photographic artists,

such as John Hartfield, and radical anti-realist strategies from the theatre as proposed by the theorist Bertolt Brecht. These theories help clarify her increasing disillusionment with the traditional documentary form. Her transition away from the use of photography as a reflection of reality to a more questioning style of photomontage can be traced between her work for the exhibition *Women and Work* and the later Hackney Flashers show *Who's Holding the Baby?* (1979).

In 1975 Photography Workshop temporarily merged with a gallery, the Half Moon, to form the Half Moon Photography Workshop, which began to publish the radical photographic magazine *Camerawork*. After disagreements, however, Dennett and Spence parted company with this new group and moved into self-publishing, producing the two influential photographic publications *Photography/Politics: One* (1979) and *Photography/Politics: Two* (1986). This involvement in publishing helped to convince Spence of the importance of contributing critical writing alongside her photographic work, and she went on to write several books and publish numerous articles. In 1979 she enrolled for a full-time degree course at the Polytechnic of Central London, where she encountered the ideas and support of the respected photographic theorist Victor Burgin. In this year she produced one of her most impressive photographic installations: *The Family Album*. This installation took as its starting point her own family album; by combining images and text she called into question the role that family photographs had played in forming her own subjectivity and identity. This early critical work on the family album was to have a significant influence on the work of many of her contemporaries. Moreover, this initial investigation of the dual identities of both gender and class was to become a central concern in her later work.

In 1982 Spence's life changed drastically when she was diagnosed with breast cancer. This news and her subsequent experiences of the medical treatment for cancer became a strong theme in her photographic work. During this period she also began to train as an art therapist; once again Spence combined this training with her past interest in the theories surrounding radical theatre to initiate a new photographic practice: photo therapy. Alongside the feminist photographer Rosy Martin she devised a way of using photography as a form of personal therapy – as she described it: "literally using photography to heal ourselves". In a collectively produced touring exhibition, *The Picture of Health* (1985), Spence combined documentary-style photographs, experimental photo-therapy images and image-text pieces to produce a powerful critique of the power relationships involved within traditional medical institutions and their treatment of breast cancer. Through her "invention" of photo therapy, Spence's work returned, once again, to the hidden and repressed elements of her family album. Photo therapy was employed as an empowering tool – where past repressed feelings, experiences and memories could be made visible by re-staging them in front of the camera.

Spence was still working with Terry Dennett on an exhibition of photographic work titled the *Final Project: A Photofantasy and Phototherapeutic Exploration of Life and Death* when she died of leukaemia. In this exhibition she aimed to challenge one of the most hidden and taboo subjects in Western culture: death itself. Finally becoming too weak to use her camera, she returned to older images and earlier work and reused them to develop yet another photographic technique, which she named photo fantasy.

Jo Spence was an influential and inspirational feminist photographer. Throughout her life she made a formidable contribution to the development of feminist photographic theory and practice. Her work was never safe, static or conventional but was always pushing the boundaries and potential of the photographic medium to its very limits. She died in the Marie Curie Hospice in London shortly after her 58th birthday.

SARAH EDGE

Spencer, Lilly Martin
American painter, 1822–1902

Born Angélique Marie Martin in Exeter, England, 26 November 1822, to French parents; nicknamed Lilly. Emigrated to USA with her family, 1830; grew up in Marietta, Ohio. Moved to Cincinnati with her father to pursue a professional career in art, 1841; studied briefly under the portrait painter John Insco Williams, 1842. Married Benjamin Rush Spencer, 1844; first of 13 children born 1845; husband died 1890. Moved to New York,

1848; attended evening drawing classes at National Academy of Design. Sold first paintings to the Western Art Union, Cincinnati, 1847, to the American Art-Union, New York, 1848, to the Cosmopolitan Art Association, New York, 1855. Moved to Newark, New Jersey, 1858; took a studio on Broadway, New York, 1867; moved to Highland, New York, 1879; returned to New York, 1900. Honorary member, National Academy of Design, 1850. Died in New York, 22 May 1902.

Principal Exhibitions

Rectory of St Luke's Episcopal Church, Marietta, OH: 1841 (individual)
Western Art Union, Cincinnati: 1847
American Art-Union, New York: 1848
National Academy of Design, New York: from 1848
Cosmopolitan Art Association, New York: 1855
Great Central Fair, Philadelphia: 1864
Women's Pavilion, Centennial Exposition, Philadelphia: 1876

Bibliography

Henrietta A. Hadery, "Mrs Lilly M. Spencer", *Sartain's Union Magazine*, ix, August 1851, pp.152–4
Elsie F. Freivogel, "Lilly Martin Spencer: Feminist without politics", *Archives of American Art Journal*, xii/4, 1972, pp.9–14
Lilly Martin Spencer, 1822–1902: The Joys of Sentiment, exh. cat., National Collection of Fine Arts, Smithsonian Institution, Washington, DC, 1973 (contains extensive bibliography)
Robin Bolton-Smith and Douglas Hyland, "*Baby Chicks*: The sentimental brush of Lilly Martin Spencer", *Register of the Spencer Museum of Art, University of Kansas*, v, Spring 1982, pp.80–93
Helen S. Langa, "Lilly Martin Spencer: Genre, aesthetics and gender in the work of a mid-nineteenth century American woman artist", *Athanor*, ix, 1990, pp.37–45
Elizabeth Johns, *American Genre Painting: The Politics of Everyday Life*, New Haven and London: Yale University Press, 1991
David M. Lubin, *Picturing a Nation: Art and Social Change in Nineteenth-Century America*, New Haven and London: Yale University Press, 1994

Manuscript collection is in the Archives of American Art, Washington, DC.

Lilly Martin Spencer is distinguished as one of the few American women artists of the 1840s and 1850s who had a successful career as a popular artist and who also had a large family. She was initially encouraged to achieve in her art and compete with mainstream male artists largely because of her enlightened parents, Angélique and Giles Martin, French socialists who came to America with hopes of organising a communal society following the ideas of Charles Fourier. Her father brought her as a teenager from the small community in Marietta, Ohio, where they lived, to the bustling city of Cincinnati, and there secured professional instruction for her while he supported them both with his tutoring. Furthermore, her husband, Benjamin Rush Spencer, also fostered her art ambitions, even devoting his own time and energies to assume the responsibilities of household manager and carer of their 13 children, of whom seven reached adulthood.

From the beginning of her career, Spencer painted spirited genre scenes inspired by her own domestic experiences. These proved popular with the Western Art Union, based in Cincinnati, which showed eight of her paintings at its first exhibition in 1847. Seeking career opportunities for Lilly, the family moved to New York in 1848, by then the art centre of the USA. In New York she perfected her craft and regularly exhibited at the National Academy of Design, the American Art-Union and the Cosmopolitan Art Association. William Schaus published many of her paintings as popular lithographs that found an audience in Europe as well as America. During the following ten years her reputation grew, although finances were often tight for the expanding family. Her ambitions and hardships are chronicled in a series of moving letters to her mother, now on file in the Archives of American Art (Washington, DC). Finally, in 1858, the Spencers moved across the Hudson River to Newark, New Jersey, where they rented a home from her patron Marcus L. Ward, but her career never prospered there as it had in New York.

Spencer painted her best work in the late 1840s and 1850s. She focused on women and children in domestic situations, but also painted "fancy pictures" of young girls and boys looking sweet and coquettish. The usual sentimental message is the devotion of mothers to their children. In *Domestic Happiness* (subtitle "*Hush: Don't Wake Them*", alternative title *Domestic Felicity*, 1849; Detroit Institute of Arts) she celebrates familial love by representing a father and mother gazing down lovingly at their baby and toddler asleep on a bed, arms intertwined. The hand of the mother reaches up to her husband to quiet his own gestures towards the two children; hence, the mother's dominance within the painting symbolically parallels Spencer's control as a painter constructing her own idealised images of women as the agents of domestic bliss. In *"This Little Pig Went to Market"* (1857; oil on composition board; Campus Martius Museum, Marietta, OH) a doll-like mother tweaks the toes of her laughing baby in the privacy of the nursery. A review in the December 1859 issue of the *Cosmopolitan Art Journal* offered typical praise: "We have here Mrs Spencer in her best mood ... The expression is very happy; the story is read at a glance. The detail is worked in with wondrous ease and beauty. Mrs Spencer elaborates, but never crowds her canvas. In this fine work all her best characteristics appear" (quoted in Washington 1973, p.169). When painting such pictures Spencer would have used herself and her own children as models. Her portrait skills are also evident in paintings she did of the children of Marcus Ward.

However, in kitchen scenes, such as *"Shake Hands?"* (1854; oil on canvas; Ohio Historical Center, Columbus), Spencer showed the humorous side of her art. Here a female servant, looking up from kneading dough, teasingly offers a flour-covered hand to the viewer. In *Young Husband: First Marketing* (1854; oil on canvas; private collection, repr. Washington 1973) Spencer pokes fun at the novice husband, hurrying along a rainy city street and unable to manage both the umbrella and the groceries and poultry spilling out of his market basket on to a wet pavement. The situations of her genre subjects tend to be unique in the history of 19th-century art, primarily because they so clearly suggest a woman's point of view about domestic life and even, at times, suggest a sinister or subversive sub-text. Although her lack of mastery of human anatomy is evident, she generally paints with a rich palette of jewel-like tones – ruby, emerald and sapphire colours – and with deft strokes detailing the fabrics of clothing and emphasising the succulence of fruits and vegetables. The retrospective exhibition of Spencer's work at the National Museum of American Art in 1973, with its catalogue that reproduced all her known paintings and drawings, revived interest in her work and made clear the parallels to the sentimental women's literature of the mid-19th century.

PATRICIA HILLS

Spero, Nancy
[fig. 57]

American artist, 1926–

Born in Cleveland, Ohio, 24 August 1926. Studied at University of Colorado, Boulder, 1944–5; School of the Art Institute of Chicago, 1945–9 (BFA); Ecole des Beaux-Arts and Atelier André Lhôte, Paris, 1949–50. Apprenticeship in scene design, Ivoryton Summer Theatre, Connecticut, 1950. Married artist Leon Golub, 1951; three sons, born 1953, 1954 and 1961. Lived in New York, 1950–51; Chicago, 1951–6; Ischia and Florence, Italy, 1956–7; Bloomington, Indiana, 1957–9; Paris, 1959–64; New York, from 1964. Joined Art Workers Coalition (AWC), 1968–9; Women Artists in Revolution (WAR), 1969; Ad Hoc Committee of Women Artists, 1970. Founder-member of AIR Gallery, New York, 1972. Recipient of Creative Artists Public Service (CAPS) grant, New York State Council of the Arts, 1976; National Endowment for the Arts (NEA) grant, 1977; NARAL/NY Pro-Choice Media award, 1995; Skowhegan medal for works on paper, 1995; Hiroshima art prize, Japan, 1996; honorary doctorate, School of the Art Institute of Chicago, 1991. Lives in New York.

Selected Individual Exhibitions

Galerie Breteau, Paris: 1962, 1965, 1968
Rhona Hoffman Gallery, Chicago: 1983, 1988
Riverside Studios, London: 1984
Burnett Miller Gallery, Los Angeles: 1985
Galerie Barbara Gross, Munich: 1986, 1991, 1995
Josh Baer Gallery, New York: 1986, 1987, 1988, 1989, 1993
Institute of Contemporary Arts, London: 1987 (touring retrospective)
Museum of Contemporary Art, Los Angeles: 1989
Schirn Kunsthalle, Frankfurt am Main: 1989
Haus am Waldsee, Berlin: 1990 (touring)
Galerie Montenay, Paris: 1990
Glyptothek am Königplatz, Munich: 1991
Galleria Stefania Miscetti, Rome: 1991
Ulmer Museum, Ulm: 1992 (retrospective)
National Gallery of Canada, Ottawa: 1993
Konsthall, Malmö: 1994
List Visual Arts Center, Massachusetts Institute of Technology, Cambridge: 1994 (with Leon Golub)
American Center, Paris: 1995 (with Leon Golub)
Vancouver Art Gallery: 1996
Hiroshima City Museum of Contemporary Art: 1996 (with Leon Golub)

Selected Writings

"Ende", *Women's Studies*, vi, 1978, pp.3–11
"The discovered uncovered", *M/E/A/N/I/N/G*, no.2, November 1987, p.32
"Sky Goddess: Egyptian acrobat", *Artforum*, xxvii, March 1988, pp.103–5
"Tracing Ana Mendieta", *Artforum*, xxx, April 1992, pp.75–7

Bibliography

Corinne Robbins, "Nancy Spero: 'Political' artist and the nightmare", *Feminist Art Journal*, Spring 1975, pp.19–22, 48
——, "Words and images through time: The art of Nancy Spero", *Arts Magazine*, liv, December 1979, pp.103–5
Donald B. Kuspit, "From existence to essence: Nancy Spero", *Art in America*, lxxii, January 1984, pp.88–96
Nancy Spero, exh. cat., Institute of Contemporary Arts, London, and elsewhere, 1987
Nancy Spero: Works since 1950, exh. cat., Everson Museum of Art, Syracuse, NY, and elsewhere, 1987
Tamar Garb, "Nancy Spero interviewed", *Artscribe International*, Summer 1987, pp.58–62
Jeanne Siegel, "Nancy Spero: Woman as protagonist (interview)", *Arts Magazine*, lxii, September 1987, pp.10–13
Jean Fulten, "A feminist resolution: The art of Nancy Spero", *New Art Examiner*, xvi/1, 1989, pp.32–5
Elizabeth Ann Dobie, "Interweaving feminist frameworks", *Journal of Aesthetics and Art Criticism*, xlviii, 1990, pp.381–94
Nancy Spero: Bilder, 1958–1990, exh. cat., Haus am Waldsee, Berlin, and elsewhere, 1990
Pamela Wye, "Freedom of movement: Nancy Spero's site paintings", *Arts Magazine*, lxv, October 1990, pp.54–8
Josephine Withers, "Nancy Spero's American-born Sheela-na-gig", *Feminist Studies*, xvii/1, 1991, pp.51–6
Jon Bird, Jo Anna Isaak and Sylvère Lotringer, *Nancy Spero*, London: Phaidon, 1996

In 1972, after two years, Nancy Spero completed the *Codex Artaud*, a work that in both form and content became the basis for her subsequent practice. *Codex Artaud* comprises 33 panels of collaged images and texts on hand-made English Bodleian paper, French vellum and Japanese rice paper, each section varying in length from 1.2 to 7.6 metres, the width (approximately 0.6 m.) being determined by the dimensions of each individual piece of paper. Spero has adhered predominantly to the horizontal format of the scroll ever since, although since the mid-1980s she has produced occasional vertical works or "Totems". The only significant deviation from this structure occurred in her development of a technique for direct printing on to interior and exterior wall surfaces in her installations from 1987 onwards. In the early 1980s the wood-backed zinc plates used for printing on to paper were supplemented by pliable polymer plates allowing the image to be reproduced also on uneven surfaces, as with *Re-Birth of Venus* (1989) on the curved interior walls and columns of the Schirn Kunsthalle, Frankfurt am Main, and *Minerva, Sky Goddess* (1991) on the roof and parapet walls of the Circulo de Bellas Artes, Madrid.

Spero trained at the Art Institute of Chicago, where she met her husband, the painter Leon Golub, and through the 1950s she produced a series of figurative paintings on the themes of lovers, prostitutes, maternity and family groups. In these powerfully expressive works, named the *Black Paris Paintings* after the five-year period the family spent in Europe, she introduced disturbing references to grotesque, nightmarish and fantastic forms in a tonal range that darkened to the point where the image barely emerged from the ground. Returning to New York in 1964, Spero continued painting but finally abandoned the medium two years later. The *War Series* followed: small-scale works on paper that employed a ferocious imaging of the Vietnam War as phallic power – helicopters and bombs ejaculating and defecating on to helpless victims with scrawled texts drawn from the official and media statements that disavowed the reality of American aggression.

The works of this period also carried the signs of Spero's increasing sense of alienation from the institutional structures of the art world – an experience of marginality and exclusion historically enacted on the grounds of gender and race. Blocked and silenced at almost every point as a woman artist whose work was primarily figurative and political, Spero turned to the tortured prose of the French poet Antonin Artaud as an analogous reference point for her own angry isolation. Artaud's desire to escape the body, made acute by the physical and emotional effects of his incarceration in the asylum at Rodez, erupts in the fractured materiality of a language pervaded by metaphors of separation and loss. Through Artaud Spero found a voice that, as her anger became politicised and historicised in the context of the Women's Movement, became a feminist voice committed to re-visioning the representation of the female body, not as the Other of the male, but as a sexual, maternal and active imaginary body dancing between the lines of histories and cultures.

With *Torture of Women* (1976; length 3.8 m.; National Gallery of Canada, Ottawa) Spero decided to concentrate solely upon representations of the female while extending the theme of language, and thus subjectivity, under duress – at the moments when the body is experienced in its extreme states as abjection or "jouissance". *Torture of Women* documents accounts of torture taken from Amnesty International. Each obscene case history is accompanied by a bestiary of fantastic and mythological creatures and figures; the pathology of oppression is given its archaic expression in the Babylonian creation myth of the battle between Marduk, the sun-god, and Tiamat, the original mother-goddess. This epic functions in *Torture of Women* not only as the symbolic representation of violence against all women, but also signifies the scope of the scrolls interspersing and repeating images from different histories, traditions and cultures, in extended and accumulative visual narratives, to displace any notion of a fixed feminine Other.

Two further major works followed: the monumental *Notes in Time on Women* (1979; 0.5 × 68.6 m.) and *The First Language* (1981; 0.5 × 57.9 m.). *Notes in Time on Women* juxtaposes images of women from prehistory to the present with the "official" texts of patriarchal culture extracted from literature, philosophy, journalism and the media. Cavorting female figures run and dance over and between the lines of print, a carnivalesque subversion by the painted and hand-printed active female bodies of the way woman is spoken of in male discourse. *Notes in Time on Women* is both document and archive; a narrativisation of the social and historical concept of woman placed "in parenthesis" by a mocking and empowered feminine presence. Formal allusions range from Egyptian wall paintings and papyrus, the Bayeux Tapestry (first seen by Spero when it was exhibited in Chicago in the 1950s), to the rebellious scrawls of urban graffiti. Reversing the usual text/image relationship where it is the literary that anchors the visual, these images up-end and fragment the discourse of power of masculine authorities. In *The First Language* Spero introduced a contemporary woman combing her hair, a Roman stone monument of a matron, a Japanese doll alongside recycled images introduced in *Torture of Women*: a roller-skating Artemis (who "heals women's pain"), the

Venus of Willendorf juxtaposed with repeated hand-stamped adaptations of the Egyptian sky-goddess and protectress, Nut. It is the female body's expressive potential that articulates a semiotics of gesture and activity, a choreographic unfolding of women's experience from victimisation to celebration privileging the maternal as a place of origin.

Paralleling her interest in the work of French feminist critical theory, particularly Julia Kristeva's notion of a semiotic "chora" as the reinscription of the maternal in the body of the text and Hélène Cixous's argument for an "écriture féminine", Spero suggested that her work could be seen as the possibility of a "peinture féminine". Through the 1980s the carnivalesque aspect, of a joyful assertion of women's sexuality and pleasure, floods the scrolls with ecstatic figures celebrating rhythmical movement in upbeat colour and tonal relations. In *Sky Goddess* (1985; 0.5 × 13.7 m.) the repeated image of the Goddess (an amalgamation of the Roman wolf nurturing the infants Romulus and Remus with the Egyptian Nut) arches over, and is interspersed with, the repeated profile of Athena, alongside schematic and abstracted dancing figures derived from Aboriginal and prehistoric sources, the whole movement concluded and then returned with the image of a Vietnamese woman, an upright, sprightly walking figure – a survivor.

Towards the end of the 1980s Spero's delineation of internal space – the gaps or "silences" between the active forms, and the external dimension – the lateral (or vertical in the case of the *Totems*) spread of the scroll across the wall, took a different turn in the installations that freed the figure–ground relation from the constraints of a framing-edge. In such works as *Waterworks* (1988), *To Soar III* (1991; Harold Washington Library, Chicago), *Minerva, Sky Goddess* (1991; Circulo de Bellas Artes, Madrid), *Ballade von der "Judenhure" Marie Sanders* (1991; Wuppertal), *Première* (1993; Ronacher Theatre, Vienne) and *To the Revolution* (1994; American Center, Paris) Spero's unbounded female figures, intermingling the mythological and the fantastic with the social and historically specific, feminise the architectural space itself. In *Vulture Goddess*, an installation at the Institute of Contemporary Art, Philadelphia (1991), the Celtic goddess of fertility and destruction – Sheela-na-Gig – defiantly displays her vagina/womb in an extended "chorus line" from the overhead beams, whereas in *To Soar I* (1988; Museum of Contemporary Art, Los Angeles) a line of dildo dancers gleefully run along the base of a wall and vanish round a corner – figures defiantly "out-of-place", defying the gaze and appearing where least expected. *Black and the Red III* (1994; Konsthall, Malmö), a scroll 60.9 metres long comprising 22 panels of dense overprinting, mixes familiar cross-cultural and historical figures from Spero's lexicon (which now approximates more than 300 individual female images) with references to heraldry, the abstract patterning of Greek vase painting and the grids of Minimal art. Interspersing vibrant areas of colour saturation within an overall scheme of red, black, gold and white vertical and horizontal squares and divisions, the textual density and surface presence here replace the open spacing and muted palette of earlier works. Interweaving the archaic with the contemporary, the mythological with the social, absence and void with density and presence, Spero's practice represents a choreographing of the liberated female body in new spatial configurations and relations in which women can act as subjects.

JON BIRD

Steger, Milly
German sculptor, 1881–1948

Born in Rheinberg, near Moers, 15 June 1881. Studied at the Kunstgewerbeschule, Elberfeld, then in the private studio of Karl Janssen in Düsseldorf, 1901–*c*.1905. Visited Florence, Paris and Belgium. Studied under Georg Kolbe in Berlin. Moved to Hagen, 1910; city sculptor of Hagen, 1914. Moved to Berlin and took over Georg Kolbe's studio, 1917. Head of sculpture class at the Zeichen- und Malschule des Vereins der Künstlerinnen zu Berlin from 1929. Several works declared "degenerate" and confiscated by the National Socialists, 1937. Apartment, studio and numerous works destroyed by bombing, 1943. Recipient of fourth prize and honourable mention, Olympic Art Competition, Berlin, 1936; Villa Romana prize, 1938 (with Georg Kolbe). Member, Arbeitsrat für Kunst (Workers Council of Art), Berlin, 1918–19; Berlin Secession, 1931. Member, 1927–43, member of executive committee, 1927–32, honorary president, 1932–43, and honorary member, 1943, Verein der Künstlerinnen zu Berlin; honorary member, 1945,

and member of honorary executive committee, 1948, Deutscher Demokratischer Frauenbund (German Democratic League of Women). Died in Berlin, 31 October 1948.

Principal Exhibitions

Individual
Prussian Academy, Berlin: 1922
Verein der Künstlerinnen zu Berlin, Galerie Archivarion, Berlin: 1949 (retrospective)

Group
Berlin Secession: 1909, 1935
Sonderbund, Düsseldorf: 1910
Internationale Ausstellung des Sonderbundes, Cologne: 1912
Museum Folkwang, Hagen: 1913 (*Hagener Künstler*), 1921 (*Die Künstler um Karl Ernst Osthaus*)
Deutscher Werkbund, Cologne: 1914
Kunsthalle, Mannheim: 1914 (*Plastiken neuzeitlicher Bildhauer*)
Freie Secession, Berlin: 1920
Grosse Berliner Kunstausstellung, Berlin: 1921
Galerie Alfred Flechtheim, Berlin: 1922 (*Frauen*)
Verein der Künstlerinnen zu Berlin: 1927–34, 1937, 1940, 1942–3 (annuals), 1929 (*Die Frau von heute*), 1930 (*Das Kind*)
Prussian Academy, Berlin: 1931
Frühjahrsausstellung, Hannover: 1933
Ausstellung des deutschen Künstlerbundes im Kunstverein Hamburg: 1936 (*Malerei und Plastik in Deutschland 1936*)
Museumsverein, Hannover: 1936
Verein der Künstlerinnen zu Berlin and Lyzeum-Club, Galerie von der Heyde, Berlin: 1939
Gäste des Vereins Berliner Künstler, Berlin: 1941
Hilfswerk für deutsche bildende Kunst in der NS-Volkswohlfahrt, Berlin: 1941
Berliner Zeughaus, Berlin: 1946 (*Erste deutsche Kunstausstellung*)

Selected Writings
"Antwort", *Ja! Stimmen des Arbeitsrates für Kunst in Berlin*, Berlin, 1919, p.65
"Begegnung mit Minne", *Kunst der Zeit*, ii/5–6, 1928–9, pp.108–9

Bibliography
Festschrift zur Einweihung des Hagener Stadttheaters, Hagen, 1911
Hans Hildebrandt, "Milly Steger", *Das Kunstblatt*, ii, 1918, pp.372–6
Alfred Kuhn, "Milly Steger", *Deutsche Kunst und Dekoration*, xxvi, 1922–3, pp.198–200
Karl Scheffler, "Ausstellungsrezensionen", *Kunst und Künstler*, no.21, 1923, p.68

Otto Grautoff, "Milly Steger", *Die Kunst für Alle*, xli, 1926, pp.321–8

Hans Hildebrandt, *Die Frau als Künstlerin*, Berlin: Rudolf Mosse, 1928

Paul Ferdinand Schmidt, "Milly Steger", *Der Kunstwanderer*, September 1931–August 1932, pp.241–3

Thorwald, "Milly Steger", *Kunst der Nation*, ii/14, July 1934, p.2

Fritz Nemitz, "Milly Steger", *Die Kunst für Alle*, l, October 1934, pp.10–15

Gertrud Richert, "Milly Steger in Memoriam", *Berliner Künstlerinnen- und Milly-Steger-Gedächtnis-Ausstellung*, Berlin, 1949, p.5

Anna Christa Funk, "Die Bildhauerin Milly Steger in Hagen", *Hagener Heimatkalender*, Hagen, 1970, pp.121–4

Herta Hesse Frielinghaus and others, *Karl Ernst Osthaus: Leben und Werk*, Recklinghausen: Bongers, 1971

Milly Steger, 1881–1948, exh. cat., Karl Ernst Osthaus-Museum, Hagen, 1981

Ulrike Evers, *Deutsche Künstlerinnen des 20. Jahrhunderts: Malerei, Bildhauerei, Tapisserie*, Hamburg: Schultheis, 1983

German Expressionist Sculpture, exh. cat., Los Angeles County Museum of Art and elsewhere, 1983

Das Verborgene Museum I: Dokumentation der Kunst von Frauen in Berliner öffentlichen Sammlungen, exh. cat., Akademie der Künste, Berlin, 1987

Werner Gerber, *Hagener Bohème: Menschen um Osthaus*, Hagen, 1990

Entartete Beeldhouwkunst: Duitse Beeldhouwers, 1900–1945 [Degenerate sculpture: German sculptors, 1900–1945], exh. cat., Commanderie van St Jan, Nijmegen, and elsewhere, 1991

Magdalena Bushart, "Der Formsinn des Weibes: Bildhauerinnen in den zwanziger und dreissiger Jahren", *Profession ohne Tradition: 125 Jahre Verein der Berliner Künstlerinnen*, exh. cat., Berlinische Galerie, Berlin, 1992, pp.135–50

Birgit Schulte, "Milly Steger: Stadtbildhauerin von Hagen", *Hagener Impuls*, no.8, September 1994, pp.27–36

Erich Ranfft, "German women sculptors, 1918–1936: Gender differences and status", *Visions of the "Neue Frau": Women and the Visual Arts in Weimar Germany*, ed. Marsha Meskimmon and Shearer West, Aldershot: Scolar Press, 1995, pp.42–61

Manuscript collections are in the Archiv des Vereins der Berliner Künstlerinnen, Berlin, and the Karl Ernst Osthaus-Archiv, Hagen.

Milly Steger was one of the first woman artists to obtain public commissions for architectural sculptures. In the early 1920s she was invariably included in texts on contemporary sculpture, and some critics considered her the most important female sculptor in Germany (Scheffler 1923, Thorwald 1934). In 1932, with Ernst Barlach and Wilhelm Lehmbruck, she was cited in *Knaurs Konversationslexikon* as an exemplary sculptor of the 20th century.

From the beginning of her career, Steger was concerned with pure form, infused with her interest in architectonic structuring. She treated specified subjects only exceptionally, as in the religious works from the 1930s onwards. Her female figures and groups of figures have terse, generic titles: *Woman*, *Girl*, *Torso*, *Group*. The poses are standing, striding, kneeling and feature every kind of movement. In addition to working in wood and bronze, she carved even the hardest stone herself in order to retain the evidence of her own hand.

Very little of her work before 1910 survives. Apart from Georg Kolbe, the crucial influences on her early work were Maillol and Bernhard Hoetger, with their full understanding of the figure. Her career was established with the move to Hagen, at the invitation of Karl Ernst Osthaus, founder of the Folkwang Museum. She created her first large architectural sculpture for this Westphalian industrial town: four over-life-size, column-like, nude female figures in sandstone for the façade of the theatre (1911; Stadttheater Hagen). Without attributes or symbolic-allegorical meaning, the nudes created a scandal that made the young artist known in Germany. The figures were saved only after a campaign of support by Osthaus.

Despite serious controversies, Steger was appointed the city sculptor of Hagen in 1914 and was employed for public commissions. She designed a series of colossal panthers above the entrance to the new town hall (1914; destroyed World War II, repr. Gerber 1990, p.25), as well as an oval relief of *Dancers* (destroyed, repr. Klaus-Jürgen Sembach, *Henry van de Velde*, London: Thames and Hudson, and New York: Rizzoli, 1989) for the theatre of the Deutsche Werkbundausstellung in Cologne, built by Henry van de Velde. Steger's plaster models (destroyed, repr. Schulte 1994, p.32) for two life-size bronze figures (unexecuted) intended for portal niches at the Folkwang Museum were exhibited in the Hagen Room, arranged by Osthaus, at the Werkbundausstellung. For her own house, built by Jan Mathieu Lauweriks, at the Hagen artists' colony of Eppenhausen, she designed a façade relief of a caryatid supporting the balcony (1911; Am Stirnband, Hagen). In Jan Thorn-Prikker's house at Eppenhausen, she executed an overmantel relief that recalls the Cologne theatre relief: three female nudes fill the oval with flowing dance movements (1910; Am Stirnband, Hagen).

The essential character of Steger's later works, its expressive gesture, is already discernible from 1910. This is largely attributable to the influence of Expressionism. Lightness and movement took the place of mass. The figures, composed of geometrical structures, are complexly intertwined, the faces are introverted and melancholy. The combination of strict composition and strong expressiveness characterises Steger's works from 1917 to the early 1920s. The nearly life-size *Rising Youth* (*c.*1919; wood; Städtische Galerie und Städelsches Kunstinstitut, Frankfurt am Main) is constructed from relating horizontals, verticals and diagonals. This close connection of expressive, stylised imitation and gestures is also visible in *Female Half-Figure* (*c.*1920; coloured plaster; Karl Ernst Osthaus-Museum, Hagen), in which spiritualised expression is pushed to its limits. More space is required by the tragic Old Testament figure *Jephtah's Daughter* (1919; bronze; private collection, repr. Hagen 1981), whose energised body language reflects contemporary expressive dance. Material weight is removed, and the fine-limbed, nearly life-size dancer is defined by the opposition of flowing arched forms. Steger understood the self-willed dynamism of her figures as the expression of emotions.

A change in style to a greater emphasis on the dynamic element, which occurred around 1920, is linked to Steger's move to Berlin. The war had prevented the realisation of other public commissions in Hagen, and her plan to establish a workshop for tombstones and monuments had failed due to lack of investment. This forced her return to Berlin in 1917. There, lacking public commissions, she executed mainly free-standing figures and portraits, and these required a different concept from architectural sculpture. Another stylistic change, replacing the Expressionist phase, began in 1922–3. It is clearly visible in the small sculpture *Sitting Woman* (*c.*1930; Karl Ernst Osthaus-Museum). Steger increasingly made reference to natural forms, and her figures gained weight. Although strong torsion and gestural language are still of central importance, the figure's emotional language is expressed in a more controlled movement. Extreme postures correspond to such attributes and titles as *The Lament*, *The Lonely*, *The Pensive*. The figures remain under-life-size, as in *The*

Austere (1928; bronze; Märkisches Museum, Berlin) and *My Ball* (1932; bronze; untraced, repr. Bushart 1992, p.139).

In 1929, when mixed classes for life-drawing and sculpture were introduced at the school of the Unterrichtsanstalt des Vereins der Berliner Künstlerinnen, Steger ran them, one of the first female artists to teach male students. Steger appears to have worked relatively undisturbed after the National Socialists seized power in 1933. She accepted a few public commissions, such as works for the Olympic Games of 1936 (*Boy Playing Ball*) and 1940 (*Relief with Rowers*; both untraced). To some extent her late work could be seen to reflect contemporary taste in art, for example *Woman Carrying a Jug* (*c.*1940; untraced, *ibid.*, p.140). Yet, *Woman Striding/Woman Carrying a Jug I* (1934; bronze; private collection, repr. Nijmegen 1991, p.243) was confiscated as "degenerate" from the Staatliche Museen, Berlin, in 1937; six works by Steger were on the list of works confiscated.

After a year's stay in Florence in 1938, in connection with the Villa Romana prize, Steger executed several small marble groups employing the *non finito*, with figures against a deliberately unfinished background, for example *Naiads* (after 1940; marble; Nationalgalerie, Berlin) and *Two Sisters* (1946; marble; private collection, repr. Hagen 1981, no.18). The sorrowful experiences of war are reflected in two late works, *Pietà 45* (1945; spruce; private collection, *ibid.*, no.16) and *In Memoriam* (*c.*1945; marble; untraced, repr. Richert 1949).

With her male clothes and manners, Steger throughout her life reinforced the legend of her innate male genius that was created about her in the writings of critics and reviewers. By presenting herself in this way, the renowned sculptor, an acknowledged outsider, united her emancipation from the traditional role of the female artist with an adaptation to the male domain she had conquered.

BIRGIT SCHULTE

Stepanova, Varvara (Fyodorovna)
Russian painter and designer, 1894–1958

Born in Kovno (now Kaunas), Lithuania, 9 October (Old Style calendar)/21 October (New Style calendar) 1894. Studied at Kovno gymnasium, graduating in 1910; Kazan Art School, 1910–13; Stroganov School of Applied Art, Moscow, 1913–14; studied in the studios of Konstantin Yuon, Ivan Dudin and Leblanc, Moscow, 1915–17. Assistant director, Art and Literature Section of IZO, Narkompros (Fine Arts Section, People's Commissariat of Enlightenment), 1919–20. Taught at the Krupskaya Academy for Communist Education, 1920–25; Vkhutemas (Higher State Artistic and Technical Workshops), Moscow, 1924–5. Member, Inkhuk (Institute of Artistic Culture), Moscow, 1920–23. Met Alexander Rodchenko at the Kazan' Art School; lived with him from 1916; one daughter; Rodchenko died 1956. Died in Moscow, 20 May 1958.

Principal Exhibitions

Moscow: 1918 (*Fifth State Exhibition*), 1919 (*Tenth State Exhibition: Non-Objective Creation and Suprematism*), 1920 (*Nineteenth State Exhibition*), 1921 (*5 x 5 = 25*, with Rodchenko, Popova, Exter and Vesnin), 1928 (*The Everyday Soviet Textile*), 1930 (*First Exhibition of the October Group*)
Galerie van Diemen, Berlin: 1922–3 (*Erste russische Kunstausstellung*, touring)
Museum of Decorative Painting, Moscow: 1923 (*Moscow's Theatrical and Decorative Art, 1918–1923*)
Venice Biennale: 1924
Exposition Internationale des Arts Décoratifs et Industriels Modernes, Paris: 1925
Academy of Arts, Leningrad: 1927 (*Graphic Art in the USSR, 1917–1927*)
State Tretyakov Gallery, Moscow: 1927 (*Russian Drawing During the Ten Years since the October Revolution*)
Cologne: 1928 (*International Pressa Exhibition*)
Park of Culture and Rest, Moscow: 1929 (*First Exhibition of Theatrical and Decorative Art*)
Petit Palais, Paris: 1931 (*International Exhibition of the Art of the Book*)
Historical Museum, Moscow: 1933 (*Artists of the Soviet Theatre over 17 Years, 1917–1934*)

Selected Writings

V. Agarykh [V. Stepanova], "O vystavlennykh grafikakh: Bespredmetnoye tvorchestvo" [About the graphic works on display: Non-objective creation], *Katalog desyatoy gosudarstvennoy vystavki: Bespredmetnoye tvorchestvo i suprematizm* [Catalogue of the Tenth State Exhibition: Non-Objective Creation and Suprematism], Moscow, 1919, pp.5–9
Untitled text in *5 x 5 = 25*, exh. cat., Moscow, 1921
Varst [V. Stepanova], "Kostyum segodnyashnego dnya prozodezhda" [The costume of the present day is working clothing], *Lef*, no.2, 1923, pp.65–8
Varst [V. Stepanova], "O rabotakh konstruktivistskoy molodyozhi" [Concerning the work of Young Constructivists], *Lef*, no.3, 1923, pp.53–6
Varst [V. Stepanova], "Rabochiy Klub: Konstruktivist A.M. Rodchenko" [The Workers' Club: The Constructivist A.M. Rodchenko], *Sovremennaya arkhitektura*, no.1, 1926, p.36
"Ot kostyuma k risunku i tkani" [From costume to drawing and the fabric], *Vechernaya Moskva*, no.49, 1929, p.3
Chelovek ne mozhet zhit bez chuda: Pisma, Poeticheskiye opyty, Zapiski khudozhnitsy [Man cannot live without miracles: Letters, poetical experiments, the artist's notes], Moscow: Izdaltelstvo Sfera, 1994

Bibliography

E. Kovtun, "Varvara Stepanova's anti-book", *Von der Flache zum Raum: Russland, 1916–1924/From Surface to Space: Russia, 1916–1924*, Cologne: Galerie Gmurzynska, 1974, pp.269–84
Varvara Fyodorovna Stepanova, 1894–1958, exh. cat., Kostroma Regional Museum of Fine Arts, 1975
Künstlerinnen der russischen Avantgarde/Women Artists of the Russian Avant-Garde, 1910–1930, exh. cat., Galerie Gmurzynska, Cologne, 1979
Angelica Zander Rudenstine, ed., *The George Costakis Collection: Russian Avant-Garde Art*, New York: Abrams, and London: Thames and Hudson, 1981
Christina Lodder, *Russian Constructivism*, New Haven and London: Yale University Press, 1983
Rodcenko e Stepanova: Alle origini del Costruttivismo, Milan: Electa, 1984
Alexander Lavrentiev, *Varvara Stepanova: A Constructivist Life*, ed. John E. Bowlt, Cambridge: Massachusetts Institute of Technology Press, and London: Thames and Hudson, 1988 (Russian original)
Art into Life: Russian Constructivism, 1914–1932, exh. cat., Henry Art Gallery, University of Washington, Seattle, 1990
M.N. Yablonskaya, *Women Artists of Russia's New Age, 1900–1935*, New York: Rizzoli, and London: Thames and Hudson, 1990
The Future Is Our Only Goal: Aleksander M. Rodchenko, Varvara F. Stepanova, exh. cat., Österreichisches Museum für angewandte Kunst, Vienna, and elsewhere, 1991

Varvara Stepanova produced some innovative work synthesising poetry and painting in the late 1910s, and from 1921 onwards played an important role in developing the theory and practice of Constructivism, notably in the areas of theatrical, costume and typographical design. From the very beginning her career was closely bound up with that of her husband, the artist Alexander Rodchenko, whom she met at the Kazan Art School around 1911.

In 1917, under the influence of the artist Olga Rozanova (q.v.), Stepanova began to write transrational poetry (*zaum*). Between 1918 and 1919 she produced a series of illustrated, collaged and handwritten books such as *Rtny khomle*, *Zigra ar*, *Globolkim*, *Gaust chaba* and *Toft*, which she categorised as "visual poetry" and "colour script graphics". In these she integrated words, phrases and lines of poetry into colourful non-objective configurations of lines and shapes, using words as pictorial elements and experimenting with collage.

She was an active participant in artistic life during the revolutionary period, working as assistant director of the Art and Literature Section of IZO, Narkompros (Fine Arts Section of the People's Commissariat of Enlightenment, 1919–20) and sitting on the council of representatives of the Union of Art Workers at IZO (1920–22). She also taught at the Krupskaya Communist Academy (1920–25), and in 1925 arranged a book evening there. A member of Moscow's Inkhuk (Institute of Artistic Culture), 1920–23, Stepanova was secretary to the Group for Objective Analysis (1920–21) and contributed to the discussions in spring 1921 that sought to define the distinction between concepts of composition and construction. As a result she, Aleksei Gan and Rodchenko founded the Working Group of Constructivists (also known as the First Working Group of Constructivists) in March 1921. The group denied the validity of art as an autonomous activity, wanting to participate in the construction of a socialist society by designing everyday objects that could be mass produced. In December 1922 Stepanova contributed a paper "On Constructivism" to Inkhuk.

In September 1921 Stepanova collaborated with Rodchenko, Lyubov Popova (q.v.), Alexander Vesnin and Alexandra Exter (q.v.) in the important exhibition 5 × 5 = 25 in Moscow. The five artists each contributed five works. Stepanova exhibited paintings based on the mechanical and geometrical analysis of the human body (e.g. *Two Figures*, 1920; Costakis Collection). In these works, which she had started making in 1919, the figure is translated into flat geometric shapes, which are organised into almost abstract compositions (e.g. *Figure with Drum*, 1921; Alexander Laurentiev Collection). The forms are imbued with a certain irregularity that is complemented by the rough textures of the painted surface. Stepanova stated in the catalogue that "Technology and industry have presented art with the problem of construction as effective action, not contemplative figuration". She subsequently used a similar, but more precise geometry for drawings and woodcuts of human figures and celebrities such as Charlie Chaplin, some of which in 1922 she contributed to Aleksei Gan's film and photographic magazine *Film-Fot*.

In 1922 Stepanova designed the set and costumes for Vsevolod Meyerkhold's production of Sukhovo-Kobylin's play *The Death of Tarelkin*. She devised a series of acting apparatuses comprising collapsible structures (made from standard planks used as slats and painted white), which reinforced the action of the play and could be adapted to perform several functions. The costumes consisted of geometrically articulated overalls (working clothes or *prozodezhda*), which were sewn in two contrasting colours to identify the actors and emphasise their movements.

In early 1924 Stepanova and Popova started to work as fabric designers at the First Textile Print Factory in Moscow (formerly the Emil Tsindel Factory). In accordance with the Constructivists' machine aesthetic and the nature of industrial manufacture, Stepanova and Popova argued that geometrically based designs had to replace traditional floral and plant patterns as part of the total rationalisation of the textile and clothing industries. By manipulating simple geometric forms and primary colours, Stepanova created 150 designs, of which 20 were actually manufactured. She also became involved with the theoretical and practical problems of dress design, particularly working clothing and sports clothing (*sportodezhda*).

Stepanova contributed articles and illustrations to the journal *Lef* and *New Lef* (1923–7). In 1925 she began to design posters with Vladimir Mayakovsky (e.g. the *Literate Man Improves the Peasant Economy*, 1925). From the mid-1920s onwards she tended to concentrate almost exclusively on typographical and graphic design, producing covers and lay-outs for such magazines as *Sovetskoye Kino* (Soviet cinema), *Kniga i revolyutsiya* (Book and Revolution), *Sovremennaya arkhitektura* (Contemporary architecture) and *Krasnoye studenchestvo* (Red students). In the 1930s she collaborated with Rodchenko on Soviet propaganda publications such as *SSSR na stroyke* (USSR in construction; e.g. no.12, 1935, on parachuting; no.8, 1936, on the wood industry; and no.7, 1940, on Mayakovsky). They also worked together on large illustrated books such as *Desyatet Uzbekistana* (Ten years of Uzbekistan; 1934) and *Pervaya Konnaya* (First cavalry; 1938). Stepanova remained active in these areas during the 1940s and 1950s, when she was involved on the design of such magazines as *Sovetskaya zhenshchina* (Soviet woman; 1945–6) and albums including the *Moskovsky metro* (Moscow Metro; 1953). She returned briefly to painting in the late 1930s, when she produced some landscapes and still lifes (e.g. *Cabbage and Onions*, 1939; artist's family collection).

CHRISTINA LODDER

Stephens, Alice Barber [fig. 67]
American painter, illustrator and graphic artist, 1858–1932

Born Alice Barber near Salem, New Jersey, 1 July 1858. Studied at Philadelphia School of Design for Women (now Moore College of Art), 1869–79; Pennsylvania Academy of the Fine Arts, Philadelphia, under Thomas Eakins, 1876–7 and 1879–81; Académie Julian, Paris, under Tony Robert-Fleury, 1886–7; Académie Colarossi, Paris, 1887. Worked as a wood-engraver and illustrator from 1873, and solely as an illustrator by 1884; also active as a painter from 1880. Contributed to numerous publications from 1878, including *Scribner's Monthly*, *Harper's Young People*, *Harper's Bazar*, *Harper's New Monthly Magazine*, *Century Illustrated Monthly*, *Cosmopolitan*, *Harper's Round Table*, *Collier's Weekly*, *Woman's Home Companion*, *New Idea Woman's Magazine*, *Ladies' Home Journal*, *Delineator*, *McCall's*, *Reader* and *Country Gentleman*; publishers included Houghton Mifflin, from 1901; Harper, New York, from 1903; and Little Brown, Boston, from 1904. Taught drawing and painting from life, crayon portraiture and illustration at the Philadelphia School of Design for Women, 1889–93. Married painter Charles Hallowell Stephens, 1890; son born 1893; husband died 1931. Founder member of The Plastic Club, Philadelphia (an art club for women), and Fellowship of the Pennsylvania Academy of the Fine Arts, 1897. Member, Society of American Wood Engravers; New Century Club. Moved to Rose Valley, Pennsylvania, 1904. Died in Philadelphia after a stroke, 13 July 1932.

Principal Exhibitions
Boston Art Club: 1880–86 (annuals), 1895 (*Original Drawings by Famous Illustrators*)
Pennsylvania Academy of the Fine Arts, Philadelphia: 1881–90 (Mary Smith prize 1890)
Museum of Fine Arts, Boston: 1881 (*American Engravings on Wood*)
Salmagundi Club, New York: 1881–3 (black and white)
Philadelphia Society of Artists: 1881–3
Paris Salon: 1887
Art Gallery and Woman's Building, World's Columbian Exposition, Chicago: 1893 (honourable mention)
Cotton States International Exposition, Atlanta: 1895 (bronze medal)
The Plastic Club, Philadelphia: 1898 (individual), 1929 (retrospective)
Earls Court, London: 1899 (*Women's Work*, gold medal)
Exposition Universelle, Paris: 1900 (bronze medal)

Bibliography
Frederick W. Webber, "A clever woman illustrator", *Quarterly Illustrator*, i, 1893, pp.174–80
"Alice Barber Stephens, illustrator", *Woman's Progress*, November 1893, p.49
Esther Singleton, "Book illustrators, xv: Alice Barber Stephens", *Book Buyer*, xii, August 1895, pp.392–4
Aimée Tourgée, "A clever woman artist", *Art Interchange*, xxxix, October 1897, pp.74–5
Regina Armstrong, "Representative American women illustrators", *Critic*, xxxvii, July 1900, pp.43–54
Elizabeth Lore North, "Women illustrators of child life", *Outlook*, lxxviii, 1 October 1904, pp.271–80
Julius Moritzen, "Some women illustrators", *Twentieth Century Home*, December 1904, p.46
"Alice Barber Stephens", *Art Digest*, vi, 1 August 1932, p.6 (obituary)
"Alice Barber Stephens", *Art News*, xxx, 13 August 1932, p.8 (obituary)
The American Personality: The Artist-Illustrator of Life in the United States, 1860–1930, exh. cat., Grunwald Center for the Graphic Arts, University of California at Los Angeles, and elsewhere, 1976
Alice Barber Stephens: A Pioneer Woman Illustrator, exh. cat., Brandywine River Museum, Chadds Ford, PA, 1984
Helen Goodman, "Alice Barber Stephens, illustrator", *Arts Magazine*, lviii, January 1984, pp.126–9
——, "Alice Barber Stephens", *American Artist*, xlviii, April 1984, pp.46–9

Unpublished correspondence is in the Archives of American Art, Smithsonian Institution, Washington, DC; an illustration scrapbook is in the Art Division, New

York Public Library; original drawings and paintings are in the Brandywine River Museum, Chadds Ford, PA; original drawings are in the Library of Congress, Washington, DC.

The wood-engraving skills that Alice Barber Stephens learned at the Philadelphia School of Design for Women were the basis for the linear qualities of her drawing style for many years. She developed a more painterly style as a result of her studies with Thomas Eakins at the Pennsylvania Academy of the Fine Arts. Stephens illustrated romances, mysteries and adventures, but as women have often been encouraged to adopt work related to their image as mothers, she became best known for her illustrations for children's literature. Stylistically, Stephens's illustrations reflect the changing technology of reproducing images as well as her observations of other artists' work.

In the late 1860s and 1870s she learned to draw in pen and ink using traditional linear and hatching methods, because linear work was easily translated into wood-engraving. As staff wood-engraver for *Women's Words* in the late 1870s, Stephens both drew and engraved her illustrations. Her portraits for the series "Eminent Women of the Past" are tightly drawn, detailed busts constructed with varying parallel lines, some broken, much as in traditional copper engraving. She experimented with slightly fluid lines and some cross-hatching in her more ambitious, half-length portrait of the German writer *Wilhelmine von Hillern* for the front page of the July 1877 edition.

Because Stephens felt that wood-engraving was confining, she entered evening classes at the Pennsylvania Academy in 1876 to study painting. Eakins, her instructor, was teaching modern French methods of painting directly from nature. Stephens learned his naturalistic techniques by painting, rather than drawing, directly from the nude model. From Eakins she probably also learned photography, which she used as a tool for composition and studying light effects. She began to paint as well as draw her illustrations. She has become particularly well known for her gouache of the *Women's Life Class* (1879; for illustration, see p.135), which accompanied a story on art schools in Philadelphia for *Scribner's Monthly* in September 1879. She also engraved the scene on wood, which required more effort than merely copying the lines on to a block – she used extremely fine, closely drawn parallel lines

to create varying shades of grey to model the figures and reproduce the tones of the gouache.

By 1880 Stephens had opened her own studio and taught wood-engraving, executed illustration and wood-engraving commissions, and painted. Her work for *Our Continent* magazine in the early 1880s included drawing and wood engraving landscapes, genre scenes and architectural views. She varied her engraving style to suit the subject. Often her engravings of her own drawings are spontaneous and free, especially landscapes, in which she portrayed naturalistic effects of light with economic and sketchy line work. In contrast, for the cover story for a memorial to Stephen Girard, a mariner and merchant, in the issue of 20 June 1883, she used a dry, traditional approach of simple parallel lines and cross-hatching.

Stephens's commissions for *Harper's Young People* of the mid-1880s were extremely detailed yet freely drawn pen-and-ink illustrations, such as the *Piano Lesson* for Lucy C. Lillie's "The household of Glen Holly" in the issue of 1 May 1888. Similar drawings for children's fiction by the well-known authors Louisa May Alcott and Kate Douglas Wiggin helped to build her reputation as one of the publisher's best artists.

In 1886–7 Stephens studied in Europe, where she viewed the new Impressionism and the work of artists participating in the Arts and Crafts movement. On her return she increasingly painted out-of-doors. Later, in an interview with Bertha Mahony and Elinor Whitney for *Contemporary Illustrators of Children's Books* (Boston, 1930), Stephens said that she wanted to capture the "pitch of color, in the swift impressionistic manner. ... I was hungry to use color and the brush; and it strengthened the illustrating". She subsequently worked more frequently in oil, exhibiting paintings at the Pennsylvania Academy and in large national exhibitions.

By 1889 photographic methods made it possible to reproduce illustrations directly. Photogravure could capture the actual qualities of the media and of the artist's hand in charcoal, colour crayon, oil, gouache and watercolour, giving the artist increased flexibility and freedom. Stephens used the painterly materials, especially washes, to create stronger, more dramatic images that particularly attracted viewers' attention with luminous sensations of colour even when reproduced in half-tone. A particularly fine example of her naturalistic style used to depict indoor light is *Buying Christmas Presents*

(1895; Library of Congress), which she painted in watercolour and gouache for *Harper's Weekly*.

The Arts and Crafts movement became an influence on Stephens's style around 1900. She flattened space and adopted decorative effects. For years she had articulated her figures with soft outline or with thicker engraving strokes to simulate an outline, but during the period 1904–5 she outlined her forms with the strong, sinuous line used by Art Nouveau artists. She then filled in the forms using oil, watercolour or charcoal. Until 1911 she continued to use linear qualities of the decorative style in such works as *I First Saw the Children with Their Mother* (1906 for *Harper's Monthly*; Library of Congress), in which she filled the forms with colour crayon. With its close-up, cut composition, *I First Saw the Children* also demonstrates how Stephens was sometimes inspired by photography.

Stephens was frequently referred to as one of America's leading illustrators, although she was usually evaluated in the context of women's work and singled out as an exemplary "woman artist". In an article for the *Quarterly Illustrator*, Frederick Webber wrote: "she stands with the foremost women painters and illustrators of the country". He claimed that she and other women were adept at illustration because they had "more delicate sensibilities and ... natural love of the beautiful ... a closer sympathy with nature and life, and a quicker perception of the poetic element" (Webber 1893). Even women writers with deeply internalised sexism, such as Esther Singleton and Elizabeth Lore North, stereotyped and trivialised women. In the *Book Buyer* (1895) Singleton wrote that Stephens "... is one of the few women who knows how to draw and who recognizes the intense importance of form and line and shading". For "Women illustrators of child life" North (1904) remarked that Stephens's work was "entirely free from prettiness or sentimentality". Julius Moritzen (1904) wrote that she ranked "with a class of illustrators who know no fashion, no vagary in art. E.A. Abbey, Smedley, Frost and those akin to them ... the aristocracy of the profession ... her presence there is an honor to her sex as well". After years of having her work or reviews of it segregated by sex, she asked the critic and former student Aimée Tourgée: "Why woman? ... If I do clever work, why not let it go at that? Can't they judge me as an artist, not as a woman?" (Tourgée 1897, p.75). Yet, as a founding member of The Plastic Club and a participating member of the New Century Club, she closely identified with and enthusiastically supported women in the arts.

PHYLLIS PEET

Stettheimer, Florine
American painter, 1871–1944

Born in Rochester, New York, 29 August 1871. Studied at Art Students League, New York, 1892–5. Moved to Europe with her mother and sisters Ettie and Carrie, 1906; toured Italy, Germany, France and Switzerland; studied art in Berlin, Munich and Stuttgart, and lived in Paris; visited Esposizione Internazionale, Venice, 1909. Returned to New York, 1914. Moved to studio apartment in Beaux Arts Building after mother's death in 1935. Died in New York, 11 May 1944.

Principal Exhibitions
M. Knoedler & Co., New York: 1916 (individual)
Society of Independent Artists, New York: 1917–26
Carnegie International Exhibition, Pittsburgh: 1924
Art Institute of Chicago: 1925 (*Modern Decorative Art*, annual)
Arts Council of the City of New York: 1929 (*One Hundred Important Paintings by Living American Artists*)
American Society of Painters, Sculptors and Gravers: from 1932
Museum of Modern Art, New York: 1930 (*Three American Romantic Painters*), 1932 (*Modern Works of Art*), 1942 (*Twentieth-Century Portraits*), 1946 (retrospective)
Whitney Museum of American Art, New York: 1932 (*First Biennial Exhibition of Contemporary American Painting*)

Selected Writings
Crystal Flowers, ed. Ettie Stettheimer, New York: privately printed, 1949

Bibliography
Adolfo Best-Maugard, *A Method for Creative Design*, New York: Knopf, 1926
Florine Stettheimer, exh. cat., Museum of Modern Art, New York, 1946
Parker Tyler, *Florine Stettheimer: A Life in Art*, New York: Farrar Straus, 1963
Anthony Bower, "Florine Stettheimer", *Art in America*, lii/2, 1964, pp.88–93

Women Artists, 1550–1950, exh. cat., Los Angeles County Museum of Art, and elsewhere, 1976

Barbara Zucker, "An 'autobiography' of visual poems", *Art News*, lxxvi, February 1977, pp.68–73

Florine Stettheimer: Still Lifes, Portraits and Pageants, 1910 to 1942, exh. cat., Institute of Contemporary Art, Boston, and elsewhere, 1980

Linda Nochlin, "Florine Stettheimer: Rococo subversive", *Art in America*, lxviii, September 1980, pp.64–83

Charlotte Streifer Rubinstein, *American Women Artists from Early Times to the Present*, Boston: Hall, 1982

Donna Graves, "'In spite of alien temperature and alien insistence': Emily Dickinson and Florine Stettheimer", *Woman's Art Journal*, iii/2, 1982–3, pp.21–7

Barbara Heins, *Florine Stettheimer and the Avant-garde American Portrait*, PhD dissertation, Yale University, 1986

Susan Waller, *Women Artists in the Modern Era: A Documentary History*, Metuchen, NJ: Scarecrow Press, 1991

Eleanor Heartney, "Saints, esthetes and hustlers: Florine Stettheimer", *Art News*, xc, May 1991, pp.95–6

Jerry Saltz, "Twilight of the Gods", *Arts Magazine*, lxvi, March 1992, pp.21–2

Roberta Smith, "Very rich hours of Florine Stettheimer", *New York Times*, 10 October 1993, p.39

Barbara J. Bloemink, *The Life and Art of Florine Stettheimer*, New Haven and London: Yale University Press, 1995

Florine Stettheimer: Manhattan Fantastica, exh. cat., Whitney Museum of American Art, New York, 1995

Manuscript collection is in the Rare Books Room, Columbia University, New York.

Florine Stettheimer was an American original whose work cannot be placed into any category. Although she was academically trained, in mid-life she adopted her own unique style, rejecting almost everything she had studied or seen. The new style was deliberately naive, the figures weightless and flat, and the perspective unconventional. In lively colours, with wit and humour, she portrayed members of her own family and the New York art world.

Born into old money wealth, Florine never had to earn a living. She lived with her mother and her two elegant sisters, Carrie and Ettie. They followed intellectual and cultural pursuits, Florine studying painting and Ettie philosophy. Father seems to have long since vanished. Florine received sound academic training. At the Art Students League, she studied under Kenyon Cox and Robert Henri, painting the customary nudes, still lifes, landscapes and portraits. Admiration for John Singer Sargent influenced her portraits, and Chinese and Japanese art,

her flowers. Her work was well executed but unremarkable. In Europe, she studied at academies in Berlin, Stuttgart and Munich. She also travelled extensively, becoming familiar with the Symbolist painters Klimt and Hodler, and with the Impressionists, Fauves and Nabis in Paris. Diaghilev's Ballets Russes made a great impression, and later paintings reflect its influence. She began to move away from the academic style, searching for something more personal and feminine, foreshadowed in *Spring Figure* (1907; Columbia University, New York), where Spring is personified as a young girl garlanded with flowers.

With the outbreak of World War I, the Stettheimers returned to New York. There they established a salon, which soon attracted their many friends in the art world: Marsden Hartley, Marcel Duchamp, Alfred Stieglitz, Virgil Thomson and the critic Henry McBride. Florine sketched her illustrious guests and painted from the sketches the following day; conversation pieces, she called them. She had not yet arrived at her mature style, but new themes and devices were evident. *Family Portrait No.1* (1915; Columbia University), for example, is viewed from above, the figures flattened, white pigment applied with a palette knife to heighten the colours, and open brushwork for the details.

In 1916 Stettheimer was persuaded to hold a solo exhibition at Knoedler's gallery in New York, but stipulated that she would arrange the installation. She wanted to recreate the environment in which the paintings had been completed – her own bedroom. Gallery walls were draped in white muslin, and the white and gold of her bed canopy duplicated. The show was not a success, and was largely ignored by the critics. After this disappointment, apart from some unjuried group shows, Stettheimer did not exhibit again. The failure helped to convince her to seek personal expression in her own way. With *Heat* (1918; Brooklyn Museum, NY) and *Lake Placid* (1919; Boston Museum of Fine Arts) she reached her mature style.

Growth continued in the 1920s. *Asbury Park South* (1920; Fisk University, Nashville), a study of a segregated New Jersey beach, was influenced by the Harlem Renaissance. Adolfo Best-Maugard introduced her to his aesthetic system of seven basic forms (*A Method of Creative Design*, 1926). Duchamp made her aware of Surrealism and Dada. She enjoyed folk art and began the use of unorthodox materials: gold, silver tassels, velvets, paste jewels and putty soaked with oil pigments. The portraits done in this period are lively, whimsical and reveal the essence of the sitter. Among the best are *Henry McBride* (1922; Smith College Museum of Art, Northampton, MA), *Portrait of My Mother* (1925; collection Mrs Julius Ochs Adler) and *Ettie, Carrie* and *Portrait of Myself* (all 1923; Columbia University). *Family Portrait No.2* (1933; Museum of Modern Art, New York) shows the family in their New York apartment, with Florine's personal motif of flowers climaxed by a huge, three-part bouquet and a selective panorama of Manhattan outside. Other pictures from this period show feminine themes, *Spring Sale at Bendels* (1922; Philadelphia Museum of Art) and *Beauty Contest* (1924; Wadsworth Atheneum, Hartford, CT). In 1934 Virgil Thomson persuaded Stettheimer to design the costumes, sets and lighting for an opera he had composed with a libretto by Gertrude Stein, *Four Saints in Three Acts*. The black singers were drenched in white light, and the costumes of brilliant colours were fashioned out of cellophane, seashells, feathers and lace. Both opera and set met with critical acclaim on Broadway, and Stettheimer, greatly encouraged, used some of the ideas in later paintings.

Stettheimer's most important works are the four "cathedral" paintings, *Cathedral of Broadway* (c.1929), *Cathedral of Fifth Avenue* (c.1931), *Cathedral of Wall Street* (c.1939) and *Cathedral of Art* (c.1942; all Metropolitan Museum of Art), left unfinished at her death. Each celebrates and satirises some aspect of the New York social and cultural scene. They are packed with action, peopled by her family and friends and mix reality with fantasy. *Cathedral of Fifth Avenue* features a society wedding, the marriage of money and power; the Rolls-Royce has a dollar sign on its grill, and Tiffany's name blazes in the sky. In *Cathedral of Wall Street*, a surprised George Washington finds himself with Rockefeller, the Roosevelts, the American eagle and the Salvation Army. *Cathedral of Art* shows the power-brokers of the art world with the paintings, artists and admiring public. The scene of action is the grand staircase of the Metropolitan Museum. Baby Art is in the foreground; portraits walk out of their frames, dealers clutch their wares, critics give the go-ahead and avid photographers swarm around. Stettheimer was part of these worlds, and she admired and criticised them all.

After her mother's death in 1935, Stettheimer moved into the Beaux Arts studios at Bryant Park. There she continued her salon, fusing life and art, and working on her cathedrals until her death. Art dealers were beginning to be interested in her, but it was too late. Florine Stettheimer was a free and ultra-feminine spirit who loved and satirised a small privileged society in New York, and its cultural and economic institutions. Her decorative, *faux-naïf* style with its radiant colour and light and feminist themes were not appreciated during her lifetime, but a memorial exhibit of her paintings was held at the Museum of Modern Art in 1946. Her poems, not meant for publication, were collected by Ettie and published under the title *Crystal Flowers* (1949). Her paintings are now in many museums and there is a resurgence of interest in her.

PATRICIA BRAUCH

Stevens, May
American painter, 1924–

Born in Quincy, near Boston, Massachusetts, 9 June 1924. Studied at Massachusetts College of Art , Boston (BFA 1946); Art Students League, New York, 1948; Académie Julian, Paris, 1948–9. Married painter Rudolf Baranik, 1948; son born 1948 (d. 1981). Taught at School of Visual Arts, New York, from 1961 (faculty member 1964); visiting artist, Syracuse University, New York, 1975; Rhode Island School of Design, Providence, 1977; Oberlin College, Ohio, 1988; distinguished visiting professor, California State University, Long Beach, 1990; faculty member, Skowhegan School of Painting and Sculpture, Maine, 1992. Co-founder of the feminist journal *Heresies*, New York, 1976. Recipient of Childe Hassam purchase awards, National Institute of Arts and Letters, 1968, 1969 and 1975; Creative Artists Public Service (CAPS) grant, New York State Council for the Arts, 1974; National Endowment for the Arts (NEA) grant, 1983; Guggenheim fellowship, 1986; Lifetime Achievement award, Women's Caucus for the Arts, 1990. Member, College Art Association. Lives in New York.

Selected Individual Exhibitions
Galerie Huit, Paris: 1951

ACA Gallery, New York: 1957

Roko Gallery, New York: 1963 (*Freedom Riders*, touring), 1968

Herbert F. Johnson Museum, Cornell University, Ithaca, NY: 1973

Douglass College, New Brunswick, NJ: 1974

SoHo 20, New York: 1974

Lerner-Heller Gallery, New York: 1975, 1976, 1978, 1981

Everson Museum, Syracuse, NY: 1976 (*Three American Realists*, with Alice Neel and Sylvia Sleigh)

Boston University Art Gallery: 1984–5 (*Ordinary, Extraordinary: A Summation, 1977–1984*, touring)

New Museum of Contemporary Art, New York: 1988

Orchard Gallery, Derry, Northern Ireland: 1988

Olin Gallery, Kenyon College, Gambier, OH: 1988

Herter Gallery, University of Massachusetts, Amherst: 1991

Colorado University Art Galleries, Boulder: 1993

Exit Art Gallery, New York: 1994 (*In Words*, with Rudolf Baranik)

Mary Ryan Gallery, New York: 1996

Selected Writings

Ordinary, Extraordinary, New York: privately printed, 1980

In Words, New York: privately printed, 1994 (with Rudolf Baranik)

Bibliography

Cindy Nemser, "Conversations with May Stevens", *Feminist Art Journal*, iii, Winter 1974–5, pp.4–7

Lucy R. Lippard, *From the Center: Feminist Essays on Women's Art*, New York: Dutton, 1976

Moira Roth, "Visions and re-visions: Rosa Luxemburg and the artist's mother", *Artforum*, xix, November 1980, pp.36–9; reprinted in Boston 1984

Lisa Tickner, "May Stevens", *Block*, no.5, 1981, pp.28–33; reprinted in Boston 1984 and *The Block Reader in Visual Culture*, London and New York: Routledge, 1996

May Stevens: Ordinary, Extraordinary: A Summation, 1977–1984, exh. cat., Boston University Art Gallery, and elsewhere, 1984

Hilary Robinson, ed., *Visibly Female: Feminism and Art: An Anthology*, London: Camden, 1987; New York: Universe, 1988

Patricia Mathews, "A dialogue of silence: May Stevens' Ordinary, Extraordinary, 1977–1986", *Art Criticism*, iii, Fall 1987, pp.34–42

Josephine Withers, "Revisioning our foremothers: Reflections on the Ordinary, Extraordinary art of May Stevens", *Feminist Studies*, xiii, Fall 1987, pp.485–512

May Stevens: One Plus or Minus One, exh. cat., Orchard Gallery, Derry, 1988

Rosa, Alice: Ordinary – Extraordinary, exh. cat., Olin Gallery, Kenyon College, Gambier, OH, 1988

Carol Jacobsen, "Two lives: Ordinary/Extraordinary", *Art in America*, lxxvii, February 1989, pp.152–7, 183, 185

Lois Tarlow, "Profile: May Stevens", *Art New England*, xii, February 1991, pp.7–9

May Stevens, exh. cat., Colorado University Art Galleries, Boulder, 1993

Norma Broude and Mary D. Garrard, eds, *The Power of Feminist Art: The American Movement of the 1970s*, New York: Abrams, and London: Thames and Hudson, 1994

Mara R. Witzling, ed., *Voicing Today's Visions: Writings by Contemporary Women Artists*, New York: Universe, 1994

Patricia Hills, "May Stevens: Painting history as lived, feminist experience", *Redefining American History Painting*, ed. Patricia M. Burnham and Lucretia Hoover Giese, New York and Cambridge: Cambridge University Press, 1995, pp.310–30, 383–7

May Stevens has held a central position within the New York art scene of activist artists since the early 1960s. Her career trajectory touches down on many of the art-and-politics events of the past three decades. In 1966 she, with Rudolf Baranik, Leon Golub, Nancy Spero (q.v.), Denise Levertov, Mitchell Goodman and Irving Petlin, organised Artists and Writers Protest Against the War in Vietnam, which in 1967 sponsored an "Angry Arts Week" – one of the earliest artists' organised protests against American involvement in the Vietnam War. In 1967 she contributed to the *Collage of Indignation* exhibition at the Loeb Student Center at New York University. She became active in feminist circles in the early 1970s, and in 1976 joined a group of New York women to found *Heresies*, a collaborative publishing venture. During 1992 and 1993 she was active in WAC – Women's Action Coalition.

Throughout her career her activist social concerns as well as her own working-class background have influenced her figurative work. In the 1960s she painted works inspired by the "Freedom Riders" – the northern Civil Rights workers who went to the South to work on voter registration campaigns; Martin Luther King, Jr wrote a foreword to the catalogue of a touring exhibition of her *Freedom Riders* paintings, which opened at the Roko Gallery in New York in 1963. In the late 1960s, as the Vietnam War escalated, she created for her paintings "Big Daddy", an iconic image of American racism and militarism. Although originally based on her own, working-class father, the figure – a middle-aged, spectacled, faintly grinning and balding male, often nude and often seated with a bulldog cradled in his lap – grew into a universalised figure, authoritarian, patriarchal. For the *Big Daddy* series she used a flat, poster style, painting in either acrylic on canvas or gouache on paper, with red, white and cobalt blue predominating, as in *Big Daddy Paper Doll* (1970; acrylic on canvas; Brooklyn Museum, NY).

By the mid-1970s the "Big Daddy" figure gave way to three large paintings (all acrylic on canvas, 182 × 304 cm.) on the theme of the artist in her studio: *Artist's Studio (After Courbet)* (1975; private collection, St Louis), *SoHo Women Artists* (1977–8; National Museum of Women in the Arts, Washington, DC) and *Mysteries and Politics* (1978; San Francisco Museum of Modern Art). Working out her ideas in these three works and their studies, she realised that she was not only drawing on the tradition of group portraiture (as Rembrandt and Courbet had done before) but infusing that tradition with the history of which she had become a part, that of contemporary feminists attempting to integrate the demands of family, radical politics and artistic creativity (Hills 1995, p.310). The flat poster style gave way to a more subtle and nuanced chiaroscuro combined with an aesthetic of montage.

In 1976 she embarked on another series, one that grew out of the images she used for two montages published as a two-page spread in the feminist journal *Heresies*, pairing the Polish Communist Rosa Luxemburg, who with Karl Liebknecht had founded the German Communist Party in 1918, with her own mother Alice Stevens, a working-class housewife from Quincy, Massachusetts. Through a dozen small mixed-media works and many large paintings, known as the *Ordinary/Extraordinary* series, she contrasted the lives of her mother (then living in a nursing home outside Boston) and her Communist heroine. The theme of her mother and Luxemburg provided the issues for Stevens to explore the implications of the social constructions of gender and class. Recalling this series, she wrote in September 1995:

> I asked myself what was the reach possible to a woman of that time and class. What avenues could she walk? What doors open? What thoughts think? What actions take? Blocked, where could she turn?
>
> The politics of women's lives in any given historical period: Could this woman have been more than she was? Is it possible to

understand what/who she was? How she felt? Was sexuality open to her? Did she choose the life she lived? Did she wish to alter it? Was she able to make changes?

> Immigrants both living in a world not ready for them. Each was out of place. Each was killed for not fitting in. Alice's world made her gentle, defenseless. Rosa's world made her powerful, then punished her for moving toward the fulfillment of that power. Alice's world destroyed her gentleness, that was not malleable, could not toughen.
>
> Rosa Luxemburg and Alice Stevens, workers both, frustrated as lovers and mothers; one fulfilled as thinker, fighter, leader; the other here fulfilled in this tribute, as mother [letter to author, 10 September 1995].

Stevens transformed the two figures into universal symbols: Alice Stevens's oblivion represents the fate of many working-class women who stifle their own intellectual interests and sink into the tedium of housekeeping. In *Go Gentle* (1983; acrylic on canvas; Museum of Fine Arts, Boston) earlier flat, photographic images of a girl, and then a woman, who might have had the potential to shape her life, contrast with a heavy-set, richly painted image of an older Alice, confused even by the most quotidian routines. By contrast *Procession* (1983; acrylic on canvas; Metropolitan Museum of Art, New York) represents a demonstration of people marching on the anniversary of Luxemburg's and Leibknecht's deaths. The reproduction of Luxemburg's face, on a placard held high by one of the marchers, dominates the scene and proclaims that Luxemburg, after death, had grown into an international heroine.

In a series of collages and small paintings done in the late 1980s Stevens drew on the imagery of a photographic project done by her son, Steven Baranik, who died in the early 1980s. That imagery was of burning horses (actually toy plastic horses that melted as they burned and which Stevens's husband, Rudolf Baranik, had also explored in his art) and symbolised the nature of representation – with elusive images of memories disappearing into the recesses of abstraction, of colour and of shadow.

In the early 1990s Stevens increasingly incorporated words into her paintings. Earlier, in *Voices* (1983; acrylic on canvas; artist's collection) from the *Ordinary/Extraordinary* series, Stevens had included layers of words spread across the canvas in the space above the coffins of Luxemburg and Leibknecht carried along during the martyrs' funeral procession; the words were those of Luxemburg. With *Sea of Words* (1991; acrylic on canvas; artist's collection) four small rowing boats with figures float across a sea of words excerpted from the writings of Virginia Woolf and Julia Kristeva. Subsequent paintings focused on young prostitutes walking the streets, women prisoners exercising in a yard or women scullers on a river. In all of these Stevens uses a limited palette of gold, silver, black, blue and green, as she merges words and elusive figures. Thus, Stevens maintains a political consciousness through oblique and subtle imagery that evokes both personal and collective memories.

PATRICIA HILLS

Stölzl, Gunta   [fig. 68]
German weaver and textile designer, 1897–1983

Born in Munich, 5 March 1897. Studied ceramics and decorative and glass painting at the Kunstgewerbeschule, Munich, 1914–16; worked as a Red Cross nurse, 1916–18; resumed studies at the Kunstgewerbeschule, 1919. Student at Bauhaus, Weimar, 1919–25 (journeyman's diploma 1922); assisted Johannes Itten in establishing Ontos Weaving Workshop near Zürich, 1925. Appointed technical director, 1925, and junior master, 1927, Weaving Workshop, Bauhaus, Dessau. Participated in 13 Bauhaus-related national and international group exhibitions, 1922–31. Married Palestinian architect Arieh Sharon, losing German citizenship, 1929; daughter born 1929; divorced 1936. Forced to resign post as director of Weaving Workshop, 1931. Established S-P-H Stoffe, a handweaving studio (with Gertrud Preiswerk and Heinrich-Otto Hürlimann) in Zürich, 1931; closed 1933. Joined Swiss Werkbund, 1932. Founded S+H Stoffe with Hürlimann, 1935. Established Handweberei (Handweaving Studio) Flora and joined Gesellschaft Schweizer Malerinnen, Bildhauerinnen und Kunstgewerblerinnen (Society of Swiss Women Painters, Sculptors and Craftsmen), 1937. Participated in interior scheme design of Swiss

Pavilion, Lyon, 1941. Married Willy Stadler and acquired Swiss citizenship, 1942; daughter born 1943. Dissolved handweaving business and executed only tapestries after *c*.1967. Weavings purchased by Museum of Modern Art, New York, and Busch-Reisinger Museum, Cambridge, Massachusetts, 1949–63; fabrics and designs purchased by Victoria and Albert Museum, London, 1967–9. Died in Zürich, 22 April 1983.

Selected Individual Exhibitions
Lyzeumclub, Zürich: 1970
Paulus-Akademie, Zürich: 1971, 1980
Bauhaus-Archiv, Berlin: 1976, 1987 (touring retrospective)

Selected Writings
"Weberei am Bauhaus", *Buch- und Weberkunst*, no.7, 1926, p.405
"Die Entwicklung der Bauhausweberei", *Bauhaus-Zeitschrift für Bau und Gestaltung*, no.2, July 1931
"Textilien im Innenraum", *Schweizer Monatszeitschrift für Architektur, Kunst und künstlerisches Gewerbe*, 1936, p.379
"Abschied von Klee", *Werk*, no.9, 1940
Text in *Über die Bauhaus-Weberei*, exh. cat., Goppinger-Galerie, Frankfurt am Main, 1964, p.110
"In der Textilwerkstatt des Bauhauses 1919 bis 1931", *Werk*, lv, 1968, pp.744–8
"Fünf Jahre Bauhaus: Grundlage für eine fünfzigjährige Freundschaft", *Benita Koch-Otte: Vom Geheimnis der Farbe*, exh. cat., Bauhaus-Archiv, Bethel and Berlin, 1972

Bibliography
Staatliches Bauhaus Weimar, 1919 bis 1923, Weimar: Bauhaus, 1923
Neue Arbeiten der Bauhauswerkstätten, no.7, Munich: Albert Langen, 1925
Wall Hangings, 2 vols, exh. cat., Museum of Modern Art, New York, 1969
Mildred Constantine and J.L. Larsen, *Beyond Craft: The Art Fabric*, New York: Van Nostrand Reinhold, 1973
Hans M. Wingler, *The Bauhaus: Weimar Dessau Berlin Chicago*, 3rd edition, Cambridge: Massachusetts Institute of Technology Press, 1976
Frank Whitford, *Bauhaus*, London: Thames and Hudson, 1984
Gillian Naylor, *The Bauhaus Reassessed: Sources and Design Theory*, New York: Dutton, and London: Herbert Press, 1985
La tessitura del bauhaus, 1919/1933, nelle collezioni della Repubblica Democratica Tedesca, Venice: Marsilio, 1985

The Bauhaus Weaving Workshop: Source and Influence for American Textiles, exh. cat., Philadelphia College of Textiles and Science, 1987

Gunta Stölzl: Weberei am Bauhaus und aus eigener Werkstatt, Bauhaus Archiv, Berlin: Kupfergraben, 1987

Bauhaus: Masters and Students, exh. cat., Barry Friedman, New York, 1988

Magdalena Droste, *Bauhaus, 1919–1933*, Bauhaus Archiv, Cologne: Taschen, 1990

Eckhard Neumann, ed., *Bauhaus and Bauhaus People*, New York: Van Nostrand Reinhold, and London: Chapman and Hall, 1993

Sigrid Wortmann Weltge, *Bauhaus Textiles: Women Artists and the Weaving Workshop*, London: Thames and Hudson, 1993; as *Women's Work: Textile Art from the Bauhaus*, San Francisco: Chronicle, 1993

Gunta Stölzl, the only female faculty member of the Bauhaus, was one of the foremost weavers and textile designers of the 20th century. Like other women students entering the Bauhaus in its founding year, she was attracted by the egalitarian principles stated in its manifesto. That these were at once disregarded was due to the unexpectedly large number of applicants who were directed into a separate Women's Department. Within a year, the scope of opportunity narrowed further when the Weaving Workshop became the sole repository for female students. Its development into one of the most successful workshops was due to Stölzl's leadership.

Stölzl studied decorative painting and ceramics at the Kunstgewerbeschule in Munich from 1914 to 1916. For the last two years of World War I she served as a Red Cross nurse behind the front lines, resuming her education in 1919 first in Munich and then at the Bauhaus in Weimar. Just as Walter Gropius believed that only the *Gesamtkunstwerk* (total work of art) could redeem society, so he envisaged a Bauhaus-trained design professional to be fully conversant in a craft as well as in the theories of design and art. Teachers capable of imparting such all-encompassing knowledge did not yet exist, and workshops, the corner-stone of Bauhaus education, were therefore staffed by both a form and a craft master. Since none was able to teach weaving, students were essentially left to their own devices.

A determined Stölzl, having discovered her unusual affinity for textiles, set out to master the medium. Although she was an auto-didact, her progress was remarkably quick, and the Bauhaus supported her in taking courses in weave and dye technology at a professional textile school in

Krefeld. This enabled her to instruct her fellow students and assume responsibility for the workshop itself. Stölzl's early textiles convey the exuberance of experimentation encouraged by the Weimar Bauhaus (1919–25). After 1925 they reflect the institution's turn towards the unity of art and technology. This evolution, analogous to the development of the Weaving Workshop itself, is evident in her collaboration with Marcel Breuer. Breuer's *African* chair (1921; destroyed), a romantic evocation of primitive art, served as Stölzl's loom for a colourful tapestry directly woven on to its rough-hewn frame. Breuer's next chair (Bauhaus Archiv Museum für Gestaltung, Berlin), although still a one-of-a-kind object, looks decidedly modern, not least because the colours of Stölzl's interlaced straps incline towards those of De Stijl. In 1926, when Breuer's tubular steel frames aligned themselves with industrial design, Stölzl's functional covers broke equally new ground, both technically and aesthetically.

The ease with which Stölzl mastered completely divergent aspects of textile design is a hallmark of her career. One of her signature pieces, the *Slit Tapestry* (1926; Bauhaus Archiv Museum für Gestaltung), although executed in the time-honoured Gobelin technique, endowed the medium with a vibrant, contemporary pictorial language. This holds true for one of her finest Jacquard hangings *5 Chöre* (1928; Museum für Kunst, Lubeck), with which she proved unequivocally that the mechanism of the industrial loom can be harnessed into communicating the rhythms of colour abstraction. Designs on paper for these and other hangings are works of art in themselves and show her mastery of watercolour, gouache, collage and mixed media. Inspired by the Bauhaus painters, especially Paul Klee, who was close to the weavers, Stölzl executed exquisite works on paper throughout her career.

Stölzl passed her journeyman's examination in 1922 and became technical director of the Weaving Workshop after the Bauhaus's move to Dessau in 1925. She was appointed junior master in 1927. In addition to administrative duties she continued to teach, establish contacts with mills and set up marketing schemes. She also revised the curriculum to implement the new policy of designing for industry. Under her direction, she and other members of the Weaving Workshop developed industrial prototypes classified as structural fabrics. These derived their visual interest not from pictorial motifs but rather from the construction of the weave and from the property of the material itself. Fabrics were designed to blend into the modern interior. As draperies they became part of the architectural scheme; as partners of new industrial products – car, train and aeroplane seats or radio covers – they integrated themselves unobtrusively. Their end use was carefully researched, taking into account easy maintenance, light and sound reflection or non-flammability. In addition, these fabrics pioneered the use of new materials such as raffia, bast and cellophane (samples in the Bauhaus-Archiv Museum für Gestaltung and the Busch-Reisinger Museum, Cambridge, MA) yet, despite their contemporary look, they were not meant as personal statements but rather as the expression of their age. The July 1931 issue of *bauhaus* magazine carried an article by Stölzl in which she eloquently described the evolution of these textiles.

After her forced resignation from the Bauhaus and emigration to Switzerland, Gunta Stölzl continued to work, often in difficult circumstances, as a hand-weaver and as a designer for industry. Her enthusiasm for weaving never abated nor did her desire to explore its myriad possibilities. As the sole woman among the Bauhaus masters, she had advanced a little-regarded workshop into becoming one of the most respected. Likewise, she never wavered in her belief that textiles should be integral to 20th-century design. The enormous influence of Bauhaus textiles world-wide, developed under her leadership, has vindicated her faith. During the last years of her life, Stölzl came full circle. After years of production weaving she turned once again to tapestry, creating hangings of great subtlety and textural beauty. Gropius's vision of the *Gesamtkunstwerk* and the ideal balance of manual and mental creativity found its perfect embodiment in Stölzl's career: she understood it, she taught it and she lived by it.

SIGRID WORTMANN WELTGE

T

Taeuber-Arp, Sophie
Swiss artist and designer, 1889–1943

Born Sophie Henriette Taeuber (or Täuber) in
Davos, 19 January 1889; father German, mother
Swiss. Studied textile design at the Gewerbeschule,
Sankt Gallen, 1908–10. Studied in experimental art
studio of Walter von Debschitz in Munich,
1911–12 and 1913–14; attended the
Kunstgewerbeschule, Hamburg, 1912–13. Became
a member of the Schweizerischer Werkbund, 1915.
Met artist Jean Arp, 1915; married him, 1922.
Active member of Dada group in Zürich, 1916–19.
Professor of textile design, Kunstgewerbeschule,
Zürich, 1916–29. Served on jury of Swiss section
for the Exposition Internationale des Arts
Décoratifs et Industriels Modernes, Paris, 1925.
Visited Italy, 1925. Became French citizen with
Arp, 1926. Moved to Meudon-Val-Fleury, near
Paris, 1928. Exhibited at the Salon des
Surindépendants, Paris, 1929–30. Member of
Cercle et Carré group founded by Michel Seuphor
and Torrès-Garcia, Paris, 1930; Abstraction-
Création group, Paris, 1931–4; Allianz (union of
Swiss painters), Zürich, 1937–43. Participated in
international Surrealist exhibitions in London
(1936), New York (1936), Paris (1938) and
Amsterdam (1938). Founder and editor of the
journal *Plastique*, 1937–9. Stayed in Grasse with
Arp and their friends Sonia Delaunay (q.v.) and
Alberto Magnelli, 1941–2. Died in Zürich as the
result of an accident, 13 January 1943.

Selected Individual Exhibitions
Libraire La Mésange, Strasbourg: 1928 (*Projets de
l'Aubette et oeuvres d'Arp, Taeuber, van Doesburg*)
Galerie des Cahiers d'Art, Paris: 1934 (with Jean Arp,
Nicolas Ghika and Jean Hélion)
Galerie Delcourt, Paris: 1937 (with Georges Vantongerloo)
Galerie Jeanne Bucher, Paris: 1939 (with Jean Arp)

Selected Writings
"Bemerkungen über den Unterricht im ornamentalen
Entwerfen", *Korrespondenzblatt des Schweiz. Vereins
der Gewerbe- und Hauswirtschaftslehrerinnen*,
no.11–12, 31 December 1922, pp.156–9
Anleitung zum Unterricht im Zeichnen für Textile Berufe,
Zürich, 1927 (with Blanche Gauchat)

Bibliography
Georg Schmidt, ed., *Sophie Taeuber-Arp*, Basel: Holbein,
1948 (includes catalogue raisonné by Hugo Weber)
Margit Staber, *Sophie Taeuber-Arp*, Lausanne: Rencontre,
1970
Elsa Honig Fine, *Women and Art: A History of Women
Painters and Sculptors from the Renaissance to the
20th Century*, Montclair, NJ: Allanheld and Schram,
and London: Prior, 1978
Germaine Greer, *The Obstacle Race: The Fortunes of
Women Painters and Their Work*, London: Secker and
Warburg, and New York: Farrar Straus, 1979
Joan M. Marter, "Three women artists married to early
modernists: Sonia Delaunay-Terk, Sophie Taüber-Arp
and Marguerite Thompson Zorach", *Arts Magazine*,
liv, September 1979, pp.88–95
Sophie Taeuber-Arp, exh. cat., Museum of Modern Art,
New York, and elsewhere, 1981
Sophie Taeuber-Arp, exh. cat., Museo Communale,
Ascona, 1983
*Hans Arp und Sophie Taeuber-Arp: Die Elemente der
Bilder und Bücher*, exh. cat., Herzog August
Bibliothek, Wolfenbüttel, 1988
Serge Fauchereau, *Arp*, New York: Rizzoli, 1988;
London: Academy, 1989
*Sophie Taeuber, Hans Arp: Künstlerpaare –
Künstlerfreunde/Dialogues d'artistes – résonances*,
exh. cat., Kunstmuseum, Bern, and elsewhere, 1988
Sophie Taeuber, exh. cat., Musée d'Art Moderne de la
Ville de Paris, and elsewhere, 1989 (contains exhibi-
tion list and extensive bibliography)
Sophie Taeuber-Arp: Zum 100 Geburtstag, exh. cat.,
Aargauer Kunsthaus, Aargau, and elsewhere, 1989
*Sophie Taeuber-Arp, Hans Arp: Besonderheiten eines
Zweiklangs*, exh. cat., Staatliche Kunstsammlungen
Albertinum, Dresden, 1991

Angela Thomas, *Mit unverstelltem Blick: Bericht zu drei Künstlerinnen: Anna Baumann-Kienast, Alis Guggenheim, Sophie Taeuber-Arp*, Bern: Benteli, 1991

Sophie Taeuber-Arp, 1889–1943, exh. cat., Bahnhof Roldandseck, and elsewhere, 1993

Renée Riese Hubert, "Sophie Taeuber and Hans Arp: A community of two", *Art Journal*, lii, Winter 1993, pp.25–32

——, *Magnifying Mirrors: Women, Surrealism and Partnership*, Lincoln: University of Nebraska Press, 1994

"One views with amazement the range of media to which Sophie Taeuber-Arp adapted her decorative genius, whether it be at l'Aubette, in her weaving, embroidery, marionettes, stage décor, furniture design, stained glass, collage, wood reliefs, or even in dancing and publishing" attests Germaine Greer in her volume on the obstacles faced by women artists. In the same paragraph, Greer laments that Taeuber's sculptor husband Jean Arp is treated as a "more significant figure...although it is perfectly well known that the innovative qualities of [his] work owed a great deal to the fruitful vision of [Taeuber]" (Greer 1979, p.43).

Sophie Taeuber was teaching applied arts and studying dance in Zürich when Jean Arp moved there in 1915 to avoid being drafted by the German army. He called their meeting "the main event of my life" and never stopped emphasising Taeuber's merits or the manner in which she influenced him. "It was Sophie who, by the example of her work and her life, both of them bathed in clarity, showed me the right way. In her world, the high and the low, the light and the dark, the eternal and the ephemeral, are balanced in perfect equilibrium" (quoted in Fauchereau 1988, p.11).

By 1916 the two artists were not only a couple, they were also members of the group that met in Hugo Ball's Cabaret Voltaire to found the Dada art movement. Dada began in Zürich largely in response to the horrors of World War I. "After the carnage, we are left with hope for a purified humanity", wrote the poet Tristan Tzara in the Dada Manifesto of 1918. Dada stressed humour and absurdity, spontaneity and chance. It debunked both conventional art media and traditional arts institutions as it celebrated a merging of the performing, literary and visual arts. Taeuber had already embraced most of these values by the time she met Arp. She composed in fabric and thread as easily as in wood and pigment, had disdain for paintings in oil on canvas, and often preferred dancing to drawing. Her dancing was a major contribution to the interdisciplinary pursuits of Swiss Dada: the entry in Hugo Ball's journal of 29 March 1917 tells of an "abstract dance" that Taeuber executed to one of his poems, wearing a mask by Arp.

Taeuber and Arp embarked on a shared life of collaboration, "in duo", as they said.

> Sophie Taeuber and I had decided to renounce completely the use of oil colors in our compositions. We wanted to avoid any references to the paintings which seemed to us characteristic of a pretentious and ostentatious world. In 1916, Sophie Taeuber and I began to work together on large compositions in fabric and paper. I embroidered with Sophie Taeuber's help a series of vertical and horizontal configurations ... In the years during which we worked exclusively with new materials, I made embroidery and configurations in paper and in fabric, and it affected us like a sort of purification, like spiritual exercises, so that finally we rediscovered painting in its original state of purity [*ibid.*, p.12].

Such purity can be seen in their *Amphora* (1917; Foundation Arp, Clamart), in which the two artists created a refined wooden sculpture by affixing one goblet atop another so as to establish rhythmic vertical symmetry and graceful horizontal balance.

Taeuber was a pioneer of geometric abstraction (although, with Arp, she preferred the term "concretion", since neither was "abstracting" from any objective source). As early as 1915, Arp wrote of their collaboration that they worked with "the simplest forms, using painting, embroidery and pasted paper. They were probably the first manifestations of their kind, pictures that were their own reality, without meaning or cerebral intentions. We rejected everything in the nature of a copy or a description, in order to give free flow to what was elemental and spontaneous" (quoted in Fine 1978, p.173). While Arp's sculpture soon moved into its characteristic biomorphic mode, Taeuber maintained a preference for the rectilinear that led to affinities with Constructivism. Fine asserted that the "pulsating rhythms and movements of [Taeuber's] 'taches quadrangulaires' of the 1920s anticipated Mondrian's 'Broadway Boogie-Woogie' (1942) by almost twenty years" (*ibid.*, p.174). In 1926–7 Taeuber collaborated with the De Stijl painter Theo van Doesburg to design the "boldly geometric" interior of the Café l'Aubette in Strasbourg. She then designed the studio-house that she shared with Arp in Meudon-Val-Fleury, in an enclave of Clamart. In 1929 she and Arp joined the Cercle et Carré group of Constructivist artists (in spite of the fact that Arp had already established ties with the Surrealists). Both were members of Abstraction-Création group; both worked on the writing staff of the *Abstraction-Création* journal. In 1937 Taeuber began publishing the Constructivist magazine *Plastique*, but due to the outbreak of World War ll could produce only five issues.

Immediately before the war, Taeuber and Arp collaborated on the book *Muscheln und Schrime* (Meudon-Val-Fleury, 1939). Renée Riese Hubert noted that the title was a surrealistic allusion to "chance encounters à la Lautréamont between a shell (not a sewing machine) and an umbrella", adding that the text and image were related as music and dance: Taeuber's drawings were "essentially a subdued and intermittent musical accompaniment" to Arp's poems (Hubert 1993, p.30). In one of the drawings, six similar curvilinear forms drift down the white page, like a scattering of shells or petals over open space. In another, seven varied forms cluster in vertical parade. Rounded contours on one side form rhythmic counterpoint to opposing straight edges (repr. Hubert 1993, figs 3 and 4). Taeuber's *Parasols* (1938; Rijksmuseum Kröller-Müller, Otterlo), created during the period of collaboration on the book, is a large wooden panel on which jigsaw-like cut-outs seem to tumble from chaos into precarious stasis. Gentle curves are answered by angles and planes in a satisfying but never static dialogue. The artist continued similar work in Meudon until the arrival of the Nazis forced her to flee with Arp to Grasse, where they were joined by their old friend Sonia Delaunay (q.v.), and they all worked on a collective series of lithographs there. In 1942 the couple took refuge in Zürich. The following year, Taeuber died in a freak accident at the home of the sculptor Max Bill. Arp was so devastated by her death that he retired for a period to a Dominican friary. When he emerged, he continued their collaboration by tearing Sophie's drawings into patches of paper and arranging them "by chance" on to his own collages (see especially his *Collage of a Torn Drawing by Sophie Taeuber*, 1946; van Doesburg Estate, The Hague).

BETTY ANN BROWN

Tanguy, Kay Sage *see* Sage

Tanning, Dorothea
American painter, sculptor and graphic artist, 1910–

Born in Galesburg, Illinois, 25 August 1910. Worked part-time at Galesburg Public Library after leaving school at age 16. Studied at Knox College, Galesburg, 1928–30, then for two weeks at the Art Institute of Chicago. Moved to New York, 1936, supporting herself by various draughtswoman jobs in advertising. Left for Paris, August 1939, hoping to meet the Surrealists, who were no longer in France; took last boat back to New York before outbreak of World War ll. Met Surrealist art dealer Julien Levy and through him Max Ernst, 1942. Married Ernst in a double ceremony with Man Ray and Juliet Browner in Beverly Hills, 1946. Exhibited with the Surrealists at Galerie Maeght, Paris, 1947. Lived in Sedona, Arizona, then in Provence and Paris until Ernst's death in 1976. Returned to USA, 1980. Lives in New York.

Selected Individual Exhibitions
Julien Levy Gallery, New York: 1944
Galerie Les Pas Perdus, Paris: 1950
Alexandre Iolas Gallery, New York: 1953
Galerie Furstenberg, Paris: 1954
Musée des Beaux-Arts, Tours: 1956 (*Trois peintres américains*, with Max Ernst and Man Ray)
Galerie Edouard Loeb, Paris: 1959
Galerie Der Spiegel, Cologne: 1963
Galerie d'Art Moderne, Basel: 1966
Casino Communal, Knokke-le-Zoute: 1967 (retrospective)
Le Point Cardinal, Paris: 1970
Centre National d'Art Contemporain, Paris: 1974 (retrospective)
Gimpel and Weitzenhoffer Gallery, New York: 1979
Stephen Schlesinger Gallery, New York: 1989
Nahan Contemporary, New York: 1990
New York Public Library: 1992 (retrospective)
Konsthall, Malmö: 1993

Selected Writings
Abyss, New York: Standard Editions, 1977 (novel, written 1947)
Birthday, Santa Monica, CA: Lapis Press, 1986 (autobiography)

Bibliography

The Astonished Gaze, film by Jean Desvilles, Paris, 1959

Alain Bosquet, *Dorothea Tanning: Peintures récentes*, Paris: Galerie Mouradian et Valloton, 1962

——, *La Peinture de Dorothea Tanning*, Paris: Pauvert, 1966

Dorothea Tanning: Oeuvre, exh. cat., Centre National d'Art Contemporain, Paris, 1974

Cindy Nemser, "'In her own image'", *Feminist Art Journal*, iii/1, Spring 1974, pp.11–18

Linda Nochlin, "Dorothea Tanning at the CNAC", *Art in America*, lxii, November–December 1974, p.128

Alain Jouffroy, "Dorothea Tanning: Le chavirement dans la joie", *XX siècle*, no.43, December 1974, pp.60–68

Gilles Plazy, *Dorothea Tanning*, Paris: Filipacchi, 1976

Daniel Abadie and others, *Dorothea Tanning: Essais, lettres, poèmes et témoignages*, Paris: XXe Siècle, 1977

Peter Schamoni, *Insomnias*, film, 1978 (on Tanning's paintings)

Dorothea Tanning: 10 Recent Paintings and a Biography, exh. cat., Gimpel and Weitzenhoffer, New York, 1979

Dorothea Tanning: Paintings, exh. cat., Stephen Mazoh Gallery, New York, 1983

Ann Gibson, "Dorothea Tanning: The impassioned double entendre", *Arts Magazine*, lviii, September 1983, pp.102–33

Whitney Chadwick, *Women Artists and the Surrealist Movement*, Boston: Little Brown, and London: Thames and Hudson, 1985

La Femme et le surréalisme, exh. cat., Musée Cantonal des Beaux-Arts, Lausanne, 1987

Dorothea Tanning: On Paper, 1948–1986, exh. cat., Kent Fine Art, New York, 1987

Eleven Paintings by Dorothea Tanning, exh. cat., Kent Fine Art, New York, 1988

Dorothea Tanning: Between Lives: Works on Paper, exh. cat., Runkel-Hue-Williams, London, 1989

Dorothea Tanning: Hail, Delirium! A Catalogue Raisonné of the Artist's Illustrated Books and Prints, 1942–1991, exh. cat., New York Public Library, 1992

Creating visionary drawings since childhood as an escape from her uneventful early life in Illinois, Dorothea Tanning discovered Surrealism at the landmark exhibition *Fantastic Art, Dada, Surrealism* held at the Museum of Modern Art in New York in 1936. The movement's enthusiastic embrace of the marvellous in art and life helped Tanning to confirm and contextualise her own artistic direction. Her association with the exiled European Surrealists in New York a few years later, however, and in particular her long marriage to Max Ernst, compromised her career. Eclipsed from art history until 1966 when the first monograph on her work was published, Tanning's oeuvre is generally understood nowadays as directly inspired by Surrealist automatic procedures. Although Tanning acknowledges her continued affinity with the works of her old Surrealist friends and acquaintances, her recurrent portrayal of the female body, whether in symbiotic merger or in violent separation towards autonomy, deliberately transcends the traditional image of woman as portrayed in Surrealism.

Tanning, unlike most other women artists who joined the Surrealists in the 1930s and 1940s, did not fit the mould of the typical Surrealist *femme-enfant*, or "child-woman". The 32-year-old American artist had already established herself as a painter of noteworthy individuality when she encountered Ernst through her art dealer Julien Levy. A self-portrait from this period, in which the artist – bare-breasted with a winged lemur at her naked feet – opens a door that reveals endless corridors of more unlocked doorways, reflects Tanning's growing confidence in her private painterly explorations. It was Ernst who christened this oil painting *Birthday* (1942; artist's collection), a title that Tanning later recycled for her autobiography in memory of her dead husband.

During the 1940s Tanning created some of the most meticulously rendered images of the Surrealist movement. In *Children's Games* (1942; collection Preminger, New York) and *Eine kleine Nachtmusik* (1944; collection Penrose, Britain) unkempt girls in ragged clothes play in formalised corridors containing magical doorways. These female models of almost perfect behaviour seem to be acting out their young erotic fantasies in a rebellious self-exploration that threatens to overthrow the existing social order. In her novel *Abyss* (written in 1947 but not published until 1977) Tanning revisited this theme once more. In an attempt to regain access to the childhood world of "perpetual astonishment" and "incomparable secrets", Albert Exodus, a painter who does not paint, is drawn into the fascinating realm of the young and beautiful Destina Meridian. Unfortunately, his path crosses Destina's destructive quest for a new trophy to include in her memory box.

Until the 1950s, Tanning's paintings such as *Palaestra* (1947; collection Filipacchi), *Interior with Sudden Joy* (1951; private collection, USA, repr. Bosquet 1962) and *Guest Room* (1950–52; private collection, Belgium, *ibid.*) continued to focus on tantalising childhood obsessions. From 1952 onwards, while not abandoning this subject matter, Tanning relinquished the exactitude of the first

Surrealist period and opted for a surer, freer form; she created a world of soft sensual shapes in perpetual interplay. The paintings of the 1950s and 1960s, directly affected by Tanning's recent ballet designs for George Balanchine (*Night Shadow*, 1946, and *Bayou*, 1952), John Cranko (*The Witch*, 1950), Ruthanna Boris (*Will-o'-the Wisp*, 1953) and Jean-Louis Barrault (*Judith*, 1961; all untraced), contain a greater sense of movement, both of materials and of the body. In *The Ill-Forgotten* (1955; collection Rosalind and Melvin Jakobs), *Insomnia* (1957) and *Two-Words* (1963; both collection Cavalio, New York) figures interweave to the point of mutation, hinting at the sheer infinite number of possible constructions. Tanning herself once described this conceptual change to Alain Jouffroy in an interview in the 1970s:

> In the first years, I was painting *our* side of the mirror – the mirror for me is a door – but I think that I've gone over, to a place where one no longer faces identities at all. One looks at them somewhat obliquely, slyly. To capture the moment, to *accept* it with all its complex identities [Jouffroy 1974].

When Tanning began sculpting in 1969 she ignored such traditional materials as bronze, marble, terracotta and wood and turned instead to upholstery and needlework to create an original series of soft sculptures. Earlier that year, while listening to Karlheinz Stockhausen's electronic piece *Hymnen* at the Maison de la Radio, the artist had actually seen her future soft sculptures in a vision. In her autobiography she described suddenly noticing "spinning among the unearthly sounds...earthy even organic shapes that I would make, had to make, out of cloth and wool...fugacious, they would be, and fragile, to please their creator and survivor". From 1969 until 1974 Tanning moulded, with the aid of her sewing machine, twisting anthropomorphous figures in tweeds and rose-coloured fabrics, sometimes growing out of a wall, or a piece of furniture. In 1974 at a retrospective at the Centre National d'Art Contemporain in Paris some of these soft sculptures were arranged in a hotel room that Tanning had created for this purpose; the *Hôtel du Pavot (Poppy Hotel), Room 202*, is now part of the permanent collection of the Centre Georges Pompidou, Paris.

The exhibition at the New York Public Library in 1992 drew overdue attention to 50 years of Dorothea Tanning's graphic work. She produced most of her lithographs with Pierre Chave, many intended to illustrate books for old friends from the Surrealist days. In her more than 100 prints, produced with Georges Visat, the artist turned once again to the female body in perpetual metamorphosis. Continuously shifting her modes of creativity, Tanning frankly challenges her public to solve her latest artistic riddles:

> We leave enigmas lying around, signs to be read ranging from knife-edge to nebulae-pleas for guesses. Having posed our riddle we hide behind a tree or a gallery wall and wait for a sign. Even a firefly radiance. We have time enough but we wait rather anxiously for a pair of eyes, any eyes, to flash pulsations to a mind, any mind that will take us on with our visual propositions.

BETTINA BRANDT

ter Borch, Gesina *see* Borch

Therbusch, Anna Dorothea *see* Lisiewska-Therbusch

Thesleff, Ellen
Finnish painter and graphic artist, 1869–1954

Born in Helsinki, 5 October 1869. Attended school in Kuopio. Studied at Adolf von Becker's academy, Helsinki, 1885–7; Finnish Art Society drawing school, Helsinki, 1887–9; Gunnar Berndtson's private academy, Helsinki, 1889–91; Académie Colarossi, Paris, under Gustave Courtois and Pascal Dagnan-Bouveret, 1891–2. In Paris, 1893–4 and 1899–1900; in Italy, 1894–1916 and 1920–39; usually spent winters in Florence, summers in Murole, Finland. Member of Septem group, 1912. Died in Helsinki, 12 January 1954.

Principal Exhibitions
Finnish Artists' Association, Helsinki: 1891–5

Stockholm: 1897 (*Allmänna konst- och industriutställnin-gen* [Universal art and industry exhibition])
Exposition Universelle, Paris: 1900 (first-class bronze medal)
Graphic Exhibition, Moscow: 1916
Finnish Art Exhibition, Petrograd: 1917
Konstsalongen, Helsinki: 1919 (woodcuts)
Liljevalchs Konsthall, Stockholm: 1929 (*Finlands nutida konst* [Contemporary Finnish art])
Nationalmuseum, Stockholm: 1944 (*Finsk nutidskonst* [Contemporary Finnish art])
Helsinki Art Hall: 1946 (Finnish Art Society centenary)

Selected Writings
Dikter och tankar [Poems and thoughts], Helsinki, 1954

Bibliography

Walter Shaw Sparrow, *Women Painters of the World*, London: Hodder and Stoughton, and New York: Stokes, 1905; reprinted New York: Hacker, 1976
Bulletin of the Cleveland Museum of Art, xiv, 1927
Leonard Bäcksbacka, *Ellen Thesleff*, Helsinki, 1955
Salme Sarajas-Korte, *Suomen varhaissymbolismi ja sen lähteet:Tutkielma Suomen maalaustiteesta, 1891–95* [Early Symbolism in Finland: A study of Finnish painting, 1891–95], Helsinki: Otava, 1966; Swedish edition as *Vid symbolismens källor* [At the source of Symbolism], Jakobstad, 1981
Ellen Thesleff, exh. cat., Ateneumin Taidemuseo, Helsinki, 1969
Markku Lahti, "Arvoitus Ellen Thesleff – Gordon Craig" [The mystery of Ellen Thesleff and Gordon Craig], *Art Museum of Ateneum Bulletin*, xviii, 1973 (also in Swedish, and with English summary)
Målarinnor från Finland/Seitsemän suomalaista taiteilijaa [Women painters from Finland], exh. cat., Nationalmuseum, Stockholm, and elsewhere, 1981
Dreams of a Summer Night: Scandinavian Painting at the Turn of the Century, exh. cat., Arts Council of Great Britain, 1986
Kirk Varnedoe, *Northern Light: Nordic Art at the Turn of the Century*, New Haven and London: Yale University Press, 1988
Salme Sarajas-Korte, "Ellen Thesleffin, 1890-luku", [Ellen Thesleff in the 1890s], *Ars: Suomen*, iv, 1989
——, *Helene Schjerfbeckin ja Ellen Thesleffin 1900-luku* [Helene Schjerfbeck and Ellen Thesleff in the 1900s], *Ars: Suomen*, v, 1990
Leena Ahtola-Moorhouse, "Löydetty Arkadia" [Arcadia discovered], *Taide*, xxxi/1, 1991, pp.45–8
Eeva Kilpi, *Ellen Thesleff: Laula rakkaudesta: Valikolma neljästä runokokoelmasta*, Helsinki: WSOY, 1991

In 1909 Ellen Thesleff wrote: "I lie deep in the sand so my heart can listen to the heartbeat of the globe, and with that rhythm I grasp colours and lines, feeling secure and free. I do not know what the result will be, but in any case it will be something wonderful." She was a painter and poet throughout her life, her family supporting her artistic ambitions. She grew up with the Symbolists and studied under the Finnish painter Gunnar Berndtson. Like several other Finnish women painters, she studied in Paris, at the Académie Colarossi from 1891. She was inspired by the French Symbolist painter Eugène Carrière, but although her works show a similarly reduced palette and the expression of airy plastic forms created by light, her technique is quite different from his. Whereas Thesleff would always add lines and paint, Carrière wiped them off. Thesleff was the first Finnish artist to paint a Symbolist work, the portrait of her sister *Thyra Elisabeth* (1892; Helsinki City Art Museum). By then she wanted her paintings to be free from realism, and have more of the curved lines of Art Nouveau. In the 1890s her portraits and landscapes were painted in dark colours, but she endeavoured to express the soul's beauty through her art.

In the Nordic countries the climate is hard to endure, with winter days that are very dark, dry and cold. But suddenly in summer outdoor life can carry on through day and night. Thesleff caught that feeling of being free and independent in the open air in the painting *Echo* (1890–91; private collection, Helsinki), which she painted before her studies abroad. *Echo* shows a girl in profile with open mouth calling or perhaps singing. True to its time, the girl in the foreground is dressed in a white blouse down to her hips. The girl's head is painted against a luminous sky and the white of her blouse contrasts with the dark forest in the background. It is a vision of youth and its uncurbed strength, which also finds a parallel in the contemporary political situation, when Finland was struggling for independence from a powerful Russia. The painting was well received when it was shown at the first exhibition of the Finnish Artists' Association in the autumn of 1891, and it was bought by the exhibition committee.

In 1894–5, on her first visit to Florence, Thesleff drew a self-portrait in full face, composed of thousands of pencil lines, a grey vision in a dreamy but clear mood (Museum of Finnish Art Ateneum, Helsinki). It looks as if the artist saw her face through a hazy glass and suddenly there was a clear spot over the centre. Thesleff's touch is both light and precise, and creates the impression of a clairvoyant's vision. Some Finnish friends of hers, the artists Ada Thilén and Helene Schjerfbeck (q.v.), also came to Florence. In the spring of 1894 Thesleff and Schjerfbeck worked together in the monastery of San Marco, copying Fra Angelico's frescoes. Thesleff's favourite Italian masters were Fra Angelico and Botticelli, with their clear, light colours, and Leonardo da Vinci, with his strong compositions. She was also inspired by theosophy, then a topical subject.

In 1906 Thesleff met the British theatre designer, writer and graphic artist Gordon Craig in Florence. He was a strong personality, and lived a long and bohemian life – he had 16 children by 11 different women, one of them the dancer Isadora Duncan. Thesleff's meeting with Craig led to a lifelong friendship, no children, but a correspondence comprising hundreds of letters. And, what is even more important, it started Thesleff's career as a graphic artist, an important complement to her work as a painter. She began to do woodcuts in 1907, initially working under Craig's influence. Her woodcut *Marionettes* (1907) was published in the journal *The Mask* in 1908. She made studies – drawings and colour notes – of the figures in the Museo Civico, Venice, both of plates with old woodcuts and of small marionette figures. In a letter of the same year she mentions this woodcut as being one of her best from the period. *Marionettes* used traditional methods, but Thesleff later tried experimental techniques of her own. She printed several colours simultaneously from the same plate and would even add colours to the print afterwards. Her monotypes were airy, often with bright, but light colours, and looked like paintings. The woodcut technique showed her the way to the unexpected and she used mild colours to create a rare lyricism.

In 1916 Thesleff wrote about her works: "No theories, no form, just colour". She worked with these ideas throughout her life. During the inter-war years she continued to live in both Italy and Finland. During World War II she stayed at home, visiting Stockholm in 1944, when she took part in the exhibition of *Finsk nutidskonst* (contemporary Finnish art).

LENA HOLGER

Thompson, Elizabeth *see* Butler

Thornycroft, Mary
British sculptor, 1809–1895

Born Mary Francis in Thornham, Norfolk, 21 May 1809. Trained by her father, the sculptor John Francis. Married one of his pupils, Thomas Thornycroft, 1840; seven children born 1841–53, of whom Alyce, Helen, Theresa and Hamo became artists; husband died 1885. Lived in London; in Rome, studying under John Gibson, 1842–3. Appointed to teach sculpture to the royal princesses, 1867. Died 1895.

Principal Exhibitions
Royal Academy, London: 1834–40, 1844, 1847–50, 1852–73, 1875, 1877
British Institution, London: 1840, 1845–64
Exposition Universelle, Paris: 1855

Bibliography
Clara Erskine Clement and Laurence Hutton, *Artists of the Nineteenth Century and Their Work*, 2 vols, Boston: Houghton Osgood, and London: Trübner, 1879; reprinted New York: Arno Press, 1969
F.G. Stephens, "The late Mrs Mary Thornycroft", *Magazine of Art*, xviii, 1895, pp.305–7
Mrs Fenwick-Miller, "The ladies' column", *Illustrated London News*, 16 February 1895
Emilie Isobel Barrington, "Mrs Mary Thornycroft", *Spectator*, 23 February 1895, pp.263–4
Elfrida Thornycroft, *Bronze and Steel: Life of Thomas Thornycroft, Sculptor and Engineer*, Long Compton: King Stone Press, 1932
Elfrida Manning, *Marble and Bronze: The Art and Life of Hamo Thornycroft*, London: Trefoil, 1982
Pamela Gerrish Nunn, *Victorian Women Artists*, London: Women's Press, 1987
Penny McCracken, "Sculptor Mary Thornycroft and her artist children", *Woman's Art Journal*, xvii/2, 1996–7, pp.3–8

Documents, correspondence and diaries are in the Thornycroft Archive, Henry Moore Centre for the Study of Sculpture, Leeds.

Mary Thornycroft was trained in the studio of her father, the sculptor John Francis, and exhibited at the Royal Academy from 1834 (she was the only woman exhibitor in 1837). Although these early career advantages were offset by her marriage and by the birth of seven children, she continued to sculpt into her eighties. In 1842 Mary went with her husband Thomas Thornycroft to Rome, where she impressed John Gibson, leader of the colony of British sculptors there, with her *Sleeping Child* (that or a similar figure was used on the *Martin* tomb at Ledbury, Herefordshire). Gibson recommended her to Queen Victoria as better able to execute portraits of the royal children than himself. Back in London, Thornycroft was commissioned to portray the children as the *Four Seasons*, beginning with Princess Alice, aged one, as *Spring* in 1845 (Royal Collection, Osborne, Isle of Wight). These so pleased the royal patrons that she was commissioned to portray four generations of the royal family, and was given her own rooms in Windsor Castle for the purpose, becoming the principal bread-winner of her family. Her last piece, exhibited at the Royal Academy in 1877, was the *Duchess of Edinburgh* (Royal Collection, Buckingham Palace, London). Although Thornycroft was fortunate in that the queen's patronage kept her constantly employed, she was left with neither time nor incentive to develop her talents and extend her repertoire; thus the artistic fashions of the day passed her by.

Thornycroft was a competent portraitist in the classical tradition, whose talent might have benefited from a more thorough study from life, then generally unavailable to women. Her *Skipping Girl* (untraced), exhibited at the Exposition Universelle, Paris, in 1855, was admired by the critic Jerichau as "one of the six most beautiful statues in the world" (Thornycroft 1932, p.55); a replica in bronze was made for Albert, the Prince Consort. But while Thornycroft enjoyed great popular success with her portraits of the rich and the royal, mainly women and children, she did not acquire the renown of the male sculptors who received the "important" commissions for heroic and equestrian statues. While the statues of *Charles I* and *James I* at the Old Bailey, London, have been attributed to both Thomas and Mary, she may have been more instrumental in the production of other statues by her husband and son Hamo than has been acknowledged. Elfrida Manning considered Mary to be a sculptor of equal worth to her husband, and, according to a studio assistant, she was his superior, because "Her heart was in it". In the family sculpture workshop, where each member contributed his or her own particular skills, Mary's speciality was portraiture, at which she excelled. An expert and delicate carver, she still had to put up with Thomas physically correcting her work. There is no evidence, however, that Mary worked on Thomas's large *Boadicea* (1902; Westminster Bridge, London), left unfinished at his death, although it has

been claimed elsewhere that she did. Other works by Mary Thornycroft include a full-length figure of *Lady Braye* reclining on her monument in Stamford Church, Lincolnshire (1862), with her dog at her feet, and a bust of *Melpomene*, the Muse of Tragedy, exhibited at the Royal Academy in 1872; her other contributions to the *Poet's Fountain* (1875; Park Lane, London; demolished 1949) are documented in Hamo's journal (Thornycroft Archive, Leeds).

According to Mrs Fenwick-Miller (1895), one of the most interesting pieces entrusted to Mary Thornycroft was a marble bust of *Alderman Pochin* (Collection Lord Aberconway, Bodnant) for Salford Corporation. The bust, exhibited at the Royal Academy in 1870, shows Pochin wearing his chain of office. The eyes are incised, and not left classically blank as in most of the artist's earlier works, demonstrating a more naturalistic influence in her work.

More typical are Thornycroft's portraits of the royal children that adorn the drawing room of Osborne House, Isle of Wight. Elfrida Thornycroft (1932) wrote: "Her child portraits were graceful without ever being merely sentimental and there is character as well as charm in her Princess Beatrice in a Nautilus Shell of 1858". *Princess Beatrice (Osborne House)* (Royal Collection) was one of many of Thornycroft's sculptures given as Christmas and birthday presents from Prince Albert to the queen; she gave the work high praise when she received it at Christmas 1858. The sculpture also received the distinction of being reproduced as a Minton porcelain figure (City Museum, Stoke-on-Trent). The conventional rendering of the princesses as passive symbolic figures representing *Peace* and *Plenty* is no less surprising than that of the young princes in the active roles of half-naked *Fisher Boy* and *Hunter*. These works were reproduced in the *Art Journal* (1864), which considered them suitable for reproduction in Parian ware, while engravings of Thornycroft's statues were popular in gift albums of the day. A macabre example of her work at Osborne is the collection of marble hands and feet of the young princes and princesses, whose names and ages were inscribed on the stumps. Casts of Mary's own hand were kept by the Thornycroft family.

An unsigned late painting, probably by her daughter Alyce (c.1890; ex-Phillips, Bath, 31 October 1994, lot 317), shows Mary with a small clay sculpture in hand, her thumb turned back from modelling. She would say: "I cannot be happy without a piece of clay to play with". She taught sculpture to Princess Louise, and passed on her enthusiasm for the art to her daughters and especially to her son Hamo, exhorting him to "stick to the clay, my boy" and not to dissipate his energy on other activities, as perhaps she and his father had.

ANDREA GARRIHY

Tintoretto, Marietta *see* Robusti

Toorop, Charley
Dutch painter, 1891–1955

[fig. 69]

Born Annie Caroline Pontifex Toorop in Katwijk, 24 March 1891. Trained by her father, the painter Jan Toorop. Married Henk Fernhout, 1912; two sons, born 1912 (the painter Edgar Fernhout) and 1913, daughter born 1916. Settled in Bergen, North Holland, 1912; moved to Laren, North Holland, 1915. Separated from Fernhout and moved to Utrecht, then Amsterdam, 1917. Frequent trips to Paris from 1918; knew Mondrian. Visited the Borinage mining district of Belgium, 1922. Worked on her studio-house, "De Vlerken", in Bergen, with the architect Piet Kramer, from 1921. Lived in Amsterdam, 1926–30; co-founded Filmliga (Film League) and met Joris Ivens. Organised exhibitions at the Stedelijk Museum, Amsterdam, with the architect J.J.P. Oud, 1928 and 1929. Studio in Paris, 1930; trip to Berlin, 1931. Settled in "De Vlerken", 1932. Died in Bergen, 6 November 1955.

Principal Exhibitions

Individual
Gallery Gerbrands, Utrecht: 1922, 1931
Stedelijk Museum, Amsterdam: 1927
Gallery d'Audretsch, The Hague: 1931, 1935
Palais des Beaux-Arts, Brussels: 1933
Gallery G.J. Nieuwenhuizen Segaar, The Hague: 1934, 1937 (*Drie Generaties* [Three generations], with Jan Toorop and Edgar Fernhout), 1939, 1945
Haags Gemeentemuseum, The Hague: 1951 (touring retrospective)
Hammer Galleries, New York: 1952
Amersfoortse Gemeenschap, Amersfoort: 1953
Gallery Huinck and Scherjon, Amsterdam: 1954

Group
Stedelijk Museum, Amsterdam: 1916–37
Venice Biennale: 1938
Kunsthalle, Bern: 1950 (*Fünf holländische Maler*)

Bibliography
H.P. Bremmer, *Beeldende Kunst*, ix, 1922, pp.57–64; xx, 1933, pp.13, 54 and 63 (in addition, at least one reproduction and comments in all volumes, 1918–37)
A.M. Hammacher, "Charley Toorop", *Beeldende Kunst*, xxvii, 1940, pp.25–32
Charley Toorop, exh. cat., Haags Gemeentemuseum, The Hague, and elsewhere, 1951
A.M. Hammacher, *Charley Toorop: Een beschouwing van haar leven en werk* [Charley Toorop: A study of her life and work], Rotterdam: Brussel, 1952
Nico J. Brederoo, *Charley Toorop: Leven en werken* [Charley Toorop: Life and work], Amsterdam: Meulenhoff, 1982 (contains bibliography)
Charley Toorop, exh. cat., Centraal Museum, Utrecht, 1982
Carel Blotkamp, "Charley Toorop over De Stijl" [Charley Toorop on De Stijl], *Jong Holland*, vi/2, 1990, pp.14–15 (with English summary)
Met verve [With verve], exh. cat., Stichting Amazone, Amsterdam, 1991
De maaltijd der vrienden [The meal with friends], exh. cat., Het Huis Kranenburgh, Bergen, North Holland, 1994
Charley Toorop: Werken in de verzameling [Charley Toorop: Works in the collection], exh. cat., Rijksmuseum Kröller-Müller, Otterlo, 1995

Charley Toorop has left behind an oeuvre that is impressive in both extent and power. Around 400 oil paintings, 120 drawings and 15 prints by her are currently in Dutch museums and private collections. Nearly one-third of these are portraits, of which many are self- and group portraits. Toorop also produced numerous still lifes (some of them churned out for dealers), besides townscapes, a few café interiors and subjects such as her garden, flowering orchards and plants. She was a well-known painter in her lifetime, and her reputation has survived up to the present day.

At around the age of 18 Toorop indicated that she wanted to become a painter. Her father Jan Toorop, one of the best-known Dutch artists at the turn of the century (his reputation is still high today), maintained many contacts with other artists, so Toorop came into contact from an early age with a circle of male and female painters, including Piet Mondrian, with whom she remained friends, Jacoba van Heemskerck (q.v.) and Jan Sluyters. Luminism and theosophy were important influences for painters at the time, as was the Parisian avant-garde. The Toorop family spent several summers at Domburg, on the island of Walcheren. At this early stage (1911), Toorop was already exhibiting in her father's exhibition room ("Het paviljoentje") there, next to many younger and older painters of repute, and, as a result, her work came to be shown elsewhere. She had learned the principles of painting from her father, who continued to advise and assist her. Thanks to her forceful personality, she nevertheless found her own direction. The fact of being a woman did not deter her from practising the profession, although bringing up three young children on her own certainly presented problems.

Toorop's earliest portraits, which date from c.1913, were painted under the influence of spiritualist ideas, for example the portrait of her baby son *John Fernhout* (1913; private collection, repr. Utrecht 1982, no.20). *Lighthouse at Evening* (1915; Rijksmuseum Kröller-Müller, Otterlo) shows clear signs of Symbolism. The spiritual element in her work began to fade after 1921, when she fell under the influence of painters from the Bergen school. This group painted in a style that had both Expressionist and Cubist elements, in which forms were emphasised by their contours. Moreover, she was also fascinated by the work of Vincent van Gogh, in particular his "profound, stark love of reality", as she recounted in an interview in 1953. In 1922 she went to the mining region of the Borinage in Belgium – as van Gogh had done 44 years earlier; her work from that time includes two double portraits of a mother and daughter: *The Owner and Her Daughter* (1922; Rijksmusem Kröller-Müller) and *Two Women Miners* (1922; Dienst Verspreide Rijkscollecties, The Hague). In these works Toorop felt that she had achieved the kind of expression that she wanted. The figures are large and positioned in the foreground. No contact is implied between the sitters, but each woman is clearly individualised, not "prettified" but keenly observed. Other paintings show a similar desire to portray Toorop's vision of things without "a blurring of the fierce and direct beauty of life", as she described it in an interview of 1951. These Borinage works reveal a strongly personal approach. Her portrait of patients from a lunatic asylum, *The Imbeciles* (1924; Stedelijk Museum, Amsterdam), shows Toorop at her best; the two seated women, rendered with a greater plasticity than in the earlier portraits, are expressively painted. In this period she also received more and

more portrait commissions from well-to-do clients. These were executed in a realistic manner, with little detail, and include her portrait of *Plasschaert* (1927; Stedelijk Museum). A striking aspect of Toorop's portraits is that she frequently depicts her subjects almost frontally; the viewer is thus directly confronted by the results of her acute observation.

After 1924 Toorop several times turned to social realism, as in the *Boarding House* (1928; Stedelijk van Abbemuseum, Eindhoven) and *Bistro, Paris* (1931; Centraal Museum, Utrecht), both produced during one of her sojourns in France. It is more than likely that the influence of the German movement Neue Sachlichkeit (New Objectivity) had its effect on her, since she maintained an awareness of avant-garde art. At the exhibition *Socialistiche kunst heden* (Socialist art today) at the Stedelijk Museum in Amsterdam (1930) she showed *Five Zeeland Peasants* (1930; Centraal Museum); the middle peasant of the five, large in stature, is shown half-length and frontally, and as if seen through a sharply focused camera lens. *Musicians and Dancing Peasants* (1927; Rijksmuseum Kröller-Müller) reveals the influence of film even more clearly. Toorop's still lifes, most of them larger than 50×50 centimetres, follow a similar progression to her portraits, moving from an Expressionist style with Cubist elements to a sturdy and powerful realism, for example *Flowers* (1919; Dordrechts Museum, Dordrecht), *Vase of Flowers Before a Stone Wall* (1924; repr. Utrecht 1982, no.249) and *Still Life with Horse's Skull* (1929; Rijksmuseum Kröller-Müller).

The years between 1930 and the outbreak of World War II were Toorop's most prolific period, and the one in which she produced her mature work; later, her health began to deteriorate. She continued to practise in different genres, to receive portrait commissions and to sell work through dealers. She carried out a number of large-scale projects, among them *Cheese Market at Alkmaar* (1933; 150×179cm.; Stedelijk Museum). These have a deep emotional resonance. Another project, *Meal with Friends* (1933; Museum Boijmans Van Beuningen, Rotterdam), a monumental group portrait, depicts some of her artist friends, among them Gerrit Rietveld of the De Stijl group and the sculptor John Rädecker. Toorop intended *Recumbent Medusa* (1938–9; Stedelijk Museum) and *Medusa Puts Out to Sea* (1941; Rijksmuseum Kröller-Müller) as laments. Her consciousness of the threat of Nazism produced this vision of beauty deceived. Medusa's head, painted after a plaster model (Toorop always used models), is beautiful and powerful, but it is as if her soul has taken temporary shelter elsewhere. The war years are reflected in *Still Life with White Jug* (private collection, *ibid.*, no.334), which bears the pointed subtitle *Meal Without Friends*. Its clearly constructed composition, characteristic of her still lifes after 1930, is brightened by the light effects and the decorative contour lines. The inner truth with which Toorop painted here comes more powerfully than ever to the fore. *Clown* (1941; Rijksmuseum Kröller-Müller) and *Female Worker among the Ruins* (1943; Stedelijk Museum) were painted after the destruction of Rotterdam in 1940.

Three Generations (Museum Boijmans Van Beuningen) is one of her last monumental canvases. She had worked on it, with interruptions, since 1941; it was eventually completed in 1950. At the upper left she painted the bronze mask made by John Rädecker after a photograph of her father, in the background at the right her son, the painter Edgar Fernhout, and in the middle herself. The work exudes a compelling power. It is the fourth from the last in the impressive series of around 35 painted and drawn self-portraits. Throughout her life she subjected herself to an unsparing scrutiny, and painted herself in many guises: open, as in *Self-Portrait Against a Wall* (1925; Museum Boijmans Van Beuningen); self-assured, as in *Self-Portrait Standing with a Palette* (1933); with a sorrowful expression, as in *Self-Portrait with a Palette* (1952; both Haags Gemeentemuseum); and *Self-Portrait with Almost Drawn Curtain* (1955; Stedelijk Museum, Alkmaar), painted when she felt herself to be at the end of her life, and capable only of looking back. Toorop was a free spirit who showed no desire to belong to a specific school. Her work is of a distinctive and penetrating expressive realism.

ROSELLA M. HUBER-SPANIER

Traquair, Phoebe

Irish artist, designer and craft worker, 1852–1936

Born Phoebe Anna Moss in Dublin, 24 May 1852. Studied at Royal Dublin Society design school, c.1869–72. Married Scots palaeontologist Ramsay Traquair, 1873; two sons, born 1874 and 1875, one daughter, born 1879; husband died 1912. Lived in Edinburgh after marriage. First woman honorary member, Royal Scottish Academy, 1920. Died in Edinburgh, 4 August 1936.

Principal Exhibitions

World's Columbian Exposition, Chicago: 1893
Arts and Crafts Society of Ireland, Dublin: 1895, 1904
Guild of Women-Binders, London: from 1898
Scottish Guild of Handicraft, Glasgow: 1898
Arts and Crafts Exhibition Society, London: 1899, 1903, 1906
Exposition Universelle, Paris: 1900 (with Guild of Women-Binders)
Royal Scottish Academy, Edinburgh: from 1902
Louisiana Purchase Exposition, St Louis: 1904

Bibliography

Gerard Baldwin Brown, "Some recent efforts in mural decoration", *Scottish Arts Review*, January 1889, pp.225–8

Margaret Armour, "Beautiful modern manuscripts", *The Studio*, 1897, pp.47–55 (special winter issue)

——, "Mural decoration in Scotland", *The Studio*, x, 1897, pp.100–06

"A Scottish lady decorator: Mrs Traquair", *Scots Pictorial*, 7 May 1898, p.10

Esther Wood, "British tooled bookbindings and their designers", *The Studio*, 1899–1900, pp.38–47 (special winter issue: *Modern Bookbindings and Their Designers*)

James Caw, "The art work of Mrs Traquair", *Art Journal*, 1900, pp.143–8

G. A. Anstruther, ed., *The Bindings of Tomorrow: A Record of the Work of the Guild of Women-Binders and of the Hampstead Bindery*, London: Guild of Women-Binders, 1902

A. F. Morris, "A versatile art worker: Mrs Traquair", *The Studio*, xxxiv, 1905, pp.339–45

Barbara Morris, "Some early embroideries of Mrs Phoebe Traquair", *Embroidery*, 1966, pp.49–53 (Diamond Jubilee edition)

Anthea Callen, *Angel in the Studio: Women in the Arts and Crafts Movement, 1870–1914*, London: Astragal, 1979; as *Women Artists of the Arts and Crafts Movement, 1870–1914*, New York: Pantheon, 1979

Arts and Crafts in Edinburgh, 1880–1930, exh. cat., Edinburgh College of Art, 1985

Elizabeth Skeoch Cumming, *Phoebe Anna Traquair HRSA (1852–1936) and Her Contribution to Arts and Crafts in Edinburgh*, PhD dissertation, University of Edinburgh, 1987

Elizabeth Cumming, "A note on Phoebe Traquair and an Edinburgh Dante", *Edinburgh Review*, 1992, pp.143–9

Phoebe Anna Traquair, 1852–1936, exh. cat., Scottish
  National Portrait Gallery, Edinburgh, 1993 (contains
  bibliography)
Nicola Gordon Bowe and Elizabeth Cumming, *The Arts
  and Crafts Movements in Dublin and Edinburgh* (in
  preparation)

In the 1890s and 1900s Phoebe Traquair was the
leading artist and craft worker of the Arts and
Crafts movement in Scotland. Working in a diverse
range of media, from mural decoration to easel
painting, manuscript illumination to book tooling,
and from embroidery to enamel work, she produced
a substantial corpus of work that was exhibited
world-wide and at the time was noted by critics in
Edinburgh and London to be romantic in its treatment of literary subjects and unique in the artist's
use of colour and texture. More recently she has
been recognised as Scotland's first professional
woman artist. Her work is in the collections of the
Victoria and Albert Museum, London, and the
Royal Museum of Scotland, Edinburgh.

Phoebe Anna Moss was born into the heart of
middle-class Ireland. Many members of her family,
including her father, were distinguished surgeons
and medical practitioners. Her earliest work
reflected this inheritance: from the early 1870s she
produced highly detailed scientific drawings of fossil
fish to illustrate the scientific research papers of the
Royal Dublin Society curator (and her future
husband), Ramsay Traquair. Dublin also offered
rich opportunities for her to study museum and
library collections. The combined use of colour and
pattern to convey spiritual values in such medieval
manuscripts as the Book of Kells (Trinity College
Library, Dublin) engaged her attention from an
early age and was subsequently to inform much of
her work in the course of a long and prolific career.

On arrival in Edinburgh in 1874, Traquair first
worked in the field of domestic embroidery, which
she worked in a simple style using crewel techniques. Surviving examples (Victoria and Albert
Museum, London), however, give little indication of
the rich imagination and technical bravura found in
her subsequent embroideries. For the first ten years
of marriage she devoted her energies to bringing up
her children, but by the mid-1880s she was determined to widen her vision beyond household duties.
Gradually her social circle expanded to include
some of the leading thinkers in Edinburgh – men
such as John Miller Gray (later the first curator of
the Scottish National Portrait Gallery), the botanist,

critic, social reformer and environmentalist Patrick
Geddes, and the art historian Gerard Baldwin
Brown – who not only introduced her to the ideas
and poetry of Rossetti and Tennyson, Blake and
Dante, but also individually helped engineer the
launch of her career.

Traquair's first professional commission came
through the Edinburgh Social Union, a philanthropic body spearheaded by Geddes. For the Union
she decorated the tiny mortuary chapel of the Royal
Edinburgh Hospital for Sick Children (1885–6).
Here, on walls measuring 2.3 × 1.5 metres, she
combined the aesthetics of medieval manuscripts
with a style much indebted to late Pre-Raphaelitism.
She used vivid blues, reds and gold leaf, and the
decoration was described by Baldwin Brown in the
Scottish Art Review as "a piece of illumination
enlarged". The central theme of Christian redemption introduced here was one that would be used
many times over the following 30 years.

While engaged on this first commission, Traquair
started the first of her ambitious panels of "artistic
embroidery". An early series of three panels was
worked on the theme of the *Salvation of Mankind*
(1886–93; City of Edinburgh Museums and Art
Galleries). When the suite was shown in Dublin in
1895, a critic commented on the "broadness of
treatment, decorative feeling, colour and dexterity
in dealing with a difficult material" (William Hunt
in *Journal and Proceedings of the Arts and Crafts
Society of Ireland*, 1896, p.26). Each measuring
over 1.8 metres in height, these embroideries neatly
illustrate her stylistic development over a seven-year
period. The density of the Aesthetic figural imagery
of the central panel (*Angel of Redemption and
Purification*, 1886–7), with its undercurrent of
medieval and Morrisian naturalism, contrasts
dramatically with the simpler design of the two side
panels (*Souls of the Blest*, 1889–91, and *Souls
Waiting on Earth*, 1891–3). This early panel shows
a similar intensity of design and imagery to a series
of illuminated manuscripts produced in 1887
(private collections) when Traquair was in correspondence with John Ruskin, who lent her medieval
manuscripts from his Brantwood library, and in turn
admired her efforts.

In the 1890s the inspiration for Traquair's work
continued to range widely from Blake and Rossetti
to medieval manuscripts and textiles. Her work,
however, had its own distinctive, strong identity and
she pursued a personal Symbolist language

expressed through a form of decorative realism. This is most obvious in her decoration of two Edinburgh buildings: the Song School at St Mary's Cathedral (1888–92) and the Catholic Apostolic Church (1893–1901). Combining portraiture with imaginative concepts, the Song School scheme was called "fresh and modern" by a London critic. The Catholic Apostolic Church decoration more obviously reflects the influence of the paintings of Botticelli and Fra Angelico, which Traquair had viewed in Florence in 1889 and 1895, and realised her primary goal of uniting the fine and decorative arts. Inspired by Renaissance ideals, Traquair here used gesso and gold leaf to give texture to the surfaces, but experimentation with the medium resulted in an original method designed to withstand (unsuccessfully) the Scottish climate: she diluted the oils with turpentine, blended beeswax with it and coated the surface with a beeswax varnish. Illuminated manuscripts of this decade, such as Elizabeth Barrett Browning's *Sonnets from the Portuguese* (1892–7; National Library of Scotland, Edinburgh), were also inspired in technique and style by Italian examples of the early Renaissance.

Recognition by London critics encouraged Traquair to produce some of her most confident and finest work during this decade. While decorating the Catholic Apostolic Church, she stitched a suite of four embroideries on the same theme of the *Progress of a Soul* (1893–1902; National Gallery of Scotland, Edinburgh), in which choice and imaginative use of traditional and modern stitches and of colour are united with powerful imagery to produce some of the finest textiles of the Arts and Crafts movement. The iconography represents the drama of a soul's development through life, from innocence through experience to ultimate salvation at the point of death. This romantic subject, at once personal and universal, may have been originally inspired by Walter Pater's tale of Denys l'Auxerrois in *Imaginary Portraits*, but it also includes iconographic references to Apollo, Orpheus and the innocent Parsifal. The underlying message supplied by Traquair, a committed Christian, was again that of man's redemption through the grace of God.

This theme continued to inform Traquair's work in a variety of media in the 1890s and 1900s. Working alongside a group of women binders who included Annie Macdonald and Jessie McGibbon at the Dean Studio in Edinburgh's West End, Traquair produced not only some of her finest manuscripts but blind-tooled and embossed, almost sculpted, monochrome leather book covers. From 1901, however, she learned the rudiments of a fashionable medium, enamelling, from Lady Gibson Carmichael, who had studied the craft in London with Alexander Fisher. Their designs were in part inspired by the medieval collections formed by Lady Carmichael's husband, Sir Thomas Gibson Carmichael. Enamelling quickly became Traquair's favoured small-scale colour craft. Here, as in illumination and mural decoration, she was able, in the true Arts and Crafts spirit, to reunite art and design. With mural painting Traquair had wrestled with the difficulties of translating small-scale designs to an "epic" architectural context, but with manuscripts and now enamels she encountered no such problem. In letters written in the 1900s to Percy Nobbs, a young architect and friend of her elder son Ramsay, she referred to such pieces as "little lyrics", commenting that these could produce "bits of lovely colour quite beautiful in themselves".

Traquair's interest in colour, always present in her work, became dominant in her work of the 1900s. When an enamelled triptych of the *Red Cross Knight* (1905; private collection, repr. *The Studio*, xxxvii, 1906, p.213) – a subject celebrating the victory of good over evil – was shown at the Arts and Crafts Exhibition Society in London in 1906, *The Studio* was quick to refer to "the charm of colour…[that] turns this triptych into a pleasant and effective, even noble, decoration" (*ibid.*, p.214). The colours she employed in enamelled jewellery, caskets and triptychs – medieval forms so well suited to the medium – were quite different from those of Fisher and his pupils. The green of land, the ultramarine of sea and the amber of an autumn sunset were conveyed in a manner that was at once harmonious and powerful. Traquair's enamels illustrated narrative scenes in which angels rescued or comforted mortals: at times sentiment was avoided only through inventive exploration of the material. Uniquely, Traquair added tiny slivers of foil to the flux to reflect light and to add texture to the surface.

Although mural decoration was primarily a craft of the 1880s and 1890s, Traquair produced two late schemes for buildings in England. The first, for the tiny church of St Peter in the village of Clayworth, Nottinghamshire (1904–5), was painted over two summers and combined portraiture with a representation of an angel choir. The other commission took her three summers to complete: painted in the apse of Detmar Blow's Manners chapel at Thorney Hill in the New Forest, Hampshire, between 1920 and 1922 it was virtually her swan-song. By the mid-1920s, with failing eyesight, Traquair had abandoned enamelling and once more took up the craft of domestic embroidery. Her career had turned almost full circle. Her achieve-ments had been many, however, and her obituaries were fullsome in their praise. According to one, she was "a little woman and sparely built but overflow-ing with nervous energy, her artistic activities were remarkable both in extent and quality" (*The Times*, 6 August 1936).

ELIZABETH CUMMING

U–V

Udaltsova, Nadezhda (Andreyevna)

Russian painter, draughtswoman and textile designer, 1886–1961

Born in Orel, 29 December 1885 (Old Style calendar)/10 January 1886 (New Style calendar); father the General of Gendarmerie, Andrei Prudkovsky. Moved to Moscow with her family, 1892; educated at a private high school for girls from aristocratic families. Attended classes in Konstantin Yuon's studio, and met Lyubov Popova (q.v.) and Vera Mukhina (q.v.). Married A.D. Udaltsov, 1908; separated after 1917. Continued her artistic education in Paris, 1912; with Popova, studied at La Palette under Henri Le Fauconnier and Jean Metzinger. Returned to Moscow, 1913. Member of Kazimir Malevich's group Supremus, 1916–17. After the Revolution, became active in the organisation of the first professional union of Russian artists, 1917–19, and joined IZO, Narkompros (Fine Arts Section, People's Commissariat of Enlightenment). Taught painting and textile design at Vkhutemas (Higher State Artistic and Technical Workshops), and Vkhutein (Higher State Artistic and Technical Institute), Moscow, 1920–30. Member of Inkhuk (Institute of Artistic Culture), Moscow, 1920–21. Explored the Russian frontiers – Ural and Altai – and worked in Armenia with her second husband, painter Alexander Drevin, late 1920s–early 1930s; son born 1921; husband executed 1938. Died in Moscow, 25 January 1961.

Principal Exhibitions

Individual

Russian Museum, Leningrad: 1928 (with Alexander Drevin)
Central Club of Artists, Moscow: 1965 (retrospective)

Group

Bubnovy valet (Jack/Knave of Diamonds), Moscow: 1914, 1917
Petrograd: 1915 (*Tramway V: First Futurist Exhibition of Paintings*), 1915 (*0.10 [Zero-Ten]: Last Futurist Exhibition of Paintings*)
Moscow: 1917 (*Verbovka: Contemporary Applied Art*), 1918 (*First Exhibition of Paintings by the Professional Union of Artists in Moscow*)
Galerie van Diemen, Berlin: 1922–3 (*Erste russische Kunstausstellung*, touring)

Selected Writings

Zhizn russkoy kubistki: Dnevniki, stati, vospominaniya [Life of a Russian Cubist woman artist: Diaries, articles, memoirs], Moscow: "RA", 1994

Bibliography

V. Denisov, "Moskovskiye zhivopistsy v Leningrade" [Moscow painters in Leningrad], *Zhizn iskusstva*, no.8, 1928, pp.6–7
O. Beskin, *Formalizm v iskusstve* [Formalism in art], Moscow, 1933
Camilla Gray, *The Great Experiment: Russian Art, 1863–1922*, London: Thames and Hudson, and New York: Abrams, 1962
J.-P. Bouillon, "Le cubisme et l'avant-garde russe", *Actes du première colloque d'histoire de l'art contemporain: Université de Saint-Étienne, 1973*, pp.153–223
Kazimir Malevich, *The Artist, Infinity, Suprematism: Unpublished Writings, 1913–1933*, ed. Troels Andersen, Copenhagen: Borgen, 1978
Künstlerinnen der russischen Avantgarde/Women Artists of the Russian Avant-Garde, 1910–1930, exh. cat., Galerie Gmurzynska, Cologne, 1979
Angelica Zander Rudenstine, ed., *The George Costakis Collection: Russian Avant-Garde Art*, New York: Abrams, and London: Thames and Hudson, 1981
E. Zavadskaya, "Moy drug zhivopisets N.A. Udaltsova" [My friend, the painter N.A. Udaltsova], *Tvorchestvo*, no.10, 1986, pp.27–8
M.N. Yablonskaya, *Women Artists of Russia's New Age, 1900–1935*, New York: Rizzoli, and London: Thames and Hudson, 1990

Alexander Drevin, Nadezhda Udaltsova, exh. cat., Union of Soviet Artists Gallery, Moscow, 1991

De grote utopie/Die grosse Utopie/The Great Utopia, exh. cat., Stedelijk Museum, Amsterdam, and elsewhere, 1992

I. Schlagheck, "Geniale Tochter der russische Revolution", *Art*, no.3, March 1992, pp.32–47

Nadezhda Udaltsova's first artistic endeavours date from her early childhood as part of a large, aristocratic and cultured family in the ancient city of Orel, under the guidance of her well-educated, gentle mother, Vera Choglokova, who was descended from one of Russia's oldest noble families. The entire collection of Udaltsova's first drawings, made in coloured pencils, was carefully kept in her archive through revolutions and two world wars. In 1905 she entered the studio of the prominent Russian painter Konstantin Yuon. After looking at her childhood drawings, one of the instructors there told Udaltsova that she was already complete as an artist and that she merely needed to find herself in art. "My art is my life. That is true. I am an artist not only deeply inside my 'ego' and not only for myself – I am an artist. How many years I was afraid to call myself an artist. It is necessary to find the joy and goodness in everything. To live in joy, to love and to create in joy" (*Zhizn russkoy kubistki ...* 1994, p.28). These words, written ten years later, in 1916, became an artistic and personal motto that Udaltsova retained throughout her long and dramatic life, a life as full of joy as of suffering and struggle, which is so beautifully reflected in her recently published diaries.

After Udaltsova realised that Yuon's traditional method of painting differed from her own feelings and innovative ideas concerning art, she moved to the studio of the Hungarian artist Carol Kish, which was oriented towards the Munich school of Art Nouveau. On several occasions in 1911 she visited the Free Collective Studio, the Tower (*Bashnya*), where she became friendly with such leaders of the Russian avant-garde as Natalya Goncharova (q.v.), Mikhail Larionov, Vladimir Tatlin and Lyubov Popova (q.v.), who had just started her artistic career. In 1912, with Popova, Udaltsova went to Paris to study painting at La Palette, in the studios of the Cubist artists Henri Le Fauconnier and Jean Metzinger, which was very popular among Russian students. She was already familiar with European art: she had visited the famous Dresden Gallery in Germany in 1908, and a visit to Shchukin's private collection of French modernism in Moscow had introduced her to the work of Cézanne, Matisse, Gauguin, van Gogh and Picasso. But, according to her own later recollection, it was Paris that left the greatest impact on her life and career. Her one year there, spent entirely dedicated to art, made her aware for the first time of her unique creative individuality.

Initially, Udaltsova thought that Cubism was just another style, another method and school, but it became her passion. She was fascinated by its strong painterly structure and its reserved colour scale combined with the deep rational logic of the compositions. From that time she became an artist who was always searching for a logical explanation of phenomena and for a mathematically calculated rational sense of harmony. Her distaste for Eastern art seems shocking for the period; it was then extremely fashionable among young modernists. Anything even vaguely mystical, visionary or sublime seemed unacceptable to her; instead, she was drawn towards clarity and rationality with a materialistic approach. Udaltsova achieved fast progress in her artistic studies in Paris, but she still did not participate in exhibitions there and composed no outstanding works in France. Only after returning to Russia in 1913 was she able to release all her new experiences gained in Europe.

Soon after her return Udaltsova worked for a while in Tatlin's studio in Moscow, and in 1914 she decided to exhibit for the first time with the Jack of Diamonds group. During the next three or four years she created her best Cubist and abstract compositions, including such masterpieces of the Russian avant-garde as *Cubist Composition* (1915; State Russian Museum, St Petersburg), *Violin* (1914–15; Tretyakov Gallery, Moscow), *At the Piano* (1914–15; Yale University Art Gallery, New Haven) and *Musical Instruments* (1915; State Russian Museum), in which she gracefully explored the theme of music and musical harmony, one of the most typical of Cubist subjects; *Red Nude* (1915; Rostovo-Yaroslavl Art Museum, Rostov), with its rich, deep texture of different tones of red and grey; *Restaurant* (1915; State Russian Museum), with its reminiscences of Paris; and *Kitchen* (1915; State Russian Museum; all oil on canvas). The quiet harmony of the very simple still life in the last work recalls the traditions of French classicism rather than Cubism. Udaltsova was the most "classicist" and traditional in spirit of the Russian avant-garde artists of her generation. In her diaries she mentions, on the same page and sometimes in the same paragraph, Veronese, Titian and Poussin, Cézanne, Matisse and Picasso. In her diary she confessed that in 1915 the most influential and strong artistic experiences for her were from icons, in which she, like Malevich, saw "autonomous form thrown into space" (*Zhizn russkoy kubistki... 1994, p.28*).

Udaltsova's works of 1915–17 were executed in different styles and genres, ranging from Cubism to Suprematism, from painting to the applied arts and theatre design. Her main interest was in mastering the painterly texture, and sometimes, as in *Blue Jar* (1915; Tretyakov Gallery), the flat painterly surface is almost transformed into relief by the use of a heavy impasto. Some of her abstract compositions of the same period are known by her title *Non-Objective Studies in Texture*.

Towards the end of 1915 and early 1916 Udaltsova experienced the strong and extensive influence of Malevich's Suprematism. She joined his group, but although she created a series of small-scale Suprematist compositions in watercolour and gouache, she never applied this style to her oil painting. These compositions (most were created as sketches for embroidery designs) are very different from Malevich's idea of Suprematism – they are still strongly linked to the Cubist tradition of depicting and analysing objects, and sometimes she called them "Plane (two–dimensional) Cubism".

Like most artists of the Russian avant-garde, Udaltsova welcomed the October Revolution and collaborated with the new government, participating in different committees on art and education and other organisational activities. In 1918 she was offered a teaching position at the newly organised Free Artistic State Studio, and between 1920 and 1930 was a professor at Vkhutemas (Higher State Artistic and Technical Workshops) and later Vkhutein (Higher State Artistic and Technical Institute).

In 1921, with her husband, the artist Alexander Drevin, she left Inkhuk (Institute of Artistic Culture), disagreeing in principle with its new orientation towards Constructivism and "productive" (or "industrial") art, proclaimed by her former comrades Rodchenko, Stepanova, Popova and others. Udaltsova and Drevin returned to traditional easel painting, hoping to collaborate with the former members of the Jack of Diamonds, the Russian "Cézannists" Ilya Mashkov, Aristarkh Lentulov and Pyotr Konchalovsky. In the 1920s Udaltsova finally abandoned abstract art, turning again to Cézanne and his principles of composition, and finding new inspiration in nature.

Udaltsova's favourite genres in the late 1920s to 1940s were still life and landscape. In the 1920s and early 1930s she created three large series of landscapes, travelling with Drevin in the most distinctive parts of the Soviet Union – ancient Armenia and the wild regions of Altai and Ural:

> My own creative exertion (tension) gave way to passive meditation, experience of the surrounding nature, study of nature. Life in the city passed during the winter and in the summer we lived in the countryside with the wild and rural untouched nature. Ural with its mountains and dales, with its fast river Chusova, bears in the pine woods, greying cliffs, blue forests and blazing sunsets, villages on river banks, the melodic speech of women and children – all that was reflected in my landscapes of the time. Colour was the main structural element in my compositions. This trip...changed my work dramatically [Moscow 1991, p.92].

This new turn in her work towards compositional structure built on perspective and colour, though still interpreted in a dry and rational rather than emotional manner, is seen at its best in such compositions as *Ural, Forest* (1926; Tretyakov Gallery), *Ural: In the Mountains* (1927; State Russian Museum), in most of the *Altai* series (artist's family collection, Moscow), in *Armenia: Landscape with Figures* (1933; Tretyakov Gallery) and *In the Garden: Village, Armenia* (1933; Tretyakov Gallery; all oil on canvas).

The crucial change in Udaltsova's career occurred after Drevin was arrested and executed in 1938. As the wife of a victim of Stalin's regime, Udaltsova was ostracised. Her own life was in danger, and it was very difficult for her to sell any work. Despite the danger, she hid and saved all of Drevin's paintings left in his studio. During World War II she remained in Moscow, working intensively. She painted realistic portraits of war heroes, but mostly still lifes. The most expressive in its solemn simplicity, *Still Life: Bread (During the War)* (1942; State Russian Museum), is one of the highlights of her late period. Among others are *Mimosa on a White Tablecloth* (1948; State Russian Museum), *Autumn:*

Onion in the Bowl (1952; Tretyakov Gallery) and *Kitchen Table* (1960; State Russian Museum).

In the late 1940s, however, Udaltsova's art and personality were again under officially sanctioned attack by Soviet art critics, who accused her of "formalism in painting" and "worshipping Western culture". Udaltsova's painterly realism of her late period never went along with the official principles of Socialist Realism. Her realistic style was influenced by the Renaissance masters and by French painting of the 19th and 20th centuries, was inspired by meditations on nature, and always existed outside the strict laws of Soviet ideology.

NINA GURYANOVA

Uranga, Remedios *see* Varo

Valadon, Suzanne   [fig. 70]
French painter and graphic artist, 1865–1938

Born Marie-Clementine Valadon in Bessines-sur-Gartempe, Haute Vienne, 23 September 1865, the illegitimate daughter of a sewing maid; grew up in Montmartre, Paris. Began working as an artist's model, *c.*1880. Son Maurice Valadon (the artist Maurice Utrillo) born 1883; Spanish journalist Miquel Utrillo y Molins claimed to be his father, 1891. Affair with composer Erik Satie, 1893. Married a well-to-do clerk, Paul Mousis, 1896; separated 1909; divorced. Lived with painter André Utter from 1909; married him, 1914. Bought château at Saint-Bernard in the Saône valley, 1923; subsequently divided time between Saint-Bernard and Paris. Exhibited at Société Nationale des Beaux-Arts, 1894; Salon d'Automne from 1909; Salon des Indépendants from 1911; Salon des Femmes Artistes Modernes, 1933–8, all in Paris. Sociétaire, Salon d'Automne, 1920; member, Femmes Artistes Modernes, 1933. Died in Paris, 7 April 1938.

Selected Individual Exhibitions
Galerie Clovis Sagot, Paris: 1911
Galerie Berthe Weill, Paris: 1915 (with André Utter), 1921 (with Utrillo), 1922 (twice, both with Utrillo), 1927 (retrospective), 1928
John Levy Gallery, Paris: 1921
Galerie Dalpayat, Limoges: 1922 (with André Utter and Utrillo)
Galerie Bernheim-Jeune, Paris: 1923 (with Utrillo), 1925 (with André Utter and Utrillo)
Galerie des Archers, Lyon: 1928
Galerie Bernier, Paris: 1929 (twice), 1937, 1939 (retrospective)
Galerie au Portique, Paris: 1931, 1932
Galerie le Centaure, Brussels: 1931 (retrospective)
Moos Gallery, Geneva: 1932 (with André Utter and Utrillo)
Galerie Georges Petit, Paris: 1932 (retrospective)

Selected Writings
Suzanne Valadon par elle-même, Paris: Promothée, 1939 (with Germain Bazin)

Bibliography
André Tabarant, "Suzanne Valadon et ses souvenirs de modèle", *Bulletin de la Vie Artistique*, 15 December 1921, pp.626–9
Robert Rey, *Suzanne Valadon*, Paris: Nouvelle Revue Française, 1922
Adolf Basler, *Suzanne Valadon*, Paris: Crès, 1929
Suzanne Valadon, exh. cat., Galerie Georges Petit, Paris, 1932
Jean Bouret, *Suzanne Valadon*, Paris: Pétridès, 1947
Robert Beachboard, *La Trinité maudite: Valadon, Utter, Utrillo*, Paris: Amiot-Dumont, 1952
John Storm, *The Valadon Drama: The Life of Suzanne Valadon*, New York: Dutton, 1958; as *The Valadon Story*, London: Longman, 1959
Suzanne Valadon, exh. cat., Musée National d'Art Moderne, Paris, 1967
Paul Pétridès, *L'Oeuvre complet de Suzanne Valadon*, Paris: Compagnie Française des Arts Graphiques, 1971
Jeanine Warnod, *Suzanne Valadon*, New York: Crown, 1981 (French original)
Sarah Bayliss, *Utrillo's Mother*, London: Pandora, 1987; New Brunswick, NJ: Rutgers University Press, 1989
Rosemary Betterton, "How do women look? The female nude in the work of Suzanne Valadon", *Looking On: Images of Femininity in the Visual Arts and Media*, ed. Rosemary Betterton, London and New York: Pandora, 1987, pp.217–34 (expanded version of article first published in *Feminist Review*, no.19, March 1985)
Patricia Mathews, "Returning the gaze: Diverse representations of the nude in the art of Suzanne Valadon", *Art Bulletin*, lxxiii, 1991, pp.415–30
Thérèse Diamond Rosinsky, *Suzanne Valadon*, New York: Universe, 1994
Gill Perry, *Women Artists and the Parisian Avant-Garde*, Manchester: Manchester University Press, and New York: St Martin's Press, 1995

Suzanne Valadon, exh. cat., Fondation Pierre Gianadda, Martigny, 1996

June Rose, *Mistress of Montmartre: A Life of Suzanne Valadon*, London: Cohen, 1997

Suzanne Valadon is now one of the best documented French women artists of the early 20th century, and her work has aroused much interest among feminist art historians, especially her bold, unconventional images of women and the female nude. Much has been written about Valadon's working-class background as the illegitimate daughter of a domestic worker, and her early art "training" in Montmartre. Without the means to pay for tuition in an art academy (many of which charged higher fees for women than for men), Valadon was partly self-taught, and gained early experience of the Parisian art world on the streets of Montmartre – in the studios where her mother worked as a cleaner, and from the artists for whom she posed from the age of 15 to 28. These included Puvis de Chavannes, Pierre-Auguste Renoir and Toulouse-Lautrec, more academic artists such as Jean-Jacques Henner and Hector Leroux, and the Realist painter Giuseppe de Nittis. Her early interest in drawing was encouraged by her friendship with Edgar Degas, who bought many of her sketches. He also taught her the technique of soft-ground etching in 1895, and over the next 20 years Valadon worked extensively on soft-ground etchings, lithographs and drawings, many of which she subsequently destroyed. Her subjects included adolescent girls and boys, for which her son Maurice Utrillo was often the model, and women and girls engaged in their toilette, a theme that echoes some of the so-called modern-life subjects of Degas and Toulouse-Lautrec. But unlike the more voyeuristic images of women bathing by these better-established male painters, Valadon's works on this theme are characterised by a strong, almost severe use of line, and candid, sometimes awkward images of bathing women and children. The harshness of her linear style and imagery led some critics to describe her works as "virile" or somehow uncharacteristic of "feminine" art (the paradigmatic example of which was generally seen to be the art of Marie Laurencin, q.v.). Such critical assumptions continued to feature in reviews of Valadon's graphic and painted work throughout her career.

She did not take up painting seriously until around 1909, and during the years leading up to the outbreak of World War I produced a series of large-scale allegorical works, several of which were shown at the Salon d'Automne and the Salon des Indépendants. These include *Joy of Life* (1911; Metropolitan Museum of Art, New York) and *The Future Unveiled; or, The Fortune-Teller* (1912; Musée du Petit Palais, Geneva). These are both works in which the nude incorporates a wide range of literal and symbolic possibilities of meaning. Both rework iconographical conventions for the representation of the female nude: in the *Joy of Life* Valadon reworks the popular bathers-in-nature theme, recalling Matisse's famous painting of 1906 with the same title; and in *The Future Unveiled* she produces an image reminiscent of the traditional "odalisque" theme in which a milky-white female body reclines horizontally across the canvas space. But both works offer possibilities for more diverse narrative interpretations. In *Joy of Life* Valadon employs a variety of seemingly unconnected poses, based on art-historical precedents, for her female protagonists, who are watched by a nude male spectator on the right (for whom her partner André Utter was the model). These female figures seem strangely separate from each other, from the male viewer and from the nature that surrounds them. Far from evoking a utopian harmony of woman and nature suggested by, for example, Matisse or Gauguin, Valadon's robust and sharply outlined women suggest a more ambiguous, dislocated relationship with both nature and the male spectator.

The Future Unveiled reveals even more complex layers of narrative and allegorical meaning. It combines the conventions of "odalisque" painting with the allegory of the card player who foretells the future as she holds up the queen of diamonds. Patricia Mathews (1991) has argued that the "symbolism of the queen of diamonds held in the hand of the fortune-teller directly related the allegory to the reading of the odalisque as a sexualized body. The card connecting the two women's bodies is a sign for the feminine principle, of physicality and the senses, and of money matters. In conjunction with the four kings in the circular arrangement of cards, it evokes a prostitute or courtesan". She suggests that the painting could thus be seen to lead to a moralising reading of the nude, as it both implicates the folly of indulgence in card-games and fortune-telling, an activity usually performed by Gypsies, and the eroticism of the courtesan. But Valadon's mode of representing this female nude could also be seen to undermine the conventional associations of the odalisque theme. The woman does not assume a passive reclining pose but seems to be actively engaged with the fortune-teller. Moreover, her heavy, sharply defined body lacks the sensual eroticism associated with 19th-century interpretations of the theme.

Valadon's interest in the nude was not confined to studies of the female body, although her painted male nudes were produced mostly for her large-scale historical and allegorical works from the period 1909–14, when she used Utter as her model. Even her male nudes were seen to disrupt convention, for she was not permitted to show her *Adam and Eve* of 1909 (Musée National d'Art Moderne, Centre Georges Pompidou, Paris) in the Salon des Indépendants of 1920 until she had painted vine leaves over Adam's genitalia. After Utter was called up on military service in 1914, depictions of the male nude disappear from her work, an absence that coincided with a move away from Valadon's ambitious, large-scale exhibition pieces.

Tensions and contradictions in both the sexual and narrative meanings of her work are also evident in some of her less ambitious, more intimate portraits of (sometimes nude) women and men that she continued to produce during the 1920s and 1930s. After receiving a contract from the dealer Bernheim Jeune in 1924 she enjoyed one of the most successful periods of her career, and gained an international reputation. Like many women artists who worked outside the established avant-garde groups of the time, she tended to be represented as an "independent" artist on the fringes of the broadly labelled "School of Paris". Her resistance to – and reworkings of – both academic and avant-garde conventions for representing the female nude have encouraged interest in her work within recent feminist art history. It has been argued that many of her images of women signal a form of resistance to some of the dominant representations of female sexuality in early 20th-century Western art. Many of her nudes painted from the 1910s onwards are heavily proportioned and sometimes awkwardly posed. They are conspicuously at odds with the svelte, elongated adolescent body that became the ideal "feminine" type to be found in the imagery of both popular and "high" art (see, for example, the imagery of women in the work of Laurencin and van Dongen) in the 1920s. In, for example, her *Nude with Striped Coverlet* (1922; Musée d'Art Moderne de la Ville de Paris) and *Reclining Nude*

(1928; Metropolitan Museum of Art) she uses strong outlines reminiscent of her earlier drawings, rich colour, and places the figures boldly across the foreground picture plane to suggest a powerful yet unerotic presence. *Reclining Nude* appears to undermine the conventions of passive, erotic display associated with the "odalisque" pose in that the woman literally shields her body; it is closed to a voyeuristic gaze.

Valadon's ability to produce some unconventional images of the female nude has been partly explained with reference to her unusual class position and background. Most successful women artists of her period came from middle-class backgrounds that could provide economic support for an art training and an often risky professional life. Unconstrained by an academic training, she may have felt better able to break with artistic conventions. Moreover, her experiences as a model may have encouraged her interest in the theme of the female nude, and enabled her to approach it from the position of a woman's experience of her own body. Unusually for a woman artist, she produced several nude self-portraits, which provide self-images from different periods of her career. These are unselfconscious images, boldly painted and free from any suggestion of "feminine" softness or available sexuality. Many of the later self-portraits reveal a frank representation of the artist's ageing in the depiction of precisely those parts of the female anatomy that could signify the ideal of youthful "feminine" beauty. She bravely depicts fallen breasts and jowls, and heavy drooping eyes, but with an air of resignation and acceptance, signified by the addition of a necklace and make-up (e.g. *Portrait with Bare Breasts*, 1931; private collection, repr. Rosinsky 1994, p.83).

Although she is better known for her portraits and studies of the female nude, still-life and landscape paintings formed an important part of Valadon's artistic output in the 1920s and 1930s. Her first known landscapes date from the 1910s, and include a series of views of the rue Cortot in Montmartre, where she lived and worked between 1914 and 1926. Scenes of Montmartre were also the subject of many of Utrillo's works from this period, which were in great demand in the 1920s, and which may have inhibited her own interest in this genre. Still lifes, especially flower paintings, began to appear in her work from around 1900. The reason that the genre does not appear earlier is probably because she had little experience of still-life painting while working as an artist's model. Thérèse Diamand Rosinsky has argued:

> As a model she never observed the artists for whom she posed painting still lifes. Therefore, she had no first-hand observation of the subject and might have thought it an unimportant genre. The images she saw on the posters, in newspaper cartoons and even the illustrations in teaching manuals focused on the human figure and physiognomy [*ibid.*, p.109].

The genre was popular with clients and patrons, however, and flower paintings feature prominently in her work from the 1920s, when they often include many personalised references. She frequently dedicated such works to close friends for whom she included inscriptions on the back of the frame, or flowers chosen for their symbolic significance. Many contemporary critics emphasised the gendered associations of this genre, seeing flower painting as a relatively superficial or "feminine" subject matter, without intellectual meaning and thus best suited to women painters. Yet flower paintings and still lifes are among the most complex of Valadon's works, often replete with symbolic meanings, personal references and possible narratives. For example, in her *Still Life with Violin* (1928; Musée d'Art Moderne de la Ville de Paris) she employs an elaborate composition dominated by a violin, its case, rich folds of red drapery and a dog-eared paperback, with flowers in a pitcher and large pot in the background. As a backdrop to these objects, she includes an autobiographical reference by reproducing the corner of her large exhibition piece *Casting of the Net* of 1914. This corner shows only the thighs and legs of her male protagonists, for whom she had used Utter as a model, with Valadon's signature and date written across the lower torso of the right-hand figure.

Although Valadon's work has recently been reassessed in terms of the unconventional imagery of women and feminine sexuality that it demonstrates, she did not espouse any feminist causes, and was sceptical of organised feminism. Such organisations were viewed with suspicion by many liberal political and social groups during the first few decades of the 20th century, despite the increasing public interest in "the woman question". Like many women painters of her era, Valadon saw herself as an "independent", engaged with a more personal aesthetic agenda and working separately from those avant-garde interests that have shaped most histories of modernism. While this representation provides a convenient framework within which to explain her position within the art history of the period, much work still remains to be done on the complex relationship of her art to the styles and culture of the early 20th-century avant-garde.

GILL PERRY

Vallayer-Coster, Anne
French painter, 1744–1818

Born Anne Vallayer in Gobelins, 21 December 1744; father a goldsmith at the royal tapestry manufactory. Moved to central Paris with her family, 1757. Nothing known of her training. Elected member of the Académie Royale, 1770. Granted title "painter to the queen", 1780. Allocated lodgings in the Louvre, 1781. Married lawyer Jean-Pierre-Silvestre Coster, 1781. Died in Paris, 28 February 1818.

Principal Exhibitions

Paris Salon: 1771, 1773, 1775, 1777, 1779, 1781, 1783, 1785, 1787, 1789, 1795, 1798, 1800–02, 1804, 1810, 1817

Bibliography

Marianne Michel, "A propos d'un tableau retrouvé de Vallayer-Coster", *Bulletin de la Société de l'Histoire de l'Art Français, 1965*, 1966, pp.185–90

Denis Diderot, *Salons*, ed. Jean Seznec and Jean Adhémar, iv, Oxford: Clarendon Press, 1967

Marianne Roland Michel, *Anne Vallayer-Coster, 1744–1818*, Paris: CIL, 1970

Les Femmes peintres au XVIIIe siècle, exh. cat., Musée Goya, Castres, 1973

French Painting, 1774–1830: The Age of Revolution, exh. cat., Grand Palais, Paris, and elsewhere, 1974

Women Artists, 1550–1950, exh. cat., Los Angeles County Museum of Art, and elsewhere, 1976

Chardin and the Still-Life Tradition in France, exh. cat., Cleveland Museum of Art, 1979

Charles Sterling, *Still-Life Painting from Antiquity to the Twentieth Century*, New York: Harper, 1981 (French original, 1952)

Anne Vallayer was born at the royal tapestry manufactory of the Gobelins. In 1757 her father, Joseph

Vallayer, having gained his mastership as a gold-smith, opened his own studio in Paris where he held the Royal Privilege for the production of military medals and the cross of the Order of St Louis. This background may help to account for the royal favour and aristocratic patronage that Vallayer-Coster was to enjoy during her career as a painter and it may also account for her admittance into the Académie Royale at the early age of 26, a month after the appointment of Jean-Baptiste Pierre, who may have been a family friend, as First Painter to the King. Anne Vallayer took the name Vallayer-Coster after her marriage in 1781 to Jean-Pierre-Silvestre Coster, an *avocat* to the Parlement of Paris and a member of a noble family of financiers and courtiers. The marriage took place at Versailles and the marriage contract includes the signature of Queen Marie-Antoinette.

Although the basic components of Vallayer-Coster's art did not vary much, her output was not restricted to paintings of still life and flowers. She produced miniatures, large decorative panels of animals and trophies of the hunt, painted *trompe-l'oeil* bas reliefs of fictive plaster sculpture and full-size portraits, including the one of the Royal medal-maker *Roettiers* (1777; Musée de Versailles). Her portraits were, however, harshly criticised by contemporary writers and she stopped producing them after 1789. She may well have suffered from the scathing comparisons that were made between her work in this genre and that of her fellow women academicians, the specialist portrait painters, Elisabeth Vigée-Lebrun (q.v.) and Adélaïde Labille-Guiard (q.v.).

It was as a painter of still life that Vallayer-Coster first achieved prominence. Somewhat exceptionally, she was approved and received into the Academy on the same day, 28 July 1770, on the basis of two imposing public pieces of virtuoso painting, *Allegory of the Arts* (1769) and *Instruments of Music* (1770; both Louvre, Paris). These subjects had been painted by Chardin and, superficially, the compositions might seem to follow the lead he had set. In manner and technique they are, however, quite different. Texture, colour and the application of paint are rich, sensuously tactile and serve to embellish the richness of the visual display. The table on which the instruments of music have been carefully posed is covered by a rich green velvet cloth fringed with a gold tassel. Against a mottled grey-brown background, the range of assorted instruments creates strong diagonals and forcefully curved forms in space. The lute, resting vertically against the pulpit and with a light blue ribbon loosely knotted round the pegs of its sound board, shows the confident marks of an individual, personal and creative contribution to the genre.

Vallayer-Coster first exhibited flower paintings at the Salon of 1775 at a time when she was cultivating a wealthy and aristocratic clientele and during the most prolific and successful decade of her career. A fine example of this type of work is her *Vase of Flowers and Shell* (1780; Metropolitan Museum of Art, New York). In the centre of the oval canvas a lavish bunch of fresh flowers has been arranged in a bronze-mounted blue vase that rests on a grey stone ledge. To the left of the vase lies a shell providing an obvious and exotic contrast in shape, form and colour. The juxtaposition of animate and inanimate objects creates much visual interest and also reflects contemporary interest in the cataloguing and recording of botanical specimens. The objects exist as isolated in themselves but are displayed so as to contribute to the unity and harmony of the composition as a whole. A cool and distanced observation of detail has been combined with a lively handling of the coloured pigment. The subtle variations and tonalities achieve the palpable effect of pastel in oil paint – a proto-Impressionist technique that precedes the flower paintings of Henri Fantin-Latour.

Vallayer-Coster was always firmly attached to the aristocratic tastes of her noble patrons. These patrons included some of the highest in the land. In 1781 she finally obtained lodgings in the Louvre through the personal interventions of the First Painter to the King, Pierre, the Director General of the King's Buildings, the Comte d'Angiviller and the queen, Marie-Antoinette. A clear mark of the queen's favour is the listing of her painting of a Vestal Virgin as belonging to the queen in the Salon catalogue of 1779. Other purchasers of her paintings included the Prince de Conti, the Comte de Merle and the Marquis and Marquise de Créqui. These patrons were courtiers of the noblest of ranks, but her works were also collected by other persons of influence and important State officials such as, for instance, M. Beaujon, Councillor of State, Receiver General to the Finances of the Generality of Rouen and Honorary Treasurer to the royal and military Order of St Louis (Roland Michel 1970, p.50).

The forms and content of Vallayer-Coster's finely crafted bravura paintings show little thematic or stylistic evolution, in spite of the turbulent times through which she lived and the high-minded Neo-classical innovations of Jacques-Louis David and his school. The same compositional patterns and motifs occur again and again, although there are subtle variations of arrangement and of detail. Dead game hang down; red coral, exotic shells and madrepore come to be juxtaposed with a small plaster statuette of an antique female deity, a bronze mounted blue vase; against a mottled grey-brown background a pink ham with a knife sticking out is set against a broken bread roll; peaches or apples are piled up into pyramids; a wicker basket is filled to overflowing with vine leaves and bunches of grapes. The elongated forms of bunches of radishes, round porcelain tea sets, glasses of water, nuts are all used in a variety of combinations so as to create sumptuous pictorial effects. *Still Life with Game* (1782) and *Lobster, Silver Tureen, Fruit and Bread on a Table* (1781; both Museum of Art, Toledo) were exhibited in the Salon of 1783 as the property of Girardot de Marigny. They form pendants; the game is strung up to hang down from a tree in the open air while the pink, cooked lobster dominates the interior scene of the richly laden table. Such subjects were not generally the province of women artists, and contemporary Salon critics such as Denis Diderot and Louis Petit de Bachaumont almost always remarked on Vallayer-Coster's achievements as a woman in a genre that was held to be the preserve of men. She was, however, much more harshly criticised for her portrait painting, especially for those she exhibited at the Salon of 1785. About a now lost portrait of an anonymous bishop, Bachaumont noted that it was vexing to see Vallayer-Coster abandon still life where she had superiority for portraiture where she was inferior to her female rivals and that the bishop looked shameful in his corner (*Mémoires secrets, deuxième lettre,* 22 September 1785). These comments are revealing for the implied comparison with Vigée-Lebrun and Labille-Guiard, for the increasing importance of the Salon and the positioning of a work of art within the Salon hang as a marker of public opinion, and for notions of genre hierarchy and of hierarchies in general at this time.

Vallayer-Coster returned to the subject of still life with a lobster in the last painting she exhibited at the Paris Salon, *A Table with Lobster, Different Fruits, Game etc.* (1817; Mobilier National, Paris). Her picture-making was far removed from the smooth finish and emblematic symbolism of a 17th-century Dutch *vanitas* painting, yet in this last Salon piece, which she appears to have donated to the king, a spray of white lilies, emblem of the now-restored Bourbon monarchy, has been carefully isolated out. The painting as a whole still serves, though, as a forceful summation of much of the oeuvre of Vallayer-Coster and of the taste and luxury, before the Revolution, of her rich patrons, which she, faithfully and with much loyalty, celebrated.

VALERIE MAINZ

van Heemskerck, Jacoba *see*

Heemskerck

van Hemessen, Catharina *see*

Hemessen

van Oosterwijck, Maria *see*

Oosterwijck

van Schurman, Anna Maria *see*

Schurman

Varo, Remedios

Spanish painter, 1908–1963

Born in Anglés, Spain, 16 December 1908. Settled in Madrid with her family, 1917. Studied at Academia de San Fernando, Madrid, 1924–30. Married (1) painter Gerardo Lizarraga, 1930; separated 1936; (2) Surrealist poet Benjamin Péret, 1940s; separated 1947; (3) businessman Walter

Gruen, 1952. Lived in Barcelona, 1932–7; moved to Paris and joined the Surrealists, 1937; settled in Mexico, 1941; became close friend of Leonora Carrington (q.v.); active in the group of European exile artists. Died in Mexico City, 8 October 1963.

Principal Exhibitions

Academia de San Fernando, Madrid: 1934

Glorieta Catalonia-Librería, Barcelona: 1936 (*Lógicofobista*)

London Gallery, London: 1937 (*Surrealist Objects and Poems*)

Nippon Salon, Tokyo: 1937 (*Exposition internationale du surréalisme*)

Galería de Arte Mexicano, Mexico City: 1940 (*Exposición internacional del surrealismo*, touring)

Galerie Maeght, Paris: 1947 (*Le Surréalisme en 1947*)

Galería Diana, Mexico City: 1955 (group), 1956 (individual)

Galería de Arte Contemporáneo, Mexico City: 1956 (*Salon Frida Kahlo*)

Galerías Excelsior, Mexico City: 1958 (*Salon de la plástica femenina*), 1959

INBA, Mexico City: 1960 (*Bienial: Pintura mexicana*)

Instituto de Arte Contemporáneo, Mexico City: 1961 (*Pintura mexicana contemporánea de la Galería de Antonio Souza de México*)

Museo Nacional de Arte Moderno, Mexico City: 1961 (*El retrato mexicano contemporáneo*)

Galería Juan Martín, Mexico City: 1961 (group), 1962 (individual)

Instituto Nacional de Bellas Artes, Mexico City: 1964 (retrospective)

Selected Writings

De homo Rodans, Mexico City: Calli-Nova, 1970 (under pseudonym Halikcio von Fuhrangschmidt)

Cartas, sueños y otros textos, ed. Isabel Castells, Mexico: Universidad Autónoma de Tlaxcala, 1994

Bibliography

Dictionnaire abrégé du surréalisme, Paris: Galerie Beaux-Arts, 1938

International Exhibition of Surrealism, exh. cat., Galería de Arte Mexicano, Mexico City, 1940

Edouard Jaguer, *Remedios Varo*, Paris: Filippachi, 1963 (contains numerous illustrations)

La obra de Remedios Varo, exh. cat., Instituto Nacional de Bellas Artes, Mexico City, 1964

Octavio Paz and Roger Caillois, *Remedios Varo*, Mexico City: Era, 1966

Ida Rodriguez Prampolini, *El surrealismo y el arte fantástico de México*, Mexico City: Universidad Nacional Autónoma de México, 1969

Obra de Remedios Varo, 1913/1963, exh. cat., Museo de Arte Moderno, Mexico City, 1971

Karen Petersen and J.J. Wilson, *Women Artists: Recognition and Reappraisal*, New York: Harper, 1976; London: Women's Press, 1978

Obliques, no.14–15, 1977 (special issue: *La Femme surréaliste*)

L'altra metà dell'avanguardia, 1910–1940: Pittrici e scultrici nei movimenti delle avanguardie storiche, exh. cat., Palazzo Reale, Milan, and elsewhere, 1980

Remedios Varo, 1913–1963, exh. cat., Museo de Arte Moderno, Mexico City, 1983

Artistic Collaboration in the Twentieth Century, exh. cat., Hirshhorn Museum, Washington, DC, 1984

Estella Lauter, *Women as Mythmakers: Poetry and Visual Art by Twentieth-Century Women*, Bloomington: Indiana University Press, 1984

Whitney Chadwick, *Women Artists and the Surrealist Movement*, London: Thames and Hudson, and Boston: Little Brown, 1985

Science in Surrealism: The Art of Remedios Varo, exh. cat., New York Academy of Sciences, 1986

Janet A. Kaplan, "Art essay: Remedios Varo", *Feminist Studies*, xiii/1, 1987

Remedios Varo, exh. cat., Fundación Banco Exterior, Madrid, 1988

Surrealismo a Catalunya, 1924–36, exh. cat., Centro Cultural Santa Mónica, Barcelona, 1988

Georgiana M.M. Colvile, "Beauty and/is the beast: Animal symbology in the work of Leonora Carrington, Remedios Varo and Leonor Fini", *Surrealism and Women*, ed. Mary Ann Caws and others, Cambridge: Massachusetts Institute of Technology Press, 1991, pp.159–81

Remedios Varo: Arte y literatura, exh. cat., Museo de Teruel, Spain, 1991

Renée Riese Hubert, *Magnifying Mirrors: Women, Surrealism and Partnership*, Lincoln: University of Nebraska Press, 1994

Janet A. Kaplan, *Unexpected Journeys: The Art and Life of Remedios Varo*, 2nd edition, New York: Abbeville, 1994 (contains extensive bibliography and illustrations)

Remedios Varo, 1908–1963, exh. cat., Museo de Arte Moderno, Mexico City, 1994

Ricardo Ovalle and others, *Remedios Varo: Catalogo Razonado*, Mexico City: ERA, 1994 (contains numerous illustrations)

Deborah J. Haynes, "The art of Remedios Varo: Issues of gender ambiguity and religious meaning", *Woman's Art Journal*, xvi/1, 1995, pp.26–32

Péret-Varo Papers are in the International Rescue Committee Archives, State University of New York, Albany; Péret Letters are in the Trotsky archives, Harvard University, Cambridge, Massachusetts; Varo Papers are in the Water Gruen archive, Mexico City.

The painter Remedios Varo was born in Spain, worked in France and gained renown after settling in Mexico. She was part of many worlds: Catholic convent schools and the Fine Arts Academy of Madrid as a young student; the artistic vanguard of Barcelona during the years of the Spanish Republic; the Parisian Surrealist group (including the French poet Benjamin Péret, who became the second of her three husbands), with whom she exhibited early experimental work, most notable among them a little oil on copper, *Double Agent* (1936; Isidore Ducasse Fine Arts, New York, repr. Kaplan 1994, p.49); the chaos of wartime Marseille and Casablanca, where she sought to arrange the many documents needed to escape from the Nazis; and finally, the hospitable refuge of Mexico where she created her mature work. Varo's startling and distinctive paintings were greeted with such resounding critical and popular success in Mexico that from her first solo exhibition in 1956 she had to establish waiting lists for her many eager patrons.

Dead of a heart attack at the age of 55, Varo left an innovative legacy of mature paintings, produced in the short span of ten years, which retains a significant position in 20th-century Mexican art. Her earlier work has recently been recognised as well, both that done in Paris and that from her earlier association with the avant-garde of pre-Civil War Barcelona. Among the most widely exhibited of these are a series of remarkable collages, including the *Anatomy Lesson* (1935; Marcel Jean, Paris, *ibid.*, p.41), and composite images created collaboratively from chance associations, as in *Cadavre exquis* (1935; Museum of Modern Art, New York, *ibid.*, p.39) – works that speak of the importance of Spain's cultural contributions to the development of modernism in Europe.

Throughout Varo's work modernism is worked out in the kitchen and the parlour, where images and ideas are brewed and stewed and cooked and knitted and embroidered. Slyly shifting the Surrealist stage from the boudoir to the kitchen, she established culinary activities as a particularly potent site for experimentation in the occult, undertaking investigations that ranged from infamous experiments with farcical recipes to serious study of alchemy, science, magic, mysticism and the occult. In *Embroidering Earth's Mantle* (1961) the art of needlework, long used as a means of acculturation for docile femininity, is transformed into a god-like act of creation and a site of subversive empowerment. Spilling forth from tower battlements is the fabric of the world, created by sequestered schoolgirls working with materials distilled in an alchemi-

cal alembic. Their embroidered cosmology, including a landscape of houses, ponds, streams and boats, is "women's work", here presented as an incantatory process that initiates transformation of the marvellous from the mundane. In many of Varo's works female characters employ alchemical methods, as in *Creation of the Birds* (1958; private collection, *ibid.*, p.180), where a female owl artist/musician uses a palette of materials synthesised through a process of alchemical distillation to create that most highly prized of magical creations, an image that comes to life, here a drawn bird that takes flight out of a window.

In Varo's fantastically constructed universe, the properties of the organic and inorganic, the scientific and magical, the natural and technological, interchange and overlap. Peopled by insect geologists (*Discovery of a Mutant Geologist*, 1961), wood nymph musicians (*Solar Music*, 1955; private collection, *ibid.*, p.127) and enchanted astronomers (*Revelation; or, The Clockmaker*, 1955; private collection, *ibid.*, p.175), it is a world that challenges preconceived assumptions about how things ought to work. In *Unexpected Presence* (1959; private collection, *ibid.*, p.158) chairbacks open to reveal human faces; in *Emerging Light* (1962; private collection, *ibid.*, p.165) bodies emerge from behind walls; in *Useless Science or the Alchemist* (1955; private collection, *ibid.*, p.126) the hard is made pliable; in *Toward the Tower* (1961; private collection, *ibid.*, p.19) the soft stiffens; and in *Farewell* (1958; private collection, *ibid.*, p.209) bodies and their shadows become interchangeable. Inspired by images from Bosch, Goya and El Greco that she had studied at the Prado in Madrid as well as the Romanesque Catalan frescoes, medieval and Renaissance architecture and veiled women of North Africa that she had seen in her early years of family travel, Varo created a world alive with the possible, the incantatory and the magical, set in the everyday.

While Surrealism was the movement within which Varo developed, the work she produced in her Mexican years is marked by an ironic, even taunting ambivalence towards Surrealist theory and practice, particularly pointed in its critique around issues related to women. Central to this stance is a challenge to authority or, in terms derived from one of Varo's paintings, a "dropping of the father". In *Woman Leaving the Psychoanalyst* (1961; private collection, *ibid.*, p.154) – rather than the son's transgression that was the Oedipal stock-in-trade of the male Surrealists – it is a daughter who, on leaving the offices of Dr FJA (representing Freud, Jung and Adler), proceeds, quite literally, to drop the head of her father into a nearby well, claiming her independence through this psychological rite of passage. Throughout her work Varo offered an alternative iconography specifically counter to the orthodoxies of male-defined Surrealist theory with its proscribed and limited role for woman as muse to male creativity. Transferring power across gender lines and conferring heroic authority on women, Varo's work is based on woman's psychology and experiences in which her access to the marvellous relies on the self as active agent.

In many paintings Varo adopted a strategy of transposition of traditionally male mythic heroes into female form. A female Minotaur holds a magical key before a mysterious floating keyhole (*Minotaur*, 1959; private collection, *ibid.*, p.184); a female Pan in the form of a woodland nymph with owlish eyes and feathery body plays a double reed (*Troubador*, 1959; private collection, *ibid.*, p.192); there is even a female Ulysses setting off in a waistcoat to explore uncharted waters (*Exploration of the Sources of the Orinoco River*, 1959; private collection, *ibid.*, p.168). Although many of the characters in Varo's paintings are androgynous or asexual, in these mythological transformations she was careful to delineate the female anatomy of her heroines.

Throughout her finely wrought compositions Varo's style carries a nostalgic echo of the illuminated manuscript, that document of obsessive belief in the transformative power of seeing the whole world in the finest moment of detail. In works such as *Mimesis* (1960; private collection, *ibid.*, p.159) she employed old master techniques of glazing and varnishing, perfected through her years of rigorous training, to create paintings, often, as here, in oil on masonite, that are masterfully rendered and painstakingly executed. Theatrical in her miniaturist vision, she created carefully constructed narrative tableaux as doll's house-like stage sets, here the fairy-tale world of a woman, immobilised in an armchair, whose skin has taken on the pallor of its fleur-de-lis upholstery, her feet and hands turned to wood. Just as fairy tales have long been used to encode subversive knowledge, so Varo used her fabulist style as a form of masking and masquerade, as a ploy to belie the power of her critique, here

directed towards the condition of women whose vitality has been enervated by domestic isolation. In both style and content, Varo's work offers a strong subversive voice within the Surrealist idiom, a subtle but forceful alternative presented from a distinctly female perspective.

JANET A. KAPLAN

Vieira da Silva, Maria Elena
Portuguese painter, 1908–1992

Born in Lisbon, 13 June 1908. Studied drawing under Emilia Santos Braga, painting under Armando Lucena, professor at the Academia de Belas-Artes, Lisbon, 1919–27; sculpture under Antoine Bourdelle at Académie de la Grande Chaumière, Paris, 1928–9; engraving under Stanley William Hayter at Atelier 17, Paris. Exhibited at Salon des Surindépendants, Paris, 1930. Married Hungarian painter Arpad Szenes, 1930; he died 1985. Lived in Paris, 1929–39; Lisbon, 1935–6 and 1939–40; Brazil, 1940–47; Paris from 1947. Naturalised French citizen, 1956. Recipient of Acquisition prize, 1953, and Grand International prize, 1962, São Paulo Bienal; Tapestry prize, University of Basel, 1954; Grand Prix National des Arts, Paris, 1963; Grand Crois de Santiago da Espada, Lisbon, 1977; Grand Prix Florence Gould, Académie des Beaux-Arts, Paris, 1986; Grand Prix Antena 1, Lisbon, 1986; Gra-Cruz da Ordem da Liberdade du Portugal, 1988; Ordre du Mérite, Paris, 1988. Chevalier, 1960, and Commandeur, 1962, Ordre des Arts et Lettres, Paris; Member, Academy of Arts, Lisbon, 1970; Chevalier, Légion d'Honneur, France, 1979; Member, Académie des Sciences, des Arts et des Lettres, Paris, 1984; honorary member, Royal Academy, London, and Art Gallery of Ontario, Canada, 1988. Fundação Arpad Szenes-Vieira da Silva founded in Lisbon, 1989. Died in Paris, 6 March 1992.

Selected Individual Exhibitions
Galerie Jeanne Bucher, Paris: 1933, 1937, 1939, 1947, 1951, 1960, 1963, 1967, 1969, 1971, 1976, 1982, 1986
Galeri UP, Lisbon: 1935
Museo Nacional de Belas Artes, Rio de Janeiro: 1942
Palacio Municipal, Belo Horizonte, Brazil: 1946 (with Arpad Szenes)

Marian Willard Gallery, New York: 1946
Galerie Pierre, Paris: 1949, 1951, 1955
Galerie Blanche, Stockholm: 1950
Redfern Gallery, London: 1952
Cadby Birch Gallery, New York: 1953
Stedelijk Museum, Amsterdam: 1955 (with Germaine Richier)
Kestner-Gesellschaft, Hannover: 1958 (touring retrospective)
Knoedler Gallery, New York: 1961, 1963, 1966, 1971
Phillips Art Gallery, Washington, DC: 1961, 1963
Kunsthalle, Mannheim: 1961
Musée de Peinture et de Sculpture, Grenoble, and Museo Civico, Turin: 1964 (retrospective)
Albert Loeb Gallery, New York: 1965
Musée National d'Art Moderne, Paris: 1969–70 (touring retrospective)
Musée Fabre, Montpellier: 1971 (retrospective)
Galerie Artel, Geneva: 1974
Musée d'Art Moderne de la Ville de Paris: 1977 (touring retrospective)
Nordjyllands Kunstmuseum, Ålborg, Denmark: 1978 (retrospective)
Galerie EMI-Valentim de Carvalho, Lisbon: 1984 (with Arpad Szenes)
Artcurial, Paris: 1986
Fondation Calouste Gulbenkian, Lisbon: 1988 (touring)
Fondation Juan March, Madrid: 1991 (retrospective)

Bibliography

Pierre Descargues, *Vieira da Silva*, Paris: Presses Littéraires de France, 1949
René de Solier, *Vieira da Silva*, Paris: Fall, 1956
José-Augusto França, *Vieira da Silva*, Lisbon: Artis, 1958
Guy Weelen, *Vieira da Silva*, Paris: Hazan, 1960
Vieira da Silva, exh. cat., Galerie Jeanne Bucher, Paris, 1967
Dora Vallier, *Vieira da Silva: La Peinture de Vieira da Silva: Chemins d'approche*, Geneva: Weber, 1971
Mario de Oliveira, *3 ensaios: Vieira da Silva e sua pintura*, Braga: Pax, 1972
Guy Weelen, *Vieira da Silva*, Paris: Hazan, 1973
Antoine Terrasse, *L'Univers de Vieira da Silva*, Paris: Scrépel, 1977
Guy Weelen, *Vieira da Silva: Les Estampes, 1926–1976*, Paris: Arts et Métiers Graphiques, Paris, 1977
Agustina Bessa-Luis, *Longas dias têm cem anos: Presença de Vieira da Silva*, Lisbon: Imprensa Nacional-Casa da Moeda, 1978
Jean Laude, "Vieira da Silva", *Cimaise*, no.145, 1978
Anne Philipe, *L'Eclat de la lumière: Entretiens avec Marie-Hélène Vieira da Silva et Arpad Szenes*, Paris: Gallimard, 1978
Jacques Lassaigne and Guy Weelen, *Vieira da Silva*, New York: Rizzoli, 1979 (French original)
Dora Vallier, *Vieira da Silva: Chemins d'approche*, Paris: Galilée, 1982
Michel Butor, *Vieira da Silva: Peintures*, Paris: L'autre Musée, 1983
Guy Weelen, *Vieira da Silva: Oeuvres sur papier*, Paris: La Différence, 1983
Mário Cesariny, *Vieira da Silva, Arpad Szenes ou o Castelo Surrealista*, Lisbon: Assírio e Alvim, 1984
Vieira da Silva, exh. cat., Fondation Calouste Gulbenkian, Lisbon, and Galeries nationales du Grand Palais, Paris, 1988
Vieira da Silva/Arpad Szenes, exh. cat., Casa de Serralves, Porto, 1989
Vieira da Silva, exh. cat., Fondation Juan March, Madrid, 1991
Jean-Luc Daval, Jean-François Jaeger and Guy Weelen, *Vieira da Silva*, 2 vols, Geneva: Skira, 1994 (contains catalogue raisonné)

"In front of the paintings of Vieira da Silva", wrote the Portuguese critic Mario de Oliveira, "the viewer experiences a reality that unites the work and its exterior, for we are ourselves transported into the desired space automatically" (Oliveira 1972). The "desired space" (*o espaço desejado*) is an ambiguous phrase. Desired by whom? By the painting itself, as appears to be Oliveira's meaning, rather than by the viewer or the artist as subjects? It is certainly a task of the work of art to assign the viewer to his or her proper place in the aesthetic relation, and it is the task of painting to orient the spectator and establish the point from which the logic of its organisation is produced and disclosed. And indeed it would be also correct to point out that a curious longing for a "home", a space of rest and repose, seems to inhabit the expressive depths of Vieira da Silva's works, these paintings obsessed with the recurrence of the void, with the mapping of tangible and intangible distances, reflecting the artist's quest for a place in the work itself as if denied or dissatisfied with a home in reality.

Maria Elena Vieira da Silva was born in Portugal in the early decades of the 20th century, and her life and career encompassed two continents, and the cities of Lisbon, Rio de Janiero and Paris. The displacements of the formative and early professional years followed those of her childhood when she travelled with her family to Britain, France and Switzerland (where her father died in 1911). Music and the visual arts were her first interests, which led, after beginning studies in the visual arts in Portugal, to a first period in Paris, from 1928 (studies with Bourdelle, later with Léger, Despiau and Bissière), with intervals in Lisbon in 1935 and 1939, and interrupted by the outbreak of World War II. From 1940 to 1946 she lived in Rio de Janeiro, returning to Paris in 1947. The period after the war coincided with the final evolution of her mature style and her participation in the developments of modern French painting, a period of formation of abstract art in France with the contributions of artists as diverse as the German-born Hartung, the Canadian Riopelle, the Russians Lanskoy and Poliakoff, the Chinese Zao Wou-ki, to name a few, as well as the Frenchmen Soulages, Manessier, Le Moal, among others. Vieira da Silva was a central figure in this "internationalised" period of the School of Paris, which was also the last international diffusion of "French-Parisian" art.

An interest in sculpture, which she studied with Bourdelle and Despiau, and the creation of textile and tapestry designs early in her career indicate the practical beginnings of two main elements of her paintings: the methodic construction of surfaces by the accumulation of small visual units and lines, and the preoccupation with space depiction and space creation on the flat surface of the canvas. The organisation of space is the main element in *Atelier* (Fundação Arpad Szenes-Maria Elena Vieira da Silva, Lisbon, repr. Daval, Jaeger and Weelen 1994, no.176), painted in Lisbon in 1934. The multiplication of geometric surface elements creates figures and ground, and guides the eye towards the depths of space, doubling the depths of human suffering in *Disaster (War)* (1942; Centre Georges Pompidou, Paris). A further development of these elements is given by *Card Players* (1947–8; private collection, France, *ibid.*, no.593). Something of the graphic, linear, dynamic and surface elements of Duchamp's early "abstract" paintings (nudes, card players) are echoed in Vieira da Silva's works – as well as, on a different level, the methodic and inspired geometry of the works of Torres Garcia (whose simplicity of form, clarity and vigorous optimism, however, are very distant from the Portuguese artist). Also combined with these elements is present also the specific recognition by the artist of the fragility of the painted surface, as if to indicate the travail of patience, love and loss that characterise the adventure of creation.

Vieira da Silva's mature works reflect the investigation of the transitions from interior to exterior space (*Three Windows*, 1972–3; Alice Pauli, Lausanne, *ibid.*, no.2681) while the patient accumulation of graphic marks, lines and colours creates imaginary vistas (*The Awakening*, 1973; *ibid.*, no.2658) and imaginary cities (*New Amsterdam II*, 1970; private collection, Portugal, *ibid.*, no.2343).

Or she presents, by the repetitive and, at times, painful weaving of marks and colours on the canvas surface, textures that stand for the "flesh" of the painted object itself (*L'Herbe*, 1973; private collection, Switzerland, *ibid.*, no.2661; *Library in Malraux*, 1974; private collection, France, *ibid.*, no.2730).

And yet, for all their accumulated elements, graphic dislocations and the apparent dynamism of their imaginary displacements, integrations and disintegrations of sites and spaces, in the end the paintings of Vieira da Silva convey the feeling of a silent return to self. This, perhaps more than the allusions to the popular and decorative art of the Portuguese *azulejos* and the occasional landscapes or cityscape drawings of Portugal, indicates a specific cultural sensibility at work beyond the elegant expressions of the visual culture of modern French art. The space in Vieira da Silva is the mask of the self, the mirror of the primary, internal space of the subject. A subjective space that reflects something of the interiority, of the self-absorbed, meditative aspects of the *alma portuguesa* (Portuguese soul).

MARCELO LIMA

Vigée-Lebrun, Elisabeth   [fig. 69]
French painter, 1755–1842

Born Marie Louise Elisabeth Vigée in Paris, 16 April 1755. Trained by her father, a portrait painter, and by Gabriel Briard. Established as a professional portrait painter by 1770; elected member of the Académie de Saint-Luc, Paris, 1774. Married painter and art dealer Jean-Baptiste-Pierre Lebrun, 1776; daughter born 1780 (d. 1819); divorced 1794. Elected member of Académie Royale de Peinture et de Sculpture, Paris, 31 May 1783. Left Paris for Rome with daughter, October 1789; elected member of the Accademia di San Luca, Rome, April 1790; stayed in Rome until April 1792, making three trips to Naples. On homeward journey through Italy, learned that her name was on the proscribed list of exiles in Paris, and decided to go to Vienna instead. Lived in Vienna until April 1795, then went to St Petersburg, Russia; stayed in Moscow, winter 1800–01; left St Petersburg in spring 1801; spent six months in Berlin before returning to Paris in January 1802. Stayed in London, 1803–5; visited Switzerland, 1807 and 1808. Divided time between country retreat at Louveciennes and Paris from 1809. Member of the academies of Paris, Rome, Parma, Bologna, St Petersburg, Berlin, Geneva, Rouen, Avignon and Vaucluse. Died in Paris, 29 May 1842.

Principal Exhibitions

Académie de Saint-Luc, Paris: 1774
Salon de la Correspondance, Paris: 1779, 1781–3
Paris Salon: 1783, 1785, 1787, 1789, 1791, 1798, 1802, 1817, 1824

Selected Writings

Souvenirs de Mme Louise-Elisabeth Vigée Lebrun, 3 vols, Paris: Fournier, 1835–7
Memoirs of Madame Vigée Lebrun, ed. Lionel Strachey, New York: Doubleday, 1903; London: Grant Richards, 1904; abridged edition with introduction by John Russell, New York: Braziller, 1989
Souvenirs, ed. Claudine Herrmann, 2 vols, Paris: Des Femmes, 1984
The Memoirs of Elisabeth Vigée-Le Brun, ed. Siân Evans, Bloomington: Indiana University Press, and London: Camden, 1989

Bibliography

Jean-Baptiste-Pierre Le Brun, *Précis historique de la vie de la citoyenne Lebrun, peintre*, Paris: Lebrun, 1794
J. T. L. F. Tripier Le Franc, *Notice sur la vie et les ouvrages de Mme Lebrun*, Paris, 1828
Charles Blanc, "Elisabeth Vigée-Lebrun", *Histoire des peintres de toutes les écoles*, ed. Charles Blanc, 14 vols, Paris: Renouard, 1861–76
Charles Pillet, *Madame Vigée-Lebrun*, Paris: Libraire de l'Art, 1890
Pierre de Nolhac, *Madame Vigée-Lebrun: Peintre de la reine Marie-Antoinette, 1755–1842*, Paris: Goupil, 1908; revised 1912
Louis Hautecoeur, *Madame Vigée-Lebrun*, Paris: Laurens, 1914
W. H. Helm, *Vigée-Lebrun: Her Life, Works and Friendships*, London: Hutchinson, and Boston: Small Maynard, 1915
André Blum, *Madame Vigée-Lebrun: Peintre des grandes dames du XVIIIe siècle*, Paris: Piazza, 1919
Lada Nikolénko, "The Russian portraits of Madame Vigée-Lebrun", *Gazette des Beaux-Arts*, 6th series, lxx, 1967, pp.91–120
Anne-Marie Passez, *Adélaïde Labille-Guiard (1749–1803): Biographie et catalogue raisonné de son oeuvre*, Paris: Arts et Métiers Graphiques, 1973
Women Artists, 1550–1950, exh. cat., Los Angeles County Museum of Art, and elsewhere, 1976
Andrzej Ryszkiewicz, "Les portraits polonais de Madame Vigée-Lebrun", *Bulletin du Musée National de Varsovie*, xx, 1979, pp.16–42
Joseph Baillio, "Le dossier d'une oeuvre d'actualité politique: *Marie-Antoinette et ses enfants par Mme Vigée LeBrun*", *L'Oeil*, no.308, March 1981, pp.34–41, 74–5; no.310, May 1981, pp.52–61, 90–91
Jean Owens Schaefer, "The souvenirs of Elizabeth Vigée-Lebrun: The self-imaging of the artist and the woman", *International Journal of Women's Studies*, iv, 1981, pp.35–49
Joseph Baillio, "Quelques peintures réattribuées à Vigée-Le Brun", *Gazette des Beaux-Arts*, 6th series, xcix, 1982, pp.13–26 (with English summary)
Elisabeth-Louise Vigée-Le Brun, exh. cat., Kimbell Art Museum, Fort Worth, TX, 1982
H. T. Douwes Dekker, "Gli autoritratti di Elisabeth Vigée-Lebrun (1755–1842)", *Antichità Viva*, xxii/4, 1983, pp.31–5
Paula Radisich, "Qui peut définer les femmes? Vigée-Lebrun's portraits of an artist", *Eighteenth-Century Studies*, xxv, 1992, pp.441–68
Susan Sontag, *The Volcano Lover: A Romance*, New York: Farrar Straus, and London: Cape, 1992
Mary Sheriff, "Woman? hermaphrodite? history painter? On the self-imaging of Elisabeth Vigée-Lebrun", *The Eighteenth Century: Theory and Interpretation*, xxxv, Spring 1994, pp.3–28
——, "The immodesty of her sex: Elisabeth Vigée-Lebrun in 1783", *The Consumption of Culture in the Early Modern Period*, ed. Ann Bermingham and John Brewer, London and New York: Routledge, 1995, pp.455–88
——, *The Exceptional Woman: Elisabeth Vigée-Lebrun and the Cultural Politics of Art*, Chicago: Chicago University Press, 1996 (contains extensive bibliography)

Elisabeth Vigée-Lebrun's life and work are split by that great cultural and political divide known as the French Revolution. She was born in Paris in 1755 and died there in 1842, but she spent the years between 1789 and 1802 in exile. Her close association with Queen Marie-Antoinette and her protégés made the artist a target for political pamphleteers, and she left France with the first wave of émigrés in 1789. Only a petition signed by 255 artists in 1801 opened the way for her repatriation. If Vigée-Lebrun's reputation was first secured in the French capital as the queen's painter, her career after 1789 was marked by travel from court to court and country to country. Even after her return to Paris in 1802, the artist continued her peripatetic life, making trips to Britain, Switzerland, Belgium and throughout France. These travels she recorded in her *Souvenirs*, published between 1835 and 1837.

The *Souvenirs* are filled with anecdotes of the artist's life before the Revolution, as well as accounts of her travels during and after her exile. Not only is it uncertain how much of the text she actually wrote, but her "memories" often depend on what others said about her, and her writing transcribes word for word flattering poems, letters and reviews. These representations, as well as the standard tropes of artistic biography and the myths of the painter's imagination, are fundamental to her *Souvenirs*. She inserted into these ready-made stories the events – remembered, fantasised or constructed – of her own life, and published this highly mediated self-representation under her name as her authorised biography. The *Souvenirs*, then, are not a factual record of her life, but a self-projection, an image as crafted as those she projected in her paintings.

The daughter of a guild painter, Louis Vigée, and a hairdresser, Jeanne Messin, Elisabeth Vigée-Lebrun did not come from an exalted social rank or wealth, but neither did she come from the poor or dispossessed. Luck of birth positioned her so she might have a chance, even if her sex made the odds of actually having one, let alone successfully seizing it, quite small. Her father taught her the trade at home, a mode of training typical for women, and she continued her education with the academic artist Gabriel Briard. From the start, Elisabeth Vigée seems to have managed her career astutely, and by 1770 she was establishing herself as a portrait painter. At 19 the artist belonged to the guild (the Académie de Saint-Luc de Paris), and she showed at its exhibition in 1774, receiving very favourable notices in the press. She married the painter and art dealer Jean-Baptiste-Pierre Lebrun in 1776, a marriage that facilitated her study of art and travel abroad. By 1780 she had the support of influential patrons, such as the Comte de Vaudreuil and the finance minister Calonne, whom she entertained at suppers. She became, most importantly, a favoured painter of Marie-Antoinette.

The path that Vigée-Lebrun took was the one that led to noble patrons and royal favour, a path familiar to French artists for more than a century. She pursued her ambitions according to the particular circumstances of the arts and the structures governing their practice. When the Revolution came, however, it would not have been easy for her to change course. Not only did she draw her clients from the aristocracy and well-to-do, but Vigée-

Lebrun was the only artist working for the crown who was calumniated in print. A highly visible public woman competing directly with men, Vigée-Lebrun was a perfect target for the fears of de-differentiation and feminisation that were played out most dramatically in the revolutionary period. In pursuing government commissions and royal favour before the Revolution, however, Vigée-Lebrun walked that well-travelled path a bit differently from her male colleagues. For them, admission into the Academy or its schools usually preceded royal favour. In her case, royal favour secured her acceptance into the privileged body of artists on 31 May 1783. That acceptance was one of the most unusual and most contested on record.

The basic story line of the controversy surrounding Vigée-Lebrun's admission is simple: because she was married to an art dealer, the Academy, represented by its Director, the Comte d'Angiviller, held her in violation of the statute forbidding artists from engaging in commerce. The reason recorded in the official records of the Academy (the *Procès verbaux*) is as follows:

> Madame Lebrun, wife of an art dealer, is very talented and would have long ago been elected to the Academy were it not for the commerce of her husband. It is said, and I believe it, that she does not mix in commerce, but in France a wife has no other station [*état*] than that of her husband.

Vigée-Lebrun's status as an art dealer's wife necessitated an exception to the statute, which the king ordered at the request of the queen. The Academy had no choice but to admit her, and on the same day also received Adélaïde Labille-Guiard (q.v.), whose acceptance as a portrait painter it conducted and recorded according to established practice. The academicians compensated themselves, however, for the forced admission by obtaining from the King an order limiting the number of women to four (since Mme Vien and Anne Vallayer-Coster, q.v., were already academicians, there were precisely four women in the Academy at the time). D'Angiviller justified the order by reasoning:

> this number is sufficient to honour their talent; women can not be useful to the progress of the arts because the modesty of their sex forbids them from being able to study after nature and in the public school established and founded by Your Majesty.

What the Director meant by progress of the arts is the progress of history painting, the grand genre he sought to revive as an instrument of state. Women could not be useful to the arts because theoretically and practically they were barred from practising as history painters. Not only were their mental talents believed inadequate, but they could attend neither the Academy's life drawing classes nor other essential training sessions (in perspective, anatomy, history). Vigée-Lebrun, however, gave the lie to d'Angiviller's claim of women's uselessness in choosing her reception piece. Because she was admitted to the Academy in such an unusual way, on the day of her acceptance the artist presented no work by which the academicians could classify her as practising a particular genre. They asked her to bring to the next meeting some painting that could stand as her reception piece. As Vigée-Lebrun was best known as a portrait painter, the Academy probably anticipated that she would bring a portrait. Thwarting this expectation, she presented instead *Peace Bringing Back Abundance* (1780; 102 × 132 cm.; Louvre, Paris), an allegorical history painting. The Academy never officially recognised this work and never positioned her within a rank or genre, but when the painting appeared in the Salon the following autumn it was listed in the guide and discussed in the press as her reception piece.

In *Peace Bringing Back Abundance* Vigée-Lebrun capitalised on the elements of history painting that did provide openings for women. Within the allegorical tradition, the idealised female body was used to represent any number of abstract ideas, and often made to stand for virtues that in the "real world" were not ordinarily ascribed to women or gendered as feminine. Those history paintings that featured the female body opened possibilities for women artists who could draw "after Nature" either by using themselves or their female friends or servants as models. In two other history paintings exhibited at the same Salon – *Juno Borrowing the Belt of Venus* and *Venus Binding Cupid's Wings* (both untraced) – and in works shown in 1785, most notably *Bacchante* (Musée Nissim de Camondo, Paris) – the artist took advantage of changes in history painting that marked the first half of the 18th century when mythological subjects of the type popularised by Boucher featured the female body. Such subjects met the criteria for history paintings in that they were drawn from literature and mythology, and demanded that the painter visualise an

event, idealise the figures, imagine their passions and choose the most appropriate artistic language. By 1783, however, some Salon critics and academic officials argued that such unedifying subjects debased history painting, eschewing its moral, serious (masculine) side and cultivating its erotic, frivolous (feminine) side. Indeed, d'Angiviller designed his reform of history painting to rescue the highest genre from the depths into which it had allegedly fallen in the hands of such painters as Boucher. Although most of Vigée-Lebrun's images could be compared to Boucher's mythologies, *Peace and Abundance* invoked a tradition of earlier royalist iconography, a tradition that in d'Angiviller's terms *could* be useful to the progress of the arts.

In *Peace and Abundance* Vigée-Lebrun deploys a standard monarchical iconography in a theme previously used for Academy reception pieces. In this iconography, Abundance is represented as a woman holding a cornucopia filled with nature's bounty, even though she is meant to refer to the financial abundance that will accrue to the arts with renewed patronage after a period of military outlay. Painted in 1780, Vigée-Lebrun's work anticipates the end of French expenditures for the American Revolution, which would bring back abundance to the arts in the sense of providing money to continue d'Angiviller's projects. Three years later, when the work appeared at the Salon, Vigée-Lebrun's contemporaries took it as a comment on the reign of Louis XVI, for the treaty ending France's involvement in the American War of Independence was signed in that year.

Salon criticism in 1783 was preoccupied with the unprecedented appearance of works by four women. Vigée-Lebrun's paintings inevitably garnered the most discussion, and much of it focused on her attempts to become a history painter. The most pointed of these addressed not a history painting, but her *Self-Portrait in a Straw Hat* (private collection; autograph copy in National Gallery, London). Published under the name Coup de Patte, this commentary presented itself as the conversation of a painter, poet and musician. The trio pauses before Vigée-Lebrun's self-portrait and the musician asks whom the work represents. The painter explains that the work is a self-portrait. "Indeed! this pretty person has painted herself!" exclaims the surprised poet. The painter, however, is troubled because the figure's hair is a little négligé. The musician takes this as a sign that she has the "taste" of great artists not focused on mundane details. Addressing himself to the painter, the musician asks: "Is she a history painter?" And the painter replies:

> No. The arms, the head, the heart of women lack the essential qualities to follow men into the lofty region of the fine arts. If nature could produce one of them capable of this great effort, it would be a monstrosity, the more shocking because there would be an inevitable opposition between her physical and mental/moral (*morale*) existence. A woman who would have all the passions of a man is really an impossible man. So the vast field of history, which is filled with vigorously passioned objects, is closed to those who would not know how to bring to it all the expressions of vigour [Coup de Patte (pseud.), *Le Triumvirat des arts* ..., Paris, 1783, p.27].

The hermaphrodite is the governing image throughout this passage. In characterising the woman history painter as a monstrosity, the text evokes the long history of considering the hermaphrodite among the mistakes of nature. As the woman history painter, Vigée-Lebrun tried to assume a man's role; if her imitation were possible, it would produce an impossible opposition between her physical and mental-moral existence. A woman who had the force to produce significant works of art would be neither woman nor man, but impossible man.

Although within the context of the Salon Vigée-Lebrun's self-image evoked the woman history painter as monstrous hermaphrodite, it also offered its viewers other associations. Based on Rubens's *Chapeau de Paille* (1620–25: National Gallery, London), the self-portrait presents Vigée-Lebrun as both beautiful woman and accomplished artist. The painting by Rubens was well-known as an excellent model for depicting beauty, but one that presented to the artist who imitated it difficult problems of colouring and light effects. Vigée-Lebrun takes up the artistic challenge but separates herself from both Rubens's beautiful model and her later *semblables* who devised their masquerade costumes after the dress shown in Rubens's painting. Vigée-Lebrun's costume – a dress *en chemise* and straw hat – evokes that sported by fashionable women of the 1780s and particularly associated with the queen and her circle at Trianon.

Vigée-Lebrun's self-image, like the one she would make in 1790 (Uffizi, Florence) for the Grand Duke of Tuscany's gallery of artists' self-portraits, advertises her association with Marie-Antoinette. Her position as a favoured painter to the queen had been won partly by social contacts, but more significantly by the approval of the queen's mother, the Habsburg empress Maria Teresa. As her correspondence indicates, throughout the 1770s Maria Teresa was exasperated by her search for an official portrait of her daughter that pleased her. When Vigée-Lebrun's portrait of the queen in her official court dress (Kunsthistorisches Museum, Vienna) arrived in Vienna in April 1779, the empress, who was finally satisfied, wrote: "Your large portrait pleases me! [The Prince de] Ligne has found it resembling, but it is enough for me that it represents your face, with which I am quite happy" (letter from Maria Teresa to Marie-Antoinette, 1 April 1779).

Vigée-Lebrun was called on over the years to make many images of the queen. The most famous was the portrait of *Marie-Antoinette with Her Children* (Palais de Versailles), a piece of royal propaganda calculated to present the queen in a positive light. The image is significant not only because executed on a monumental scale, but also as the first and only work from Vigée-Lebrun commissioned through official channels – through the Bâtiments du Roi. In fact, this portrait was the only work in the 18th century that the Bâtiments commissioned from a woman. Thoroughly politicised, the image appeared at the Salon of 1787, where it was praised by royalist supporters and denounced by many oppositional critics. Less obviously political, but more controversial, was the image of the queen *en chemise* shown four years earlier (private collection, Germany; autograph copy, National Gallery of Art, Washington, DC). This portrait so outraged a segment of the public that Vigée-Lebrun was forced to remove it from the Salon. What shocked that public was the costume *en chemise*.

Imported from England in the 1780s, the robe *en chemise* was made from sheer white muslin fastened down the back and caught at the waist with a sash. The underskirt and corset, which ordinarily showed through the transparent muslin, were often of blue or pink silk, as in Vigée-Lebrun's *Self-Portrait* shown in 1783. Although the style was immensely popular in Britain, where it suggested the "natural woman", in France formalities of court made it less acceptable. For public appearances the *robe en chemise* was considered immodest, even though it revealed far less of the body than traditional court dresses. More significantly, the portrait *en chemise* shows Marie-Antoinette not as the king's consort, or in relation to a position at court, but as the queen of Trianon, her private domain in the grounds of Versailles. Indeed, the dress *en chemise* signalled the circle of women that Marie-Antoinette drew around her at Trianon, and whom libels such as the *Portefeuille d'un talon rouge* characterised as the "tribades of Trianon". In fact, slurs directed at Vigée-Lebrun's portrait articulated the most common themes of the libels emanating from the court: the queen's foreign character, her extravagant spending and uncontrolled sexuality. The portrait opened itself to these libels not simply because it showed Marie-Antoinette *en chemise* but because it showed the queen in an official public setting – the king's art exhibition – in a private role. If at the Salon of 1783 Vigée-Lebrun claimed a public role as a history painter, she allowed the queen the right to pose publicly as a private individual.

Although she aspired to a public role, it is as a painter of private individuals that Vigée-Lebrun has become best known. During her lifetime she was sought precisely because she made pleasing images of women both as society ladies and good mothers. Her most convincing works of the first sort include the *Lady Folding a Letter* (1784; Toledo Museum of Art, OH) and the portraits of the *Duchesse de Polignac* (1783; National Trust, Waddesdon Manor) and *Marquise de Jaucourt* (1789; Metropolitan Museum of Art, New York); and among her most striking representations of motherhood are the portrait of the *Marquise de Pezé and the Marquise de Rouget with Her Two Children* (1787; National Gallery of Art, Washington, DC) and her self-portrait called *Maternal Tenderness* (1787; Louvre); the last was Vigée-Lebrun's most popular painting at the Salon of 1787, and critics praised the work lavishly for the sentiment it expressed. The artist also represented women in coquettish allegorical disguise, as in the portrait of the *Duchesse de Gramont as a Grape Gatherer* (1784; Nelson-Atkins Museum of Art, Kansas City). Although reputed to be a painter of women, Vigée-Lebrun throughout her career executed compelling, lively and original portraits of men, as her images of *Alexandre Charles Emmanuel de Crussol-Florensac* (1787; Metropolitan Museum of Art), *Hubert Robert* (1787; Louvre) and the *Count Shuvaloff* (North

Carolina Museum of Art, Raleigh) so well demonstrate.

Indeed, Vigée-Lebrun worked for private patrons both in France before the Revolution and during her years of exile. Her years of exile, moreover, repeatedly challenged her to locate new clients, establish new studios and find her place in social and artistic circles as she moved from Italy to Germany to Austria to Russia. Her works during these years sometimes repeat paradigms that she had already established in France; for example, her portrait of Marie-Antoinette's sister, *Marie-Thérèse* (Musée Condé, Chantilly), painted in Italy in 1790, strongly recalls in costume, pose and bearing her images of the French queen, while her portrait of the *Princess A.P. Golitsyna with Her Son* (Pushkin Museum, Moscow), executed in Vienna in 1794, is modelled on the highly succesful *Maternal Tenderness*. Other images made in France are reconstituted for elite women of all nationalities for whom it was fashionable to masquerade in the imagined dress of a culture thought exotic. With some changes here and there, the *Portrait of a Lady* (1789; National Gallery of Art, Washington, DC), which shows a turbaned woman in costume *à la turque* seated on a divan, her right arm bent and resting on a pillow, her left arm extended, becomes her image of the *Comtesse Skavronskaia* (Musée Jacquemart-André, Paris), painted in Naples in 1790. In addition to repeating these portrait-types while in exile, Vigée-Lebrun also established more "modern" sorts of representations, some of which had been presaged by work in France.

By 1790 many of her portraits were set out of doors, and early on Vigée-Lebrun worked with a type that would become a norm in later Romantic portrait painting. Her portrait of the *Comtesse de Buquoi* (1793; Minneapolis Art Institute), for example, positions the sitter on a hillock in an autumnal landscape suggestive of scenery along the Danube, and her earlier portrait of *Madame du Barry* (1789; Musée Lambinet, Versailles) shows the ageing royal mistress reading in an overgrown garden setting. With works such as the portraits of *Countess Golovine* (c.1798; Barber Institute of Fine Arts, University of Birmingham) and *Varvara Ivanovna Narishkine* (1800; Gallery of Fine Arts, Columbus, OH), Vigée-Lebrun also developed the close-up portrait focused on the sitter's intense gaze and expression, a type that became popular in the first half of the 19th century.

Vigée-Lebrun's most ambitious "romantic" portrait, however, is her representation of Madame de Staël as the title character of her novel *Corinne; ou, L'Italie* (1807). The peripatetic Vigée-Lebrun journeyed to Switzerland (one of many trips after her repatriation), to Madame de Staël's château at Coppet, to render her subject from life. In the final portrait (1808; Musée d'Art et d'Histoire, Geneva) Madame de Staël plays the improvisational poet-sibyl Corinne in the midst of an inspired performance. The work evokes a specific moment in the story when Corinne performs an improvisation in the Neapolitan countryside, but it also represents the dramatic tensions evident in the novel. Like her character Corinne, the expressive Madame de Staël embodies what much late 18th-century thinking conceptualised as a natural, sublime force – a singular genius.

Madame de Staël as Corinne is one of Vigée-Lebrun's most challenging works, and the challenge comes not only from showing a female poet in conventions usually reserved for the male genius (and especially Homer and Ossian), but also – and perhaps more forcefully – from offering viewers a flawed and expressive Madame de Staël where they expect a perfect and idealised woman. Vigée-Lebrun presents the sitter as a monumental figure with sculptural limbs, large, expressive features – and a markedly individualised physiognomy that is distinctly unlike the one Staël gives the beautiful Corinne. In the face of Corinne, Vigée-Lebrun's portrait suggests that Staël could have a profound influence on her audience, on her culture, even on history, without that quintessential signifier of femininity. Moreover, Vigée-Lebrun's monumental portrait reveals the effect of situating a woman in the pantheon of genius. This representation unmasks, without perhaps realising it, those grand illusions that have seemed natural idealisations when donned by men and ridiculous vanities when worn by women. Those illusions are not only inscribed on the sitter; they also mark the artist who conceptualised the image.

Vigée-Lebrun's portrait of Staël, like her struggle with the Academy and her reception by Salon critics, makes visible the barriers that prevented women who practised the arts at an extraordinary level of achievement from positioning themselves in the canon of great masters. For better or worse, their work could only spur other exceptional women. The father of Rosa Bonheur (q.v.) challenged his daughter not to compete with Poussin or David, but to surpass the most talented woman painter – Elisabeth Vigée-Lebrun.

MARY D. SHERIFF

See also Academies of Art survey

Vigri, Caterina [St Catherine of Bologna]

Italian painter and illuminator, c.1413–1463

Born in Bologna, c.1413; grew up in Ferrara. Entered Corpus Christi, Ferrara, a convent of Poor Clares, c.1427; professed c.1429–30. Appointed abbess of Corpus Domini, Bologna, 1456. Died in Bologna, 9 March 1463. Canonised 1712.

Selected Writings

Le sette armi spirituali (completed after 1456), ed. S. d'Aurizio, Bologna, 1981
Le sette armi spirituali (completed after 1456), ed. Cecilia Foletti, Padua: Antenore, 1985

Bibliography
Illuminata Bembo, *Lo specchio di illuminazione* (15th century), ed. S. d'Aurizio, Bologna, 1983
G.B. Melloni, *Atti o memorie degli uomini illustri in santità nati, o morti in Bologna*, i and iii, Bologna, 1818
I.B. Supino, *L'arte nelle chiese di Bologna, secoli XV–XVI*, ii, Bologna, 1838
Laura M. Ragg, *The Women Artists of Bologna*, London: Methuen, 1907
P. Lucius M. Nuñez OFM, "Descriptio breviarii manuscripti S. Catharinae Bononiensis O.S.CL", *Archivum Franciscanum Historicum*, iv, 1911, pp.732–47
La santa nella storia, nelle lettere e nell'arte, Bologna: Garagnani, 1912
F. Wormald, "A saint identified in a Lee picture", *Journal of the Warburg and Courtauld Institutes*, xxv, 1962, pp.129–30
R. Ricciardi, *Santa Caterina da Bologna*, Padua, 1963
Serena Spanò, "Per uno studio su Caterina da Bologna", *Studi Mediaevali*, 3rd series, xii, 1971, pp.713–59
Teodosio Lombardi, *I francescani a Ferrara*, iv, Bologna, 1975
Serena Spanò Martinelli, "La Biblioteca del 'Corpus Domini' bolognese: L'inconsueto spaccato di una cultura monastica femminile", *Bibliofilia*, lxxxviii, 1986, pp.1–23

J. Berrigan, "Catherine of Bologna: Franciscan mystic", *Women Writers of the Renaissance and Reformation*, ed. Katharina M. Wilson, Athens: University of Georgia Press, 1987, pp.81–95

F. Cardini, "Santa Caterina da Bologna e il trattato *Le sette armi spirituali*", *Studi Francescane*, lxxxvi, 1989, pp.53–64

Jeryldene M. Wood, *Women, Art and Spirituality: The Poor Clares of Early Modern Italy*, Cambridge: Cambridge University Press, 1996

Known to posterity as St Catherine of Bologna, Caterina Vigri actually spent most of her life in Ferrara. While she was born in Bologna and died there in 1463, she lived in Ferrara from early childhood until 1456 when she became abbess at the Corpus Domini, a Bolognese convent of Poor Clares. According to her first biographer Sister Illuminata Bembo, who knew the saint from about 1432, her father Giovanni Vigri was employed at the court of Niccolò d'Este in Ferrara, and Catherine served as a lady-in-waiting to Niccolò's daughter Margarita (Bembo 1983, p.100). After Margarita's marriage in 1427, Catherine entered a house of Poor Clares at Ferrara, the Corpus Christi, where she professed her vows *c.*1429–30 (for a recent study of the saint's life and writings, see *Le sette armi spirituali*, ed. Foletti 1985, pp.1–76). A series of visions and ecstasies established her reputation for sanctity; several of these were incorporated into her treatise *Le sette armi spirituali*, which was completed after her transfer to the Corpus Domini in Bologna and made public only on her death-bed.

Eighteen days after Catherine's burial, a sweet odour emanating from her grave led to the exhumation of her corpse. Probably sketched at this time, a portrait attributed to Bembo records the pale, ascetic features of the abbess (chalk and gold on paper; Corpus Domini, Bologna, repr. Ricciardi 1963, fig.12). A popular cult soon developed around Catherine's incorrupt body, which was exhibited to visitors at the nun's communion window in the Corpus Domini until the construction of a separate chapel (see Wormald 1962, p.129). The present Cappella della Santa in the same church dates to the late 17th century, when the chamber was remodelled in anticipation of Catherine's long-awaited canonisation in 1712.

Whether Catherine received her artistic training at court or in the convent is uncertain. Bembo claimed that she was educated at the d'Este court; like other upper-class young women of this era, she would have studied grammar, history, poetry, scripture, Latin, some rhetoric and perhaps music (she played a small violin) and drawing (see M. King and A. Rabil, *Her Immaculate Hand*, Binghamton, NY, 1983, p.15). Yet it may well be that Catherine learned her craft in the scriptorium of the Corpus Christi; for according to Bembo, she chanted poems of her own composition as she painted numerous images of the swaddled Infant Christ on the walls of the convent. These murals are lost, but some sense of their appearance can be gleaned from the haloed *bambini* drawn in the margins of the breviary decorated during this period (*c.*1438–52; conserved as a relic in Cappella della Santa, Corpus Domini, Bologna, repr. *La Santa nella storia* 1912, p.57), and from a painted wooden plaque of the Christ Child wrapped in rich fabric (*c.*1456–63; Corpus Domini, repr. *Le sette armi spirituali*, ed. d'Aurizio 1981).

St Catherine's artistic practice cannot be separated from her experiences as a nun and a mystic, or from her work as a writer and a musician. She did not pursue a "professional" career like her contemporary, the Dominican friar Fra Angelico, who often worked on projects outside his friary in Florence. As a nun cloistered in an Observant Franciscan convent that followed a strict interpretation of St Clare's monastic rule, Catherine's activities were restricted. Her production cannot be evaluated by the criteria developed for male artists because she remained essentially an "amateur" painter: she did not undergo an apprenticeship, oversee a workshop or participate in ambitious commissions. Her style does not evolve; it retains the same direct and somewhat naive character throughout her career. Her oeuvre is relatively limited: four independent paintings (two on paper and two on panel); an illumination in *Le sette armi spirituali*, and the many decorated pages of her 519-page breviary; and the wooden *Christ Child* (the *St Ursula and Four Saints* formerly attributed to her in the Accademia, Venice, is now listed as workshop of Giovanni Bellini). Although Catherine was later named the patron saint of painters in Bologna, it is unclear whether her paintings were seen by outsiders during her lifetime. As far as we know, she did not create altarpieces for the public space of the Poor Clares' churches at either Ferrara or Bologna; she provided instead personal works for herself and her sisters.

St Catherine's art is best considered as a devotional activity akin to prayer. Bembo discloses that the abbess prayed and shed tears as she worked on her breviary, and that spiritual edification rather than artistic decoration was her purpose. The merging of text and image in the breviary fosters "the memory of the sweet Jesus", as on folio 10r, where the head of Christ appears in the capital letter of "Fratres" and a boy Christ in the V of "Verbum", as well as a chalice and host emerging at the centre of the simple foliage enframing the page (repr. *La santa nella storia* 1912, p.51). On the page for the feast of her patron saint, Catherine of Alexandria, the crowned head of the virgin-martyr in the capital letter of "Deus" resembles a 15th-century lady more than the Early Christian queen famed for her mystical marriage with Christ (fol.465r; repr. Nuñez 1911, p.746), and annotations referring to the "Most happy spouse of Christ" express the abbess's identification with her namesake. Catherine's approach fuses painting, writing and spirituality, as on the vellum sheet inserted in *Le sette armi spirituali* (after fol.49v; Corpus Domini, repr. d'Aurizio 1981), where yearning for mystical union with Jesus informs the historiated capital letter of "Deus". There the tiny Poor Clare (perhaps a self-portrait) gazing at the Crucified Saviour offers a visual parallel to a line in one of Catherine's poems: "O sweet Fruit of Mary, when I am finally lost in You, making melody within your side ...".

Despite the vivid recollections of visions in *Le sette armi spirituali*, Catherine does not reproduce specific mystical events in her visual art. Her paintings focus on the epiphanies experienced during ecstasy (especially the doctrine of the Incarnation, which was clarified for her in a vision) and thereby function as devotional guides to assist spiritual enlightenment. The medium, small scale and delicate brushwork of her paintings promote personal study and meditation. In her *Redeemer* (tempera on paper; Corpus Domini, repr. Ricciardi 1963, fig.4) roundels containing the angel Gabriel and the Annunciate Virgin denote the Incarnate Christ, who stands below blessing with one hand and displaying an open book with the other. Encircled by golden rays and attired in a white dalmatic sprinkled with gold stars, the Redeemer embodies the light of wisdom inscribed on his book: "In me is all the grace of the way and of the truth; in me is all hope of life and of virtue" (Ecclesiasticus, xxiv:25).

The lavish gold, bright colours and flat, stylised figures of Catherine's paintings indicate that even after three decades of claustration she continued to assimilate memories of secular life into her monastic experience. The affection shared by Mary and Christ in a half-length *Virgin and Child* (Convent of Corpus Domini, Bologna) charms in spite of the awkward anatomies; indeed, the courtly elegance of the panel resembles the Gothic style of the north Italian artists Pisanello and Jacopo Bellini, who worked for the d'Este in the first half of the 15th century.

Catherine's paintings offer a glimpse of female monastic attitudes towards the visual arts in early modern Italy. Exhibited in the Cappella della Santa, her *Madonna del Pomo* (repr. *Le sette armi spirituali*, ed. d'Aurizio 1981) represents Mary and her Son garbed in expensive brocade and wearing gold crowns. The paradoxical juxtaposition of their royal splendour and the humble brown habit worn by the miraculously preserved Catherine intimates that through their denial of material comforts in this life, the nuns hoped to enjoy eternal bliss in a celestial court.

JERYLDENE M. WOOD

WalkingStick, Kay

American painter, 1935–

Born in Syracuse, New York, 2 March 1935.
Studied at Beaver College, Glenside, Pennsylvania
(BFA 1959); Pratt Institute, Brooklyn, New York
(MFA 1975). Assistant professor of art, Cornell
University, Ithaca, 1988–90 and from 1992; State
University of New York, Stony Brook, 1990–92;
visiting artist, Vermont Studio Center, Johnson,
1995. Artist-in-residence at MacDowell Colony,
Peterborough, New Hampshire, 1970–71; Yaddo
Artists' Colony, Saratoga Springs, New York,
1976; William Flanagan Memorial Creative
Persons Center, Albee Foundation, Montauk, New
York, 1983; Rockefeller Conference and Study
Center, Bellagio, Italy, 1992. Recipient of National
Endowment for the Arts (NEA) grant, 1983; Joan
Mitchell Foundation award, 1995; National Honor
award for Achievement in the Arts, Women's
Caucus for Art, 1996. Member of Cherokee
Nation of Oklahoma. Lives in Ithaca, New York.

Selected Individual Exhibitions

SoHo Center for the Visual Arts, New York: 1976
Bertha Urdang Gallery, New York: 1978, 1981, 1984
M-13 Gallery, New York: 1987, 1990
Wenger Gallery, Los Angeles: 1988
Hillwood Art Museum, Long Island University,
    Brookville, NY: 1991 (touring retrospective)
Elaine Horwitch Gallery, Scottsdale, AZ: 1991
Galerie Calumet, Heidelberg, Germany: 1993
June Kelly Gallery, New York: 1994

Selected Writings

"Democracy, Inc.: Kay WalkingStick on Indian law",
    Artforum, xxx, November 1991, pp.20–21
"Native American art in the postmodern era", *Art
    Journal*, li, Fall 1992, pp.15–17 (guest editor, with
    Jackson Rushing)

Bibliography

Contemporary Native American Art, exh. cat., Gardiner
    Art Gallery, Oklahoma State University, Stillwater,
    and elsewhere, 1983
Signale: Indianischer Kunstler, exh. cat., Gallery Akmak,
    Berlin, and elsewhere, 1984
Pat Malarcher, "The meaning of 'duality' in art", *New
    York Times*, 22 December 1985
*The Painting and Sculpture Collection: Acquisitions since
    1972*, Buffalo, NY: Albright-Knox Art Gallery, 1987
We the People, exh. cat., Artists Space, New York, 1987
Judy Kay Collischan van Wagner, *Lines of Vision:
    Drawings by Contemporary Women*, New York:
    Hudson Hills Press, 1989
Kellie Jones, "Kay WalkingStick", *Village Voice*, 16 May
    1989
The Decade Show: Frameworks of Identity in the 1980s,
    exh. cat., New Museum of Contemporary Art, New
    York, and elsewhere, 1990
Lucy R. Lippard, *Mixed Blessings: New Art in a
    Multicultural America*, New York: Pantheon, 1990
Phyllis Braff, "A special regard for nature's forces", *New
    York Times*, 14 April 1990
Kay WalkingStick: Paintings, 1974–1990, exh. cat.,
    Hillwood Art Museum of Long Island University,
    Brookville, NY, and elsewhere, 1991
*Shared Visions: Native American Painters and Sculptors
    in the Twentieth Century*, exh. cat., Heard Museum,
    Phoenix, and
    elsewhere, 1991
*Land, Spirit, Power: First Nations at the National Gallery
    of Canada*, exh. cat., National Gallery of Canada,
    Ottawa, and elsewhere, 1992
Nicole Vogtlin, "Landschaften und deren Spiegelbilder",
    Rhein-Neckar-Main, 7 April 1993
Robin Lawrence, "Native tradition spoken in language of
    post-modernism", *The Weekend Sun/Saturday Review*
    (Vancouver), 31 December 1993
Lawrence Abbott, ed., *I Stand in the Center of the Good:
    Interviews with Contemporary Native American
    Artists*, Lincoln: University of Nebraska Press, 1994
Erin Valentino, "Mistaken identity: Between death and
    pleasure in the art of Kay WalkingStick", *Third Text*,
    no.26, Spring 1994, pp.61–73

H. W. Janson, *History of Art*, 5th edition, revised by
    Anthony F. Janson, New York: Abrams, 1995
Richard Vine, "Kay WalkingStick", *Art in America*,
    lxxxiii, January 1995, p.106
Anne Barclay Morgan, "Kay WalkingStick", *Art Papers*,
    November–December 1995, pp.12–15

The art of Kay WalkingStick expresses issues of duality and complexity, especially as those issues derive from personal experience and identity. Her paintings of the 1980s and 1990s have usually contained two distinct components that speak to both estrangement or separateness and reconciliation or unification. The role of nature is paramount in her art. While her imagery is concerned in part with primal forces, her style – which has been described as both Neo-abstract and Neo-expressionist – is a sophisticated, informed one that uses a highly developed formal language to deal with fundamental, mythic matters. At times, her work has made direct statements about the situation, past and present, of Native Americans.

WalkingStick was the daughter of a Cherokee father and a European-American mother. Although there was little direct contact with her father and his culture (based in Tahlequah, Oklahoma) during her childhood, her Native American heritage was impressed upon her by her mother and siblings. Her primary experience growing up was the dominant white culture of New York State, and only in adulthood did she come to terms with and begin to express the Native American aspect of her heritage. After receiving a BFA in 1959, she delayed graduate school to raise her family, receiving a MFA from the Pratt Institute in 1975. During those years, she dealt with realist treatments of the nude, then in the early 1970s produced a series of "apron" paintings with hand-applied markings that indicated her shift towards abstraction as well as a new approach to the process of painting.

Her first major artistic statement about her Cherokee heritage, *Messages to Papa* (artist's collection), came in 1975. The new piece was both object and experience: the interior of a conical tipi form large enough to contain only the artist was hung with feathers and paper strips on which were written "messages" in the Cherokee language. (The Cherokee was unique among the tribes in the USA in that one of its members, Sequoyah, developed a syllabary specifically for their language.) Describing the construction of this sculpture as a "ritual activity", WalkingStick used wooden poles and canvas that she sewed and then painted with brightly coloured abstractions. Although the tipi was not used by the Cherokee (their origins were in the mountains and woodlands of the southeastern USA; the tipi is a Plains dwelling form), she recognised that the tipi was "a symbol of the Native Americans to non-Native Americans" (quoted in Valentino 1994, p.64).

In subsequent work she continued to explore imagery that spoke of both aspects of her heritage and that, in addition, developed further layers of meaning. The arcing forms found in both the apron paintings and *Messages to Papa* were developed in several ways, especially in the 36-piece *Chief Joseph* series (*c*.1974–7; artist's collection). Other paintings used a variety of linear forms such as a single line or an equilateral cross. The restraint and deliberation of these poised compositions were balanced by the earthiness and emotion of the process. Precise lines were incised into a deep impasto so that layers of colour were revealed. The surface was worked by hand, added to and reworked again until it literally built up its own history, at the same time suggesting markings on an ancient surface. In much of her work, the use of her own hands in applying and manipulating the material has been a central technique for WalkingStick. In 1983 she stated: "I apply the paint (acrylic and wax) with my hands to give the painting energy, excitement and a 'handedness'; the paint is dense; it is layered, scratched, and scraped" (Stillwater 1983). Later on, she elaborated: "I redraw, repaint, repeat, and layer until the painting seems to me to reach a kind of significant level of meaning. The message is as much in the paint as in the imagery" (Brookville 1991, p.34).

In the mid-1980s WalkingStick embarked on a long series of two-panelled paintings in which one side carries abstract, emblematic, usually geometric shapes while the other is a recognisable but highly expressionist depiction of land features such as a river, waterfall or rocky cliffs, as in *Four Directions: Stillness* (1994), *On the Edge* (1989) and *Remnant of Cataclysm* (1992; all artist's collection). Both sides are thickly painted and often presented on deep frames so that they have a strong, three-dimensional presence. WalkingStick has explained that these paintings are seated in her own identity as a bi-racial woman in the dominant white culture. In her writings she has noted the "double life" of many Indians who draw on tribal identities as well as experiences in the broader culture. Her paintings give form to such notions of separateness but at the same time speak to the possibility of transcendence and unity. In these searches and struggles, the role of land is seminal, as WalkingStick has explained: "The two portions represent two kinds of knowledge of the earth. One is visual, immediate and particular, the other is spiritual, long-term, and non-specific" ("Native American art in the postmodern era", 1992). Retaining the idea of the sacredness of the land that is a tenet in tribal beliefs, WalkingStick joins it to contemporary ecological concerns, both personal and societal. This inclusionary quality is typical of the multi-layered nature of her work both in imagery and technique. In a statement of 1991 WalkingStick discussed the purpose of her work and the role of duality in that purpose:

> My paintings show two different perceptions of the world in two different methods of painting: to some viewers these are diametrically opposed methods. Yet, I believe in the possibility of unity, of wholeness. My goal is to make meaningful, intuitive connections between these different, but mythically related, views [Brookville 1991, p.34].

In other work of the 1990s WalkingStick has dealt with Native American issues, including historical events such as the Massacre at Wounded Knee (*The Wizard Speaks, the Cavalry Listens, December 29th, 1890*, 1992; artist's collection). She has used her personal history in a book of drawing and commentary, *Talking Leaves* (1993; artist's collection), in which she records and reflects upon offensive and presumptuous remarks made to her over the years about being an Indian. She is a prominent spokesperson on matters concerning Native American artists and served as co-editor of the College Art Association *Art Journal* issue on "Recent Native American art" (Fall 1992). She has taught at colleges, universities and museums and is currently Associate Professor of Art at Cornell University.

LEA ROSSON DELONG

Ward, Henrietta (Mary Ada)

British painter, 1832–1924

Born in London, 1 June 1832, into a family of artists. Taught drawing by her mother, Mary Webb, and from 1843 by future husband Edward Matthew Ward. Married Ward, causing family estrangement, 1848; eight children. Attended art classes at Sass's, then lectures at the Royal Academy; own studio at home at 33 Harewood Square, London. Taught various royal children after 1854, when living near Windsor. Set up art school for girls after husband's death in 1879, in order to support her family. Signed petition for the admission of women to the Royal Academy Schools, 1859. Honorary member, Society of Female Artists, 1877; member of Central Committee of the National Society for Women's Suffrage, 1897. Died 12 July 1924.

Principal Exhibitions

Royal Academy, London: occasionally 1846–1921
Society of Female (later Lady) Artists, London: occasionally 1857–83
Dudley Gallery, London (oil): 1872

Selected Writings

Mrs E.M. Ward's Reminiscences, ed. Elliott O'Donnell, London: Pitman, 1911
Memories of Ninety Years, ed. Isabel McAllister, London: Hutchinson, 1924; New York: Holt, 1925

Bibliography

James Dafforne, "British artists: Their style and character, lxxvii: Henrietta Ward (Mrs E.M. Ward)", *Art Journal*, 1864, pp.357–9
Sarah Tytler, *Modern Painters and Their Paintings*, London: Strahan, 1873; Boston: Roberts, 1874
Ellen C. Clayton, *English Female Artists*, 2 vols, London: Tinsley, 1876
Clara Erskine Clement and Laurence Hutton, *Artists of the Nineteenth Century and Their Work*, 2 vols, Boston: Houghton Osgood, and London: Trübner, 1879; reprinted New York: Arno Press, 1969
R.W. Maude, "Mrs E.M. Ward: 'Royalties as Artists'", *Strand Magazine*, xvi, October 1898, pp.366–71
Connoisseur, lxx, 1924, p.57 (obituary)
Pamela Gerrish Nunn, "The case history of a woman artist: Henrietta Ward", *Art History*, i, 1978, pp.293–308
Charlotte Yeldham, *Women Artists in Nineteenth-Century France and England*, 2 vols, New York: Garland, 1984
Pamela Gerrish Nunn, ed., *Canvassing Women: Recollections by Six Victorian Women Artists*, London: Camden, 1986
——, *Victorian Women Artists*, London: Women's Press, 1987
Paula Gillett, *The Victorian Painter's World*, New Brunswick, NJ: Rutgers University Press, and Gloucester: Sutton, 1990

Deborah Cherry, *Painting Women: Victorian Women Artists*, London and New York: Routledge, 1993

Henrietta Ward was a prolific and successful Victorian painter of historical subjects with a domestic flavour. In her own long lifetime she saw her work win royal patronage and critical acclaim, and then go completely out of fashion. Today few of her pictures can be located, although her subjects are well recorded in contemporary reviews, the exhibition records of the Royal Academy and elsewhere, and in her own memoirs, *Reminiscences* (1911), which were more or less republished in *Memories of Ninety Years* in the year of her sparsely recorded death.

Born into a dynasty of British artists (grandfather James Ward, RA, father George Raphael Ward, a painter and engraver, and mother Mary Webb, a miniature painter) and married to the artist Edward Matthew Ward, Henrietta enjoyed both the educational advantages and suffered the public disadvantages of her connections. Ward's work was never reviewed without some comparative reference to her male relatives, especially as her husband also specialised in historical genre painting. Henrietta Ward feminised her art, preferring female protagonists and often concentrating on the depiction of emotions, for which reasons she was seen by some to be domesticating history. Much of her work emphasised female virtues and the happiness of family life. For example, in *George III and His Family at Windsor* (1872; Walker Art Gallery, Liverpool), exhibited at the Royal Academy as *The Queen's Lodge, Windsor in 1786*, she shows a visit paid by the artist Mary Delany to the king and queen. Ward depicts a scene of domestic tranquillity, with the queen and lady artist engaged in conversation while the king plays on the floor with Princess Amelia and the other royal children paint and draw at the table. This work, because of its theme and compositional similarity, could have been intended as a companion piece to E. M. Ward's picture of the *Royal Family of France* (1872; Harris Museum and Art Gallery, Preston), which shows the disruption of a happy family brought about by Revolution.

In the 1850s Ward specialised in domestic scenes for which her own home life, servants included, was the model. The Wards lived near Windsor, so that her husband could work on his royal commissions. Queen Victoria and Prince Albert visited the artists in their studios and Henrietta's paintings and draw-

ings of her own brood won her a number of commissions to paint the royal children. Ward writes frankly about her own domestic arrangements in *Memories*, in which she describes a harmonious working partnership, but with the business and housekeeping responsibilities falling heavily on to her shoulders. Although she praises her husband for his "broadmindedness" in allowing his wife to be a career woman, it would appear from her account of daily life in the Ward household, where both had their studios, that his work was rarely interrupted while she was often faced with "some knotty problem that could only be solved by the mistress of the house". She often used her own children as models in her domestic subject pictures, such as *Morning Lesson* (1855), *The Bath* (1858), *A First Step in Life* (1871) and *God Save the Queen* (1857; repr. *Art Journal*, 1875). This was a sometimes hazardous practice, such as the occasion recorded by Ward when her two-year-old daughter, modelling for *The Birthday*, "industriously removed all my painting, having vigorously rubbed it all over with a paint rag" while the artist's back was turned.

In the 1860s Ward shifted her interest from purely domestic subjects to depictions of women in history. Her particular source was Agnes Strickland's book *The Lives of the Queens of Scotland* (1850), in which she found the basis for her paintings of women of courage, fortitude and assertive action. At the Royal Academy in 1863 she exhibited *Queen Mary Quitted Stirling Castle on the Morning of Wednesday, April 23...*, in which the scene is set in the nursery at Stirling Castle, with the dignified figure of Mary Queen of Scots standing over the cradle of her sleeping child as she prepares to leave and meet her unhappy fate. Celebrated by the critics as "thoroughly a woman's subject, which a woman's heart and hand may best understand and paint" (*Illustrated London News*, 11 July 1863), this work is now lost, as is the case with much of Ward's oeuvre. Ward's history pictures, meticulously researched in details of costume and setting, focused on her heroines in the roles of wife and mother, but never to detract from their dignity and courage. Other subjects include *Scene at the Louvre in 1649: The Despair of Henrietta Maria at the Death of Her Husband Charles I* (1862), *Sion House, 1553* (1868), an episode in the life of Lady Jane Grey, *Scene from the Childhood of the Old Pretender* (1869), *Defence of Latham House* (1874), which records the cool heroism of the Countess of Derby and her daughters when her house was under siege, and *Princess Charlotte of Wales* (1877), chronicling the princess's motherly kindness to a wounded waif. French history was also a popular source for Ward, for example *Scene from the Childhood of Joan of Arc* (1867) and *First Interview of the Divorced Empress Josephine with the King of Rome* (1870).

The Victorian picture-viewing public expected history painters to provide them with a readable narrative and complete historical accuracy. In her autobiography Ward recorded one occasion on which the pursuit of artistic truth almost put her life in danger. Engaged in an unchaperoned sitting with a soldier-model for *Scene from the Camp at Chobham, in the Encampment of the 79th Highlanders* (1854) – her husband out of earshot in his own studio – she was alarmed to realise that the queen's piper model had been drinking, and even more horrified when he lunged at her with a knife. Ward remained calm, the soldier collapsed after his frenzy and the picture was rewarded with a fine review in the *Art Journal* (1854, p.170).

From more recent history, Ward took the subject of one of her best-known works, *Newgate 1818* (1876; original probably in the USA; replica of 1895 in Friends' House, London), in which she depicts Elizabeth Fry, the great Quaker philanthropist, conducting her young friend Mary Sanderson around the grim female prison. Ward professed great admiration for Fry, describing her as a woman who "was determined to probe the depths of humanity's miseries, not from any curiosity, but because she had realised the truth of vital Christianity".

The death of her husband in 1879 left Ward in her late forties with a family to support on her own. Like many other women artists in her situation she turned to teaching to boost her income, opening an art school for girls in 1880, much patronised by royalty and the aristocracy and with distinguished visiting teachers such as Sir Lawrence Alma-Tadema, Marcus Stone, William Powell Frith and Sir Luke Fildes. Ward's own daughters, Eva, Flora, Beatrice and Enid, studied with her and themselves became artists. Despite Ward's own steely professionalism, on the whole her pupils were confirmed amateurs in search of no more than an attractive feminine accomplishment. The work of running the school prevented Ward from exhibiting so often and, in the latter part of her life, her art out of fashion, she turned to landscape and domestic scenes.

Ward was one of the few Victorian women artists to find success, albeit in constant comparison with that of her male family members, within the art establishment. She exhibited regularly at the Royal Academy for much of her life (her drawing of *Elizabeth Woodville Parting from the Duke of York* was accepted when she was only 14; collection of artist's descendants), and supported the Society of Female Artists by showing her studies and sketches there from 1857. Although many of her most significant works are now inaccessible, her painting *Palissy the Potter* (1866) is in Leicester City Art Galleries, and *Chatterton* (1873), one of a number of scenes from the lives of poets, is in Bristol City Museum and Art Gallery. Although criticism of Ward constantly noted the "feminine" defects of her art, equally her skills of pictorial composition and her natural figure relationships were always admired. Speaking for herself, Ward wrote: "personally I feel that the RA-ship should be open to women equally with men, for there is no sex in Art, and it is pure selfishness that has excluded women from this honour, with the exception of Mary Moser and Angelika Kauffmann".

JANE SELLARS

Warrick, Meta Vaux *see* Fuller

Watson, Caroline
British printmaker, 1760 or 1761–1814

Born in London, 1760 or 1761; daughter of printmaker James Watson. Appointed Engraver to Queen Charlotte, 1785. Died in Pimlico, London, 10 June 1814.

Bibliography
G. Goodwin, *Thomas Watson, James Watson and Elizabeth Judkins*, London: Bullen, 1904

Freeman O'Donoghue and Henry M. Hake, *Catalogue of Engraved British Portraits...in the British Museum*, 6 vols, London, 1908–25

Gerald Eades Bentley, *Blake Records*, Oxford: Clarendon Press, 1969

Richard and Maria Cosway: Regency Artists of Taste and Fashion, exh. cat., Scottish National Portrait Gallery, Edinburgh, and National Portrait Gallery, London, 1995

Caroline Watson, stipple engraver, primarily of portraits, engraved two or three plates a year between 1780 and 1810, and was the only Englishwoman to have had an extended career as an independent engraver in 18th-century Britain. Other women certainly worked as professional engravers, but they all belonged to families headed by male engravers. It is true that Watson's father, James, was an engraver, but he worked exclusively in mezzotint, whereas his daughter worked primarily in stipple, the technique that suddenly became fashionable in the mid-1770s with the demand for "furniture prints" after pictures and drawings by Angelica Kauffman (q.v.) and others; the prints, generally ovals or circles, were often printed in red or in colours and close-framed in gilt. James Watson had done well enough to retire to Welwyn in Hertfordshire by 1781.

It is not known who taught Watson to engrave in the new technique, but she was signing plates by 1780 and soon began working for the leading print publisher John Boydell, for whom her father had engraved many plates. In 1781 Boydell published her *Boy and Dog* after a painting by Murillo, the first of at least seven plates by her that he issued. Another early commission was from the painter Robert Edge Pine to engrave his pictures of Shakespearian scenes of which he held a special exhibition; these were unusual in being imaginative depictions rather than stage scenes. Pine's venture failed and the plates, such as Watson's *Miranda* (1782), were bought by Boydell, who soon after developed Pine's idea and launched his Shakespeare Gallery.

Perhaps because she was seen as a woman on her own, Watson attracted support from a number of influential people. Her father engraved many pictures by Sir Joshua Reynolds, who was one of the first to help Watson's career, allowing her to engrave and publish two pictures in his possession: in 1788 *St Matthew* after Rubens, and in 1786 a miniature of the poet *John Milton*. In the inscription on the latter Reynolds praises the way in which she had preserved the likeness with "the utmost exactness". The extreme delicacy of her modelling was well suited to the reproduction of miniatures and she engraved at least 20, including seven after Samuel Shelley.

In the 1780s Watson herself published a number of prints from Fitzroy Street, London, where she probably lived with her barrister brother. It is possible that she had the help of her father with print selling; he was living with her at the time of his death in 1790. Her reputation increased rapidly, not least because of her appointment as Engraver to Queen Charlotte in 1785; she had engraved a portrait of *Prince William* for Boydell in 1781, and in 1786 engraved portraits by Hoppner of the princesses *Sophia* and *Mary*, which she published with dedications to the king and queen. This appointment seems to have brought prestige rather than employment from the queen, who had begun to collect prints, and no doubt her example encouraged others to buy Watson's productions. A more valuable association was the one she formed with the diplomat and collector Lord Mountstuart, later 4th Earl and 1st Marquess of Bute, and his wife; for the rest of her career she engraved pictures and family portraits belonging to the Bute family. Some of these plates have her name as publisher, but they were probably more in the nature of private plates, with the family paying handsomely for copies to distribute to friends and relations.

The end of the 1780s, when the print market was buoyant, must have been the busiest period of Watson's career. According to the *Monthly Magazine* (1803, p.48), it was at the specific request of Reynolds that she engraved a large plate of the *Death of Cardinal Beaufort*, the picture he painted for Boydell's Shakespeare Gallery, of which proofs were published in 1790. It was unfortunate for her that this was such an unsatisfactory picture; alterations had to be made to the print in order to make it less ludicrous. During the 1790s Watson published very few prints herself; this may have been because of the difficulties that any sole engraver had in distributing prints, but it was also probably because the print market contracted as a result of hostilities with France. Instead Watson began to engrave plates for the printseller Molteno, and she also began to work for the book trade. In 1804 Ackermann published a set of 12 aquatints by her after drawings by Maria Cosway (q.v.) illustrating Mary Robinson's poem *The Winter Day*. This appears to be her only major project in aquatint, and the etched outlines give the subjects a vivacity that was not obtainable with the softness of stipple.

The next major commission that she secured was for seven plates in William Hayley's *Life of William Cowper*, published in 1809. Despite the adverse views expressed by the sculptor John Flaxman about Watson's abilities (Flaxman to Hayley, 16 June 1804), Hayley was keen to employ her; another friend, who had heard she was in need of work, visited her on Hayley's behalf in Furnival's Inn Court, Holborn, and reported that he "found her a very interesting, diffident woman ... Her reputation is so high, & her powers of art so delightful, that I rejoice you have employed her" (John Carr to Hayley, 28 March 1805, quoted in Bentley 1969, p.161). This work was the last major undertaking she finished; her health began to deteriorate, her output dropped off after 1810 and she did not entirely complete her last plate, the *Annunciation* by Murillo in the Bute collection at Luton Hoo, Bedfordshire.

DAVID ALEXANDER

Werefkin, Marianne [fig. 72]
Russian painter, 1860–1938

Born in Tula, 29 August 1860, into a military family. Received drawing lessons from a woman Academy instructor, 1874. Trained in portrait painting by the Warsaw-based artist P. Heinemann in Lublin, Poland, 1876. Studio established in summer residence "Gut Blagodat" in Kovno (now Kaunas), Lithuania, 1879. Became a private student of Ilya Repin, 1880. Trained under Illarion Pryanishnikov at the Moscow Academy, 1883. Moved to St Petersburg, 1886. Right hand injured in a shooting accident, 1888. Met the artist Alexej Jawlensky, 1891. Inherited an annuity on the death of father, enabling her to move to Munich with Jawlensky, 1896; devoted herself to developing Jawlensky's career for the next ten years. Founded the St Luke Artists Association, which held meetings at her Munich residence, 1897. Visited Venice with Jawlensky and other Russian painters from Anton Ažbè's studio, 1899. Started journal *Lettres à un inconnu* (completed 1905) and travelled to Russia, 1901–2. Visited Normandy and Paris with Jawlensky and was impressed by work of Neo-Impressionists and van Gogh, 1903. Accompanied Jawlensky on extended trip to Brittany, Paris,

Provence and Switzerland, visiting the artist Ferdinand Hodler, 1905. Under the impact of the French avant-garde, began to sketch again, 1906. Visit of the Nabis Jan Verkade and Paul Sérusier to studio, 1907. Painted alongside Jawlensky, Gabriele Münter (q.v.) and Kandinsky in Murnau, 1908–10. Founder member, Neue Künstlervereinigung München, 1909; left the association after publication of Otto Fischer's book *Das Neue Bild* to participate in exhibitions of Der Blaue Reiter, 1912. Extended visit to Russia, 1914; emigrated to St Prex, Switzerland, at outbreak of World War I. Established contact with exponents of Dada and attended sessions of the Cabaret Voltaire in Zürich; cessation of payment of tsarist pension after the October Revolution, 1917. Settled in Ascona, Switzerland, 1918. Returned to Munich to arrange storage of possessions and paintings, 1920. Separated from Jawlensky, 1922. With seven other artists, founded the group Der grosse Bär in Ascona, 1924. Visited major sites of Italy, 1926. Died 6 February 1938; buried according to Russian Orthodox rites.

Principal Exhibitions
Neue Künstlervereinigung München, Galerie Thannhauser, Munich: 1909–11
Galerie Der Sturm, Berlin: 1912 (*Der Blaue Reiter*), 1913 (*Erster deutscher Herbstsalon*), 1914 (with Jacoba van Heemskerck)
Sonderbund, Cologne: 1912
Kunstsalon Wolfsberg, Zürich: 1919 (with Alexej Jawlensky, Arthur Segal and Robert Genin)
Venice Biennale: 1920
Kunsthalle, Bern: 1925 (*Der grosse Bär*)
Galerie Nierendorf, Berlin: 1928 (with Christian Rohlfs, Karl Schmidt-Rottluff and Der grosse Bär, touring)

Selected Writings
Briefe an einen Unbekannten 1901–1905, ed. Clemens Weiler, Cologne: DuMont Schauberg, 1960
"Lettres à un inconnu, 1901–1905", *Voicing Our Visions: Writings by Women Artists*, ed. Mara R. Witzling, New York: Universe, 1991; London: Women's Press, 1992, pp.132–46

Bibliography
Otto Fischer, *Das Neue Bild*, Munich: Delphin, 1912
Gustav Pauli, *Erinnerungen aus sieben Jahrzehnten*, Tübingen: Wunderlich, 1936
F. Stöckli, *Marianne Werefkin, Otillie Roederstein, Hans Brühlmann*, Zürich: Kunsthaus, 1938
Marianne Werefkin, 1860–1938, exh. cat., Städtisches Museum, Wiesbaden, 1958

Elisabeth Erdmann-Macke, *Erinnerung an August Macke*,
Stuttgart: Kohlhammer, 1962

Jelena Hahl-Koch, "Marianne Werefkin und der russische
Symbolismus: Studien zur Ästhetik und Kunsttheorie",
Slavistische Beiträge, xxiv, 1967

Rosel Gollek, *Der Blaue Reiter im Lenbachhaus
München: Katalog der Sammlung in der Städtischen
Galerie*, Munich: Prestel, 1974; 4th edition, 1988

Monte Verità: Berg der Wahrheit, exh. cat.,
Gemeindemuseum, Ascona, and Kunsthaus, Zürich,
1978

Alessandra Comini, "State of the field, 1980: The woman
artists of German Expressionism", *Arts Magazine*, lv,
November 1980, pp.147–53

Marianne Werefkin: Gemälde und Skizzen, exh. cat.,
Städtische Museum, Wiesbaden, 1980

Renate Berger, *Malerinnen auf dem Weg ins 20.
Jahrhundert: Kunstgeschichte als Sozialgeschichte*,
Cologne: DuMont, 1982

Ulrike Evers, *Deutsche Künstlerinnen des 20.
Jahrhunderts: Malerei, Bildhauerei, Tapisserie*,
Hamburg: Schultheis, 1983

Bernd Fäthke, "Die Werefkin im Profil", *Alexej
Jawlensky, 1864–1941*, exh. cat., Städtische Galerie im
Lenbachhaus, Munich, 1983, pp.67–71

B. Weidle (Pörtener), *Die Malerin Marianne Werefkin in
München (1896–1914) und ihr Beitrag zur Entstehung
der abstrakter Malerei in Deutschland*, MA thesis,
Bonn University, 1986

Shulamith Behr, *Women Expressionists*, Oxford: Phaidon,
and New York: Rizzoli, 1988

Marianne Werefkin: Leben und Werk, 1860–1938, exh.
cat., Museo Comunale d'Arte Moderna, Ascona, and
elsewhere, 1988

S. Heinlein, *Gabriele Münter und Marianne Werefkin:
Die Rollen zweier Frauen im "Blauen Reiter"*, MA
thesis, Hamburg University, 1989

C. Ashjian, *Primitivism and Modernity in Marianne
Werefkin's 1907–1914 Works*, MA thesis, Courtauld
Institute of Art, University of London, 1992

Bernd Fäthke, "Die Wiedergeburt der 'Blaue Reiter –
Reiterin' in Berlin: Von der Diskriminierung der Frau
in der Kunst am Beispiel Marianne Werefkin",
*Profession ohne Tradition: 125 Jahre Verein der
Berliner Künstlerinnen*, exh. cat., Berlinische Galerie,
Berlin, 1992, pp.237–48

While Marianne Werefkin's pivotal role within Munich-based Expressionism was acknowledged by contemporary commentators, her contribution has been woefully neglected in accounts of early modernism. In post-World War II Germany her works surfaced publicly at an exhibition in Wiesbaden in 1958. Interestingly, however, she was excluded from the ambitious exhibition *Women Artists, 1550–1950* at the Los Angeles County Museum of Art in 1976 and only mentioned in passing in the accompanying catalogue (p.282). This possibly attests to the difficulty of contextualising her production in relation to either German or Russian avant-garde art and yet, even in a groundbreaking article of 1980, Alessandra Comini queried whether Werefkin's work measured up to that of her fellow Russians Alexej Jawlensky and Wassily Kandinsky (Comini 1980, p.147).

Surprisingly, then, unlike other women practitioners in her circle such as Gabriele Münter (q.v.) and Erma Bossi, Werefkin's intellectual preoccupations have received far more focused attention than her artistic abilities. In comparison to their training in Germany, women artists were not excluded from academies in Russia, and Werefkin's confident interaction in public life was considered unusual in the Munich context (Pauli 1936, p.264). By virtue of her family's military background and her independent means, she was accorded aristocratic status and was indubitably the initiator of cultural discourse at the salons organised at her Giselastrasse residence in Schwabing.

To date, however, there has been no comprehensive publication of Werefkin's writings, notes or reminiscences. In 1960 Clemens Weiler published an abridged German translation of her diaries, *Lettres à un inconnu, 1901–5*, in which he stressed Werefkin's direct influence on Kandinsky's theoretical formulations and move towards abstraction (Weiler 1960, p.71). By 1967 serious academic attention was paid to the artist's Russian symbolist heritage in Jelena Hahl-Koch's doctoral dissertation and subsequent publications. This was supplemented by Bernd Fäthke's findings on the significance of French symbolist theory to Werefkin's early intellectual maturity; titles, excerpts and commentaries on key authors and poets (Rimbaud, Mallarmé, Verlaine, Baudelaire and Edgar Allan Poe) were listed in a notebook dating from 1889 (Wiesbaden 1980, p.7). Since 1970 Fäthke and his wife have been responsible for initiating a Werefkin Archive of source material and documentation and his publication accompanying the major retrospective of her works in 1988 (Munich, Hannover and Ascona) is enriched by quotations from primary evidence; these, however, are invariably undated and unclassified.

Werefkin chose to write her journals in French, the language of elite circles in tsarist Russia. The manner of addressing the inner, unique self (*Letters to an Unknown*) acknowledges the impact of

Charles Baudelaire's intimate journals *Mon coeur mis à nu* ("My heart laid bare", 1869), but Werefkin's interest in the divided being is compounded by her awareness of societal constructions of the terms "woman" and "artist": "Am I a true artist? Yes, yes, yes. Am I a woman? Alas, yes, yes, yes. Are the two able to work as a pair? No, no, no" (vol.i: abridged English translation in Witzling 1991, p.136). Hence, while the journals record the private frustrations caused by her lack of personal creative fulfilment and domestic trauma, they also divulge a calculated attempt to construct an artistic personality. In this she was informed by Nietzsche's beliefs – she read his *Birth of Tragedy* (1872) in 1900 – in the visionary role of the artist and the salvationary power of art to transform society (Weidle 1986, pp.60–64). Werefkin's aspirations to this status are well conveyed in her *Self-Portrait* of *c.*1910 (tempera on board; Städtische Galerie im Lenbachhaus, Munich, repr. Behr 1988, pl.6), which radiates the intensity of her personality, the startling colour of the piercing red eyes investing the image with prophetic qualities.

It is therefore understandable that in her journal Werefkin declared the autonomy of art from imitating nature: "Art is a Weltanschauung...which finds its expression in those forms, which inspire its technical means: sound, colour, form, line, word" (vol.ii: abridged German translation in Hahl-Koch 1967, p.94). This prescription for abstraction, transmitted in a forceful declamatory style, places Werefkin's journals at the forefront of Expressionist treatises and indicates that her formulations were intended for a wider and initiated audience. It was not without some familiarity with her writings that Otto Fischer could claim: "For this spiritual woman, art is the essential expression of an inner life, that is totally accessible...possibly only to those tuned to the same pitch. The large gouaches that she paints are for her the confessions of a journal" (Fischer 1912, p.42). Evidently, by 1912, critical reception had little difficulty in accepting Werefkin's "visionary" status even though she had devoted herself exclusively to nurturing Jawlensky's artistic talent between 1896 and 1906.

The lack of consistency in Werefkin's development as a painter can be attributed to this hiatus in her career, to the complexity of her situation as a Russian expatriate in Munich and Switzerland and to her unsystematic practice. Her major paintings were left undated and unsigned, while her studies

were only occasionally dated. For various reasons, Werefkin did not have access to her pre-1914 Russian and Munich oeuvre which was only retrieved by her close friend in Ascona, Ernst Alfred Aye, after her death (see Fäthke 1992, pp.247–8). There is no catalogue raisonné of her works and the mostly uncatalogued state of her sketchbooks prevents systematic examination of her production. One can, however, distinguish the major features of her thematic departures, process and style from a chronological breakdown of her output in the three geographic locations: Russia (1880–96), Munich (1906–14) and Ascona (1918–38).

Werefkin's concern for figure painting was inherited from her training with Pryanishnikov in Moscow and Repin in St Petersburg. As members of the Wanderers (*Peredvizhniki*), a realist movement associated with radical social comment, their iconography included portraiture, landscape and depictions of peasant life. Werefkin's early oils on canvases, focusing on depictions derived from her domestic and military environment, reveal a considerable talent in capturing likeness within an overall monumentality of form. The formal qualities of the ambitious, full-length portrait of her *Father's Orderly* (1883) and bust-length portrait of her *Mother* (1886; both collection of Dr C. Artzibushev, Odessa/Florida, repr. Ascona 1988, pls 1 and 2) rely on a tradition of Dutch and Spanish naturalism. Employing a limited tonal palette, Werefkin highlights the facial and gestural characterisation against a neutral background, seizing on the impact of red for dramatic detail.

Her paintings of the 1890s confirm that the permanent crippling of her right-hand thumb and index finger in 1888 represented more of a challenge than a threat to her career. She continued to portray figural types – Jews, peasants, servants – drawn from the margins of society that she encountered at the Werefkin summer estate in Kovno, Lithuania. In the painting *Jewish Day-Labourer* (*c.*1890; oil on canvas; private collection, *ibid.*, fig.27) Werefkin attempted to reach beyond the tattered shabbiness of the man's attire in representing the quiet dignity of the bearded worker. Abandoning the tight control of realistic modelling, her brushwork became looser and less descriptive, allowing the figure to emerge more effectively from an atmospheric background. She received positive endorsement of her progress when her works were exhibited with the Wanderers in St Petersburg in 1891; comparing the impact to that of Velázquez, Repin admired the freedom of the modelling and expressive forcefulness of the portraits (Fäthke in Ascona 1988, pp.30–31). It is worth noting, however, that photographs of Werefkin's studio in St Petersburg (*ibid.*, fig.30) indicate that she was a prolific artist and adept at painting studies of the nude, still-life, landscape and multi-figured compositions.

Werefkin began sketching in 1906 after spending approximately a decade in Munich. By the time that she resumed painting, she revised her understanding of what constituted high art. She abandoned the earthy tonalities and medium of oil painting on canvas, favouring the primary significance of colours and quicker drying processes of a mixed technique: watercolour, gouache and/or tempera on paper or board. It would be misleading to suggest that she was working in a more *alla prima*, intuitive style, since Werefkin always retained a complex method of producing ink and graphite sketches or fully developed studies in colour before executing final paintings. Undoubtedly, the impact of her second visit to Paris in 1905 and viewing of the launch exhibition of the Salon d'Automne confirmed her theoretical departure from naturalistic form and colour. Indeed, Werefkin proclaimed: "I went to France for a year, started everything afresh and in a few months I had found the direction that I am now going in" (quotation undated; Stöckli 1938, p.5). Werefkin's subject matter embraced modern experience, and her work of this period expresses the city/country paradigm and other issues that were fiercely debated in the cultural politics of the 1900s (see Ashjian 1992, pp.21, 38–9).

Equating the spectacles of Paris and Munich, Werefkin declared in her journal:

> The everyday man relishes life and it is always the same to him, if he wanders on the Parisian boulevard or drinks beer in the Munich Hofbräu. The life he creates around himself, is always the same. Here and there more sociable or elegant, here and there stiffer and more boring for the most part though always the same [quotation undated; Fäthke in Ascona 1988, p.80].

Inspired by the works of Toulouse-Lautrec, the Nabis and Intimists, she pursued themes of modernity derived from the extremes of social entertainment, from sophisticated salon, ballroom and soirée interiors (Behr 1988, pp.28 and 40) to scenes from popular culture – the circus, cabaret and low life (for Werefkin's role as *flâneuse*, see Ashjian 1992, p.24). The uniformity engendered by urban capitalism is most suitably portrayed in the tempera on board *In the Café* (1909; Fondazione Marianne Werefkin, Ascona, repr. Ascona 1988, pl.32). The rhythmic positioning of the four male figures close to the picture plane, in a frieze-like arrangement, is complemented by a sinuous flow of contour that defines the downcast facial expressions and hand movements. A symbolist use of blue dominates the composition, from the dark shapes of the figures to the transparency of the table top, relieved only by the pastel shades of green and pink in the wine glasses.

Werefkin's distinctive stylistic and thematic interests are equally pronounced in her country works; her concern for social topics was unusual both in the context of the Neue Künstlervereinigung München and in relation to the Murnau works produced by Jawlensky, Kandinsky and Münter between 1908 and 1910. In its focus on genre-like detail of costume and daily ritual, *The Washerwomen* (1909; tempera on paper mounted on board; 50.5 × 60 cm.; Städtische Galerie im Lenbachhaus, repr. Behr 1988, pl.3) has much in common with the paintings of the school of Pont-Aven, Brittany. In other works on this theme, however, as in the larger scale *Black Women* (1909; Sprengel Museum, Hannover), the depiction of processions of darkly clad women, burdened by white bundles, indicate a less-than-idealised commentary on peasant life in the changing economy of the region. The stylising process is more accentuated, and dramatic use is made of silhouette, spatial distortion and mood-evoking coloration.

The encroachment of industrialisation on the traditionally romantic, Alpine setting is consistently dealt with in Werefkin's Murnau landscapes. In *Roof-tile Factory* (1910; tempera on board; 105 × 80 cm.; Museum Wiesbaden, repr. Behr 1988, pl.11) the tall smokestack of the factory in Oberau competes with the mountain peaks, while a peasant portrayed in the foreground appears displaced in this compressed and unstable composition. Yet, as in the paintings of the community of artists in the Blaue Reiter, Werefkin was not immune to investing nature with mystical and spiritual importance. The iconic value of the motifs and verticality of the composition in the *Red Tree* (1910; tempera on board; 76 × 57 cm.; Fondazione Marianne Werefkin, *ibid.*, pl.8) belie its source of inspiration in a Japanese print by Hokusai, *Pine in front of Mount Fuji* (1835; repr. Ascona 1988, fig.150). The dominating, blue ice-capped mountain, vivid red foliage of the centrally placed tree, the seated contemplative figure and thatched chapel suggest a hermetic reading of the visual components. Moreover, Werefkin dismissed plein-airism (local colour has been heavily overpainted and obscured in this painting), focusing attention on the emotional and expressive power of the colours. Recognising the value of these ideas, Franz Marc communicated to Maria Franck in a letter of 12 December 1910: "Miss Werefkin said ... that colour is totally different [to illumination] and has little to do with light."

In Ascona Werefkin entered into the spirit of the international artistic community and her anthroposophist leanings became more pronounced. Mystical and religious associations were prevalent in her themes and titles and, as in her Murnau works, the motifs of steep mountain ranges and hilltop villages of the Italian-Swiss Alps were employed as systematic metaphors for spiritual evocation. In the painting *Sacred Fire* (1919; tempera on board; 74 × 56 cm.; Fondazione Marianne Werefkin, *ibid.*, pl.90) Werefkin exploits the use of rhythmic, organic line and a harmony of red colours to sweep the eye towards the centrally placed summit, haloed by stars and luminosity.

Interestingly, the artist does not allow one to forget the centres of metropolitan power even at a distance from the materialism of city life. In a painting entitled *The Victor* (c.1929; tempera on board; 68 × 96 cm.; Fondazione Marianne Werefkin, *ibid.*, pl.99) a train track penetrates the idyll, as cranes load quarried stone on to the rail cars, threatening the anthropomorphically shaped, cowering images of the mountain range. Ceaselessly exploring variations of facture and colour orchestration, Werefkin invested each of her mature paintings with a power of suggestion, imagination and mystery. As one cannot say this of the late works of many avant-garde male painters who reach the age of 78, it is evident that a more rigorous contextual study of her contribution is both urgent and overdue.

SHULAMITH BEHR

Wheeler, Candace

American embroiderer and designer,
1827–1923

Born Candace Thurber in Delhi, New York, 1827; father a farmer, Presbyterian deacon and abolitionist. Married stockbroker Thomas M. Wheeler, 1844; four children, including painter and textile designer Dora (born 1856). Moved to Brooklyn, New York, after marriage; to Hollis, Long Island, 1854. Studied painting in Europe, 1860s. Visited Philadelphia Centennial Exposition and saw work of the Royal School of Art Needlework, 1876. Co-founder and vice-president, Society of Decorative Art of New York City, 1877; founder, Woman's Exchange, for the sale of crafts and foodstuffs, 1878. Partner and textile specialist of Associated Artists, 1879–83; continued to produce textiles under the name Associated Artists after dissolution of original partnership, 1883–1907. Designed wallpapers for Warren, Fuller and Company from 1881; textiles for Cheney Brothers, Connecticut, from c.1884. Colour (i.e. interior) director for Woman's Building and director of Bureau of Applied Arts for State of New York display, World's Columbian Exposition, Chicago, 1893. Awarded first prize, Society of Decorative Art of New York City, 1879. Died in New York, 5 August 1923.

Principal Exhibitions
World's Columbian Exposition, Chicago: 1893

Selected Writings
Editor, *Columbia's Emblem: Indian Corn: A Garland of Tributes*, Boston: Houghton Mifflin, 1893
Editor, *Household Art*, New York: Harper, 1893
"Applied arts in the Woman's Building", *Art and Handicraft in the Woman's Building of the World's Columbian Exposition, Chicago, 1893*, ed. Maud Howe Elliott, Chicago and New York: Rand McNally, 1894, pp.59–67
"Decorative art", *Architectural Record*, iv, 1895, pp.409–13
"Art education for women", *Outlook*, lv, 2 January 1897, pp.81–7
Content in a Garden, Boston: Houghton Mifflin, 1901
How to Make Rugs, New York: Doubleday, 1902
Principles of Home Decoration with Practical Examples, New York: Doubleday, 1903
Yesterdays in a Busy Life, New York: Harper, 1918 (autobiography)
The Development of Embroidery in America, New York: Harper, 1921

Bibliography

Constance Cary Harrison, *Woman's Handiwork in Modern Homes*, New York: Scribner, 1881

——, "Some work of the Associated Artists", *Harper's New Monthly Magazine*, lxix, August 1884, pp.343–51

Wilson H. Faude, "Associated Artists and the American renaissance in the decorative arts", *Winterthur Portfolio*, x, 1975, pp.101–30

——, "Candace Wheeler: Textile designer", *Magazine Antiques*, cxii, 1977, pp.258–61

Karal Ann Marling, "Portrait of the artist as a young woman: Miss Dora Wheeler", *Bulletin of the Cleveland Museum of Art*, lxv, February 1978, pp.46–57

Anthea Callen, *Angel in the Studio: Women in the Arts and Crafts Movement, 1870–1914*, London: Astragal, 1979; as *Women Artists of the Arts and Crafts Movement, 1870–1914*, New York: Pantheon, 1979

Virginia Williams, "Candace Wheeler: Textile designer for Associated Artists", *Nineteenth Century*, vi, Summer 1980, pp.60–61

Jeanne Madeline Weimann, *The Fair Women*, Chicago: Academy, 1981

Isabelle Anscombe, *A Woman's Touch: Women in Design from 1860 to the Present Day*, London: Virago, and New York: Viking, 1984

In Pursuit of Beauty: Americans and the Aesthetic Movement, exh. cat., Metropolitan Museum of Art, New York, 1986 (contains bibliography)

Lamia Doumato, *Candace Wheeler and Elsie de Wolfe: A Bibliography*, Monticello, IL: Vance, 1989

Gillian Moss, "Textiles of the American Arts and Crafts movement", *William Morris and the Arts and Crafts Movement: A Sourcebook*, ed. Linda Parry, London: Studio, 1989, pp.16–22

Susan Waller, *Women Artists in the Modern Era: A Documentary History*, Metuchen, NJ: Scarecrow, 1991

Candace Wheeler's 45-year career as artist and writer began when she was 50 years of age, and well established as a wealthy society matron in New York. The Royal School of Art Needlework (London) exhibit in the Main Building of the Philadelphia Centennial Exposition in 1876 provided the impetus for the activities of the rest of her life. The exhibit, a set of British art needlework pieces based on designs inspired by William Morris and others, was a revelation to American needleworkers who were immersed in Berlin woolwork and other "fancy work" of the period. Wheeler, whose motives were charitable as well as artistic, was also impressed with the Royal School's scheme for assisting impoverished gentlewomen who were in need of remunerative work but limited by social custom from seeking employment. Wheeler saw art needlework as a means of providing work for seamstresses displaced by mechanisation and as an opportunity to improve artistic taste among the needleworkers of America.

Her first attempt at organisation, the Society of Decorative Art of New York City (1877), was an amalgamation of socialites and artist advisers. Although it proved a successful model for similar societies in other American cities, its artistic goals were not as successful. Americans did not care for British designs and, having a less sophisticated art tradition, tended to produce work that failed to meet the standards of the socialites who selected work for the Society's sales. Wheeler was forced to resign when she formed the Woman's Exchange, deemed by her associates to be a competing organisation. She took advantage of her disaffiliation, however, to enter her wool and silk embroidered and painted velvet portières based on British examples, *Consider the Lillies of the Field* (Mark Twain House, Hartford, CT), in the Society's competition of 1879 and took first prize.

In 1879 she took the unusual step for a woman of that period of going into business with three men. She joined Louis Comfort Tiffany, Samuel Colman and Lockwood de Forest as textile specialist in their interior decorating firm, Associated Artists, a group now recognised as a major influence in the American Aesthetic movement. Their first commission, an embroidered drop-curtain for the new Madison Square Theatre in New York, was designed by the partners and executed under Wheeler's direction. The curtain, a realistic landscape in velvet and silks, was unfortunately burned on 26 February 1880 in a gas-lighting accident during the theatre's first season (it was replaced with a copy that has not survived). Wheeler's work as textile designer for Associated Artists during this period included decoration of the 7th Regiment Armory in New York (1880–81), the Mark Twain house in Hartford (1881) and redecoration of the White House in Washington, DC (1882–3).

Although textiles were Wheeler's major interest, she ventured into wallpaper design for a competition sponsored by the firm of Warren, Fuller and Company in October 1881. She and her students submitted designs and swept the four prizes, with Wheeler taking first for her bees and honeycomb pattern. Some of Wheeler's designs were used by Cheney Brothers, a large silk manufacturer of

Manchester and Hartford, Connecticut. She did a series of designs based on American flora and fauna including a popular carp pattern and a bees and honeycomb design similar to her prize-winning wallpaper pattern. Much of her work drew on British and Japanese precedents. She also greatly admired the work of Walter Crane and the British pre-Raphaelite painters. Because she wanted her fabric designs to be affordable by less affluent consumers, she had them printed on cotton as well as silk. Representative samples of her work are now in the Metropolitan Museum of Art, New York, and the Mark Twain Memorial.

In 1883 the Associated Artists firm was dissolved by mutual agreement. Tiffany's group, Louis C. Tiffany and Company, moved into Art Nouveau and became one of the leading exponents of the Art Nouveau style in America. Wheeler retained the name of Associated Artists and stayed with the naturalistic plant and animal forms that had characterised her work from the beginning. She rejected the British embroidery designs of the South Kensington school as too conventional and pursued pictorial representations as being more typically American. She continued as director of Associated Artists until shortly before 1900 when her son, Dunham Wheeler, took over. The firm produced textiles until 1907.

Wheeler and her associates experimented with needle-weaving, a technique that simulated tapestry weaving. In 1883 she patented an "American tapestry" method combining embroidery with weaving on a silk canvas. The tapestries included portraits and copies of other works of art, in particular a copy of Raphael's tapestry cartoon, the *Miraculous Draught of Fishes* (c.1519; Victoria and Albert Museum, London), executed by the staff of Associated Artists in the 1880s. It was greatly admired, and exhibited at the Chicago World's Columbian Exposition in 1893.

The major appointment of Wheeler's career was that of colour director of the Woman's Building at the World's Columbian Exposition. The idea of a Woman's Building had been put forward by Mrs Potter Palmer of Chicago and others who felt that women's achievements would be overshadowed if they were placed with those of men in exhibits dispersed throughout the fair. Wheeler was in charge of the interior decoration of the building, particularly the New York State Room, a library devoted to books written by women. Her responsi-

bilities included selecting art works for the many national and state exhibits. The great success of the Woman's Building lay in the overwhelming impression created by an entire building of exhibits devoted to women's achievements.

Wheeler wrote prolifically on interior decoration and related topics. Of her books, *The Development of Embroidery in America* (1921), published when she was 94, is the best known. It has more significance as the pioneering work on the history of American needlework than as a scholarly study. Although it has some value for its description of extant pieces, the text was not well researched, and contains many historical inaccuracies.

CONSTANCE A. FAIRCHILD

Wieland, Joyce

Canadian painter, film-maker and multi-media artist, 1931–1998

Born in Toronto, 30 June 1931. Studied at the Central Technical School, Toronto, under Carl Schaeffer, Doris McCarthy and Bob Ross. Married artist Michael Snow, 1956; divorced. Animator, Graphic Films, Toronto, 1957–9. Lived in New York, 1962–71. Instructor, Nova Scotia College of Art and Design, 1971; San Francisco Art Institute, 1985–6; artist-in-residence, University of Toronto, Architecture School, 1988–9. Recipient of Canada Council grants, 1966, 1968, 1984 and 1986; second prize, Ann Arbor Film Festival, for *A & B in Ontario*, 1986; Canada Council Victor M. Staunton award, 1972; Toronto Arts award, 1987; YWCA Woman of Distinction award, 1987. Member, Royal Academy, London, 1973. Officer, Order of Canada, 1983. Ceased working when affected by Alzheimer's disease, c.1990. Died in Toronto, 27 June 1998.

Selected Individual Exhibitions

Isaacs Gallery, Toronto: 1960, 1962, 1963, 1967, 1972, 1974, 1981, 1983
Hart House Gallery, University of Toronto: 1962 (with Michael Snow, touring)
Museum of Modern Art, New York: 1968, 1969
Vancouver Art Gallery: 1968 (retrospective)
Glendon College Art Gallery, York University, Toronto: 1969 (retrospective)

National Gallery of Canada, Ottawa: 1971, 1978
(touring)
Pauline McGibbon Cultural Centre, Toronto: 1979
Powerhouse Gallery, Montreal: 1980 (with Judy Chicago)
Forest City Gallery, London, Ontario: 1982 (touring)
Concordia University, Montreal: 1985
Alma Gallery, Toronto: 1986
Art Gallery of Ontario, Toronto: 1987–8 (touring retro-
spective)
Canada House Gallery, London: 1988
Agnes Etherington Art Centre, Queen's University,
Kingston, Ontario: 1995

Bibliography

Michel Sanouillet, "The sign of Dada", *Canadian Art*,
xix, March–April 1962, p.111
Jonathan Holstein, "New York's vitality tonic for
Canadian artists", *Canadian Art*, xxi,
September–October 1964, pp.270–79
Barrie Hale, "Joyce Wieland: Artist, Canadian, soft,
tough woman!", *The Telegram* (Toronto), 11 March
1967
P. Adams Sitney, "There is only one Joyce", *Artscanada*,
April 1970, pp.43–5
*True Patriot Love/Véritable amour patriotique: Joyce
Wieland*, exh. cat., National Gallery of Canada,
Ottawa, 1971
Hugo McPherson, "Wieland: An epiphany of north",
Artscanada, xxviii, August–September 1971, pp.17–27
Regina Cornwell, "True patriot love: The films of Joyce
Wieland", *Artforum*, x, September 1971, pp.36–40
Toronto Painting, 1953–1965, exh. cat., National Gallery
of Canada, Ottawa, 1972
William J. Withrow, *Contemporary Canadian Painting*,
Toronto: McClelland and Stewart, 1972
Kay Armatage, "Kay Armatage interviews Joyce
Wieland", *Take One*, iii, February 1972, pp.23–5
Joyce Wieland: Drawings for "The Far Shore", exh. cat.,
National Gallery of Canada, Ottawa, 1978
Lauren Rabinovitz, "Issues of feminist aesthetics: Judy
Chicago and Joyce Wieland", *Woman's Art Journal*,
i/2, 1980–81, pp.38–41
——, "An interview with Joyce Wieland", *Afterimage*,
viii, May 1981, pp.8–12
Martha Fleming, "Joyce Wieland", *Parachute*, no.23,
Summer 1981, p.45
Lauren Rabinovitz, "The development of feminist strate-
gies in the experimental films of Joyce Wieland", *Film
Reader 5*, Evanston, IL: Northwestern University
Press, 1982, pp.132–9
Toronto Painting of the 1960s, exh. cat., Art Gallery of
Ontario, Toronto, 1983
John Porter, "Artists discovering film: Post-war Toronto",
Vanguard, xiii, 1984, pp.24–6
Toronto Painting '84, exh. cat., Art Gallery of Ontario,
Toronto, 1984
Cache du Cinéma: Discovering Toronto Filmmakers, exh.
cat., Funnel Experimental Film Theater, 1985
Joyce Wieland: A Decade of Painting, exh. cat.,
Concordia University, Montreal, 1985
Kass Banning, "Textual excess in Joyce Wieland's *Hand-
Tinting*", *Cine-Action*, no.5, May 1986
Kay Armatage, *Artist on Fire: The Work of Joyce
Wieland*, documentary film, Toronto: Canadian
Filmmakers Distribution Centre, and New York:
Women Make Movies, 1987
Kass Banning, "The mummification of mommy: Joyce
Wieland as the Art Gallery of Ontario's first living
other", *C Magazine*, no.13, 1987, pp.32–9; reprinted
in *Sightlines: Reading Contemporary Canadian Art*,
ed. Jessica Bradley and Lesley Johnstone, Montreal:
Artextes, 1994
Joyce Wieland, exh. cat., Art Gallery of Ontario,
Toronto, and elsewhere, 1987 (contains extensive
bibliography)
Kay Armatage, "The feminine body: Joyce Wieland's
Water Sark", *Canadian Women's Studies/Cahiers de la
Femme*, viii, Spring 1987, pp.84–8
Susan M. Crean, "Notes from the language of emotion:
A conversation with Joyce Wieland", *Canadian Art*,
Spring 1987, pp.64–5
Jay Scott, "Full circle: True patriot womanhood: The
thirty year passage of Joyce Wieland", *ibid.*, Spring
1987, pp.56–63
Kay Armatage, "Joyce Wieland: Feminist documentary
and the body of work", *Canadian Journal of Political
and Social Theory*, xiii/1–2, 1989
Linda Hutcheon, *Splitting Images: Contemporary
Canadian Ironies*, Toronto: Oxford University Press,
1991
Lauren Rabinovitz, *Points of Resistance: Women, Power
and Politics in the New York Avant-Garde Cinema,
1943–71*, Urbana: University of Illinois Press, 1991
Joyce Wieland: Twilit Record of Romantic Love, exh.
cat., Agnes Etherington Art Centre, Queen's
University, Kingston, Ontario, 1995

Joyce Wieland was one of the most prominent
artists of her generation in Canada, and one of the
earliest women to develop an art practice deliberately woman-centred and political in its concerns. In
the heyday of Pop Art she asserted a female viewpoint on eroticism and on the sexual body, and drew
not only on mass media but on women's traditions
of creativity. She worked collaboratively with other
women artists and craft workers, and from the
1970s focused increasingly on political issues. Her
art, however, was never didactic. Throughout her
career Wieland cultivated a sensibility that revelled
in humorous playfulness and a baroque exuberance
of colour and of sensuous reference to the physical
world. With her constant attention to the formal
possibilities of her media and to the social nature of
sign systems, her persistent concern with embodi-

ments of a feminine desire and her courage to work outside current fashions, Wieland produced a body of work that remains compelling, if often controversial, to younger feminist artists and critics.

Born in Toronto to English immigrant working-class parents, and orphaned young, Wieland moved directly from the art department of the Central Technical School, Toronto, to work for commercial art and advertising companies, including Graphic Films, a commercial company whose director George Dunning later made the Beatles' film *Yellow Submarine*. Here she learned film animation techniques and story-boarding, and met a lively group of fellow artists, including Michael Snow, whom she would marry in 1956. Wieland drew on this experience as she joined a generation of Toronto artists who inherited the formal legacy of the Canadian Abstract Expressionist-inspired Painters Eleven, while opening their art to the imagery of urban consumer culture under the stimulus of Dada, Surrealism and Pop Art.

The remarkable body of painting that Wieland produced during the years 1956–66, the first decade of her artistic career, has been discussed by Sandra Paikowsky (Montreal 1985). Her earliest figure paintings proclaimed her admiration for the work of Willem de Kooning (*Morning*, 1956; oil on canvas; repr. Montreal 1985, p.16). She made several series of informal, playful drawings of nude lovers, responding to Picasso's erotica, but focusing on the male as love object, or wryly noting women's vulnerability in the power structure of the heterosexual couple (Allen in Kingston 1995, pp.6–10). From 1959 Wieland developed a distinctive abstract language in which coloured shapes, suggestive of anatomical fragments or organic forms, cluster together or disperse as areas of brushed pigment over richly stained grounds (see *Redgasm*, 1960; oil on canvas; repr. Montreal 1985, p.19). Working often on a very large scale, Wieland went beyond conventional sexual symbols to evoke the rhythms of sexual intercourse and the cycles of female sexuality through large spontaneously drawn circular forms, loops and paint splashes. She also made lyrical collages of found materials that referred abstractly to water and sky, breasts, belly and penis, to sexual activity and to nature eroticised (*Summer Blues – Ball*, 1961; mixed media; *ibid.*, p.29).

From 1962 to 1971 Wieland lived and worked in New York with Michael Snow. Experimental film now became a major part of their output, as they became members of the "New York underground" of independent film-makers around Jonas Mekas, organiser of the Film-Makers' Cooperative and Cinematheque. Wieland collaborated with a number of its members (notably Hollis Frampton, Shirley Clarke, George and Mike Kuchar), and delighted in the freedom offered by the deliberately primitive "home-movie" aesthetic. Unfortunately, Mekas would exclude her from his Anthology Film Archives set up in 1970, in marked contrast to the treatment given to Snow, whose films became classics of the structural film movement (Rabinovitz in Toronto 1987, pp.166–7).

Wieland's early New York works in film, painting and multi-media introduced a woman's voice into an aesthetic current that explored the vernacular of commercial imagery and the mass media's fascination with eroticism and sensational disasters. The film *Patriotism, Part II* (1964; 16 mm., 5 minutes, silent, colour), with its Pop imagery of hot dogs, cigarettes and aeroplanes, parodied "a world ruled by the phallus", while *Water Sark* (1964–5; 16 mm., 14 minutes, colour) explored "a woman's familiar domestic space as the site for feminine self-discovery...the kitchen table as domestic altar and a world of aesthetic beauty" (Rabinovitz in *ibid.*, p.120). In *Hand Tinting* (1967–8; 16 mm., $5^1/_2$ minutes, colour) Wieland used footage she had shot for a film, commissioned by Xerox, about a Job Corps Center for young women. She turned this into an abstract and rhythmic study of their gestures, expressions and movements, using repetition and reversal of short sequences of incomplete action, and varying sections by using negative prints, or dyeing or puncturing the film. Recent critics have found specifically feminist textual qualities in Wieland's manipulations. For Kass Banning, *Hand Tinting* displays "an unspeakable excess, a space of contradiction, an inscription of difference, through the rhythmic play not only of the female forms which shape the image but of the rhythmic oscillation of the film material itself..." (cited in Armatage, "The feminine body", 1987, p.84). Armatage finds in *Water Sark*, with its refractions of water, breast and mirror captured through circling and evasive movement, Wieland's "'discovery' of the feminine body", and a mode that "bears close links with and certainly shares the significance of what we have come to know as *l'écriture feminine*" (*idem*).

In her New York paintings and assemblages Wieland employed the sequential units of the story-board and the film-frame as a structural grid. The pervasive sexual imagery is sometimes humorous; sometimes lyrical, as in *Nature Mixes* (1963; oil on canvas; repr. Toronto 1987, pl.38) where a hand metamorphoses into a flower and then into a limp penis; and sometimes playfully parodic, in the scenes of romantic encounter of the *First Integrated Film with a Short on Sailing* (1963; oil on canvas; *ibid.*, p.49). In several paintings a distant sailboat or ocean liner moves erratically through the frames to end in a sudden sinking, or aeroplanes cross blue skies and plummet to earth. Wieland's assemblages of 1964–5 used discarded wooden boxes as framing units in which phallic planes and boats (children's toys) appear in counterpoint with articles coded as feminine. The lipstick-stained coffee cups and heart-shaped bodice of a red ball-gown pegged on a washing line in *Cooling Room II* (1964; mixed media construction; National Gallery of Canada, Ottawa), for example, are suggestively juxtaposed with a crashed toy aeroplane, and with an ocean liner represented by a red plastic bath toy.

From 1966 Wieland turned to women's craft traditions, designing sewn images in the form of quilts executed by her sister Joan Stewart, and composing wall hangings or "home totems" of vertically arranged pouches and frames that she made of coloured transparent celluloid, stuffed with cotton wads or found objects and images. Their imagery paid fond or ironic homage to the dominance of the cine camera and the news media in current consciousness. At a time of political upheaval in the USA, triggered by the Vietnam war and by racial and social conflicts, Wieland increasingly incorporated political references in her assemblages – press reports and photographs of the Vietnam war in *N.U.C.* (1966; mixed media; *ibid.*, p.67) and images of the American, British and Canadian flags that question the ethics of patriotic identification. In the film *Rat Life and Diet in North America* (1968; 16 mm., 14 minutes, colour) Wieland deals with the exodus of draft resisters to Canada. The protagonists, a group of pet gerbils in a Beatrix Potter-like narrative, flee from terror and confinement to idyllic flower-festivals and organic gardening in Canada. Wieland's treatment ironically combines the pleasures and playfulness of a children's tale with allusions to the fears and desires of the contemporary world.

From 1967 Wieland turned to issues of Canadian identity and politics. Her interest was triggered by a number of factors: distress at the invisibility of Canada in the USA; the mood of Canadian national celebration and self-examination unleashed by the Canadian Centennial in 1967; and the vexed problems of Quebec separatism and of American domination of the Canadian economy. A rail trip across Canada for a retrospective of her work at the Vancouver Art Gallery triggered her major film *Reason over Passion/La Raison avant la passion* (1967–9; 16 mm., 90 minutes, colour). This is a romantic-ironic exploration of the Canadian landscape and of national icons such as the flag (instituted in 1964) and the image of Pierre Trudeau, whose election as Prime Minister at the Liberal leadership convention of April 1968 appears as a balletic, dream-like freeze frame sequence at the centre of the film. Using a hand-held camera, Wieland crosses the country from sea to sea, shooting from the train and through the windscreen of a car, provoking visual discoveries through the physical constraints, accidents and perceptions of a particular journey. The resulting footage is re-filmed and rendered more abstract, structured into segments punctuated with regular electronic beeps, while Trudeau's catchword "reason over passion" appears superimposed at the centre of the screen in endless computer-generated permutations.

In 1971 Wieland was the first woman artist to be invited to mount a large solo exhibition at the National Gallery of Canada. As she worked on this, relations between Quebec and the rest of Canada were polarised by the FLQ terrorist kidnappings. Wieland turned the show into an affirmation of Canadian national identity and of its defining symbols, titling it *True Patriot Love* from the words of the Canadian national anthem. Echoing the earlier Canadianism of the Group of Seven, whom she admired, Wieland emphasised imagery of the wilderness, now endangered, and of the Arctic. She constructed an Arctic environment with fir trees and hatchling Canada geese, and an "Arctic Passion Cake", whose sugar-icing landscape held a female personification of "the Spirit of Canada suckling the French- and English-Canadian beavers" and a polar bear, mortally wounded by hunters. A large number of quilted, knitted and embroidered works were executed for her by women craft experts, their content asserting the French, English and aboriginal presences in Canadian history and culture, through works such as *Montcalm's Last Letter/Wolfe's Last Letter* (1971; embroidery on cloth; repr. Toronto

1987, pl.54) and *Eskimo Song: The Great Sea* (1970–71; cloth assemblage; Canada Council Art Bank). While her work was highly sophisticated in its use of formal structure and its concern with the implications of symbol systems, Wieland sought to overcome the alienation of the public from avant-garde art by involving collaborators, by using down-to-earth media, and by addressing issues of common concern, often inspired by the political critiques published at that time by members of the socialist Waffle Group. An example is *Water Quilt* (1970–71; Art Gallery of Ontario, Toronto). Wieland's political activism was further seen in her work for CAR, the Canadian artists' union, and in strikingly idiosyncratic political films such as *Solidarity* (1973; 16 mm., 11 minutes, colour), which records a rally of striking women factory workers while the camera allows us to see only the protagonists' feet, and *Pierre Vallières* (1972; 16 mm., 45 minutes, colour), an interview with the Quebec nationalist and socialist leader, in which the sole image is a close-up of the speaker's active mouth with the English subtitles to his text. In 1976 Wieland embodied her nationalist and ecological themes, with qualified success, in a full-length commercial feature film, *The Far Shore* (35 mm.; 106 minutes, black and white).

During the 1980s Wieland again turned her attention to painting and drawing, working in coloured pencils, in watercolour and oil, and appropriating what she found most eloquent in the artistic traditions of the West, particularly in the painting and music of the Baroque period. Her allegorical images offer glimpsed intuitions of transcendence, showing humans, animals and fragments of the Canadian landscape infused with energy and harmonised by freely brushed lines and patches of radiant prismatic colour. The eroticism in Wieland's work of the early 1960s re-emerges as a vital force that is shown pervading not only human life but the growth of plants and the movement of the elements, for example in *Victory of Venus* (1981; coloured pencil on paper; *ibid.*, p.94). She has cited the mystical writings of Teilhard de Chardin and of Hildegard of Bingen (q.v.) as inspiration for her attempts to picture a redemptive mode of emotional experience. This imagery has distressed some feminist observers in its turn away from immediate political issues, while others have seen in it "a tenacious expression of faith in love" in the face of the contemporary "eviction of love from social discourse" (Fleming 1981; Allen in Kingston 1995, p.13).

GERTA MORAY

Z

Zorach, Marguerite Thompson

American painter and textile artist,
1887–1968

Born Marguerite Thompson in Santa Rosa,
California, 25 September 1887; grew up in Fresno,
California. Enrolled at Stanford University, autumn
1908, but left to accompany her aunt on a trip to
Paris; saw paintings by the Fauves at Salon
d'Automne; met Gertrude Stein, Pablo Picasso and
Ossip Zadkine. Toured Europe, 1908–11. Studied
painting at La Palette, Paris, 1911; painted in
southern France with Jessica Dismorr, summers
1910–11. Travelled to Near and Far East,
1911–12; returned to USA, 1912. Married artist
William Zorach in New York, 1912; son born
1915, daughter born 1917; husband died 1966.
Lived in New York; later resided mainly in
Robinhood Cove, Maine, spending winters in
Brooklyn. Taught at the Modern Art School, New
York, 1915–16. Founder and first president, New
York Society of Women Artists, 1925. Visiting
artist (with William) at Skowhegan School of
Painting and Sculpture, Maine, summers 1946–66;
member of board of governors, 1960–68. Recipient
of silver medal, California Palace of the Legion of
Honor, 1919; honorary doctorate, Bates College,
Lewiston, Maine, 1964. Died in Brooklyn, New
York, 27 June 1968.

Principal Exhibitions

Individual

Royar Galleries, Los Angeles: 1912
Playhouse, Cleveland: 1913 (with William Zorach)
Charles Daniel Gallery, New York: 1915–16 (touring),
    1916, 1918 (all with William Zorach)
Tenth Street studio (Zorach studio), New York: 1918,
    1919 (both with William Zorach)
Dayton Museum of Arts, OH: 1922 (with William
    Zorach)

Montross Gallery, New York: 1923 (touring)
Downtown Gallery, New York: 1928, 1930, 1934
Brummer Gallery, New York: 1935 (retrospective)
Knoedler Galleries, New York: 1944
California Palace of the Legion of Honor, San Francisco:
    1946 (with William Zorach)
Kraushaar Galleries, New York: 1953, 1957, 1962, 1968
Colby College Art Museum, ME: 1968–9 (touring retro-
    spective, with William Zorach)

Group

American Women's Art Association, Paris: 1910
Salon des Indépendants, Paris: 1911
Salon d'Automne, Paris: 1911
International Exhibition of Modern Art, "Armory
    Show", New York: 1913
Panama-Pacific International Exhibition, San Francisco:
    1915
Anderson Galleries, New York: 1916 (*Forum Exhibition
    of Modern American Painters*)
Society of Independent Artists, New York: 1917
Whitney Museum of American Art, New York: 1932
    (annuals)

Selected Writings

"When is an American artist?", *Space*, i, March 1930,
    pp.28–30
"A painter turns craftsman", *Craft Horizons*, iv, February
    1945, pp.2–3
"Embroidery as art", *Art in America*, xliv, Fall 1956,
    pp.48–51, 66–7

Bibliography

Marya Mannes, "The embroideries of Marguerite
    Zorach", *International Studio*, xcv, March 1930,
    pp.29–33
"Mrs Zorach's new art, pictures in wool, make bow at
    exhibition here", *New York Herald Tribune*, 23
    October 1935
Louis M. Starr, "Reminiscences of William Zorach",
    typescript, Butler Library, Columbia University Oral
    History Collection, New York, 1957 (includes inter-
    views with Marguerite Zorach, pp.247–83)
William Zorach, *Art Is My Life: The Autobiography*,
    Cleveland: World Publishing, 1967

Marguerite Zorach: The Early Years, 1908–1920, exh. cat., National Collection of Fine Arts, Smithsonian Institution, Washington, DC, and elsewhere, 1973

Roberta K. Tarbell, "Early paintings by Marguerite Thompson Zorach", *American Art Review*, l, March–April 1974, pp.43–57

Joan M. Marter, "Three women artists married to early modernists: Sonia Delaunay-Terk, Sophie Taüber-Arp and Marguerite Thompson Zorach", *Arts Magazine*, liv, September 1979, pp.88–95

William and Marguerite Zorach: The Maine Years, exh. cat., William A. Farnsworth Library and Art Museum, Rockland, ME, and elsewhere, 1980

Charlotte Streifer Rubinstein, *American Women Artists from Early Times to the Present*, Boston: Hall, 1982

Marguerite and William Zorach: The Cubist Years, 1915–1918, exh. cat., Currier Gallery of Art, Manchester, NH, and elsewhere, 1987

Companions in Art: William and Marguerite Zorach, exh. cat., Williams College Museum of Art, Williamstown, MA, 1991

Marguerite Zorach: Cubism and Beyond, exh. cat., Kraushaar Galleries, New York, 1991

Susan Waller, *Women Artists in the Modern Era: A Documentary History*, Metuchen, NJ: Scarecrow Press, 1991

Nicola J. Shilliam, "Emerging identity: American textile artists in the early twentieth century", *Early Modern Textiles: From Arts and Crafts to Art Deco*, exh. cat., Museum of Fine Arts, Boston, 1993, pp.28–44

Hazel Clark, "The textile art of Marguerite Zorach", *Woman's Art Journal*, xvi/1, 1995, pp.18–25

Marguerite Zorach Papers are in the Library of Congress manuscript division and Archives of American Art, Washington, DC.

Marguerite Thompson Zorach was one of a small group of American artists who brought modernism to New York in the early 20th century. In her work, much of which still remains in private collections, she bridged the conventional divisions between the so-called fine and decorative arts. Throughout her long career as a painter, printmaker, woodcarver and textile artist, Zorach's subject matter – human figures, animals, idyllic sea- and landscapes – was a celebration of everyday life interpreted through a sophisticated synthesis of modern styles. Yet, like her contemporary Sonia Delaunay (q.v.), Zorach explored some of her main artistic themes and theories through the medium of textiles, which conventional art historians have tended to hold in lower esteem.

Marguerite Thompson's early work was deeply influenced by her travels abroad in Europe and the Far East. At the invitation of an aunt living in Paris, she abandoned her studies at Stanford University to study art in France. Based in Paris from 1908 to 1911, she visited much of western Europe, including Belgium, the Netherlands, Italy and Germany, where she viewed some of the most recent developments in modern art, as well as painting and sketching from nature. In 1911 she studied painting under John Duncan Fergusson and Jacques-Emile Blanche at La Palette, an informal, progressive Parisian art school that attracted many foreign students, including William Zorach, her future husband. The expressive use of colour and vigorous brushwork of her early paintings, such as *Café in Arles* (1911; private collection, repr. Washington 1973, p.25), reflected her admiration for the Fauves, especially Matisse, and her interest in the early work of the Cubists. Before returning to the USA in 1912, she spent seven months travelling through Egypt, Palestine, India, Burma, Malaysia, Indonesia, China, Korea and Japan, painting, sketching and making notes. These experiences provided the inspiration for many of her later works, including textiles. In works such as *Judea Hill in Palestine* (1911; private collection, *ibid.*, p.27), a landscape composed of bands of flattened forms and abstracted shapes outlined in blue, in the Fauve manner, she interpreted an exotic landscape in the style she had evolved in Paris.

On her return to California, she spent two months in the Sierra Mountains, where, inspired by the beauty of the rugged landscape, she produced a series of boldly executed paintings, including *Man Among the Redwoods* (1912; private collection, *ibid.* p.33), and delicate calligraphic drawings, reminiscent of Japanese scroll paintings. In late 1912 she moved to New York, married William Zorach and established what the Zorachs referred to as their "Post Impressionist" studio. In the 1910s both artists were at the forefront of American modernism, exhibiting paintings at the Armory Show, where Marguerite Zorach's Fauvist portrait of a woman (untraced) received the distinction of being vilified in the conventional art press. The Zorachs lived and worked mainly in New York, but spent summers in the country, where Marguerite Zorach sought rejuvenation through her contact with nature. Between 1915 and 1920 she experimented with Cubist devices, including faceted planes, in such paintings as the *Deserted Mill* (1917; private collection, repr. Manchester 1987, p.24) and

Sunrise – Moonset, Provincetown (1916; Nebraska Art Association, Lincoln).

Around 1913 Zorach began to make pictorial embroideries, which she referred to as embroidered tapestries. She wrote:

> In 1912 when I returned from Paris full of enthusiasm over the world of lively color the Fauves had discovered, paint seemed dull and inadequate to me. The wealth of beautiful and brilliant color available in woolen yarns so fascinated me that I tried to paint my pictures in wool. ... But almost immediately they became divorced from the painting viewpoint and developed life and form in their own medium. Yet were I not a painter my embroideries would never be what they are or have the stature that they possess ["Embroidery as art", 1956, p.48].

In her first embroideries, Zorach often reinterpreted works that she had already executed in paint, for example an embroidery entitled *The Sea* (1917–18; private collection, repr. Washington 1973, p.12) was based on a picture known as *The Swimmers* (1917; private collection). William Zorach collaborated on some of these early projects, including *The Sea* and *Maine Islands* (1919; National Museum of American Art, Smithsonian Institution, Washington, DC), and the two artists often shared motifs in their works in different media. In the later embroideries only portions or particular motifs related to existing paintings or sketches. Marguerite Zorach's working method was to make only the simplest sketch of the forms on the fabric before working them up freely in brightly hued wool yarns, without the use of an embroidery frame, in inventive stitches that created a rich surface texture resembling brush strokes. Zorach's textiles, with their rhythmical compositional devices, flat patterning and expressive use of non-naturalistic colour, were the ideal medium for her art of this time. They appear to have been better received than her paintings of the same period. One critic wrote: "It happens that many who reject cubist art in painting accept it readily enough in decorative productions, and so more unanimous praise is heard for the Zorach rugs and embroideries than for the pictures."

Zorach concentrated on the creation of textiles throughout the 1910s and 1920s, when she divided her time between art and her young family. In these works she explored the familiar connotations of traditional domestic textiles, such as the 18th-century embroidered pictures, bedcovers and later hooked rugs that were beginning to become highly collectible as American folk art. Yet her textiles also reveal her experience of European modernism, as is evident in a hooked rug with a figure of a reclining nude in the style of Matisse (c.1925; private collection, repr. Rockland 1980, p.15). In common with other young American textile designers in this period, Zorach was also interested in ancient and non-European sources of design. She was one of the first Americans to practise batik, a resist-dyeing technique, primarily used to decorate fabrics, that she probably learned during her visit to Indonesia, where she acquired batik-making implements. Although Zorach's batiks won prizes in the Art Alliance of America's competitions of 1916–20, which were intended to attract the attention of progressive textile manufacturers, her designs do not appear to have been produced industrially. Some of her batiks were made into artistic dress, such as a silk scarf with horses and nude riders (c.1918; Museum of Fine Arts, Boston). Others functioned as decorative wall hangings, for example, a set of three hangings (1918–20; Metropolitan Museum of Art, New York) with stylised nudes and animals reminiscent of African sculpture that Zorach and other artists interested in Cubism studied. Zorach exhibited batiks with her paintings in 1919 at the height of the fashion for batiks in New York.

Although Zorach made decorative textiles and dress for her own and her family's use, she was also commissioned to make textiles by collectors of modern art. Major patrons were Helen and Lathrop Brown, for whom she made many items, including an embroidered bedcover (1925–8; Museum of Fine Arts, Boston). The cover is decorated with whimsical figures of God and angels and scenes from Provincetown, where the Zorachs worked with the Provincetown Players, an avant-garde theatre group, in 1916 and 1921–3, and the Browns summered in the seaside community of artists. Embroidered portraits of other patrons included that of the *Jonas Family* (1925–6; private collection, repr. Mannes 1930, p.32) and the *Family of John D. Rockefeller, Jr, Seal Harbor, Maine* (1929–32; private collection, repr. "Embroidery as art". 1956, facing p.67). These pictorial embroideries, with iconic figures piled against a high horizon line, were executed in a denser manner than the bedcovers, the stitches almost entirely covering the linen ground fabric. Reviewers of the major retrospective of most of the embroideries at the Brummer Gallery in 1935 generally concurred with a critic who wrote: "She has never before approached, in any medium, the quality of work she now publishes" (H[enry] McB[ride], "Mrs Zorach steps forward", *New York Sun*, 26 October 1935).

Zorach continued to paint throughout her life, and after 1923, when the Zorachs purchased a house in Maine, local landscapes and characters, such as *Maine Sheriff* (1930; Whitney Museum of American Art, New York), featured prominently in her paintings. Powerful portraits, such as *Guy Lowe – The Last of Lowe's Point, Maine* (1928; private collection, repr. New York 1991), with their flattened forms and deliberate naïveté to emphasise character traits, suggest the influence of American folk painting on her work of this period. Some of the last embroideries that she executed were family portraits, including *Robinhood Farm, Georgetown Island, Maine* (1937; private collection, repr. Rockland 1980, p.19), depictions of her children, Tessim Zorach and Dahlov Ipcar with their families in domestic settings, both executed in the 1940s, and the retrospective *My Home in Fresno Around the Year 1900* (1949; National Museum of American Art). Having made more than 20 embroidered pictures and four bedcovers, Zorach was forced to abandon the more exacting work of embroidery completely in 1953 as a result of an eye condition, but was still able to paint, teach and exhibit into the 1960s. In her later paintings, which were mainly landscapes, Zorach's palette became purer, almost acidic, as is evident in *Maine Fishing Village* (1950; private collection, *ibid.*, p.26).

NICOLA J. SHILLIAM

Zürn, Unica
[fig. 73]

German artist and writer, 1916–1970

Born in Grunewald, Berlin, 6 July 1916. Worked for Universum-Film AG (UFA), Berlin, as secretary, editor, archivist and artistic adviser, 1933–mid-1940s. Married Eric Laupenmühlen, 1942; daughter born 1943, son born 1945; divorced 1949; lost custody of children. Began career as a creative writer for German and Swiss magazines. Met the artist Hans Bellmer in Berlin, and moved with him to Paris, where she met the Surrealists, 1953. First nervous breakdown, 1957; subsequent internments of varying lengths in psychiatric hospital of Sainte-Anne, Paris. Committed suicide in Paris, 19 October 1970.

Principal Exhibitions

Galerie Le Soleil dans la Tête, Paris: 1953, 1957 (both individual)
Galerie Daniel Cordier, Paris: 1959 (*EROS: Exposition inteRnatiOnale du Surréalisme*)
Galerie Point Cardinal, Paris: 1962, 1964 (both individual)
Galerie Dieter Brunsberg, Hannover: 1967 (with Hans Bellmer)
Galerie Werner Kunze, Berlin: 1975 (retrospective)

Selected Writings

Hexentexte, Berlin: Galerie Springer, 1954 (appendix by Hans Bellmer); as *Oracles et Spectacles*, Paris: Visat, 1967
Der Mann in Jasmin, 1965; as *L'Homme jasmin*, Paris: Gallimard, 1971; as *The Man of Jasmine*, London: Atlas, 1994
Dunkler Frühling, Hamburg: Merlin, 1969; as *Sombre printemps*, ed. Ruth Henry and Robert Valanay, Paris: Belfond, 1971
Gesamtausgabe, Berlin: Brinkmann und Böse, 1988
The House of Illnesses, London: Atlas, 1993
Lettres au Docteur Ferdière, Paris: Séguier, 1994 (with Hans Bellmer)

Bibliography

Obliques, 1975 (special issue: Hans Bellmer)
Obliques, no.14–15, 1977 (special issue: *La Femme surréaliste*)
Jean-François Rabain, "Le démembrement de la figure chez Bellmer, Zürn, Schreber", *Confrontation*, Autumn 1980
Peter Webb and Robert Short, *Hans Bellmer*, London: Quartet, 1985
Luce Irigaray, "Une lacune natale", *Le Nouveau Commerce*, no.62–3, Autumn 1985, pp.39–45
Renée Riese Hubert, "Portrait d'Unica Zürn en anagramme", *Pleine Marge*, no.7, June 1988, pp.61–73
Leonora Carrington, *The House of Fear*, New York: Dutton, 1988; London: Virago, 1989
John M. MacGregor, *The Discovery of the Art of the Insane*, Princeton: Princeton University Press, 1989
Thérèse Lichtenstein, "Behind closed doors", *Artforum*, xxix, March 1991, pp.119–22
Renée Riese Hubert, *Magnifying Mirrors: Women, Surrealism and Partnership*, Lincoln: University of Nebraska Press, 1994

Unica Zürn does not fit easily into the category of Woman-Surrealist. She was the muse and obsession of the Surrealist artist Hans Bellmer for the last two decades of his life; she was a *Nadja retrouvée* in the eyes of André Breton; she did practise Surrealist "psychic automatism" in her automatic writing and drawing. Such aspects of her career seem to locate her within the genre of the *femme-enfant* ("child-woman"), but Zürn's is a difficult case because her art is inseparable from – indeed interdependent with – her mental instability. Her most creative periods were also her most schizophrenic. The Surrealists, ever since their first Manifesto of 1924, had a highly romanticised concept of insanity, but for Zürn the imagined became the real "whether she wants it or not ... the most incredible, hitherto unseen things become reality ..." (*The Man of Jasmine* 1994, pp.32–3). Zürn, not unlike Antonin Artaud before her, was "adopted" by the Surrealists, who "heralded the benefits that would accrue from unlocking the gates of reason, and ignored the abominations" (Susan Sontag, "Artaud", *Antonin Artaud: Selected Writings*, New York: Farrar Straus, 1976, p.xxvi).

Zürn's career began in the field of film in 1933, working for Universum-Film AG in Berlin, seemingly unaware of Nazi atrocities and only finding out the truth late in the war. It was not until the end of her marriage in 1949 that she began her life as an artist, writing short stories and radio plays for newspapers and journals, and painting in a fluid, automatic style, already coined – unknown to her – as the technique of "chance" or "decalomania" by the Surrealists in Paris. Zürn's writings were consistently haunted by a father figure, an ethereal presence whom she referred to as the "Man of Jasmine". He symbolised both her creative side and her mental instability; when she felt his presence she was enraptured and dominated by a faceless force: "Someone travelled inside me, crossing from one side to the other ... From his gaze the circle closes around me" (*The Man of Jasmine* 1994, p.26). Several figures represented this force for Zürn: Herman Melville, Henri Michaux, Hans Bellmer. It was Bellmer, whom Zürn met and became infatuated with in Berlin in 1953, who played the greatest role in her career, however, and who introduced her to the Surrealists in Paris that year.

The anagram provides the best key to Zürn's work (examples were published in *Panorama*, *Panderma* and *Der Monat*, 1959–61). In 1953 she produced both her first written anagram-poems and her first collection of anagram-drawings (i.e. automatic drawings that also involved a subversion of signs). The written and drawn are inseparable in Zürn's work, for in the mode of Art Brut she etched and erased lines, whether figurative or linguistic, filling up every section of paper with a fragmentary collage of bizarre sparks of thought. This link between writing and drawing had been celebrated by Breton in his essay "Le Message automatique" (1934), wherein Surrealism was discussed alongside the iconography of the insane/schizophrenic (André Breton, *Oeuvres complètes*, ed. Marguerite Bonnet and others, i, Paris: Gallimard, 1988). In his preface to Zürn's *Hexentexte* of 1954 Bellmer also romanticised this word-image interplay peculiar to the anagram as one born of "a violent, paradoxical conflict, a conflict that presupposes the need for the greatest strain of the imaginative will and at the same time insists on the exclusion of all preconceived intention" (*Obliques* 1975, p.111; my translation).

Working in indian ink on paper, Zürn would begin with one blot and end up with a fusion of forms, hybrids of self and subconscious portraits, as in her illustrations in *The House of Illnesses*. Here the narrative is both linguistic and formalistic. We read of a Dr Mortimer, Zürn's imagined personal death who has the bearing of an army (Nazi?) officer and who denies her any hope or traditional last wish. His presence and his effect on Zürn's persecuted mind come across not from her brief narration of this encounter, but from her accompanying image: *Portrait of a Whispered Message*. Here art and psychosis merge in a frenzy of black ink strokes that build up a hawk-like portrait of prey. We see that the artist herself only read this image when it had been completed, writing around its form on 8 May 1958: "This is the portrait of a whispered message; apparently it represents 'the trapper', but that must not necessarily be true because no one saw him come or go." The following day she added: "No, now I know who it is – it's Dr Mortimer".

This hawk-like form recurs in her imagery when she describes her enemy in *The Man of Jasmine* (1994, p.30) as one who "describes circles" preying over her, the "masochistic chicken" and portraying him, Phoenix-like, stealing her heart in *The House of Illnesses* (1993, p.20). Hers is not an inner bestiary, however, like that of her Surrealist counterpart Leonora Carrington (q.v.). Zürn dissolves rather than seeks a mythical identity (cf. Leonora Carrington's *The House of Fear* with *The House of Illnesses*). While Carrington found refuge in Shamanism and the occult, Zürn denied herself spiritual recompense and throughout her periods of breakdown continued to be plagued with images of death, torture and murder.

Two biographical factors contributed to this obsession and the resultant iconography: the loss of her children and maternal identity (on her divorce in 1949 and the subsequent abortions she chose to have), and the loss of a sense of national (i.e. German) identity. Both crises, personal and political, led to a guilt in Zürn that could not be exorcised: hence her foetal-like self-portraits and embryo-faces and her militant enemies. As she wrote herself: "I am obsessed by faces when I draw" (*The Man of Jasmine* 1994, p.40). She feared men in white coats, suspecting that they wanted to torture her "here on this bed" because she came from "the race which had set up the concentration camps" (*ibid.*, p.137).

This schizophrenic approach is constant in all Zürn's art: she both creates in a frenzy and analyses her inner and outer self. This automatic delirium was embraced by the Surrealists who invited her to exhibit with them (albeit in the section "Invention neuve" with the visionary artist Friedrich Schröder Sonnenstern) in 1959 at Galerie Daniel Cordier, Paris. Her ink drawing *Zoobiologie* (repr. *Exposition internationale du surréalisme, 1959–1960*, exh. cat., Galerie Daniel Cordier, Paris, 1959, p.116) embodies a nest of chimerical beasts, with bird legs, sagging breasts, male and female heads, and scribbled words – a fantastic creature that may be compared to Henri Michaux's *Meidosems* (1948).

Most recent interpretations of Zürn's work have misread this complex woman as a failed woman. She has been simplistically dismissed as a protégée of Bellmer (Webb and Short 1985), and as a woman who failed to be both a woman and an artist, lacking both a female and/or an artistic identity. The latter critique, by Luce Irigaray (1985), argues that Zürn's lack of an "ideal self" and the fragmentary nature of her imagery is due to the fact that she is lost in a metaphorical "passage between her selves", that her imagery represents a nostalgia for a "self", a body threshold. Yet Surrealism, especially in post-war Paris, was no longer searching for this mythological self, it focused on the experience of experiencing (see Maurice Blanchot, "Le demain joueur", *Nouvelle Revue Française*, April 1967, pp.863–88). Jean Schuster identified this shift as consciously pessimistic: "at the present time its main ambition is to establish a balance between revolt and despair" (Jean Schuster, *Entretiens sur le surréalisme*, ed. F. Alquié, The Hague: Mouton, 1968).

Zürn's "plight" was not one of a miscarried identity, of a loss of the female self, of a "failure to be born". Rather in accepting her self as a medium between the supposedly sane and insane universes, Zürn accepted that at times she felt "ashamed that she herself is a woman", that she is mad "she takes it quite for granted – she likes this word: crazy" (*Man of Jasmine*, 1994, pp.144 and 42). She gave a voice to Artaud's assertion, that the artist, or in this case the woman-artist, is inevitably suicided by society.

On 19 October 1970 Zürn threw herself from the sixth floor of the apartment she had shared for 17 years with Bellmer in Paris. The previous day she had been released from Sainte-Anne psychiatric clinic in Paris and had visited Bellmer only to find that he was determined to end their relationship. In "Le Printemps noir" she had described a childhood vision of her own suicide: "'It is finished', she says in a quiet voice and she feels herself already dead before her feet leave the window-sill. She falls on her head and breaks her neck". Ruth Henry, her close friend, concluded: "For her, who no longer had the will to live, wakefulness had become intolerable. The Black Spring of the little girl had become her life and her suicide hers" (Ruth Henry, "Le printemps noir d'Unica", *Obliques* 1977, p.259; my translation). In her poem of 1965, "Das leben, ein schlechter Traum" (Life is a bad dream), however, Zürn had also foretold this final departure, one that pushed the paradigm of the creative subject to its ultimate foreclosure: "I break everything in the middle: nose,/belly, right arm,/Miserable list/of love! Martyr! Oh the glow/of the pale dream – it laughed/at me, life deceiver,/and provided nothing. Poor soul" (translated in Hubert 1994, p.145).

ALYCE MAHON

NOTES ON CONTRIBUTORS

Adler, Kathleen Head of Education, National Gallery, London. Author of *Manet* (1986), *Berthe Morisot* (with Tamar Garb, 1987) and *Unknown Impressionists* (1988); editor of *The Body Imaged: The Human Form and Visual Culture since the Renaissance* (with Marcia Pointon, 1993). Book review editor, *Art History* (1991–5). **Essay:** Morisot (with Tamar Garb).

Alexander, David Independent scholar. Author of *Painters and Engraving: The Reproductive Print from Hogarth to Wilkie* (with Richard T. Godfrey, catalogue, 1980); contributor to *Affecting Moments* (catalogue, 1993). Member of the editorial board for the journal *Print Quarterly*. **Essays:** Watson; Printmakers survey.

Arnold, Bruce Literary editor, political columnist and art critic of the *Irish Independent* newspaper. Author of numerous books including *A Concise History of Irish Art* (1969), *Orpen: Mirror to an Age* (1981), *The Art Atlas of Britain and Ireland* (1991), *William Orpen* (1991) and *Mainie Jellett and the Modern Movement in Ireland* (1991); maker of the film *To Make It Live: Mainie Jellett, 1897–1944*. **Essay:** Jellett.

Bearor, Karen A. Associate Professor, Florida State University, Tallahassee. Author of *Irene Rice Pereira: Her Paintings and Philosophy* (1993) and *Irene Rice Pereira's Early Work: Embarking on an Eastward Journey* (1994). **Essay:** Pereira.

Behr, Shulamith Bosch Lecturer in 20th-Century German Art, Courtauld Institute of Art, University of London. Author of *Women Expressionists* (1988), *Conrad Felixmüller: Works on Paper* (catalogue, 1994), *Women and Expressionist Culture* (in preparation); co-editor of *Expressionism Reassessed* (1993); contributor to *Gabriele Münter, 1877–1962: Retrospektive* (catalogue, 1992), *Sigrid Hjertén* (catalogue, 1995), *Visions of the "Neue Frau": Women and the Visual Arts in Weimar Germany* (1995) and to the journals *Art History*, *Burlington Magazine*, *National Arts Collection Fund: Annual Review* and *Oxford Art Journal*. **Essays:** Heemskerck; Münter; Werefkin.

Belz, Carl Director, Rose Art Museum, Brandeis University, Waltham, Massachusetts. Contributor to the catalogues *Frank Stella: Metallic Reliefs* (1978), *Frankenthaler: The 1950s* (1981), *William Beckman and Gregory Gillespie* (1984), *Katherine Porter: Paintings, 1969–1984* (1985), *Stephen Antonakos: Neons and Drawings* (1986), *Jake Berthot* (1988), *Stanley Boxer, 45 Years* (1992) and *Joan Snyder, Painter: 1969 to Now* (1994). **Essay:** Snyder.

Berardi, Marianne Independent scholar. Author of *Catlin's Indians: The Kemper Portfolio* (1990) and *Under the Influence: The Students of Thomas Hart Benton* (1993). Contributor to *Sculpture by Women in the Eighties* (catalogue, 1985), *Mel Bochner: Paintings and Drawings, 1973–1985* (1985), *Memorial Art Gallery: An Introduction to the Collection* (1988), *American Paintings in the Collection of the Carnegie Museum of Art* (1992), *American Drawings and Watercolors from the Kansas City Region* (1992) and *Women's Studies Encyclopedia* (in preparation), and to the journal *Porticus*. **Essays:** Oosterwijck; Ruysch.

Berger, Renate Professor of Art History, Hochschule der Künste, Berlin. Author of *Malerinnen auf dem Weg ins 20. Jahrhundert: Kunstgeschichte als Sozialgeschichte* (1982) and *"Und ich sehe nichts, nichts als die Malerei": Autobiographische Texte von Künstlerinnen des 18.–20. Jahrhunderts* (1987). Editor of *Camille Claudel, 1864–1943* (catalogue, 1990). Co-editor of *Weiblichkeit und Tod in der Literatur* (1987) and *Frauen-Kunst-Geschichte, Forschungsgruppe Marburg, Feministische Bibliographie zur Kunst- und Kulturgeschichte von Frauen* (1993). Contributor to *Die Weibliche und die Männliche Linie* (1993). **Essay:** Training and Professionalism survey: Germany, Austria and Switzerland.

Bird, Jon Reader in Visual Culture, Middlesex University. Co-author of *Nancy Spero* (1996). Co-editor of *Mapping the Futures: Local Cultures, Global Change* (1993), *Traveller's Tales: Narratives of Home and Displacement* (1994), *The Block Reader in Visual Culture* (1996) and *FutureNatural: Nature, Science, Culture* (1996). Contributor to the journals *Art in America, Block, New Socialist, Artscribe International, Art Monthly, Control Magazine, Frameworks Journal* and *Studio International*. **Essays:** Bourgeois; Spero.

Bloem, Marja Curator, Stedelijk Museum, Amsterdam. Contributor to *Agnes Martin: Prints and Drawings* (catalogue, 1991), *Rini Hurkmans* (catalogue, 1991), *Lood om Oud ijzer* (1992), *Sadness, Sluices, Mermaids, Delay* (catalogue, 1994), *De lijmstokman* (1995) and to the periodicals *Museumjournaal* and *Forum International*. **Essay:** Martin.

Bomford, Kate Currently studying for a PhD on English and Flemish 17th-century friendship portraiture at the Courtauld Institute of Art, London; has worked at the Dulwich Picture Gallery, the Wallace Collection and the University College Art Collections, London. **Essay:** Schurman.

Bourne, Patrick Art dealer and editor at Atelier Books, Edinburgh. Author of *Anne Redpath: Her Life and Works* (1989) and *The Clydesdale Bank Collection* (1991). **Essay:** Redpath.

Bowe, Nicola Gordon Lecturer and art and design historian. Author of *Harry Clarke* (1979), *20th-Century Irish Stained Glass* (1983), *Harry Clarke: His Graphic Art* (1983), *The Dublin Arts and Crafts Movement* (1985), *Cork Glass Art* (1986), *The Life and Work of Harry Clarke* (1989), *My Tender Shell: Maud Cotter* (1991) and *The Arts and Crafts Movements in Dublin and Edinburgh* (with Elizabeth Cumming, in preparation). Editor of *A Gazetteer of Irish Stained Glass* (1988) and *Art and the National Dream: The Search for Vernacular Expression in Turn of the Century Design* (1993). Contributor to a wide variety of journals. **Essay:** Geddes.

Bowlt, John E. Professor, Department of Slavic Languages and Literature, University of Southern California, Los Angeles. Author of *Russian Avant-Garde: Theory and Criticism, 1902–34* (1988), *20th-Century Russian and East European Painting* (with Nicoletta Misler, 1993), *Artists of the Russian Theater* (in Russian, 1994) and *The Salon Album of Vera Stravinsky* (1995). Contributor to the *Journal of Decorative and Propaganda Arts*. Member of the editorial board of *Experiment: A Journal of Russian Culture*. **Essays:** Delaunay; Exter; Mukhina.

Brandt, Bettina Visiting Assistant Professor of German Studies, Columbia University, New York. Contributor to *Der Imaginierte Findling: Studien zur Kaspar-Hauser-Rezeption* (1995). Co-editor, *Tijdschrift voor Vrouwenstudies*. **Essays:** Oppenheim; Tanning.

Brauch, Patricia Associate Librarian for Information Services, Brooklyn College of the City University of New York. Contributor to *Magazines for Libraries* (1986 and 1988), *Books for College Libraries* (1988), *Reference Librarian* (1988), *Research Guide to American Historical Biography* (1990), *St James Guide to Biography* (1991) and *Dictionary of American Biography*. **Essay:** Stettheimer.

Brooke, Xanthe Curator, European Fine Art, Walker Art Gallery, Liverpool. Author of *Murillo in Focus* (1990), *Lady Lever Art Gallery: Catalogue of Embroideries* (1992) and *Face to Face: Three Centuries of Artists' Self-Portraiture* (1994). **Essay:** Ayala de Óbidos.

Brown, Betty Ann Art historian, critic and curator; Professor, Department of Art, California State University, Northridge. Author of *Exposures: Women and Their Art* (with Arlene Raven, 1989),

Roland Reiss: A Seventeen Year Survey (1991) and *Communitas: The Feminist Art of Community Building* (1992). Contributor to *Behind the Mask in Mexico* (1988), *Smoke and Mist: Mesoamerican Studies in Memory of Thelma D. Sullivan* (1988), *Californian Women Artists* (1989) and *Forty Years of California Assemblage* (catalogue, 1989). Contributor to *Art Scene, Arts Magazine, Los Angeles Reader, New Art Examiner, InSpain* and *Artweek*. Founding editor of *Visions: The Los Angeles Art Quarterly*. **Essays:** Cunningham; Kozloff; Sleigh; Taeuber-Arp.

Budick, Ariella Adjunct Professor, Department of Fine Arts, New York University. Contributor to the journal *History of Photography*. **Essay:** Arbus.

Bumpus, Bernard Ceramic historian. Author of *Charlotte Rhead: Potter and Designer* (1988) and *Pâte-sur-Pâte: The Art of Ceramic Relief Decoration, 1849–1992* (1992). Contributor to *Rhead: Artists and Potters* (catalogue, 1986), *The Rheads of Staffordshire* (catalogue, 1989) and to the periodicals *Antique Collector, Decorative Arts Society Journal, Dossier de l'Art, Sèvres, Arts Ceramica, Arts and Crafts, Collector's World* and *Antique Dealer and Collector's Guide*. **Essay:** Robineau.

Cameron, Vivian P. Independent scholar. Author of *Woman as Image and Image-Maker in Paris During the French Revolution* (PhD dissertation, 1983). Contributor to *Eroticism and the Body Politic, College Art Journal, Woman's Art Journal* and *Studies in Eighteenth-Century Culture*. **Essays:** Benoist; Labille-Guiard.

Carmean, E.A., Jr Director, Memphis Brooks Museum of Art, Memphis. Author of *Helen Frankenthaler: A Paintings Retrospective* (catalogue, 1989) and catalogues on David Smith, Robert Motherwell, Picasso, Mondrian and other artists. Contributor to the journals *Art Présent, Separata, Macula, Art in America, Art International, Arts* and *Studio International*. **Essays:** Frankenthaler; Graves.

Caroli, Flavio Professor of the History of Art, Politecnico, Milan. Author of *Sofonisba Anguissola e le sue sorelle* (1987), *Fede Galizia* (1989 and 1991) and numerous other publications. **Essay:** Galizia (with Domenica Spadaro).

Carr, Annemarie Weyl Professor and Chair of Art History, Southern Methodist University, Dallas. Author of *Byzantine Illumination, 1150–1250: The Study of a Provincial Tradition* (1987) and *A Masterpiece of Byzantine Art Recovered: The Thirteenth-Century Murals of Lysi, Cyprus* (1991), and numerous articles and papers on Byzantine art. Editor of *Gesta* (1994–7). **Essay:** Women as Artists in the Middle Ages survey.

Casteras, Susan P. Member of the department of Art History, University of Washington, Seattle. Author of *The Victorian Cult of Childhood* (1986), *Images of Victorian Womanhood in English Art* (1987), *English Pre-Raphaelitism and Its Reception in America in the 19th Century* (1990), *Pocket Cathedrals: Pre-Raphaelite Book Illustration* (1991) and *James Smetham: Artist, Author, Pre-Raphaelite Associate* (1995); co-author of *Richard Redgrave* (1988), *Breaking the Rules: Audrey Flack: A Retrospective, 1950–1990* (catalogue, 1992), *A Struggle for Fame: Victorian Women Artists and Authors* (catalogue, 1994) and *Pre-Raphaelite Art and Its European Context* (1995). Co-editor of *The Grosvenor Gallery: A Palace of Art in Victorian England* (1996). **Essays:** Eakins; Marisol.

Caviness, Madeline H. Mary Richardson Professor and Professor of Art History, Tufts University, Medford, Massachusetts. Author of *The Early Stained Glass of Canterbury Cathedral, ca.1175–1220* (1977), *The Windows of Christ Church Cathedral, Canterbury* (1981), *Stained Glass Before 1540: An Annotated Bibliography* (1983) and *Sumptuous Arts at the Royal Abbeys in Reims and Braine* (1990). Editor of *Medieval and Renaissance Stained Glass from New England Collections* (catalogue, 1978) and *Studies in Medieval Stained Glass* (1985). Contributor to *Stained Glass Windows* (1993), *Women's Literary and Artistic Patronage in the Middle Ages* (1996), *Translation Theory and Practice in the Middle Ages* (1997) and to the periodicals *Art Bulletin, La Revue de l'Art, Journal of the Warburg and Courtauld Institutes, Antiquaries Journal, Österreichische Zeitschrift für Kunst und Denkmalpflege, Walpole Society Publications, Gesta* and *Speculum*. **Essay:** Hildegard of Bingen.

Caws, Mary Ann Distinguished Professor of English, French and Comparative Literature, Graduate School, City University of New York.

Author of *The Eye in the Text* (1980), *Reading Frames in Modern Fiction* (1985), *The Art of Interference* (1989), *Women of Bloomsbury* (1990) and *Robert Motherwell: What Art Holds* (1996). Editor of *Surrealism and Women* (with others, 1991) and *Joseph Cornell's Theater of the Mind* (1993). **Essay:** Bell.

Chan, Mary Curatorial assistant, Department of Drawings, Museum of Modern Art, New York. **Essay:** Sage.

Chandler, Robin M. Assistant Professor, Northeastern University, Boston, and artist. Contributor to *African American Women: A Biographical Directory* (1993), *A Very Strange Society? Comparative Perspectives on South Africa* (in preparation) and to the journals *International Review of African-American Art, American Political Science Review, Journal of Arts Management, Law and Society, Third Text* and *Black Issues in Higher Education*. **Essays:** Fuller; Sligh.

Cheney, Liana De Girolami Professor of Art History and Chair of Art Department, University of Massachusetts, Lowell. Author of *Religious Architecture of Lowell* (1984), *The Paintings of the Casa Vasari* (1985), *Quattrocento Neoplatonism and Medici Humanism in Botticelli's Mythological Paintings* (1985), *Andrea del Verrocchio's Celebration, 1435–1488* (1990), *Pre-Raphaelitism and Medievalism in the Arts* (1992), *Symbols of Vanitas in the Arts, Literature and Music* (1992) and *Readings in Italian Mannerism* (1995). Contributor to the periodicals *Emblematica, Woman's Art Journal, Italian Culture, Studies in Iconography, Sixteenth-Century Journal, Artibus et Historiae* and *Journal of Pre-Raphaelite Studies*. **Essay:** Longhi.

Coatts, Margot Exhibition curator and writer. Author of *A Weaver's Life: Ethel Mairet* (1983), *The Oxshot Pottery* (catalogue, 1984), *Heywood Sumner* (1986), *Lucie Rie* (1992), *Robert Weldy* (1995) and *Marianne de Trey* (1995). Features writer for the periodical *Crafts* and Associate Editor of *Craft History* (1989–91). **Essay:** Rie.

Colvile, Georgiana M.M. Professor of French Film and Comparative Literature, University of Colorado, Boulder. Author of *Vers un langage des arts autour des années vingt* (1977), *Beyond and Beneath the Mantle: On Thomas Pynchon's The Crying of Lot 49* (1988), *Blaise Cendrars, Ecrivain Protéiforme* (1994) and of many articles on French, American and Canadian literature, film and painting, with emphasis on Surrealism and women. Editor of *Women's Voices from the Other Americas* (1995) and *Cendrars, la Provence et la Seduction du Sud* (with Monique Chefdor, 1996). **Essays:** Leonora Carrington; Fini.

Cooper, Emmanuel Writer. Author of *A History of World Pottery* (1988), *The Sexual Perspective: Homosexuality and Art in the Last 100 Years in the West* (2nd edition, 1994) and *Fully Exposed: The Male Nude in Photography* (2nd edition, 1995). Contributor to the journals *Time Out, Creative Camera* and *Crafts Magazine*. Co-editor of *Ceramic Review*. **Essay:** Lempicka.

Cropper, Elizabeth Professor, History of Art, Johns Hopkins University, Baltimore. Author of *Pietro Testa, 1612–1650: Prints and Drawings* (catalogue, 1988) and *Nicolas Poussin: Friendship and the Love of Painting* (with Charles Dempsey, 1996). **Essay:** Gentileschi.

Cumming, Elizabeth Lecturer in Design History, Edinburgh College of Art. Author of *The Arts and Crafts Movement* (with Wendy Kaplan, 1991), *Glasgow 1900: Art and Design* (1992), *Phoebe Anna Traquair, 1852–1936* (1993) and *The Arts and Crafts Movements in Dublin and Edinburgh* (with Nicola Gordon Bowe, in preparation). **Essay:** Traquair.

Curtis, Penelope Curator, Henry Moore Institute, Leeds. Author of *Julius Gonzalez: Sculptures and Drawings* (catalogue, 1990) and *Barbara Hepworth: A Retrospective* (catalogue, 1994); contributor to *Archives de l'Art Français, Woman's Art Journal* and *Gazette des Beaux-Arts*. **Essay:** Hepworth.

Dahmen, Sabine Doctoral candidate, Bonn University. Author of MA thesis on Charlotte Salomon. **Essay:** Salomon.

Damian, Carol Assistant Professor, Art History, Florida International University, Coral Gables. Author of *The Virgin of the Andes: Art and Ritual in Colonial Cuzco* (1995). Editor of *Tribal Arts Newsletter*. **Essay:** Amaral.

Danilowitz, Brenda   Curator, Josef and Anni Albers Foundation, Orange, Connecticut. Author of *Josef Albers at Marfa* (1991); contributor to *Josef Albers Photographien, 1928–55* (1991) and *Constance Stuart Larrabee: Adventures with a Camera* (catalogue, 1995). Contributor to the journal *African Arts*. **Essays:** Albers; Matthiasdóttir.

Day, John A.   Dean, College of Fine Arts, University of South Dakota, Vermillion. Contributor to *Understanding Undergraduate Education* (1990) and to the journals *Plains Anthropologist*, *Southwest Art*, *Choice* and *Caduces*. **Essay:** Quick-to-See Smith.

Deepwell, Katy   Trustee of Women's Art Library, London (Chair, 1990–94). Author of *Ten Decades: Careers of Ten Women Artists Born 1897–1906* (catalogue, 1992); editor of *New Feminist Art Criticism: Critical Strategies* (1995) and *Women and Modernism* (in preparation). Contributor to *Women's Art Magazine*. **Essays:** Agar; Training and Professionalism survey: Britain and Ireland, 20th century.

DeLong, Lea Rosson   Adjunct Professor, Drake University, Des Moines, Iowa. Author of *Nature's Forms/Nature's Forces: The Art of Alexandre Hogue* (1984) and *New Deal Art of the Upper Midwest* (1988). Contributor to *Chemistry Imagined: Reflections on Science* (1993) and to the *Woman's Art Journal*. **Essay:** WalkingStick.

Diego, Estrella de   Professor of Contemporary Art History, Universidad Complutense, Madrid. Author of *La mujer y la pintura del XIX español* (1987), *El andrógino sexuado: Eternos ideales, nuevas estrategias de género* (1992) and *Leonardo* (1994). Contributor to the journals *Lápiz, Revista de Occidente, La Balsa de la Medusa, ArtPress, Art Journal, Contemporanea* and *Art Magazine*. **Essay:** Mallo.

Diggory, Terence   Professor of English, Skidmore College, Saratoga Springs, New York. Author of *William Carlos Williams and the Ethics of Painting* (1991) and *Grace Hartigan and the Poets: Paintings and Prints* (catalogue, 1993). Contributor to *Art Journal*. **Essay:** Hartigan.

Doherty, Claire   Exhibitions co-ordinator, Ikon Gallery, Birmingham. Contributor to *Re-Presenting Barbara Hepworth* (1996) and to the journal *Untitled*. **Essay:** Messager.

Dreishpoon, Douglas   Curator of Collections, Weatherspoon Art Gallery, University of North Carolina at Greensboro. Contributor to *Art Journal* and *Art News*. **Essays:** Abakanowicz; Hesse.

Eastmond, Elizabeth   Senior Lecturer, Art History, University of Auckland. Author of *Women and the Arts in New Zealand: Forty Works, 1936–86* (with Merimeri Penfold, 1986) and *Frances Hodgkins: Paintings and Drawings* (with Iain Buchanan and Michael Dunn, 1994). **Essays:** Angus; Hodgkins.

Edge, Sarah   Exhibition organiser and performance artist; Lecturer in Media Studies, University of Ulster, Coleraine. Contributor to the journals *Feminist Review, Women's Art Magazine* and *Film Ireland*. Member of editorial board, *Irish Journal of Feminist Studies*. **Essay:** Spence.

Elliott, Bridget   Associate Professor of Visual Arts, University of Western Ontario, London. Author of *Women Artists and Writers: Modernist (Im)positionings* (with Jo-Ann Wallace, 1994); contributor to *On Your Left: New Historical Materialism in the 1990s* (1996) and to the periodicals *Genders, Feminist Review, Feminist Art News, Victorian Studies, Oxford Art Journal* and *Art History*. **Essay:** Modernism and Women Artists survey.

Evans, Michael   Fellow of the Warburg Institute, University of London. Author of *Medieval Drawings* (1969), *Herrad of Hohenbourg: Hortus Deliciarum* (with Rosalie Green and others, 1979) and *Basic Grammar for Medieval and Renaissance Studies* (1995). Contributor to *Studies in Church History: Subsidia. 1: Medieval Women* (1978), *Manuscripts in the Fifty Years after the Invention of Printing* (1983), *Sight and Insight: Essays on Art and Culture in Honour of E.H. Gombrich at 85* (1994) and to the periodicals *Architectural Association Quarterly, Source: Notes on the History of Art* and *Journal of the Warburg and Courtauld Institutes*. **Essay:** Herrad.

Facos, Michelle   Assistant Professor, History of Art, Indiana University, Bloomington. Contributor to *Domesticity and Modernism* (1995) and to the journals *Gazette des Beaux-Arts, Arts Magazine, Zeitschrift für Kunstgeschichte, Konsthistorisk*

Tidskrift and *Woman's Art Journal*. **Essays:** Backer; Kielland.

Fahlman, Betsy   Associate Professor of Art History, Arizona State University, Tempe. Author of *Pennsylvania Modern: Charles Demuth of Lancaster* (1983), *The Spirit of the South: The Sculpture of Alexander Galt* (1992) and *John Ferguson Weir: The Labor of Art* (in preparation). **Essay:** Lange.

Fairchild, Constance A.   Assistant Professor of Library Administration (Emerita), University of Illinois, Urbana. Contributor to *American Mass Market Magazines* (1990) and *Reference and Information Services: An Introduction* (2nd edition, 1995). Book reviewer in decorative arts for *Library Journal*. **Essay:** Wheeler.

Faxon, Alicia Craig   Rhode Island Regional Editor of *Art New England* and Professor of Art History (Emerita), Simmons College, Boston. Author of *The Prints of Jean-Louis Forain: A Catalogue Raisonné* (1982), *Jean-Louis Forain: Artist, Realist, Humanist* (1982) and *Dante Gabriel Rossetti* (1989). Editor of *Pilgrims and Pioneers: New England Women in the Arts* (with Sylvia Moore, 1987) and contributor to the periodicals *Art Bulletin*, *Master Drawings*, *Metropolitan Museum of Art Journal*, *Journal of Pre-Raphaelite Studies* and *Art New England*. **Essays:** Hawarden; Jones.

Floyd, Phylis   Associate Professor, Michigan State University, East Lansing. Author of *The Prints of Frank Stella: A Catalogue Raisonné* (with Richard Axsom, 1983). Contributor to *Treasures of the Hood Museum of Art* (1985), *The Prints of Ellsworth Kelly: A Catalogue Raisonné* (1987), *The Ivan Albright Collection* (catalogue, 1988), *St James Guide to Biography* (1991), *The Dictionary of Art* (1996) and to the journals *Kresge Art Museum Bulletin* and *Art Bulletin*. **Essays:** Kruger; Saar.

Foley, Jeana K.   Curatorial Assistant, Department of Photographs, National Portrait Gallery, Smithsonian Institution, Washington, DC. Author of thesis on the photography of Lee Miller, University of North Carolina (1995). **Essay:** Miller.

Francey, Mary F.   Associate Professor of Art History and Associate Dean, College of Fine Arts, University of Utah, Boise. Author of *Depression*

Printmakers as Workers: Re-Defining Traditional Interpretations (1988) and *American Women at Work: Prints by Women Artists of the 1930s* (1991). Contributor to *Dutch Art: An Encyclopedia* (1997). **Essay:** Schapiro.

Garb, Tamar   Reader in History of Art, University College, London. Author of *Women Impressionists* (1986), *Berthe Morisot* (with Kathleen Adler, 1987) and *Sisters of the Brush* (1994). Review editor, *Oxford Art Journal*. **Essays:** Bashkirtseff; Bertaux; Bracquemond; Morisot (with Kathleen Adler).

Garrihy, Andrea   Sculptor, writer and lecturer. Contributor to *Feminist Art News*, *Fan* and *Circumspice*. **Essay:** Thornycroft.

Gellman, Lola B.   Professor and Chair, Department of Art and Photography, Queensborough Community College, City University of New York. Editor of *Women's Studies and the Arts* (with Elsa Honig Fine and Judy Loeb, 1978). Contributor to *Outside the City Limits: Landscape by New York City Artists* (catalogue, 1977) and to the journals *Burlington Magazine*, *Women's Studies in Art and Art History* and *Simiolus*. Member of the Editorial Board, *Woman's Art Journal*. **Essay:** Hemessen.

Giacometti, Margherita   Freelance art historian. Contributor to the catalogues *Drawings from Venice: Masterworks from the Museo Correr* (1985), *Italian Art in the 20th Century* (1989), *I Tiepolo e il Settecento Vincentino* (1990), *The Glory of Venice* (1994) and to the journals *Art Newspaper* and *RA Magazine*. **Essay:** Carriera.

Goodman, Helen   Lecturer, Fashion Institute of Technology, New York. Author of *The Art of Rose O'Neill* (catalogue, 1989); contributor to the periodicals *Arts Magazine*, *American Artist*, *History of Photography* and *Woman's Art Journal*. **Essay:** Johnston.

Grove, Jeffrey D.   Assistant Curator, Akron Art Museum, Ohio, and PhD candidate, Case Western Reserve University, Cleveland. Co-author of *Lee Krasner: A Catalogue Raisonné* (1995). Contributor to *Ohio Selections X* (catalogue, 1991) and *Creating in a Crisis: Making Art in the Age of AIDS* (catalogue, 1994). **Essay:** Krasner.

Guryanova, Nina   Lecturer, Columbia University, New York. Author of *Russian Futurists and Their*

Books (1993). Contributor to *Unknown Russian Avant-Garde* (1992) and to the journals *Elementa*, *Russian Literature, Art e Dossier* and *Iskusstvo*. **Essays:** Rozanova; Udaltsova.

Hall-van den Elsen, Catherine Independent scholar. Contributor to *Archivo Hispalense, Boletín del Museo e Instituto Camón Aznar, Goya* and *Revista de Arte*. **Essay:** Roldán.

Harding, Catherine Assistant Professor, University of Victoria, British Columbia. Contributor to *Florence and Italy: Renaissance Studies in Honour of Nicolai Rubenstein* (1988) and to *Dumbarton Oaks Papers*. Member of advisory board, *Racar*. **Essay:** Robusti.

Harris, Rosemary Curator, NatWest Group Art Collection, London. Contributor to *Tate Gallery Illustrated Catalogue of Acquisitions, 1982–84* (1986), *Tate Gallery Illustrated Catalogue of Acquisitions, 1984–86* (1989), *Within These Shores: A Selection of Works from the Chantrey Bequest* (catalogue, 1989) and the *Guinness Encyclopedia* (1990). **Essay:** Mitchell.

Heer, Lisa Independent scholar. Author of *Problems in Copies: The Production, Consumption and Criticism of Copies after the Old Masters in Eighteenth-Century England* (PhD dissertation, 1995). **Essays:** Amateur Artists (18th and 19th centuries) and Copyists surveys.

Helland, Janice Associate Professor of Art History, Concordia University, Montreal. Author of *The Studios of Frances and Margaret Macdonald* (1995). Contributor to *Glasgow Girls: Women in Art and Design, 1880–1920* (1990 and 1993), *Charles Rennie Mackintosh* (1996) and the periodicals *Art History* and *Woman's Art Journal*. **Essay:** Margaret Macdonald.

Hill, Jane Freelance writer, lecturer and consultant. Author of *The Art of Dora Carrington* (1994) and curator of *Dora Carrington: A Retrospective* (London, 1995). Contributor to the journals *World of Interiors* and *The Artist*. **Essay:** Carrington.

Hills, Patricia Professor of Art History, Boston University. Author of *The Painters' America: Rural and Urban Life, 1810–1910* (1974), *Turn of the Century America: Paintings, Graphics, Photographs, 1890–1910* (1977), *Alice Neel* (1983), *John Singer Sargent* (1986) and *Stuart Davis* (1996). Co-editor of *Eastman Johnson* (1972) and contributor to *Oxford Art Journal* and *Art New England*. **Essays:** Catlett; Neel; Savage; Spencer; Stevens.

Hilton, Alison Associate Professor, Fine Arts Department, Georgetown University, Washington, DC. Author of *New Art from the Soviet Union: The Known and the Unknown* (with Norton Dodge, 1977), *Kasimir Malevich* (1992) and *Russian Folk Art* (1995). Contributor to the periodicals *Art Bulletin, Art Journal, Art in America, Arts Magazine, Art News, Woman's Art Journal, Studies in Iconography, Journal of Decorative and Propaganda Arts* and *Slavica Tamperensia*. **Essays:** Golubkina; Serebryakova.

Hochstrasser, Julie Berger Independent scholar. Author of *Life and Still Life: A Cultural Inquiry into Seventeenth-Century Dutch Still-Life Painting* (PhD dissertation, 1995). Contributor to *Center 12: Record of Activities and Research Reports June 1991–May 1992, National Gallery of Art, Washington, DC* (1992) and *Dutch Art: An Encyclopedia* (1997). **Essay:** Peeters.

Holger, Lena Chief Curator, Nationalmuseum, Stockholm. Author of *Helene Schjerfbeck: Liv och konstnärskap* (1987), *Helene Schjerfbeck* (catalogue, 1994), *Åsa Herrgård, Sculptor* (1994) and *Bo Andersson, Sculptor* (1995). **Essays:** Churberg; Schjerfbeck; Thesleff.

Hooker, Denise Author of *Nina Hamnett: Queen of Bohemia* (1986) and editor of *Art of the Western World* (1989). Series consultant to Channel 4/WNET television series *Art of the Western World*. **Essay:** Hamnett.

Huber-Spanier, Rosella M. Art teacher. Author of *Over moderne kunst* (1994); contributor to *Bloemen uit de kelder* (catalogue, 1989). **Essay:** Toorop.

Huneault, Kristina PhD candidate, University of Manchester. Contributor to *Journal of Canadian Art History*. **Essay:** Greenaway.

Iversen, Margaret Reader, Department of Art History and Theory, University of Essex, Colchester. Author of *Alois Riegl: Art History and Theory* (1993); contributor to the journals *Psychoanalysis and Art History* and *Art History*. **Essay:** Kelly.

Jacobs, Fredrika H. Associate Professor, Virginia Commonwealth University, Richmond. Contributor to *Word and Image, Renaissance Quarterly, Art Bulletin* and *Artibus et Historiae*. **Essays:** Anguissola; Rossi.

Johnson, Deborah Jean Associate Professor of Art and Art History, Providence College, Rhode Island. Author of *Mabel Ducasse: Artist, Critic, Woman of Her Time* (1991) and *Joe Norman: Fantasia Del Tugurio* (1992). Editor of *A Century of Black Photographers* (1983) and *Students on Gender* (1994 and 1995). Contributor to the catalogues *Whistler to Weidenaar: American Prints, 1870–1950* (1987), *The Rise of Landscape Painting in France: Corot to Monet* (1991), *Roberta Paul* (1991) and *Joseph Norman* (1991), and to the periodicals *Burlington Magazine, Photographic InSight, Mosaic, Choice* and *Source: Notes on the History of Art*. **Essay:** Training and Professionalism survey: North America, 20th century.

Jones, Amelia Member of the Department of History of Art, University of California, Riverside. Author of *Postmodernism and the En-Gendering of Marcel Duchamp* (1994); editor of *Sexual Politics: Judy Chicago's Dinner Party in Feminist Art History* (1996). Contributor to the journals *Art History, Camera Obscura, Art+Text* and *Artscribe*. **Essay:** Chicago.

Kaiser-Schuster, Britta Museum Assistant, Bauhaus-Archiv, Berlin. Author of *Kunstkarikatur im Deutschen Kaiserreich* (doctoral thesis, 1992) and *Das frühe Bauhaus und Johannes Itten* (1994), of catalogue essays on the Bauhaus and articles in the periodicals *Neues Glas* and *Museumsjournal*. **Essay:** Brandt.

Kaplan, Janet A. Professor of Art History and Chair of Liberal Arts, Moore College of Art and Design, Philadelphia. Author of *Unexpected Journeys: The Art and Life of Remedios Varo* (1988 and 1994). Contributor to *Women Artists in History: From Antiquity to the 20th Century* (1985), *A Woman's Thesaurus: An Index of Language Used to Describe and Locate Information About Women* (1989), *Mexican Journeys: Myth, Magic and Mummies* (catalogue, 1990), *Artists Choose Artists* (catalogue, 1991), *Beyond Aesthetics: Artworks of Conscience* (catalogue, 1991) and *Remedios Varo: Catalogo Razonado*

(1994). Contributor to the periodicals *Woman's Art Journal, Feminist Studies, Art News, Choice, Times Higher Education Supplement, New Statesman and Society* and *M/E/A/N/I/N/G*. **Essay:** Varo.

Kettering, Alison McNeil Professor of Art History, Carleton College, Northfield, Minnesota. Author of *The Dutch Arcadia: Pastoral Art and Its Audience in the Golden Age* (1983) and *Drawings from the Ter Borch Studio Estate in the Rijksmuseum* (1988). Contributor to the journal *Art History*. **Essay:** ter Borch.

King, Catherine Head of Art History, Open University, Milton Keynes. Author of *Gender and Art in Renaissance Italy, c.1300–c.1570* (1997); editor of *Women as Consumers and Users of Art and Architecture in the Italian Renaissance* (in preparation). Contributor to the periodicals *Journal of the Warburg and Courtauld Institutes, Wiener Jahrbuch für Kunstgeschichte, Zeitschrift für Kunstgeschichte, Gazette des Beaux-Arts, Pantheon, Art Christiana* and *Renaissance Studies*. **Essay:** Nelli.

King, Elaine A. Associate Professor of Critical Theory and Art History, Carnegie Mellon University, Pittsburgh. Contributor to *Beyond Walls and Wars: Art, Politics and Multiculturalism* (1992), *The Architect's Dream* (catalogue, 1993), *Peggy Cyphers: Lexicon of Paradise* (catalogue, 1993), *Alfred DeCredico: Drawings, 1985-1993* (catalogue, 1994), *Light Into Art: From Video to Virtual Reality* (1994), *The Figure as Fiction* (catalogue, 1994) and *The Post-Modern Enigma: Who and What Is Killing Art?* (1995). **Essay:** Abbott.

Knox, George Professor Emeritus, University of British Columbia, Vancouver. Author of *Giambattista and Domenico Tiepolo: The Chalk Drawings* (1980), *Giambattista Piazzetta, 1682–1754* (1992) and *Antonio Pellegrini, 1675–1741* (1995). **Essay:** Lama.

Krebs, Ute Picture researcher, AKG London. **Essay:** Duparc (with Esmé Ward).

Langdale, Cecily Partner, Davis & Langdale Co. Inc., New York. Author of *Gwen John: Paintings and Drawings from the Collection of John Quinn and Others* (catalogue, with Betsy G. Fryberger, 1982), *Monotypes by Maurice Prendergast in the*

Terra Museum of Art (1984), *Gwen John: An Interior Life* (with David Fraser Jenkins, 1985) and *Gwen John: With a Catalogue Raisonné of the Paintings and a Selection of the Drawings* (1987). Contributor to the *Dictionary of National Biography* and to the journals *Drawing*, *Connoisseur* and *Antiques*. **Essay:** John.

Lewis, Mary Tompkins Visiting Assistant Professor, Trinity College, Hartford, Connecticut. Author of *Cézanne's Early Imagery* (1989); contributor to *Cézanne: The Early Years, 1858–1872* (1988) and to the *Art Journal*. **Essay:** Gonzalès.

Lidén, Elisabeth Curator, Millesgården, Stockholm. Author of *Albin Amelin* (1975), *Between Water and Heaven: Carl Milles' Search for American Commissions* (1986) and *Kalle Hedberg* (1989); contributor to the journal *Konsten i Sverige*. **Essay:** Nilsson.

Lima, Marcelo Assistant Professor, Visual Arts Department, Sangamon State University, Springfield, Illinois. Contributor to the journals *New Art Examiner*, *Psychohistory Review* and *Revista do Museu de Arte Contemporanea*. **Essays:** Malfatti; Vieira da Silva.

Lincoln, Evelyn Assistant Professor of the History of Art, Brown University, Providence, Rhode Island. Author of *Art in Transition: Post Impressionist Prints and Drawings from the Achenbach Foundation for Graphic Arts* (with Robert Flynn Jonson, 1988). Contributor to *Art History*. **Essay:** Mantuana.

Lloyd, Stephen Assistant Keeper, Scottish National Portrait Gallery, Edinburgh. Editor of *Richard and Maria Cosway: Regency Artists of Taste and Fashion* (catalogue, 1995). Contributor to *Journal of Anglo-Italian Studies*. **Essay:** Cosway.

Lodder, Christina Reader in Art History, University of St Andrews, Scotland. Author of *Russian Constructivism* (1983) and *Russian Painting of the Avant-Garde, 1906–1924* (1993); co-author of *Catalogue Raisonné of the Constructions and Sculptures of Naum Gabo: Sixty Years of Constructivism* (1985). Contributor to *Art into Life: Russian Constructivism, 1914–1932* (1990), *The Great Utopia: The Russian Soviet Avant-Garde, 1915–1932* (catalogue, 1992) and *The Avant-Garde*

Frontier: Russia Meets the West, 1910–1930 (1992). **Essays:** Popova; Stepanova.

Lowe, Sarah M. Independent curator and writer. Author of *Frida Kahlo* (1991), *Consuelo Kanaga: An American Photographer* (with Barbara Head Millstein, 1992), *Tina Modotti: Photographs* (catalogue, 1995) and *The Diary of Frida Kahlo: An Intimate Self Portrait* (1995). Contributor to the catalogues *Herman Cherry: Monotypes* (1985) and *The House That Jack Built: The Politics of Domesticity* (1987), and to the journals *History of Photography* and *Center Quarterly*. **Essay:** Kahlo.

Lucchesi, Joe PhD candidate and instructor, University of North Carolina, Chapel Hill. **Essays:** Brooks; Gluck.

Ludwig, Heidrun Museums assistant. Author of *Nürnberger naturgeschichtliche Malerei im 17. und 18. Jahrhundert* (PhD dissertation, 1993). Contributor to *Der Franken Rom: Nürnbergs Blütezeit in der zweiten Hälfte des 17. Jahrhunderts* (1995) and *Archives of Natural History*. **Essay:** Merian.

MacKenzie, Catherine Chair, Department of Art History, Concordia University, Montreal. Previously editor of *University Art Association of Canada Women's Caucus Newsletter*. **Essay:** Bishop.

Mahon, Alyce PhD candidate (post-war Surrealism in Paris), Courtauld Institute of Art, London. **Essays:** Maar; Zürn.

Mainz, Valerie Associate Lecturer, Fine Art Department, University of Leeds. Contributor to *The Dictionary of Art* (1996), *The Companion Encyclopaedia to the Making of Western Art* and to the journal *Interfaces*. **Essays:** Charpentier; Vallayer-Coster.

Marter, Joan M. Professor of Art History, Rutgers University, New Brunswick, New Jersey. Author of *Alexander Calder* (1991) and *Theodore Roszak: The Drawings* (1992). Contributor to the catalogues *Vanguard American Sculpture, 1913–1939* (1979), *Beyond the Plane: American Constructions, 1930–1965* (1983) and *Dorothy Dehner, Sixty Years of Art* (1993). Guest editor of a sculpture issue of *Art Journal* (1994). **Essay:** Dehner.

Mathews, Nancy Mowll Eugénie Prendergast Curator, Williams College Museum of Art, Williamstown, Massachusetts. Author of *Cassatt and Her Circle: Selected Letters* (1984), *Mary Cassatt* (1987), *Mary Cassatt: The Color Prints* (1989), *Maurice Prendergast* (1990) and *Mary Cassatt: A Life* (1994); contributor to *Maurice Brazil Prendergast, Charles Prendergast: A Catalogue Raisonné* (1990). **Essays:** Cassatt; Training and Professionalism surveys: France, 19th century; North America, 19th century.

Meskimmon, Marsha Lecturer in History of Art and Design, Staffordshire University. Author of *Domesticity and Dissent: The Role of Women Artists in Germany, 1918–1938* (with Martin Davies, 1992) and *The Art of Reflection: Women Artists' Self-Portraiture in the Twentieth Century* (1996). Editor of *Visions of the "Neue Frau": Women and the Visual Arts in Weimar Germany* (with Shearer West, 1995). **Essay:** Höch.

Michaels, Barbara L. Art historian, writer and lecturer. Author of *Gertrude Käsebier: The Photographer and Her Photographs* (1992) and contributor to the journals *Art Bulletin*, *History of Photography*, *Afterimage* and *New York Times*. Series Editor, Perspectives on Photography, Cambridge University Press. **Essay:** Käsebier.

Miller, Lillian B. Historian of American Culture, Smithsonian Institution, and Editor, The Peale Family Papers, National Portrait Gallery, Washington, DC. Author of *Patrons and Patriotism: The Encouragement of Fine Arts in the United States, 1790–1860* (1966, 1974) and *In Pursuit of Fame: Rembrandt Peale, 1778–1860* (1992); editor of *The Collected Papers of Charles Willson Peale and His Family* (microfiche edition, 1980; book edition, 1983–). **Essay:** Peale.

Mitchell, Claudine Associate Lecturer, University of Leeds. Author of *Auguste Rodin* (in preparation); contributor to *On the Brink? Women Sculptors in Yorkshire* (1992), *Reflections of Revolution* (1993) and to the journals *Art History* and *Feminist Review*. **Essay:** Claudel.

Modesti, Adelina Lecturer, History and Theory of Art, Gippsland School of Art, Monash University, Australia. Co-author of *Art in Diversity* (1988); contributor to *Pilgrimage: Works by Julie Adams,*

Kaye Green and Susan Purdy (catalogue, 1991), *David Hazelwood "Collages"* (catalogue, 1993), *Identità ed appartenza: Donne e relazioni di genere dal mondo classico all'età contemporanea* (1995) and to the journal *Arts Gippsland*. **Essay:** Sirani.

Monahan, Laurie J. Doctoral candidate, Harvard University, Cambridge, Massachusetts. Author of articles on Surrealism, Claude Cahun, Matisse and Robert Rauschenberg. **Essay:** Cahun.

Moray, Gerta Associate Professor of Fine Art, University of Guelph, Ontario. Author of *Mary Pratt* (with Sandra Gwynn, 1989) and *Northwest Coast Native Culture and the Early Indian Paintings of Emily Carr, 1899–1913* (PhD dissertation, 1993); contributor to *Textual Studies in Canada*. **Essays:** Carr; Wieland.

Mulley, Elizabeth PhD candidate in art history and part-time lecturer at McGill University, Montreal. Contributor to *Journal of Canadian Art History*. **Essay:** Garzoni.

Murphy, Caroline P. Author of *Lavinia Fontana: An Artist and Her Society in Late Sixteenth-Century Bologna* (PhD dissertation, 1996); contributor to *Women of the Golden Age* (1994) and *Picturing Women in Renaissance and Baroque Italy* (in preparation). **Essay:** Fontana.

Nunn, Pamela Gerrish Senior Lecturer, School of Fine Arts, University of Canterbury, Christchurch, New Zealand. Author of *Canvassing Women: Recollections by Six Victorian Women Artists* (1986), *Victorian Women Artists* (1987) and *Women Artists and the Pre-Raphaelite Movement* (with Jan Marsh, 1989). **Essays:** Butler; Rae; Solomon; Training and Professionalism survey: Britain and Ireland, 19th century.

Öhrner, Annika Curator of Riksutställningar (Swedish Travelling Exhibitions). Contributor to *Porträtt, porträtt, studier i Statens porträttsamling på Gripsholm* (1987), *Den goda fröken och huset* (1989), *Fogelstadkvinnor: En porträttutställning Gripsholms slott* (1990) and *Gabriele Münter, 1877–1962: Retrospektive* (catalogue, 1992), and to the journals *Dagens Nyheter*, *INDEX/Contemporary Scandinavian Images*, *Tidskriften 90* and *Kvinnovetenskaplig Tidskrift*. **Essay:** Klint.

Parton, Anthony Director, Hatton Gallery, University of Newcastle upon Tyne. Author of *Mikhail Larionov and the Russian Avant-Garde* (1993); contributor to *Nathalie Gontcharova, Michel Larionov* (catalogue, 1995); editor and translator of *Women Artists of Russia's New Age, 1900–1935* by M.N. Yablonskaya (1990). **Essay:** Goncharova.

Peacock, Martha Moffitt Assistant Professor, Brigham Young University, Provo, Utah. Editor of *Rembrandt as Printmaker: An Exhibition at Brigham Young University* (catalogue, 1988) and contributor to the periodicals *Woman's Art Journal, Dutch Crossing* and *Konsthistorisk Tidskrift*. **Essay:** Roghman.

Peers, Juliet Lecturer, Art and Design History, RMII, Melbourne. Author of *Completing the Picture: Women Artists and the Heidelberg Era* (with Victoria Hammond, 1992), *More Than Just Gumtrees: A Personal, Social and Artistic History of the Melbourne Society of Women Painters and Sculptors* (1993), *A l'ombre des jeunes filles et des fleurs: A Guide to Women Artists in the Benalla Art Gallery Collection, pre-1960* (catalogue, 1995). Contributor to *Pre-Raphaelite Sculpture* (1991) and *Heritage: The National Women's Art Book* (1995). Editor of the *Women's Art Register*, Melbourne. **Essay:** Preston.

Peet, Phyllis Director/Professor of Women's Programs and Women's Studies, Monterey Peninsula College, Monterey, California. Author of *American Women of the Etching Revival* (catalogue, 1988), *American Paintings and Sculpture in the Collection of the High Museum of Art, Atlanta* (with Donelson Hoopes and Judy Larson, 1994). Contributor to *Life Sources: Multiple Visions* (catalogue, 1990), several reference books and *American Society of Wood Engravers Journal, Woman's Art Journal, Journal of the Print World* and *Imprint*. **Essay:** Stephens.

Perry, Gill Senior Lecturer in Art History, Open University, Milton Keynes. Author of *Paula Modersohn-Becker: Her Life and Work* (1979) and *Women Artists and the Parisian Avant-Garde* (1995). Co-editor of *Femininity and Masculinity in 18th-Century Art and Culture* (1994). Contributor to *Primitivism, Cubism Abstraction: The Early Twentieth Century* (1993). Reviews editor for the

journal *Art History*. **Essays:** Laurencin; Modersohn-Becker; Valadon; Training and Professionalism survey: France, 20th century (with Sarah Wilson).

Prelinger, Elizabeth Associate Professor and Chair, Department of Art, Music and Theatre, Georgetown University, Washington, DC. Author of *Edvard Munch: Master Printmaker* (1983) and *Käthe Kollwitz* (catalogue, 1992); contributor to *Seymour Slive Festschrift* (1995) and the journal *Print Quarterly*. **Essay:** Kollwitz.

Proctor, Nancy Art history lecturer, Saint Mary's College, Rome Program; PhD candidate, University of Leeds. Author of articles on American women sculptors in Rome, Mary Kelly and Frank Faulkner. Also experimental film-maker, with exhibitions in Leeds and São Paolo. **Essay:** Lewis.

Ranfft, Erich Henry Moore Scholar in the Study of Sculpture, Department of Fine Art, University of Leeds. Co-editor of *Sculpture and Its Reproductions* (in preparation); contributor to *Expressionism Reassessed* (1993), *Visions of the "Neue Frau": Women and the Visual Arts in Weimar Germany* (1995), *The Dictionary of Art* (1996) and to the journals *Art History, Burlington Magazine* and *Women's Art Magazine*. **Essay:** Roeder.

Reeve, Christopher Keeper of Fine and Decorative Art, St Edmundsbury Borough Council, Suffolk. Author of *Something to Splash About: Sybil Andrews in Suffolk* (1991) and *Mrs Mary Beale, Paintress* (catalogue, 1994); contributor to the *Burlington Magazine*. **Essay:** Beale.

Robinson, Roxana Writer. Author of *Georgia O'Keeffe: A Life* (1989) and fiction. Contributor to *Arthur Dove* (1984), *William Harnett* (1992) and to *Arts Magazine, Art News* and *American Art and Antiques*. **Essay:** O'Keeffe.

Roworth, Wendy Wassyng Professor of Art History, University of Rhode Island, Providence. Author of *"Pictor Succesor": A Study of Salvator Rosa as Satirist, Cynic and Painter* (1978); editor of *Angelica Kauffman: A Continental Artist in Georgian England* (1992). Contributor to *Eighteenth-Century Women and the Arts* (1988), *Femininity and Masculinity in Eighteenth-Century Art and Culture* (1994) and to the periodicals *Burlington Magazine, Art Bulletin, Metropolitan*

Museum Journal, *Muse* and *The Seventeenth Century*. **Essays:** Kauffman; Academies of Art survey (with Mary D. Sheriff).

Salmond, Wendy R. Associate Professor and Chair, Department of Art, Chapman University, Orange, California. Author of *Arts and Crafts in Late Imperial Russia: Reviving the Kustar Art Industries, 1870–1917* (1996) and contributor to the journals *Decorative and Propaganda Arts* and *Studies in Decorative Arts*. **Essay:** Training and Professionalism survey: Russia.

Saunders, Gill Curator of Documentation, Collection of Prints, Drawings and Paintings, Victoria and Albert Museum, London. Author of *The Nude: A New Perspective* (1989), *Recording Britain: A Pictorial Domesday of Pre-War Britain* (with David Mellor and Patrick Wright, 1990) and *Picturing Plants: An Analytical History of Botanical Illustration* (1995). **Essay:** Riley.

Scales, Alette Rye Freelance lecturer and linguist. **Essay:** Ancher.

Schoeneck, Edith Freelance art historian. Author of *Anna Rosina Lisiewska-Matthieu-de Gasc* (dissertation, in preparation); contributor to *Arx, Burgen und Schlösser in Bayern Österreich und Südtirol* (1994). **Essay:** Lisiewska-Therbusch.

Schulte, Birgit Curator at the Karl Ernst Osthaus-Museum, Hagen, Germany. Author of catalogues on *Christian Rohlfs* (1989), *Eberhard Viegener* (1990), *Ruth Biller* (1990), *Henry van de Velde* (1992), *Emil Rudolf Weiss* (1992), *Druckgrafik des Expressionismus* (1993), *Bruno Taut* (1994), *Egon Wilden* (1994), *Milly Steger* (1994) and *Herbert Bardenheuer* (1995); contributor to *Das Kunstwerk*. **Essay:** Steger.

Seidel, Miriam Philadelphia corresponding editor, *Art in America*. Contributor to *Art in America*, *New Art Examiner* and *Philadelphia Inquirer*. **Essay:** Schneemann.

Sellars, Jane Curator, Harewood House Trust, Leeds. Author of *Women's Works: Paintings, Drawings, Prints and Sculpture by Women* (1988) and *The Art of the Brontës* (with Christine Alexander, 1995). Contributor to the periodicals *Feminist Art News*, *Transactions of the Brontë*

Society, *Museums Journal* and *Art Review*. **Essays:** De Morgan; Ward.

Senie, Harriet F. Director of Museum Studies and Professor of Art History, City College, City University of New York. Author of *Contemporary Public Sculpture: Tradition, Transformation and Controversy* (1992). Co-editor of *Critical Issues in Public Art* (1992); contributor to *Encyclopedia of New York City* (1995) and to *Art Journal* and *Art News*. **Essay:** Nevelson.

Sheriff, Mary D. Professor, University of North Carolina, Chapel Hill. Author of *Fragonard: Art and Eroticism* (1990) and *The Exceptional Woman: Elisabeth Vigée-Lebrun and the Cultural Politics of Art* (1996). Co-editor of *Eighteenth Century Studies*. **Essays:** Collot; Gérard; Vigée-Lebrun; Academies of Art survey (with Wendy Wassyng Roworth).

Shilliam, Nicola J. Assistant Curator, Textile and Costume Collection, Department of European Decorative Arts and Sculpture, Museum of Fine Arts, Boston. Author of *Early Modern Textiles: From Arts and Crafts to Art Deco* (with Marianne Carlano, 1993). Contributor to the periodicals *Magazine Antiques*, *Textile and Text* and *Journal of the Museum of Fine Arts, Boston*. **Essay:** Zorach.

Smith, Elizabeth A.T. Curator, Museum of Contemporary Art, Los Angeles; Adjunct Professor, School of Fine Arts, University of Southern California, Los Angeles. Editor of the catalogues *Rebecca Horn: Diving Through "Buster's Bedroom"* (1990), *Blueprints for Modern Living: History and Legacy of the Case Study Houses* (1989) and *Urban Revisions: Current Projects for the Public Realm* (1994). **Essay:** Bontecou.

Smith, Richard J. Freelance researcher. Author of a forthcoming biography and catalogue raisonné on Margaret Carpenter; contributor to the *Hatcher Review*. **Essay:** Carpenter.

Spadaro, Domenica Lecturer at the Politecnico in Milan, Italy. **Essay:** Galizia (with Flavio Caroli).

Stevenson, Lesley Senior Lecturer, Thames Valley University, London. **Essay:** Moillon.

Stighelen, Katlijne Van der Member of the faculty, Catholic University, Leuven, Belgium. Author of

Anna Maria van Schurman (1607–1678) of *"Hoe hooge dat een maeght kan in de konsten stijgen"* (1987), *De portretten van Cornelis de Vos* (1990) and many articles and catalogue essays on Flemish and Netherlandish art. Co-editor of *Pictura nova*, a series on Flemish painting and drawing. **Essay:** Amateur Artists survey (16th and 17th centuries).

Stober, Karin Scientific employee, University of Karlsruhe. Contributor to *Buchobjekte* (catalogue, 1980), *Von allen Seiten betrachtet: 4 Heiligenfiguren von Ignaz Günther* (catalogue, 1988), *Klar und lichtvoll wie eine Regel: Planstädte der Neuzeit* (catalogue, 1990), *Mitteilungsblatt des Ministeriums für Kultus und Wissenschaft* (1990), *"...und hat als Weib unglaubliches Talent" (Goethe): Angelika Kauffmann (1741–1807), Marie Ellenrieder (1791–1863)* (catalogue, 1992), *Palmanova–Fortezza d'Europa, 1593-1993* (catalogue, 1993), *Handbuch der deutschen Kunstdenkmäler* (1993) and *Faszination eines Klosters: 750 Jahre Kloster Lichtenthal* (catalogue, 1995), and to *Studi Piemontesi*. **Essay:** Ellenrieder.

Tappert, Tara Leigh Independent scholar. Author of *The Emmets: A Generation of Gifted Women* (1993) and *Out of the Background: Cecilia Beaux and the Art of Portraiture* (in preparation). Contributor to *Revivals! Diverse Traditions, 1920–1945* (1994), *Craft in the Machine Age: European Influence on American Modernism, 1920-45* (1995) and to *Women's Studies: An Interdisciplinary Journal*. **Essay:** Beaux.

Taylor, Dorcas Curatorial assistant, Centre for the Study of Sculpture, Henry Moore Institute, Leeds, and graduate student researching Katharine Read and professional women artists in 18th-century Britain at the University of Manchester. Author of *Michael Kidner: Making Maps, Looking for Landmarks* (1997); contributor to the *Encyclopedia of Interior Design* (1997). **Essay:** Read.

Terra Cabo, Paula PhD candidate, Department of Art Theory and History, University of Essex, Colchester. Author of *Casa França-Brasil* (1991) and contributor to *Hélio Oiticica* (catalogue, 1992) and to *The Independent* newspaper. **Essay:** Clark.

Thompson, Margo Hobbs PhD candidate, Art History Department, Northwestern University, Evanston, Illinois. **Essay:** Rainer.

Thornberry, Joanna Exhibitions Assistant, Anthony D'Offay Gallery, London. **Essay:** Saint Phalle.

Vaizey, Marina. Editor of Publications, National Art Collections Fund. Author of *100 Masterpieces of Painting* (1980), *The Artist as Photographer* (1982), *Peter Blake* (1985), *Christo* (1990) and *Christiane Kubrick* (1990). Contributor to *Connoisseur, Art International, Antique Collector, New Statesman, Times Literary Supplement, Times Educational Supplement, Tatler, Vogue, The Sunday Times* and other periodicals. **Essay:** Cameron.

Wacks, Debra PhD candidate in Art History, Graduate Center, City University of New York. **Essay:** Chryssa.

Walker, Neil Keeper of Fine Art, Nottingham Castle Museum and Art Gallery. Contributor to *Richard Parkes Bonington, Paul Sanby: Wegbereiter der Aquarellmalerei* (catalogue, 1989) and *The Staithes Group* (catalogue, 1993). **Essay:** Knight.

Waller, Susan PhD candidate in art history, Northwestern University, Evanston, Illinois. Author of *Women Artists in the Modern Era* (1991); contributor to *Women Artists News* and *Woman's Art Journal*. **Essay:** Bonheur.

Ward, Esmé Freelance gallery and museum educator. Contributor to *Dulwich Picture Gallery Children's Art Book* (1997) and *Dulwich Picture Gallery Activity Book* (1997). **Essay:** Duparc (with Ute Krebs).

Weibull, Nina Curator of the Stockholm University Art Collection; editor of *Divan*. Co-author of *Channa Bankier* (1994) and *Liv Derkert* (1994); contributor to the catalogues *Carlssons* (1995), *Liljevalchs* (1995) and *Sigrid Hjertén* (1995). **Essay:** Hjertén.

Weltge, Sigrid Wortmann Professor, History of Art and Design, Philadelphia College of Textiles. Author of *Die Ersten Maler in Worpswede* (1979 and 1987), *Bauhaus Textiles: Women Artists and the Weaving Workshop* (1993) and *Women's Work: Textile Art from the Bauhaus* (1993). Contributor to *International Dictionary of Women Artists Born Before 1900* (1985), *The Bauhaus Weaving Workshop: Source and Influence for American Textiles* (catalogue, 1987) and *Sonja Flavin: Weavings and Computer Drawings* (catalogue,

1989). Contributor to the journals *Tiller*, *Update*, *Women's Studies Quarterly*, *Portfolio*, *Interweave Magazine*, *Arts Exchange Magazine* and *Women's Caucus for Art News*. **Essay:** Stölzl.

Welu, James A. Director, Worcester Art Museum, Worcester, Massachusetts. Contributor to the catalogues *Seventeenth-Century Dutch Painting: Raising the Curtain on New England Private Collections* (1979), *The Collector's Cabinet: Flemish Paintings from New England Private Collections* (1983) and *Judith Leyster: A Dutch Master and Her World* (1993), and to the journal *Art Bulletin*. **Essay:** Leyster.

Werkmäster, Barbro Author, art critic and Senior Lecturer in Art History, Uppsala University. Author of *Frihet jämlikhet systerskap* (with Maud Hägg, 1971), *Kvinnor och sex* (with Maud Hägg, 1973), *Bilden som Handling* (with J. Rosell, 1984), *Möte med bilderboken* (with Lena Kåreland, 1985), *Anna Nordlander och hennes samtid* (1993) and *Livsvandring i tre akter* (with Lena Kåreland, 1994). Editor of *Kvinnor som konstnärer* (with Anna Lena Lindberg, 1975). Contributor to *Kvinnor och skapande* (1983) and *Visual Paraphrases: Studies in Mass Media Imagery* (1984) and to the periodicals *Författaren*, *Hertha*, *Konsthistorisk Tidskrift*, *Kvinnovetenskaplig Tidskrift*, *Ord & Bild*, *Paletten*, *Phaedrus* and *Valör*. **Essay:** Nyström.

Weston, Helen Senior Lecturer, History of Art Department, University College, London. Contributor to *Burlington Magazine*, *Oxford Art Journal*, *Art Monthly* and *RES: Journal of Anthropology and Aesthetics*. **Essay:** Mayer.

Wiggins, Colin Member of the Education Department, National Gallery, London. Author of *Working After the Masters: Frank Auerbach and the National Gallery* (1995) and *Now We are 64: Peter Blake at the National Gallery* (1996). Contributor to *Paula Rego: Tales from the National Gallery* (catalogue, 1991). **Essay:** Rego.

Wilson, Beth Elaine Adjunct Professor, State University of New York at New Paltz. Contributor to *Geometries of Color: American Post-Painterly Abstraction* (catalogue, 1991), and to the journals *Arts Magazine*, *Tema Celeste* and *FAD Magazine*. Text editor, *Blind Spot* photography magazine. **Essay:** Bourke-White.

Wilson, Sarah Lecturer in 20th-Century Art, Courtauld Institute of Art, University of London. Author of *Matisse* (1992), *Max Ernst* (1994), *When Modernism Failed: Art and Politics of the Left in France, 1935–1955* (in preparation) and *Intellectual Revolution: Art and Politics in France, 1958–1981* (in preparation). Contributor to *Orlan* (1996), *Critical Introductions to Art: Portraiture* (1996), *Face à l'histoire* (1996) and *Rrose is a Rrose is a Rrose: Gender Performance in Photography* (catalogue, 1997). **Essays:** Richier; Training and Professionalism survey: France, 20th century (with Gill Perry).

Witzling, Mara R. Professor, Art History and Women's Studies, University of New Hampshire, Durham. Author of *Voicing Our Visions* (1991), *Mary Cassatt: A Private World* (1991) and *Voicing Today's Visions* (1994); contributor to *Woman's Art Journal* and *NWSA Journal*. **Essays:** Flack; Ringgold; Feminism and Women Artists survey.

Wood, Jeryldene M. Assistant Professor of Art History, University of Illinois, Urbana. Author of *Women, Art and Spirituality: The Poor Clares of Early Modern Italy* (1996) and contributor to the periodicals *Konsthistorisk Tidskrift*, *Art History* and *Renaissance Quarterly*. **Essay:** Vigri.

Yarrington, Alison Senior Lecturer, History of Art, Leicester University. Author of *The Commemoration of the Hero, 1800–1864* (1988). Editor of *Reflections of Revolution: Images of Romanticism* (with Kelvin D. Everest, 1993) and *An Edition of the Ledger of Sir Francis Chantrey, RA, at the Royal Academy, 1809–1841* (with others, 1994). Contributor to *Art and Artists: Painters, Sculptors, Terms and Techniques* (1981), *The Thames and Hudson Encyclopedia of British Art* (1985) and *Patronage and Practice: Sculpture on Merseyside* (1989), and to the journals *Art History*, *Parametro* and *Women's Art Magazine*. **Essays:** Damer; Hosmer.

PHOTOGRAPHIC ACKNOWLEDGMENTS

The Publishers, the editor and the picture researchers would like to thank all the organisations, agencies and individuals who have kindly provided photographic material and given permission for the use of the illustrations in this book. The locations of the works are given in the captions. All illustrations are reproduced by courtesy and by kind permission of the sources given in the captions, and the following:

© the Artist: All artists' copyright in their works is acknowledged

© DACS, London: Fig. 9, Fig. 21, Fig. 25, Fig. 34, Fig. 40, Fig. 48, Fig. 51, Fig. 56, Fig. 68, Fig. 69

© ACA Galleries, New York/Munich: Fig. 28

© Alinari: Fig. 5

© Art Gallery of Ontario, Toronto: (photo Carlo Catenazzi) Fig. 14

photo © 1996 Art Institute of Chicago, All Rights Reserved: Fig. 53

Art Resource, New York: Fig. 11

© Charlotte Salomon Foundation: Fig. 63

photo: Courtauld Institute of Art, London: Fig. 66

photo: David Reynolds: Fig. 57

photo © 1994 Detroit Institute of Arts Founders Society: Fig. 60

© Estate of Barbara Hepworth, Sir Alan Bowness: Fig. 27

Hirschsprung Collection, Copenhagen (photo Hans Pedersen): Fig.2

© Instituto Nacional Bellas Artes y Literatura, Mexico: Fig. 38

photo: Jean Bernard, Marseille: Fig. 20

Landesbibliotek Wiesbaden/Rheinisches Bildarchiv, Cologne: Fig. 32

© Margaret Bourke-White Collection, George Arents Research Library, Syracuse University: Fig. 8

Marlborough Fine Art, London: Fig. 54

photo © 1996 Metropolitan Museum of Art, New York. All Rights Reserved: Fig. 6, Fig. 17

Nasjonalgalleriet Oslo (photo: J. Lathion) Fig. 37

photo © 1996 Board of Trustees, National Gallery of Art, Washington, DC: Fig. 39

By Courtesy of the Trustees, The National Gallery, London: Fig. 29, Fig. 70

National Trust Photo Library: Fig. 36

New York Public Library, Office of Special Collections: Fig. 18, Fig. 22

Osvaldo Böhm, Venice: Fig. 42

© Photo RMN: Fig. 3, Fig. 4, Fig. 41

Courtesy Robert Miller Gallery, New York: Fig. 7, Fig. 31

Sächsische Landesbibliothek, Abteilung Deutsche Fotothek: Fig. 44

Staatliche Museen zu Berlin, Preussiche Kuturbesitz: Fig. 30

photo © 1996 Whitney Museum of American Art, New York: Fig. 61

Every effort has been made to contact copyright holders and sources of permission for illustrations in this book. Where any have been overlooked, the publisher acknowledges their right to be credited.